INTERNATIONAL FINANCE AND ACCOUNTING HANDBOOK

THIRD EDITION

Subscriber
Update
Service

BECOME A SUBSCRIBER!

Did you purchase this product from a bookstore?

If you did, it's important for you to become a subscriber. John Wiley & Sons, Inc. may publish, on a periodic basis, supplements and new editions to reflect the latest changes in the subject matter that you ***need to know*** in order to stay competitive in this ever-changing industry. By contacting the Wiley office nearest you, you'll receive any current update at no additional charge. In addition, you'll receive future updates and revised or related volumes on a 30-day examination review.

If you purchased this product directly from John Wiley & Sons, Inc., we have already recorded your subscription for this update service.

To become a subscriber, please call **1-800-225-5945** or send your name, company name (if applicable), address, and the title of the product to:

mailing address: **Supplement Department**
John Wiley & Sons, Inc.
One Wiley Drive
Somerset, NJ 08875

e-mail: **subscriber@wiley.com**
fax: **1-732-302-2300**
online: **www.wiley.com**

For customers outside the United States, please contact the Wiley office nearest you:

Professional & Reference Division
John Wiley & Sons Canada, Ltd.
22 Worcester Road
Rexdale, Ontario M9W 1L1
CANADA
(416) 675-3580
Phone: 1-800-567-4797
Fax: 1-800-565-6802
canada@jwiley.com

John Wiley & Sons, Ltd.
Baffins Lane
Chichester
West Sussex, PO19 1UD
ENGLAND
Phone: (44) 1243 779777
Fax: (44) 1243 770638
cs-books@wiley.co.uk

Jacaranda Wiley Ltd.
PRT Division
P.O. Box 174
North Ryde, NSW 2113
AUSTRALIA
Phone: (02) 805-1100
Fax: (02) 805-1597
headoffice@jacwiley.com.au

John Wiley & Sons (SEA) Pte. Ltd.
2 Clementi Loop #02-01
SINGAPORE 129809
Phone: 65 463 2400
Fax: 65 463 4605; 65 463 4604
wiley@singnet.com.sg

INTERNATIONAL FINANCE AND ACCOUNTING HANDBOOK
THIRD EDITION

Edited by

FREDERICK D.S. CHOI

WILEY

JOHN WILEY & SONS, INC.

This book is printed on acid-free paper.♾

Published simultaneously in Canada

For general information on our other products and services, or technical support, please contact our Customer Care Department within the United States at 800-762-2974, outside the United States at 317-572-3993 or fax 317-572-4002.

Wiley also publishes its books in a variety of electronic formats. Some content that appears in print may not be available in electronic books.

For more information about Wiley products, visit our Web site at *www.wiley.com.*

Library of Congress Cataloging-in-Publication Data:
International finance and accounting handbook / edited by Frederick D.S. Choi.—3rd ed.
p. cm.
Rev. ed. of: International accounting and finance handbook. 2nd ed. New York: Wiley, ©1997.
Includes bibliographical references and index.
ISBN 0-471-22921-0 (cloth)
1. International business enterprises—Accounting. 2. International business enterprises—Accounting—Standards. 3. Comparative accounting. I. Choi, Frederick D.S., 1942– II. International accounting and finance handbook.
HF5686.I56H36 2003
657′.96—dc21 2002192266

Printed in the United States of America

10 9 8 7 6 5 4 3 2 1

To Lois—
Thank you for being there
always and all ways.

ABOUT THE EDITOR

Frederick D.S. Choi, is the Abraham L. Gitlow Professor of Accounting and International Business and Dean of the Undergraduate College at the Stern School of Business at New York University. He has served as chairman of NYU's Department of Accounting, Taxation, and Business Law and its International Business Area and is former Director of the Vincent C. Ross Institute of Accounting Research.

He has lectured at such institutions as the Cranfield School of Management (England), I.N.S.E.A.D. (France), University of Washington, Japan America Institute of Management Science, University of Bocconi (Italy), and the Stockholm School of Economics (Sweden) and served as a member of the First American Visiting Team to establish the National Center for Industrial Science and Technology Management Development in the People's Republic of China.

Professor Choi has contributed more than 100 pieces to the scholarly and professional literature including 20 books on the subject of international accounting and financial control. The first edition of this Wiley publication, the *Handbook of International Accounting*, received the Most Outstanding Book Award, having been judged the best work on law and accounting for 1991 by the American Association of Publishers. A Fellow of the Academy of International Business, he is a recipient of the Citibank Excellence in Teaching Award and the American Accounting Association's Outstanding International Accounting Educator Award.

Currently serving as co-editor of the specialist journal, *The Journal of International Financial Management and Accounting*, Professor Choi joined NYU in 1981.

ABOUT THE CONTRIBUTORS

Carol Adams is a Professor of Accounting and Head of School of Business and Economics—Gippsland at Monash University. She is a Council Member and Director of the Institute of Social and Ethical AccountAbility.

Linda Allen is a professor of finance at the Zicklin School of Business at Baruch College, City University of New York, and Adjunct Professor of Finance at the Stern School of Business New York University. She is also the author of *Capital Markets and Institutions: A Global View* (Wiley) and co-author of *Credit Risk Measurement: New Approaches to Value at Risk and Other Paradigms*, 2nd edition (Wiley). She is an associate editor of the *Journal of Banking and Finance*, *Journal of Economics and Business*, *Multinational Finance Journal*, *Journal of Multinational Financial Management*, and *The Financier*, and has published extensively in top academic journals in finance and economics.

Edward I. Altman, MBA, PhD, is the Max L. Heine Professor of Finance at the Stern School of Business, New York University. He is the Vice Director of the NYU Salomon Center and an international authority on credit risk management, corporate distress analysis, and fixed income valuation.

Paul M. Bodner, Esq., CPA, is an attorney with offices in Great Neck, New York. He has written and spoken extensively on international tax matters.

Paul Brunner, CPA, BCA (Hons), is a Partner in the Global Capital Markets Group of PricewaterhouseCoopers LLP and provides U.S. accounting advice to non-U.S. companies registered with the United States Securities and Exchange Commission and to companies seeking to undertake securities offerings, cross-border mergers and acquisitions, and structured transactions.

Mikelle A. Calhoun, J.D., received her undergraduate degree and a master's degree in speech communications and later obtained an MBA and a JD from the University of North Carolina. As the result of her experience practicing law for ten years, Ms. Calhoun's interests are primarily in the areas of service and financial industry corporate strategy decisions and international operations.

Ya-Ru Chen, PhD, is currently an assistant professor of management and international business at New York University. Her research has examined how fundamental processes of organizational behavior, such as feedback, intergroup processes, and conflict resolution, operate in various cultural settings. She has published numerous articles in these areas. She has also begun work exploring the social psychology of status, particularly with respect to its effects on behavior in negotiations.

Marcia Millon Cornett, PhD, is a professor of finance at Southern Illinois University, Carbondale. She has written several articles in the areas of bank performance, bank regulation, corporate finance, and investments. She has served as an associate editor for *Financial Management* and is currently an associate editor for the *Multinational Finance Journal.* She is a member of the Board of Directors of the Southern Illinois University Credit Union.

Aswath Damodaran is a professor of finance at the Stern School of Business at New York University, and teaches the corporate finance and equity valuation courses in the MBA program. He has published in the *Journal of Financial and Quantitative Analysis*, the *Journal of Finance*, the *Journal of Financial Economics*, and the *Review of Financial Studies*, and has written three books on equity valuation (*Damodaran on Valuation*, *Investment Valuation*, *The Dark Side of Valuation*) and two on corporate finance (*Corporate Finance: Theory and Practice* and *Applied Corporate Finance: A User's Manual*). He has co-edited a book on investment management with Peter Bernstein (*Investment Management*). He was profiled in *BusinessWeek* as one of the top 12 business school professors in the United States in 1994.

William E. Decker, CPA, is the senior partner and founder of PricewaterhouseCoopers LLP's Global Capital Markets Group. He has served on the AICPA's International Practices Task Force and is the author of *The Coopers & Lybrand SEC Manual*, 7th ed. (John Wiley & Sons, 1997).

Gunter Dufey, DBA (University of Washington, Seattle), is an adjunct professor in banking and finance at Nanyang Technological University, Nanyang Business School, Singapore. He also serves as a senior advisor with McKinsey and Company, supporting the corporate governance practice of the firm in Asia.

David K. Eiteman, PhD, is emeritus professor in international finance at the John E. Anderson Graduate School of Management at UCLA. He has been a visiting professor at the National University of Singapore and the Hong Kong University of Science and Technology. He is a past president of the Western Finance Association and the International Trade and Finance Association. He is a co-author of *Multinational Business Finance*, *Fundamentals of Multinational Finance*, and *Essentials of Investing*.

Edwin J. Elton, PhD, is a Nomura Professor of Finance at the Stern School of Business at New York University. Professor Elton has authored or co-authored six books and over 90 articles, and is a former president of the American Finance Association.

Robert Feinschreiber is an attorney and counselor in Miami. His firm, Feinschreiber & Associates, concentrates on international transfer pricing. He has written and edited many books on taxation, including *Transfer Pricing Handbook*, *Transfer Pricing International: A Country-by-Country Guide*, and *International Mergers: A Country-by-Country Tax Guide*. He is the editor of *Interstate Tax Report* and the founding editor of the *International Tax Journal*.

Lisa Filomia-Aktas is a partner in Ernst & Young's New York Financial Services office. She leads the On-Call Advisory Services group, which assists with evaluating the accounting, tax, and regulatory aspects of derivative, securitization, corporate finance, M&A, leasing, compensation, and structured product transactions. Lisa has advised a significant number of leading investment banks, global financial institutions, and *Fortune* 1000 corporations on capital market transactions. She is a member of the accounting subcommittee for the American Securitization Forum and is a frequent speaker at conferences.

Carol A. Frost, PhD, is president of Global Capital Markets Access, LLC, a consulting and research company based in Hanover, New Hampshire. Prior to forming GCMA LLC, she was on the faculties of the Tuck School of Business at Dartmouth College and the Olin School of Business at Washington University (St. Louis). She also is a member of the Nasdaq Listing and Hearing Review Council.

Geoff Frost is a senior lecturer in accounting at the University of Sydney. His major research interests are environmental accounting and reporting.

Ian H. Giddy, PhD, is a visiting associate professor of finance at New York University's Stern School of Business and a consultant to multinational companies and banks.

Sidney J. Gray is Professor of International Business and Associate Dean (Postgraduate) in the Faculty of Commerce and Economics at the University of New South Wales, Sydney, Australia. He is also currently President of the Australia and New Zealand International Business Academy (ANZIBA).

Martin J. Gruber, PhD, is the past president of the American Finance Association, and the author of more than seven books and 75 articles. The sixth edition of his book, *Modern Portfolio Theory and Investment Analysis*, has recently been published by John Wiley & Sons.

Sara Hanks is a partner with the international law firm Clifford Chance, where she practices international securities law. She was formerly chief of the SEC's Office of International Corporate Finance.

Seymour Jones is Clinical Professor of Accounting at the Stern School of Business, New York University. Previously, he was a senior partner of Coopers & Lybrand (now PricewaterhouseCoopers). He teaches auditing, accounting, tax and legal issues for entrepreneurs, and international financial statement analysis. Mr. Jones has written several books and publications on accounting subjects and is also associate director of the Ross Institute of Accounting Research, New York University.

Margaret Kent is an attorney and counselor at Feinschreiber & Associates in Miami, Florida.

Stephen J. Mezias, PhD, is a professor in the Department of Management at New York University. His current research focuses on institutional processes, especially as they apply to public policy regarding financial reporting standards, simulation of organizational learning processes, and cultural differences and similarities in multinational corporations.

James L. Mills, PhD, is a professor of international finance and banking at Thunderbird—The American Graduate School of International Management. He has served as visiting faculty at the Institute of International Studies and Training (Japan), McMaster University (Canada), and Stichting Nijenrode (Netherlands). In addition to teaching courses in international treasury management and financial engineering, he is co-author of *Prime Cash: First Steps in Treasury Management* (McGraw-Hill, 1993).

Michael H. Moffett, PhD, is a professor of international finance at Thunderbird—The American Graduate School of International Management. He has served as visiting faculty and researcher at the Helsinki School of Economics (Finland), the International Center for Public Enterprises (Slovenia), Handelsjoskoen I Aarhus (Denmark), the University of Michigan, Ann Arbor (USA), and the Brookings Institution (USA). In addition to teaching classes in international corporate financial management, he is the co-author of *Multinational Business Finance* (Addison-Wesley, 1994) and *International Business* (Dryden, 1995).

Patrice Murphy, PhD, holds degrees in business, labor relations, and political science. Her research interests include cross-cultural issues in performance management, and the effects of diversity on intragroup processes. She is a consultant with Robert H. Shaffer and Associates, Stamford, Connecticut.

Paul Narayanan is an independent financial consultant. He co-authored one of the pioneering works in business failure classification models, the Zeta score model (1977).

Belverd E. Needles Jr., PhD, CPA, is the Anderson LLP Distinguished Professor of Accountancy at DePaul University. He is the author of many publications in the field of international accounting and auditing. He has served as chair of the International Section of the American Accounting Association, has been on the Executive Committee of the European Accounting Association, and served on the Education Committee of the International Federation of Accountants. He is currently president of the International Association for Accounting Education and Research and is senior vice chair of the Illinois CPA Society.

Paul Pacter, PhD, CPA, is director of the Global IAS Office of Deloitte Touche Tohmatsu. He is based in Hong Kong. His primary responsibilities at Deloitte are developing his firm's responses to IASB proposals; responding to client technical questions; writing an IAS newsletter called IASPlus; managing the Website *www.iasplus.com*; training; and a project to assist the Ministry of Finance of China in developing accounting standards. From 1996 to 2000 he was International Accounting Fellow at the International Accounting Standards Committee, London. Previously, he worked for the U.S. Financial Accounting Standards Board from its inception in 1973 and, for seven years, was Commissioner of Finance of the City of Stamford, Connecticut. Paul was vice chairman of the Advisory Council to the U.S. Governmental Accounting Standards Board (1984–1989) and a member of GASB's pensions task force and FASB's consolidation task force.

Lee H. Radebaugh, DBA, is the KPMG Peat Marwick Professor of Accounting at Brigham Young University and Co-Director of the BYU–University of Utah Center for International Business Education and Research. He is the author of *International Business Environments Operations*, 7th ed. (Addison-Wesley) with John D. Daniels, *International Accounting and Multinational Enterprises* (John Wiley & Sons, 3rd Edition) with S. J. Gray, and *Introduction to Business: International Dimensions* (South-Western Publishing Company) with John D. Daniels.

Kurt P. Ramin, MBA, CPA, CEBS, is commercial director, International Accounting Standards Committee Foundation, in London. He is a former partner of PricewaterhouseCoopers LLP, New York. He currently also acts as vice chair for XBRL International, a worldwide consortium to improve worldwide financial reporting.

James R. Ratliff is a retired professor of accounting at the Leonard N. Stern School of Business at New York University. His professional interests include financial accounting, not-for-profit auditing, auditing, and ERISA.

Anthony Saunders is John M. Schiff Professor of Finance and Chair of the Department of Finance at the Stern School of Business at New York University. He holds positions on the Board of Academic Consultants of the Federal Reserve Board of Governors and the Council of Research Advisors for the Federal National Mortgage Association. He is an editor of the *Journal of Banking and Finance* and *Financial Markets, Instruments and Institutions.*

Tony Shieh, PhD, is an assistant professor in the Department of Accountancy at the City University of Hong Kong.

Roy C. Smith is the Kenneth Langone Professor of Entrepreneurship and Finance, and Clinical Professor of International Business and of Professional Responsibility at the Stern School of Business, New York University. Prior to joining the faculty at Stern in 1987, he was a general partner of Goldman, Sachs & Co., specializing in international investment banking and corporate finance. During his career at Goldman Sachs he served as President of Goldman Sachs International Corp. while resident in the firm's London office. In addition to various articles in professional journals and op-ed pieces, he is the author of several books on financial topics.

Richard C. Stapleton is professor of accounting and finance at Strathclyde University, Glasgow, United Kingdom. Formerly, he taught at Lancaster University, University of Cambridge, Manchester Business School, and New York University. He is a past president of the European Finance Association. He has advised several global financial institutions in the area of derivatives. He has also published extensively on asset pricing and financial markets, with particular reference to derivatives.

Donna L. Street, PhD, is the Mahrt Chair in Accounting at the University of Dayton. She is Vice President of Publications for the International Association for Accounting Education and Research and Secretary of the International Accounting Section of the American Accounting Association. Professor Street has published several papers on segment reporting in journals including Journal of International Accounting Research; Accounting Horizons; Journal of International Accounting, Auditing, and Taxation; Accountancy; and Journal of Accountancy.

Marti G. Subrahmanyam is the Charles E. Merrill Professor of Finance, Economics, and International Business at the Stern School of Business, New York University. He has been a visiting professor at leading schools in France, England, Germany, and India. He has served as a consultant to several financial institutions in the United States and abroad, and sits on many board of directors. He has a number of publications in leading academic journals in the areas of corporate finance, financial markets, asset pricing, and international finance.

Judy Tsui, PhD, is the Dean, Faculty of Business and Information Systems, and Chair Professor of Accounting at the Hong Kong Polytechnic University.

Jon A. Turner, PhD, is Professor of Information Systems at the Stern School of Business, New York University, and Deputy Department Chair of the Information, Operations, and Management Sciences Department. His current research involves studies of new forms of organizing work enabled by technology and studies of technology infrastructure.

Norman R. Walker is a partner in the National Auditing Services Group for PricewaterhouseCoopers LLP. He is a former director of MNC Client Services for Price Waterhouse World Firm.

Jeffrey B. Wallace, CPA, is managing partner of Greenwich Treasury Advisors LLC, which he founded in 1992. GTA provides international treasury consulting, and is best known for its treasury benchmarking programs and risk management consulting. He wrote *The Group of 31 Report: Core Practices for Managing Multinational FX Risk* (Association for Finance Professionals, 1999), which may be freely downloaded at *www.greenwichtreasuryc.com.* Formerly, he was Vice President–International Treasury at American Express, an assistant treasurer at both Seagram and Dun & Bradstreet, and a CPA with PricewaterhouseCoopers.

Ingo Walter, PhD, is the Charles Simon Professor of Applied Financial Economics and director of the New York University Salomon Center, Leonard N. Stern School of Business, New York University. He has also held an appointment as Professor of International Management at INSEAD in Fontainbleau, France. He has been a consultant to a number of corporations and banks and has authored some 27 books on international economics and finance as well as articles in various professional journals.

Peter Walton, PhD, FCCA, is a professor of accounting at ESSEC Business School, Paris, France. His research centers on international accounting and comparative regulation of financial reporting. He is editor of *World Accounting Report* and a founder and former co-editor of the *European Accounting Review.* He is a consultant to the United Nations Intergovernmental Working Group of Experts in International Standards of Accounting and Reporting (ISAR).

Harold E. Wyman, PhD, is a retired professor of accounting and former dean of the College of Business Administration at Florida International University. He was a Peat Marwick Fellow and head of the accounting department at the University of Connecticut.

PREFACE

This handbook is intended as a reference for financial managers, credit and security analysts, bankers, lawyers, accountants, auditors, and educators, whose decisions encompass the international dimensions of financial analysis, reporting, and control. It expands and updates the topical coverage of its award-winning predecessor, *The Handbook of International Accounting*, and, in its second edition, the *International Accounting and Finance Handbook.*

Its new title, *International Finance and Accounting Handbook*, emphasizes the fact that many of the decision models for accounting, auditing, and financial reporting come from finance. As financial decisions are premised to a large extent on accounting data, providers of financial information cannot add value unless they are cognizant of the operating processes, products, and decision needs of the user.

The key ingredient of any successful handbook is the expertise of its contributors. On this score, the element that binds the authors of this collaborative effort is their commitment to excellence. It has been, and continues to be, a pleasure and a privilege to be associated with this elite group of authors who combine both technical know-how with practical experience. Indeed, a distinctive feature of this work is the balance between academic and practicing contributors, with many chapters being a collaboration between *town and gown.*

This volume is divided into the following parts:

- *Part I: Globalization of Financial Markets.* A comprehensive examination of current trends in the international markets for financial capital, services, and regulation.
- *Part II: Financial Analysis.* Examines the decision models of users in the areas of foreign investments, treasury management, risk management, corporate valuation, bankruptcy prediction, and portfolio analysis.
- *Part III: World Scene of Accounting and Reporting Practices.* Details the diversity that characterizes accounting measurements, corporate financial disclosure, and auditing standards.
- *Part IV: International Accounting Harmonization.* Describes the institutional responses to international accounting diversity at the regional and international levels.
- *Part V: Reporting Issues.* Covers standards and practices applying to multinational consolidations, financial derivatives, changing prices, asset securitization, segmental and foreign operations, social and environmental disclosures, corporate governance, financial control, performance measurement, and information systems.
- *Part VI: International Transfer Pricing and Taxation.* Comprehensive treatment of objectives, policies, worldwide regulations, and practice treatments.

- *Part VII: International Auditing.* Provides insights into both internal and external auditing requirements in a post-Enron world.

I wish to thank Sheck Cho, Executive Editor at John Wiley & Sons, Inc., who has been with this volume from its inception, and whose encouragement, support, and patience is much appreciated. I also thank Ms. Mary-Grace Tomecki for her assistance in riding herd on late manuscripts. Above all, I am indebted to the select group of contributors who unselfishly gave of their time to contribute to this distinctive undertaking and who add immeasurably to the success of this wonderful team effort.

FREDERICK D.S. CHOI

New York, New York
July 2003

IMPORTANT NOTE:
Because of the rapidly changing nature of information in this field, this product may be updated with annual supplements or with future editions. **Please call 1-877-762-2974 or e-mail us at subscriber@wiley.com to receive any current update at no additional charge.** We will send on approval any future supplements or new editions when they become available. If you purchased this product directly from John Wiley & Sons, Inc., we have already recorded your subscription for this update service.

CONTENTS

INTERNATIONAL FINANCE AND ACCOUNTING HANDBOOK

THIRD EDITION

PART I

GLOBALIZATION OF FINANCIAL MARKETS

CHAPTER 1

INTEGRATION OF WORLD FINANCIAL MARKETS: PAST, PRESENT, AND FUTURE

Roy C. Smith
New York University

CONTENTS

1.1 INTRODUCTION. Financial people know in their bones that their profession goes back a long way. Its frequent association with "the world's oldest profession" may simply be because it is almost as old. After all, the essential technology of finance is simple, requiring little more than arithmetic and minimal literacy, and the environment in which it applies is universal—that is, any situation that involves money, property, or credit, all of which are commodities that have been in demand since humankind's earliest days.

These financial commodities have been put to use to facilitate trade, commerce, and investment and to accommodate the accumulation, preservation, and distribution of wealth by states, corporations, and individuals. Financial transactions can occur in an almost infinite variety, yet they always require the services of banks, whether acting as principal or as agent, and financial markets in which they can operate. Banks have predominantly been local institutions throughout their history, but many have sought international expansion to follow clients abroad or to offer services not available in other countries.

Banks have a long history: a history rich in product diversity, international scope, and continuous change and adaptation. Generally, change has been required to adjust to shifting economic and regulatory conditions, which have on many occasions been drastic. On such occasions banks have collapsed, only to be replaced by others eager to try their hand in this traditionally dangerous but profitable business. New competitors have continually appeared on the scene, especially during periods of rapid economic growth, opportunity, and comparatively light governmental interference. Competitive changes have forced adaptations, too, and in general have improved the level and efficiency of services offered to clients, thereby increasing transactional volume. The one constant in the long history of banking is, perhaps, the sight of new stars rising and old ones setting. Some of the older ones have been able to transform themselves into players capable of competing with the newly powerful houses, but many have not. Thus, the banking industry has much natural similarity to continuous economic restructuring in general.

It is doubtful, however, that there has ever been a time in the long history of banking that the pace of restructuring has been greater than the present. Banking and securities markets during the 1980s and 1990s in particular have been affected by a convergence of several exceptionally powerful forces—deregulation and re-regulation, disintermediation, the introduction of new technology and product innovation, cross-border market integration, and greatly increased competition and consolidation—all of which have occurred in a spiraling expansion of demand for financial services across the globe. Bankers today live in interesting—if exhausting and hazardous—times. In this chapter we will have a look at how we got to where we are today, at the characteristics of the wholesale financial services markets in the early twenty-first century, and some of the unresolved issues that will affect the industry's future.

1.2 ROOTS OF MODERN BANKING. Our modern economic and financial heritage begins with the coming of democratic capitalism, around the time of Adam Smith (1776). Under this system, the state does not intervene in economic affairs unnecessarily, removes barriers to competition and subsidies to favored persons to allow competition to develop freely, and, in general, does not prevent or discourage anyone willing to work hard enough—and who also has access to capital—from becoming a capitalist.

A hundred years after Adam Smith, England was at the peak of its power. Politically, it ruled 25% of the Earth's surface and population. The British economy was by far the strongest and most developed in the world. Its traditional competitors were still partly asleep. France was still sorting itself out after a century of political chaos and a war with Prussia that had gone wrong. Germany was just starting to come together politically, but still had a way to go to catch up with the British in industrial terms. The rest of Europe was not all that important economically. There was a potentially serious problem, however, from reckless and often irresponsible competition from America that fancied itself as a rising economic power. Otherwise, the horizon was comparatively free of competitors. British industry and finance were very secure in their respective positions of world leadership in the 1870s.

English financial markets had made it all possible according to Walter Bagehot, the editor at the time of *The Economist*, who published a small book in 1873 titled *Lombard Street,* which described these markets and what made them tick. England's economic glory, he suggested, was based on the supply and accessibility of capital. After all, he pointed out, what would have been the good of inventing a railroad back in Elizabethan times if there was no way to raise the capital to build it? In poor countries there were no financial resources anyway, and in most European countries money stuck to the aristocrats and the landowners and was unavailable to the market. But in England, Bagehot boasted, there was a place in the City of London—called Lombard Street—where "in all but the rarest of times, money can be always obtained upon good security, or upon decent prospects of probable gain." Such a market, Bagehot continued, was a "luxury which no country has ever enjoyed with even comparable equality before."

However, the real power in the market, Bagehot went on to suggest, is its ability to offer the benefits of leverage to those working their way up in the system, whose goal is to displace those at the top. "In every district," Bagehot explained, "small traders have arisen who discount their bills largely, and with the capital so borrowed, harass and press upon, if they do not eradicate, the old capitalist." The new trader has "obviously an immense advantage in the struggle of trade":

> If a merchant has £50,000 all his own, to gain 10% on it he must make £5,000 a year, and must charge for his goods accordingly; but if another has only £10,000 and borrows £40,000 by discounts (no extreme instance in our modern trade), he has the same capital of £50,000 to use, and can sell much cheaper. If the rate at which he borrows be 5%, he will have to pay £2,000 a year [in interest]; and if, like the old trader he makes £5,000 a year, he will still, after paying his interest, obtain £3,000 a year, or 30% on his own £10,000. As most merchants are content with much less than 30%, he will be able, if he wishes, to forego some of that profit, lower the price of the commodity, and drive the old-fashioned trader—the man who trades on his own capital—out of the market.

Thus, the ambitious "new man," with little to lose and access to credit through the market, can earn a greater return on his money than a risk-averse capitalist who borrows little or nothing. The higher return enables the new man to undercut the other man's prices and take business from him. True, the new man may lose on the venture, and be taken out of the game, but there is always another new man on his way up who is eager to replace him. As the richer man has a lot to lose, he risks it less, and thus is always in the game, continually defending himself against one newcomer or another until finally he packs it in, retires to the country, and invests in government securities instead.

"This increasingly democratic structure of English commerce," Bagehot continued, "is very unpopular in many quarters." On one hand, he says, "it prevents the long duration of great families of merchant princes . . . who are pushed out by the dirty crowd of little men."

> On the other hand, these unattractive democratic defects are compensated for by one great excellence: no other country was ever so little "sleepy," no other was ever so prompt to seize new advantages. A country dependent mainly on great 'merchant princes' will never be so prompt; there commerce perpetually slips more and more into a commerce of routine. A man of large wealth, however intelligent, always thinks, "I have a great income, and I want to keep it. If things go on as they are, I shall keep it, but if they change I *may* not keep it." Consequently he considers every change of circumstance a bore, and thinks of such changes as little as he can. But a new man, who has his way to make in the world, knows that such changes are his opportunities; he is always on the lookout for them, and always heeds them when he finds them. The rough and vulgar structure of English commerce is the secret of its life . . .[1]

---

[1]Walter Bagehot, *Lombard Street, A Description of the Money Market* (London: Henry S. King & Co., 1873), 1–20.

In 1902, a young American named Bernard Baruch took Bagehot's essay to heart and made himself the first of many millions in a Wall Street investment pool, buying control of a railroad on borrowed money. The United States had come of age financially around the turn of the century, and Wall Street would soon displace Lombard Street as the world's center of finance.

(a) The Rise of the Americans. Early in the century, J.P. Morgan organized the United States Steel Corporation, having acquired Carnegie Steel and other companies in a transaction valued at $1.5 billion—an amount worth perhaps $30 billion today. This was the largest financial deal ever done, not surpassed until the RJR–Nabisco leveraged buyout transaction in 1989, and it occurred in 1902 during the first of six merger booms to take place in the United States during the twentieth century and first years of the twenty-first century. Each of these booms was powered by different factors. But in each, rising stock markets and easy access to credit were major contributors.

By the early 1900s New York was beginning to emerge as the world's leading financial center. True, many American companies (especially railroads) still raised capital by selling their securities to investors in Europe—they also sold them to American investors. These investors, looking for places to put their newly acquired wealth, also bought European securities; perhaps thinking they were safer and more reliable investments than those of American companies. By the early years of the twentieth century it was commonplace to find European, Latin American, and some Asian issues in the New York market. This comparatively high level of market integration proved especially beneficial when World War I came—both sides in the conflict sought funds from the United States, both by issuing new securities and by selling existing holdings, though the Allied Powers raised by far the larger amounts.

After World War I, America's prosperity continued while Europe's did not. Banks had a busy time, raising money for corporations, foreign governments, and investment companies and making large loans to investors buying securities. Banks were then "universal." That is, they were free to participate in commercial banking (lending) and investment banking, which at the time meant the underwriting, distribution, and trading of securities in financial markets. Many of the larger banks were also involved in a substantial amount of international business. There was trade to finance all over the world, especially in such mineral-rich areas as Latin America and Australia. There were new securities issues (underwritings) to perform for foreign clients, which in the years before the 1929 crash aggregated around 25% of all business done. There were correspondent banking and custodial (safekeeping) relationships with overseas counterparts and a variety of overseas financial services to perform for individuals, both with respect to foreigners doing business in the United States and the activities abroad of Americans.

The stock market crash in 1929 was a global event—markets crashed everywhere, all at the same time, and the volume of foreign selling orders was high. The Great Depression followed, and the banks were blamed for it, although the evidence has never been strong to connect the speculative activities of the banks during the 1920s with either the crash or the subsequent depression of the 1930s. Nonetheless, there were three prominent results from these events that had great effect on American banking. The first was the passage of the Banking Act of 1933 that provided for the Federal Deposit Insurance system and the Glass–Steagall provisions that completely separated commercial banking and securities activities. Second was the depression itself, which led in the end to World War II and a 30-year period in which banking was confined to basic, slow-growing deposit taking and loan making within a limited local market only. And third was the rising importance of the government in deciding financial matters, especially during the post-war recovery period. As a consequence, there was comparatively little for banks or securities firms to do from the early 1930s until the early 1960s.

By then, world trade had resumed its vigorous expansion and U.S. banks, following the lead of First National City Bank (subsequently Citicorp, now part of Citigroup), resumed their activities abroad. The successful recovery of the economies of Western Europe and Japan led to pressures on the fixed-rate foreign exchange system set up in 1944. The Eurodollar market emerged from a surplus of U.S. currency available outside the country; then the Eurobond market followed and the reattraction of banks and investment banks to international capital market transactions.

(b) Global Banking Reemerges. Next came the 1971 collapse of the fixed exchange rate system in which the dollar was tied to gold and other currencies were tied to the dollar. Floating exchange rates set by the market replaced this system, obviating the need for government capital controls. In turn, this led to widespread removal of restrictions on capital flows between countries, and the beginnings of the global financial system that we have today.

This system, which is based on markets setting prices and determining the flow of capital around the world, has drawn many new players—both users and providers of banking and capital market services. Competition among these players for funds, and the business of providing them, has greatly increased both the stakes and the risks of the banking and securities businesses. But the volume and size of transactions increased steadily through the 1970s and 1980s.

The effects of competitive capitalism have been seen and appreciated during the past decades as they have not been since 1929. The 1980s witnessed further rounds of deregulation and privatization of government-owned enterprises, indicating that governments of industrial countries around the world found private-sector solutions to problems of economic growth and development preferable to state-operated, semi-socialist programs. Massive deregulation of financial markets occurred in the United Kingdom and several other countries. The Single Market Act and Economic and Monetary Union initiatives of the European Union (EU) promised stimulating effects on European business and finance. Deregulation in Japan has (rather more gradually) freed vast sums of capital to seek investment overseas and to create active global securities markets in Tokyo.

Most large businesses are now effectively global, dealing with customers, suppliers, manufacturing, and information centers all over the world. Many corporations are repositioning themselves strategically because of changes in their industry and in traditional markets and among their competitors. In Europe, for example, most sizeable firms must consider themselves as at least continental players, not just national players. The European market, in aggregate, is as large as the market for goods and services in the United States; indeed, it is larger if you include Eastern Europe. No important competitor in any industry can afford not to be active in such a market, but neither can it neglect the markets in the United States. And all competitors seem interested in the emerging markets for goods and services that are developing in India, China, South Asia, and Latin America since these regions began to adopt market economies in a capitalistic form. Global companies have thus become active in world markets as never before, and as a result have become major consumers of international financial services of many types: for capital raising, mergers and acquisitions, and foreign direct investments; for foreign exchange and commodity brokerage; and for investment and tax advice. Governments and financial institutions also have become major users of these financial services for the investment of reserves, the issuance of debt securities, the privatization of state-owned enterprises, the sale of deposits and other bank liabilities, mutual funds, and a variety of investment and hedging services.

1.3 BANKING TODAY: SURVIVAL OF THE FITTEST. Global banking and capital market services proliferated during the 1980s and 1990s as a result of a great increase in demand from companies, governments, and financial institutions, but also because financial market conditions were buoyant and, on the whole, bullish. Interest rates in the United States declined from about 15% for two-year U.S. Treasury notes to about 5% during the 20-year period, and the Dow Jones Index increased nearly 14-fold, driving prices higher in financial markets all over the world. Indeed, financial assets grew then at a rate approximately twice the rate of the world economy, despite significant and regular setbacks in the markets in 1987, 1990, 1994, 1998, and 2001. Such growth and opportunity in financial services, however, entirely changed the competitive landscape—some services were rendered into commodities, commissions and fees were slashed, banks became bold and aggressive in offering to invest directly in their clients' securities without the formation of a syndicate, traditional banker–client relationships were shattered, and, through all this, a steady run of innovation continued—new products, practices, ideas, and techniques for improving balance sheets and earnings. As a result, many firms were unable to remain competitive, some took on too much risk and failed, and others were taken up in mergers or consolidations. Great banking houses such as Baring Brothers, Chase Manhattan, Dillon Read, Dresdner Bank, First Boston, Industrial Bank of Japan, Kidder Peabody, Kuhn Loeb, Midland Bank, J.P. Morgan, National Westminster Bank, Salomon Brothers, Union Bank of Switzerland, and Yamaichi Securities all disappeared into mergers or liquidation. The 1980–2000 years were a difficult time for many banks, but a time of great opportunity for others. For their clients, however, it was a time of prosperity in which the pendulum of profitability swung from favoring the manufacturers of financial services to their users.

(a) Market Integration in 2000. Market integration has been accelerated by several factors that have occurred during the past 20 years. The end of the need for foreign exchange controls has resulted in a free flow of capital between markets of industrially developed countries. Deregulation has removed barriers that impeded access to markets in different parts of the world, by both issuers and financial service providers. Massive improvements in telecommunications capability has made it possible for information available in one part of the world (such as bond prices) to be simultaneously available in many other places. And advances in financial technology (and the infrastructure to support it), such as swaps and other derivatives, have made it possible to take advantage of many new financing opportunities. For example, in 1997, the U.S. Federal National Mortgage Association (FNMA) issued five-year notes denominated in Australian dollars that were sold in the United States, Europe, Asia, and Australia. These notes were priced at a rate very close to the Australian government bond rate, taking advantage of very strong market conditions in Australia at the time. FNMA, advised by a Swiss bank (UBS-Warburg), was able to arrange a simultaneous U.S. dollar/Australian dollar currency swap that enabled FNMA to convert its forward payment obligations in Australian dollars into U.S. dollars. Because the terms of the new issue were very attractive to FNMA, and the cost of the swap was also, the borrower was able to secure funds from an entirely new source at an all-in cost somewhat less than (or certainly no greater than) the cost of funds available to it in the New York market. The swap had been a form of arbitrage that linked the Australian and U.S. bond markets and made a global distribution of the new bonds to international investors possible. FNMA had in the past issued its securities in the Eurobond market also, where investors there must "bid" for the paper in competition with U.S. investors. This continuous stream of new issues (which are frequently accompanied by currency or interest rate swaps) that harness the investment demands of institutional investors all over the world has created a highly integrated world market for debt securities.

Bond market investors, after all, see bonds partly as commodities with two distinctive characteristics only—they represent a certain credit quality (defined by bond ratings) and they extend for a certain duration. An AA bond with a maturity of 12 years and fairly standard call provisions will be expected to provide a certain yield to investors. The bond may be packaged with a swap and sold to investors in any number of different currencies. But in all major bond markets the price of such bonds, translated into home market currency through the swap market, will be about the same, thus indicating a high degree of correlation of returns and therefore of market integration.

There is a much lesser degree of market integration in the case of equities. Each stock is unique, representing not a fixed income return for a specified time but only the prospect of future dividends for an indefinite time. These prospects are still significantly differentiated by national economic conditions (such as labor and capital costs) and other factors that make DaimlerChrysler different from Ford and Toyota. Stock market returns in different countries are not highly correlated as a result, though with increasing international and cross-border investment these correlations are rising, and within certain regions (such as the eurozone within the EU) equity market correlations are starting to become significant.

The merger and acquisition market (sometimes thought of as the market for corporate control) has also experienced considerable integration since the mid-1980s, when mergers outside the United States first came to be significant. In 1985, for example, 89.4% of all global merger and acquisition transactions occurred within the United States or involved either a U.S. buyer or seller. In 1995 that percentage had decreased to 58.8%, and by 2001 to 48.8%. Indeed, after 1999, more mergers occurred outside the United States than within. For the entire period from 1985 through 2001, $12.8 trillion of global mergers and acquisitions have been completed, of which $5.5 trillion were within the United States, $1.9 trillion involved crossborder deals in which one side was a U.S. company, and $5.3 trillion of completed transactions occurred outside the United States, of which $5.0 trillion occurred within Europe.

The merger market requires a healthy supply of willing parties, an availability of capital to finance the deals, transactional know-how and an environment free of impediments to takeovers in order for deals to be done. For international deals, these requirements must apply globally, which, for the most part, they have. The last set of conditions, freedom from barriers to takeovers, does not exist everywhere—nor does it exist anywhere in completely pure form—but many countries, such as Japan, Germany, and several emerging markets in which cross-shareholdings are considerable, access to corporate control is not always available in the market. Over the years, however, barriers to takeovers have been falling and specific barriers to takeovers by foreign corporations are disappearing quickly.

(b) Competitive Issues. The effects of wide-scale market integration, together with greatly increased demand for sophisticated financial services, put great pressure on banks and investment banks seeking to secure a significant share of this rapidly growing and lucrative market. Chief financial officers (CFOs) quickly learned that there were many possibilities for creative, beneficial financing available to them, but they could not expect to receive all of the best ideas and lowest quotes from just one firm. The days of the so-called traditional, "exclusive" investment banking relationship were numbered. Large companies with undisputed access to capital markets around the world would receive frequent proposals from bankers, and before long they began to deal with several. Competitive biddings for conventional new issues became common; exclusive relationships were abandoned, especially after the Securities and Exchange Commission (SEC) adopted Rule 415 that provided for instant access to markets by issuers using a "shelf registration." "Proprietary" financing ideas, however, were reserved for the bank first submitting the idea, such as the global Australian dollar bond issue proposed to FNMA by UBS-Warburg. Of course, once a proprietary idea was revealed, anyone could copy it, and in such cases the mandates would go to the bank bidding the highest price. Banks now had to compete on the basis of best ideas or highest prices even for their traditional clients' business. To be competitive meant opening offices in London, Tokyo, and other locations; developing very advanced trading skills; and being willing to acquire and manage large positions in securities to accommodate clients. Firms must also be able to collect price information from all over the world and analyze it effectively before a competitor was able to in order to stay competitive with the best players. It was difficult, expensive, and risky to do all of these things, and some firms stumbled along the way. However, for those who succeeded, the enormous increase in transactional volume—in stocks, bonds, derivatives, and mergers—provided adequate room for fees and commissions to be compressed and still leave plenty for those able to land the mandates.

Throughout the last 20 years of the last century, however, there was continuous turmoil in and deregulation of the banking industry that changed that industry profoundly. Rapidly rising interest rates in the 1970s squeezed savings and loan organizations, and certain banks in the United States and Europe accustomed to mortgage lending, to the point of a crisis in the industry. Too many low fixed-interest-rate mortgage loans had been made with money obtained by the bank from the short-term deposit market. To offset the problem, some banks made riskier loans in order to gain higher interest rate returns. An ensuing credit crunch was very painful to many such banks, and many failed or nearly failed during the 1980s. Regulators were required to intervene extensively, limiting the freedom of banks and their capacity for growth. During this period, many corporate clients abandoned banks as a source of finance and turned instead to capital markets. In the early 1990s, banks argued that they had survived the worst and were ready to compete for business again, but banking regulations prevented them from keeping up with their investment banking competitors for business in the wholesale market. Regulators were sympathetic, believing that more competition in financial markets would lower costs of capital and stimulate industrial growth and restructuring. As a result, in the United States the McFadden Act restricting banks' interstate activities was repealed. So was the Glass-Steagall Act, which since 1933 had separated commercial and investment banking. The United States also participated in the Basel Agreement (among 12 leading financial countries) to require banks to maintain a minimum amount of capital relative to their risk-weighted assets. In Europe, the EU adopted the Second Banking Directive that allowed banking operations to extend to any member country. In Japan, provisions similar to Glass-Steagall were also repealed. So banks were now free to plunge into the investment banking business to win back their clients from the capital markets to which they had migrated in such large numbers.

But investment banking was risky and involved entirely different skills from the deposit-taking and loan-making commercial banking business they knew well, despite many changes related to credit cards, automated teller machines (ATMs), and a variety of different consumer products. As a result, most American, European, and Asian banks chose to stay focused on consumer and small business finance (including all companies with no or limited access to capital markets) within their national markets and to ignore (or at least deemphasize) the more complex, global wholesale sector which comprised syndicated bank loans, securities underwriting and placements, and merger and acquisition advisory work.

But, of course, a handful of the largest banks with the longest history of corporate banking relationships—in the United States, Europe, and Japan—elected to compete for a fair share of their clients' lending, securities, and merger businesses. But it was difficult for many of them to develop the necessary product skills and support capabilities. It was also necessary to project those capabilities into markets in the United States, Europe, and Asia in competition always with firms with greater product expertise and regional knowledge. This task was especially difficult for Japanese banks, hugely powerful at the end of the 1980s, but very diminished by the Japanese stock market decline, loan write-offs, and the many bank failures and forced mergers that occurred during the 1990s.

Finally, the period of the 1980s and 1990s saw many changes in the competitive alignments within the financial services industry. Many banks demonstrated a preference for the "universal banking" model so prevalent in Europe. Universal banks were free to engage in all forms of financial services, make investments in client companies, and function as much as possible as a "one-stop" supplier of both retail and wholesale financial services. (Others would say that these banks had become financial "conglomerates" and the end of the 1990s had become unwieldy and inefficient.) Even then, however, some European universal banks chose to rid themselves of some of their activities that siphoned off profits, especially their securities businesses and investing in the shares of their industrial clients. Many of these banks would be better off, they thought, specializing in either retail or wholesale services, but not both. Others took an opposite view, so there were many different strategic alignments. Many such possible alignments could be accomplished only by large acquisitions, and there were many of them. As a result, the process narrowed the field of competition in wholesale services considerably. By the end of 2000, a year in which a record level of financial services transactions with a market value of $10.5 trillion occurred, the top ten banks commanded a market share of more than 80% and the top five, 55%. Of the top ten banks ranked by market share, seven were large universal-type banks (three American and four European), and the remaining three were large U.S. investment banks who between them accounted for a 33% market share.

1990			2001		
1	Industrial Bank of Japan	57.1	1	Citigroup	259.7
2	Fuji Bank	52.0	2	American International Group	207.4
3	Mitsui Taiyo Kobe Bank	46.3	3	HSBC Holdings	109.7
4	Sumitomo Bank	46.0	4	Berkshire Hathaway	100.2
5	Dai-Ichi Kangyo Bank	44.8	5	Bank of America	99.0
6	Mitsubishi Bank	44.0	6	Fannie Mae	79.5
7	Sanwa Bank	41.2	7	Wells Fargo	73.7
8	Nomura Securities	25.5	8	J.P. Morgan Chase	71.7
9	Long-Term Credit Bank	24.8	9	Royal Bank of Scotland	69.4
10	Allianz	24.6	10	UBS	67.1
11	Tokai Bank	21.3	11	Allianz	62.9
12	Mitsubishi Trust & Banking	17.2	12	Morgan Stanley Dean Witter	61.4
13	Deutsche Bank	16.4	13	Lloyds TSB	60.3
14	American International Group	16.3	14	Barclays	55.2
15	Bank of Tokyo	15.9	15	Credit Suisse	51.3

Source: Morgan Stanley Capital International.

Exhibit 1.1. Top Financial Firms, Market Capitalization, End Year ($billion).

Consolidation in the industry and concentration of market share had already achieved substantial levels by the year 2000. (See Exhibit 1.1.)

But not all financial service providers were banks. Large corporate players were beginning to find their way into the financial service community, offering competition to established banks. Many of these players had been ignored before their businesses began to overlap. Most prominent among these corporate players were finance subsidiaries of large industrial companies, such as General Electric Capital Services, General Motors Acceptance Corporation, Ford Motor Credit, and others. There were further disturbances in the competitive force by such insurance giants as American International Group, Berkshire Hathaway, and Allianz and such mortgage finance giants as FNMA and its siblings. Indeed, by the end of 2001 the market capitalization of the world's 15 largest financial services providers included four nonbanks (though Allianz, which is included, has since acquired Dresdner Bank). The top 15 such companies included eight U.S. firms and seven Europeans—four British, two Swiss, and one German). By comparison, at the end of 1990, the 15 largest financial firms by market capitalization contained 12 Japanese firms, two German, and one American. The Japanese firms, within the decade, disappeared from the list entirely. (See Exhibit 1.2.)

1.4 FACING THE FUTURE. It is difficult to predict the future and this chapter is not going to attempt it, except to note that there are now certain conditions in place that will affect how the future develops, and we can rely on these conditions to remain in place for some time.

(a) Market Integration is Irreversible. Certainly, the market integration that has developed among the United States, Europe, and Japan will continue to send both borrowers and investors to the cheapest markets, and their experience will reinforce the

Rank	Firm (Rank 2000)	Market Share	Syndicated Bank Loans	Global Debt U/W & Private Placement	Global Equity U/W & Private Placements	M&A Advisory Announced	MTNs Arranged	Total
1	Citigroup (4)	10.81%	278,375	429,342	48,789	476,149	640,797	1,873,452
2	JP Morgan Chase (1)	10.35%	514,476	299,192	14,644	428,011	538,515	1,794,838
3	Merrill Lynch (5)	9.65%	37,987	367,429	61,324	597,350	608,608	1,672,698
4	Goldman Sachs (3)	8.43%	43,953	238,695	60,928	748,990	369,735	1,462,301
5	Morgan Stanley (2)	8.20%	20,060	225,691	44,446	626,839	505,256	1,422,292
6	Credit Suisse Group (6)	6.99%	42,485	303,724	44,225	426,358	395,483	1,212,275
7	UBS-Warburg (9)	5.58%	33,870	220,815	29,662	212,449	470,308	967,104
8	Deutsche Bank (12)	5.29%	83,423	206,799	16,946	119,269	491,265	917,702
9	Lehman Brothers (11)	4.99%	32,760	237,902	18,428	172,180	403,508	864,778
10	Bank of America (8)	3.83%	238,057	151,205	5,746	67,116	202,344	664,468
11	Dresdner Bank (10)	3.12%	48,339	49,202	29,729	343,353	69,822	540,445
12	Barclays (15)	2.38%	58,742	72,722			281,110	412,574
13	ABN AMRO (7)	2.34%	30,869	83,018	4,824	29,173	258,323	406,207
14	BNP Paribas (16)	2.22%	28,938	49,829	4,767	36,599	264,007	384,140
15	Bear Stearns (17)	2.17%	4,492	130,706	3,650	90,569	146,269	375,686

Exhibit 1.2. Global Wholesale Banking Rankings: 2001: Full Credit to Book—Running Manager Only ($ million).

international character of the wholesale market place. This market nexus will encourage other countries and regions to tie into it (e.g., as the countries of the EU have done by allowing the transnational Euromarket to become the principal wholesale financial market for the entire region) and to integrate their own markets to it. Much of this has already happened and will no doubt continue in more advanced emerging market countries.

(b) Regulation Will Continue to Converge. The wholesale market largely consists of institutions, corporations, governments, and sophisticated investors. This group does not need much protection from government securities regulators (in Europe there is no government body that regulates the Euromarkets, and in the United States securities sold to qualified investors may be exempt from registration requirements), and the absence of such regulation is a considerable economic benefit to the market. However, regulation of financial exchanges and of conduct of professional operators is developing in the EU and following established American principles. Regulation of minimum levels of capital for banking institutions, though a continuing work in progress, has developed to embrace all major capital market countries. Surely, these regulatory matters will continue along the paths they are now committed to. The result, however, suggests a moderate amount of reasonable regulation, which is healthy for an integrated, global financial marketplace.

(c) Competition Will Continue to Provide Benefits to Users of Financial Services. The bigger, more robust the market, the more attractive it will be to competitors. There are still many competitors large enough to attempt to secure a prominent position in the market, though the identity of these competitors has changed considerably over time. No doubt this will continue, as will the ongoing debate over whether universal banks with large balance sheets will dominate, or whether quick-adapting, flexible, smaller specialist firms will. European banks have already demonstrated the ability to become competitive in capital markets, recovering somewhat from an earlier period in which American firms were especially prominent. Will Japanese banks and securities firms accomplish the same competitive recovery in the decade ahead? They very well may do so, and we may also see nonbanking enterprises become much more aggressive in stripping business away from the traditional players. But the volume of transactions should continue to rise, providing the base for the motivation by all the competitors to secure a larger market share. Time will tell.

CHAPTER 2

GLOBALIZATION OF THE FINANCIAL SERVICES INDUSTRY

Ingo Walter
New York University

CONTENTS

2.1 INTRODUCTION. Few industries have encountered as much "strategic turbulence" in recent years as has the financial services sector. In response to far-reaching regulatory and technological change, together with important shifts in client behavior and the de facto globalization of specific financial functions, the organizational structure of the industry has been profoundly displaced and there remains a great deal of uncertainty about the nature of any future equilibrium in the industry's contours. At the same time, a major part of the industry has been effectively globalized, linking borrowers and lenders, issuers and investors, risks and risk takers around the world. This chapter deals with the issue of globalization in the context of a coherent analytical framework and spells out the key consequences for the strategic positioning and implementation for financial firms worldwide.

Section 2.2 considers the generic processes and linkages that comprise financial intermediation—the basic "financial hydraulics" that ultimately drive efficiency and innovation in the financial system and its impact on real-sector resource allocation and economic growth. Maximum economic welfare demands a high-performance financial system. What does this actually mean? We also document some of the structural changes that have occurred in both national and global financial systems and suggest how the microeconomics of financial intermediation work. These can have an enormous impact on the industrial structure of the financial services industry and on individual firms. Sequentially, financial channels that exhibit greater static and dynamic efficiency have supplanted less efficient ones. Competitive distortions can retard this process, but they usually extract significant economic costs and at the same time divert financial flows into other venues, either domestically or elsewhere.

Section 2.3 described the specific financial activities that have become most heavily globalized, notably the "wholesale" end of the financial spectrum that links end users through increasingly seamless global financial market structures.

Finally, Section 2.4 examines the consequences of this process in terms of financial sector reconfiguration, both within and between the four major segments of the industry (commercial banking, securities and investment banking, insurance, and asset management) as well as within and between national financial systems.

2.2 A STYLIZED PROCESS OF FINANCIAL INTERMEDIATION. The central component of any model of a modern financial system is the nature of the conduits through which the financial assets of the ultimate savers flow through to the liabilities of the ultimate users of finance, both within and between national economies. This involves alternative and competing modes of financial intermediation, or "contracting," between counterparties in financial transactions.

A guide to thinking about financial contracting and the role of financial institutions and markets is summarized in Exhibit 2.1. The exhibit depicts the financial process (flow-of-funds) among the different sectors of the economy in terms of underlying

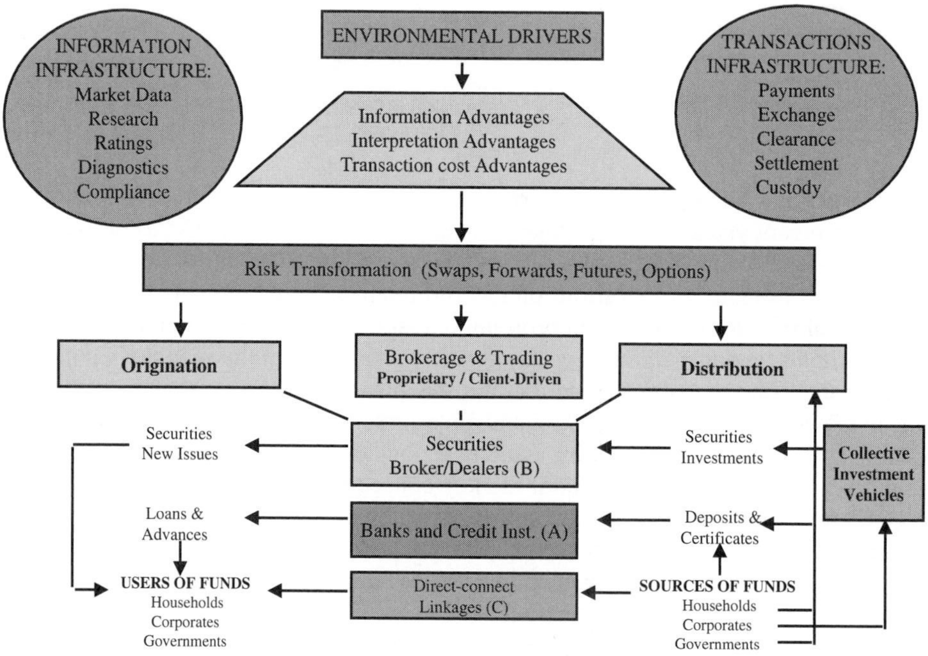

Exhibit 2.1. Intermediation Dynamics.

environmental and regulatory determinants or drivers as well as the generic advantages needed to profit from three primary linkages:

1. *Fully intermediated financial flows.* Savings (the ultimate sources of funds in financial systems) may be held in the form of deposits or alternative types of claims issued by commercial banks, savings organizations, insurance companies, or other types of financial institutions that finance themselves by placing their liabilities directly with the general public. Financial institutions ultimately use these funds to purchase assets issued by nonfinancial entities such as households, firms, and governments.
2. *Investment banking and securitized intermediation.* Savings may be allocated directly or indirectly via fiduciaries and collective investment vehicles, to the purchase of securities publicly issued and sold by various public- and private-sector organizations in the domestic and international financial markets.
3. *Direct-connect mechanisms between ultimate borrowers and lenders.* Savings surpluses may be allocated to borrowers through various kinds of direct-sale mechanisms, such as private placements, usually involving fiduciaries as intermediaries.

Ultimate *users* of funds comprise the same three segments of the economy—the household or consumer sector, the business sector, and the government sector.

1. Consumers may finance purchases by means of personal loans from banks or by loans secured by purchased assets (hire-purchase or installment loans). These may appear on the asset side of the balance sheets of credit institutions for the duration of the respective loan contracts on a revolving basis, or they may be sold off into the financial market in the form of various kinds of securities backed by consumer credit receivables.
2. Corporations may borrow from banks in the form of unsecured or asset-backed straight or revolving credit facilities and/or may sell debt obligations (e.g., commercial paper, receivables financing, fixed-income securities of various types) or equities directly into the financial market.
3. Governments may likewise borrow from credit institutions (sovereign borrowing) or issue securities directly.

Borrowers such as corporations and governments also have the possibility of privately issuing and placing their obligations with institutional investors, thereby circumventing both credit institutions and the public debt and equity markets. Consumer debt can also be repackaged as asset-backed securities and sold privately to institutional investors.

In the first mode of financial contracting in Exhibit 2.1, depositors buy the "secondary" financial claims or liabilities issued by credit institutions, and benefit from liquidity, convenience, and safety through the ability of financial institutions to diversify risk and improve credit quality by means of professional management and monitoring of their holdings of primary financial claims (both debt and equity). Savers can choose from among a set of standardized contracts and receive payments services and interest.

In the second mode of financial intermediation in Exhibit 2.1, investors can select their own portfolios of financial assets directly from among the publicly issued debt and equity instruments on offer. This may provide a broader range of options than standardized bank contracts and permit the larger investors to tailor portfolios more closely to their objectives while still achieving acceptable liquidity through rapid and cheap execution of trades—aided by linkages with banks and other financial institutions that are part of the domestic payments mechanism. Investors may also choose to have their portfolios professionally managed, for a fee, through various types of mutual funds and pension funds—designated in Exhibit 2.1 as collective investment vehicles.

In the third mode of financial intermediation, institutional investors buy large blocks of privately issued securities. In doing so, they often face a liquidity penalty—due to the absence or limited availability of a liquid secondary market—for which they are rewarded by a higher yield. However, directly placed securities can be specifically "tailored" to more closely match issuer and investor requirements than can publicly issued securities. Market and regulatory developments (such as Securities and Exchange Commission [SEC] Rule 144A in the United States) have added to the liquidity of some direct-placement markets.

Value to ultimate savers and investors, inherent in the financial processes described here, accrues in the form of a combination of yield, safety, and liquidity. Value to ultimate users of funds accrues in the form of a combination of financing cost, transactions cost, flexibility, and liquidity. This value can be enhanced through credit backstops, guarantees, and derivative instruments such as forward rate agreements, caps, collars, futures, and options. Furthermore, markets can be linked functionally and geographically, both domestically and internationally. Functional linkages permit bank receivables, for example, to be repackaged and sold to nonbank securities investors. Privately placed securities, once they have been seasoned, may be able to be sold in public markets. Geographic linkages make it possible for savers and issuers to gain incremental benefits in foreign and offshore markets, thereby enhancing liquidity and yield or reducing transaction costs.

(a) Static and Dynamic Efficiency Characteristics of Financial Systems. *Static efficiency* properties of the three alternative financial processes can be measured by the all-in, weighted average spread (differential) between rates of return provided to ultimate savers and the cost of funds to users. This spread is a proxy for the total cost of using a particular type of financial process, and is reflected in the monetary value of resources consumed in the course of financial intermediation. In particular, it reflects direct costs of financial intermediation (operating and administrative costs, cost of capital, etc.). It also reflects losses incurred in the financial process, as well as any excess profits earned and liquidity premiums. Financial processes that are considered "statically inefficient" are usually characterized by high all-in margins due to high overhead costs, high losses, concentrated markets and barriers to entry, and so on.

Dynamic efficiency is characterized by high rates of financial product and process innovation through time:

- *Product innovations* usually involve creation of new financial instruments along with the ability to replicate certain financial instruments by bundling or rebundling existing ones (synthetics). There are also new approaches to contract pricing, new investment techniques, and other innovations that fall under this rubric.

- *Process innovations* include contract design and methods of trading, clearance and settlement, custody, techniques for efficient margin calculation, and so on. Successful product and process innovation broadens the menu of financial services available to ultimate issuers, ultimate savers, or other participants in the various financial channels described in Exhibit 2.1.

It is against a background of continuous pressure for static and dynamic efficiency that financial markets and institutions have evolved and converged. Global financial markets for foreign exchange, debt instruments, and, to a lesser extent, equity have developed various degrees of "seamlessness," and it is arguable that the most advanced of the world's financial markets are approaching a theoretical, "complete" optimum wherein there are sufficient financial instruments and markets, and combinations thereof, to span the whole state-space of risk and return outcomes. Financial systems that are deemed inefficient or incomplete tend to be characterized by a limited range of financial services and obsolescent financial processes.

Exhibit 2.2 gives some indication of recent technological change in financial intermediation, particularly leveraging the properties of the Internet. Although not all of these initiatives have been successful or will survive, some have enhanced financial intermediation efficiencies. Internet applications have already dramatically cut information and transaction costs for both retail and wholesale end users of the financial system as well as for financial intermediaries themselves. The examples of online banking and insurance and retail brokerage given in Exhibit 2.2 are well known and continue to evolve and change the nature of the process, sometimes turning prevailing business models on their heads. For example, financial intermediaries have traditionally charged for transactions and provided advice almost for free, but increasingly are forced to provide transaction services almost for free and to charge for advice. The new models are often far more challenging for market participants.

At the same time, online distribution of financial instruments such as commercial paper, equities, and bonds in primary capital markets not only cuts the cost of market access but also improves and deepens the distribution and book-building process—including providing issuers with information on the investor base. And as Exhibit 2.1 suggests, it is only one further step to cutting out the intermediary altogether by putting the issuer and the investor or fiduciary into direct electronic contact. The same is true in secondary markets, as shown in Exhibit 2.2, with an increasing array of alliance-based competitive bidding utilities (FXall) and reverse auctions (Currenex) in foreign exchange and other financial instruments as well as interdealer brokerage, cross-matching and electronic communications networks (ECNs). When all is said and done, Internet-based technology overlay is likely to have turbocharged the cross-penetration story depicted in Exhibit 2.1.

A further development consists of attempts at automated end-user platforms such as CFOWeb (now defunct) for corporate treasury operations and Quicken 2002 for households, with real-time downloads of financial positions, risk profiles, market information, research, and so on. By allowing end users to "cross-buy" financial services from best-in-class vendors, such utilities could upset conventional thinking that focuses on "cross-selling," notably at the retail end of the end-user spectrum. If this is correct, financial firms that are following Allfinanz or bancassurance (universal banking) strategies may end up trapped in the wrong business model, as open-architecture approaches facilitating easy access to best-in-class suppliers begin to gain market share.

Retail banking:
On-line banking (CS Group, Bank-24, E*loan, Amex Membership *B@nking*, ING Direct, Egg)

Insurance:
ECoverage (P&C) *[defunct 2002]*
EPrudential term and variable life

Retail brokerage:
E-brokerage (Merrill Lynch, MSDW, Fidelity, Schwab, E*trade, DJL Direct, Consors)

Primary capital markets:
E-based CP & bond distribution (UBS Warburg, Goldman Sachs)

E-based direct issuance:
Governments (TreasuryDirect, World Bank)
Municipals (Bloomberg Municipal, MuniAuction, Parity)
Corporates (CapitaLink (defunct), Intervest)
IPOs (W.R. Hambrecht, Wit Soundview, Schwab, E*Trade)

Secondary Financial Markets
Forex (***Atriax*** [defunct 2002], Currenex, FXall, FX Connect)
Governments (Bloomberg Bond Trader, QV Trading Systems, Trade Web EuroMTS)
Municipals (QV Trading Systems, Variable Rate Trading System)
Corporates (QV Trading Systems)
Government debt cross-matching (Automated Bond System, Bond Connect, Bondnet)
Municipal debt cross-matching (Automated Bond System)
Corporate debt cross-matching (Automated Bond System, Bond Connect, Bondlink, Bondnet Limitrader, *BondBook* [defunct 2001])
Debt interdealer brokerage (Brokertec, Primex)
Equities—ECNs (Instinet, Island, Redi-Book, B-Trade, Brut, Archipelago, Strike, Eclipse)
Equities—cross-matching (Barclays Global Investors, Optimark)
Research (Themarkets.com)

End-user Platforms:
Corporate finance and end-user platforms (CFOWeb.com—now defunct)
Institutional investor utilities
Household finance utilities (Quicken 2002, Yodlee.com)

Exhibit 2.2. E-Applications in Financial Services (January 2002).

Both static and dynamic efficiency in financial intermediation are of obvious importance from the standpoint of national and global resource allocation. That is, since financial services can be viewed as inputs to real economic processes, the level of national output and income—as well as its rate of economic growth—are directly or indirectly affected. A "retarded" financial services sector can be a major impediment to a nation's overall economic performance. Financial-system retardation represents a burden on the final consumers of financial services and potentially reduces the level of private and social welfare. It also represents a burden on producers, by raising their cost of capital and eroding their competitive performance in domestic and global markets. These inefficiencies ultimately distort the allocation of labor as well as capital.

(b) The Facts: Shifts in Intermediary Market Shares. Developments over the past several decades in intermediation processes and institutional design across both time and geography are striking. In the United States, "commercial banks"—institutions that accept deposits from the public and make commercial loans—have seen their market share of domestic financial flows between end users of the financial system decline from about 75% in the 1950s to under 25% today. In Europe the change has been much less dramatic, and the share of financial flows running though the balance sheets of banks continues to be well over 60%—but declining nonetheless. And in Japan, banks continue to control in excess of 70% of financial intermediation flows. Most emerging market countries cluster at the highly intermediated end of the spectrum, but in many of these economies there is also factual evidence of declining market shares of traditional banking intermediaries. Classic banking functionality, in short, has been in long-term decline more or less worldwide.

Where has all the money gone? Disintermediation as well as financial innovation and expanding global linkages have redirected financial flows through the securities markets. Exhibit 2.3 shows developments in the United States from 1970 to 2000, highlighting the extent of commercial bank market share losses and institutional investor gains. While this may be an extreme case, even in highly intermediated financial systems like Germany (Exhibit 2.4) direct equity holdings and managed funds have increased from 9.6% to 22.7% in just the 1990–2000 period.

Ultimate savers increasingly use the fixed-income and equity markets directly and through fiduciaries, which, through vastly improved technology, are able to provide substantially the same functionality as classic banking relationships—immediate access to liquidity, transparency, safety, and so on—coupled to a higher rate of return. The one thing they cannot guarantee is settlement at par, which in the case of transactions balances (e.g., money market mutual funds) is mitigated by portfolio constraints mandating high-quality, short-maturity financial instruments. Ultimate users

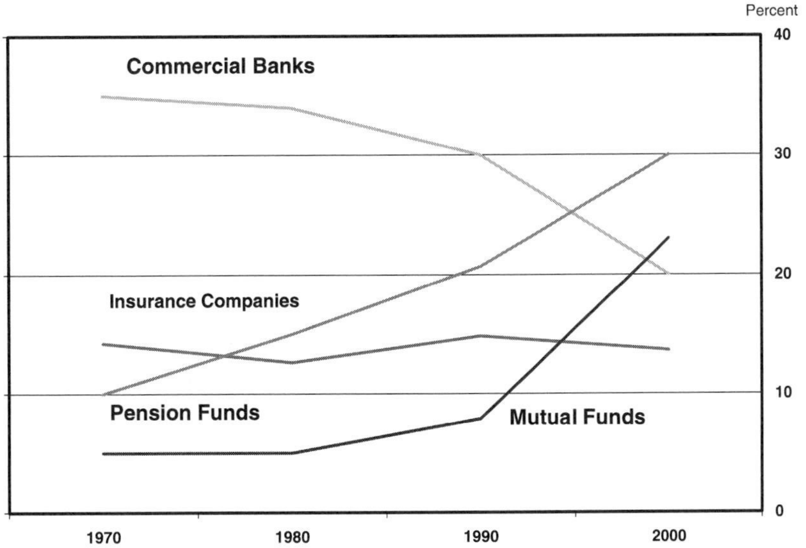

Source: Federal Reserve.

Exhibit 2.3. U.S. Financial Assets, 1970–2000.

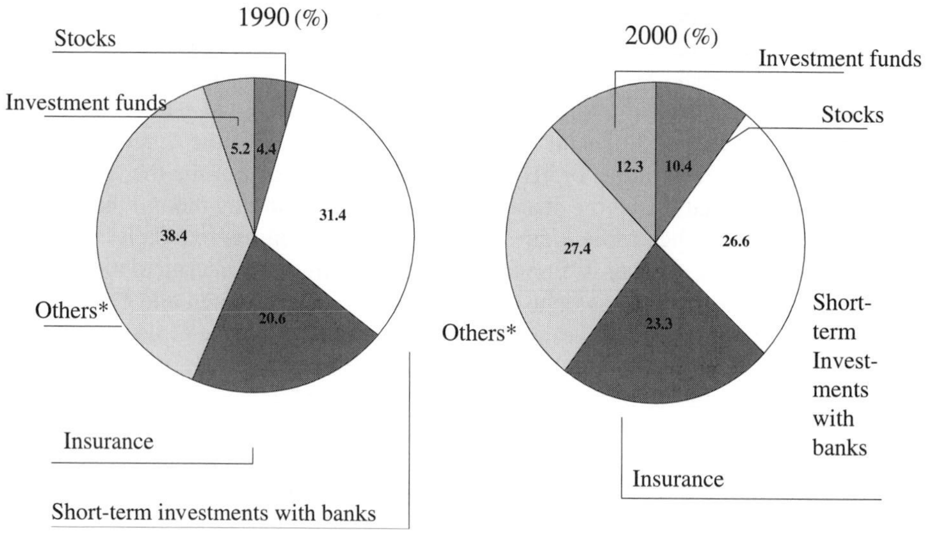

**Includes fixed interest deposits, long-term investments with banks and building society deposits.*

Sources: Tecis; J.P. Morgan.

Exhibit 2.4. Private Asset Allocation in German Households.

of funds have benefitted from enhanced access to financial markets across a broad spectrum of maturity and credit quality using conventional and structured financial instruments. Although market access and financing cost normally depend on the current state of the market, credit and liquidity backstops can be easily provided.

At the same time, a broad spectrum of derivatives overlays the markets, making it possible to tailor financial products to the needs of end users with increasing granularity, further expanding the availability and reducing the cost of financing on the one hand and promoting portfolio optimization on the other. And as the end users have themselves been forced to become more performance oriented in the presence of much greater transparency and competitive pressures, it has become increasingly difficult to justify departures from highly disciplined financial behavior on the part of corporations, public authorities, and institutional investors.

In the process, two important and related differences are encountered in this generic financial-flow transformation. Intermediation shifts, in the first place, from book-value to market-value accounting and, in the second place, from more intensively regulated to less intensively regulated channels, generally requiring less oversight and less capital. Both have clear implications for the efficiency properties of financial systems and for their transparency, safety, and soundness. Regulatory focus in this context has migrated from institutions to markets.

2.3 GLOBALIZED BANKING ACTIVITIES. The globalized part of the financial services industry comprises the so-called wholesale sector and is today serviced by both commercial banks and investment banks, although both of these types of banks also provide a wide range of retail and mid-sized corporate services. Clients of wholesale finance providers are governments, corporations, banks, and investment managers of many types. The services offered by wholesale finance firms include bank lending, securities market transactions, mergers and corporate restructuring advisory services, and asset management. In this chapter we refer to wholesale financial service providers as *investment banks*, although traditional investment banks now engage in many other services, and other types of financial service firms (such as traditional commercial banks and universal banks) also offer wholesale market services.

Investment banking is among those financial-sector activities that have had important catalytic effects on the global economy. Investment banks are key facilitators. They help reduce information and transaction costs, help raise capital, bring buyers and sellers together, improve liquidity, and generally make a major contribution to both the static (resource-allocation) and dynamic (growth-related) dimensions of economic efficiency. In terms of their impact on overall economic development and restructuring, in advanced and emerging-market economies alike, investment banks have an interesting and important role to play. The overall market for financial instruments within which wholesale financial services forms operate can be illustrated by the schematic appearing as Exhibit 2.5.

At the core of the market are foreign exchange and money market instruments. There is virtually complete transparency in these markets, high liquidity, large numbers of buyers and sellers—probably as close to the economists' definition of perfect competition as one gets in global financial markets.

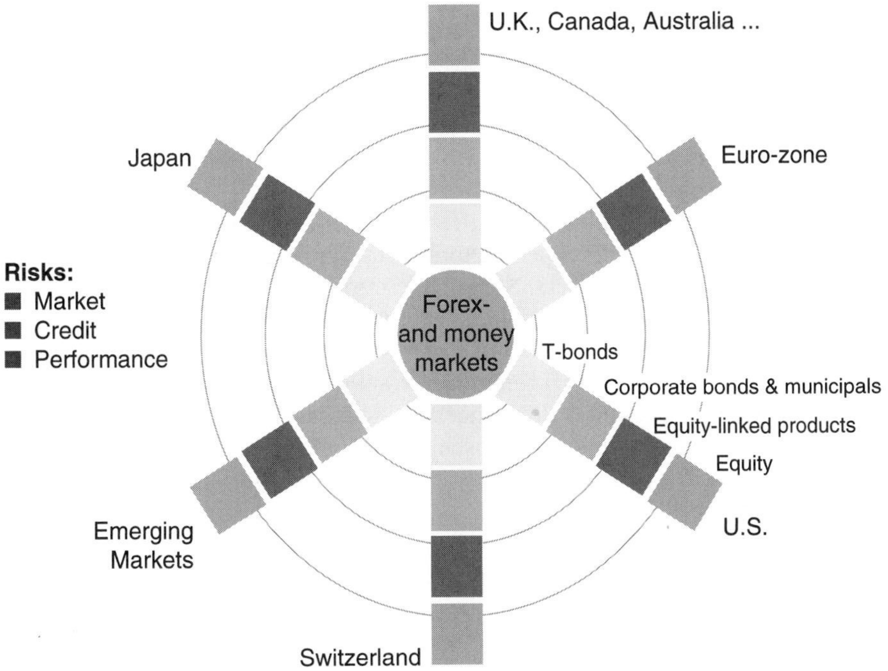

Exhibit 2.5. Global Financial Markets.

Moving out from the center of the diagram, the next most perfect market comprises sovereign debt instruments in their respective national markets, which carry no credit risk (only market risk) and usually are broadly and continuously traded. Sovereign debt instruments purchased by foreign investors, of course, also carry foreign exchange risk and the (arguably minor) risk of repudiation of sovereign obligations to foreign investors. If these sovereign debt instruments are denominated in foreign currencies, they carry both currency risk and country risk (the risk of inability or unwillingness to service foreign-currency debt). Sovereign debt instruments run the gamut from AAA-rated obligations that may be traded in broad and deep markets all the way to non-investment-grade, highly speculative "country junk."

Next come state, local, and corporate bonds, which range across the quality spectrum from AAA-rated corporate and municipal securities that trade in liquid markets fractionally above sovereigns, all the way to high-yield non-investment-grade and nonrated bonds. Also included in this category are asset-backed securities and syndicated bank loans, which may be repackaged and resold once issued.

Then there are common stocks of corporations that trade in secondary markets and constitute the brokerage business. Equity securities are also issued, underwritten and distributed by investment banks. Between corporate bonds and equities lie hybrid financial instruments such as convertible bonds and preferred stocks and warrants to buy securities at some time in the future, which in turn can sometimes be "stripped" and sold in the "covered warrant" market. Well out on the periphery of Exhibit 2.5 is venture capital and private equity, which tends to be speculative with little or no liquidity until an exit vehicle is found through sale to another company or an initial public offering (IPO).

As one moves from the center of Exhibit 2.5 to the periphery in any given financial market environment, information and transaction costs tend to rise, liquidity tends to fall, and risks (e.g., market risk, credit risk, and/or performance risk) tend to rise. Along the way, there are a host of "structured" financial products and derivatives that blend various characteristics of the underlying securities in order to better fit into investors' portfolio requirements and/or issuer/borrower objectives. There are also index-linked securities and derivatives, which provide opportunities to invest in various kinds of asset baskets.

Finally, each geographic context is different in terms of size, liquidity, infrastructure, market participants, and related factors. Some have larger and more liquid government bond markets than others. Some have traditions of bank financing of business and industry, while others rely more heavily on public and private debt markets. Some have broad and deep equity markets, while others rely on permanent institutional shareholdings. Some are far more innovative and performance oriented than others. In addition to structural differences, some—such as the euro-zone since its creation in 1999—may be subject to substantial and rapid shift.[1] Such discontinuities can be highly favorable to the operations of wholesale and investment banking firms, and provide rich opportunities for arbitrage. But they can also involve high levels of risk.

Financial intermediaries that perform well tend to have strong comparative advantages in the *least perfect* corners of the global financial market. Banks with large market shares in traditional markets that are not easily accessed by others are exam-

[1]See Smith & Walter, 2000(b).

ples of this. Sometimes, intermediaries specialize in particular sectors, types of clients, regions, or products. Some have strong businesses in the major wholesale markets and as a result are able to selectively leverage their operating platforms to access markets that are less efficient. They may also be able to cross-link on a selective basis both the major and peripheral markets as interest rates, exchange rates, market conditions, and borrower or investor preferences change, for example, by financing the floating-rate debt needs of a highly rated American corporation by issuing fixed-rate Australian dollar bonds at an especially good rate, and then swapping the proceeds into floating rate U.S. dollars. These cross-links—permitting the intermediary to creatively marry opportunistic users of finance to opportunistic investors under ever-changing market conditions—are what in many cases separate the winners from the losers.

(a) Wholesale Finance Market Activity Segments. Global wholesale banking involves a range of businesses that service the financial and strategic needs of corporate and institutional clients, trading counterparties, and institutional investors. In this section of the chapter we characterize the key wholesale and investment banking product lines, and in the appendix indicate where data are available and which were the leading firms in 1999 in each segment. In subsequent sections of the chapter we attempt to explain the underlying reasons for the wide differences that appear to prevail in competitive performance among firms in the industry.

(i) Wholesale Lending. Loan syndication comprises an important wholesale finance activity. It involves the structuring of short-term loans and "bridge" financing, credit backstops and enhancements, longer-term project financing, and standby borrowing facilities for corporate, governmental, and institutional clients. The loan syndicate manager often "sells down" participation to other banks and institutional investors. The loans may also be repackaged through special-purpose vehicles into securities that are sold to capital market investors. Syndicated credit facilities are put together by lead managers who earn origination fees, and jointly with other major syndicating banks earn underwriting fees for fully committed facilities. These fees usually differ according to the complexity of the transaction and the credit quality of the borrower, and there are additional commitment, legal, and agency fees involved as well.

Global lending volume increased rapidly in the 1990s and the early 2000s. The business is very competitive, with loan spreads often squeezed to little more than 10 to 20 basis points. Wholesale loans tend to be funded in the interbank market, usually in Eurocurrencies. In recent years investment banks, such as Goldman Sachs & Co., Lehman Brothers, and Merrill Lynch, have moved into what was once almost exclusively the domain of commercial banks, and many commercial banks, such as Citibank, Crédit Suisse, NatWest, and J.P. Morgan, have backed away from lending in this sector to focus on structuring deals and trying to leverage their lending activity into fee-based services. The firms coming in find it important to be able to finance client requirements with senior bank loans (at least temporarily) as well as securities issues, especially in cases of mergers and acquisitions on which they may be advising. Those departing the business are concerned about the high costs of doing business and the low returns.

(ii) Securities Underwriting. The securities market new-issue activity usually involves an underwriting function that is performed by investment banks. Corporations

or government agencies issue the securities. Sovereign governments tend to issue bonds to the markets directly, without underwriting. The U.S. securities market accommodates the greatest volume of new issues, and the international securities markets based in Europe comprise most of the rest. Domestic market issues of corporate stocks and bonds have historically been comparatively modest outside the United States.

Underwriting of securities is usually carried out through domestic and international syndicates of securities firms with access to local investors, investors in various important foreign markets such as Japan and Switzerland, and investors in offshore markets (Eurobonds), using one of several distribution techniques. In some markets "private placements" occur in cases in which securities are directed not at public investors but only at selected institutional investors. Access to various foreign markets is facilitated by means of interest-rate and currency swaps (swap-driven issues). Some widely distributed, multimarket issues have become known as "global issues." In some markets, intense competition and deregulation have narrowed spreads to the point that the number of firms in underwriting syndicates has declined over time, and in some cases a single participating firm handles an entire issue—in a so-called bought deal.

Commercial paper and medium-term note (MTN) programs maintained by corporations, under which they can issue short-term and medium-term debt instruments on their own credit standing and more or less uniform legal documentation, have become good substitutes for bank credits. Financial institutions provide services in designing these programs, obtaining agency ratings, and dealing the securities into the market when issued. In recent years, MTN programs have become one of the most efficient ways for borrowers to tap the major capital markets.

Underwriting of equity securities is usually heavily concentrated in the home country of the issuing firm, which is normally where the investor base and the secondary-market trading and liquidity is to be found. Corporations periodically issue new shares for business capital, but the principal source of new supplies of stocks to the market has come from government privatization programs. New issues of stocks may also involve companies issuing shares to the public for the first time (IPOs), existing shareholders of large positions selling their holdings, and issues by companies of new shares to existing shareholders (rights issues).

(iii) Privatizations. Sales of state-owned enterprises (SOEs) to the private sector became a major component of global wholesale financial services in the early 1980s. Privatizations generally involve the sale of the IPO of a large corporation, but they have also involved the sale of SOEs to corporate buyers, and substantial advice giving on how the processes should work to satisfy the public interests. They have run the gamut from state-owned manufacturing and service enterprises to airlines, telecommunications, infrastructure providers, and so on, using various approaches such as sales to domestic or foreign control groups, local market flotations, global equity distributions, sales to employees, and the like.

(iv) Trading. Once issued, bonds, notes, and shares become trading instruments in the financial markets, and the underwriters remain active as market makers and as proprietary investors for their own accounts. Secondary-market trading is also conducted by investment bankers in other instruments including foreign exchange, derivative securities of various types, and commodities and precious metals. Trading

activities include market making (executing client orders, including block trades), proprietary trading (speculation for the firm's own account), "program trading" (computer-driven arbitrage between different markets), and "risk arbitrage," usually involving speculative purchases of stock on the basis of public information relating to pending mergers and acquisitions—a market traditionally dominated by commercial banks but increasingly penetrated by insurance companies and investment banking firms as well.

(v) Brokerage. Agency business is an important and traditional part of the securities and investment banking industry. Its key area is brokerage, involving executing buy or sell orders for customers without actually taking possession of the security or derivative contract, sometimes including complex instructions based on various contingencies in the market. Brokerage tends to be highly oriented to retail as opposed to wholesale business, although many of the financial market utilities discussed below are aimed at providing more efficient vehicles for classic brokerage functions as they affect institutional investors.

(vi) Investment Research. Research into factors affecting the various financial markets, as well as individual securities and derivatives, specific industries, and macroeconomic conditions, has become an important requirement for competitive performance in investment banking. Research is made available to clients by more or less independent analysts within the firm. Research analysts' reputation and compensation depend on the quality of their insights, usually focused on specific industries or sectors in the case of equity research. The value of research provided to clients depends critically on its quality and timeliness, and is often compensated by business channeled though the firm, such as brokerage commissions and underwriting or advisory mandates. Closely allied are other research activities—often highly technical modeling exercises—involving innovative financial instruments that link market developments to value-added products for issuer-clients and/or investor-clients. Over the years, research carried out by investment banks (called "sell-side" research) has become increasingly important in soliciting and retaining investment banking clients, a condition that has increasingly placed their objectivity in question.

(vii) Hedging and Risk Management. Hedging and risk management mainly involves the use of derivative instruments to reduce exposure to risk associated with individual securities transactions or markets affecting corporate, institutional, or individual clients. These include interest-rate caps, floors and collars, and various kinds of contingent contracts, as well as futures and options on various types of instruments. It may be quicker, easier, and cheaper, for example, for an investor to alter the risk profile of a portfolio using derivatives than by buying and selling the underlying instruments. In modern wholesale financial markets, the ability to provide risk management services to clients depends heavily on a firm's role in the derivatives market, particularly over-the-counter (OTC) derivatives that allow structuring of what are frequently highly complex risk management products.

(viii) Advisory Services. Corporate finance activities of investment banks predominantly relate to advisory work on mergers, acquisitions, divestitures, recapitalizations, leveraged buyouts, and a variety of other generic and specialized corporate transactions. They generally involve fee-based assignments for firms wishing to ac-

quire others or firms wishing to be sold (or to sell certain business units) to prospective acquirers.

This business sector (usually called "M&A business") is closely associated with the market for corporate control, and may involve assistance to and fund-raising efforts for hostile acquirers or plotting defensive strategies for firms subjected to unwanted takeover bids. It may also involve providing independent valuations and "fairness opinions" for buyers or sellers of companies to protect against lawsuits from disgruntled investors alleging that the price paid for a company was either too high or too low. Such activities may be domestic, within a single national economy, or cross-border, involving parties from two different countries. The global M&A marketplace has been extraordinarily active in recent years, with a majority of the transactions in it being outside the United States.

(ix) Principal Investing. So-called merchant banking (a term used by U.S. investment banks) involves financial institutions' placing their clients' and their own capital on the line in private placement investments of (usually) nonpublic equity securities (e.g., venture capital, real estate, and leveraged buyouts) and certain other equity participations. It may sometimes involve large, essentially permanent stakeholdings in business enterprises, including board-level representation and supervision of management. Or it may involve short-term subordinated lending (bridge loans or mezzanine financing) to assure the success of an M&A transaction. Firms began to participate in these investments in the late 1980s to take advantage of the opportunity to participate in the high expected returns that were a natural part of their natural "deal flow."

An important dimension of merchant banking today involves greater emphasis on venture capital with the idea that the firms would not only benefit from the success of the investment per se, but they would also arrange the IPO and any other financial services needed afterward. Virtually all of the global investment banks have now established private equity or venture capital units.

(x) Investment Management and Investor Services. There are a variety of asset-allocation services provided to institutional and individual investors, as well as technology-intensive investor services that reduce transactions costs, improve market information and transparency, and facilitate price discovery and trading. Key activities are institutional asset management and private banking. With respect to institutions, major investors such as pension funds and insurance companies may allocate blocks of assets to be managed against specific performance targets or "bogeys" (usually stock or bond indexes). Closed-end or open-end mutual funds or unit trusts may also be operated by broker-dealers, banks, or fund management firms and either marketed to selected institutions or mass-marketed to the general investor community either as tax-advantaged pension holdings or to capture general household savings. Private banking for high-net-worth individuals usually involves assigning discretionary or active asset management to financial institutions within carefully structured parameters. These may link asset management to tax planning, estates and trusts, and similar services in a close personal relationship with an individual private banking officer that involves a high level of discretion. Many (notably offshore) private clients are confidentiality driven, which makes them comparatively less sensitive to normal risk–return considerations and more sensitive to trust vested in the bank and the banker.

Top asset managers are dispersed worldwide, based in part on the location of the major savings pools and insurance markets. The United States is heavily represented based on firms managing the assets of classic defined-benefit pension funds as well as mutual fund companies and large life insurers. Europe's presence is mainly represented by the insurance sector and the major universal banks—which dominate mutual fund distribution in most countries—plus the private banking assets of the Swiss banks. The fact that much of the reconfiguration with respect to global pension programs will be centered in Europe points to significant future developments in this industry, including strong penetration of the European environment by U.S. asset managers.

(xi) Infrastructure Services. There are an array of services that lies between buyers and sellers of securities, domestically as well as internationally, which are critical for the effective operation of securities markets. These center on domestic and international systems for trading (notably, electronic communication networks [ECNs]) and for clearing and settling securities transactions via efficient central securities depositories (CSDs). These are prerequisites for a range of services, often supplied on the basis of quality and price by competing private-sector vendors of information services, analytical services, trading services and information processing, credit services, securities clearance and settlement, custody and safekeeping, and portfolio diagnostics.

Investor services represent financial market utilities that tend to be highly scale and technology intensive. Classic examples include Euroclear, a Belgian cooperative that was pioneered by and had a long-standing operating agreement with J.P. Morgan. Many banks and securities firms have stakes in investor services utilities, which can generate attractive risk-adjusted returns for financial services firms if all-important costs and technologies are well managed.

All of these activities have to be organized in an effective structure that in most cases has come to form a so-called full-service global wholesale banking capability, which comprises market-access services (debt and equity originations); trading and brokerage; and corporate advisory services, including M&A activities, principal investing, asset management, and (sometimes) investor services. Such a structure may be reflected in an independent investment bank or (at least in part) the investment banking division of a universal bank or financial conglomerate.

2.4 CONSEQUENCES FOR GLOBAL INSTITUTIONAL COMPETITIVE ADVANTAGE. The basic microeconomics of financial intermediation covering the financial services enumerated in the previous section have, to a significant extent, been reflected in the process of financial-sector reconfiguration summarized in Exhibit 2.6.

Moreover, in retail financial services, extensive banking overcapacity in some countries has led to substantial consolidation—often involving M&A activity. Excess retail production and distribution capacity has been slimmed down in ways that usually release redundant labor and capital. In some cases this process is retarded by large-scale involvement of public-sector institutions and cooperatives that operate under less rigorous financial discipline. Also at the retail level, commercial banking activity has been linked strategically to retail brokerage, retail insurance (especially life insurance), and retail asset management through mutual funds, retirement products, and private-client relationships. Sometimes, this linkage process has occurred selectively and sometimes using simultaneous multilinks coupled to aggressive

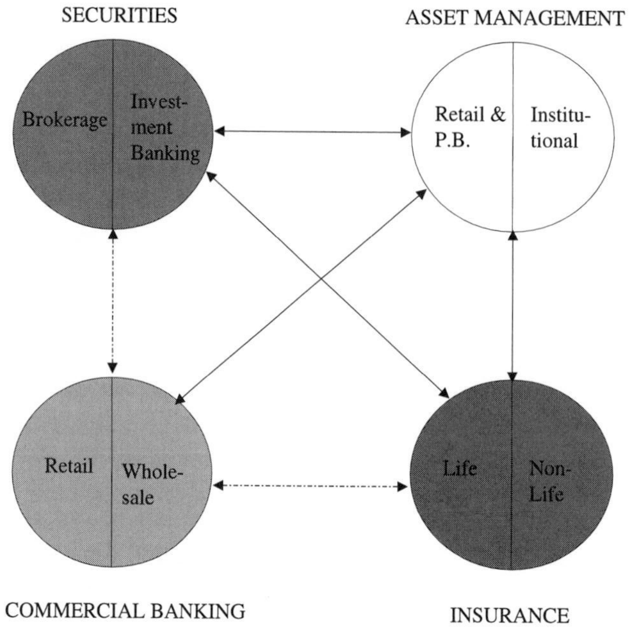

Exhibit 2.6. Multifunctional Financial Linkages.

cross-selling efforts. At the same time, relatively small and focused firms have sometimes continued to prosper in each of the retail businesses, especially where they have been able to provide superior service or client proximity while taking advantage of outsourcing and strategic alliances where appropriate.

In wholesale financial services, similar links have emerged. Wholesale commercial banking activities, such as syndicated lending and project financing, have often been shifted toward a greater investment banking focus, while investment banking firms have placed growing emphasis on developing institutional asset management businesses in part to benefit from vertical integration and in part to gain some degree of stability in a notoriously volatile industry.

Exhibit 2.7 shows the global volume of financial services restructuring through merger and acquisition (M&A) activity from 1986 through 2001—roughly two thirds of which occurred in the banking sector, one quarter in insurance, and the remainder in asset management and investment banking.

Exhibit 2.8 indicates that the vast bulk of this activity occurred on an in-sector basis. Worldwide, 78% of the dealflow (by value) was in-sector—85% in the United States (where line-of-business restrictions existed for most of the period) and 76% in Europe (where there were no such barriers). So cross-sector M&A deals, including banking–insurance, were a small part of the picture—only 11.4% even in Europe, home of bank assurance.

In addition to being largely in-sector, restructuring via M&A transactions was also largely domestic, as Exhibit 2.9 shows. Worldwide in commercial banking, less than 23% (by value) was cross-border. Only 12.7% and 20.2% of the U.S. and European banking dealflow, respectively, was cross-border (mostly European banks buying

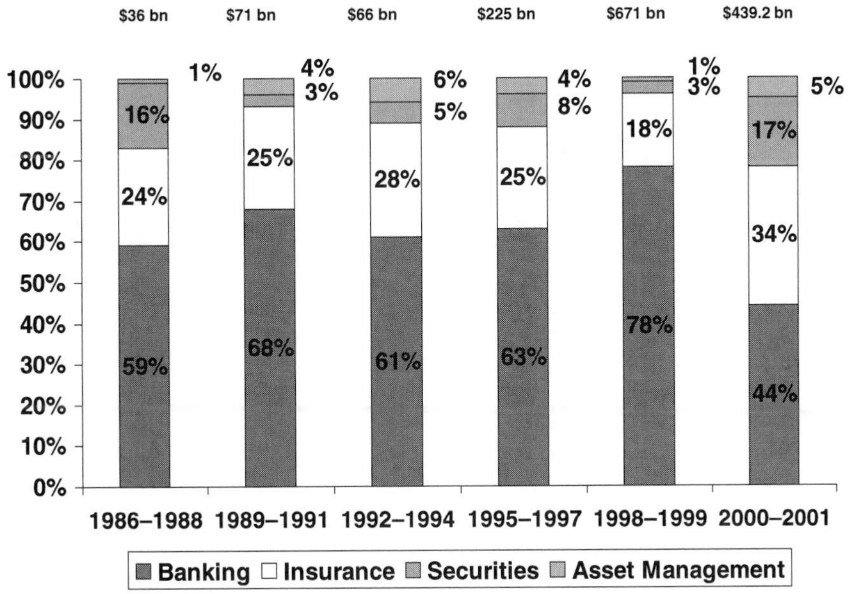

Exhibit 2.7. Worldwide Financial Services Merger Volume, 1986–2001.

U.S. banks). Cross-border intra-European banking deals amounted to 25.8% of the European total. The share of cross-border activity in the insurance sector has been roughly twice that of banking, which possibly suggests somewhat different economic pressures at work. With a few exceptions like HSBC and Citigroup globally, and Fortis, Nordea, ABN AMRO, ING, BSCH, and BBVA as parts of regional or interregional strategies, the aggressive development of cross-border platforms seems to be the exception in the banking sector. In insurance, however, global initiatives by firms like AXA, AIG, Zurich, AEGON, ING, Allianz, Generali, and GE Capital seem to be a more important part of the M&A picture.

Industrial economics suggests that structural forms in any sector, or between sectors, should follow the dictates of institutional comparative advantage. If there are significant economies of scale that can be exploited, it will be reflected in firm size. If there are significant economies of scope, either with respect to costs or revenues (cross-selling), then that will be reflected in the range of activities in which the dominant firms are engaged. If important linkages can be exploited across geographies or client segments, then this too will be reflected in the breadth and geographic scope of the most successful firms.

It seems clear, from a structural perspective, that a broad array of financial services firms may perform one or more of the roles identified in Exhibit 2.1—commercial banks, savings banks, postal savings institutions, savings cooperatives, credit unions, securities firms (e.g., full-service firms and various kinds of specialists), mutual funds, insurance companies, finance companies, finance subsidiaries of industrial companies, and others. Members of each strategic group compete with each other, as well as with members of other strategic groups. Assuming it is allowed to do so, each organization elects to operate in one or more of the financial channels

	Target Institution								
	World Total			U.S.			Europe		
Acquiring Institution	Banks	Securities	Insurance	Banks	Securities	Insurance	Banks	Securities	Insurance
Commercial banks	1260 (52.2%)	71 (2.9%)	63 (2.6%)	594 (50.9%)	30 (2.6%)	0.3 (0.0%)	307 (47.5%)	24 (3.1%)	52 (6.7%)
Securities firms	111 (4.6%)	282 (11.7%)	96 (4.0%)	14 (1.2%)	182 (15.6%)	49 (4.2%)	53 (6.8%)	48 (6.2%)	39 (5.0%)
Insurance companies	128 (5.3%)	36 (1.5%)	365 (15.1%)	73 (6.3%)	19 (1.6%)	200 (17.2%)	50 (6.4%)	12 (1.5%)	131 (16.8%)
			79			83.7			70.4

Source: Thomson Financial Securities Data.

Exhibit 2.8. Volume of In-Market Mergers and Acquisitions in the United States and Europe, 1985–2001 (US $ million and percent).

	Target Institution											
	World Total			U.S.–non-U.S.			Intra-Europe			Europe–Non-Europe		
Acquiring Institution	Banks	Securities	Insurance	Banks	Securities	Insurance	Banks	Securities	Insurance	Banks	Securities	Insurance
Commercial banks	185 (25.9)%	68 (9.5)%	11 (1.5)%	58 (19.1)%	44.0 (14.5)%	4 (1.3)%	79 (28.3)%	18 (6.5)%	4 (1.4)%	63.0 (22.7)%	40.0 (14.4)%	4.0 (1.4)%
Securities firms	31 (4.3%)	98.0 (13.7)%	17.0 (2.4)%	10 (3.3)%	61.0 (20.1)%	6.0 (1.8)%	8 (2.9)%	19.0 (6.8%)	4 (1.4)%	7 (2.5)%	40 (14.4)%	11 (4.0)%
Insurance companies	26 (3.6)%	28.0 (3.9)%	249 (34.9)%	1 (0.3)%	22 (7.2)%	98 (32.3)%	24 (8.6)%	3 (1.1)%	121 (43.4)%	2 (0.7)%	19 (6.9)%	90 (32.5)%

Sources: DeLong, Smith and Walter (1998) and Thomson Financial Securities Data. The first figure is the dollar value(in billions) of M&A activity and the second number in parentheses is the percentage of the total (these sum to 100 for each 3 × 3 matrix). Figures reported are the sum of the equity values of the target institutions.

Exhibit 2.9. Volume of Cross-Market Mergers and Acquisitions in the United States and Europe, 1985–2001 (US $ billion and percent).

according to its own competitive advantages. Institutional evolution therefore depends on how these comparative advantages evolve, and whether regulation permits them to drive institutional structure. In some countries, commercial banks, for example, have had to "go with the flow" and develop competitive asset management, origination, advisory, trading, and risk management capabilities under constant pressure from other banks and, most intensively, from other types of financial services firms.

Take the United States as a case in point. With financial intermediation distorted by regulation—notably the Glass-Steagall provisions of the Banking Act of 1933—banks half a century ago dominated classic banking functions, broker-dealers dominated capital market services, and insurance companies dominated most of the generic risk management functions, as shown in Exhibit 2.10. Cross-penetration among different types of financial intermediaries existed mainly in savings products.

Some 50 years later this functional segmentation had changed almost beyond recognition despite the fact that full *dejure* deregulation was not implemented until the end of the period with the Gramm-Leach-Bliley Act of 1999. Exhibit 2.11 shows a virtual doubling of strategic groups competing for the various financial intermediation functions. Today, there is vigorous cross-penetration among them in the United States. Most financial services can be obtained in one form or another from virtually every strategic group, each of which is, in turn, involved in a broad array of financial intermediation services. If cross-competition among strategic groups promotes both static and dynamic efficiencies, then the evolutionary path of the U.S. financial structure probably served macroeconomic objectives—particularly growth and economic restructuring—very well indeed. And line-of-business limits in force since 1933 have probably contributed, as an unintended consequence, to a much more heterogeneous financial system—certainly more heterogeneous than existed in the United States of the 1920s or in most other countries today. This structural evolution has been accompanied in recent years by higher concentration ratios in various types of financial services, although not in retail banking, wherein concentration ratios have actually fallen. None of these concentrations are yet troublesome in terms of antitrust concerns, and markets remain vigorously competitive.

A similar coverage analysis for Europe is not particularly credible because of the wide intercountry variations in financial structure. One common thread, however, given the long history of universal banking, is that banks dominate most intermediation functions in many European countries, with the exception of insurance. And given European bancassurance initiatives, some observers think a broad-gauge banking–insurance convergence is likely. Except for the penetration of continental Europe by U.K. and U.S. specialists, many of the relatively narrowly focused firms seem to have found themselves sooner or later acquired by major banking groups. Exhibit 2.12 may be a reasonable approximation of the continental European financial structure, with substantially less "density" of functional coverage by specific strategic groups than in the United States and correspondingly greater dominance of major financial firms that include banking as a core business.

The structural evolution of national and regional financial systems seems to have an impact on global market-share patterns. With about 28.9% of global gross domestic product (GDP), U.S. banking assets and syndicated bank loans are well underweight (they are overweight in Europe and Japan), whereas both bond and stock market capitalizations, capital market new issues, and fiduciary assets under management are overweight (they are underweight in Europe and Japan). One result is

Function / Institution	Payment Services	Savings Prod.	Fiduc. Services	Lending		Underwriting Issuance of		Insurance and Risk Mgt. Products
				Business	Retail	Equity	Debt	
Insured depository institutions	✔	✔	✔	✔	✔			
Insurance companies		✔		✔				✔
Finance companies				✔	✔			
Securities firms		✔	✔			✔	✔	
Pension funds		✔						
Mutual funds		✔						

✔ minor involvement.

Exhibit 2.10. U.S. Financial Services Sector, 1950.

Institution \ Function	Payment Services	Savings Prod.	Fiduc. Services	Lending		Underwriting Issuance of		Insurance and Risk Mgt. Products
				Business	Retail	Equity	Debt	
Insured depository institutions	✔	✔	✔	✔	✔	✔	✔	✔
Insurance companies	✔	✔	✔	✔	✔	✔	✔	✔
Finance companies	✔	✔	✔	✔	✔	✔	✔	✔
Securities firms	✔	✔	✔	✔	✔	✔	✔	✔
Pension funds		✔	✔	✔	✔			
Mutual funds	✔	✔	✔		✔	✔		✔
Diversified financial firms	✔	✔	✔	✔	✔	✔	✔	✔
Specialist firms	✔	✔	✔	✔	✔	✔	✔	✔

✔ Selective involvement of large firms via affiliates.

Exhibit 2.11. U.S. Financial Services Sector, 2001.

Institution \ Function	Payment Services	Savings Prod.	Fiduc. Services	Lending		Underwriting Issuance of		Insurance and Risk Mgt. Products
				Business	Retail	Equity	Debt	
Insured depository institutions	✔	✔	✔	✔	✔	✔	✔	✔
Insurance companies		✔	✔					✔
Finance companies				✔	✔			✔
Securities firms			✔			✔	✔	✔
Pension funds			✔					
Mutual funds		✔	✔					
Diversified financial firms								
Specialist firms	✔	✔	✔	✔	✔	✔	✔	✔

✔ Selective involvement of large firms via affiliates.

Exhibit 2.12. European Financial Services Sector, 2001.

that U.S. financial firms have come to dominate various intermediation roles in the financial markets—over half of global asset management mandates, over 77% of lead manager positions in wholesale lending, two thirds of bookrunning mandates in global debt and equity new issues, and almost 80% of advisory mandates (by value of deal) in completed M&A transactions. Indeed, it is estimated that in 2000 U.S.-based investment banks captured about 70% of the fee-income on European capital markets and corporate finance transactions (see Smith and Walter, 2000a).

Why? The reasons include the size of the U.S. domestic financial market (accounting for roughly two thirds of global capital-raising and M&A transactions in recent years), early deregulation of markets (but not of institutions) dating back to the mid-1970s, and performance pressure bearing on institutional investors, as well as corporate and public-sector clients, leading to an undermining of client loyalty in favor of best price and best execution. Perhaps as an unintended consequence of separated banking since 1933, institutions dominating disintermediated finance—the U.S. full-service investment banks—evolved from close-knit partnerships with unlimited liability to large securities firms under intense shareholder pressure to manage their risks well and extract maximum productivity from their available capital. At the same time it was clear that, unlike the major commercial banks, regulatory bailouts of investment banks in case of serious trouble were highly unlikely. Indeed, major firms like Kidder Peabody and Drexel Burnham (at the time the seventh-largest U.S. financial institution in terms of balance sheet size) were left to die by the regulators. Subsequently, the capital-intensity and economic dynamics of the investment banking business has caused most of the smaller and medium-size independent firms in both the United States, the United Kingdom and elsewhere (e.g., Paribas in France and MeesPierson in the Netherlands) to disappear into larger banking institutions.

It is interesting to speculate what the European matrix in Exhibit 2.12 will look like in 10 or 20 years' time. Some argue that the impact of size and scope is so powerful that the financial industry will be dominated by large, complex financial institutions—not only for Europe but also for other markets. Others argue that a rich array of players, stretching across a broad spectrum of strategic groups, will serve financial systems better than a strategic monoculture based on massive universal banking organizations. Some argue that the disappearance of small community banks, independent insurance companies in both the life and nonlife sectors, and a broad array of financial specialists is probably not in the public interest, especially if, at the end of the day, there are serious antitrust concerns in this key sector of the economy.

2.5 SUMMARY. Major parts of the financial services industry have become globalized over the years, linking borrowers and lenders, issuers and investors, risks and risk takers around the world. In this chapter we have considered the generic processes and linkages that comprise financial intermediation and the characteristics of high-performance financial systems, and reviewed some of the structural changes that have occurred in both national and global financial systems. We noted that financial channels that exhibit greater static and dynamic efficiency have supplanted less efficient ones as part of a generic process of financial evolution.

We then described a range of specific financial activities that have become most heavily globalized, notably the "wholesale" end of the financial spectrum that links end users through increasingly seamless global financial market structures. This was followed by an examination of the consequences in terms of financial-sector reconfiguration, both within and among the four major segments of the industry (commer-

North America		Europe	
Citigroup	250,143	HSBC	140,693
AIG	206,084	Allianz	86,530
GECS	194,636	ING	77,806
Berkshire Hathaway	105,238	UBS	73,497
J.P. Morgan Chase	103,133	RBS Group	60,865
Morgan Stanley	99,055	Lloyds TSB	60,663
Bank of America	82,745	Munich Re	60,532
American Express	72,069	AXA	58,235
Merrill Lynch	60,883	CS Group	57,719
Goldman Sachs	54,297	Barclays	53,630
Banc One	46,395	Deutsche	51,047
Schwab	41,609	Aegon	50,753
Bank of New York	41,466	Zurich	50,194
MBNA	33,007	BSCH	48,310
Marsh & McLennan	30,457	BBVA	46,774

Source: Financial Times, May 11, 2001.

Exhibit 2.13. 15 Most Valuable Financial Services Businesses in North America and Europe (market capitalization in US $ million, May 4, 2001).

cial banking, securities and investment banking, insurance, and asset management) as well as within and among national financial systems.

At least so far, the most valuable financial services franchises in the United States and Europe in terms of market capitalization seem far removed from a financial-intermediation monoculture, as Exhibit 2.13 suggests. In fact, each presents a rich mixture of banks, asset managers, insurance companies, and specialized players. How the institutional structure of the financial services sector will evolve is anybody's guess. Those who claim to know often end up being wrong. Influential consultants sometimes convince multiple clients to do the same thing at the same time, and this spike in strategic correlation can contribute to the wrongness of their vision. What is clear is that the underlying economics of the industry's microstructure depicted in Exhibit 2.1 will ultimately prevail, and finance will flow along conduits that are in the best interests of the end users of the financial system. The firms that comprise the financial services industry will have to adapt and readapt to this dynamic in ways that profitably sustain their *raison d'être.*

SOURCES AND SUGGESTED REFERENCES

Cumming, C. M., and B. J. Hirtle. *The Challenges of Risk Management in Diversified Financial Companies.* Federal Reserve Bank of New York Policy Review, EPR7.01 (01), 2001.

Dermine, J., and P. Hillion (eds.). *European Capital Markets with a Single Currency.* Oxford: Oxford University Press, 1999.

Kane, E. J. Competitive Financial Reregulation: An International Perspective, in *Threats to International Financial Stability.* Edited by R. Portes and A. Swoboda. London: Cambridge University Press, 1987.

Lamfalussy Report. *Final Report on the Regulation of European Securities Markets.* Brussels, February 2001.

Smith, R. C., and I. Walter. *Street Smarts: Leadership, Professional Conduct and Shareholder Value in the Securities Industry*. Boston: Harvard Business School Press, 2000.

Smith, R. C., and I. Walter. *High Finance in the Euro-zone*. London: Financial Times–Prentice Hall, 2000.

Smith, R. C., and I. Walter. *Global Wholesale Finance: Structure, Conduct, Performance*. Paper presented at the 22nd Annual Colloquium of the Société Universitaire Européenne de Recherches Financières (SUERF), Vienna, April 27–29, 2000(a).

Smith, R. C., and I. Walter. *High Finance in the Euro-zone*. London: Financial Times–Prentice Hall, 2000(b).

Story, J., and I. Walter. *Political Economy of Financial Integration in Europe*. Manchester: Manchester University Press, and Cambridge: MIT Press, 1998.

Walter, I. *Global Competition in Financial Services: Market Structure, Protection and Trade Liberalization*. New York: Ballinger–Harper & Row for the American Enterprise Institute, 1988.

Walter, I. "Financial Integration Across Borders and Across Sectors: Implications for Regulatory Structures," in *Financial Supervision in Europe*. Edited by Jeroen Kremers, Dirk Schoenmaker and Peter Wierts. London: Edward Elgar Publishing Ltd., 2002.

CHAPTER 3

BIS BASEL INTERNATIONAL BANK CAPITAL ACCORDS*

Linda Allen
Baruch College, CUNY
Anthony Saunders
New York University

CONTENTS

3.1 INTRODUCTION. The 1988 Basel[1] Captial Accord (BIS I) was revolutionary in that it sought to develop a single capital requirement for credit risk across the major banking countries of the world.[2] A major focus of BIS I was to distinguish the credit risk of sovereign, bank, and mortgage obligations (accorded lower risk weights) from nonbank private sector or commercial loan obligations (accorded the highest risk weight). There was little or no attempt to differentiate the credit risk exposure within the commercial loan classification. All commercial loans implicitly required an 8% total capital requirement (Tier 1 plus Tier 2),[3] regardless of the inher-

---

*This chapter is excerpted from A. Saunders and L. Allen, *Credit Risk Measurement: New Approaches to Value at Risk and Other Paradigms.* New York: John Wiley & Sons, Second Edition, 2002.

[1]The Basel Committee consists of senior supervisory representatives from Belgium, Canada, France, Germany, Italy, Japan, Luxembourg, Netherlands, Sweden, Switzerland, United Kingdom, and the United States. It usually meets at the Bank for International Settlements in Basel, where its permanent Secretariat is located.

[2]More than 100 countries have adopted BIS I.

[3]Tier 1 consists of the last, residual claims on the bank's assets, such as common stock and perpetual preferred stock. Tier 2 capital is slightly more senior than Tier 1, e.g., preferred stock and subordinated debt.

ent creditworthiness of the borrower, its external credit rating, the collateral offered, or the covenants extended.[4] Since the capital requirement was set too low for high-risk/low-quality business loans and too high for low-risk/high-qualtiy loans, the mispricing of commercial lending risk created an incentive for banks to shift portfolios toward those loans that were more underpriced from a regulatory risk capital perspective; for example, banks tended to retain the most credit risky tranches of securitized loan portfolios.[5] Thus, the 1988 Basel Capital Accord had the unintended consequence of encouraging a long-term deterioration in the overall credit quality of bank portfolios.[6] The proposed goal of the new Basel Capital Accord of 2002 (BIS II)—to be fully introduced, if approved as proposed, in 2006—is to correct the mispricing inherent in BIS I and incorporate more risk sensitive credit exposure measures into bank capital requirements.[7]

Hammes and Shapiro (2001)[8] delineate several key drivers motivating BIS II:

- *Structural changes in the credit market.* Regulatory capital must reflect the increased competitiveness of credit markets, particularly in the high-default-risk categories; the trading of credit risk through credit derivatives or collateralized loan obligations; modern credit risk measurement technology; and increased liquidity in the new credit risk markets.
- *Opportunities to remove inefficiencies in the lending market.* In contrast to the insurance industry, which uses derivatives markets and reinsurance companies to transfer risk, the banking industry is dominated by the "originate and hold" approach in which the bank fully absorbs credit risk.
- *Ballooning debt levels during the economic upturn, with a potential debt servicing crisis in an economic downturn.* For example, in 1999, debt-to-equity ratios at Standard & Poor's (S&P) 500 companies rose to 115.8% (as compared to 84.4% in 1990) and to 95% (as compared to 72% in 1985) ratio of household debt to personal disposable income.[9]

BIS II follows a three-step (potentially evolutionary) paradigm. Banks can choose among (or, for less sophisticated banks, are expected to evolve from) the basic (1) Standardized Model to the (2) Internal Ratings–Based (IRB) Model Foundation Approach to the (3) Advanced Internal Ratings–Based Model. The Standardized Approach is based on external credit ratings assigned by independent ratings agencies

---

[4]An indication of BIS I's mispricing of credit risk for commercial loans is obtained from Flood (2001) who examines the actual loan loss experiences for U.S. banks and thrifts from 1984–1999. He finds that in 1984 (1996) 10% (almost 3%) of the institutions had loan losses that exceeded the 8% Basel capital requirement. Moreover, Falkenheim and Powell (2001) find that the BIS I capital requirements for Argentine banks were set too low to protect against the banks' credit risk exposures. See ISDA (1998) for an early discussion of the need to reform BIS I.

[5]For a discussion of these regulatory capital arbitrage activities, see Jones (2000).

[6]However, Jones (2000) and Mingo (2000) argue that regulatory arbitrage may not have been all bad because it set the forces of innovation into motion that will ultimately correct the mispricing errors inherent in the regulations.

[7]The original timeline has been pushed back. The final draft of the proposals is scheduled for 2003, with possible implementation in 2006.

[8]p. 102.

[9]The Federal Housing Authority reported that the percentage of homeowners whose mortgage payments were more than 30 days late exceeded 10% for the first time ever as of the first quarter of 2001 (Leonhardt, 2001).

(such as Moody's, S&P, and Fitch IBCA). Both internal ratings approaches require the bank to formulate and use its own internal credit risk rating system. The risk weight assigned to each commercial obligation is based on the ratings assignment (either external or internal), so that higher (lower) rated, high (low) credit quality obligations have lower (higher) risk weights and therefore lower (higher) capital requirements, thereby eliminating the incentives to engage in risk shifting and regulatory abitrage.

Whichever of the three models is chosen, the BIS II proposal states that overall capital adequacy after 2005 will be measured as follows:[10]

Regulatory Total Capital	=	Credit Risk Capital Requirement	+	Market Risk Capital Requirement	+ Operational Risk Capital Requirement

where:

1. The Credit Risk Capital Requirement depends on the bank's choice of either the Standarized or the Internal Ratings–Based (Foundation or Advanced) Approaches.
2. The Market Risk Capital Requirement depends on the bank's choice of either the Standardized or the Internal Model Approach (e.g., RiskMetrics, historical simulation, or Monte Carlo simulation). This capital requirement was introduced in 1996 in the European Union (EU) and in 1998 in the United States.
3. The Operational Risk Capital Requirement (as proposed in 2001) depends on the bank's choice among a basic Indicator Approach, a Standardized Approach, and an Advanced Measurement Approach (AMA).[11] While part of the 8% ratio under BIS I was viewed as capital allocated to absorb operational risk, the proposed new operational risk requirement (to be introduced in 2006) aims to separate out operational risk from credit risk and, at least for the basic Indicator Approach, has attempted to calibrate operational risk capital to equal 12% of a bank's total regulatory capital requirement.[12] Specifically, on November 5, 2001, the BIS released potential modifications to the BIS II proposals that reduced the proposed target of operational risk capital as a percent of minimum regulatory capital requirements from 20% to 12%.

BIS II incorporates both expected and unexpected losses into capital requirements, in contrast to the market risk amendment of BIS I, which is concerned only with unexpected losses. Thus, loan loss reserves are considered the portion of capital that cushions expected credit losses, whereas economic capital covers unexpected losses. BIS (2000)[13] sound practices for loan accounting state that allowances for loan losses (loan

---

[10]McKinsey estimates that operational risk represents 20%, market risk comprises 20%, and credit risk 60% of the overall risk of a typical commercial bank or investment bank. See Hammes and Shapiro (2001), p. 106.

[11]The Basic Indicator Approach levies a single operational risk capital charge for the entire bank, the Standardized Approach divides the bank into eight lines of business, each with its own operational risk charge, and the Advanced Measurement Approach (AMA) uses the bank's own internal models of operational risk measurement to assess a capital requirement. See BIS (2001c).

[12]For more details on the market and operational risk components of regulatory capital requirements, see the BIS Web site www.bis.org.

[13]p. 4.

loss reserves) should be sufficient to "absorb estimated credit losses." However, loan loss reserves may be distorted by the stipulation that they are considered eligible for Tier 2 capital up to a maximum 1.25% of risk-weighted assets.[14] That is, if expected credit losses exceed 1.25% of risk-weighted assets, then some portion of loan loss reserves would not be eligible to meet the bank's capital requirement, thereby requiring excess capital to meet some portion of expected losses and leading to redundant capital charges. In November 2001, the BIS proposed modifications that would relax these constraints and permit the use of "excess" provisions to offset expected losses. While capital requirements for credit and operational risk can be satisfied by Tier 1 and Tier 2 capital only, part of the market risk capital requirement can be satisfied by Tier 3 capital which includes subordinated debt of more than two years' maturity.[15]

The new capital requirements in BIS II are applied on both a consolidated and unconsolidated basis to holding companies of banking firms.[16] When BIS II is completely adopted, overall regulatory capital levels, on average, are targeted (by the BIS) to remain unchanged for the system as a whole.[17] However, recent tests conducted by 138 banks in 25 countries have led to a downward calibration of the capital levels required to cover credit risk (under the Internal Ratings–Based Foundation Approach) and operational risk (under the standardized model, basic indicator model and advanced measurement approach).[18]

3.2 STANDARDIZED MODEL FOR CREDIT RISK. The Standardized Model follows the same methodology as BIS I, but makes it more risk sensitive by dividing the commercial obligor designation into finer gradations of risk classifications (risk buckets), with risk weights that are a function of external credit ratings. Under the current system (BIS I), all commercial loans are viewed as having the same credit risk (and thus the same risk weight). Essentially, the book value of each loan is multiplied by a risk

---

[14]Moreover, accounting rules differ from country to country so that oftentimes the loan loss reserve is a measure of current or incurred losses, rather than expected future losses. See Wall and Koch (2000) and Flood (2001). Indeed, Cavallo and Majnoni (2001) show that distorted loan loss provisions may have a pro-cyclical effect that exacerbates systemic risk. In particular, many Latin American countries require large provisions for loan losses (averaging 8% of gross financing), raising the possibility of excessive capital requirements in these countries due to double counting of credit risk [see Powell (2001)].

[15]BIS II makes no changes to the Tier I and Tier 2 definitions of capital. Carey (2001b) suggests that since subordinated debt is not useful in preserving soundness (i.e., impaired subordinated debt triggers bank insolvency), there should be a distinction between equity and loan loss reserves (the buffer against credit risk, denoted Tier A) and subordinated debt (the buffer against market risk, denoted Tier B). Jackson, et al. (2001) also show that the proportion of Tier I capital should be considered in setting minimum capital requirements.

[16]The one exception to this is with regard to insurance subsidiaries. Banks' investments in insurance subsidiaries are deducted for the purposes of measuring regulatory capital. However, this distinction ignores the diversification benefits from combining banking and insurance activities; see Gully, et al. (2001).

[17]Capital requirements are just the first of three pillars comprising the BIS II proposals. The second pillar consists of a supervisory review process that requires bank regulators to assess the adequacy of bank risk management policies. Several issues, such as interest rate risk included in the banking book, have been relegated to the second pillar (i.e., supervisory oversight) rather than to explicit capital requirements. The third pillar of BIS II is market discipline. The Accord sets out disclosure requirements to increase the transparency of reporting of risk exposures so as to enlist the aid of market participants in supervising bank behavior. Indeed, the adequacy of disclosure requirements is a prerequisite for supervisory approval of bank internal models of credit risk measurement.

[18]See BIS (2001c, d).

External Credit Rating	AAA to AA–	A+ to A–	BBB+ to BB–	Below BB–	Unrated
Risk Weight under BIS II	20%	50%	100%	150%	100%
Capital Requirement under BIS II	1.6%	4%	8%	12%	8%
Risk Weight under BIS I	100%	100%	100%	100%	100%
Capital Requirement under BIS I	8%	8%	8%	8%	8%

Exhibit 3.1. Total Capital Requirements on Corporate Obligations under the Standardized Model of BIS II

weight of 100% and then by 8% in order to generate the Tier 1 plus Tier 2 minimum capital requirement of 8% of risk-adjusted assets, the so-called 8% rule. Exhibit 3.1 compares the risk weights for corporate obligations under the proposed new Standardized Model to the old BIS I risk weights. Under BIS II, the bank's assets are classified into each of the five risk buckets shown in Exhibit 3.1 according to the credit rating assigned the obligor by independent rating agencies, such as S&P, Moody's and Fitch. Appendix A shows how credit ratings provided by the three major rating agencies are mapped on a comparable basis. In order to obtain the minimum capital requirement for credit risk purposes, all credit exposures (known as the exposure at default EAD)[19] in each risk weight bucket are summed up, weighted by the appropriate risk weight from Exhibit 3.1, and then multiplied by the overall total capital requirement of 8%.

The Standardized Approach takes into account credit risk mitigation by adjusting the transaction's EAD to reflect collateral, credit derivatives or guarantees, and offsetting on-balance-sheet netting. However, any collateral value is reduced by a haircut to adjust for the volatility of the instrument's market value. Moreover, a floor capital level assures that the credit quality of the borrower will always impact capital requirements.

The risk weights for claims on sovereigns and their central banks are shown in Exhibit 3.2. The new weights allow for differentiation of credit risk within the classification of Organization for Economic Cooperation and Development (OECD) nations. Under BIS I, all OECD nations carried preferential risk weights of 0% on their government obligations. BIS II levies a risk weight that depends on the sovereign's external rating, not on its political affiliation.[20] However, claims on the BIS, the IMF, the European Central Bank, and the European Community all carry a 0% risk weight.

---

[19]The *EAD* for on-balance-sheet items is the nominal outstanding amount, whereas *EAD* for off-balance-sheet items is determined using most of the same credit conversion factors from BIS I, with the exception of loan commitments maturing in less than one year that now have a 20% conversion factor rather than the 0% under BIS I.

[20]Korea and Mexico (both OECD members) will move under the proposals from a zero risk weight to a positive risk weight corresponding to their credit ratings. Powell (2001) uses the Standardized Approach to estimate that capital requirements for banks lending to Korea (Mexico) will increase by $3.4 billion ($5 billion) resulting in an estimated incease in bond spreads of 74.8 basis points for Korea and 104.5 basis points for Mexico. If the IRB Approach is used, the impact is even greater.

External Credit Rating	AAA to AA– or ECA Rating 1	A+ to A– or ECA Rating 2	BBB+ to BBB– or ECA Rating 3	BB+ to B– or ECA Rating 4 to 6	Below B– or ECA Rating 7
Risk Weight under BIS II	0%	20%	50%	100%	150%
Capital Requirement under BIS II	0%	1.6%	4%	8%	12%

Notes: ECA denotes Export Credit Agencies. To qualify, the ECA must publish its risk scores and use the OECD methodology. If there are two different assessments by ECAs, then the higher risk weight is used. Sovereigns also have an unrated category with a 100 percent risk weight (not shown). Under BIS I, the risk weight for OECD government obligations is 0 percent. OECD interbank deposits and guaranteed claims, as well as some non-OECD bank and government deposits and securities carry a 20 percent risk weight under BIS I. All other claims on non-OECD governments and banks carry a 100 percent risk weight under BIS I. (See Saunders and Cornett, 2002.)

Exhibit 3.2. Total Capital Requirements on Sovereigns under the Standardized Model of BIS II

There are two options for Standardized risk weighting of claims on banks and securities firms. Under option 1, all banks incorporated in a given country are assigned a risk weight one category less favorable than the sovereign country's risk weight. Thus, the risk weights for option 1 shown in the heading in Exhibit 3.3 pertain to the *sovereign's* risk weight. For example, a bank that is incorporated in a country with an AAA rating will have a 20% risk weight under option 1, resulting in a 1.6% capital requirement.[21] Option 2 uses the external credit rating of the bank itself to set the risk

[21]That is, an AAA rating would normally warrant a 0% risk weight, but instead the risk weight is set one category higher at 20%.

External Credit Rating	AAA to AA–	A+ to A–	BBB+ to BBB–	BB+ to B–	Below B–	Unrated
Risk Weight under BIS II Option 1	20%	50%	100%	100%	150%	100%
Capital Requirement under BIS II Option 1	1.6%	4%	8%	8%	12%	8%
Risk Weight under BIS II Option 2	20%	50%	50%	100%	150%	50%
Risk Weight for short-term claims under BIS II Option 2	20%	20%	20%	50%	150%	20%

Notes: The capital requirements for option 2 can be calculated by multiplying the risk weight by the 8 percent capital requirement.

Exhibit 3.3. Total Capital Requirements on Banks under the Standardized Model of BIS II

weight. Thus, the risk weights for option 2 shown in the heading in Exhibit 3.3 pertain to the *bank's* credit rating. For example, a bank with an AAA rating would receive a 20% risk weight (and a 1.6% capital requirement) no matter what the sovereign's credit rating. Exhibit 3.3 also shows that BIS II reduced the risk weights for all bank claims with original maturity of three months or less.[22] The choice of which option applies is left to national bank regulators and must be uniformly adopted for all banks in the country.

3.3 ASSESSMENT. BIS II is a step in the right direction in that it adds risk sensitivity to the regulatory treatment of capital requirements to absorb credit losses. However, Altman and Saunders (2001a, b) and the Institute of International Finance (2000) find insufficient risk sensitivity in the proposed risk buckets of the Standardized Model, especially in the lowest-rated bucket for corporates (rated below BB-), which will require a risk weight three times greater than proposed under BIS II to cover unexpected losses based on empirical evidence on corporate bond loss data.[23] By contrast, the risk weight in the first two corporate loan buckets may be too high. Exhibit 3.4 shows the historical actual one year losses on a bond portfolio using a loss distribution (default mode) at the 99.97% confidence level (i.e., credit losses will exceed the capital amounts as a percent of assests (loans) shown in Exhibit 3.4 in just three out of 10,000 years).[24] The 1.6% capital charge for the first risk bucket (AAA to AA-ratings) is too high given the 0% historical loss experience. However, the historical one-year loss experience for the lowest-risk bucket (ratings below BB-) is significantly larger than the 12% capital requirement. Thus, capital regulation arbitrage incentives will not be completely eliminated by the BIS II credit risk weights.[25]

The unrated risk bucket (of 100%) has also been criticized (see Altman and Saunders (2001a, b)). Exhibit 3.5 shows that more than 70% of corporate exposures were unrated in the 138 banks that participated in a BIS survey (the Quantitative Impact

[22]However, if the contract is expected to roll over upon maturity (e.g., an open repo), then its effective maturity exceeds three months and the bank supervisor may consider it ineligible for the preferential risk weights shown in Exhibit 3.3.

[23]Similary, Powell (2001) finds insufficient convexity in the Standarized Approach for sovereign debt.

[24]It should be noted that since actual loss data are used and the samples are finite, there are standard errors around these estimates. Moreover, BIS II is calibrated to a 99.9% level, not the higher 99.97% used in the Altman and Saunders (2001b) study.

[25]One year has become the common time horizon for credit risk models since one year is perceived as being of sufficient length for a bank to raise additional capital (if able to do so). However, Carey (2001b) contends that this time horizon is too short.

	AAA to AA–	A+ to A–	BBB+ to BB–	Below BB–
BIS II Risk Weight	20%	50%	100%	150%
BIS II Capital Requirement	1.6%	4%	8%	12%
All Bonds 1981–1999	0%	14.988%	54.837%	97.228%
Senior Bonds 1981–1999	0%	0%	91.862%	93.185%
All Bonds 1981–2000	0%	14.989%	74.749%	97.309%
Year 2000	0%	0%	91.187%	93.762%

Source: Altman and Saunders (2001b)

Exhibit 3.4. Comparison of BIS II Proposed Risk Buckets to Actual Loss Values

	AAA–AA	A	BBB–BB	Below B	Higher risk loans	Unrated
Large banks in G10 countries	6%	9%	11%	1%	1%	72%
Small banks in G10 countries	11%	9%	6%	2%	2%	70%
Large banks in the EU	6%	8%	8%	1%	1%	75%
Small banks in the EU	8%	10%	5%	2%	2%	73%
Developing countries	7%	3%	4%	2%	3%	81%

Source: "Results of the Second Quantitative Impact Study," November 5, 2001a.

Exhibit 3.5. Quality Distribution of Corporate Exposures (138 Banks from 25 Countries Participating in the QIS2 Survey)

Study QIS2). Since the majority of obligations held by the world's banks are not rated (see Ferri, et al. (2001)), for example, it is estimated that less than 1,000 European companies are rated,[26] the retention of an unrated risk bucket is a major lapse that threatens to undermine the risk sensitivity of BIS II.[27] Specifically, actual default data on nonrated loans puts them closer to the 150% bucket risk weight than the specified 100% risk weight. In addition, low-quality borrowers that anticipate receiving an external credit rating below BB- have an incentive to eschew independent rating agencies altogether, choosing to reduce their costs of borrowing by remaining unrated, but thereby reducing the availability of credit information available to the market.[28]

On a more fundamental basis, concern has been expressed about tying capital requirements to external ratings produced by rating agencies. Ratings are opinions about the overall credit quality of an obligor, not issue-specific audits.[29] There is a certain

[26]For less developed countries, the proportion of companies with external credit ratings is much lower than for developed countries. Powell (2001) reports that only 150 corporates in Argentina are rated, although the central bank's credit bureau lists 25,000 corporate borrowers. Thus, Ferri et al. (2001) surmise that borrowers in less developed countries are likely to suffer a substantial increase in borrowing costs relative to those in developed countries upon adoption of BIS II.

[27]Linnell (2001) and Altman and Saunders (2001b) suggest that, at the very least, the unrated classification risk weight should be 150%. There is evidence that the failure ratio on nonrated loans is similar to the failure ratio in the lowest (150%) rated bucket; see Altman and Saunders (2001b).

[28]To mitigate this problem, Griep and De Stefano (2001) suggest that more unsolicited ratings be used. German bank associations plan to pool credit data so as to address the problem of unrated small and medium sized businesses. Because of the importance of this market sector to the German economy, Chancellor Schroder has threatened to veto the BIS II proposal. (See *The Economist*, November 10, 2001.) Allen (2002b) surveys the special problems of credit risk measurement for middle market firms.

[29]Moody's in its ratings of about 1,000 banks worldwide uses a complex interaction of seven fundamental factors: (1) operating environment (competitive, regulatory, institutional support); (2) ownership and governance; (3) franchise value; (4) recurring earning power; (5) risk profile (credit, market, liquidity risks, and asset-liability management, agency, reputation, operational, etc.) and risk management; (6) economic capital analysis; (7) management priorities and strategies. See Cunningham (1999) and Theodore (1999).

amount of heterogeneity within each rating class, since a single letter grade is used to represent a multidimensional concept that includes default probability, loss severity, and transition risk. Moreover, since ratings agencies try to avoid discrete jumps in ratings classifications, the rating may be a lagging, not a leading indicator of credit quality (see Reisen and von Maltzan (1999) and Reinhart (2001) for discussions of lags in sovereign credit ratings, Kealhofer (2000) and Altman and Saunders (2001a) for lags in publicly traded corporate ratings, and Bongini et al. (2001) for lags in credit ratings of banks). As ratings change over time, the transaction may be shifted from one risk bucket to another, thereby injecting excessive volatility into capital requirements (see Linnell (2001)) and may lead to an increase in systemic risk since, with increased downgrades in a recession, banks may find their capital requirements peaking at the worst time (i.e., in the middle of a recession when earnings are relatively weak). Indeed, there is evidence (see Ferri et al. (2001), Monfort and Mulder (2000), Altman and Saunders (2001a)) that ratings agencies behave procyclically since ratings are downgraded in a financial crisis, thereby increasing capital requirements at just the point in the business cycle that stimulation is required (see Reisen (2000)). Thus, pegging capital requirements to external ratings may exacerbate systemic risk concerns. Concern about systemic risk may lead to regulatory attempts to influence ratings agencies, thereby undermining their independence and credibility.[30] (See Allen and Saunders (2002) for a survey of cyclical effects in credit risk measurement models.)

Although an important advantage of external ratings is their validation by the market, the credit rating industry is not very competitive. There are only a handful of well-regarded rating agencies. This leads to the risk of rating shopping.[31] Since the obligors are free to choose their rating agency, moral hazard may lead rating agencies to shade their ratings upward in a bid to obtain business. Moreover, since there is no single, universally accepted standard for credit ratings, they may not be comparable across rating agencies and across countries. (See discussions in White (2001), Cantor (2001), Greip and De Stefano (2001).) This is likely to distort capital requirements more in less developed countries, because of greater volatility in less developed countries (LDC) sovereign ratings, less transparent financial reporting in those countries, and the greater impact of the sovereign rating as a de facto ceiling for the private sector in LDCs.[32]

Finally, banks are also considered "delegated monitors" (see Diamond (1984)) who have a comparative advantage in assessing and monitoring the credit risk of their borrowers. Indeed, this function is viewed as making banks "special." This appears to be inconsistent with the concept underlying the Standardized Model, which essentially attributes this bank monitoring function to external rating agencies for the purposes of setting capital requirements. Adoption of this approach may well reduce bank incentives to invest time and effort in monitoring, thereby reducing the availability of information and further undermining the value of the banking franchise.

---

[30]Moreover, the usefulness of external ratings for regulatory purposes is questionable since the rating incorporates the likelihood that the firm will be bailed out by the government in the event of financial distress. Only Fitch IBCA and Moody's provide stand-alone creditworthiness ratings, but these cannot be used to calculate the probability of default (PD); see Jackson et al. (2001).

[31]Jewell and Livingston (1999) find that Fitch ratings are slightly higher on average than ratings from S&P and Moody's. Fitch is the only rating agency that explicitly charges for a rating.

[32]Moreover, contagious regional financial crises in confidence may lead to excessive downgradings of sovereign ratings, see Cantor and Packer (1996), Ferri, et al. (2001), and Kaminsky and Schmukler (2001).

3.4 INTERNAL RATINGS–BASED MODELS FOR CREDIT RISK. Under the IRB approaches,[33] each bank is required to establish an internal ratings model to classify the credit risk exposure of each activity (e.g., commercial lending, consumer lending, etc.), whether on or off the balance sheet. For the Foundation IRB Approach, the required outputs obtained from the internal ratings model are estimates of one-year[34] probability of default (PD) and EAD for each transaction. In addition to these estimates, independent estimates of both the loss given default (LGD) and maturity (M)[35] are required to implement the Advanced IRB Approach. The bank computes risk weights for each individual exposure (e.g., corporate loan) by incorporating its estimates of PD, EAD, LGD, and M obtained from its internal ratings model and its own internal data systems. The model also assumes that the average default correlation among individual borrowers is between 10 and 20% with the correlation a decreasing function of PD; see BIS (2001e).[36]

Expected losses upon default can be calculated as follows:

$$\text{Expected Losses} = \text{PD} \times \text{LGD}$$

where PD is the probability of default and LGD is the loss given default.[37] However, this considers only one possible credit event—default—and ignores the possibility of losses resulting from credit rating downgrades. That is, deterioration in credit quality caused by increases in PD or LGD will cause the value of the loan to be written down—in a mark-to-market sense—even prior to default, thereby resulting in portfolio losses (if the loan's value is marked to market). Thus, credit risk measurement models can be differentiated on the basis of whether the definition of a "credit event" includes only default (the default mode or DM models) or whether it also includes nondefault credit quality deterioration (the mark-to-market or MTM models). The mark-to-market approach considers the impact of credit downgrades and upgrades on market value, whereas the default mode is only concerned about the economic value of an obligation in the event of default. There are five elements to any IRB approach:

1. A classification of the obligation by credit risk exposure—the internal ratings model.

---

[33]In this article, we focus on the BIS II regulations as applied to on-balance-sheet activities. See Chapter 15 in Saunders and Allen (2002) for a discussion of the BIS II proposals for off-balance-sheet activities.

[34]As noted earlier, the use of a one year time horizon assumes that banks can fully recapitalize any credit losses within a year. Carey (2001b) argues that a two- to three-year time horizon is more realistic.

[35]Maturity is the Weighted Average Life of the loan (i.e., the percentage of principal repayments in each year times the year(s) in which these payments are received). For example, a two year loan of \$200 million repaying \$100 million principal in year 1 and \$100 million principal in year 2 has a Weighted Average Life (WAL) = $[1 \times (100/200)] + [2 \times (100/200)] = 1.5$ years.

[36]According to Carey (2001b), the January 2001 IRB proposal is calibrated to a 4.75% Tier 1 capital ratio with a Tier 2 subordinated debt multiplier of 1.3 and a PD error multiplier of 1.2. This results in a target capital ratio minimum of $4.75 \times 1.3 \times 1.2 = 7.4\%$. Since the BIS I 8% ratio incorporates a safety factor for operational risk, it makes sense that the pure credit risk IRB minimum capital requirement would be calibrated to a number less than 8%.

[37]The format of the IRB approaches is to use PD, LGD and M to determine the loan's risk weight and then to multiply that risk weight times the EAD times 8% in order to determine the loan's capital requirement.

2. Risk components—PD and EAD for the Foundation model and PD, EAD, LGD, and M for the Advanced model.
3. A risk weight function that uses the risk components to calculate the risk weights.
4. A set of minimum requirements of eligibility to apply the IRB approach (i.e., demonstration that the bank maintains the necessary information systems to accurately implement the IRB approach).
5. Supervisory review of compliance with the minimum requirements.

(a) Foundation IRB Approach. The bank is allowed to use its own estimate of PD over a one-year time horizon, as well as each loan's EAD. However, there is a lower bound on PD that is equal to three basis points, so as to create a nonzero floor on the credit risk weights (and hence capital required to be held against any individual loan). The average PD for each internal grade is used to calculate the risk weight for each internal rating. The PD may be based on historical experience or even potentially on a credit scoring model (see Saunders and Allen (2002) for discussions of traditional credit scoring models as well as newer, more theory-based models). The EAD for on-balance-sheet transactions is equal to the nominal (book) amount of the exposure outstanding. Credit mitigation factors (e.g., collateral, credit derivatives or guarantees, on-balance-sheet netting) are incorporated following the rules of the Standardized IRB Approach by adjusting the EAD for the collateral amount, less a haircut determined by supervisory advice under Pillar II. The EAD for off-balance-sheet activities is computed using the BIS I approach of translating off-balance-sheet items into on-balance-sheet equivalents mostly using the BIS I conversion factors (see Saunders (1997), Chapter 20).[38] The Foundation IRB Approach sets a benchmark for M, Maturity (or Weighted Average Life of the loan) at three years (in November 2002, this was changed to 2.5 years). Moreover, the Foundation Approach assumes that Loss Given Default for each unsecured loan is set at LGD = 50% for senior claims and LGD = 75% for subordinated claims on corporate obligations.[39] However, in November 2001, the Basel Committee on Banking Supervision presented potential modifications that would reduce the LGD on secured loans to 45% if fully secured by physical, non–real estate collateral and 40% if fully secured by receivables.

Under the January 2001 proposal, the Foundation Approach formula for the risk weight on corporate obligations (loans) is:[40]

$$\text{RW} = (\text{LGD}/50) \times \text{BRW or } 12.50 \times \text{LGD, whichever is smaller} \qquad (1)$$

where the benchmark risk weight (BRW) is calculated for each risk classification using the following formula:

$$\text{BRW} = 976.5 \times \text{N}(1.118 \times \text{G}(\text{PD}) + 1.288) \times 1 + .0470 \times (1 - \text{PD})/\text{PD}^{0.44} \qquad (2)$$

---

[38]However, there is now a 20% conversion factor for loan commitments maturing in less than one year. Under BIS I this conversion factor was 0%.

[39]The Foundation Approach assumes a constant LGD. Altman and Brady (2001) find that LGD is directly related to PD.

[40]PD is expressed in decimal format in all formulas.

The term $N(y)$ denotes the cumulative distribution function for a standard normal random variable (i.e., the probability that a normal random variable with mean zero and variance of one is less than or equal to y) and the term $G(z)$ denotes the inverse cumulative distribution function for a standard normal random variable (i.e., the value y such that $N(y) = z$). The BRW formula is calibrated so that a three-year corporate loan with a PD equal to 0.7% and a LGD equal to 50% will have a capital requirement of 8%, calibrated to an assumed loss coverage target of 99.5% (i.e., losses to exceed the capital allocation occur only 0.5% of the time, or five years in 1,000).[41] Appendix B shows the calibration of equation (2) for retail loans, demonstrating that the BRW for retail loans is set lower than the BRW for corporate loans for all levels of PD. Exhibit 3.6 shows the continuous relationship between the BRW and the PD. Note that this continuous function allows the bank to choose the number of risk categories in the internal risk rating system, as long as there is a minimum of six to nine grades for performing borrowers and two grades for nonperforming borrowers.[42]

Consultation between the Basel Committee on Banking Supervision and the public fueled concerns about the calibration of the Foundation Approach as presented in equations (1) and (2). This concern was galvanized by the results of a Quantitative Impact Study (QIS2) that examined the impact of the BIS II proposals on the capital requirements of 138 large and small banks from 25 countries. Banks that would have adopted the IRB Foundation Approach would have seen an unintended 14% increase in their capital requirements. Potential modifications were released on November 5,

[41]Historical insolvency for AA (A) rated bonds corresponds to a 99.97% (99.5%) target loss percentile, Jackson et al. (2001) use CreditMetrics to show that BIS I provides a 99.9% solvency rate (equivalent to a BBB rating) for a high-quality bank portfolio and 99% (BB rating) for a lower-quality bank portfolio.

[42]Treacy and Carey (2000) document that bank internal ratings systems generally have more than 10 rating classifications.

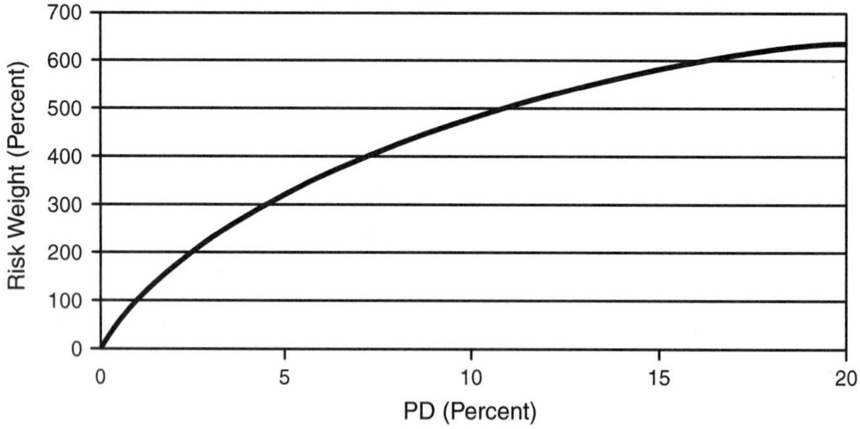

Source: BIS (2001), "The Internal Ratings–Based Approach."

Exhibit 3.6. Proposed IRB Risk Weights for Hypothetical Corporate Exposure Having LGD Equal to 50 Percent.

2001, to lower the risk weights and make the risk weighting function less steep for the IRB Foundation Approach only. Moreover, the potential modifications (if incorporated into the BIS II proposals) would make the correlation coefficient a function of the PD, such that the correlation coefficient between assets decreases as the PD increases. Finally, the confidence level built into the risk weighting function would be increased from 99.5% to 99.9%.

The potential modifications to equations (1) and (2) corporate loan risk weight curves are as follows:

$$\begin{aligned} \mathrm{BRW} &= 12.5 \times \mathrm{LGD} \times \mathrm{M} \times \mathrm{N}[(1 - \mathrm{R})^{-0.5} \times \mathrm{G(PD)} \\ &\quad + (R/(1 - R))^{0.5} \times G(0.999)] \end{aligned} \tag{3}$$

where

$$M = 1 + 0.047 \times ((1 - \mathrm{PD})/\mathrm{PD}^{0.44}) \tag{4}$$

$$\begin{aligned} R &= 0.10 \times [(1 - \exp^{-50\mathrm{PD}})/(1 - \exp^{-50})] + 0.20 \\ &\quad \times [1 - (1 - \exp^{-50\mathrm{PD}})/(1 - \exp^{-50})] \end{aligned} \tag{5}$$

and

$$\mathrm{RW} = (\mathrm{X}/50) \times \mathrm{BRW} \tag{6}$$

where $X = 75$ for a subordinated loan, $X = 50$ for an unsecured loan, $X = 45$ for a loan fully secured by physical, non–real estate collateral, and $X = 40$ for a loan fully secured by receivables. In equations (3) through (6), *exp* stands for the natural exponential function, $N(.)$ stands for the standard normal cumulative distribution function and $G(.)$ stands for the inverse standard normal cumulative distribution function.

Equation (4) denotes the maturity factor M. This is reportedly unchanged from the BIS II proposals shown in equation (2) in that it is still benchmarked to a fixed three-year Weighted Average Life of the loan.[43] The correlation coefficient R is computed in equation (5). The correlation ranges from 0.20 for the lowest PD value to 0.10 for the highest PD value. This inverse relationship appears to be somewhat counterintuitive in that empirically asset correlations increase during systemic crises when PDs also tend to increase, thereby implying a direct positive (rather than inverse) relationship between correlation and PD.

Using the potential modifications of November 2001, the BRW is calculated from equations (3) through (5). The actual risk weight (RW) is then calculated in equation (6) where $RW = (X/50)\ x\ BRW$ and $X =$ the stipulated fixed LGD for each type of loan. For example, under the potential modifications of November 2001, the LGD takes on a value of either 40% (if the loan is fully secured by receivables), 45% (if fully secured by physical, non–real estate collateral), 50% (if unsecured but senior) or 75% (if subordinated). Risk-weighted assets are then computed by multiplying the risk weight times the exposure at default. Finally, the minimum capital requirement is computed by multiplying the risk-weighted assets times 8%; that is, the minimum capital requirement on the individual loan $= RW \times EAD \times 8\%$.

---

[43]In contrast to the Advanced IRB Approach, the Foundation IRB Approach does not input the loan's actual maturity into the risk weight calculation.

Probability of Default	Jan. 2001 BIS II Proposal Capital Requirements	Nov. 2001 BIS Modified Capital Requirements
3 basis points	1.1%	1.4%
10	2.3	2.7
25	4.2	4.3
50	6.4	5.9
75	8.3	7.1
1%	10.0	8.0
1.25	11.5	8.7
1.50	12.9	9.3
2.00	15.4	10.3
2.50	17.6	11.1
3.00	19.7	11.9
4.00	23.3	13.4
5.00	26.5	14.8
10.00	38.6	21.0
20.00	50.0	30.0

Notes: The minimum capital requirements shown are a percent of EAD (exposure at default) assuming LGD = 50%.

Source: BIS (November 5, 2001b).

Exhibit 3.7. Comparison of BIS II Proposals and Potential Modifications: Capital Requirements under the IRB Foundation Approach

Exhibit 3.7 shows the impact of the November 2001 modified risk weighting function on the capital requirements under the IRB Foundation Approach. For example, an unsecured $100 million loan with a PD of 10% would have s 262% benchmark risk weight under the November 2001 modifications, computed using equations (3) through (6). Since the loan in our example is unsecured, using equation (1) the $RW = (50/50) \times BRW = 2.62$. Thus, the loan's minimum capital requirement would be $\$100\text{m} \times .08 \times 2.62 = \$21$ millon. In contrast, Exhibit 3.7 shows that the same loan's minimum capital requirement under the January 2001 proposals would have been $38.6 million. Moreover, under BIS I the capital requirement would have been $\$100$ million $\times$ 8% = $8 million. Exhibit 3.7 also shows that the capital requirement for the highest-quality (lowest PD) exposures increases slightly in the modified proposals, whereas the capital requirement for the lowest quality (highest PD) exposures decreases significantly as compared to the January 2001 BIS II proposals.[44]

(b) Advanced IRB Approach. Sophisticated banks are encouraged to move from the Foundation to the Advanced Approach. A primary source for this incentive is the result of the use of the bank's *actual* LGD experience in place of the fixed assumption

[44]This example is for a single loan. Adjustments for the concentration of the loan portfolio (granularity adjustments) that would measure the portfolio's level of diversification have been dropped from pillar 1 of the BIS II proposals.

of a 40, 45, 50, or 75% LGD. Evidence suggests that historical LGD for bank loans is significantly lower than 50%[45] and therefore, the shift to the advanced approach is expected to reduce bank capital requirements by 2 to 3%. However, the quid pro quo for permission to use actual LGD is compliance with an additional set of minimum requirements attesting to the efficacy of the bank's information systems in maintaining data on LGD.

Another adjustment to the Foundation Approach's BRW is the incorporation of a maturity adjustment reflecting the transaction's effective maturity, defined as the greater of either one year or nominal maturity, which is the weighted average life (= $\sum_t tP_t/\sum_t P_t$ where P_t is the minimum amount of principal contractually payable at time t) for all instruments with a predetermined, minimum amortization schedule. The maturity is capped at seven years in order to avoid overstating the impact of maturity on credit risk exposure.

The Advanced IRB Approach allows the bank to use its own credit risk mitigation estimates to adjust PD, LGD, and EAD for collateral, credit derivatives, guarantees, and on-balance sheet netting. The risk weights for the mark-to-market Advanced IRB Approach are calculated as follows:

$$\mathrm{RW} = (\mathrm{LGD}/50) \times \mathrm{BRW}(\mathrm{PD}) \times [1 + \mathrm{b}(\mathrm{PD}) \times (\mathrm{M} - 3)] \quad (7)$$

$$\text{where } \mathrm{b}(\mathrm{PD}) = [.0235 \times (1 - \mathrm{PD})]/[\mathrm{PD}^{0.44} + .0470 \times (1 - \mathrm{PD})] \quad (8)$$

and *BRW* is as defined in the Foundation IRB Approach.

The effect of the $[1 + \mathrm{b}(\mathrm{PD}) \times (\mathrm{M} - 3)]$ term in equation (7) is to adjust the risk of loans for its maturity.[46] For longer maturity instruments, the maturity adjustments increase for low PD rated borrowers (i.e., higher quality borrowers). The intuition is that maturity matters most for low PD borrowers since they can move only in one direction (downward) and the longer the maturity of the loan, the more likely this is to occur. For high PD (low quality) borrowers who are near default, the maturity adjustment will not matter as much since they may be close to default regardless of the length of the maturity of the loan.[47]

The Advanced IRB Approach entails the estimation of parameters requiring long histories of data that are unavailable to most banks.[48] Given the costs of developing these models and databases, there is the possibility of dichotomizing the banking in-

---

[45]Carty (1998) find the mean LGD for senior unsecured (secured) bank loans is 21% (13%). Carey (1998) finds mean LGD of 36% for a portfolio of private placements. Asarnow and Edwards (1995) find a 35% LGD for commercial loans. Gupton (2000) find a 30.5% (47.9%) LGD for senior secured (unsecured) syndicated bank loans. Gupton et al. (2000) obtain similar estimates for expected LGD, but find substantial variance around the mean.

[46]This may incorporate a mark to market adjustment. However, the mark to market adjustment in BIS II does not incorporate the transition risk (deterioration in credit quality) and spread risk (change in the market price of credit risk) components of a fully mark to market model. There is also an alternative specification of the *b*(PD) adjustment based on the default mode assumption.

[47]That is, for loans with maturities longer than three years, the increase in the capital requirement relative to the BRW decreases as the loan quality deteriorates. This could increase the relative cost of long term bank credit for low risk borrowers. See Allen (2002a).

[48]See the Basel Committee on Banking Supervision (1999a) for a survey of current credit risk modeling practices at 20 large international banks located in ten countries.

dustry into "haves and have-nots." For example, some anecdotal estimates suggest that no more than 15 U.S. banks will choose to use either of the IRB approaches. Moreover, capital requirements are highly sensitive to the accuracy of certain parameter values; in particular, estimates of LGD and the granularity in PD are important (see Gordy (2000) and Carey (2000)). Since credit losses are affected by economic conditions, the model parameters should also be adjusted to reflect expected levels of economic activity. Thus, the data requirements are so substantial that full implementation of the Advanced IRB Approach lies far in the future even for the most sophisticated banks. And when that date comes, regulators will have commensurate challenges in obtaining the necessary data to validate the banks' models.

3.5 ASSESSMENT. BIS II is a potential improvement over BIS I in its sophistication in measuring credit risk. Moreover, it moves regulatory capital in the direction of economic capital. However, it is far from an integrated portfolio management approach to credit risk measurement. Focus on individual ratings classifications (whether external or internal) prevents an aggregated view of credit risk across all transactions, and regulatory concerns about systemic risk prevent full consideration of cross-asset correlations that might reduce capital requirements further.[49] Thus, capital requirements are likely to be higher than economically necessary when considering actual portfolio correlations[50] Moreover, incompatible approaches to assessing the capital adequacy of insurance companies and other nonbanking firms may obscure their impact on financial system instability. In the United States, the insurance industry and government-sponsored enterprises (such as Fannie Mae and Freddie Mac), and the Financial Services Authority in the United Kingdom all use a variety of models, ranging from minimum ratios and stress test survivorship requirements to dynamic risk-of-ruin scenario analysis, that include both the asset and liability sides of the balance sheet in order to measure capital requirements.

The Advanced IRB Approach also contains some properties that may distort bank incentives to manage their credit risk exposure. For example, Allen (2002a) finds that the maturity adjustment in the Advanced IRB Approach (see equation(7)) creates perverse incentives when dealing with loans with maturities greater than three years such that the loan adjustment factor *decreases* the loan's risk weight as the loan quality (credit rating) declines. Moreover, the Advanced IRB Approach penalizes increases in LGD more than increases in PD. Exhibit 3.8 uses data from Altman and Saunders (2001b) to determine the impact of increases in LGD on the Advanced IRB risk weights for loans with maturity of three years keeping expected losses (i.e., LGD $\times$ PD) constant. For all risk buckets (for illustrative purposes only, the Standardized Approach's risk classifications are used), the Advanced IRB risk weights increase as

[49]Hoggarth, et al. (2001) show that cumulative output losses during systemic crises average 15 to 20% of annual GDP.

[50]That is, the IRB frameworks are calibrated to an asset correlation of 0.20, which is higher than actual correlations that averaged 9 to 10% for eurobonds; see Jackson et al. (2001). The November 2001 potential modifications to BIS II proposals incorporate a correlation coefficient that is inversely related to the PD. However, Freixas et al. (2000) show that systemic crises may occur even if all banks are solvent.

BIS II Risk Buckets (1)	Actual LGD Altman & Saunders (2)	PD% Altman & Saunders (3)	Increased LGD (4)	Decreased PD% (5)	Advanced IRB Risk Weight Altman & Saunders	Advanced IRB Risk Weight using cols. (4) & (5)
AAA–AA–	0	0	0	0	0	0
A+ A–	20.714	0.058	25	0.048	3.585	4.327
BBB+ BB–	18.964	0.857	20	0.813	16.315	17.206
Below BB–	28.321	9.787	35	7.919	153.063	189.160

Notes: The LGD and PD values in columns (2) and (3) are taken from Altman and Saunders (2001b). The LGD and PD values in columns (4) and (5) are adjusted to increase LGD while keeping expected losses (LGD × PD) constant).

Exhibit 3.8. The Impact of Increases in LGD on Advanced Internal Ratings–Based Risk Weights under BIS II Holding Expected Losses Constant

the LGD increases, although the PD decreases offset the LGD increases so as to keep expected losses constant.

BIS II is based on a prespecified threshold insolvency level; that is, capital levels are set so that the estimated probability of insolvency of each bank is lower than a threshold level such as 99.9% (or 0.1% probability of failure per year, or one bank insolvency every 1,000 years).[51] However, there are two potential shortcomings to this approach from the regulator's point of view. First, without considering the relationship between individual banks' insolvency probabilities. BIS II cannot specify an aggregate, system-wide insolvency risk threshold (see Acharya (2001)). Second, there is no information about the magnitude of loss given bank insolvency. The deposit insurer, for example, may be concerned about the cost to the deposit insurance fund in the event that the bank's capital is exhausted. (See Gordy (2000) for a discussion of the estimation of the "expected tail loss.") BIS II addresses neither of these concerns. However, there is evidence (see Jackson et al. (2001)) that banks hold capital in excess of the regulatory minimum in response to market pressure; for example, in order to participate in the swap market, the bank's credit quality must be higher than would be induced by complying with either BIS I or II.[52] Thus, regulatory capital requirements may be considered lower bounds that do not obviate the need for more precise credit risk measurement.

3.6 SUMMARY. The new Basel Accord on bank capital (BIS II) makes capital requirements more sensitive to credit risk exposure. Regulations governing minimum capital requirements allow the bank to evolve through three steps: (1) The Standard-

[51]Jackson et al. (2001) show that BIS II is calibrated to achieve a confidence level of 99.96% (i.e., an insolvency rate of 0.4%), whereas banks choose a solvency standard 99.9% in response to market pressures. This conforms to observations that banks tend to hold capital in excess of regulatory requirements.

[52]Jackson et al. (2001) find that a decrease in the bank's credit rating from A+ to A would reduce swap liabilities by approximately £2.3 billion.

ized Model, (2) The Internal Ratings-Based (IRB) Foundation Approach, and (3) The Advanced IRB Approach. In the Standardized Model, credit risk weights are determined using external ratings assigned by independent credit rating agencies. For commercial loans, there are four risk buckets (plus an unrated classification) corresponding to prespecified corporate credit ratings.

The IRB approaches require banks to formulate their own internal ratings models in order to classify the credit risk of their activities. The Foundation Approach requires that the bank estimate only the probability of default (PD) and the exposure at default (EAD). There are two additional parameter estimates required to implement the Advanced Approach: the loss given default (LGD) and the maturity (M). BIS II requires supervisors to validate the internal models developed by the banks, in conjunction with enhanced disclosure requirements that reveal more detailed credit risk information to the market.

APPENDIX A: MAPPING OF S&P, MOODY'S, AND FITCH IBCA RATINGS

Exhibits 3A.1 through 3A.5 use Standard & Poor's credit ratings in order to derive the risk weights under the Standardized Approach. Exhibit 3A.1 shows how Standard & Poor's ratings can be mapped onto comparable Moody's and Fitch IBCA ratings.

Standard & Poor's Credit Rating	Moody's Credit Rating	Fitch IBCA Credit Rating
AAA	Aaa	AAA
AA+	Aa1	AA+
AA	Aa2	AA
AA–	Aa3	AA–
A+	A1	A+
A	A2	A
A–	A3	A–
BBB+	Baa1	BBB+
BBB	Baa2	BBB
BBB–	Baa3	BBB–
BB+	Ba1	BB+
BB	Ba2	BB
BB–	Ba3	BB–
B+	B1	B+
B	B2	B
B–	B3	B–
CCC+	Caa1	CCC+
CCC	Caa2	CCC
CCC–	Caa3	CCC–
CC	Ca	CC
C	C	C
D		D

Source: BIS (April 30, 2001)

Exhibit 3A.1 Mapping of Standard & Poor's, Moody's, and Fitch IBCA Credit Ratings

APPENDIX B: BIS II TREATMENT OF RETAIL EXPOSURES UNDER THE INTERNAL RATINGS-BASED APPROACH

The retail portfolio is defined as a "large number of small, low value loans with either a consumer or a business focus, in which the incremental risk of any particular exposure is small."[53] (BIS, 2001a), "The Internal Ratings-Based Approach," p. 59.) This includes: credit cards, installment loans (e.g., personal finance, education loans, auto loans, leasing), revolving credits (e.g., overdrafts, home equity lines of credit), residential mortgages, and small business facilities. To be considered "retail," the loans must be managed by the bank as a large pool of fairly homogeneous loans. The retail loan portfolio is typically divided into segments based on each segment's PD, LGD, and EAD. For each loan, the bank determines the EAD and multiplies that by the risk weight,[54] which in turn is dependent on a benchmark risk weight following the methodology shown in equation (2), but calibrated to different constants as follows:

$$\text{BRW} = 976.5 \times N(1.043 \times \text{G(PD)}\ 0.766) \times (1 + .0470 \times (1 - \text{PD})/\text{PD}^{0.44}) \tag{B1}$$

The term $N(y)$, where y reflects the variables in equation (4), denotes the cumulative distribution function for a standard normal random variable (i.e., the probability that a normal random variable with mean zero and variance of one is less than or equal to y) and the term $G(z)$, where z reflects the term in brackets in equation (B1), denotes the inverse cumulative distribution function for a standard normal random variable (i.e., the value y such that $N(y) = z$). The risk weight formula is calibrated to a three year retail loan maturity with a LGD = 50%. As for corporate loans, the BRW is substituted into equation (1) to determine the retail loan's risk weight. In Exhibit B.1, the benchmark risk weights for retail loans are compared to the BRW for corporate loans; both sets of loans assume a three-year maturity and a LGD = 50%. As shown in Exhibit 3B.1, retail loans have lower benchmark risk weights for every value of PD reflecting lower minimum captial requirements for the retail sector.[55]

In July 2002, the Basel Committee on Banking Supervision published potential modifications to the BIS II proposals for retail obligations. Under the modifications (if adopted) residential mortgages would have a higher risk weight curve than other retail exposures, but both retail risk weight curves would be lower than the one specified in equation (B1) under the BIS II proposals.

The residential mortgage risk weight curve under the IRB Approach is:[56]

$$\text{BRW} = 12.50 \times \text{LGD} \times \text{N}[(1 - \text{R})^{-.0.5} \times \text{G(PD)} + (\text{R}/(1 - \text{R}))^{0.5} \times \text{G}(0.999)] \tag{B2}$$

---

[53]BIS 2001, "The Internal Ratings-Based Approach," p. 59.

[54]If EAD cannot be determined, the bank can use an estimate of expected losses, or PD × LGD.

[55]The lower retail capital charges reflect BIS concern that certain retail portfolios may generate expected margin income sufficient to cover expected losses (EL). Thus, the proposed risk weights, which cover both EL and UL, may overstate capital requirements.

[56]There is no distinction between IRB Foundation and Advanced for retail credits.

Probability of Default PD (%)	Corporate Loan Benchmark Risk Weight	Retail Loan Benchmark Weight
0.03	14	6
0.05	19	9
0.1	29	14
0.2	45	21
0.4	70	34
0.5	81	40
0.7	100	50
1	125	64
2	192	104
3	246	137
5	331	195
10	482	310
15	588	401
20	625	479

Notes: Both the corporate and retail loans are calibrated to a 3 year maturity and a LGD = 50 percent.

Source: BIS (2001a), "The Internal Ratings–Based Approach."

Exhibit 3B.1 Comparison of Benchmark Risk Weights under BIS Internal Ratings–Based Foundation Approach for Corporate versus Retail Loans: January 2001 Proposal

where the correlation R is calibrated to equal 0.15. As in the BIS II proposals, the LGD is set at 50% for the IRB Foundation Approach.

The other retail exposures risk weight curve is:

$$\begin{aligned} \text{BRW} = 12.50 \times [&\text{LGD} \times \text{N}[(1 - \text{R})^{-.0.5} \times \text{G(PD)} + (\text{R}/(1 - \text{R}))^{0.5} \\ &\times \text{G}(0.999)] \end{aligned} \tag{B3}$$

where

$$\begin{aligned} \text{R} = &\ 0.02 \times (1 - e^{-35 \times \text{PD}})/(1 - e^{-35}) \\ &+ 0.17 \times [1 - (1 - e^{-35 \times \text{PD}})/(1 - e^{-35})] \end{aligned} \tag{B4}$$

The impact of the correlation expression in equation (B4) is to decrease the correlation coefficient at higher levels of PD. Thus, the risk weight for other retail credits is slightly above the risk weight for residential mortgages at low levels of PD (below 0.50%), but decreases (relative to the risk weight for residential mortgages) at higher levels of PD, as a result of the assumed inverse relationship between correlation and PD in equation (B4). That is, as PD exceeds 0.50%, the correlation on other retail credits calculated using equation (B4) falls below 0.15, thereby lowering the risk weight and the bank's capital requirement for other retail credit as compared to residential mortgages.

The July 2002 proposal introduced a third model for the measurement of bank capital requirements for revolving credit. Revolving credit has the lowest capital requirement of all three retail credits under the proposed July 2002 IRB. The lower capital requirements for revolving credit reflect a belief that although retail products have higher rates of estimated default and higher loss given default (LGD), the correlation among retail products is lower than among wholesale products. This assumption is reflected in the proposed regulations in two ways. First, the correlation expression for revolving credits is lower (at each level of PD) than the correlation for other retail credits (and lower than the correlation for residential mortgages at most levels of PD). Second, the capital requirement is lowered for revolving exposures to allow 90% of expected losses to be covered by future income. Thus, the July 2002 IRB proposals for risk weights for revolving credit are:

$$\begin{aligned} \mathrm{BRW} = {} & 12.50 \times \mathrm{LGD} \times \mathrm{N}\,[1/\sqrt{1-\mathrm{R}} \times \mathrm{G(PD)} + (\mathrm{R}/\sqrt{1-\mathrm{R}} \times \mathrm{G}(0.999))] \\ & - (0.90\mathrm{PD} \times \mathrm{LGD}) \end{aligned} \tag{B5}$$

For revolving exposures, the correlation is:

$$\begin{aligned} \mathrm{R} = {} & 0.02 \times (1 - e^{-50 \times \mathrm{PD}})(1 - e^{-50}) + 0.15 \\ & \times [1 - (1 - e^{-50 \times \mathrm{PD}})/(1 - e^{-50})] \end{aligned} \tag{B6}$$

The last term in equation (B5) reduces the capital requirement on revolving credits by 90% of expected losses (PD × LGD). Comparing equation (B6) to (B4) shows the lower correlation (at each level of PD) for revolving credits as compared to other retail credits.

SOURCES AND SUGGESTED REFERENCES

Acharya, V. V. "A Theory of Systemic Risk and Design of Prudential Bank Regulation." NYU, Dissertation Thesis, January 2001.

Allen, L. "Discussion," in *Ratings, Rating Agencies, and the Global Financial System.* Edited by R. Levich. Kluwer Academic Press, 2002(a) (forthcoming).

Allen, L. "Credit Risk Modeling of Middle Markets." Presented at the Wharton Conference on Credit Risk Modeling and Decisioning, May 29–30, 2002b.

Allen, L., and A. Saunders. "A Survey of Cyclical Effects in Credit Risk Measurement Models." NYU Stern School Department of Finance working paper, May 2002.

Altman, E. I. with B. Brady. "Explaining Aggregate Recovery Rates on Corporate Bond Defaults." Salomon Center Working Paper, November 2001.

Altman, E. I., and A. Saunders. "An Analysis and Critique of the BIS Proposal on Capital Adequacy and Ratings." *Journal of Banking and Finance*, January 2001(a), pp. 25–46.

Altman, E. I., and A. Saunders. "Credit Ratings and the BIS Reform Agenda." Paper presented at the Bank of England Conference on Banks and Systemic Risk, London, May 23–25, 2001(b).

Asarnow, E., and D. Edwards. "Measuring Loss on Defaulted Bank Loans: A 24-Year Study." *The Journal of Commercial Lending*, March 1995, pp. 11–23.

Bank for International Settlements. *Standardized Model for Market Risk.* Basel, Switzerland: Bank for International Settlements. 1996.

Bank for International Settlements. "Credit Risk Modeling: Current Practices and Applications." Basel Committee on Banking Supervision, Document No. 49, April 1999(a).

Bank for International Settlements. "Sound Practices for Loan Accounting and Disclosure." Basel Committee on Banking Supervision, Document No. 55, July 1999(b).

Bank for International Settlements. "Range of Practice in Banks' Internal Ratings Systems." Basel Committee on Banking Supervision, Document No. 66, January 2000.

Bank for International Settlements. "The New Basel Capital Accord," January 2001(a).

Bank for International Settlements. "Long-term Rating Scales Comparison," April 30, 2001(b).

Bank for International Settlements. "Working Paper on the Regulatory Treatment of Operational Risk," September 2001(c).

Bank for International Settlements. "Results of the Second Quantitative Study," November 5, 2001(c).

Bank for International Settlements. "Potential Modifications to the Committee's Proposals," November 5, 2001(e).

Bongini, P., L. Laeven, and G. Majnoni. "How Good is the Market at Assessing Bank Fragility: A Horse Race Between Different Indicators." World Bank, Working Paper, January 2001.

Cantor, R. "Moody's Investors Service Response to the Consultative Paper Issued by the Basel Committee on Bank Supervision 'A New Capital Adequacy Approach'." *Journal of Banking and Finance*, January 2001, pp. 171–186.

Cantor, R., and F. Packer. "Determinants and Impacts of Sovereign Credit Ratings." *Economic Policy Review*. Federal Reserve Bank of New York, October, 1996, pp. 37–53.

Carey, M. "Credit Risk in Private Debt Portfolios." *Journal of Finance*, August 1998, pp. 1363–1387.

Carey, M. "Dimensions of Credit Risk and Their Relationship to Economic Capital Requirements." NBER, Working Paper 7629, March 2000.

Carey, M. "Consistency of Internal versus External Credit Ratings and Insurance and Bank Regulatory Capital Requirements." Federal Reserve Board, Working Paper, February 2001(a).

Carey, M. "A Policymaker's Guide to Choosing Absolute Bank Capital Requirements." Federal Reserve Board Working Paper, June 3, 2001(b), Presented at the Bank of England Conference on Banks and Systemic Risk, May 23–25, 2001(b).

Carey, M. and M. Hrycay. "Parameterizing Credit Risk Models with Rating Data." *Journal of Banking and Finance*, Vol. 25, No. 1, 2001, pp. 197–270.

Carty, L. V. "Bankrupt Bank Loan Recoveries." Moody's Investors Service, *Rating Methodology*, June 1998.

Cavallo, M., and G. Majnoni. "Do Banks Provision for Bad Loans in Good Times? Empirical Evidence and Policy Implications." World Bank, Working Paper 2691, June 2001.

Cunningham, A. "Bank Credit Risk in Emerging Markets." Moody's Investors Service, *Rating Methodology*, July 1999.

Diamond, D. "Financial Intermediation and Delegated Monitoring." *Review of Economic Studies*, Vol. 51, 1984. pp. 393–414.

The Economist. "The Basel Perplex," November 10, 2001, pp. 65–66.

Falkenheim, M., and A. Powell. "The Use of Credit Bureau Information in the Estimation of Appropriate Capital and Provisioning Requirements." Central Bank of Argentina, Working Paper, 2001.

Ferri, G., L. G. Liu, and G. Majnoni. "The Role of Rating Agency Assessments in Less Developed Countries: Impact of the Proposed Basel Guidelines." *Journal of Banking and Finance*, January 2001, pp. 115–148.

Flood, M. "Basel Buckets and Loan Losses: Absolute and Relative Loan Underperformance at Banks and Thrifts." Office of Thrift Supervision, Working Paper, March 9, 2001.

Freixas, X., B. Parigi, and J. C. Rochet. "Systemic Risk, Interbank Relations, and Liquidity Provision by the Central Bank." *Journal of Money, Credit and Banking*, Vol. 32, No. 3, Part II, August 2001.

Gordy, M. B. "A Comparative Anatomy of Credit Risk Models." *Journal of Banking and Finance*, January 2000, pp. 119–149.

Gordy, M. B. "A Risk-Factor Model Foundation for Ratings-Based Bank Capital Rules." Board of Governors of the Federal Reserve System, Working Paper, February 5, 2001.

Griep, C., and M. De Stefano. "Standard & Poor's Official Response to the Basel Committee's Proposal." *Journal of Banking and Finance*, January 2001, pp. 149–170.

Gully, B., W. Perraudin, V. Saporta. "Risk and Economic Capital for Combined Banking and Insurance Activities." Paper presented at the Bank of England Conference on Banks and Systemic Risk, London, May 23–25, 2001.

Gupton, G. M. "Bank Loan Loss Given Default." Moody's Investors Service, *Special Comment*, November 2000.

Gupton, G. M., D. Gates, and L. V. Carty. "Bank-Loan Loss Given Default." Moody's Investors Service, *Global Credit Research*, November 2000.

Hammes, W., and M. Shapiro. "The Implications of the New Capital Adequacy Rules for Portfolio Management of Credit Assets." *Journal of Banking and Finance*, January 2001, pp. 97–114.

Hoggarth, G., R. Reis, and V. Saporta. "Costs of Banking System Instability: Some Empirical Evidence." Paper presented at the Bank of England Conference on Banks and Systemic Risk, London, May 23–25, 2001.

Institute for International Finance/International Swap Dealers Association (IIF/JSDA). "Modeling Credit Risk: Joint IIF/JSDA Testing Program," February 2000.

International Swaps and Derivatives Association (ISDA). *Credit Risk and Regulatory Capital.* New York/London, March 1998.

Jackson, P., W. Perraudin, and V. Saporta. "Setting Minimum Capital for Internationally Active Banks." Paper presented at the Bank of England Conference on Banks and Systemic Risk, London, May 23–26, 2001.

Jewell, J., and M. Livingston. "A Comparison of Bond Ratings from Moody's, S&P, and Fitch." *Financial Markets, Institutions, and Instruments*, Vol. 8, No. 4, 1999.

Jones, D. "Emerging Problems with the Basel Capital Accord: Regulatory Capital Arbitrage and Related Issues." *Journal of Banking and Finance*, Vol. 24, 2000, pp. 35–58.

Kaminsky, G., and S. Schmukler. "Emerging Markets Instability: Do Sovereign Ratings Affect Country Risk and Stock Returns?" World Bank, Working Paper, February 28, 2001.

Kealhofer, S. "The Quantification of Credit Risk." KMV Corporation, January 2000, (unpublished).

Leonhardt, D. "More Falling Behind on Mortgage Payments." *New York Times*, June 12, 2001, pp. A1, C5.

Linnell, I. "A Critical Review of the New Capital Adequacy Framework Paper Issued by the Basel Committee on Banking Supervision and its Implications for the Rating Agency Industry." *Journal of Banking and Finance*, January 2001, pp. 187–196.

McQuown, J. A., and S. Kealhofer. "A Comment on the Formation of Bank Stock Prices." KMV Corporation, April 1997.

Mingo, J. J. "Policy Implications of the Federal Reserve Study of Credit Risk Models at Major US Banking Institutions." *Journal of Banking and Finance*, January 2000, pp. 15–33.

Monfort, B., and C. Mulder. "Using Credit Ratings for Capital Requirements on Lending to Emerging Market Economies—Possible Impact of a New Basel Accord." International Monetary Fund, Working Paper WP/00/69, 2000.

Powell, A. "A Capital Accord for Emerging Economies?" World Bank working paper, July 11, 2001.

Reinhart, C. "Sovereign Credit Ratings Before and After Financial Crises." Dept. of Economics, University of Maryland. February 21, 2001, presented at the Conference on Rating Agencies in the Global Financial System, Stern School of Business NYU, June 1, 2001.

Reisen, H. "Revisions to the Basel Accord and Sovereign Ratings." In R. Hausmann and U. Hiemenz (eds.), *Global Finance From a Latin American Viewpoint.* IDB/OECD Development Centre, 2000.

Reisen, H., and J. von Maltzan. "Boom and Bust and Sovereign Ratings." *International Finance*, Vol. 2.2, July 1999, pp. 273–293.

Saunders, A., and L. Allen. *Credit Risk Measurement: New Approaches to Value at Risk and Other Paradigms*, 2nd edition. New York: John Wiley & Sons, 2002.

Saunders, A., and M. M. Cornett. *Financial Institutions Management: A Risk Management Approach*, 4th edition. John Wiley & Sons, New York, 2002.

Theodore, S. S. "Rating Methodology: Bank Credit Risk (An Analytical Framework for Banks in Developed Markets.)" Moody's Investors Service, *Rating Methodology*, April 1999.

Treacy, W., and M. Carey. "Internal Credit Risk Rating Systems at Large U.S. Banks." *Federal Reserve Bulletin*, November 1998.

Treacy, W. F., and M. Carey. "Credit Risk Rating Systems at Large U.S. Banks." *Journal of Banking and Finance*, January 2000, pp. 167–201.

Wall, L. D., and T. W. Koch. "Bank Loan-Loss Accounting: A Review of the Theoretical and Empirical Evidence." *Federal Reserve Bank of Atlanta Economic Review*, Second Quarter 2000, pp. 1–19.

White, L. "The Credit Rating Industry: An Industrial Organization Analysis." Presented at the Conference on Rating Agencies in the Global Financial System. Stern School of Business NYU, June 1, 2001.

PART II

FINANCIAL ANALYSIS

CHAPTER 4

FOREIGN INVESTMENT ANALYSIS

David K. Eiteman
University of California, Los Angeles

CONTENTS

4.1 INTRODUCTION. Foreign investment analysis is the procedure for analyzing expected cash flows for a proposed direct foreign investment to determine if the potential investment is worth undertaking. In finance literature, foreign investment analysis is also called capital budgeting. Foreign investment analysis is concerned with direct (as distinct from portfolio) investments. Examples range from purchase of new equipment to replace existing equipment, to an investment in an entirely new business venture in a country where, typically, manufacturing or assembly has not previously been done. The technique is also useful for decisions to disinvest, that is, liquidate or simply walk away from an existing foreign investment.

The overall foreign investment decision has two components: the quantitative analysis of available data ("capital budgeting" proper) and the decision to invest abroad as part of the firm's strategic plans. Investments of sufficient size as to be important are usually conceived initially because they fit into a firm's strategic plan. The quantitative analysis which follows is usually done to determine if implementation of the strategic plan is financially feasible or desirable.

This chapter deals with the quantitative aspects of foreign investment analysis. It treats, first, the general methodology of capital budgeting, second, the international complexities of that procedure, and third, the implications of international accounting for conclusions reached by that methodology. For convenience, the United States will be regarded as "home." However, the principles discussed have relevance for any home company investing in a foreign land.

An example of the foreign capital budgeting process appears in Appendix A to illustrate how an international project might be evaluated.

4.2 GENERAL METHODOLOGY FOR ONE-COUNTRY CAPITAL BUDGETING. Capital budgeting is essentially concerned with three types of data: (1) cash outflows (i.e., project costs) and (2) project cash inflows, both of which are measured over a period of time, and (3) the marginal cost of capital. This chapter will follow the typical procedure of using annual time periods, but an analysis could be based on cash flows for quarters, months, or even days.

(a) Project Cash Outflows (Costs). Project cash outflows refers to the *cash* cost paid out to start the project. Usually the outflow for an investment occurs at the time when the investment is made, which is to say in "year 0" if the project is to be analyzed in annual time periods. However, other time squences are possible; for example, the cash outlay could occur over several years, as when a very large hydroelectric plant is being constructed.

Cash outflows include:

- Cash paid for all new assets purchased.
- Cash paid to prepare a new site. These outlays might be for such costs as grading, building access roads, or installing utilities.
- Cash paid to dispose of, remove, or destroy old equipment or other assets, or, alternatively, net cash received from the sale of old assets. Cash disbursed or received, net of any tax effect, is the relevant flow.
- Cash cost of additional storage and/or transportation facilities needed because of the new investment. If the new venture necessitates additional warehousing space or additional transportation equipment (e.g., a new fleet of trucks), these additional costs must be included as part of the required supporting investment for the project.

- Cash payment for any *additional* engineering or design work to be incurred if a decision is made to invest. Care must be taken not to include "sunk costs" which reflect cash outflows already incurred in the process of preparing for the investment decision. The relevant cash outflows are those incurred from the decision day forward and only if the project is undertaken.
- The cash opportunity cost of any existing equipment or space allocated to the project. If a section of a factory is currently idle but would be used for the new project, the relevant cost is the alternate cash flow that section might generate. (Could it be subleased to another firm?) If no alternative use exists for the section (i.e., it will otherwise sit idle), it has no cash opportunity cost. An accounting allocation of overhead to departments or divisions on the basis of floor space occupied is not a relevant cost, because it does not involve cash flow.
- Investment in additional working capital necessitated by the new project, such as larger cash balances, more inventory, or expanded receivables. These items might be negative (i.e., a cash recovery) if a replacement project enables the firm to operate with less cash, inventory, or receivables.
- Outlays in future years needed to supplement the original investment. Examples are periodic major overhauls of key assets and costs incurred at the end of the project to close it. Examples of the latter are the cost of disposing of nuclear waste or restoring an open pit mining site to a natural state by regrading and replanting.

The essence of determining what cash outflows are relevant to the investment decision is to look only at those future cash outflows that will take place because of the investment decision, and to ignore both earlier cash outflows undertaken for analytical purposes (sunk costs) and accounting overhead charges which do not represent additional new cash outflows.

(b) Project Cash Inflows. The relevant cash inflows for any project are those that will be received by the firm in each future year from the investment. This set of cash flows must be identified by specific year.

Each annual cash inflow differs from net income for that same period for two general reasons:

1. The cash inflows are calculated ignoring noncash expenses, such as depreciation of assets, or amortization of earlier costs, such as research and development (R&D) or prior-service pension costs.
2. The calculation is usually made on the hypothetical assumption that the entire venture is financed with equity (stockholder) funds and that taxes are thus based upon such an "all-equity" assumption. Consequently, the income tax calculation is a hypothetical amount, unless the firm is, in fact, financed without any debt. (The tax shelter consequences of interest payments are incorporated into the cost-of-capital calculation.)

A simplified view of a single year's cash flow calculations is illustrated below.

Projected Income Statement with New Investment		Projected Cash Flow Statement with New Investment	
New Sales	$ 2,000	New Sales	$ 2,000
Cost of goods sold	–1,000	Cost of goods sold	–1,000
Administrative expenses	–200	Administrative expenses	–200
Amortization of prior service pension costs	–50	Amortization of prior service pension costs	0
Depreciation	–150	Depreciation	0
Total expenses	$–1,400	Total cash outflow	$–1,200
Earnings before interest and taxes (EBIT)	600	Cash flow before taxes	800
Interest expense	–200		
Pretax earnings	$ 400	Less hypothetical tax on EBIT (.34) (600)	$ –204
Income taxes @ 34%	–136		
Net earnings	$ 264	Net cash flow to equity investors	$ 596

The project cash flow of $596 can be calculated from the income statement (above left) by either a top-down or a bottom-up approach.

Top-Down Approach

Cash flow = EBIT – (TAX RATE) (EBIT) + DEPRECIATION + AMORTIZATION
= 600 – (.34) (600) + 150 + 50
= 596

Bottom-Up Approach

Cash flow = NET INCOME + DEPRECIATION + AMORTIZATION + (1 – TAX RATE) (INTEREST)
= 264 + 150 + 50 + (.66) (200)
= 596

The top-down or bottom-up simplification is important, because, in practice, one or the other is often applied to pro forma income statements for a project as the fastest way to estimate likely cash flows. Hence, the person doing the calculations is often an unconscious slave to the accounting methods used in the pro forma analysis, and, when those methods differ from home country methods, errors are made.

The all-equity method just illustrated is justified for domestic capital budgeting because the tax shelter created by interest expense is incorporated into the cost-of-capital calculation. However when this all-equity method is used for an international project, the project analyst must be aware that only actual foreign taxes paid can be used as a credit against U.S. taxes levied on grossed up dividends received from the foreign subsidiary.[1] The hypothetical tax used for the cash flow calculation is not a valid base for credit against U.S. taxes.

[1]The grossing up of dividends from foreign affiliates to calculate taxable income for U.S. taxes is treated more fully in Chapter 30 of this book. Suffice it to say that dividends received from foreign operating affiliates are increased ("grossed up") by the amount of foreign tax paid on the income which generated that dividend, a tenative U.S. tax is calculated on this grossed up income, and the actual tax paid

(c) Cost of Capital. Cost of capital is the discount rate used to equate present and future cash flows. This discount rate is more properly called the "weighted-average cost of capital" (WACC). It is found by combining the cost of the firm's equity with the cost of its debt in proportion to the relative weight of each in the firm's optimal long-term financial structure. More specifically:

$$K = K_e\frac{E}{V} + K_d(1 - t)\frac{D}{V}$$

where

K = weighted-average cost of capital (WACC), after tax
K_c = risk-adjusted cost of equity
K_d = before-tax cost of debt
t = marginal income tax rate
E = market value of the firm's equity
D = market value of the firm's debt
V = total market value of the firm's securities ($E + D$).

The essence of this calculation is that the firm determines a mix of debt and equity for its capital structure such that the resulting weighted average of the costs of equity and debt are minimized. With interest costs adjusted for the fact that interest is deducted before calculating income taxes, the resultant WACC indicates the minimum rate of earnings on any project necessary if the value of the firm is to be maintained. The WACC thus becomes an acceptable "hurdle" rate, usable as a cutoff criteria for evaluating new projects.

(d) Combining Cash Outflows, Cash Inflows, and the Cost of Capital. Traditionally, cash outflows, cash inflows, and the weighted-average cost of capital are combined in one of two ways to determine the feasibility of an investment proposal. The two approaches are net present value (NPV) and internal rate of return (IRR). The interaction of cash outflows, cash inflows, and the cost of capital is shown in Exhibit 4.1.

The operating rule for the net present value (NPV) approach is:

If present value (cash inflows discounted at the cost of capital) is greater than project cost (cash outflows discounted at the cost of capital), make the investment because net present value is positive.

The operating rule for the internal rate of return (IRR) approach is:

If the internal rate of return (the discount rate which equates cash inflows and cash outflows) is greater than the firm's weighted-average cost of capital, make the investment.

in the foreign country is deducted from the tentative U.S. charge in determining the actual additional U.S. tax paid. The effect of this is that annual earnings retained in foreign countries are taxed only at the foreign rate, but the income from which dividends are declared back to the United States is taxed at the higher of the foreign or the U.S. rate.

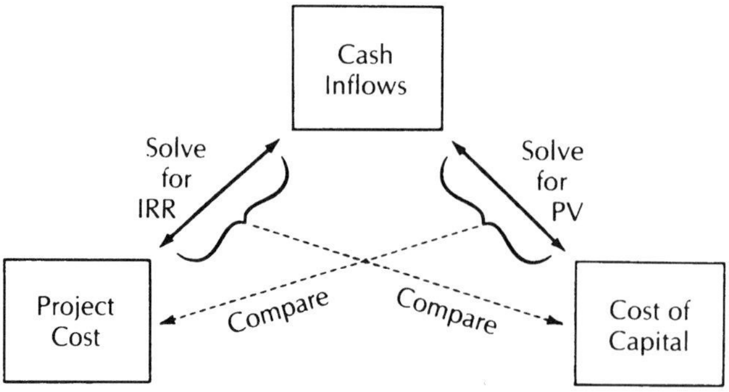

Exhibit 4.1. Interaction of Project Cost, Cash Inflows, and Cost of Capital in Capital Budgeting Analysis.

Under most conditions, NPV and IRR lead to the same decision. However, different decisions may result under certain circumstances, such as when projects of substantially different lifetimes are compared or when cash flows fluctuate sharply from year to year. If NPV and IRR give different decisions, NPV is preferable on theoretical grounds.[2] Hence, NPV is used in the illustrative example at the end of this chapter.

4.3 INTERNATIONAL COMPLEXITIES. Capital budgeting for a foreign project uses the one-country framework just described, but with certain adjustments to reflect the greater complexities in an international situation. Many of the adjustments arise because of the fact that two separate sovereign nations are involved and the operating cash flows in the host country are in a different currency than those desired by the parent company.

(a) Project versus Parent Cash Flows. Project (e.g., host country) cash flows must be distinguished from parent (e.g., home country) cash flows. Project cash flows generally follow the domestic, or one-country model, described earlier. However, parent cash flows reflect all cash flow consequences for the parent company.

(b) Parent Cash Flows Tied to Financing. Because of the above, parent cash flows depend, in part, on financing. Unlike the domestic situation, financing cannot be kept separate from operating cash flows. In fact, "clever" financing is often the key to making an otherwise unattractive foreign investment proposal attractive to the parent firm. Cash may flow back to the parent because the venture is structured from a financial point of view to provide such flows. Fund flows back to the parent on international projects arise from any of the following, which must be incorporated into the original investment agreement:

- Dividends.
- Royalties.

[2]Readers should consult a standard domestic financial management text for an explanation of why NPV is theoretically superior to IRR.

- License fees.
- Interest on parent-supplied debt.
- Principal repayment of parent-supplied debt.
- Liquidating dividends.
- Transfer prices paid on goods supplied by the parent.
- Transfer prices paid on goods sent to the parent.
- Overhead charges.
- Recovery of assets at project end (i.e., terminal value).

Note that depreciation is not a cash flow to the parent.

(c) Foreign Exchange Forecasts Needed. An explicit forecast is needed for future exchange rates. Future cash flows in a foreign currency have value to the parent only in terms of the exchange rates existing at the time funds are repatriated, or valued if they are not repatriated. Hence, an exchange rate forecast is necessary. In addition, the investment decision must consider the possibility, if not the probability, of unanticipated deviations between actual ending exchange rates and the original forecast.

(d) Long-Range Inflation Must Be Considered. Over the extended period of years anticipated by most investments, inflation will have three effects on the value of the operation: (1) inflation will influence the amount of local currency cash flows, both in terms of the amount of local money received for sales and paid for expenses and in terms of the impact local inflation will have on future foreign competition: (2) inflation will influence the future foreign exchange rates used to measure the parent company's value of local currency cash flows; and (3) inflation will influence the real cost of financing choices between domestic and foreign sources of capital.

(e) Subsidized Financing Must Be Explicitly Treated. Subsidized financing available from the host government must be explicitly treated. If a host country provides subsidized financing at a rate below market rates, the value of that subsidy must be considered. If the lower rate is built into a cost-of-capital calculation, the firm is making an implicit assumption that the subsidy will continue forever. It is preferable to build subsidized interest rates into the analysis by adding the present value of the subsidy rather than by changing the cost of capital.

(f) Political Risk Must Be Considered. The host government may change its attitude towards foreign influence or control over some segments of the local economy. This may be through sudden revolution, or it may result from a gradual evolution in the political objectives of the host goverment. Political risk is also important in determining the terminal value, because politics may impose a specific ending date which negates use of an infinite horizon for valuation purposes. If a specific ending date is mandated, the value received on that date may be extremely difficult to anticipate. In the context of premiums for political risk, diversification among countries may create a portfolio effect such that no single country need bear the higher return that would otherwise be imposed if that country were the only location of a foreign investment.

4.4 ACCOUNTING IMPLICATIONS FOR THE METHODOLOGY. The key concept in this section is that accounting principles and policies that are used in a particular country are likely also to be used in developing pro forma financial statements for a particular project. These pro forma financial statements, in turn, are likely to be the database from which financial executives estimate future cash flows as they try to determine whether or not the proposed project has a positive or a negative net present value. If financial executives are not aware of how the foreign accounting system differs from the home system, they may base their analysis on faulty cash flow data.

Accounting differences can be grouped by type. Specifically, we can think of (1) asset costs which become expenses as they are allocated to specific time periods, (2) operating costs of the current time period which do not flow through in the calculation of current income, (3) changes in the recorded amount of debt not matched by cash payments, and (4) basic differences in underlying accounting principles and methods.

Some of these differences are relevant only when estimating cash flows for a physical investment, such as a new machine or a building. Others are relevant only when investing in an entire foreign corporation, in which case past and pro forma financial statements may be the base for estimating future cash flows.

Accounting differences, by type, are discussed in the following paragraphs.

(a) Asset Cost Allocation to Income Periods

(i) Fixed Asset Depreciation. Variations between historical cost depreciation and some types of replacement cost depreciation lead to different net income calculations. The difference in depreciation method may influence income tax payments and consequently cash flow after taxes.

(ii) Inventory Costing. Variations between historical costing and replacement costing, and also between first in, first out (FIFO) and last in, first out (LIFO) as alternative methods of historical costing, have an influence on reported income, on taxes on that reported income, and on income allocation between time periods. The first two of these influence measures of cash flow, and the third influences the timing of total cash flow, with a possible consequence for any valuation method based on discounting.

(iii) Amortization of Purchased Goodwill. In some countries, purchased goodwill is amortized, reducing net income and possibly income taxes. However, goodwill amortization is not a cash cost. In other countries, purchased goodwill cannot be amortized. In either case, cash flow must be adjusted to account for the amortization or nonamortization of goodwill, or any similar cost. Such amortization, it will be noted, is a noncash expense similar to depreciation.

(iv) Asset Revaluation. In some high-inflation countries, such as Argentina, Brazil, and Israel, fixed assets are revalued upward to bring accounts closer to reality. The related expenses, such as depreciation, are also restated. Care must be taken not to let such revaluations influence estimates of cash flow.

(b) Nonallocation of Current Operating Costs

(i) Charges of Expenses to Reserves. In many countries, arbitrary reserves are created, against which certain expenses are charged. Examples are reserves for bad debts and

reserves for pensions or other unfunded retirement obligations. In some cases a nonspecific "reserve for contingencies" is created against very vague future uncertainties. The intent is often to manipulate income (called "income smoothing") by arbitrarily subtracting from good years and adding to bad years. The creation of such reserves reduces reported net income without reducing cash flow, and the charging of expenses to the reserves usually involves a cash outflow not recorded in the current year.

(ii) Deferred Taxes Shown as a Liability. Treatment varies among countries between reported incomes taxes for accounting purposes and actual income taxes paid. The difference usually arises when additional expenses (such as extra depreciation or a credit for taxes paid) are allowed by the government as a "tax incentive" but are not recognized as current income by the accounting process. In any case, a bottom-up calculation which approximates cash flow from the sum of net income and noncash expenses must include as additional cash flow any increase in the deferred tax liability, because actual payments are less than the accrued expense. The capital-budgeting process must recognize the possibility of different treatment of actual and accrued taxes in various countries.

(iii) Flow Through of Translation Gains. Translation gains which flow through income statements or which are taken directly to a cumulative translation reserve must be subtracted because they do not reflect cash flows. In the United States, under Statement of Financial Accounting Standards (SFAS) No. 8, which was issued in 1975, translation gains or losses were recognized in current quarterly income. This rule was replaced by SFAS No. 52 in 1981, under which translation gains and losses are charged to a reserve account and *not* passed through the income statement. Each country has its own approach, not only as to *how* to measure such gains and losses but also where to record the gains and losses. An analyst evaluating a foreign project from past financial records must be sure that measures of cash flow exclude that impact of translation gains and losses.

(iv) Severance Pay If the Foreign Affiliate Is Closed. In many countries, local social laws require severance pay of up to several years' annual earnings for workers who are released. Thus, if a firm decides to close a foreign operation, it may face a large cash outflow related to severance benefits to workers who lose their jobs. Such severance payments represent a large cash outflow in the last year of a project and must be considered carefully, not only when a decision to stop operations is made but also when an operation that has some risk of economic failure is started.

(c) Debt Changes Not Matched by Cash Payments

(i) Foreign Exchange Translation Gains or Losses on Long-Term Debt. If a project is financed with foreign currency debt, the book amount of that debt will change as foreign exchange rates change. The resulting charge or gain may show as a decrease or an increase in current income, depending upon the translation rules in effect. However, restatement of the book amount of debt has no cash flow implications until the year in which the debt is repaid.

(ii) Noncapitalization of Financial Leases. Some countries in the world, such as the United States, require that financial leases be capitalized as debt on the balance sheet. In other countries, financial leases are not capitalized. A change in accounting proce-

dure, under which both assets and debts are increased by the present value of a financial lease, will change the apparent cash outflow (amount of assets required) without any real change being needed. Amortization of a financial lease obligation may also vary from a strict measurement of the cash needed for lease payments. An awareness of such variations is essential.

(d) Other

(i) Changes in Accounting Principles and Methods Without Prior Year Change. Many countries switch from one accounting principle to another, say, from one type of depreciation assumption to another, without adjusting financial statements for the prior year. Under these conditions, measures of both income and cash flow from one year to another are not meaningful. Because depreciation is a noncash expense which is often added back to obtain cash flow, as in the bottom-up example given earlier, and because income taxes paid depend in part on the depreciation approach used, a change in depreciation method in future years may have cash flow implications. If the change is made to augment ("dress up") reported income, the cash flow implication may be negative because of the tax impact.

(ii) Treatment of Unconsolidated Subsidiaries. Unconsolidated subsidiaries are recorded differently in different countries. In some countries, unconsolidated subsidiaries are carried at original historical cost (rather than at equity, as in the United States). Hence, earnings of the foreign subsidiary are reported only when received as dividends, rather than when earned. Retained earnings in the subsidiaries, and thus subsidiary cash flow less cash dividends, are concealed. This has two consequences: (1) some cash flow from a consolidated perspective is kept secret, and (2) variations in dividend payments from nonconsolidated subsidiaries can be used to conceal variations in earnings and/or cash flow in the parent entity. In periods when the parent entity itself has abnormally low earnings, dividends from subsidiaries may be used to bolster reported earnings.

The 2001–2002 scandal at Enron Corporation in the United States was a separate type of misstatement. Nonconsolidated subsidiaries were written up, creating a nonrealized increase in earnings that was used to justify pumped-up stock prices.

(iii) Blocked Funds. If cash flow in the host country is blocked so that it is not available for dividends and consequently for reinvestment elsewhere in the world system, the value of that cash flow in a capital budgeting context can be questioned. Although no treatment can necessarily be considered "correct," often blocked cash is valued as if it were reinvested in the local economy at a nominal risk-free rate and then repatriated at a much later date. If repatriation of blocked cash flows is not expected, those funds should have no value in the capital budgeting analysis.

4.5 SUMMARY International investment analysis is based on analysis of expected future cash flows from a foreign direct investment. The database for estimating future cash flows is often current and recent past financial statements. In addition, future cash flows depend on local accounting and tax treatment of profits and expenses.

The essential difference between domestic and international investment analysis is that estimates of future cash flows are in different currencies and depend on local accounting methods. Those methods often differ from one country to another.

This chapter has described the investment analysis, or capital budgeting process, for both a home country and an international project, and it has explained how different accounting procedures will influence the cash flow estimate.

To illustrate the process, an example is given in Appendix A. A more detailed summary of principal accounting differences around the world is provided in Chapter 12.

APPENDIX A: ILLUSTRATIVE INTERNATIONAL CAPITAL BUDGETING EXAMPLE

To illustrate complexities than can arise in the analysis of a foreign investment proposal, a capital budgeting analysis for Cacau do Brasil, S.A., a proposed investment in a chocolate factory in Belém, Brazil. is presented. The U.S. parent will invest the entire equity of R$56,000,000, or US$20,000,000 at the current exchange rate of R$2.80 = US$1.00. ("R$" is the symbol for Brazil's currency, the *real.*)

If established, Cacau do Brasil, S.A. will have an initial balance sheet as shown in Exhibit 4A.1.

Cacau do Brasil is expected to operate as follows:

- *Sales.* Unit sales will grow at 3% per annum. Initial unit sales will be 25,000 tons, and the initial sales price will be R$5,000 per ton. Initial labor cost is R$2,000 per ton and initial local material will cost R$200 per ton. Cacau do

CACAU DO BRASIL, S.A.
Initial Balance Sheet, Year 0
(In Thousands of Brazilian Reals)

Cash	R$ 5,685	Long-term debt	R$ 24,000
Accounts receivable	6,250		
Inventory	8,065		
Net plant & equipment	60,000	Common stock equity	56,000
	R$ 80,000		R$ 80,000

Note 1: Net plant and equipment will be depreciated on a straight line basis over eight years, with no salvage value.

Note 2: Long-term debt of R$24,000,000 will be the sole obligation of Cacau do Brasil and will not be guaranteed by the U.S. parent. The regular market interest rate for a Brazilian real debt of this type is 14%, but Cacau do Brasil is borrowing at a subsidized interest rate of 5% per annum arranged by Brazilian development authorities. The debt will be paid off in five equal annual installments of R$5,543,000, payable at the end of each year, calculated as follows (rounded to one thousand reals):

End of year	Principal	Interest at 5% per Annum	Total Service	Principal Reduction	Remaining Balance
1	24,000	1,200	5,543	4,343	19,657
2	19,657	983	5,543	4,560	15,097
3	15,097	755	5,543	4,788	10,309
4	10,309	515	5,543	5,028	5,281
5	5,281	262	5,543	5,281	–0–

Exhibit 4A.1. Initial Balance Sheet.

Brasil will import material from the United States having an initial cost of R$360 per ton of output. Administrative expenses in the first year will be R$20 million.

- *Customers.* All production will be sold to unaffiliated buyers in Europe and the United States at sales prices denominated in Brazilian reals.
- *Brazilian inflation.* Brazilian prices are expected to rise as follow:

Raw material costs:	+2% per annum
Labor costs:	+5% per annum
General Brazilian prices:	+4% per annum
Cacau do Brasil sales prices	+4% per annum

- *Exchange rate forecasting.* U.S. inflation is expected to be 2% per annum. Using the theory of purchasing power parity, the U.S. parent expects the real to drop in U.S. dollar value steadily in proportion to the ratio of Brazilian to U.S. inflation, calculated as follows: 1.04/1.02 = 1.0196078, or approximately 1.96% per annum greater inflation in Brazil. Consequently the exchange rate forecast, by purchasing power parity, is:

Year 0:	R$ 2.8000/$
Year 1:	R$ 2.8000 × 1.0196 = R$ 2.8549/$
Year 2:	R$ 2.8549 × 1.0196 = R$ 2.9109/$
Year 3:	R$ 2.9109 × 1.0196 = R$ 2.9680/$
Year 4:	R$ 2.9680 × 1.0196 = R$ 3.0262/$
Year 5:	R$ 3.0262 × 1.0196 = R$ 3.0855/$
Year 6:	R$ 3.0855 × 1.0196 = R$ 3.1460/$

- *Discount rate.* The U.S. parent has determined that the appropriate discount rate for the Brazilian project is 24% per annum. It will use this rate both within Brazil (project evaluation) and from its own U.S. point of view (parent evaluation).
- *Working capital.* Year-end accounts receivable will be equal to 5% of sales of the year just finished. Year-end inventory balances will be maintained at 10% of expected variable costs for the following year. The initial cash balance of R$5,685,000 will be allowed to increase with retained cash flow in Brazil.
- *Terminal value.* The U.S. parent expects to sell the subsidiary as a going concern after five years for a price equal to the remaining net book value of fixed assets plus the full value of ending working capital (cash, receivables, and inventory).
- *Royalties.* A royalty fee of 5% of sales revenue will be paid by Cacau do Brasil to the U.S. parent each year. This fee creates taxable income in the United States.
- *Taxes.* Brazilian corporate income taxes are 40%, with no additional dividend withholding tax. The U.S. corporate tax rate is 34%.
- *Parent exports.* Components imported by Cacau do Brasil from its U.S. parent have a direct manufacturing cost in the United States equal to 90% of their transfer price to Cacau do Brasil. Hence, the U.S. parent earns a dollar cash profit and cash flow in the United States equal to 10% of all sales to Cacau do Brasil. Brazilian production and sales will not cause any loss of sales by the U.S. parent from any other operation elsewhere in the world.
- *Dividends.* The U.S. parent intends to have Cacau do Brasil declare 75% of its accounting profit as dividends each year. Brazilian authorities have approved this level of remittance.

CACAU DO BRASIL, S.A.
Revenue, Expenses, and Profit for Years 1 Through 5
(In Thousands of Brazilian Reals, Except for Unit Costs)

	Year 1	Year 2	Year 3	Year 4	Year 5
Revenue					
1. Unit volume (g = 3%)	25,000	25,750	26,522	27,318	28,138
2. Unit price (g = 4%)	5,000	5,200	5,408	5,624	5,849
3. Total sales revenue	125,000	133,900	143,431	153,636	164,579
Unit variable costs					
4. Local labor (g = 5%)	2,000	2,100	2,205	2,315	2,431
5. Local material (g = 2%)	200	204	208	212	216
6. U.S. parent (note 1)	1,028	1,068	1,113	1,156	1,203
7. Variable cost/unit	3,228	3,372	3,526	3,683	3,850
8. Total variable costs	80,700	86,829	93,517	100,612	108,331
Cost and Profit Data					
9. Gross profit (3–8)	44,300	47,071	49,914	53,024	56,248
10. Royalties (5% × Sales)	6,250	6,695	7,172	7,682	8,229
11. Administration (g = 4%)	20,000	20,800	21,632	22,497	23,397
12. Depreciation	7,500	7,500	7,500	7,500	7,500
13. Earnings before interest and taxes (EBIT)	10,550	12,076	13,610	15,375	17,122
14. Interest expense	1,200	983	755	515	262
15. Pretax income	9,350	11,093	12,855	14,860	16,860
16. 40% Brazilian tax	–3,740	–4,437	–5,142	–5,944	–6,744
17. Net income	5,610	6,656	7,713	8,916	10,116
18. Cash dividends @75%	4,207	4,992	5,785	6,687	7,587

Note 1: U.S. raw material supplied will rise in dollar price at 2% per annum with U.S. inflation. The real equivalent on a per unit basis is calculated as follows. The sixth-year calculation is necessary for forecasting fifth year inventory.

	Year 1	Year 2	Year 3	Year 4	Year 5	Year 6
Unit sales price in \$ (g = 2%)	\$360	\$367	\$375	\$382	\$390	\$397
Exchange rate	2.8549	2.9109	2.9680	3.0262	3.0855	3.1460
Unit cost in reals	1,028	1,068	1,113	1,156	1,203	1,249

Exhibit 4A.2. Revenue, Expense, and Profit Report: Five Years.

Cacau do Brasil's pro forma income statement for the first year of operations is shown as column 1 of Exhibit 4A.2. The remainder of Exhibit 4A.2 shows expected income accounts over the following five years in accordance with the expectations and guidelines described above.

Exhibit 4A.2 shows a growing annual revenue, accompanied by increased costs. Line 17 indicates that the project is profitable in every year, and line 18 shows the expected cash dividend to the U.S. parent.

Exhibit 4A.3 shows the annual increase in accounts receivable, inventory, and cash balances. Note that receivables levels are based on sales of the past year, while inventory levels depend on expected sales for the following year. This means that variable costs for the sixth year must be calculated to determine inventory required at the end of the fifth year.

Exhibit 4A.4 shows the current asset balances after five years of operations—balances that are necessary to calculate the terminal value.

Exhibit 4A.5 shows the calculation of terminal value at the end of five years. Terminal value is equal to the ending net book value of plant and equipment, plus ending current assets. Obviously a terminal value many years in the future is subjective, and other methods of estimating this future value are possible. At the end of five years the U.S. parent expects to sell Cacau do Brazil for R$65,753,000 as derived in Exhibit 4A.5.

The present value of the subsidized loan is calculated in Exhibit 4A.6. The essence of the calculation is that the actual payments, based on equal annual payments that amortize the principal and that pay interest at 5%, are discounted at 14%, the interest rate that would have been paid on a similar nonsubsidized loan. The present value of the subsidy (in year 0) is R$4,970,000.

PROJECT VALUATION

Exhibit 4A.7 shows that the present value of operating inflows, calculated on an all-equity basis, is R$61,671,000. To this must be added the net present value of the subsidized loan, calculated in Exhibit 4A.6, which is R$4,970,000. Subtracting the original outlay of R$56,000,000 leaves a positive net present value of R$10,641,000. From the point of view of the project, the investment is worthwhile.

The fact that Cacau do Brasil has a positive net present value of R$10,641,000 as a domestic project means that the project is a reasonable use of economic resources within Brazil. It also suggests that a domestic Brazilian corporation would find the project worthwhile, although of course a domestic corporation might not be able to sell production outside of Brazil as easily as the subsidiary of a foreign corporation with worldwide operations. In other words, the technology and marketing ability of the U.S. parent add to the cash generating ability of Cacau do Brasil.

A positive project net present value, however, does not mean that the investment is worthwhile from the parent's perspective. A separate calculation based on cash flows from and to the parent company is necessary. Such a calculation is shown in Exhibit 4A.8.

PARENT VALUATION

The value of Cacau do Brasil, S.A. to its U.S. parent is calculated in Exhibit 4A.8 to be a *negative* US$1,567,000. As designed, the investment is not worthwhile from the point of view of the U.S. parent.

CACAU DO BRASIL, S.A.
Working Capital and Cash Accumulation
(In Thousands of Brazilian Reals)

	Year 1	Year 2	Year 3	Year 4	Year 5
Accounts Receivables					
1. Sales revenue	125,000	133,900	143,431	153,636	164,579
2. Required A/R @ 5% of past year's sales	6,250	6,695	7,172	7,682	8,229
3. Increase over prior balance	None	445	477	510	547
Inventory					
4. Variable costs	80,700	86,829	93,517	100,612	108,331
5. Required inventory @ 10% of next year's variable costs[1]	8,683	9,352	10,061	10,833	11,657
6. Increase over prior year's balance	618	669	709	772	824
Cash Balances					
7. Net income (Exhibit 4A.2,line 17)	5,610	6,656	7,713	8,916	10,116
8. Earnings retained (25% of net income)	1,403	1,664	1,928	2,229	2,529
9. Plus depreciation	+7,500	+7,500	+7,500	+7,500	+7,500
10. Less increase in accounts receivable (line 3 above)	None	−445	−477	−510	−547
11. Less increase in inventory (line 6 above)	−618	−669	−709	−772	−824
12. Addition to cash balance from operations	8,285	8,050	8,242	8,447	8,658
13. Less repayment of debt principal, from Note 2, Exhibit 4A.1	−4,343	−4,560	−4,788	−5,028	−5,281
14. Net addition to cash balance	3,942	3,490	3,454	3,419	3,377

Note 1: Variable costs in the sixth year are calculated as follows:

Sixth year labor	(1.05)(2,431) =	$2,553
Sixth year local material.	(1.02)(216) =	220
Sixth year U.S. material, from Note 1, Exhibit 4A.2		1,249
Total unit variable costs		$4,022
Times volume (1.03(28,138)		× 28,982
Total sixth year variable costs		$116,566

Exhibit 4A.3. Working Capital and Cash Accumulation.

CACAU DO BRASIL, S.A.
Current Asset Balances After Five Years
(In Thousands of Brazilian Reals)

	Cash	A/R	Inventory
1. Initial balance	5,685	6,250	8,065
2. Year 1 addition	3,942	0	618
3. Year 2 addition	3,490	445	669
4. Year 3 addition	3,454	477	709
5. Year 4 addition	3,419	510	772
6. Year 5 addition	3,377	547	824
7. Ending balances	23,367	8,229	11,657

Note 1: Initial operating cash balance is from Exhibit 4A.1. Additions to cash balances are from line 14 of Exhibit 4A.3. Additions to receivables and inventory balances are from lines 3 and 6 of Exhibit 4A.3.

Exhibit 4A.4. Current Asset Values After Five Years.

CACAU DO BRASIL, S.A.
Terminal Value at the End of Five Years

1. Original cost of net plant and equipment:	R$ 60,000,000
2. Less depreciation for five years @ R$7,500,000/yr.	–37,500,000
3. Net book value of plant and equipment	R$ 22,500,000
3. Plus ending cash balance (Exhibit 4A.4, line 7)	+23,367,000
4. Plus ending receivable balance (Exhibit 4A.4, line 7)	+ 8,229,000
5. Plus ending inventory (Exhibit 4A.4, line 7)	+11,657,000
6. Terminal value at end of year 5	R$ 65,753,000

Exhibit 4A.5. Terminal Value at the End of Five Years.

CACAU DO BRASIL, S.A.
Present Value (PV) of Subsidized Loan
(In Thousands of Brazilian Reals)

	Year 0	Year 1	Year 2	Year 3	Year 4	Year 5
1. Principal	+24,000					
2. Loan payments from Note 2 of Exhibit 4A.1:		–5,543	–5,543	–5,543	–5,543	–5,543
3. 14% PV factor:	1.0000	0.8772	0.7695	0.6750	0.5921	0.5194
4. PV of each payment	+24,000	–4,862	–4,265	–3,742	–3,282	–2,879
5. Net PV of all payments	+ 4,970					

Exhibit 4A.6. Present Value of Subsidized Loan.

CACAU DO BRASIL, S.A.
Project Net Present Value, All-Equity Basis
(In Thousands of Brazilian Reals)

	Year 0	Year 1	Year 2	Year 3	Year 4	Year 5
1. Earnings before interest and taxes Exhibit 4A.6, line 13)		10,550	12,076	13,610	15,375	17,122
2. Less 40% income taxes[1]		–4,220	–4,830	–5,444	–6,150	–6,849
3. All-equity net income		6,330	7,246	8,166	9,225	10,273
4. Plus depreciation		+7,500	+7,500	+7,500	+7,500	+7,500
5. Less increase in receivable balance Exhibit 4A.5,line 6)		None	–445	–477	–510	–547
6. Less increase in inventory balance(Exhibit 4A.5,line 9)		–618	–669	–709	–772	–824
7. Plus terminal value (Exhibit 4A.5,line 6)						65,753
8. Net project cash flow		13,212	13,632	14,480	15,443	82,155
9. 24% P.V. factor		0.8065	0.6504	0.5245	0.4230	0.3411
10. PV of annual inflows		10,655	8,866	7,595	6,532	28,023
11. Sum of PV of inflows	+61,671					
12. PV of subsidized loan (Exhibit 4A.6,line 5)	+4,970					
13. Original outflow	–56,000					
14. Net present value	+10,641					

Note 1: Brazilian income taxes shown on line 2 are not actual taxes paid, but are rather the taxes that would have been paid had Cacau do Brasil, S.A. been financed entirely with equity. However only actual taxes paid, rather than hypothetical taxes based on an all-equity assumption, are allowable as a credit against U.S. taxes on dividends received.

Exhibit 4A.7. Project Net Present Value, All-Equity Basis.

This value is different both in amount and, in this instance, in sign, from value as a project because different cash flows are being measured. The major differences are:

- *Total cash flow versus dividends.* From a project point of view, all cash generated contributes to value because it is available within Brazil. From a parent point of view, cash in Brazil has no value until received by the U.S. parent in the United States. That is, retained earnings and funds equal to depreciation charges are valued at once in the host country, Brazil, but only when and if recovered (or completely available to be recovered) in the parent country, the United States.
- *Free cash flow.* Free cash flow (cash flow greater than needed for day-to-day operations) is valued at the time received in the project approach, but only when remitted to the parent company as a liquidating dividend from a parent point of view.
- *Royalties.* Royalties and similar charges paid by Cacau do Brasil to its U.S. parent are not part of cash flow in the project valuation (in fact, they are an outflow), but are an important portion of the value to the U.S. parent. This suggests that if the parent exports sufficient items of value to its foreign subsidiary, the

CACAU DO BRASIL, S.A.
Net Present Value—Parent Perspective
(In Thousands of Brazilian Reals or U.S. Dollars)

	Year 0	Year 1	Year 2	Year 3	Year 4	Year 5
In Brazilian Reals						
1. Brazilian royalties (Exhibit 4A.2, line 10)		6,250	6,695	7,172	7,682	8,229
2. U.S. tax @ 34%		–2,125	–2,276	–2,438	–2,612	–2,798
3. Net royalty		4,125	4,419	4,734	5,070	5,431
4. Brazilian dividend (Exhibit 4A.2, line 18)		4,207	4,992	5,785	6,687	7,587
5. Terminal value Exhibit 4A.5,line 6)						65,753
6. Total cash flow to parent		8,332	9,411	10,519	11,757	78,771
8. Forecast exchange rate		2.8549	2.9109	2.9680	3.0262	3.0855
In U.S. Dollars						
9. Cash flow from Brazil		2,918	3,233	3,544	3,885	25,529
10. Export contribution[1]		594	624	657	688	724
11. Total dollar inflow.		3,512	3,857	4,201	4,573	26,253
12. 24% PV factor		0.8065	0.6504	0.5245	0.4230	0.3411
13. Present value of inflows		2,832	2,509	2,203	1,934	8,955
14. Sum of present value of inflows	+18,433					
15. Less original outflow	–20,000					
16. Net present value	–1,567					

Note 1: U.S. parent's dollar profit on exports to Brazil:

	Year 1	Year 2	Year 3	Year 4	Year 5
Unit sales price in dollars(g = 2%)	$ 360	$ 367	$ 375	$ 382	$ 390
Unit volume	25,000	25,750	26,522	27,318	28,138
Dollar revenue	$ 9,000	$ 9,450	$ 9,946	$10,435	$10,974
Contribution to pretax profit (10%)	900	945	995	1,043	1,097
Less U.S. 34% tax	–306	–321	–338	–355	–373
Net cash contribution to parent	$ 594	$ 624	$ 657	$ 688	$ 724

Exhibit 4A.8. Net Present Value: Parent Perspective.

project may be worthwhile to the parent even if it should fail to pass the project net present value criteria.

- *Subsidized loan.* The present value of the subsidized loan does not show as a cash flow to the parent because the loan is reflected in increased cash retention by the subsidiary over the five years. The parent benefits only from the higher terminal value and free cash recovered.

Other significant factors, not present in this case but nevertheless important from an overall point of view in considering foreign capital investments are:

- *Foreign exchange rate forecast.* A long forecast of future foreign exchange rates is necessary, and various predictions are possible.
- *Income grossed up for parent country taxation.* In the present case in which the Brazilian corporate income tax rate is 40% and the U.S. rate is only 34%, no grossed-up calculation is needed. No additional U.S. income tax liabilities are incurred on dividends from Brazil.

In many instances, however, parent overall cash flow may be influenced by how the project interacts with other international ventures. Under present U.S. tax law (which could be changed), dividends from operations in countries where the income tax rate is above the U.S. tax rate generate "excess" (i.e., lost) tax credits. These excess tax credits can be used only if dividends of a similar nature are declared from other subsidiaries operating in jurisdictions where the tax rate is below the U.S. tax rate. Thus the high taxes of one foreign jurisdiction can be combined with the low taxes of another foreign jurisdiction to minimize overall total U.S. taxes levied on the total post-tax dividends received from all foreign countries.[3]

Because the negative net present value of US$1,567,000 is comparatively small, relative to the overall size of the project, management's task might be to seek out some other combination of investment costs (perhaps subcontracting part of production), revenue (perhaps raising sales prices in some markets), or operating costs (perhaps using a different degree of technology or automation to reduce costs) that will generate a positive net present value. Another possibility would be to increase the transfer price on items sold by the U.S. parent to Cacau do Brazil.

Any such steps would have cash flow consequences for Cacau do Brazil as well as its U.S. parent. However a finance manager should be a "doer" rather than just a passive analyst of data collected from others, so the finance manager should participate actively in the search for another combination of cash flows that would lead to expected positive net present values for both project and parent.

Management might also decide to go ahead, in spite of the calculated negative net present value, for reasons of global strategy. One way of expressing this in financial terms is to acknowledge that some long-run global advantage can be achieved with the Brazilian subsidiary that can not be quantified as estimated cash flows. Some will argue that the introduction of such subjectivity destroys the rigor of the net present value approach to capital budgeting. Others will argue that recognition of long-run nonquantifiable strategic goals is an important part of management's judgment and hence is vital to success. The latter will say one should not be a slave to a quantitative approach, but should use it only as a valuable guide.

---

[3]For a detailed explanation of this pooling of tax credits, see pp. 497–501 of David K. Eiteman, Arthur I. Stonehill, and Michael H. Moffett, *Multinational Business Finance*, 9th ed. Boston: Addison-Wesley-Longman, 2001.

CHAPTER 5

INTERNATIONAL TREASURY MANAGEMENT*

Michael H. Moffett

Thunderbird—The American Graduate School of International Management

James L. Mills

Thunderbird—The American Graduate School of International Management

CONTENTS

5.1 INTRODUCTION. The financial management of the nonfinancial firm is traditionally divided between treasury activities and controller activities. Simplistically, this is a distinction between *cash flow* (treasury) and *financial reporting* (controller). Controller activities such as end-of-month closings, internal reporting and forecasting, and external financial reporting have become increasingly automated. Continuing advances in the field of information technology, combined with the increasing focus by management on the future rather than the historical details of the accounting past, have led to a larger role for treasury within financial management.

---

*Additional research assistance was provided by Timothy Magnusson.

As firms have expanded the global scope of their operations, and as global financial markets have increased their pace and volatility, the complexity of international treasury has expanded exponentially. Globalization, combined with the expanding scope of business reengineering, including the financial functions of the firm, have placed new demands on treasury to add value to the business. Many working in the field of treasury management today might argue that it is an area of significantly underdeveloped potential; the treasury function in many firms today is often understaffed and underinvested. To use the business parlance of the day, the treasury which is not keeping pace with the best practices of the day may be leaving a lot of money on the table.

This chapter provides a detailed overview of the principle purpose and practices of *international treasury management.* Although it is increasingly difficult to differentiate international from domestic treasury, understanding the unique responsibilities and challenges presented by multinational operations for treasury management is our primary goal. After explaining the basic dimensions of treasury in practice, we focus on the two areas of most general application: multinational cash management and multinational currency management. Throughout this chapter we suggest maintaining a classical financial focus: Cash flow is king.

5.2 TREASURY MANAGEMENT. The treasury function of the firm might well be best explained in the context of its issue of identification, cash flow. Treasury operations have traditionally focused on two dimensions of business, the settlement of cash flows associated with sales, and the funding of the firm's general operations. This is in essence a balance sheet focus. A more comprehensive treasury organization has, however, evolved in the past decade in which the focus of management activity has followed the economic factors which drive firm value, corporate-wide cash flow. This modern treasury organization focuses on a different financial statement, the statement of cash flows, and is now in the process of adapting to the complex environment and cash flows of the global business.

(a) Traditional Treasury. Treasuries have historically focused their organizational form and manpower needs on the labor-intensive process of collections. As illustrated in Exhibit 5.1, the organization devoted significant resources to the conversion of collections into cash, a constant substitution of one liquid current asset into pure cash. This functional role was passive and reacted to the cash flows which were created by the business; treasury's role was quite clearly that of an overhead body for funding and settlement. There was no expectation of value-added activity from the treasury organization.

In addition to the basic cash management settlement function, treasury was charged with the funding of the firm. This meant that treasury would plan for and gain access to the funds necessary for the continued growth of the firm. Treasuries therefore worked closely with banking institutions and other credit-granting organizations which would create and maintain adequate access to affordable funding. Capital structure goals were basically the maintenance of a maturity match, the balancing of maturity of the useful life of assets with the funding of the individual obligations. An *aggressive treasury organization* was one which managed the maturity of the debt portfolio for interest expense—accepting repricing and refunding risks along the way—in the hopes of any competitive advantages which might accrue to the firm through lower capital costs.

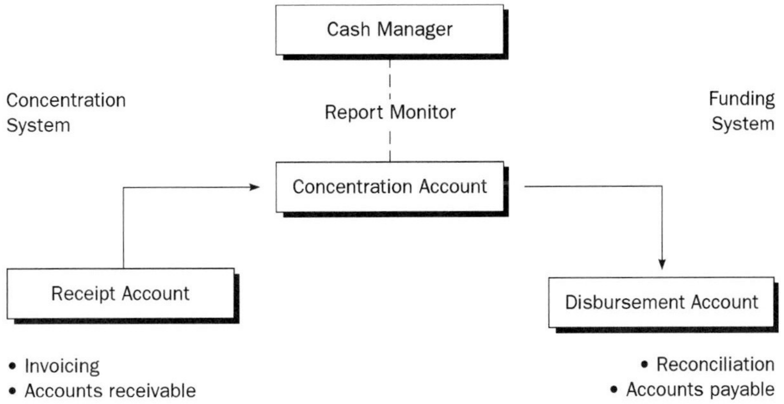

Exhibit 5.1. The Traditional Treasury Function of Cash Management Settlement.

Efficient treasury operations consider every element that affects the operating unit's ability to collect, disburse, and manage the cash resources available to it. This includes the whole cash cycle, from sales to the payment of trade obligations. The following steps must be taken to minimize interest and administration costs:

1. Conserve cash resources.
2. Ensure adequate liquidity at the lowest overall cost for payments.
3. Invest surplus funds for highest return.
4. Protect operating returns from fluctuations in the foreign exchange market.

All within the constraints of maintaining good customer, bank, and supplier relations.

(b) Treasury Implementation. Implementation of treasury is a three-step process: (1) planning; (2) processing and control; and (3) investment and financing.

(i) Planning. Cash planning is short- and long-term forecasting encompassing everything that may affect cash flow. It requires timely collection of a great deal of information about inflows expected from recurring and nonrecurring sources, and about obligations that have to be met in the immediate and more distant future. The aim is to match inflows and outflows, thus reducing dependence on borrowed funds to meet maturing obligations. This is particularly important for organizations that are sensitive to daily cash flow and the cost and frequency of borrowing.

Good cash organization is based directly on the time value of money and recognizes that a dollar received and put to use today is worth more than a dollar tomorrow. In practice it means maximum acceleration of inflows, stringent regulation of outflows, and constant diversion of spare cash into profitable investment—not periodically but routinely, every day, and occasionally overnight. Good cash organization makes it normal to meet obligations with funds that were earning interest up to the last moment before disbursement. It also means having funds ready to gain every available advantage by prompt payment.

An integral component of the planning process is a thorough understanding of the firm's cash flow conversion cycle. The three components of the cycle, days payments outstanding (DPO), days of inventory outstanding (DIO), and the days sales outstanding (DSO), are all indicators of how cash flows move through the business process from cash to sales back to cash.[1]

The cash management process involves the forecasting, timing, and management of receipts and disbursements. With the receipts or cash inflow established, sales and accounts receivable are forecasted. In the disbursement process, analysis is pursued to pinpoint the timing and value of cash outflows. The inflows and outflows are matched as accurately as possible before surpluses of either are used by the financing or investment functions. The firm's information and control system is integral to this process; timely information is critical for accurate planning of cash flows. The role of information technology in treasury, either domestic or international, is likely the single largest area of concern to treasury organizations today.

(ii) Processing and Control. Planning and organization depend heavily on timely, accurate, and detailed information. The first step in matching receipts and disbursements is a detailed and itemized knowledge of transactions. The next stage is to ensure that things happen as they should. That is control. The type of control required depends on whether the treasury function is centralized or decentralized. The degree of centralization is dependent on the size and complexity of the corporate structure as well as the degree of computerization of the financial data. Whether to centralize or decentralize is generally based on considerations such as: (1) industry characteristics, type of business and cash flow; (2) corporation size, type of sale, diversification of business, products, operating locations; (3) complexity of the firm's organizational structure; and (4) the corporate financial policy.

(iii) Investment and Financing. To approach an ideal cash management system, it is necessary to devise and maintain a corporate investment policy that is the best compromise between yield and liquidity. In order to position funds properly, a cash manager must: (1) know the amounts of incoming cash from recurring and nonrecurring sources; (2) match cash requirements to sources of funds; (3) arrange to acquire funds if necessary; and (4) formulate short-term investment programs for surplus funds. The basic objective is to put all cash, over all time periods, long and short, to the best active use. It is easy to lose sight of this overall objective because there are so many factors in a complete treasury management program, and it is easy to become preoccupied with one or two.

Once a consolidated cash position is achieved, timely decision must be made about surplus funds and/or obligations to be met. Concerning surplus receipts, the main criteria are the type of investments (e.g., treasury bills, foreign exchange), date of maturity (24 hours to 6 months), and yield. With regard to disbursement requirements, the Treasurer must decide whether funds are to be generated from the corporate cash flow or externally sourced. The exact nature of the financial vehicle, period of time, and interest rates must be determined.

---

[1]An example of how important simple planning of cash flow needs can be is that of the United States Postal Service. Through cash forecasting, the U.S. postal service was able to reduce average cash on hand from $7 billion to between $1 and $2 billion in 1995. This, in conjunction with significant changes such as allowing customers to use credit cards and electronic transfers, has resulted in a significant downsizing in the postal balance sheet, and a 1995 profit of $1.8 billion.

These investment and financing decisions must be viewed in terms of financial risk, flexibility, and opportunity cost. Financial risk measures the ability of the firm to meet future debt service obligations. Flexibility is the company's ability to alter a course of action in order to meet future unspecified financial requirements in an undefined financial market. In today's quick changing economic conditions, opportunity cost is an uncompromising yardstick, that is, the maximum profit that could have been obtained had cash been applied to some other use.

Although adequate for the time, the disassociation between the two functions—the lack of a theoretical or managerial linkage between asset management and funding strategy, and the lack of a general financial strategy focus for the firm—have proven inadequate for the modern multinational.

(c) Modern Treasury. Whereas the traditional treasury activities focused solely on the conversion of collections into cash, the modern view of treasury is a much more proactive management of the entire business process, the management of the cash flows which *create* firm value. This is an assertive managerial approach akin to a view of the firm as a statement of cash flows. An indirect statement of cash flows divides the cash flows of the firm into three distinct areas: *operating cash flows, investing cash flows,* and *financing cash flows.* This singular document captures the essence of the modern cash management cum treasury management activities.

- *Operating cash flows* are those arising from the true business line. In an indirect statement of cash flows, this is net income from operations plus depreciation less net additions to net working capital (current asset changes less current liability changes). The principal source of cash for investing in long-lived assets is from operations.

  The fundamental requirement for creating corporate value is by making good investment in long-lived assets. When firms do not generate enough cash internally—through their operations, they either cut investment more drastically than their competitors do or they are forced to turn to external markets for the requisite funding (financing cash flows). The effective management of the company's operating cash flows is called working capital management.
- *Investing cash flows* arise from the capital investment analysis and acquisition needs of the firm. Firms evaluating new capital asset acquisitions (capital budgeting), mergers, or other independent business unit valuations (much of which historically was out-sourced to the investment banking sector) are conducted within this functional treasury area.
- *Financing cash flows* are those arising from the funding of the firm. Funding decisions such as debt issuance, form, maturity structure, restructuring, and dividend policies would all fall within the analytical and management capabilities of this treasury function.

The statement of cash flow highlights the modern view of the treasurer as a *working capital manager*. The modern view of treasury extends beyond funding to the full gamut of working capital management, including collections and concentration accounts, debt restructuring, financial risk management, to integrating data systems into the production processes of the firm. Working capital is the money invested by the business in those things—products, services—which are to be sold, and includes money spent on the purchase of materials, the processing of goods, and the overhead incurred for the period that the goods are being processed. In fact, business itself represents the investment of cash.[2] The business therefore recycles cash, turning it into goods, labor, and overhead, so that it can cycle back into cash. The more time it takes to complete the cash-revenue cycle, and the more working capital that is invested during this period, the greater the financing costs and the lower the profits of the firm.[3]

Working capital management is therefore the management and funding of a physical/financial process. Mechanically, working capital management is the conversion of:

Contract **Manufacture** **Booking/AR** **Settlement**

|——————————————————————————————>

Cash **Materials** **Work-in-progress** **Final goods** **Shipping** **Cash**

Although traditionally described as the cash conversion cycle, modern treasury management requires that the activities described here in the cycle of cash to sales to cash be simultaneously managed with the short-term funding cycle on the right hand side of the balance sheet. This integration of asset and liability management in the context of maximizing value-enhanced sales of the business line is the emerging challenge to treasury as a *strategic business partner.*

This emerging strategic role is a departure from traditional resource commitment in the treasury organization. The traditional functions of treasury have expanded to three with the addition of strategic value; the three treasury activities today are *administrative, transaction*, and *strategic*. The *administrative activity* of treasury, the record keeping and financial statement contribution, has been greatly reduced in recent years by the reengineering of business and financial processes, the redefinition of what data and financial records are essentially needed for record keeping of the past and for record/plankeeping for the future, and the introduction of technology which eliminates much of the work. *Transactions activity*, the time, manpower, and other resources devoted to the processing and completion of managerial treasury activities on an ongoing basis, is also seeing substantial reduction as a result of the integration of technology into the financial process. It is the third treasury activity, the *strategic function*, which is as yet the most undeveloped, yet most promising in providing additional value to the firm.

As illustrated in Exhibit 5.2, administration was the consuming activity in treasury in the recent past. Currently, the introduction of technology for the documentation of treasury activities has resulted in a significant reduction in administrative activity burdens, but transaction activity has not been as successfully computerized. A contributing factor to the current dominance of transaction activity has been the expansion of risk management activities of all kinds—foreign exchange, interest, and commodity prices—which in times past was not widespread. The challenge for the

---

[2]The concept that a business is basically the investment of cash is highlighted by the Ethnic Chinese expression for investment which roughly translates the concept of "investment" as "cash which is asleep;" the problem is always the reconversion of an investment back into cash (waking it up).

[3]One example of this in practice is American Standard, a U.S.-based multinational which has established a goal of zero net working capital in order to minimize the size of its balance sheet and reduce capital needs to the bare minimum.

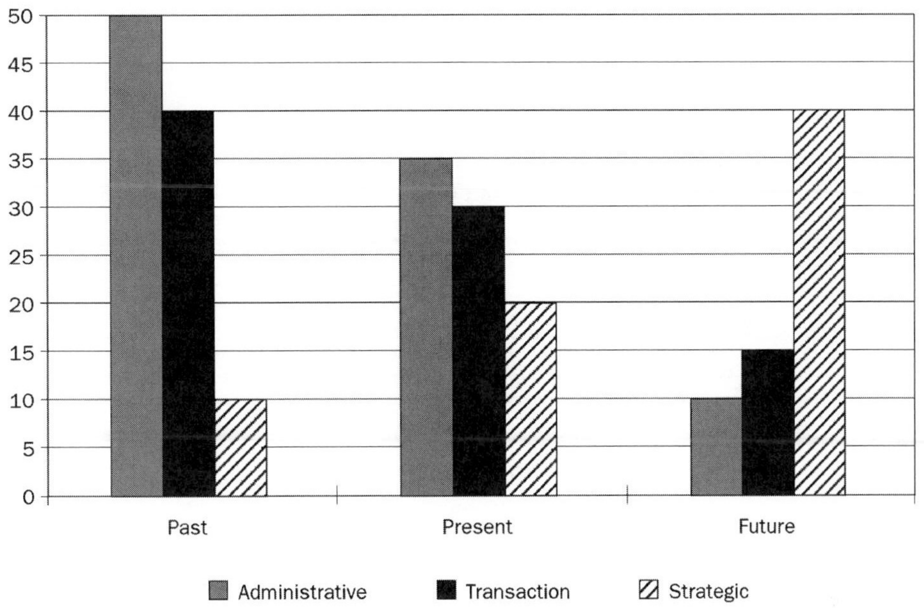

Exhibit 5.2. The Changing Resource Use of Treasury Activities: The Evolution of Administrative, Transaction, and Strategic Activity in Treasury Management.

treasury of the future is to achieve the goal of increased resource utilization for the benefit of the business—strategic activity—while the total treasury burden continues to contract (the sum of the three activities). The shifting of resources from the traditional administrative and transaction roles to strategic activities will put treasury staff and functions into a business partnership with the other business units of the firm. This is the ideal, and is the goal of treasury managers worldwide.

(d) Treasury Organization. Although people manage, not organizational structures (or charts), the generic organizational structure used by multinational firms to organize their financial management activities is a good place to start in understanding the multitude of activities required of management. The "typical" organizational chart of a multinational firm's treasury department—if there is such a thing as typical—might appear as that in Exhibit 5.3, illustrating the functional vice presidents and frequent staffing below the vice president level. The international treasury is actually more "typical" than the superstructure in which it falls.

In principle and in order, the activities focus on the financial strategy and decision-making of the firm (corporate finance), the management of the cash flows of the firm (cash management), the funding of the firm (capital markets), the tax planning functions of the firm as they are understood across all functional areas (tax management), and the international financial activities of the firm (international treasury). Obviously there are as many organizational charts and combinations of vice presidents, directors, managers, and assistants, as there are firms, but this minimum requirement list serves as representative of the underlying functional areas required of all treasury departments.

Exhibit 5.3 also illustrates a fairly typical mix of function and geography in the in-

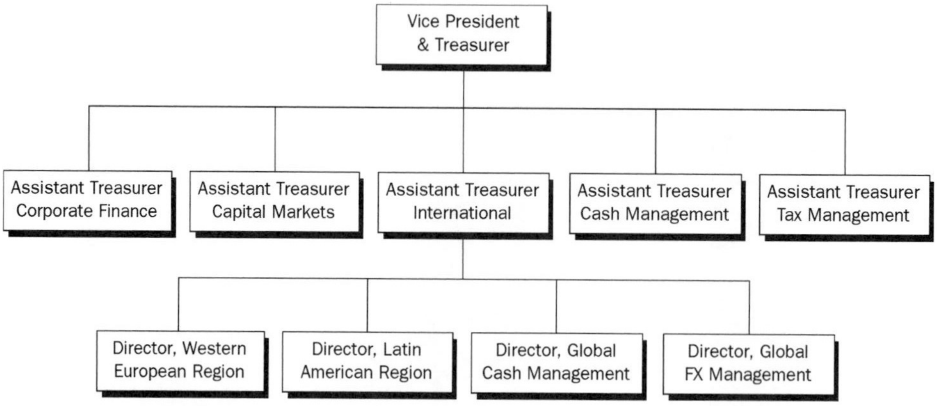

Exhibit 5.3. Modern Treasury Organization.

ternational treasury. Larger multinational firms will often possess such a large number of foreign subsidiaries and affiliates that they are frequently managed both on the regional level (in this case Western Europe and Latin America) as well as by the basic functions (cash management, foreign exchange, and foreign exchange risk management). Regional treasuries are often needed as an intermediate step between the sparsely staffed foreign affiliate, its dependence on other regional affiliates, and the needs of the parent to coordinate and centrally manage financial and operational activity.[4] However, there is frequently a duplication in responsibility and activity, both between the regional treasury offices and global cash and foreign exchange management, as well as between international treasury and the other first level treasury management activities such as cash management and capital markets.

As firms expand and evolve, the nature of the individual industry of the firm, or the corporate goals of the specific firm, may require that specific treasury functions evolve and expand more rapidly than others.

- U.S.-based multinationals with manufacturing operations in the U.S. territory of Puerto Rico, a special office or director of Section 936 tax management regarding the specific tax benefits under the U.S. internal revenue service code section 936 often are required.
- Firms with substantial cross-border trade or payments with firms domiciled in nonconvertible currency environments may require a full-time staff member devoted to countertrade and other nonmonetary exchange business lines.
- Firms involved in large scale capital intensive projects financed with heavy participations of debt, may create entire treasury staff expertise in project finance.

[4]For North American-based multinational firms, it is not uncommon to have intensive subsidiary operations in Western Europe and Latin or South America. Regional treasuries representing these activities are therefore common and heavily utilized due to commonality of time zones and market activity. The Far East or Asian Pacific, however, is uneven in industrial and financial market developments, causing many of these same multinationals to manage these individual affiliates on a selective basis, although rarely from the parent office direct.

- Firms that are searching for value-added activities within the firm (spinoffs, restructuring) or from outside the firm (mergers and acquisitions) are developing in-house expertise in valuation and investment banking which was previously outsourced.
- Cash flow can be disrupted by movements in external factors such as exchange rates, commodity prices, and interest rates. Ensuring that these external prices do not adversely impact the firm's ability to make value-enhancing investments is the domain of *financial risk management.*

All of these examples reflect the treasury services required of an increasingly strategic, proactive, value-added role for treasury.

(e) Treasury Drivers. A number of trends have emerged in the 1990s that are driving change in the treasury function. The reexamination of business processes, *reengineering*, the adoption of new technology and electronically linked business partnering, and the changing view of finance's role in the global firm are now causing drastic changes in the way treasury looks and works.

Activities can be subdivided into three major classifications: administrative, transaction, and strategic. Administrative activities focus on the reporting dimensions. Transaction activities include working capital concerns (A/R, A/P, etc.), and have themselves fallen under considerable scrutiny in the past few years as firms have reengineered many of their financial functions. The strategic dimensions of treasury activities, for example, treasury operating as an internal consultant to line functions or business units, treasury acting as a focal point for intelligence gathering regarding the currency and interest rate positions and sensitivities of major competitors, are all relatively new additions to the role of treasury. They are, however, the primary future direction of treasury managerial resource use and attention.

Treasury may be treated as a cost center, a service center, or a profit center, though the latter is relatively rare and of considerable debate as to its appropriateness.[5] Because most treasury departments are cost centers, they are typically small in manpower resources and large in capital/technology commitments. This point cannot be overstated; treasury organizations today are attempting to expand the scope and sophistication of their activities with higher-powered people, and higher-powered processes. For example, many of the transaction-based activities which have occupied manpower in the past such as the processing of accounts receivable and payable have now been automated. An efficient treasury function today requires sophisticated human and capital resources alike.[6]

Technology is also having real functional and organizational impacts on treasury. The development of real-time systems has had a profound impact on the cash manager's ability to execute the three-step implementation process outlined above. The

---

[5]A 1995 survey by Price Waterhouse of 386 corporate treasuries indicated that 7 percent considered their treasury a profit center, 67 percent a service center, 19 percent a cost center, and 7 percent not defined.

[6]WT Grace & Company, a $5.8 billion U.S.-based multinational, restructured treasury operations in 1993, expanding treasury staff to 17 from a mere 3 in 1990. In addition to the restructuring of reporting guidelines (tax management now reports to the treasurer instead of the controller), the scope of activity has been expanded to include both foreign exchange and interest rate risk management, requiring new highly trained staff and computerized system support.

most important real-time system innovation is that of electronic data interchange (EDI), a cross-industry standard format for data transmission between customers, suppliers, and firms. EDI involves the conversion of paper documents such as purchase orders, invoices, checks, to electronic form. This electronic transmission expedites the processing of all stages of not only the settlement process, but more comprehensively the entire business process. In addition, EDI allows for more accurate and timely information on interfirm transactions, as well as for traditional financial and market data for balance reporting and cash management between the firm and its domestic and foreign banking business partners. Most importantly, EDI has allowed many firms to reduce funds invested in inventory, improve cash disbursement forecasting through more accurate and timely shipping notices, and allowed more disbursement forecasting through more accurate and timely shipping notices, and allowed more precise prenegotiated payment terms with suppliers and customers.

The second real-time innovation is that of electronic funds transfer (EFT) systems. These systems, such as the automated clearing house (ACH) and the corporate trade payments (CTP) systems, allow a much more efficient use of capital resources. These systems, in conjunction with the Society for Worldwide Interbank Financial Telecommunications (SWIFT), allow efficient utilization of financial resources regardless of their physical or time-zone locale. The ability to routinely access and manipulate capital market information and balances—although still somewhat an ideal rather than a reality—can potentially allow the modern treasury to add value by allowing the business to support the same basic operating cash flows with fewer financial resources (financing cash flows).

The final force driving treasury change is *globalization;* the globalization of the organization, the business, and the financial markets themselves. Outside of the previously identified risks associated with international operations—currency risks—the financial management requirements of the multinational enterprise have essentially doubled the stakes of adequate treasury management.

5.3 INTERNATIONAL TREASURY MANAGEMENT. Multinational firms develop their international treasuries as business demands. As the scope of the firm's global operations expand, so do the specific functions and structures of international treasury. Again, although there are no rules as to the stages of global treasury development, a simple three-stage approach captures much of the variety of developments.

(a) Stage 1. Representative of firms with active exporting and/or importing of goods, the early stages of dealing with international operations typically includes two primary areas:

1. Foreign exchange management
2. Basic international cash management

The establishment of only one or two foreign affiliates initiates the need to pursue improved cash management as the firm explores repatriation of profits and other cash flow-based decisions. International tax management is often added to the scope of work of the domestic tax management division of treasury, although issues of international taxation are complex and material to the firm's financial results. (For more on international taxation, see Chapter 30.)

(b) Stage 2. As multinational operations expand, international treasury continues to expand so that it is often duplicating all domestic treasury functional areas.

- Foreign exchange risk management, reporting and analysis of derivative positions
- Multinational cash management, netting, pooling, and bank relations
- International tax management and earnings repatriation
- International capital markets, subsidiary funding, capital structure

It is often at this stage, prior to the firm truly addressing the organizational and functional conflicts, in which many of the worst treasury management practices arise. The firm has outgrown the effectiveness of its managerial structure.

(c) Stage 3. A large multinational firm now reflects both the scope of its global activities through functional areas (foreign exchange, cash management, etc.) but is also highly regionalized, requiring regional treasury specialists or managers in addition to a redefinition of the functional financial overlap and duplication problems arising under Stage #2.[7]

Although foreign currency management, foreign exchange risk management, and international tax management are the most widely recognized unique features of international treasury, managing the cash flow process within the multinational firm is first priority. The fact that many of the cash flows are denominated in multiple currencies (the subject of the following section on currency management) complicates the process significantly.

But the complexity of issues in international treasury defies simple categorization. Note the variety of functional areas which are working in combination in the following sample of an international treasury problem:

> In countries such as Italy and Switzerland withholding tax rules will strongly influence the choice of technique. A Dutch company, for example, was confronted with recurring deficit situations of its subsidiaries in Italy. A zero balancing structure would result in intercompany loans from the treasury (located in the Netherlands) to the Italian subsidiaries. The average lending amount over a year would be US$2,000,000 on which 10% debit interest would be charged. On the US$200,000 interest payment, 10% withholding tax (according to the treaty between Italy and the Netherlands) would be deducted. This US$20,000 would result in an actual cost for the treasury because the loan would be financed by a credit facility in the Netherlands, which would lead to the unavailability of settlement opportunities within the Dutch corporate income tax system. Faced with this scenario the company decided to re-evaluate their original zero balancing structure.[8]

It is readily apparent that all the financial functions—cash management, foreign exchange management, centralized versus decentralized management and control

---

[7]Westinghouse recently restructured Treasury from one which had grown international to one which is international. Prior to restructuring, Westinghouse's treasury had six primary areas: banking, credit and collections, corporate finance, domestic cash management, pension, and international. After restructuring, treasury was reduced to five areas, global capital markets, global cash management, pension, project finance, corporate finance, and had reduced total positions from 109 to 40.

[8]"International Liquidity Management: Efficiency Through Creativity," by Marcel Van Eijk, *Treasury Management International*, Special Report, 1995.

(the whole, the region, the individual affiliate), disbursements, tax—influence the management process.

5.4 INTERNATIONAL CASH MANAGEMENT. The typical multinational firm possesses cash flows between the parent and its subsidiaries, the subsidiaries and their suppliers, the subsidiaries and their customers, and between subsidiaries themselves, all of which are generally processed through banking institutions.

(a) International Cash Management Goals. The theory of international cash management is the same as that of domestic cash management: the maximization of the firm's financial resources is achieved by effectively receiving payments as fast as possible while taking advantage of all liability provisions, payable periods, which are low in cost. Simply put, the business would prefer to conduct the same level of business activity with an ever-decreasing balance sheet. The complex part is not the theory, but the practice.

There are two primary reasons why cash is transferred across national boundaries. First, for the payment for resources used such as materials, technology (fees), property rights (royalties), financing and debt service (principal and interest), or invested capital (dividends). The second reason is for the effective deployment or repositioning of funds in order to obtain higher rates of return, assure accessibility to funds, minimize currency risk, minimize total capital invested in working capital forms, and to minimize the global tax bill of the firm.

(b) Mechanics of International Cash Management. The international cash management techniques employed for the payments depend on whether the payment is to be associated with a related or unrelated third party. The primary distinction arises from the ability of the parent to dictate or coordinate cash flow payment methods and timing between internal units, often without true market incentives (such as discounts), as opposed to third-party payments which are obviously less controllable.

The sample U.S.-based multinational in Exhibit 5.4 illustrates a common "map" to the cash flow structure of a global firm. The subsidiaries in France and Spain are each individually faced with the common cash management and working capital management all firms everywhere face—traditional domestic treasury. The primary conduit for cash management in each country is the utilization of local banking and cash management services.[9] International treasury, either through a regional treasurer or through a representative of the parent company, would typically consider and evaluate any of the following potential techniques for the management of payments with unrelated parties:

- Timing of billing
- Use of lockboxes or intercept points
- Negotiated value dates

---

[9]The electronic data interchange (EDI) and electronic funds transfer (EFT) systems in Western Europe are relatively sophisticated compared to the majority of similar systems worldwide. The barrier is often not the linkage of real time cash management between the customers and suppliers in the local market with the subsidiary, but rather the cross-border linkages, including the parent.

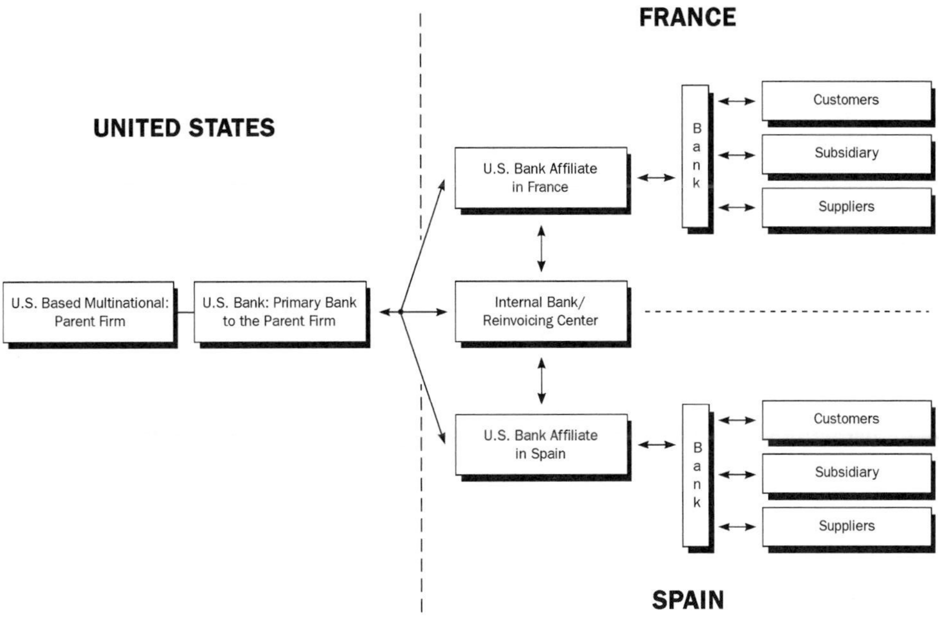

Exhibit 5.4. International Cash Management: U.S.-Based Multinational with French and Spanish Subsidiaries.

- EDI and EFT avenues
- Same-day value basis transfers

The parent firm, its treasury staff, and bank representatives would in turn also be responsible for gaining whatever scale and scope benefits which may be derived from managing the related-party payments, the cash flows that are intrafirm:

- Leading and lagging of payments
- In-house factoring
- Bilateral or multilateral netting of payments
- EDI and EFT avenues
- In-house banking/reinvoicing

The last item on the list requires additional discussion. The multinational framework illustrated in Exhibit 5.4 includes the potential creation of an in-house bank, a unit that could borrow and lend between units of the firm, offering competitive market rates for credit/investment that could be managed more effectively given proper cash planning throughout the multinational.

Each of the two cash management goals could be more effectively achieved with this type of structure, more effective cash management by either using excess cash flow from some units to supplement cash needs in other units (in-house banking), and to reposition funds for tax and foreign exchange management through repricing and invoicing (reinvoicing center). This comes at varying degrees of cost; in-house banking can often be achieved with acceptable separable costs, the savings often easily justifying the independent structure. The reinvoicing center, however, is not for everyone, given its separate incorporation needs and staffing if it is going to be effective in the repricing and taking title to intrafirm goods flows.

The sample firm in Exhibit 5.4 also illustrates one of the primary complexities of international cash management—the need to work through and manage a dual- or multiple-bank system. The payments by customers to the subsidiaries are typically processed through a local bank. Payments between the subsidiary and the parent, however, are frequently processed through branches, correspondents, or affiliates of the parent's primary bank back in the United States.[10] The U.S. bank affiliate structure serves as the primary conduit for real-time information regarding the cash flows and balances within the foreign markets. Typically, the U.S.-based parent will monitor cash balances in its foreign local banks (French and Spanish in Exhibit 5.4) through the electronic reporting systems of its U.S.-parent bank. There is at present a highly competitive marketplace for cash management system sales by many banks in New York and London to provide these services to the corporate public. Unfortunately, the systems are still years away from providing the technological and real-time accuracy, access, and comprehensiveness which the ideal multinational treasury system would require.

(c) Techniques for Effective Deployment of Funds. The firm of Exhibit 5.4 would, depending on the magnitude of cash flow differences between the two foreign subsidiaries and the operational and financial linkages between subsidiaries and parent, make varying levels of effort to reduce the total cash stock and cost within the system. This international cash management/banking activity might take one of two forms, *cash concentration* or *cash pooling*.

Cash pooling is exactly what it sounds like, a commingling of cash flows or balances between affiliate operations. Pooling is often readily available in-country, but can be quite complex to establish and run cross-country. Cash pooling can take a variety of forms, including *notional pooling* and *zero balancing*, each of which requires the establishment of a master account in each country over the individual affiliate accounts. *Notional pooling* (also commonly referred to as interest compensation) is when interest charges are calculated on a notional pool of cash—the master account, although the individual balances are not intermixed. Individual balances are mathematically pooled for the calculation of master account interest expense/charges. *Zero balancing* refers to a structure in which funds are transferred from the subsidiary accounts each day to the master account in order to maintain an end-of-day zero-balance on the affiliate level. Although many treasurers prefer a structure in which no physical transfer is made, the notional pooling approach, both techniques are financially equivalent.

Cash concentration is the establishment of a cross-border master account to which all individual foreign affiliates have access. Essentially the creation of an internal bank, the cash concentration account can be constructed to allow access to funds, and accept payment of funds, in a variety of currencies. It may be constructed within the framework of a cash pooling structure, or independently formed so that multiple currencies are accessible to multiple units in multiple markets. Although beyond the

---

[10]There is a growing consensus among international treasurers that an established local bank generally provides better services for processing of payments with domestic firms.

scope of this chapter on international treasury management, the complexity of establishing a truly cost-effective cross-border cash concentration system would require a combination of tax management, cash management, and foreign exchange management. At the heart of such a system would be the minimization of cross-border cash payments, by currency, achieved through either bilateral or multilateral netting of obligations. Aside from the complexity of terminology involved, the complexity of gaining real-time access to the information necessary for the attainment of true efficiencies is frequently prohibitive.

The reporting and monitoring system for global cash management should be designed to ensure that the firm, on a global basis, can hold overall cash balances to a minimum, avoid political and foreign exchange risk, minimize net interest expense, and minimize costs associated with transactions, bank float, and the general movement of funds. Transaction costs associated with global cash management are generally minimized by minimizing the number of transactions. The reports should include the following from the overseas operations: daily bank account records, activity schedules and fees, disbursements and collections, deposits and payments, negotiated bank arrangements (value dates), intragroup receivables and payables, and a cash budget for the appropriate time period ahead (including anticipated use of overdraft facilities). From the overseas banks, ledger balances and value balances should be available.

(d) Barriers to Effective International Cash Management. What are the factors that make a comprehensive and effective international cash management system difficult to implement and manage? A partial list would include the following:

- Differences and discrepancies in national bank rules, regulations, and practices
- National restrictions on netting, leads and lags, and hedging practices
- Limited local banking services
- Few standards for pricing of banking services
- Chronic informational failures such as confirmation delays
- National differences in corporate payment practices and customs
- Local credit restrictions, rationing of access to local borrowing or investing alternatives

This formidable list is the playing field of the international cash manager. Although new and sophisticated electronic services are introduced daily by banks, the firm with multinational operations in far-flung parts of the globe faces a difficult and often time-consuming task of efficiently managing the firm's source of value—cash flow.

5.5 FOREIGN EXCHANGE MANAGEMENT. Foreign exchange management and international cash management share the same basic goals, *centralization* and *concentration*. The multinational firm's foreign affiliates and subsidiaries (similar to those shown in Exhibit 5.4) possess their own individual currencies of cash flow (functional currency). Many of these affiliates are often not equipped, both in staffing and expertise, to effectively manage the currency transactions and risks which arise. The consensus in industry today is that the international treasury of the parent company, through *centralization*, can provide value-added processing and expertise to the subsidiary without absolving the subsidiary from responsibility of aiding in the effective management of currency exposures. The international treasury is a combination internal consultant, banker, and parent.

Concentration is the effective use of techniques for handling the everyday and not so everyday currency transaction and exposure management needs of the firm as a whole. Techniques such as netting of cross-border currency cash flows can significantly reduce the frequency of transactions, allowing fewer and larger individual currency purchases and hedge purchases. The economies of scale are appreciable, and the increased control results in better company-wide reporting, forecasting, and subsequent management of cash flows by currency in the short to medium term.

The components to the design and implementation of an international currency management program in the multinational involves

- Establishing risk management guidelines (exposure identification, list of authorized instruments, required minimum or maximum hedge coverage)
- Separation of front-office and back-office roles, responsibilities, and personnel
- Position monitoring and performance measurement

Treasury today is expected to take a much more proactive role in the management of the firm's multinational cash flows. This concerns not only the more efficient use of cash as a whole, but in the management of the currency of denomination of those cash flows within the multinational—all in the context of adding value to the internal and external customer. Once the currency risk management system within the multinational is designed, management and control of operations is critical to its success. Many of the derivative-related fiascos in recent years are traceable to nonexistent or inadequate specification of procedures and controls or simply management discipline in the implementation of risk management. Recent surveys indicate that still over 20 percent of major multinationals have no formal controls over treasury operations.

(a) Risk Management Guidelines. Senior management of the firm, from the treasurer's office to the chief financial officer, to the senior management group, to board and audit committee, must establish clear and simple guidelines by which currency risk management must abide.[11] (For a detailed treatment of this subject, see Chapter 6.)

These guidelines should include the requirements for exposure identification, allowable instruments for use, and required exposure coverage. Exposure identification, the specification of which types of exposures are to be managed (backlogs, balance sheet-related, translation, economic exposures, foreign currency-denominated bids, anticipated exposures, etc.) is fundamental to control of a risk management pro-

[11]PricewaterhouseCoopers' recent treasury survey indicated varying degrees of formal controls in treasury operations among major multinational firms. Foreign currency exposure management seems to be actually controlled more often than interest rate risk management. Among survey respondents, 87 percent indicated currency transaction exposure management controls, 63 percent on translation exposure management, and 43 percent on economic exposure management. Interest rate risks, however, were not as diligently watched. Only 74 percent of survey respondents indicated explicit controls over interest rate risk management, while investment management was explicitly controlled by over 84 percent of the firms.

gram. By isolating what will and will not be the subject of hedging will effectively limit the scale of the exposure management program. A list of accepted financial instruments which treasury is authorized to use for risk management is also important to control of operations given the ever-growing list of second-generation risk management products, many of which have complex valuation and exposure profiles. Even a short list today would need to determine the firm's policy toward the use of forwards, purchased options, written options, complex options, structured products, and straight interest rate swaps and cross-currency interest rate swaps. (See Chapter 7.) Finally, the firm's risk management guidelines should address the desirability of any minimum or maximum exposure coverage, by exposure size (amount), or by percentage required forward cover (e.g., 50% forward cover required on all booked exposures of $100,000 or more).

(b) Front-Office/Back-Office Division. There is little debate among treasury managers worldwide that the one critical element to preventing risk management system failures is the separation of front office activities, the design and construction of currency-related activities (transactions, hedging strategies), and back-office activities, the booking and settlement of transactions and hedging activity. Many treasuries are now outsourcing their back-office activities as an additional physical and fiduciary step in preventing any conflict or system failure. Regardless of whether these duties are carried out by internal or external personnel, it is fundamental that the duties be carried out by different personnel, with different upward-reporting requirements in the organization, and be physically separated if at all possible.[12]

(c) Position Monitoring and Performance Measurement. Once a currency risk management program is under way, treasury must monitor all positions and periodically measure its own performance against some benchmark.

Position monitoring is a critical issue facing many treasuries today as a result of the increased use of derivative products, many of which are difficult to mark-to-market on a frequent basis. This difficulty is a combination of the complexity of the instrument's valuation, and the timeliness and appropriateness of critical inputs, such as market volatilities, which are integral to the determination of true value. Position monitoring must be pursued in parallel for all outstanding (identified) exposures, and for the structured instruments, positions, or derivatives used for the hedging of such exposures. For decentralized multinationals with foreign exchange risk management at the subsidiary or regional level, it is necessary for the parent and the subparent to be aware of these position values on a daily basis if possible. This requires the ability by treasury to mark-to-market all outstanding positions with contemporaneous market data. A number of major information vendors such as Reuters now provide the software and information linkages that allow constant mark-to-market valuation of all positions.

Performance measurement is a topic of some debate. Recent surveys indicate that nearly 30% of all treasuries do not consider performance measurement or other

[12]The subject of separation of strategy and confirmation/settlement has of course gained enormous attention after the fall of Baring Brothers which was nearly single-handedly the result of Mr. Nick Leeson's control over both front- and back-office job duties, allowing fraud and abuse and, in the case of the oldest investment bank in London, failure.

benchmarking activities as important. Given the increasing role of treasury, and its ability to leverage its activities for the betterment or detriment of the firm's overall profitability, performance measurement is critical to adequate controls and effective management. Foreign exchange benchmarks such as fully covered and no-cover indicators allow international treasury a continuing set of metrics which may be used to reevaluate hedging policies. Treasury, once accepted as a value-added component of the firm, must be held to similar standards and industry practices (best practices) if it is to truly contribute to the value of the business.

5.6 SUMMARY: THE EMERGING VALUE-ADDED ROLE OF TREASURY. As domestic and international treasury operations evolve, reducing redundancy and focusing increasingly on efficiencies which are cross-border, cross-currency, and cross-function, the role of treasury expands as a source of value to the company as a whole. But there are many managerial challenges ahead, as many treasuries today are as yet unprepared for true global treasury effectiveness, requiring rethinking and restructuring treasury operations. Redundancy between domestic and international treasury functions, the need to add staff prepared for the expanding complexity of risk management activities and instruments, as well as the continuing impact of global telecommunications and technological support are continuing items on the treasury to-do list.

SOURCES AND SUGGESTED REFERENCES

Alfonsi, Michael J. "Best Practices in International Treasury Management." *AFP Exchange*. Bethesda, November/December 1999.

Bedell, Denise. "Choosing a Global Treasury Strategy." *Corporate Finance*. London, May 2001.

Corporate Finance, Crunching the Payments Problem: Technology in Treasury Management 1995. A Supplement to *Corporate Finance*, October 1995.

Corporate Finance. "Regional Pooling and Netting in Europe." March 1992, pp. 18–25.

Eiteman, David K., Arthur I. Stonehill, and Michael H. Moffett. *Multinational Business Finance*, 9th ed. Boston, MA: Addison-Wesley Publishing, 2001.

Frank, Nicholas. "Solving Treasurers' Troubles: Regional Treasury Centres," *Corporate Finance Guide to Asian Treasury*, February 1996, pp. 2–5.

Giannotti, John B., and Richard W. Smith. *Treasury Management: A Practitioner's Handbook*. New York: John Wiley & Sons, 1981.

Greifer, Nicholas, and Jeffery Vieceli. "Best Practices in Treasury Management." *Government Finance Review*, Vol. 16, No. 2, April 2000, p. 19.

Kuhlmann, Arkadi, F. John Mathis, and James L. Mills. *Prime Cash: First Steps in Treasury Management*. New York: McGraw-HIll, Inc., 1993.

Masson, Dubos J., and David A. Wickoff. *Essentials of Cash Management*, 5th ed. Bethesda, MD: Treasury Management Association, 1995.

Millar, Bill. *Global Treasury Management*. Business International Corporation. New York: Harper Business, 1991.

Mulligan, Emer. "Treasury Management Organisation: An Examination of Centralised versus Decentralised Approaches." *Irish Journal of Management*. Dublin, 2001.

Teigen, Lee E. "Treasury Management: An Overview." *Business Credit*, New York, July 2001.

Thurston, Charles W. "Integrating Treasury Management." *Global Finance*. New York, July 2000.

Van Eijk, Marcel. "International Liquidity Management: Efficiency Through Creativity." Special Report, *Treasury Management International*. 1995, pp. 17–23.

CHAPTER 6

MANAGEMENT OF CORPORATE FOREIGN EXCHANGE RISK

Gunter Dufey

University of Michigan and McKinsey & Co.

Ian H. Giddy

New York University

CONTENTS

6.1 INTRODUCTION. "Corporate" exchange risk refers to the adverse effects that unanticipated exchange rate changes can have on the value of the firm. This chapter explores the impact of currency fluctuations on cash flows, on assets and liabilities, and on the real business of the firm. At the onset, some basic questions must be answered: What is exchange risk, how does exposure relate to it, and why is it of importance to corporates at all? If foreign exchange risk is an issue that corporations have to deal with, we need to know how they identify and measure their currency exposure and, based on the nature of the exposure and the firm's ability to forecast currencies, what exchange risk management strategy they should employ. Finally, guidance is necessary regarding which of the various tools and techniques of the foreign exchange market they should employ: forwards and futures; options or the specification of debt and assets? The chapter concludes by suggesting a framework that can be used to find the appropriate hedging instrument for a certain type of exposure.

In order to lay the foundations for the following sections, it is important to understand what foreign exchange risk in the context of a corporation is, and how it relates to the concept of exposure. Exchange risk originates from the (random) fluctuations of foreign exchange rates. It can be measured by the variance of the value of monetary as well as real assets and liabilities and the operating income of a company that is caused by unanticipated changes in the exchange rates. The emphasis here is on unexpected changes, as anticipated changes in the foreign exchange rate—as well as all other available information—are already reflected in market prices. In most currencies there exist futures or forward exchange contracts whose prices give firms an indication of where the market expects currencies to go. And these contracts offer the ability to lock in the anticipated change.

Exchange rate volatility is by itself a necessary, but not sufficient, condition for foreign exchange risk: Indeed, some firms may not be affected by foreign exchange rate changes at all. Thus, what is required is to assess foreign exchange exposure that quantifies the sensitivity of the value of assets, liabilities, and operating income with respect to exchange rate variations. The concept of exposure describes the effect that exchange rate changes have on these values: It is the value at risk. Therefore, it is ultimately foreign exchange exposure that is relevant for each individual corporation. One of the consequences of this conclusion is that a corporation may decide to take operating measures that alter its exposure as one way to manage the underlying exchange risk (Levi, 1996).

From this notion of exchange risk, several complex issues arise. First, the right perspective has to be determined: From the company's point of view, it could well be that there are offsetting positions elsewhere in the firm, so exchange risk might not matter because there is no exposure. But how about future cash flows that are not yet contractually fixed but anticipated? For nonfinancial firms these future cash flows reflect the basis of their current value! Thus, they should surely be part of the analysis, too, when determining the corporate risk profile.

Last but not least, the company belongs to its shareholders. Therefore, it might be appropriate to look at the issue from their perspective, that is, maximization of shareholder wealth, as postulated by modern finance. Yet the impact of any given currency change on shareholder value is difficult to assess; and frankly, the empirical evidence linking exchange rate changes to stock prices is weak.

Moreover, the shareholder who has a diversified portfolio may find that the negative effect of exchange rate changes on one firm is offset by gains in other firms; in other words, exchange risk is diversifiable. Thus, an investor may be concerned with such a risk. This means that one has to investigate whether—and if so, why—it makes sense to deal with foreign exchange risk on the corporate level at all.

6.2 SHOULD FIRMS MANAGE FOREIGN EXCHANGE RISK? Some firms refrain from active management of their foreign exchange, even though they understand that exchange rate fluctuations can affect their earnings and value. They make this decision for a number of reasons.

First, managers do not take time to understand the issue. They consider any use of risk management tools, such as forwards, futures, and options, as speculative. Or they argue that such financial manipulations lie outside the firm's field of expertise. "We are in the business of manufacturing slot machines, and we should not be gambling on currencies." Perhaps they are right to fear abuses of hedging techniques, but refusing to use forwards and other instruments may expose the firm to substantial speculative risks.

Second, managers claim that exposure cannot be measured. They are right—currency exposure is complex and can seldom be gauged with precision. But, as in many business situations, imprecision should not be taken as an excuse for indecision.

Third, they say that the firm is hedged. All transactions such as imports or exports are covered with forward contracts, and foreign subsidiaries finance in local currencies. This ignores the fact that the bulk of the firm's value comes from transactions not yet completed, so that transactions hedging is a very incomplete strategy.

Fourth, they say that the firm does not have any exchange risk because it does all its business in dollars (or yen, or whatever the home currency is). But a moment's thought will make it evident that even if you invoice French customers in dollars, when the euro drops, your prices will have to adjust or you'll be undercut by local competitors. So revenues are influenced by currency changes.

Fifth, they argue that doing business is risky and the firm gets rewarded for bearing risks, business and financial. What this argument overlooks is that investors may reward the firm for risks in which the outcome, while uncertain, is expected to be positive. That is rarely the case in financial market bets in which the outcome tends to reflect odds that are 50–50.

Finally, they assert that the balance sheet is hedged on an accounting basis—especially when the "functional currency" is held to be the dollar. The misleading signals that balance sheet exposure measures can give are documented in later sections of this paper.

But is there any economic justification for a "doing nothing" strategy? Modern principles of the theory of finance suggest prima facie that the management of corporate foreign exchange exposure may neither be an important nor a legitimate concern for corporate managers. More specifically, Modigliani and Miller have demonstrated that in the absence of taxes, information asymmetries, transactions cost, and other market imperfections, a company's investment and financing decisions are independent of each other. Consequently, since value creation takes place on the asset side of the balance sheet (namely through realization of positive net present value projects), risk management as part of the firm's financing policies cannot create value per se. These lines of thought suggest that the investor, who might be able to manage exposure to financial risks more efficiently by properly diversifying his or her investment portfolio, should do risk management. Unless firms have a comparative advantage in the management of exposure relative to investors, for example, on the basis of transactions or information costs, there is no reason why firms should deal with this issue.

Furthermore, foreign exchange risk management might simply not matter because of certain equilibrium conditions in international markets for both financial and real assets as another line of reasoning suggests. These conditions include the relationship between relative price levels of goods in different markets and exchange rate changes, also known as Purchasing Power Parity (PPP), and between interest rates and foreign exchange rates, usually referred to as the International Fisher Effect (IFE) (see next section).

However, this view of corporate risk management is at odds with reality as well as recent theoretical insights into corporate finance. Empirically, many firms, financial as well as nonfinancial, can be observed to devote efforts and resources to the reduction of risk. Obviously, corporations do concern themselves with the variability of their earnings or market value. As documented by a survey of derivatives usage, U.S. nonfinancial firms quite often even employ derivatives in order to hedge primarily anticipated (77%) or firm–commitment (80%) transactions with the overall objective of minimizing the fluctuations in the company's cash flows (67%) (Bodnar, Hayt, Marston, and Smithson, 1995). Also, there is some evidence (Jorion, 1990, and Barton, Bodnar, and Kaul, 1994) suggesting that stock prices are adversely affected by foreign exchange changes.

The observed relevance and importance of risk management to corporations has led also to the development of positive theories that try to explain this phenomenon. Turning the classic Modigliani-Miller Theorem around, one can argue that if financial policies affect corporate value, it must be because of their impact on transaction costs, taxes, information asymmetries, or investment decisions. Thus it is that the model's assumptions may not hold that establishes the case for corporate risk management.

There are two conditions that a corporate hedging strategy has to meet in order to be justified on economic grounds: There have to be benefits to the company's shareholders greater than the cost of that hedging strategy; and risk management on the corporate level must be the way to realize these benefits at least cost. In general, this can be the case if risk management increases the expected cash flows from the firm to shareholders and/or if the discount rate that is applied to calculate the cash flow's present value is lowered. As will be shown most of the value of hedging is generated from an increase in cash flows rather than a decrease in the discount rate.

Analyzing first the risks shareholders bear and the benefits that can be derived from corporate hedging, it follows that there are arguments that do justify risk management at the corporate level for the benefit of shareholders (although the potential gain might in most cases be quite small). Assuming (domestically) well-diversified investors, most of the value to shareholders will come from corporate hedging in case it functions as a means to substitute for international diversification: Corporate risk management can have the effect of international diversification in that certain risks, for example, oil price risk, could be transferred abroad, thus reducing the exposure in both countries. If this hedging transaction is associated with a fixed cost, the firm will be able to accomplish the hedge at a lower cost than the individual investors, that is, the firm has to take some action anyway in the course of its normal business. Also risk sharing with privately held companies might be beneficial for investors if they could not trade these firms otherwise.

Apart from these direct effects on shareholders' wealth—often difficult to prove because of the diversity of individual investors' interests and preferences—there are several benefits that come from corporate hedging that affect the value of the company and thus the wealth of all shareholders. The existence of taxes represents one argument in favor of corporate hedging, provided the tax code is nonlinear. At first shown in detail by Smith and Stulz (1985), expected corporate after tax income and thus cash flows to the shareholders increase with lower volatility of pretax income in the presence of convex tax structures. Since risk management policies aim at the reduction in earnings variance, they effectively reduce the company's average long tax rate and create gains that shareholders could not realize otherwise.

A reduction in corporate income variability is a value-creating activity for another reason. The idea is that higher volatility of firm value implies a higher probability of situations where financial distress or even bankruptcy are encountered. Wages, debt service, and other fixed claims have to be met by the corporation regardless of its profitability. With higher variance of corporate earnings it is therefore more likely that situations arise where income is too low to serve fixed financial commitments, thus getting the company into financial distress. These negative events, however, have special, discrete costs associated with them. There are direct cost such as bankruptcy proceeding and legal cost, as well as indirect cost that come in many different manifestations. They result in higher contracting costs with suppliers, customers, and employees. Management's attention will be less focused on value-creating operations; profitable investment opportunities may be passed up due to increased difficulties in raising the necessary funds. By stabilizing the income stream to the corporation, corporate hedging activities reduce the probability of financial distress. Thus, as with taxes, expected corporate value is increased to the advantage of shareholders. Risk management, by reducing the firm's costs of financial distress, also increases the corporation's debt capacity. This leads to a higher optimal debt–equity ratio which means benefits from increased tax shields.

Another important argument to support the concept of corporate hedging has been brought forth: Under often realistic conditions of additional costs, such as underwriting fees, and so on, the variability of funds generated by the company will have undesirable effects on its investment and/or financing policies in that it increases their volatility, too (Froot, Scharfstein, and Stein, 1993). As a result, investment opportunities with positive net present values (NPVs) might be passed up as a result of a shortage of funds available or outside financing will be necessary. A corporate risk management program creates value to shareholders in that it ensures that the company always has sufficient funds to make value-enhancing investments independent of otherwise disrupting movements of external factors.

Risk management can also mitigate the problem of conflicting interests between shareholders and bondholders of the firm. If the company is highly leveraged and firm value is low, profitable investment opportunities might be passed up because shareholders have little interest in undertaking these projects since their benefits accrue to bondholders (this is known as the "underinvestment problem"). They might, however, be interested in taking on high-risk, high-return projects as this will transfer wealth from bondholders to shareholders. Higher variability of firm value will increase the value of the shareholders' claims because the value of their call option increases with higher volatility of the underlying assets' value. Bondholders try to limit such behavior via bond covenants. As hedging can reduce the variability of firm value, it is apt to mitigate the conflicts between shareholders and bondholders, because situations where firm value is low are avoided or appear less frequently (Levi and Serecu, 1991).

Two additional aspects arise in the context of employee compensation and its linkage to the performance of the employing firm: Whereas the dependence of the employees' income on corporate performance basically represents a hedge for owners of small corporations, this effect is rather negligible for large corporations in which shareholders hold diversified portfolios. On the contrary, if the company has more stable income streams due to its hedging activities and does not have to link its employees' income to its revenue, it does not have to compensate its employees for taking on some of its risks either. Thus, the savings in the wage bill goes to the shareholders.

Tying management compensation to the firm's performance raises yet a second issue. Various measures of corporate performance (such as earnings of the stock price) often represent a basis for upper-management compensation. As hedging reduces the impact of risks that are not under management control on these measures, it makes the incentive structure more effective. By the same token, managers have only limited ways to diversify their personal stake given their large interest in the performance of the company. Moreover, since managerial success or ability is hard to estimate, corporate performance measures will almost by necessity serve as proxies for management evaluation. As a consequence, managers will favor lower variability of firm value (unless their compensation increases with higher volatility, as for example with stock options) in order not to lose the present value of their future income from their current employer. This however may raise the problem that the optimal risk management strategy to managers is not necessarily the best for the firm, an issue which can be solved by separating the actually implemented risk management policy from that used as a base for management compensation (Fite and Pfleiderer, 1995).

Finally, there usually exist information asymmetries between the firm's management and the market. Hedging can help securities analysts to get a more precise estimate of the value of the firm's assets assuming that the firm's exposure is not entirely known to market participants. It then represents an alternative to information disclosure which has the advantage that investors do not have to go through the difficulty of analyzing all relevant information in order to get a comprehensive picture of the company's exposure. Also, the higher quality of information about the firm enables management to do a much better job at risk management than the individual investor could do. As will be shown in the material that follows, the assessment of exposure to exchange rate fluctuations requires detailed estimates of the susceptibility of net cash flows to unexpected rate changes (Dufey and Srinivasulu, 1984).

All the above considerations basically rest on the assumptions that equilibrium such as PPP and IFE do not hold, since if they did, hedging would not be necessary. Whereas these equilibriums tend to persist in the long run, they do not in the short run. Therefore, risk management does matter to corporations if shareholder value is to be maximized. An important result and consequence is that a passive strategy toward risk can be quite costly in that it means to take on certain risks on purpose. Hedging considerations are at the same time interdependent with general business planning, as there are different ways to affect exposure: measures that affect exposure per se and measures that reduce risk by establishing offsetting (financial) positions. In addition, companies are now focused more on consolidated measures of risk, including interest rate and commodity and credit risk, instead of segmenting currency risk into a bucket of its own. The most popular methods are variants on value-at-risk (VaR) or its flow equivalent, cash flow-at-risk (Smithson, 1998, and Jorion, 2000).

6.3 ECONOMIC EXPOSURE, PURCHASING POWER PARITY, AND THE INTERNATIONAL FISHER EFFECT. Exchange rates, interest rates, and inflation rates are linked to one another through a classical set of relationships at the level of the economy that have import for the nature of foreign exchange risk at the level of the firm also. These relationships are: the Purchasing Power Parity Theorem, which describes the linkage between inflation rates differentials and exchange rates changes; the International Fisher Effect, which ties interest rate differences to exchange rate expectations; and the Unbiased Forward Rate Theory, which relates the forward exchange rate to exchange rate expectations. These relationships, along with two other "parity" linkages, are illustrated in Exhibit 6.1.

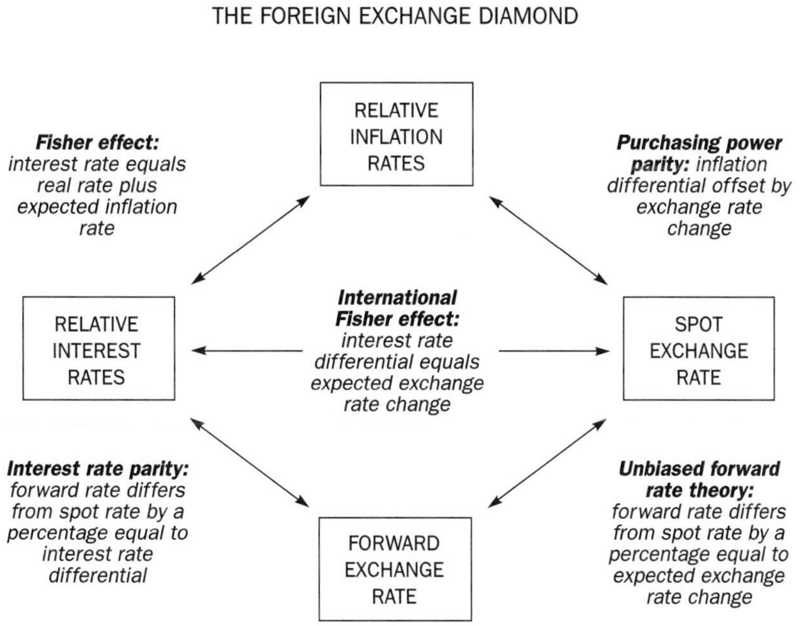

Exhibit 6.1. Key Parity Relationship of International Finance that Affect Corporate Exchange Risk Exposure.

The Purchasing Power Parity (PPP) theorem can be stated in different ways, but the most common representation links the changes in exchange rates to those in relative price indices in two countries:

$$\text{Rate of change of exchange rate} = \text{Difference in inflation rates}$$

The relationship is derived from the basic idea that, in the absence of trade restrictions, changes in the exchange rate mirror changes in the relative price levels in the two countries. Therefore, under conditions of free trade, prices of similar commodities cannot differ between two countries by more than the transfer cost, because arbitrageurs will take advantage of such situations until price differences are eliminated. This "Law of One Price" leads logically to the idea that what is true of one commodity should be true of the economy as a whole—the price level in two countries should be linked through the exchange rate—and hence to the notion that exchange rate changes are tied to inflation rate differences.

The International Fisher Effect (IFE) states that the interest rate differential will exist only if the exchange rate is expected to change in such a way that the advantage of the higher interest rate is offset by the loss on the foreign exchange transaction.

The IFE can be written as follows:

$$\text{Expected rate of change of the exchange rate} = \text{Interest rate differential}$$

In practical terms, the IFE implies that while an investor in a low-interest country can convert his funds into the currency of the high-interest country and get paid a higher rate, his gain (the interest rate differential) will be offset by his expected loss because of foreign exchange rate changes.

The Unbiased Forward Rate Theory asserts that the forward exchange rate is the "best" estimate of the expected future spot rate. While it is consistent with the efficient market theory that asserts that all relevant information is reflected in prices, including forwards and futures, market efficiency allows the existence of factors that can introduce a "bias" in the forward price of foreign exchange. However, in the absence of such factors, it is difficult to claim that systematic and regular biases exist that would not be taken advantage of by professional market participants and, thus, eliminated. Indeed, the best empirical evidence of ex post data demonstrates that risk premiums exist, but they are time variant, exhibiting a largely random pattern.

For risk management, therefore, there is little choice but to act as if ex ante, the forward is an unbiased predictor of the expected future spot rate in all those currencies where there are no factors such as exchange controls, excess external indebtedness, or other identifiable reasons that would rationalize a reasonably systematic risk premium. In the absence of such influences, the unbiased forward rate theory can be stated simply:

$$\text{Expected exchange rate} = \text{Forward exchange rate}$$

Now we can summarize the impact of unexpected exchange rate changes on the internationally involved firm by drawing on these parity conditions. Given sufficient time, competitive forces and arbitrage will neutralize the impact of exchange rate changes on the returns to assets; due to the relationship between rates of devaluation and inflation differentials, these factors will also neutralize the impact of the changes on the value of the firm. This is simply the principle of Purchasing Power Parity and the Law of One Price operating at the level of the firm. On the liability side, the cost of debt tends to adjust as debt is repriced at the end of the contractual period, reflecting (revised) expected exchange rate changes. And returns on equity will also reflect required rates of return; in a competitive market, these will be influenced by expected exchange rate changes. Finally, the unbiased forward rate theory suggests that locking in the forward exchange rate offers the same expected return as remaining exposed to the ups and downs of the currency—on average, it can be expected to err as much above as below the forward rate.

In the long run, it would seem that a firm operating in this setting will not experience net exchange losses or gains. However, because of contractual or, more importantly, strategic commitments, these equilibrium conditions rarely hold in the short and medium term. Moreover, the preceding equilibrium conditions refer to economic relationships across all markets in the entire economy, which does not necessarily mean that they hold for the individual firm that operates in a specific segment of the market. Therefore, the essence of foreign exchange exposure and, significantly, its management, are made relevant by these deviations, which may be temporary or structural.

6.4 IDENTIFYING EXPOSURE. The first step in management of corporate foreign exchange risk is to acknowledge that such risk does exist and that managing it is in the interest of the firm and its shareholders. The next step, however, is much more difficult: the identification of the nature and magnitude of foreign exchange exposure. In other words, identifying what is at risk, and in what way. The focus here is on the exposure of nonfinancial corporations, or rather the value of their assets. This reminder is necessary because most commonly accepted notions of foreign exchange risk hedging deal with assets; that is, they are pertinent to (relatively simple) financial institutions where the bulk of the assets consists of (paper) assets that have contractually fixed returns (i.e., fixed income claims, not equities). Clearly, such time-honored hedging rules as "finance your assets in the currency in which they are denominated" applies in general to banks and similar firms. However, nonfinancial business firms have, as a rule, only a relatively small proportion of their total assets in the form of receivables and other financial claims. Their core assets consist of inventories, equipment, special-purpose buildings, and other tangible assets, often closely related to technological capabilities that give them earnings power and thus value. Unfortunately, real assets (as compared to paper assets) are not labeled with currency signs that make foreign exchange exposure analysis easy. Most importantly, the location of an asset in a country is, as we shall see, an all too fallible indicator of their foreign exchange exposure.

The task of gauging the impact of exchange rate changes on an enterprise begins with measuring its exposure, the amount, or value, at risk. This issue has been clouded because financial results for an enterprise tend to be compiled by methods based on the principles of accrual accounting. Unfortunately, this approach yields data that frequently differ from those relevant for business decision making, namely future cash flows and their associated risk profiles. As a result, considerable efforts are expended, both by decision makers as well as students of exchange risk, to reconcile the differences between the point-in-time effects of exchange rate changes on the enterprise in terms of accounting data, referred to as accounting or translation exposure, and the ongoing cash flow effects, which are referred to as economic exposure. (See also Coppe, Graham, and Koller, 1996.) Both concepts have their grounding in the fundamental concept of transactions exposure. The relationship between the three concepts is illustrated in Exhibit 6.2. While exposure concepts have been aptly analyzed elsewhere in this Handbook, some basic concepts are repeated here to make the present chapter self-contained.

Measures of translation exposure have a grounding in simple transactions exposure. But economic exposure deals with exchange rate effects on future transactions.

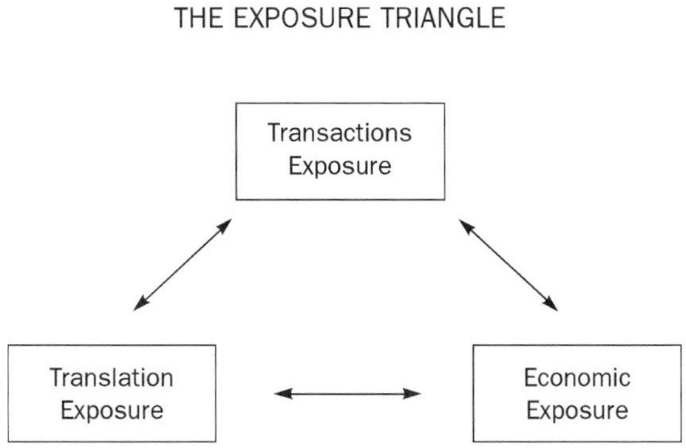

Exhibit 6.2. Three Concepts of Exposure. Measures of translation exposure have a grounding in simple transactions exposure, but economic exposure deals with exchange rate effects on future transactions.

(a) Transaction Exposure. The typical illustration of transaction exposure involves an export or import contract giving rise to a foreign currency receivable or payable. On the surface, when the exchange rate changes, the value of this export or import transaction will be affected in terms of the domestic currency. However, when analyzed carefully, it becomes apparent that the exchange risk results from a financial investment (the foreign currency receivable) or a foreign currency liability (the loan from a supplier) that is purely incidental to the underlying export or import transaction; it could have arisen in and of itself through independent foreign borrowing and lending. Thus, what is involved here are simply foreign currency assets and liabilities, whose value is contractually fixed in nominal terms. While this traditional analysis of transactions exposure is correct in a narrow, formal sense, it is really relevant for financial institutions only. With returns from financial assets and liabilities being fixed in nominal terms, they can be shielded from losses with relative ease through cash payments in advance (with appropriate discounts), through the factoring of receivables, or more conveniently via the use of forward exchange contracts, unless unexpected exchange rate changes have a systematic effect on credit risk. However, the essential assets of nonfinancial firms have noncontractual returns, that is, revenue and cost streams from the production and sale of their goods and services that can respond to exchange rate changes in very different ways. Consequently, they are characterized by foreign exchange exposure very different from that of firms with contractual returns.

(b) Accounting Exposure. The concept of accounting exposure arises from the need to translate accounts that are denominated in foreign currencies into the home currency of the reporting entity. Most commonly the problem arises when an enterprise has foreign affiliates keeping books in the respective local currency. For purposes of consolidation, these accounts must somehow be translated into the reporting currency of the parent company. In doing this, a decision must be made as to the exchange rate that is to be used for the translation of the various accounts. While income statements of foreign affiliates are typically translated at a periodic average rate, balance sheets pose a more serious challenge.

To a certain extent this difficulty is revealed by the struggle of the accounting profession to agree on appropriate translation rules and the treatment of the resulting gains and losses. A comparative historical analysis of translation rules may best illustrate the issues at hand. Over time, U.S. companies have followed essentially four types of translation methods, summarized in Exhibit 6.3. These four methods differ with respect to the presumed impact of exchange rate changes on the value of individual categories of assets and liabilities. Accordingly, each method can be identified by the way in which it separates assets and liabilities into those that are "exposed" and are, therefore, translated at the current rate, that is, the rate prevailing on the date of the balance sheet, and those whose value is deemed to remain unchanged, and which are, therefore, translated at the historical rate.

The current/noncurrent method of translation divides assets and liabilities into current and noncurrent categories, using maturity as the distinguishing criterion; only the former are presumed to change in value when the local currency appreciates or depreciates vis-à-vis the home currency. Supporting this method is the economic rationale that foreign exchange rates are essentially fixed but subject to occasional adjustments that tend to correct themselves in time. This assumption reflected reality to some extent, particularly with respect to industrialized countries during the period of

MEASURES OF ACCOUNTING EXPOSURE

	Current/ Noncurrent	Monetary/ Nonmonetary	Temporal	Current
ASSETS				
Cash	C	C	C	C
Marketable Securities (At Market Value)	C	C	C	C
Accounts Receivable	C	C	C	C
Inventory (At Cost)	C	H	H	C
Fixed Assets	H	H	H	C
LIABILITIES				
Current Liabilities	C	C	C	C
Long Term Debt	H	C	C	C
Equity	Residual Adjustment	Residual Adjustment	Residual Adjustment	Residual Adjustment

Note: In the case of Income Statements, sales revenues and interest are generally translated at the average historical exchange rate that prevailed during the period; depreciation is translated at the appropriate historical exchange rate. Some of the general and administrative expenses as well as cost-of-goods-sold are translated at historical exchange rates, others at current rates.

"C" = Assets and liabilities are translated at the current rate,or rate prevailing on the date of the balance sheet.

"H" = Assets and liabilities are translated at the historical rate.

Exhibit 6.3. Methods of Translation for Balance Sheets.

the Bretton Woods system. However, with subsequent changes in the international financial environment, this translation method has become outmoded; only in a few countries is it still being used.

Under the monetary/nonmonetary method all items explicitly defined in terms of monetary units are translated at the current exchange rate, regardless of their maturity. Nonmonetary items in the balance sheet, such as tangible assets, are translated at the historical exchange rate. The underlying assumption here is that the local currency value of such assets increases (decreases) immediately after a devaluation (revaluation) to a degree that compensates fully for the exchange rate change. This is equivalent of what is known in economics as the Law of One Price, with instantaneous adjustment.

A similar but more sophisticated translation approach supports the so-called temporal method. Here, the exchange rate used to translate balance sheet items depends on the valuation method used for a particular item in the balance sheet. Thus, if an item is carried on the balance sheet of the affiliate at its current value, it is to be translated using the current exchange rate. Alternatively, items carried at historical cost are to be translated at the historical exchange rate. As a result, this method synchronizes the time dimension of valuation with the method of translation. As long as foreign affiliates compile balance sheets under traditional historical cost principles, the temporal method gives essentially the same results as the monetary/nonmonetary method. However, when "current value accounting" is used, that is, when accounts are adjusted for inflation, then the temporal method calls for the use of the current exchange rate throughout the balance sheet. The temporal method provided the conceptual base for the first influential translation standard, Financial Accounting Standard Board's (FASB's) Standard 8 (FAS 8).

The temporal method points to a more general issue: the relationship between translation and valuation methods for accounting purposes. When methods of valuation provide results that do not reflect economic reality, translation will fail to remedy that deficiency, but will tend to make the distortion very apparent. To illustrate this point: companies with estate holdings abroad financed by local currency mortgages found that under FAS 8 their earnings were subject to considerable translation losses and gains. This came about because the value of their assets remained constant, as they were carried on the books at historical cost and translated at historical exchange rates, while the value of their local currency liabilities increased or decreased with every twitch of the exchange rate between reporting dates.

In contrast, U.S. companies whose foreign affiliates produced internationally traded goods (e.g., minerals or oil) felt comfortable valuing their assets on a dollar basis. Indeed, this latter category of companies was the one that did not like the transition to the current/current method at all. Here, all assets and liabilities are translated at the exchange rate prevailing on the reporting date. They found the underlying assumption that the value of all assets (denominated in the local currency of the foreign affiliate) would change in direct proportion to the exchange rate change did not reflect the economic realities of their business.

In order to accommodate the conflicting requirements of companies in different situations and still maintain a semblance of conformity and comparability, in the early 1980s the FASB issued Standard 52, replacing Standard 8. FAS 52, as it is commonly referred to, uses the current/current method as the basic translation rule. At the same time, it mitigates the consequences by allowing companies to move translation losses directly to a special subaccount in the net worth section of the balance sheet, instead of adjusting current income. This latter provision may be viewed as a mere gimmick without much substance, providing at best a signaling function, indicating to users of accounting information that translation gains and losses are of a nature different from items normally found in income statements.

A more significant innovation of FAS 52 is the "functional" currency concept, which gives a company the opportunity to identify the primary economic environment and select the appropriate (functional) currency for each of the corporation's foreign entities. This approach reflects the official recognition by the accounting profession that the location of an entity does not necessarily indicate the currency relevant for a particular business. Thus, FAS 52 represents an attempt to take into account the fact that exchange rate changes affect different companies in different ways, and that rigid and general rules treating different circumstances in the same manner will provide misleading information. In order to adjust to the diversity of real life, FAS 52 had to become quite complex. The following provides a brief road map to the logic of that standard.

In applying FAS 52, a company and its accountants must make two decisions in sequence. First, they must determine the functional currency of the entity whose accounts are to be consolidated. For all practical purposes, the choice here is between local currency and the U.S. dollar. In essence, there are a number of specific criteria that provide guidelines for this determination. As usual, extreme cases are relatively easily classified: A foreign affiliate engaged in retailing local goods and services will have the local currency as its functional currency, while a "border plant" that receives the majority of its inputs from abroad and ships the bulk of the output outside of the host country will have the dollar as its functional currency. If the functional currency is the dollar, foreign currency items on its balance sheet will have to be restated into dollars and any gains and losses are moved through the income statement. If the functional currency is determined to be the local currency, however, a second issue arises: whether the entity operates in a high-inflation environment. High-inflation countries are defined as those whose cumulative three-year inflation rate exceeds 100%. In that case, essentially the same principles as in FAS 8 are followed. In the case in which the cumulative inflation rate falls short of 100%, the foreign affiliate's books are to be translated using the current exchange rate for all items, and any gains or losses are to go directly as a charge or credit to the equity accounts.

FAS 52 and subsequent edicts on hedge accounting and accounting for derivatives contain a number of other fairly complex provisions regarding the treatment of hedge contracts, the definition of transactional gains and losses, and the accounting for intercompany transactions. In essence, it allows management much more flexibility to present the impact of exchange rate variations in accordance with perceived economic reality; by the same token, such flexibility provides greater scope for manipulation of reported earnings, and it reduces comparability of financial data for different firms. Companies' abuse of derivatives in the 1990s led to a revised standard, called FAS 133. This statement established accounting and reporting standards for derivative instruments, including certain derivative instruments embedded in other contracts (collectively referred to as derivatives), and for hedging activities. It requires that an entity recognize all derivatives as either assets or liabilities in the statement of financial position and measure those instruments at fair value. If certain conditions are met, a derivative may be specifically designated as (a) a hedge of the exposure to changes in the fair value of a recognized asset or liability or an unrecognized firm commitment, (b) a hedge of the exposure to variable cash flows of a forecasted transaction, or (c) a hedge of the foreign currency exposure of a net investment in a foreign operation. The purpose of this is simple—to clarify situations in which a company's earnings are fluctuating as a result of what is, in effect, speculation—but its application has proved controversial. See Exhibit 6.4 and the chapter on this subject.

(c) Critique of the Accounting Model of Exposure. Even with the stronger logic of FAS 52 and the discipline of FAS 133, users of accounting information must be aware that there are three systemic sources of error that can mislead those responsible for exchange risk management:

1. Accounting data do not capture all commitments of the firm that give rise to exchange risk.
2. Because of the historical cost principle, accounting values of assets and liabilities do not reflect the respective contribution to total expected net cash flow of the firm.
3. Translation rules do not distinguish between expected and unexpected exchange rate changes.

Conceptually, though, it is important to determine the time frame within which the firm cannot react to (unexpected) rate changes by raising prices; changing markets for inputs and outputs; and/or adjusting production and sales volumes. Sometimes, at

[1]The accounting for changes in the fair value of a derivative (that is, gains and losses) depends on the intended use of the derivative and the resulting designation.

- For a derivative designated as hedging the exposure to changes in the fair value of a recognized asset or liability or a firm commitment (referred to as a fair value hedge), the gain or loss is recognized in earnings in the period of change together with the offsetting loss or gain on the hedged item attributable to the risk being hedged. The effect of that accounting is to reflect in earnings the extent to which the hedge is not effective in achieving offsetting changes in fair value.
- For a derivative designated as hedging the exposure to variable cash flows of a forecasted transaction (referred to as a cash flow hedge), the effective portion of the derivative's gain or loss is initially reported as a component of other comprehensive income (outside earnings) and subsequently reclassified into earnings when the forecasted transaction affects earnings. The ineffective portion of the gain or loss is reported in earnings immediately.
- For a derivative designated as hedging the foreign currency exposure of a net investment in a foreign operation, the gain or loss is reported in other comprehensive income (outside earnings) as part of the cumulative translation adjustment. The accounting for a fair value hedge described above applies to a derivative designated as a hedge of the foreign currency exposure of an unrecognized firm commitment or an available-for-sale security. Similarly, the accounting for a cash flow hedge described above applies to a derivative designated as a hedge of the foreign currency exposure of a foreign-currency-denominated forecasted transaction.
- For a derivative not designated as a hedging instrument, the gain or loss is recognized in earnings in the period of change.

Under this Statement, an entity that elects to apply hedge accounting is required to establish at the inception of the hedge the method it will use for assessing the effectiveness of the hedging derivative and the measurement approach for determining the ineffective aspect of the hedge.

Source: Financial Accounting Standards Board.

Exhibit 6.4. FAS 133, Accounting for Derivative Instruments and Hedging Activities.

least one of these reactions is possible within a relatively short time; at other times, the firm is "locked in" through contractual or strategic commitments extending considerably into the future. Indeed, those firms that are free to react instantaneously and fully to adverse (unexpected) rate changes are not subject to exchange risk. A further implication of the time-frame element is that exchange risk stems from the firm's position when its cash flows are, for a significant period, exposed to (unexpected) exchange rate changes, rather than the risk resulting from any specific international involvement. Thus, companies engaged purely in domestic transactions but who have dominant foreign competitors may feel the effect of exchange rate changes in their cash flows as much or even more than some firms that are actively engaged in exports, imports, or foreign direct investment.

Regarding the first point, it must be recognized that, normally, commitments entered into by the firm in terms of foreign exchange (e.g., a purchase or a sales contract) will not be booked until the merchandise has been shipped. At best, such obligations are shown as contingent liabilities. More importantly, accounting data reveal very little about the ability of the firm to change costs, prices, and markets quickly. Alternatively, the firm may be committed by strategic decisions such as investment in plant and facilities. Such "commitments" are important criteria in determining the existence and magnitude of exchange risk.

The second point surfaced in our discussion of the temporal method: whenever asset values differ from market values, translation, however sophisticated, will not redress this original shortcoming. Thus, many of the perceived problems of FAS 8 had their roots not so much in translation, but in the fact that in an environment of inflation and exchange rate changes, the lack of current value accounting frustrates the best translation efforts.

Finally, translation rules do not take account of the fact that exchange rate changes have two components: (1) expected changes that are already reflected in the prices of assets and the cost of liabilities (relative interest rates); and (2) the unexpected deviations from the expected change that constitute the true sources of risk. The significance of this distinction is clear: Managers have already taken account of expected changes in their decisions. The basic rationale for corporate foreign exchange exposure management is to shield net cash flows, and thus the value of the enterprise, from unanticipated exchange rate changes.

This thumbnail sketch of the economic foreign exchange exposure concept has a number of significant implications, some of which seem to be at variance with frequently used ideas in the popular literature and apparent practices in business firms. Specifically, there are implications regarding the question of whether exchange risk originates from monetary or nonmonetary transactions, a reevaluation of traditional perspectives such as "transactions risk," and the role of forecasting exchange rates in the context of corporate foreign exchange risk management.

(d) Contractual versus Noncontractual Cash Flows. An assessment of the nature of the firm's assets and liabilities and their respective cash flows shows that some are contractual, that is, fixed in nominal, monetary terms. Such returns, earnings from fixed interest securities and receivables, for example, and the negative returns on various liabilities are relatively easy to analyze with respect to exchange rate changes: when they are denominated in terms of foreign currency, their terminal value changes directly in proportion to the exchange rate change. Thus, with respect to financial items, the firm is concerned only about net assets or liabilities denominated in foreign currency, to the extent that maturities (actually, "durations" of asset classes) are matched.

What is much more difficult, however, is to estimate the impact of an exchange rate change on assets with noncontractual return. While conventional discussions of exchange risk focus almost exclusively on financial assets, for trading and manufacturing firms at least, such assets are relatively less important than others. Indeed, equipment, real estate, buildings, and inventories make the decisive contributions to the local cash flow of those firms (in fact, companies frequently sell financial assets to banks, factors, or "captive" finance companies in order to leave banking to bankers and instead focus on the management of core assets!). And returns on such assets are affected in quite complex ways by changes in exchange rates. The most essential consideration is how the prices and costs of the firm will react in response to an unexpected exchange rate change. For example, if prices and costs react immediately and fully to offset exchange rate changes, the firm's cash flows are not exposed to exchange risk since they will be affected in terms of the base currency. Thus, the value of noncontractual assets is not affected.

Inventories may serve as a good illustration of this proposition. The value of an inventory in a foreign subsidiary is determined not only by changes in the exchange rate, but also by a subsequent price change of the product—to the extent that the underlying cause of this price change is the exchange rate change. Thus, the dollar value of an inventory destined for export may increase when the currency of the destination country appreciates, provided its local currency prices do not decrease by the full percentage of the appreciation.

The effect on the local currency price depends, in part, on competition in the market. The behavior of foreign and local competitors, in turn, depends on capacity utilization, market share objectives, likelihood of cost adjustments, and a host of other factors. Of course, firms are not only interested in the value change or the behavior of cash flows of a single asset, but rather in the behavior of all cash flows. Again, price and cost adjustments need to be analyzed. For example, a firm that requires raw materials from abroad for production will usually find its streams of cash outlays going up when its local currency depreciates against foreign currencies. Yet the depreciation may cause foreign suppliers to lower prices in terms of foreign currencies for the purpose of maintaining market share.

(e) Currency of Denomination versus Currency of Determination. One of the concepts of modern international corporate finance is the distinction between the currency in which cash flows are denominated and the currency that determines the size of the cash flows. In the example in the previous section, it does not matter whether, as a matter of business practice, the firm may contract, be involved in, and pay for each individual shipment in its own local currency. If foreign exporters do not provide price concessions, the cash outflow of the importer behaves just like a foreign currency cash flow; even though payments are made in local currency, they occur in greater amounts. As a result, the cash flow, even while denominated in local currency, is determined by the relative value of the foreign currency. The functional currency concept introduced in FAS 52 is similar to the "currency of determination, " but not exactly the same. The currency of determination refers to revenue and operating expense flows, respectively; the functional currency concept pertains to an entity as a whole and is, therefore, less precise.

To complicate things further, the currency of recording, that is, the currency in which the accounting records are kept, is yet another matter. For example, any debt contracted by the firm in foreign currency will always be recorded in the currency of the country where the corporate entity is located. However, the value of its legal obligation is established in the currency in which the contract is denominated.

It is possible, therefore, that a firm selling in export markets may record assets and liabilities in its local currency and invoice periodic shipments in a foreign currency and yet, if prices in the market are dominated by transactions in a third country, the cash flows received may behave as if they were in that third country. To illustrate: A Brazilian firm selling coffee to West Germany may keep its records in reals, invoice in European euros, and have euro-denominated receivables, and physically collect euro cash flow, only to find its revenue stream behaves as if it were in U.S. dollars! This occurs because euro prices for each consecutive shipment are adjusted to reflect world market prices which, in turn, tend to be determined in U.S. dollars. The significance of this distinction is that the currency of denomination is (relatively) readily subject to management discretion, through the choice of invoicing currency. Prices and cash flows, however, are determined by competitive conditions which are beyond the immediate control of the firm.

Yet another dimension of exchange risk involves the element of time. In the very short run, virtually all local currency prices for real goods and services (although not necessarily for financial assets) remain unchanged after an unexpected exchange rate change. However, over a longer period of time, prices and costs move inversely to spot rate changes; the tendency is for Purchasing Power Parity and the Law of One Price to hold.

In reality, this price adjustment process takes place over a great variety of time patterns. These patterns depend not only on the products involved, but also on market structure, the nature of competition, general business conditions, government policies such as price controls, and a number of other factors. Considerable work has been done on the phenomenon of "pass-through" of price changes caused by (unexpected) exchange rate changes. And yet, because all the factors that determine the extent and speed of pass-through are very firm-specific and can be analyzed only on a case-by-case basis at the level of the operating entity of the firm (or strategic business unit), generalizations remain difficult to make. Exhibit 6.5 summarizes the firm-specific effects of exchange rate changes on operating cash flows.

WHAT IS ECONOMIC EXPOSURE?

Let us offer an example. PDVSA, the Venezuelan state-owned oil company, recently set up an oil refinery near Oslo, Norway, for shipment to Germany and other continental European countries. The firm planned to invoice its clients in euros, the currency unit of the European Union. The treasurer is considering sources of long term financing. In the past all long-term finance has been provided by the parent company, but working capital required to pay local salaries and expenses has been financed in Norwegian kroner. The treasurer is not sure whether the short-term debt should be hedged, or in what currency to issue long term debt.

This is an example of a situation where the definition of exposure has a direct impact on the firm's hedging decisions.

Translation exposure has to do with the location of the assets, which in this case would be a totally misleading measure of the effect of exchange rate changes on the value of the unit. After all, the oil comes from Venezuela and is shipped to Germany: its temporary resting place, be it a refinery in Oslo or a tanker en route to Germany, has no import. Both provide value added, but neither determine the currency of revenues. So financing should definitely not be done in Norwegian kroner.

Transactions exposure has to do with the currency of denomination of assets like accounts receivable or payable. Once sales to Germany have been made and invoicing in euros has taken place, PDVSA Norway has contractual, euro-denominated assets that should be financed or hedged with euros. For future sales, however, PDVSA Norway does not have exposure to the euro. This is because the currency of determination in the oil business is the U.S. dollar.

Economic exposure is tied to the currency of determination of revenues and costs. Since the world market price of oil is dollars, this is the effective currency in which PDVSA's future sales to Germany are made. If the euro rises against the dollar, PDVSA must adjust its euro price down to match those of competitors like Aramco. If the dollar rises against the euro, PDVSA can and should raise prices to keep the dollar price the same, since competitors would do likewise. Clearly the currency of determination is influenced by the currency in which competitors denominate prices.

The conclusion is, therefore, that the Norwegian subsidiary of a Venezuelan company whose sales to Germany are invoiced in euros should do its long term financing in U.S. dollars, to hedge the effective currency of exposure.

Exhibit 6.5. Exposure Concepts: Currency of Location versus Currency of Denomination versus Currency of Determination.

6.5 MANAGING ECONOMIC EXPOSURE

(a) Economic Effects of Unanticipated Exchange Rate Changes on Cash Flows. From this analytical framework, some practical implications emerge for the assessment of economic exposure. First of all, the firm must project its cost and revenue streams over a planning horizon that represents the period of time during which the firm is "locked in," or constrained from reacting to (unexpected) exchange rate changes. It must then assess the impact of a deviation of the actual exchange rate from the rate used in the projection of costs and revenues.

Subsequently, the effects on the various cash flows of the firm must be netted over product lines and markets to account for diversification effects wherein gains and losses could cancel out, wholly or in part. The remaining net loss or gain is the subject of economic exposure management. For a multiunit, multiproduct, multinational corporation, the net exposure may not be very large at all because of the many offsetting effects. By contrast, enterprises that have invested in the development of one or two major foreign markets are typically subject to considerable fluctuations of their net cash flows, regardless of whether they invoice in their own or in the foreign currency.

Normally, the executives within business firms who can supply the best estimates of these effects of unanticipated currency changes in future operating cash flows tend to be those directly involved with purchasing, marketing, and production. Finance managers who focus exclusively on credit and foreign exchange markets may easily miss the essence of corporate foreign exchange risk (see Exhibit 6.6).

(b) Financial versus Operating Strategies for Hedging. When operating (cash) inflows and (contractual) outflows from liabilities are affected by exchange rate changes, the general principle of prudent exchange risk management is: any effect on cash inflows and outflows should cancel out as much as possible. This can be achieved by maneuvering assets, liabilities, or both. Copeland and Yoshi, whose study of currency hedging found transactions hedging to be of little value, assert, "relocating plants and adjusting pricing often provide the best hedge against foreign exchange risk" (Copeland and Yoshi, 1996). When should operations—the asset side—be used?

We have demonstrated that exchange rate changes can have tremendous effects on operating cash flows. Does it not therefore make sense to adjust operations to hedge

---

For practical purposes, four questions capture the extent of a company's foreign exchange exposure:

1. How quickly can the firm adjust prices to offset the impact of an unexpected exchange rate change on profit margins?
2. How quickly can the firm change sources for inputs and markets for outputs? Or, alternatively, how diversified are a company's factor and product markets?
3. To what extent does the firm have the ability to switch markets and sources quickly?
4. Do changes in the volume of sales, associated with unexpected exchange rate changes, have an impact on the value of assets?

Exhibit 6.6. Practical Measures of FX Exposure.

against these effects? Many companies, such as Japanese auto producers, are now seeking flexibility in production location, in part to be able to respond to large and persistent exchange rate changes that make production much cheaper in one location than another. Among the operating policies are the shifting of markets for output, sources of supply, product lines, and production facilities as a defensive reaction to adverse exchange rate changes. Put differently, deviations from purchasing power parity provide profit opportunities for the operations-flexible firm. This philosophy is epitomized in the following quotation.

> It has often been joked at Philips that in order to take advantage of currency movements, it would be a good idea to put our factories aboard a supertanker, which could put down anchor wherever exchange rates enable the company to function most efficiently . . . In the present currency markets . . . [this] would certainly not be a suitable means of transport for taking advantage of exchange rate movements. An airplane would be more in line with the requirements of the present era.

The problem is that Philips's production could not fit into either craft. It is obvious that such measures will be very costly, especially if undertaken over a short span of time. It follows that operating policies are not the tools of choice for exchange risk management. Hence, operating policies that have been designed to reduce or eliminate exposure will be undertaken only as a last resort, when less expensive options have been exhausted.

As firms face foreign exchange risk, they try to reduce this cause of cash flow volatility through either financial or operative hedging. The strengths of financial hedging are the great ease with which the hedge can be modified according to the changing exposure of the firm. However, liquid markets for financial hedging instruments in some currencies exist for short maturities only. Operative hedging is clearly more costly to implement and less flexible, but it provides the company with a natural hedging mechanism that is very appealing: if revenues and their costs are generated in the same currency and move in tandem because they are determined by the same factors, exchange risk is eliminated "automatically" (Logue, 1995). Last but not least, within the political environment of the firm's management, conflicts of responsibility and blame for hedging losses between treasury and operating departments (production, purchasing, sales) are being minimized. Firms seem to be using financial instruments more frequently in order to hedge exposures in the short run, whereas operative hedging is used to insure against long run exposures (Chowdhry and Howe, 1996).

It is not surprising, therefore, that risk management focuses not on the asset side, but primarily on the liability side of the firm's balance sheet. Exhibit 6.7 provides a summary of the steps involved in managing economic exposure. Whether and how these steps should be implemented depends first on the extent to which the firm wishes to rely on currency forecasting to make hedging decisions, and second on the range of hedging tools available and their suitability to the task. These issues are addressed in the next two sections.

6.6 GUIDELINES FOR CORPORATE FORECASTING OF EXCHANGE RATES. Academics and practitioners have sought to discover the determinants of exchange ever since there were currencies. Many students have learned about the balance of trade and that the more a country exports, the more demand there is for its currency, and the stronger is its exchange rate. In practice, the story is a lot more complex. Re-

STEPS IN MANAGING ECONOMIC EXPOSURE

1. Estimation of planning horizon as determined by reaction period (time dependence of exposure).
2. Determination of expected future spot rate (depending on state of FX market, usually forward rate).
3. Estimation of expected revenue and cost streams, given the expected spot rate.
4. Estimation of effect on revenue and expense streams for unexpected exchange rate changes (exposure estimation).
5. Choice between hedging and positioning (depending on state of FX market)
6. Choice of appropriate type of hedging instrument/strategy (cash market, derivatives, arbitrage considerations).
7. Determination of specific characteristics of hedging instrument (duration, denomination, options)
8. Estimation of amount of hedging instrument required.
9. Decision about "residual" risk: consider adjusting business strategy/operations.

Exhibit 6.7. Steps in Managing Economic Exposure.

search in the foreign exchange markets has come a long way since the days when international trade was thought to be the dominant factor determining the level of the exchange rate. Monetary variables, capital flows, rational expectations, and portfolio balance are all now understood to factor into the determination of currency values in a floating exchange rate system. Many models have been developed to explain and to forecast exchange rates. No model has yet proved to be the definitive one, probably because the worlds' economies and financial markets are undergoing constant rapid evolution.

Corporations nevertheless avidly seek ways to predict currencies, in order to decide when to hedge and when not to hedge. The models typically fall into one of the following categories: political event analysis, fundamental, or technical analysis.

Academic studies in international finance, in contrast, find strong empirical support for the role of arbitrage in global financial markets, and for the view that exchange rates exhibit behavior that is characteristic of other speculative asset markets: They react to news. Rates are far more volatile than changes in underlying economic variables; they are moved by changing expectations, and hence are difficult to forecast. In a broad sense they are "efficient" but tests of efficiency face inherent obstacles in testing the precise nature of this efficiency directly.

The simplistic "efficient market" model is the unbiased forward rate theory introduced earlier. It says that the forward rate equals the expected future level of the spot rate. Because the forward rate is a contractual price, it offers opportunities for speculative profits for those who correctly assess the future spot price relative to the current forward rate. Specifically, risk neutral players will seek to make a profit if their forecast differs from the forward rate, so if there are enough such participants, the forward rate will always be bid up and down until it equals the expected future spot. Because expectations of future spot rates are found on the basis of presently available information (historical data) and an interpretation of its implication for the future, they tend to be subject to frequent and rapid revision. The actual future spot rate

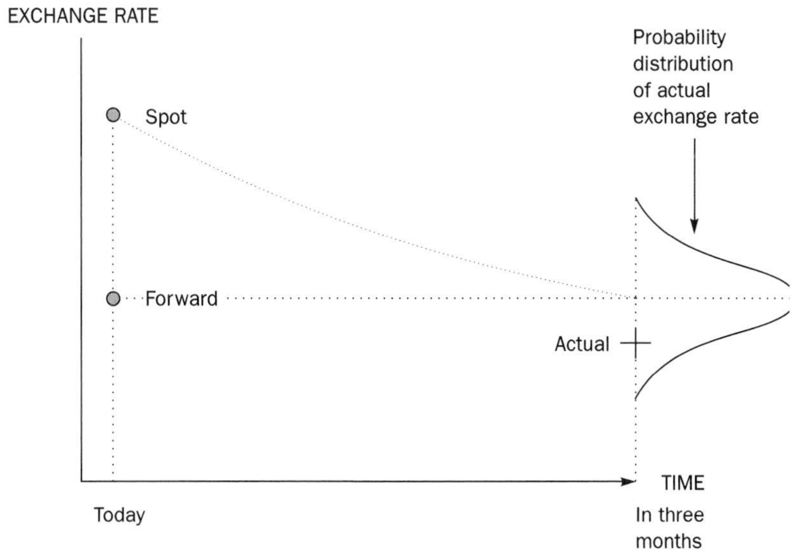

Exhibit 6.8. The Unbiased Forward Rate Theory. This theory says, in effect, that the forward rate follows a random walk; this implies that the spot rate follows a random walk with drift.

may therefore deviate markedly from the expectation embodied in the present forward rate for that maturity.

As is indicated in Exhibit 6.8, in an efficient market the forecasting error will be distributed randomly, according to some probability distribution, with a mean equal to zero. An implication of this is that today's forecast, as represented by the forward rate, is equal to yesterday's forward plus some random amount. In other words, the forward rate itself follows a random walk.[1]

Another way of looking at these is to consider them as speculative profits or losses: what you would gain or lose if you consistently bet against the forward rate. Can they be consistently positive or negative? A priori reasoning suggests that this should not be the case. Otherwise, one would have to explain why consistent losers do not quit the market, or why consistent winners are not imitated by others or do not increase their volume of activity, thus causing adjustment of the forward rate in the direction of their expectation. Barring such explanation, one would expect that the forecast error is sometimes positive, sometimes negative, alternating in a random fashion, driven by unexpected events in the economic and political environment.

Rigorously tested academic models have cast doubt on the pure unbiased forward rate theory of efficiency, and demonstrated the presence of speculative profit oppor-

---

[1]Note that when we say the forward rate follows a random walk, we mean the forward for a given delivery date, not the rolling three-month forward. Since the only published measure of a forward rate for a given delivery date is the price of a futures contract, the latter serves as a proxy to test the proposition that the forward rate should fluctuate randomly.

tunities for certain currencies during specified periods (for example, by the use of "filter rules "). However it is also logical to suppose that speculators will bear foreign exchange risk only if they are compensated with a risk premium. Are the above zero expected returns excessive in a risk-adjusted sense? Given the small size of the bias in the forward exchange market and the magnitude of daily currency fluctuations, the answer is "probably not."

As a result of their finding that the foreign exchange markets are among the world's most efficient, academics argue that exchange rate forecasting by corporations, in the sense of trying to beat the market, plays a role only under very special circumstances. Indeed, few firms actively decide to commit real assets in order to take currency positions. Rather, they get involved with foreign currencies in the course of pursuing profits from the exploitation of a competitive advantage. Instead of being based on currency expectations, this advantage is based on expertise in such areas as production, marketing, the organization of people, or other technical resources. If someone does have special expertise in forecasting foreign exchange rates, such skills can usually be put to use without incurring the risks and costs of committing funds to other than purely financial assets. Most managers of nonfinancial enterprises concentrate on producing and selling goods; they should find themselves acting as speculative foreign exchange traders only because of an occasional opportunity encountered in the course of their normal operations.

Only when foreign exchange markets are systematically distorted by government controls on financial institutions do the operations of trading and manufacturing firms provide an opportunity to move funds and gain from purely financial transactions. Exhibit 6.9 offers a flowchart of criteria for forecasting and hedging decisions.

Forecasting exchange rate changes, however, is important for planning purposes. To the extent that all significant managerial tasks are concerned with the future, anticipated exchange rate changes are a major input into virtually all decisions of enterprises involved in and affected by international transactions. However, the task of forecasting foreign exchange rates for planning and decision-making purposes, with the purpose of determining the most likely exchange rate, is quite different from attempting to beat the market in order to derive speculative profits.

Expected exchange rate changes are revealed by market prices when rates are free to reach their competitive levels. Organized futures or forward markets provide inexpensive information regarding future exchange rates, using the best available data and judgment. Thus, whenever profit-seeking, well-informed traders can take positions, forward rates, prices of future contracts, and interest differentials for instruments of similar risk (but denominated in different currencies) provide good indicators of expected exchange rates. In this fashion, an input for corporate planning and decision making is readily available in all currencies where there are no effective exchange controls. The advantage of such market-based rates over "in-house" forecasts is that they are both less expensive and more likely to be accurate. Those who tend to have the best information and track record determine market rates; incompetent market participants lose money and are eliminated.

The nature of this market-based expected exchange rate should not lead to confusing notions about the accuracy of prediction. In speculative markets, all decisions are made on the basis of interpretation of past data; however, new information surfaces constantly. Therefore, market-based forecasts rarely will come true. The actual price of a currency will either be below or above the rate expected by the market. If the market knew which would be more likely, any predictive bias quickly would be

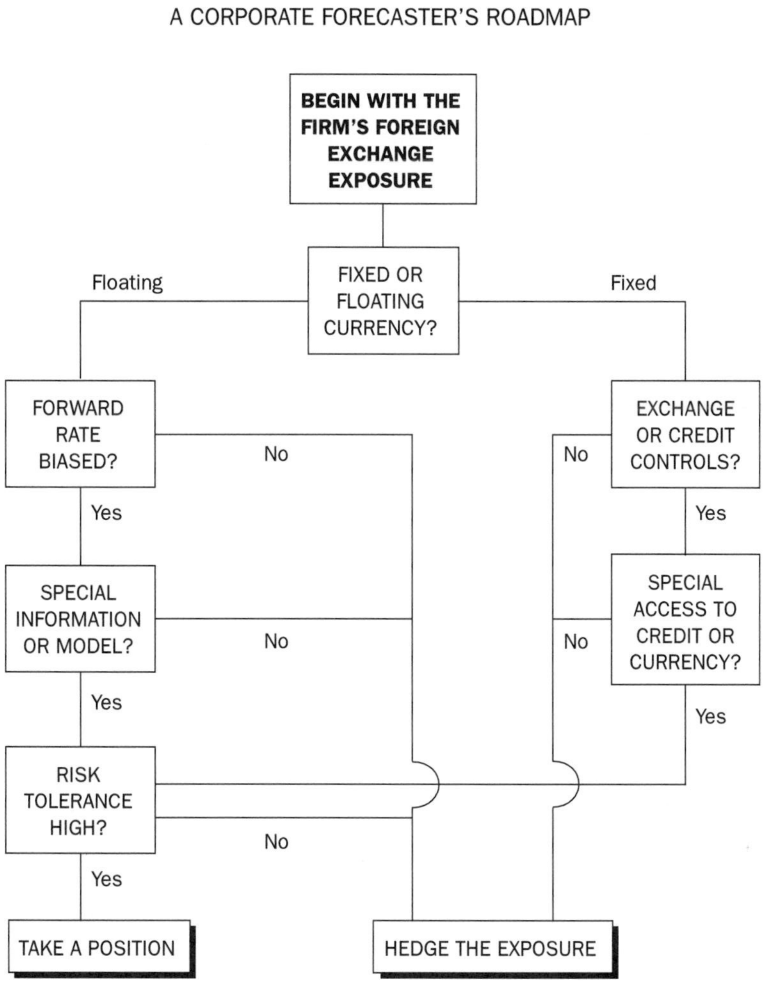

Exhibit 6.9. Decision Criteria for Currency Forecasting and Hedging.

corrected. Any predictable, economically meaningful bias would be corrected by the transactions of profit-seeking transactors.

The importance of market-based forecasts for a determination of the foreign exchange exposure of the firm is that of a benchmark against which the economic consequences of deviations must be measured. This can be put in the form of a concrete question: How will the expected net cash flow of the firm behave if the future spot exchange rate is not equal to the rate predicted by the market when commitments are made? The making of this kind of forecast is completely different from trying to outguess the foreign exchange markets.

6.7 TOOLS AND TECHNIQUES FOR THE MANAGEMENT OF FOREIGN EXCHANGE RISK. In this section we consider the relative merits of several different tools for hedging exchange risk, including forwards, futures, debt, swaps, and options. We will use the following criteria for contrasting the tools.

First, there are different tools that serve effectively the same purpose. Most currency management instruments enable the firm to take a long or short position to hedge an opposite short or long position. Thus, one can hedge a yen payment using a forward exchange contract, or debt in yen, or futures or perhaps a currency swap. In equilibrium the cost of each will be the same, according to the fundamental relationships of the international money market as illustrated in Exhibit 6.1. They differ in details like default risk or transactions costs, or if there is some fundamental market imperfection.

Second, tools differ in that they hedge different risks. In particular, symmetric hedging tools like futures cannot easily hedge contingent cash flows: options may be better suited for the latter.

(a) Foreign Exchange Forwards. Foreign exchange is, of course, the exchange of one currency for another. Trading or "dealing" in each pair of currencies consists of two parts, the spot market, where payment (delivery) is made right away (in practice this means usually the second business day), and the forward market. The rate in the forward market is a price for foreign currency set at the time the transaction is agreed to but with the actual exchange, or delivery, taking place at a specified time in the future. While the amount of the transaction, the value date, the payments procedure, and the exchange rate are all determined in advance, no exchange of money takes place until the actual settlement date. This commitment to exchange currencies at a previously agreed exchange rate is usually referred to as a forward contract.

Forward contracts are the most common means of hedging transactions in foreign currencies, as the example in Exhibit 6.10 illustrates. The trouble with forward contracts, however, is that they require future performance, and sometimes one party is unable to perform on the contract. When that happens, the hedge disappears, sometimes at great cost to the hedger. This default risk also means that many companies do not have access to the forward market in sufficient quantity to fully hedge their exchange exposure. For such situations, futures may be more suitable.

(b) Currency Futures. Outside of the interbank forward market, the best-developed market hedging exchange rate risk is the currency futures market. In principle, currency futures are similar to foreign exchange forwards in that they are contracts for delivery of a certain amount of a foreign currency at some future date and at a known price. In practice, they differ from forward contracts in important ways.

One difference between forwards and futures is standardization. Forwards are for

---

Janet Fredericks, Foreign Exchange Manager at Murray Chemical, was informed that Murray was selling 25,000 tons of naphtha to Canada for a total price of C$11,500,000, to be paid upon delivery in two months' time. To protect her company, she arranged to sell 11.5 million Canadian dollars forward to the Royal Bank of Montreal. The two-month forward contract price was US$0.6785 per Canadian dollar. Two months and two days later, Fredericks received US$7,802,750 from RBM and paid RBM C$11,500,000, the amount received from Murray's customer.

Exhibit 6.10. Hedging with a Forward Contract.

any amount, as long as it's big enough to be worth the dealer's time, while futures are for standard amounts, each contract being far smaller than the average forward transaction. Futures are also standardized in terms of delivery date. The normal currency futures delivery dates are March, June, September, and December, while forwards are private agreements that can specify any delivery date that the parties choose. Both of these features allow the future contract to be tradable.

Another difference is that forwards are traded by phone and telex and are completely independent of location or time. Futures, on the other hand, are traded in organized exchanges such as the LIFFE in London, SIMEX in Singapore, and the IMM in Chicago.

The most important feature of the futures contract is not its standardization or trading organization but the time pattern of the cash flows between parties to the transaction. In a forward contract, whether it involves full delivery of the two currencies or just compensation of the net value the transfer of funds takes place once: at maturity. With futures, cash changes hands every day during the life of the contract, or at least every day that has seen a change in the price of the contract. This daily cash compensation feature largely eliminates default risk.

Thus, forwards and futures serve similar purposes, and tend to have identical rates, but differ in their applicability. Most big companies use forwards; futures tend to be used whenever credit risk may be a problem.

(c) Foreign Currency Debt. Debt, borrowing in the currency to which the firm is exposed or investing in interest-bearing assets to offset a foreign currency payment, is a widely used hedging tool that serves much the same purpose as forward contracts. Consider an example.

In Exhibit 6.10, Fredericks sold Canadian dollars forward. Alternatively, she could have used the Eurocurrency market to achieve the same objective. She would borrow Canadian dollars, which she would then change into francs in the spot market, and hold them in a U.S. dollar deposit for two months. When payment in Canadian dollars was received from the customer, she would use the proceeds to pay down the Canadian dollar debt. Such a transaction is termed a "money market hedge."

The nominal (not the expected) cost of this money market hedge is the difference between the Canadian dollar interest rate paid and the U.S. dollar interest rate earned. According to the Interest Rate Parity Theorem, the interest differential equals the forward exchange premium, the percentage by which the forward rate differs from the spot exchange rate. So the cost of the money market hedge should be the same as the forward or futures market hedge, unless the firm has some advantage in one market or the other. Indeed, in an efficient market, one would expect even the anticipated cost of hedging to be zero. This follows from the unbiased forward rate theory.

The money market hedge suits many companies because they have to borrow anyway, so it simply is a matter of denominating the company's debt in the currency to which it is exposed. That is logical but if money market hedge is to be done for its own sake, as in the example just given, the firm ends up borrowing from one bank and lending to another, thus losing on the spread. This is costly, so the forward hedge would probably be more advantageous except where the firm had to borrow for ongoing purposes anyway.

(d) Currency Options. Many companies, banks, and governments have extensive experience in the use of forward exchange contracts, whereas currency options—or option contracts in general— are still used far less frequently. However, as market participants have developed a better understanding of option pricing, trading, and hedging of options positions over the last couple of years, the use of options has become more frequent. But when comparing options with forwards and futures, one has to be aware of the fact that these types or categories of financial instruments have very different characteristics and hence serve very different purposes.

With a forward contract, one can lock in an exchange rate for the future. There are a number of circumstances, though, where it may be desirable to have more flexibility than a forward contract provides. For example, a computer manufacturer in California may have sales priced in U.S. dollars or in euros in Europe. Depending on the relative strength of the two currencies, revenues may be realized in either euros or dollars. In such a situation, the use of forward and futures would be inappropriate: There is no point in hedging a position that does not exist. What is needed in this situation is a foreign exchange option that represents the right to exchange currency at a predetermined rate.

A foreign exchange option is a contract for future delivery of a currency in exchange for another, where the holder of the option has the right, but not the obligation to buy (or sell) the currency at an agreed price, the strike or exercise price. The right to buy is a call; the right to sell is a put. For such a right the option buyer pays a price called the option premium. The option seller receives the premium and is obliged to make (or take) delivery at the agreed-upon price if the buyer exercises his option. In some option contracts, the instrument being delivered is the currency itself; in others, a futures contract on the currency. American options permit the holder to exercise at any time before the expiration date; European options only on the expiration date; Asian options have an exercise price that represents an average rate.

Futures and forwards are contracts in which two parties oblige themselves to exchange an asset under specified conditions in the future, which makes them useful to hedge or to convert known currency or interest rate exposures. An option, in contrast, offers flexibility in that its holder can decide at any point in time whether he wants to exercise the option now or later, sell it, or let it expire without exercise. Options are often compared to insurance because of their asymmetric payoff structure that "keeps the upside potential while eliminating downside risk." This view, however, represents a misconception of the true nature of this type of financial instrument. Options can be properly used for hedging purposes, that is, for risk reduction, only if the exposure the firm faces has been an option-type character, too. In the above example, the computer manufacturer has effectively granted a currency option to his European customers, giving them the choice to pay in U.S. dollars or euros. Therefore, he can offset his exposure to unanticipated changes in the exchange rate by an equivalent currency option.

In the presence of currency exposures, however, for example, caused by foreign currency receivables or liabilities, the use of options has to be regarded as position taking, that is, speculating. Although there may be nothing wrong about speculating per se, it should not, but often is, done under the guise of hedging. Speculating means taking a position against the market; thus, a person who speculates puts money at risk under the premise that he or she has superior information than professional market makers. In contrast to linear instruments like futures and forwards, the value of an option does not depend on the price of the underlying instrument alone, but also on its volatility and the remaining time to expiration. As a consequence, using currency options in the absence of a matching exposure means speculation with respect to one or more of these determinants. Therefore, just having a view on the currency's direction that is different from the forward rate would simply suggest taking a position via the forward or futures market. But if one's expectation of volatility deviates from the market, futures do not work any more, but options are needed. Indeed, currency options provide the only convenient means of hedging or positioning "volatility risk," as their price is directly influenced by the outlook for a currency's volatility: the more volatile, the higher the price of the option.

Corporate uses of currency options vary widely. Some multinational companies use options to hedge transaction exposures, that is, currency risk from transactions that have already been booked as payables or receivables. Others use them as a shield against currency risk of future transactions (economic exposure). If companies bid for overseas contracts, they face what is called "contingent exposures," a risk with respect to unexpected currency changes that arises only in case the company wins the contract. Still other companies try to bet against the market by taking a position with respect to the direction of currency changes or the expectation of volatility. A general obstacle to the use of options might still be the fact that the purchase of an option—as opposed to futures and forwards which are just mutual agreements—has to be paid for, thus drawing management's attention to the employment of this financial instrument and requiring justification of its usefulness. An attempt to hide or avoid outlays for such option premiums leads treasury departments to adopt more risky strategies that involve the simultaneous sale of an option—with the concomitant downside risks.

6.8 CONCLUSION. This chapter offers the reader an introduction to the complex subject of the measurement and management of foreign exchange risk. We began by noting some problems with interpretation of the concept, and entered the debate as to whether and why companies should devote active managerial resources to something that is so difficult to define and measure.

Accountants' efforts to put an objective value on a firm involved in international business has led many to focus on the translated balance sheet as a target for hedging exposure. As was demonstrated, however, there are numerous realistic situations where the economic effects of exchange differ from those predicted by the various measures of translation exposure. In particular, we emphasized the distinctions between the currency of recording, the currency of denomination, and the currency of determination of a business.

After giving some guidelines for the management of economic exposure, the chapter addressed the thorny question of how to approach currency forecasting. We suggested a market-based approach to international financial planning, and cast doubt on the ability of the corporation's treasury department to outperform the forward exchange rate.

The chapter then turned to the tools and techniques of hedging, contrasting the applications that require forwards, futures, money market hedging, and currency options. In Exhibit 6.11, we present a sketch of how a company may approach the exchange management task, based on the principles laid out in this chapter.

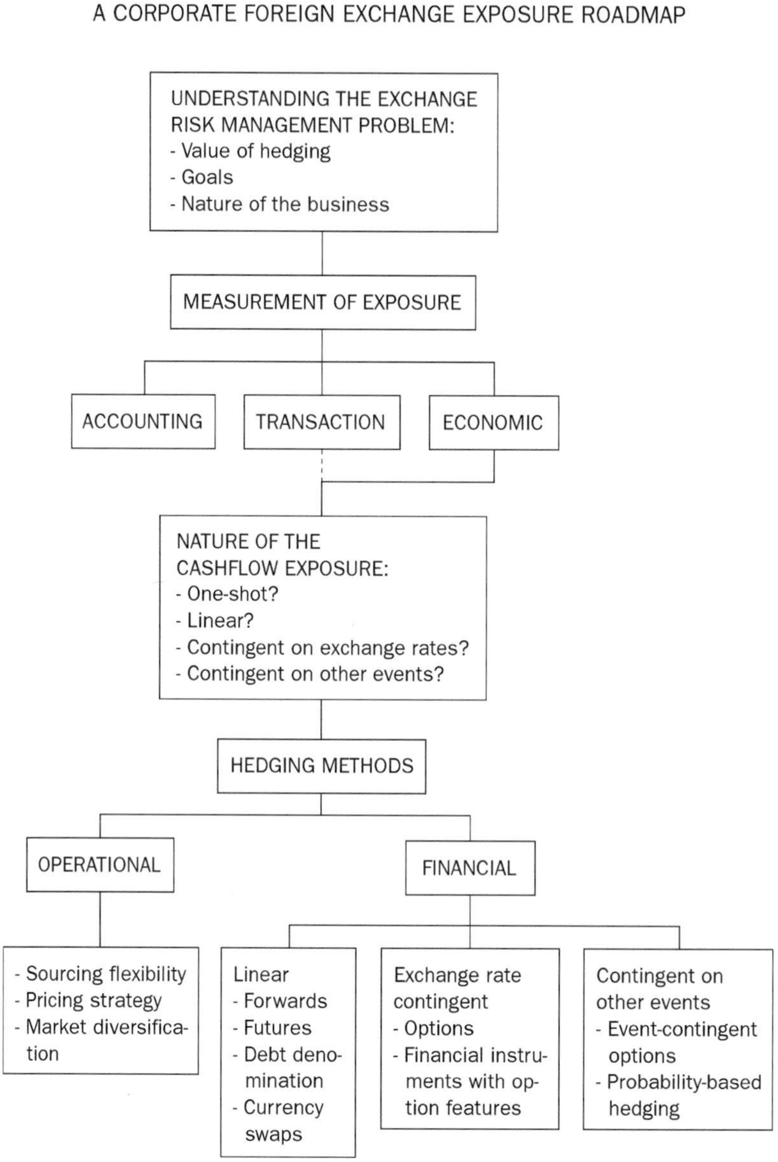

Exhibit 6.11. Management of Corporate Foreign Exchange Exposure.

SOURCES AND SUGGESTED REFERENCES

Adler, M. "Translation Methods and Operational Foreign Exchange Risk Management" in *International Financial Management.* Edited by G. Bergendahl. Stockholm: Norstedts, 1982.

Aliber, R. Z. *Exchange Risk and Corporate International Finance.* New York: John Wiley & Sons, 1979.

Bartov, E., G. M. Bodnar, and A. Kaul. *Exchange Rate Variability and the Riskiness of U.S. Multinational Firms: Evidence from the Breakdown of the Bretton Woods System.* Working Paper 94-6. Wharton Weiss Center, 1994.

Bodnar, G. M., G. S. Hayt, R. C. Marston, and C. W. Smithson. "Wharton Survey on Derivatives Usage by U.S. Non-Financial Firms." *Financial Management*, Vol. 24, No. 2, 1995, pp. 104–114.

Brealey, R. A., and S. C. Myers. *Principles of Corporate Finance*, 5th ed. New York: McGraw-Hill, 1996.

Breeden, D., and S. Viswanathan. *Why Do Firms Hedge? An Asymmetric Information Model.* Working paper. Duke University, 1996.

Chowdhry, B., and J. T. B. Howe. *Corporate Risk Management Corporations: Financial and Operational Hedging Policies.* Working paper No. 20-95. UCLA, 1996.

Copeland, T., and Y. Joshi. "Why Derivative Don't Reduce FX Risk." *The McKinsey Quarterly*, No. 1, 1996, pp. 66–79.

Coppé, B., M. Graham, and T. M. Koller. "Are You Taking the Wrong FX Risk?" *The McKinsey Quarterly*, No. 1, 1996, pp. 81–89.

Cornell, B. "Inflation, Relative Price Changes, and Exchange Risk." *Financial Management,* Autumn 1980, pp. 30–44.

Culp, C. L. "The Revolution in Corporate Risk Management: A Decade of Innovations in Process and Products." *Journal of Applied Corporate Finance*, Vol. 14, No. 4, Winter 2002, pp. 8–26.

Culp, C. L., and M. H. Miller. "Hedging in the Theory of Corporate Finance." *Journal of Applied Corporate Finance*, Spring 1995, pp. 121–127.

Dufey, G. "Corporate Finance and Exchange Rate Variations." *Financial Management*, Summer 1972, pp. 51–57.

Dufey, G., and I. H. Giddy. "International Financial Planning: The Use of Market-Based Forecast." *California Managment Review*, Vol. 21, Fall 1978, pp. 69–81.

——. "Uses and Abuses of Currency Options." *Journal of Applied Corporate Finance*, Vol. 8, No. 3, 1995, pp. 49–57.

Dufey, G., and S. L. Srinivasulu. "The Case for Corporate Management of Foreign Exchange Risk." *Financial Management*, Vol. 12, No. 4., 1984, pp. 54–62.

Duke, R. *An Empirical Investment of the Effects of Statement of Financial Accounting Standards No. 8 on Security Return Behavior.* Stamford, CT: Financial Accounting Standards Board, 1978.

Eaker, M. R. "The Numeraire Problem and Foreign Exchange Risk." *Journal of Finance*, May 1981, pp. 419–427.

Feiger, G. B., and Jacquillat. *International Finance: Text and Cases.* Boston: Allyn & Bacon, 1981.

Financial Accounting Standards Board. *Statement No. 133, Accounting for Derivative Instruments and Hedging Activities.*

Fite, D., and P. Pfleiderer. "Should Firms Use Derivatives to Manage Risk?" in *Risk Management Problems and Solutions.* Edited by W. Beaver and G. Parker. New York: McGraw-Hill, 1995.

Foreign Currency Translation: Understanding and Applying FASB 52. New York: Price Waterhouse, 1981.

Froot, K. A., D. S. Scharfstein, and J. C. Stein. "Risk Management: Coordinating Corporate Investment and Financing Policies." *Journal of Finance*, Vol. 48, No. 5, 1993, pp. 1629–1658.

——. "A Framework for Risk Management." *Harvard Business Review*, November/December 1994. pp. 91–102.

Giddy. I. H. "Why It Doesn't Pay to Make a Habit of Forward Hedging." *Euromoney*, December 1976, pp. 96–100.

——. *Global Financial Markets.* Lexington, MA: D. C. Heath, 1994.

Hekman, C. R. "Foreign Exchange Exposure: Accounting Measures and Economic Reality." *Journal of Cash Management*, February/March 1983, pp. 34–45.

Hodder, J. E. *Hedging International Exposure: Capital Structure Under Flexible Exchange*

Rates and Expropriation Risk. Unpublished working paper. Stanford University, November 1982.

Jacque, L. L. "Management of Foreign Exchange Risk: A Review Article." *Journal of International Business Studies*, Spring/Summer 1981, pp. 81–101.

——. *Management and Control of Foreign Exchange Risk.* Norwell, MA: Kluwer Academic Publishers, 1996.

Jesswein, K., C. C. Y. Kwok, and W. R. Folks Jr. "What New Risk Products Are Companies Using and Why?" *Journal of Applied Corporate Finance*, Vol. 8, No. 3, 1995, pp. 103–114.

Jorion, P. "The Exchange-Rate Exposure of U.S. Multinationals." *Journal of Business*, Vol. 63, No. 3, 1990, pp. 31–45.

——. "The Pricing of Exchange Rate Risk in the Stock Market." *Journal of Financial and Quantitative Analysis*, Vol. 26, No. 3, 1990, pp 363–376.

Jorion, P. *Value at Risk.* New York: McGraw-Hill, 2000.

Lessard, D. R. *International Financial Management.* Boston: Warren, Gorham and Lamont, 1979.

Levi, M. D. *International Finance*, 3d ed. New York: McGraw-Hill, 1996.

Levi, M. D., and P. Sercu. "Erroneous and Valid Reasons for Hedging Foreign Exchange Rate Exposure." *Journal of Multinational Financial Management*, Vol. 1, No. 2, 1991, pp. 25–37.

Logue, D. E. "When Theory Fails: Globalization as a Response to the (Hostile) Market for Foreign Exchange." *Journal of Applied Corporate Finance*, Vol. 8, No. 5, 1995, pp. 39–48.

Logue, D. E., and G. S. Oldfield. "Managing Foreign Assets When Foreign Exchange Markets Are Efficient." *Financial Management*, Summer 1997, pp. 16–22.

Makin, J. "Discussion." *Journal of Finance*, May 1981, pp. 440–442.

Makin, J. H. "Portfolio Theory and the Problem of Foreign Exchange Risks." *Journal of Finance*, May 1978, pp. 517–534.

Mathur, I. "Managing Foreign Exchange Risk Profitably." *Columbia Journal of World Business*, Winter 1982, pp. 23–30.

Mauer, D. C., and A. J. Triantis. "Interactions of Corporate Financing and Investment Decisions: A Dynamic Framework." *Journal of Finance*, Vol. 49, No. 4, 1994, pp. 1253–1277.

Miller, K. D. "A Framework for Integrated Risk Management in International Business." *Journal of International Business Studies*, 1992, pp. 311–331.

Modigliani, F., and M. H. Miller. "The Cost of Capital Corporate Finance and the Theory of Investment." *American Economic Review*, Vol. 48, No. 3, 1992, pp. 262–297.

Nance, D. R., C. Smith, and C. W. Smithson. "On the Determinants of Corporate Hedging." *Journal of Finance*, Vol. 48, No. 1, 1993. pp. 267–284.

Naumann-Etienne, R. *Exchange Risk in Foreign Operations of Multinational Corporations.* Doctoral dissertation. University of Michigan, 1977.

——. "A Framework for Financial Decisions in Multinational Corporations—A Summary of Recent Research." *Journal of Financial and Quantitative Analysis*, November 1974, pp. 859–874.

Peat, Marwick, Mitchell and Co. *Foreign Currency Translation.*

Rodriguez, R. M. "Corporate Exchange Risk Management: Theme and Aberrations." *Journal of Finance*, May 1981. pp. 427–439.

——. *Foreign Exchange Management in U.S. Multinational.* Lexington, MA: D. C. Heath, 1980.

Santomero, A. M. "Financial Risk Management: The Whys and Hows." *Financial Markets, Institutions & Instruments*, Vol. 4, No. 5, 1995, pp. 1–14.

Sercu, P., and R. Uppal. *International Financial Markets and the Firm.* London: Chapman & Hall Ltd., 1995.

Shapiro, A. C. *Currency Risk and Relative Price Risk.* Unpublished working paper. Los Angeles, University of Southern California, November 1982.

Shapiro, A. C., and D. P. Rutenberg. "Managing Exchange risks in a Floating World." *Financial Management*, Summer 1976. pp. 48–58.

Smith, W. S. Jr. "Corporate Risk Management: Theory and Practice." *Journal of Derivatives*, Vol. 2, No. 4, 1995.

Smith, W. S. Jr., and R. M. Stulz. "The Determination of Firms' Hedging Policies." *Journal of Financial and Quantitative Analysis*, Vol. 20, No. 4, 1985, pp. 341–406.

Smithson, C. W. *Managing Financial Risk*. New York: McGraw-Hill, 1998.

Snijders, D. "Global Company and World Financial Markets," in *Financing the World Economy in the Nineties*. Edited by J. J. Sijben. Dordrecht, Netherlands: Kluwer Academic Publishers, 1989.

Srinivasulu, S. L. "Strategic Response to Foreign Exchange Risk." *Columbia Journal of World Business*, Spring 1981, pp. 13–23.

Stulz, R. "Managerial Discretion and Optimal Financing Policies." *Journal of Financial Economics*, Vol. 26, 1990, pp. 3–27.

——. *Rethinking Risk Management*. Working paper. Ohio State University, 1995.

Stulz, R. M. "Optimal Hedging Policies." *Journal of Financial and Quantitative Analysis*, Vol. 19, No. 2, 1994, pp. 127–140.

"Survey on Corporate Risk Management." *Economist*, February 10, 1996.

Waters, S. R. "Exposure Management Is a Job for All Departments." *Euromoney*, December 1979, pp. 79–82.

Williams, J. J. *Capital Market Reaction to Financial Accounting Standards Board Statement No. 8*. PhD dissertation, Pennsylvania State University, 1978.

Yeater, D. S. *The Impact of Statement of Financial Accounting Standard No. 8 on Corporate Value*. PhD dissertation. Cornell University, 1978.

CHAPTER 7

INTEREST RATE AND FOREIGN EXCHANGE RISK MANAGEMENT PRODUCTS: OVERVIEW OF HEDGING INSTRUMENTS AND STRATEGIES

Richard C. Stapleton

Strathclyde University, United Kingdom

Marti G. Subrahmanyam

New York University

CONTENTS

7.1 INTRODUCTION. Most economic agents, such as firms and investors, face foreign exchange or interest rate risk when they have future cash inflows or outflows arising from their capital investments, operations, and financing. The main factors that determine the magnitude of these flows, foreign exchange rates, and interest rates, both real (i.e., net of inflation) and nominal, are volatile. Indeed, there is a close correspondence between foreign exchange and interest rates. Hence, one of the important tasks of financial management is to reduce the exposure of the agent to foreign exchange and interest rate risk using various financial instruments.

For instance, if a firm needs to convert its foreign currency inflows or borrow money at a future point in time, it can *hedge* its exposure to an increase in these rates in a number of ways. The principal instruments available for the hedging of foreign exchange and interest rate risk are discussed in the following subsections.

(a) Forward Contracts. A foreign exchange *forward contract* is an agreement made today to deliver or take delivery of a specified amount of foreign currency in exchange for domestic currency, on a future date at a fixed exchange rate. An interest rate forward or a *forward rate agreement* (FRA) is a contract made now to pay or receive the difference between the future rate of interest and a fixed interest rate on a specified principal amount, over a given loan period. In the absence of changes in credit risk, an FRA can be thought of as an agreement to borrow or lend money in the future at a fixed agreed rate of interest.

(b) Futures Contracts. *Futures contracts* are standardized contracts on foreign exchange and interest rates that are traded on a futures exchange. They are based on the delivery of a specified amount of foreign currency or an interest-bearing security at a future date. Thus, both forward and futures contracts are agreements to deliver or take delivery of a specified quantity of an asset on a future date at a prespecified price. However, the important difference between forward and futures contracts is that the latter are marked-to-market on every trading day.

(c) Option Contracts. Interest rate *options* give the holder the *right* to receive the difference between the future rate of interest and a fixed interest rate, known as the *strike rate*, on a specified principal amount, over a given loan period. Again, in the absence of credit risk, an interest rate option can be thought of as the *right* to borrow or lend at a fixed rate. Note that in contrast to forward contracts, the holder of the option is not *obliged* to borrow or lend at the agreed rate, if market interest rates change to a level that is unfavorable to the holder of the option.

Foreign exchange options confer on the holder the right to buy or sell a specified amount of foreign currency at a fixed exchange rate, the strike rate, in exchange for domestic currency. As in the case of interest rate options, the option holder would exchange the foreign currency only if the previously fixed strike rate is favorable in relation to the prevailing market rate.

Many firms and investors have cash flows denominated in multiple currencies. For firms involved in transnational trade, manufacture, and financing, these cash flows may be related to the purchase of capital equipment or raw materials, and the sale of finished products, or financing flows relating to borrowing and lending. In the case of investors, these cash flows may be related to their investments and the return from the investments, as well as the cash flows for consumption. Cash flows in various foreign currencies may be hedged using forward/futures or option contracts, for short horizons. For longer maturities, it may be necessary to use *foreign currency swaps*, *caps*, and *floors*. A foreign currency swap is a portfolio, or a series, of foreign currency forward contracts over multiple periods. Similarly, a foreign currency cap or floor can be defined in terms of a series of call or put options on the foreign currency.

Borrowers often require money over longer periods of time (e.g., from 5 years to as long as 100 years). To hedge over longer periods, borrowers can use an *interest rate swap contract* or an *interest rate cap* or *floor contract*. A swap is a portfolio, or series, of interest rate forward contracts covering successive borrowing periods. Likewise, an interest rate cap or floor is a series of interest rate option contracts. Most interest rate risk management is done with FRA/futures and swap, cap and floor contracts.

Many hedging contracts, such as forward contracts and swaps, are made between financial institutions, such as banks, and corporate clients on what is known as the over-the-counter (OTC) market. These contracts are often specially structured to suit the needs of the corporate client. Many are known as *exotic* or *complex derivatives*. Examples are knockout options and swaps, quanto options and differential (diff) swaps, Asian swaps and options, binary or digital options, and compound options. Other contracts, such as futures contracts and some option contracts, are exchange traded (ET). The principal differences between OTC and ET contracts are that the latter are marked-to-market each trading day, are usually standardized contracts, and have less counterparty or credit risk.

7.2 FOREIGN EXCHANGE AND INTEREST RATE VOLATILITY. There are many different interest rates in each currency. Interest rates differ according to the maturity of the loan involved, the credit status of the borrower, and the currency that is being lent. Of all these rates, perhaps the most important single rate is the three-month \$LIBOR. \$LIBOR stands for London Interbank Offer Rate and is the (truncated) average quote from several major international banks, lending U.S. dollars, in the London interbank market. Many corporate loan agreements are linked to \$LIBOR, and most interest rate derivative contracts have payoffs that depend on this rate. Similar interest rates are quoted in all the major currencies and various maturities of less than one year. Collectively, these rates are referred to as *money market rates*. More recently, Euribor has become the benchmark interest rate in Euros based on rates quoted by banks across Euroland (the countries that use Euros as their currency) that is also commonly used.

The development in the 1980s and early 1990s of the markets for interest rate and foreign currency derivatives owes much to the volatility of these rates. Exhibit 7.1 illustrates this for interest rate volatility, recording the \$LIBOR rate at quarterly intervals over the period 1992–2001.

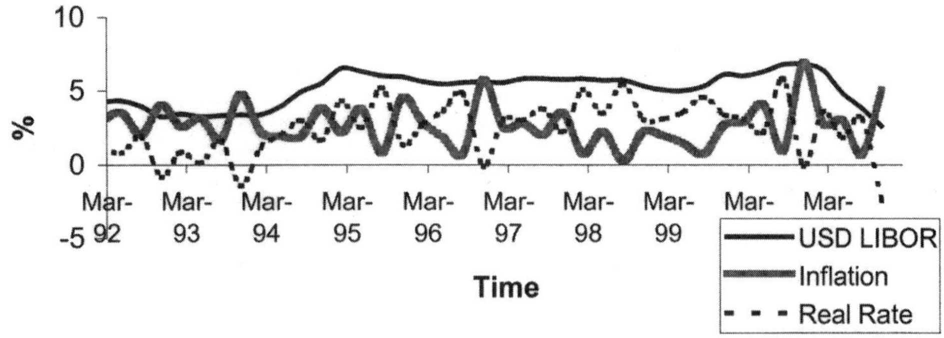

Exhibit 7.1. Real and Nominal Interest Rates.

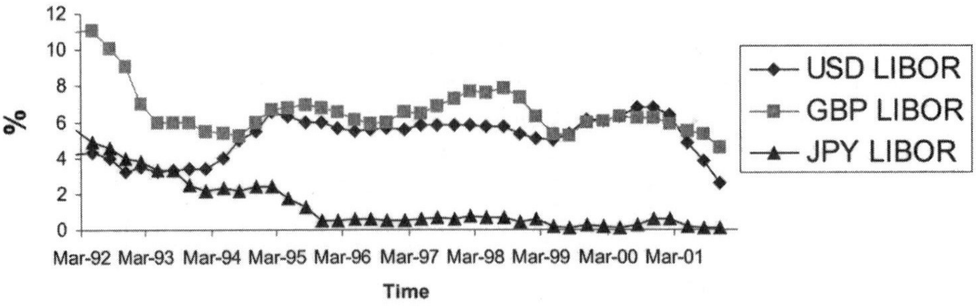

Exhibit 7.2. Short Term Interest Rates in Major Currencies.

Exhibit 7.1 also shows the inflation rate that occurred over the subsequent three-month period. The inflation rate is measured by the consumer price index (CPI) in the United States. The third line in Exhibit 7.1 shows the real interest rate, defined conventionally as follows:

$$\text{Real \$ Interest Rate} = \text{\$LIBOR} - \text{\$ CPI Inflation rate}$$

The real interest rate is an *ex-post* measure of the real rate of return earned by investors from investing $LIBOR for each three-month period, given the inflation that subsequently occurred over that period.

Exhibit 7.2 shows the three-month LIBORs in three major currencies—dollar, yen, and pound sterling—during the period 1992–2001. It is evident from the graph that these key rates have fluctuated considerably in all three currencies.

The volatility of short-term interest rates is closely related to the volatility of foreign exchange rates. Exhibit 7.3 shows the foreign exchange rates against the U.S. dollar of key currencies, the yen, the euro, and the pound sterling, over the period 1999–2001.

The historical volatility of a financial variable is normally measured by the standard deviation of the observations of the logarithm of the variable, stated on an annualized basis. The standard deviation of the quarterly observations of $LIBOR

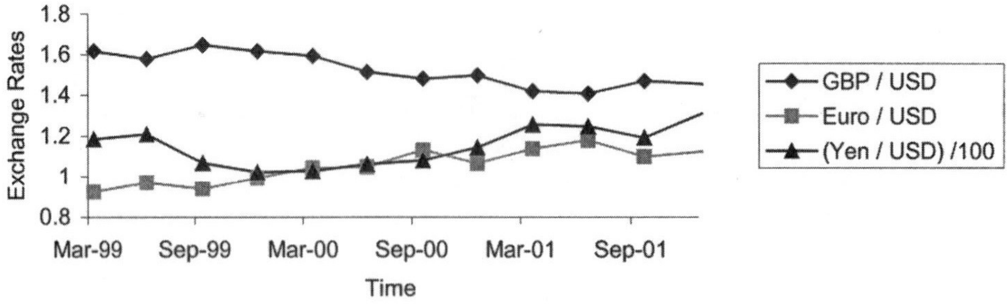

Exhibit 7.3. Foreign Exchange Rate.

recorded in Exhibit 7.1 on an annualized basis is:

$$\sigma_L(\text{volatility of LIBOR}) = \sqrt{\frac{\text{var}[\ln(\text{LIBOR})]}{1/4}} = 22.54\%$$

The volatility of foreign exchange rates can be computed on a similar basis.

7.3 HEDGING FOREIGN EXCHANGE AND INTEREST RATE RISK. The basic ideas underlying the management of foreign exchange and interest risk are quite similar. First, consider the position of a company that borrows at a rate of $LIBOR + π to finance its operations. The premium, π, (above LIBOR) that it has to pay depends upon its credit status. A large company with a sound balance sheet should be able to borrow, for example, at say $LIBOR + 25 basis points. If $LIBOR is 3%, it will pay 3.25% on its borrowings. Such a firm would have seen its borrowing cost vary considerably over the period shown in Exhibit 7.1: even recently, from 6.80 + 0.25 = 7.05% in December 2000 to 2.60 + 0.25 = 2.85% in December 2001.

Now, consider the position of an investor who invests a proportion of his or her portfolio in three-month $Treasury bills (T bills), purchasing these bills every three months. Since the price of three-month T bills closely follows the three-month $LIBOR, the return on this investment strategy, net of transaction costs of say 0.5%, turns out to be $LIBOR – 0.50%. Again, an investor who followed this strategy over recent the period in Exhibit 7.1 would have seen a return varying from 6.80 – 0.50 = 6.30% in December 2000 to 2.60 – 0.50 = 2.10% in December 2001.

A similar example can be given for the case of foreign exchange risk. Consider a firm that exports its products at prices denominated in a foreign currency. If the firm does not hedge its exposure, its export earnings would be very volatile, given the uncertainty of foreign exchange rates. For example, a company importing goods worth $1 million would have paid about 100 million yen for it in September 2000 and nearly 125 million yen in March 2001.

These examples show that foreign exchange and interest rates have varied considerably over time and are likely, therefore, to vary in the future. For example, if a firm is committed to investment expenditures in the future, or has working capital requirements that will need to be financed, it faces the prospect of uncertain future cash flows, both for capital and operating items. Similarly, investors face the prospect of uncertain future returns on their investments.

The financial management of foreign exchange and interest rate risk often takes the form of hedging. Hedging these risks involves placing a bet that pays off when the foreign exchange rate or interest rate goes against the agent. For example, an appropriate hedge for the borrowing company in the above example would be to place a bet on the interest rate rising in the future. The bet will pay off if interest rates rise and the resulting profit would offset, to some extent, the rise in the firm's borrowing costs. Similarly, a firm exporting goods denominated in a foreign currency will be able to hedge its foreign currency exposure by selling its inflows with forward or options contracts. It is the purpose of foreign currency and interest rate futures/forward and options markets to provide a simple way of betting on changes in foreign exchange and interest rates.

(a) Forward and Long-Term Loan Contracts. Before considering the use of options and futures markets, we look at the traditional ways of hedging foreign exchange and interest rate risk. An extreme form of risk management is to "lock in" the foreign exchange and interest rates over the future period. In the case of foreign exchange risk, this can be done with forward contracts, which can be entered into, either for long maturities, where possible, or for shorter maturities, but on a "rolling" basis, that is a new contract is purchased just as the previous one expires. For instance, a Japanese firm that regularly buys crude oil, whose price is usually stated in U.S. dollars, can hedge its foreign exchange exposure by buying dollars forward. Similarly, a Japanese exporter of goods invoiced in dollars could hedge its risk by selling dollars forward. The problem with this approach is that long-term forward contracts were not available until recent years, and even today, are available only between the major currencies. In the case of foreign exchange forward contracts, longer-dated instruments have relatively poorer liquidity compared to those with shorter maturities. Hence, in some cases, only a rolling hedging is feasible for hedging long-term risks.

In the case of interest rate risk, the equivalent method would be to lock in the interest rates, again either over a long horizon or on a rolling basis. Thus, the traditional way of hedging against changes in the short-term interest rates is to borrow or lend on a long-term contract at a fixed rate. A company could issue a 20-year, fixed-interest-rate bond, for example. On the other side of the transaction, an individual investor could lend money by buying such a bond. However, two important problems arise with this type of hedging. First, it may be difficult or costly for the investor to sell the bond if it turns out that the money is needed for other purposes at some future date. Second, buying a long-term bond involves taking an increased default risk: the risk that the borrower may not be able to repay the promised capital at the maturity date. Long-term loans, even when made by governments, tend to require higher rates of interest because of these risks. This discourages borrowers from raising loans in this manner. Moreover, in a world of uncertain inflation, a long-term, fixed-rate loan becomes a highly risky security in terms of real purchasing power. From the lender's point of view, supposing that the bond promises to pay back \$100 in 25 years' time, the real purchasing power of this \$100 is highly uncertain in an inflationary world. Long-term loans that may be almost riskless in *nominal* or money terms are often highly risky in *real* terms.

Long-term forward contracts and bonds represent the traditional method by which companies, investors, and governments hedge their future foreign exchange and interest rate exposure. However, they have to be viewed in relation to other hedging alternatives that offer different trade-offs of risk versus cost/return. In particular, derivative contracts, broadly defined, provide a range of possibilities for managing foreign exchange and interest rate risk.

7.4 HEDGING WITH FOREIGN EXCHANGE AND INTEREST RATE DERIVATIVES. A *derivative* security or contract is one whose payoff and value depends on the price of some underlying asset. In the present context, we are concerned with foreign exchange and interest rate derivatives. These are contracts whose payoff and value depend on an underlying foreign exchange or interest rate (or bond price). The forward contracts, futures contracts, and option contracts mentioned in the overview are all examples of derivatives. One of the main features of a derivative is that the contract is detachable from the underlying asset. If an agent desires to speculate on the movement of a future foreign exchange or interest rate, it can use a derivative as a stand-alone bet. However, if it wishes to hedge an existing borrowing or lending commitment, it must add the derivative payoff to its loan costs or returns. The market for derivatives allows hedgers and speculators such as corporations, investors, banks, brokers, and other institutions involved in providing these services to compete in the same market, using the instruments for whatever purpose they desire. For example, in the case of interest rate risk, the loan cost, including the payoff from the derivative will be:

Net Cost of Borrowing/Return on Lending

= Market interest rate at future date $\pm$ Payoff on interest rate derivative

For example, if a borrower hedges, and interest rates rise, they might end up paying a market rate of interest of $x\%$, having a payoff from the derivative of $y\%$ and a net borrowing cost of x-$y\%$. A similar definition in terms of costs versus prices in terms of domestic currency can be made in the case of foreign exchange derivatives.

7.5 HEDGING WITH FUTURES/FORWARD AND OPTION CONTRACTS. *Forward* contracts have been common in commodity and foreign exchange markets for centuries. In the middle ages, for example, the monks from the abbeys in Yorkshire, England, bought their wool forward on continental markets. Forward and futures contracts on rice warehouse receipts were traded in Japan since the late seventeenth century. Forward contracts to buy and sell commodities and foreign exchange and interest rate instruments are in widespread use today and are growing at a rapid rate. Indeed, most of the trading in foreign exchange is still in the form of forward contracts, and currently exceeds $1.5 trillion a day. However, public futures markets have evolved to overcome some of the moral hazard problems associated with forward markets (i.e., the incentive for one of the parties to the contract to default). Futures contracts are made between a hedger/speculator and the *clearing corporation* of a *futures exchange*. Also, the default risk problem is minimized by requiring the contract holder to put up margin: a form of deposit against adverse price movements. Futures contracts are also of a standard size. For example, in the case of short-term interest rate futures, one standard eurodollar futures contract represents a bet on the future short-term (three-month) interest rate on a face amount of $1 million. Note that the holder of a *long* futures contract receives the difference between the market rate of interest and the futures rate agreed in the contract. The holder of a *short* futures contract pays the difference between the market interest rate and the agreed futures rate. Note that a forward or futures contract has no up-front cost that is, at the time the contract is made, so that it is initially a zero-value contract. In the case of futures contracts, the marking-to-market ensures that the contract has zero value at the end of each trading day.

In contrast, an *option* contract can be thought of as a one-sided futures contract. For example, a call option on euro confers the right, but not the obligation on the holder to exchange dollars for euro at a prescribed exchange rate.

The difference between the payoffs on the futures and the option contract is illustrated by the examples shown in Exhibits 7.4 and 7.5 respectively. The futures con-

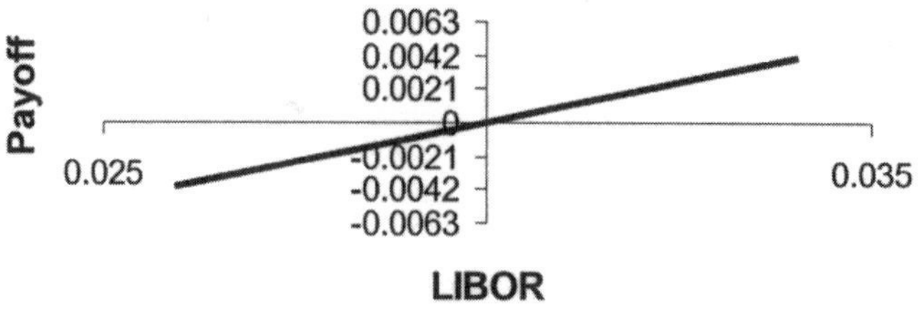

Exhibit 7.4. Net Profit from a Futures Contract.

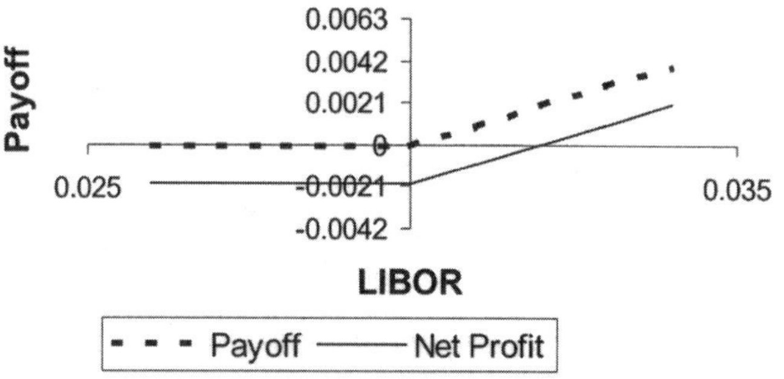

Exhibit 7.5. Net Profit from an Options contract.

tract is simply an agreement to buy or sell in the future. In Exhibit 7.4, this is indicated by a horizontal line on the LIBOR axis. The payoff on the long futures is the difference between the LIBOR rate and 0.03 or 3%, the assumed futures rate. If LIBOR rises to 0.034 or 3.4%, a profit of 0.004 (40 basis points) is made, but if LIBOR falls to 0.026 or 2.6%, a loss of 0.004 (40 basis points) is made. In the case of the call option contract, however, in Exhibit 7.5 a positive payoff is received if LIBOR rises, but the payoff is zero if LIBOR falls. Since the option payoff can only be non-negative, the call option contract must have a positive price. In other words, it must cost money to enter the options contract. This entry price is called the option premium. In Exhibit 7.5, we assume the premium is 0.002 (20 basis points). Then, the dashed line and solid line in Exhibit 7.5 indicate payoff and the net profit, that is, [payoff – premium], respectively, from the contract. Similar examples can be constructed for the case of foreign exchange risk.

Foreign exchange and interest rate risk can be hedged either by entering into a futures/forward contract or an option contract. The difference is that the purchase of an appropriate number of the futures/forward contracts can result in the borrower or lender completely fixing the rate to be paid or received in the future. The option is more akin to an insurance contract. It protects the borrower, for example, against an increase in rates, in return for an insurance premium. However if rates fall, he or she can still benefit from lower market rates. In Exhibit 7.5, for example, with an interest rate option, the maximum interest rate is capped at 0.032 or 3.2%, but when interest rates go down, the borrower gets the benefit.

7.6 HEDGING FOREIGN EXCHANGE AND INTEREST RATE RISK WITH FORWARD CONTRACTS. Firms and other large organizations often hedge their foreign exchange and interest rate exposure by making forward contracts directly with dealers, mainly banks, rather than by using publicly traded futures contracts. The market where these contracts with banks are arranged is the over-the-counter OTC market. The two most important contracts in this market are *forward contracts* and *foreign currency swaps* in the case of foreign exchange rates and *forward rate agreements* (FRAs) and *interest rate swaps* for interest rates.

A foreign exchange forward contract is an agreement to receive the difference (positive or negative) between the foreign exchange rate, say between U.S. dollars and euros, on a given future date, and a preset fixed rate, based on a given face amount. A foreign currency swap is a series of FRAs covering several future dates.

7.7 FOREIGN EXCHANGE FORWARD CONTRACTS. An example of the contract details of a forward contract are as follows:

Contract Type	Forward Contract
Maturity	90 days
Underlying foreign exchange rate	Euro/USD(€/US$)
Forward rate agreed	0.98 $/€ or (about) 1.02 €/$
Face value	$100 million
Position	Long

In this example, the forward contract will pay the difference between €/$ exchange rate in three months' time and a fixed rate of 1.02 €/$ on a face value of $100 million. The contract holder is "long" the contract, so that he or she receives euro and pays dollars. This results in the following cash flows for each dollar of face value:

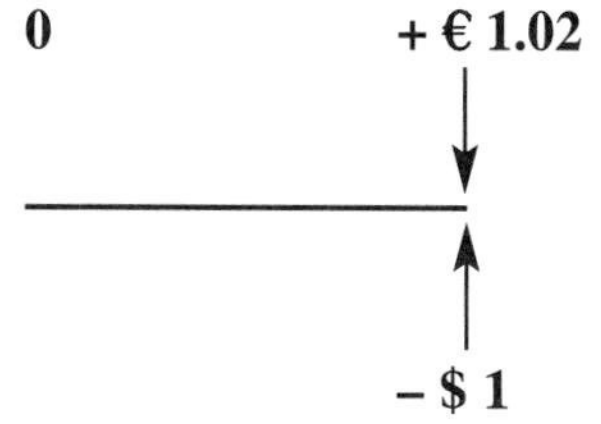

If the €/$ exchange rate turns out to be 0.92 €/$, the contract holder gains 0.10 € per $ of face value. If it turns out to be 1.12 €/$, however, the contract holder loses 0.10 €. The cash flows actually received or paid under the contract have to be adjusted for the underlying face value. For example, the actual cash flow from this contract will be:

$$\text{Payoff from forward contract} = (\text{€}/\$ - 1.02) \times \$100 \text{ million}$$

The payoff will be received or paid in 90 days' time.

Notice that the payoff from the forward, by itself, is a pure gamble on the future exchange rate. However, the foreign exchange forward contract is akin to many other derivatives: If it is held along with an underlying foreign currency cash flow, it is an effective hedge. For example, if a firm needs to pay €102 million in 90 days' time, the contract would be a perfect hedging instrument. On the other hand, the contract may be used purely as a speculative play on the future exchange rate, if the transaction is not directly related to the underlying euro cash flow.

7.8 FORWARD RATE AGREEMENTS. An example of the contract details of an FRA are:

Contract Type	Forward Rate Agreement
Maturity	12 months
Underlying interest rate	3 month LIBOR
Forward rate agreed	3%
Face value	$10 million
Position	Long

In this example, the FRA will pay the difference between $LIBOR in 12 months' time and a fixed rate of 3% on a principal of $10 million. The contract holder is "long" the contract, so that he or she receives LIBOR and pays 3%. This results in the following cash flow diagram:

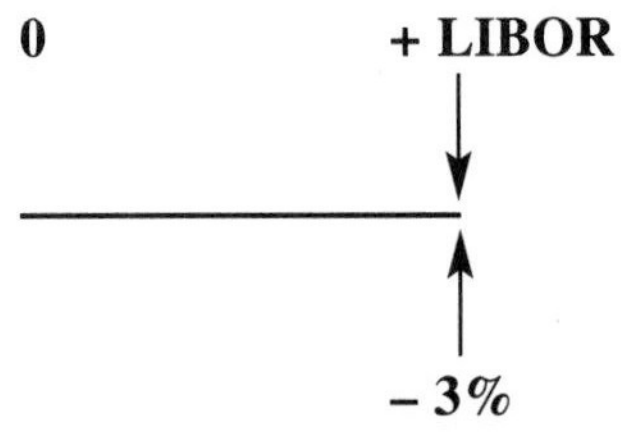

If LIBOR turns out to be 5%, the contract holder gains 2%. If it turns out to be 2%, however, the contract holder loses 1%. The cash flows actually received or paid under the contract have to be adjusted for the underlying principal and the precise number of days of the underlying loan. For example, the actual cash flow from this contract will be:

$$\text{FRA payoff} = (\$\text{LIBOR} - 3\%) \times \$10 \text{ million} \times \frac{91}{360}$$

assuming that the loan period is 91 days. Also the payoff will be received or paid in 15 months' time. Typically, the cash flow takes place on a discounted basis, when the FRA expires in 12 months' time, in this case. Note that, in the case of US $LIBOR, the notional number of days in the year is 360. This is referred to in the markets as the "day count" convention. Note that the convention of dividing by 360 rather than 365 days is because of the meaning of the $LIBOR quote and is also true of most other currencies. In the case of the Canadian dollar and the £ sterling, the day count convention is 365 days.

Notice that the FRA payoff is like the difference between the cash flows from borrowing at 3% and lending at $LIBOR in 12 months' time. Similar to the foreign exchange forward contract, it is a pure gamble on the future LIBOR rate, when held by itself. Again, like other derivatives, if it is held together with a borrowing requirement, it is an effective hedge. For example, if a firm needs to borrow $10 million in 12 months' time, the contract would be a perfect hedging instrument. However, the contract may be used purely as a gamble on the future interest rate, since it is legally separate from any loan that is required.

So far, we have considered a long position in an FRA contract, which is appropriate for hedging a borrowing requirement. In contrast, a lender might be interested in a *short* position in an FRA. As an example, a short FRA at the rate of 3% will pay 3% *minus* the future LIBOR rate. The short holder of the FRA contract makes a profit on the contract if interest rates *fall.* It follows that the profits or losses of the short contract, added to the rate of return from the lending arrangement can be used to guarantee a future lending return of 3%.

7.9 FOREIGN EXCHANGE OPTIONS. We now consider in more detail the foreign exchange option contract, that is, the "one-sided" contract, where the holder receives the payoff, in case it is positive, and zero, otherwise. The option contract can be illustrated using the previous example of forward contracts. Suppose that in the foreign exchange example in the previous section, instead of a forward contract, the firm buys an option to receive the difference between the €/$ foreign exchange rate and 1.02 €/$. We will assume, in the following example that the cost of this option is 0.05 €. We have the following contract details:

Contract Type	Foreign Exchange Dollar Call/Euro Put Option
Maturity	90 days
Underlying foreign exchange rate	Euro/USD (€/US$)
Strike rate	1.02 €/$
Face value	$100 million
Position	Long
Option premium	0.05 €/$

Here the option payoff is again the difference between €/$ exchange rate in 90 days and 1.02 €/$. However, it is paid only if the difference is positive. The payoff diagram in the case of the long $ call/€ put option is:

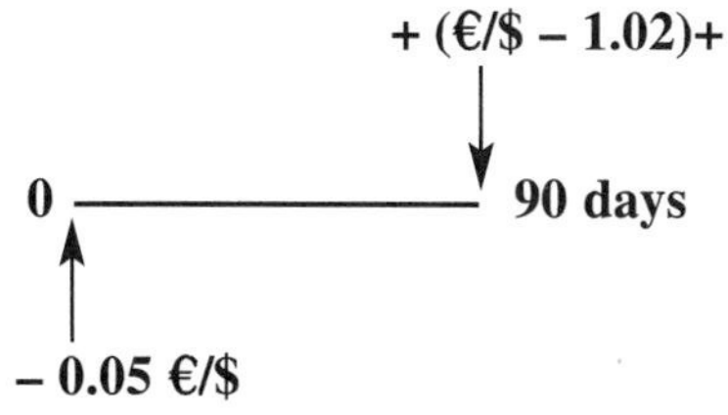

Here, the notation (......)+ means that the payoff is only received if it is positive. As in the case of the forward contract, the actual cash flow will be:

$$\text{Option payoff} = (\text{€}/\$ - 1.02)^{+} \times \$100 \text{ million}$$

and it is receivable in 90 days' time, only if it is positive. Similarly, the cash cost of the option payable at time 0 is:

$$\text{Option premium} = 0.05 \times \$100 \text{ million} = \text{€ } 5 \text{ million}$$

Note that the option premium can be set in either dollars or euros, with the conversion being made at the current exchange rate. It should be emphasized that a call option on the €/$ rate is a bet on the euro going down or the dollar going up. In market parlance, this is referred to as a dollar call/euro put. Hence, it gives the holder the same payoff as a put option on the euro, which is a bet on the euro going down. Both these options give the holder protection against an appreciation of the \$ relative to the €. It is an appropriate hedge for an agent whose numeraire currency is the euro and who has a dollar cash outflow in 90 days' time. In contrast to a forward contract, the option contract is a form of insurance. The holder pays a premium of 0.05, which confers the right to get dollars for euros at 1.02 euro/dollar. Effectively, this means that the agent's costs are capped at approximately 1.07 euro/dollar, if the euro appreciates to say 1.15 euro/dollar, since the payoff from the option would offset the appreciation of the dollar. However, if exchange rates go down, in 90 days' time, to say 1.00 euro/dollar, the option contract is worthless at maturity, but the borrower can take advantage of the low market exchange rate. The 0.05 euro/dollar option premium is the cost of the insurance purchased. The argument in the above example can be modified for the case of an investor with a future dollar inflow (or euro outflow). In this case, the appropriate hedge would be a dollar put/euro call.

(a) Interest Rate Options. Next, consider the case of interest rate options, which are similar to the case discussed above except that the payoff is based on an interest rate. Suppose in the earlier example, in contrast to the FRA contract, the firm negotiates an option to receive the difference between \$LIBOR and 3%. We will assume, in the following example, that the cost of this option is 0.5%. We have the following contract details:

Contract Type	Interest Rate Call Option
Maturity	12 months
Underlying interest rate	3-month \$LIBOR
Strike rate	3%
Face value	\$10 million
Position	Long
Option premium	0.5%

Here the option payoff is again the difference between LIBOR and 3%. However, it is paid *only* if the difference is positive. The payoff diagram in the case of the long call option is:

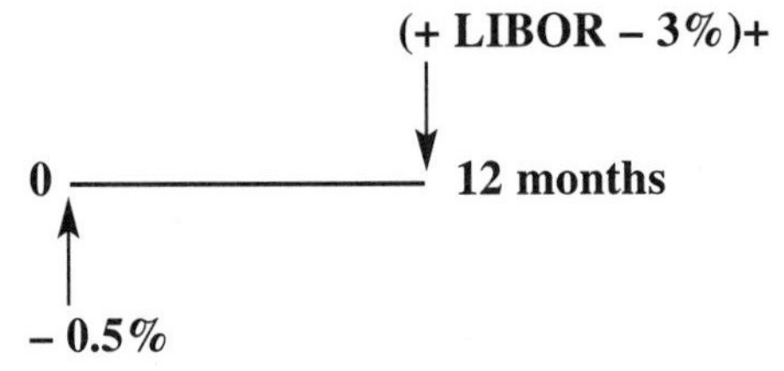

Here, the notation (...)+ means that the payoff is only received if it is positive. As in the case of the FRA, the actual cash flow will be:

$$\text{IRO payoff} = (\$\text{LIBOR} - 3\%) + \times \$10 \text{ million} \times \frac{91}{360}$$

and it is receivable in 15 months' time. Similarly, the cash cost of the option payable at time 0 is:

$$\text{IRO premium} = 0.5\% \times \$10 \text{ million} \times \frac{91}{360}$$
$$= \$12{,}639$$

Note that both the strike rate (3%) and the option premium (0.5%) are quoted using the $LIBOR convention. They both, therefore, have to be adjusted by multiplying by the number of days of the loan contract (assumed here to be 91 days) and divided by the day count convention (360). The interest rate option also gives a protection to the borrower against a rise in interest rates. In the case of the option, however, the contract is a form of insurance. The borrower pays a premium of 0.5%, which confers the right to borrow at 3%. This means that the borrower's loan costs are capped at approximately 3.5%. If interest rates go down, in 12 months' time, to say 2%, the option contract is worthless at maturity, but the borrower can take advantage of the lower market borrowing costs. The 0.5% option premium is the cost of the insurance purchased.

The interest rate option (IRO) or *caplet* pays the difference between the future interest rate and the fixed, preset rate of 3%. This instrument is known as a caplet since a string of caplets is known as a *cap*, as discussed later on. It is, therefore, suitable for a borrower who will need to raise funds at or related to the $LIBOR rate in the future. The borrower can go into the market, borrow at or near the LIBOR rate that exists in 12 months' time and use the proceeds from the IRO contract to reduce the net borrowing costs, if interest rates have risen in the meantime. As in the case of the FRA, the IRO is usually a legally separate contract from the actual loan raised by the borrower. It is used, together with a separate loan contract to achieve a capped borrowing cost of approximately 3.5% in the above example.

So far, we have considered just a borrower's position, where the borrower is faced with an uncertain future borrowing cost. IRO's can be arranged also to protect a lender's position, where the lender faces an uncertain future return. Typically, consider the position of a portfolio manager who will be receiving funds for investment in 12 months' time, and will then be in a position to lend the funds at an interest rate which is related to three month $LIBOR. Such a lender can protect against a *fall* in LIBOR by buying an interest rate put option or *floorlet.* The floorlet pays a fixed rate (say 3%) *minus* the $LIBOR rate in the market in 12 months' time. It provides insurance against a fall in market rates. The portfolio manager can add the proceeds from the floorlet to his or her investment returns in order to guarantee a floor level of approximately 3% to the return received on the investment less the cost of the floorlet. Note that the payoff diagram for the floorlet is:

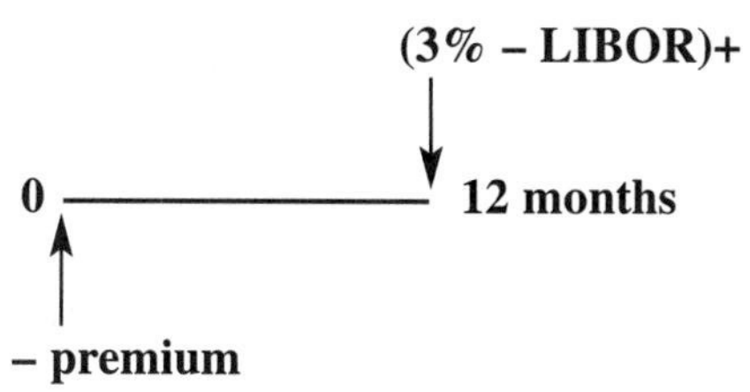

Again, the notation (...)+ means that the difference between 3% and LIBOR is paid if and only if it is positive. A string of floorlets is known as a *floor.*

7.10 INTEREST RATE SWAP. Firms often borrow money on a rolling or *floating rate* basis. Under a floating rate contract, every three months, say, the interest rate is *reset* in line with market rates, but the money will be outstanding for a longer period of, say, five years. A firm with this sort of financing in place is obviously exposed, much like a adjustable-rate mortgage borrower, to increases in the LIBOR at future points in time. A possible strategy for a firm in this position is to arrange an interest rate swap. This is a contract whereby the firm agrees to pay a fixed rate of interest and receive LIBOR at the end of each three-month period over the five-year term of the loan. Note that the interest rate swap is essentially a series of forward rate agreements extending over the whole five-year term, since on each reset date over the period, the firm pays or receives the difference between the fixed and floating interest rates.

The contract details of the interest rate swap are:

Contract Type	Interest Rate Swap
Term	5 years
Underlying interest rate	3 month LIBOR
Rest period	3 months
Swap rate agreed	3%
Face value	$10 million
Position	Long

In this example, the swap pays the difference between $LIBOR and 3%, on an underlying principal (face value) of $10 million, every three months for a total period of five years. The payoff diagram in the case of the long position in the swap is as follows:

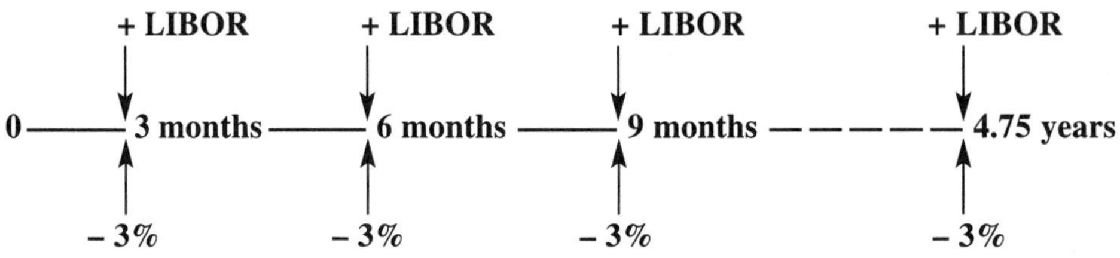

If LIBOR fluctuates above and below 3% over the term of the contract, the swap will pay positive amounts in some periods and negative amounts in others. Looked at in isolation, the swap is a series of future gambles on the interest rate. However, when it is combined with a long term LIBOR related rolling or floating rate loan agreement, it can be used to create a fixed rate loan of 3%. The swap is a flexible contract, which allows the LIBOR borrower to switch from a variable to a fixed rate of interest on their loans.

The interest rate swap is a series of forward rate agreements made to cover each of the three-month periods of the total five-year term of the loan. For a lender, as opposed to a borrower, a series of short forward contracts could be arranged. These would involve *paying* LIBOR and *receiving* a fixed rate of interest. This arrangement would be what is called a *short* interest rate swap contract. It has the reverse payments to those shown above. The short position receives 3% and pays LIBOR-related interest.

7.11 INTEREST RATE CAPS AND FLOORS. An alternative way to hedge a long-term borrowing need is to buy an interest rate *cap*. This contract is a portfolio of interest rate options with maturities coinciding with future rollover dates for the LIBOR-related loans. For example, a five-year cap on three-month LIBOR consists of nineteen individual IRO's covering each three-month period over the five-year term, except the first period, when the interest rate is already known, and there is no optionality involved. Each option gives the right to exchange LIBOR payments for the strike rate, on a specified principal amount. The contract details for a typical cap are as follows:

Contract Type	Interest Rate Cap
Term	5 years
Underlying interest rate	3-month LIBOR
Strike rate	3%
Face value	$10 million
Position	Long
Option premium	2.5%

In this example, the cap pays the difference between LIBOR and 3%, if it is positive, at the end of each three-month period from now until the end of the five-year term. The cost of the option, in this case, is assumed to be 2.5% of the face value or $250,000, representing the aggregate cost of the 19 option payments in the cap. The payoff diagram for the long position (i.e., for the buyer) of the cap is:

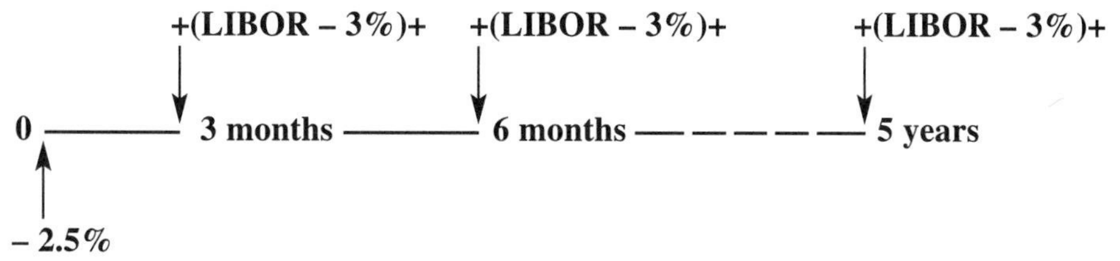

Note that all the payments are based on LIBOR, adjusted for the day count and for the underlying principal of $10 million.

An interest rate cap is an alternative to a swap for hedging LIBOR borrowing requirements. It provides a series of insurance contracts, placing a maximum on the rate to be paid on any three-month loan, while at the same time allowing the borrower to benefit from lower market rates, if and when they occur. Similarly, an interest rate floor is a portfolio of interest rate put options, each of which gives the right to receive a fixed rate and pay LIBOR. The floor can be used by a lender who wishes to ensure a minimum return on a LIBOR-related investment.

In addition to interest rate caps and floors, there is another instrument that is closely related, known as the *swap option* or *swaption*. This contract is the right to go long or short a swap at a date in the future. A *payer swaption* is the right to pay a fixed interest rate and receive the floating interest rate (i.e., go long the swap). Similarly, a *receiver swaption* is the opposite—the right to go short the swap by receiving fixed payments and making floating-rate payments. These instruments are useful for hedging a current swap position or to create or cancel one in the future. Note that a swaption is an option on a portfolio of forward contract, while caps/floors can be thought of as portfolios of options on forward contracts.

(a) Foreign Currency Swaps, Caps, and Floors. Corporations and investors often have cash flows denominated in foreign currencies that arise over multiple time periods in the future. For example, a Japanese corporation may have negotiated a contract for the supply of crude oil at a fixed-dollar price over the next three years. Similarly, a U.S. investor may have purchased a bond denominated in Swiss francs. In such cases, there are cash inflows and outflows, the amounts of which are known in foreign currency terms, but are uncertain when converted into the domestic currency, the currency of account. In order to hedge the foreign currency exposure, the agent has to enter into a multiperiod hedge instrument such as a foreign currency swap.

Consider the case of a U.S. corporation that has issued a five-year euro-bond denominated in euros with a face value of €100 million and a coupon of 6%. If the corporation wishes to eliminate foreign exchange risk and fix its funding cost in dollar terms, it could enter into a five-year dollar/euro swap.

This transaction is basically a series of forward contracts on the dollar/euro exchange rate, where the company pays dollars and receives euros.

Contract Type	Foreign Currency Swap
Term	5 years
Underlying foreign exchange rate	Fixed $/Fixed €
Reset period	Annual
Swap rate (fixed) and position	Pay 5% in $, receive 6% in €
Face value	€100 million

In this example, the swap pays the difference between 5% in $ and 6% in €, at the prevailing exchange rate at the end of each year over the next five years, on an underlying principal (face value) of € 100 million. The payoff diagram in this case is as follows:

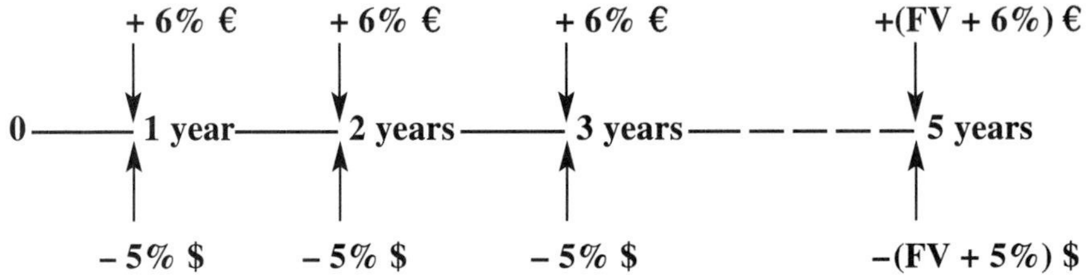

At the €/$ exchange rate fluctuates over the term of the contract; the swap will pay positive amounts in some periods and negative amounts in others. Note that in contrast to the interest rate swap discussed previously, there is an exchange of principal on the maturity date of the swap. This is because, unlike the interest rate swap, where the face amounts on the fixed and floating sides are identical in value, in the case of the foreign currency swap, the face amounts are in different currencies, and hence would be worth different amounts depending on the exchange rate on the maturity date. This currency swap, when combined with a similar-term euro borrowing, eliminates the foreign exchange exposure of the borrower in dollar terms. Hence, this contract allows the euro borrower to switch to a dollar obligation.

There are several variations of the above transactions in practice. The main ones relate to the interest rates used. In contrast to the above example, where fixed euros are exchanged for fixed dollars, other variations would be fixed €/floating $, floating €/fixed $, and floating €/floating $. As in the case of interest rate derivatives, there are foreign currency version of caps, floors, and swaptions, which are defined in an analogous manner.

7.12 FOREIGN EXCHANGE AND INTEREST RATE RISK AND HEDGING INSTRUMENTS. Foreign exchange and interest rate risks are an ever-present and important problem facing both individuals and companies. We have discussed various methods by which these risks can be hedged by using derivatives. These derivatives may be used to fix future borrowing or lending rates (using futures, forwards/FRAs or swaps) or to insure against adverse movements (using IRO's or caps/floors).

As mentioned earlier, many of the deals in the interest rate derivatives market are done "over the counter," that is, between banks and counterparties such as other firms and institutional investors, rather than on organized exchanges. This has led to the development of customized deals between the counterparties. These contracts take account of the particular circumstances of the hedging firm. Detailed description of these customized or "exotic" derivatives is beyond the scope of this chapter. However, the following list provides a brief definition of a selection of these hedging instruments. This gives some idea of the range of products available.

Diff swap	Pays the difference between the interest rate in one currency and the interest rate in another, on a principal amount denominated in one currency.
American/Bermudan swaption	An American swaption is an option on a swap exercisable at any time up to the maturity of the option. A Bermudan swaption is exercisable on specified dates before maturity.
Asian option	An option on the average interest rate over a specified period.
Barrier option	An option that is valid only if the interest rate stays above or below a particular level or within a specified range, e.g., knockout and knockin options.
Pay-as-you-go option	An option where an additional premium is required at a series of points of time to maintain a valid option on the interest rate.

The diff swap has been used by U.S. firms that have views about rates in one foreign currency, (e.g., euros) compared to U.S. dollar rates. Asian options have been particularly popular in Japan and Europe, where many loan contracts depend on the average of interest or foreign exchange rates, over a specified period. Barrier options such as knockout options, and "pay-as-you-go" options have been popular with corporations that wish to reduce the cost of caps or floors and are prepared to take the risks of certain events occurring. These products show both the innovative ability and the complexity of the derivatives industry's solutions to the problem of interest rate and foreign exchange risk.

7.13 SUMMARY. Foreign exchange and interest rate risk are among the most important risks facing most economic agents, whether they are corporations, institutional investors, or households. In recent times, the volatility of these rates has increased substantially and, as a result, agents have a greater need to hedge against these risks. A number of hedge instruments have been developed to manage these risks effectively. Broadly speaking, there are forward and futures contracts, which represent agreements to deliver a specified quantity of these assets at a prespecified price on a future date, and option contracts, which confer on the holder the right to deliver the assets at a prespecified price, only if it is worthwhile to do so on the future date. Many contracts such as swaps, caps, floors, and swaptions are variations on these basic contracts and provide the ability to hedge multiperiod cash flows. Other customized contracts, often referred to as "exotics," provide a vast array of hedging possibilities to agents facing interest rate and foreign exchange risk.

SOURCES AND SUGGESTED REFERENCES

Manson, B. *Interest Rate Risk Management.* Graham and Trotman, 1992.

Stapleton, R. C., and Subrahmanyam, M. G. "Interest Rate Caps and Floors." Chapter 6 in Figlewski, S., W. L. Silber and M. G. Subrahmanyam (eds.), *Financial Options: From Theory to Practice.* Business One Irwin, 1990.

Stapleton, R. C., and C. Thanassoulas. "Options of Foreign Currencies." Chapter 7 in Figlewski, S., W. L. Silber and M. G. Subrahmanyam (eds.), *Financial Options: From Theory to Practice.* Business One Irwin, 1990.

CHAPTER 8

MARKET RISK*

Anthony Saunders
New York University
Marcia M. Cornett
Southern Illinois University

CONTENTS

8.1 INTRODUCTION. In recent years, the trading activities of financial institutions have raised considerable concern among regulators and FI analysts alike. Major FIs such as Merrill Lynch, Citigroup, and J.P. Morgan Chase have taken big hits to their profits from losses in trading.[1] Moreover, in February 1995, Barings, the U.K. merchant bank, was forced into insolvency as a result of losses on its trading in Japanese stock index futures. In September 1995, a similar incident took place at the New York branch of a leading Japanese bank, Daiwa Bank. The largest trading loss in recent history involving a "rogue trader" occurred in June 1996 when Sumitomo Corp. (a Japanese bank) lost $2.6 billion in commodity futures trading. 1997 was another rel-

---

*Reprinted with permission. Anthony Saunders and Marcia Millon Cornett, *Financial Institutions Management: A Risk Management Approach.* New York: McGraw-Hill, 2002.

[1]For example, one trader cost Merrill Lynch over $370 million in 1987 by taking a position in mortgage-backed security strips.

	Assets	Liabilities
Banking Book	Loans	Capital
	Other illiquid assets	Deposits
Trading Book	Bonds (long) Commodities (long) FX (long) Equities (long)	Bonds (short) Commodities (short) FX (short) Equities (short)
	Derivatives (long)	Derivatives (short)

Exhibit 8.1. The Investment (Banking) Book and Trading Book of a Commercial Bank.

atively turbulent year that featured considerable currency and financial market volatility in Eastern Europe and Asia. This volatility was magnified further throughout 1998 with additional losses on Russian bonds as the ruble fell in value and the prices of Russian bonds collapsed. The problems in Russia forced big U.S. banks like Bank of America and Chase Manhattan (now J.P. Morgan Chase) to write off hundreds of millions of dollars in losses on their holdings of Russian government securities. As traditional commercial and investment banking franchises shrink and markets become more complex (e.g., emerging country equity and bond markets and new sophisticated derivative contracts), concerns are only likely to increase regarding the threats to FI solvency from trading.

Conceptually, an FI's trading portfolio can be differentiated from its investment portfolio on the basis of time horizon and liquidity. The trading portfolio contains assets, liabilities, and derivative contracts that can be quickly bought or sold on organized financial markets. The investment portfolio (or in the case of banks, the so-called "banking book") contains assets and liabilities that are relatively illiquid and held for longer holding periods. Exhibit 8.1 shows a hypothetical breakdown between banking book and trading book assets and liabilities. Note that capital produces a cushion against losses on either the banking or trading books. As can be seen the banking book contains the majority of loans and deposits plus other illiquid assets. The trading book contains long and short positions in instruments such as bonds, commodities, foreign exchange (FX), equities, and derivatives.

With the increasing securitization of bank loans (e.g., mortgages), more and more assets have become liquid and tradable (e.g., mortgage-backed securities). Of course, with time, every asset and liability can be sold. While bank regulators have normally viewed tradable assets as those being held for horizons of less than one year, private FIs take an even shorter-term view. In particular, FIs are concerned about the fluctuation in value—or value at risk (VAR)—of their trading account assets and liabilities for periods as short as one day [so-called daily earnings at risk (DEAR)]—especially if such fluctuations pose a threat to their solvency.

Market risk (or value at risk) can be defined as the risk related to the uncertainty of an FI's earnings on its trading portfolio caused by changes in market conditions such as the price of an asset, interest rates, market volatility, and market liquidity.[2]

[2]J.P. Morgan, *Introduction to RiskMetrics* (New York: October 1994), p. 2.

Market risk arises whenever FIs actively trade assets and liabilities (and derivatives) rather than holding them for longer term investment, funding, or hedging purposes. Income from trading activities is increasingly replacing income from traditional FI activities of deposit taking and lending. The resulting earnings uncertainty can be measured over periods as short as a day or as long as a year. Moreover, market risk can be defined in absolute terms as a *dollar* exposure amount or as a relative amount against some benchmark. The sections that follow concentrate on absolute dollar measures of market risk. We look at three major approaches that are being used to measure market risk: RiskMetrics, historic or back simulation, and Monte Carlo simulation.

So important is market risk in determining the viability of an FI, since 1998 U.S. regulators have included market risk in determining the required level of capital an FI must hold.[3] The link between market risk and required capital levels is also discussed in the chapter.

8.2 MARKET RISK MEASUREMENT. There are at least five reasons why market risk measurement (MRM) is important:

1. *Management information.* MRM provides senior management with information on the risk exposure taken by FI traders. Management can then compare this risk exposure to the FI's capital resources. Such an information system appears to have been lacking in the Barings failure.
2. *Setting limits.* MRM considers the market risk of traders' portfolios, which will lead to the establishment of economically logical position limits per trader in each area of trading.
3. *Resource allocation.* MRM involves the comparison of returns to market risks in different areas of trading, which may allow the identification of areas with the greatest potential return per unit of risk into which more capital and resources can be directed.
4. *Performance evaluation.* MRM, relatedly, considers the return-risk ratio of traders, which may allow a more rational bonus (compensation) system to be put in place. That is, those traders with the highest returns may simply be the ones who have taken the largest risks, It is not clear that they should receive higher compensation than traders with lower returns and lower risk exposures.
5. *Regulation.* With the Bank for International Settlements (BIS) and Federal Reserve currently regulating market risk through capital requirements (discussed later in this chapter), private sector benchmarks are important since it is possible that regulators will overprice some risks. MRM conducted by the FI can be used to point to potential misallocations of resources as a result of prudential regulation. As a result, in certain cases regulators are allowing banks to use their own (internal) models to calculate their capital requirements.[4]

---

[3]This requirement was introduced earlier (in 1996) in the EU.

[4]Since regulators are concerned with the social costs of a failure or insolvency, including contagion effects and other externalities, regulatory models will normally tend to be more conservative than private sector models that are concerned only with the private costs of failure.

8.3 CALCULATING MARKET RISK EXPOSURE. Large commercial banks, investment banks, insurance companies, and mutual funds have all developed market risk models. In developing these models—so-called internal models—three major approaches have been followed:

1. RiskMetrics (or the variance/covariance approach)
2. Historic or back simulation
3. Monte Carlo simulation

We consider RiskMetrics[5] first and then compare it to other internal model approaches, such as historic or back simulation.

8.4 RISKMETRICS MODEL. The ultimate objective of market risk measurement models can best be seen from the following quote by Dennis Weatherstone, former chairman of J.P. Morgan (JPM), now J.P. Morgan Chase: "At close of business each day tell me what the market risks are across all businesses and locations." In a nutshell, the chairman of J.P. Morgan wants a single *dollar* number at 4:15 PM New York time that tells him J.P. Morgan's market risk exposure the next day—especially if that day turns out to be a "bad" day.

This is nontrivial, given the extent of JPM's trading business. As shown in Exhibit

[5]J.P. Morgan (JPM) first developed RiskMetrics in 1994. In 1998 the development group formed a separate company, partly owned by JPM. The material presented in this chapter is an overview of the RiskMetrics model. The details, additional discussion and examples are found in "Return to RiskMetrics: The Evolution of a Standard," April 2001, available at the J.P. Morgan Chase website, *www.jpmorganchase.com* or *www.riskmetrics.com.*

	Fixed Income	Foreign Exchange STIRT*	Commodities	Derivatives	Equities	Emergency Markets	Proprietary	Total
Number of active locations	14	12	5	11	8	7	11	14
Number of independent risk-taking units	30	21	8	16	14	11	19	120
Thousands of transactions per day	>5	>5	<1	<1	>5	<1	<1	>20
Billions of dollars in daily trading volume	>10	>30	1	1	<1	1	8	>50

*Short-term interest rate instruments.

Source: J.P. Morgan, *Introduction to RiskMetrics* (New York: October 1994). *www.jpmorganchase.com.*

Exhibit 8.2. JPM's Trading Business.

8.2, when JPM developed its RiskMetrics Model it had 14 active trading locations with 120 independent units trading fixed income securities, foreign exchange, commodities, derivatives, emerging-market securities, and proprietary assets, with a total daily volume exceeding $50 billion. This scale and variety of activities is typical of the major money center banks, large overseas banks (e.g., Deutsche Bank and Barclays), and major insurance companies and investment banks.

Here, we will concentrate on measuring the market risk exposure of a major FI on a daily basis using the RiskMetrics approach. As will be discussed later, measuring the risk exposure for periods longer than a day (e.g., five days) is under certain assumptions a simple transformation of the daily risk exposure number.

Essentially, the FI is concerned with how much it can potentially lose if market conditions move adversely tomorrow; that is:

$$\text{Market risk} = \text{Estimated potential loss under adverse circumstances}$$

More specifically, the market risk in terms of the FI's *daily earnings at risk (DEAR)* has three measurable components:

$$\begin{aligned}\text{Daily earnings at risk} &= (\text{Dollar market value of the position}) \\ &\quad \times (\text{Price sensitivity of the position}) \\ &\quad \times (\text{Potential adverse move in yield})\end{aligned} \qquad (1)$$

Since price sensitivity multiplied by adverse yield move measures the degree of price volatility of an asset, we can also write Equation (1) as Equation (2):

$$\text{Daily earnings at risk} = (\text{Dollar market value of the position}) \times (\text{Price volatility}) \qquad (2)$$

How price sensitivity and an "adverse yield move" will be measured depends on the FI and its choice of a price-sensitivity model as well as its view of what exactly is a potentially "adverse" price (yield) move.

We concentrate on how the RiskMetrics model calculates daily earnings at risk in three trading areas—fixed income, foreign exchange (FX), and equities—and then how it estimates the aggregate risk of the entire trading portfolio to meet Dennis Weatherstone's objective of a single aggregate dollar exposure measure across the whole bank at 4:15 PM each day.[6]

(a) Market Risk of Fixed-Income Securities. Suppose an FI has a $1 million market value position in zero-coupon bonds of seven years to maturity with a face value of

---

[6]It is clear from the above discussion that interest rate risk (see Chapter 7) is part of market risk. However, in market risk models we are concerned with the interest rate sensitivity of the fixed-income securities held as part of an FI's active trading portfolio. Many fixed-income securities are held as part of an FI's investment portfolio. While the latter are subject to interest rate risk, they will not be included in a market risk calculation.

\$1,631,483.[7] Today's yield on these bonds is 7.243% per annum. These bonds are held as part of the trading portfolio. Thus,

$$\text{Dollar market value of position} = \$1 \text{ million}$$

The FI manager wants to know the potential exposure the FI faces should interest rates move against the FI due to an adverse or reasonably bad market move the next day. How much the FI will lose depends on the bond's price volatility. We know that:

$$\begin{aligned}\text{Daily price volatility} &= (\text{Price sensitivity to a small change in yield}) \\ &\quad \times (\text{Adverse daily yield move}) \\ &= (-MD) \times (\text{Adverse daily yield move}) \qquad (3)\end{aligned}$$

The modified duration (MD) of this bond is:[8]

$$MD = \frac{D}{1 + R} = \frac{7}{(1.07243)} = 6.527$$

given that the yield on the bond is $R = 7.243\%$. To estimate price volatility, multiply the bond's MD by the expected adverse daily yield move.

Suppose we define "bad" yield changes such that there is only a 5% chance that the yield changes will exceed this amount in either direction—or, since we are concerned only with bad outcomes, and we are long in bonds, that there is 1 chance in 20 (or a 5% chance) that the next day's yield increase (or shock) will exceed this given adverse move.

If we assume that yield changes are normally distributed,[9] we can fit a normal distribution to the histogram of recent past changes in seven-year zero-coupon interest rates (yields) to get an estimate of the size of this adverse rate move. From statistics, we know that 90% of the area under the normal distribution is to be found within ±1.65 standard deviations (σ) from the mean—that is, 1.65σ. Suppose that during the last year the mean change in daily yields on seven-year zero-coupon bonds was 0%[10]

---

[7]The face value of the bonds is \$1,631,483—that is, \$1,631,483/(1.07243)^7 = \$1,000,000 market value. In the original model prices were determined using a discrete rate of return, R_j. In the 2001 document, "Return to RiskMetrics: The Evolution of a Standard," April 2001, prices are determined using a continuously compounded return, e^{-rf}. The change was implemented because continuous compounding has properties that facilitates mathematical treatment. For example, the logarithmic return on a zero-coupon bond equals the difference of interest rates multiplied by the maturity of the bond. That is:

$$\log\left(\frac{e^{-\tilde{r}t}}{e^{-rt}}\right) = -(\tilde{r} - p)t$$

where $\tilde{r}$ is the expected return.

[8]Assuming annual compounding for simplicity.

[9]In reality, many asset return distributions—such as exchange rates and interest rates—have "fat tails." Thus, the normal distribution will tend to underestimate extreme outcomes. This is a major criticism of the RiskMetrics modeling approach. (See later footnote and references.)

[10]If the mean were nonzero (e.g., –1 basis point), this could be added to the 16.5 bp to project the

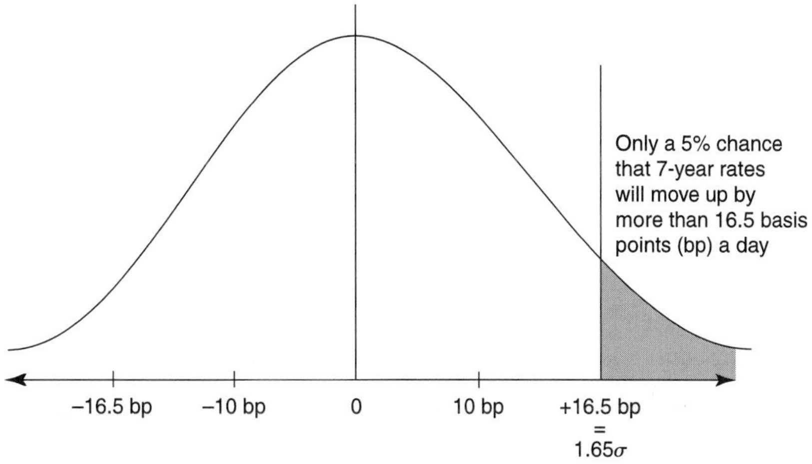

Exhibit 8.3. Adverse Rate Move, Seven-Year Rates.

while the standard deviation was 10 basis points (or 0.001). Thus, 1.65σ is 16.5 basis points (bp).[11] In other words, over the last year, daily yields on seven-year, zero-coupon bonds have fluctuated (either positively or negatively) by more than 16.5 bp 10% of the time. Adverse moves in yields are those that decrease the value of the security (i.e., the yield increases). These occurred 5% of the time, or 1 in 20 days. This is shown in Exhibit 8.3.

We can now calculate the potential daily price volatility on seven-year discount bonds using Equation (3) as:

$$\begin{aligned} \text{Price volatility} &= (-MD) \times (\text{Potential adverse move in yield}) \\ &= (-6.527) \times (.00165) \\ &= -.01077 \text{ or } -1.077\% \end{aligned}$$

Given this price volatility and the initial market value of the seven-year bond portfolio, then Equation (2) can be used to calculate the daily earnings at risk as:[12]

$$\begin{aligned} \text{Daily earnings at risk} &= (\text{Dollar market value of position}) \times (\text{Price volatility}) \\ &= (\$1{,}000{,}000) \times (.01077) \\ &= \$10{,}770 \end{aligned}$$

That is, the potential daily loss on the \$1 million position is \$10,770 if the one bad day in 20 occurs tomorrow.

---

[11] RiskMetrics weights more recent observations more highly than past observations (this is called *exponential weighting*). This allows more recent news to be more heavily reflected in the calculation of σ. Regular σ calculations put an equal weight on all past observations.

[12] Since we are calculating loss, we drop the minus sign here.

We can extend this analysis to calculate the potential loss over 2, 3 . . . N days. If we assume that yield shocks are independent and daily volatility is approximately constant,[13] and that the FI is "locked in" to holding this asset for N number of days, then the N-day market value at risk (VAR) is related to daily earnings at risk ($DEAR$) by:

$$VAR = DEAR \times \sqrt{N}$$

That is, the earnings the FI has at risk, should interest rate yields move against the FI, is a function of the value or earnings at risk for one day ($DEAR$) and the (square root of the) number of days that the FI is forced to hold the securities because of an illiquid market. Specifically, $DEAR$ assumes that the FI can sell all the bonds tomorrow, even at the new lower price. In reality, it may take many days for the FI to unload its position. This relative illiquidity of a market exposes the FI to magnified losses (measured by the square root of N).[14] If N is five days, then

$$VAR = \$10{,}770 \times \sqrt{5} = \$24{,}082$$

If N is 10 days, then:[15]

$$VAR = \$10{,}770 \times \sqrt{10} = \$34{,}057$$

In the above calculations, we estimated price sensitivity using modified duration. However, the RiskMetrics model generally prefers using the present value of cash flow changes as the price sensitivity weights over modified durations. Essentially, each cash flow is discounted by the appropriate zero-coupon rate to generate the daily earnings at risk measure. If we used the direct cash flow calculation in this case, the loss would be $10,771.2.[16] The estimates in this case are very close.

---

[13]The assumptions that daily volatility is constant and there is no autocorrelation in yield shocks are strong assumptions. Much recent literature suggests that shocks are autocorrelated in many asset markets over relatively long horizons. To understand why we take the square-root of N, consider a 5-day holding period. The σ_5^2, or five-day variance of asset returns, will equal the current one-day variance σ_1^2 times 5 under the assumptions of constant daily variance and no autocorrelation in shocks, or:

$$\sigma_5^2 = \sigma_1^2 \times 5$$

The standard deviation of this equation is:

$$\sigma_5 = \sigma_1 \times \sqrt{5}$$

or in the terminology of RiskMetrics, the five-day value at risk (VAR_5)is:

$$VAR_5 = DEAR \times \sqrt{5}.$$

[14]In practice, a number of FIs calculate N internally by dividing the position it holds in a security by the median daily volume of trading of that security over recent days. Thus, if trading volume is low because of a "one-way market" in that most people are seeking to sell rather than buy, then N can rise substantially (i.e., N = ($ position in security/median daily $ volume of trading)).

[15]Under the BIS 1998 market risk capital requirements, a 10-day holding period ($N = 10$) is assumed to measure exposure.

[16]The initial market value of the seven-year zero was $1,000,000 or $\$1{,}631{,}483/(1.07243)^7$. The (loss) effect on each $1 (market value) invested in the bond of a rise in rates by 1 bp from 7.243% to 7.253% is .0006528. However, the adverse rate move is 16.5 bp. Thus,

$$DEAR = (\$\ 1 \text{ million}) \times (.0006528) \times (16.5) = \$\ 10{,}771.2$$

(b) Foreign Exchange. Like other large FIs, J.P. Morgan Chase actively trades in foreign exchange (FX). Remember that:

$$DEAR = (\text{Dollar value of position}) \times (\text{Price volatility})$$

Suppose the FI had a Swf 1.6 million trading position in spot Swiss Francs at the close of business on a particular day. The FI wants to calculate the daily earnings at risk from this position (i.e., the risk exposure on this position should the next day be a "bad" day in the FX markets with respect to the value of the Swiss franc against the dollar).

The first step is to calculate the dollar value of the position:

$$\begin{aligned}\text{Dollar equivalent value of position} &= (\text{FX position}) \times (\text{Swf/\$ spot exchange rate})\\ &= (\text{Swf } 1.6 \text{ million})\\ &\quad \times (\text{\$ per unit of foreign currency})\end{aligned}$$

If the exchange rate is Swf 1.60/$1 or $0.625/Swf at the daily close, then

$$\begin{aligned}\text{Dollar value of position} &= (\text{Swf } 1.6 \text{ million}) \times (\$0.625/\text{Swf})\\ &= \$1 \text{ million}\end{aligned}$$

Suppose that, looking back at the daily changes in the Swf/$ exchange rate over the past year, we find that the volatility or standard deviation (σ) of daily changes in the spot exchange rate was 56.5 bp. However, suppose that the FI is interested in adverse moves—that is, bad moves that will not occur more than 5% of the time, or 1 day in every 20. Statistically speaking, if changes in exchange rates are historically "normally" distributed, the exchange rate must change in the adverse direction by 1.65σ (1.65×56.5 bp) for this change to be viewed as likely to occur only 1 day in every 20 days:[17]

$$\text{FX volatility} = 1.65 \times 56.5 \text{ bp} = 93.2 \text{ bp or } 0.932\%$$

In other words, during the last year, the Swiss franc declined in value against the dollar by 93.2 bp 5% of the time. As a result:

$$\begin{aligned}DEAR &= (\text{Dollar value of position}) \times (\text{FX volatility})\\ &= (\$1 \text{ million}) \times (.00932)\\ &= \$9{,}320\end{aligned}$$

This is the potential daily earnings exposure to adverse Swiss franc to dollar exchange rate changes for the FI from the Swf 1.6 million spot currency holdings.

---

[17]Technically, 90% of the area under a normal distribution lies between $\pm 1.65\sigma$ from the mean. This means that 5% of the time, daily exchange rate changes will increase by more than 1.65σ, and 5% of the time, will decrease by 1.65σ. This case concerns only adverse moves in the exchange rate of Swiss francs to dollars (i.e., a depreciation of 1.65σ).

(c) Equities. Many large FIs also take positions in equities. As is well known from the Capital Asset Pricing Model (CAPM), there are two types of risk to an equity position in an individual stock i:[18]

$$\text{Total risk} = \text{Systematic risk} + \text{Unsystematic risk}$$
$$(\sigma_{it}^2) = (\beta_i^2 \sigma_{mt}^2) + (\sigma_{eit}^2)$$

Systematic risk reflects the comovement of that stock with the market portfolio (reflected by the stock's *beta* (β_i) and the volatility of the market portfolio (σ_{mt}), while unsystematic risk is specific to the firm itself (σ_{eit}).

In a very well-diversified portfolio, unsystematic risk (σ_{eit}^2) can be largely diversified away (i.e., will equal zero), leaving behind systematic (undiversifiable) market risk ($\beta_i^2 \sigma_{mt}^2$). If the FI's trading portfolio follows (replicates) the returns on the stock market index, the β of that portfolio will be 1 since the movement of returns on the FI's portfolio will be one to one with the market,[19] and the standard deviation of the portfolio, σ_{it}, will be equal to the standard deviation of the stock market index, σ_{mt}.

Suppose the FI holds a $1 million trading position in stocks that reflect a U.S. stock market index (e.g., the Wilshire 5000). Then $\beta = 1$ and the *DEAR* for equities is:

$$\begin{aligned} DEAR &= (\text{Dollar market value of position}) \times (\text{Stock market return volatility}) \\ &= (\$1{,}000{,}000) \times (1.65\ \sigma_m) \end{aligned}$$

If over the last year, the σ_m of the daily returns on the stock market index was 2%, then 1.65 σ_m = 3.3% (i.e., the adverse change or decline in the daily return on the stock market exceeded 3.3% only 5% of the time). In this case:

$$\begin{aligned} DEAR &= (\$1{,}000{,}000) \times (0.033) \\ &= \$33{,}000 \end{aligned}$$

That is, the FI stands to lose at least $33,000 in earnings if adverse stock market returns materialize tomorrow.

In less well diversified portfolios or portfolios of individual stocks, the effect of unsystematic risk σ_{eit} on the value of the trading position would need to be added. Moreover, if the CAPM does not offer a good explanation of asset pricing compared to, say, multi-index arbitrage pricing theory (APT), a degree of error will be built into the *DEAR* calculation.[20]

(d) Portfolio Aggregation. The preceding sections analyzed the daily earnings at risk of individual trading positions. The examples considered a seven-year, zero-coupon, fixed-income security ($1 million market value), a position in spot Swf ($1

---

[18] This assumes that systematic and unsystematic risks are independent of each other.

[19] If $\beta \neq 1$, as in the case of most individual stocks, *DEAR* = dollar value of position × β_j × $1.65\sigma_m$, where β_j is the systematic risk of the ith stock.

[20] As noted in the introduction, derivatives are also used for trading purposes. To calculate its *DEAR*, a derivative has to be converted into a position in the underlying asset (e.g., bond, FX, or equity).

million market value), and a position in the U.S. stock market index ($1 million market value). The individual *DEAR*s were:

- Seven-year zero-coupon bonds = $10,770
- Swf spot = $9,320
- U.S. equities = $33,000

However, senior management wants to know the aggregate risk of the entire trading position. To calculate this, we *cannot* simply sum the three *DEAR*s—$10,770 + $9,320 + $33,000 = $53,090—because this ignores any degree of offsetting covariance or correlation among the fixed-income, FX, and equity trading positions. In particular, some of these asset shocks (adverse moves) may be negatively correlated. As is well known from modern portfolio theory, negative correlations among asset shocks will reduce the degree of portfolio risk.

Exhibit 8.4 shows a hypothetical correlation matrix between daily seven-year zero-coupon bond yield changes, Swf/$ spot exchange rate changes, and changes in daily returns on a U.S. stock market index (Wilshire 5000). From the correlation between the seven-year zero-coupon bonds and Swf/$ exchange rates, $\rho_{z,swf}$, is negative (–.2), while the seven-year zero-coupon yield changes with, respectively, U.S. stock returns, $\rho_{z,U.S.}$, (.4) and Swf/$ shocks, $\rho_{U.S.,Swf,}$ (.1) are positively correlated.

Using the correlation matrix along with the individual asset *DEAR*s, we can calculate the risk or standard deviation of the whole (three-asset) trading portfolio as:[21]

$$DEAR\text{ portfolio} = \begin{bmatrix} [DEAR_z)^2 + (DEAR_{Swf})^2 + (DEAR_{U.S.})^2 \\ + (2 \times \rho_{z,Swf} \times DEAR_z \times DEAR_{Swf}) \\ + (2 \times \rho_{z,U.S.} \times DEAR_z \times DEAR_{U.S.}) \\ + (2 \times \rho_{U.S.Swf} \times DEAR_{U.S.} \times DEAR_{Swf}) \end{bmatrix}^{1/2} \quad (4)$$

This is a direct application of modern portfolio theory (MPT) since *DEAR*s are directly similar to standard deviations. Substituting into this equation the calculated in-

[21]This is a standard relationship from modern portfolio theory in which the standard deviation or risk of a portfolio of three assets is equal to the square root of the sum of the variances of returns on each of the three assets individually plus two times the covariance among each pair of these assets. With three assets there are three covariances. Here we use the fact that a correlation coefficient times the standard deviations on each pair of assets equals the covariance between each pair of assets. Note that *DEAR* is measured in dollars and has the same dimensions as a standard deviation.

	Seven-Year Zero	Swf/$1	U.S. Stock Index
Seven-year zero	—	–.2	.4
Swf/$1		—	.1
U.S. stock index			—

Exhibit 8.4. Correlations (ρ_{ij}) among Assets.

dividual *DEAR*s (in thousands of dollars), we get

$$\begin{aligned} DEAR \text{ portfolio} &= \begin{bmatrix} [(10.77)^2 + (9.32)^2 + (33)^2 + 2(-.2)(10.77)(9.32) \\ + 2(.4)(10.77)(33) + 2(.1)(9.32)(33)] \end{bmatrix}^{1/2} \\ &= \$39{,}969 \end{aligned}$$

The equation indicates that considering the risk of each trading position as well as the correlation structure among those positions' returns results in a lower measure of portfolio trading risk ($39,969) than when risks of the underlying trading positions (the sum of which was $53,090) are added. A quick check will reveal that had we assumed that all three assets were perfectly positively correlated (i.e., $\rho_{ij} = 1$), *DEAR* for the portfolio would have been $53,090. Clearly, even in abnormal market conditions, assuming that asset returns are perfectly correlated will exaggerate the degree of actual trading risk exposure.

Exhibit 8.5 shows the type of spreadsheet used by FIs such as J.P. Morgan Chase to calculate *DEAR*. As you can see, in this example positions can be taken in 15 different country (currency) bonds in eight different maturity buckets.[22] There is also a column for FX risk (and, if necessary, equity risk) in these different country markets, although in this example the FI has no FX risk exposure (all of the cells are empty).

In the example in Exhibit 8.5, while the FI is holding offsetting long and short positions in both German and French bonds, it is still exposed to trading risks of $48,000 and $27,000, respectively (see the column Interest *DEAR*). This happens because the French yield curve is more volatile than the German and shocks at different maturity buckets are not equal. The *DEAR* figure for a U.S. bond position of long $20 million is $76,000. Adding these three positions yields a *DEAR* of $151,000. However, this ignores the fact that German, French, and U.S. yield shocks are not perfectly correlated. Allowing for diversification effects (the "portfolio effect") results in a total *DEAR* of only $89,000. This would be the number reported to the FI's senior management. Exhibit 8.6 reports the average, minimum, and maximum daily earnings at risk for several large U.S. commercial banks at year-end 2000. J.P. Morgan Chase was exposed to a maximum of $43 million in 2000.

Currently, the number of markets covered by J.P. Morgan Chase's traders and the number of correlations among those markets require the daily production and updating of over 450 volatility estimates (σ) and correlations (ρ). These data are updated daily.

---

[22]Bonds held with different maturity dates (e.g., six years) are split into two and allocated to the nearest two of the eight maturity buckets (here, five years and seven years) using three criteria:

1. The sum of the current market *value* of the two resulting cash flows must be identical to the market value of the original cash flow.
2. The market *risk* of the portfolio of two cash flows must be identical to the overall market risk of the original cash flow.
3. The two cash flows have the same *sign* as the original cash flow.

See J.P.Morgan, RiskMetrics—Technical document, November 1994 and Return to RiskMetrics: The Evolution of a Standard, April 2001. *www.jpmorganchase.com* or *www.riskmetrics.com*.

	Interest Rate Risk Notional Amounts (U.S. $millions equivalents)									FX Risk		Total	
	1 Month	1 Year	2 Years	3 Years	4 Years	5 Years	7 Years	10 Years	Interest DEAR	Spot FX	FX DEAR	Portfolio Effect	Total DEAR
Australia										AUD			
Belgium										BEF			
Canada										CAD			
Denmark										DKK			
France	19			–30				11	48	FFR			48
Germany	–19			30				–11	27	DEM			27
Italy										LIR			
Japan										YEN			
Netherlands										NLG			
Spain										ESB			
Sweden										SEK			
Switzerland										CHF			
United Kingdom										GBP			
ECU										ECU			
United States						10		10	76	USD			76
Total						10		10	151				151
								Portfolio effect	(62)				(62)
RISK	DATA	PRINT CLOSE						Total *DEAR* ($000s)	89				89

Source: J.P. Morgan, *RiskMetrics* (New York: 1994). *www.jpmorgan.com, www.riskmetrics.com.*

Exhibit 8.5. Portfolio *DEAR* Spreadsheet.

Name	Average DEAR for the year 2000	Minimum DEAR during 2000	Maximum DEAR during 2000
Bank of America	$42	$25	$53
Bank One	14	8	19
Citicorp	45	28	96
First Union	10	5	16
FleetBoston Financial	40	28	59
J.P. Morgan Chase	28	18	43

*The figures are based on these banks' internal models, i.e., they may be based on methodologies other than RiskMetrics—see below.

Source: Year 2000 10-K reports for the respective companies.

Exhibit 8.6. Daily Earnings at Risk for Large U.S. Commercial Banks, 2000* (in millions of dollars).

8.5 HISTORIC OR BACK SIMULATION APPROACH. A major criticism of RiskMetrics is the need to assume a symmetric (normal) distribution for all asset returns.[23] Clearly, for some assets, such as options and short-term securities (bonds), this is highly questionable. For example, the most an investor can lose if he or she buys a call option on an equity is the call premium; however, the investor's potential upside returns are unlimited. In a statistical sense, the returns on call options are nonnormal since they exhibit a positive skew.[24]

Because of these and other considerations discussed below, the large majority of FIs that have developed market risk models have employed a historic or back simulation approach. The advantages of this approach are that (1) it is simple, (2) it does not require that asset returns be normally distributed, and (3) it does not require that the correlations or standard deviations of asset returns be calculated.

---

[23]Another criticism is that *VAR* models like RiskMetrics ignore the (risk in the) payments of accrued interest on an FI's debt securities. Thus, *VAR* models will underestimate the true probability of default and the appropriate level of capital to be held against this risk (see P. Kupiec, "Risk Capital and VAR," *The Journal of Derivatives*, Winter 1999, pp. 41–52). Also, Johansson, Seiles, and Tjarnberg find that because of the distributional assumptions, while RiskMetrics produces reasonable estimates of downside risk of FIs with highly diversified portfolios, FIs with small, undiversified portfolios will significantly underestimate their true risk exposure using RiskMetrics (see, F. Johansson, M. J. Seiles, and M. Tjarnberg, "Measuring Downside Portfolio Risks," *The Journal of Portfolio Management*, Fall 1999, pp. 96–107). Finally, a number of authors have argued that many asset distributions have "fat tails" and that RiskMetrics, by assuming the normal distribution, underestimates the risk of extreme losses. See, for example, Salih F. Neftci, "Value at Risk Calculations, Extreme Events and Tail Estimations," *Journal of Derivatives*, Spring 2000, pp. 23–37. One alternative approach to dealing with the "fat-tail" problem is extreme value theory. Simply put, one can view an asset distribution as being explained by two distributions. For example, a normal distribution may explain returns up to the 95% threshold, but for losses beyond that threshold another distribution such as the generalized Pareto distribution may provide a better explanation of loss outcomes such as the 99% level and beyond. In short, the normal distribution is likely to underestimate the importance and size of observations in the tail of the distribution which is after all what value at risk models are meant to be measuring (see, also, Alexander J. McNeil, "Extreme Value Theory for Risk Managers," Working Paper, Department of Mathematics, ETH Zentrom, Ch-8092, Zurich, Switzerland, May 17, 1999).

[24]For a normal distribution, its skew (which is the third moment of a distribution) is zero.

The essential idea is to take the current market portfolio of assets (FX, bonds, equities, etc.) and revalue them on the basis of the actual prices (returns) that existed on those assets yesterday, the day before that, and so on. Frequently, the FI will calculate the market or value risk of its current portfolio on the basis of prices (returns) that existed for those assets on each of the last 500 days. It will then calculate the 5% worst case, that is, the portfolio value that has the 25th lowest value out of 500. That is, on only 25 days out of 500, or 5% of the time, would the value of the portfolio fall below this number based on recent historic experience of exchange rate changes, equity price changes, interest rate changes, and so on.

Consider the following simple example in Exhibit 8.7 where a U.S. FI is trading two currencies: the Japanese yen and the Swiss franc. At the close of trade on December 1, 2003, it has a long position in Japanese yen of 500,000,000 and a long position in Swiss francs of 20,000,000. It wants to assess its *VAR*. That is, if tomorrow is that one bad day in 20 (the 5% worst case), how much does it stand to lose on its total foreign currency position? As shown in Exhibit 8.7, six steps are required to calculate the *VAR* of its currency portfolio. It should be noted that the same methodological approach would be followed to calculate the *VAR* of any asset, liability, or derivative (bonds, options, etc.) as long as market prices were available on those assets over a sufficiently long historic time period.

- *Step 1: Measure exposures.* Convert today's foreign currency positions into dollar equivalents using today's exchange rates. Thus, in evaluating the FX position of the FI on December 1, 2003, it has a long position of $3,846,154 in yen and $14,285,714 in Swiss francs.
- *Step 2: Measure sensitivity.* Measure the sensitivity of each FX position by calculating its delta, where delta measures the change in the dollar value of each FX position if the yen or the Swiss franc depreciates (declines in value) by 1% against the dollar. As can be seen from Exhibit 8.7, line 6, the delta for the Japanese yen position is –$38,081, and for the Swiss franc position it is –$141,442.
- *Step 3: Measure risk.* Look at the actual percentage changes in exchange rates, yen/$ and Swf/$, on each of the past 500 days. Thus, on November 30, 2003, the yen declined in value against the dollar over the day by 0.5% while the Swiss franc declined in value against the dollar by 0.2%. (It might be noted that if the currencies were to appreciate in value against the dollar, the sign against the number in row 7 of Exhibit 8.7 would be negative; that is, it takes fewer units of foreign currency to buy a dollar than it did the day before). As can be seen in row 8, combining the delta and the actual percentage change in each FX rate means a total loss of $47,328.9 if the FI had held the current ¥500,000,000 and Swf 20,000,000 positions on that day (November 30, 2003).
- *Step 4: Repeat Step 3.* Step 4 repeats the same exercise for the yen and Swiss franc positions but uses actual exchange rate changes on November 29, 2003; November 28, 2003; and so on. That is, we caluclate the FX losses and/or gains on each of the past 500 trading days, excluding weekends and holidays, when the FX market is closed. This amounts to going back in time over two years. For each of these days the actual change in exchange rates is calculated (row 7) and multiplied by the deltas of each position (the numbers in row 6 of Exhibit 8.7). These two numbers are summed to attain total risk measures for each of the past 500 days.

	Yen	Swiss Franc
Step 1. Measure Exposures		
1. Closing position on December 1, 2003	500,000,000	20,000,000
2. Exchange rate on December 1, 2003	¥130/$1	Swf 1.4/$1
3. U.S. $ equivalent position on December 1, 2003	3,846,154	14,285,714
Step 2. Measure Sensitivity		
4. 1.01 × current exchange rate	¥131.3	Swf 1.414
5. Revalued position in $s	3,808,073	14,144,272
6. Delta of position ($s) (measure of sensitivity to a 1% adverse change in exchange rate, or row 5 minus row 3)	–38,081	–141,442

Step 3. Measure risk of December 1, 2003, closing position using exchange rates that existed on each of the last 500 days

November 30, 2003	Yen	Swiss Franc
7. Change in exchange rate (%) on November 30, 2003	0.5%	0.2%
8. Risk (delta × change in exchange rate)	–19,040.5	–28,288.4
9. Sum of risks = –$47,328.9		

Step 4. Repeat Step 3 for each of the remaining 499 days

November 29, 2003

⋮

April 15, 2002

⋮

November 30, 2001

⋮

Step 5. Rank days by risk from worst to best

DATE	RISK ($)
1. May 6, 2002	–$105,669
2. Jan 27, 2003	–$103,276
3. Dec 1, 2001	–$ 90,939
⋮	
25. Nov, 30, 2003	–$ 47,328.9
⋮	
499. April 8, 2003	+$ 98,833
500. July 28, 2002	+$108,376

Step 6. VAR (25th worst day out of last 500)

VAR = –$47,328.9 (November 30, 2003)

Exhibit 8.7. Hypothetical Example of the Historic or Back Simulation Approach Using Two Currencies as of December 1, 2003.

- *Step 5: Rank days by risk from worst to best.* These risk measures can then be ranked from worst to best. Clearly the worst-case loss would have occurred on this position on May 6, 2002, with a total loss of $105,669. While this "worst-case scenario" is of interest to FI managers, we are interested in the 5% worst case, that is, a loss that does not occur more than 25 days out of the 500 days (25 ÷ 500 equals 5%). As can be seen, in our example, the 25th worst loss out of 500 occurred on November 30, 2003. This loss amounted to $47,328.9.
- *Step 6: VAR.* If it is assumed that the recent past distribution of exchange rates is an accurate reflection of the likely distribution of FX rate changes in the future—that exchange rate changes have a "stationary" distribution—then the $47,328.9 can be viewed as the FX value at risk (*VAR*) exposure of the FI on December 1, 2003. That is, if tomorrow (in our case December 2, 2003) is a bad day in the FX markets, and given the FI's position of long yen 500 million and long Swf 20 million, the FI can expect to lose $47,328.9 (or more) with a 5% probability. This *VAR* measure can then be updated every day as the FX position changes and the delta changes. For example, given the nature of FX trading, the positions held on December 5, 2003, could be very different from those held on December 1, 2003.[25]

(a) Historic (Back Simulation) Model versus RiskMetrics. One obvious benefit of the historic or back simulation approach is that we do not need to calculate standard deviations and correlations (or assume normal distributions for asset returns) to calculate the portfolio risk figures in row 9 of Exhibit 8.7.[26] A second advantage is that it directly provides a worst-case scenario number, in our example, a loss of $105,669—see step 5. RiskMetrics, since it assumes asset returns are normally distributed—that returns can go to plus and minus infinity—provides no such worst-case scenario number.[27]

The disadvantage of the back simulation approach is the degree of confidence we have in the 5% *VAR* number based on 500 observations. Statistically speaking, 500 observations are not very many, and so there will be a very wide confidence band (or standard error) around the estimated number ($47,328.9 in our example). One possible solution to the problem is to go back in time more than 500 days and estimate the 5% *VAR* based on 1,000 past daily observations (the 50th worst case) or even 10,000 past observations (the 500th worst case). The problem is that as one goes back farther in time, past observations may become decreasingly relevant in predicting *VAR* in the future. For example, 10,000 observations may require the FI to analyze FX data going back 40 years. Over this period we have moved through many very different FX

---

[25]As in RiskMetrics, an adjustment can be made for illiquidity of the market, in this case, by assuming the FI is locked into longer holding periods. For example, if it is estimated that it will take 5 days for the FI to sell its FX position then it will be interested in the weekly (i.e., 5 trading days) changes in FX rates in the past. One immediate problem is that with 500 past trading days only 100 weekly periods would be available, which reduces the statistical power of the *VAR* estimate (see below).

[26]The reason for this is that the historic or back simulation approach uses actual exchange rates on each day that implicitly include correlations or comovements with other exchange rates and asset returns on that day.

[27]The 5% number in RiskMetrics tells us that we will lose more than this amount on 5 days out of every 100; it does not tell us the maximum amount we can lose. As noted in the text, theoretically, with a normal distribution, this could be an infinite amount.

regimes: from relatively fixed exchange rates in the 1950–1970 period, to relatively floating exchange rates in the 1970s, to more managed floating rates in the 1980s and 1990s, to the abolition of exchange rates and the introduction of the European Currency Unit in 11 European countries in January 2002. Clearly, exchange rate behavior and risk in a fixed exchange-rate regime will have little relevance to an FX trader or market risk manager operating and analyzing risk in a floating-exchange rate regime.

This seems to confront the market risk manager with a difficult modeling problem. There are, however, at least two approaches to this problem. The first is to weight past observations in the back simulation unequally, giving a higher weight to the more recent past observations.[28] The second is to use a Monte Carlo simulation approach that generates additional observations that are consistent with recent historic experience. The latter approach in effect amounts to simulating or creating artificial trading days and FX rate changes.

(b) Monte Carlo Simulation Approach. To overcome the problems imposed by a limited number of actual observations, additional observations (in our example, FX changes) can be generated. Normally, the simulation or generation of these additional observations is structured so that returns or rates generated reflect the probability with which they have occurred in recent historic time periods. The first step is to calculate the historic variance—covariance matrix (Σ) of FX changes. This matrix is then decomposed into two symmetric matrices, A and A'. The only difference between A and A' is that the numbers in the rows of A become the numbers in the columns of A'. This decomposition[29] then allows us to generate "scenarios" for the FX position by multiplying the A' matrix by a random number vector z: 10,000 random values of z are drawn for each FX exchange rate.[30] The A' matrix, which reflects the historic correlations among FX rates, results in realistic FX scenarios being generated when multiplied by the randomly drawn values of z. The *VAR* of the current position is then caluculated as in Exhibit 8.7, except that in the Monte Carlo approach the *VAR* is the 500th worst simulated loss out of 10,000.[31]

8.6 REGULATORY MODELS: THE BIS STANDARDIZED FRAMEWORK The development of internal market risk models by FIs such as J.P. Morgan Chase was partly in response to proposals by the Bank for International Settlement (BIS) in 1993 to measure and regulate the market risk exposures of banks by imposing capital requirements on their trading portfolios.[32] The BIS is a organization encompassing the largest central banks in the world. After refining these proposals over a number of years, the BIS (including the Federal Reserve) decided on a final approach to measuring market risk and the capital reserves necessary for an FI to hold to withstand and

---

[28]See J. Boudoukh, M. Richardson, and X. R. Whitelaw, "The Best of Both Worlds: A Hybrid Approach to Calculating Value at Risk," New York University Finance Department, Working Paper, 1998.

[29]The technical term for this procedure is the Cholesky decomposition, where $\Sigma = AA'$.

[30]Technically, let y be an FX scenario; then $y = A'z$. For each FX rate, 10,000 values of z are randomly generated to produce 10,000 values of y. The y values are then used to revalue the FX position and calculate gains and losses.

[31]See, for example, J.P. Morgan, *RiskMetrics*, Technical Document, 4th ed., 1997.

[32]BIS, Basel Committee on Banking Supervision, "The Supervisory Treatment of Market Risks," Basel, Switzerland, April 1993; and "Proposal to Issue a Supplement to the Basel Accord to Cover Market Risks," Basel, Switzerland, April 1995.

survive market risk losses. Since January 1998[33] banks in the countries that are members of the BIS can calculate their market risk exposures in one of two ways. The first is to use a simple standarized framework (to be discussed below). The second, with regulatory approval, is to use their own internal models, which are similar to the models described above. However, if an internal model is approved for use in calculating capital requirements for the FI, it is subject to regulatory audit and certain constraints. Before looking at these constraints, we examine the BIS standardized framework for, respectively, fixed-income securities, foreign exchange, and equities. Additional details of this model can be found at the BIS Website, *www.bis.org*.

(a) Fixed Income. We can examine the BIS standardized framework for measuring the market risk on the fixed-income (or debt security) trading portfolio by using the example for a typical FI provided by the BIS (see Exhibit 8.8). Panel A in Exhibit 8.8 lists the security holdings of an FI in its trading account. The FI holds long and short positions in—column (3)—various quality debt issues—column 2—with maturities ranging from one month to over 20 years—column (1). Long positions have positive values; short positions have negative values. To measure the risk of this trading portfolio, the BIS uses two capital charges: (1) a specific risk charge—columns (4) and (5)—and (2) a general market risk charge —columns (6) and (7).

(i) Specific Risk Charge. The specific risk charge is meant to measure the risk of a decline in the liquidity or credit risk quality of the trading portfolio over the FI's holding period. As column (4) in panel A of Exhibit 8.8 indicates, treasuries have a zero risk weight, while junk bonds (e.g., 10–15 year nonqualifying "Non Qual" corporate debt) have a risk weight of 8%. As shown in Exhibit 8.8, multiplying the absolute dollar values of all the long and short positions in these instruments—column (3)—by the specific risk weights— column (4)—produces a specific risk capital or requirement charge for each position—column (5). Summing the individual charges for specific risk gives the total specific risk charge of $229.[34]

(ii) General Market Risk Charge. The general market risk charges or weights—column (6)—reflect the product of the modified durations and interest rate shocks expected for each maturity.[35] The weights in Exhibit 8.8 range from zero for the 0–1 month Treasuries to 6% for the long-term (longer than 20 years to maturity) quality corporate debt securities. The positive or negative dollar values of the positions in each instrument—column (3)—are multiplied by the general market risk weights—

---

[33]The requirements were introduced earlier in 1996 in the European Union.

[34]Note that the risk weights for specific risks are not based on obvious theory, empirical research, or past experience. Rather, the weights are based on regulators' perceptions of what was appropriate when the model was established.

[35]For example, for 15–20 year Treasuries in Exhibit 8.8 the modified duration is assumed to be 8.75 years, and the expected interest rate shock is 0.60%. Thus, $8.75 \times 0.6 = 5.25$, which is the general market risk weight for these securities shown in Exhibit 8.8. Multiplying 5.25 by the $1,500 long position in these securities results in a general market risk charge of $78.75. Note that the shocks assumed for short-term securities, such as 3-month T-bills, are larger (at 1%) than those assumed for longer maturity securities. This reflects the fact that short-term rates are more impacted by monetary policy. Finally, note that the standardized model combines unequal rate shocks with estimated modified durations to calculate market risk weights. Technically, this violates the underlying assumptions of the duration model which assumes parallel yield shifts at each maturity.

Panel A: FI Holdings and Risk Charges

(1) Time Band	(2) Issuer	(3) Position ($)	Specific Risk (4) Weight (%)	Specific Risk (5) Charge	General Market Risk (6) Weight (%)	General Market Risk (7) Charge
0–1 month	Treasury	5,000	0.00%	0.00	0.00%	0.00
1–3 months	Treasury	5,000	0.00	0.00	0.20	10.00
3–6 months	Qual Corp	4,000	0.25	10.00	0.40	16.00
6–12 months	Qual Corp	(7,500)	1.00	75.00	0.70	(52.50)
1–2 years	Treasury	(2,500)	0.00	0.00	1.25	(31.25)
2–3 years	Treasury	2,500	0.00	0.00	1.75	43.75
3–4 years	Treasury	2,500	0.00	0.00	2.25	56.25
3–4 years	Qual Corp	(2,000)	1.60	32.00	2.25	(45.00)
4–5 years	Treasury	1,500	0.00	0.00	2.75	41.25
5–7 years	Qual Corp	(1,000)	1.60	16.00	3.25	(32.50)
7–10 years	Treasury	(1,500)	0.00	0.00	3.75	(56.25)
10–15 years	Treasury	(1,500)	0.00	0.00	4.50	(67.50)
10–15 years	Non Qual	1,000	8.00	80.00	4.50	45.00
15–20 years	Treasury	1,500	0.00	0.00	5.25	78.75
>20 years	Qual Corp	1,000	1.60	16.00	6.00	60.00
Specific risk				229.00		
Residual general market risk						66.00

Panel B: Calculation of Capital Charge

(1)	(2)	(3)	(4)	(5)	(6)	(7) Charge
1. Specific Risk						229.00
2. Vertical Offsets within Same Time Bands						
Time Band	Longs	Shorts	Residual*	Offset	Disallowance	Charge
3–4 years	56.25	(45.00)	11.25	45.00	10.00%	4.50
10–15 years	45.00	(67.50)	(22.50)	45.00	10.00	4.50
3. Horizontal Offsets within Same Time Zones						
Zone 1						
0–1 month	0.00					
1–3 months	10.00					
3–6 months	16.00					
6–12 months		(52.50)				
Total zone 1	26.00	(52.50)	(26.50)	26.00	40.00%	10.40
Zone 2						
1–2 years		(31.25)				
2–3 years	43.75					
3–4 years	11.25					
Total zone 2	55.00	(31.25)	23.75	31.25	30.00%	9.38
Zone 3						
4–5 years	41.25					
5–7 years		(31.50)				
7–10 years		(56.25)				
10–15 years		(22.50)				
15–20 years	78.75					
>20 years	60.00					
Total zone 3	180.00	(111.25)	68.75	111.25	30.00%	33.38

(continued)

Exhibit 8.8. BIS Market Risk Calculation (Debt Securities, Sample Market Risk Calcula-

Time Band	Longs	Shorts	Residual*	Offset	Disallowance	Charge
4. Horizontal Offsets between Time Zones						
Zones 1 and 2	23.75	(26.50)	(2.75)	23.75	40.00%	9.50
Zones 1 and 3	68.75	(2.75)	66.00	2.75	150.00%	4.12
5. Total Capital Charge						
Specific risk						229.00
Vertical disallowances						9.00
Horizontal disallowances						
Offsets within same time zones						53.16
Offsets between time zones						13.62
Residual general market risk after all offsets						66.00
Total						370.78

*Residual amount carried forward for additional offsetting as appropriate.
Note: Qual Corp is an investment grade debt issue (e.g., rated BBB and above). Non Qual is a below investment grade debt issue (e.g., rated BB and below), that is, a "junk bond."

Exhibit 8.8. (Continued)

column 6—to determine the general market risk charge of $66 for the whole fixed-income portfolio.

(iii) Vertical Offsets. The BIS model assumes that long and short positions, in the same maturity bucket but in different instruments, cannot perfectly offset each other. Thus, the $66 general market risk charge tends to underestimate interest rate or price risk exposure. For example, the FI is short $1,500 in 10–15 year U.S. Treasuries producing a market risk charge of $67.50 and is long $1,000 in 10–15 year junk bonds (with a risk charge of $45). However, because of basis risk—that is, the fact that the rates on Treasuries and junk bonds do not fluctuate exactly together—we cannot assume that a $45 short position in junk bonds is hedging an equivalent ($45) risk value of U.S. Treasuries of the same maturity. Similarly, the FI is long $2,500 in three- to four-year Treasuries (with a general market risk charge of $56.25) and short $2,000 in three- to four-year quality corporate bonds (with a risk charge of $45). To account for this, the BIS requires additional capital charges for basis risk, called *vertical offsets* or disallowance factors. We show these calculations in part 2 of panel B in Exhibit 8.8

In panel B, column 1 lists the time bands for which the bank has both a long and short position. Columns (2) and (3) list the general market risk charges—from column (7) of panel A—resulting from the positions, and column (4) lists the difference (or residual) between the charges. Column (5) reports the smallest value of the risk charges for each time band (or offset). As listed in column (6), the BIS disallows 10%[36] of the $45 position in corporate bonds in hedging $45 of the Treasury bond position. This results in an additional capital charge of $4.50 ($\$45 \times 10\%$).[37] The total charge for all vertical offsets is $9.

[36]Note again that the disallowance factors were set subjectively by regulators.

[37]Intuitively, this implies that long-term U.S. Treasury rates and long-term junk bond rates are approximately 90% correlated. However, in the final plan, it was decided to cut vertical disallowance factors in half. Thus, a 10% disallowance factor becomes a 5% disallowance factor, and so on.

(iv) Horizontal Offsets within Time Zones. In addition, the debt trading portfolio is divided into three maturity zones: 1 (1 month to 12 months), 2 (more than 1 year to 4 years), and 3 (more than 4 years to 20 years plus). Again because of basis risk (i.e., the imperfect correlation of interest rates on securities of different maturities), short and long positions of different maturities in these zones will not perfectly hedge each other. This results in additional (horizontal) disallowance factors of 40% (zone 1), 30% (zone 2), and 30% (zone 3),[38] Part 3 of the bottom panel in Exhibit 8.8 shows these calculations. The *horizontal offsets* are calculated using the sum of the general market risk charges from the long and short positions in each time zone—columns (2) and (3). As with the vertical offsets, the smallest of these totals is the "offset" value against which the disallowance is applied. For example, the total zone 1 charges for long positions is $26.00 and for short positions is ($52.00). A disallowance of 40% of the offset value (the smaller of these two values), $26.00 is charged, that is, $10.40 ($26 × 40%). Repeating this process for each of the three zones produces additional (horizontal offset) charges totaling $53.16.

(v) Horizontal Offsets between Time Zones. Finally, because interest rates on short maturity debt and long maturity debt do not fluctuate exactly together, a residual long or short position in each zone can only partly hedge an offsetting position in another zone. This leads to a final set of offsets or disallowance factors between time zones, part 4 of panel B of Exhibit 8.8. Here the BIS model compares the residual charges from zones 1 ($26.50) and 2 ($23.75). The difference, $2.75, is then compared to the residual from zone 3 ($68.75). The smaller of each zone comparison is again used as the "offset" value against which a disallowance of 40% for adjacent zones[39] and 150%[40] for non-adjacent zones, respectively, is applied. The additional charges here total $13.62.

Summing the specific risk charges ($299), the general market risk charge ($66), and the basis risk or disallowance charges ($9.00 + $53.16 + $13.62) produces a total capital charge of $370.78 for this fixed income trading portfolio.[41]

(b) Foreign Exchange. The standardized model or framework requires the FI to calculate its net exposure in each foreign currency—yen, DM, and so on—and then convert this into dollars at the current spot exchange rate. As shown in Exhibit 8.9, the FI is net long (million dollar equivalent) $50 yen, $100 DM, and $150 £s while being short $20 French francs and $180 Swiss francs. Its total currency long position is $300, and its total short position is $200. The BIS standardized framework imposes a capital requirement equal to 8% times the maximum absolute value of the aggregate long or short positions. In this example, 8% times $300 million = $24 million. This method of calculating FX exposure assumes some partial but not complete offsetting of currency risk by holding opposing long or short positions in different currencies.

(c) Equities. As discussed in the context of the RiskMetrics market value model, the two sources of risk in holding equities are (1) a firm specific, or unsystematic, risk el-

[38]The zones were also set subjectively by regulators.

[39]For example, zones 1 and 2 are adjacent to each other in terms of maturity. By comparison zones 1 and 3 are not adjacent to each other.

[40]This adjustment of 150% was later reduced to 100%.

[41]This number can also be recalculated in risk-adjusted asset terms to compare with risk-adjusted assets on the banking book. Thus, if capital is meant to be a minimum of 8% of risk-adjusted assets, then $370.78 × (1/1.08), or $370.78 × 12.5 = $4,634.75 is the equivalent amount of trading book "risk-adjusted assets" supported by this capital requirement.

Once a bank has calculated its net position in each foreign currency, it converts each position into its reporting currency and calculates the risk (capital) measure as in the following example, in which the position in the reporting currency (dollars) has been excluded:

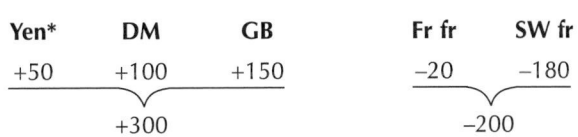

Yen*	DM	GB	Fr fr	SW fr
+50	+100	+150	–20	–180
	+300		–200	

The capital charge would be 8 percent of the higher of the longs and shorts (i.e., 300).

*All currencies in $ equivalents.

Source: BIS, 1993. *www.bis.org.*

Exhibit 8.9. Example of the BIS Standardized Framework Measure of Foreign Exchange Risk (in millions of dollars).

ement and (2) a market, or systematic, risk element. The BIS charges for unsystematic risk by adding the long and short positions in any given stock and applying a 4% charge against the gross position in the stock (called the x factor). Suppose stock number 2, in Exhibit 8.10, is IBM. The FI has a long $100 million and short $25 million position in that stock. Its gross position that is exposed to unsystematic (firm-specific) risk is $125, which is multiplied by 4% to give a capital charge of $5 million.

Market or systematic risk is reflected in the net long or short position (the so-called y factor). In the case of IBM, this risk is $75 million ($100 long minus $25 short). The capital charge would be 8% against the $75 million, or $6 million. The total capital charge (x factor + y factor) is $11 million for this stock.

This approach is very crude, basically assuming the same systematic risk factor (β) for every stock. It also does not fully consider the benefits from portfolio diversification (i.e., that unsystematic risk is not diversified away).

8.7 BIS REGULATIONS AND LARGE BANK INTERNAL MODELS. As discussed previously, the BIS capital requirement for market risk exposure introduced in January 1998 allows large banks (subject to regulatory permission) to use their own internal models to calculate market risk instead of the standardized framework. However, the required captial calculation has to be relatively conservative compared to that produced internally. A comparison of the BIS requirement for large banks using their internal models with RiskMetrics indicates the following in particular.

- In calculating DEAR, the FI must define an adverse change in rates as being in the 99th percentile rather than in the 95th percentile (multiply σ by 2.33 rather than by 1.65 as under RiskMetrics).
- The FI must assume the minimum holding period to be 10 days (this means that RiskMetrics' daily DEAR would have to be multiplied by $\sqrt{10}$).

The FI must consider its proposed captial charge or requirement as the *higher* of:

- The previous day's VAR (value at risk or DEAR × $\sqrt{10}$).
- The average daily VAR over the previous 60 days times a multiplication factor

Under the proposed two-part calculation, there would be separate requirements for the position in each individual equity (i.e., the gross position) and for the net position in the market as a whole. Here we show how the system would work for a range of hypothetical portfolios, assuming a capital charge of 4 percent for the gross positions and 8 percent for the net positions.

			x Factor		*y* Factor		
Stock	Sum of Long Positions	Sum of Short Positions	Gross Position (sum of cols. 1 and 2)	4 Percent of Gross	Net Position (difference between cols. 1 and 2)	8 Percent of Net	Capital Required (gross + net)
1	100	0	100	4	100	8	12
2	100	25	125	5	75	6	11
3	100	50	150	6	50	4	10
4	100	75	175	7	25	2	9
5	100	100	200	8	0	0	8
6	75	100	175	7	25	2	9
7	50	100	150	6	50	4	10
8	25	100	125	5	75	6	11
9	0	100	100	4	100	8	12

Source: BIS, 1993. *www.bis.org.*

Exhibit 8.10. BIS Capital Requirement for Equities (Illustration of *x* plus *y* Methodology).

with a minimum value of 3 (i.e., Capital charge = (DEAR) × ($\sqrt{10}$) × (3)). In general, the multiplication factor makes required capital significantly higher than VAR produced from private models.

However, to reduce the burden of capital needs, an additional type of capital can be raised by FIs to meet the capital charge (or requirement). For example, suppose the portfolio *DEAR* was $10 million using the 1% worst case (or 99th percentile).[42] The minimum capital charge would be:[43]

$$\text{Capital charge} = (\$10 \text{ million}) \times (\sqrt{10}) \times (3) = \$94.86 \text{ million}$$

Capital provides an internal insurance fund to protect an FI, its depositors and other liability holders, and the insurance fund (e.g., the FDIC fund) against losses. The BIS permits three types of capital to be held to meet this capital requirement: Tier 1, Tier 2, and Tier 3. Tier 1 capital is essentially retained earnings and common stock, Tier 2 is essentially long-term subordinated debt (over five years), and Tier 3 is short-term subordinated debt with an original maturity of at least two years. Thus, the $94.86 million in the example above can be raised by any of the three capital types subject to the two following limitations: (1) Tier 3 capital is limited to 250% of Tier 1 capital, and (2) Tier 2 capital can be substituted for Tier 3 capital up to the same 250% limit. For example, suppose Tier 1 capital was $27.10 million and the FI issued short-term Tier 3 debt of $67.76 million. Then the 250% limit would mean that no more Tier 3 (or Tier 2) debt could be issued to meet a target above $94.86 ($27.1 × 2.5 = $67.76) without additional Tier 1 capital being added. This capital charge for market risk would be added to the capital charge for credit risk and operational risk to get the FI's total capital requirement.

Exhibit 8.11 lists the market risk capital requirement to the total capital requirement for several large U.S. bank holding companies as of the first quarter of 2000. Notice how small the market risk capital requirement is relative to the total capital requirement for these banks. Only J.P. Morgan (prior to its merger with Chase) and CIBC have ratios greater than 10%. The average ratio of market risk capital required to total capital required for the 16 bank holding companies is only 4%.[44] Moreover, very few banks, other than the very largest (above), report market risk exposures at all.

---

[42]Using 2.33σ rather than 1.65σ.

[43]The idea of a minimum multiplication factor of 3 is to create a scheme that is "incentive compatible." Specifically, if FIs using internal models constantly underestimate the amount of capital they need to meet their market risk exposures, regulators can punish those FIs by raising the multiplication factor to as high as 4. Such a response may effectively put the FI out of the trading business. The degree to which the multiplication factor is raised above 3 depends on the number of days an FI's model underestimates its market risk over the preceding year. For example, an underestimation error that occurs on more than 10 days out of the past 250 days will result in the multiplication factor being raised to 4.

[44]D. Hendricks and B. Hirtle, in "Bank Capital Requirements for Market Risk: The Internal Models Approach," *Federal Reserve Bank of New York Economic Policy Review*, December 1997. pp. 1–12, also finds that the impact of the market risk capital charges on required capital ratios using internal models are small. They calculate an increase in the level of required capital from the general market risk component to range between 1.5 and 7.5% for the banks they examined. B. Hirtle, in "What Market Risk Capital Reporting Tells Us about Bank Risk," Federal Reserve Bank of New York, Working Paper, July 2001, finds that since the implementation of the market risk capital standards at the beginning of 1998, the bank holding companies that were subject to the market capital requirements accounted for more than 98% of the trading positions held by all U.S. banking organizations. For these banks, market risk capital represented just 1.9% of overall capital requirements of the median bank.

Name	Market Risk Capital Requirement to Total Capital Requirement (%)
KeyCorp	0.19974%
Bank One	0.53955
Wells Fargo	0.60787
Mellon Financial	1.03772
Bank of New York	1.25022
First Union	1.52644
Bankmont Financial	1.56739
Chase Manhattan	1.57258
FleetBoston Financial	2.14923
HSBC North America	2.22723
State Street	2.94050
Taunus	3.47091
Bank of America	4.83992

Exhibit 8.11. Ratio of Market Risk Capital Required to Total Capital Required for Bank Holding Companies Using Internal Models, First Quarter 2000.

8.8 SUMMARY. In this chapter we analyzed the importance of measuring an FI's market risk exposure. This risk is likely to continue to grow in importance as more and more loans and previously illiquid assets become marketable and as the traditional franchises of commercial banks, insurance companies, and investment banks shrink. Given the risks involved, both private FI management and regulators are investing increasing resources in models to measure and track market risk exposures. We analyzed in detail three different approaches FIs have used to measure market risk: RiskMetrics, the historic (or back simulation) approach, and the Monte Carlo simulation approach. The three different approaches were also compared in tems of simplicity and accuracy. Market risk is also of concern to regulators. Beginning in January 1998, banks in the United States have had to hold a capital requirement against the risk of their trading positions. The novel feature of the regulation of market risk is that the Federal Reserve and other central banks (subject to regulatory approval) have given large FIs the option to calculate capital requirements based on their own internal models rather than based on the regulatory model.

CHAPTER 9

VALUATION IN EMERGING MARKETS

Aswath Damodaran
New York University

CONTENTS

9.1 INTRODUCTION. The principles of valuation do not change when you are valuing emerging market companies. In particular, the value of an asset or a business is the present value of the expected cash flows, discounted back at a rate that reflects the riskiness of the cash flows. It is true that many inputs that we take for granted in developed markets, such as risk-free rates may not be easily accessed in emerging markets, and other inputs, such as risk parameters and premiums, are much more difficult to estimate because of the paucity of historical data. In addition, the information provided in financial statements may fall well short of what we need to know to value a firm. We will begin by considering the estimation issues associated with discount rates first, then examine cash flow estimation, and close with some general caveats about emerging market valuation.

9.2 ESTIMATING DISCOUNT RATES. While there are several competing risk and return models in finance, most of them require three inputs to come up with an expected return. The first is a riskless rate, which acts as a floor on your required return and measures what you would make on a guaranteed investment. The second is a risk premium, which looks at the extra return you would require as an investor for investing in the average risk investment. The third is a risk parameter or parameters (depending on the model you use) that captures the relative risk of the specific investment that you are evaluating.

(a) Risk-Free Rate. Most risk and return models in finance start off with an asset that is defined as risk-free and use the expected return on that asset as the risk-free rate. The expected returns on risky investments are then measured relative to the risk-free rate, with the risk creating an expected risk premium that is added on to the risk-free rate. But what makes an asset risk free? And what do we do when we cannot find such an asset?

(i) Requirements for an Asset to Be Risk Free. An asset is risk free if we know the expected returns on it with certainty (i.e., the actual return is always equal to the expected return). Under what conditions will the actual returns on an investment be equal to the expected returns? There are two basic conditions that have to be met. The first is that *there can be no default risk.* Essentially, this rules out any security issued by a private firm, since even the largest and safest firms have some measure of default risk. The only securities that have a chance of being risk free are government securities, not because governments are better run than corporations, but because they control the printing of currency. At least in nominal terms, they should be able to fulfill their promises. There is a second condition that riskless securities need to fulfill that is often forgotten. For an investment to have an actual return equal to its expected return, *there can be no reinvestment risk.* To illustrate this point, assume that you are trying to estimate the expected return over a five-year period and that you want a risk-free rate. A six-month Treasury bill rate, while default free, will not be risk free, because there is the reinvestment risk of not knowing what the treasury bill rate will be in six months. Even a five-year treasury bond is not risk free, since the coupons on the bond will be reinvested at rates that cannot be predicted today. The risk-free rate for a five-year time horizon has to be the expected return on a default-free (government) five-year zero coupon bond. This clearly has painful implications for anyone doing corporate finance or valuation, where expected returns often have

to be estimated for periods ranging from one to ten years. A purist's view of risk-free rates would then require different risk-free rates for each period and different expected returns. Here again, you may run into a problem with emerging markets, since governments often borrow only short term.

(ii) Risk-Free Rates When There Is No Default-Free Entity. The assumption that you can use a government bond rate as the risk-free rate is predicated on the assumption that governments do not default, at least on local borrowing. There are many emerging market economies in which this assumption might not be viewed as reasonable. Governments in these markets are perceived as capable of defaulting even on local borrowing. When this is coupled with the fact that many governments do not borrow long term locally, there are scenarios in which obtaining a local risk-free rate, especially for the long term, becomes difficult. In these cases, there are compromises that give us reasonable estimates of the risk-free rate:

- Look at the largest and safest firms in that market and use the rate that they pay on their long-term borrowings in the local currency as a base. Given that these firms, in spite of their size and stability, still have default risk, you would use a rate that is marginally lower[1] than the corporate borrowing rate.
- If there are long-term dollar-denominated forward contracts on the currency, you can use interest rate parity and the treasury bond rate (or riskless rate in any other base currency) to arrive at an estimate of the local borrowing rate.

$$\text{Forward rate}^t_{FC,\$} = (\text{Spot rate}_{FC,\$})\left(\frac{1 + \text{Interest rate}_{FC}}{1 + \text{Interest rate}_{\$}}\right)^t$$

where,

$\text{Forward Rate}_{FC,\$}$ = Forward rate for foreign currency units/ \$
$\text{Spot Rate}_{FC,\$}$ = Spot rate for foreign currency units/ \$
$\text{Interest Rate}_{FC}$ = Interest rate in foreign currency
$\text{Interest Rate}_{\$}$ = Interest rate in U.S. dollars

For instance, if the current spot rate is 38.10 Thai baht per U.S. dollar, the 10-year forward rate is 61.36 baht per dollar and the current 10-year U.S. treasury bond rate is 5%, the 10-year Thai risk-free rate (in nominal baht) can be estimated as follows.

$$61.36 = (38.1)\left(\frac{1 + \text{Interest rate}_{\text{Thai baht}}}{1 + 0.05}\right)^{10}$$

Solving for the Thai interest rate yields a 10-year risk free rate of 10.12%. The biggest limitation of this approach, however, is that forward rates are difficult to

[1] I would use 0.50% less than the corporate borrowing rate of these firms as my risk-free rate. This is roughly an AA default spread in the United States.

obtain for periods beyond a year[2] for many of the emerging markets, where we would be most interested in using them.

- You could adjust the local currency government borrowing rate by the estimated default spread on the bond to arrive at a riskless local currency rate. The default spread on the government bond can be estimated using the local currency ratings[3] that are available for many countries. For instance, assume that the Indian government bond rate is 12% and that the rating assigned to the Indian government is A. If the default spread for A-rated bonds is 2%, the riskless Indian rupee rate would be 10%.

$$\begin{aligned}\text{Riskless Rupee rate} &= \text{Indian Government Bond rate} - \text{Default Spread}\\ &= 12\% - 2\% = 10\%\end{aligned}$$

(iii) Cash Flows and Risk-Free Rates: Consistency Principle. The risk-free rate used to come up with expected returns should be measured consistently with how the cash flows are measured. Thus, if cash flows are estimated in nominal U.S. dollar terms, the risk-free rate will be the U.S. Treasury bond rate. This also implies that it is not where a project or firm is domiciled that determines the choice of a risk-free rate, but the currency in which the cash flows on the project or firm are estimated. Thus, Ambev, a Brazilian company, can be valued using cash flows estimated in Brazilian real, discounted back at an expected return estimated using a Brazilian risk-free rate or it can be valued in U.S. dollars, with both the cash flows and the risk-free rate being the U.S. Treasury bond rate. Given that the same firm can be valued in different currencies, will the final results always be consistent? If we assume purchasing power parity, then differences in interest rates reflect differences in expected inflation rates. Both the cash flows and the discount rate are affected by expected inflation; thus, a low discount rate arising from a low risk-free rate will be exactly offset by a decline in expected nominal growth rates for cash flows and the value will remain unchanged.

If the difference in interest rates across two currencies does not adequately reflect the difference in expected inflation in these currencies, the values obtained using the different currencies can be different. In particular, projects and assets will be valued more highly when the currency used is the one with low interest rates relative to inflation. The risk, however, is that the interest rates will have to rise at some point to correct for this divergence, at which point the values will also converge.

(iv) Real versus Nominal Risk free Rates. Under conditions of high and unstable inflation, valuation is often done in real terms. Effectively, this means that cash flows are estimated using real growth rates and without allowing for the growth that comes

[2]In cases in which only a one-year forward rate exists, an approximation for the long-term rate can be obtained by first backing out the one-year local currency borrowing rate, taking the spread over the one-year treasury bill rate, and then adding this spread onto the long-term treasury bond rate. For instance, with a one-year forward rate of 39.95 on the Thai bond, we obtain a one-year Thai baht riskless rate of 9.04% (given a one-year T-bill rate of 4%). Adding the spread of 5.04% to the 10-year treasury bond rate of 5% provides a 10-year Thai baht rate of 10.04%.

[3]Ratings agencies generally assign different ratings for local currency borrowings and dollar borrowing, with higher ratings for the former and lower ratings for the latter.

from price inflation. To be consistent, the discount rates used in these cases have to be real discount rates. To get a real expected rate of return, we need to start with a real risk-free rate. While government bills and bonds offer returns that are risk free in nominal terms, they are not risk free in real terms, since expected inflation can be volatile. The standard approach of subtracting an expected inflation rate from the nominal interest rate to arrive at a real risk-free rate provides at best an estimate of the real risk-free rate.

Until recently, there were few traded default-free securities that could be used to estimate real risk-free rates, but the introduction of inflation-indexed treasuries has filled this void. An inflation-indexed treasury security does not offer a guaranteed nominal return to buyers, but instead provides a guaranteed real return. Thus, an inflation-indexed treasury that offers a 3% real return will yield approximately 7% in nominal terms if inflation is 4% and only 5% in nominal terms if inflation is only 2%.

The only problem is that real valuations are seldom called for or done in the United States, which has stable and low expected inflation. The markets where we would most need to do real valuations, unfortunately, are markets without inflation-indexed default-free securities. The real risk free rates in these markets can be estimated by using one of two arguments:

1. The first argument is that as long as capital can flow freely to those economies with the highest real returns, there can be no differences in real risk free rates across markets. Using this argument, the real risk free rate for the United States, estimated from the inflation-indexed treasury, can be used as the real risk-free rate in any market.
2. The second argument applies if there are frictions and constraints in capital flowing across markets. In that case, the expected real return on an economy, in the long term, should be equal to the expected real growth rate, again in the long term, of that economy, for equilibrium. Thus, the real risk-free rate for a mature economy like Germany should be much lower than the real risk free rate for an economy with greater growth potential, such as Hungary.

(b) Equity Risk Premiums. The notion that risk matters and that riskier investments should have a higher expected return than safer investments to be considered good investments is intuitive. Thus, the expected return on any investment can be written as the sum of the risk-free rate and an extra return to compensate for the risk. The disagreement, in both theoretical and practical terms, remains on how to measure this risk and how to convert the risk measure into an expected return that compensates for risk. This section looks at the estimation of an appropriate risk premium to use in risk and return models, in general, and in the capital asset pricing model, in particular.

(i) Competing Views on Risk Premiums. While competing models for risk and return in finance come to different conclusions about how best to measure an asset's risk, they all share some common views about risk. First, they all define risk in terms of variance in actual returns around an expected return; thus, an investment is riskless when actual returns are always equal to the expected return. Second, they all argue that risk has to be measured from the perspective of the marginal investor in an asset and that this marginal investor is well diversified. Therefore, the argument goes, it is only the risk that an investment adds on to a diversified portfolio that should be meas-

ured and compensated. In fact, it is this view of risk that leads models of risk to break the risk in any investment into two components. There is a firm-specific component that measures risk that relates only to that investment or to a few investments like it and a market component that contains risk that affects a large subset or all investments. It is the latter risk that is not diversifiable and should be rewarded.

While all risk and return models agree on these fairly crucial distinctions, they part ways when it comes to how to measure this market risk. The capital asset pricing model assumes that you can measure it with one beta, whereas the arbitrage pricing and multifactor models measure market risk with multiple betas. In all of these models, the expected return on any investment can be written as:

$$\text{Expected return} = \text{Risk-free Rate} + \sum_{j=1}^{j=k} \beta_j(\text{Risk Premium}_j)$$

where,

$$\beta_j = \text{Beta of investment relative to factor } j$$
$$\text{Risk Premium}_j = \text{Risk Premium for factor } j$$

Note that in the special case of a single-factor model, such as the capital asset pricing model (CAPM), each investment's expected return will be determined by its beta relative to the single factor.

Assuming that the risk-free rate is known, these models all require two inputs. The first is the beta or betas of the investment being analyzed, and the second is the appropriate risk premium(s) for the factor or factors in the model. We would like to measure how much market risk (or nondiversifiable risk) there is in any investment through its beta or betas. As far as the risk premium is concerned, we would like to know what investors, on average, require as a premium over the risk-free rate for an investment with average risk, for each factor. Without any loss of generality, let us consider the estimation of the beta and the risk premium in the CAPM. Here, the beta should measure the risk added on by the investment being analyzed to a portfolio, diversified not only within asset classes but across asset classes. The risk premium should measure what investors, on average, demand as extra return for investing in this portfolio relative to the risk-free asset.

In practice, however, we compromise on both counts. We estimate the beta of an asset relative to the local stock market index, rather than a portfolio that is diversified across asset classes. This beta estimate is often noisy and a historical measure of risk. We estimate the risk premium by looking at the historical premium earned by stocks over default-free securities over long time periods. These approaches might yield reasonable estimates in markets like the United States, with a large and diversified stock market and a long history of returns on both stocks and government securities. We will argue, however, that they yield meaningless estimates for both the beta and the risk premium in emerging markets, where the equity markets represent a small proportion of the overall economy and the historical returns are available only for short periods.

(ii) Historical Premium Approach: An Examination. The historical premium approach, which remains the standard approach when it comes to estimating risk premiums, is simple. The actual returns earned on stocks over a long time period is es-

timated and compared to the actual returns earned on a default-free asset (usually government security). The difference, on an annual basis, between the two returns is computed and represents the *historical risk premium.*

While users of risk and return models may have developed a consensus that historical premium is, in fact, the best estimate of the risk premium looking forward, there are surprisingly large differences in the actual premiums we observe being used in practice. For instance, the risk premium estimated in the U.S. markets by different investment banks, consultants, and corporations range from 4% at the lower end to 12% at the upper end. Given that we almost all use the same database of historical returns, provided by Ibbotson Associates,[4] summarizing data from 1926, these differences may seem surprising. There are, however, three reasons for the divergence in risk premiums. The first is that the premium will be different, depending on how far back in time you go. Statistically, the more reliable estimates come from going back longer—estimates in the United States often are based on going back to 1926. The second is that the premium will be different depending on your definition of a risk-free rate—it is generally larger when you use the T-bill rate as your riskless rate. The third reason for differences is that the premium is different when you look at the arithmetic average return earned over time as opposed to the geometric average, since the latter considers compounding. Exhibit 9.1 summarizes premiums for the United States, using three different slices of history, different risk-free rates, and arithmetic versus geometric averages. Note that the premiums can range from 4.52% to 12.67%, depending on the choices made. In fact, these differences are exacerbated by the fact that many risk premiums that are in use today were estimated using historical data three, four, or even ten years ago.

Given how widely the historical risk premium approach is used, it is surprising how flawed it is and how little attention these flaws have attracted. Consider first the underlying assumption that investors' risk premiums have not changed over time and that the average risk investment (in the market portfolio) has remained stable over the period examined. We would be hard-pressed to find anyone who would be willing to sustain this argument with fervor. The obvious fix for this problem, which is to use a shorter and more recent time period, runs directly into a second problem, which is the large noise associated with risk premium estimates. While these standard errors may be tolerable for very long time periods, they clearly are unacceptably high when shorter periods are used.

[4]See "Stocks, Bonds, Bills, and Inflation," an annual edition that reports on the annual returns on stocks, treasury bonds and bills, as well as inflation rates from 1926 to the present. (*www.ibbotson.com*).

	Stocks—Treasury Bills		Stocks—Treasury Bonds	
	Arithmetic	Geometric	Arithmetic	Geometric
1928–2000	8.41%	7.17%	6.53%	5.51%
1962–2000	6.41%	5.25%	5.30%	4.52%
1990–2000	11.42%	7.64%	12.67%	7.09%

Exhibit 9.1. Historical Risk Premia for the United States.

If it is difficult to estimate a reliable historical premium for the U.S. market, it becomes doubly so when looking at markets with short and volatile histories. This is clearly true for emerging markets, but it is also true for the European equity markets. While the economies of Germany, Italy, and France may be mature, their equity markets do not share the same characteristic. They tend to be dominated by a few large companies; many businesses remain private; and trading, until recently, tended to be thin except on a few stocks.

(iii) Modified Historical Risk Premium. While historical risk premiums for markets outside the United States cannot be used in risk models, we still need to estimate a risk premium for use in these markets. To approach this estimation question, let us start with the basic proposition that the risk premium in any equity market can be written as:

Equity risk premium = Base premium for mature equity market + Country premium

The country premium could reflect the extra risk in a specific market. This boils down our estimation to answering two questions:

1. What should the base premium for a mature equity market be?
2. Should there be a country premium, and if so, how do we estimate the premium?

To answer the first question, we will make the argument that the U.S. equity market is a mature market and that there is sufficient historical data in the United States to make a reasonable estimate of the risk premium. In fact, reverting back to our discussion of historical premiums in the U.S. market, we will use the geometric average premium earned by stocks over treasury bonds of 5.51% between 1928 and 2000. We chose the long time period to reduce standard error, for the Treasury bond to be consistent with our choice of a risk-free rate, and geometric averages to reflect our desire for a risk premium that we can use for longer-term expected returns.

On the issue of country premiums, there are some who argue that country risk is diversifiable and that there should be no country risk premium. We will begin by looking at the basis for their argument and then consider the alternative view that there should be a country risk premium. We will present two approaches for estimating country risk premiums, one based on country bond default spreads and one based on equity market volatility.

(iv) Should There Be a Country Risk Premium? Is there more risk in investing in a Malaysian or Brazilian stock than there is in investing in the United States? The answer, to most, seems to be obviously affirmative. That, however, does not answer the question of whether there should be an additional risk premium charged when investing in those markets.

Note that the only risk that is relevant for the purpose of estimating a cost of equity is market risk or risk that cannot be diversified away. The key question then becomes whether the risk in an emerging market is diversifiable or nondiversifiable risk. If, in fact, the additional risk of investing in Malaysia or Brazil can be diversified away, then there should be no additional risk premium charged. If it cannot, then it makes sense to think about estimating a country risk premium.

But diversified away by whom? Equity in a Brazilian or Malaysian firm can be held by hundreds or thousands of investors, some of whom may hold only domestic stocks in their portfolio, whereas others may have more global exposure. For purposes of analyzing country risk, we look at the marginal investor—the investor most likely to be trading on the equity. If that marginal investor is globally diversified, there is at least the potential for global diversification. If the marginal investor does not have a global portfolio, the likelihood of diversifying away country risk declines substantially. Stulz[5] made a similar point using different terminology. He differentiated between segmented markets, where risk premiums can be different in each market because investors cannot or will not invest outside their domestic markets, and open markets, where investors can invest across markets. In a segmented market, the marginal investor will be diversified only across investments in that market; whereas in an open market, the marginal investor has the opportunity (even if he or she does not take it) to invest across markets.

Even if the marginal investor is globally diversified, there is a second test that has to be met for country risk to not matter. All or much of country risk should be country specific. In other words, there should be low correlation across markets. Only then will the risk be diversifiable in a globally diversified portfolio. If the returns across countries have significant positive correlation, however, country risk has a market risk component and is not diversifiable and can command a premium. Whether returns across countries are positively correlated is an empirical question. Studies from the 1970s and 1980s suggested that the correlation was low and this was an impetus for global diversification. Partly because of the success of that sales pitch and partly because economies around the world have become increasingly intertwined over the last decade, more recent studies indicate that the correlation across markets has risen. This is borne out by the speed at which troubles in one market, say Russia, can spread to a market with little or no obvious relationship, say Brazil.

So where do we stand? We believe that, while the barriers to trading across markets have dropped, investors still have a home bias in their portfolios and that markets remain partially segmented. While globally diversified investors are playing an increasing role in the pricing of equities around the world, the resulting increase in correlation across markets has resulted in a portion of country risk being nondiversifiable or market risk. In the next section, we will consider how best to measure this country risk and build it into expected returns.

(v) Measuring Country Risk Premiums. If country risk matters and leads to higher premiums for riskier countries, the obvious follow-up question becomes how we measure this additional premium. In this section, we will look at two approaches. The first builds on default spreads on country bonds issued by each country, whereas the second uses equity market volatility as its basis.

DEFAULT RISK SPREADS. While there are several measures of country risk, one of the simplest and most easily accessible is the rating assigned to a country's debt by a ratings agency (Standard & Poor's [S&P], Moody's, and Fitch all rate countries). These ratings measure default risk (rather than equity risk), but they are affected by many

---

[5]R. M. Stulz, Globalization, Corporate Finance, and the Cost of Capital, *Journal of Applied Corporate Finance*, Vol. 12, 1999.

Country	Rating[a]	Typical Spread[b]	Market Spread[c]
Argentina	B1	450	433
Bolivia	B1	450	469
Brazil	B2	550	483
Colombia	Ba2	300	291
Ecuador	Caa2	750	727
Guatemala	Ba2	300	331
Honduras	B2	550	537
Mexico	Baa3	145	152
Paraguay	B2	550	581
Peru	Ba3	400	426
Uruguay	Baa3	145	174
Venezuela	B2	550	571

[a]Ratings are foreign currency ratings from Moody's.

[b]Typical spreads are estimated by looking at the default spreads on bonds issued by all countries with this rating and are over and above a riskless rate (U.S. treasury or German Euro rate).

[c]Market spread measures the spread difference between dollar-denominated bonds issued by this country and the U.S. treasury bond rate.

Exhibit 9.2. Ratings and Default Spreads: Latin America.

of the factors that drive equity risk—the stability of a country's currency, its budget and trade balances, and its political stability, for instance[6] The other advantage of ratings is that they come with default spreads over the U.S. Treasury bond. For instance, Exhibit 9.2 summarizes the ratings and default spreads for Latin American countries in June 2000. The market spreads measure the difference between dollar-denominated bonds issued by the country and the U.S. Treasury bond rate. While this is a market rate and reflects current expectations, country bond spreads are extremely volatile and can shift significantly from day to day. To counter this volatility, we have estimated typical spreads by averaging the default spreads of all countries in the world with the specified rating over and above the appropriate riskless rate. These spreads tend to be less volatile and more reliable for long-term analysis.

Analysts who use default spreads as measures of country risk typically add them on to both the cost of equity and debt of every company traded in that country. For instance, the cost of equity for a Brazilian company, estimated in U.S. dollars, will be 4.83% higher than the cost of equity of an otherwise similar U.S. company. If we assume that the risk premium for the United States and other mature equity markets is 5.51%, the cost of equity for an average Brazilian company can be estimated as follows (with a U.S. Treasury bond rate of 5% and a beta of 1.2).

$$\text{Cost of equity} = \text{Risk-free rate} + \text{Beta} * (\text{U.S. Risk premium}) + \text{Default spread}$$
$$= 5\% + 1.2(5.51\%) + 4.83\% = 16.34\%$$

[6]The process by which country ratings are obtained is explained on the S&P Web site at *www.ratings.standardpoor.com/criteria/index.htm.*

In some cases, analysts add the default spread to the U.S. risk premium and multiply it by the beta. This increases the cost of equity for high-beta companies and lowers them for low-beta firms.

While ratings provide a convenient measure of country risk, there are costs associated with using them as the only measure. First, ratings agencies often lag markets when it comes to responding to changes in the underlying default risk. Second, the fact that the ratings agency focus on default risk may obscure other risks that could still affect equity markets. What are the alternatives? There are numerical country risk scores that have been developed by some services as much more comprehensive measures of risk. *The Economist*, for instance, has a score that runs from 0 to 100, where 0 is no risk, and 100 is most risky, that it uses to rank emerging markets. Alternatively, country risk can be estimated from the bottom up by looking at economic fundamentals in each country. This, of course, requires significantly more information than the other approaches. Finally, default spreads measure the risk associated with bonds issued by countries and not the equity risk in these countries. Since equities in any market are likely to be more risky than bonds, you could argue that default spreads understate equity risk premiums.

RELATIVE STANDARD DEVIATIONS. There are some analysts who believe that the equity risk premiums of markets should reflect the differences in equity risk, as measured by the volatilities of these markets. A conventional measure of equity risk is the standard deviation in stock prices; higher standard deviations are generally associated with more risk. If you scale the standard deviation of one market against another, you obtain a measure of relative risk.

$$\text{Relative standard deviation}_{\text{Country X}} = \frac{\text{Standard deviation}_{\text{Country X}}}{\text{Standard deviation}_{\text{U.S.}}}$$

This relative standard deviation when multiplied by the premium used for U.S. stocks should yield a measure of the total risk premium for any market.

$$\text{Equity risk premium}_{\text{Country X}} = \text{Risk premium}_{\text{U.S.}} {*} \text{Relative standard deviation}_{\text{Country X}}$$

Assume, for the moment, that you are using a mature market premium for the United States of 5.51% and that the annual standard deviation of U.S. stocks is 20%. If the annual standard deviation of Indonesian stocks is 35%, the estimate of a total risk premium for Indonesia would be as follows.

$$\text{Equity risk premium}_{\text{Indonesia}} = 5.51\% {*} \frac{35\%}{20\%} = 9.64\%$$

The country risk premium can be isolated as follows:

$$\text{Country risk premium}_{\text{Indonesia}} = 9.64\% - 5.51\% = 4.13\%$$

While this approach has intuitive appeal, there are problems with using standard deviations computed in markets with widely different market structures and liquidity. There are very risky emerging markets that have low standard deviations for their equity markets because the markets are illiquid. This approach will understate the equity risk premiums in those markets. The second problem is related to currencies since the standard deviations are usually measured in local currency terms; the standard deviation in the U.S. market is a dollar standard deviation, whereas the standard deviation in the Indonesian market is a rupiah standard deviation. This is a relatively simple problem to fix, though, since the standard deviations can be measured in the same currency—you could estimate the standard deviation in dollar returns for the Indonesian market.

DEFAULT SPREADS PLUS RELATIVE STANDARD DEVIATIONS. The country default spreads that come with country ratings provide an important first step, but still measure only the premium for default risk. Intuitively, we would expect the country equity risk premium to be larger than the country default risk spread. To address the issue of how much higher, we look at the volatility of the equity market in a country relative to the volatility of the bond market used to estimate the spread. This yields the following estimate for the country equity risk premium:

$$\text{Country risk premium} = \text{Country default spread}*\left(\frac{\sigma_{\text{Equiy}}}{\sigma_{\text{Country bond}}}\right)$$

To illustrate, consider the case of Brazil. In March 2000, Brazil was rated B2 by Moody's, resulting in a default spread of 4.83%. The annualized standard deviation in the Brazilian equity index over the previous year was 30.64%, while the annualized standard deviation in the Brazilian dollar denominated C-bond was 15.28%. The resulting country equity risk premium for Brazil is as follows:

$$\text{Brazil's country risk premium} = 4.83\%\left(\frac{30.64\%}{15.28\%}\right) = 9.69\%$$

Note that this country risk premium will increase if the country rating drops or if the relative volatility of the equity market increases.

Why should equity risk premiums have any relationship to country bond spreads? A simple explanation is that an investor who can make 11% on a dollar-denominated Brazilian government bond would not settle for an expected return of 10.5% (in dollar terms) on Brazilian equity. Playing devil's advocate, however, a critic could argue that the interest rate on a country bond, from which default spreads are extracted, is not really an expected return, since it is based on the promised cash flows (coupon and principal) on the bond rather than the expected cash flows. In fact, if we wanted to estimate a risk premium for bonds, we would need to estimate the expected return based on expected cash flows, allowing for the default risk. This would result in a much lower default spread and equity risk premium.

Both this approach and the previous one use the standard deviation in equity of a market to make a judgment about country risk premium, but they measure it relative to different bases. This approach uses the country bond as a base, whereas the previous one uses the standard deviation in the U.S. market. This approach assumes that investors are more likely to choose between Brazilian bonds and Brazilian equity, whereas the previous one approach assumes that the choice is across equity markets.

(vi) Choosing between the Approaches. The three approaches to estimating country risk premiums will generally give you different estimates, with the bond default spread and relative equity standard deviation approaches yielding lower country risk premiums than the melded approach that uses both the country bond default spread and the equity and bond standard deviations. We believe that the larger country risk premiums that emerge from the last approach are the most realistic for the immediate future, but that country risk premiums will decline over time. Just as companies mature and become less risky over time, countries can mature and become less risky as well.

One way to adjust country risk premiums over time is to begin with the premium that emerges from the melded approach and to adjust this premium down towards either the country bond default spread or the country premium estimated from equity standard deviations. Another way of presenting this argument is to note that the differences between standard deviations in equity and bond prices narrow over longer periods and the resulting relative volatility will generally be smaller.[7] Thus, the equity risk premium will converge to the country bond spread as we look at longer-term expected returns. As an illustration, the country risk premium for Brazil would be 9.69% for the next year but decline over time to either the 4.83% (country default spread) or 4.13% (relative standard deviation).

(vii) Estimating Asset Exposure to Country Risk Premiums. Once country risk premiums have been estimated, the final question that we have to address relates to the exposure of individual companies within that country to country risk. There are three alternative views of country risk.

1. *Assume that all companies in a country are equally exposed to country risk.* Thus, for Brazil, where we have estimated a country risk premium of 9.69%, each company in the market will have an additional country risk premium of 9.69% added to its expected returns. For instance, the cost of equity for Aracruz Celulose, a paper and pulp manufacturer listed in Brazil, with a beta of 0.72, in U.S. dollar terms would be (assuming a U.S. Treasury bond rate of 5% and a mature market (U.S.) risk premium of 5.59%):

$$\text{Expected cost of equity} = 5.00\% + 0.72(5.51\%) + 9.69\% = 18.66\%$$

Note that the risk-free rate that we use is the U.S. Treasury bond rate, and that the 5.51% is the equity risk premium for a mature equity market (estimated from historical data in the U.S. market). To convert this dollar cost of equity into a cost of equity in the local currency, all that we need to do is to scale the estimate by relative inflation. To illustrate, if the BR inflation rate is 10% and the U.S. inflation rate is 3%, the cost of equity for Aracruz in BR terms can be written as:

$$\text{Expected cost of equity}_{BR} = 1.1866\left(\frac{1.10}{1.03}\right) - 1 = 0.2672 \text{ or } 26.72\%$$

[7]Jeremy Siegel reports on the standard deviation in equity markets in his book *Stocks for the Very Long Run: The Definitive Guide to Financial Market Returns and Long-Term Investment Strategies*, (McGraw-Hill, 2002), and notes that they tend to decrease with time horizon.

This will ensure consistency across estimates and valuations in different currencies. The biggest limitation of this approach is that it assumes that all firms in a country, no matter what their business or size, are equally exposed to country risk.

2. *Assume that a company's exposure to country risk is proportional to its exposure to all other market risk, which is measured by the beta.* For Aracruz, this would lead to a cost of equity estimate of:

$$\text{Expected cost of equity} = 5.00\% + 0.72(5.51\% + 9.69\%) = 15.94\%$$

This approach does differentiate between firms, but it assumes that betas which measure exposure to market risk also measure exposure to country risk as well. Thus, low-beta companies are less exposed to country risk than high-beta companies.

3. *The most general, and our preferred approach, is to allow for each company to have an exposure to country risk that is different from its exposure to all other market risk.* We will measure this exposure with λ and estimate the cost of equity for any firm as follows:

$$\text{Expected return} = R_f + \text{Beta (Mature equity risk premium)} + \lambda(\text{County risk premium})$$

How can we best estimate λ? You could argue that commodity companies which get most of their revenues in U.S. dollars[8] by selling into a global market should be less exposed than manufacturing companies that service the local market. Using this rationale, Aracruz, which derives 80% or more of its revenues in the global paper market in U.S. dollars, should be less exposed[9] than the typical Brazilian firm to country risk. Using a λ of 0.25, for instance, we get a cost of equity in U.S. dollar terms for Aracruz of:

$$\text{Expected return} = 5\% + 0.72(5.51\%) + 0.25(9.69\%) = 11.39\%$$

Note that the third approach essentially converts our expected return model to a two-factor model, with the second factor being country risk as measured by the parameter λ and the country risk premium. This approach also seems to offer the most promise in analyzing companies with exposures in multiple countries like Coca-Cola and Nestlé. While these firms are ostensibly developed market companies, they have substantial exposure to risk in emerging markets and their costs of equity should reflect this exposure. We could estimate the country risk premiums for each country in which they operate and a λ relative to each country and use these to estimate a cost of equity for either company.

(viii) An Alternative Approach: Implied Equity Premiums. There is an alternative to estimating risk premiums that does not require historical data or corrections for coun-

[8]While I have categorized the revenues into dollar, the analysis can be generalized to look at revenues in other stable currencies and revenues in "risky currencies."

[9]$$\text{Aracruz} = \frac{\%\text{ from local market}_{\text{Aracruz}}}{\%\text{ from local market}_{\text{average Brazilian firm}}} = \frac{0.20}{0.80} = 0.25$$

try risk, but does assume that the market overall is correctly priced. Consider, for instance, a very simple valuation model for stocks.

$$\text{Value} = \frac{\text{Expected dividends next period}}{\text{Required Return on Equity} - \text{Expected Growth Rate in Dividends}}$$

This is essentially the present value of dividends growing at a constant rate. Three of the four variables in this model can be obtained externally—the current level of the market (i.e., value), the expected dividends next period and the expected growth rate in earnings and dividends in the long term. The only "unknown" is then the required return on equity; when we solve for it, we get an implied expected return on stocks. Subtracting out the risk-free rate will yield an implied equity risk premium.

To illustrate, assume that the current level of the S&P 500 Index is 900, the expected dividend yield on the index for the next period is 2% and the expected growth rate in earnings and dividends in the long term is 7%. Solving for the required return on equity yields the following:

$$900 = \frac{900(0.02)}{r - 0.07}$$

Solving for r,

$$r - 0.07 = 0.02$$
$$= 0.09 = 9\%$$

If the current risk-free rate is 6%, this will yield a premium of 3%.

This approach can be generalized to allow for high growth for a period and extended to cover cash flow–based, rather than dividend-based, models. To illustrate this, consider the S&P 500 Index, as of December 31, 1999. The index was at 1469, and the dividend yield on the index was roughly 1.68%. In addition, the consensus estimate[10] of growth in earnings for companies in the index was approximately 10% for the next 5 years. Since this is not a growth rate that can be sustained forever, we employ a two-stage valuation model, where we allow growth to continue at 10% for 5 years and then lower the growth rate to the treasury bond rate of 6.50% after the 5 year period.[11] Exhibit 9.3 summarizes the expected cash flows for the next 5 years of high growth and the first year of stable growth thereafter. If we assume that these are reasonable estimates of the cash flows and that the index is correctly priced, then

$$\text{Level of the index} = 1469 = \frac{27.15}{(1+r)} + \frac{29.86}{(1+r)^2} + \frac{32.85}{(1+r)^3} + \frac{36.13}{(1+r)^4} + \frac{39.75 + \dfrac{42.33}{r - 0.065}}{(1+r)^5}$$

[10]We used the average of the analyst estimates for individual firms (bottom-up). Alternatively, we could have used the top-down estimate for the S&P 500 earnings.

[11]The Treasury bond rate is the sum of expected inflation and the expected real rate. If we assume that real growth is equal to the real rate, the long-term stable growth rate should be equal to the Treasury bond rate.

Year	Cash Flow on Index
1	27.15[a]
2	29.86
3	32.85
4	36.13
5	39.75
6	42.33

[a]Cash flow in the first year = 1.68% of 1469 (1.10)

Exhibit 9.3. Estimating an Implied Equity Risk Premium.

Note that the term with 42.33 in the last term of the equation is the terminal value of the index, based on the stable growth rate of 6.5%, discounted back to the present. Solving for r in this equation yields us the required return on equity of 8.56%. The Treasury bond rate on December 31, 1999, was approximately 6.5%, yielding an implied equity premium of 2.06%.

The advantage of this approach is that it is market-driven and current and it does not require any historical data. Thus, it can be used to estimate implied equity premiums in any market. It is, however, bounded by whether the model used for the valuation is the right one and the availability and reliability of the inputs to that model. For instance, the equity risk premium for the Argentine market on September 30, 1998, was estimated from the following inputs. The index (Merval) was at 687.50 and the current dividend yield on the index was 5.60%. Earnings in companies in the index are expected to grow 11% (in U.S. dollar terms) over the next 5 years and 6% thereafter. These inputs yield a required return on equity of 10.59%, which when compared to the treasury bond rate of 5.14% on that day results in an implied equity premium of 5.45%. For simplicity, we have used nominal dollar expected growth rates[12] and Treasury bond rates, but this analysis could have been done entirely in the local currency.

(c) Betas. In the CAPM, the beta of an investment is the risk that the investment adds to a market portfolio. In the APM and multifactor model, the betas of the investment relative to each factor have to be measured. There are two approaches available for estimating these parameters. The first is to use historical data on market prices for individual investments. The second is to estimate the betas from the fundamental characteristics of the investment.

(i) Historical Market Betas. With historical market betas, we use past data on stock returns and returns on a market index to estimate the beta for a firm. In this section, we will first describe the standard approach and then talk about some of the limitations of using it in emerging markets.

[12]The input that is most difficult to estimate for emerging markets is a long term expected growth rate. For Argentine stocks, I used the average consensus estimate of growth in earnings for the largest Argentine companies that have listed American Depository Receipts (ADRs). This estimate may be biased, as a consequence.

STANDARD APPROACH. The conventional approach for estimating the beta of an investment is a regression of the historical returns on the investment against the historical returns on a market index. For firms that have been publicly traded for a length of time, it is relatively straightforward to estimate returns that an investor would have made on investing in stock in intervals (such as a week or a month) over that period. In theory, these stock returns on the assets should be related to returns on a market portfolio (i.e., a portfolio that includes all traded assets, to estimate the betas of the assets). In practice, we tend to use a stock index, such as the S&P 500, as a proxy for the market portfolio, and we estimate betas for stocks against the index. When we regress stock returns (R_j) against market returns (R_m):

$$R_j = a + bR_m$$

where

$$a = \text{Intercept from the regression}$$

$$b = \text{Slope of the regression} = \frac{\text{Cov}(R_j, R_m)}{\sigma_m^2}$$

The *slope* of the regression corresponds to the beta of the stock and measures the riskiness of the stock.

HISTORICAL BETA ESTIMATE FOR COMPANIES IN SMALLER OR EMERGING MARKETS. The process for estimating betas in markets with fewer stocks listed on them is no different from the process described above, but the estimation choices on return intervals, the market index and the return period can make a much bigger difference in the estimate. The historical beta is likely to be flawed for the following reasons:

- When liquidity is limited, as it often is in many stocks in emerging markets, the betas estimated using short return intervals tend to be much more biased. In fact, using daily or even weekly returns in these markets will tend to yield betas that are not good measures of the true market risk of the company.
- In many emerging markets, both the companies being analyzed and the market itself change significantly over short periods of time. Using five years of returns, as we did for Boeing, for a regression may yield a beta for a company (and market) that bears little resemblance to the company (and market) as it exists today.
- Finally, the indices that measure market returns in many smaller markets tend to be dominated by a few large companies. For instance, the Bovespa (the Brazilian index) was dominated for several years by Telebras, which represented almost half the index. Nor is this just a problem with emerging markets. When an index is dominated by one or a few companies, the betas estimated against that index are unlikely to be true measures of market risk. In fact, the betas are likely to be close to one for the large companies that dominate the index and wildly variable for all other companies.

ILLUSTRATION 1: BETA ESTIMATES FOR TITAN CEMENTS.

Consider, for instance, the beta estimated for Titan Cements, a cement and construction company in Greece. Exhibit 9.4 is the beta estimate for Titan obtained from a beta service (Bloomberg) from January 1996 to December 2000. Note that the index

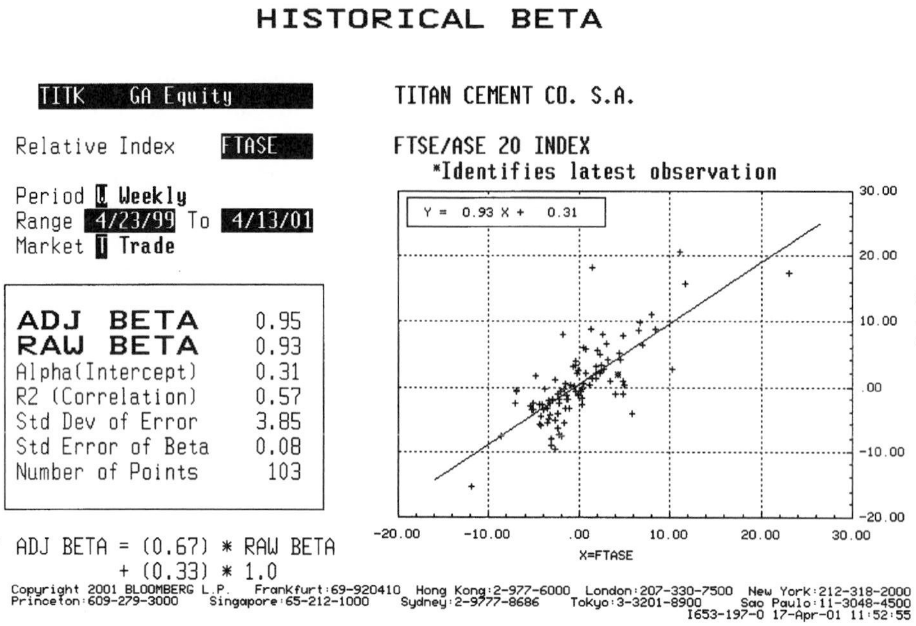

Exhibit 9.4. Beta Estimate for Titan Cement: Athens Stock Exchange Index.

used is the Athens Stock Index. This is a fairly conventional choice since most services estimate betas against a local index. Based on this regression, we arrive at the following equation.

$$\text{Returns}_{\text{Titan Cement}} = 0.31\% + 0.93\text{Returns}_{\text{ASE}} \qquad R \text{ squared} = 57\%$$
$$(0.08)$$

The beta for Titan Cements, based upon this regression, is 0.93. The standard error of the estimate, shown in brackets below, is only 0.08, but the caveats about narrow indices apply to the Athens Stock Exchange Index.

Drawing on the arguments in the previous section, if the marginal investor in Titan Cements is, in fact, an investor diversified across European companies, the appropriate index would have been a European stock index. The Bloomberg beta calculation with the MS European Index is reported in Exhibit 9.5. Note the decline in beta to 0.33 and the increase in the standard error of the beta estimate.

In fact, if the marginal investor is globally diversified, Titan Cement's beta (as well as Boeing's beta in the previous illustration) should have been estimated against a global index. Using the Morgan Stanley Capital Index (MSCI), we get the regression beta of 0.33 in Exhibit 9.6. In fact, the beta estimate and the standard error look very similar to the ones estimated against the European index.

In short, regression betas will almost always be either too noisy or skewed by estimation choices to be useful measures of the equity risk in a company. The cost of equity is far too important an input into a discounted cash flow valuation to be left to statistical chance.

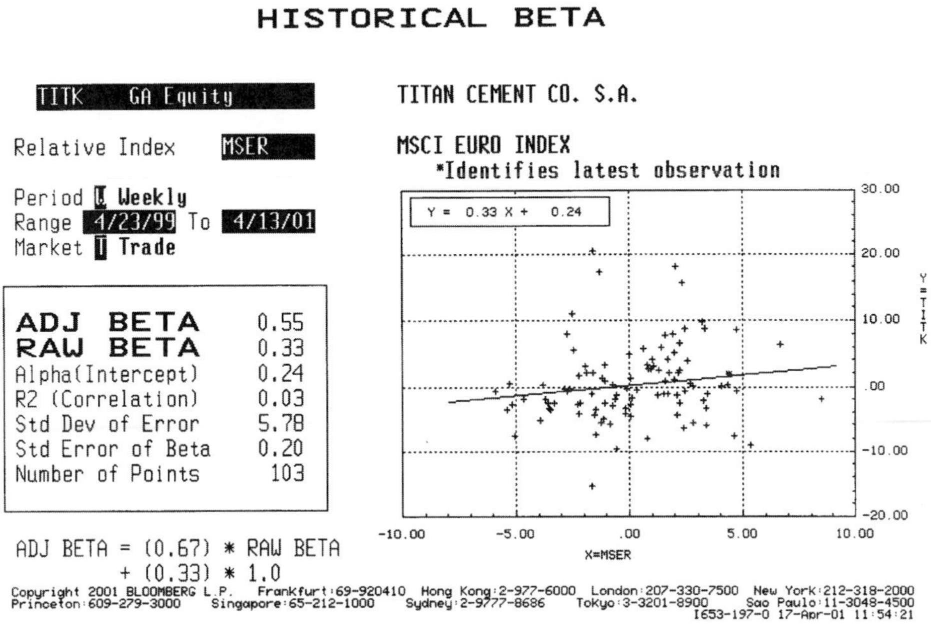

Exhibit 9.5. **Beta Estimate for Titan: MSCI Euro Index.**

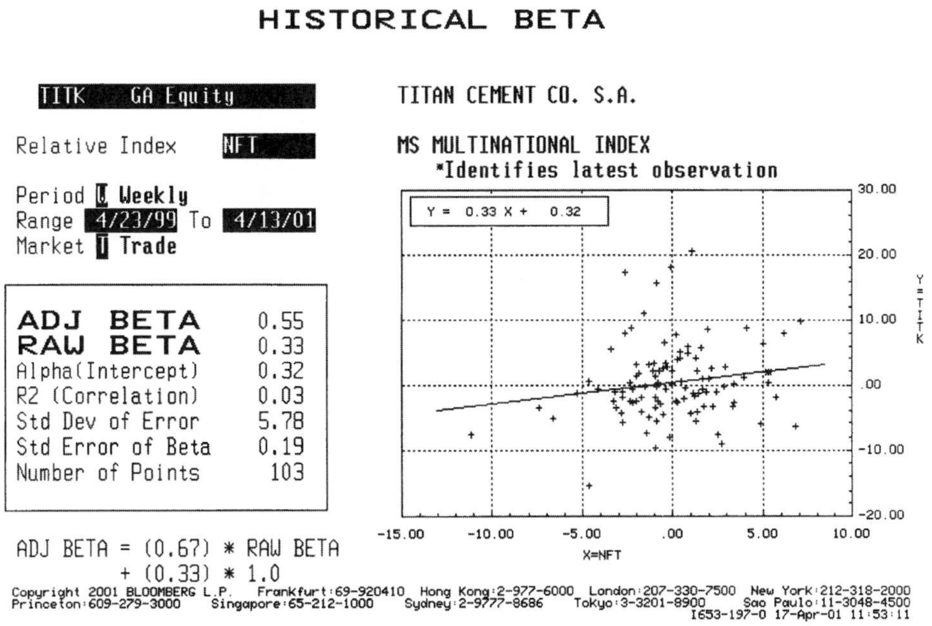

Exhibit 9.6. **Beta Estimate For Titan: MSCI Global Index.**

(ii) Fundamental Betas. A second way to estimate betas is to look at the fundamentals of the business. The beta for a firm may be estimated from a regression, but it is determined by decisions the firm has made on what business to be in, how much operating leverage to use in the business, and the degree to which the firm uses financial leverage. In this section, we will examine an alternative way of estimating betas for firms, where we are less reliant on historical betas and more cognizant of their fundamental determinants.

DETERMINANTS OF BETAS. The beta of a firm is determined by three variables: (1) the type of business or businesses the firm is in, (2) the degree of operating leverage of the firm, and (3) the firm's financial leverage. Although we will use these determinants to find betas in the CAPM, the same analysis can be used to calculate the betas for the arbitrage pricing and the multi-factor models as well.

TYPE OF BUSINESS. Since betas measure the risk of a firm relative to a market index, the more sensitive a business is to market conditions, the higher its beta. Thus, other things remaining equal, cyclical firms can be expected to have higher betas than non-cyclical firms. Companies involved in housing and automobiles, two sectors of the economy that are very sensitive to economic conditions, should have higher betas than companies in food processing and tobacco, which are relatively insensitive to business cycles.

We can extend this view to a company's products. The degree to which a product's purchase is discretionary will affect the beta of the firm manufacturing the product. Firms whose products are much more discretionary to their customers should have higher betas than firms whose products are viewed as necessary or less discretionary. Thus, the beta of Procter & Gamble, which sells diapers and daily household products, should be lower than the beta of Gucci, which manufactures luxury products.

DEGREE OF OPERATING LEVERAGE. The degree of *operating leverage* is a function of the cost structure of a firm and is usually defined in terms of the relationship between fixed costs and total costs. A firm that has high fixed costs relative to total costs is said to have high operating leverage. A firm with high operating leverage will also have higher variability in operating income than would a firm producing a similar product with low operating leverage. Other things remaining equal, the higher variance in operating income will lead to a higher beta for the firm with high operating leverage.

Can firms change their operating leverage? While some of a firm's cost structure is determined by the business it is in (an energy utility has to build expensive power plants, and airlines have to lease expensive planes), firms in the United States have become increasingly inventive in lowering the fixed cost component in their total costs. For instance, firms have made cost structures more flexible by:

- Negotiating labor contracts that emphasize flexibility and allow the firm to make its labor costs more sensitive to its financial success
- Entering into joint venture agreements, where the fixed costs are borne or shared by someone else
- Subcontracting manufacturing and outsourcing, which reduce the need for expensive plant and equipment

While the arguments for such actions may be couched in terms of offering competitive advantage and flexibility, they do also reduce the operating leverage of the firm and its exposure to market risk.

While operating leverage affects betas, it is difficult to measure the operating leverage of a firm, at least from the outside, since fixed and variable costs are often aggregated in income statements. It is possible to get an approximate measure of the operating leverage of a firm by looking at changes in operating income as a function of changes in sales.

$$\text{Degree of operating leverage} = \%\text{Change in operating profit}/\%\text{Change in sales}$$

For firms with high operating leverage, operating income should change more than proportionately when sales change.

Generally, smaller firms with higher growth potential are viewed as riskier than larger, more stable firms. While the rationale for this argument is clear when talking about total risk, it becomes more difficult to see when looking at market risk or betas. Should a smaller software firm have a higher beta than a larger software firm? One reason to believe that it should is operating leverage. If there is a set-up cost associated with investing in infrastructure or economies of scale, smaller firms will have higher fixed costs than larger firms, leading in turn to higher betas for these firms.

DEGREE OF FINANCIAL LEVERAGE. Other things remaining equal, an increase in financial leverage will increase the beta of the equity in a firm. Intuitively, we would expect that the fixed interest payments on debt result in high net income in good times and low or negative net income in bad times. Higher leverage increases the variance in net income and makes equity investment in the firm riskier. If all the firm's risk is borne by the stockholders (i.e., the beta of debt is zero)[13] and debt has a tax benefit to the firm, then

$$\beta_L = \beta_u\left(1 + (1 - t)\left(\frac{D}{E}\right)\right)$$

where

β_L = Levered beta for equity in the firm
β_u = Unlevered beta of the firm (i.e., the beta of the firm without any debt)
t = Corporate tax rate
D/E = Debt/Equity ratio

---

[13]This formula was originally developed by Hamada in 1972. There are two common modifications. One is to ignore the tax effects and compute the levered beta as:

$$\beta_L = \beta u\left(1 + \frac{D}{E}\right)$$

If debt has market risk (i.e., its beta is greater than zero), the original formula can be modified to take it into account. If the beta of debt is β_D, the beta of equity can be written as:

$$\beta_L = \beta_u\left(1 + (1 - t)\left(\frac{D}{E}\right)\right) - \beta_D(1 - t)\left(\frac{D}{E}\right)$$

Intuitively, we expect that as leverage increases (as measured by the debt to equity ratio), equity investors bear increasing amounts of market risk in the firm, leading to higher betas. The tax factor in the equation measures the tax deductibility of interest payments.

The *unlevered beta* of a firm is determined by the types of the businesses in which it operates and its operating leverage. It is often also referred to as the *asset beta* since it is determined by the assets owned by the firm. Thus, the *levered beta*, which is also the beta for an equity investment in a firm or the *equity beta*, is determined both by the riskiness of the business it operates in and by the amount of financial leverage risk it has taken on.

Since financial leverage multiplies the underlying business risk, it stands to reason that firms that have high business risk should be reluctant to take on financial leverage. It also stands to reason that firms that operate in stable businesses should be much more willing to take on financial leverage. Utilities, for instance, have historically had high debt ratios but have not had high betas, mostly because their underlying businesses have been stable and fairly predictable.

BOTTOM UP BETAS. Breaking down betas into their business risk and financial leverage components provides us with an alternative way of estimating betas in which we do not need past prices on an individual firm or asset.

To develop this alternative approach, we need to introduce an additional property of betas that proves invaluable. The beta of two assets put together is a weighted average of the individual asset betas, with the weights based upon market value. Consequently, the beta for a firm is a weighted average of the betas of all the different businesses it is in. We can estimate the beta for a firm in five steps.

- Step 1: We identify the business or businesses the firm operates in.
- Step 2: We find other publicly traded firms in these businesses and obtain their regression betas, which we use to compute an average beta for the firms, and their financial leverage.
- Step 3: We estimate the average unlevered beta for the business, by unlevering the average beta for the firm by their average debt to equity ratio. Alternatively, we could estimate the unlevered beta for each firm and then compute the average of the unlevered betas. The first approach is preferable because unlevering an erroneous regression beta is likely to compound the error.

$$\text{Unlevered beta}_{\text{Business}} = \frac{\text{Beta}_{\text{comparable firms}}}{1 + (1 - t)(D/E \text{ ratio comparable firms})}$$

- Step 4: To estimate an unlevered beta for the firm that we are analyzing, we take a weighted average of the unlevered betas for the businesses it operates in, using the proportion of firm value derived from each business as the weights. If values are not available, we use operating income or revenues as weights. This weighted average is called the bottom-up unlevered beta.

$$\text{Unlevered beta}_{\text{firm}} = \sum_{j=1}^{j=k} \text{Unlevered beta}_j * \text{Value weight}_j$$

where the firm is assumed to operating in k different businesses.

- Step 5: Finally, we estimate the current market values of debt and equity of the firm and use this debt-to-equity ratio to estimate a levered beta.

The betas estimated using this process are called *bottom-up betas*.

THE CASE FOR BOTTOM-UP BETAS. At first sight, the use of bottom-up betas may seem to leave us exposed to all of the problems we noted with regression betas. After all, the betas for other publicly traded firms in the business are obtained from regressions. Notwithstanding these bottom up betas represent a significant improvement on regression betas for the following reasons:

- While each regression beta is estimated with standard error, the average across a number of regression betas will have much lower standard error. The intuition is simple. A high standard error on a beta estimate indicates that it can be significantly higher or lower than the true beta. Averaging across these errors results in an average beta that is far more precise than the individual betas that went into it. In fact, if the estimation errors on individual firm betas are uncorrelated across firms, the savings in standard error can be stated as a function of the average standard error and the number of firms in the sample.

$$\text{Standard error}_{\text{Bottom-up beta}} = \frac{\text{Average standard error}_{\text{Comparable firms}}}{\sqrt{n}}$$

  where n is the number of firms in the sample. Thus, if the average standard error in beta estimates for software firms is 0.50 and the number of software firms is 100, the standard error of the average beta is only 0.05 ($0.50/\sqrt{100}$).
- A bottom-up beta can be adapted to reflect actual changes in a firm's business mix and expected changes in the future. Thus, if a firm divested a major portion of its operations last week, the weights on the businesses can be modified to reflect the divestiture. The same can be done with acquisitions. In fact, a firm's strategic plans to enter new businesses in the future can be brought into the beta estimates for future periods.
- Firms do change their debt ratios over time. While regression betas reflect the average debt-to-equity ratio maintained by the firm during the regression period, bottom-up betas use the current debt to equity ratio. If a firm plans to change its debt-to-equity ratio in the future, the beta can be adjusted to show these changes.
- Finally, bottom-up betas wean us from our dependence on historical stock prices. While we do need these prices to get betas for comparable firms, all we need for the firm being analyzed is a breakdown of the businesses it is in. Thus, bottom-up betas can be estimated for private firms, divisions of business and stocks that have just started trading in financial markets.

COMPUTATIONAL DETAILS. While the idea behind bottom-up betas is fairly simple, there are several computational details that are deserving of attention:

- *Defining comparable firms*. First, we have to decide how narrowly we want to define a business. Consider, for instance, a firm that manufactures entertainment software. We could define the business as entertainment software and consider only companies that primarily manufacture entertainment software to be comparable firms. We could go even further and define comparable firms as firms manufacturing entertainment software with revenues similar to that of the company being analyzed. While there are benefits to narrowing the comparable firm definition, there is a large cost. Each additional criterion added on to the definition of comparable will mean that fewer firms make the list and the savings in standard error that comprise the biggest benefit to bottom-up betas become smaller. A common sense principle should therefore come into play. If there are hundreds of firms in a business, as there are in the software business, you can afford to be more selective. If there are relatively few firms, not only do you have to become less selective, you might have to broaden the definition of comparable to bring in other firms into the mix.

- *Estimating Betas.* Once the comparable firms in a business have been defined, you have to estimate the betas for these firms. While it would be best to estimate the regressions for all of these firms against a common and well diversified equity index, it is usually easier to use service betas that are available for each of these firms. These service betas may be estimated against different indices. For instance, if you define your business to be global telecommunications and obtain betas for global telecom firms from Bloomberg, these betas will be estimated against their local indices. This is usually not a fatal problem, especially with large samples, since errors in the estimates tend to average out.
- *Averaging Method.* The average beta for the firms in the sector can be computed in one of two ways. We could use market-weighted averages, but the savings in standard error that we touted in the earlier section will be muted, especially if there are one or two very large firms in the sample. We could estimate the simple average of the betas of the companies, thus weighting all betas equally. The process weighs in the smallest firms in the sample disproportionately but the savings in standard error are likely to be maximized. There is also the issue of whether the firm being analyzed should be excluded from the group when computing the average. While the answer is yes, there will make little or no difference in the final estimate if there are more than 15 or 20 comparable firms.
- *Controlling for differences.* In essence, when we use betas from comparable firms, we are assuming that all firms in the business are equally exposed to business risk and have similar operating leverage. Note that the process of levering and unlevering of betas allows us to control for differences in financial leverage. If there are significant differences in operating leverage—cost structure—across companies, the differences in operating leverage can be controlled for as well. This would require that we estimate a business beta, where we take out the effects of operating leverage from the unlevered beta.

$$\text{Business beta} = \frac{\text{Unlevered beta}}{1 + (1 - \text{tax rate})(\text{Fixed costs/Variable costs})}$$

Note the similarity to the adjustment for financial leverage; the only difference is that both fixed and variable costs are eligible for the tax deduction and the tax rate is therefore no longer a factor. The business beta can then be relevered to reflect the differences in operating leverage across firms.

HOW WELL DO BETAS TRAVEL? Often, when analyzing firms in small or emerging markets, we have to estimate betas by looking at firms in the same business but traded on other markets. This is what we did when estimating the beta for Titan Cement. Is this appropriate? Should the beta for a steel company in the United States be comparable to that of a steel company in Indonesia? We see no reason why it should not. But the company in Indonesia has much more risk, you might argue. We do not disagree, but the fact that we use similar betas does not mean that we believe that the costs of equity are identical across all steel companies. In fact, using the approach described earlier in this paper, the risk premium used to estimate the cost of equity for the Indonesian company will incorporate a country risk premium, whereas the cost of equity for the U.S. company will not. Thus, even if the betas used for the two companies are identical, the cost of equity for the Indonesian company will be much higher.

There are a few exceptions to this proposition. Recall that one of the key determinants of betas is the degree to which a product or service is discretionary. It is entirely possible that products or services that are discretionary in one market (and command high betas) may be nondiscretionary in another market (and have low betas). For instance, phone service is viewed as a nondiscretionary product in most developed markets, but is a discretionary product in emerging markets. Consequently, the average beta estimated by looking at telecom firms in developed markets will understate the true beta of a telecom firm in an emerging market. Here, the comparable firms should be restricted to include only telecom firms in emerging markets.

ILLUSTRATION 2: ESTIMATING A BOTTOM-UP BETA FOR TITAN CEMENTS—JANUARY 2000.

To estimate a beta for Titan Cement, we began by defining comparable firms as other cement companies in Greece but found only one comparable firm. When we expanded the list to include cement companies across Europe, we increased our sample to nine firms. Since we did not see any reason to restrict our comparison to just European firms, we decided to look at the average beta for cement companies globally. There were 108 firms in this sample with an average beta of 0.99, an average tax rate of 34.2% and an average debt to equity ratio of 27.06%. We used these numbers to arrive at an unlevered beta of 0.84.

$$\text{Unlevered beta for cement companies} = \frac{0.99}{1 + (1 - 0.342)(0.2706)} = 0.84$$

We then used Titan's market values of equity (566.95 million Gdr) and debt (13.38 million GDr) to estimate a levered beta for its equity:

$$\text{Levered beta} = 0.84\left(1 + (1 - 0.2414)\left(\frac{13.38}{566.95}\right)\right) = 0.86$$

We used a tax rate of 24.14% in this calculation.

(d) From Cost of Equity to Cost of Capital. While equity is undoubtedly an important and indispensable ingredient of the financing mix for every business, it is but one ingredient. Most businesses finance some or much of their operations using debt or some security that is a combination of equity and debt. The costs of these sources of financing are generally very different from the cost of equity and the cost of financing for a firm should reflect their costs as well, in proportion to their use in the financing mix. Intuitively, the *cost of capital* is the weighted average of the costs of the different components of financing—including debt, equity and hybrid securities—used by a firm to fund its financial requirements. In this section, we examine the process of estimating the cost of financing other than equity and the weights for computing the cost of capital.

(i) Calculating the Cost of Debt. The *cost of debt* measures the current cost to the firm of borrowing funds to finance projects. In general terms, it is determined by the following variables:

- *The riskless rate.* As the riskless increases, the cost of debt for firms will also increase.
- *The default risk (and associated default spread) of the company.* As the default risk of a firm increases, the cost of borrowing money will also increase.
- *The tax advantage associated with debt.* Since interest is tax deductible, the after-tax cost of debt is a function of the tax rate. The tax benefit that accrues from paying interest makes the after-tax cost of debt lower than the pretax cost. Furthermore, this benefit increases as the tax rate increases.

$$\text{After-tax cost of debt} = \text{Pretax cost of debt}\ (1 - \text{tax rate})$$

The simplest scenario for estimating the cost of debt occurs when a firm has long term bonds outstanding that are widely traded. The market price of the bond, in conjunction with its coupon and maturity can serve to compute a yield that we use as the cost of debt. Alternatively, for firms that have bonds that are rated, we can estimate their costs of debt by using their ratings and associated default spreads. Thus, a firm with a AA rating can be expected to have a cost of debt approximately 0.50% higher than the treasury bond rate, since this is the spread typically paid by AA rated firms.

What happens when, as is often the case with emerging market companies, when you have firms that have neither bonds outstanding nor a bond rating. You have two choices.:

1. *Recent borrowing history.* Many firms that are not rated still borrow money from banks and other financial institutions. By looking at the most recent borrowings made by a firm, we can get a sense of the types of default spreads being charged the firm and use these spreads to come up with a cost of debt.
2. *Estimate a synthetic rating.* An alternative is to play the role of a ratings agency and assign a rating to a firm based on its financial ratios; this rating is called a *synthetic rating*. To make this assessment, we begin with rated firms and examine the financial characteristics shared by firms within each ratings class. To illustrate, Exhibit 9.7 lists the range of interest coverage ratios for small manufacturing firms in each S&P ratings class for the United States.

Now consider a small firm that is not rated but has an interest coverage ratio of 6.15. Based on this ratio, we would assess a "synthetic rating" of A for the firm.

In general, there are two problems we run into when we use this approach to esti-

Interest Coverage Ratio	Rating	Spread
>12.5	AAA	0.75%
9.5–12.5	AA	1.00%
7.5–9.5	A+	1.50%
6–7.5	A	1.80%
4.5–6	A–	2.00%
3.5–4.5	BBB	2.25%
3–3.5	BB	3.50%
2.5–3	B+	4.75%
2–2.5	B	6.50%
1.5–2	B–	8.00%
1.25–1.5	CCC	10.00%
0.8–1.25	CC	11.50%
0.5–0.8	C	12.70%
<0.5	D	14.00%

[a]This table was developed in 1999 and 2000, by listing out all rated firms, with market capitalization lower than $2 billion, and their interest coverage ratios, and then sorting firms based on their bond ratings. The ranges were adjusted to eliminate outliers and to prevent overlapping ranges.

Exhibit 9.7. Interest Coverage Ratios and Ratings: Low Market Cap Firms.[a]

mate the synthetic ratings for emerging market firms. The first is that the synthetic ratings may be skewed by differences in interest rates between the emerging market and the United States. Interest coverage ratios will usually decline as interest rates increase and it may be far more difficult for a company in an emerging market to achieve the interest coverage ratios of companies in developed markets. This can be fixed fairly simply by either modifying the tables developed using U.S. firms or restating the interest expenses (and interest coverage ratios) in dollar terms. The second problem is the existence of country default risk overhanging the cost of debt of firms in that market. Conservative analysts often assume that companies in a country cannot borrow at a rate lower than the country can borrow at. With this reasoning, the cost of debt for an emerging market company will include the country default spread for the country.

$$\begin{aligned}\text{Cost of debt}_{\text{Emerging market company}} &= \text{Riskless rate} + \text{Country default spread}\\ &\quad + \text{Company default spread}_{\text{Synthetic rating}}\end{aligned}$$

The counter to this argument is that companies may be safer than the countries that they operate in and that they bear only a portion or perhaps even none of the country default spread.

ILLUSTRATION 3: ESTIMATING A COST OF DEBT FOR EMBRAER.

As an example, consider Embraer, the Brazilian aerospace company. To estimate Embraer's cost of debt, we first estimate a synthetic rating for the firm. Based upon its operating income of $810 million and interest expenses of $28 million in 2000, we arrived at an interest coverage ratio of 28.93 and an AAA rating. While the default spread for AAA rated bonds in the United States was only 0.75%, there is the added consideration that Embraer is a Brazilian firm. Since the Brazilian government bond traded at a spread of 5.37% at the time of the analysis, you could argue that every Brazilian company should pay this premium, in addition to its own default spread. With this reasoning, the pretax cost of debt for Embraer in U.S. dollars (assuming a Treasury bond rate is 5%) can be calculated:

$$\text{Cost of Debt} = \text{Risk-free rate} + \text{Default spread for country} + \text{Default spread for firm}$$

$$= 5\% + 5.37\% + 0.75\% = 11.12\%$$

Using a marginal tax rate of 33%, we can estimate an after-tax cost of debt for Embraer:

$$\text{After-tax cost of debt} = 11.12\%(1 - .33) = 7.45\%$$

With this approach, the cost of debt for a firm can never be lower than the cost of debt for the country in which it operates. Note, though, that Embraer gets a significant portion of its revenues in dollars from contracts with non-Brazilian airlines. Consequently, it could reasonably argue that it is less exposed to risk than the Brazilian government and should therefore command a lower cost of debt.

(ii) Calculating the Weights of Debt and Equity Components. The final step in computing a cost of capital is to compute the weights of debt and equity components in a firm's capital. Before we discuss how best to estimate weights, we define what we include in debt. We then make the argument that weights used should be based upon market value and not book value. This is so because the cost of capital measures the cost of issuing securities—stocks as well as bonds—to finance firms and these securities are issued at market value, not at book value.

(iii) What is debt? The answer to this question may seem obvious since the balance sheet for a firm shows the outstanding liabilities of a firm. There are, however, limitations with using these liabilities as debt in the cost of capital computation. The first is that some of the liabilities on a firm's balance sheet, such as accounts payable and supplier credit, are not interest bearing. Consequently, applying an after-tax cost of debt to these items can provide a misleading view of the true cost of capital for a firm. The second is that there are items off the balance sheet that create fixed commitments for the firm and provide the same tax deductions that interest payments on debt do. The most prominent of these off-balance-sheet items are rental and lease commitments. In most emerging markets, leases are treated as operating expenses rather than financing expenses. Consider, though, what an operating lease involves. A retail firm leases a store space for 12 years and enters into a lease agreement with the owner of the space agreeing to pay a fixed amount each year for that period. We do not see much difference between this commitment and borrowing money from a bank and agreeing to pay off the bank loan over 12 years in equal annual installments.

There are therefore two adjustments we will make when we estimate how much debt a firm has outstanding:

1. We will consider only interest bearing debt rather than all liabilities. We will include both short term and long term borrowings in debt.

2. We will also capitalize operating leases and treat these expenditures as financing expenses.

(iv) Book Value versus Market Value Debt Ratios. There are three standard arguments against using market value and none of them are convincing. First, there are some financial managers who argue that book value is more reliable than market value because it is not as volatile. While it is true that book value does not change as much as market value, this is more a reflection of book value's weakness rather than its strength since the true value of the firm changes over time as both firm-specific and market information is revealed. We would argue that market value, with its volatility, is a much better reflection of true value than book value.[14]

Second, the defenders of book value also suggest that using book value rather than market value is a more conservative approach to estimating debt ratios. This assumes that market value debt ratios are always lower than book value debt ratios, an assumption not based on fact. Furthermore, even if the market value debt ratios are lower than the book value ratios, the cost of capital calculated using book value ratios will be lower than those calculated using market value ratios, making them less conservative estimates, not more. To illustrate this point, assume that the market value debt ratio is 10%, while the book value debt ratio is 30%, for a firm with a cost of equity of 15% and an after-tax cost of debt of 5%. The cost of capital can be calculated as follows:

$$\text{With market value debt ratios: } 15\%(0.9) + 5\%(0.1) = 14\%$$

$$\text{With book value debt ratios: } 15\%(.7) + 5\%(.3) = 12\%$$

Third, it is claimed that lenders will not lend on the basis of market value, but this claim again seems to be based more upon perception than fact. Any homeowner who has taken a second mortgage on a house that has appreciated in value knows that lenders do lend on the basis of market value. It is true, however, that the greater the perceived volatility in the market value of an asset, the lower is the borrowing potential on that asset.

(v) Estimating the Market Values of Equity and Debt. The market value of equity is generally the number of shares outstanding times the current stock price. If there are other equity claims in the firm such as warrants and management option, these should also be valued and added on to the value of the equity in the firm.

The market value of debt is usually more difficult to obtain directly, since very few firms have all their debt in the form of bonds outstanding trading in the market. Many firms have nontraded debt, such as bank debt, which is specified in book value terms but not market value terms. A simple way to convert book value debt into market value debt is to treat the entire debt on the books as one coupon bond, with a coupon set equal to the interest expenses on all the debt and the maturity set equal to the face-value weighted average maturity of the debt, and then to value this coupon bond at

---

[14]There are some who argue that stock prices are much more volatile than the underlying true value. Even if this argument is justified (and it has not conclusively been shown to be so), the difference between market value and true value is likely to be much smaller than the difference between book value and true value.

the current cost of debt for the company. Thus, the market value of $1 billion in debt, with interest expenses of $60 million and a maturity of 6 years, when the current cost of debt is 7.5% can be estimated as follows:

$$\text{Estimated market value of debt} = 60\left(\frac{1 - \dfrac{1}{1.075^6}}{0.075}\right) + \frac{1{,}000}{1.075^6} = \$\,930 \text{ million}$$

(vi) Gross Debt versus Net Debt. Gross debt refers to all debt outstanding in a firm. Net debt is the difference between gross debt and the cash balance of the firm. For instance, a firm with $1.25 billion in interest bearing debt outstanding and a cash balance of $1 billion has a net debt balance of $250 million. The practice of netting cash against debt is common in both Latin America and Europe, and the debt ratios are usually estimated using net debt.

It is generally safer to value a firm based on gross debt outstanding and to add the cash balance outstanding to the value of operating assets to arrive at the firm value. The interest payment on total debt is then entitled to the tax benefits of debt and we can assess the effect of whether the company invests its cash balances efficiently on value.

In some cases, especially when firms maintain large cash balances as a matter of routine, analysts prefer to work with net debt ratios. If we choose to use net debt ratios, we have to be consistent all the way through the valuation. To begin, the beta for the firm should be estimated using a net debt ratio rather than a gross debt ratio. The cost of equity that emerges from the beta estimate can be used to estimate a cost of capital, but the market value weight on debt should be based upon net debt. Once we discount the cash flows of the firm at the cost of capital, we should not add back cash. Instead, we should subtract the net debt outstanding to arrive at the estimated value of equity.

Implicitly, when we net cash against debt to arrive at net debt ratios, we are assuming that cash and debt have roughly similar risk. While this assumption may not be outlandish when analyzing highly rated firms, it becomes much shakier when debt becomes riskier. For instance, the debt in a BB rated firm is much riskier than the cash balance in the firm and netting out one against the other can provide a misleading view of the firm's default risk. In general, using net debt ratios will overstate the value of riskier firms.

(vii) Estimating the Cost of Capital. Since a firm can raise its money from three sources—equity, debt, and preferred stock —the cost of capital is defined as the weighted average of each of these costs. The cost of equity (k_e) reflects the riskiness of the equity investment in the firm, the after-tax cost of debt (k_d) is a function of the default risk of the firm and the cost of preferred stock (k_{ps}) is a function of its intermediate standing in terms of risk between debt and equity. The weights on each of these components should reflect their market value proportions since these proportions best measure how the existing firm is being financed. Thus, if E, D, and PS are the market values of equity, debt, and preferred stock, respectively, the cost of capital can be written as follows:

$$\text{Cost of capital} = k_e\left(\frac{E}{D + E + PS}\right) + k_d\left(\frac{D}{D + E + PS}\right) + k_{ps}\left(\frac{PS}{D + E + PS}\right)$$

ILLUSTRATION 4: ESTIMATING A BOTTOM-UP BETA FOR TITAN CEMENTS—JANUARY 2000.

To estimate a cost of capital for Embraer, we again draw on the estimates of cost of equity and cost of debt we obtained in prior illustrations. The cost of capital will be estimated using net debt all the way through (for the levered betas, interest coverage ratios and debt ratios) and in U.S. dollars:

- Cost of equity = 18.86%
- After-tax cost of debt = 7.45%
- Market value of debt = 1,328 million BR
- Cash and marketable securities = 1,105 million BR
- Market value of equity = 9,084 million BR

The cost of capital for Embraer is estimated below:

$$\text{Net Debt} = 1{,}328 \text{ million} - 1{,}105 \text{ million} = 223 \text{ million}$$

$$\text{Cost of Capital} = 18.86\%\left(\frac{9084}{9084 + 223}\right) + 7.45\%\left(\frac{223}{9084 + 223}\right) = 18.59\%$$

To convert this into a nominal real cost of capital, we would apply the differential inflation rates (10% in Brazil and 2% in the United States):

$$\text{Cost of capital}_{\text{Nominal BR}} = (1 + \text{Cost of Capital}_{\$})\left(\frac{\text{Inflation rate}_{\text{Brazil}}}{\text{Inflation rate}_{\text{U.S.}}}\right) - 1$$

$$= (1.1859)\left(\frac{1.10}{1.02}\right) - 1 = 27.89\%$$

9.3 ESTIMATING CASH FLOWS. To estimate cash flows for a firm, we usually begin with its accounting earnings and adjust their earnings for noncash charges and reinvestment needs. While the equation for computing free cash flows to the firm may be identical for emerging market and developed companies, there are a few more roadblocks that we run into when we look at emerging market companies.

(a) Earnings. The income statement for a firm provides measures of both the operating and equity income of the firm in the form of the earnings before interest and taxes (EBIT) and net income. When valuing firms, there are two important considerations in using this measure. One is to obtain as updated an estimate as possible, given how much these firms change over time. The second is that reported earnings at these firms may bear little resemblance to true earnings because of limitations in accounting rules and the firms' own actions. On both measures, you may have special problems when valuing emerging market firms.

(i) Importance of Updating Earnings. Firms reveal their earnings in their financial statements and annual reports to stockholders. Annual reports are released only at the end of a firm's financial year, but you are often required to value firms all through the year. Consequently, the last annual report that is available for a firm being valued can contain information that is sometimes six or nine months old. In the case of firms that

are changing rapidly over time, it is dangerous to base value estimates on information that is this old. Instead, use more recent information. While you have the option of using quarterly reports in the United States, there are many emerging markets when accounting statements are provided semiannually or annually. When valuing firms in these markets, analysts may have to draw on unofficial sources to update their valuations.

(ii) Correcting Earnings Misclassification and for Differences in Accounting Standards. The expenses incurred by a firm can be categorized into three groups:

1. Operating expenses are expenses that generate benefits for the firm only in the current period. For instance, the fuel used by an airline in the course of its flights is an operating expense, as is the labor cost for an automobile company associated with producing vehicles.
2. Capital expenses are expenses that generate benefits over multiple periods. For example, the expense associated with building and outfitting a new factory for an automobile manufacturer is a capital expense, since it will generate several years of revenues.
3. Financial expenses are expenses associated with nonequity capital raised by a firm. Thus, the interest paid on a bank loan would be a financial expense.

The operating income for a firm, measured correctly, should be equal to its revenues less its operating expenses. Neither financial nor capital expenses should be included in the operating expenses in the year that they occur, though capital expenses may be depreciated or amortized over the period that the firm obtains benefits from the expenses. The net income of a firm should be its revenues less both its operating and financial expenses. No capital expenses should be deducted to arrive at net income. It is at this stage that differences in accounting standards come into play. Practices vary widely across countries on how items are categorized. As noted above, leases are treated as operating expenses in most emerging markets. In addition, the treatment of research and development (R&D) expenses, which are really capital expenses, varies across countries. In some countries, the practice is similar to the United States and all R&D expenses are treated as operating expenses. In other countries, some R&D expenses are capitalized. If you are doing discounted cash flow valuation, you often have to recategorize these expenses to come up with a measure of true operating income. If you are comparing earnings multiples across companies in different markets, you have to correct for differences in accounting standards before making comparisons.

(iii) Correcting for Earnings Manipulation. Firms try to manage their earnings and in some cases manipulate them. While this is true for both developed market and emerging market companies, the weakness of accounting standards and the laxity of the legal system make earnings management and manipulation a much more serious problem in emerging markets. To the extent that firms manage or manipulate earnings, you have to be cautious about using the current year's earnings as a base for projections. In particular, you have to look at two issues:

1. *Extraordinary, recurring and unusual items.* The rule for estimating both operating and net income is simple. The operating income that is used as a base for

projections should reflect continuing operations and should not include any items that are one-time or extraordinary. Putting this statement to practice is often a challenge because there are four types of extraordinary items:

i. *One-time expenses or income that is truly one time.* A large restructuring charge that has occurred only once in the last 10 years would be a good example. These expenses can be backed out of the analysis and the operating and net income calculated without them.

ii. *Expenses and income that do not occur every year but seem to recur at regular intervals.* Consider, for instance, a firm that has taken a restructuring charge every 3 years for the last 12 years. While not conclusive, this would suggest that the extraordinary expenses are really ordinary expenses that are being bundled by the firm and taken once every three years. Ignoring such an expense would be dangerous because the expected operating income in future years would be overstated. What would make sense would be to take the expense and spread it out on an annual basis. Thus, if the restructuring expense for every 3 years has amounted to $1.5 billion, on average, the operating income for the current year should be reduced by $0.5 billion to reflect the annual charge due to this expense.

iii. *Expenses and income that recur every year but with considerable volatility.* The best way to deal with such items is to normalize them by averaging the expenses across time and reducing this year's income by this amount.

iv. *Items that recur every year that change signs—positive in some years and negative in others.* Consider, for instance, the effect of foreign currency translations on income. For a firm in the United States, the effect may be negative in years in which the dollar gets stronger and positive in years in which the dollar gets weaker. The most prudent thing to do with these expenses would be to ignore them. This is because income gains or losses from exchange rate movements are likely to reverse themselves over time, and making them part of permanent income can yield misleading estimates of value.

To differentiate among these items requires that you have access to a firm's financial history. For young firms in emerging markets, this may not be available, making it more difficult to draw the line between expenses that should be ignored, expenses that should be normalized and expenses that should be considered in full.

2. *Income from Investments and Cross Holdings.* Emerging market companies often have complex cross holding structures and substantial holdings of marketable securities. The income from such holdings can often exceed the operating income of the firm, and in some cases, the two types of income are mingled. Investments in marketable securities generate two types of income. The first takes the form of interest or dividends and the second is the capital gains (losses) associated with selling securities at prices that are different from their cost bases. In our view, neither type of income should be considered part of the earnings used in valuation for any firm other than a financial service firm that defines its business as the buying and selling of securities (such as a hedge fund). The interest earned on marketable securities should be ignored when valuing the firm, since it is far easier to add the market value of these securities at the end of the process rather than mingle them with other assets. Firms that have a substantial number of cross holdings in other firms will often report increases or decreases to earnings reflecting these holdings. The effect on earnings will vary depending on how the holding is categorized. Often, you will see them categorized into one of the following:

- A minority, passive holding, where only the dividends received from the holding are recorded in income.
- A minority, active interest, where the portion of the net income (or loss) from the subsidiary is shown in the income statement as an adjustment to net income (but not to operating income).
- A majority, active interest, where the income statements are consolidated and the entire operating income of the subsidiary (or holding) are shown as part of the operating income of the firm. In such cases, the net income is usually adjusted for the portion of the subsidiary owned by others (minority interests).

The safest route to take with the first two types of holdings is to ignore the income shown from the subsidiary when valuing a firm, to value the subsidiary separately and to add it on to the value obtained for the parent. As a simple example, consider a firm (Holding Inc.) that generates \$100 million in after-tax cash flows from its operating assets and assume that these cash flows will grow at 5% a year forever. In addition, assume that the firm owns 10% of another firm (Subsidiary Inc.) with after-tax cash flows of \$50 million growing at 4% a year forever. Finally, assume that the cost of capital for both firms is 10%. The firm value for Holding Inc. can be estimated as follows.

$$\text{Value of operating assets of Holding Inc.} = 100\left(\frac{1.05}{0.10 - 0.05}\right) = \$\,2{,}100 \text{ million}$$

$$\text{Value of operating assets of Subsidiary Inc.} = 50\left(\frac{1.04}{0.10 - 0.04}\right) = \$\,867 \text{ million}$$

$$\text{Value of Holding company's share of Subsidiary Inc} = \$\,2{,}100 + 0.10(867)$$

$$= \$\,2{,}187 \text{ million}$$

When earnings are consolidated, you can value the combined firm with the consolidated income statement and then subtract out the value of the minority holdings. To do this, though, you have to assume that the two firms are in the same business and are of equivalent risk since the same cost of capital will be applied to both firm's cash flows. Alternatively, you can strip the entire operating income of the subsidiary from the consolidated operating income and follow the process laid out above to value the holding.

(iv) Warning Signs in Earnings Reports. The most troubling thing about earnings reports is that we are often blindsided not by the items that get reported (such as extraordinary charges) but by the items that are hidden in other categories. The following checklist should be reviewed regarding any earnings report to gauge the possibility of such shocks:

- Is earnings growth outstripping revenue growth by a large magnitude year after year? This may well be a sign of increased efficiency, but when the differences are large and continue year after year, you should wonder about the source of these efficiencies.

- Do one-time or nonoperating charges to earnings occur frequently? The charge itself might be categorized differently each year—an inventory charge one year, a restructuring charge the next, and so on. While this may be just bad luck, it may also reflect a conscious effort by a company to move regular operating expenses into these non-operating items.
- Do any of the operating expenses, as a percent of revenues, swing wildly from year to year? This may suggest that the expense item (say sales, general and administrative [SG&A]) includes nonoperating expenses that should really be stripped out and reported separately.
- Does the company manage to beat analyst estimates quarter after quarter by a cent or two? Not every company is a Microsoft. Companies that beat estimates year after year are involved in earnings management and are moving earnings across time periods. As growth levels off, this practice can catch up with them.
- Does a substantial proportion of the revenues come from subsidiaries or related holdings? While the sales may be legitimate, the prices set may allow the firm to move earnings from one unit to the other and give a misleading view of true earnings at the firm.
- Are accounting rules for valuing inventory or depreciation changed frequently?
- Are acquisitions followed by miraculous increases in earnings? An acquisition strategy is difficult to make successful in the long term. A firm that claims instant success from such as strategy requires scrutiny.
- Is working capital ballooning out as revenues and earning surge? This can sometimes let us pinpoint those firms that generate revenues by lending to their own customers.

None of these factors, by themselves, suggest that we lower earnings for these firms but combinations of the factors can be viewed as a warning signal that the earnings statement needs to be held up to higher scrutiny.

(b) Reinvestment Needs. The cash flow to the firm is computed after reinvestments. Two components go into estimating reinvestment. The first is *net capital expenditures*, which is the difference between capital expenditures and depreciation. The other is *investments in noncash working capital*. With technology firms, again, these numbers can be difficult to estimate. For emerging market firms, these numbers can sometimes be difficult to find in the financial statements and even when found, they are often volatile.

(i) Net Capital Expenditures. In estimating net capital expenditures, we generally deduct depreciation from capital expenditures. The rationale is that the positive cash flows from depreciation pay for at least a portion of capital expenditures and it is only the excess that represents a drain on the firm's cash flows. With emerging market companies, forecasting these expenditures can be difficult for three reasons. The first is that many emerging market companies provide little or very diffuse information about their capital expenditures. Many provide no or very sketchy statements of cash flows, bundling capital expenditures with investments in financial assets. The second is that firms often incur capital spending in chunks—a large investment in one year can be fol-

lowed by small investments in subsequent years. The third is that acquisitions are not classified by accountants as capital expenditures. For firms that grow primarily through acquisition, this will result in an understatement of the net capital expenditures.

Firms seldom have smooth capital expenditure streams. Firms can go through periods when capital expenditures are very high (as is the case when a new product is introduced or a new plant built) followed by periods of relatively light capital expenditures. Consequently, when estimating the capital expenditures to use for forecasting future cash flows, you should normalize capital expenditures. The simplest normalization technique is to average capital expenditures over a number of years. For instance, you could estimate the average capital expenditures over the last four or five years for a manufacturing firm and use that number rather than the capital expenditures from the most recent year. By doing so, you could capture the fact that the firm may invest in a new plant every four years. If instead, you had used the capital expenditures from the most recent year, you would either have overestimated capital expenditures (if the firm built a new plant that year) or underestimated it (if the plant had been built in an earlier year). There are two measurement issues that you will need to confront. One relates to the number of years of history that you should use. The answer will vary across firms and will depend upon how infrequently the firm makes large investments. The other is on the question of whether averaging capital expenditures over time requires us to average depreciation as well. Since depreciation is spread out over time, the need for normalization should be much smaller. In addition, the tax benefits received by the firm reflect the actual depreciation in the most recent year, rather than an average depreciation over time. Unless depreciation is as volatile as capital expenditures, it may make more sense to leave depreciation untouched.

In estimating capital expenditures, you should not distinguish between internal investments (which are usually categorized as capital expenditures in cash flow statements) and external investments (which are acquisitions). The capital expenditures of a firm, therefore, need to include acquisitions. Since firms seldom make acquisitions every year and each acquisition has a different price tag, the point about normalizing capital expenditures applies even more strongly to this item.

ILLUSTRATION 5: ESTIMATING NORMALIZED NET CAPITAL EXPENDITURES—RELIANCE INDIA.

Reliance Industries is one of India's largest firms and is involved in a multitude of businesses ranging from chemicals to textiles. The firm makes substantial investments in these businesses and Exhibit 9.8 summarizes the capital expenditures and depreciation for the period 1997–2000.

The firm's capital expenditures have been volatile but its depreciation has been trending upward. There are two ways in which we can normalize the net capital expenditures. One is to take the average net capital expenditure over the four year period, which would result in net capital expenditures of INR 13,639 million. The problem with doing this, however, is that the depreciation implicitly being used in the calculation is INR 8,027 million, which is well below the actual depreciation of INR 12,784. A better way to normalize capital expenditures is to use the average capital expenditure over the four-year period (INR 21,166) and depreciation from the current year (INR 12,784) to arrive at a normalized net capital expenditure value of

$$\text{Normalized net capital expenditures} = 21{,}166 - 12{,}784 = \text{INR } 8{,}882 \text{ million}$$

Year	Capital Expenditures	Depreciation	Net Capital Expenditures
1997	INR 24,077	INR 4,101	INR 19,976
1998	INR 23,247	INR 6,673	INR 16,574
1999	INR 18,223	INR 8,550	INR 9,673
2000	INR 21,118	INR 12,784	INR 8,334
Average	INR 21,666	INR 8,027	INR 13,639

Exhibit 9.8. Capital Expenditures and Depreciation: Reliance India (Millions of Indian Rupees).

Note that the normalization did not make much difference in this case because the actual net capital expenditures in 2000 amounted to INR 8,334 million.

(ii) Investment in Working Capital. Increases in working capital tie up more cash and hence generate negative cash flows. Conversely, decreases in working capital release cash and positive cash flows. Working capital is usually defined to be the difference between current assets and current liabilities. However, we will modify that definition when we measure working capital for valuation purposes.

- We will back out cash and investments in marketable securities from current assets. This is because cash, especially in large amounts, is invested by firms in Treasury bills, short-term government securities, or commercial paper. While the return on these investments may be lower than what the firm may make on its real investments, they represent a fair return for riskless investments. Unlike inventory, accounts receivable, and other current assets, cash then earns a fair return and should not be included in measures of working capital. Are there exceptions to this rule? When valuing a firm that has to maintain a large cash balance for day-to-day operations or a firm that operates in a market in a poorly developed banking system, you could consider the cash needed for operations as a part of working capital.
- We will also back out all interest-bearing debt—short-term debt and the portion of long-term debt that is due in the current period—from the current liabilities. This debt will be considered when computing cost of capital and it would be inappropriate to count it twice.

While we can estimate the noncash working capital change fairly simply for any year using financial statements, this estimate has to be used with caution. Changes in noncash working capital are unstable, with big increases in some years followed by big decreases in the following years. To ensure that the projections are not the result of an unusual base year, you should tie the changes in working capital to expected changes in revenues or costs of goods sold at the firm over time. The noncash working capital as a percent of revenues can be used, in conjunction with expected revenue changes each period, to estimate projected changes in noncash working capital over time. You can obtain the non-cash working capital as a percent of revenues by looking at the firm's history or at industry standards.

9.4 CONCLUSION. The value of a firm is a function of the same inputs—cash flows and discount rates—for an emerging market firm as it is for a developed market firm. There are, however, thorny estimation issues that can make emerging market firm valuation much more complicated than the valuation of developed market firms. We considered first the estimation of a discount rate in absence of a riskfree rate and the paucity of historical information. When the local government has default risk, you can either try to estimate a riskless rate or do your valuation in a different currency—one in which a riskless rate does exist. To estimate risk premiums, you can also fall back on a premium estimated for a mature market and adjust it for country risk or you can estimate an implied premium. For betas, the best solution is to use the betas of comparable firms, even though they might be traded on other markets. In the second part of this paper, we examined how best to estimate cash flows. The earnings reported by emerging market firms may have to be adjusted both for the misclassification of items (like leases) and for manipulation. To estimate reinvestment needs, when both net capital expenditures and working capital needs are volatile, you should look at normalized values.

SOURCES AND SUGGESTED REFERENCES

Booth, L. "Estimating the Equity Risk Premium and Equity Costs: New Way of Looking at Old Data." *Journal of Applied Corporate Finance*, Vol. 12, No. 1, 1999, pp. 100–112.

Bruner, R. F., K. M. Eades, R. S. Harris, and R. C. Higgins. *Best Practices in Estimating the Cost of Capital: Survey and Synthesis*. Financial Practice and Education, 1998, pp. 14–28.

Chan, K. C., G. A. Karolyi, and R. M. Stulz. "Global Financial Markets and the Risk Premium on U.S. Equity." *Journal of Financial Economics*, Vol. 32, 1992, pp. 132–167.

Damodaran, A. *Investment Valuation* (2nd ed.). New York: John Wiley & Sons, Inc., 2000.

Fama, E. F., and K. R. French. "The Cross-Section of Expected Returns." *Journal of Finance*, Vol. 47, 1992, pp. 427–466.

Godfrey, S., and R. Espinosa. "A Practical Approach to Calculating the Cost of Equity for Investments in Emerging Markets." *Journal of Applied Corporate Finance*, Vol. 9, No. 3, 1996, 80–81.

Ibbotson, R. G., and G. P. Brinson. *Global Investing*. New York: McGraw-Hill, 1993.

Indro, D. C., and W. Y. Lee. " Biases in Arithmetic and Geometric Averages as Estimates of Long-run Expected Returns and Risk Premium." *Financial Management*, Vol. 26, 1997, pp. 81–90.

Mamada, R. S. "The Effect of the Firm's Capital Structure on the Systematic Risk of Common Stock." *Journal of Finance*, Vol. 27, 1972, pp. 435–452.

Stocks, Bonds, Bills and Inflation. Chicago: Ibbotson Associates, 1999.

Stulz, R. M. "Globalization, Corporate Finance, and the Cost of Capital." *Journal of Applied Corporate Finance*, Vol. 12, 1999, pp. 8–25.

CHAPTER 10

BUSINESS FAILURE CLASSIFICATION MODELS: AN INTERNATIONAL SURVEY

Edward I. Altman

New York University

Paul Narayanan

Consultant

CONTENTS

10.1 INTRODUCTION. Business failure identification and early warnings of impending financial crisis are important not only to analysts and practitioners in the United States. Indeed, countries throughout the world, even noncapitalist nations, have been concerned with individual entity performance assessment. Developing countries and smaller economies, as well as the larger industrialized nations of the world, are vitally concerned with avoiding financial crises in the private and public sectors. Some policy makers in smaller nations are particularly concerned with financial panics resulting from failures of individual entities.

From the late 1960s to the present day, numerous studies in the United States were devoted to assessing one's ability to combine publicly available data with statistical classification techniques in order to predict business failure. Studies by Beaver (1966) and Altman (1968) provided the stimulus for numerous other papers. One of the first attempts at modern statistical failure analysis was performed by Tamari (1964). We will not discuss his work here, but we point out its pioneering status. A steady stream of failure prediction papers have appeared in the English literature, and numerous textbooks and monographs include a section or chapter on these models. What has gone relatively unnoticed is the considerable effort made to replicate and extend these models to environments outside the United States. With the exception of two special issues of the *Journal of Banking and Finance* (1984 and 1988), edited by one of the authors of this article, there is no work with which we are familiar that attempts to survey these studies and to comment on their similarities and differences. The purpose of this paper is to do just that.

We survey the works by academics and practitioners in 21 countries and give references to several other studies. This survey will bring together these myriad studies and highlight study designs, innovations, and outcomes that will be of practical value to researchers and practitioners. While the economic forces shaping the outcomes in various countries may diverge, the researchers share a striking similarity in their approach to distress prediction. For example, nearly every study contrasts the profile of failed firms with that of healthier firms to draw conclusions about the coincident factors of failure. Causal studies of failure appear to be comparatively rare.

In several of the countries studied, notably Brazil, France, Canada, Australia, Korea, Mexico, and Italy, one of the authors of this article has participated directly in the construction of a failure classification model. In many cases, we can present an in-depth discussion of the models including individual variable weights. In others, we present the models in more general terms due to the lack of precise documentation in the original article. In general, to make this survey useful to researchers and practitioners alike, we attempt to summarize the contents of the models under the following headings:

- *Modeling techniques used.* While multiple discriminant analysis (MDA) continues to be the most popular technique, researchers have tried other techniques such as multi-nomial logit analysis, probit analysis, recursive partitioning (decision tree analysis), Bayesian discriminant analysis, survival analysis, and neural networks. For a variety of reasons, MDA appears to be a *de facto* standard for comparison of distress prediction models. Where the authors have used a technique other than MDA, they usually have compared its results with those from MDA. It is interesting to note that MDA results continue to compare favorably with the other techniques.
- *Data issues.* The size of the sample used and the sources of data are oftentimes critical in assessing the statistical validity of results as well as in the planning of replication or extension type studies. As in many areas of empirical research, the sophistication of the techniques is often not matched by the availability of good data, especially data on failed firms. This problem tends to be more pronounced in the smaller economies of some of the developed countries and in the case of most developing countries. As is common in all empirical research, the randomness and the size of the sample used are mentioned because they are generally indicative of the degree of confidence that may be placed in the conclusions being drawn.
- *Definition of "failure" and "nonfailure".* Most models employ a sample of two *a priori* groups consisting of "failed" and "nonfailed" firms. Depending on the inclination of the researcher or on the local conditions, the definition of a failure may vary. Some examples are bankruptcy filing by a company, bond default, bank loan default, delisting of a company, government intervention via special financing, and liquidation. Closely tied to the failure event is the date of the event. The quality of almost all conclusions drawn about how "early" the distress prediction was depends upon where the analyst placed the date of failure. The healthy firms' data is, by definition, "censored" data because all that can be said of the healthy firms is that they were healthy at the time the sample was taken. It has been found, for example, that some firms that appear to be Type II errors by a model (healthy firms classified as failures) turned out to have failed at a later time.
- *Test results.* It is customary to expect test statistics (such as the t and F statistics) to indicate the statistical significance of the findings. While this is done to establish a baseline for measurement, it is important to note that useful conclusions may be drawn from even small sample studies. In-sample and Out-of-sample or hold-out results, Type I and Type II results, and analyst-modified results are also reported where available.

(a) Developing and Developed Country Models. The failure prediction models reviewed in this chapter may be broadly grouped into two homogeneous categories: developed country models and developing country models. The classification of a country as a "developing" or a "developed" country in this survey is in the context of failure prediction and may deviate somewhat from the traditional grouping of the country.

The main characteristics of developed country models are: (1) failure prediction studies have a long history, (2) corporate financial data are more readily available, (3) failure is easier to identify because of the existence of bankruptcy laws and banking infrastructures, (4) government intervention is somewhat less, but not nonexistent, and (5) there is a more sophisticated regulation of companies to protect investors. The developing country models are characterized by the relative absence of the above factors. In developing countries, where free market economies have not taken hold, a company's failure is harder to see because of the degree of protection provided by the government. However one may also point to similar practices in developed countries, notably the United Kingdom, Germany, Japan, to a lesser extent, and even the United States on some rare occasions, for example, the case of Chrysler in 1980.

Exhibit 10.1 summarizes the 39 studies from 21 countries included in this survey. We have not included summaries of nonpublished studies although we are aware of several, for example, two from South Africa and several in languages other than English (e.g., Korean).

While we believe this international treatment of failure prediction models is the most comprehensive effort to date, we recognize that some relevant works will possibly be overlooked in this survey and apologize for any omission. Note: The term "author" or "authors" in the succeeding paragraphs pertains to the authors of the respective articles, not to the authors of this review.

(b) Emerging Markets Application. One of the models presented in this chapter was developed by Altman, Hartzell, and Peck (1995) to rate the credit quality of emerging markets corporate debt. We discuss it below in the context of Mexico—one of the prime countries whose companies have tapped the international bond markets in recent years. This application has particular relevance since the vast majority of Mexican, Latin American, and emerging market countries' corporate debt in general, is as yet still unrated by the major rating agencies. The model is a variation on the original Z-Score model developed by Altman (1968).

(c) Altman, Hartzell, and Peck, (1995). Most of the models presented in this chapter are based on data from individual firms in a specific country and the resulting model is unique for that country. The one exception is the model discussed in 10.1 (b) where, as noted, we used a variation on the original Z-Score model to predict distress and bond rating equivalents for emerging market corporate debt. In this case, we advocated that a single model (Altman, Hartzell, and Peck, 1995) could be used in any developing country and possibly for nonmanufacturing industrial firms in the United States, as well.

In all cases, the models discussed are used to analyze individual firms. These models and the techniques used in their development (e.g., discriminant, probit, logit regressions) have become extremely important and relevant as the Bank for International Settlements (BIS) is in the process of recommending that most banks develop internal rate–based models (IRBs) for rating their customers' credit risk. The so-called Basel-2 accords are being debated as we update this article, but it is clear that the resulting IRBs for most banks will be variations of the types of models presented in this chapter.

A potentially important extension of these models is to use them to assess country or

Developed Countries	Japan	Takahashi, Kurokawa & Watase (1979)
		Ko (1982)
	Germany	Stein (1968)
		Beermann (1976)
		Weinrich (1978)
		Gebhardt (1980)
		Fischer (1981)
		von Stein & Ziegler (1984)
		Baetge, Huss & Niehaus (1988)
	England	Taffler & Tisshaw (1977)
		Marais (1979)
		Earl & Marais (1982)
	France	Altman, et al (1973)
		Mader (1975, 1979, 1981)
		Collongues (1977)
		Bontemps (1981)
	Canada	Knight (1979)
		Altman & Lavallee (1981)
	The Netherlands	Bilderbeek (1977)
		van Frederikslust (1978)
		Fire Scoring System (de Breed—1996)
	Spain	Briones, Marín & Cueto (1988)
		Fernández (1988)
	Italy	Cifarelli, Corielli, Foriestieri (1988)
		Altman, Marco & Varetto (1994)
	Australia	Castagna & Matolcsy (1981)
		Izan (1984)
	Greece	Gloubos & Grammatikos (1988)
		Theodossiou & Papoulias (1988)
Developing Countries	Argentina	Swanson & Tybout (1988)
	Brazil	Altman, et al (1979)
	India	Bhatia (1988)
	Ireland	Cahill (1981)
	South Korea	Altman, Kim & Eom (1995)
	Malaysia	Bidin (1988)
	Singapore	Ta and Seah (1988)
	Finland	Suominen (1988)
	Mexico	Altman, Hartzell, and Peck (1995)
	Uruguay	Pascale (1988)
	Turkey	Unal (1988)

Exhibit 10.1. List of International Studies Surveyed.

sovereign risk as well as the classical application for individual firms. Indeed, a 1998 World Bank study analyzed Asian countries after the crisis and concluded that a number of standard financial measures (e.g., firm financial ratio) and the Z-Score model (Altman, 1968) could have been used to aggregate the credit risk of the corporate sectors in each country and realize an effective early warning of the coming financial crisis. The corporate data that was used to calculate Z-Scores was derived from year-end 1996 financials. Countries like South Korea, Thailand, and Indonesia showed unmistakable signs of distress considerably before their meltdown in July 1997 and thereafter. As such, the World Bank study concluded that corporate and sovereign governance were the primary causes of the sovereign risk problems in that era. This "bottom-up" approach to assess country risk, as opposed to the more traditional "top-down" measures (e.g., macroeconomic variable), was, in our opinion, an important contribution.

10.2 JAPAN. In Japan, bankruptcies are concentrated in the small- and medium-size firms, especially those that do not enjoy the protection of an affiliated group of companies. These groups, known as "Keiretsu," usually involve a leading commercial bank and a number of firms in diverse industries. Still, a number of larger firms listed on the first section of the Tokyo Stock Exchange have succumbed to the negative economic reality of failure. A comparison of the business failures in Japan and the United States may be made based on these statistics appearing in the *Failure Record* published by Dun & Bradstreet and *Tokyo Shoko Koshinso*, among others. There have been a number of studies concentrating on failure prediction in Japan—most were built prior to 1984. Although we will discuss just two, the reader can find reference and discussion to at least a half dozen more in Altman (1983).

(a) Takahashi, Kurokawa, and Watase (1984). Using multiple discriminant analysis, over 130 measures on individual firms, 36 pairs of failed and non-failed manufacturing firms listed on the Tokyo Stock Exchange in the period 1962–1976 and 17 different model types, the authors have constructed a failure prediction model using the following measures:

- Net worth/fixed assets
- Current liabilities/assets
- Voluntary reserves plus unappropriated surplus/total assets
- Borrowed expenses (interest)/sales
- Earned surplus
- Increase in residual value/cash sales
- Ordinary profit/total assets
- Value added (sales—variable costs)

The authors suggest that their model could be more accurate than Altman's (1968) because of (1) its simultaneous consideration of data from one, two, and three years prior to failure, (2) its combination of ratios and absolute numbers from financial statements, (3) its utilization of the cash basis of accounting from financial statements as well as the accrual base, and (4) its adjustment of the data when the firm's auditors express an opinion as to the limitations of the reported results (window dressing problem).

It was found that models with several years of data for each firm outperformed a similar model with data from only one year prior to failure. Further, absolute financial statement data contributed to the improved classification accuracy and data from financial reports prepared external to the firm on an accrual basis were more predictive than those prepared from an "investment effect" or cash basis method. Adjusting the data to account for auditor opinion limitations improved the information content of the reported numbers and ratios. A holdout sample of four failed and 44 nonfailed firms was tested with the selected model. The four failed firms went bankrupt in 1977, that is, the year after the last year used in the original model.

One problem with the above model might be the use of several years of data for the same firm in order to construct a model. The authors apparently were aware of this problem but felt it was not serious. While this technique may be superior to the sometimes-advocated technique of utilizing several models, each based on a different year's data (e.g., Deakin [1972]), it still remains that the observations are not independent from each other. That is, while the 36 firms are independently drawn observations, the three years of data for each firm are not.

The accuracy of this model on the original and holdout samples was simulated based on various cutoff score criteria. The Type I error was found to be quite low for the original sample (range of 0.0% to 16.7% error rates) and virtually nil on the very small four-firm holdout failed firm sample. The Type II error rates ranged greatly, from 0.0% to 52.8%, indicating the tradeoff between Type I and Type 11 errors as one varies the cutoff score.

The authors spend considerable effort to discuss the derivation of cutoff scores based on various assumptions of prior probabilities and cost of errors. In essence, Takahashi et al. simulate various assumptions and leave the choice of a cutoff score up to the individual user.

(b) Ko (1982). Ko's sample included 41 pairs of bankrupt and nonbankrupt entities from 1960 through 1980. Several accounting corrections, adjustments, and transformations, in addition to variable trends, were applied to the data set in order to reduce the biases held to be inherent in conventional Japanese reporting practices. He compared the standard linear model design against a model with first order interactions and, also, a quadratic model. He also examined a discriminant model using factor analysis for orthogonal variable transformation. On the basis of classification results, a five-variable linear independent model, without the orthogonal transformations, was selected as the best model; it yielded a 82.9% correct classification rate by Lachenbruch (1967) tests versus a 90.8% for the original sample set. It is interesting to note that the linear interaction design appeared best on the basis of group separations potential, but not for classification accuracy.

Ko found, with respect to the variables of the model, that each sign was in agreement with each variable's economic meaning and that three of the variables are similar to those in Altman's 1968 model. They are: EBIT/sales, working capital/total debt, and market equity/total debt. A fourth variable in this model is an inventory turnover change ratio. His last ratio was the standard deviation of net income over four periods. The final standardized coefficient model is of the form:

$$Z_j = 0.868X_1 + 0.198X_2 - .048X_3 + 0.436X_4 + 0.115X_5$$

where

X_1 = EBIT/sales
X_2 = inventory turnover two years prior/inventory turnover three years prior
X_3 = standard error of net income (four years)
X_4 = working capital/total debt
X_5 = market value equity/total debt
Z_j = Z-score (Japanese model)

The standardized form results in a zero cutoff score; that is, any score greater than zero indicates a healthy situation, with probability of classification of bankruptcy less than 0.5, and probabilities greater than 0.5 for negative scores.

10.3 SWITZERLAND

(a) Weibel (1973). While bankruptcy classification and its many implications have interested researchers in Germany for many years, the earliest major work published in German was performed in Switzerland by Weibel (1973). He constructed a sample of 36 failed Swiss firms from 1960 to 1971 and matched them to a like number of non-failed firms in terms of age, size, and line of business. Using univariate statistical parametric and nonparametric tests, Weibel analyzed ratios of these two groups in much the same way that Beaver (1967) did. He found that many of the individual ratios were non-normal and so he abandoned multivariate tests [We have often referred (Altman et al., 1977) to the non-normality problem which exists in many economic and financial data sets but we prefer to test the robustness of models using such data rather than abandoning the tests. We do observe that some European researchers have found multivariate studies suspect due to the non-normality properties of financial measures].

Out of 41 original ratios, Weibel selected 20 for dichotomous comparisons. He utilized cluster analysis to reduce collinearity and arrived at the conclusion that six ratios were especially effective in discriminating among the paired groups. Three ratios were types of liquidity measures with one (near monetary resource assets-current liabilities/operating expenditures prior to depreciation) performing best. He also found that inventory turnover and debt/asset ratios were good individual predictors. He examined the overlapping range of individual ratios for the two groups and presented some *ad hoc* rules for identifying failures. He then divided the observations into three risk groups. The low-risk group had all six ratios in the interdecile range of good firms; high-risk firms had at least three ratios in the interdecile range of failed companies; and a final category was identified where the firm does not fall into either of the other two groupings. Weibel's results were quite accurate in the classification stage; we have no documentation on how his "model" performed on holdout tests and what has been the evolution of models in Switzerland since his original work.

10.4 GERMANY

(a) Beerman (1976). Many studies in Germany have investigated the causes and problems of insolvencies, especially for financial organizations. Beerman (1976) published one of the first German statistical classification models for insolvency analysis. He examined matched groups of 21 firms that operated or failed in 1966 through 1971. Applying dichotomous and linear discriminant tests, he analyzed 10 ratios encompassing profitability, cash flow, fixed asset growth, leverage, and turnover. His results, using the difference in means dichotomous test, were mixed, with one ratio type (profitability) yielding quite respectable results. The other ratios were far less impressive on a univariate basis.

Beerman advocates using discriminant analysis, and his 10-ratio model yielded classification error rates of 9.5%, 19.0%, 28.6%, and 38.1% for the four years prior to failure. He does not indicate which model to use, and the coefficients of each measure were quite unstable in the four different year models. Also, we are given no indication of holdout test results or predictive accuracy and, due to the small sample, we do not have confirming evidence of the model(s) reliability.

(b) Weinrich (1978). Weinrich's (1978) book, from his dissertation, attempted to construct risk classes in order to predict insolvency. His sample of failed firms was considerably larger (44) than Beerman's, concentrating on small and intermediate-size firms, with average sales of DM 4 million (less than $2 million), that failed from 1969 through 1975. Weinrich considered three consecutive annual financial statements (Years 2 through 4 prior to failure) but did not utilize the one statement closest to insolvency. This is a marked difference from most of the other models we have studied.

Weinrich abandoned the use of parametric classification techniques because of his feeling that many assumptions were violated (normality, variance homogeneity of groups, and high correlation amongst the variables). His linear discriminant models were quite good in terms of classification accuracy (11% error for Year 2, 15.7% and 21.9% for Years 3 and 4, respectively).

Weinrich did use factor analysis and found the technique useful, indicating at least six different factors that explained 80% of the variance of the ratios. He then devised a model of credit-worthiness that contained eight relatively independent ratios and utilized both univariate and multivariate methods. A point evaluation system was devised based on quartile values of good and bad firms. For example, a net worth/debt ratio over 43.3% receives the best (lowest) point value. A firm with significant insolvency potential is one with 24 points or more (an average of three for each of the eight ratios). This arbitrary point system correctly classified over 90% of the failed firms two years prior to failure, but was only 60% accurate three years prior. The Type II error rate was quite high, averaging well over 20% in each year. Weinrich advocated the use of trend analysis of the point system as well as the point estimate.

(c) Gebhardt (1980). Gebhardt (1980) compared dichotomous and multivariate classification tests of samples of failed and nonfailed firms based on models constructed before and after the 1965 Financial Statement Reform Law. The earlier model contained 13 matched pairs of industrial firms and the post-1965 model contained 28 pairs. He utilized a very large number of possible financial indicators which were reduced to 41 ratios for the dichotomous tests. He also incorporated crude measures of misclassification costs and tested his results with the Lachenbruch (1967) holdout test procedure. Gebhardt, like others, felt that the non-normality of some ratios implied the use of nonparametric procedures but found those results unsatisfactory. The multivariate results were far superior. Gebhardt concluded that the pre-1965 models' results were actually better than the ones following the reform law.

(d) Fischer (1981). Fischer's work concentrates on non-numerical data for forecasting failure. He is particularly interested in methods of credit evaluation for suppliers who do not have the ability or the data to perform comprehensive conventional analysis on their existing and potential customers. He advocates an electronic data processing system which can retrieve and analyze such non-numerical information as reports from newspapers, magazines, inquiry agencies, and credit information from other sellers. Unfortunately, according to Fischer, commercial rating agencies and banks are constrained as to how honest and revealing they choose to be with regard to their reports. In addition, the information provided may be outdated and certainly contains subjective elements. More than one source of credit information is therefore desirable.

Fischer advocates combining the permanent and transitory information on enterprises with microeconomic and sociopolitical data. Five arbitrary rating categories are devised based on non-numerical data and the delphi technique (numerous experts in various areas) is also recommended. Each characteristic is rated over time into the five categories. The sum of development patterns from varying sources of information builds the basis for a final classification. Clustering techniques are also used by Fischer to clarify information types.

(e) von Stein and Ziegler (1984). This is an ambitious attempt to identify bankruptcy risk from three separate, yet inter-related perspectives. They are: (1) balance sheet analysis using financial ratios; (2) analysis of the bank accounts of firms, and (3) analysis of the behavioral characteristics of company management. The study thus addresses criticism leveled at relying exclusively on one of the three approaches in assessing failure risk.

The balance sheet analysis considers medium-sized firms in Germany. The failure dates for the "bads" covered the years from 1971 to 1978. The date for all the "goods" was fixed (1977). There were 119 failed companies; the failure date was defined as the date of the first value adjustment or write-off, or only in a few cases, the date of the bankruptcy or composition petition. The "goods" consisted of 327 companies. The companies in the "bad" sample were from the following industries: manufacturing and processing (54.5%), building (17.7%), trade (22.7%), others (5.1%). The companies in the "goods" sample were comparably distributed across industries.

Thirteen financial ratios were identified as the most discriminating of the 140 ratios initially considered. These ratios are:

1. Capital borrowed/total capital
2. (Short-term borrowed capital × 360)/total output
3. (Accounts payable for purchases and deliveries × 360)/material costs
4. (Bill of exchange liabilities + accounts payable for purchases and deliveries × 360)/total output
5. (Current assets – short-term borrowed capital)/total output
6. Equity/(total assets – liquid assets – real estates and buildings)
7. Equity/(tangible property – real estates and buildings)
8. Short-term borrowed capital/current assets
9. (Working expenditure – depreciation on tangible property)/(liquid assets + accounts receivable for sales and services – short-term borrowed capital)
10. Operational result/total capital
11. (Operational result + depreciation on tangible property)/net turnover
12. (Operational result + depreciation on tangible property)/short-term borrowed capital
13. (Operational result + depreciation on tangible property)/capital borrowed

Three nonparametric methods (Nearest-Neighbor Classifications: Fix/Hodges, Loftsgaarden/Quiesenberry and Parzen) and two parametric methods (linear and quadratic multiple discriminant analysis) were tested. The method of Fix and Hodges was found to be the most discriminating. The results of the tests on the development sample are given in Exhibit 10.2.

In the second phase of the analysis, 45 bad and 37 good cases were examined using the following account characteristic variables:

Group	Year Before Fixed Date	Correct Classification
	5	71.4%
	4	78.2
Bad cases	3	86.6
	2	89.9
	1	95.0
Good cases	1977	83.7

Exhibit 10.2. Classification Results—Fix/Hodges Nonparametric Model.

- Average balance with regard to value dates
- Most favorable balance for the borrower
- Most unfavorable balance for the borrower
- Credit turnover
- Debit turnover
- Bill of exchange credits
- Check credits
- Transfer credits
- Cash deposits
- Bill of exchange debits
- Check debits
- Transfer debits
- Cash payouts
- Limit

Profile analysis, dichotomous classification, and linear discriminant analysis were the three techniques applied on the data. All three methods revealed important differences between the bad and the good companies. Linear discriminant analysis provided the best results. The function contained the following variables:

- (Most favorable balance for the borrower)/limit
- (Most favorable balance for the borrower)/debit turnover
- Check debits/debit turnover
- Debit turnover/limit
- Bill of exchange debits/debit turnover
- Transfer credits/credit turnover

The classification results (from von Stein and Zeigler [1984]) on the development sample are shown in Exhibit 10.3

The third phase of the study attempted to identify the characteristics and concrete behavioral indications that distinguish the failed firms from the solvent ones. The authors used a psychological technique named "nomethetical assessment" and the "principle of simultaneous vision." The latter term is taken to mean that the authors looked for factors consistently found in the failed group that are consistently absent

Semiannual Period before Fixed Date	Correct Classification	Correct Classification of Good Cases
8	73.3%	89.2%
7	66.7	83.8
6	75.6	81.1
5	80.0	89.2
4	82.2	78.4
3	91.1	78.4
2	88.9	83.8
1	88.9	83.8

Exhibit 10.3. Classification Results on the Development Sample.

in the nonfailed groups. The investigation was based on 135 bad companies and 25 good companies and consisted of (1) an examination of the functional areas of the companies leading to their weak points and (2) partly standardized interviews of bank lending personnel most familiar with the history and behavioral characteristics of the owner/managers.

The qualities found to set the failed company management apart were the following:

- Being out of touch with reality
- Large technical knowledge but poor commercial control
- Great talents in salesmanship
- Strong-willed
- Sumptuous living and unreasonable withdrawals
- Excessive risk-taking

The management of the solvent companies was found to be more homogeneous than the failed companies and seldom showed a lack of consciousness of reality. The authors recommend all three components of analysis (balance sheet, account behavior, and management) be pursued to assess a company.

(f) Baetge, Huss, and Niehaus (1988). This study reports the results of a multiple discriminant analysis model whose aim is to identify at least 80% of the endangered corporate borrowers three years before they become distressed.

The bad borrowers were defined as those that resulted in a final credit loss to the bank or wherever a temporal delay occurred or was feared in the payment of the obligations of the borrower as stipulated by contract. Good borrowers were those that did not possess the above characteristics. Samples were drawn from both bad and good enterprises representative of the line of business, legal form, and size. Principal component analysis was used to reduce the initial universe of 42 financial ratios to seven factors. These factors in turn led to a three variable MDA model consisting of the following ratios:

1. Capital structure: Net worth/(total assets – quick assets – property and plant [without equipment])

2. Profitability: (operating income + ordinary depreciation + addition to pension reserves)/total assets
3. Financial Strength: (cash income including extraordinary income – cash expense including extraordinary expense)/short term liabilities

Rather than using the cutoff point as the basis for separating the firms into good and bad groups, the authors created a gray area around the cutoff point where the probability of assigning to either group was low. By doing so they were able to put the predictive accuracy of the model in a clearer perspective. The discriminant function was subsequently tested with about 40,000 financial statements of all corporate customers of the bank. The results of the tests were quite similar to that found on the analysis sample. The model proved very stable when tested using a simulation model developed at Gottingen University.

10.5 ENGLAND

(a) Taffler and Tisshaw (1977). Taffler and Tisshaw (1977) have approached the corporate distress problem primarily from the viewpoint of security analysis and adaptations of their work, and that of Taffler and Houston (1980) and Taffler (1976). They indicate that their model is also relevant for accounting firms to assess the going concern capability of clients and in their work as receivers and liquidators of firms that have already failed.

(b) Research Design. To construct their solvency model, Taffler and Tisshaw (T&T, 1977) utilized linear discriminant analysis on a sample of 46 failed firms and 46 financially sound manufacturing companies. The latter sample was matched to the failed sample by size and industry (no information on these characteristics is available), from the period 1969 through 1975. Failed firms were those entering into receivership, creditors' voluntary liquidation, compulsory winding up by order of the court, or government action (bailouts) undertaken as an alternative to the other unfortunate fates. Eighty different ratios were examined for the two samples with a resulting model utilizing only four measures. These four were:

X_1 = profit before tax/current liabilities

X_2 = current assets/total liabilities

X_3 = current liabilities/total assets

X_4 = no-credit interval

The first three ratios are taken from the balance sheet and measure profitability, liquidity, and a type of leverage, respectively. The no-credit interval is the time for which the company can finance its continuing operations from its immediate assets if all other sources of short term finance are cut off. More directly it is defined as immediate assets-current liabilities/operating costs excluding depreciation. T&T state that the no-credit interval is "something akin to the acid-test ratio" (p. 52).

(c) Empirical Results. Both the model described above and an "unquoted model" (for non-listed companies) appeared to be quite accurate in classifying correctly over 97% of all observations. Another model by Taffler (1976), supposedly the one being used by practitioners in the U.K. investment community, had accuracies of 96%, 70%, 61%, and 35% for the four years prior to failure.

The nearly perfect one-year-prior accuracy that T&T observe utilizing their model contrasts sharply with the relatively small percentage of quoted and unquoted firms that were assessed to have a going concern problem by their auditors. In fact, T&T report that just 22% of the 46 quoted firms (and none of the 31 unquoted manufacturing bankrupt firms) had been qualified on-going concern grounds prior to failure.

(d) Implications. The drop-off in accuracy is quite noticeable as earlier year data are applied. For investment purposes, however, one needs less of a lead time, versus credit risk models, before failure in order to disinvest without losing a major amount of his investment. It is fair to say, however, that as failure approaches, stock prices tend to move downward in a rather continuous manner. Taffler and Houston (1980) indicated that 12% of large quoted industrial firms had Z scores indicating high failure risk. This is a comparable figure to results we observed utilizing our own ZETA model (Altman, Haldeman, and Narayanan, 1977) in the United States.

The authors also point out that about 15% to 20% of those firms which display a profile similar to failed companies will actually fail. In addition, the British government appeared to them to be keeping many ailing firms alive. Although this type of paternalism is less common in the United States, examples like Lockheed and Chrysler Corp. periodically crop up. Finally, T&T conclude that accountants are too defensive when it comes to considering the value of conventional published historic statements. When several measures of a firm, described from a set of accounts, are considered together the value of the information derived is enhanced dramatically. Essentially, T&T advocate a multivariate approach to financial analysis, and we certainly agree. It is unfortunate that they did not share with readers a more complete description of their findings and the data used in their analysis. Their results are certainly provocative and appear to be of some practical use in England.

In his latest attempt to revise the company failure discriminant model (Taffler, 1982), a smaller sample of 23 failed companies (1968–1973) and 45 nonfailed entities displaying financially healthy profiles were examined first within a principal component analysis framework. A large list of almost 150 potential variables was reduced to just five. These five are:

1. Earnings before interest and taxes/total assets
2. Total liabilities/net capital employed
3. Quick assets/total assets
4. Working capital/net worth
5. Stock inventory turnover

The variables were discussed in terms of their discriminant standardized coefficients and other relative measures of contribution, but no function weights were provided. Taffler did utilize prior probability and cost-of-error estimates in his classification procedures. He concludes that such an approach is best used in an operational context as a means of identifying a short list of firms that might experience financial distress (p. 15). Another conclusion is that the actual bankruptcy event is essentially determined by the actions of the financial institutions and other creditors and cannot strictly be predicted by using a model approach.

(e) Other U.K. Studies. Marais (1979), while on a short-term assignment for the Industrial Finance Unit of the Bank of England, also utilized discriminant analysis to quantify relative firm performance. He too concentrated on U.K. industrials and incorporated flow of funds variables with conventional balance sheet and income statement measures. Using a sample of 38 failed and 53 nonfailed companies (1974–1977), he tested several previously published models from the United States and the United Kingdom using both univariate and multivariate techniques.

He then went on to develop his own model, of which space does not permit a full discussion. His model included the following variables:

X_1 = current assets/gross total assets

X_2 = 1/gross total assets

X_3 = cash flow/current liabilities

X_4 = funds generated from operations minus net change in working capital to total debt

His results were considered "satisfactory" and his conclusions modest. He mainly advocated that firms whose scores fell below a certain cutoff point should be regarded as possible future problems; "that all Z scores can hope to do is act as a sophisticated screening device to those firms most urgently in need of analysis" (p. 29).

A later work, by Earl and Marais (1982), expanded upon this work with more enthusiastically reported results and implications. Classification results of 93%, 87%, and 84% respectively for the three years prior to failure are reported. The authors felt that funds flow data improved their classification accuracy. The single ratio of cash flow/current liabilities was a successful discriminator. Subsequent tests on failures and nonfailures in 1978 revealed a very low Type I error but an unacceptably high Type II error assessment.

10.6 CANADA. Canada, like Australia, is a relatively small country in terms of business population, yet it too is concerned with the performance assessment of individual entities. The economy is very much tied to the fortunes of the United States and its financial reporting standards are often derived from the same accounting principles. Like many other environments, the key constraint in Canada is the availability of a large and reliable database of failed companies. This requires both a sufficient number of failures and publicly available data on those firms. Both attributes do exist in Canada, but just barely.

(a) Knight (1979). Knight (1979) analyzed the records of a large number of small business failures as well as conducting interviews with the key persons involved. The author contends that his study supplies information "to answer the question, why do small businesses fail in Canada and also generates certain guidelines as to how the failure rate in Canada may be decreased from its recent increasing level." Not surprisingly, Knight finds that a firm usually fails early in its life (50% of all failed firms do so within four years and 70% within six) and that some type of managerial incompetence accounts for almost all failures.

Knight also attempted to classify failure using a discriminant analysis model. He amassed a fairly large sample of 72 failed small firms with average sales and assets of about \$100,000. A five-variable discriminant function realized disappointing results, however. Only 64% of the original sample of 36 failed and 36 nonfailed firms and 54% of the test sample of a like number of firms were correctly classified. He concluded that the discriminant analysis procedure was not successful. Knight did combine firms in many different industries, including manufacturing, service, retail, and construction and this will contribute to estimation problems, especially if the data are not adjusted to take into consideration industry differences and/or accounting differences, for instance, lease capitalization. We discuss this industry effect at length in the Australian situation.

(b) Altman and Lavallee (1981). The results of Altman and Lavallee (1981) were more accurate when manufacturing and retailing firms are combined but they do not advocate a single model for both sectors. Indeed, the holdout tests of this study indicate that nonmanufacturers cannot be confidently measured when the model contains variables which are industry sensitive.

The Altman and Lavallee (A&L) study was based on a sample of 54 publicly traded firms, half failed and half continuing entities. The failures took place during the ten years 1970–1979 and the average tangible asset size of these 27 failures was \$12.6 million at one statement date prior to failure (average lag was 16 months). Manufacturers and retailer-wholesalers were combined although the data did not enable them to adjust assets and liabilities for lease capitalization. The continuing firms were stratified by industry, size, and data period and had average assets of \$15.6 million. One can observe, therefore, that the Canadian model for the 1970s decade consisted of firms with asset sizes similar to those of the previously reported U.S. models (e.g., Altman, 1968) constructed from the 1950s and 1960s data period.

A&L examined just 11 ratios, and their resulting model contained five based on a forward stepwise selection procedure. The model for Canada (ZC) is

$$Z_C = -1.626 + 0.234(X_1) - 0.531(X_2) + 1.002(X_3) + 0.972(X_4) + 0.612(X_5)$$

where

Z_C = Canadian Z-score
X_1 = sales/total assets
X_2 = total debt/total assets
X_3 = current assets/current liabilities
X_4 = net profits after tax/total debt
X_5 = rate of growth of equity − rate of asset growth

(c) Classification Results. The overall classification accuracy of the Canadian Z model on the original 54-firm sample was 83.3%, which is quite high, although not as impressive as that reported in some of the other economic environments discussed in this international review article. Practically speaking, classification criteria are based on a zero cutoff score with positive scores indicating a nonfailed classification and negative scores a failed assignment. Reliability, or holdout tests, included Lachenbruch (1967) test replications, the original sample broken into randomly chosen classification and test samples, and testing the model on prior years data, for example years 2 through 4 before failure. The Lachenbruch and replication holdout results showed accuracies very similar to those of the original sample results and the prior year accuracies were 73% (Year 2), 53% (Year 3), and only 30% (Year 4).

Therefore, the model appears reasonably accurate for up to two statements prior to failure but not accurate for earlier periods. These findings are quite similar to those of Altman's (1968) model and we can suggest that the similarities in accuracies are partially related to the similarities of the data quality and the somewhat diverse industries represented in the sample.

A&L also simulated their results for various assumptions of prior probabilities of group membership and costs of error. Their findings were that Type I errors could be reduced, even eliminated, but that the resulting Type II error was unacceptably high and vice versa for eliminating the Type II error. The Z model's results were also compared to a naive classification strategy of assigning all observations to the nonbankrupt category or assuming that the resulting errors would be realized in proportion to the actual experience of bankrupts and nonbankrupts (proportional chance model. They concluded that, in every case, the Canadian Z model was more efficient; that is, it had a lower expected cost than a naive model.

Finally, A&L observe that the industry affiliations of the misclassified firms were predominantly retailers amongst the failed group and manufacturers among the nonfailed. It appeared that one of the variables, sales/assets (X_1), was particularly sensitive to industry effects, with the misclassified failed retailers all having high asset turnovers and the misclassified manufacturers all with low turnovers.

(d) Implications. A&L attempted to reestimate the model without the sales/assets variable, but the results actually were worse. One can conclude that the Canadian investigations are at an early stage and follow-up work is needed in subdividing a larger sample into manufacturers and retailers-wholesalers and/or improving the information on critical industry differences, such as lease usage and capitalization. Only additional time will permit analysts to construct models with sufficiently large samples or to witness an improvement in the quality of reported data. We are aware of a move with the Canadian government to set up an early warning system to identify potential large publicly traded firm crisis situations, for instance, Massey-Ferguson. Authorities are currently considering available models such as Altman (1968) and A&L (1980) as alternatives to building their own model.

10.7 THE NETHERLANDS

(a) Bilderbeek (1977). Bilderbeek (1977) analyzed a sample of 38 firms which went bankrupt from 1950 through 1974 and 59 ongoing companies. They found that 85 firms had sufficient data for analysis. Bilderbeek analyzed 20 ratios within a stepwise discriminant framework and arrived at a five-variable model of the form:

$$Z = 0.45 - 5.03X_1 - 1.57X_2 + 4.55X_3 + 0.17X_4 + 0.15X_5$$

where

Z = Z-score (Netherlands, Bilderbeek)
X_1 = retained earnings/total assets
X_2 = added value/total assets
X_3 = accounts payable/sales
X_4 = sales/total assets
X_5 = net profit/equity

Two of the five signs (coefficients), X_4 and X_5, are positive and contrary to expectations since, for this model, negative scores indicate a healthy situation and positive scores indicate a failure classification. His model was based on observations over five reporting periods prior to failure and is not based on one-year intervals. His results were only mildly impressive, with accuracies ranging from 70% to 80% for one year prior and remaining surprisingly stable over a five-year period prior to failure. He explains in his book (1979) that the stability is due to the facts that there are no liquidity variables and the stable role of the value-added measure. Subsequent tests of Bilderbeek's model have been quite accurate (80% over five years). Apparently, several institutions are now using his model for practical purposes.

(b) Van Frederikslust (1978). Van Frederikslust's (1978) model included tests on a sample of 20 failed and a matched nonfailed sample of observations for 1954 through 1974. All firms were quoted on The Netherlands Stock Exchange. In addition to the now traditional research structure, that is, linear discriminant analysis, single year ratios, and equal *a priori* probability of group membership assumptions, the author performed several other tests. Those included (1) looking at the development of ratios over time (temporal model) as well as analyzing ratio levels, (2) varying the *a priori* assumption of group membership likelihood to conform with a specific user of the model (e.g., lending officer), and (3) varying the expected costs of the models, taking into consideration the specific user's utility for losses.

Van Frederikslust attempts to provide a theoretical discussion for his choice of variables. He concludes that traditional measures of firm performance, that is, liquidity, profitability, solvency, and variability of several of these categories, are the correct indicators. Industry affiliation and general economic variables are also thought to be important but are not included in his model. In fact, the primary model only contained two variables representing liquidity and profitability.

Van Frederikslust's primary model analyzed the level of ratios. His definition of failure included many different types but essentially involved the failure to pay fixed obligations. His sample included textile, metal processing, machinery, construction, retailing, and miscellaneous firms. The nonfailed group (20) were randomly selected from the same industries, size categories (assets), and time periods as was the failed group. His first model was:

$$Z_{NF} = 0.5293 + 0.4488X_1 + 0.2863X_2$$

where

Z_{NF} = Z-score (Netherlands, Van Frederikslust)
X_1 = liquidity ratio (external coverage)
X_2 = profitability ratio (rate of return on equity)

The author distinguishes between the *internal coverage* ratio (cash balance + resources earned in the period/short-term debt) and the *external coverage* ratio (short-term debt in period *t* plus available short-term debt [$t - 1$]). The external coverage measures what can be expected from the renewal of existing debt and additional debt. "Failure at moment (*t*) is completely determined by the values of internal and external coverage at that moment" (p. 35). Van Frederikslust uses only the external coverage measure in his "simple" model.

Separate models are developed for each year, as Deakin (1972) did. The arguments for this are that a separate model is necessary to assess failure probabilities for different time periods and that the distributions of ratios vary over time. While we do not necessarily agree that separate models are desirable—indeed, they could be confusing—the discussion on timing of failure prediction is a useful one. The classification program utilized was actually a 0.1 multiple regression structure and not the discriminant analysis model used in most other studies. Fisher (1936) has shown that the coefficients of these structures are proportional when dealing with a two-group model.

The results for the one-period model indicate that the estimated chances of misclassification into the two groups are 5% for the failed group and 10% for the nonfailed group. The expected accuracy falls as time prior to failure increases. For example, the error rates are 15% and 20% respectively for two years prior.

A revised model, analyzing the development of ratios over time, yielded an equation that utilized the liquidity ratio in the latest year before failure, the profitability ratio two years prior, the coefficient of variation of the liquidity ratio over a seven-year period, and the prediction error of the profitability ratio in the latest year before failure. Again, separate models were developed for each year prior to failure. Using Lachenbruch's procedure for estimating error rates, the results were quite similar to those of the first set of equations based on the two variable, "levels" ratios. Accuracies for earlier years did show slight improvements.

(c) The Fire Scoring System: de Breed and Partners (1996). A small consulting firm in the Netherlands recently developed specialized credit scoring models for specific industries in Holland. Utilizing discriminant analysis techniques, like many of the other studies discussed earlier, the unique aspect of these models is their specific industry orientation and the very large databases of failed and unfailed companies maintained and updated. In 1996, the firm published a type of "Michelin Guide" for rating the health of Dutch companies, using a zero to four star system. Since the models are proprietary, we cannot comment further.

10.8 FRANCE

(a) Altman, Margaine, Schlosser and Vernimmen (1974); Mader (1975, 1979); Collongues (1977); and Bontemps (1981). Altman et al. (1973) first attempted to apply credit scoring techniques to problem firms, many of which filed for bankruptcy (*faillite*). Working with a sample of textile firms and data provided by Banque de France, this study applied principal component analysis to a large number of financial indicators and proceeded to utilize the most important ones in a linear discriminant model. Their results were at best mediocre on test samples and, while the model did provide insights into that troublesome sector, it was not implemented on a practical basis.

A more recent study by Bontemps (1981), using a large sample of industrial companies and data from the Centrale de bilans of Credit National (supplier of long-term debt capital to French firms), achieved high accuracy on original and holdout tests. His results are quite interesting in that as little as three variables were found to be useful indicators. Bontemps combined both the univariate technique developed by Beaver (1967) with arbitrary, qualitative weightings of the three most effective measures to classify correctly as much as 87% of his holdout sample of 34 failed and 34 nonfailed firms. The original function was built based on a matched (by industry, size, and year) sample of 50 failed and nonfailed entities from 1974 through 1979.

Collongues (1977), Mader (1975 and 1979) also have attempted to combine financial ratios with data from failed and nonfailed French firms. Mader's studies were descriptive of firms in difficulty and the utility of ratios as risk measures. These have led to several multivariate studies performed by the Banque de France in their "centrale de bilans" group. Collongues did utilize discriminant analysis in his analysis of small- and medium-size firms with some success.

The application of statistical credit scoring techniques in the French environment appears to be problematic, but the potential remains. One problem usually is the quality of data and the representativeness of them. But this is a problem in all countries and is not unique to France. The government has gone on record on several occasions as intending not to keep hopelessly insolvent firms alive artificially but to try to assist those ailing firms prior to total collapse. An accurate performance predictor model could very well help in this endeavor.

10.9 SPAIN

(a) Fernández (1988). This study describes an empirical model to objectively evaluate and screen credit applicants. The work consists of the determination of the model with two objectives: (1) to check the validity of financial ratios as prediction tools, and (2) to predict a firm's collapse.

The research sample consisted of 25 failed and 25 non-failed firms, with an additional 10 each being set aside for validation testing. Data pertaining to two years preceding the failure was collected. Only data pertaining to 1978–1982 was permitted in order to eliminate the possible distortion caused by the natural changes in ratios caused by the business cycle. The ratios were examined using three techniques:

1. Univariate analysis
2. Factor analysis by principal components
3. Discriminant analysis

The author concludes that univariate analysis is not practical given the volume of the ratios to be considered and the possible interactions among the ratios. In addition, the univariate ratio analysis has to be performed in the context of the market in which the firm operates, thus the ratios show only relative position of the company. Lastly, multivariate ratios can improve analyst productivity and free him/her to concentrate on other equally important matters such as the credit terms, maturity, guarantees, and so on.

When there are a large number of variables to be considered, principal component analysis is a way to eliminate the variables that carry the same information and reduce the observation to a handful of factors or "principal components." Each principal component is a linear combination of one or more of the underlying variables. The coefficient of the underlying variable in the factor equation is called the "factor loading." In this study the author conducted factor analysis in two ways: (1) without rotation of the factors and (2) using varimax rotation to ensure the independence of the resulting factors.

The second way is believed to produce more desirable (i.e., stabler) results when used as independent variables in regression or discriminant analysis.

The author found that eight factors existed that account for 79.3% of the information contained in the initial set of ratios. Just two factors provide for 42.1% of the information. The eight factors are:

1. Capacity to repay debt
2. Liquidity
3. Fixed assets financing
4. Efficiency of the firm
5. Rotation of fixed assets
6. Profitability of permanent funds
7. Structure of working capital
8. Structure of short-term debt

Fourteen ratios with a higher loading from the principal components were selected as input for the discriminant analysis procedure. A six variable discriminant function emerged as the best, with an overall classification accuracy of 84% in the original sample. The discriminant function is as follows:

$$\begin{aligned} Z1 = & -0.26830V3 + 0.54666*V4 + 0.55483*V6 + 0.62925*V9 \\ & -0.514119*V12 + 0.43665*V17 \end{aligned}$$

where

V3 = (Permanent funds/Net fixed assets)/Industry value
V4 = Quick ratio/Industry value
V6 = Cash-flow/Current liabilities
V9 = Return on investment
V12 = Earnings before taxes/sales
V17 = Cash-flow/sales

The results of the model on the development sample and the hold out sample are given in Exhibit 10.4. As expected, there is a slight drop in performance of the model in the hold out sample. Of greater concern is where the drop in performance is: normally the Type I accuracy will be maintained and the Type II accuracy will be lower. In this case, the Type I accuracy has dropped from 84 to 70%. Some follow-up analy-

		Predicted Group Membership	
Actual Group	No. of Cases	1	2
Group 1	25	21 84.0%	4 16.0%
Group 2	25	4 16.0%	21 84.0%

Exhibit 10.4. Classification Results.

sis of the Type I and Type II errors by individual case may have been useful. The author compared the discriminant model using the underlying ratios (described in the foregoing) with a discriminant model using the factor scores and found that the percentage accuracy of classification was the same in both cases. This is an interesting result for future researchers.

(b) Briones, Marín, and Cueto (1988). This study presents the results of empirical research undertaken to build a multivariate model to forecast the possible failure of financial institutions in Spain and their takeover by the monetary authorities or regulatory agencies.

During the period 1978–1983, Spain underwent a serious crisis in its financial institutions. Roughly 47% of all Spanish banks failed during this period; 21.4% of the equity and 18.7% of the deposits were affected by the problem banks. Banco de Espana (the Spanish equivalent of the Federal Reserve) working through Fondo de Garantía de Depósitos (the Spanish equivalent of the Federal Deposit Insurance Corporation) carried out the resolution of the banks through "administrative solutions." Legal solutions such as bankruptcy procedures were not used for fear of causing a panic. A bank may thus be technically insolvent when it has a liquidity crisis or it may be definitively insolvent when there is negative net worth. Since a "failed" institution can operate indefinitely with assistance from the regulators, the authors have defined a bank to have failed if there was an intervention by Fondo de Garantía Depósitos.

The sample consisted of 25 failed banks and an equal number of nonfailed banks paired up based on the five-year average size of deposits during the period prior to intervention. The data sources were Anuario Estadístico la Banca Privada published by the Consejo Superior Bancario and the memorandum of the Fondo de Garantía de Depósitos. Both a univariate and multivariate approach were used in classifying the failed and nonfailed groups.

In the univariate approach, the authors found that the mean values for the ratios maintain a logical correspondence (the actual mean values obtained are not mentioned in the study, however). They also found that standard deviations of the failed bank ratios tended to be generally higher. Profitability and liquidity measures were found to be the most significant variables for forecasting failures in a univariate analysis. The cutoff point for the individual ratio was fixed in a heuristic way, by a process of trial and error. The costs of Type I and Type II errors were assumed to be equal.

In the multivariate approach, discriminant analysis was used to develop models using data of j year prior as the development sample ($j = 1, 2, 3, 4, 5$) and testing the model on the data for all the years j. Since the ratios for a bank tend to be correlated from one year to the next, the classification test on the other years does not constitute a true out-of-sample (hold out) test. Some of the classification results presented are nonsensical because if you used data for $j = 2$ to develop the model, you can not test it on data of $j = 1$ because in real time that information would be nonexistent; only $j = 3$, 4, and 5 would be!

The multiple discriminant analysis produced three and four variable models for each year prior, resulting in a total of 10 alternative models to choose from. The comparison of the prediction accuracy using univariate analysis and the discriminant analysis showed that univariate analysis actually did better than the discriminant function in the first and the fifth year (Exhibit 10.5)—a surprising result. Most re-

Years	Ratios	Functions
1	90/95%	80/85%
2	75/80	80/85
3	75/80	75/80
4	75/80	75/80
5	80/85	75/80

Exhibit 10.5. Overall Accurate Predictions—Comparison of Single Ratios with Discriminant Functions.

search using multivariate methods appears to come to the opposite conclusion because it is believed that the interaction or the substitution effects of one variable with others provide better information than if the variables are considered sequentially.

The authors conclude that there is a close balance between the univariate ratio approach and the function approach and that both types of analysis can be viewed as complementary.

More rigorous testing using a holdout sample will be needed to confirm that univariate approach has predictive power comparable to the multivariate approach. Coming to this conclusion based solely on original sample test results is premature because of sampling bias in the results.

10.10 ITALY

(a) Altman, Marco, and Varetto (1994). This study presents the results of two interesting innovations in the diagnosis of corporate financial distress. The first is the use of a two-stage decision process employing two discriminant analysis models to fine-tune the process used to grade companies into groups of healthy, vulnerable, and unsound companies. The second innovation is the application of neural networks (NN) to solve the same problem. The study is also of interest because of the access of the authors to a large and well-developed database of financial information on over 37,000 companies in Italy, as much as to the pooling of this data by a consortium of banks that have thereupon been able to use the diagnostic system developed for medium- and small-sized businesses in Italy. After trying various alternative approaches in neural network modeling, the authors conclude that the linear discriminant model compares well relative to neural networks. The main advantages of the discriminant model are its consistency of performance and the modest cost in fine-tuning the model. Having said that, the authors state that neural networks continue to hold promise especially in situations where the complexity of the problem can be handled well by the flexibility of NN systems and the capacity to structure them into simple, integrated families.

The study was carried out in the Centrale dei Bilanci (CB) in Turin, Italy. CB is an organization established by the Banca d'Italia, the Associazione Bancaria Italiana and over forty leading banks and special credit institutions in Italy. CB develops and distributes tools for the member banks to use. One product was a linear discriminant analysis-based model that is used in practice to improve credit analyst productivity by pre-selecting the credits and for monitoring the uniformity of the judgments made about businesses by the various branches of the bank.

The first part of the study describes the results of the new release of the system

F1 Discriminant Model Results

	Test Period	Healthy Firms	Unsound Firms
Estimation sample (404 companies in each group)			
Estimation period	T-3	90.3%	86.4%
Control period	T-1	92.8	96.5
Holdout sample (150 companies in each group)	T-1	90.3	95.1

F2 Discriminant Model Results

	Test Period	Healthy Firms	Unsound Firms
Estimation sample (404 companies in each group)			
Estimation period	T-3	99.0%	60.1%
Control period	T-1	97.8	82.7
Holdout sample (150 companies in each group)	T-1	96.8	81.0

Exhibit 10.6. Test Results.

that improves on predictive accuracy by splitting the estimation/classification problems into two steps. In the first step, the two group sample consists of healthy firms on the one hand and unsound and vulnerable companies on the other. "Vulnerable" companies are those that are not at the point being considered "Unsound" but are borderline cases. The second step was to develop another discriminant analysis model to classify the vulnerable companies on the one hand and the unsound companies on the other. Estimation of the model was done based on data three years prior to distress and tested on original and control (hold-out) sample for one and three years prior. The results of the tests of the two models are as shown in Exhibit 10.6.

(b) Neural Networks. Neural networks consist of a potentially large number of elementary processing units. Every unit is interconnected with other units and each is able to perform relatively simple calculations. The processing behavior of the network is derived from the collective behavior of the units each of which is capable of altering its responses to stimuli from the external environment as well as from the other neurons with which it is linked. Obviously, the change of response is the learning process that the NN goes through as revisions are introduced to the weightings that drive the response. Neural networks can range in complexity from the simple single-layer network to multilayer networks. In general, the more complex the network, the greater is the promise that it will have a genuine capacity to solve a problem, but also greater is the difficulty associated with understanding its sometimes anomalous behavior. And, more complex networks take longer to train.

The Altman et al. (1994) experiment with neural network progressed through four steps:

1. Attempt to replicate the scores generated by multiple discriminant analysis using ratios different from those used in discriminant analysis. The objective in

doing so was to verify the network's capacity to do at least as well as discriminant analysis but using a different set of ratios.

2. Train the network using data three years prior and test it in one year prior data in its ability to separate the healthy and bankrupt companies.
3. Attempt to integrate the knowledge implicit in observing the evolution of the various ratios and indicators over time. In other words teach the network to learn from both point-in-time data and trend data.
4. Check the capacity of the network to separate the healthy, vulnerable and unsound companies in the same way as the two stage discriminant analysis models presented earlier.

(c) Results. The best results were obtained with a three-layer network in replicating the scores generated by discriminant analysis. The initial layer of ten neurons, a second layer of four neurons, and an output layer consisting of a single neuron. The input consisted of ten financial ratios. The resulting profile after 1000 learning cycles on 808 companies was extremely close to the desired level.

In the second stage (classifying healthy and bankrupt companies) a 15, 4, 1 network provided the best recognition rate, with a classification accuracy of 97.7% for the healthy companies and 97% for the unsound companies. However the authors noted two concerns with the network: it was able to obtain that accuracy using a much higher number of indicators, that is, fifteen as opposed to nine used by discriminant analysis. Second, its behavior became erratic as the learning progressed—initially the model makes rapid strides in its capacity to identify the groups but as it moves forward there are often points where its performance actually deteriorates. This led the authors to suggest that neural networks may suffer from "overfitting," a phenomenon encountered with quadratic discriminant functions that do very well in the development sample but fail in hold-out testing.

In the third stage the authors fed the same ratios used in discriminant analysis to the neural network using the argument that it is common for analysts and systems to receive a standard information base. The objective was to check the network's capacity to replicate the knowledge base produced by discriminant analysis, using the same inputs. The results of this, obtained using a 9, 5, 1 network are as shown in Exhibit 10.7.

The next experiment, involving the synthesis of historical information by the network, also produced impressive classification results, but here again, the behavior of the network became at times unexplainable and unacceptable due to frequent inversion of output values when the inputs were modified uniformly or in limited subsets.

	Discriminant Analysis			
	Neural Network		Linear Discriminant Function (F1)	
Sample size = 404 in each group	Healthy	Unsound	Healthy	Unsound
Estimation T-3 period	89.4%	86.2%	90.3%	86.4
Control T-1 period	91.8	95.3	92.8	96.5

Exhibit 10.7. Comparison of Classification Rates: Neural Network vs. Linear.

In conclusion, the authors note that while complex networks may produce better classification results, they take longer to train and are more difficult to control in terms of illogical behavior. However, they have shown enough promising features to provide an incentive for better implementation techniques and more creative testing.

(d) Cifarelli, Corielli, and Forestieri (1988). These authors propose a Bayesian variant to the classical discriminant analysis which takes explicit care of the uncertainty with which the parameters of the diagnostic distribution are known when classifications are made. In particular, in "out-of-sample" cases, the classical method uses an estimate density of future observables, whereas the method suggested by the authors uses a predictive density calculated using Bayes theorem.

The sample used to test develop the model came from a large Italian bank's loan portfolio. Unsound companies were selected among cases of formal declaration of bankruptcy. The sound firm sample was formed by a random selection from the bank loan portfolio. Fourteen financial ratios descriptive of growth, profitability, productivity, liquidity, and financial structure were used. The authors report that the classification accuracy of the Bayesian model is very close to that obtained with different versions of the classical discriminant analysis model.

10.11 AUSTRALIA. Australia has certain unique characteristics, with huge development potential (like Brazil) but with an already established industrial base but a relatively small population (under 20 million people). While the influence of multinational firms is quite important, the local corporate structure is large enough to support a fairly substantial capital market.

(a) Castagna and Matolcsy (1982). The active financial environment in Australia is a motivation for rigorous individual firm analysis. A series of studies by A. Castagna and Z. Matolcsy (C&M), culminating in their published work (1982), have analyzed corporate failures in Australia and have concluded that there is a strong potential for models like those developed in the United States to assist analysts and managers.

(b) Research Design. One of the difficult requirements for failure analysis found in just about every country in the world outside the United States is assembling a database of failed companies large enough to perform a reliable discriminant analysis model. Despite a relatively large number of liquidations, Australian data on failed firms are quite restricted. C&M were able to assemble a sample of only 21 industrial companies (the number of firms would have been much larger if mining companies were included). The failure dates spanned the years from 1963 through 1977, with the date determined by the appointment of a liquidator or receiver. An alternative criterion date might have been the time of delisting from the stock exchange or the liquidation/receiver date, whichever comes first. For every failed company in the sample, there is a randomly selected surviving quoted industrial firm from the same period. Industries represented include retailers, manufacturers, builders, and service firms.

(c) Empirical Results. Prior studies by C&M reduced the number of potential discriminating variables to 10 that were then analyzed in a linear and quadratic discriminant structure. The authors also attempted to test their results for various *a priori* group membership probabilities. The results suggest that it is difficult to identify a unique model to predict corporate failures and that some specification of user preferences is desirable. Still, they do indicate 10-variable linear and 5-variable quadratic classification models.

As noted, the results of C&M's work are not definitive. For example, if one is concerned with minimizing the misclassification of failed companies, then the linear model using equal priors outperforms all other models tried. This model also had the best overall results, except in the fourth year prior to failure. However, the linear model does not perform better than other models in the classification of surviving companies. A stepwise procedure indicated that a five-variable model did not perform as well as the models based on the ten-ratio set in the overall classification tests. All of their comparisons are based on the Lachenbruch validation tests.

The C&M study does not address prediction accuracy per se. All of the tests are on the original sample of 21 firms. In order for the tests to be predictive in nature, their model(s) should be applied to subsequent firm performance in Australia. The authors do note that they expect to monitor their findings on samples of continuing companies listed on the Australian Stock Exchange.

(d) Izan (1984). Izan (1984) and Altman and Izan (1983), in subsequent attempts to address the failure classification problem in Australia, analyzed a larger sample of firms (50 failed and an industry-failure-year-matched sample of 50 nonfailed firms). Perhaps the most distinctive aspect of this model is the attempt to standardize the ratios by the respective firms' industry medians.

The argument put forward by the authors to use industry-relatives is to point to the significant differences that exist among industries of the key financial ratios. As for the counterargument that some industries are indeed riskier than others, the authors respond by stating that a near-bankrupt situation of any of the industries represented in the study is extremely remote. Having made the argument for using the industry relatives, the authors proceed to derive the value of this variable by dividing the failed and the nonfailed firm's raw ratio by the industry median.

The 10 candidate ratios chosen for analysis were:

1. Ordinary earnings/shareholder funds
2. Earnings before interest and taxes (EBIT)/total assets
3. Earnings after interest and taxes/total assets
4. Cash flow/borrowings
5. EBIT/interest
6. Current assets/current liabilities
7. Current assets stocks/current liabilities–overdrafts
8. Funded debt/shareholder funds
9. Market value of equity/total liabilities
10. Book value of equity/market value of equity

The final model was quite similar to the Altman (1968) model. The ratios in the model and their relative contributions are as shown in Exhibit 10.8.

The classification accuracy of the models on the development sample one year prior to failure is presented in Exhibit 10.9.

The industry relative ratios model showed a Type I accuracy of 94.1%, 75%, and 63.5% respectively on data one, two, and three years prior to failure. Type II accu-

Variable	Univariate F Amount	Univariate F Rank	Standardized Coefficient Amount	Standardized Coefficient Rank	Wilk's Lambda Amount	Wilk's Lambda Rank	Forward Stepwise
EBIT/TA	26.4	3	0.79	3	0.23	5	3
EBIT/Interest	49.2	1	0.66	1	0.53	1	1
CA/CL	4.3	5	0.96	5	0.24	4	5
FD/SF	21.6	4	0.82	4	–0.25	3	4
MV/TL	36.9	2	0.72	2	0.44	2	2

Exhibit 10.8. Relative Contribution Tests and Ranks of Variables in the Distress Model.

Actual Group	No of Cases	Industry Relative Ratios Classified Failed	Industry Relative Ratios Classified Nonfailed	Raw Ratios Classified Failed	Raw Ratios Classified Nonfailed
Failed	51	48 (94.1%)	3 (7.8%)	46 (90.2)	5 (9.8%)
Nonfailed	48	5 (10.4%)	43 (89.6%)	5 (10.4%)	43 (89.6%)

Exhibit 10.9. Classification Accuracy of the Industry Relative and the Raw Ratio Models.

racy for the same periods was 89.6%, 89.6%, and 85.4% respectively. The prediction accuracy on a small secondary sample (holdout) of ten failed firms was 100% one year prior to failure, 70% two years prior and 40 percent three years prior. In the absence of the corresponding Type II accuracy, this result is difficult to interpret, however. The authors believe that the model is sufficiently robust as to be applicable to a cross-section of firms and industries.

10.12 GREECE

(a) Gloubos and Grammatikos (1988). Companies in regulated economies are often sustained in operation long after they have become economically bankrupt. This causes taxonomic problems for the researcher because to treat such companies as healthy is clearly wrong, while including them in the bankrupt group causes biases because of the difficulties in identifying the date of the bankruptcy. The authors suggest that estimated models in such economies as Greece may be expected to have a higher degree of misclassification than similar models estimated in market-driven economies. In this study the authors compare four techniques on a "new" sample of healthy and bankrupt firms. The four techniques used are:

1. Linear Probability Model (LPM)
2. Probit Analysis (PROBIT)

3. Logit Analysis (LOGIT)
4. Multiple Discriminant Analysis (MDA)

The LPM model is a multiple linear regression model where the dependent variable is a 0–1 variable which is regressed against a set of independent variables. One problem with this approach is that the error terms' distribution is not normal. Also when the predicted value lies outside the 0–1 range, it is difficult to interpret the result. This difficulty is overcome by applying suitable transformations that would restrict the probability predictions to the 0–1 interval. This is done in the PROBIT model where P is the conditional probability of failure expressed in terms of a cumulative standard normal distribution function. As to be expected, the introduction of the standard normal distribution involved nonlinear estimation. The LOGIT model uses a computationally simpler function based on the cumulative logistic probability function. In multiple discriminant analysis, the function is linear or quadratic in the variables.

The sample consisted of 30 Greek industrial firms that went bankrupt during the period 1977–1981. Each failed firm was paired with a healthy firm of similar size in the same year and from the same industry. Data was gathered for one year prior to bankruptcy and was obtained from various issues of the *Government Gazette*. Seventeen accounting ratios were used in the analysis and the final models with all four techniques had the same variables. The group statistics for these ratios along with the T-statistics are presented in Exhibit 10.10.

The model results on the development sample are as reproduced in Exhibit 10.11. It was found that the MDA and LPM have the greater accuracy overall and also in the Type I and Type II categories. The authors note that the MDA model's coefficients for two of the variables had counterintuitive signs but go on to suggest that because of the interdependencies inherent in a multivariate model, this may be acceptable.

Variable	Group Mean Bankrupt	Group Mean Nonbankrupt	T-value
Current assets/current liabilities	0.932	1.579	–3.95
Net working capital/total assets	–0.092	0.196	–5.20
Total debt/total assets	0.813	0.595	5.69
Gross income/total assets	0.077	0.253	–4.51
Gross income/current liabilities	0.106	0.607	6.16

Exhibit 10.10. Group Statistics.

A. One year prior to bankruptcy	Overall	Bankrupt	Nonbankrupt
MDA	91.7%	96.7%	86.7%
LPM	91.7	93.3	90.0
PROBIT	85.0	83.3	86.7
LOGIT	86.7	83.3	90.0

Exhibit 10.11. Correct Classifications on the Original Sample.

A. One year prior to bankruptcy	Overall	Bankrupt	Nonbankrupt
MDA	66.7%	66.7%	66.7%
LPM	72.9	70.8	75.0
PROBIT	72.9	70.8	75.0
LOGIT	77.1	66.7	87.5
B. Two years prior to bankruptcy			
MDA	71.7	60.9	82.6
LPM	71.7	60.9	82.6
PROBIT	71.7	60.9	82.6
LOGIT	71.7	60.9	82.6
C. Three years prior to bankruptcy			
MDA	75.0	64.3	85.7
LPM	71.4	64.3	78.6
PROBIT	60.7	42.9	78.6
LOGIT	64.3	50.0	78.6

Exhibit 10.12. Correct Classifications on a New Sample.

The models were tested on 24 new paired samples of bankrupt and healthy firms for the period 1982–1985. As to be expected, the classification performance of the models drops off somewhat in the holdout sample as shown in Exhibit 10.12.

The performance differences among the four models are marginal. The authors recommend using probability models because they are more successful slightly before bankruptcy and their dependent variables can be interpreted directly as probabilities. The fact that the Type I accuracy of these models, which is more critical, is less than Type II accuracy is of some concern, however.

(b) Theodossiou and Papoulias (1988). The problematic firms in Greece are typically moribund firms kept alive by government assistance. The assistance is provided by banks in the form of external financing under pressure from the government anxious to minimize unemployment that would ensue if these firms are allowed to fail. The 1979 oil crisis, the entrance of Greece into the European Economic Community, and resulting competition, as well as the worldwide recessions in the 1980s brought about the minicollapse of the industrial sector. Irresponsible lending policies of banks and the improper management of the capital structure by the firms were also, according to the authors, contributing factors. The purpose of the study was to demonstrate, using a corporate failure prediction model developed by the authors, that the prevailing state of problematic firms in Greece could have been anticipated years before the problem became an issue. The models employed are logit, probit, and a Bayesian approach to discriminant analysis. In the Bayesian discriminant analysis, the coefficients are identical to those of traditional discriminant analysis. However, the discriminant score is scaled by an intercept in such a way that its distributional assumptions are invariant to either the sample size or the industries. Moreover, this technique is said to be free from the problem of differential firm size and yields probabilities in the 0–1 interval.

The sample used by the authors contained 33 failed firms and 68 nonfailed firms for the year 1983. To adjust the timing of failure for the bankrupt firms kept alive by government interventions beyond their natural span of existence, the data for such firms was collected as of two years prior to the time their net worth became negative. For others, data was gathered for one year prior.

The authors found that the performance scores generated by the three models were highly correlated and ranked the problematic firms similarly. Because the models appeared to be equivalent, the authors chose just the probit model for presenting the results. It was found that the probabilities of failure increased for the problematic firms from 0 in 1973–1974 to more than 0.5 in the mid-seventies, with complete deterioration of performance of about two-thirds of the problematic firms in the sample by 1979.

While there is no doubt that the models anticipated the problematic firms quite well, the results would be more compelling had the authors published the Type I accuracy of the models. A model may have 100% Type I accuracy, but if it has 0 Type II accuracy, then it is of no value.

10.13 ARGENTINA

(a) Swanson and Tybout (1988). This paper analyzes the determinants of industrial bankruptcy on Argentina on three levels. First, the importance of macroeconomic variables on the business failures is considered. Real interest rate, credit stock, manufacturing output, real wage rate and the peso exchange rate are regressed on business failures two variables at a time using a multivariate regression with third order polynomial distributed lag terms. Second, sectoral failure rates are examined to determine whether reform policies had a differential effect on highly protected industries. The data is divided into high protection and low protection industries and the differential impact of economic policies is evaluated by adding the degree of protection as a dummy variable in a regression of the number of business failures against the real interest rate and credit stock. The authors then consider the firm-level anatomy of failure by creating a probit regression model on a sample of 19 to 22 failures and 190 to 324 survivors. Measures of financial structure consisting of cash flow indices, firm financial structure variables, firm size, and the degree of protection were utilized. The firm failure model was estimated for the pre- and post-maxi devaluation period of the Argentinian peso, that is, 1979–1981 and the period following 1981, respectively.

Following the military coup that ousted Isabel Peron in 1976, Argentina passed through a reform period. The reform started with selective tariff reductions. Soon, contractionary monetary policies and temporary wage and price controls were imposed to combat hyperinflation. In late 1978, an exchange rate regime was introduced. The end result of all these policies led to a maxi devaluation of the peso that threw the economy into a recession similar to the Mexican peso crisis precipitated by the December 1994 devaluation. The authors examine the effects of the reform polices with the hope that policymakers will evaluate future policy options in terms of the stress they place on the corporate sector. Their results were obviously ignored or, more than likely, unknown in the more recent Mexican crisis.

Using quarterly data on the macroeconomic variables (24 data points), 10 regressions were estimated using a different combination of two macro variables. Although the business failure *rate*, rather than the absolute number of business failures would have been more appropriate as the dependent variable, the authors did not have the data on the total number of businesses in each time period, and therefore they were forced to use the absolute number of failures. The authors also note the other shortcomings: limited size of the data sample, conceptual problems with measuring expected devaluation rates, and the distortions in measuring the time of failure by lags in court processing time. The authors conclude, based on the results of the regressions, that of all the factors considered, interest rates and credit stocks are the most important factors in explaining business failures.

The second question examined by the authors is the issue of whether all industries were *uniformly* affected by the Argentine reforms. The authors' hypothesis is that the high protection industries suffer considerably higher failure levels than the low protection industries when the protection is reduced. Each subsample for the study consisted of 12 industries with data for 20 quarters. To account for interindustry difference in the number of firms, the authors included the logarithm of the number of establishments in the industry as an explanatory variable. The authors report statistically significant evidence to support their hypothesis that high protection leads to higher failures when protection is removed.

In order to test their third question, that is, what are the firm-level variables that predict failure, the authors favor the use of a probit regression instead of discriminant analysis for two stated reasons: that assumptions necessary for statistical inference are typically not satisfied and that the individual influences of the predictors cannot be isolated. The criticism of discriminant analysis by the authors is not compelling because the authors appear to tolerate even more serious limitations caused by the smallness of the sample. Also the standardized discriminant function does show the relative importance of the variables.

The models were estimated for the predevaluation period and postdevaluation period. The final model contained ratios with total assets as the best normalizing variable (as opposed to total debt or net worth). The resulting model included the following ratios: the protection (0, 1) index, quick ratio, real financial cost, EBIT, sales, debt, Ln(Assets), and foreign exchange.

In the post-devaluation period, the role of financial costs, foreign currency exposure and firm size become more marked as expected. In both pre-devaluation and post-devaluation periods, the dummy variable for protection has the expected sign but is not statistically significant. The authors conclude based on this outcome, and because sectoral regressions reflect contrasts among firms not listed in the stock exchange, that higher failure rates for protected firms are concentrated among smaller, privately held firms.

Although by using probit regression, the authors could evaluate and present the statistical significance of individual variables, the published statistics (log-likelihood and the chi-square) do not tell us anything about the classification/misclassification accuracy among fails and nonfails respectively. In addition, the published results are in-sample values. Despite the problems with the data, this article is impressive in the broad sweep of the issues considered in both macroeconomic and microeconomic terms and in explicitly modeling trade protection and foreign currency exposure. As we move further into a truly global economy, these variables take on added significance in assessing risk.

10.14 BRAZIL. Brazil is an example of an economy where the end result of a series of economic setbacks would put severe pressure on private enterprises. For example, tightening of credit for all firms—especially smaller ones—can jeopardize financial institutions and undermine government efforts to promote economic development.

Most observers would agree that action to detect and avoid critical pressures of this type is highly desirable in an economy like Brazil, which has enjoyed extraordinary growth followed by severe inflation, maxi devaluations and recessions. And, as a result of the very recent significant reduction in inflation, banks are now making loans again and are therefore concerned with credit risk issues. Based on the results in 1994–1996, these concerns are valid as the number of business failures escalated, computed to the days of hyperinflation and little borrowing.

(a) Altman, Baidya, and Ribeiro-Dias (1979). Altman, Baidya, and Ribeiro-Dias (1979) examined two *a priori* groups of firms categorized as serious-problem (SP) and no-problem (NP) companies. A small number of variables were then calculated for each observation (firm) in each of the two samples. Data covered the period from one to three annual reporting statements prior to the problem date. The data from one year prior (and the corresponding year for the control sample) were then analyzed through the use of linear discriminant analysis.

The serious-problem firms were defined as those filing formal petitions for court-supervised liquidations, legal reorganizations in bankruptcy (*concordatas*), and out-of-court manifestations of serious problems. In all but two of the 23 serious-problem cases, the problem became manifest during the 30 months from January 1975 to June 1977. Industry categories represented include textiles, furniture, pulp and paper, retail stores, plastics, metallurgy, and others. The average asset size of the serious-problem firms was surprisingly high at 323 million cruzeiros (U.S. $25–30 million). Therefore, the model, if accurate, has relevance over a wide range of companies in terms of size. The control (or no-problem) sample was actually somewhat smaller in terms of average asset size.

One or two firms were selected for the control sample from each of the same industrial categories as those represented by the serious-problem group, and data were gathered from the year corresponding to the year prior to the problem date. Since there were more than 30 industrial categories to choose from, the number of firms in each industrial group was often quite small. Whenever possible, privately owned, domestic companies were selected since we felt that a state-owned or multinational affiliation reduced, in general, the possibility of failure.

The classification procedure used in this study is based on the failure model developed in the United States (Altman, 1968), with modifications that allow for consideration of Brazilian standards and reporting practices. In this Brazilian study, the same variables were utilized but X_2 and X_4 were modified. With respect to X_2, the retained earnings account on U.S. balance sheets reflects the cumulative profits of a firm less any cash dividends paid out and stock dividends. In most instances, the small, young firm will be discriminated against because it has not had time to accumulate its earnings. In Brazil, however, due to different financial reporting practices and adjustments for inflation, there is no exact equivalent to retained earnings. The nearest translation to retained earnings is "*lucros suspetisos*," which refers to those earnings retained in the business after distribution of dividends, This amount is usually transferred, however, within a short time (perhaps two years) through stock dividends to the account known as capital.

In addition, reserves that were created to adjust for monetary correction on fixed assets and the maintenance of working capital were deducted from profits and thereby decrease those earnings which are reported to be retained in the firm. These reserves, however, increase both the assets and the firm's equity and they too are transferred to capital. In essence, then, that amount of capital which represents funds contributed by the owners of the firm is the only part of equity that is not considered in the Brazilian equivalent to retained earnings. X_2 was calculated as:

$$(\text{Total equity} - \text{Capital contributed by shareholders (CCS)})/\text{Total assets}$$

A more precise expression of the numerator would be the cumulative yearly retained earnings plus the cumulative reserves created over the life of the firm, but this information is very difficult to obtain outside the firm and was not available to the authors.

Since most Brazilian firms' equity was not traded, there cannot be a variable which measures the market value of equity (number of shares outstanding times the latest market price). To derive the new values for X_4, the book value of equity (*patrimonio liquido*) was substituted and divided by the total liabilities. The remaining three variables were not adjusted, although we are aware of the fact that certain financial expenses are also adjusted for inflation in Brazilian accounting.

(b) Empirical Results. The empirical results will be discussed in terms of two separate but quite similar models. The first model, referred to as Z_1, includes variables X_2 to X_5 (four measures) of the original Z-Score model. Model Z_1 does not include X_1 because the stepwise discriminant program indicated that it did not add any explanatory power to the model and the sign of the coefficient was contrary to intuitive logic. Once again, as so often is found in multivariate failure classification studies, the liquidity variable is not found to be particularly important. The second model, referred to as Z_2, does not include X_2, because X_2 is quite difficult to derive with just one set of financial statements and it is similar to X_4. Model Z_2 can therefore be applied without supplementary data.

The models are as follows:

$$Z_1 = 1.44 + 4.03X_2 + 2.25X_3 + 0.14X_4 + 0.42X_5$$

$$Z_2 = 1.84 - 0.51X_1 + 6.23X_3 + 0.71X_4 + 0.56X_5$$

In both cases, the critical cutoff score is zero. That is, any firm with a score greater than zero is classified as having a multivariate profile similar to that of continuing entities and those with a score less than zero are classified as having characteristics similar to those of entities that experienced serious problems.

Results from the two models are essentially identical based on one year prior data. Model Z_1 performed better for Years 2 and 3; therefore, only the results of that model are discussed. Of the 58 firms in the combined two samples, seven are misclassified, yielding an overall accuracy of 88%. The Type I error (that of classifying a serious-problem firm as a continuing entity) was 13% (3 out of 23 misclassified) and the Type II error (that of misclassifying a continuing entity) was slightly lower at 11.4% (4 of 35). These results are impressive since they indicate that published financial data in Brazil, when correctly interpreted and rigorously analyzed, do indeed possess important information content.

Due to the potential upward bias involved in original sample classification results, further tests of the models were performed with several types of holdout or validation samples. The accuracy of the SP sample is unchanged after applying the Lachenbruch test. Several replication tests also showed high accuracy levels. Finally, the accuracy of the model is examined as the data become more remote from the serious problem date. The SP sample results, as expected, show a drop in the accuracy of the models. We utilized the weights from the model constructed with Year 1 data and inserted the variable measures for Years 2 and 3 prior to the SP date. Year 2 data provided accuracy of 84.2% (16 of 19 correct). Year 3 data provided lower accuracy of 77.8% (14 of 18 correct) classifications. Therefore, in only four cases were errors observed in classification based on data from three (or more in some cases) years prior to the SP date.

(c) Implications of Results for Brazil. The implications and applications of models designed for assessing the potential for serious financial problems in firms are many. This is especially true in a developing country, where an epidemic of business failures could have drastic effects on the strength of the private sector and on the economy as a whole. Most observers of the Brazilian situation would agree on the merit of preserving an equilibrium among private enterprises, state-owned firms, and multinationals. Such equilibrium would be jeopardized if the domestic private sector were weakened by an escalation of liquidations. If a model such as the one suggested is used to identify potential problems, then in many cases preventive or rehabilitative action can be taken. This should involve a conscious internal effort, by the firms themselves, to prevent critical situations as soon as a potential problem is detected. Besides internal efforts, a program of financial and managerial assistance, more than likely from official external sources, is a potential outcome.

Many economists, including the writers, have argued that significant government assistance for the private sector is an unwise policy except where the system itself is jeopardized. One can rationalize government agencies' attempts to stabilize those industries where a significant public presence or national security is involved, for instance, commercial and savings banks or the steel industry. In developing countries, the distinction between high public interest sectors and the fragile private sector is more difficult to make, and limited early assistance is advocated.

10.15 INDIA

(a) Bhatia (1988). The author has developed a discriminant analysis model for identifying "sick" companies. Sick companies in India refer to companies that continue to operate (or more accurately are kept in operation even after their economic value is in question) even after incurring losses. The definition used by the Industrial Development Bank of India for sickness is if a company suffers from any of the following ills:

- Cash losses for a period of two years, or if there is a continuous erosion of net worth, say 50%
- Four successive defaults on its debt service obligations
- Persistent irregularity in the use of the credit lines
- Tax payments in arrears for one to two years

The sample consisted of 18 sick and 18 healthy companies all of which are publicly traded. Data used pertained to the period 1976–1995. The healthy companies were paired with the sick ones based on the type of product and gross fixed assets.

	Standardized Coefficient	Rank	Unstandardized Coefficient
X_1	0.56939	2	1.64621
X_2	0.23186	6	0.03071
X_3	0.34543	4	0.004271
X_4	0.50499	3	0.8169
X_5	0.64154	1	0.05372
X_6	0.14993	7	−0.007024
X_7	0.34498	5	0.006616

X_1 = Current ratio
X_2 = Stock of finished goods/sales
X_3 = Profit after tax/net worth
X_4 = Interest/value of output
X_5 = Cash flow/total debt
X_6 = Working capital management ratio
X_7 = Sales/total assets

Exhibit 10.13. Discriminant Function Coefficients.

The companies were drawn from the cement, electrical, engineering, glass, paper, and steel industries.

The seven ratios in the final discriminant function, along with the standardized discriminant function coefficient are presented in Exhibit 10.13.

The Type I accuracy was 87.1% and the Type II accuracy was 86.6% on the development sample. A holdout test was performed on 20 healthy companies and 28 sick companies. The test results generally validated the efficacy of the model.

10.16 IRELAND. In Ireland, Cahill (1981) presents some exploratory work on a small sample of 11 bankrupt, listed companies covering the period from 1970 through 1980. Three primary issues are explored: (1) identification of those ratios which showed a significant deterioration as failure approaches, (2) whether the auditors' reports expressed any reservations or uncertainty about the continuance of the firms as going concerns, and (3) whether there were any other unique aspects of the failed companies' conditions.

Cahill's analysis revealed a number of ratios indicating clear distress signals one year prior to failure. These ratios compared unfavorably with aggregate norms and ratios for the comparable industrial sector. Although several measures continued to show differences in earlier years, the signals were less clear in year 2 prior and it was difficult to detect strong signals from ratios prior to year 2.

Only one of the 11 auditors' reports was qualified on the basis of going concern. Five other less serious qualifications were present in the auditor's reports. Cahill speculates that the low frequency of auditor qualifications on a going concern basis was due to auditor reluctance and accounting convention in Ireland as well as their feeling of being part of a "small society." We observed similar circumstances in Australia. Still, according to Cahill, since deterioration was quite apparent, those close to the situation should have been aware of the seriousness of the situations and earlier remedial action taken or qualification given.

Unsuccessful merger activity and significant investment and asset expansion financed by debt were the major causes of Irish failures. Several of the firms continued to pay dividends right up to the year prior to failure. On the other hand, only one company actually made payments to unsecured creditors after insolvency, indicating that asset value had deteriorated beyond repair and only then was failure declared.

10.17 KOREA

(a) Altman, Kim, and Eom (1995). As a growing and potentially overheated economy, Korea may be following in the footsteps of its neighbor, Japan, which had a period of rapid economic growth only to be followed by increased business failures. For this reason, the authors suggest, that a failure prediction model for Korea is timely, even given the 1995 robustness of the South Korean economy. In particular, because of the increased deregulation and greater autonomy in decision-making by financial institutions, the availability of predictive models is relevant.

The distress classification model described in this study consists of two versions: the K1 model is applicable for both public and private firms, whereas the K2 model, which uses the market value of equity in one of its ratios, may be used only for publicly traded firms.

Linear discriminant analysis was the technique used in building the model. The sample of failed firms consisted of 34 publicly traded industrial and trading companies with assets ranging from $13 million to $296 million. Failure and failure dates were defined based on technical insolvency or liquidation whichever came first. Technical insolvency is defined as the condition when the credit of a company is no longer accepted. Most of the failures in the sample occurred in 1991–1992. It is significant to note that 30 of the 34 distressed firms had their shares publicly traded only since 1988, and 23 of the 30 were listed during the explosion of new IPO listings in 1988 and 1989. For this reason, the results of the model may be of interest to investors and regulators of new issues in the Korean stock market.

Because the nondistressed group of firms tended to be significantly larger in size on average, the pairing of the healthy firm with the failed firm was based mainly on industry sector grouping. For 34 distressed firms a larger sample of 61 nonfailed entities was chosen, with the actual one to one pairing done by random selection from the universe of 61 firms during model building.

The time series analysis of the individual ratio averages revealed that some early warning financial indicators such as book value of equity to total liabilities do not behave in the same way as they do for U.S. firms. This ratio, contrary to expectations, actually improves for failed firms until just before bankruptcy. However, the same ratio based on market value behaves as expected. For this reason, the authors have proceeded with two different models: one employing the book equity leverage variable and the other with a market equity variable.

The criteria for selecting the final variable set were:

- High univariate significance test (see Exhibit 10.14).
- Expected sign for all the model coefficients.
- Original (in-sample) and holdout (out-of-sample) test results.
- Reasonable accuracy levels over time.

The K1 model had the following variables:

Years Prior to Failure	No of Firms	% Correctly Classified
1	34	97.1
2	34	88.2
3	33	69.7
4	32	50.0
5	16	68.8
Year	No of Firms	% Correctly Classified
1988	57	77.2
1989	58	81.0
1990	59	83.1
1991	47	89.4
1992	29	93.1
Total	250	83.6

Exhibit 10.14. Classification Results—Bankrupt Firms K1 Model.

- LOG(Total assets)
- LOG(Sales/total assets)
- Retained earnings/total assets
- Book value of equity/total liabilities

The classification results on the original sample for the K1 and K2 models are presented in Exhibit 10.14.

The K2 model contained the following ratios:

- LOG(Total assets)
- LOG(Sales/total assets)
- Retained earnings/total assets
- Market value of equity/total liabilities

The classification results on the original sample for the K2 models are presented in Exhibit 10.15.

The authors note two major limitations of these models. First, because of lack of data, the authors were unable to perform hold-out testing. Second, the Type II accuracy of 70% is perceived to be rather low. Both limitations will be removed if future tests of the model yield usable predictions.

10.18 MALAYSIA

(a) Bidin (1988). The New Economic Policy launched by the Malaysian Government in the early 1980s was aimed at increasing and redistributing corporate ownership among the races in that country. The indigenous races in which the Malays form the majority have a disproportionately small share of the corporate wealth. The government has set up a number of public corporations and enterprises to directly involve the indigenous races in terms of ownership and the development of managerial skills. Permodalan Nasional Berhad (PNB) is a corporation whose objective is to evaluate, select, and acquire shares in corporations with good potential with the intention of ultimately selling them to a unit trust fund. PNB is thus an investment in-

Years Prior to Failure	No of Firms	% Correctly Classified
1	29	96.6
2	23	85.2
3	15	71.4
4	4	40.0
5	3	75.0
Year	No of Firms	% Correctly Classified
1988	40	75.0
1989	51	86.3
1990	57	86.0
1991	47	89.4
1992	29	93.1
Total	224	85.7

Exhibit 10.15. Classification Results: Bankrupt Firms K2 Model.

stitution which has developed some expertise in financial analysis and monitoring the operations of companies. In 1985, the government entrusted PNB with the additional task of monitoring the performance of *all government companies*, not just those in PNB's portfolio. This led to the formation of CICU, the Central Information Collection Unit, the unit within PNB that performs this function. CICU is charged with the task of identifying companies in distress at an early stage so that the necessary remedial action may be taken by the authorities. A multivariate discriminant analysis model has been built with applicability mainly for manufacturing companies, and also for companies in the transportation and service sector.

The sample consisted of 21 companies known to have been in distress paired with financially sound companies which were entirely Malaysian with business activities in Malaysia. Forty-one ratios were defined for inclusion in the analysis. Stepwise selection yielded a discriminant function that had seven variables ranked by the level of contribution to the F statistic as shown in Exhibit 10.16.

Variable	R**2	F-Statistic
R1	0.5307	45.230
R2	0.3921	30.250
R3	0.2388	12.506
R4	0.2275	10.898
R5	0.1360	5.665
R6	0.0333	3.181
R7	0.0795	2.935

R1 = Operating profit/total liabilities
R2 = Current assets/current liabilities
R3 = EAIT/paid-up capital
R4 = Sales/working capital
R5 = Current assets – Stocks – Current liabilities/EBIT
R6 = Total shareholders' fund/total liabilities
R7 = Ordinary shareholders' fund/employment of capital

Exhibit 10.16. Discriminant Function Variables.

The authors present three case studies where the PNB-Score was able to correctly predict the outcome in advance. They also note that the test of the model on over 600 companies showed that the results predicted by the model were found to be relatively consistent with the actual performance of the companies. The model is very sensitive to the liabilities of the company, because failure is most often caused when the companies' cash flows are relatively low compared to its fixed debt commitments. The study does not present any information on Type II accuracy. It is also not clear whether the 600 companies tested are all problem companies or they included some healthy ones as well. To the best of our knowledge, a revised PNB model is still actively used.

10.19 SINGAPORE

(a) Ta and Seah (1988). Singapore was and still is a dynamic and growing economy that has attracted a large amount of foreign investment. A business failure prediction model is justified both for preserving Singapore's image as a major financial and manufacturing center and as a way to assist rational investment in Singapore companies by investors and creditors. This study examines 24 financial ratios using linear discriminant function analysis.

The failed firm sample consists of 22 firms with failure dates in the period 1975–1983. The failure characteristics of the firms in the sample are as follows: 9% went into receivership, 18% went into creditors' voluntary liquidation, while the rest were involuntary "winding up" by the order of the court. The matched sample consists of 21 nonfailed entities. Only industrial and commercial firms are considered in the samples. The mean asset size of the firms in the sample is S$89.5 million. The data sources for the sample are:

- Singapore Registry of Companies and Businesses
- Singapore Stock Exchange
- National University of Singapore's Financial Database

The discriminant analysis process produced a four-variable model consisting of:

1. Total debt/equity
2. Profit before tax/sales
3. Profit before tax/equity
4. Interest payment/profit before interest and taxes

The results of the model on the original sample and a validation (holdout) sample are reported in Exhibit 10.17. The results for the original sample are based on data from one year prior to failure. The validation test results are for one and two years prior.

Although the sample size is relatively small, the results of the model are fairly good, and its performance is assured as good quality data is available on a larger number of Singapore companies. The model does suffer from several variables measuring similar firm attributes (e.g. profits).

	Original Sample			Holdout Sample		
Year Prior	Type I Accuracy	Type II Accuracy	Overall Accuracy	Type I Accuracy	Type II Accuracy	Overall Accuracy
1 year	77.3%	93.5%	86.8%	75.0%	90.5%	86.2%
2 years				62.5	85.7	79.3

Exhibit 10.17. Summary of Results.

10.20 FINLAND

(a) Suominen (1988). The author employs a multinomial logit model (MNL) to classify firms into two groups: failing and nonfailing and to assess the relative importance of each financial ratio variable. The second part of the study classifies failed firms further into two groups: firms failed within one year of prediction and firms that failed later. Both models employ the same set of three financial ratios indicative of profitability, liquidity and leverage. The ratios are:

PROF = (Quick flow – Direct taxes)/Total assets, where Quick flow = (Net turnover – Materials and supplies – Wages and salaries – Rent and leases – Other expenses + Other revenues)

LIQU = Quick/Total assets, where Quick = (Current assets – Inventories/Current liabilities)

LEVE = Liabilities/Total assets

The author favors the MNL technique, corrected for the constant term, because concerns that the assumptions of equal covariance matrices and normal distribution of the variables are not usually prevalent or tested when using discriminant analysis. In addition, the coefficients from a MNL model are easily testable. Suominen's sample consists of two sets of data. The first set covers the period 1964–1973 and consists of 49 failed firms and 87 healthy firms, both from manufacturing industries. The second set consists of data for a different set of failed and healthy firms covering the period 1981–1982.

The PROF ratio was not found to be significant in the models for one and two years prior to failure. In the three years prior model, only LEVE was significant. In the four years prior model only LIQU was significant. The classification results on the first sample and the second sample are summarized in Exhibit 10.18. It should be noted that both results are for the sample space and not for holdouts. The results of the one-year model are comparable to those obtained using discriminant analysis using the same variables. The Type I errors are reported to be fewer in the discriminant model, however.

The purpose behind the second part of the study is not entirely clear. Here the objective is to predict correctly the firms that failed within one year of the prediction as

	Data From 1964–1973		Data From 1981–1982	
Years Prior	Type I Accuracy %	Type II Accuracy %	Type I Accuracy %	Type II Accuracy %
1	67–71	85–86	65–74	61–65
2	53–57	84	61	70
3	31–33	87–89	65	70
4	26	93–95		

Exhibit 10.18. Classification Accuracy.

	Sample No. 1	Sample No. 2*
Years of Failure	Accuracy %	Accuracy %
1 vs. 2, 3, 4	73–75	65–70
2 vs. 3, 4	60–67	57–65
3 vs. 4	50–52	

*There are no firms with data extending beyond 3 years prior to failure.

Exhibit 10.19. Classification Accuracy.

distinct from those failed later. The results suggest that the MNL model is able to classify the firms into the two groups with overall accuracies as indicated in Exhibit 10.19 for the first and the second sample sets. Type I and Type II accuracy rates could not be reported here because this information is not available in the study.

10.21 MEXICO

(a) Altman, Hartzell, and Peck (1995). The authors assert that emerging markets credits should be initially analyzed in a manner similar to traditional analysis of U.S. corporates. Once a quantitative risk assessment has emerged out of traditional analysis, it can then be modified by the qualitative assessments of an analyst for other risks, such as currency risk and industry risk characteristics of the industry itself as well as the firm's competitive position in that industry. It is not often possible to build a model specific to an emerging country based on a sample from the country itself because of the lack of credit experience in that country. To deal with this problem, the authors have modified the Altman Z-Score model and renamed the resulting model as the EMS model (Emerging Market Scoring Model). The revised model utilized the first four of the original five variable Z-score (1988) model, with weightings determined by a new set of computer runs.

The process of deriving the rating for a Mexican corporate credit is:

1. EMS score is calculated and equivalent U.S. bond rating is obtained based on the calibration of the EMS scores with U.S. bond rating equivalents.
2. The company's Eurobond bond is then analyzed for the issuing firm's vulnerability to servicing its foreign currency denominated debt. This is based on the relationship between the nonlocal currency revenues minus costs compared to nonlocal currency expenses. Then, the level of nonlocal currency cash flow is compared with the debt coming due in the next year. Depending on the degree of vulnerability seen by the analyst, the rating is adjusted downward, or remains the same in the case of little vulnerability.
3. The rating is further adjusted (up or down) if the company is in an industry considered to be relatively different from the bond equivalent rating attained in step 1.
4. The rating is further adjusted up or down depending upon the dominance of the firm's position in its industry.

5. If the debt has special features such as collateral or a bona fide guarantor, the rating is adjusted accordingly.

For relative value analysis, the corresponding U.S. corporates' credit spread is added to the sovereign bond's option adjusted spread. Only a handful of the Mexican companies are rated by the rating agencies. Thus the risk assessments such as those provided by EMS are often the only reliable indicators of credit risk to overseas investors in Mexico. The author reports that the ratings have proven accurate in anticipating both downgrades and defaults (e.g., Grupo Synkro in May 1995) and upgrades.

10.22 URUGUAY

(a) Pascale (1988). The economic situation in Uruguay had gone through a major transformation, starting from a period of deep economic intervention during the period 1950–1974 that led to high inflation, low real growth and frequent balance of payments crises. Starting in 1974 there was gradual reduction in the controls for capital flows, government intervention in economic affairs was reduced, and a new tax policy implemented. The change in the economic environment provided a new set of shocks to Uruguayan firms. They had to face new market conditions and decreased protection. It is in this setting that this model was developed to predict financial problems in firms.

The sample consisted of 44 failed firms (FP's; Financial Problems), and 41 healthy firms (NPs; No problems). The criterion for failure was any one of the following: liquidation, bankruptcy, (forbearance/restructuring) agreement with creditors, arrangements with bank syndicates or other financial backers which did not always involve special formalities but entailed substantial changes in financial structure, and cessation of activities owing to financial problems. The firms were in food, beverage, footwear and apparel, leather, chemical, and metal products. All the firms selected had no less than 10 workers each, with most firms (both failed and healthy) employing 50 or more workers. Healthy firms were matched with failures based on size and industry, although an exact correspondence was not always possible due to lack of data. Both groups of firms were studied for the period from 1978 to 1982. Of the firms with problems, 77% experienced their difficulties in 1980 and 1981, and 11% in 1982.

The adjustments performed on the sample data are worth mentioning because normally nominal values of the ratios are used in such studies rather than those based on constant term or inflation-adjusted financials:

- The data was cross-checked with published reports.
- All amounts were restated in a common currency.
- Fixed assets were valued in accordance with tax regulations.
- Current assets and liabilities in local currency were deflated by the wholesale price index applicable to the industry.
- Investments other than fixed assets were deflated using the general consumer price index.
- Fixed assets were computed at their value for tax purposes for the first year of data. In subsequent years the adjustments to the value were deflated by the implicit price index for fixed gross investment.

Variable	FP Mean	NP Mean	F
Asset turnover	1.11932	1.64829	16.397
Current ratio	1.02636	2.29415	39.594
Changes in working capital	0.03091	0.46927	4.514
Sales/nonbank working capital	2.94295	4.78073	10.433
Leverage	1.33432	3.03975	54.260
Inventory/bank debt	0.98568	4.58146	21.548
Bank debt/total debt	1.68295	2.84097	8.735
Long-term debt/total debt	0.07455	0.12659	2.912
(Accounts receivable + inventories/accounts payable + spontaneous sources)	3.85841	3.06780	2.070
Inventory turnover	3.90432	7.68439	16.656
Rate of return on assets	–0.25068	0.23341	6.414
Sales/debts	1.53454	4.67829	68.243
Net earnings/total assets	–0.08705	0.10756	27.057

$F_{1.60}(0.05) = 4.00$, $F_{1.120}(0.05) = 3.92$
$F_{1.60}(0.01) = 7.08$, $F_{1.120}(0.01) = 6.85$

Exhibit 10.20. Means of the Variables and Significance Tests.

- Net worth was calculated in constant terms as the difference between assets and liabilities.
- Sales were deflated using the wholesale price index for the industry.

The variables used in the model along with the means and univariate F statistics are presented in Exhibit 10.20.

The resulting discriminant function using the F value as the criterion to enter contained the following three variables:

1. Sales/debt
2. Net Earnings/total assets
3. Long-term debt/total debt

The classification accuracy of the model in the original sample was 98% for Type I and 85% for Type II. In the Lachenbruch holdout test, the corresponding values were 98% and 83% respectively. The Lachenbruch test (sometimes called the "jack-knife" test) is used to eliminate the sample bias, by estimating the model with one observation held out and then classifying that observation. This process is repeated as many times as there are cases which virtually eliminates any potential bias. The author performed holdout tests by validating the model with random sub-samples.

The classification accuracy in the holdout subsample ranged from 79% to 100%. Finally the accuracy of the model was tested on data two and three years prior to failure. The Type I accuracy for two and three years prior was 83% and the Type II accuracy was 79% for two years prior and 81% for three years prior, indicating that the model had an impressive ability to predict failure.

10.23 TURKEY

(a) Unal (1988). In this study, the author argues in favor of conducting principal component and congruency analysis on the universe of financial ratios in order to reduce the dimensions of the variables selected and minimize multicollinearity in the discriminant analysis by the use of highly correlated variables. This in turn leads to insufficient discriminating ability and possibly also lack of stability. His research on the Turkish Food sector employs these two techniques to reduce the number of variables that best separate failing and stable firms.

In the second phase, cluster analysis, principal factor analysis and Q factor analysis were conducted to determine the basic financial ratios that will appear in the early warning model. Varimax rotation was applied to the principal factors to obtain a more meaningful interpretation of the principal factors. The basic financial ratios that were obtained were then subjected to discriminant analysis to formulate a failure prediction model for the industry during the period 1979–1984.

The failed firm sample consisted of 33 firms. The definition of a failed firm was: (1) a firm that reported continuous losses after a certain period of time; (2) firms whose capital profitability was below that provided by risk-free government bonds; (3) those firms that had standing debts after the date they were due; and (4) those firms that could not be considered successful because they did not exhibit a positive correlation between the ratios representing risk and profitability respectively. Sixty-two firms registered in the Turkish Capital Market Roster were used in the study. The data was comprised of 50 financial ratios.

The author discussed the pros and cons of adjusting the financial numbers for inflation (i.e., use ratios derived from constant dollar data) versus using the nominal amounts. In the end, he used the nominal values because of the limited scope of the research. There are other limitations in a study of this nature, according to the author. The first is the existence of correlations among the financial ratios. This can be addressed through factor analysis. The effect of economic change brought about by the business cycle cannot be evaluated by looking at data for a narrow band of time. A time series analysis of data from 1979–1984 was performed to take account of this problem. To address the question of the distribution of the financial ratios, normalcy tests were conducted on the ratios. Although the attempts to normalize through transformations the nonnormal ratios proved to be unsuccessful, the normalcy tests did bring about the rejection of outliers that appeared to cause right skewness in the sample data.

After conducting factor analysis to identify principal components, time series analysis to look for ratio stability, and cluster analysis and Q factor analysis to group "like" ratios, the final model was determined.

The ratios satisfying the normalcy conditions, low correlations, and stability were:

X_1: Earnings before interest and tax/total assets

X_2: Net working capital/sales

X_3: Long-term debt/total assets

Ratio	Coefficient	Coefficient (absolute value of the difference of the means)	The Relative Importance of the Ratio (%)
X_1	18.11	5.4029	52.04
X_2	1.64	1.0365	9.98
X_3	−1.21	0.1078	1.04
X_4	1.21	0.1806	1.74
X_5	−0.96	0.3890	3.75
X_6	5.85	3.2663	31.45

Exhibit 10.21. Discriminant Function Coefficients.

X_4: Total debt/total assets

X_5: Quick assets/inventory

X_6: Quick assets/current debt

The standardized discriminant function coefficients and the discriminant function are as shown in Exhibit 10.21. The classification accuracy of the model on the development sample was 97% overall. With the same level of accuracy for Type I and II. Tests on data 2 years prior yielded a Type I accuracy of 91% and Type II accuracy of 93%. No hold-out test results were reported.

10.24 SUMMARY. We have attempted to review and compare a relatively large number of empirical failure classification models from over twenty countries. Much of the material is derived from little-known sources and as such we hope that the study will stimulate a greater transnational discussion. Indeed, as financial institutions and government agencies in countries such as Canada, the United States, Brazil, France, and England wrestle with the specter of large firm failures in the future, the knowledge that prior work has been done with respect to early warning models may help obviate the consequences or reduce the number of these failures.

We expect the quality and reliability of models constructed in many of the aforementioned countries to improve (1) as the quality of information on companies is expanded and refined, (2) as the number of business failures increase, thereby providing more data points for empirical analysis, and (3) as researchers and practitioners become more aware of the problems and potential of such models. Where sufficient data do not exist for specific sector models, for instance, manufacturing, retailing, and service firms, the application of industry relative measures, for example, Altman and Izan (1983), can perhaps provide a satisfactory framework for meaningful analysis. Of course, this requires that government or private agencies build reliable industry databases for comparison purposes.

SOURCES AND SUGGESTED REFERENCES

Abrahams, A., and R. A. I. van Frederikslust. "Discriminant Analysis and the Prediction of Corporate Failure." *European Finance Association 1975 Proceedings*. R. Brealey and G. Rankine (eds.). Amsterdam: North Holland, 1976.

Altman, E. I. *Corporate Financial Distress*. New York: John Wiley & Sons, 1993.

———. "Financial Ratios, Discriminant Analysis and the Prediction of Corporate Bankruptcy." *Journal of Finance,* Vol. 23, No 4, 1968, pp. 589–609.

Altman, E. I., T. Baidya, and L. M. Riberio-Dias. "Assessing Potential Financial Problems of Firms in Brazil." *Journal of International Business Studies*, Fall 1979.

Altman, E. I., R. G. Haldeman, and P. Narayanan. "ZETA Analysis: A New Model to Identify Bankruptcy Risk of Corporations." *Journal of Banking and Finance*, Vol. 1, No. 1, 1977, pp. 29–51.

Altman, E. I., D. W. Kim, and Y. H. Eom. "Failure Prediction: Evidence from Korea." *Journal of International Financial Management and Accounting*, Vol. 6, No. 3, 1995, pp. 230–249.

Altman, E. I., J. M. Hartzell, and M. B. Peck. *Emerging Markets Corporate Bonds Scoring System—Mexican 1995 Review and 1996 Outlook*. New York: Salomon Brothers Inc., 1995.

Altman, E. I., and H. Y. Izan. *Identifying Corporate Distress in Australia; An Industry Relative Analysis*. Sydney: Australian Graduate School of Management, 1983.

Altman, E. I., and M. Lavallee. "Business Failure Classification in Canada." *Journal of Business Administration*, Summer 1981.

Altman, E. I., G. Marco, and F. Varetto. "Corporate Distress Diagnosis: Comparisons Using Linear Discriminant Analysis and Neural Networks (The Italian Experience)." *Journal of Banking and Finance*, Vol. 18, 1994, pp. 505–529.

Altman, E. I., M. Margaine, M. Schlosser, and P. Vernimmen. "Statistical Credit Analysis in the Textile Industry: A French Experience." *Journal of Financial and Quantitative Analysis*, March 1974.

Appetti, S. "Identifying Unsound Firms in Italy." *Journal of Banking and Finance*, Vol. 8, 1984, pp. 269–279.

Argenti, J. "Predicting Corporate Failure, Institute of Chartered Accountants in England and Wales." *Accountants Digest*, No. 138, 1983.

Ashton, R. H. "Some Indications of Parameter Sensitivity Research for Judgment Modelling in Accounting." *Accounting Review*, Vol. 54, No. 1, 1979, pp. 170–179.

Baetge, J., M. Muss, and H. Niehaus. "The Use of Statistical Analysis to Identify the Financial Strength of Corporations in Germany." *Studies in Banking & Finance*, Vol. 7, 1988, pp. 183–196.

Beaver, William. "Financial Ratios as Predictors of Failure." Empirical Research in Accounting: Selected Studies, 1966, supplement to *Journal of Accounting Research*, 1966, pp. 71–102.

Beerman, K. *Possible Ways to Predict Capital Losses with Annual Financial Statements*. Dusseldorf, Germany: n.p., 1976.

Betts, J. "The Identification of Companies at Risk of Financial Failure." *Working Environment Research Group, Report No. 5*. Bradford: University of Bradford, U.K., 1983.

Bhatia, U. "Predicting Corporate Sickness in India." *Studies in Banking & Finance*, 1988.

Bidin, A. R. "The Development of a Predictive Model (PNB-Score) for Evaluating Performance of Companies Owned by the Government of Malaysia." *Studies in Banking & Finance*, Vol. 7, 1988, pp. 91–103.

Bilderbeek, J. "An Empirical Study of the Predictive Ability of Financial Ratios in the Netherlands." *Zeitschrift fur Betriebswirtschaft*, No. 5, May 1977.

Bontemps, P. O. "La Notation du Risque de Credit." *Credit National*, Paris, 1981.

Briones, J. J., J. L. Martin Marín, and M. J. Vazquez Cueto. "Forecasting Bank Failures: The Spanish Case." *Studies in Banking & Finance*, Vol. 7, 1988, pp. 127–139.

Cahill, E. "Irish Listed Company Failure Ratios: Accounts and Auditors' Opinions." *Journal of Irish Business and Administrative Research*, April 1981.

Castagna, A. D., and Z. P. Matolcsy. "The Prediction of Corporate Failure; Testing the Australian Experience." *Australian Journal of Management*, June 1982.

Cifarelli, D. M., F. Corielli, and G. Forestieri. "Business Failure Analysis." A Bayesian Approach with Italian Firm Data." *Studies in Banking & Finance*, Vol. 7, 1988, pp. 73–89.

Collongues, Y. "Ratios, Financiers et Prevision des failites des Petites et Moyennes Enterprises (Financial Ratios and Forecasting of Small and Medium Size Enterprises). *Review Banque*, No. 365, 1977.

Deakin, E. B. "A Discriminant Analysis of Predictors of Business Failure." *Journal of Accounting Research*, Spring 1972, pp. 167–179.

Earl, M. J., and D. Marais. "Predicting Corporate Failure in the U.K. Using Discriminant Analysis." *Accounting and Business Research*, 1982.

Fernåndez, A. I. "A Spanish Model for Credit Risk Classification." *Studies in Banking & Finance*, Vol. 7, 1988, pp. 115–125.

Fischer, J. "Forecasting Company Failure by Using Non-Numerical Data." EISAM Workshop on Bank Planning Models, Brussels, April 6/7, 1981.

Gebhardt, G. "Insolvency Prediction Based on Annual Financial Statements According to the Company Law—An Assessment of the Reform of Annual Statements by the Law of 1965." In *Bochumer Beitrage Zur Untennehmungs und Unternehmens-forschung,* Volume 22. Edited by H. Besters et al., Wiesbaden, Germany: n.p. 1980.

Ghesquiere, S., and B. Micha. "L'analyses des defaillances d'enterprises." *Rapport de la Journee d'etude des Centrales de Bilans*, 1983.

Gloubos, S., and T. Grammatikos. "The Success of Bankruptcy Prediction Models in Greece." *Studies in Banking & Finance*, Vol. 7, 1988, pp. 37–46.

Grammatikos, T., and G. Gloubos. "Predicting Bankruptcy in Industrial Firms in Greece." *Spoudai*, Vol. 33, No. 3–4, (1988): p. 421.

Izan, H. Y. "Corporate Distress in Australia, 1984." *Journal of Banking and Finance*, Vol. 8, No. 2, 1984, pp. 303–320.

Knight, R. M. "The Determination of Failure in Canadian Firms." ASA Meetings of Canada, Saskatoon, May 28–30, 1979. Working paper. University of Western Ontario, May 1979.

Ko, C. J. "A Delineation of Corporate Appraisal Models and Classification of Bankruptcy Firms in Japan." Thesis. New York University, 1982.

Lachenbruch, P. A. "An Almost Unbiased Method of Obtaining Confidence Intervals for the Probability of Misclassification in Discriminant Analysis." *Biometrics* Vol. 23, 1967.

Lincoln, M. "An Empirical Study of the Usefulness of Accounting Ratios to Describe Levels of Insolvency Risk." *Journal of Banking and Finance*, Vol. 8, No. 2, 1984.

Mader, F. "Les Ratios et l'analyse du risque (Ratios and Analysis of Risk)." *Analyse Financiere*, Zeme Trimestre, 1975.

——. "Un Enchantillon d'Enterprises en Difficulte (A sample of Enterprises in Difficulty)." *Journee des Centrales der Bilans*, 1979.

Mallo, F. "FINPLAN—A Model of Credit Rating in Finland." Helsinki: Kansellis-*Osake Pakki Bank*, Helsinki, 1976.

Marais, D. A. J. "A Method of Quantifying Companies' Relative Financial Strength." Working Paper No. 4, Bank of England, London, 1979.

Micha, B. "Analysis of Business Failures in France." *Journal of Banking and Finance*, Vol. 8, No. 2, 1984, p. 281.

Papoulias, C., and P. Theodissiou. "Corporate Failure Prediction Models for Greece." Working paper. Fordham University, 1987.

Pascale, R. "A Multivariate Model to Predict Firm Financial Problems: The Case of Uruguay." *Studies in Banking & Finance*, Vol. 7, 1988, pp. 171–182.

Prihti, A. "Konkunssin Ennustaminen Kaseinformation Avulla (with English summary; The Prediction of Bankruptcy with Published Financial Data)." *Acta Academiae Oeconomica Helsingiensis A*, No. 13 (Helsinki).

Schimidt, R. "Early Warning of Debt Rescheduling." *Journal of Banking and Finance*, Vol. 8, No. 2, 1984, p. 357.

Suominen, S. I. "The Prediction of Bankruptcy in Finland." *Studies in Banking & Finance 7*, 1988, pp. 27–36.

Swanson, E., and J. Tybout. "Industrial Bankruptcy Determinants in Argentina." *Studies in Banking & Finance*, Vol. 7, 1988, pp. 1–25.

Ta, H. P., and L. H. Seah. "Business Failure Prediction in Singapore." *Studies in Banking & Finance*, Vol. 7, 1988, pp. 105–113.

Taffler, R. J. "Empirical Models for the Monitoring of U.K. Corporations." *Journal of Banking and Finance*, Vol. 8, No. 2, (1976): p. 199.

——. "Forecasting Company Failure in the U.K. Using Discriminant Analysis and Financial Ratios Data." *Journal of Royal Statistical Society*, 1982.

Taffler, R., and C. Houston. "How to Identify Failing Companies Before It Is Too Late." *Professional Administration*, April 1980.

Taffler, R. J., and H. Tisshaw. "Going, Going, Going—Four Factors Which Predict." *Accountancy*, 1977, p. 50.

Takahashi, K., Y. Kurokawa, and K. Watase. "Corporate Bankruptcy Prediction in Japan." *Journal of Banking and Finance*, Vol. 8, No. 2, 1984, pp. 229–247.

Tamari, M. "Financial Ratios as a Means of Forecasting Bankruptcy." *Economic Review* (Bank of Israel, Jerusalem), 1964.

"Techniques for Assessing Corporate Financial Strength." *Bank of England Quarterly Bulletin*, June 1982, pp. 221–223.

Theodossiou, P., and C. Papoulias. "Problematic Firms in Greece: An Evaluation Using Corporate Failure Prediction Models." *Studies in Banking & Finance*, Vol. 7, 1988, pp. 47–55.

Unal, T. "An Early Warning Model for Predicting Firm Failure in Turkey." *Studies in Banking & Finance*, Vol. 7, 1988, pp. 141–170.

van Frederikslust, R. A. I. *Predictability of Corporate Failure.* Leiden: Martinus Nijhoff Social Science Division, 1978.

von Stein, J. H. *Identifying Endangered Firms*. Stuttgart-Hohenheim: Hohenheim University, 1981.

von Stein, J. H., and W. Ziegler. "The Prognosis and Surveillance of Risks from Commercial Credit Borrowers." *Journal of Banking and Finance*, Vol. 8, No. 2, 1984, pp. 249–268.

Webb, L. "Predicting Australian Corporate Failures." *Charteres Accountant in Australia*, September 1980.

Weibel, P. F. *The Value of Criteria to Judge Credit Worthiness in the Lending of Banks.* Stuttgart: Bern, 1973.

Weinrich, G. *Predicting Credit Worthiness, Directions of Credit Operations by Risk Class.* Galder, Weisbaden: Galder, 1978.

CHAPTER 11

INTERNATIONAL DIVERSIFICATION

Edwin J. Elton
New York University
Martin J. Gruber
New York University

CONTENTS

11.1 INTRODUCTION. Portfolio managers in France, Germany, and England have for decades routinely invested a large fraction of their portfolio in securities that were issued in other countries. In contrast only in the last decade has there been a significant amount of foreign securities held by U.S. investors. Was the historical emphasis on U.S. securities by U.S. investors provincialism that is now disappearing, or are there sound economic reasons for the historical differences in the behavior of managers in different countries and for the current changes on the part of U.S. managers? In this chapter we attempt to present sufficient evidence for the readers to decide for themselves.

In section 11.2 we examine the market value of equities and debt worldwide. It turns out that no country comprises most of the world's wealth. Given the great number of opportunities worldwide, we discuss whether international diversification is a sensible strategy for investors. To analyze this question, we first show how returns on foreign assets are computed. The reasonableness of international diversification depends on the correlation coefficient across markets, the risk of each market, and the

---

returns in each market. This is the subject of the next section of the chapter. One of the major sources of risk in international investment are changes in exchange rates. The impact of exchange risk on international diversification and the possibility of eliminating part of the risk through hedging is examined next. Sections 11.3 and 11.4 examine the key role of return expectations in determining the benefits of international diversification. Break-even returns are derived and evidence is presented from actively managed international portfolios. After discussing the reasonableness of international diversification, we focus on active and passive strategies for international investment.

11.2 WORLD PORTFOLIO. In discussing the size of capital markets it is interesting to employ the concept of world portfolio. The world portfolio represents the total market value of all stocks (or bonds) that an investor would own if he or she bought the total of all marketable stocks on all the major stock exchanges in the world. Exhibit 11.1 shows the percentage that each nation's equity securities represented of the

Area or Country	Percent of Total[a]
Austria	0.1%
Belgium	0.4%
Denmark	0.4%
Finland	1.6%
France	5.5%
Germany	4.3%
Ireland	0.2%
Italy	2.1%
Netherlands	2.5%
Norway	0.2%
Portugal	0.2%
Spain	1.3%
Sweden	1.6%
Switzerland	2.8%
U.K.	9.7%
Europe	32.8%
Australia	1.1%
Hong Kong	1.0%
Japan	12.6%
Malaysia	0.5%
New Zealand	0.1%
Singapore	0.4%
Pacific	15.5%
Canada	2.1%
United States	49.5%
North America	51.6%
Total	100.0%

Source: From *Morgan Stanley Capital International Perspectives,* June 2000.

[a]Since the Morgan Stanley index does not include all shares traded in a market the proportions are approximate. Column sums may not equal totals because of rounding.

Exhibit 11.1. Comparative Sizes of World Equity Markets 2000.

Area or Country	Percent of Total
United States	47.0%
Euroland	22.9%
Japan	18.3%
United Kingdom	3.0%
Canada	1.7%
Switzerland	0.9%
Denmark	0.8%
Australia	0.6%
Sweden	0.6%
Norway	0.2%
New Zealand	0.1%
Asia	2.3%
Latin America	0.8%
Eastern Europe/Middle East/Africa	0.7%
Total	100.0%

Source: From Salomon Brothers.

Exhibit 11.2. Comparative Sizes of Major Bond Markets 1999.

world portfolio in 2000. Exhibit 11.2 shows similar percentages for the various publicly traded bond markets in 1999.

In 2000 the largest equity market was the United States, which represented 50% of the total. The second largest was Japan with 13% of the world market. All of the European markets combined accounted for about 33% of the world market.[1] Exhibit 11.2 shows that the U.S. bond market represented 47% of the world value and the European Monetary Union bond market was 23% of world value. Next was Japan with 18.3% of the world market.

Even for U.S. investors a large part of the investment opportunities lie outside the domestic market. For investors from any other country the opportunities (in terms of the market value of securities) outside the home country are much greater than those within the country of domicile. Thus for all investors a large part of the world's wealth lies outside the investor's home country. International assets could be duplicates of those found in the home country, in which case they do not offer new opportunities, or they could represent opportunities not duplicated in the home country. Which of these possibilities holds needs to be analyzed in order to determine whether international diversification should be an important part of each investor's portfolio. To examine this question we need to analyze the correlation between markets and the risk and return of each market. But before we do this we must first examine how to calculate returns on foreign investments.

11.3 CALCULATING THE RETURN ON FOREIGN INVESTMENTS. The return on a foreign investment is affected by the return on the assets within its own market and the change in the exchange rate between the security's own currency and the currency

[1]The percentage shown for Japan is an overstatement since Japanese companies have a greater tendency to own other companies than do companies in other countries and thus have more double counting.

of the purchaser's home country. Thus the return on a foreign investment can be quite different than simply the return in the asset's own market and can differ according to the domicile of the purchaser. From the viewpoint of an American investor, it is convenient to express foreign currency as costing so many dollars.[2] Thus it is convenient to express an exchange rate of 2 marks to the dollar, or the cost of 1 mark is \$0.50. Assume the following information:

Time	1 Cost of 1 Mark	2 Value of German Shares	Value in Dollars (1 × 2)
0	\$0.50	40 DM	0.50 × 40 = \$20
1	\$0.40	45 DM	0.40 × 45 = \$18

Furthermore assume that there are no dividends paid on the German shares. In this case the return to the German investor expressed in the home currency (marks) is

$$(1 + R_H) = \frac{45}{40} \quad \text{or} \quad R_H = 0.125 \text{ or } 12.5\%$$

However, the return to the U.S. investor is

$$(1 + R_{\text{US}}) = \frac{0.40 \times 45}{0.50 \times 40} = \frac{18}{20} \quad \text{or} \quad R_{\text{US}} = -0.10 \text{ or } -10\%$$

The German investor received a positive return, whereas the U.S. investor lost money because marks were worth less at time one than at time zero. It is convenient to divide the return to the American investor into a component due to return in the home or German market and the return due to exchange gains or losses. Letting R_x be the exchange return we have

$$(1 + R_{\text{US}}) = (1 + R_x)(1 + R_H)$$

$$1 + R_x = \frac{0.40}{0.50} = 1 - 0.20 \quad \text{or} \quad R_x = -0.20$$

$$1 + R_H = \frac{45}{40} = 1 - 0.125 \quad \text{or} \quad R_H = 0.125$$

$$(1 + R_{\text{US}}) = (1 - 0.20)(1 + 0.125) = 1 - 0.10 \quad \text{or} \quad R_{\text{US}} = -0.10$$

Thus the $12\frac{1}{2}\%$ gain on the German investment was more than offset by the 20% loss on the change in the value of the mark. Restating the preceding equation

$$(1 + R_{\text{US}}) = (1 + R_x)(1 + R_H)$$

[2]Foreign currency exchange rates can be quoted in two ways. If an exchange rate is stated as the amount of dollars per unit of foreign currency, the exchange rate is quoted in direct (or American) terms. If the exchange rate is given as the amount of foreign currency per dollar, the quote is in indirect (or foreign) terms. The form of quotes differs across markets. In the interbank market indirect quotes are used, whereas direct quotes are the norm in futures and options markets.

Simplifying

$$R_{\text{US}} = R_x + R_H + R_x R_H$$

In the example

$$\begin{aligned} -0.10 &= -0.20 + 0.125 + (-0.20) \times (0.125) \\ &= -0.20 + 0.125 - 0.025 \end{aligned}$$

The last term (the cross-product term) will be much smaller than the other two terms, so that return to the U.S. investor is approximately the return of the security in its home market plus the exchange gain or loss. Using this approximation, we have the following expressions for expected return and standard deviation of return on a foreign security.

Expected return

$$\overline{R}_{\text{US}} = \overline{R}_x + \overline{R}_H$$

Standard deviation of return

$$\sigma_{\text{US}} = [\sigma_x^2 + \sigma_H^2 + 2\sigma_{Hx}]^{1/2}$$

As will be very clear when we examine real data, the standard deviation of the return on foreign securities (σ_{US}) is much less than the sum of the standard deviation of the return on the security in its home country (σ_H) plus the standard deviation of the exchange gains and losses (σ_x). This relationship results from two factors. First, there is very low correlation between exchange gains (or losses) and returns in a country (and therefore the last term σ_{Hx} is close to zero). Second, squaring the standard deviations, adding them, and then taking the square root of the sum is less than adding them directly. To see this, let

$$\begin{aligned} \sigma_x &= 0.10 \\ \sigma_H &= 0.15 \\ \sigma_{Hx} &= 0 \qquad \text{(to make the covariance zero)} \end{aligned}$$

then

$$\sigma_{\text{US}}^2 = 0.10^2 + 0.15^2$$

and

$$\sigma_{\text{US}} = 0.18$$

Thus, the standard deviation of the return expressed in dollars is considerably less than the sum of the standard deviation of the exchange gains and losses and the standard deviation of the return on the security in its home currency. The reader should be conscious of this difference in the tables that follow.

Having developed some preliminary relationships it is useful to examine some actual data on risk and return.

11.4 RISK OF FOREIGN SECURITIES. Exhibit 11.3 presents the correlation between the equity markets of several countries for the period 1991–2000. These correlation coefficients have been computed using monthly returns on market indexes. The indexes are computed by Morgan Stanley Capital International. They are market-weighted indexes with each stock's proportion in the index determined by its market value divided by the aggregate market value of all stocks in that market. The indexes include securities representing approximately 60% of the aggregate market value of each country. All returns were converted to U.S. dollars at prevailing exchange rates before correlations were calculated. Thus, Exhibit 11.3 presents the correlation from the viewpoint of a U.S. investor. These are very low correlation coefficients relative to those found within a domestic market. The average correlation coefficient between a pair of U.S. common stocks is about 0.40, and the correlation between U.S. indexes is much higher. For example, the correlation between the S&P index of 425 large stocks and the rest of the stocks on the New York Stock Exchange is about 0.97. The correlation between a market-weighted portfolio of the 1,000 largest stocks in the U.S. market and a market-weighted portfolio of the next 2,000 largest stocks is approximately 0.92. Finally, the correlation coefficient between two 100-security portfolios drawn at random from the New York Stock Exchange is on the order of 0.95. The numbers in the table are much smaller than this, with the average correlation being 0.48.

The correlations between international indexes are only slightly larger than the correlation between two securities in the United States and less than the correlation between two securities in most other markets. The correlations shown in Exhibit 11.3 are very similar to those found in other studies. Thus Exhibit 11.3 is representative of typical correlation coefficients.[3] The numbers in Exhibit 11.3 are somewhat higher than those found five years earlier, 0.48 rather than 0.40. This is primarily due to the increased correlation among countries within the European Monetary Union because of the elimination of exchange rates charges and greater integration of the economies.

Exhibit 11.4 shows the correlation between the Salomon Brothers long-term bond indexes of eight countries for the years 1990–2000. These indexes are value-weighted indexes of the major issues in each country. Once again the correlations are very low relative to the correlations of two intracountry indexes or bond portfolios. The average correlation between countries shown in Exhibit 11.4 is 0.54. In contrast, Kaplanis and Schaefer show an average correlation between countries of 0.43 for long-term bond indexes in their sample period, and Chollerton, Pieraerts, and Solnik (1986) find 0.43. This can be contrasted with the correlation between two typical American bond mutual funds of 0.94 and the correlation between the U.S. government and corporate bond index of 0.98.

Finally, Exhibit 11.5 shows correlation coefficients for short-term bonds, in particular, monthly returns of three-month debt. The average correlation for the same eight countries shown in Exhibit 11.4 is 0.34. The low correlation across markets for stocks, bonds, and Treasury bills (T-bills) is the strongest evidence in favor of inter-

---

[3]Similar results have been found by other researchers. For example, Solnik (1974a) studied the 15-year period 1971–1986 and found an average correlation of 0.35 between countries. Similarly, Kaplanis and Schaefer (1996), studying the period February 1978–June 1987, found an average correlation of 0.32. Furthermore, Eun and Resnick (1988), studying the period 1973–1982, found an average correlation of 0.41.

	Australia	Austria	Belgium	Canada	France	Germany	Hong Kong	Italy	Japan	Netherlands	Spain	Sweden	Switzerland	United Kingdom	United States
Australia															
Austria	0.279														
Belgium	0.304	0.459													
Canada	0.608	0.316	0.299												
France	0.400	0.505	0.677	0.465											
Germany	0.393	0.671	0.612	0.454	0.749										
Hong Kong	0.501	0.350	0.225	0.572	0.387	0.395									
Italy	0.248	0.358	0.396	0.361	0.487	0.495	0.231								
Japan	0.430	0.245	0.317	0.355	0.415	0.307	0.289	0.330							
Netherlands	0.480	0.578	0.738	0.514	0.758	0.740	0.424	0.429	0.432						
Spain	0.460	0.422	0.523	0.455	0.681	0.606	0.415	0.575	0.482	0.599					
Sweden	0.490	0.364	0.348	0.486	0.600	0.639	0.393	0.480	0.461	0.577	0.693				
Switzerland	0.363	0.530	0.610	0.410	0.598	0.537	0.327	0.304	0.465	0.697	0.567	0.494			
United Kingdom	0.543	0.519	0.577	0.460	0.642	0.594	0.437	0.313	0.474	0.722	0.602	0.523	0.494		
United States	0.505	0.281	0.504	0.709	0.534	0.489	0.491	0.301	0.348	0.592	0.530	0.466	0.523	0.646	
Average Correlation Coefficient				0.475											

Exhibit 11.3. Correlations Among Stock Indexes Measured in U.S. Dollars.

	Canada	France	Germany	Japan	Netherlands	Switzerland	U.K.
Canada							
France	0.191						
Germany	0.157	0.910					
Japan	0.112	0.391	0.495				
Netherlands	0.217	0.917	0.960	0.408			
Switzerland	0.076	0.697	0.803	0.540	0.751		
U.K.	0.433	0.599	0.580	0.314	0.614	0.467	
United States	0.567	0.456	0.357	0.177	0.430	0.257	0.478

Exhibit 11.4. Correlations Among Bond Indexes Measured in U.S. Dollars.

	Canada	France	Germany	Japan	Netherlands	Switzerland	United Kingdom
Canada							
France	–0.178						
Germany	–0.163	0.978					
Japan	–0.015	0.393	0.426				
Netherlands	–0.167	0.983	0.998	0.422			
Switzerland	–0.146	0.915	0.933	0.477	0.931		
United Kingdom	–0.006	0.696	0.697	0.282	0.695	0.660	
United States	0.097	–0.073	–0.073	0.113	–0.068	–0.060	–0.106

Exhibit 11.5. Correlations for Three-Month Bond Indexes Measured in U.S. Dollars.

national diversification. The low correlation suggests that international diversification could reduce the risk on an investor's portfolio.

Risk depends not only on correlation coefficients but also on the standard deviation of return. Exhibits 11.6 through 11.8 show the standard deviation of return for an investment in the common equity indexes, the long-term bond indexes, and the short-term bond indexes discussed earlier. It should be emphasized once again that the standard deviation is calculated on market indexes and is therefore a measure of risk for a well-diversified portfolio, consisting only of securities traded within the country under examination.

As shown in the last section, there are two sources of risks. The return on an investment in foreign securities varies because of variation of security prices within the securities home market and because of exchange gains and losses. Note that in some cases the total risk is less than the domestic risk. The reduction in correlation when exchange rates are taken into account comes about because for these countries in this period exchange fluctuations were negatively correlated with movements in the local market.

The column headed "Domestic Risk" in Exhibits 11.6 through 11.8 shows the standard deviation of return when returns are calculated in the indexes' own currency. Thus the standard deviation of 20.41 for Germany is the standard deviation when returns on German stocks are calculated in marks. The second source of risk is exchange risk. Exchange risk arises because the exchange rate between the mark and dollar

Stocks	Domestic Risk	Exchange Risk	Total Risk
Australia	13.94	8.66	17.92
Austria	24.80	10.59	24.50
Belgium	16.15	10.21	15.86
Canada	15.02	4.40	17.13
France	18.87	10.61	17.76
Germany	20.41	10.55	20.13
Hong Kong	29.75	0.43	29.79
Italy	24.55	11.13	25.29
Japan	22.04	12.46	25.70
Netherlands	16.04	10.59	15.50
Spain	22.99	11.18	23.27
Sweden	24.87	11.18	24.21
Switzerland	17.99	11.61	17.65
United Kingdom	14.45	10.10	15.59
United States	13.59	0.00	13.59
Equally Weighted Index (Non-U.S.)	21.57	10.03	23.43
Value-Weighted Index (Non-U.S.)			16.70

Exhibit 11.6. Risk for U.S Investor in Stocks 1990–2000.

Stocks	Domestic Risk	Exchange Risk	Total Risk
Canada	8.67	4.40	10.75
France	8.71	10.61	12.61
Germany	5.38	10.55	11.20
Japan	9.18	12.46	15.10
Netherlands	7.03	10.59	11.68
Switzerland	6.64	11.61	12.06
United Kingdom	9.23	10.10	12.78
United States	7.89	0.00	7.90
Equally Weighted Index (Non-U.S.)	7.95	10.33	12.38
Value-Weighted Index (Non-U.S.)			9.45

Exhibit 11.7. Risk for U.S Investor in Bonds 1990–2000.

Stocks	Domestic Risk	Exchange Risk	Total Risk
Canada	0.77	4.40	4.42
France	0.86	10.61	10.53
Germany	0.72	10.55	10.49
Japan	0.79	12.46	12.42
Netherlands	0.72	10.59	10.52
Switzerland	0.82	11.61	11.52
United Kingdom	0.82	10.10	10.04
United States	0.35	0.00	0.35
Equally Weighted Index (Non-U.S.)	0.79	10.33	10.27
Value-Weighted Index (Non-U.S.)			6.77

Exhibit 11.8. Risk for U.S Investor in Three-Month Securities 1990–2000.

changes over time, affecting the return to a U.S. investor on an investment in German securities. The variability of the exchange rate for each currency converted to dollars is shown in the column titled "Exchange Risk." As discussed in the last section, the exchange risk and the within country risk are usually relatively independent (in this period they were negatively correlated for many countries) and standard deviations are not additive. Thus total risk to the U.S. investor is much less than the sum of exchange risk and within country risk. For example, the standard deviation of German stocks in marks is 20.41%. The standard deviation of changes in the mark dollar exchange rate is 10.55%. However, the risk of German stocks in dollars when both fluctuations are taken into account is 20.13%. It should be emphasized that the variability of exchange rates is calculated by examining the variability of each currency in dollars. Thus the total risk is measured from a U.S. investor's point of view.

As shown in Exhibit 11.6 over the 1990–2000 time period, the standard deviation of an index of the U.S. equity market was less than the standard deviation of other market indexes when the standard deviation of returns was calculated in its own currency (domestic risk). When the effect of exchange risk is taken into account, the higher risk of foreign markets was even more pronounced. These results are not atypical. Solnik (1988), Kaplanis and Schaefer, and Eun and Resnick (1989) find the same results for different periods.

For long-term bonds, the standard deviation of the U.S. bond index is about average when the standard deviation of each index is calculated in its own currency. When returns are adjusted for changes in exchange rates and all returns are expressed in dollars, the risk for the U.S. bond index is much lower than for any foreign index. This illustrates the importance of exchange rate fluctuations on returns and risk. Finally, for short-term bonds (Exhibit 11.8) the effect of exchange rates is even more dramatic. The exchange rate risk is by far the largest component of total risk. When the standard deviation is calculated for a U.S. investor, the standard deviation of U.S. T-bills is much less than the standard deviation for non-U.S. investments. For the case of T-bills and perhaps bonds, although the relatively low correlation strongly suggests that international diversification pays, the higher standard deviation suggests it may not.

Exhibit 11.9 shows the combination of a value-weighted index of non-U.S. markets and the corresponding U.S. index. The numbers in the table are standard deviations of this combination when various percentages are invested in the international portfolio. When considering equities the minimum risk is achieved with 74% in the U.S. portfolio and 26% in the market-weighted world portfolio (excluding U.S. securities), and total risk is reduced by 3.7% compared with exclusive investment in the U.S. market. The risk reduction for long-term bonds is much less dramatic because the relative risk of a non-U.S. market-weighted international bond portfolio is much higher and the correlation slightly higher. Nevertheless a slight risk reduction is achieved. Finally, for T-bills some international diversification lowers risk (slightly less than 1%). Because of exchange risk the standard deviation of a value-weighted non-U.S. international short-term bond portfolio is dramatically higher than the standard deviation of U.S. T-bills. In this time period, however, the correlation of U.S. T-bills and a value-weighted index of foreign T-bills was about zero. Thus, even with the high standard deviation, a modest amount of international diversification lowered risk.

These results were derived using data from 1990 to 2000. An interesting question to analyze is whether the results are unique to the period examined or if we can safely generalize them. The conclusions depend on the correlation between the world portfolio

X Proportion in World Index (%)	Value-Weighted Index Stocks	Long-Term Bonds	T-Bills
0%	13.59	7.90	0.35
10%	13.28	7.63	0.75
20%	13.12	7.45	1.38
30%	13.10	7.37	2.05
40%	13.23	7.39	2.72
50%	13.51	7.52	3.39
60%	13.93	7.75	4.06
70%	14.47	8.06	4.74
80%	15.12	8.46	5.42
90%	15.87	8.93	6.09
100%	16.70	9.45	6.77

Exhibit 11.9. Risk from Placing *X* Percent in a World Index Excluding U.S. Securities and the Rest in U.S. Index 1990–2000.

and the U.S. index and the standard deviation of each index. As discussed earlier, the correlations used in this analysis are very similar to the correlations other researchers have found in other periods and somewhat higher than the correlations found in earlier periods. The variability of return for foreign markets during this period is higher than the variability of return that most other researchers have found.

Thus, the risk reduction shown in Exhibit 11.9 would hold if data from other periods were used and the results are likely to be robust across periods. Furthermore, for stocks, rather substantial errors in selecting the optimal mix could be made and risk would still be reduced. Therefore, using data from a prior period to decide on a mixture of an international and domestic portfolio would likely result in a less risky portfolio than pure domestic investment. For long-term bonds and T-bills, the risk reduction via international diversification is so small that errors in determining the risk-minimizing mix of international and domestic portfolios could easily result in a portfolio more risky than the domestic one held alone.

11.5 RETURNS FROM INTERNATIONAL DIVERSIFICATION. The decade of the 1990s was an especially favorable time for U.S. markets relative to foreign markets. Exhibits 11.10 and 11.11 show the average annual returns from January 1990 to December 2000 on several international markets. The "Exchange Gain" column is the difference between the return in the assets home country and the assets return in the United States.[4] The average non-U.S. equity index had a return of 12.54% in its home country compared with 16.17% for the U.S. market with an exchange loss averaging −2.212%, when converted to dollars the average non-U.S. equity index returned 10.31%.

The column in Exhibit 11.10 that presents returns in U.S. dollars shows only three countries, Hong Kong, Netherlands, and Sweden, that had returns above the United

[4]Earlier we showed that the expected return to a U.S. investor is not the sum of exchange gains and losses and the return in the investor's home country. Thus, column two includes not only the exchange return but also includes all joint effects of the country and exchange return.

Stocks	Own Country	Exchange Gain	To U.S. Investor
Australia	10.51	−2.82	7.69
Austria	2.37	−1.55	0.82
Belgium	11.85	−1.39	10.46
Canada	13.53	−2.29	11.24
France	14.78	−1.40	13.37
Germany	13.89	−1.56	12.32
Hong Kong	16.90	0.02	16.92
Italy	12.55	−4.34	8.22
Japan	−4.80	2.47	−2.32
Netherlands	17.38	−1.55	15.83
Spain	16.13	−4.17	11.96
Sweden	21.22	−3.40	17.81
Switzerland	15.81	−0.43	15.38
United Kingdom	12.71	−0.42	12.28
United States	16.17	0.00	16.17
Equally Weighted Index (Non-U.S.)	12.54	−2.22	10.31
Value-Weighted Index (Non-U.S.)			8.77

Exhibit 11.10. Return to U.S. Investor in Stocks 1990–2000 (percent per annum).

Bonds	Own Country	Exchange Gain	To U.S. Investor
Canada	11.50	−2.08	9.42
France	11.08	−1.77	9.31
Germany	7.89	−1.89	6.00
Japan	8.13	3.62	11.75
Netherlands	8.84	−1.93	6.91
Switzerland	6.63	−0.55	6.08
United Kingdom	12.21	−0.54	11.67
United States	8.93		
Equally Weighted Index (Non-U.S.)	9.47	−0.73	8.73
Value-Weighted Index (Non-U.S.)			9.59
Three-Month Securities			
Canada	6.34	−2.16	4.18
France	6.44	−1.63	4.81
Germany	5.73	−1.82	3.91
Japan	2.72	3.67	6.39
Netherlands	5.58	−1.80	3.78
Switzerland	4.35	−0.38	3.97
United Kingdom	7.65	−0.44	7.21
United States	4.92		
Equally Weighted Index (Non-U.S.)	5.54	−0.65	4.89
Value-Weighted Index (Non-U.S.)			6.77

Exhibit 11.11. Return to U.S. Investor in Bonds 1990–2000 (percent per annum).

States. Thus, most internationally diversified equity portfolios would have had a lower return than the U.S. market index over this period. During this period international diversification had the advantage of lowering risk but resulted in lower average returns.

The results for long-term bonds are similar. The equally weighted portfolio of country return indexes (excluding the United States) did slightly worse than the U.S. market index. The value-weighted portfolio performed better. This was due primarily to the performance of Japanese bonds. In yen, Japanese bonds returned about 8.13% but over this period, the dollar value of the yen increased by 3.62% resulting in an 11.75% return to U.S. investors. A fair number of countries underperformed the U.S. bond market. Thus many international portfolios would have also underperformed a portfolio of U.S. bonds.

For three-month T-bills the return on the equally weighted index was slightly worse and value-weighted index was slightly better than the return on U.S. T-bills. Given the higher risk discussed earlier, many international portfolios would have been inferior to an exclusive U.S. portfolio.

Although these results are appropriate for the period discussed, it is useful to examine other periods. Solnik (1988) studied equity indexes for 17 countries for the years 1971–1985. For all but two countries the return on the foreign index expressed in dollars was greater than the return on the U.S. equity index. The exchange gain from holding foreign equities added 0.2% on average to this return. For long and short bonds only, Canada and the United Kingdom had a lower return when return was expressed in U.S. dollars. For bonds, however, a major factor contributing to the return being above the U.S. return was exchange gains. The 1980s was a better period for non-U.S. markets and many international portfolios would have outperformed their U.S. counterparts.

For portfolio decisions, estimates of future values of mean return, standard deviation, and correlation coefficients are needed. The correlation coefficients between international markets have been very low historically relative to intracountry correlations. As Europe integrates its markets and as all countries move toward greater integration, these coefficients are likely to rise.[5] However, they are still likely to be low relative to intracountry correlation. For example, the correlation coefficient between countries whose economies are relatively highly integrated, such as Canada and the United States, the Benelux countries, or the Scandinavian countries is still much lower than the intracountry correlation coefficients. Thus international diversification is likely to continue to lead to risk reduction in the foreseeable future. However, we know of no economic reason to argue that returns in foreign markets will be higher or lower than for domestic markets.

11.6 EFFECT OF EXCHANGE RISK. Earlier we showed how the return on a foreign investment could be split into the return in the security's home market and the return from changes in exchange rates. In each of the prior tables we separated out the effect of changes in the exchange rate on return and risk. In Exhibit 11.11, the column entitled "Exchange Return or Exchange Risk" calculated the effect of converting all currencies into dollars. Obviously if we were presenting the same tables from a French

---

[5]In particular, exchange rates between European currencies are fixed. Although European currencies will continue to fluctuate with the U.S. currency, any advantage in diversifying across currencies will be eliminated.

or Norwegian point of view, the "Exchange Rate Expected Return" and "Risk" columns would be different, because they would contain results as if all currencies were converted to francs (for the French investor) or kroner (for the Norwegian investor). Because francs and kroner have not fluctuated perfectly with the dollar, these columns would be different. Thus, the country of domicile affects the expected returns and risk (including correlation coefficients) from international diversification.

Exhibit 11.12 illustrates this by computing expected return and risk from the U.S. investor's point of view (which is a repeat of prior exhibits) and from the French point of view. The numbers are clearly quite different. It is possible to protect partially against exchange rate fluctuations. An investor can enter into a contract for future delivery of a currency at a price that is fixed now. For example, an American investor purchasing German securities could simultaneously agree to convert marks into dollars at a future date and at a known rate. If the investor knew exactly what the security would be worth at the end of the period, he or she would be completely protected against rate fluctuations by agreeing to switch an amount of marks exactly equal to the value of the investment. However, given that, in general, the end of period value of the investment is random, the best the investor can do is protect against a particular outcome (e.g., its expected value).[6]

As shown earlier, the standard deviation of foreign investments generally increases as a result of exchange risk. If exchange risk was completely hedged, then the "Domestic Risk" column in Exhibits 11.6 through 11.8 would be the relevant column used to measure risk.

When examining risk for common stocks in most periods, total risk is higher for most countries. However, in the period of the 1990s, this was not true. Therefore, in the 1990s, hedging increased risk for many countries. The increase in risk due to ex-

[6]Procedures exist for changing the hedge through time in order to eliminate most of the exchange risk. See Kaplanis and Schaefer.

	Mean Return		Variance	
Country	In Francs	In Dollars	In Francs	In Dollars
Australia	9.15	7.69	21.58	17.92
Austria	2.29	0.82	25.62	24.50
Belgium	11.92	10.46	16.77	15.86
Canada	12.70	11.24	21.73	17.13
France	14.78	13.37	18.87	17.76
Germany	13.79	12.32	21.02	20.13
Hong Kong	18.38	16.92	32.72	29.79
Italy	9.68	8.22	27.91	25.29
Japan	−0.86	−2.32	26.67	25.70
Netherlands	17.29	15.83	16.44	15.50
Spain	13.42	11.96	25.08	23.27
Sweden	19.28	17.81	26.37	24.21
Switzerland	16.84	15.38	18.67	17.65
United Kingdom	13.74	12.28	17.03	15.59
United States	17.63	16.17	18.45	13.59

Exhibit 11.12. The Effect of Country of Domicile on Mean Return and Risk.

change fluctuations is clearest for long- and short-term bonds. Although we will not present the tables, the correlation coefficients are somewhat lower when we calculate the correlation between returns assuming exchange risk is fully hedged away. Exchange movement increases the correlation among countries' returns. The average correlation coefficient between two countries is 0.46 assuming exchange risk is hedged away for the countries shown in Exhibit 11.3. This contrasts with 0.48 when exchange risk is fully borne. Similarly, Kaplanis and Schaefer found an average correlation of 0.37 when including the effect of exchange risk and 0.32 when exchange risk was fully hedged. Risk in international stock portfolios is normally reduced if exchange risk is hedged away and always reduced in bond markets.

The effect on expected return is less clear. Exhibits 11.10 and 11.11 show that during the 1990–2000 period, exchange movements caused losses to U.S. investors for most countries. The same table in the 1970s would have shown mostly gains. Also, the loss to the U.S. investor is the gain to the foreign investor, so that a different table would hold if we expressed returns in, for example, Swiss francs. Thus the effect of eliminating exchange gains or losses on expected return varies from country to country and period to period.

One way to determine whether international diversification will be a useful strategy in the future is to analyze how low expected returns in foreign countries would have to be for an investor not to gain via international diversification.

11.7 RETURN EXPECTATIONS AND PORTFOLIO PERFORMANCE. Most of the literature on domestic and international diversification tells us that history is a much better guide in forecasting risk than it is in forecasting returns. If we accept the historical data on risk as indicative of the future, for any assumed return on the U.S. market we can solve for the minimum return that must be offered by any foreign market to make it an attractive investment from the U.S. standpoint.

We did this under two assumptions: that the U.S. market would return 12% and that it would return 16%. These numbers were selected because 16% is approximately the return for the U.S. equity market in the 1990s and 12% is roughly the historical long-term return on U.S. equities. The calculations used the correlation coefficients shown in Exhibit 11.3 and the standard deviations shown in Exhibits 11.6 through 11.8, and a risk-free rate of 6%. These numbers are shown in Exhibit 11.13. The basic formula to determine these numbers is as follows:

Hold non-U.S. securities as long as[7]

$$\frac{\bar{R}_N - R_F}{\sigma_N} > \frac{\bar{R}_{\text{US}} - R_F}{\sigma_{\text{US}}} \rho_{N,\text{US}} \tag{11.1}$$

---

[7]From Chapter 4 the first-order conditions are

$$\bar{R}_N - R_F = Z_N \sigma_N^2 + Z_{\text{US}} \rho_{N,\text{US}} \sigma_{\text{US}} \sigma_N$$

$$\bar{R}_{\text{US}} - R_F = Z_N \rho_{N,\text{US}} \sigma_{\text{US}} \sigma_N + Z_{\text{US}} \sigma_{\text{US}}^2$$

Setting Z_N equal to zero and eliminating Z_{US} results in the preceding equation as an equality. Increasing $\bar{R}_N$ would cause Z_N to be greater than zero. For a more detailed derivation see Elton, Gruber, and Rentzler (1987).

This analysis assumes foreign securities cannot be shorted. If they can be shorted, then markets for which Equation (11.1) doesn't hold are candidates for short sales.

	U.S. Return	
Country	12%	16%
Australia	9.99	12.66
Austria	9.04	11.07
Belgium	9.53	11.88
Canada	11.36	14.94
France	10.19	12.98
Germany	10.35	13.24
Hong Kong	12.46	16.76
Italy	9.36	11.60
Japan	9.95	12.58
Netherlands	10.05	12.75
Spain	11.44	15.07
Sweden	10.98	14.30
Switzerland	10.08	12.79
United Kingdom	10.45	13.41
Equally Weighted Index (Non-U.S.)		
Value-Weighted Index (Non-U.S.)	10.17	12.95

Exhibit 11.13. Minimum Returns on Foreign Markets Necessary for International Diversification to Be Justified.

where

$\bar{R}_N$ is the expected return on the non-U.S. securities in dollars
$\bar{R}_{US}$ is the expected return on U.S. securities
σ_N is the standard deviation of the non-U.S. securities in dollars
σ_{US} is the standard deviation of U.S. securities
$\rho_{N,US}$ is the correlation between U.S. securities and non-U.S. securities
R_F is the risk-free rate of interest

Although this equation is written from a U.S. investor's point of view, a similar equation holds true for investors in any country considering foreign investment. The reader would simply redefine the symbols presently subscripted U.S. to the country of interest.

Note that in Exhibit 11.13 the return required on a foreign investment is, for most markets, considerably less than the return on the U.S. investment. For an assumed U.S. expected return of 12%, Austrian securities would have to have an expected return of less than 9.04% for it not to pay to invest in Austrian securities at all. Diversification into Canada and Spain requires higher expected returns than diversification into other countries and Hong Kong would have to have an expected return above U.S. securities. For Canadian securities this result is caused by high correlation of the U.S. and Canadian markets. For Spain and Hong Kong it is primarily very high standard deviation that makes diversification less attractive. Thus, the expected return in these markets must be higher or almost as high as the U.S. market for diversification to pay.

If we rearrange the expression (11.1), we have hold non-U.S. securities as long as[8]

$$\overline{R}_N - R_F > [\overline{R}_{\text{US}} - R_F]\left[\frac{\sigma_N \rho_{N,\text{US}}}{\sigma_{\text{US}}}\right] \tag{11.2}$$

As long as the expression in the last bracket is less than one, foreign securities should be held even with expected returns lower than those found in the domestic market. For all the countries except Hong Kong, the expression in the last bracket was less than one so the expected return on non-U.S. securities could be less than U.S. securities and international diversification would still pay. Thus, for the period studied, expected returns in non-U.S. countries could have been considerably less than in U.S. countries and international diversification would still have paid.

All the entries in Exhibit 11.13 with the exception of those in the last row showed the minimum expected return when one country was added to the U.S. portfolio. Thus the portfolio was composed of two countries' securities. The last row shows the expected return on a value-weighted index necessary to justify adding it to U.S. securities. Although not the lowest return, it is less than most countries' return considered separately. If the expected return on U.S. securities is 16%, a value-weighted portfolio should be added if its expected return is greater than 12.95%. This is a general result. Portfolios of securities from many countries will be less risky than portfolios of a single country's securities. Examining Equation (11.2) shows that for a given correlation, the lower the standard deviation the lower the expected return on a foreign portfolio can be and still have international diversification pay.

We argued in the first section that international diversification lowers risk. In this section we have shown that returns in foreign markets would have to be much lower than returns in the domestic market or international diversification pays. What is foreign to one investor is domestic to another, however. Are there any circumstances where international diversification does not pay for investors of all countries?

To understand this issue, consider the U.S. and U.K. markets and refer to Exhibit 11.13. This table shows that if the return in the U.K. market is not less than 13.41% when returns in the U.S. market are 16%, a U.S. investor should purchase some U.K. securities. Furthermore, it is easy to show that if a U.K. investor believed expected returns in the U.K. would be less than in the U.S., then the U.K. investor should purchase U.S. stocks. If investors in the two markets agree on expected returns, we have one of three situations: both gain from diversification, the U.S. investor gains, or the U.K. investor gains. In all three cases, however, at least one investor should diversify internationally. If the investors do not agree on returns in the two markets, then it is possible that neither the U.S. investor nor the U.K. investor will benefit from international diversification. For example, assume U.S. investors believe that U.K. markets have an expected return of 5%, whereas U.S. markets would have an expected return of 10%. Further assume that U.K. investors believe U.K. markets have an expected return of 10%, whereas U.S. markets have an expected return of 5%. Under this set of expected returns neither U.S. nor U.K. investors would wish to diversify internationally. Are there any circumstances where investors in all countries could ra-

---

[8]Multiplying the numerator and denominator of the expression in the brackets by σ_{US} shows that the expression in the brackets is the Beta of the non-U.S. markets on the U.S. index.

tionally believe that returns are higher in their country relative to the rest of the world? The answer is *yes*!

If governments tax foreign investments at rates very different from domestic investments, then the pattern just discussed would be possible for aftertax returns. Differential taxation has occurred in the past, continues to occur today, and will likely persist into the future.[9] Second, many countries impose a withholding tax on dividends. Taxable investors may receive a domestic credit for the foreign tax withheld and thus not have lowered returns. However, for nontaxable investors (or for a nontaxable part of an investor's portfolio such as pension assets), the withholding is a cost that lowers the return of foreign investment. A third situation that could cause foreign investments to have a lower return than domestic investments for all investors is if there were differential transaction costs for domestic and foreign purchases. This could occur if there was difficulty in purchasing foreign securities or currency controls existed. For example, there may be restrictions in converting domestic to foreign currency that could affect returns. The exchange of currency A for B might take place at an official rate higher than the free market rate, and there might be an expectation of a later reversal. A fourth situation that can result in investors in all countries having an expectation of higher returns from domestic investments relative to foreign, is a danger of a government restricting the ability of foreigners to withdraw funds. Governments can and do place such restrictions on foreigners, and this can reduce returns to foreigners. The considerations just discussed are real and can affect the returns from international diversification.

Before leaving this section, one other issue needs to be discussed. It has been suggested that investors could confine themselves to a national market and receive most of the benefits of international diversification by purchasing stocks in multinational corporations. Jacquillat and Solnik (1978) have tested this for the American investor. They found that stock prices of multinational firms do not seem to be affected by foreign factors and behave much like the stocks of domestic firms. The American investor cannot gain much of the advantage of international diversification by investing in the securities of the multinational firm.

11.8 OTHER EVIDENCE ON INTERNATIONALLY DIVERSIFIED PORTFOLIOS. In prior sections we have presented the considerations that are important in deciding on the reasonableness of international diversification. Obviously, we feel that the type of analysis we have presented is the relevant way to analyze the problem. However, several studies analyze the reasonableness of international diversification by examining the characteristics of international portfolios selected using historical data. The most common approach attempts to show the advantages of international diversification by forming an optimal portfolio of international and domestic securities using historical data and comparing the return to an exclusively domestically held portfolio over the same time period. It should not surprise the reader that knowing the exact values of mean returns, variance, and covariances for international markets allows construction of portfolios that dominate investment exclusively in the domestic portfolio. A variant of this analysis presents the efficient frontier using historical data with and without international securities and "shows" that adding international securities improves the efficient frontier.

---

[9]A government's ability to enforce payment of taxes may be lower on foreign than domestic securities. Tax cheating could mitigate tax rate differentials.

	1990–1999			
	Mean Return Monthly	Standard Deviation	Beta	Correlation with Market
Canada General Fund	1.05	4.27	0.92	0.93
Keystone International Fund	0.76	3.96	0.58	0.63
Japan Fund	0.76	7.08	0.41	0.25
Scudder International Fund	1.12	4.30	0.62	0.62
G.T. Pacific Fund	0.23	6.52	0.81	0.53
Alliance International Fund/A	0.65	4.55	0.66	0.62
Templeton Foreign Fund	0.98	3.88	0.60	0.66
T. Rowe Price International Stock Fund	1.00	4.30	0.63	0.64
Fidelity Overseas Fund	0.97	4.36	0.64	0.63
Vanguard World—International Growth	0.89	4.40	0.61	0.60
Managers Funds: International	1.06	3.68	0.56	0.66
Morgan Stanley Instl. Fund—International Eq.	1.12	3.93	0.53	0.58
Warburg Pincus International Equity	1.09	4.72	0.64	0.59
G.T. Global Growth—Europe Growth	0.78	4.90	0.71	0.62
T. Rowe Price International Discovery	1.17	5.41	0.54	0.43
Schroder Captial Funds: International	0.84	4.24	0.56	0.57
Smith Barney World Funds International	1.19	4.86	0.72	0.64
Thompson McKinnon Invest Trust Global	0.84	4.67	0.76	0.71
Fidelity International Growth and Income	1.01	4.05	0.58	0.62
Ivy Fund International	1.03	4.40	0.67	0.66
Average	0.93	4.62	0.64	0.61
S&P	1.48	3.58	1.00	1.00

Exhibit 11.14. Performance Data on Stock Funds.

While examining historical data is interesting, the real of test of international diversification is the performance of funds that hold internationally diversified portfolios. Exhibit 11.14 shows data for 20 of the largest international mutual funds (funds that invest only in international securities) that existed in the 1990s together with data on the Standard & Poor's (S&P) index.

Exhibit 11.14 shows data for a random sample of 20 international funds (funds that invest only in international securities) that existed in the 1990s together with data on the S&P index.

The major promise of international diversification is the low correlation between domestic securities and foreign securities. As shown in Exhibit 11.14, the average correlation between the fund return and the S&P index was 0.61. These correlations are somewhat higher than the correlations between the international stock indexes and the U.S. indexes presented in Exhibit 11.3.

Correlations this low would never be found for a U.S. mutual fund investing primarily in common stock. Rather, the average correlation with the S&P index would be above 0.90. This is strong evidence that the extensive analysis discussed earlier concerning low correlation among countries can be reflected in actual performance of international mutual funds. Similarly, the column entitled "Beta" shows the responsiveness of international funds to a change in the S&P index. The Beta for the common stock portion of a fund invested in U.S. securities would be close to one.

For the 20 funds the average beta is 0.64. For a similar sample in the 1980s the average beta was 0.71. Thus, there is a fair amount of stability in historical risk numbers.

As shown in Exhibit 11.6 through 11.8, the U.S. market is less risky than other national markets from a U.S. perspective. Given the low correlation between non-U.S. markets, however, the relative riskiness of U.S. portfolios and an internationally diversified portfolio is less clear.

Exhibit 11.14 shows that the average standard deviation of an international portfolio was somewhat higher than the S&P index. This evidence would suggest that the higher risk of individual countries relative to U.S. markets was balanced by low correlation between countries, and the interaction of these two effects produced a portfolio with risk somewhat higher than that of a U.S. portfolio.

The realized return on international portfolios relative to U.S. portfolios is very dependent on the time period studied.

This 10-year period had very high returns in the U.S. market. There were other 10-year periods where international portfolios outperformed U.S. portfolios.

There are many fewer international bonds funds than there are stock funds, and their history is much more limited. Exhibit 11.15 shows summary statistics for the six funds for which data were available. The last column is the correlation coefficient of each fund with the Shearson–Lehman bond index, which is the standard index used to calculate the performance of U.S. bond funds. It is the bond market equivalent of the S&P index. For U.S. domestic bond funds the correlation with the Shearson– Lehman index would be 0.85 to 0.90. Examining the last column shows that once again the promise of low correlation is met. The average correlation of 0.51 is considerably less than for U.S. bond funds. The standard deviation of a bond fund is very dependent on the maturity of the portfolio. Portfolios of bonds with long maturities have a higher standard of deviation than portfolios of short-maturity bonds. We have no information on the maturity of the foreign bond funds relative to the Shearson–Lehman index. Thus, it is not meaningful to compare standard deviations.

The risk structure between various countries has been studied for 20 years, and the result of low correlation among international markets relative to intracountry portfo-

		Fund			
Fund Name	Sample Period (years)	Mean Return Monthly	Standard Deviation	Beta	Correlation with Shearson–Lehman Index
Fidelity Global Bond Fund	10	0.42%	1.85%	0.76	0.48
T. Rowe Price International Bond Fund	10	0.60%	2.41%	0.80	0.38
PaineWebber Master Global Income Fund	10	0.50%	1.32%	0.66	0.58
Putnam Global Governmental Income Trust	10	0.52%	1.85%	0.87	0.54
Scudder International Bond Fund	10	0.58%	2.05%	0.87	0.49
Morgan Stanley Dean Witter World Wide Inc.	10	0.46%	1.50%	0.78	0.60
Average	10.00	0.51%	1.83%	0.69	0.51

Exhibit 11.15. Performance Data on Bond Funds.

Return on International Portfolio Relative to U.S. Portfolio	15-Year Data Optimal Proportions		10-Year Data Optimal Proportions	
	U.S.	International	U.S.	International
+3	27%	73%	40%	60%
+2	40%	60%	53%	47%
+1	53%	47%	66%	34%
0	68%	32%	80%	20%
−1	85%	15%	96%	4%
−2	99%	1%	100%	0%
−3	100%	0%	100%	0%

R_f = the return on the riskless and = 6%,
$R_{S\&P}$ = the total return on the Standard & Poor's index = 12%.

Exhibit 11.16. Optimal Investment Proportions.

lios has been consistently found. Thus the risk characteristics of international funds that have been found in the past are likely to be found in the future. It is hard, however, to develop a convincing economic case that the U.S. market will outperform or underperform other markets consistently in the future. Thus, once again, we believe the relevant way to utilize mutual fund data to examine the reasonableness of international diversification is to examine the proportions to invest in the United States and an international portfolio at various levels of assumed differences between returns in the United States and returns in other countries. Exhibit 11.16 shows the optimal investment proportions for a portfolio of the S&P index and the typical international fund.

In calculating the proportions, the standard deviations shown in Exhibit 11.14 for the S&P index and the average international fund were used as well as the average correlation coefficient. An expected return of 12% was assumed for the S&P index and a 6% riskless lending and borrowing rate.

Using data for the typical fund in the 10-year sample shows that international diversification pays as long as the return on the international portfolio is no less than $1\frac{1}{4}$% below the return on the S&P index.[10] With equal expected return, the optimum is 80% United States and 20% international.

11.9 MODELS FOR MANAGING INTERNATIONAL PORTFOLIOS. Prior sections present analysis that suggests that a portfolio of international equities should be a part of an optimum portfolio. Furthermore, examining the performance of international funds shows that the analysis is confirmed by actual performance. The conclusions were less clear for international bond funds.

---

[10] One consideration an investor in an international portfolio needs to be aware of is that there is some evidence that international managers underperform domestic managers. At a number of conferences the authors have listened to industry speakers who specialize in evaluating international portfolios. They estimate a U.S. manager of a portfolio of foreign securities (such as Japanese) underperforms the foreign (Japanese) manager. The estimates we have heard range from 2% to 4%. The underperformance may well hold. Estimates of the exact amount should be treated with some skepticism.

The obvious strategy for an investor deciding to diversify internationally but not wishing to determine how to construct an international portfolio is to hold an international index fund. The parallel to holding a domestic index fund is to hold a value-weighted portfolio of international securities. The Morgan Stanley Capital International index excluding the United States is a value-weighted index, and an investment matching this index would be a value-weighted index fund.[11]

If expected return is related to a market index and if securities are in equilibrium, then bearing nonmarket or unique risk does not result in additional compensation. The way to eliminate nonmarket risk is to hold an index fund. Even an investor who believes that securities are out of equilibrium but does not profess to know which securities give a positive or negative nonequilibrium return (has no forecasting ability) should hold the index fund. In this case, bearing nonmarket risk on average does not improve expected return because the investor on average selects securities with zero nonmarket return. Thus the investor should eliminate nonmarket risk by holding an index fund. If there was good evidence that individual securities' expected returns were determined by an international equilibrium model, and if a value-weighted index was the factor affecting expected returns, a parallel argument could be presented for holding an international value-weighted index fund. However, the evidence in favor of any international model determining expected return is still controversial.

A disturbing aspect of an international index fund is the proportion that Japan represents of the world excluding the United States (about 25%). If one believes in an international equilibrium asset pricing model and Japan represents about 25% of the market portfolio, then this is appropriate. Otherwise it makes sense only if Japan is expected to have an abnormally high return; for diversification or risk arguments it is clearly inappropriate. The authors have heard a number of presentations suggesting other weighting schemes, such as trade or gross national product (GNP) that lower the percentage in Japan. The correct justification for any weighting should come from equilibrium arguments; otherwise any weighting is as arbitrary as another.

If one is not willing to accept an international equilibrium model that partitions risk into that part that results in higher expected return and that part that is unique, it is appropriate for an investor without an ability to forecast expected returns to minimize total risk. The risk structure is reasonably predictable through time. The low correlation on average among country portfolios, and the pattern of relatively high correlation among countries with close economic links (such as the United States and Canada) is likely to continue in the future. Both Jorion (1985) and Eun and Resnick (1989) have examined the stability of the correlation structure and have found predictability. Thus the past correlation matrices can be used to predict the future. Similarly, Jorion (1985) has shown that standard deviations are predictable, and thus a low-risk international portfolio can be developed.

If one wishes to develop an active international portfolio, then many of the same considerations are involved as are present in developing an active domestic portfolio. However, international investment adds two elements to the investment process

[11]Although the Morgan Stanley index is the most widely used index, differences by country in the cross holdings of securities (one company owning shares in another) means that its weighting is very different than an index using the value of a country's equity assets. Japan in particular is very much overweighted. In addition, the Morgan Stanley index is a sample of each country's securities and the proportion sampled varies from country to country. Thus it is not an appropriately weighted market index.

not present in pure domestic investment—country selection and exchange exposure.[12]

The decision concerning how much to invest in each country depends on the factors discussed earlier, namely, intercountry correlation, the variance of return for each country's securities, and the expected return in each country. There is good evidence that the past standard deviations and correlations are useful in predicting the future.

Recently a number of researchers have also found predictable in returns. Harvey (1995), Solnick (1998), and Campbell and Hammo (1992) find predictability in many country's returns. The predictability is low with 1% to 2% of the variation in returns explained by past variables. However, Kandel and Stambaugh (1996) provide evidence that even with this low explanatory power, improvement in portfolio allocation can be achieved. What variables seem to predict returns? Lagged returns, price levels (dividend price, earnings price, and book price ratios), interest rate levels, yield spreads, and default premiums have all been used. How is this done?

There are several ways to estimate the coefficients in a multi-index model. For example, we could estimate the relationship between return in a country (e.g., France) and some of the variables that have been found to predict return. Performing this analysis we could find the relationship

$$\text{Return} = -1 + 1\,(\text{return in the prior period}) + \tfrac{1}{2}\,(\text{interest rate in the prior period})$$

The coefficients, -1, 1, and $\frac{1}{2}$, are estimated by running a time series regression. To forecast return in the next period, one simply substitutes the current value of this period's return and interest rates in the right side of the equation.

These predictions of return plus past values of correlations and standard deviations can be used as input to the portfolio optimization process.

A second possibility for predicting expected returns is to utilize a valuation model. For example, the infinite constant growth model states that

$$\text{Expected return} = \frac{\text{Dividend}}{\text{Price}} + \text{Growth}$$

Estimates of next period's dividend could be obtained by estimating earnings and estimating the proportion of earnings paid out as dividends (the payout rate). The payout ratio for a country portfolio is very stable over time, and forecasts of earnings are widely available and at an economy level quite accurate. Estimates of growth rates in earnings are also widely available internationally. Thus valuation models are a feasible way to estimate expected returns.[13]

One of the few studies that examines some alternative ways of estimating expected return is Arnott and Henriksson (1989). They forecast the relative performance of

---

[12]Technically the amount to invest in any security should depend on securities selected in other countries. Thus our treatment of first selecting each portfolio within a country and then doing country selection is nonoptimal. However, it captures much of practice. Furthermore, intercountry factors are relatively unimportant in determining each securities' return, so this assumption may be a simplification that improves performance.

[13]Testing of the accuracy of forecasts produced by these models is unavailable, so all we can do is to suggest types of analysis; we cannot report results.

each country's stocks compared to the country's bonds on the basis of current risk premiums and economic variables. They define the risk premium as the difference in expected return between common equity and bonds. They measure expected return on bonds by using the yield to maturity. They measure expected return on equity by calculating the earnings divided by price. Comparing this measure with the valuation model just presented shows that growth should be added and differences in payout taken into account. These differences, as well as differences in accounting conventions across countries and the impact of this on earnings, could affect risk premium comparisons across countries. They recognize these influences and instead of using risk premiums directly, they use current risk premiums relative to past risk premiums. Their forecast equation states that future performance is related to current risk premiums divided by average risk premiums in the past. In equation form this is

Future returns on equities relative to debt =

Constant + Constant (Current risk premium/average risk premium prior two years)

They find for many countries that this equation is a useful predictor and that for some countries it can be improved by adding other macroeconomic variables, such as prediction of trade and production statistics. This model could be used to estimate which countries have higher expected future returns on equities by using current bond yields as expected returns for bonds, and the preceding equation to estimate the difference between bond and equity returns. Clearly, further testing of all of these models is necessary. However, they are suggestive of the type of analysis that can be done in active international asset allocation.

The second new consideration that international investment introduces is exchange risk. As discussed earlier, entering into futures contracts can reduce the variability because of the exchange risk. Considering only risk, this is generally useful. Entering into futures contracts can also affect expected return; however, entering into a futures contract could lower expected returns. Furthermore, the investor may have some beliefs about changes in exchange rates different from those contained in market prices.[14] In this case the sacrifice in expected return may lead the investor to choose not to eliminate exchange risk.

Finally, Black (1989) has shown that taking some exchange risk can increase expected return. Thus exchange rate exposure involves a risk return tradeoff.

Risk-free interest rates differ from country to country. For example, the interest rate on six-month government issues could be 7% in England and 4% in the United States. The expected return for a U.S. investor buying an English bond would be the expected return to a British investor plus the exchange gains and losses.

Theory says the exchange gain or loss should be related to the interest rate differential. Thus the U.S. investor should expect to lose about 3% in exchange rate changes by buying the British bond. However, empirical evidence does not support the claim that exchange rate changes have a close relationship to interest rate differentials.

The empirical evidence strongly supports that investment in the high interest rate country gives the higher return.[15] Three explanations have been suggested: a peso ex-

---

[14]Levich (1970 and 1979) has shown that some forecasters are able to predict exchange rate movements.

[15]For example, Cumby (1990) finds on average that exchange rate changes increase the return of buying the higher interest rate counting (e.g., British bonds would be expected to return more than 7%).

planation, extra risk, and an investment opportunity. The peso explanation is named after the investors who invested their money in Mexican government bonds. For a number of years they earned a return greater than they would have earned in the United States. When the devaluation occurred, however, it more than eliminated all past gains. The peso argument is that although the empirical evidence suggests gains by investing in the higher interest rate countries, some future devaluation will eliminate all gains. The return gains have been so persistent that the size of a devaluation necessary to eliminate past gains seems too large to be plausible. Thus, most analysts reject this explanation.

The second explanation is that the extra return is simply compensation for risk. Although some of the extra return may be compensation for risk, studies to date do not support this as a complete explanation. Thus, there seems to be an investment opportunity and there are a number of funds that follow the strategy of investing in the higher-yielding country (Cho, Eun, and Senbet (1986).[16]

11.10 CONCLUSION. In this chapter we have discussed the evidence in support of international diversification. The evidence that international diversification reduces risk is uniform and extensive. Given the low risk, international diversification is justified even if expected returns are less internationally than domestically. Unless there are mechanisms such as taxes or currency restrictions that substantially reduce the return on foreign investment relative to domestic investment, international diversification has to be profitable for investors of some countries, and possibly all.

SOURCES AND SUGGESTED REFERENCES

Adler, Michael. "The Cost of Capital and Valuation of a Two-Country Firm." *Journal of Finance*, XXIX, No. 1, March 1974, pp. 119–132.

Adler, Michael, and Reuven Horesh. "The Relationship Among Equity Markets: Comment on [3]." *Journal of Finance*, XXIX, No. 4, September 1974, pp. 1131–1317.

Adler, Michael, and Bernard Dumas. "International Portfolio Choice and Corporate Finance: A Synthesis." *Journal of Finance*, Vol. 38, No. 3, June 1983, pp. 925–984.

Adler, Michael, and Bhaskar Prasad. "On Universal Currency Hedges." *Journal of Financial and Quantitative Analysis*, Vol. 27, No. 1, March 1992, pp. 19–38.

Agmon, Tamir. "The Relations Among Equity Markets: A Study of Share Price Co–Movements in the United States, United Kingdom, Germany and Japan." *Journal of Finance*, XXVII, No. 3, June 1972, pp. 839–855.

---

[16]There is a variation in this strategy that some funds follow. Assume we observe the following interest rates on six-month government debt:

$$\text{U.S. rate} = 4\%$$
$$\text{English rate} = 7\%$$
$$\text{German rate} = 5\%$$

In this scenario, one investment strategy is to buy English bonds and hedge exchange risk by buying a futures contract of Deutsche marks for dollars. The investor will lose 1% on the futures contract since there is a 1% difference in T-bill rates and empirical evidence supports that the interest rate differential is reflected in the futures contract. If the English-deutsche mark exchange rate stays constant, the investor will earn 7% on the bond less 1% on the futures contract or 6%, which is superior to the return on U.S. bills.

——. "Country Risk: The Significance of the Country Factor for Share-Price Movements in the United Kingdom, Germany, and Japan." *Journal of Business*, Vol. 46, No. 1, January 1973, pp. 24–32.

——. "Reply to [2]." *Journal of Finance*, XXIX, No. 4, September 1974, pp. 1318–1319.

Agmon, Tamir, and Donald Lessard. "Investor Recognition of Corporate International Diversification." *Journal of Finance*, XXXII, No. 4, September 1977, pp. 1049–1055.

Arnott, A., and N. Henriksson. "A Disciplined Approach to Global Asset Allocation." *Financial Analyst Journal*, March–April 1989, pp. 17–28.

Baxter, Marianne. "The International Diversification Puzzle Is Worse Than You Think." *The American Economic Review*, Vol. 87, No. 1, March 1997, pp. 170–180.

Bennett, James A. "International Stock Market Equilibrium with Heterogenous Tastes." *The American Economic Review*, Vol. 89, No. 3, June 1999, pp. 639–648.

Black, F. "International Capital Market Equilibrium with Investment Barriers." *Journal of Financial Economics*, Vol. 1, No. 4, December 1974, pp. 337–352.

Black, F. "Equilibrium Exchange Rate Hedging." National Bureau of Economic Research (NBER) Working Paper, No. 2947, April 1989.

Branch, Ben. "Common Stock Performance and Inflation: An International Comparison." *Journal of Business*, Vol. 47, No. 1, January 1973, pp. 48–52.

Campbell, J., and Y. Hammo. "Predictable Stock Returns in the United States and Japan: A Study of Long-Term Capital Market Integration." *Journal of Finance*, Vol. 47, 1992, pp. 43–70.

Cho, Chinhyung D., Cheol S. Eun, and Lemma Senbet. "International Arbitrage Pricing Theory: An Empirical Investigation." *Journal of Finance*, Vol. 41, No. 2, June 1986, pp. 313–329.

Chollerton, Kenneth, Pierre Pieraerts, and Bruno Solnik. "Why Invest in Foreign Currency Bonds?" *Journal of Portfolio Management,* Vol. 22, Summer 1986, pp. 4–8.

Cumby, Robert. "Is It Risk? Explaining Deviations from Uncovered Interest Rate Parity." *Journal of Monetary Economics,* Vol. 22, No. 2, 1988, pp. 297–300.

Cumby, Robert, and Jack Glen. "Evaluating the Performance of International Mutual Funds." *Journal of Finance,* Vol. 24, 1990, pp. 408–435.

Elton, Edwin J., Martin J. Gruber, and Joel Rentzler. "Professionally Managed, Publicly Traded Community Funds." *The Journal of Business*, Vol. 60, No. 2, April 1987, pp. 175–199.

Eun, Cheol, Richard Kolodny, and Bruce Resnick. "U.S. Based International Mutual Funds: A Performance Evaluation." *Journal of Portfolio Management,* forthcoming.

Eun, Cheol S., and Bruce G. Resnick. "Exchange Rate Uncertainty, Forward Contracts, and International Portfolio Selection." *The Journal of Finance*, Vol. 43, No. 1, March 1988, pp. 197–215.

Eun, Cheol, and Bruce Resnick. "Exchange Rate Uncertainty, Forward Contracts and International Portfolio Selection." *Journal of Finance,* Vol. 43, No. 8, 1988, pp. 197–215.

Fama, Eugene, and Kenneth French. "Business Conditions and Expected Return on Stocks and Bonds." *Journal of Financial Economics*, Vol. 25, 1993, pp. 23–50.

Farber, Andre L. "Performance of Internationally Diversified Mutual Funds." In Edwin J. Elton and Martin J. Gruber (eds.), *International Capital Markets.* Amsterdam: North-Holland, 1975.

Fatemi, Ali M. "Shareholder Benefits from Corporate International Diversification." *Journal of Finance*, Vol. 39, No. 5, December 1984, pp. 1325–1344.

French, Kenneth R., and James M. Poterba. "Investor Diversification and International Equity Markets." *The American Economic Review*, Vol. 81, No. 2, May 1991, pp. 222–226.

Grauer, R., and Nils Hakansson. "Gains from Internation Diversification: 1968–85 Returns on Portfolios of Stocks and Bonds." *Journal of Finance*, July 1987, pp. 721–738.

Grauer, Robert R., Nils H. Hakansson, and Michel Crouhy. "Gains from International Diversification: 1968–85 Returns on Portfolios of Stocks and Bonds/Discussion." *The Journal of Finance*, Vol. 42, No. 3, July 1987, pp. 721–741.

Grauer, F., R. Litzenberger, and R. Stehle. "Sharing Rules and Equilibrium in an International Capital Market Under Uncertainty." *Journal of Financial Economics*, Vol. 3, No. 3, June 1976, pp. 233–256.

Grubel, Herbert. "Internally Diversified Portfolios: Welfare Gains and Capital Flows." *American Economic Review*, LVIII, No. 5, Part 1, December 1968, pp. 1299–1314.

Grubel, G. Herbert, and Kenneth Fadner. "The Interdependence of International Equity Markets." *Journal of Finance*, XXVI, No. 1, March 1971, pp. 89–94.

Gultekin, N. Bulent. "Stock Market Returns and Inflation: Evidence from Other Countries." *The Journal of Finance*, Vol. 38, No. 1, March 1983, pp. 49–68.

Guy, J. "The Performance of the British Investment Trust Industry." *Journal of Finance*, May 1978, pp. 443–455.

Harvey, Campbell R. "Predictable Risk and Returns in Emerging Markets." *Review of Financial Studies*, Vol. 8, No. 3, 1995, pp. 773–816.

Ibbotson, Roger, Lawrence Siegal, and Kathryn Love. "World Wealth: Market Values and Returns." *Journal of Portfolio Management*, Vol. 4, No. 2, Fall 1985, pp. 4–23.

Jacquillat, Bertrand, and Bruno Solnik. "Multi-Nationals Are Poor Tools for Diversification." *Journal of Portfolio Management*, Vol. 11, No. 1, Winter 1978, pp. 8–12.

Jorion, Philippe. "International Diversification with Estimation Risk." *Journal of Business*, Vol. 12, No. 1, July 1985, pp. 259–278.

Joy, Maurice, Don Panton, Frank Reilly, and Stanley Martin. "Co-Movements of International Equity Markets." *The Financial Review*, Vol. 58, No. 3, 1976, pp. 1–20.

Kandel, Shmuel, and Robert Stambaugh. "On the Predictability of Stock Returns: An Asset-Allocation Perspective." *Journal of Finance*, Vol. 51, 1996 pp. 385–424.

Kaplanis, C. E., and Stever Schaefer. "Exchange Risk and International Diversification in Bond and Equity Portfolios." Unpublished manuscript, London Business School.

Lessard, Donald. "International Portfolio Diversification: A Multivariate Analysis for a Group of Latin American Countries." *Journal of Finance*, XXVIII, No. 3, June 1973, pp. 619–633.

——. "World, National and Industry Factors in Equity Returns." *Journal of Finance*, XXIV, No. 2, May 1974, pp. 379–391.

——. "The Structure of Returns and Gains from International Diversification: A Multivariate Approach." In Edwin J. Elton and Martin J. Gruber (eds.), *International Capital Markets*. Amsterdam: North-Holland, 1975.

Levich, Richard. "On the Efficiency of Markets for Foreign Exchange." In Frenkel, J. and Dornbusch, R. (eds.), *International Economic Policy: Theory and Evidence* 42. Baltimore, MD: Johns Hopkins Press, 1970.

——. "The Efficiency of Markets for Foreign Exchange: A Review and Extension." In Donald Lessard (ed.), *International Financial Management: Theory and Application*. New York: Warren, Gorham and Lamont, 1979.

Levich, Richard, and Jacob Frenkel. "Covered Interest Arbitrage: Unexplored Profits?" *Journal of Political Economy*, April, 1975, pp. 325–338.

——. "Transaction Costs and Interest Arbitrage: Tranquil versus Turbulent Periods." *Journal of Political Economy*, December 1977, pp. 1209–1286.

Levy, Haim, and Marshall Sarnat. "International Diversification of Investment Portfolios." *American Economic Review*, LX, No. 4, September 1970, pp. 668–675.

——. "Devaluation Risk and the Portfolio Analysis of International Investment." In Edwin J. Elton and Martin J. Gruber (eds.), *International Capital Markets*. Amsterdam: North-Holland, 1975.

Makin, John. "Portfolio Theory and the Problem of Foreign Exchange Risk." *Journal of Finance*, XXXIII, No. 2, May 1978, pp. 517–534.

McDonald, John. "French Mutual Fund Performance: Evaluation of Internationally-Diversified Portfolios." *Journal of Finance*, XXVIII, No. 5, December 1973, pp. 1161–1180.

Obstfeld, Maurice. "Risk-Taking, Global Diversification, and Growth." *The American Economic Review*, Vol. 84, No. 5, December 1994, pp. 1310–1329.

Panton, Don, Parket Lessig, and Maurice Joy. "Co-Movement of International Equity Markets: A Taxonomic Approach." *Journal of Financial and Quantitative Analysis*, XI, No. 3, September 1976, pp. 415–432.

Ripley, Duncan. "Systematic Elements in the Linkage of National Stock Market Indices." *Review of Economics and Statistics*, LV, No. 3, August 1973, pp. 356–361.

Robicher, Alexander, and Mark Eaker. "Foreign Exchange Hedging and the Capital Asset Pricing Model." *Journal of Finance*, XXXIII, No. 3, June 1978, pp. 1011–1018.

Severn, Alan. "Investor Evaluation of Foreign and Domestic Risk." *Journal of Finance*, XXIX, No. 2, May 1974, pp. 545–550.

Sharma, J. L., and Robert Kennedy. "A Comparative Analysis of Stock Price Behavior on the Bombay, London, and New York Stock Exchanges." *Journal of Financial and Quantitative Analysis*, XII, No. 3, September 1977, pp. 391–413.

Solnik, Bruno. "The International Pricing of Risk: An Empirical Investigation of the World Capital Market Structure." *Journal of Finance*, XXIX, No. 2, May 1974, pp. 365–378.

——. "Why Not Diversify Internationally?" *Financial Analysts Journal*, Vol. 20, No. 4, July/August 1974, pp. 48–54.

——. "An Equilibrium Model of the International Capital Market." *Journal of Economic Theory*, Vol. 8, No. 4, August 1974, pp. 500–524.

——. "An International Market Model of Security Price Behavior." *Journal of Financial and Quantitative Analysis*, IX, No. 4, September 1974, pp. 537–554.

——. "The Advantages of Domestic and International Diversification." In Edwin J. Elton and Martin J. Gruber (eds.), *International Capital Markets*, Amsterdam: North-Holland, 1975.

——. "Testing International Asset Pricing: Some Pessimistic Views." *Journal of Finance*, XXXII, No. 2, May 1977, pp. 503–512.

Solnik, Bruno. *International Investments*. Reading, MA: Addison-Wesley, 1988.

Solnick, Bruno. "The Performance of International Asset Allocations Strategies Using Conditioning Information." *Journal of Empirical Finance*, Vol. 1, No. 1, June 1993, pp. 33–55.

——. "Global Asset Management." *The Journal of Portfolio Management*, Summer 1998, pp. 43–51.

Solnik, Bruno, and B. Noetzlin. "Optimal International Asset Allocation." *Journal of Portfolio Management*, Vol. 2, Fall 1982, pp. 11–21.

Stehle, Richard. "An Empirical Test of the Alternative Hypotheses of National and International Pricing of Risky Assets." *Journal of Finance*, XII, No. 2, May 1977, pp. 493–502.

Subrahmanyam, Marti. "International Capital Markets, Equilibrium, and Investor Welfare with Unequal Interest Rates." In Edwin J. Elton and Martin J. Gruber (eds.), *International Capital Markets*. Amsterdam: North-Holland, 1975.

——. "On the Optimality of International Capital Market Integration." *Journal of Financial Economics*, Vol. 2, No. 1, March 1975, pp. 3–28.

Uppal, Raman. "A General Equilibrium Model of International Portfolio Choice." *The Journal of Finance*, Vol. 48, No. 2, June 1993, pp. 529–553.

PART III

WORLD SCENE OF ACCOUNTING AND REPORTING PRACTICES

CHAPTER 12

SUMMARY OF ACCOUNTING PRINCIPLE DIFFERENCES AROUND THE WORLD*

William E. Decker, Jr.

PricewaterhouseCoopers LLP

Paul Brunner

PricewaterhouseCoopers LLP

CONTENTS

12.1 INTRODUCTION. The major objectives of this chapter are to illustrate, by example, how and why accounting measurement practices differ from country to country and to discuss current developments and trends in the "globalization" of accounting practices around the world. After reading this chapter, the reader should better appreciate the potential significance of differences from a financial statement per-

*The authors would like to thank Samying Huie for her assistance.

spective and the difficulty of getting all countries to agree to a single set of internationally accepted accounting principles. Emphasis is given to discussing the role of International Financial Reporting Standards (IFRS), formerly known as International Accounting Standards (IAS), and the policies and activities of the U.S. Securities and Exchange Commission (SEC) as they relate to the international capital markets.

12.2 GLOBALIZATION OF FINANCIAL DECISIONS. The world is constantly changing, and it is important to identify the forces generating change and the pressures they create when evaluating differences in accounting measurement between countries. The increase in the number of multinational companies, combined with floating foreign exchange markets, globalization of the capital markets, and the opening up of markets in previously centrally planned economies (e.g., Russia and China) to foreign direct investment have important implications for financial reporting. These factors indicate that business and investment decisions are becoming increasingly international in scope.

The continuing trend toward a single "global" marketplace reflects the results of the economic policies many countries are pursuing to increase the opportunities for international trade by reducing barriers to trade such as tariffs and quotas, to reduce the size of government by privatizing certain government-owned businesses such as telecommunications and postal services, to encourage the growth of competitive markets, and to minimize market regulation. One of the most recent examples of this type is China's entry to the World Trade Organization in 2001. Changes in the accessibility and competitiveness of markets and in the regulatory environment have led to an increase in the overall number of multinational companies and have resulted in many multinationals' relocating manufacturing and service operations to developing economies to obtain efficiencies. Multinationals need to consolidate accounting data that is sourced from many different countries. Depending on whether the parent entity is located in Chile, Germany, or the United States, for example, a different basis of accounting may apply at the group level. In a time when multinationals had a predominantly national identity, with creditors and shareholders who shared that identity, this situation was tolerable. Multinationals are increasingly seeking to define an international identity, with investors and creditors from several countries, and the national accounting rules are frequently a barrier to achieving this objective.

There are many reasons for the globalization of the capital markets. From an investor's perspective, the relatively unregulated and open foreign exchange markets in most currencies facilitate cross-border capital flows. In this environment, subject to foreign investment constraints in some industries within some countries (e.g., television and media), investors are free to acquire existing businesses, to establish new businesses, and to form joint ventures and other alliances in many countries around the world. Also, mutual funds, pension funds, and insurance companies are able to allocate capital to publicly traded equities, debt, and derivatives in other countries. … a large pool of capital when aggregated globally that is allocated … ment decisions that reflect an assessment of prospective returns and … investment relative to other opportunities on a cross-border or …

… pective of an issuer of securities (i.e., a company seeking to raise … ability of investor funds in other markets creates new sources of … l is to access the capital markets for funds with terms that match their requirements, and that can be accessed efficiently at a reasonable price or cost of capital when compared to the next best alternative. The size of the flotation sometimes necessitates an international offering, as has been the case, for example, with certain privatizations such as British Telecom in 1984, the Royal PTT Nederland NV in 1995 and Petro China Company Limited in 2000. In other cases, internationally diversified companies from relatively small countries outgrow their home country's capital market and/or desire an international presence, for example, Nokia from Finland. There are now 40 non-U.S. banks registered with the SEC, reflecting their desire, in some cases, for access to competitively priced debt finance in a liquid and sophisticated market that affords them greater financial flexibility. A high percentage of cross-border capital raisings involve simultaneous offerings in each enterprise's home country and in the United States, as well as an "international" offering which in practice could mean Canada or Japan, but most probably Europe. This structure forces the senior management of the enterprise, and its accountants, lawyers, and investor relations people to deal simultaneously with the conflicting demands of investors, analysts, and regulators in different countries. As a result there is now a much greater appreciation of the strengths and weaknesses of different approaches to market regulation (e.g., insider trading and preoffering advertisements), corporate governance, disclosure, and financial reporting regimes.

The trend toward globalization of the capital markets can be illustrated by the recent developments in the United States. By December 31, 2001, there were 1,344 non-U.S. enterprises registered with the SEC, representing some 59 countries from around the world. Approximately 77 non-U.S. enterprises entered the U.S. public markets for the first time in 2001, down from levels experienced in 1999 and 2000. In 2001, non-U.S. enterprises raised more than US$40.0 billion of debt and equity capital and over the past six years have raised over US$300 billion. Of the 1,344 non-U.S. registrants, approximately 600 or 45%, entered the United States during the last six years. Because the accounting principles of so many countries are involved and as the volume of transactions has increased, so too has the pressure to simplify the financial reporting process where possible.

Cross-border mergers and acquisitions have skyrocketed in this past decade, exemplified by the fact that, in 2001 alone, foreign investors spent over US$158 billion to buy American businesses, while American buyers spent over US$156 billion in acquiring foreign companies. These amounts of foreign investments were even higher during the mid to late 1990s.

The exchanges in the United States and London are highly internationalized. The volume of trade in foreign shares on the New York Stock Exchange and London Stock Exchange reached US$787 billion and US$2,651 billion respectively in 2001. Approximately 11% of listings on major exchanges throughout the world in 2001 were foreign (see Exhibit 12.1).

With all of this international activity taking place, creditors, investors, regulators, and others in the business world need to better understand cross-border financial information. A multinational firm's management needs to be able to compare the performance of each of its operations in other countries. Management also must accurately assess its competition. In addition, lenders and investors need comparable and consistent information to make informed decisions. Therefore, the financial information generated by an enterprise serves as a basis for making critical business decisions.

	NO OF COMPANIES WITH SHARES LISTED				VALUE OF SHARE TRADING in Billion of US$			
Exchange	Domestic	%	Foreign	%	Domestic	%	Foreign	%
North America								
NYSE	1,939	81%	461	19%	9,602	92%	787	8%
NASDAQ	4,176	89%	493	11%	10,465	96%	469	4%
Toronto	1,261	97%	38	3%	459	99.9%	0.4	0.1%
South America								
Sao Paulo	438	99%	3	1%	64	99%	0.4	1%
Europe								
Deutsche Borse	748	76%	235	24%	1,306	91%	136	9%
Euronext	1,132	72%	432	28%	3,150	99%	19	1%
London	1,923	82%	409	18%	1,877	41%	2,651	59%
Madrid	1,458	99%	22	1%	839	99.6%	3	0.4%
Swiss Exchange	263	64%	149	36%	577	97%	15	3%
Asia, Pacific								
Australia	1,334	95%	76	5%	241	99%	3	1%
Hong Kong	857	99%	10	1%	238	99.9%	0.2	0.1%
Korea	688	100%	0	0%	381	100%	—	0%
Taiwan	584	99.7%	2	0.3%	544	100%	0.3	0%
Tokyo	2,103	98%	38	2%	1,656	100%	0.4	0%

Source: Federation Internationale des Bourses de Valeurs (International Federation of Stock Exchanges)

Exhibit 12.1. Domestic and Foreign Listings and U.S. Dollar Trading Volume by Major Exchange.

12.3 INTERNATIONAL ACCOUNTING DIVERSITY. As businesses become more international, there is a more pressing need for financial information to be prepared by businesses on a comparable basis. Unfortunately, although many financial statement users may find it surprising, international financial data are frequently not comparable. The rules of financial accounting often differ from one country to another, which adds another dimension to the complexity of the accounting puzzle. Exhibit 12.2 illustrates that accounting conventions established by one nation's accounting rule makers are not necessarily consistent with those established elsewhere. The continued existence of differences is also illustrated in an extensive survey completed in 2001 entitled *GAAP 2001: A Survey of National Accounting Rules Benchmarked against International Accounting Standards. GAAP 2001* concluded that investors continue to be handicapped by variations between national accounting rules in the world's leading economies. Of the 65 countries surveyed, almost half revealed significant differences but showed no signs of convergence. Some prevalent differences noted in the study were in the following areas:

- Recognition and measurement of financial assets and derivatives, impairment losses, provisions, employee benefit obligations, income taxes
- Business combinations
- Related-party and -segment disclosure

There are promising signs that many countries will harmonize based on IFRS, as is illustrated in Exhibit 12.3. The most concrete example is the fact that the European Parliament has mandated the use of IFRS for all listed companies in the European Union by 2005. This will impact Germany, France, and the United Kingdom and other countries within the European Community. Countries such as Australia, Brazil, Canada, and Singapore, which have had a long-standing practice of adopting IAS as local standards with few exceptions, will likely also increase their efforts to adopt new IFRS. For example, Australia has recently announced the adoption of IFRS by 2005, an announcement that in part reflects the need for Australia to "catch up" and issue comprehensive standards in areas such as pensions and derivatives.

In the short to medium term, it is important to note that the IFRS may increase rather than reduce differences through issuing new standards. IAS 39, "Financial Instruments: Recognition and Measurement," is an example of a standard that increased comparability with the equivalent U.S. standard Statement of Financial Accounting Standards (SFAS) No. 133, while perhaps getting ahead of various national standard-setting efforts. IAS 40, "Investment Property," also sets a new standard that is not merely a "cut and paste" from a comparable U.S. standard, and for most countries the fair value model it employs presents many challenges.

Similarly, developments in the major capital markets may also increase differences. In the United States, the change to eliminate goodwill amortization charges and introduce a fair value impairment model diverge from IAS and have resulted in billions of dollars of impairment charges. Additionally, chang rounding the consolidation of special purpose vehicles have beer

Because of this inconsistency in accounting rules, investors, financial statement users whose scope has broadened beyond tl borders are at a disadvantage when they analyze foreign compa differences in accounting principles that exist internationally, tw ferent countries may experience identical economic results during significantly different results in their financial statements.

	United States	Japan	United Kingdom	France	Germany	The Netherlands	Switzerland	Canada	Italy	Brazil	International: Benchmark	International: Allowed Alternative
Capitalization of research and development	Not allowed	Allowed in certain circumstances	Allowed in certain circumstances	Allowed in certain circumstances	Not allowed	Allowed in certain circumstances	Allowed in certain circumstances	Allowed in certain circumstances	Allowed in certain circumstances	Allowed	Required in certain circumstances	None
Fixed asset revaluation stated at amount in excess of cost	Not allowed	Not allowed	Allowed	Allowed	Not allowed	Allowed in certain circumstances	Allowed in certain circumstances	Not allowed	Required in certain circumstances	Allowed	Not allowed	Allowed
Inventory valuation using LIFO	Allowed	Allowed	Allowed but rarely done	Allowed	Allowed in certain circumstances	Allowed	Allowed	Allowed	Allowed	Allowed but rarely done	Not allowed	Allowed
Finance leases capitalized	Required	Allowed in certain circumstances	Required	Allowed	Allowed in certain circumstances	Required	Allowed	Required	Not allowed	Allowed in certain	Required	None
Pension expense accrued during period of service	Required	Allowed	Required	Allowed	Required	Required	Allowed	Required	Allowed	Allowed	Required	None
Book and tax timing differences presented on the balance sheet as deferred tax	Required	Allowed in certain circumstances	Required in certain circumstances	Required	Allowed in certain circumstances	Required	Allowed	Required	Generally required	Required	Allowed	None
Current rate method used for foreign currency translation	Required for foreign operations whose functional currency is other than the reporting currency	Generally required	Required	Required for self-sustaining foreign operations	Allowed	Required for self-sustaining foreign operations	Allowed	Required for self-sustaining foreign operations	Required	Required	Required for self-sustaining foreign operations	None
Pooling method used for mergers	Required in certain circumstances	Allowed	Required in certain circumstances	Not allowed	Allowed in certain circumstances	Allowed but rarely done	Allowed but rarely done	Allowed in rare circumstances	Allowed in rare circumstances	Allowed but rarely done	Required in certain circumstances	None
Equity method used for 20–50% ownership	Required	Required	Required	Required	Required	Required	Allowed in certain circumstances	Required	Allowed	Required	Required	None

Exhibit 12.2. Comparative Analysis of Accounting Differences Around the World.

Country	IAS Transition Plan
United States	As U.S. GAAP is an internationally accepted body of accounting principles, there is no immediate plan to adopt IAS as United States' national accounting standards. However, there has been increased pressure to simplify U.S. GAAP to adopt a more principles-based approach and to revisit its requirements for non-U.S. filers, especially for those that report under IAS.
United Kingdom	As part of the European Union (EU), IAS will be required for listed companies in the United Kingdom beginning in 2005. IAS are expected to be introduced as national standards in 2005.
Germany	As part of the EU, IAS will be required for listed companies in Germany beginning in 2005. The German stock exchanges currently allow IAS an alternative to German GAAP. However, reporting under IAS is not compulsory under German law, and there is no indication that IAS will replace its national standards.
Japan	There has been enormous pressure for structural reform of the Japanese financial system during the recent economic downturn. The reform initiatives led to the establishment of a new independently funded commission, the Accounting Standards Board of Japan (ASBJ). The ASBJ will continue to focus on reshaping the Japanese standard-setting system in line with the International Accounting Standards Board and Japanese GAAP in line with IAS. While there is growing support for convergence and improved transparency, the practical implications are proving difficult for Japanese companies to accept.
China	Even though the exchanges in China still require Peoples Republic of China (GRC) GAAP, the Ministry of Finance has established transition rules to gradually reduce the differences between PRC GAAP and IAS. Before 1997, there were different accounting standards for different industries and enterprises with different legal forms. with the 16 accounting standards issued in 1997 and the new accounting regulation for financial institutions issued in 2001. The Chinese accounting regulators have made significant steps toward unifying the accounting standards in China across industries and with IAS. How rigorous these standards are applied/interpreted will be critical in achieving harmonization with IAS.
Brazil	The professional bodies and the regulators in Brazil support harmonization with IAS. New standards have been developed based on IAS and the old standards are being reviewed to bring them into line. To support this initiative, the corporate law is being reviewed by Congress and there is a project, supported by the Brazilian Securities Commission, to create a Brazilian Accounting Standard Board.

Exhibit 12.3. Countries IAS Transition Plans.

12.4 CONSEQUENCES OF INTERNATIONAL ACCOUNTING DIVERSITY. Users who are not sensitive to international accounting differences may make less-than-prudent business decisions. For example, an analyst may have certain "rules of thumb" or benchmarks against which to measure a company's price/earnings ratio, debt-to-equity ratio, or working-capital ratio. These benchmarks were likely developed by the analyst on the basis of ratios of comparable companies in the local environment prepared under accounting rules existing in that country. If the analyst were to apply the same nominal benchmarks to a company whose balance sheet was prepared under a different set of rules, it is not inconceivable that the analyst could arrive at an inappropriate conclusion in the absence of any additional effort to interpret that information properly.

Furthermore, the capital market's inability to understand efficiently a company's performance could have a detrimental effect on the entity's ability to raise capital at competitive prices. For example, pricing inefficiencies may arise because the company has adopted unique accounting policies that are unfamiliar to investors and creditors, the display of financial information in the primary statements and the footnotes does not follow accepted reporting conventions, and/or the company provides relatively less extensive or transparent disclosure compared with other companies in the market. Other things being equal, pricing inefficiencies may imply that a company's cost of capital will be relatively higher and that the price of its equity and debt will be relatively lower. Pricing inefficiencies could become evident in the domestic, foreign, or international markets and, while this is not only a cross-border issue, the area of greatest variation is perceived to exist between the reporting of companies from different countries. However, the existence of inefficiencies implies that there will be pressure on companies to improve their financial reporting in ways that lower their cost of capital. To illustrate this point, anecdotal evidence from certain Swiss companies has indicated that the adoption of more comprehensive and internationally accepted financial reporting and disclosure standards resulted in significant increases in their stock prices.

Perceptions about the reliability of financial reporting and disclosure made by companies from a particular country also affect the cost of capital. This is because the release of inaccurate information will lead to pricing errors and because a lack of full disclosure will lead to pricing inefficiencies as well as leaving the door open for insider trading and other forms of price manipulation. To protect the public, the issuer and other parties (underwriters, lawyers, accountants, etc.) associated with a U.S. prospectus must ensure that the statements made in the prospectus are accurate and that material facts have not been omitted. Full disclosure is believed to enhance the credibility of the markets, to improve their efficiency, and to make the capital markets attractive to the public. Given the liability standard associated with SEC filings, fulfilling these requirements demands a high standard of honesty and integrity. Companies from countries that place relatively less emphasis on complete and accurate reporting and disclosure may be penalized unless they take steps to adhere to more internationally accepted reporting and disclosure practices.

In addition to the negative impact on an entity's capital-raising ability and cost of capital, disharmony in accounting principles makes it difficult to monitor competitive factors. Officers whose responsibility it is to develop competitive strategies may not fully understand the accounting rules of their foreign competitors and thus cannot effectively assess their competitors' performance. Differences in accounting principles have a large impact on many business decisions for other reasons as well. For example, some have suggested that one of the reasons for the continuing wave of mergers and acquisitions by British companies of American companies may be the differences in accounting for goodwill in the two countries. Furthermore, accounting differences have apparently affected the investment decisions of institutional investors from many countries. The concerns of institutional investors typically relate to their lack of understanding of a specific country's accounting principles and disclosures, and concerns about the reliability of financial statements.

Another example of a business decision that might be affected by accounting information is a bank's credit extension decision. For credit appraisals, banks rely on accounting information in deciding whether to lend funds. If the bank is not familiar with the implications of accounting differences, it runs the risk of making the wrong decision. An example of this is a bank's use of the interest coverage ratio for lending decisions. The components of this ratio are interest expense and pretax income before interest expense. If a company is located in a country whose standards require goodwill to be amortized or research and development (R&D) costs to be expensed as incurred, its pretax income may be significantly different from what it would be if the company were in a country where the accounting standards allow goodwill to be written off directly against equity or the deferral of R&D expense. As a result, the ratios between two nearly identical companies could be drastically different solely because of the application of different accounting principles.

12.5 ENVIRONMENTAL INFLUENCES ON ACCOUNTING. One might ask why the accounting standards in two countries would differ. After all, aren't accountants simply supposed to keep track of a company's assets, liabilities, revenues, and expenses? Should not there be only one right answer? The truth is that the "right" answer depends a great deal on one's perspective. A given country's accounting standards can be influenced by a multitude of factors. The objectives of an accounting system are very much a function of the economic, social, and political environment of the country in which the system exists. The objectives are often linked, from an historical perspective, to the goals and objectives of the perceived end users of the financial statements (e.g., lenders, investors, or the government). Accounting standards in a particular country are often influenced by the standards followed in other countries for one reason or another; for example, Canadian accounting principles are strongly influenced by U.S. principles (and vice versa) because of geographic proximity and economic interdependence.

The volume of accounting standard codification that countries have developed differs greatly. Certain countries have promulgated elaborate sets of rules and regulations that govern the manner in which financial information is to be presented and disclosed. Economically developed countries have established institutional structures, including professional accounting societies, stock exchanges, securities regulators, and national legislative bodies, to create national standards. The objective has generally been to resolve accounting issues and to ensure consistency in accounting practices within a single nation. A national accounting system promotes one set of accounting standards that makes the system useful to investors, creditors, auditors, and companies' management within the given country. The United States uniformly is looked on as having developed the most extensive set of accounting standards and disclosures. This exhaustive set of rules was developed in response to what was arguably the most advanced economic system in the world–an economy that has given rise to extensive markets for both equity and debt securities. The SEC was called on to be the watchdog for the large population of investors and creditors. Consequently, the SEC has overseen the development of an elaborate set of rules and regulations. Similarly, while not as comprehensive and detailed as those in the United States, the accounting standards in Canada and the United Kingdom are becoming more and more codified—a trend due, in large part, to the growth of the economies and capital markets in these countries. Post-Enron, the preeminence of the U.S. standard-setting model has been challenged and the pendulum is swinging more toward a greater desire for principles rather than rules. In this regard, IFRS is considered principles based whereas U.S. GAAP are more rules orientated through being more prescriptive, detailed, and comprehensive.

Other countries have somewhat less extensive bodies of promulgated standards. One explanation for this may be found in those countries where companies are required to conform their accounting books and statements to the books and records utilized for income tax-reporting purposes. Examples of countries in which there exists a high degree of book and tax conformity are France, Germany, and Japan. The standards in these countries require companies to take book deductions for items such as reserves, write-offs, and accelerated depreciation that are deducted on their tax returns. As a result, given the natural bias to minimize taxes, their reported earnings are generally less than if the book and tax conformity requirement did not exist. Over the past five years, globalization of the capital markets has continued to exert its influence forcefully on financial reporting. In relation to the United States, this debate is focused on the SEC's financial reporting requirements and, in particular, the requirement that non-U.S. registrants either prepare their financial statements in accordance with U.S. GAAP or reconcile them thereto. Some argue that these regulations are acting as a barrier to the formation of capital as evidenced by the fact that there are apparently more than 2,000 companies that have not yet entered the U.S. public markets, even though they would meet the listing criteria of the New York Stock Exchange (NYSE). Shares in many of these companies, which include Bayer of Germany and Nestle of Switzerland, are actively traded in an over-the-counter "pink" sheet market in the United States for which there is no volume reporting and no real time quotes. Thus, there is an enormous number of high-quality companies that may find the U.S. public markets attractive.

With so much cross-border activity, strong pressures have emerged for there to be one financial language around the world. This goal has been embraced by the International Accounting Standards Committee (IASC), the predecessor to the International Accounting Standards Board (IASB), which has clearly emerged with the leadership role in the international standard-setting process. The IASB and the International Organization of Securities Commissions (IOSCO) have announced that their mutual goal is for financial statements prepared in accordance with IAS to be accepted worldwide (including the United States) in cross-border offerings and listings as an alternative to the use of national accounting standards. This promises to be a very significant development having important worldwide ramifications from a financial reporting standpoint.

12.6 FINANCIAL STATEMENT EFFECTS OF DIFFERENCES IN ACCOUNTING PRINCIPLES. In this section, we will discuss, evaluate, and assess 12 specific areas of accounting where diversity exists, and we will discuss the differences in accounting principles practiced in a representative group of countries. As can be seen in Exhibit 12.2, there is a good deal of diversity among countries' standards even in light of the recent efforts toward the achievement of financial reporting harmonization. In addition, we will examine the theoretical bases for the different methods adopted, and we will explore why countries use certain rules. The accounting principles that will be discussed are:

- Research and development expenditures
- Fixed assets
- Inventory valuation
- Leases
- Pensions
- Accounting for income taxes
- Foreign currency translation
- Accounting for mergers and acquisitions (including goodwill)
- Consolidation
- Impairment
- Transfer of financial assets and special purpose vehicles
- Derivatives

This chapter is not intended to provide a comprehensive analysis of differences in accounting standards but, rather, a decision framework.

(a) Research and Development Expenditures. The first issue we will discuss is the accounting treatment for R&D expenditures. Though the definitions vary from country to country, "research" is generally thought of as the planned efforts of a company to discover new information that will help create a new product, service, process, or technique, or will improve one that is already in use. "Development" takes the findings generated by research and formulates a plan or design for the production of a new product or to improve an existing one substantially. The costs incurred during each accounting period by a company on R&D activities are generally thought to be a discretionary expenditure, which will not translate into significant revenue generation or expense reduction in that period, and may or may not result in future revenue generation. Rule makers in each country, and at the IASB, have been called upon to establish a policy governing the accounting for R&D costs.

The two basic ways to account for R&D are capitalizing the costs or expensing them when they have been incurred. Those who support immediate expense recognition argue that there is a great deal of uncertainty as to whether the R&D will benefit future periods. To expense the costs is conservative, since income will be lower in the current year than if the cost is amortized over future years. Several countries' standards (including those of Germany and the United States) require immediate expense recognition under all circumstances.

However, the more popular approach is to allow capitalization under specified circumstances. Those who support this approach believe that, if it can be determined that there is a strong chance that the new product will be successful, capitalization provides a better matching of future revenue and expense. By allowing capitalization, companies are encouraged to spend money now for the future, without worrying about the impact on their current reported income. Canada, France, the Netherlands, Switzerland, the United Kingdom, and IAS all allow capitalization under certain circumstances. Each of the countries' criteria for capitalization focus primarily on whether the technical feasibility of a product or process has been established combined with a judgmental assessment of the economic likelihood of product success.

Some countries take the approach that research costs should be expensed, while development costs can be capitalized. Such is the case, for example, in Canada and the United Kingdom, and under IAS 38, "Intangible Assets." The theory is that the development costs eventually will turn the "researched idea" into action and generate revenue. Therefore, these are the only costs that should be capitalized. Countries that advocate this approach generally stipulate that the product should have a high likelihood of success before development costs may be capitalized. In Brazil, Italy, and Japan, the constraints on capitalization of R&D are less restrictive than in the other countries. IAS 38 requires that:

- The product or process is clearly defined and the costs attributable to the product or process can be separately identified and measured reliably.
- The technical feasibility of the product or process *can* be demonstrated.
- The enterprise intends to produce, and market or use, the product or process.
- The market exists for the product or process or, if it is to be used internally rather than sold, its usefulness to the enterprise can be demonstrated.
- Adequate resources exist, or their availability can be demonstrated, to complete the project, and market or use the product or process.

The key considerations from an IAS perspective revolve around technical feasibility and the enterprise's intention to produce and market/use the product or process. To illustrate, if IAS 38 required that technical feasibility *has been* (as opposed to *can be*) demonstrated before permitting capitalization, then it would be clear that most development activities (e.g., costs of constructing and operating a pilot plant) would not satisfy the criterion because the activity have not been completed and technical feasibility would remain unproven. Demonstrating technical feasibility for a new product or process would appear to necessitate that all R&D aspects of a product or process have been completed because, until their completion, feasibility would not have actually been demonstrated. On the other hand, it can be argued that the "can" in IAS 38 leaves room for management to take the position that it will be able to demonstrate technical feasibility in the future.

Another criterion that must be met under IAS 38 before development costs can be capitalized is that the enterprise must intend to produce and market the product or process. In cases in which the enterprise is still evaluating alternative products or processes, this test will arguably not be satisfied, and certain development costs will not qualify for capitalization. However, once the particular product or process has been selected to take to market, and assuming that the other tests have been satisfied, the enterprise may no longer be engaged in an R&D activity. Furthermore, until these criteria are made clear, debate will be inevitable as to whether an identifiable asset exists.

(b) Fixed Assets. Fixed assets consist of land, building, machinery, and equipment. These assets are used by an enterprise in its business for a number of years, and they generally require a significant expenditure at the time of acquisition. The two critical issues raised in accounting for fixed assets are: (1) In what periods should these expenditures be charged to the income statement for accounting purposes? (2) At what amount, if any, should the assets be carried on the company's balance sheet?

Enterprises in all countries are required to capitalize and to depreciate fixed assets. The reasoning is that this large expenditure will benefit the enterprise in future years;

depreciating the costs over time yields a better matching of costs to the periods in which the related assets are used to generate revenues. Depreciation is essentially a rational allocation of the costs over the estimated useful life of an asset. There are many methods of depreciation used in the various countries, including straight-line, units-of-output, sum-of-the-years' digits, and accelerated methods. The major difference between the various methods lies in how the costs are allocated among the years. The units-of-output method tries to match the costs against revenues generated. The accelerated method allocates more of the costs to expense in the early years, on the theory that an asset will usually be more efficient and lose a higher percentage of its value in the early years of its life. In this way, higher revenue is matched against higher costs. The simplest and most commonly used method of depreciation is the straight-line method. This method allocates cost equally over the estimated life of the asset. In many countries, a specific depreciation method is not required to be used. However, for countries with accounting standards that are heavily influenced by tax rules, such as Japan, Germany, and France, the general rule is that a company must use the same depreciation method for both book and tax purposes.

Depreciation schedules for a 10-year asset costing 1,000 ECUs under the straight-line, sum-of-the-years' digits, and double-declining-balance-depreciation methods can be seen in Exhibit 12.4.

Another factor that must be considered in this area is whether a fixed asset should be reflected in the balance sheet at historical cost or current fair value. Historical cost comprises the original recorded cost less accumulated depreciation; no revaluation is allowed under this approach for amounts in excess of the original cost. (However, if the value of an asset has been impaired below its depreciated historical cost, a write-down is required.) This usually is viewed as a conservative balance sheet approach

	SL	SYD[a]	DDB[b]
Year 1	100	182	200
Year 2	100	164	160
Year 3	100	145	128
Year 4	100	127	102
Year 5	100	109	82
Year 6	100	91	66
Year 7	100	73	66
Year 8	100	55	65
Year 9	100	36	65
Year 10	100	18	65
	1,000	1,000	1,000

[a]SYD—calculates each year's percent depreciation by dividing the number of years remaining at the beginning of the year by the sum of the years' digits (e.g., in year one, the percent is computed as 10 divided by 10 + 9 + 8 + 7 . . . 1).

[b]DDB—completed by applying a rate of double the straight-line rate to the remaining undepreciated balance. Once a straight-line method for the remaining life yields a higher depreciation amount, a switch is usually made to straight-line.

Exhibit 12.4. Sensitivity of Depreciable Expense to Choice of Depreciation Method.

that results in an asset's book value falling below its current market value during periods of moderate to high inflation. Countries whose accounting standards follow the historical cost approach include Canada, Germany, Japan, and the United States.

The alternative is to allow upward or downward revaluation of fixed assets to the most current fair (appraised) value. Downward revaluation may be used under this approach even to value the asset below its cost similar to reporting a write down under the historical cost method. Those who advocate upward revaluation contend that the balance sheet should, whenever possible, present the fair value of the company's assets, provided that the increase in value is not determined to be temporary. Revaluation gives management more flexibility to improve the appearance of its balance sheet when it is most advantageous. Countries where the accounting rules allow some form of revaluation include Brazil, France, Italy, the Netherlands, Switzerland, and the United Kingdom. IAS 16, "Property, Plant and Equipment," establishes historical cost as the benchmark standard, but permits revaluations as an allowed alternative, albeit that the IASB is proposing to eliminate the allowed alternative when IAS 16 is adopted as an IFRS.

(c) Inventory. Inventory valuation is an extremely important area of accounting. For many commercial companies, inventory is one of the largest assets on the balance sheet. Inventory consists of goods owned and held for sale in the normal course of business operations, and raw materials and goods in the process of being produced. Inventory is normally recorded at acquired cost, which includes the purchase price plus any additional costs needed to bring the product to a salable state. The critical accounting question regarding inventory is how to allocate costs between the cost of goods sold in the income statement and the goods yet to be sold (i.e., the inventory) on the balance sheet. The three main acceptable methods most often used to account for inventory are first in, first out (FIFO), the average cost method, and last in, first out (LIFO), all of which are applied on a lower-of-cost-or-market-value basis.

The LIFO method allocates the cost on the premise that the last goods purchased are the first ones sold. The ending inventory that remains on the balance sheet under this approach represents the inventory that was purchased first. This is considered conservative for income statement purposes, since the resulting cost of goods sold (expense) is generally higher (assuming rising prices). However, the majority of accountants around the world argue that LIFO has no conceptual basis in accounting theory in most industries. The inventory on the balance sheet, they argue, is valued at "inaccurate" old prices when LIFO is applied. The main advantage for a company using LIFO is that it can provide large tax savings when used for tax purposes. This is because, under conditions of rising prices, taxable income will be lower under the LIFO method than under the FIFO method. In addition, LIFO allows for a more current cost to flow through the income statement. As can be seen from Exhibit 12.2, all countries listed allow the LIFO method to be used under certain circumstances. However, countries' standards differ on the circumstances under which it can be used, and from a worldwide perspective it is rarely used in practice, other than by companies in the United States.

In certain countries, such as Germany, LIFO can be used for tax purposes if there is a corresponding physical flow of goods, which would be unusual, and consequently LIFO is not widely used. In Brazil and the United Kingdom, LIFO is not often used for book purposes, since it is not allowed to be used for tax purposes. IAS permits LIFO as an allowed alternative but a proposed amendment has been announced to eliminate the use of LIFO.

The principal justification for using the FIFO method for inventory valuation is that under FIFO the cost of goods sold on the income statement is valued more accurately and FIFO is thought to better parallel the physical flow of goods. As a general rule, there is a better matching of the costs incurred to produce the inventory with its revenues. Additionally, the balance sheet will be presented more accurately, because the inventory stated on the balance sheet will be valued at the most recent prices. The FIFO method is permitted in all countries and is accepted under the IAS benchmark approach.

(d) Leases. Leasing has become quite popular in recent years due to the high degree of financial and tax flexibility it gives both the lessor and the lessee. Leasing often affords the parties tax advantages not available in the purchase of fixed assets. In contrast to an outright purchase, the rights and risks in a leasing transaction can be assumed by either party in a number of different combinations; leases essentially allow a company to "buy" an asset for a specified period of time. Depending on the specifics of the leasing contract, differences arise among the countries' accounting rules as to how such transactions should be accounted for. The basic accounting issue regarding leases is whether a leased item can or should be capitalized as an asset as if owned or whether the lease payments should be treated as periodic rent expense.

When a company (lessee) leases an item from another entity (the lessor), the transaction could be viewed as an acquisition of an asset if the lease term is the majority of the useful life of the item or if the price paid is significant when compared with the fair market value of the item. When these criteria, among others, are met, some would argue that substantially all the risks and benefits of ownership of the leased property have been transferred from the lessor to the lessee, thus calling for capital lease treatment. Those who view a lease in this manner would argue that the lease contract ought to be accounted for as a purchase of an asset on the lessee's books. Generally, the same people would also argue that the lessor should treat the lease as the sale of the underlying asset. Under a capital lease, the lease is accounted for as if the lessee borrowed money and acquired the asset and the lease payments represent payments of principal and interest on the borrowing.

Many countries' principles, including those in Australia, Canada, the Netherlands, the United Kingdom, and the United States, require capital lease treatment if certain criteria are met. Similarly, IAS 17, "Accounting for Leases," requires leases to be capitalized if certain criteria are met.

The alternative method is to expense the lease payments as they occur, which is referred to as an operating lease treatment. As shown in Exhibit 12.2, there are some countries, such as Japan, where standards permit all leases to be accounted for as operating leases, provided there is footnote disclosure of capital leases. Under this method, the leased property remains an asset on the lessor's books. The rationale behind this treatment is that the asset has not legally changed hands.

Depending on whether leases are on- or off- balance sheet, their treatment can be quite controversial as it may have a significant impact on certain debt covenants, leverage, interest coverage and other financial data and ratios. There continues to be concern that many operating leases contain non-cancelable obligations that are not being given accounting recognition as liabilities. Some argue that all non-cancelable lease commitments should be recognized as liabilities to better reflect the substance of the rights and obligations leases embody. While sophisticated analysts may arguably not be "fooled" by the off-balance-sheet accounting, there is no substitute for getting the treatment right.

(e) Pensions. Over the past couple of decades, pension plans have received a great deal of attention from standard setters and regulators worldwide. Historically, government-sponsored pension plans bore the greatest burden of providing postretirement benefits. However, many employees contended that these types of pension plans did not provide sufficient retirement income. Therefore, as time passed, the sufficiency of pension benefits became a prime area of importance for collective-bargaining negotiations, and eventually, in many countries, firms instituted or enhanced private pension plans. As the privately handled pension plans grew in popularity throughout the 1980s, the accounting rule-making bodies were called upon to address the accounting for these plans.

A pension plan is an arrangement under which an employer agrees to continue to provide its employees with an income stream after their retirement. Accountants are faced with the question of whether this promise should give rise to an expense and a corresponding liability at the time an employee provides the underlying service or whether the expense should be recorded as the pension payments are made (many years later).

Enterprises that have defined benefit pension plans know that their promise to the employee will ultimately result in a cost to the company; however, the enterprise does not know the precise amount or timing of the ultimate costs. Many countries apply the principle that, if the liability can be reasonably estimated on the basis of various actuarial assumptions, then it should be accrued in some manner during the period of employee service. This provides the best matching of revenues and expenses. Countries where the standards require this treatment include Canada, Germany, the Netherlands, the United Kingdom, and the United States. In Germany, although this accounting requirement did not come into effect until 1987, many enterprises had accrued for pension plan liabilities before that time, since they could not take a tax deduction for such amount unless they recorded the expense for book purposes. In Italy, a "termination indemnity," representing a calculation of the amount that would be payable if all employees were terminated on the balance sheet date, is required to be shown as a liability on a company's balance sheet.

An alternative approach is to record pension expense as the pension payments are made. Those who support this view argue that reasonably estimating the pension liability is impossible because of the many variables involved (such as years of service, salary, and discount-rate assumptions). However, the debate in those countries that allow, but do not require, pension expense to be accrued is now focused more on the determination of appropriate measurement principles (actuarial methods, etc.) than on whether there should be any accrual. IAS 19, "Employee Benefits", has recently been revised to prevent the recognition of gains solely as a result of actuarial losses or past service cost and the recognition of losses solely as a result of actuarial gains. This standard provides comprehensive coverage of this topic. The likelihood exists that IAS 19 will stimulate other countries to improve their local standards in this area.

In the United States, a troublesome area has been the requirement that each assumption reflect the best estimate solely with respect to that assumption. For example, under SFAS No. 87, "Employers' Accounting for Pensions," the discount rate needs to be reassessed each year to reflect changes in current settlement rates. Settlement rates generally match the duration of the benefit obligation and are therefore long-term rates. However, these rates change each year according to changes in general interest rates and other factors. Changes in the discount rate have consequential effects on the present values of accumulated and projected benefit obligations. Under IAS 19, however, the emphasis is on selecting "compatible" assumptions even though the absolute values used may not reflect current experience. Due to the emphasis on long-term considerations in IAS 19, the assumptions selected may differ significantly from those that would be selected in the United States, which in turn means that the present values of accumulated and projected benefit obligations will differ.

In the wake of the burst of the technology bubble in the U.S. and an economic recession, stock prices have fallen dramatically. Now just as unrealized gains during the bull market were deferred to be recognized as an adjustment to pension expense over future accounting periods, the downturn in stock prices has witnessed the deferral of significant unrealized losses. The result is that pension expense may be measured assuming investment returns of 7% or more when stock markets returns are nil or negative. There is little doubt that further reforms are needed to remove complexity of the deferral and smoothing provisions from pension accounting and improve the transparency of reporting through timely recognition of pension investment performance.

(f) Accounting for Income Taxes. All developed countries have some form of income tax system that calls for companies to pay to the government a certain portion of their earnings, as defined. For income tax purposes, the definition of taxable income will differ from the definition of "pretax book income" for financial-accounting purposes in countries that do not require book-to-tax conformity. In some cases, these differences are due to the timing of revenue or expense recognition for tax versus financial-reporting purposes. This situation gives rise to an issue as to whether the effect associated with a given item of revenue or expense should be recognized during the period in which the item appears on the income statement or during the period in which it appears on the tax return. To recognize the expense during the period in which the item appears on the income statement gives rise to an associated asset or liability (referred to as deferred tax) on the balance sheet. In theory, it also results in a stabilized effective tax rate.

For certain countries, the issue of whether deferred taxes should appear on the balance sheet does not arise, because financial reporting of revenues and expenses generally follows the tax recognition in the financial statements; consequently, relatively few timing differences arise. Examples of countries that historically have generally not been required to deal with the issue of deferred taxes are Germany and Japan. However, a major shift in reporting by enterprises in these countries has been toward the presentation of consolidated financial statements. Because the book/tax conformity rules do not normally apply on consolidation, deferred taxes are increasingly becoming part of the financial landscape in these countries too. In Japan, recognition of deferred taxes has been required since 1999.

In most countries, timing differences do arise between book and tax recognition of certain items of revenue and expense. An example of this is different depreciation methods used for book and tax purposes. When the variations are caused by items of revenue or expense included in the determination of book income in one period and taxable income in another period, the two most often used methods to record deferred taxes are the deferral method and the liability method. The objective of the deferral method is to match tax expense with pretax book income. Deferred taxes are based on the effect of past tax differences; they are not updated for subsequent events or changes in tax rates. This approach was most prevalent in Canada. However, Canadian entities must use the liability method (as discussed below) in determining deferred tax beginning in 2002. The alternative is the liability method. The focus of deferred tax accounting under this method is the balance sheet, whereas the focus of the deferral method is the income statement. The objective of the liability method is to determine the amount of future taxes payable or receivable on the basis of cumulative temporary differences between the book and tax basis of assets and liabilities at the balance sheet date. Deferred taxes on temporary differences are accrued on the basis of tax rates expected to be in effect when the differences reverse. Amounts previously deferred are subsequently adjusted when tax rates change. Countries in which variations of this method are followed include the Netherlands, the United Kingdom, Italy, and the United States. It is interesting to note that standard setters have taken different approaches to limiting the recognition of deferred taxes. For example, in the United Kingdom, a deferred tax provision is required to be recorded when it is reasonable to assume that the circumstances that gave rise to these differences will reverse in the foreseeable future.

The original IAS 12, "Accounting for Taxes on Income," permitted either the deferral method or the liability method to be applied, but the revised IAS 12, "Income Taxes," approved in 1996, mandates a comprehensive liability method.

The revised IAS 12 is similar to U.S. GAAP. However, certain differences will arise, for example, with respect to the determination of the enactment date of a change in tax rates and with respect to intercompany profit eliminations. The revised IAS indicates that deferred tax assets and liabilities should be measured according to tax rates that have been enacted or substantively enacted at the balance sheet date. The substantively enacted concept is intended to acknowledge that in some jurisdictions, such as Australia, Canada, and the United Kingdom, announcements by the government have the substantive effect of actual enactment even though the tax rate change may not occur for several months. This is because in their systems of parliamentary democracy, the party with the majority in parliament has a high degree of certainty that the tax rate change it announces will be passed. While final outcome of the U.S. legislative process may not always be so easily predicted, there have been instances where, through announcements of support, it is virtually certain that a tax bill will be passed by Congress and signed into law by the president. Under U.S. GAAP, however, the tax rate change must have been enacted before it is booked. Actual enactment does not occur until an act is finally passed into law (i.e., signed into law by the president or given Royal Assent in a commonwealth country). Thus, substantive enactment and actual enactment may occur in two different reporting periods. Conceptually, there are strong arguments for and against the substantive-enactment-date concept, and few would take the position that the IAS approach is unreliable.

Intercompany profit eliminations give rise to temporary differences in cases where the gain is recognized for tax purposes but deferred for book purposes until realized. The issue is whether the tax effect of the temporary difference should be measured by reference to the seller's tax rate or the buyer's tax rate. Using the seller's tax rate removes any income statement effect of the sale in the period in which it occurs by eliminating the gain and deferring the tax paid on the gain in the seller's tax jurisdiction. Of course, the temporary difference actually reverses in the buyer's tax jurisdiction when the buyer sells (or uses) the asset. For example, if the sale proceeds equal the buyer's tax basis, then for book purposes the buyer realizes the deferred gain and the associated tax benefit of the temporary difference. Conceptually, since the tax basis of the asset is deductible in the buyer's tax jurisdiction, the buyer's tax rate is a better measure of the tax consequences of the temporary difference. But if the temporary difference is set up at the buyer's tax rate, any difference between the tax rates of the seller and the buyer would result in a credit or debit in the income statement in the year of sale, despite the fact that the gain was unrealized for book purposes. Under the revised IAS approach, the temporary difference would be measured at the buyer's tax rate. This approach was previously adopted in the United States under SFAS No. 96, "Accounting for Income Taxes," but was ultimately rejected when SFAS No. 109 replaced SFAS No. 96 in 1992. Under SFAS No. 109, the tax effect of the intercompany profit is measured at the seller's tax rate. The FASB referred to this issue as giving rise to a "conflict of concepts" and decided to prohibit recognition in the buyer's tax jurisdiction. The weight of technical and practical issues makes it easy to see how different standard-setters could reach different conclusions on this matter.

The area of income tax accounting clearly illustrates the difficulty of harmonizing standards among different countries when the economic substance of the event is similar across all countries but the standards were determined at different times, by different groups of people, that had different objectives and constituencies to satisfy. Conversely, the issues described in this section also illustrate why greater cooperation between the major standard-setting bodies and the IASB (e.g., on joint projects) may provide a forum for a reduction of unnecessary differences.

(g) Foreign Currency Translation. Enterprises that operate in more than one economy and engage in businesses in currencies other than the currency in which they present their financial statements are confronted with the issue of how to address the effects of fluctuating currency exchange rates in their financial statements. These companies must present their financial statements in a single currency as the common denominator. The fundamental questions that arise in accounting for changes in foreign currency exchange rates are which exchange rate (current or historical) should be used to translate the statements of foreign subsidiaries, or assets or liabilities denominated in foreign currencies and how gains and losses arising from these foreign currency translations should be accounted for. With the recent trend toward an increased level of international business, it is no wonder that the issue of foreign currency translation has increased importance.

There are essentially two methods that are used to translate statements denominated in foreign currencies. The first method is the current rate method. Under this method, assets and liabilities are translated at the rate current at the balance sheet date, with the adjustment recorded as a direct charge or credit to equity. For income statement items, the weighted-average exchange rate for the period is used. Examples of countries whose accounting rules generally apply this method are the Netherlands, the United Kingdom, and the United States. Recognizing the effects of translation gains and losses on investments in foreign subsidiaries as a direct adjustment to equity avoids cluttering net income with an unrealized gain or loss that has remote and uncertain effects on future cash flows. In a recent development, the United Kingdom has introduced a statement of gains and losses that provides a measure of comprehensive income. Foreign currency gains and losses enter into the determination of comprehensive income, which reflects the premise that they do have economic consequences for the value of an enterprise.

Another accounting method used for foreign currency translation is the temporal method. Under this method, the financial assets and liabilities are translated at the current rate. All assets that are stated at historical prices, such as fixed assets and common stock investments, are translated at the historical rate (i.e., the rate in effect when the asset was acquired). The principal advantage of this method is that it best reflects what the balance sheet would have looked like had the company always operated using only one currency. Under this approach, translation gains and losses on foreign currency–denominated monetary items are recorded in the income statement. Several countries, and IAS 21, "The Effects of Changes in Foreign Currency Exchange Rates," require the use of the temporal method for integrated foreign operations.

(h) Accounting for Mergers and Acquisitions (Including Goodwill). The volume of mergers and acquisitions over the past two decades has risen exponentially. This is attributed to many factors, not the least of which are the ever-growing appetite for international expansion and the recognition of synergies that can be realized. Also, the relatively high prices at which certain companies have been trading make stock-for-stock mergers attractive. It seems as if almost every time you pick up a newspaper there is at least one story about a company merging with or acquiring another company. The major accounting question that arises is at what value the assets and liabilities of the acquired company should be carried in the consolidated financial statements. In most circumstances, accountants agree that the acquired company's assets and liabilities should be carried at their fair value at the date of acquisition. In certain limited circumstances, however, where the shareholders of the acquired company end up owning shares of the acquiror, some believe that the acquiree's assets and liabilities should not be revalued, since the two companies have simply "merged" or "pooled."

Accounting principles in Japan, the United Kingdom, Germany, the Netherlands, and until recently, the United States, all allowed (or required) so-called pooling (uniting) or merger accounting when certain specific criteria are met. However, the conditions vary from one country to another and, depending upon which country's GAAP are applied, a given transaction may be accounted for as either a purchase-acquisition or a pooling-merger. For many years the criteria for using pooling accounting in the United States were considered to be much more stringent than the criteria in the United Kingdom. However, in 1994, FRS 6, "Acquisitions and Mergers," was issued in the United Kingdom. Among other things, FRS 6 introduced stringent criteria that must be satisfied before merger accounting can be used, and included within these criteria is the requirement that the relative sizes of the parties must not be so disparate that one party dominates the other by virtue of its size. A similar criterion is contained in IAS 22, "Business Combinations," which was revised in 1993 and 1998. The size test requirement was perceived to be extremely restrictive when FRS 6 and IAS 22 were issued and subsequently led the SEC in the United States to revise its reconciliation requirements to the effect that a non-U.S. issuer that complies with the criteria in IAS 22 may deem an acquisition under IAS 22 to be an acquisition for the purposes of its reconciliation to U.S. GAAP, notwithstanding that it may meet the U.S. pooling rules. Similarly, a pooling under IAS 22 would be deemed a pooling for the purposes of the reconciliation to U.S. GAAP even though it may fail the U.S. pooling rules. The SEC's expectation when making this rule was that a pooling under IAS 22 would be extremely rare because of the size test. In theory, the purchase method is favored because it gives accounting recognition to the values transacted in the business combination, which is considered to be relevant to investors and creditors and appropriate in a transaction-based historical cost model. Enterprises, however, generally prefer to use pooling accounting whenever possible because it avoids the earnings drag associated with the depreciation and amortization of the fair-value write-up, including goodwill, in future periods.

Now the stage is set for another international accounting controversy and debate. The controversy unfolds because the IAS 22 criteria are not being uniformly interpreted in the restrictive way that the SEC staff had expected. The key issues in the debate are as follows: (1) IAS 22 does not provide quantitative guidance on what is meant by a "significant difference in size"; (2) IAS 22's size test is actually contained in a discussion paragraph of IAS 22 instead of a black letter standard, so its authoritative standing is unclear; (3) the relevance of the size test is questionable in stock-for-stock transactions in which the pooling concept is otherwise satisfied (i.e., notwithstanding its relevance when a grocery store purports to merge with a supermarket chain); (4) FRS 6 provides that a party should be presumed to dominate if it is more than 50% larger than another as judged by reference to ownership interests; (5) FRS 6 explicitly states that the size test can be rebutted on the basis of specific facts and under certain circumstances; (6) FRS 6 indicates that it is consistent with IAS 22; and (7) the size test has no history in the United States, where big companies have historically managed to swallow up small companies without violating the U.S. pooling rules. select

As a practical matter, the SEC staff interpret similar size to mean virtually the same size or that the fair value of each entity is approximately 50% of the combined enterprise. In contrast, the Ontario Securities Commission in Canada has indicated that under Canadian GAAP it would be extremely difficult for pooling to occur if one entity was more than 55% of the combined enterprise, which would imply that one party may be approximately 22% larger than the other. Under U.K. GAAP, one party may be 50% larger than the other as noted above. This divergence is of great concern to standard setters and regulators. A former chief accountant of the SEC, Michael H. Sutton, addressed the subject of IAS 22 at the annual American Institute of Certified Public Accountants (AICPA) SEC conference in February 1996, when he noted that the SEC staff has addressed several proposals by non-U.S. registrants that in the staff's view were clearly inconsistent with the explicit requirements, as well as the spirit, of the standard. He also indicated that the staff will insist that the core international standards be applied "rigorously":

> By that we mean that the standards, though they may be different than U.S. standards, should be applied with the same degree of adherence to the spirit and intent of the standard that we now expect of U.S. registrants applying U.S. standards.

Although the SEC is perceived as rule driven, it is clear that the Chief Accountant couched his concern as being with the application of the "spirit" of non-U.S. standards. In fact the SEC staff has not accepted any business combinations as qualifying for pooling accounting under IAS 22 and one may question whether the elimination of unitings of interests was the IASC's intention when they drafted IAS 22. More recently, the United States has issued SFAS No. 41, "Business Combinations," which eliminates the pooling method and requires all business combinations to be accounted for under the purchase method. This development is in line with the SEC's position in support of purchase accounting and similar developments at the IASB are expected.

For transactions accounted for as purchases, the fair value of consideration paid often exceeds the aggregate fair value of the identifiable net assets acquired. The difference is referred to as "goodwill." The question of how to record this goodwill from an accounting perspective is also an issue of considerable debate among accountants. Some accountants believe that goodwill is a real, albeit nonidentifiable, asset; if it were not, they argue, the acquiring enterprise would not have paid for it. However, even among those who believe that goodwill is an asset, there is disagreement as to whether the asset should be amortized and, if so, over what period of years.

Accountants in some countries take the position that, since goodwill is not a "real" identifiable asset, it does not necessarily belong on the balance sheet. For example, the United Kingdom permits companies either to write goodwill off directly against reserves in the year of acquisition or to capitalize and amortize such amount. Many believed that this accounting gives British companies an advantage in the merger and acquisition arena, because income statements of British companies did not suffer from the earnings drag impact of goodwill amortization in years subsequent to the acquisition. Some British companies found difficulty in certain acquisitions, however, in relation to absorbing substantial amounts of goodwill against reserves. As an example of the continuing trend towards harmonization of accounting standards, this special accounting treatment is no longer allowed under FRS 10, "Goodwill and Intangible Assets." Under this new standard, goodwill and intangibles are now required to be capitalized, as in most other countries, and may be either amortized over the useful life, which is presumed not to exceed 20 years, or tested for impairment annually if an indefinite life is used. In Germany, however, purchased goodwill may be capitalized and amortized or charged to the income statement in the current period. In the United States, under a recently issued standard, SFAS No. 142, "Goodwill and Other Intangibles," goodwill and indefinite lived intangibles should be capitalized and tested for impairment at least annually, but should not be amortized. Impairment is measured based on the asset's fair value.

The recent severe downturn in technology and certain other stocks has seen impairment write-downs under the new standards of unprecedented size.

(i) Consolidation. We will discuss accounting for long-term investments in equity securities in this section. When one enterprise invests significantly in another enterprise, the investment can be accounted for in different ways. The two basic methods used to record an investment are the equity method (accounting for the net investment in the investee as one line on the balance sheet) and the consolidation method (adding all of the investee's individual assets and liabilities to the company's individual assets and liabilities and backing out a "minority interest" for the percentage of the net asset not owned by the parent company's shareholders). In most countries, the accounting rules require the equity method to be used when the investor can exercise significant influence over the affairs of the investee but cannot unilaterally "control" the investee's affairs. As a general rule, the standards specify that an investor that has approximately 20 to 50% ownership in another company meets this criterion.

When an investor has a controlling voting interest in another enterprise, most countries' standards require that the investee be consolidated. One major disagreement between accounting standard setters in various countries is whether nonhomogeneous or dissimilar subsidiaries should be consolidated, even where control exists. Standards that support consolidation of nonhomogeneous or dissimilar subsidiaries, such as IAS and U.S. GAAP, are based on the premise that the financial statements of an enterprise should present all the assets and liabilities under the enterprise's control. Alternatively, some countries, such as Italy and China, have taken the position that consolidation of dissimilar subsidiaries may be misleading and confusing to the reader of the financial statements. Ironically, in those countries that have required nonhomogeneous operations to be consolidated, analysts have sought more extensive disaggregated disclosure.

The most difficult aspect of the consolidation standards concerns the definition of control and its application to specific facts and circumstances. U.S. GAAP currently embodies what may be described as a legal concept of control. That is, to obtain control of the enterprise usually requires that the controlling entity have the direct or indirect ability to elect or appoint a majority of the members of another company's governing board. In the United States, the notion of control encompasses control obtained by ownership or by agreement with other shareholders. IAS 27, "Consolidated Financial Statements," also requires controlled entities to be consolidated but relies on a definition of effective control. Thus, it is likely that more entities would qualify for consolidation under IAS 27 because of the IASB's emphasis on effective control rather than on ownership of a majority voting interest. The U.S. standard setters have proposed changes to the accounting rules relating to consolidated financial statements that would, if adopted, broaden the notion of control to include situations where an enterprise has effective control over another. The effective-control concept significantly extends the circumstances under which consolidation would be required and, in particular, has the potential to eliminate certain off-balance-sheet finance structures. Let's look at one condition that might give rise to effective control under the proposals. First, absent evidence to the contrary, ownership of a large minority interest (approximately 40%) of a publicly traded company in circumstances under which no other party or organized group of parties has a significant interest would be said to give rise to effective control. Accountants have criticized this outcome because the enterprise's ability to retain control in these circumstances is reliant on the existence of conditions that may be temporary and beyond the so-called controlling enterprise's "control." For example, another party may suddenly emerge on the stock register as a significant minority shareholder and seek to assert its will on the company in question. That party may subsequently sell down its interest, leaving the first enterprise with effective control once again. For the enterprise to continually consolidate, then deconsolidate only to subsequently reconsolidate the same target is not viewed by everyone to be either desirable or to be resolving an existing practice problem that anyone can point to. Further, it seems to be contrary to the notion of control that an enterprise may lose control without relinquishing any rights.

Another set of circumstances that may give rise to effective control are those instances in which special-purpose vehicles (SPVs) are employed by an enterprise to obtain structured finance. The party providing or organizing for substantially all of the funding is typically an investment bank. The enterprise may provide collateral in the form of noncancelable lease commitments or through a variety of other mechanisms. In these arrangements, the enterprise may control all of the residual benefits and be exposed to all of the residual risks. But in more subtle arrangements, some of the upside and downside (generally outside the range of expected returns) may be transferred to other parties through puts and calls. These types of structures merit international debate because the structures that achieve off-balance-sheet accounting are commonly replicated around the world. Australia, the United Kingdom, and other major economies have already moved to tackle some of these problems through broadening their definition of control.

(j) Impairment. Under the historical cost convention of accounting, assets should be stated at their respective acquisition cost basis. When it is determined that such assets cannot be recovered fully, all accounting standards allow the write-down for impairment losses. However, there is diversity in practice as to when and how to measure impairment losses. In the United States, SFAS No. 5, "Accounting for Contingencies," and SFAS No. 114, "Accounting by Creditors for Impairment of a Loan," provides guidance on impairment on loans, SFAS No. 144, "Accounting for the Impairment or Disposal of Long-Lived Assets," provides guidance on impairment of long-lived assets held for use and long-lived assets held for sale, SFAS No. 142, "Goodwill and Other Intangible Assets," provides guidance on impairment of goodwill and other intangible assets, while SFAS No. 115, "Accounting for Certain Investments in Debt and Equity Securities," and related implementation guides provide guidance on impairment of investments in marketable securities. Even with the proliferation of rules in the United States, impairment remains an area that requires significant management judgment.

Impairment write downs have a significant impact on absolute accounting earnings and earnings per share, but it may not necessarily trigger changes in the prices of the shares as observed in the open market. This is arguably because the market anticipated the loss and because impairment losses are sometimes perceived to be one-time noncash charges. This is most evident in the case of goodwill impairment. Almost US$200 billion of goodwill was impaired in the 2001/2002 reporting periods because of the new impairment rules that became effective on January 1, 2002, for just nine companies in the media and entertainment, telecommunication, and technology sector. The day after the announcement of the impairment charges, however, the stock prices of many of those companies actually increased!

U.S. GAAP requires detailed impairment analysis of long-lived assets held for use if there is a "triggering event." IAS requires entities to assess assets, without distinction for long-lived assets or goodwill, at each balance sheet date to determine whether there is any "indication" that an asset may be impaired. *Triggering event* and *indication* have similar definitions, and both sets of accounting standards provide similar examples. This approach was mainly adopted to reduce the burden incurred by preparers that would otherwise need to prepare fair value assessments. Under a different pronouncement, U.S. GAAP requires impairment of goodwill to be performed at least annually. The FASB considered it necessary to distinguish the timing of impairment reviews for goodwill and other long-lived assets because of the inherent difference in assets with a definite life and those with an indefinite life. With SFAS No. 142 disallowing the amortization of goodwill, the FASB believe adequate and timely reviews for impairment has increased importance. Would the US$200 billion goodwill impairment loss recognized under U.S. GAAP as mentioned above also be recognized under different sets of accounting standards?

Under U.S. GAAP, when impairment has occurred, it is measured based on the fair value of the asset. Fair value is defined as the amount at which "an asset could be bought or sold in a current transaction between willing parties, other than a forced liquidation sale." Under IAS and U.K. accounting standards, the asset's carrying amount is compared to its recoverable amount, which is defined as the higher of the net selling price or value in use, to identify impairment of long-lived assets, including goodwill. Value in use is defined as the present value of the expected future cash flows of the asset. The U.S. concept of fair value is akin to the net selling price concept, which may coincide with the value in use measure in some cases. In a recession or other market downturn it may be expected that illiquid and volatile markets will indicate that net selling prices are much lower than value in use, thus increasing the magnitude of write-downs for similar assets.

After an impairment loss has been recognized, not only is the amount of annual depreciation or amortization affected, but the future appreciation of the asset's fair value can also be treated differently under the various accounting standards. Certain countries require an impairment loss to be reversed in future periods when the asset's fair value appreciates while other countries deem the impaired value to be the new cost basis and the reversal of prior impairment losses is not allowed.

Even though the concept of impairment is basically the same around the world, differences in the timing and the amount of impairment recognized under different countries' accounting standards could vary significantly. These differences will lead to continuing confusion and concern with the reliability of financial reporting.

(k) Transfer of Financial Assets and Special Purpose Vehicles. Transfers of financial assets are daily occurrences, especially as part of the operational strategies of many financial services institutions. Companies may enter into complex structures to transfer financial assets with the objective of (1) improving certain financial ratios (e.g., nonperforming loan ratios, return on asset or equity, and profit margins), (2) minimizing (or sharing) risk in the recoverability of the financial assets, (3) enhancing liquidity, (4) improving asset/liability management, or (5) completing borrowing arrangements. Over the past decade, there has been increased scrutiny in the accounting treatment for the transfer of financial assets involving complex structures. This is especially true with transfers involving securitizations, the process by which financial assets are transformed into securities, or SPVs, entities that are set up for a specified unique purpose. The complexity of securitizations has evolved such that the nature of a transferor's continuing involvement makes it unclear whether control has been relinquished and whether the risks and rewards have been retained by the transferor.

Generally, the accounting framework provides for derecognization when the transferred asset is isolated from the transferor and the transferor no longer controls the asset *and* does not retain any of the risks and rewards of the transferred asset. However, differences may exist depending on the focus of the respective accounting standards. Additionally, standards in various nations do not provide specific guidance for derecognition of financial assets and practice may vary as a result of the lack of specific guidance. Because of this diversity, the IASB joined with national standard setters, including the FASB and Canadian Institute of Chartered Accountants, in a Joint Working Group to develop, integrate, and harmonize international accounting standards on financial instruments beginning in 1997. As a result of such efforts, the FASB and IASB have adopted a similar approach in accounting for the derecognition of financial assets. However, despite the efforts to harmonize accounting for the transfer of financial assets, diversity continues to exist. Two of the more commonly used models for derecognition of financial assets are the risk-and-rewards model and the financial components model.

Under the risk-and-rewards model, assets are derecognized when risks and rewards related to the asset are surrendered to the transferee. Variations on that approach attempt to choose which risks and rewards are most critical and whether all or some major portion of those risks and rewards must be surrendered to allow derecognition. The risk-and-rewards approach may allow for more management judgment, as the concept of risk and rewards is subjective in nature. Such an approach focuses on the substance of a transaction rather than its legal form. The asset is derecognized where the transaction transfers to others the significant rights or other access to benefits relating to that asset, and the significant exposure to the risks inherent in those benefits. The risk-and-rewards approach could sometimes result in an entity continuing to recognize assets even though it had surrendered control over the assets to a successor entity.

The United Kingdom adopted a variation of the risk and rewards model with FRS 5, "Reporting the Substance of Transactions." FRS 5 requires the surrender of substantially all risks and rewards for derecognition of financial assets but permits, in limited circumstances, the use of a *linked presentation.* Use of the linked presentation is restricted to circumstances in which an entity borrows funds to be repaid from the proceeds of pledged financial assets, any excess proceeds go to the borrower, and the lender has no recourse to other assets of the borrower. In those circumstances, the pledged assets remain on the borrower's statement of financial position, but the unpaid borrowing is reported as a deduction from the pledged assets rather than as a liability; no gain or loss is recognized. The question of whether it is appropriate for an entity to offset restricted assets against a liability or to derecognize a liability merely because assets are dedicated to its repayment remains a point of further debate.

The IASB originally issued an exposure draft based on the risk and rewards model. After consideration of the comments received and FASB's issuance of SFAS No. 140, the IASB determined that a financial components approach based on control is more consistent with its accounting framework. Accordingly, a financial components approach was adopted in IAS 39. This approach analyzes a transfer of a financial asset by examining the different components of assets (controlled economic benefits) and liabilities (present obligations for probable future sacrifices of economic benefits) that exist after the transfer. According to the FASB in the United States, the financial components approach is designed to:

1. Be consistent with the way participants in the financial markets deal with financial assets, including the combination and separation of components of those assets
2. Reflect the economic consequences of contractual provisions underlying financial assets and liabilities
3. Conform to the FASB conceptual framework

Under the financial component approach, the economic benefits provided by a financial asset (generally, the right to future cash flows) are derived from the contractual provisions that underlie that asset, and the entity that controls those benefits should recognize them as its asset. The concept of control led to the following criteria to be established in SFAS No. 140 (similar conditions required under IAS 39):

1. Transferred assets have been isolated from the transferor.
2. Transferees have obtained the right to pledge or exchange either the transferred assets or beneficial interests in the transferred assets.
3. The transferor does not maintain effective control over the transferred assets through an agreement to repurchase or redeem them before their maturity or through the ability to unilaterally cause the holder to return specific assets.

Proponents of the financial component approach believe that the aspect of control is the most relevant factor in determining whether financial assets should be recorded on an entity's books . This discussion masks the fact that frequently the sale of financial assets to an SPV is via an equitable assignment rather than a legal sale. Thus, the bank retains a legal right or receivable, continues to maintain the customer relationship, and continues to collect cash flows from the debtor. The bank incurs an obligation to pass cash flows through to the SPV and may assume other roles with respect to the SPV (e.g., trustee, manager, or service agent). Importantly, the bank may enter into currency and interest rate swaps with the SPV to enable the SPV to issue securities with a different term structure than the underlying financial assets (e.g., the SPV might issue US$-denominated securities secured against euro-denominated financial assets). As described in SFAS No. 140, a legal vehicle that has a standing at law distinct from the transferor and whose activities are permanently limited by the legal documents establishing it as a qualifying SPV under SFAS No. 160, qualifying SPVs should not be consolidated.

Certain countries do not have specific accounting standards for SPVs and apply the consolidation concepts applicable to operating entities. Others, like the United States, have complex accounting rules surrounding SPVs, with different rules applying to *qualifying* versus *nonqualifying* SPVs. Nonqualifying SPVs are not required to be consolidated if certain conditions are met. Problems in this area are alleged to underlie some of Enron's problems. The relevant conditions for nonconsolidation include (1) the independent owners must take a substantive equity investment of at least 3% of the SPV's assets throughout the entire life of the SPV, and (2) the independent owners must exercise control of the SPV. Although the official line of the FASB and the SEC has been that the literal application of such rules should result in an accounting treatment that is not misleading, practice has adhered closely to the 3% equity condition regardless of the risks in the structure. The FASB currently has a project to promulgate new standards to address these issues.

(l) Derivatives. A particularly controversial current topic concerns accounting for financial instruments that generally have no net initial investment (i.e., no initial cost) and are sometimes entered into to hedge interest rate, exchange rate, and commodity price risks. Recent standards have moved to require all derivatives to be recognized at fair value in the balance sheet with immediate recognition of gains and losses in the income statement unless the instrument qualifies for hedge accounting.

The concept of hedge accounting is an important one because derivatives held for speculative purposes are conceptually and inherently different from those derivatives held to hedge an identified risk. Companies hold speculative derivatives to take advantage of potential market movements, while they hold hedging derivatives to minimize the potential loss on existing assets or expected future cash flows. Because of this fundamental difference, separate accounting rules should be applicable based on the company's intent and the derivative's use. Both IAS and U.S. GAAP contain explicit requirements for designation of derivatives as hedging instruments and require specific documentation before hedge accounting can be applied. Most other countries still do not specify when hedge accounting can be applied and do not specify how hedge accounting should be applied. Most countries are quickly developing their own derivative accounting rules or looking towards the IAS for guidance on accounting for derivatives. For example, an accounting standard similar to FASB No. 133 was developed under Japanese GAAP and became effective for fiscal years beginning after March 31, 2000. Even though the two most influential and well-regarded standard setters have adopted similar approaches, hedge accounting remains a topic of continual deliberation. In December 2000, the Joint Working Group of standard setters was formed to develop a long-term solution for recognition and measurement of all financial instruments at fair value. Gains and losses arising from changes in fair value would generally be included in the income statement. No "deferral" or hedge accounting would be permitted.

12.7 BENEFITS OF ACCOUNTING HARMONIZATION. Having explored some of the ways in which countries' accounting practices may differ, we can better appreciate the benefits that can be obtained from harmonization. However, harmonization is not an end in itself. The goal of harmonization should be for like transactions and events to be given the same financial reporting treatment by different enterprises in different countries. Similarly, harmonization should accommodate differences in accounting treatment for different transactions and events.

Harmonization is even more important in today's marketplace than at any time in the past. As explained in the introduction to this chapter, an ever-increasing number of companies are becoming international in scope. Technology is reducing barriers to the exchange of information on a global basis. Furthermore, investors and lenders are focusing their attention more and more on international companies and international markets. The most accurate way for investors or creditors to make a business decision is to ensure that they are able to make cross-country company comparisons on a level playing field and with comparable information.

Many feel that steps must be taken to minimize this diversity in accounting standards. If such an effort is going to be successful, the entire global business community must be involved. The various securities regulators from each country must work together so that there is no preference given to either a domestic or a multinational company as far as accounting treatment or disclosure requirements are concerned. The regulators must ensure that they fulfill their responsibility of providing comparable information to their domestic investors.

The impetus for the change is already here. It is coming from the business communities of Germany, France, and China and other countries whose large and powerful companies face increasing pressure to obtain greater access to financial capital and to lower their cost of capital. It is being accompanied by changes in corporate governance and in the relationships between the enterprise and its management, its employees, its shareholders, and its creditors. These companies need access to international investors and creditors, and there is an increasing understanding that a capital market will only attract investors if it is open, fair, and transparent. Because so many companies are entering the world's capital markets simultaneously, they have a strong incentive to push for a reduction of accounting diversity to minimize the complexity and costs of this task. Unsurprisingly, a number of organizations are now involved in the quest for a harmonized set of international standards.

12.8 OBSTACLES TO ACCOUNTING HARMONIZATION. There are many obstacles present in the global environment that make harmonization difficult to achieve. Each country's own nationalism and pride serve as a deterrent to reaching this goal. As demonstrated previously, there are many alternative methods to account for particular transactions. Each method can reasonably be considered the "best" or "correct" way, depending on one's perspective. It will be difficult to get a country's standard setters to accept alternative principles when they clearly believe that the standards they have developed provide the best information from their national perspective. Countries' standard setters have different objectives and users. For example, the primary objective of financial reporting in the United States is to meet the needs of shareholders, while in Germany the creditors' perspective is the main concern of the financial reporting process. Finally, a country's legal tradition also influences its perspective. The United Kingdom has a common-law tradition, so it naturally prefers more flexibility and less codification in its standards. Germany has a Roman law tradition, which emphasizes stricter interpretation of the rules.

There are a number of costs in achieving harmonization. The level of costs to be incurred depends upon the manner in which harmonization is achieved. If harmonization is achieved by developing a loose, flexible framework into which a country's accounting standards fit, the costs would be far less than if a specific, rigid set of accounting standards were imposed uniformly on all companies in all countries. Also, the level of costs would vary, depending upon the specific standards required.

Another alternative is to require all companies to reconcile their financial statements to one set of internationally accepted principles, similar to the requirement in the United States for non-U.S. registrants to reconcile shareholders' equity and net income to U.S. GAAP for SEC filings. Under the reconciliation approach, the primary financial statements may continue to be prepared under the relevant company's national accounting principles. Thus, harmonization is achieved through reconciliation to an agreed benchmark such as IAS or U.S. GAAP. An advantage of the reconciliation approach is that, with the exception of IAS, it is clear which country's accounting profession or standard setters have the standing to resolve accounting issues. Thus, the German profession resolves issues that arise under German GAAP and the U.S. profession resolves issues that arise under U.S. GAAP. In many instances, companies coming to the United States for the first time will adopt accounting policies that, to the extent permissible by their home country standards, minimize any differences from U.S. GAAP that actually need to be calculated. European companies, for example, are currently anticipating the move to IAS by selecting options that eliminate any difference between their home country GAAP, IAS, and U.S. GAAP, where feasible. This is obviously a difficult task to manage given the rate of change but, overall, the practical issues are generally resolved in a sensible manner.

In our experience, the major obstacle reconciliation presents non-U.S. companies is that it frequently contains sensitive information. Generally, the potentially sensitive information in the reconciliation detracts from an otherwise rosy picture of healthy management performance. For example, we aware of situations where a bank has accounted for transfers of nonperforming loans to related parties at book value rather than reporting the impairment loss as would be required under U.S. GAAP. Other situations have involved significant capitalized preoperating and start-up costs that would need to be expensed to adhere to SEC staff views. But perhaps the most salient reason for requiring the reconciliation came with the Daimler-Benz offering in 1994. Under German GAAP, Daimler-Benz reported a profit of almost DM 200 million in 1993 after an undisclosed release of DM 1.5 billion in provisions to income. In its reconciliation to U.S. GAAP, the company revealed a loss of just under DM 1 billion. Without the reconciliation, the amount of the release would not have been evident.

The mechanics involved in preparing the reconciliation are generally manageable tasks, sometimes with the exception of pensions and taxes. Further, a lot of the mystery associated with the process has been eliminated by the SEC staff's willingness to go to extraordinary lengths to arrive at sensible solutions to burdensome practical problems. For example, the SEC staff has in a number of cases agreed to accept fresh-start fair-value accounting to be applied by newly privatized companies in situations where reliable historical cost records are not available. The SEC staff are also permitting companies that are unable to apply the U.S. pension standards retroactively (i.e., going back to 1987 to calculate the transition liability) to approximate application of that standard under alternative methods.

There are strong grounds for the view that the reconciliation requirement best meets the needs of investors and creditors, since the primary financial statements provide the reader with an insight into the home country's understanding of the enterprise's performance, financial position, and cash flows, while highlighting any major departures from U.S. GAAP. Nevertheless, the SEC is facing a great deal of pressure to permit non-U.S. companies to enter the U.S. capital markets without reconciliation to U.S. GAAP. Multinational companies, in particular, appear to favor the move to comprehensive acceptance of financial statements prepared under internationally accepted accounting principles. To this end, the IASB/International Organization of Securities Commissions (IOSCO) plan is for IAS to be accepted for all cross-border offerings, including the United States. In the following section of this chapter, the potential issues associated with moving toward internationally accepted principles are discussed in more detail.

12.9 INTERNATIONALLY ACCEPTED ACCOUNTING PRINCIPLES. Since its formation in 1973, International Accounting Standards Committee, known as the International Accounting Standards Board since 2001, has gained worldwide recognition. Together with the International Financial Reporting Interpretations Committee (IFRIC), formerly the Standing Interpretations Committee (SIC), IASs are currently being developed with a view to gaining acceptance for cross-border offerings. As stated in the Preface to International Financial Reporting Standards, the objectives of IASB are:

- To develop, in the public interest, a single set of high-quality, understandable and enforceable global accounting standards that require high-quality, transparent, and comparable information in financial statements and other financial reporting to help participants in the various capital markets of the world and other users of the information to make economic decisions
- To promote the use and rigorous application of those standards
- To work actively with national standard setters to bring about convergence of national accounting standards and IFRSs to high-quality solutions.

One issue that needs to be considered is whether the acceptance of IAS also embraces the broader concept of global GAAP and, if so, how the issues of general acceptance and substantive support should be addressed within this framework. It has been a feature of the SEC's approach to enforcement since 1938 that it will object to financial statements prepared in accordance with accounting policies for which there is no *substantive authoritative* support and that such statements would be presumed to be misleading and inaccurate. Indeed, the concept of GAAP is predicated on there being agreement among accountants on the existence of a body of GAAP, and that accountants are knowledgeable about these principles and in the determination of their general acceptance. This concept is also integral to the legal liability of the issuer and of accountants with respect to financial reporting. The issues of substantive authoritative support and general acceptance are difficult to resolve in relation to a body of international accounting standards that by definition have no frame of reference to any particular country.

The IASB's Statement of Principles, "Presentation of Financial Statements," effective 1998, would require the enterprise's accounting policies to be selected and applied so that the financial statements meet the objective of financial statements and the qualitative characteristics of the IASB's Framework. The framework emphasizes relevance and reliability, but there is no requirement for the enterprise to establish substantive authoritative support or any guidance on the critical issues of selecting and justifying accounting policies when a range of alternatives may be available. By definition, international standards should be capable of consistent international interpretation, and it is contradictory that enterprises purporting to comply with global generally accepted accounting standards and principles will basically be working with different information sets as regards what is acceptable.

Under the current framework of SEC rules and procedures, the significance of these problems is mitigated by the fact that the enterprise will need to quantify this difference from U.S. GAAP in the required reconciliations of net income and stockholders' equity. Thus, users of the financial statements could not be misled or confused by either accounting treatment. If, however, the reconciliation requirement were to be removed, the issue about the general acceptance of the accounting treatment would increase in importance. The SEC staff would need to consider how such a policy could be supported under generally accepted international principles. While the SEC staff arguably do not have jurisdiction over the interpretation of the enterprise's home country GAAP, the determination of accepted global principles will be a different matter. If the SEC staff disagrees with an enterprise's IAS interpretation, then the enterprise would need to restate the financial statements. This will give rise to awkward situations when the enterprise has previously issued financial statements in its home country over many years under a different concept of what it considered to be generally accepted international accounting principles.

Historically, there has been strong criticism of the lack of implementation guidance under IAS, especially from the standpoint of U.S. regulators. However, recently, there has been increased dissatisfaction with the proliferation of rules in the U.S. environment indicating that such rules may not always result in a "true and fair" view as evidenced by Enron, Worldcom, and other recent events. The IASB has received strong backing globally from many different constituents who prefer its primarily principle-based standards. The SEC's former chairman, Harvey Pitt, has called for a "move toward principle-based set of accounting records" in his speech before the Federal Bar Council in 2002, while the President of the United States spoke of the need for tighter disclosures and more transparency in corporate financial reporting. The global financial reporting environment has changed dramatically in recent years, even in recent months, and there is a clear move toward a principle-based set of internationally accepted accounting standards.

The issues and perceived obstacles associated with moving toward internationally accepted principles must be weighed against the perceived benefits of harmonization. The most significant benefit will be enhanced financial comparability. The diverse multinational users of the financial statements will have a better understanding of statements, and a harmonized approach will ostensibly provide more useful information to them. A better understanding of foreign companies could lead to more stable and efficient international stock markets and more international business activity, which could stimulate all foreign economies.

12.10 CONCLUSION. As discussed previously, the diversity in accounting principles worldwide is significant. Important progress is being made within Europe and in other countries that are moving to embrace IFRSs by 2005, and these efforts are being closely supported by the SEC and the FASB. But while progress is being made, it needs to be recognized that deciding what financial information is relevant and should be reported in the current environment is difficult. Volatile and unpredictable markets will continue to challenge management, to destroy value, and to cause financial performance measurement and reporting issues. There has never been a stronger signal that the markets need a credible body of global GAAP that provides for the reporting of relevant and reliable information.

SOURCES AND SUGGESTED REFERENCES

Andersen, BOD, Deloitte Touche Tohmastsu, Ernst & Young, Grant Thornton, KPMG, and PricewaterhouseCooper. *GAAP 2001: A Survey of National Accounting Rules Benchmarked against International Accounting Standards.*

Back, Christopher L. *U.S. International Transactions, Fourth Quarter and Year 2001.* Bureau of Economic Analysis, April 2002

Breeden, Richard C. *Fordham International Law Journal: Foreign Companies and U.S. Securities Markets in a Time of Economic Transformation.* New York: Fordham University School of Law, 1994.

China Securities Regulatory Commissions, Statistics, 2001.

Choi, Frederick, Carol Frost, and Gary Meek. *International Accounting.* Upper Saddle River, NJ: Prentice Hall, 2002.

Cochrane, James L. *Fordham International Law Journal: Are U.S. Regulatory Requirements for Foreign Firms Appropriate?* New York: Fordham University School of Law, 1994.

Conference Summary, International Accounting Standards: The Challenges and the Future. Paris, September 22, 1995.

DiPiazza Jr., Samuel A., and Robert G. Eccles. *Building Public Trust.* New York: John Wiley & Sons, 2002.

Gebhardt, Gunther. "The Evolution of Global Standards in Accounting." In Robert E. Litan and Anthony M. Santomero (eds.), Brookings-Wharton Papers on Financial Services 2000. Washington, DC: Brookings Institution, 2000, pp. 341–376.

Harris, Trevor S. *International versus U.S.-GAAP Reporting: Empirical Evidence Based on Case Studies.* Mason, Ohio: Southwestern College Publishing, 1995.

Herdman, Robert K. Chief Accountant, U.S. Securities & Exchange Commission. "Moving Toward the Globalization of Accounting Standards." Speech at the Schmalenback Institute for Business Administration Conference, April 18, 2002, Cologne, Germany.

Hertig, Gerard. "Regulatory Competition for EU Financial Services." In Daniel C. Estery and Damien Geradin, (eds.), *Regulatory Competition and Economic Integration: Comparative Perspectives.* Oxford: Oxford University Press, 2001, pp. 218–240.

International Accounting Standards Committee. *International Accounting Standards 1996.* London: Authors, 1996.

International Organization of Securities Organizations. *Objectives and Principles of Securities Regulation*, February 2002.

Leutz, Christian. *IAS versus US GAAP, A Market Based Comparison.* Philadelphia: Wharton School, June 2001.

Pownall, Grace, and Katherine Schipper. *Implications of Accounting Research for the SEC's Consideration of International Accounting Standards for U.S. Securities Offerings.* Accounting Horizons, September 1999.

Securities and Futures Commissions. Quarterly Bulletin, Winter 2001.

Simmons, Beth A. "The International Politics of Harmonization: The Case of Capital Market Regulation." International Organization, Autumn 2001.

Singer, David Andrew. *Regulatory Harmonization and Competition: Domestic Interests and International Pressures in a World of Global Finance.* Department of Government, Harvard University, September 2001.

Statistics, Federation Internationale des Bourses de Valeurs (International Federation of Stock Exchanges).

Tarca, Ann. *International Convergence of Accounting Practices: Choosing Between IASs and US GAAP.* Thesis, University of Western Australia.

Thomas, William C. "The Rise and Fall of Enron." *Journal of Accountancy*, April 2002.

U.S. Bureau of International Transactions, 2001.

CHAPTER 13

CORPORATE FINANCIAL DISCLOSURE: A GLOBAL ASSESSMENT*

Carol A. Frost

Global Capital Markets Access LLC

Kurt P. Ramin

International Accounting Standards Committee Foundation

CONTENTS

*The authors appreciate the generous research support provided by the Tuck School of Business at Dartmouth College Center for Asia and emerging Economies, and are indebted to Howard L. Blum, III, for his excellent research assistance. Thanks are also due to Karen Sluzenski (Feldberg Library at Dartmouth College) for providing invaluable technical assistance.

13.1 INTRODUCTION. Corporate disclosure practices are rapidly changing. More than ever, they are the focus of attention for policy makers, investors, financial professionals, and corporate managers worldwide. The U.S. Securities and Exchange Commission (SEC) and other securities regulators have been increasing required disclosure levels for regulated companies, and monitoring and enforcement activities have become more intense. Following the widely publicized financial scandals of Enron, WorldCom, Tyco International Ltd., and other large corporations in 2001 and 2002, investors, lenders, regulators, and lawmakers are closely scrutinizing the level and quality of corporate disclosure.[1]

Individual investors are concerned about the consequences to their portfolios of inadequate and fraudulent disclosure. Share prices plummet when corporate fraud or other types of disclosure failures are uncovered.[2] The U.S. Congress and the SEC view corporate disclosure practices in terms of their impact on U.S. capital markets and the economy, in addition to their impact on shareholder protection. Analysts at the Brookings Institution estimate that the recent wave of scandals will cost the U.S. economy at least US$35 billion. Many commentators blame these scandals, which have seriously undermined the credibility of U.S. capital markets, for the disappointing performance of the U.S. equities markets during 2002.

The Sarbanes-Oxley Act, enacted by the U.S. Congress in July 2002, was designed to improve the credibility of U.S. capital markets, in part by improving disclosure by U.S. and non-U.S. companies active in these markets. However, already it is clear that Sarbanes-Oxley's requirements are unacceptable to many foreign companies active in U.S. capital markets. If criminal sanctions and other aspects of this law deter foreign issuers from entering U.S. markets, access of U.S. investors to overseas investment opportunities will decrease and become more expensive. Thus, it is difficult to evaluate the tradeoffs involved in imposing more stringent disclosure rules, monitoring and enforcement.[3]

Exposure of corporate disclosure-related scandals and increasing stringency by securities regulators are not confined to the United States. As one conspicuous example, during 2002, securities regulators in France aggressively investigated Vivendi Universal for fraudulent financial reporting, including a highly publicized raid on its corporate offices.[4]

Although public attention has focused on scandals involving fraud and misleading disclosure, the general trend in recent years has been one of dramatic improvements

---

[1]Refer to *Accountancy* (August, 2002) for a summary of some of the most serious scandals and allegations involving U.S., U.K., French, and Anglo-Dutch companies during 2002.

[2]See William R. Kinney, Jr. (2000) for discussion of two types of financial statement fraud: misappropriation fraud and misrepresentation fraud. Misappropriation fraud is the intentional misstatement of recorded amounts by employees, ordinarily accompanied by theft of company assets. Misrepresentation fraud is the intentional overstatement of recorded assets, understatement of recorded liabilities, or use of improper accounting methods or biased accounting estimates with the intent of overstating a performance measure such as net income.

[3]Some U.S.-listed companies already have announced that they may delist from U.S. stock exchanges if some of the new law's rules are not relaxed for foreign issuers. Non-U.S. governments and business organizations, including in the United Kingdom and Japan, have been pushing for exemptions from the new legislation. For example, Porsche, the German sports car company, announced that it was canceling its plan to list on the New York Stock Exchange, in response to concerns about the new legislation. For discussion, see David Ibison and Adrian Michaels (2002), Robert Bruce (2002), Wassener (2002), and *Accountancy* (September, 2002).

[4]See Jo Johnson (2002).

in voluntary disclosure (from a financial statement user's perspective), and more stringent disclosure rules, monitoring, and enforcement. Use of the Internet has become an integral part of many companies' disclosure strategy, and many of these disclosures are strictly voluntary in nature. Companies' growing interest in eXtensible Business Reporting Language (XBRL), and the strong endorsement of XBRL by the International Accounting Standards Board and other international organizations, suggest that financial reporting is on the verge of revolutionary change. Corporate managers are moving toward the view that increased voluntary disclosure increases shareholder value.

This chapter has two main purposes. First, it briefly lays out a framework for thinking about disclosure. This framework links regulators' goals of investor protection (of which disclosure is a key element) and market quality. Recent empirical evidence is discussed which supports the view that disclosure is positively associated with market liquidity in global equity markets. Second, the chapter discusses selected corporate disclosure practices and regulations, and analyzes what that evidence implies for financial statement users and corporate managers.

To illustrate the similarities and differences in corporate disclosure worldwide, we present results from an analysis of disclosures made by six automobile manufacturers: Fiat S.p.A. (Italy), Ford Motor Company (United States), Hyundai Motor Co. (South Korea), Jaingling Motor Corporation (China), Toyota Motor Corporation (Japan), and Volkswagen AG (Germany). These companies vary greatly in terms of characteristics expected to influence their disclosure. They represent both developed (United States, Italy, Japan, and Germany) and emerging (China and South Korea) economies, range from very large to moderate size, and cover the range from global to more local production and capital market activities. The evidence is anecdotal, but highly representative of what is found in practice.

13.2 SUMMARY OF MAIN RESULTS. The evidence and discussion presented in this chapter suggest the following:

- Capital markets drive corporate disclosure practices. To know what to expect a company to disclose and to understand managers' disclosure incentives, one must be familiar with the (global) capital markets in which the company operates, its ownership structure, and the corporate finance and governance characteristics of its home market.
- Empirical evidence supports regulators' and managers' assumptions that increased disclosure improves market liquidity.
- Global norms for many types of mandated corporate disclosure now exist. For example, disclosure about cash flows and industry and geographic segments is now almost universal among large public companies. Similarly, securities regulators and stock exchanges increasingly are adopting international benchmarks for non-financial disclosures made in connection with the public offering of securities.
- However, vast differences in mandatory disclosure for listed companies remain (depending on the capital markets in which they operate). For example, U.S. financial statement users should not expect all "world-class" non-U.S. companies to disclose "sensitive" information, such as details about directors and corporate officers' compensation, share ownership, and related party transactions. Such

disclosures simply are not required in many jurisdictions outside the United States, where it is generally believed that the potential costs to companies in making such disclosures outweigh the capital market benefits of making the disclosures.

- Finally, there are vast differences in companies' voluntary disclosure practices. Managers' disclosure incentives vary dramatically, as do cultural norms and established business practices, and there can be large differences in opinion as to the relative costs and benefits of voluntary disclosures.

13.3 CORPORATE DISCLOSURE, LIQUIDITY, AND THE COST OF CAPITAL. A key theme in this chapter is that corporate disclosure is best understood as it relates to capital markets. Capital market participants have demanded change in disclosure practices in recent years; regulators respond to these demands, and managers' disclosure incentives are influenced by these demands (as well as legal requirements).

A distinct but closely related link between disclosure and capital markets is that research has shown that expanded disclosure is associated with important capital market-related benefits such as increased share liquidity and reduced cost of capital.[5] Enhanced disclosure reduces information differences (asymmetries) between corporate insiders (management) and outsiders. These information differences lead to greater transaction costs and reduced liquidity in the secondary markets for a company's equity shares.

If corporate managers' incentives were perfectly aligned with those of their company's shareholders, they would select disclosure policies providing maximum capital market benefits.[6] However, corporate managers' incentives are not perfectly aligned with those of shareholders.[7] Moreover, investors, creditors, regulators and other capital market participants may desire disclosure that is not in the company's best interest. For example, shareholders might desire that information leading to a drop in share prices not be disclosed.

Several solutions to these disclosure incentive problems have evolved. These include contracts between managers and their shareholders to ensure proper alignment between these parties' incentives and the use of information intermediaries (such as financial analysts) to search for private information, and regulation. These mechanisms are highly imperfect.[8] For example, even stringent regulation (such as that in the United States and the United Kingdom) has failed to prevent catastrophic and highly publicized disclosure failures. Ultimately, managers choose whether and how much to disclose, even where laws and regulation dictate particular types of disclosure.

(a) Disclosure and Capital Market Quality: A Regulatory Perspective. Exhibit 13.1 presents the broad objectives for the regulation of investor-oriented equity markets,

---

[5]See for example, Amihud and Mendelson (1989, 1986); Botosan (1997); Botosan and Frost (1999); Diamond and Verrecchia (1991); Healy and Palepu (1993); Healy, Hutton and Palepu (2002); Leuz and Verrecchia (2000); King, Pownall and Waymire (1990); and Welker (1995). See Healy and Palepu (2001) for a review of research on information asymmetry, corporate disclosure, and capital markets.

[6]Of course, capital market advantages are not the only consideration in developing a corporate disclosure strategy. For example, the capital market benefits of a disclosure may be more than offset by competitive disadvantages resulting from the disclosure.

[7]See, for example, Carol A. Frost (1997), Lewellen et al. (1996), and Lennox (2001).

[8]See Healy and Palepu (1993, 2001).

Objectives:

Investor Protection

Investors are provided with material information, and are protected through monitoring and enforcement.

Market Quality

Markets are fair, orderly, efficient, and free from abuse and misconduct.

Specifically:

Investor Protection

1. Provide investors with material information.
2. Monitor and enforce market rules.
3. Inhibit fraud in the public offering, trading, voting and tendering of securities.
4. Seek comparability of financial information (allow investors to compare companies across industries and domiciles).

Market Quality

1. Promote equitable access to information and trading opportunities (market fairness).
2. Enhance liquidity and reduce transaction costs (market efficiency).
3. Contribute to freedom from abuse through monitoring and enforcement.
4. Foster investor confidence.
5. Facilitate capital formation.
6. Seek conditions in which prices reflect investor perceptions of value without being arbitrary or capricious (market orderliness).

Principles:

1. *Cost Effectiveness.* The cost of market regulation should be proportionate to the benefits it secures.
2. *Market Freedom and Flexibility.* Regulation should not impede competition and market evolution.
3. *Transparent Financial Reporting and Full and Complete Disclosure.*
4. *Equal Treatment of Foreign and Domestic Firms.*

Source: Frost and Lang (1996).

Exhibit 13.1. Broad Objectives for the Regulation of Investor-Oriented Equity Markets.

and shows that the two main regulatory objectives are investor protection and market quality.[9] Investor protection means that investors are provided with material information, and are protected through monitoring and enforcement. (IOSCO [2002] argues that the most important means for ensuring investor protection is to require full disclosure of information material to investors' decisions.) High-quality markets are fair, orderly, efficient, and free from abuse and misconduct. Regulators have long recognized that investor protection and market quality are linked. However, the optimal disclosure system for a particular stock exchange is not obvious, since disclosure

[9]For further discussion of these concepts, see International Organization of Securities Commissions (IOSCO, 2002), U.S. Securities and Exchange Commission (1987), and Securities and Investment Board (1994). IOSCO includes the reduction of systematic risk as a third regulatory objective. Also refer to Meier (1998), who introduces a conceptual model of "stock exchange excellence." The model consists of 12 stock exchange quality factors, including liquidity, cost-effectiveness, disclosure, market regulation, clearing and settlement, and market architecture.

regulation should not impede competition and investor access to trading opportunities, and must pass the test of cost effectiveness.[10]

International organizations such as the International Organization of Securities Commissions (IOSCO) and the Organization of Economic Cooperation and Development (OECD) are seeking to harmonize and improve disclosure standards. These efforts assume that such initiatives will reduce the regulatory barriers to cross-border capital raising efforts, and improve investor protection and market quality. IOSCO has published international disclosure standards for cross-border offerings and initial listings by foreign issuers (IOSCO, 1998), and a recent report by the Multidisciplinary Working Group on Enhanced Disclosure (2001) notes that disclosure can play an important role in maintaining capital market stability.[11]

(b) Environmental Factors that Influence Disclosure and Market Liquidity. National differences in systems of corporate governance and finance are associated with different levels of equity market development and information asymmetry, and therefore probably lead to different levels of demand for public disclosure by external parties, and in turn, differences in market liquidity.[12]

In the United States, the United Kingdom, and other English (common) law countries, equity markets are highly developed, share ownership is widely dispersed, and investor protection is emphasized. France, Germany, and other countries with non-English law systems rely more heavily on debt financing, equity cross-holdings, and ownership by family members; banks and other members of interlocking shareholder groups are closely informed about corporate financial position and activities. As a result, external demand for disclosure in these countries may be lower than in the United States and the United Kingdom.[13]

Related to the legal system are features of legal protection of investors, which might be associated with differences in financing and ownership across countries.[14] These, in turn, are associated with different levels of equity market development, information asymmetries, and demand for information, implying that the external de-

---

[10]For discussion of this and closely related issues, see, for example, Cox (1999); Fox (1999, 2000); Romano (1998, 2001); and Coffee (2002).

[11]The Multidisciplinary Working Group was formed in June of 1999 to provide advice to its sponsoring organizations on steps that would advance the state of financial institutions' disclosures of financial risks. The four sponsoring organizations are IOSCO, Basel Committee on Banking Supervision, International Association of Insurance Supervisors, and the Committee on the Global Financial System of the G-10 Central Banks.

[12]For discussions of factors shaping accounting and disclosure development, see Choi, Frost, and Meek (2002). Frost (1999) analyzes disclosure systems (rules, monitoring and enforcement, and information dissemination) in effect at 50 international stock exchanges during 1998. In correlation analyses involving 17 different disclosure system characteristics, she reports that (1) the extent of annual report disclosure is positively associated with stock exchange size, and (2) the level of monitoring and enforcement is positively associated with extent of investor protection, external financing, and legal system in the exchange's country. Adhikari and Tondkar (1992) investigate institutional factors associated with a stock exchange disclosure index based on 40 items. They find five country-specific factors to be significantly related to the index: market size, dispersion of stock ownership, activity on the equity market, degree of economic development, and type of economy.

[13] See, for example, Organization for Economic Cooperation and Development (OECD) (1998b) and Jacobson and Aaker (1993).

[14]See La Porta et al. (1997).

mand for disclosure in markets with greater legal protection of investors should be greater, and market liquidity higher.[15]

Emerging markets are by definition not well developed, and outside equity investors are not their primary sources of finance.[16] Therefore, both the external demand for disclosure and market liquidity in emerging market countries are expected to be lower than in developed economies.

(c) Disclosure and Liquidity: Empirical Evidence. A recent academic study strongly supports the view that disclosure is positively associated with market liquidity.[17] The study examines associations between measures of stock exchange disclosure and market liquidity at the 50 member stock exchanges of the World Federation of Exchanges (WFE) during 1998. It focuses on stock exchange disclosure systems (rather than actual company disclosures) because this approach links stock exchange and government policy with desired outcomes related to market quality factors, such as liquidity. In the study, "disclosure system" refers to: requirements for disclosure of company information imposed by stock exchanges and government regulators, monitoring and enforcement of disclosure requirements, and stock exchange mechanisms for disseminating and making publicly available information about listed companies.[18] Using survey evidence and data from public sources, the authors develop a measure of overall disclosure and measures of disclosure system components such as enforcement, level of sensitive disclosures, and innovations in stock exchange and government disclosure systems.

The authors find that all disclosure measures are positively and significantly related to market liquidity. This result is consistent with the theoretical prediction that higher levels of disclosure reduce differences in information between corporate managers and outsiders, and result in increased share liquidity. The analysis controls for the influences of: legal protection of investors, external financing, legal system (English law versus non-English law), stock exchange size, whether the country is an emerging market country, the CIFAR[19] index (an alternative measure of corporate disclosure), analyst following, and importance of the media. Further, the authors find that, beyond the influence of stock exchange disclosure level, only the emerging market and media variables are significantly associated with market liquidity.

13.4 OVERVIEW OF AUTOMOBILE COMPANY DISCLOSURE SURVEY. Sections 13.4 through 13.9 present results from a survey of disclosure practices of six automobile manufacturing companies, focusing on: periodic financial reports, cash flow

---

[15]Frost (2002) presents evidence supporting the view that legal environment influences company disclosures of forward-looking information in five countries. Ball, Kothari, and Robin (2000); Ali and Hwang (2000); Hung (2000); Francis, Khurana, and Pereira (2001); Bushman, Piotroski, and Smith (2001); Hope (2002); and several other studies provide evidence on the associations among institutional characteristics and the properties of accounting numbers, financial transparency, and other accounting- and auditing-related characteristics.

[16]National governments have provided much of the financing in some countries, families and lenders in others. For detailed discussion, see Beim and Calomaris (2001).

[17]Frost, Gordon, and Hayes (2002).

[18]The study focuses on stock exchange disclosure systems as related to domestic companies with equity listed in primary markets. To keep analysis manageable, it does not examine disclosure systems related to companies with equities traded over the counter or on other secondary markets.

[19]Center for International Financial Analysis and Research, Inc.

statements and segment disclosures, special disclosures for non-domestic financial statement users, disclosures of forward-looking information, corporate governance disclosures, and Internet financial reporting and disclosure. Companies from four developed economies, (Germany, Italy, Japan, and the United States) and two developing countries (South Korea and Peoples' Republic of China) are investigated: Fiat S.p.A. (Italy), Ford Motor Company (U.S.), Hyundai Motor Company (South Korea), Jaingling Motor Corporation (China), Toyota Motor Corporation (Japan), and Volkswagen AG (Germany).[20]

Exhibit 13.2 presents profile information about the companies. It shows that the companies vary greatly in terms of sales revenue, market capitalization, number of employees, and extent of activity in nondomestic equity and product markets. For example, sales revenue for fiscal year 2001 ranges from US$487 million (Jiangling Motors Corp.) to US$87,776 million (Toyota Motor Corp.). Hyundai and Jiangling are listed only on their domestic stock exchanges. In contrast, Toyota's equity is officially listed in Japan, the United Kingdom, and the United States, and Fiat, Ford, and Volkswagen all have equity listed on international stock exchanges in four or more countries. Fiat, Ford, and Toyota are SEC registrants listed on the New York Stock Exchange (NYSE). Hyundai, Jiangling, and Volkswagen do not have equity listed on U.S. stock exchanges. These considerations, along with home market characteristics, are expected to influence the companies' disclosure practices.

13.5 PERIODIC FINANCIAL REPORTS

(a) Types, Frequency, and Content of Reports. This section discusses three types of periodic report: (1) annual reports, (2) interim reports, and (3) announcements of annual general meetings.[21] Securities regulators generally require that listed companies file annual reports once yearly, and interim reports at least half-yearly. Beyond this basic requirement, there is much variation in periodic reporting requirements. Some regulators require certain types of reports (e.g., quarterly financial reports, announcements of annual general meetings) while others do not. Requirements vary concerning the distribution and forms of publication of the information contained in the report, and the nature of the information the reports are required to contain. For example, the U.S. SEC is unique in requiring domestic companies to provide highly detailed information disclosures in their proxy statements. Finally, companies may voluntarily publish reports beyond the required minimums.

---

[20]This analysis is from Frost and Blum (2002).

[21]This chapter does not discuss other types of periodic reports, such as current reports on Forms 6-K and 8-K required by the U.S. SEC, and extraordinary reports in Japan, as specified in the Japanese Securities and Exchange Law. Announcements and other materials related to annual general meetings are not generally considered "periodic reports." However, because of their importance to investors and other financial statement users, we include discussion of them here. The names by which periodic reports are identified vary widely among companies and national jurisdictions. Many annual reports, although distributed to shareholders, are not titled as such, and their contents follow statutory and regulatory guidelines. The greatest variation is in announcements and reports related to forthcoming shareholders' meetings, also referred to as annual general meetings. For convenience, we refer to this type of report as "announcement of annual general meeting."

The most reliable sources of information on financial reporting and disclosure requirements are stock exchange and government publications. Many stock exchange Web sites provide detailed information and Web links to relevant regulatory authorities. Stock exchange handbooks, such as Palmiero and Lobo (2002) also provide useful summaries.

	Fiat S.p.A.	Ford Motor Company	Hyundai Motor Company	Jiangling Motors Corp.	Toyota Motor Corp.	Volkswagen AG
Home Country	Italy	United States	South Korea	People's Republic of China	Japan	Germany
Trading Market in the United States	New York Stock Exchange (NYSE)	NYSE	Over-the-counter (OTC)	OTC	NYSE	OTC
Most Recent Fiscal Year Sales ($US, millions)	$55,963	$162,412	$32,837	$419	$124,022	$89,179
Market Capitalization (September, 2002, $US, millions)	$6,591	$19,413	$6,047	$487	$87,776	$18,060
Number of Employees	198,764	354,431	48,831	5,802	246,702	322,070
Stock Exchange Official Listings	Italy, France, Germany, NYSE (U.S.)	NYSE (U.S.), Belgium, France, Germany, Switzerland, London	South Korea	Shenzhen (China)	Tokyo, NYSE (U.S.), London	Germany, Netherlands, Belgium, London, Switzerland, Tokyo, Luxembourg
Principal Business Segments	Automotive, Agriculture and Construction Equip., Commercial Vehicles	Automotive Manufacturing, Financial Services	Automotive Manufacturing Financial Services	Automotive Manufacturing	Automotive Manufacturing Financial Services	Automobiles, Financial Services
Principal Geographic Segments	Europe (Excluding Italy), Italy, North America	North America, Europe, Other	South Korea, North America, Asia	People's Republic of China	North America, Europe, Japan	Western Europe, North America, South America/ Africa

Note: Information is from Annual Reports and SEC filings, with the exception of (1) market capitalization and number of employees, which are from Wright Investors' Services (http://profiles/wisi.com/profiles), and (2) U.S. trading market, which is from several sources.

Exhibit 13.2. Profile Information—Six Automobile Manufacturing Companies.

Exhibit 13.3 illustrates the variations seen in practice, from the perspective of a U.S.-based financial statement user. Three sources were used to gather the financial documents tabulated in the exhibit: the Global Access Database (Primark, Inc.), the U.S. SEC's Electronic Data Gathering, Analysis, and Retrieval (EDGAR) system, and company Web sites. The exhibit shows that SEC filers publish far more English language information (in terms of pages of information), and more documents (due to the SEC filing requirements for U.S. and non-U.S. registrants).

Evidence in the exhibit reflects a fact well-known in practice: U.S. SEC minimum reporting requirements are set at a high level relative to those in non-U.S. jurisdictions. SEC registrants file more reports, and more detailed reports than non-SEC registrants. Managers' incentives (in terms of whether to file the reports, and to a large extent, the content of the reports) are clear: If the required reports are not filed, the company may have serious legal and disciplinary difficulties with the SEC and U.S. stock exchanges on which the companies are listed. For this reason, the automobile companies that are *not* SEC registrants disclose less.

The exhibit also gives evidence about voluntary disclosure practices. In particular, in the absence of SEC requirements (for quarterly reports and detailed announcements of annual general meetings), great variation is observed. For example, Volkswagen is a "world-class" company (2001 sales revenue of US$89 billion, with 322,060 employees), but has chosen not to list on a U.S. stock exchange, and therefore has avoided SEC registration. This decision is reflected in Volkswagen's periodic reports. The company does not voluntarily disclose information in its annual report that is required in the Form 20-F (or 10-K) required of Fiat, Toyota, and Ford.[22]

(b) Annual Reports. Exhibit 13.3 shows that Fiat, Ford, and Toyota (all SEC filers) publish both "regular" annual reports and annual reports on U.S. SEC Forms 20-F (Fiat and Toyota) or Form 10-K (Ford). Fiat's annual report ("Consolidated and Statutory Financial Statements") is the most lengthy of the nine annual reports in our data set, reflecting Italy's highly detailed statutory annual reporting requirements.[23] Hyundai's and Jiangling's annual reports are the briefest, at 81 and 54 pages, respectively, compared to an average of 156 pages for the other seven annual reports.

(c) Interim Reports. The United States and South Korea are the only two countries represented in our sample that require the filing of quarterly reports by domestic firms listed on primary markets.[24] Germany's Neuer Markt, a specialized market for young, high growth companies, required the filing of quarterly reports, and Japan's high growth equity market, Mothers, requires that listed companies publish quarterly results.[25] The U.S. SEC's interim reporting requirements are by far the most stringent. Non-U.S. securities regulators are increasingly implementing a quarterly reporting requirement for

---

[22]Page length of annual reports is a crude proxy, but reflects the underlying disclosures. As shown in Exhibit 13.3, page lengths of Forms 20-F filed by Fiat and Toyota (279 and 185, respectively) exceed the page length of Volkswagen's annual report (144).

[23]Our sample reports do not include non-English language reports filed in non-U.S. home countries and not translated into English and distributed in the United States. These include, for example, the highly detailed Japanese Language Securities Report filed by Toyota with the Ministry of Finance in Japan.

[24]Consistent with the SEC's acceptance of home country practice, the NYSE and NASDAQ do not require non-U.S. listed companies to file quarterly financial reports.

[25]The Neuer Markt, plagued by problems related to fraud and financial distress of its listed companies, ceased to exist at the end of 2002.

	Fiat S.p.A.	Ford Motor Company	Hyundai Motor Company	Jiangling Motors Corp.	Toyota Motor Corp.	Volkswagen AG
Home Country	Italy	United States	South Korea	People's Republic of China	Japan	Germany
U.S. SEC registrant?	Yes	Yes	No	No	Yes	No
Total number of pages in documents	614	371	117	75	351	189
Documents Analyzed (page length shown in parentheses)						
Annual Reports—fiscal period-end (page length)						
Annual Report	Dec. 31, 2001 (184)	Dec. 31, 2001 (80)	Dec. 31, 2001 (81)	Dec. 31, 1999 (54)	March 31, 2001 (96)	Dec. 31, 2001 (144)
Form 10K	—	Dec. 31, 2001 (127)	—	—	—	—
Form 20F	Dec. 31, 2001 (279)	—	—	—	March 31, 2002 (185)	—
Interim Reports—fiscal period-end (page length)						
First Fiscal Quarter	March 31, 2002 (17)	March 31, 2002 (12)	None	March 31, 2002 (6)	June 30, 2002 (13)	March 31, 2002 (14)
Half-year	Second Quarter Report–June 30, 2002 (16) Half-year Report–June 30, 2001 (91)	June 30, 2002(13)	June 30, 2002 (non-consolidated) (25)	June 30, 2002 (15)	Sept. 30, 2001 (23)	June 30, 2002 (16)

(*continued*)

Exhibit 13.3. Periodic Reports Widely Available for Six Auto Companies (English Language) Fiscal 2001/2002.

	Fiat S.p.A.	Ford Motor Company	Hyundai Motor Company	Jiangling Motors Corp.	Toyota Motor Corp.	Volkswagen AG
Interim Reports—fiscal period-end (page length) (*continued*)						
Form 10Q	—	March 31, 2002 (27), June 30, 2002 (53)	—	—	—	—
Does half-year report include financial statements for second quarter?	Yes (separate second quarter report published)	Yes	No	No	No	Yes
Annual General Meeting Announcements						
Announcement/ invitation	September 10–12, 2002 (27)		February 21–March 15, 2002	Not Avail.	June 11, 2001 (34)	April 3, 2002 (15)
Proxy Statement		May 9, 2002 (59)				

Notes: Document Search was limited to English language documents only.

Notes: "Not Available" means not available from the company's investor relations Web site, the U.S. Securities and Exchange Commission Edgar Web site, or from the Global Vantage (Primark) Database as of September 16, 2002. Unless otherwise noted, financial reports contain consolidated (versus non-consolidated) financial statements.

Notes: Fiat: For semi-annual periods, Fiat publishes separate second quarter and more detailed half-year reports. Half-year report for fiscal 2002 not available on Fiat Web site as of 14 September, 2002. Annual General Meeting information published in large number of individual one-page announcements posted on company's Web site.

Ford: Half-year and second quarter results are reported in the second quarter report.

Hyundai: Quarterly reports are not published. However, Web site provides information on quarterly sales revenue, gross profit, operating income, ordinary income, net income, assets, liabilities, shareholders' equity, and liabilities to equity, all in billion won.

Jiangling: "Not Available" means no English language report available, and existence of Chinese language report can not be determined using the data sources listed in general note, above. For June 30, 2002, only six-month results are available (no figures for the second quarter).

Toyota: Publishes quarterly consolidated financial results (not reports as such), and "complete" half-yearly interim reports.

Volkswagen: Half-year and second quarter results are reported in a single "Interim" report.

Exhibit 13.3. (*continued*)

listed companies. In addition, world-class non-U.S. companies increasingly are choosing voluntarily to publish quarterly financial reports. For example, Pricewaterhouse-Coopers Consulting found in a recent survey of 160 large European multinationals that managers in continental Europe are aware of pressures for quarterly reporting.[26]

However, many world-class companies continue to publish half-year reports only, and there have been controversies in some non-U.S. jurisdictions about requiring quarterly reporting. (For example, as discussed in a recent news article,[27] Porsche has long refused to publish quarterly reports.) Exhibit 13.3 shows that one of the six auto companies surveyed (Hyundai) did not publish a first-quarter financial report. Note that although quarterly reporting *is* required in Hyundai's home market, the company does not choose to publish English language quarterly reports on its Internet Web site. Also, Hyundai's half-year financial statements are nonconsolidated. Finally, three companies (Hyundai, Jaingling, and Toyota) do not include second quarter results in their half-year reports.

(d) Announcements of Annual General Meetings and Proxy Statements. Corporate disclosures in announcements of annual meetings and proxy solicitations vary dramatically worldwide, both in terms of information disclosed and method of information distribution. U.S. investors are accustomed to the highly detailed disclosures contained in proxy statements published by U.S. companies, and sometimes assume that such information is available for non-U.S. companies as well. However, foreign companies registered with the SEC are exempt from many proxy-related disclosures, and in general, many types of disclosure found in U.S. proxy statements are simply not made by non-U.S. companies, whether or not they are listed in the United States. Exhibit 13.3 does show that all of our sample auto companies except Jiangling publish at least some English language information before their annual general meetings.

Exhibits 13.4 through 13.7 illustrate the wide range of detail provided in such announcements. Exhibit 13.4 presents Hyundai's one-page report announcing its annual general meeting of shareholders held on March 13, 2002. The primary item (consisting of a brief outline, less than one page in length), presents dividend information, financial statement items approved at the meeting, and a list of resolutions (topics, not details). A public announcement released by Hyundai on February 21, 2002, shown in Exhibit 13.5, announced the forthcoming meeting, providing very sketchy information. Hyundai's Internet Web site also contained seven brief announcements related to annual general meeting matters, including preliminary announcements of earnings and sales revenue, and a dividend increase.

Volkswagen's Invitation to the Annual General Meeting of Shareholders on April 16, 2002, is far more detailed. The document contains the following items:

- Agenda
- Resolutions on dividend payments and other supervisory board and management board actions
- Information about persons proposed to be elected to the supervisory board
- Detailed information about resolutions to be voted on at the meeting
- Proposal for appointment of auditors for financial year 2002

---

[26]See *Accountancy* (May 2002).

[27]"Porsche Pulls NY Listing Plan," *Financial Times*, October 17, 2002, p. 19.

Title	Resolution of the Annual General Meeting of Shareholders (AGM)	Count	1907	Date	03-15-2002

1. Approval of the financial statements of the 34th business year:

			(unit: million KRW)
Total assets	19,632,846	Sales	22,505,093
Total liabilities	10,535,035	Ordinary income	1,666,018
Capital stock	1,476,454	Net income	1,165,399
Total shareholders' Equity	9,097,811	*Earnings per share	KRW 5,164

   *Opinion of outside auditor: appropriate

2. Details of dividends:
   1) Dividends per share:
      Common shares KRW 750
      Series 1 preferred shares KRW 800
      Series 2 preferred shares KRW 850
      Series 3 preferred shares KRW 800
   2) Total cash dividends: KRW 215,145,000,000
   3) Dividend ratio to market value: 3.03%
   4) Dividend ratio to face value: 15%
   5) Dividend payout ratio: 18.5%
3. Current status of directors and audit committee:
   1) Appointees: Mong-Koo Chung, Byung-In Park, Rudiger Grube, Kwang-Nyun Kim
   2) Total number of registered directors: 8
   3) Total number of outside directors: 4
   4) Percentage of outside directors appointed: 50%
   5) Total number of audit committee: 3 outside auditors
4. Other resolutions:
   1) Approval of the financial statements of 34th business year;
   2) Amendment of the Articles of Incorporation;
   3) Appointment of directors;
   4) Appointment of a member of audit committee; and,
   5) Approval of the limit on compensation for directors.

   *The agenda was passed as proposed.
5. Date of AGM: March 15, 2002
6. Others: Total cash dividend in No. 2-2) above is rounded up to KRW 1,000,000.

Exhibit 13.4. Annual General Meeting Disclosure Hyundai Motor Company.

- Excerpts from the 2001 Annual Report
- Counter-motions to the annual general meeting of shareholders

Exhibit 13.6 shows the cover page of the notice of Toyota's annual general meeting, which presents the meeting agenda, and reports contained in the Toyota shareholders' meeting document. Toyota's document is more detailed than Volkswagen's. For example, it presents a discussion of the company's progress and management's objectives for the future, information about the company, major shareholders, status of main subsidiaries and affiliates, and more detailed information about the 53 members of the board of directors than is disclosed by Volkswagen.

Exhibit 13.7 presents the table of contents of Ford's Proxy Statement. The proxy statement includes Ford's Audit Committee Report, details on director and executive officer compensation, information on relationships and related transactions, management stock ownership, and many other types of information.

Title	Resolution of the Board of Directors on Convocation of General Meeting of Shareholders	Count	1429	Date	02-21-2002

1. Date of Board Resolution: February 21, 2002
   (four out of four outside directors were present)
2. Reason for Convocation of BOD Meeting: To discuss the date of convocation of general meeting of shareholders and the agenda.
3. Expected Date of General Meeting of Shareholders: March 15, 2002 10:00 a.m.
4. Expected Place of General Meeting of Shareholders:
   Grand conference room of the 2nd floor of Hyundai Motor Company, 231 Yangjae-dong, Seochoku, Seoul, Korea
5. Agenda:
   1) Approval of the financial statements of the 34th business year (1/1/2001~12/31/2001)
   2) Amendment of the Articles of Incorporation of the Company
   3) Appointment of director(s)

Nominees	Name	Position
Outside Director	Kwang-Nyun Kim	Outside Director of HMC
Inside Director	Mong-Koo Chung	Representative Director of HMC
	Jung-In Park	Representative Director of Hyundai MOBIS
	Rudiger Grube	Deputy Member of the Board of Management of DaimlerChrysler AG

   4) Appointment of member(s) of Audit Committee
   5) Approval of the limit of directors' remuneration
6. Result: Agenda approved as proposed

Attachment There is no record.

Exhibit 13.5. Announcement of Forthcoming Annual General Meeting Hyundai Motor Company.

The evidence in the periodic report exhibits suggests that there is a strong association between U.S. SEC registration status and the amount of information published. This difference reflects the highly detailed U.S. disclosure requirements.

13.6 CASH FLOW STATEMENTS AND SEGMENT DISCLOSURES. Cash flow statements and industry and geographic segment disclosures are two types of financial statement disclosure where practices have changed dramatically in recent years in response to strong demand by capital market participants and changes in accounting regulation. Minimum required disclosures in these areas have increased, and many companies disclose information beyond the required minimums.

To illustrate the dramatic changes that have occurred in cash flow and segment disclosures, consider international practices from less than 10 years ago. Exhibits 13.8 and 13.9 present results from an analysis of the 1993/94 annual reports of 200 of the largest companies in France, Germany, Japan, the United Kingdom, and the United States (40 companies from each country).[28] Exhibit 13.8 shows that the majority of U.K. and U.S. companies disclosed segment revenues, assets and profits, consistent

[28]Refer to Frost and Ramin (1997) for sample selection details and empirical results. The mean market capitalization for each country subsample of 40 companies ranged from US$2.48 billion (Japan) to US$2.76 billion (France).

June 11, 2001

To All Shareholders:

President Fujio Cho
TOYOTA MOTOR CORPORATION
1, Toyota-cho, Toyota City, Aichi Prefecture

Notice of Convocation of FY2001
Ordinary General Shareholders' Meting
(All financial information has been prepared in accordance with generally accepted accounting principles in Japan)
English translation from the original Japanese-language document

Dear Shareholder,

Please refer to the following for information about the upcoming FY2001 Ordinary General Shareholders' Meeting. We hope that you will be able to attend this Meeting.

If you are unable to attend the Meeting, we would appreciate it if you could find the time from your busy schedule to vote "yes" or "no" as appropriate on the enclosed ballot form, sign the form, and return it to us after reviewing the enclosed documents. Thank you very much for your assistance.

Sincerely yours,

Fujio Cho

1. **Date and time:** June 27, 2001 (Wednesday), 10:00 AM
2. **Venue:** Toyota Head Office, 1, Toyota-cho, Toyota City, Aichi Prefecture
3. **Meeting Agenda**

Reports:

(1) Report on Business Review, balance sheet, and statement of income for the FY2001 term (covering April 1, 2000 through March 31, 2001)

(2) Report on treasury share repurchases under the provisions of Article 3 of the Law for Special Exceptions to the Commercial Code Concerning Procedures of Cancellation of Shares.

Resolutions:

Proposed Resolution 1:	Approval of Proposed Appropriation of Retained Earnings
Proposed Resolution 2:	Election of 12 Directors
Proposed Resolution 3:	Election of 1 Corporate Auditor
Proposed Resolution 4:	Acquisition of treasury shares to be awarded to Toyota Directors and employees A summary of this resolution appears among the "Reference Documents Pertaining to Exercise of Voting Rights," on pages 28–32 to follow
Proposed Resolution 5:	Award of Bonus payments to retiring members of Directors and Corporate Auditor

Note: If you decide to attend the meeting in person, we would appreciate it if you would submit the enclosed voting ballot to the reception desk as your admission pass. Thank you.

Exhibit 13.6 Notice of Toyota Motor Corporation's Ordinary General Shareholders' Meeting.

TABLE OF CONTENTS

Notice of Annual Meeting of Shareholders
Defined Terms
Proxy Statement

QUESTIONS AND ANSWERS ABOUT THE PROXY MATERIALS
AND THE ANNUAL MEETING

- What is a proxy?
- What is a proxy statement?
- What is the purpose of the meeting?
- What is the record date and what does it mean?
- Who is entitled to vote at the meeting?
- What are the voting rights of the holders of common stock and Class B stock?
- What is the difference between a shareholder of record and a "street name" holder?
- How do I vote my shares?
- Are votes confidential? Who counts the votes?
- Can I vote my shares in person at the meeting?
- What are my choices when voting?
- What are the Board's recommendations?
- What if I do not specify how I want my shares voted?
- Can I change my vote?
- What vote is required for a proposal to be approved?
- How can I attend the meeting?
- Are there any rules regarding admission?
- Are there any other matters to be acted upon at the meeting?

Election of Directors
Committees of the Board of Directors
Audit Committee Report
Management Stock Ownership
Section 16(a) Beneficial Ownership Reporting Compliance
Compensation of Directors
Certain Relationships and Related Transactions
Compensation Committee Report on Executive Compensation (How Ford Determines Executive Compensation)
Compensation Committee Interlocks and Insider Participation
Compensation of Executive Officers
Stock Options
Performance Stock Rights and Restricted Stock Units
Stock Performance Graphs
Retirement Plans
Proposals Requiring Your Vote
Shareholder Proposals for 2003
Annual Report and Other Matters
Multiple Shareholders Sharing the Same Address
Expenses of Solicitation
Directions to the Annual Meeting Site
Appendix Amendment to Ford Motor Company 1998 Long-Term Incentive Plan

Exhibit 13.7 Table of Contents from Ford Motor Company's Notice of Annual Meeting of Shareholders and Proxy Statement (released May 9, 2002).

	France	Germany	Japan	U.K.[b]	U.S.[c]
Number of Companies	40	40	40	40	40
A. Industry Segments					
Firms Disclosing Revenues, Assets and Profits	9	2	0	33	16
Revenues, Assets and Profits not all disclosed					
Firms Disclosing Profits	4	4	7	2	0
Firms Do Not Disclose Profits But Do Disclose—					
Revenue Only	21	31	25	1	0
Assets Only	0	0	0	0	0
Assets and Revenue	1	0	0	0	0
Firms Disclosing Some Segment Information	35	37	32	36	16
B. Geographic Segments					
Firms Disclosing Revenues, Assets and Profits	12	1	0	34	25
Revenues, Assets and Profits not all disclosed					
Firms Disclosing Profits	1	3	1	2	0
Firms Do Not Disclose Profits But Do Disclose—					
Revenue Only	18	31	6	1	0
Assets Only	0	0	0	0	0
Assets and Revenue	3	1	0	0	1
Firms Disclosing Some Segment Information	34	36	7	37	26

Exhibit 13.8. Industry and Geographic Segment Disclosures in 1993/94 Annual Reports.[a]

[a]Refer to Frost and Ramin (1997) for sample selection details and empirical results. The mean market capitalization for each country subsample of 40 companies ranged from US$ 2.48 billion (Japan) to US$ 2.76 billion (France).

[b]Two U.K. firms stated that disclosure of segment net assets (and, for one firm, segment profits) would seriously prejudice their interests. A third U.K. firm stated that analysis of net assets would not be meaningful.

[c]One U.S. firm stated that disclosure of geographic segment profits would not provide meaningful information.

	France	Germany	Japan	U.K.	U.S.
Number of Companies	40	40	40	40	40
Number of Firms Presenting Cash Flow Statement	18	5	17	40	40
Number of Firms Presenting Funds (Noncash) Flow Statement	12	21	1	0	0
Number of Firms Presenting Neither Cash nor Funds Flow Statement	10	14	22	0	0
Number of Firms Presenting Definition of Cash (or Funds)	16	1	11	2	35

Exhibit 13.9. Cash Flow and Funds Flow Statements in 1993/94 Annual Reports[a]

[a]Refer to Frost and Ramin (1997) for sample selection details and empirical results. The mean market capitalization for each country subsample of 40 companies ranged from US$ 2.48 billion (Japan) to US$ 2.76 billion (France).

with accounting requirements in those countries.[29] In contrast, only 9 of the 40 French companies, 2 of the 40 German companies, and none of the 40 Japanese companies disclosed industry segment revenues, assets, and profits. However, 35 French, 37 German, and 32 Japanese companies disclosed *some* type of industry segment information. A similar pattern was observed for geographic segment disclosures, which were even less common. For example, only 7 Japanese companies made any type of geographic segment disclosure apparently due to their sensitive nature.

Exhibit 13.9 presents information on cash flow and funds flow statements in the annual reports of the 200 companies from the same study. The exhibit shows that all 40 U.K. companies and all 40 U.S. companies presented cash flow statements, in conformance with U.S. and U.K. accounting standards. In contrast, only 18 French companies, 5 German companies, and 17 Japanese companies presented cash flow statements. Even more striking is that 46 of the 120 French, German, and Japanese companies did not even disclose funds flow information.

Exhibit 13.10 shows dramatic change in disclosures since 1993/94. All six of the auto companies present segment revenues, assets, and sales, except for Jiangling, which states that it operates in a single industry segment (automobile manufacturing) and geographic region (China). All six companies also present cash flow statements. (As shown in Exhibit 13.10, Jiangling and Volkswagen use International Accounting Standards [IAS] for their consolidated financial reports, Toyota and Ford both use U.S. GAAP, Hyundai uses Korean GAAP, and Fiat's financial statements are prepared in conformance with Italian regulations.)[30]

Refer to Exhibit 13.11 for Volkswagen's Cash Flow Statement. Cash flow disclosures are new for Volkswagen, reflecting its recent adoption of International Accounting Standards. Exhibit 13.12 presents Volkswagen's Funds Flow statement from its December 31, 2000, Annual Report based on German accounting standards.

13.7 SPECIAL DISCLOSURES FOR NONDOMESTIC FINANCIAL STATEMENT USERS AND ACCOUNTING PRINCIPLES USED. Annual reports often include special disclosures to accommodate nondomestic financial statement users. Such disclosures include: convenience restatements of financial information to a nondomestic currency, limited restatements of financial results and position to a second set of accounting standards, a complete set of financial statements prepared in conformance with a second set of accounting principles, and discussion of differences between accounting principles used in the primary financial statements and some other set of accounting principles. Many firms in countries where English is not the primary language also translate entire annual reports from the home country language to English; such is the

---

[29]Companies with no reportable segments do not make these disclosures.

[30]For convenience, we use the term International Accounting Standards (IAS) to refer to standards promulgated by the International Accounting Standards Board (IASB) and the Board of the International Accounting Standards Committee (IASC). More precisely, the IASB publishes its Standards in a series of pronouncements called International Financial Reporting Standards (IFRS). It has also adopted the body of Standards issued by the Board of the IASC. Those pronouncements are designated as "International Accounting Standards" (IAS) in this chapter. Refer to the IASB Web site (*www.iasb.org.uk*) and Deloitte Touche Tohmatsu's Web site on International Accounting Standards (IAS Plus, at *www.iasplus.com*) for detailed information about IAS. IAS Plus publishes highly useful country updates that report on financial reporting, accounting standards, and related developments.

Volkswagen is required to use German accounting standards for nonconsolidated statutory reports, however.

	Fiat S.p.A.	Ford Motor Company	Hyundai Motor Company	Jiangling Motors Corp.	Toyota Motor Corp.	Volkswagen AG
Home Country	Italy	United States	South Korea	People's Republic of China	Japan	Germany
Trading Status in the United States	NYSE	NYSE	OTC	OTC	NYSE	OTC
Accounting principles used	Italian Law	U.S.	Korean	International Accounting Standards	U.S.	International Accounting Standards
Auditing principles used	U.S.	U.S.	Korean	International Standards on Auditing	U.S.	German Audit Regulations and Standards
Cash Flow Statement	Yes	Yes	Yes	Yes	Yes	Yes
Segment disclosures						
Geographic						
Sales	Yes	Yes	Yes	Not Applic.	Yes	Yes
Capital Expenditures	Yes	Yes		Not Applic.	Yes	
Profits (or net income, or similar item)	Yes	Yes	Yes	Not Applic.	Yes	Yes

Total assets (or something similar)	Yes	Yes	Yes	Not Applic.	Yes	Yes
Industry						
Sales	Yes	Yes	Yes	Not Applic.	Yes	Yes
Capital Expenditures	Yes	Yes		Not Applic.	Yes	Yes
Profits	Yes	Yes	Yes	Not Applic.	Yes	Yes
Total assets	Yes	Yes	Yes	Not Applic.	Yes	Yes
Disclosures for Nondomestic Users						
Convenience Restatements to Nondomestic currency	Yes	—	Yes	—	Yes	—
Limited restatement to nondomestic accounting principles	Yes	—	—	—	—	—
Use of non-Domestic Accounting Standards	—	—	—	Yes (IAS)	Yes (U.S. GAAP)	Yes (IAS)
Discussion of Differences Between Accounting Principles Used and Domestic Accounting Standards	Yes	—	—	—	Yes	Yes

Note: Jiangling states that it operates in a single business segment (auto manufacturing), and a single geographic segment, its domestic market.

Exhibit 13.10. Annual Report Disclosures—Six Auto Companies.

million €	2001	2000
Cash and cash equivalents at beginning of period	**2,156**	**3,016**
Profit before tax	4,409	3,719
Income taxes paid	–1,362	–1,304
Depreciation of tangible and intangible assets*	4,668	4,052
Amortization of capitalized development costs*	917	852
Depreciation of financial assets*	18	45
Depreciation of leasing and rental assets*	1,159	632
Change in provisions	620	1,659
Loss on disposal of non-current assets	60	95
Share of retained earnings of Group companies accounted for using the equity method	–170	–226
Other expenses/income not affecting cash flow	358	315
Change in inventories	–597	–742
Change in receivables (excluding financial services)	–169	–713
Change in liabilities (excluding borrowings)	127	826
Cash flows from operating activities	**10,038**	**9,210**
Acquisition of tangible and intangible assets	–6,617	–6,130
Additions to capitalized development costs	–2,180	–1,258
Acquisition of investments	–82	–1,766
Investments in other financial assets	–28	–267
Changes in leasing and rental assets (excluding depreciation)	–3,428	–2,464
Change in financial services receivables	–3,396	–3,354
Proceeds from disposal of non-current assets (excluding leasing and rental assets)	540	676
Cash flows from investing activities	**–15,191**	**–14,563**
Net cash flow	**–5,153**	**–5,353**
Change in investments in securities	**266**	**–297**
Investing activities including investments in securities	**–14,925**	**–14,860**
Capital contributions	135	24
Acquisition of treasury shares	—	–2,285
Dividends paid/compensation for loss	–465	–333
Other changes in equity	–345	–1,430
Take-up of bonds	4,319	2,859
Repayment of bonds	–3,232	–1,463
Change in other borrowings	6,917	7,495
Finance lease payments	–27	25
Change in loans to Group companies	–319	–141
Cash flows from financing activities	**6,983**	**4,751**
Cash flows from changes to the scope of consolidation	29	15
Cash flows from exchange rate changes	4	24
Change in cash and cash equivalents	**2,129**	**–860**
Cash and cash equivalents at end of period	**4,285**	**2,156**
Securities and loans	**4,581**	**4,932**
Gross liquidity	**8,866**	**7,088**
Total third-party borrowings	**–42,794**	**–34,584**
Net liquidity	**–33,928**	**–27,496**

*Offset against reversals

Explanatory notes on cash flow statement are provided in note (30). *(continued)*

Exhibit 13.11. Cash Flow Statement of the Volkswagen Group for the period of January 1 to December 31, 2001.

Other information

(30) Cash flow statement

The cash flow statement comprises only Cash and cash equivalents shown in the balance sheet.

Cash flows for the 2001 financial year with prior year comparatives are presented in the cash flow statement analysed into cash inflows and outflows from operating activities, investing activities and financing activities. The cash effects of changes to the scope of consolidation and exchange rate changes are shown separately in the statement.

The change in Cash and cash equivalents from changes in consolidation relates to companies consolidated for the first time that were recorded at cost in previous years.

Cash flows from investing activities include additions to Tangible assets and long-term financial assets as well as to Capitalized development costs. The changes in Leasing and rental assets and in Financial services receivables are also shown here.

Cash flows from financing activities include outflows of funds resulting from dividend payments and redemption of bonds as well as inflows from the Issue of bonds and from the change in other financial liabilities.

Exhibit 13.11. ***(continued)***

case for the five non-U.S. firms in our survey. Some firms prepare financial statements that conform to accounting standards more widely accepted than domestic standards (primarily IAS or U.S. GAAP), or that conform both to domestic standards and to a second set of accounting principles.

Exhibit 13.10 shows that Fiat, Hyundai, Toyota, and Volkswagen all provide special disclosures for nondomestic users. Jiangling does not, consistent with its limited international capital market geographic activities. (However, Jiangling does prepare financial statements in conformance with IAS, which might be viewed as an accommodation.) For example, Fiat, Hyundai, and Toyota provide many of their financial results in both domestic currency and U.S. dollars. Fiat provides a detailed reconciliation between key financial statement items as reported in its financial statements and what those amounts would be under U.S. GAAP as required in its annual report on Form 20-F filed with the SEC. Refer to Exhibit 13.13 for Fiat's footnote disclosure of reconciliation to U.S. GAAP from its December 31, 2001, Form 20-F.

13.8 DISCLOSURE OF FORWARD-LOOKING INFORMATION. Corporate disclosures of forward-looking information vary dramatically within and across national jurisdictions, reflecting differences in regulatory requirements and, more importantly, managers' voluntary disclosure incentives. Exhibit 13.14 presents results from a survey of forward-looking disclosures made in 1993/94 annual reports by 200 large companies from France, Germany, Japan, the United Kingdom, and the United States.[31] As shown in the exhibit, relatively more French and German companies disclosed quantitative forecasts of earnings and sales than did U.K. and U.S. companies, reflecting the less stringent legal and regulatory climates in France and Germany.[32]

[31]Frost and Ramin (1997).

[32]U.S. managers long have argued that disclosure of forward-looking information exposes them to legal and regulatory risk if their forecasts turn out to be inaccurate. In the United Kingdom, the Financial Services Act creates legal liability for managers responsible for untrue or misleading statements in listing particulars or prospectuses. See Frost (2002) for detailed discussion and evidence.

Development of short-term liquidity of the Volkswagen Group from January 1 to December 31, 2000 (million DM)

	Automotive Division	Financial Services	Volkswagen Group
Net earnings before extraordinary expenses	5,577	146	5,423
Depreciation and write-up of fixed assets[1]	8,935	157	9,131
Depreciation and write-up of leasing and rental assets	—	7,870	8,198
Change in medium and long-term provisions	644	73	871
Other expenses and income not affecting payments	–432	–11	–443
Cash flow	**14,724**	**8,235**	**23,180**
Change in short-term provisions	1,226	69	98
Change in inventories and trade receivables	–6,582	–6,915	–10,267
Change in liabilities (excluding credit liabilities)	797	1,338	–90
Other internal financing	**–4,559**	**–5,508**	**–10,259**
Inflow of funds from current operations	**10,165**	**2,727**	**12,921**
Disposals of fixed assets and leasing and rental assets	233	7,714	8,022
Capital investments in tangible fixed assets[1]	–12,284	–293	–11,935
Capital investments in financial assets[2]	–4,689	–76	–4,026
Additions to leasing and rental assets	—	–20,604	–20,603
Adjustments resulting from consolidation	317	190	507
Inpayments/outpayments for acquisition of consolidated companies	—	29	–432
Capital investments	**–16,423**	**–13,040**	**–28,467**
Net cash flow	**–6,258**	**–10,313**	**–15,546**
Capital increases	46	750	46
Share buyback	–4,469	—	–4,469
Dividends/profit transfers	–913	–1,159	–644
Capital repayments to retired stockholders	–348	—	–348
Other equity changes	–226	–376	–204
Change in financial liabilities	10,284	10,228	19,835
Inflow/outflow of funds in respect of financing operations	**4,374**	**10,195**	**14,216**
Change in gross liquidity	**–1,884**	**–118**	**–1,330**
Gross liquidity at start of period	**13,486**	**1,575**	**13,202**
Gross liquidity at end of period	**11,602**	**1,457**	**11,872**
Liquid funds	3,475	982	4,204
Securities (excluding treasury stock)	3,403	475	3,499
Long-term financial investments	4,724	—	4,169
Total third-party borrowings	**–18,241**	**–62,967**	**–67,610**
Net liquidity	**–6,639**	**–61,510**	**–55,738**

[1]Including intangible assets.
[2]Excluding part of the long-term financial investments and excluding equity valuation of the companies not fully consolidated into the Group financial statements.

Note: The development of short-term liquidity is for the first time presented according to the DRS 2 breakdown as specified by the German Accounting Standards Committee (DRS).

Exhibit 13.12. Volkswagen AG Funds Flow Statement for December 31, 2000.

THE FIAT GROUP
NOTES TO CONSOLIDATED FINANCIAL STATEMENTS
at December 31, 2001, 2000 and 1999

(24) Reconciliation to Generally Accepted Accounting Principles in the United States

The consolidated financial statements of the Fiat Group are prepared in accordance with the accounting policies described above in the notes entitled "Form and content of the consolidated financial statements" and "Principles of consolidation and significant accounting policies" (hereinafter also referred to as collectively "Italian GAAP") which differ in certain respects from accounting principles generally accepted in the United States of America ("U.S. GAAP"). The significant differences and their effect on consolidated net income and stockholders' equity are set out below.

(i) Net income

	Note 24 Reference	2001 (in millions of U.S. Dollars) (*) (note 22)	2001	2000	1999
			Years ended December 31, (in millions of euros)(*)		
Net income (loss) as reported in the consolidated statements of operations		(393)	(445)	664	353
Items increasing (decreasing) reported net income, net of the effects of minority interest:					
Reversal of depreciation of revalued property, plant and equipment	(d)	16	18	12	23
Capital gains on the sale of revalued property, plant and equipment	(d)	35	40	78	26
Amortization of goodwill	(e)	(40)	(46)	(55)	(60)
Difference of amortization period of Case goodwill	(e)	46	52	37	—
Elimination of goodwill amortization	(e)	26	30	—	—
Difference in gains/losses on disposal of investments in subsidiaries	(f)	—	—	31	(16)
Accounting for Case acquisition	(g)	1	1	1	(41)
Deferred revenue recognition	(h)	(145)	(164)	—	—
Deferral of gain on real estate sale-leaseback transactions	(i)	(41)	(47)	3	3
Write-off of start up costs, net of effect on amortization	(j)	(41)	(47)	61	(52)
Adjustments to financial instruments	(k)	—	—	(358)	—
Difference in accounting for postretirement benefits	(m)	(21)	(24)	(24)	(6)
Accounting for pensions	(m)	(7)	(8)	(1)	(2)
Adjustments to restructuring provisions	(n)	(152)	(172)	443	(19)
Accounting for deferred income taxes	(o)	(64)	(72)	(48)	(24)
Treasury stock transactions	(p)	8	9	2	(31)
Other accounting differences	(q)	34	38	34	(32)
Approximate net income (loss) in accordance with U.S. GAAP, before cumulative effect of a change in accounting principle, except as permitted by Item 18		(738)	(837)	880	122
Cumulative effect of a change in accounting principle, net of tax	(j)	—	—	—	(91)
Approximate net income (loss) in accordance with U.S. GAAP, except as permitted by Item 18		(738)	(837)	880	31
Approximate per ordinary share amounts in accordance with U.S. GAAP:	(a)				
Basic					
Income (loss) before cumulative effect of change in accounting principle		(1.38)	(1.56)	1.58	0.20
Cummulative effect of change in accounting principle		—	—	—	(0.17)
Net income (loss) per share		(1.38)	(1.56)	1.58	0.03
Diluted					
Income (loss) before cumulative effect of change in accounting principle		(1.38)	(1.56)	1.58	0.20
Cumulative effect of change in accounting principle		—	—	—	(0.17)
Net income (loss) per share		(1.38)	(1.56)	1.58	0.03
Per ordinary share amounts in accordance with Italian GAAP:	(a)				
Basic					
Net income (loss) per share		(0.74)	(0.84)	1.19	0.62
Diluted					
Net income (loss) per share		(0.74)	(0.84)	1.19	0.62

(*) Except per share data, which is in Euros and Dollars.

Exhibit 13.13. Reconciliation Footnote Disclosure—Fiat S.p.A. Form 20-F for December 31, 2001.

THE FIAT GROUP
NOTES TO CONSOLIDATED FINANCIAL STATEMENTS (continued)
at December 31, 2001, 2000 and 1999

(ii) Stockholders' equity

	Note 24 Reference	At December 31, 2001	At December 31, 2001	2000
		(in millions of U.S. Dollars) (note 22)	(in millions of euros)	
Stockholders' equity as reported in the consolidated balance sheets		10,736	12,170	13,320
Items increasing (decreasing) stockholders' equity:				
Elimination of revaluation of fixed assets	(d)	(284)	(322)	(375)
Reinstatement of goodwill previously written-off	(e)	729	826	872
Difference in amortization period of Case goodwill	(e)	85	96	37
Elimination of goodwill amortization	(e)	26	30	—
Accounting for Case acquisition	(g)	(34)	(39)	(40)
Deferred revenue recognition	(h)	(145)	(164)	—
Deferral of gain on real estate sale-leaseback transactions	(i)	(105)	(119)	(67)
Write-off of start up costs	(j)	(158)	(179)	(127)
Adjustments to financial instruments	(k)	(562)	(637)	(419)
Accounting for derivatives instruments and hedging activities	(k)	(187)	(212)	—
Difference in accounting for post-retirement benefits	(m)	19	21	43
Accounting for pensions	(m)	(98)	(111)	92
Adjustments to restructuring provisions	(n)	261	296	452
Accounting for deferred income taxes	(o)	(94)	(107)	(104)
Treasury stock recorded as an asset	(p)	(249)	(282)	(50)
Other accounting differences	(q)	(39)	(44)	(120)
Approximate stockholders' equity in accordance with U.S. GAAP, except as permitted by Item 18		9,901	11,223	13,514

Exhibit 13.13. ***(continued)***

Quantitative earnings and sales forecasts among Japanese companies commonly are made in the form of press releases (a requirement of the Tokyo Stock Exchange) and so are not reflected in Exhibit 13.14.

Exhibit 13.15 presents a summary of forward-looking disclosures of the six auto companies. As shown in the exhibit, the types of forward-looking disclosure made, and the kinds of report in which they appear, vary widely. Exhibit 13.16 presents excerpts of forward-looking information presented in Volkswagen's 2001 Annual Report. Exhibit 13.17 shows the highly detailed forward looking disclosures presented in Toyota's press release of unconsolidated half year results for the period ending September 30, 2001.

13.9 CORPORATE GOVERNANCE DISCLOSURES. Here we discuss corporate disclosures relevant for evaluating critical aspects of a company's governance. Recent research claims that 35% of investor decisions are now based on nonfinancial indicators,[33] and information about corporate governance practices is widely considered to be useful for assessing corporate integrity. Many such disclosures are mandated by securities regulators; in addition, more and more companies are voluntarily disclosing corporate governance information.

[33]The research was published by Ernst & Young Strategic Finance Group, as discussed in Christina Buckingham (2001).

THE FIAT GROUP
NOTES TO CONSOLIDATED FINANCIAL STATEMENTS (continued)
at December 31, 2001, 2000 and 1999

(iii) Changes in U.S. GAAP stockholders' equity for the years ended December 31, 2001, 2000 and 1999

	Capital stock	Additional paid-in capital	Retained earnings and reserves	Accumulated other comprehensive income (loss): Cumulative translation adjustment	Accumulated other comprehensive income (loss): Available for sale securities	Accumulated other comprehensive income (loss): Derivative financial instruments	Accumulated other comprehensive income (loss): Minimum pension liability	Treasury stock	Total
	(in millions of euros)								
Balance at January 1, 1998 . .	2,844	2,619	7,809	346	212	—	(17)	(124)	13,689
Net income	—	—	31	—	—	—	—	—	31
Other comprehensive income (loss)	—	—	—	(82)	(109)	—	17	—	(174)
Total comprehensive income									(143)
Changes in treasury stock . . .	—	—	—	—	—	—	—	97	97
Dividends	—	—	(350)	—	—	—	—	—	(350)
Other	(91)	—	121	—	—	—	—	—	30
Balance at December 31, 1999	2,753	2,619	7,611	264	103	—	—	(27)	13,323
Net income	—	—	880	—	—	—	—	—	880
Other comprehensive income (loss)	—	—	—	125	(316)	—	1	—	(190)
Total comprehensive income									690
Changes in treasury stock . . .	—	—	—	—	—	—	—	(23)	(23)
Dividends	—	—	(352)	—	—	—	—	—	(352)
Other	—	—	(124)	—	—	—	—	—	(124)
Balance at December 31, 2000	2,753	2,619	8,015	389	(213)	—	1	(50)	13,514
Net income	—	—	(837)	—	—	—	—	—	(837)
Other comprehensive income (loss)	—	—	—	(367)	(143)	(192)	(111)	—	(813)
Total comprehensive income								—	(1,650)
Changes in treasury stock . . .	—	—	—	—	—	—	—	(232)	(232)
Dividends	—	—	(352)	—	—	—	—	—	(352)
Other	—	—	(57)	—	—	—	—	—	(57)
Balance at December 31, 2001	2,753	2,619	6,769	22	(356)	(192)	(110)	(282)	11,223

Exhibit 13.13. (*continued*)

THE FIAT GROUP
NOTES TO CONSOLIDATED FINANCIAL STATEMENTS (continued)
at December 31, 2001, 2000 and 1999

Comments on the above and other differences between the Group's accounting policies and U.S. GAAP are as follows:

(a) *Earnings per share*—The approximate net income (loss) per share amounts in accordance with U.S. GAAP for each of the years ended December 31, 2001, 2000 and 1999 have been calculated in accordance with the provisions of SFAS No. 128, "Earnings Per Share" ("SFAS No. 128"), using the method for two-class ordinary shares and participating securities, as prescribed therein. Under this method for the earnings per share computation, income remaining after dividends allocated to ordinary, preference and savings shares was allocated equally to the aggregate weighted average number of ordinary, preference and savings shares outstanding (approximately 542 million in 2001, 549 million in 2000 and 546 million in 1999). Dividends allocated to ordinary, preference and savings shares, in the aggregate, were 178 million euros in 2001, 352 million euros in 2000, and 350 million euros in 1999.

The net income per share amounts in accordance with Italian GAAP have been determined by reference to the provisions of IAS No. 33, "Earnings Per Share" ("IAS No. 33"). The provisions of IAS No. 33 and, accordingly, the method for calculating net income per share amounts in accordance therewith, are substantially the same as those of SFAS No. 128 previously described.

Both SFAS No. 128 and IAS No. 33 require the presentation of both basic and diluted earnings per share. Due to the limited number of stock options outstanding during the years ended December 31, 2000 and 1999, the dilutive effect of stock options calculated using the treasury stock method has resulted in diluted earnings per share data being the same as basic earnings per share amounts for those years. As the year ended December 31, 2001 resulted in a net loss, any effect from stock options outstanding would result in reducing the loss per share; therefore diluted earnings per share is reported as being the same as basic earnings per share amounts for that year.

(b) *Estimates*—The preparation of financial statements in conformity with U.S. GAAP requires explicit statement of the fact that, as under Italian GAAP, management is required to make estimates and assumptions that effect the reported amounts of assets and liabilities and disclosure of contingent assets and liabilities at the date of the financial statements and the reported amounts of revenues and expenses during the reporting period. Actual results could differ from such estimates.

(c) *Translation of financial statements of subsidiaries operating in highly inflationary economies*—The financial statements of the subsidiaries operating in highly inflationary economies have been adjusted in accordance with inflation accounting procedures (consistent with IAS No. 29, "Financial Reporting in Hyperinflationary Economies"), restating historical costs on the basis of indices deemed representative of the real change in the purchasing power of the local currencies; consistent with this procedure, the financial statements thus restated are translated into the Group's reporting currency at year-end exchange rates. Economies are defined as being highly inflationary when cumulative inflation exceeds 100% over the latest three-year period. The Group's inflation accounting policy and procedures differ from the U.S. GAAP requirements of SFAS No. 52, "Foreign Currency Translation" with respect to the translation of financial statements of entities operating in highly inflationary economies. Under U.S. GAAP, the translation of financial statements of subsidiaries operating in highly inflationary economies is based on local currency financial statements on a historical cost basis after reversing all adjustments made to take account of inflation. These financial statements are then translated into the Group's reporting currency by applying historical exchange rates to non-monetary items and current exchange rates to monetary items. All exchange adjustments arising in this remeasurement process are recorded in income.

As permitted by Item 18 of Form 20-F, the differences between accounting for operations in highly inflationary economies using international and U.S. accounting principles have not been presented in the reconciliations to net income and stockholders' equity. Accordingly, the amounts presented for such periods, while in conformity with International Accounting Standards and Italian GAAP, are not in conformity with U.S. GAAP.

(d) *Revaluation of fixed assets*—In 1983 and prior years, Fiat revalued certain property, plant and equipment to amounts in excess of historical cost, as permitted by law (see "Principles of consolidation and significant accounting policies"). Additionally, in 1991, Italian legislation (Law 413/91) re-

Exhibit 13.13. *(continued)*

THE FIAT GROUP
NOTES TO CONSOLIDATED FINANCIAL STATEMENTS (continued)
at December 31, 2001, 2000 and 1999

quired the obligatory revaluation of industrial and commercial land and buildings for all Italian companies, using coefficients as set forth by the law. Revaluations were credited to stockholders' equity and the revalued assets are depreciated over their remaining useful lives.

U.S. GAAP does not permit the revaluation of fixed assets. The capital gain differences arising upon the sale of such fixed assets are stated separately in the caption "Capital gains on the sale of property, plant and equipment." The gross asset increase due to revaluation was 645 million euros and 707 million euros at December 31, 2001 and 2000, respectively.

(e) *Goodwill*—The Group's accounting policy related to accounting for goodwill is described in the notes "Principles of consolidation and significant accounting policies." These policies differ in certain respects from those required under U.S. GAAP, as further described below.

(e.*i*) *Accounting for goodwill*—Prior to December 31, 1994, the Group accounted for goodwill on acquisitions as a direct reduction of equity. Under U.S. GAAP, goodwill is recorded on the balance sheet as an intangible asset of the acquiring company and then through December 31, 2001 was amortized to income over a period not in excess of 40 years. For the adjusted U.S. GAAP results in the tables above, goodwill previously charged to equity has been reinstated and is amortized over a 30-year period. This item also includes other differences on goodwill recorded in purchase accounting subsequent to 1994 due to U.S. GAAP adjustments applicable to acquired companies. The total amount of adjustments to goodwill, gross of accumulated amortization, was 1,323 million euros and 1,360 million euros at December 31, 2001 and 2000, respectively.

(e.*ii*) *Difference of amortization period of Case goodwill*—For U.S. GAAP financial reporting purposes, the goodwill recorded by CNH Global N.V., the purchaser of Case Group, is being amortized over a 30-year period, whereas under Italian GAAP the amortization period for goodwill is limited to 20 years. CNH Global N.V. reports separate U.S. GAAP consolidated financial statements.

(e.*iii*) *Elimination of goodwill amortization*—In June 2001, the FASB issued SFAS No. 142, "Goodwill and Other Intangible Assets." SFAS No. 142 addresses financial accounting and reporting for intangible assets and goodwill. The Statement requires that goodwill and intangible assets having indefinite useful lives not be amortized, but rather be tested at least annually for impairment. Intangible assets that have finite useful lives will continue to be amortized over their useful lives. Italian GAAP, on the other hand, requires that "goodwill and other intangible assets" be amortized over their remaining useful lives. As required by SFAS No. 142, for U.S. GAAP purposes the Group has adopted this standard for goodwill acquired after June 30, 2001. For goodwill existing as of June 30, 2001, on the other hand, the standard became effective on January 1, 2002. The complete application of the non-amortization provision of SFAS No. 142 is expected to result in a pretax increase in earnings of approximately 240 million euros per year related to goodwill and an insignificant amount per year related to the intangible assets with indefinite lives. The Group is currently defining its reporting units and performing the required transitional impairment tests of goodwill and indefinite-lived intangible assets. The Group has not yet determined the financial impact, if any, of these transitional impairment tests. During 2001, the Group continued to evaluate the recoverability of goodwill in compliance with SFAS No. 121, "Accounting for the Impairment of Long-Lived Assets and for Long-Lived Assets to be Disposed Of" (SFAS No. 121), for U.S. GAAP purposes only. The Group did not record any impairment in accordance with the requirements of SFAS No. 121.

(f) *Difference in gains/losses on disposal of investments in subsidiaries*—Gains or losses on disposals of investments arising from the sale of interests in subsidiaries as recorded in the Group's consolidated statement of operations are adjusted to reflect the higher or lower U.S. GAAP basis of the underlying equity of the disposed interest. Negative adjustments primarily relate to unamortized goodwill which has been reinstated in the U.S. GAAP value of the subsidiary's net equity, thereby resulting in lower gains on sale on a U.S. GAAP basis; positive adjustments relate primarily to the effect of reversal of the revaluation of fixed assets which is included in the Italian GAAP value of the subsidiary's net equity.

(g) *Accounting for Case acquisition*—As described in the note "Form and content of the consolidated financial statements," Fiat's Italian GAAP consolidated financial statements as of December 31, 1999 did not consolidate the financial statements at that date of the Case Group, which was acquired on

Exhibit 13.13. ***(continued)***

THE FIAT GROUP
NOTES TO CONSOLIDATED FINANCIAL STATEMENTS (continued)
at December 31, 2001, 2000 and 1999

November 12, 1999, on the grounds that it would not have been practicable to obtain the necessary information on a timely basis without disproportionate expense; accordingly for Italian GAAP purposes, the Case Group was consolidated and related purchase accounting entries were recorded with effect from January 1, 2000. U.S. GAAP does not permit the exclusion of controlled companies from consolidation unless control is temporary. Accordingly, for U.S. GAAP purposes, the net loss incurred by the Case Group from the date of acquisition to December 31, 1999, has been included in determining net income and stockholders' equity of the Group in accordance with U.S. GAAP as of December 31, 1999. The adjustments reflected in the reconciliation for the two years ended December 31, 2001 relate to the effect of this difference on the calculation of goodwill arising on the acquisition of the Case Group, which was determined in the Italian GAAP consolidated financial statements as of January 1, 2000. Additional information required by U.S. GAAP related to this acquisition is provided in (v) *Business combinations.*

(h) *Deferred revenue recognition*—Certain transactions which are recognized as sales under Italian GAAP on the basis of passage of title are accounted for under U.S. GAAP as financing transactions or operating lease arrangements until the buyer resells or subsequently consumes or uses the product, and the risks and rewards of ownership are effectively transferred, thus deferring the moment at which revenues and margins are recognized.

(i) *Real estate sale-leaseback transactions*—In December 1998, the Group entered into sale-leaseback transactions involving certain of its real estate subject to the terms of an operating lease which extends for approximately 22 years. The lease does not contain any purchase or renewal options. At December 31, 1998, buildings with a total book value of 107 million euros have been removed from the balance sheet and, after giving effect to minority interest, the gains realized on the sale transaction totaling 73 million euros, before taxes of approximately 31 millions euros, have been fully realized in accordance with the accounting principles applied by the Group. The approximate annual lease payments over the lives of the leases are 15 million euros for the above mentioned buildings.

During 2001, the Group entered into two sets of sale-leaseback transactions. The first involved the sale of certain property and its leaseback, has a term of 12 years and includes a purchase option. As a result of the sale, assets with a value of 6 million euros were removed from the balance sheet. Under Group accounting principles, a gain of 16 million euros was recognized in 2001. The total rental cost for the property over the life of the lease is approximately 22 million euros.

The second set of 2001 sale-leaseback transactions involved the sale of property under three contracts with lease terms of 5, $5\frac{1}{2}$ and 6 years. As a result of this transaction, 53 million euros of assets were removed from the balance sheet. The net gain realized on this set of transactions under Group accounting principles was 35 million euros. The total annual lease payments are approximately 34 million euros. Under these agreements, if the Group chooses not to repurchase the assets, the purchaser has the option to compel the Group to continue to lease the property for an additional five years.

U.S. GAAP requires that, where certain conditions are met, such gain be deferred and be recognized in proportion to the related gross rental charges to expense over the term of the operating lease.

(j) *Start-up costs*—In accordance with the Group's accounting policies, the costs of start-up activities are capitalized and amortized over their estimated useful lives. Effective January 1, 1999, however, U.S. GAAP Statement of Position 98-5, "Reporting on the Costs of Start-Up Activities" (SOP 98-5), requires that these costs be expensed as incurred. The initial adoption of SOP 98-5 as of January 1, 1999 has been reported as a cumulative effect of a change in accounting principle, as required for U.S. GAAP purposes. Such costs incurred after that date have also been expensed for U.S. GAAP purposes and, consequently, amortization expense deriving from amounts capitalized in accordance with the Group's accounting policies is reversed.

(k) *Financial instruments*—The Group's accounting policies related to financial receivables, financial payables and derivative financial instruments are described in the notes, "Principles of consolidation and significant accounting policies" and "Memorandum accounts." These policies and the related disclosures included in the Group's consolidated financial statements differ in certain respects from those required under U.S. GAAP, as further described below.

Exhibit 13.13. *(continued)*

	France	Germany	Japan	U.K.	U.S.
Number of Sample Firms	40	40	40	40	40
Firms making no forward-looking disclosures	3	0	5	3	0
Firms making one or more forward-looking disclosures	37	40	35	37	40
A. Firms disclosing Management's Plans or Objectives	29	28	33	25	39
B. Firms disclosing Forecasts:					
Earnings	4	16	2	2	3
Sales	7	14	1	1	2
Capital Expenditures	2	6	0	4	22
Other	2	3	0	9	18
At least one forecast	11	22	2	11	31
C. Firms disclosing "softer" prospective information	29	36	6	31	36

Exhibit 13.14. Number of Firms Disclosing Forward-Looking Information in 1993/94 Annual Reports[a]

[a]Refer to Frost and Ramin [1997] for sample selection details and empirical results. The mean market capitalization for each country subsample of 40 companies ranged from US$ 2.48 billion (Japan) to US$ 2.76 billion (France).

The term *corporate governance* is used loosely in practice, but often refers to the structure of relationships and responsibilities among shareholders, board members and managers designed to meet corporate objectives. For example, the OECD provides the following definition:[34]

> The definition of governance as the interaction between owners and managers in controlling and directing a company is commonly accepted and used. A broader definition would include "stakeholders" in addition to owners. Good governance has traditionally been framed as an issue of what systems and procedures best ensure that managers are accountable for, and act responsibly with, the assets they hold in trust. The contemporary governance debate continues to attribute great importance to the issue of accountability though it increasingly focuses on what systems of governance best promote economic efficiency and generate "Shareholder value" or returns for owners.

Corporate governance disclosures are receiving close scrutiny as the public focuses attention on perceived weaknesses in how companies are governed. Violations of required corporate governance disclosures, or failure to disclose potentially inflammatory information, have received wide publicity in the United States. For example, when it was revealed in 2002 that General Electric failed to disclose specific information about remarkably generous retirement benefits granted to Jack Welch, its former CEO, Welch and the company were so embarrassed that the benefits were

[34]Variation in topics covered by different corporate governance codes further illustrates the range in (implicit) definitions of governance. For example, the OECD's Principles of Corporate Governance address five areas: (1) The rights of shareholders; (2) The equitable treatment of shareholders; (3) The role of stakeholders; (4) Disclosure and transparency; and (5) The responsibilities of the board. In contrast, the United Kingdom's Combined Code focuses on (1) Company directors; (2) Directors' remuneration; (3) Relations with shareholders; (4) Accountability and audit; and (5) Institutional shareholders.

	Fiat S.p.A.	Ford Motor Company	Hyundai Motor Company	Jiangling Motors Corp.	Toyota Motor Corp.	Volkswagen AG
Home Country	Italy	United States	South Korea	People's Republic of China	Japan	Germany
Trading Status in the United States	NYSE	NYSE	OTC	OTC	NYSE	OTC
A. Discussion of Mgmt's plans or objectives						
in Annual Report, Form 10K or 20F	x	x	x		x	x
in Interim Report		x				
in Proxy						
B. Quantitative forecasts in Ann'l Report, Form 10K or 20F						
Earnings		x				
Sales			x	x	x	
Capital Expenditures	x			x	x	x
Units to be manufactured		x			x	
Other (earnings of subsidiaries, cash flows, market share)	x					x
C. Quant. Forecasts in Interim Report or Proxy?				Sales, profits	Sales, expenditures, production	Sales, production, profits
D. Disclosure of "softer" forward-looking information						
in Annual Report, Form 10K or 20F	x	x	x	x	x	x
in Interim Report	x	x				
in Proxy or Invitation to Annual General Meeting					x	x

Exhibit 13.15. Disclosures of Forward-Looking Information—Six Auto Companies.

Earnings Prospects

The Volkswagen Group will build further on its success of recent years in 2002. We will greatly expand and renew our continuously improving range of high-quality vehicles, with the aim of entering new segments and further enhancing our position in established segments. Consequently, we again expect to see our share of the world automobile market rise in 2002. We will counter the competitive pressures, as previously, with our strategy of product value retention, and will continue to reject the option of a discount-driven pricing policy.

We also aim to make further progress on the cost side. Measures in this area will extend across the entire process chain, based on a unified IT infrastructure. The focus of the measures will be on development and material costs and the cost of procurement, production and distribution logistics, delivering a boost to productivity, product quality and customer satisfaction.

Earnings development overall will, however, depend on automobile demand in the various market regions. The German and U.S. markets will be key. The downward sales trend in those two countries which took hold in the second half of 2001 still persists. It is not yet possible to forecast whether and when the trend will be reversed. Consequently, no reliable forecast with regard to earnings development can yet be made at present.

Outlook for Volkswagen Passenger Cars

The Volkswagen Passenger Cars brand expects to safeguard its high level of unit sales and achieve further improvements in profits in 2002 despite continuing weak markets, based on continuous optimization of revenues and costs. With a wide product range, the brand will extend its lead over the competition.

Outlook for Volkswagen Commercial Vehicles

2002 profits will be burdened by expenditure on the new model generations. On the other hand, all growth opportunities in international markets in commercial and leisure vehicles will be taken up. The targeted investments in the modernization of the brand's sites will form a sound basis for an attractive, refreshed and expanded product range—for the greater benefit of customers worldwide.

Exhibit 13.16. Excerpts from Volkswagenwerk AG's Annual Report Discussing Financial Prospects.

drastically reduced. Also during 2002, Tyco International Ltd. admitted its failure to disclose information about secret bonus payments (compensation) for top executives, which were compensation-related disclosures required by the U.S. SEC in U.S. companies' proxy statements.[35]

Stock exchange corporate governance disclosure requirements vary dramatically around the world, but are becoming more stringent in many jurisdictions. At one extreme, the U.S SEC, NYSE, and NASDAQ impose stringent corporate governance requirements on domestic listed companies.[36] At the other extreme is the Tokyo

---

[35] See Maremont and Cohen (2002) and *Financial Times* (September 18, 2002).

[36] Within the last two years, the NYSE and NASDAQ have implemented the recommendations contained in the *Report and Recommendations of the Blue Ribbon Committee on Improving the Effectiveness of Corporate Audit Committees* (Blue Ribbon Committee, 1999). In early 2002, Harvey Pitt, the Chairman of the U.S. SEC, requested the U.S. stock exchanges to consider further changes to improve the quality of corporate governance of U.S. companies.

Highlights of Unconsolidated Financial Results for FY 2002 Interim (Six months ended September 30, 2001)

(All financial information has been prepared in accordance with accounting principles generally accepted in Japan)

(Billions of yen unless otherwise specified)

	FY2001 Interim	FY2002 Interim		FY2002 Forecast (Apr. 2001 through Mar. 2002)		
	(Apr. 2000 through Sep. 2000)	(Apr. 2001 through Sep. 2001)	% of change from previous interim	Revised Forecast	% of change from FY2001	Initial forecast
Domestic vehicle production (Thousand units)	1,637	1,644	0.5%	3,420	–0.1%	3,390
Overseas vehicle production (Thousand units)	874	890	1.9%	1,820	3.9%	1,890
Domestic vehicle sales (Thousand units)	835	850	1.8%	1,820	0.2%	1,890
Exports (Thousand units)	866	824	–4.8%	1,680	–1.4%	1,580
Net sales	3,708.7	4,011.9	8.2%	8,200.0	3.8%	8,000.0
Domestic	1,682.3	1,767.3	5.1%			
Export	2,026.4	2,244.5	10.8%			
Operating income <Income ratio>	191.3 <5.2%>	354.2 <8.8%>	85.1%	660.0 <8.0%>	30.2%	610.0
Ordinary income <Income ratio>	226.7 <6.1%>	347.1 <8.7%>	53.0%	660.0 <8.0%>	6.2%	630.0
Income before income taxes <Income ratio>	171.6 <4.6%>	347.1 <8.7%>	102.3%	660.0 <8.0%>	17.4%	630.0
Net income <Income ratio>	104.3 <2.8%>	203.5 <5.1%>	95.0%	380.0 <4.6%>	13.9%	370.0
Factors contributing to increases and decreases in operating income		Operating income increased by 162.9 billion yen (Increase) Effects of exchange rate fluctuations 150.0 Cost reduction efforts 90.0 Impact from sales 10.0 (Decrease) Increases in R&D and IT related expenses, etc. –87.1		Operating income is expected to increase by 153.2 billion yen (Increase) Effects of exchange rate fluctuations 230.0 Cost reduction efforts 190.0 (Decrease) Impact from sales –70.0 Increases in R&D and IT related expenses, etc. –196.8		
Exchange rates	¥107/US$ ¥99/Euro	¥122/US$ ¥108/Euro		¥121/US$ ¥106/Euro		¥115/US$ ¥105/Euro
Capital investment	83.2	81.8		250.0		240.0
Depreciation expenses	136.8	131.6		260.0		260.0
R&D expenses	201.2	226.7		490.0		460.0
Interest-bearing debt	514.1	514.7				
Performance evaluation		Increases in sales and ordinary income				
Number of employees	65,907	65,029				

Exhibit 13.17. Forecast Disclosure Published by Toyota Motor Corporation.

Stock Exchange, whose only corporate governance requirement is related to the independence of *internal* auditors.[37]

Governance became an issue in the United States in the 1980s during a period of extensive corporate restructuring. Often the impact of corporate reorganization was profound, with protracted take-over battles, sale and closing of business units, extensive layoffs, and so on. Many conflicts among shareholders, creditors, and managers arose. Corporate boards, institutional investors, stock exchange regulators and the public began to examine their roles in the strategic decision-making process of corporations.

In the United Kingdom, the creation of the Cadbury Committee, the first group to draft governance guidelines, was a consequence of serious mismanagement in a number of Britain's large firms. Cadbury's recommendations focused on the function of boards, and in the United Kingdom, listed companies now face stringent disclosure requirements concerning corporate governance.

Continental Europe has been becoming more investor-oriented in recent years due to privatizations, pension reform, economic expansion, the success of the European Monetary Union, and increasing involvement by individual investors. Continental European companies have voluntarily started to increase their disclosure levels and improve their financial reporting to attract new capital and increase investor interest. However, many Continental European companies, including some of the world's largest, remain secretive, make misleading disclosures, and retain anti-investor rules.

In emerging financial markets such as Brazil, corporate governance has become critically important because weak corporate governance and inadequate disclosure have been linked to financial crises. Many have argued that the Asian financial crisis of 1997–1998 in part reflected weaknesses in corporate governance throughout East Asia.

Exhibit 13.18 presents a summary of corporate governance disclosures made in annual and interim reports and annual general meeting materials published by the six auto companies. As with other disclosures examined in this chapter, the six companies vary widely in their disclosures. The most important observation from the exhibit is that of the six companies surveyed, the three companies listed in the United States (Fiat, Ford, and Toyota) provide the most detailed disclosure, in conformance with SEC requirements.

13.10 INTERNET DISCLOSURE

(a) Overview and Regulatory Initiatives. Technology advances have revolutionized information dissemination and business management, so that businesses and consumers now have access to much more information than ever before. The World Wide Web increasingly is being used to disseminate information, with print-based media often playing a secondary role. Electronic information dissemination often is less ex-

---

[37]Beim and Calomiris (2001) argue that corporate governance can be evaluated only in the context of corporate goals, and these vary. The primary models of corporate governance found around the world are: State ownership and control, Family ownership and control, Bank-centered control systems, and Control by dispersed shareholders. In the United States, most agree that the goal of private enterprise is to maximize shareholder value. However, in much of Continental Europe, there has been concern for the welfare of employees. Germany, for example, institutionalizes employee goals in corporate governance with its policy of *Mitbestimmung*, under which unions have a right to several seats on large corporate boards.

	Fiat S.p.A.	Ford Motor Company	Hyundai Motor Company	Jiangling Motors Corp.	Toyota Motor Corp.	Volkswagen AG
Home Country	Italy	United States	South Korea	People's Republic of China	Japan	Germany
Trading Status in the United States	NYSE	NYSE	OTC	OTC	NYSE	OTC
A. Directors and Senior Management						
Company Directors						
1. Names of company directors	20F, ARS, Int Rep	Proxy, 10Q, ARS, AGM	AGM (limited information)	ARS, Int Rep	AGM, ARS, 20F, Int Rep	AGM, ARS
2. Business experience of company directors	20F	Proxy, ARS, AGM	AGM-only limited information given—for directors only		20F	
Senior Management						
3. Names of senior managers	20F	Proxy, ARS		ARS, Int	AGM, 20F	ARS
				Rep	ARS, Int Rep	
4. Business experience of senior managers	20F	Proxy, ARS			20F	
5. Functions and areas of experience in the Company (applicable to senior management)	20F	Proxy, ARS		ARS, Int Rep	AGM, 20F	ARS
6. Nature of any family relationship between any directors and senior management						
7. Any arrangements or understanding with major shareholders, customers, suppliers or others, pursuant to which any person referred to above was selected as a director or member of senior management.					20F: "None were appointed pursuant to (such) an arrangement or understanding"	
B. Compensation						
Provide the following information for the last full financial year for the company's directors and members of its administrative, supervisory or management bodies:						

8. Compensation paid and benefits granted	20F	Proxy, 10Q, AGM		ARS	General info. in: 20F	ARS
9. The total amounts set aside or accrued by the company or its subsidiaries to provide pension, retirement or similar benefits.	20F	Proxy, 10Q ARS, AGM				ARS
C. Board Practices						
10. Date of expiration of Directors' current term, and the period during which the person has served in that office.	20F	Beginning dates of terms provided in: Proxy, 10Q, AGM		Dates of terms provided in: ARS	20F	Beginning dates of terms provided in: ARS
11. Details of directors' service contracts with the company		Proxy, 10Q, AGM				
12. Details relating to the company's audit committee and remuneration committee, including the names of committee members and a summary of the terms of reference under which the committee operates	Names provided in: ARS, 20F	Names provided in: Proxy, AGM			Names provided in: AGM, ARS,20F	
D. Share Ownership (Management and Board)						
13. Provide share ownership in the company as of the most recent practicable date (including disclosure on an individual basis of the number of shares and percent of shares outstanding of that class, and whether they have different voting rights) held by the persons listed and options granted to them on the company's shares.	ARS, 20F: "Ownership by directors and senior managers as a group is immaterial."	Proxy, AGM (highly detailed)		ARS	20F	
14. Describe any arrangements for involving the employees in the capital of the company, including any arrangement that involves the issue or grant of options or shares or securities of the company.	Option info. in 20F, ARS	Option info. Available in: Proxy, ARS, AGM	Small amount of option info. Available in: ARS, Int. Rep.		AGM, option info. Available in: ARS, 20F	Option info. In: ARS, AGM

Exhibit 13.18 Corporate Governance Disclosures—Six Auto Companies.

pensive than a print-based medium, and is instantaneous. The Web also allows interactive information dissemination in a manner not possible in print.[38] Securities trading using the Internet has increased the demand for Web-based business and financial reporting. Individual investors increasingly use the Web as an important information source, and to trade and make investment decisions.

Securities regulators recognize the importance of technology in providing investors timely access to company information. For many years, the London Stock Exchange has made press releases filed by listed companies publicly available through its Regulatory News Service. Recently, many other stock exchanges have adopted similar practices. For example, media announcements released by listed companies now are published on the Web sites of Euronext (formerly the Paris, Brussels and Amsterdam stock exchanges), the Italian Exchange and the Johannesburg Stock Exchange.

The U.S. SEC recently issued new rules designed to encourage the dissemination of information electronically, with the goal of increasing investor access to timely company information. Generally, "accelerated filers" are now required to disclose in their Forms 10-K the company's Internet Web site address, if it has one; whether the company makes its periodic and current reports available, free of charge, on its Web site as soon as reasonably practicable after those reports are electronically filed with or furnished to the Commission; and if the company does not make its filing available on its Web site, the reasons it does not do so and whether it will voluntarily provide electronic or paper copies of its filings free of charge upon request.[39]

Regulatory initiatives designed to increase investor access to information published on listed companies' websites are underway in non-U.S. jurisdictions, as well. The European Commission recently began to consider rules on basic ways that information must be made available, such as on the listed companies' Web sites.[40]

(b) eXtensible Business Reporting Language. One important development that will greatly facilitate Web-based reporting is eXtensible Business Reporting Language (XBRL). XBRL is a new medium that allows computer applications—including ERP systems, financial reporting applications and even spreadsheet programs—to "understand" and "re-use" business information in a common yet robust manner. XBRL is the technology that will eliminate much of the ambiguity that is prevalent in business information.[41]

---

[38]See International Accounting Standards Committee, *Business Reporting on the Internet, A Discussion Paper Issued by the IASC Staff.* London: November 1999, 103 pages; Mike Willis, *Corporate Communications for the 21st Century: How E-Business is Redefining the Business Information Supply Chain.* PricewaterhouseCoopers, October 2000; and Samual A. DiPiazza, Jr. and Robert G. Eccles, *Building Public Trust: The Future of Corporate Reporting*, New York: John Wiley & Sons, Inc., 2002.

[39]See U.S. Securities and Exchange Commission Final Rule: Acceleration of Periodic Report Filing Dates and Disclosure Concerning Website Access to Reports, Release No. 34-46464, September 11, 2002 (*www.sec.gov/rules/final/33-8128.htm*), and Thacher, Proffitt, and Wood, *Corporate and Financial Institutions Bulletin, SEC Accelerates Filing Deadlines for Annual and Quarterly Report*, September 19, 2002. An "accelerated filer" is a domestic company reporting with the SEC that has a public float of at least $75 million that has been subject to the Exchange Act's reporting requirements for at least 12 calendar months and that previously has filed at least one annual report.

[40]For discussion, refer to the Commission's Europa Web site at: *http://europa.eu.int/comm/internal_market/en/finances/mobil/transparency/htm*, and the European Commission Internal Market DG's "Seeking Common Ground on Market Information Requirements," *Single Market News*, June 2002.

[41]See Ramin and Prather (2002), Ramin (2000); and Zarowin and Harding (2000).

Staunch supporters of this universal business language include the AICPA and the International Accounting Standards Committee Foundation (IASCF), both of whom recognize the tremendous benefits that a standardized digital financial reporting protocol will bring to the business world. Many other firms and organizations understand the advantages of having a single widely-used standard that provides clear data definitions. They support XBRL by actively participating in XBRL International (*www.xbrl.org*), the organization that coordinates XBRL efforts worldwide.

The strength of XBRL is its simple approach: Tag the information that is commonly used in business reporting in a way with which computer applications can work. The IASCF, for example, has assigned XBRL "tags" to the International Accounting Standards. The IASB concept of "Property, Plant and Equipment" in XBRL is <PropertyPlantEquipment>; the brackets allow an application to "read" the XBRL tag (see Exhibits 13.19 and 13.20). When entity-specific information, such as

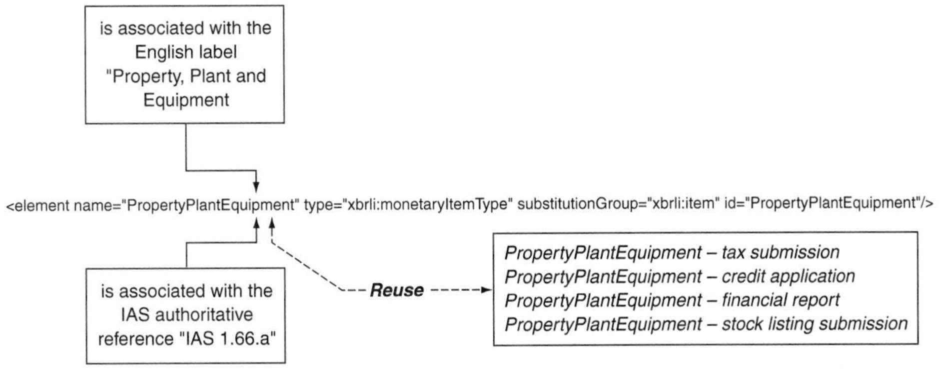

Exhibit 13.19 IAS Information "Tagged" in XBRL.

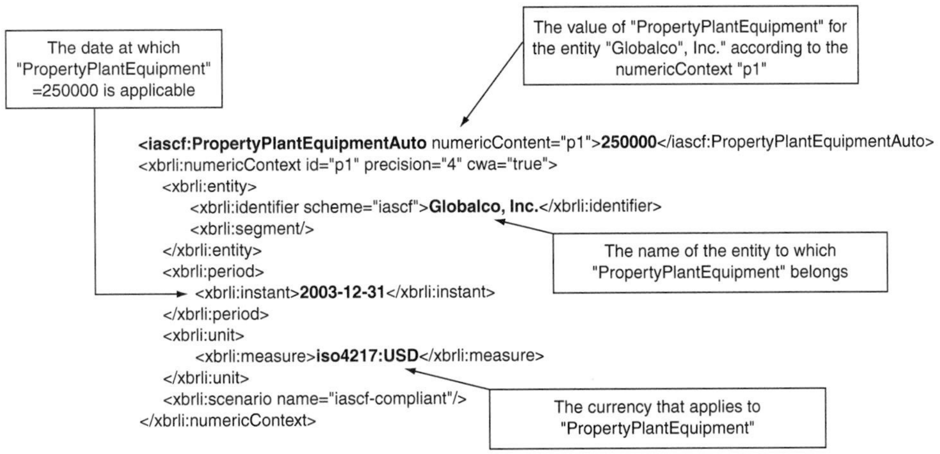

Exhibit 13.20 An Entity Reporting IAS Information in an XBRL Report.

"Globalco, Inc.", "US Dollars", "250,000" and "December 31, 2003", accompanies the XBRL tag, this creates reusable business information that can be consolidated and deconsolidated and aggregated and de-aggregated. Mapping an entity's quantitative data to the appropriate XBRL tags will undoubtedly enhance the overall transparency of financial disclosures.

(c) Survey of Auto Companies' Internet Disclosures. Our survey of auto companies' Web based disclosures strongly supports the view that the World Wide Web is now a critical method of information dissemination.

Exhibit 13.21 presents a tabular summary of information available from the Web sites of Fiat, Ford, Hyundai, Jiangling, Toyota, and Volkswagen. It shows that all of the companies except Jiangling make extensive information available on their Web sites, including press releases, information from analyst meetings and presentations, and information for shareholders (related to the annual general meeting), as well as providing access to periodic financial reports (including SEC filings). Exhibit 13.22 presents a qualitative comparison of information about the Web sites.

13.11 SUMMARY AND IMPLICATIONS FOR FINANCIAL STATEMENT USERS AND MANAGERS. The discussion and illustrations in this chapter have important implications for financial statement users and for corporate managers responsible for financial reporting and disclosure. First, it appears that global standards in financial reporting are developing. Up to only a few years ago, many jurisdictions (including France, Germany, and Japan) did not require such financial disclosures as those related to cash flows and segments. Managers at many large multinational companies did not think that the benefits of disclosing such information would justify the costs. Now, most countries require such disclosures.

Vast differences in mandatory disclosure for listed companies remain. For example, U.S. financial statement users should not expect all "world-class" non-U.S. companies to disclose "sensitive" information, such as details about directors and corporate officers' compensation and share ownership. Such disclosures simply are not required in many jurisdictions outside the United States, where it is generally believed that the potential costs to companies in making such disclosures outweigh the capital market benefits of making the disclosures. The high cost of disclosure continues to persuade many non-U.S. companies to stay out of U.S. capital markets.

Empirical evidence supports the view that increased disclosure improves the market liquidity of a company's shares. It is widely accepted that managers who decide to provide enhanced disclosures in areas considered important to investors and analysts might obtain a competitive advantage over firms with narrower disclosure policies. Further study of the costs and benefits of enhanced disclosure in international settings should provide important evidence in this area.

To know what to expect a company to disclose and to understand managers' disclosure incentives, one must be familiar with the (global) capital markets in which the company operates, its ownership structure, and the corporate finance and governance characteristics of its home market. Therefore, financial statement users should continue to expect wide variation in disclosure levels, financial reporting practices, and free availability of information on company Web sites.

	Fiat S.p.A.	Ford Motor Company	Hyundai Motor Company	Jiangling Motors Corp.	Toyota Motor Corp.	Volkswagen AG
Home Country	Italy	United States	South Korea	People's Republic of China	Japan	Germany
Trading Status in the United States	NYSE	NYSE	OTC	OTC	NYSE	OTC
English Language Investor Relations Page	Yes	Yes	Yes	—	Yes	Yes
Periodic Financial Reports						
Annual Reports	Yes	Yes	Yes	—	Yes	Yes
Interim Reports	Yes	Yes	Yes	—	Yes	Yes
Forms 10K, 10Q, 20F, 6K, if applicable	Yes	Link Provided	Not Applic.	Not Applic.	—	Not Applic.
Special Information for Shareholders						
Notice of Annual General Meeting and Related Information	Yes	Yes	—	—	—	Date Given
Results of Annual General Meeting	—	—	Yes	—	—	Yes
Press Releases—Date range available	9/15/01–9/14/02	10/2/01–9/9/02	3/29/99–9/2/02	—	1/26/00–9/10/02	11/24/00–9/6/02
Analyst Meetings and Presentations						
Webcasts	Yes	Yes	—	—	Yes	Yes
Presentation Slides	Yes	—	—	—	Yes	Yes
Additional Textual Information	Yes	Yes	—	—	—	—

Exhibit 13.21. Corporate Disclosures (English Language) Available on Company Web Sites.

Fiat S.p.A

www.fiatgroup.com/eng/finanza.ef9finanza.htm

The Fiat Group's Web site is comprehensive. It provides financial press releases going back to September 15, 2001, notices of Annual General Meetings, shareholder reports and official filings. It also has a comprehensive section of webcasts and presentations.

Ford Motor Company

www.ford.com/en/ourCompany/investorInformation/default.htm

Ford's investor relations Web site lacks only one section—presentation slides—found on the Fiat Group site. Ford provides a wealth of financial data for shareholders and links to SEC documents. The section containing webcasts is relatively small.

Hyundai

www.hyundai-motor.com/eng/investment/index.html

Hyundai provides a fair amount of financial data, but not the Notice of Annual General Meeting. Its archive of news and press releases goes back to early 1999. Hyundai does not give shareholders information about analyst meetings or presentation slides.

Jiangling

www.jiangling.com

Jiangling does not provide English-language information on its Web site.

Toyota

http://global.toyota.com/ir.html

Toyota's investor relations Web site ranks fairly well for comprehensiveness and archived information, but has no official filings. Press releases go back to 2000. One must download 12 separate files to recreate Toyota's annual report in PDF format. Toyota archives webcasts for 30 days and keeps presentation slides available for download.

Volkswagen

http://ir.volkswagen-ir.de/english/default.asp

Volkswagen has a very well-done site complete with annual reports, interim reports, and dates for upcoming shareholder events. Volkswagen also provides information about the results of annual meetings. Press releases go back to late 2000, and Volkswagen provides webcast archives of recent meetings and presentation materials from shareholder meetings and roadshows.

Exhibit 13.22. Qualitative Comparison of Information Available on Company Websites.

SOURCES AND SUGGESTED REFERENCES

"UK Companies Fearful of Sarbanes-Oxley Obligations." *Accountancy*, September, 2002, p. 20.

"Accounting Crisis." *Accountancy*, August 2002, p. 13.

"Chasing the Goalposts." *Accountancy*, May 2002, pp. 57–58.

Adhikari, A., and R. H. Tondkar. "Environmental Factors Influencing Accounting Disclosure Requirements of Global Stock Exchanges." *Journal of International Financial Management and Accounting*, Summer 1992, pp. 75–105.

Ali, A., and L. S. Hwang. "Country-Specific Factors Related to Financial Reporting and the Value Relevance of Accounting Data." *Journal of Accounting Research*, Spring 2000, pp. 1–21.

Amihud, Y., and H. Mendelson. "Asset Pricing and the Bid-Ask Spread." *Journal of Financial Economics*, 1986, pp. 223–249.

Amihud, Y., and H. Mendelson. "The Effects of Beta, Bid-Ask Spread, Residual Risk, and Size on Stock Returns." *Journal of Finance*, June 1989, pp. 479–487.

Ball, R., S. P. Kothari, and A. Robin. "The Effect of International Institutional Factors on Properties of Accounting Earnings." *Journal of Accounting and Economics*, 2000, pp. 1–51.

Beattie, Alan. "Corporate Scandals Will Cost the U.S. $35bn." *Financial Times*, September 5, 2002, p. 4.

Beim, D. O., and C. W. Calomaris. *Emerging Financial Markets*. Boston: McGraw-Hill Irwin, 2001.

Blue Ribbon Committee on Improving the Effectiveness of Corporate Audit Committees. *Report and Recommendations of the Blue Ribbon Committee on Improving the Effectiveness of Corporate Audit Committees*, 1999.

Botosan, C. A. "Disclosure Level and the Cost of Equity Capital." *The Accounting Review*, July 1997, pp. 323–349.

Botosan, C. A., and C. A. Frost. "Regulation, Disclosure and Market Liquidity (An Examination of Foreign Issuers in Regulated versus Less-regulated U.S. Equity Markets)." Washington University and Dartmouth College Working Paper, January 1999.

Bruce, Robert. "Europeans Protest over U.S. Fraud Law." *Financial Times*, September 15, 2002, *www.FT.com.*

Buckingham, Christina."After the Gold Rush." *Accountancy*, February 2001, p. 39.

Bushman, R., J. Piotroski, and A. Smith. "What Determines Corporate Transparency?" Working paper, University of Chicago and University of North Carolina, 2001.

Chang, J., T. Khanna, and K. Palepu. "Analyst Activity Around the World." Working paper, Harvard University and University of Pennsylvania, 2000.

Choi, F. D. S., C. A. Frost, and G. K. Meek. *International Accounting*, 4th ed. Upper Saddle River, NJ: Prentice Hall, 2002.

Coffee, John C., Jr. "Competition Among Securities Markets: A Path Dependent Perspective." Columbia Law School, The Center for Law and Economic Studies working paper, April 2002.

Cox, James D. "Regulatory Duopoly in U.S. Securities Markets." *Columbia Law Review*, Vol. 99, 1999.

Diamond, D. W., and R. E. Verrecchia. "Disclosure, Liquidity, and the Cost of Capital." *Journal of Finance*, September 1991, pp. 1325–1359.

DiPiazza, Jr., Samual A., and Robert G. Eccles. *Building Public Trust: The Future of Corporate Reporting*. New York: John Wiley & Sons, Inc., 2002.

European Commission, Internal Market DG. "Seeking Common Ground on Market Information Requirements: Commission Consults Regulators, Stock Issuers and Investors." *Single Market News*, No. 29, June 2002, p. 12.

"Tyco Reveals Kozlowski's Long Litany of Excesses." *Financial Times*, September 18, 2002, p. 13.

"Europe Plans Big Shake-Up for Stock Exchanges." *Financial Times*, September 27, 2002, p. 1.

Fox, Merritt B. "The Securities Globalization Disclosure Debate." The University of Michigan Law School working paper, April 2000.

Fox, Merritt B. "Required Disclosure and Corporate Governance." *Law and Contemporary Problems*, Summer 1999, pp. 113–127.

Francis, J. R., I. K. Khurana, and R. Pereira. "Investor Protection Laws, Accounting and Auditing Around the World." University of Missouri-Columbia working paper, October 2001.

Frost, C. A. "Characteristics and Information Value of Corporate Disclosures of Forward-

Looking Information in Global Equity Markets." Global Capital Markets Access LLC and Dartmouth College Center for Asia and Emerging Economies working paper, August 2002.

Frost, C. A. *Stock Exchange Disclosure Systems: A Comparative Analysis of 50 Member Exchanges of the FIBV—International Federation of Stock Exchanges*. Paris, France: FIBV, 1999.

Frost, C. A. "Disclosure Policy Choices of U.K. Firms Receiving Modified Audit Reports." *Journal of Accounting and Economics*, Vol. 23, 1997, pp. 163–187.

Frost, Carol A., and Howard L. Blum, III. "International Corporate Disclosure and Equity Market Consequences: An Analysis of Eight Automobile Companies." Global Capital Markets Access LLC and Tuck School of Business at Dartmouth Center for Asia and Emerging Economies working paper, October 2002.

Frost, Carol A., Elizabeth Gordon, and Andrew Hayes. "Stock Exchange Disclosure and Market Liquidity:An Analysis of 50 International Exchanges." Rutgers University, Ohio State University, Dartmouth College Center for Asia and Emerging Economies, and Global Capital Markets Access LLC working paper, October 2002.

Frost, Carol A., and Kurt Ramin. "Corporate Financial Disclosure: A Global Assessment." In Choi, F.D.S. (ed.), *International Accounting and Finance Handbook, Second Edition*. New York: John Wiley and Sons, 1997.

Frost, Carol A., and Kurt Ramin. "Global Trends in Corporate Disclosure: Implications for Financial Statement Users." Global Capital Markets LLC and Tuck School of Business at Dartmouth College working paper, September 2002.

Healy, P. M., and K. G. Palepu. "The Effect of Firms' Financial Disclosure Strategies on Stock Prices." *Accounting Horizons*, March 1993, pp. 1–11.

Healy, P. M., A. Hutton, and K. G. Palepu. "Information Asymmetry, Corporate Disclosure, and the Capital Markets: A Review of the Empirical Disclosure Literature." *Journal of Accounting and Economics*, Vol. 31, 2001, pp. 405–440.

Healy, P. M., A. Hutton, and K. G. Palepu. "Stock Performance and Intermediation Changes Surrounding Sustained Increases in Disclosure." *Contemporary Accounting Research*, Vol. 16, 1999, pp. 485–520.

Hope, O. "Accounting Policy Disclosures and Analysts' Forecasts." Contemporary Accounting Research, Vol. 20, forthcoming in 2003.

Hung, M. "Accounting Standards and Value Relevance of Financial Statements: An International Analysis." *Journal of Accounting & Economics*, Vol. 30, 2000, pp. 401–420.

Ibison, David, and Adrian Michaels. "Japan Pushes for U.S. Company Act Exemption." *Financial Times*, September 25, 2002.

International Accounting Standards Committee. "Business Reporting on the Internet, A Discussion Paper Issued by the IASC Staff." London: November 1999, 103 pages.

International Organization of Securities Commissions, Objectives and Principles of Securities Regulation. February 2002, *www.iosco.org*, 66 pages.

Jacobson, R., and D. Aaker. "Myopic Management Behavior with Efficient, but Imperfect, Financial Markets." *Journal of Accounting and Economics*, October 1993, pp. 383–405.

Johnson, Jo. "Regulator Seizes Messier Messages." *Financial Times*, September 11, 2002, p. 16.

King, R., G. Pownall, and G. Waymire. "Expectations Adjustment Via Timely Management Forecasts: Review, Synthesis and Suggestions for Future Research." *Journal of Accounting Literature*, 1990, pp. 113–144.

Kinney, Jr., William R. *Information Quality Assurance and Internal Control for Management Decision Making*. Boston: Irwin McGraw-Hill: 2000.

La Porta, R., F. Lopez-de-Silanes, A. Shleifer, and R. W. Vishny. "Legal Determinants of External Finance." *Journal of Finance*, July 1997, pp. 1131–1150.

Lennox, C. "Self-Serving Disclosures by Chairpersons of Failing UK Companies." *Asia-Pacific Journal of Accounting and Economics* Vol. 8, 2001, pp. 63–81.

Leuz, C., and R. Verrecchia. "The Economic Consequences of Increased Disclosure." *Journal of Accounting Research*, Supplement 2000, pp. 91–124.

Lewellen, Wilbur G., Taewoo Park, and Byung T. Ro. "Self-serving Behavior in Managers'

Discretionary Information Disclosure Decisions." *Journal of Accounting and Economics*, April 1996, pp. 227–251.

Maremont, Mark, and Laurie P. Cohen. "Tyco Probe Expands to Include Auditor PricewaterhouseCoopers." *The Wall Street Journal*, September 30, 2002, A1, A12.

Meier, R. T. *Benchmarking Analysis of Stock Exchange Trading (With the FIBV Model of Stock Exchange Excellence)*. Paris/Zurich: FIBV—International Federation of Stock Exchanges, September 1998.

Organization for Economic Cooperation and Development. "Background and Issues Paper for the OECD Symposium on the Role of Disclosure in Strengthening Corporate Governance." February 12–13, 1998a.

Organization for Economic Cooperation and Development. "Background and Issues Paper for the OECD Symposium on the Role of Disclosure in Strengthening Corporate Governance." OECD, February 12–13, 1998b.

Palmiero, Teresa, and Jacqueline Grosch Lobo (eds.). *The Euromoney Guide to World Equity Markets 2002*. London: Euromoney Books, 2002.

Ramin, Kurt P., and David A. Prather. "Fair Values." *Business Excellence for the Intellectual Capital Investor*, Vol. 1, Summer 2000, pp. 13–15.

Ramin, Kurt P. "Building an XBRL IFRS Taxonomy: New Tools for Corporate Reporting." *IASB Insight*, October 2002.

Romano, Roberta. "Empowering Investors: A Market Approach to Securities Regulation." *The Yale Law Journal*, Vol. 107, June 1998, pp. 2359–2430.

Romano, Roberta. "The Need for Competition in International Securities Regulation." *Theoretical Inquiries in Law*, Vol. 2, July 2001, pp. 387–562.

Securities and Investments Board. *Regulation of the United Kingdom Equity Markets—Discussion Paper*. London: 1994.

Thacher Proffitt & Wood. *SEC Accelerates Filing Deadlines for Annual and Quarterly Reports*. Corporate and Financial Institutions Bulletin, September 19, 2002.

U.S. Securities and Exchange Commission (SEC). *Internationalization of the Securities Markets: Report of the Staff of the U.S. Securities and Exchange Commission to the Senate Committee on Banking, Housing and Urban Affairs and the House Committee on Energy and Commerce*. Washington, D.C., July 17, 1987.

U.S. Securities and Exchange Commission Final Rule: Acceleration of Periodic Report Filing Dates and Disclosure Concerning Website Access to Reports, Release No. 34-46464, September 11, 2002, *www.sec.gov/rules/final/33-8128.htm*).

Wassener, Bettina. "Porsche Pulls NY Listing Plan." *Financial Times*, October 17, 2002, p. 19.

Welker, M. "Disclosure Policy, Information Asymmetry, and Liquidity in Equity Markets." *Contemporary Accounting Research*, Spring 1995, pp. 801–827.

Willis, Mike. *Corporate Communications for the 21st Century: How E-Business is Redefining the Business Information Supply Chain*. PricewaterhouseCoopers, 2000.

Zarowin, Stanley, and Wayne E. Harding. "Finally, Business Talks the Same Language." *Journal of Accountancy*, August 2000, pp. 24–30.

CHAPTER 14

GLOBALIZATION OF WORLD FINANCIAL MARKETS: PERSPECTIVE OF THE U.S. SECURITIES AND EXCHANGE COMMISSION

Sara Hanks

Clifford Chance

CONTENTS

14.1 INTRODUCTION. Why should a handbook on international finance and accounting include an in-depth discussion of only one regulatory agency? The easy answer is that the U.S. Securities and Exchange Commission (SEC or the Commission) is the largest regulator of securities markets in the world and that it oversees the accounting disclosure of corporations in the world's largest and most liquid single capital market. Moreover, it oversees standards that have traditionally been considered the most thorough, and arguably the most burdensome. This is not the only reason, however. Because of the rigor of its standards and the importance of the markets it oversees, the SEC has been intrinsically involved in every attempt to promote global standards, every effort to make the international capital markets more accessible to all issuers, and every discussion of what investors who depend on financial statements really need.

14.2 FUNCTION AND ORGANIZATION. The SEC was founded in 1934 to administer the federal securities legislation introduced in 1933 and 1934 after the Wall Street crash of 1929. It is an independent agency rather than a department of the U.S. government, which means that the White House does not have the same influence over the Commission's policies as it does over, for example, the Commerce Department. The Administration does, however, appoint the five commissioners of the SEC to five-year terms of office. All commissioners are subject to Senate confirmation, and Congress additionally exercises supervision of the Commission, among other things, by having control of its budget.

The SEC has four principal operating divisions, with numerous support and specialist offices. The largest division is the Division of Corporation Finance, which reviews disclosure documents filed by domestic and foreign issuers. The Division of Market Regulation deals with the conduct of trading on the secondary securities markets and the regulation of broker dealers. The Division of Investment Management regulates the management of investment companies or mutual funds and the offering of securities by such institutions. The Division of Enforcement investigates violations of securities laws and regulations. The Office of the Chief Accountant develops policies on accounting issues. The Office of the General Counsel is the Commission's chief legal office and represents the Commission in judicial and legislative matters. Through these divisions and offices, the SEC regulates all aspects of capital raising through the sale of securities in the United States and the conduct of intermediaries in the U.S. securities markets.

The capital raising process in the United States, which is the primary focus of this chapter, is regulated by the SEC on the basis of "full disclosure," rather than by applying "merit regulation," which is the case in many U.S. states (which also regulate securities offerings) and foreign countries; that is, rather than reviewing disclosure documents in order to ascertain whether a particular offering is a good investment or not, the SEC permits investors to make up their own minds as to the merits of an offering and concentrates on whether all information material to such investors is set forth in the disclosure document. Provided that all information that an investor needs in order to make an informed investment decision is made public (through the SEC's registration and prospectus delivery requirements), the SEC permits even securities representing dubious investments to be offered to the public. This in part accounts for the emphasis that the Commission places on the provision of financial information and compliance with auditing standards. In fact, SEC staff often refer to financial disclosure requirements and accounting standards as being "at the heart" of the full disclosure program. If an investor is to be able to make an informed investment decision, it is essential that he or she be able to compare alternative investment opportunities. Thus, meaningful comparison depends on accounting standards being as complete as possible.

It should be noted that the SEC's full disclosure requirements apply principally to public offerings. The Commission cannot directly influence disclosures made to potential investors in private offerings to sophisticated investors, which are not subject to the SEC registration process. It is noticeable, however, that disclosure practices in private placements made pursuant to Rule 144A, discussed in section 14.5(b)(ii), are heavily influenced by disclosure practices in the U.S. public markets.

(a) Division of Corporation Finance. When a public offering is made in the United States, the issuer of the securities generally is required under the Securities Act of 1933 (the Securities Act) to file a registration statement with the SEC. This comprises the prospectus or offering circular and other documents regarding the issuer or the offering, such as important contracts, the underwriting agreement, and indentures relating to the securities offered, which are not part of the prospectus but which are required to be provided to the SEC as exhibits. The entire registration statement, including exhibits, is available for public inspection. Each registration statement is subject to review by both attorneys and accountants in the Division of Corporation Finance. Nearly half of the division's review staff is made up of accountants. The reviewers note any deficiencies and request further information, clarification, or amendment to the registration statement by means of "comment letters" to the issuer or its counsel. When the staff is satisfied that all material disclosure has been made, the registration statement is "declared effective" and the securities described in it can be sold (offers, but not sales, may be made as soon as the registration statement is filed).

The staff of the division also reviews, in a similar way, the periodic disclosure documents required by the Securities Exchange Act of 1934 (the Exchange Act) of all issuers that have securities listed on a U.S. securities exchange, that have made a recent public offering, or that have a certain number of shareholders. The Division of Corporation Finance additionally reviews proxy solicitations, trust indentures relating to publicly offered debt securities, and the conduct of tender offers (including the disclosure made in such offers and the substantive rights granted to offerees).

Within the division, the Office of International Corporate Finance deals with issues that arise in connection with offerings by foreign issuers in the United States and offerings made outside the United States by issuers with links to the jurisdiction. It is this office together with the division's chief accountant, and head of accounting operations, that is principally involved when accommodations must be made to permit foreign issuers to make offerings in the United States or to permit multinational offerings to take place without undue interference by the SEC. Accommodations to foreign issuers may be made either through formal rules adopted by the Commission or on a case-by-case basis through informal waivers or "no-action letters" (in which the SEC staff, without expressing a legal conclusion, agrees not to recommend enforcement action if an offering is conducted in a specified way).

Where accommodations to foreign issuers involve accounting issues, the chief accountant of the Division of Corporation Finance will also become involved. Despite the similarity of names, this individual is different from the Commission's chief accountant or any staff in the Office of the Chief Accountant. The division's chief accountant is concerned with implementation of the policies developed by the Office of the Chief Accountant.

(b) Office of the Chief Accountant. The Office of the Chief Accountant is concerned more with the development of accounting policy than with its application to specific companies' disclosure documents, which function is performed by the Division of Corporation Finance, as discussed above. The Chief Accountant's office is also responsible for issues relating to the independence and qualifications of accountants and auditors practicing before the Commission, including foreign accountants and auditors.

14.3 RELATIONSHIP WITH U.S. ACCOUNTING BODIES. The method used for establishing accounting principles and standards differs from country to country. Accounting standards, for the most part, are established either by governmental bodies, by private standard-setting bodies, or by a combination of the two. Different approaches to standard setting may be the result of legal, cultural, political, or economic differences among countries.

Generally, if corporate ownership in a country is concentrated in the hands of only a few institutional investors and small family businesses predominate in the country, accounting standards will be set mainly by governmental agencies, because there is no need for a comprehensive or sophisticated financial reporting system. In a country where corporate ownership is diverse, however, the need for a sophisticated financial reporting system increases, and, correspondingly, the influence of the private sector, through the accounting professions, usually becomes greater.

The standard-setting process in the United States, where corporate ownership is diverse, is a clear illustration of private-sector standard setting. Although the government, through the SEC, does have the authority to establish accounting standards, U.S. generally accepted accounting principles, (U.S. GAAP), are principally set by the private sector. These standards are currently set by the Financial Accounting Standards Board (FASB). The SEC has historically recognized and relied on the FASB's authority to promulgate accounting standards and generally refrains from prescribing accounting methods to be used in the presentation of financial statements.

The SEC first established this policy of looking to the private sector to establish accounting principles and standards in Accounting Series Release (ASR) No. 4, dated April 25, 1938. An ASR is an interpretive release issued by the SEC to develop uniform standards and practices in connection with major accounting questions. In ASR No. 4, the SEC stated that any financial statements prepared in accordance with accounting principles for which there is no authoritative support will be considered misleading.

As a result, the Committee on Accounting Procedure of the American Institute of Accountants (now the American Institute of Certified Public Accountants, or AICPA) began to issue pronouncements known as Accounting Research Bulletins (ARBs). This committee's effectiveness began to be questioned, however, and, as a result, the Accounting Principles Board (APB), which functioned under the guidance of the AICPA, was created in 1959. The APB functioned until 1972, when the FASB, an independent accounting standard-setting body, was established. The establishment of the FASB was supported by the SEC in ASR No. 150 (December 20, 1973), in which the SEC stated that principles, standards, and practices promulgated by the FASB in its Statements and Interpretations would be considered by the Commission as having substantial authoritative support and those contrary to such FASB promulgations would be considered to have no such support. In 1984, the FASB established the Governmental Accounting Standards Board (GASB) to set standards for state and local governmental accounting and reporting, but the FASB remains the key standard setter.

The FASB is a seven-member body which is the operating part of a larger body, including both the Financial Accounting Foundation and the Financial Accounting Standards Advisory Council. The process by which accounting standards are promulgated by the FASB is very similar to the rulemaking procedures employed by governmental agencies. This is because the FASB's Rules of Procedure require it to follow a process that is based on the Administrative Procedures Act (which governs the SEC's conduct) and is open to public observation and accommodation.

For major projects, the board typically appoints an advisory task force of outside experts and studies existing literature on the subject. In addition, the FASB conducts or commissions any additional research that is needed on the subject. A "Discussion Memorandum" may then be published. The purpose of the Discussion Memorandum is to define the problem and the scope of the accounting and reporting issues involved, to discuss any relevant literature and research findings, and to present some possible solutions to the issue under consideration and describe the implications of each proposed solution. The Discussion Memorandum then serves as the basis for both written comments and oral presentations at public hearings.

Once written comments have been received and public hearings have been held, the FASB circulates an "Exposure Draft," which sets forth the new proposed standards of financial accounting and reporting with a proposed effective date and explanation of the board's conclusions. After the exposure draft has been circulated, an additional comment period, generally at least 60 days, is provided.

Throughout this standard-setting process, the meetings of the FASB are open to the public and a public record is kept. For smaller projects, the procedures employed by the FASB are less extensive; for example, there may be no task force or public hearings.

Although the SEC, for the most part, relies on the accounting standards promulgated by the FASB, the SEC also significantly influences the standard-setting process by overseeing the private sector's efforts to establish accounting standards; for example, the SEC staff consults regularly with the FASB staff concerning any opinions or concerns which it may have and meets regularly to review the FASB's agenda and discuss items of mutual interest. Every project on the FASB's agenda is assigned to an SEC staff member. That staff member follows developments in the FASB project, reviews comments received by the FASB concerning the project, attends FASB meetings and public hearings throughout the project, and confers regularly with the FASB staff. Additionally, a senior staff member of the SEC's Office of the Chief Accountant ordinarily serves as an observer on each task force commissioned by the FASB. As a result of these procedures, the SEC is involved to some extent in most steps of the standard-setting process.

At times, guidance on an accounting issue may be needed more quickly than the FASB can respond. In circumstances such as these, the SEC will usually take action to encourage uniformity or comparability in reporting among companies until the FASB has time to address the issue. Such actions by the SEC are usually intended to be temporary measures taken until the private sector can fully address the issue and resolve it appropriately.

Since 1984, additional guidance on new accounting issues has been provided by the Emerging Issues Task Force (EITF) of the FASB. The EITF addresses, within the framework of existing generally accepted accounting principles, accounting issues not covered by current standards. EITF consists of 13 voting members from major and regional accounting firms and large corporations. It meets six times a year to tackle complex existing or new issues arising in the accounting industry. SEC and AICPA representatives attend its meetings as observers. In fact, the SEC's chief Accountant is a regular observer with privilege of the floor. The SEC's Chief Accountant has stated that the Commission will challenge accounting that differs from a consensus position adopted by the EITF. Issues before the EITF are resolved by consensus of the members of the task force. A consensus is considered to exist if no more than two of the 13 voting members object to a proposed solution. If no consensus exists, the Chief Accountant is left to implement his or her own views. Prior to 1988, EITF consensuses were not published. However, in 1988, FASB began publishing the highly condensed summaries of the issues and their resolutions. These summaries are provided as a public service because the outcome of the EITF meetings are not necessarily the opinion of the majority of the board. However, these consensuses may be followed with respect to SEC filings as long as the Office of the Chief Accountant does not have a serious objection to the consensus.

While the FASB is currently the sole entity to which the SEC looks for U.S. GAAP accounting standards, there is no statutory requirement that this remain the case. As indicated earlier in this section, the FASB is a successor to two former entities upon which the SEC relied for accounting standards. At the time of writing, and especially with respect to some highly publicized corporate failures, such as that of Enron, the SEC has been critical of the efficiency and responsiveness of the FASB. Although it is unlikely that the FASB will be replaced, reforms are likely. In addition, the SEC may eventually begin to rely upon additional standard setters in the quest for acceptable international accounting standards, although currently there are no other entities constituted in such a way that the SEC could rely on them as it relies on the FASB.

The SEC itself also influences the promulgation of accounting standards by taking rulemaking initiatives which supplant accounting standards, implementing financial disclosure requirements, establishing independence criteria for accountants, bringing enforcement actions which encourage registrants and accountants to consider accounting issues with greater care, and identifying potential accounting issues through the review and comment process discussed above.

Additionally, the SEC's Regulation S-X also establishes the form and content of financial statements required to be filed as part of registration statements or other disclosures under the Securities Act, the Exchange Act, the Public Utility Holding Company Act of 1935, and the Investment Company Act of 1940. The requirements of Regulation S-X generally address the format and style of financial statements, specify the content of certain financial statement footnotes, and prescribe schedules that should be filed with financial statements.

14.4 CHALLENGES POSED TO THE SEC BY INTERNATIONAL DEVELOPMENTS. The SEC has traditionally been viewed as having, if not the "best" disclosure requirements, at least the most rigorous, and this has meant that its disclosure rules have often been looked on as the "gold standard" for regulators. Although competing capital markets have existed for many years, the U.S. markets (together with their regulators) have been leery of competing for the business of issuers and investors lest the competition result in a "race to the bottom."

Contrary to what those regulators may have believed in the early 1990s, the "race to the bottom" has not in fact occurred, and competition for listings and trading today is among markets that offer more transparency, more and better regulation, and more stringent disclosure requirements than they did a decade ago. Whereas at that time the SEC may well have been justified in refraining from responding to the challenge from competing capital markets on the basis that the Commission enforced a quality not available in other markets, today that argument is less tenable, and other markets offer credible competition.

Another challenge to the SEC is presented by the continuing growth of cross-jurisdictional and multijurisdictional offerings. Five of the ten largest U.S. initial public offerings (IPOs) of all time were by non-U.S. companies. The U.S. securities market is so large that extremely large offerings are forced to access it for the time being, but they will only continue to do so if the SEC can continue to make the registration process attractive for such offerings.

Additionally, at the time of writing, the SEC and the rules it enforces are under challenge by U.S. and international critics. Several large companies have failed or have been forced to restate their financial results while the critics ask whether the rules the SEC has been enforcing, especially as they relate to financial disclosures, are indeed the standard to which other regulators should aspire.

(a) Development of Competing Capital Markets. In recent years we have seen several important developments that affect the competitiveness of the U.S. capital markets. Many European markets have been restructured or deregulated to improve efficiency, and some markets where foreign ownership of securities was traditionally prohibited or restricted have opened up to foreign investment. These markets are becoming more competitive with the United States as they become more attractive to investors and to issuers seeking capital.

Markets are additionally becoming increasingly integrated, leading to the development of supranational markets that are more attractive than their component domestic markets. The most obvious example of this is the European Union's (EU's) effort to develop a single capital market, without obstacles to the freedom of movement for capital. In 1985, the EU passed a directive designed to achieve completion of a single internal market by 1992, spurred on by a perception that the fragmented European markets were not competitive with their international competitors. The EU has adopted or has proposed a number of directives that harmonize regulation of the securities markets in Europe. Harmonization of disclosure requirements, and listing standards in particular, has made substantial progress. In 1994, the EU adopted a new directive designed to facilitate stock exchange listings in one member state by companies listed in the other member states. This directive exempts issuers that have listed in one state for at least three years from the requirement of publishing full listing particulars in the other EU member state. The same also applies to public offers; the same documents may be used to offer securities simultaneously to the public in all member countries. In addition, Directive 2001/34 sets forth minimum standards for the admission of securities to official stock exchange listings in each of the member states in an attempt to harmonize listing standards. That directive also prescribes the information to be published with respect to those securities. Directive 89/298 (the Prospectus Directive) provides that where public offers are made within a short interval of one another in two or more member states, a public offer prospectus prepared and approved in one state must be recognized as a public offer prospectus in other member states. In addition, in 1998, the European Council adopted the Financial Services Action Plan with the aims of completing a single wholesale market, developing open and secure markets for retail financial services, ensuring the continued stability of EU financial markets and eliminating tax obstacles to financial market integration. The plan consists of a series of legislative and non-legislative initiatives. There are still wrinkles to be ironed out. For example, some have argued that proposed amendments to the Prospective Directive could be burdensome to issuers by requiring them to follow the regulations of their home country rather than their listing country. In addition to being burdensome, these provisions could increase issuer liability by requiring issuers to maintain a shelf prospectus at all times, and to be updated annually.

The efficiencies in time and cost offered by this procedure are obvious, though: an integrated market comparable in size in population and capitalization to that of the United States is being created. A European or U.S. issuer can reach investors in several European countries without any additional regulatory burdens or costs. This should make the European capital markets more attractive to issuers and thus more competitive with the United States.

(b) Cross-Border and Multijurisdictional Offerings. Over the last two decades, there has been substantial growth in cross-border securities transactions. These include both the purchase of foreign securities by U.S. investors (whether in the primary or secondary markets) and the offering of securities outside the United States by U.S. issuers. Part of the growth in these transnational securities transactions has resulted from an increase in the number of offerings made simultaneously in two or more countries. Such "multijurisdictional" offerings may be made for several reasons. Issuers may find that their home market is not large enough to absorb a large offering of securities. Examples of this would be offerings by large issuers from the comparatively small Latin American or Scandinavian markets or the huge offerings made in recent years pursuant to the privatization of nationalized industries by European, Latin American, and Asian issuers. Issuers may wish to expand the geographic base of their security holders or to increase the market for their securities internationally. Issuers may also wish to acquire foreign shareholders for strategic purposes, such as to protect against takeover attempts. (Many issuers have found that the existence of U.S. shareholders is an effective delaying mechanism, or deterrent, to tender offers for their securities.)

In 1989, the Technical Committee of the International Organization of Securities Commissions (IOSCO) produced a report on "International Equity Offerings." The Working Party that produced the report analyzed current practices and issues that had arisen in the making of multijurisdictional equity offerings. Several major areas of problems encountered in both equity and debt offerings were identified.

Problems are caused in multijurisdictional offerings by differing underwriting practices; different disclosure requirements (including continuous disclosure); different registration and regulatory requirements; and processing delays, stabilization, and other regulatory controls over dealings; and widely differing clearance and settlement procedures.

Differing underwriting practices cause timing problems. The price of issues is set at different times under the U.S. and U.K. models, for example. Additional timing problems are caused when it is necessary to obtain regulatory clearances or approvals. Settlement procedures for the securities offered may differ from country to country, with no clearly established principle of immediate delivery on payment to avoid credit risks, financing costs, and the costs of settling failed transactions. Additionally, settlement dates for primary and secondary trades also vary from country to country, although settlement dates are fast becoming conformed.

The problems identified that most affected the United States, however, were in the areas of disclosure and regulation of stabilization and similar controls over dealings. While, as discussed below, the SEC has made significant accommodations to mitigate the effects of its stabilization rules, its disclosure requirements, particularly financial disclosure, are as much an issue now as they were in 1989. Since the United States is one of the largest capital markets in the world, it should be an obvious candidate when companies decide that they have to raise capital outside their own home market. The United States, however, also arguably has the most detailed disclosure requirements in the world, and issuers offering securities simultaneously in the United States and overseas have often found that compliance with U.S. disclosure regulations adds a considerable burden to structuring an offering and to the preparation of offering documents. SEC concern for investor protection dictates that more detailed and additional disclosures and different formats must be added to selling documents prepared in accordance with another jurisdiction's rules.

Under the SEC's rules, although an issuer's financial statements may be prepared in accordance with its home country's GAAP, those financial statements must be reconciled to U.S. GAAP. Reconciliation, showing what financial results would have looked like under U.S. GAAP, can be a difficult and expensive process. Although the SEC has made some concessions to its requirements (discussed below), many companies have chosen to forego accessing the U.S. public markets rather than undergo reconciliation.

(c) Tarnish on the "Gold Standard". The collapse of Enron in a sea of red ink and undisclosed liabilities has led to a reexamination of the standards that the SEC enforces. Critics have asked whether U.S. GAAP, by becoming increasingly rule intensive, does in fact produce the "true and fair" view of a company's performance that financial statements are supposed to provide. Some of the criticism leveled at the SEC and the FASB is no doubt unjustified, and at the time of writing it is unclear how U.S. GAAP and the SEC's reliance on them, will be affected. It is clear, however, that the Enron scandal has created a climate more open to changes with respect to U.S. GAAP than ever before.

14.5 RESPONSE TO GLOBALIZATION. The SEC's response to the challenges of globalization have taken three forms, broadly speaking: adaptation, reciprocity, and harmonization. First, the Commission has modified many of its rules to respond to the requirements of non-U.S. issuers and cross-border offerings. Second, with respect to some rules affecting non-U.S. issuers and cross-border transactions, the Commission has accepted the rules of regulators from other countries as providing the same level of investor support as its own. In some cases, these modifications have been made at the SEC's own initiative and in others, such as the multijurisdictional disclosure system, made on a reciprocal basis with other regulators. Third, the Commission has worked with other regulators to harmonize their rules or create rules common across several jurisdictions. In order to understand how the SEC has approached the challenges of globalization, it is important to be aware of the policies underlying the SEC's approach.

(a) Policy Statements. In November 1988, the SEC published a Policy Statement on the regulation of international securities markets. The SEC stated that the challenge facing regulators of global securities markets, which had become increasingly automated and linked, was to "ensure efficiency and honesty." The Policy Statement is important because it sets out the basis for some of the SEC's actions over the last decade and provides a blueprint for the direction that the SEC may take in this area in the future.

The Commission stated that an effective regulatory structure for an international securities market system would include the following features:

- Efficient structures for quotation, price, and volume information and dissemination; order routing; order execution; clearance; settlement and payment; and strong capital adequacy standards
- Sound disclosure systems, including accounting principles, auditing standards, auditor independence standards, registration and prospectus provisions, and listing standards that provide investor protection yet balance costs and benefits for market participants
- Fair and honest markets, achieved through regulation of abusive sales practices; prohibitions against fraudulent conduct; and high levels of enforcement cooperation

The SEC urged securities regulators in other nations to work closely with their foreign counterparts and to seek coordinated international solutions to world market problems.

On the subject of "sound disclosure systems," the SEC stated that investors participating in the international securities markets should be protected through a sound disclosure system based on mutually agreeable accounting principles, auditing standards, auditor independence standards, registration and prospectus provisions, and listing standards. The Commission expressed its opinion that the goal in addressing international disclosure and registration problems should be to minimize regulatory impediments without compromising investor protection. Differences in disclosure requirements, accounting principles, auditing standards, and auditor independence standards between countries are impediments to multijurisdictional offerings, and securities regulators should, therefore, in the SEC's view, seek ways to accommodate and, to the extent possible, minimize these differences in order to facilitate transnational capital formation, while at the same time ensuring adequate disclosure for the protection of investors. The SEC suggested that regulators consider the multijurisdictional registration mechanism, the SEC prototype for which—the multijurisdictional disclosure system with Canada—is discussed below, as a means of facilitating transnational capital formation.

The SEC opined that mutually acceptable international accounting standards are desirable, because they will reduce the unnecessary regulatory burdens resulting from current disparities between the various national accounting standards. Accordingly, therefore, securities regulators and members of the accounting profession were urged by the SEC to continue efforts to revise and adjust international accounting standards with the aim of increasing comparability and reducing costs.

The SEC's position with respect to accounting disclosure requirements was refined in further public statements by the Commission and its commissioners, who have stated that any such standards, to be acceptable to the SEC, must constitute a core set of accounting standards that:

- Constitute a comprehensive basis of accounting
- Are of a high quality (i.e., result in transparency and comparability and provide for full disclosure)
- Are capable of being, and actually be, vigorously interpreted and applied

(b) Adaptation of Rules Regarding Non-U.S. Issuers

(i) Changes to Rules Relating to Public Offerings. Over the years, the SEC has made several important concessions adapting its rules to the needs of non-U.S. issuers. In April 1994, the SEC adopted several rule changes that affect offerings by non-U.S. issuers. While none of these changes had a major effect in and of itself, together they made U.S. public offerings by non-U.S. issuers easier and more attractive, and marked the SEC's continuing commitment that, provided U.S. issuers are protected, U.S. regulations should not deter foreign companies from making offerings in the United States. The most noteworthy development was the SEC's acceptance of cash flow statements prepared in accordance with IASC standards (IAS 7) without reconciliation to U.S. GAAP. In addition, the SEC amended its rules to require reconciliation to U.S. GAAP of financial statements and selected financial data only for the two most recently completed fiscal years and any interim periods; relaxed its requirements relating to reconciliation of financial statements of non-U.S. issuers' smaller acquisitions and equity investees; made accommodation for pro rata consolidation for certain joint ventures that would be accounted for under the equity method pursuant to U.S. GAAP; and eliminated certain supplemental financial schedules as part of the reconciling information.

The Commission also adopted further changes relating to registration and reporting by foreign issuers, including registration on Form F-3. Form F-3 is a "short form," permitting incorporation by reference of filings made previously with the SEC. Prior to the change in 1994, that form generally could be used only if the public float of voting stock was $300 million or more and the issuer had been reporting for at least 36 months. The Commission amended Form F-3 to lower the public float requirement from US$300 million to US$75 million and to reduce the reporting history provision from 36 to 12 months.

In December 1994, the SEC again relied on the IAS standards as an alternative to U.S. GAAP when it permitted non-U.S. issuers to account for their operations in hyperinflationary economies in accordance with IAS 21, and to determine the manner in which to account for business combinations in accordance with IAS 22. The Commission streamlined and reduced other accounting disclosures applying to non-U.S. issuers at the same time.

(ii) Non-Public Offerings under Rule 144A. Rule 144A under the Securities Act was adopted in April 1990 after a two-year proposal and comment period. While Rule 144A applies equally to domestic and foreign companies, a substantial part of the SEC's intention in the rule's adoption was to attract foreign companies to the U.S. capital markets. The rule did this by providing a new alternative for the resale of privately placed securities, thus increasing the liquidity of the secondary market for privately placed securities in the United States. This, in turn, reduces the cost of capital in the private markets in the United States.

Prior to the adoption of Rule 144A, foreign investors were reluctant to raise capital in the United States in either the public or the private markets. Public offerings must be registered with the SEC, which can be an expensive and time-consuming process, involving large legal and accounting costs incurred in preparing the required information in the format in which it must be presented to the SEC. Registration also may involve the issuer in disclosing information (such as segment information) which it has no interest in revealing to the outside world or to its competitors. Foreign issuers were similarly disinclined to raise capital in the U.S. private markets because of the "illiquidity premium" involved in raising capital there. The fact that securities placed privately could be resold only in limited circumstances meant that investors demanded that they be recompensed in the pricing of the securities for those securities' lack of liquidity.

There were, prior to the adoption of Rule 144A, two principal ways pursuant to which privately placed securities could be resold in the United States. The first was to hold the securities for a two- to three-year period and resell them publicly, pursuant to Rule 144 under the Securities Act. Restricted securities could be sold subject to restrictions, including volume limitations, after two years and freely after three years, pursuant to Rule 144. The second was to resell the securities privately in a transaction, developed by the securities bar and never formally blessed by the SEC, referred to as a "Section 4 ($1\frac{1}{2}$)" resale. This involved the provisions of letters of investment intent from the purchaser of the securities and was typically undertaken only after the provision of an opinion of counsel.

Rule 144A added a third alternative. Under the rule, restricted securities may be resold without registration and without any holding period if they are sold only to specified institutional buyers who are "qualified institutional buyers," that is, investors who have portfolios of at least $100 million of eligible securities (certain types of securities are excluded from the $100 million). The other requirements of the rule are straightforward: The seller must notify the buyer that the seller is relying on Rule 144A; the securities resold may not be investment company securities or those of the same class as securities listed on a U.S. securities exchange or quoted on NASDAQ; and there must be at least some minimal information available about the issuer of the securities. Provided these conditions are met, securities can be traded actively among qualified institutional buyers from the date of their placement.

While Rule 144A is on its face applicable to resales only, the fact that it adds liquidity to the secondary market for privately placed securities makes private placements in the United States of securities that may be resold in reliance on Rule 144A (referred to as "Rule 144A offerings") a more attractive option.

It was the SEC's intention that the new market created in the United States by Rule 144A should provide a U.S. complement to the Euromarkets. Foreign and U.S. issuers considering a Euromarket offering now routinely include a Rule 144A tranche.

Looking at the rule from the point of view of the investor (at least those large enough to be "qualified institutional buyers"), the SEC intended to attract foreign issuers to the U.S. markets so that U.S. investors would have access to foreign securities without having to buy them overseas, unprotected by U.S. securities antifraud laws.

The rule permits the market (i.e., the investors themselves) to determine what information in the way of a prospectus or offering circular is necessary for them to make an informed investment decision. It is therefore open to issuers to provide as much or as little information as they choose or the market dictates. Market practice in Rule 144A offerings by non-U.S. companies is to provide financial statements prepared in accordance with home country GAAP, and not to reconcile those financial statements to U.S. or international GAAP. In most cases, however, a summary of material differences between home country and U.S. GAAP is provided.

(c) Multijurisdictional Disclosure System and other Reciprocal Initiatives.

(i) Concept Release. In February 1985, in response to the multijurisdictional securities offerings discussed above and the increasing internationalization of the securities markets, the SEC published a "concept release," soliciting public comment on efforts to harmonize disclosure and distribution practices for multinational offerings. The SEC suggested two possible approaches that would facilitate such offerings. The first, referred to as the "reciprocal" approach, would involve agreement by two or more participating regulating bodies that disclosure documents prepared in accordance with the disclosure standards of other participating regulators would be automatically accepted as meeting their own disclosure requirements. The second, described as the "common prospectus" approach, would involve participating regulators agreeing upon common disclosure standards for a prospectus that would be simultaneously filed with the regulator of each jurisdiction in which an offer was made. The SEC suggested in the concept release that Canada and the United Kingdom were the most obvious partners in the development of such a system, on the grounds that their disclosure requirements and their accounting standards were largely comparable to those of the United States. Comments received by the SEC in response to the concept release overall were in favor of the idea of facilitating multinational offerings. Most commenters thought that, while a common prospectus would be ideal in theory, it would be difficult to work with in practice, so the reciprocal approach was hailed as a more practical solution.

Many of the commenters on the concept release expressed views on accounting issues in a wider context (i.e., with respect to countries other than the United Kingdom and Canada). Of those commenters expressing a view as to whether reconciliation to U.S. GAAP was necessary for financial statements used in multinational offerings, opinion was split. Approximately half favored reconciliation to U.S. GAAP, although some of these comments were founded on the fact that some countries' GAAP do not conform to IASC standards. Others felt that no reconciliation would be necessary (a view that came to be held by a majority of commenters on the U.S.–Canadian system discussed below). Several stated that IASC standards should serve as the GAAP for multinational offerings. Most commenters expressing an opinion on the subject were in favor of some indication or warning in disclosure documents that foreign issuers' accounting standards were different from those of the United States.

The concept release asked commenters what the role of the SEC should be in encouraging multinational offerings. The majority of commenters on this point favored a proactive role by the SEC, with the Commission either taking a leading role in actively encouraging such offerings or identifying and removing barriers to multinational offerings without compromising investor protection. It is important to note, then, that the SEC has not yet been taking action in this area without significant backing and encouragement from U.S. securities issuers, intermediaries, and professional advisers.

(ii) U.S.-Canadian Multijurisdictional Disclosure System. Subsequent to the concept release, the SEC began two years of discussions with the securities commissions of

Ontario and Quebec (which provinces regulate the majority of offerings in Canada) to develop an integrated disclosure system that would permit Canadian issuers to access the U.S. capital markets using their home-country disclosure documents and offering practices and that would permit U.S. issuers to raise capital in Canada using U.S. documents and practices. In 1989, the SEC proposed for public comment the rules, schedules, and forms that would form a basis for a multijurisdictional disclosure system (MJDS). At the same time, the two Canadian provinces proposed that a similar system be adopted in Canada for U.S. issuers. In 1990, the SEC reproposed its rules, and in 1991, the MJDS was adopted by the SEC and the two Canadian provinces (some adjustments were made to the system in 1993). The MJDS goes further than just providing a framework for public offerings to be made simultaneously in two or more jurisdictions. It also permits periodic disclosure requirements of one of the participating countries to be met by the provision of disclosure documents prepared in accordance with the other country's requirements and additionally covers cross-border tender offers and rights offers.

The system is a hybrid between the "common prospectus" approach and the "reciprocal prospectus" approach. While it looks like a reciprocal system in that, in most cases, documents prepared in accordance with the issuer's home country's requirements would be automatically accepted as having met the disclosure requirements of the country into which the offering was made, the SEC stated in the proposing release that Canada was chosen as the initial partner for the experiment because its requirements were so close to those of the United States. In other words, some degree of harmonization (the first steps towards the development of a common prospectus) had already taken place.

Multijurisdictional and cross-border offerings by Canadian issuers in the United States on the basis of Canadian documents is permitted in order to encourage cross-border public offers and to facilitate the free flow of capital. The system also covers specified rights and exchange offers in order to encourage Canadian issuers to extend such offers to U.S. shareholders. At the time the MJDS was adopted, U.S. shareholders were frequently "cashed out" of such offers and denied the investment opportunities they represent. The multijurisdictional disclosure system also permits tender offers that are primarily Canadian in character to comply with the provisions of the Williams Act (the portion of the Exchange Act that regulates tender offers) by complying with the applicable Canadian tender offer regulations, again in order to encourage such offers to be made to U.S. investors. The SEC stated that, given the extensive Canadian regulator provisions that it discussed in its proposing release, the United States did not have an overriding investor protection interest in insisting on compliance with the specific regulatory provisions of the Williams Act.

An eligible issuer using the system may prepare a disclosure document according to the requirements of its home jurisdiction and use that document for securities or cash offerings in the other jurisdiction. Review of the document is as prescribed by the issuer's home country, and the home country's regulatory authorities are responsible for applying disclosure standards. Thus, documents prepared in accordance with Canadian requirements generally are subject to no review by the SEC. Except where the SEC has reason to believe that there is a problem, it does not independently review the filings made under the MJDS by Canadian issuers but relies on the review conducted in Canada. Prospective investors in the United States receive the Canadian disclosure document, plus a brief "wraparound" form that identifies the issuer's agent for service in the United States, lists the documents regarding the issuer of the securities on file with the Commission, and incorporates a warning legend regarding the potential tax consequences of an investment, the fact that remedies for securities law violations may have to be pursued outside the United States, and the fact that financial statements were not prepared in accordance with U.S. GAAP.

In order to be eligible to participate in the multijurisdictional system, an issuer must have a one-year history of reporting to Canadian securities regulators and be in compliance with the periodic reporting requirements of those authorities at the time of filing with the SEC. In offerings of securities other than investment-grade nonconvertible securities, or pursuant to rights offerings, the issuer must have a minimum capitalization of US$75 million. Where securities are offered in a rights, exchange, or tender offer, that offer must be primarily of a Canadian nature; that is, no more than a specified percentage of offerees may be U.S. residents. In the case of rights and exchange offers, or when investment grade debt (rated by either U.S. or Canadian rating agencies) or preferred stock is offered, the system is at its simplest. The SEC allows such offerings to be made in the United States entirely on the basis of Canadian disclosures. This is because such rights and exchange offerings are of a Canadian nature, and investment grade securities generally trade on the basis of yield and rating. For investment grade debt and preferred securities, the financial statements filed as incorporated by reference under cover of Form F-9 need not be reconciled to U.S. GAAP. The financial information pertaining to liquidity and capital resources, which in the SEC's view is not substantially different from U.S. and Canadian GAAP, is most relevant to the decision to invest in such securities.

In the case of offerings of securities other than investment grade debt and preferred stock, reconciliation of financial statements to U.S. GAAP is required. While the SEC stated that financial statements prepared in accordance with Canadian GAAP are "relevant and reliable," it stated that financial statement reconciliation would increase comparability of financial information, which is of greater importance to investment decisions with respect to equity and other investment-grade securities. It should be noted that the Commission in its original proposal expressly asked for comment as to whether such reconciliation is necessary or whether Canadian financial statements would provide investors with adequate information for comparative analysis purposes in some or all cases. A majority of commenters felt that financial information in accordance with Canadian GAAP provided a sufficient basis for an informed investment decision and that reconciliation was not necessary. The SEC, however, retained the requirement to reconcile.

(iii) Cross-Border Tender and Exchange Offers. The Commission has long expressed its concern that, where U.S. investors comprise a small portion of a foreign company's security holders, foreign bidders and issuers in tender and exchange offers may try to avoid U.S. jurisdiction and may exclude U.S. investors from multinational offerings because the cost of compliance with U.S. laws and regulations outweighs the benefits of extending the offer to U.S. security holders. U.S. investors may thus be denied investment opportunities.

The Commission particularly noted that, in the case of exchange offers, which must be registered under the Securities Act, one of the most significant barriers to inclusion of U.S. security holders in an offshore exchange offer has been the need for adherence to, or reconciliation with, U.S. GAAP and auditing standards.

The Commission has traditionally addressed the practice of excluding U.S. security holders in such cases in two principal ways. First, it has asserted its regulatory jurisdiction, which is in many cases extraterritorial in scope. The SEC has pointed out that, in tender offers for securities regulated by the Williams Act, use of the jurisdictional means to sell into the market by the security holders themselves, even where the offeror has avoided such jurisdictional means, will result in the SEC's having authority over the offer. However, having asserted jurisdiction, the SEC has attempted to accommodate foreign tender offers where necessary and consistent with the protection of U.S. investors.

In 1999, the Commission adopted new rules to make it easier for non-U.S. companies to make rights offerings into the United States and for any person (U.S. or non-U.S.) to extend into the United States tender offers and exchange offers for securities of non-U.S. companies that are made primarily outside the United States.

The tender offer rules exempt tender offers for the securities of non-U.S. issuers from most provisions of the Williams Act when U.S. holders own 10% or less of the subject class of the securities. The rules provide more limited exemptions from some of those provisions when U.S. holders own more than 10% but no more than 40% of the subject class of securities.

The rules also exempt from registration under the Securities Act exchange offers for the securities of non-U.S. issuers and rights offers by non-U.S. issuers where 10% or less of the subject class of securities is owned by U.S. holders. In both these cases, public offers of securities may now be made into the United States on the basis of the information documents (if any) distributed overseas. These must be in English, and distributed to U.S. holders on the same basis as they are distributed in the issuer's home jurisdiction.

In contrast to the MJDS, no reconciliation of financial statements is required, and the rules are entirely neutral as to the jurisdiction under whose rules disclosure, if indeed there is any, is required. The offering documents are furnished to (not officially "filed with") the SEC, and they must bear a legend regarding the non-U.S. nature of the transaction and the difficulty of enforcing rights against foreign companies. The anti-fraud rules still apply, and the offeror (if not a U.S. person) is required to file a consent to service of process in the United States. On the whole, however, this is a fairly revolutionary ceding of regulation on the part of the SEC.

(iv) Regulation M. In the adoption of Regulation M in 1997, the SEC codified much of the relief it had granted over the years with respect to its antimanipulation rules where U.S. and overseas regulations conflicted. In particular, it granted blanket relief for transactions governed by the United Kingdom's City Code on Takeovers, on the grounds that U.K. rules provided adequate investor protection.

(d) IOSCO, IASC and Harmonization

(i) IOSCO. The SEC's participation in the International Organization of Securities Commission, (IOSCO), whose membership includes securities administrators from nearly 50 countries, demonstrates the SEC's commitment to the development of international standards. In its 1988 Policy Statement, the SEC stated that securities regulators should utilize bilateral and multilateral relationships in the securities areas and that cooperative efforts through multilateral organizations such as IOSCO should be continued and strengthened.

The Commission has played a major part in IOSCO committees and task forces. One important result of this is the IOSCO report on international equity offerings discussed above. This report not only identified the problems encountered by multinational offerings but also made recommendations to facilitate such offerings. The IOSCO committee, echoing the conclusions reached by the Commission in its Concept Release on Multinational Offerings (discussed above), stated that efficiency of the capital-raising process would be greatly enhanced by permitting an issuer to prepare one disclosure document for use in each jurisdiction in which it sells securities and recommended that securities regulators facilitate the use of single disclosure documents, whether by harmonization of standards, reciprocity, or otherwise. The committee also recommended that timeliness and period of financial reporting should either be harmonized or accommodations made to foreign issuers. Since in many jurisdictions the making of a public offering leads to the imposition of continuous disclosure requirements, the committee also recommended further study to develop internationally acceptable continuous disclosure documents. Additionally, the committee recommended further study with respect to harmonization of rules relating to stabilization and other controls over dealings, and codification of accommodations already made in this area.

The SEC's participation in this report does not necessarily imply agreement with all its conclusions, but it gives some indication of the direction in which IOSCO, an organization heavily influenced by the SEC as its largest and most experienced member, is moving as a whole. The SEC has generally complied with IOSCO recommendations, as it did in the 1994 rule changes discussed above—the acceptance of IAS cashflow statements was an IOSCO recommendation,—and as it did in the adaption of the IOSCO International Disclosure Standards discussed in the next section.

(ii) IOSCO International Disclosure Standards. In 1999, the SEC adopted a series of amendments to the nonfinancial disclosure requirements of registration statements and annual reports filed by foreign private issuers. These changes of affected non-U.S. companies that register their securities with the Commission in connection with a public offering in the United States or a listing on a U.S. national securities exchange and make annual reports under the Exchange Act thereafter. The Commission made these changes by modifying Form 20-F, which is the form used for registration and annual reports under the Exchange Act, and the contents of which are incorporated by reference into the forms used by non-U.S. issuers to register offerings under the Securities Act.

The amendments represent an effort by the SEC to conform U.S. disclosure requirements for foreign private (i.e., nongovernmental) issuers to a core set of international disclosure standards endorsed by IOSCO. The IOSCO international disclosure standards were developed to reflect current international disclosure practices and are intended to facilitate the ability of companies to conduct cross-border offerings of equity securities (The SEC actually went further than mandated in the standards since it applies them to periodic reports too.) IOSCO intended its members implement as much as possible of the core disclosure standards in their jurisdictions with the hope that broad acceptance of the disclosure standards will allow issuers to prepare one disclosure document that, with a minimum amount of tailoring, may be accepted in multiple jurisdictions.

The SEC modified Form 20-F to replace most of the nonfinancial statement disclosure requirements with the international disclosure standards adopted by IOSCO; revised the registration forms under the Securities Act applicable to foreign private issuers to cross-reference revised Form 20-F whenever necessary; and incorporated into Form 20-F the provisions of the international disclosure standards addressing the age of financial statements. While wholesale adoption of IOSCO's disclosure requirements may seem radical, the IOSCO disclosure provisions were very heavily influenced by the SEC's requirements, and resulted in very few substantive changes to the existing Form 20-F.

The SEC's implementation of the IOSCO international disclosure standards will help provide a more consistent base of disclosure requirements for cross-border offerings in the United States and other jurisdictions adopting the IOSCO standards. However, the approach of IOSCO members of promoting the adoption of IOSCO standards in each of their individual jurisdictions, but without a concept of reciprocity allowing for the acceptance in all IOSCO member jurisdictions of one disclosure document review by one regulator, will limit what can be achieved with the IOSCO standards. Disclosure is likely to continue to vary from market to market, as each regulator's review and interpretation of the disclosure for a cross-border offering will be based on its own laws and practices, and the standards of legal liability relating to securities offerings will continue to vary from market to market. Consequently, the need to reconcile disclosure in a cross-border transaction is very likely to continue to exist despite the fact that all relevant jurisdictions are applying the same basic IOSCO disclosure standards.

More important, while implementation of the IOSCO standards brings at least the foundation for nonaccounting disclosure closer together in different markets, it will not promote significant movement toward the goal of producing a single disclosure document for use in multiple jurisdictions until agreement is reached on a core set of international accounting standards. It should also be noted that the "Management's Discussion and Analysis" (called "Operating and Financial Review and Prospects" in the 20-F), which the SEC regards as being at the heart of any corporate disclosure, and which includes a quantitative and qualitative discussion of market risk, is viewed by the SEC as being financial, rather than nonfinancial disclosure. Thus, the apparent movement toward harmonization in this area is somewhat limited.

(iii) International Accounting Standard Committee. As a result of the problems associated with differences in accounting standards and principles among different countries, the United States and various other countries have become involved in a number of projects with a goal of encouraging harmonization of accounting standards. The first such project, the International Accounting Standards Committee (IASC), an arm of International Federation of Accountants (IFAC), discussed below, was formed in 1973 by the United States and eight other countries. The purpose of the organization was primarily to articulate international accounting standards. There are approximately 100 organizational members of the IASC, representing accountants from more than 74 countries. The IASC has issued many international accounting standards dealing with topics of major importance to the presentation of financial statements worldwide. SEC accountants and other professional staff participate in IASC projects. (See Chapter 16 for a further description of the IASC.)

Adoption of IASC standards would result in a reduction of the alternate measurement and recording standards that currently exist. Being a private sector organization, the IASC has no effective means to enforce compliance with its pronouncements. As a result, the IASC must rely on its members, who are pledged to use their best efforts to achieve compliance with, and acceptance of, the international accounting standards worldwide. Voluntary implementation has achieved a certain amount of success. Many members of the Toronto Stock Exchange, for example, have been persuaded to comply with IASC standards; listed companies in Italy are required, in the absence of local requirements, to comply with IASC standards; and the listing requirements of the London Stock Exchange include compliance with IASC standards or disclosure explaining any deviation from such standards.

A second project aimed at harmonization of international standards, the establishment of the IFAC, began in 1977, and U.S. accountants also participate in this body. The IFAC has a membership similar to that of IASC. IFAC's purpose is the development and coordination of worldwide auditing standards. Like the IASC, the IFAC must also rely on voluntary acceptance of its guidelines, and successful completion of IFAC's goal is dependent on its members being able to have the IFAC pronouncements implemented in their respective countries. (See Chapter 16 for a further description of IFAC.) In October 1982, the IASC and IFAC entered into an agreement to create a formal relationship between the two bodies. According to the terms of the agreement, the membership of the two bodies was unified in January 1984, and the IFAC was given the authority to nominate the 13 countries chosen for the IASC's Board. The agreement also provided that the IASC would be the only party with authority to issue or promulgate international accounting standards or to promote worldwide compliance or acceptance of these standards.

Since the agreement, IASC has continued to make a great deal of progress. In an article by IASC's secretary general, David Cairns, in December 1989, entitled "IASC's Blueprint for the Future," Cairns stated that there had not been enough progress to ensure that financial statements of companies from different countries would be readily comparable by users worldwide. In an attempt to better achieve this goal, in 1989 the IASC published Exposure Draft 32, *Comparability of Financial Statements* (the "Comparability Project"), which addressed the different choices of accounting treatment for like transactions and events which are available under international accounting standards and result in a loss of comparability and understandability of financial statements.

The basic purpose of IASC's Comparability Project was to provide a set of accounting standards that can either be used to reconcile multinational prospectuses or to prepare financial statements for multinational prospectuses. In other words, it was the beginning of an attempt to formulate global GAAP. A new set of IAS standards, with fewer options than was previously the case, came into effect in 1995.

Comments of the SEC and other regulating bodies made at the annual meeting of IOSCO in Paris on July 11, 1995, indicated that harmonization of international accounting standards is most likely a process that will continue to evolve over a number of years. Former SEC commissioner Steven M. H. Wallman said, responding to a question relating to the SEC's reaction to IOSCO's and IASC's plan to set up international accounting standards, "Our goal is to have the highest level of standards possible. The closer [the IASC] comes to that, the better." On August 3, 1995, IOSCO and IASC announced that they had reached an agreement on a work plan to establish an international set of accounting standards by 1999. The IASC subsequently announced a "fast-track work program" to complete a core set of standards by 1998, a year ahead of schedule. The IASC completed the core set in December 1998 with the approval of IAS 39 and IOSCO began reviewing those standards in 1999.

In 2000, IOSCO recommended that its members allow multinational issuers to use 30 IASC standards in cross-border offerings and listings. The European Union voted in the summer of 2002 to require all publicly listed EU companies to use IAS for quarterly and annual filings.

Throughout this time, the IASC (now known as the International Accounting Standards Board, or IASB, since a reorganization in 2001) and the FASB have been working closely together to produce similar standards on an ongoing basis. In early 1996 the two bodies produced exposure drafts on earnings per share that were substantially identical. In addition, since the adoption of IASC's core standards, the FASB has attempted to educate the public about the core standards and has undertaken to compare the standards to U.S. GAAP (the "IASC–U.S. Comparison Project: A Report on the Similarities and Differences between IASC Standards and U.S. GAAP"). The next big project for the IASB will be "global accounting convergence," specifically the alignment of U.S. and international standards. It remains to be seen whether the Enron scandal might help hasten this process.

(iv) Concept Release on International Accounting Standards. In 2000, the SEC issued a "concept release" on the subject of international accounting standards. The release asked for feedback from U.S. and non-U.S. parties regarding the establishment of a globally accepted, high-quality financial reporting framework. Most significantly, the SEC asked whether it should modify its requirement that the financial statements of non-U.S. issuers should be reconciled to U.S. GAAP, as discussed above, the single biggest reason why more non-U.S. companies have not chosen to access the U.S. public securities markets. The SEC asked whether it should accept the International Accounting Standards (IASs) promulgated by the IASC for use in filings by non-U.S. issuers. The Commission asked whether these standards are of a sufficiently high quality, whether they can be vigorously interpreted and applied, and the implications for the U.S. markets of accepting an alternative set of standards. Despite what the cynics say, this was a genuine initiative that may well evolve into rule making, although it may take some considerable time. For many years, various constituencies have attempted to persuade the SEC to accept financial statements that have been prepared in accordance with the accounting practices of non-U.S. jurisdictions. These attempts have all failed. The reason for this is that the SEC has taken the view that non-U.S. accounting regimes do not produce the same quality of financial statements as U.S. GAAP. A particular bugbear has been the ability of companies under some European regimes to "smooth out" their earnings by creating hidden reserves that can be drawn on later to disguise decreases in revenues. International accounting standards were mooted as a possible alternative to national standards, but for a long time international standards were insufficiently detailed and allowed too many alternative treatments for the SEC to accept them.

It had thus become an article of faith that the SEC will never accept non-U.S. GAAP financial statements. This ignored the leading role the SEC has taken in recent years in shaping international standards and the framework that will support and enforce those standards.

There are differences between U.S. GAAP and IASs, some of them significant. The financial results of a company may well look different when prepared under the two systems. This of course does not necessarily mean that one is better than the other (in fact, the SEC's chief accountant has stated that some international standards are better than their U.S. equivalents.) It does mean, however, that it is harder for a user of financial statements to compare the financial statements of a company using U.S. GAAP with the financials of a company using IASs and make an informed investment decision on the basis of that comparison.

The FASB produced a report on the similarities and differences between IASC standards and U.S. GAAP. The report states that "conclusions about the acceptability of IASC standards for cross-border securities listings and other purposes are mixed and often are supported by fragmentary evidence." The FASB points out that in particular, there are few studies that have focused on comparability among the financial statements of enterprises following IASC standards (i.e., whether the financial statements of a French company following IASs are comparable to those of a Japanese company following IASs). The FASB report is over 500 pages long and its discussion is objective rather than judgmental. It does, however, identify some significant differences between IAS and U.S. GAAP. While some differences are merely differences rather than shortcomings, there are other areas identified that the SEC may be expected to have reservations about. One such area is permitting alternative treatments. Comparability is harmed if issuers are able to choose among accounting treatments, and the SEC cares very much about comparability.

The SEC received numerous comments, ranging from enthusiastic acceptance of IASs to total rejection of the idea. In general, however, comments were supportive of the concept but uncertain as to whether IASs would be capable of the rigorous enforcement the SEC sought.

When the SEC considers changes to its accounting and disclosure requirements, it must evaluate the impact of potential changes on capital formation, including the possible impact on the cost of capital for domestic companies, and the impact on investor protection, the SEC's prime directive. In 1996, the SEC set out the criteria that must be met if it were ever to accept financial statements prepared under standards other than U.S. GAAP. The standards must:

- Constitute a comprehensive basis of accounting
- Be of a high quality, that is, result in transparency and comparability and provide for full disclosure
- Be capable of being, and actually be, rigorously interpreted and applied

The SEC is concerned that there should be a body with sufficient power to interpret international standards and enforce those interpretations. Consistency of interpretations is very important if investors are to be able to make informed investment decisions on the basis of comparable financial statements. If there are no mechanisms or structures in place promoting consistent interpretations of the IASC standards, then national regulators may develop interpretations that are inconsistent with each other.

Before the SEC could reduce or remove the current reconciliation requirement, several things would need to happen. First, the SEC staff would need to conclude, after assessment of the IASC core standards (which includes evaluating comments received on the concept release), that the standards are of a sufficiently high quality, and will be rigorously enforced. The other members of IOSCO would have to come to the same conclusion. (The SEC would never accept standards rejected by other regulators and would presumably make changes only within the context of the IOSCO International Disclosure Standards project.) The SEC would then propose rule changes for public comment. The SEC staff would then analyze the comments received on the proposals and develop final recommendations, which, if approved by the SEC's Commissioners, would be issued in a final release.

Assuming the SEC even gets to the rule proposal stage, it is not clear what form the proposals would take. Since this initiative is related to the IOSCO International

Disclosure Standards project, it is quite likely that the SEC would propose changes to Form 20-F, and, as it did with the adoption of the nonfinancial statement International Disclosure Standards, apply the changes to all non-U.S. companies accessing the U.S. public markets, not just those involved in cross-border equity offerings. Even within that context however, the SEC may waive only some of its requirements, require supplemental information in addition to IAS financials, impose additional requirements or reconciliation for particular industries, or remove the reconciliation requirement only for issuers that meet certain tests of size, liquidity, listing, or disclosure history.

If the SEC does decide to accept financial statements prepared in accordance with IASs, non-U.S. companies filing registration statements can still expect to receive substantial SEC comments on their financials in the review process. Just as the SEC rigorously tests financial statements prepared under U.S. GAAP, and enforces the standards established by FASB, the SEC will enforce IASC principles and interpretations when reviewing IAS statements.

(e) Other SEC Initiatives. Other than the participation in the aforementioned multilateral measures, the SEC has been involved in a number of bilateral efforts to integrate the capital markets. The SEC has assisted or promised to assist many emerging markets in formulating and/or streamlining their securities regulations in conformity with international standards. The SEC's Office of International Affairs (OIA) has primary responsibility for the negotiation and implementation of information-sharing arrangements, and for developing legislative and other initiatives to facilitate international cooperation. The OIA coordinates and assists in making requests for assistance to, and responding to requests for assistance from, foreign authorities. The OIA also addresses other international issues that arise in litigated matters, such as effecting service of process abroad and gathering foreign-based evidence under various international conventions, freezing assets located abroad, and enforcing judgments obtained by the SEC in the United States against foreign parties. In addition, the OIA operates in a consultative role regarding the significant ongoing international programs and initiatives of the SEC's other divisions and offices. Since August 1993, the OIA has been responsible for coordinating the SEC's technical assistance program for training and advice in countries with developing securities markets. The OIA also consults with and provides technical assistance to other federal agencies regarding trade-related issues relevant to the regulation of securities markets in the United States.

The SEC has signed comprehensive Memoranda of Understanding (MOUs) for consultation and cooperation in enforcement-related matters with a number of regulators. These MOUs usually entail providing consultation, technical assistance, and mutual assistance of exchange of information. The SEC International Institute for Securities Market Development (the SEC Institute) is the SEC's flagship technical assistance program. The SEC Institute is a two-week, management-level training program covering a full range of topics relevant to the development and oversight of securities markets. The SEC's technical assistance efforts in Eastern Europe have included sending SEC staff as advisers to several countries in the region under a program funded by the United States Agency for International Development. The SEC has also participated in a number of short-term assistance projects for the countries of Latin America and the Caribbean, as well as several countries in other regions. The SEC also invites foreign securities regulators to participate in the SEC's Annual Enforcement Training Program held in the fall.

14.6 THE FUTURE. Over the next few years, the SEC is likely to be faced repeatedly with demands that it recognize and accept foreign disclosure, especially financial statements, prepared otherwise than in accordance with U.S. GAAP. There are several reasons for this. First, multinational offerings are unlikely to diminish. The British privatization of several industries in the 1980s were in the multibillion-dollar range, and five of the top ten IPOs of all time in the United States were made by non-U.S. companies, mostly in recent years. Such offerings cannot be absorbed in the home market. As the newly capitalist countries of Eastern Europe and some emerging markets move to market economies, they are privatizing state-owned industries in much the same way as their Western European counterparts. Again, these offerings have to be made, at least in part, outside their domestic markets. If they have to exclude the United States or limit U.S. offerings to private placements because U.S. requirements, including disclosure standards, cannot conveniently be met, U.S. investors are likely to increase pressure on the SEC to encourage such offers to be made in the United States.

In the interests of competitiveness, the U.S. securities exchanges are likely to continue to pressure the SEC to accept foreign accounting standards. By 2005, all European regulators will accept accounts prepared according to IASs. Increased competition among stock exchanges is likely to result in those exchanges that have the least accommodating attitudes to foreign issuers being at a disadvantage. The SEC can be accommodating with regard to the needs of the exchanges to attract foreign issuers, as has been demonstrated in the past, when the Commission approved rule changes by the New York Stock Exchange and the American Stock Exchange, permitting them to waive rules that were otherwise applicable to foreign issuers, including quarterly earnings reporting.

There will be competition, not only among the world's exchanges, but also among the markets themselves: Newly deregulated markets may prove to be more attractive to issuers than the United States, especially as smaller markets integrate into larger entities, as is happening in Europe and will increase as technological advances, such as a much debated pan-European trading system, are developed.

At the same time as the U.S. authorities are being urged to make accommodations to their standards, they are, in effect, being met halfway, as non-U.S. countries that in the past had less rigorous disclosure requirements develop more stringent disclosure. This process can be seen in the European Union, where the EC directives prescribe minimum standards to be met in all countries, some of which previously had less onerous national requirements. International standards, too, as prescribed by IOSCO and IASC, have become much more stringent.

However, it is possible that domestic issuers in the United States will become more sensitive to the fact that the disclosure standards that they are being held to are stricter and perhaps more expensive than those being applied to foreign issuers. The SEC's challenge will be to hold domestic issuers to U.S. GAAP, while at the same time attempting to encourage a substantial number of foreign issuers to access the U.S. markets, which will depend on relief from strict compliance with the SEC's requirements, especially U.S. GAAP reconciliation, being available.

SOURCES AND SUGGESTED REFERENCES

EU Directive 80/390 (Listing Particulars).

EU Directive 89/298 (Prospectus Directive).

EU Directive 2001/34.

Statement of John S. R. Shad, Chairman of the Securities and Exchange Commission, before the House Subcommittee on Oversight and Investigations of the Committee on Energy and Commerce, March 6, 1985.

"International Equity Offers." International Organization of Securities Commissions, September 1989.

"International Equity Offerings: Changes in Regulation since April, 1990." International Organization of Securities Commissions, September 1991.

"SEC Statement re: International Accounting Standards." SEC Press Release 96-61, April 11, 1996.

"Facilitation of Multinational Securities Offerings." Securities Act Release No. 6568, February 28, 1985.

"Multijurisdictional Disclosure." Securities Act Release No. 6841, July 26, 1989.

"Resale of Restricted Securities." Securities Act Release No. 6862, April 23, 1990.

"Multijurisdictional Disclosure and Modifications to the Current Registration and Reporting System for Canadian Issues." Securities Act Release No. 6879, October 16, 1990.

"Multijurisdictional Disclosure and Modifications to the Current Registration and Reporting System for Canadian Issuers." Securities Act Release No. 6902, June 21, 1991.

"Simplification of Registration and Reporting Requirements for Foreign Companies; Safe Harbor for Public Announcements & Unregistered Offerings and Broker-Dealer Research Reports." Securities Act Release No. 7053, April 19, 1994.

"Reconciliation of the Accounting by Foreign Private Issuers for Business Combinations." Securities Act Release No. 7056, April 1994.

"Cross-Border Tender and Exchange Offers, Business Combinations and Rights Offerings." Securities Act Release No. 7759, October 26, 1999.

"International Accounting Standards." Securities Act Concept Release No. 7801, February 16, 2000.

"Regulation of the International Securities Markets." Policy statement of the United States Securities and Exchange Commission, November 14, 1988.

"Internationalization of the Securities Markets." Report of the Staff on the U.S. Securities and Exchange Commission to the Senate Committee on Banking, Housing and Urban Affairs and the House Committee on Energy and Commerce, July 27, 1987.

CHAPTER 15

TAXONOMY OF AUDITING STANDARDS

Belverd E. Needles, Jr.

DePaul University

CONTENTS

15.1 INTRODUCTION. This chapter provides an overview of similarities and differences in auditing standards in 18 countries. It focuses on broad legal and professional characteristics, as well as selected auditing procedures. Although the study surveys mostly major industrialized countries throughout the world, choices were made to represent countries on six continents and a cross-section of the contrasting

The author wishes to thank Thomas McDermott, retired partner of Ernst & Young, and Robert Temkin, partner of Ernst & Young, for their assistance with the previous edition of this chapter. The author also wishes to thank the following individuals who provided assistance in updating the current text: Juan Carlos Seltzer, Kennedy University (Argentina); Morley Lemon, University of Waterloo (Canada); Salvador Ruiz-de-Chavez , National Center of Evaluation (Mexico); Martin Hoogendoorn, University of Amsterdam (the Netherlands); Pauline Weetman, University of Strathclyde (United Kingdom); Giuseppe Galassi, University of Parma (Italy); Alain Mikol, Groupe ESCP (France); Peter Moeller, Aachen University of Technology (Germany); Gunilla Arvidsson, Swedish Supervisory Board of Public Accountants (Sweden); Sven-Arne Nilsson, Lund University (Sweden); Nonna Martinov, University of New South Wales (Australia); Kazuo Hiramatsu, Kwansei Gakuin University (Japan); Zhijun Lin, University of Hong Kong (China); In Ki Joo, Yonsei University (Korea); Teresita Nadurata, De la Salle University (Philippines); Tan Teck Meng, Singapore Management University (Singapore).

legal, social, and economic systems that exist in the world. The countries represented are Argentina, Canada, Mexico, and the United States in North and South America; France, Germany, the Netherlands, Italy, Sweden, and the United Kingdom in Europe; Australia, Hong Kong, Japan, Korea, the Philippines, and Singapore, in Asia and the Pacific area; and Kenya and Saudi Arabia in Africa and the Middle East. Due to the rapid changes taking place there, no country from Eastern Europe is included in the survey. After a short discussion of the importance of auditing standards and their international harmonization, this chapter examines the auditing standards of the identified countries in regard to the auditor, the attest function, ethical standards and enforcement, independence, audit reports, and auditing procedures. The chapter concludes with a summary of the results.

15.2 IMPORTANCE OF AUDITING STANDARDS AND THEIR HARMONIZATION. The Securities and Exchange Commission (SEC) in its discussion document on "International Accounting Standards" emphasizes that

> While the accounting standards used must be high quality, they also must be supported by an infrastructure that ensures that the standards are rigorously interpreted and applied, and that issues and problematic practices are identified and resolved in a timely fashion.[1]

The SEC goes on to say that the elements of this infrastructure must include:

- Effective, independent, and high-quality accounting and auditing standard setters
- High-quality auditing standards
- Audit firms with effective quality controls worldwide
- Profession-wide quality assurance
- Active regulatory oversight[2]

It is evident from this position that not only must accounting and auditing move in tandem but also the development of high-quality auditing standards and the application of those standards under conditions of quality assurance must be of equally high priority. Accounting identifies, measures, and generates value-relevant financial information for the capital markets; auditing validates and adds credibility to such externally reported information. Independent auditors should create the credibility that is the foundation of capital markets. Effective auditing standards and practices worldwide are necessary for global investors to discriminate among desirable and suspect accounting practices and judge the overall quality of financial reporting. Consequently, the development of both international *accounting* and *auditing* standards should be suitably aligned and keep pace with each other for optimal harmonization results.[3]

The International Forum on Accountancy Development (IFAD) was established in 1999 based on the premise that the expertise and resources of the accounting profession (represented by the International Federation of Accountants [IFAC] and the

---

[1]SEC, 2000.
[2]SEC, 2000.
[3]Needles et. al., 2002.

seven largest accounting firms) and the institutional muscle of the World Bank and other international institutions such as IOSCO (the International Organization of Securities Commissions), the Organization of Economic Cooperation and Development (OECD), and the International Monetary Fund (IMF), when combined and utilizing both their contacts, could be harnessed in the interests of enhancing accounting capacity and capabilities in developing and emerging nations (see *www.ifad.net*). Initial meetings lead to a significant broadening of IFAD's objectives to focus on common worldwide issues. Currently, IFAD provides a mechanism through which more than 30 international organizations work in an informal "partnership" to fulfill a common mission of improving financial reporting, accountability, and transparency worldwide. In addition to those noted above, IFAD members include the International Accounting Standards Board (IASB), the Basel Committee on Banking Supervision, and the International Association for Accounting Education and Research (IAAER).[4] Key components of IFAD's Vision hold that:

> all general purpose financial information must be prepared using a single world-wide framework using common measurement criteria and fair and comprehensive disclosure.... The Vision will not be achieved overnight and will require significant long-term efforts. National accounting standards of most countries should be raised with IAS as the benchmark ... a strong world-wide audit profession must be developed. The Vision is for all general purpose financial statements to be audited in compliance with a single world-wide framework of auditing standards that provides users with assurance regarding the results, financial position and changes in financial position of entities and that is applied rigorously and consistently. The implementation of international standards on auditing will result in significant enhancement in national standards in many countries. The common high standards on ethics and specifically on independence required in the profession will be obtained through implementing new global standards developed by IFAC.

The Vision also discusses the significance of other crucial areas that must be addressed if change is to materialize. These include corporate governance, financial accountability and reporting laws, and education. IFAD's Vision is detailed on its Web site (*www.ifad.net*).

In the context of this chapter, *auditing* refers to the examination of financial statements primarily of business organizations by an independent, qualified auditor for the purpose of expressing an opinion on how well the financial statements meet certain established criteria, often called "accounting standards" or "principles." This function is usually referred to as the "attest function." The users of financial statements may rely on the representations in the statements if they are accompanied by a positive or unqualified opinion from the qualified auditor. This relationship between the auditor and the financial statements lends credibility to the statements and makes possible much of the flow of capital throughout the world. Auditing standards, the criteria that guide the conduct of the audit, are usually promulgated by professional or legislative bodies. They are intended to ensure that the external auditors are qualified and that certain procedures and guidelines are followed in all audits.

Interpreting the results of an external audit as represented by the auditor's report can be difficult or impossible if the standards that apply to the preparation of financial statements and to the conduct of the audit differ from country to country. Har-

[4] Smith, 2002.

monization refers to efforts to achieve, through cooperation among national accounting organizations, greater uniformity of practice in accounting and auditing, particularly in the financial reporting of business organizations, so that the problems of interpretation will become less difficult. The principal advantages of harmonization of accounting and auditing standards are that (1) the increased comparability of international financial information would eliminate possible misunderstandings as to the reliability of financial statements from other countries, thus removing one of the leading impediments to the flow of international investment; (2) time and money currently spent in consolidating divergent financial information, when more than one set of reports is required to comply with national laws or practice, would be saved; and (3) the quality of audits throughout the world may be improved.

Harmonization of auditing standards has been an objective of several international organizations. One of the most important of these is the IFAC, whose members are the professional accounting organizations of more than 80 countries. The IFAC's broad objectives include the "development and enhancement of a coordinated worldwide accountancy profession with harmonized standards." The International Auditing Practices Committee (IAPC) of the IFAC, which has responsibility for issuing International Standards on Auditing (ISAs), has been a positive force in the harmonization of auditing standards, even though the IFAC does not have the power of enforcement. An ISA issued by IAPC does not override local regulations governing the audit of financial statements in a particular country, but, although local regulations differ from, or conflict with, the ISA, each member country has agreed to work toward the implementation of the guidelines issued by the IAPC whenever practicable.

The IAPC has accelerated its activities in recent years to meet the increasing global demands for high-quality standards. Most of these standards have tended to focus on specific matters related to the audit, such as planning, the use of the work of another auditor, audit evidence, and documentation; however, several have dealt with broader issues, such as the objective of the audit, basic principles governing an audit, and the responsibility of the auditor for the detection of fraud. Some of these guidelines are relevant to this paper and will be presented at appropriate points.

Efforts at harmonization have also taken place among the European states. For example, the Company Law Directives (legislative instruments adopted by the European Economic Commission's (EEC) Council of Ministers) have encouraged harmonization. Member states are required to implement the provisions of directives in their national legislation within a specific time limit, usually three years. Several directives deal with accounting matters: the Fourth Directive concerns the layout of annual accounts, valuation methods, contents of annual reports, and provisions for publication of the accounts; the Seventh Directive deals with consolidated financial statements; more closely related to auditing standards, the Eighth Directive deals with the qualifications of professionals who may legally be authorized to perform audits. The coordinating organization for the accountancy profession in Europe is the Federation des Experts Comptables Europeens, known as FEE. The members of FEE are national professional bodies. Professional bodies from 26 countries including all European Union (EU) states were represented. The influence of FEE as the spokesbody for European accountants has grown rapidly, and although it is not a standard-setting body, it has considerable influence in promoting harmonization with IFAC International Auditing Standards. The pressure to improve auditing standards in Europe will intensify as the EU moves to international accounting standards in 2005. "In summary, a large group of up to 30 countries will have to comply with IAS and probably ISA by 2005 or soon thereafter. But the infrastructure and regulation problems are yet to be resolved. Even within the current 15 EU members, there are large differences in infrastructure, particularly regulation, as well as differences in education and professional structure."[5]

Other regional organizations of accountants are not as active in setting international auditing standards.

15.3 THE AUDITOR. A fundamental consideration in comparing auditing standards among countries is the definition of who may be an auditor with power to attest to financial statements. Among the countries in this survey, there is wide variation in defining the auditor's identity and qualifications. Exhibit 15.1 summarizes essential information related to the auditor in five areas: title of auditor, source of authority, licensing procedures, training, and foreign reciprocity. The paragraphs below discuss broad conclusions that may be reached on the basis of Exhibit 15.1. They are not intended to repeat detailed information supplied by the exhibit. (This statement is also applicable to subsequent exhibits in this chapter.)

(a) Title of Auditor and Source of Authority. There are two basic types of auditors who may perform the attest function: statutory accountants and public accountants. Because statutory accountants are defined in the law, they are, in a sense, an extension of the legal system. Auditing standards in these cases are usually part of the legal system. Examples of countries with statutory auditors are France, Italy, and Mexico. Public accountants, while also authorized in the law, are defined through their membership in independent professional associations of accountants. Examples are public accountants in Argentina, certified public accountants in the United States, registered accountants in the Netherlands, and chartered accountants in the United Kingdom. The source of authority for the attest function in most countries comes from national laws and commercial or companies' laws, but, in some cases, such as the United States and Canada, the individual states or provinces have considerable control over who the auditor is and the qualifications for becoming one. In Canada, three groups of professional accountants have evolved, while, in the United States, the American Institute of Certified Public Accountants (AICPA) is the main determiner of auditing standards. Most countries have strong organizations of professional accountants that establish auditing standards and may also influence who may become an auditor. However, the fact that auditing and auditors are deeply rooted in the laws of most countries is a principal impediment to the international harmonization of auditing standards.

(b) Licensing Procedures and Training. In most countries, the auditor is trained in an academic program and must meet certain licensing requirements. Licensing procedures may cover areas such as personal characteristics, education, examinations, and experience. Most countries have a minimum age requirement that ranges from 21 to 25 years of age, as well as a citizenship requirement. Although most countries require the equivalent of a university degree, not all do. For instance, Korea and Kenya do not require university degrees, and in Canada certified general accountants and members

[5] Smith, 2002.

Country	Title of Auditor	Source of Authority	Licensing Procedures	Training
North and South America				
Argentina	Public Accountant	Law and government; Argentine Federation of Professional Councils in Economic Sciences (FACPCE); Center of Scientific and Technical Research (DECyT); and Professional Councils Of Economic Sciences (CPCE)	Applicant must: hold a Contador Publico (Public Accountant) degree that has been issued by an officially recognized national, provincial, or private university and falls within the framework of laws 14557 & 17604; be licensed to practice in the country by (1) filing application, (2) registering his or her name, and (3) paying an annual fee at any jurisdiction.	Applicant must hold a Contador Publico degree from a university within the framework of laws 14557 & 17604. Continuing professional education not required but recommended.
Canada	Chartered Accountant (CA); Certified General Accountant (CGA); and Certified Management Accountant (CMA)	Provincial governments	To become a CA, applicant must hold a degree with at least two years' experience and pass a national exam, administered by the CICA. In some provinces, a nonCA may perform an audit. CGAs and SMAs have to meet education and experience requirements and pass courses or a national examination.	A university degree is normally required to become a CA, CGA or CMA.

Mexico	Contador Publico (Public Accountant); Comisario (statutory auditor); *Licenciado en Contaduna (B.S. in Accounting); Contador Publico Certificado (Certified Public Accountant)*	Regulatory law; The Mexican Institute of Public Accountants; and the Secretary of Public Education	A license is granted by the Secretary of Public Education after the applicant has completed the academic requirements set forth in the law. To be a member of one of the Societies of Public Accountants, the applicant must: (1) hold the professional title of Public Accountant; (2) *be recommended by two members of the society; and* (3) *be approved by the membership committee.*	The academic requirements are set forth in the law. Continuing professional education is required for the members of the Societies of Public Accountants. *Since 1999, optional certification by the Mexican Institute of Public Accountants.*
United States	Certified Public Accountant (CPA)	American Institute of Certified Public Accountants (AICPA)	To obtain the title of CPA, the applicant must have completed a minimum number of hours of education at an accredited college or university and work experience (as established by the state where the applicant wishes to be licensed) and pass the uniform CPA examination, which is given nationwide under the direction of the AICPA.	A minimum number of hours of education at an accredited college or university (usually four years at present but becoming five years in most states by the year 2002) and continuing professional education requirements (as established by the state where the applicant is licensed).

Exhibit 15.1. The Auditor.

Country	Title of Auditor	Source of Authority	Licensing Procedures	Training
Europe				
The Netherlands	Registeraccountant (RA), Accountant-*administratie-consulent* (AA)	Nederlands Instituut van *Registeraccountants* (NivRA) Nederlands Orde van Accountant-administratie consulenten (NOVAA)	After passing either a *university or AA* examination, the applicant must show that he or she is 1. Not bankrupt 2. Not under court guardianship; and 3. Not under a court order preventing practice.	There is a requirement for continuing education—minimum of 40 hours of continuing professional education every year.
United Kingdom	Registered Auditors	*Companies Acts 1985 and 1989. (other legislation may require auditors to hold Registered Auditor status and to have additional experience relevant to specific application, e.g. financial services, banking)*	*A person must be registered with a Recognized Supervisory Body (RSB) recognized under CA 1989 and must meet that RSB's rules for carrying out audit work. The RSB must have arrangements for monitoring and enforcing compliance with Statements of Auditing Standards (SASs).*	*Must meet standards for membership of RSB, plus specific auditing requirements, and must carry out continuing professional education. University education in accounting/auditing is not essential.*
Italy	*Revisore Contabile; Auditing Firm*	*Law and government; Ministry of Justice; Law and government; Ministry of Justice; National Commission of Companies and Stock Exchange (CONSOB)*	*One must be admitted to membership in the Official List of Auditors (Registro dei Revisori Contabili) regulated by the ministry of Justice, after passing a public examination held twice every year. The majority of partners of the firm must have achieved the title of Revisore Contabile and have passed an examination by CONSOB.*	*A period of three years of practical experience tutored by a Revisore Contabile. A degree from a five-year business secondary school plus a three or four-year university degree. Continuing professional education is not formally required; Training is not applicable. However, all such auditing firms are subject to continuous control by CONSOB.*

France	Commissaire aux Comptes (Statutory Auditor)	Laws, beginning with the Companies Act 1863; now Companies Act 1966. This act has been modified many times but still kept the date of 1966.	The applicant is placed on an official list after meeting the following conditions: 1. be 25 years of age; 2. be a citizen in France or the European Union; 3. successfully complete the examination cycle; and 4. have three years' practical experience in auditing.	Academic diploma, which qualifies one for the professional examination cycle.
Germany	Wirtschaftsprüfer (Independent Public Accountants)	Commercial Law and Federal Wirtschaftsprüfer-ordnung Law of 1961, awarded in 1995.	The applicant must be publicly appointed and sworn in after meeting personal and professional qualifications following a government-regulated admission and examination procedure, which includes a heavy experience requirement (minimum of four years).	A university course in business economics, economics, law, engineering, or agriculture. Experience may be substituted.
Sweden	Authorized Public Accountant (Aukand Approved Public Accountant (*Godkaend* Revisor (GR))	Law and government; *The Supervisory Board of Public Accountants (SBPA)*	To be licensed as an AR, one must meet the following basic requirements: 1. Hold a *master* of commerce degree from a Swedish university, with honor grades in business administration and law; 2. have five years of experience in the accounting field, under supervision of an authorized public accountant; and	A degree from a *4*-year Swedish university or school of economics (*3* years for a GR); 5 years of experience (*3 years for a GR*). Continuing professional education is not required but recommended.

Exhibit 15.1. ***(Continued)***

Country	Title of Auditor	Source of Authority	Licensing Procedures	Training
Europe (Continued)				
Sweden (Continued)				
			3. have residency in Sweden *or in another country in the European economic area,* with no restrictions on personal property. The requirements for GR status are the same as for an AR, except that the necessary knowledge of accounting can be acquired through a *three*-year study program at the university level.	
Asia and Pacific				
Australia	*Companies:* Registered Company Auditor *Noncompanies:* Auditor	Companies: *Corporation Law, Australian Securities and Investment Commission (ASIC)* Noncompanies: Either legislation or the documents establishing the entity being audited	Companies: Generally those accepted by *ASIC* are members of the Institute of Chartered Accountants in Australia	Companies: Approved degree followed by the courses and examinations of either the ICAA or the ASCPA. After qualifications, *120* hours of continuing professional education *over each three year period*
Japan	Professional Accountants or Independent Auditors (Certified Public Accountant)	Commercial Law Code; Securities and Exchange Act; and CPA Law	An applicant must pass three levels of examinations and show general knowledge of accounting sufficient expertise as a junior CPA, and professional competency.	A university degree is *not* required. *Continuing professional education is commonly provided by the JICPA and its regional chapters and by training programs offered by the firms.*

Hong Kong	Certified Public Accountant	Companies Ordinance: Hong Kong Society of Accountants (HKSA), established in 1973 by the Professional Accountants Ordinance	The applicant must be 21 years of age and of good character, belong to an approved institute or have completed successfully the prescribed examinations in accountancy and other subjects, and have accumulated five years of practical experience. Graduates of approved universities or colleges may have the experience requirement reduced by as much as two years.	Practicing certificates are issued by the General Council of the HKSA to registered accountants with not less than 30 months of full-time experience in the office of a professional accountant or not less than four years of experience as a registered accountant.
Korea (South)	Certified Public Accountant	*The Ministry of Finance and the Securities and Exchange Commission*	All applicants are eligible to take the first part of the CPA examination. Those who pass it may take the second part, which enables them to become junior CPAs. After serving for two years for a CPA firm *or three years for a* government agency, or bank, applicants are able to *register with the Ministry of Finance to become a CPA*. Applicants with qualifying experience with the government, the military, or bank do not have to sit for the *first part* of the examination.	There are no educational requirements for becoming a CPA. Thirty hours of continuing education are required each year. *Especially, Junior CPAs should complete 200 hours of training at the Accounting Education Institute of KICPA before becoming a CPA.*

Exhibit 15.1. ***(Continued)***

Country	Title of Auditor	Source of Authority	Licensing Procedures	Training
Asia and Pacific (Continued)				
Philippines	Certified Public Accountant	*Revised Accountancy Law (Presidential Decree No. 692) and supervision of the Professional Regulation Commission through the Board of Accountancy*	The applicant must be a citizen of the Philippines or of a country granting reciprocal privileges, 21 years of age, of good moral character, and the holder of a B.S. Degree in Commerce or the equivalent from a recognized college or university. *At present only holders of Bachelor of Science of Accountancy can take the Board Examination.*	*After graduation, graduates can take the Board Examination immediately.*
Singapore	Certified Public Accountant, Singapore (CPA)	The Accountants Act of 1987 and the Companies Act of 1994	Applicants must be 21 years of age, of good character, and not engaged in an occupation inconsistent with the integrity of the Institute of Certified Public Accountants of Singapore (ICPAS). They must have passed examinations in accountancy at the National University of Singapore/Nanyang Technological University or its recognized equivalent or be a member of a recognized accounting association of another country, with at least two years of structured practical experience in areas of accounting, auditing, and taxation.	To qualify for registration, public accountants without structured practical experience must have three years of experience in a public accountant's office before gaining membership in the Institute or else five years of experience in areas of accounting, auditing, and taxation in a public accountant's office, of which at least two years are obtained after passing the qualifying examination.

Africa and Middle East				
Saudi Arabia	Registered Accountant	Ministry of Commerce; Accountants' Regulations (1394/1974)	Application is made to the Ministry of Commerce by the following: (1) for Saudis with I.D., a university degree certificate (for business or accounting degree), and pass examination of the Saudi Organization of CPAs (SOCPA); (2) for non-Saudis, professional qualification plus a business or accounting university degree certificate and pass the SOCPA examination.	Professional accounting experience is recommended.
Kenya	Certified Public Accountant; Kenya-ICPA (K); and External Auditor	The Accountants Act (Chapter 53) of the Laws of Kenya; registration of Accountants' Board at the Ministry of Finance	To obtain the title of ICPA (K), the applicant must be admitted to membership in the Council of the Institute of Certified Public Accountants of Kenya-ICPA (K), must pass the final examination of the Kenya Accountants and Secretaries National Examination Board (KASNEB), or obtain an equivalent qualification recognized by the Institute.	A university degree is not necessary, but admission by ICPA (K) is necessary before the applicant can practice as a Certified Public Accountant. Continuing professional education is offered, although not required.

Exhibit 15.1. ***(Continued)***

of the Society of Management Accountants are not required to hold degrees. Completion of a qualifying examination is also common, but the content and rigor of the examinations vary. The amount of experience required and the extent to which experience can be substituted for education also vary greatly. Germany, the United Kingdom, and Sweden, for example, have experience requirements of three to five years; however, the United States requires only one or two years, and in some states it is possible to become certified without experience. Professional experience is recommended but not required in Saudi Arabia. It is common for individuals in the United States and Canada to become professional accountants in their early twenties, but in Germany, the Netherlands, and Japan, many do not attain the position until their mid-thirties. After receiving qualified status, auditors are required to pursue continuing professional education in less than half the countries. The number of individuals who become professional auditors also varies widely, from a few hundred in Saudi Arabia to a few thousand in Germany to more than 350,000 in the United States.

(c) Reciprocity. The following paragraphs provide an update on the current status of reciprocity in the European Community and the Americas and on the effect of the General Agreement on Tariffs and Trade (GATT) and the General Agreement on Trade of Service (GATS).[6]

(i) European Community. The legal foundation for the philosophy of mutual recognition was the 1957 Treaty of Rome, but it took a number of decades to develop the necessary political will. This happened with the Single European Act of 1986, which enshrined the philosophy of mutual recognition. The general system of mutual recognition of diplomas seeks to permit professionals in the EC to be able to circulate more freely and easily from one member state to another. This system concerns only individuals and ignores firms that may be part of the relevant profession. In addition, the directive relates only to establishment-based provision of services, and does not address the question of cross-border provision of services. The end result sought is the right of the professional to practice his or her profession in the host member state or provide services there under the same conditions as those to which professionals in that country are subject. The progressive implementation of the first directive in member states and the effective organization of local knowledge examinations for the accountancy profession should result in a significant increase in the number of accountants who benefit from the mutual recognition of diplomas.

(ii) Americas. The North American Free Trade Agreement (NAFTA) establishes basic rules and obligations to facilitate cross-border trade in services. NAFTA, while recognizing the need for regulation, encourages broader market access by providing that licensing requirements must be based on objective and transparent criteria, such as professional competence, and must be no more burdensome than is necessary to ensure the quality of service provided.

In 1991, an agreement was entered into between the CICA, the AICPA, and the National Association of State Boards of Accountancy (NASBA), which became effective in some, but not all, states in November 1993. A holder of one designation may qualify for the other by passing local knowledge examinations and by meeting

---

[6] "Discussion Paper on Reciprocity," International Federation of Accountants, 1994.

certain experience requirements. Candidates for reciprocal recognition, who qualify by passing the local knowledge examinations of one of the bodies, will be exempt from the obligation to write the final qualification examination of that body.

(iii) GATT/GATS. The Uruguay Roundtable package, negotiated under the auspices of the General Agreement on Tariffs and Trade (GATT), included the first multilateral agreement removing obstacles to accountants who wish to practice across borders. Some of these hurdles, such as exchange controls and visa restrictions, are faced in common with other service industries and providers. Others, notably difficulties in obtaining certification to practice in foreign jurisdictions, are unique to the professions.

The multilateral agreement, the General Agreement on Trade in Services (GATS), addresses these problems in qualifying to practice in foreign jurisdictions in two ways. First, its provisions on domestic regulation require countries to administer their licensing or certification rules in a reasonable, objective, and impartial manner, and forbids using them as disguised barriers to trade. To carry out this broad mandate, the agreement envisions the development of more specific binding disciplines in the future. Countries are also required to establish specific procedures for verifying the competence and credentials of professionals from other countries. Second, the agreement encourages countries to recognize other countries' qualifications, either autonomously or through mutual recognition agreements. It further sets out guidelines to assure that such mutual recognition agreements are not used simply to discriminate against professionals from countries that are not party to them.

15.4 THE ATTEST FUNCTION.

Exhibit 15.2 addresses some basic characteristics of the attest function. It indicates by country which organizations are required to be audited, how the auditor is elected or appointed, the objective or purpose of the audit, and the source of auditing standards.

(a) Organizations Audited. Generally, auditing is seen as an important function in most countries, as indicated by the broad requirements for organizations to be audited. Most countries require public companies and companies with limited liability to be audited. Some countries are very comprehensive in their requirements. For example, Canada, in addition to requiring audits of public companies, requires private corporations meeting certain size requirements and most nonprofit organizations to be audited. In most countries, there are tests of size below which organizations do not have to be audited.

(b) Election of Auditor. In nearly every country, the auditor is elected or approved by the shareholders of the company. The only exception is Korea, where the auditor is appointed by management or the audit committee.

(c) Objective or Purpose of Audit. The IAPC addresses the objective of an audit in ISA No. 1, as follows: "The objective of an audit of financial statements is to enable the auditor to express an opinion whether the financial statements are prepared, in all material respects, in accordance with an identified financial reporting framework".[7] The guideline does not discuss the wording of the opinion, but states that the

---

[7]International Federation of Accountants, 2001, p. 46.

Country	Required to Be Audited	Election of Auditor	Objective or Purpose of Audit	Sources of Auditing Standards
North and South America				
Argentina	An independent audit is required by *Argentinean legal control authorities like Inspeccion General de Justicia, Taxes Departments, Central Bank, etc.*	Appointed by the board of directors or by the shareholders at the annual meeting for the period subject to review, so as to increase the reliability of accounting information	To issue a technical opinion as to whether the statement present fairly the entity's financial position and results for the period subject to review, according to *Professional Accounting Standards* so as to increase the reliability of accounting information.	*Professional Auditing Standards* are issued by the professional organizations. The Argentinean GAAS are similar to U.S. GAAS.
Canada	Public corporations, private corporations meeting certain tests of size, municipalities, universities, hospitals, and most nonprofit organizations	Elected by the shareholders in the case of corporations; elected by the board in the case of other organizations	To attest to the fairness of financial statements presented by the organization's management.	*Federal and provincial incorporating acts require auditing to follow* GAAS (covered in the CICA Handbook).
Mexico	Every company registered with the Comision Nacional de Falores (National Securities Commission), *all companies filing a consolidated tax return and for tax purposes all companies with income of Pesos 2,412,000 or more than 300 employees in the previous fiscal year*	Generally appointed by the general manager, the board of directors, or the shareholders	*The objective of an audit is to express an opinion regarding the company's financial statements.* The purpose of an audit of a small company would include providing financing, tax and social security services and meeting the requirements of the National Securities Commission. The general law of commercial companies requires all corporations to appoint at least one statutory auditor or (comisario), who is required to submit an annual report to the shareholders on accounting and administrative matters.	Set forth in technical bulletin issued by the Comision de Normas y Procedimiento de Auditoria of the Mexican Institute of Public Accountants, and summarized and classified in the publication *Auditing Standards and Procedures*, issued by the Mexican Institute of Public Accountants.

United States	Companies traded on a national stock exchange, companies that have over 500 shareholders and assets of over $5 million (amounts vary depending on applicable state laws), and certain types of financial services industries (if required to file with the Securities and Exchange Commission or regulated or funded by federal agencies)	Recommendation by the audit committee or a board of directors and approved by the shareholders	The expression of an opinion on the fairness with which the financial statements presents fairly, in all material respects, financial position, results of operations, and its cash flows in conformity with generally accepted accounting principles.	Statements on Auditing Standards are issued by the Auditing Standards Board, the senior technical body of the AICPA designated to issue pronouncements on auditing matters.
Europe				
The Netherlands	All public companies, private companies, cooperative societies, and mutual guarantee associations if they meet at least two of the following criteria: Assets exceed 7.5 million guilders; net turnover exceeds 15 million guilders; average number of employees exceeds 49. All insurance companies and institutions registered under Dutch Credit System Supervision Act and investment companies under Dutch Investment Companies Supervision Act.	Appointed by shareholders at the annual meeting or by the supervisory board of the board of directors	To ensure that balance sheets and accompanying notes present a true and fair view of the financial position; and that profit and loss statements and notes give a true and fair view of the results of operations of a company for the fiscal year under review.	NIvRA has adopted International Standards on Auditing issued by IFAC. They have been translated to the Dutch with specific modifications as necessary.

Exhibit 15.2. The Attest Function.

Country	Required to Be Audited	Election of Auditor	Objective or Purpose of Audit	Sources of Auditing Standards
Europe (Continued)				
United Kingdom	*All limited companies above a specified size limit. Small companies may request audit; separate requirements exist for charities; other bodies/interested parties may request "audit" service for a wide range of enterprises*	*Appointed/reappointed annually by shareholders' majority vote at annual general meeting; in exceptional circumstances casual vacancies may be appointed by Secretary of State for Trade and Industry*	*An independent examination and opinion, for shareholders, on whether the financial statements give a true and fair view of the state of the company's affairs as at the balance sheet date and of the profit and loss for the year then ended and have been properly prepared in accordance with the Companies Act 1985.*	*The Auditing Practices Board (APB) established in 1991 by the Consultative Committee of Accountancy Bodies (CCAB) comprising the six principal accountancy bodies in the United Kingdom and Republic of Ireland*
Italy	*In Italy there are two bodies charged with auditing: The Board of Statutory Auditors* (Collegio Sindacale) *and the Auditing Firm. The first is composed of three to five members and it is compulsory for all companies in the legal form of Stock Company and for Limited Liability Companies that have a capital above 200 million lira. However, a board is required also if, in two consecutive financial years, the company exceeds two of the following limits: a) assets—4.70 million lira b) earnings from sales and provisions of services—9.500 million lira; average*	Proposed by the board of directors and elected by the general *meeting* of shareholders	*To ensure that the financial statements taken as a whole* give a true and fair view of the financial position and result in compliance with the civil code.	Auditing standards are issued by the Dottori Commercialisti and the Ragionieri Collegialisti; and approved by the National Association of Auditors' Firms (ASSIREVI) and by CONSOB. *Similar to International Standards on auditing.*

	staff employed during the financial years—50 units. The Auditing Firm is compulsory for listed companies and other entities that operate in particular economic sectors. A recent decree specifies the regulation concerning appointments for the Board of Statutory Auditors and for Audit firms in listed companies. Particularly: –Auditing firms are in charge of the independent audit of financial statements (and some additional financial information); –Statutory			
France	The following are required to be audited; public limited companies, some limited companies (size >), and some nonprofit organizations (associations, football leagues, political parties, etc.)	Elected or reelected by the shareholders for a six-year term	To certify that all reports and financial statements conform to existing rules and regulations and give a fair and true view.	Companies Act of 1966 and standards published by the Compagnie Nationale des Commissaires aux Comptes (CNCC). These standards are in accordance with IFAC's standards (IAPC).

Exhibit 15.2. (*Continued*)

Country	Required to Be Audited	Election of Auditor	Objective or Purpose of Audit	Sources of Auditing Standards
Europe (Continued)				
Germany	Public companies (including cooperatives), and stock corporations, insurance companies, banks, and government-directed enterprises, audits provided by disclosure law, special audits of relations with affected companies. Small companies are exempted.	Elected by shareholders at annual meetings in case of statutory audit	To determine that financial statements comply with the company's status under legal regulations (German Law) and give a true and fair view.	Commercial laws and jurisdiction are the primary basis, but the Institute of Wirtschaftsprüfers issues professional standards and guidelines.
Sweden	Any company with limited liability status. This includes limited liability companies, branches of foreign companies, cooperative units, and banks.	The Companies Act requires appointment of at least one auditor by the shareholders.	To satisfy the requirements of the Companies Act and to determine if a company's accounts are fairly presented.	The Companies Act states that the audit should be carried out in accordance with generally accepted auditing standards. SBPA recommendations and sections of the Companies Act are the main sources of the auditing standards. These standards are much less detailed than U.S. standards and professionals rely on judgment when applying specific standards.
Asia and Pacific				
Australia	*All public and "large" entities have to be audited. A Company is "large" if it has two of the following three attributes: consolidated gross revenue of $10 million; consolidated gross assets of $5 million; 50 or more employees*	Board of directors with shareholders' approval; client's management; or Auditor General; and at the choice of the body to be audited	*Corporation Law* requires that accounts show a true and fair view and comply with the *Accounting Standards and the Corporation Regulations;* accounts should be presented fairly and be in accordance with the trust deed.	Auditing standards (AUS) and guidelines (AUG) approved by the ICAA and ASCPA.

Japan	Corporations with more than 500 million yen in capital stock or more than 20 billion in liability stocks; public stock and debentures exceeding 500 million yen; stocks registered for the stock exchange or over the counter; plans to list on the exchange; and *labor* unions and educational institutions *receiving a subsidy from governmental bodies; corporations applying for financing from the Small Business Investment Development Corporation*	Under the Commercial Law Code, the auditor and auditing officer are appointed at the stockholders' general meeting. Under the Securities and Exchange Act, the auditor (CPA or corporate) is appointed by the board of directors.	The Commercial Law Code does not specify the purposes of an audit; the Securities and Exchange Act specifies that it is to protect *indirectly public interests and investors,* to confirm that the financial statements fairly and appropriately show the financial position and results, and that they are prepared in conformity with accounting principles.	No Commercial Law Code; the Auditing Standards require: (1) experience, ability, independence; (2) a fair, impartial attitude; (3) due care; (4) refusal to use or reveal confidential information; (5) sufficient evidence for a reasonable basis for an opinion; (6) planning, execution; and (7) audit procedure, timely, and extent of tests based on internal controls, materiality and audit risk.
Hong Kong	All companies incorporated and registered under the Companies Ordinance except certain private companies.	Appointed by the shareholders at the annual meeting.	To show a true and fair view at the balance sheet date and of profit and loss for the financial year and compliance with the Companies Ordinance, certain private companies must show a true and correct view.	Statements of Auditing Standards of the HKSA; regulations of the Companies Ordinance.
Korea (South)	All companies above certain minimum sizes.	Selected by management or audit committee is required to be set up for large listed companies.	To give an opinion on the fairness of the client's financial position, results of operations, and cash flow, and to satisfy statutory requirements.	Pronouncements on GAAS and GAAP issued by the Korean Institute of CPAs and, in certain cases, by the Securities and Exchange Commission.

Exhibit 15.2. ***(Continued)***

Country	Required to Be Audited	Election of Auditor	Objective or Purpose of Audit	Sources of Auditing Standards
Asia and Pacific (Continued)				
Philippines	*Financial statements of sole proprietorships, partnerships and corporations with a minimum quarterly gross sales of P150,000*	*In corporations, elected by the Board of Directors or the shareholders; in unincorporated entities, selected by the general or the sole proprietor*	*Express an independent opinion on the fairness or propriety of the financial statements.*	*GAAS and additional standards promulgated by the Auditing Standards and Practices Council as approved by the Board of Accountancy and the Professional Regulation Commission.*
Singapore	All incorporated companies, both public and private.	Appointed by the shareholders at the annual meeting	To determine whether accounts give a true and fair view of the company's affairs in accordance with provisions of the Companies Act.	Statements of Auditing Guidelines and Practices of the Institute of Certified Public Accounts of Singapore. Closely follow international standards.

Africa and Middle East				
Saudi Arabia	All businesses whose owners enjoy limited liability; all banks, public companies, multinational companies	By shareholders and/or owners	To enhance the credibility of the financial statements and to state if the financial statements: (1) present fairly the financial position and results of a business; (2) comply with the requirements of the regulations for companies and with the company's articles of association insofar as they affect the preparation and presentation of the financial statements.	Saudi Arabian Auditing Standards. In the absence of Saudi standards, U.S. standards are applied.
Kenya	Companies registered and governed by the Companies Act (Chapter 486 of the Laws of Kenya). For companies, the audit is a statutory requirement. In practice, however, audits are a predominant practice for most enterprises.	Auditors of companies registered under the Companies Act (Chap 486 of the Laws of Kenya) must be appointed by the members of the company. In the case of banks and financial institutions, the Central Bank of Kenya must be notified of a change of auditor and approval of the change must be sought.		Member of ICPA(K) are under an obligation to serve Kenyan Accounting Standards and observe approved auditing guidelines. In addition, members of ICPA(K) are obliged by their regulations, where no Kenyan Accounting Standard exists, to observe international accounting standards issued by the IASC.

Exhibit 15.2. (*Continued*)

phrases "present fairly" or "give a true and fair view" are equivalent terms. As can be seen in Exhibit 15.2, both phrases are widely used.

ISA No. 1 does not address what may be a major difference in the objectives of audits in determining whether the financial statements are prepared according to requirements prescribed by law or whether they are presented solely in accord with a set of accounting standards. France, Germany, Sweden, and Italy require both determinations, whereas the United States, the Netherlands, Canada, Mexico, Japan, and the Philippines require only the latter.

(d) Source of Auditing Standards. Most countries rely on professional bodies of accountants for the establishment of auditing standards. Only in a few countries are auditing standards significantly influenced by national laws. An example of the latter practice is Germany, although the professional body issues standards and guidelines; examples of the former include Argentina, the United States, Italy, and Australia. Other countries, such as the United Kingdom and Hong Kong, rely on a combination of legal and professional standards. Sweden and the Netherlands seem to have less detailed auditing standards, relying to a great extent on the basic competence, judgment, and knowledge of the auditor. The wide differences in the establishment of auditing standards in the countries surveyed would seem to point to the practical difficulties of achieving international harmonization of auditing standards.

15.5 ETHICAL STANDARDS AND ENFORCEMENT. Two areas often mentioned as possible obstacles to harmonization are the enforcement of ethical standards and the application of the concept of independence. This section and the next are devoted to these topics. Exhibit 15.3 summarizes ethical standards, enforcement, legal liability, and responsibility of the detection of fraud for each country in this survey.

(a) Ethical Standards and Enforcement. In most countries, the establishment of ethical standards is a complex process. In some countries, such as France and Kenya, the code of ethical conduct is a matter of law, and enforcement involves penalties under the law. Most countries set and enforce ethical standards through a process that involves both a legal basis in law and a code of ethics adopted by a professional body of accountants. In Canada and the United States, ethical standards are established in each province or state both by law and by professional bodies. While there are similarities among these codes, differences do arise, especially during periods when changes are adopted at differing rates.

The effectiveness of enforcing ethical standards varies from country to country. In most of the countries studied, an auditor who violates the ethical standards may be disciplined either by law or by the professional organization, with the penalties ranging from a reprimand to a fine or expulsion. In the United Kingdom, professional bodies have difficulty obtaining evidence because they lack subpoena power. In the United States, expulsion from a state society or the AICPA does not necessarily prevent the expelled member from practicing public accounting, because only the state boards of public accountancy have the authority to revoke a license and the boards often fail to act. In other countries, such as Japan, France, Germany, the Netherlands, and Kenya, the government often takes a formal role in the enforcement of standards. Because the enforcement of national standards is uneven, international enforcement can be expected to be even more difficult.

International organizations, such as the IFAC, depend on the individual countries

Country	Ethical Standards	Enforcement	Legal Liability	Responsibility for Detection of Fraud
North and South America				
Argentina	Argentinean Code of Ethics issued by the FACPCE, which aims to safeguard the public against careless or unscrupulous professionals.	A disciplinary court elected by the direct vote of all registered professionals	Failure by an auditor to perform his or her duties, with regard to the examination of financial statements, may lead to monetary, criminal, professional, or other consequences applicable under the regulations of the control authorities involved. Due to negligence by the auditor, in the event of deception or fraud, the auditor may be responsible for paying damages to the client or another party.	An auditor may be held criminally responsible, not necessarily for the perpetration of crimes, but rather for complicity or concealment, such as providing false or misleading examinations of financial statements.
Canada	The chartered accountants for each province have their own codes, but the codes *are being harmonized. The certified general accountants have a national code. The certified management accountants have provincial codes*	In Ontario, for example, the *provincial institute's* Professional Conduct Committee is partially responsible; the Disciplinary Committee presides over more serious breaches of ethics and the Practice Inspection Commission ensures that practice meets the standards set in codes.	Liability under common law to third parties *was defined for statutory audits by a Supreme court decision. There is some uncertainty* due to recent U.K. and Canadian court decisions.	*GAAS requires the auditor to be skeptical and consider whether* material fraud and error are present in the financial statements. There are no other responsibilities, but management has its own responsibilities.

(*continued*)

Exhibit 15.3 Ethical Standards and Enforcement.

Country	Ethical Standards	Enforcement	Legal Liability	Responsibility for Detection of Fraud
North and South America (Continued)				
Mexico	The Mexican Institute of Public Accountants has issued a code of professional ethics to guide its members in moral conduct and to declare its intentions to serve society with trust, diligence, *and self-respect.*	The Mexican Institute of Public Accountants	*The auditor may be sued if the audit is not conducted according to the standards and procedures issued by the Mexican Institute of Public Accountants and a third party is affected.*	*A statutory auditor is responsible for the vigilance of the company and the administrations*
United States	The bylaws of the AICPA require that members adhere to the Rules of Code of Professional Conduct. These Principles of the Code of Professional Conduct of the AICPA express the profession's recognition of its responsibilities to the public, to clients, and to colleagues, They guide members in the performance of their professional responsibilities and express the basic tenets of ethical and professional conduct.	Council of the AICPA is authorized to designate bodies to promulgate technical standards under the Rules, and the bylaws require adherence to those Rules and Standards. Compliance with the Code of Professional Conduct depends primarily on members' understanding and voluntary actions, secondarily on reinforcement by peers and on public opinion, and, ultimately, on disciplinary proceedings, when necessary, against members who fail to comply with the rules.	The auditor may be held legally and professionally liable when he or she fails to apply due professional care in the application of the required auditing standards.	The auditor should assess the risk that errors and irregularities may cause the financial statements to contain a material misstatement. Based on that assessment, the auditor should design the audit to provide reasonable assurance of detecting errors and irregularities due to fraud that are material to the financial statements.

Europe				
The Netherlands	The Rules of Conduct for accountants (GBS) prohibit discrediting the profession, the use of information for one's own gain. They require preserving records of evidence and keeping information about a client confidential. Key issues addressed are impartiality, confidentiality, quality of work, and independence.	Complaints received by the Disciplinary Board and the Board of Appeal	Criminal and civil liability for criminal offense (fines to imprisonment), for negligence, acts discrediting the profession; the latter part is enforced by the Disciplines Board, not by the law; for violating professional rules (resulting in written warning, written reprehension, suspension (maximum 6 months), and expulsion).	In principle, management bears responsibility for the financial statements; however, auditors can also be taken to court if they fail to detect errors, Auditors are not responsible for irregularities (intentional distortions of financial statements) if they have performed their audit with due and professional care. Material fraud that is detected, but not redressed, must be reported to the authorities.
United Kingdom	*Each RSB has an ethical guide; all stress integrity, objectivity, independence, professional competence and due care, professional behavior, and confidentiality*	*Each RSB must have rules for enforcing compliance with SASs; penalties may include withdrawal of registration so that person becomes ineligible to perform company audits. Monitoring is carried out, e.g. by the Joint Monitoring Unit of the ICAEW/ICAS*	*Rule of "joint and several" liability means that auditors may carry the full cost of negligence even where this is partly the fault of directors; liability to third party exists at common law where loss is clearly attributable to reliance on a report prepared negligently and the party preparing the report knew (or should have known) it would be relied upon.*	*Required to plan audit so as to obtain sufficient evidence to give reasonable assurance that the financial statements are free from material misstatement, whether caused by fraud or other irregularity or error.*

Exhibit 15.3 (*Continued*)

Country	Ethical Standards	Enforcement	Legal Liability	Responsibility for Detection of Fraud
Europe (Continued)				
Italy	The rules of association of the Ordine Nazionale del Dottori Commercialisti and of the Collegio Nazionale dei Ragionieri include specific ethics requirements relating to independence and competence. Auditing Standard No. 1 of the Consiglio Nazionale del Dottori Commercialisti specifies the following re-requirements for the auditor: Competence as a condition for acceptance of the auditor's work, exercise of due professional care in the conduct of the audit, integrity, and independence.	Ethical standards are enforced by the professional associations.	The auditor is legally and professionally liable only when he or she fails to apply, or incorrectly applies, the required auditing standards.	No specific requirements. According to the ISA, the auditor is not resopnsible for failure to detect fraud or illegal acts if the auditing procedures appropriate in the circumstances have been competently performed.
France	Set both by law and the Code of Professional Ethics adopted by the Compagnie Nationale, including rules on independence, incompatible functions, advertising, use of title or firm name, relationships with colleagues, connection between predecessor and successor.	Penalties are set by law, and in several cases by the Compagnie Nationale des Commissaires aux Comptes, which may take disciplinary action.	Violation of laws that regulate the profession are subject to Penal Code. Requirements are stated by law. Auditors are required to carry liability insurance.	No responsibility, but liable to client and third parties for fraud and negligence; must report known illegal acts by client to government authorities and/or public prosecutor.

Germany	A code of ethics covers legally required audits. Detailed guidelines issued by the Institute of CPAs, and by the Chamber of Auditors include independence, professional care, partial responsibility, discretion, impartiality, professional conduct, and elimination of incompatible duties.	A self-regulated body can warn, reprimand, fine, or expel an auditor who is guilty of not performing duties in accordance with professional laws and standards.	Unlimited liability to clients and third parties for false statements or other intentional violations. Liability is limited in case of negligence. Breach of confidentiality is a criminal offense.	Expected to conduct the examination in an impartial and conscientious manner. Liable if failure to discover fraud results from negligence.
Sweden	The FAR has developed rules of professional ethics similar to those followed by U.S. CPAs.	Sanctions may be imposed by the Supervisory Board of Public Accountants.	The auditor can be held liable for client damages that were intentional or caused by carelessness.	The auditor is responsible for fraud only if the failure to detect it was intentional or caused by carelessness.
Asia and Pacific				
Australia	*Code of Professional Conduct (CPC) of the ICAA and ASCPA*	Disciplinary committees in the profession	The ethical standards per se do not give rise to legal liability. However, under the *Corporation Law*, criminal sanctions may be invoked against dishonest auditors, and deregistration may be a remedy against inappropriate conduct. Civil remedies for auditors; negligence are also available.	The auditor has no responsibility for reporting on control structures, *other than reporting significant problems in the management letter to the Board or Audit Committee on a timely basis*. Specific requirements to see and detect fraud do not at present exist.

Exhibit 15.3 (*Continued*)

Country	Ethical Standards	Enforcement	Legal Liability	Responsibility for Detection of Fraud
Asia and Pacific (Continued)				
Japan	The CPA law and the JICPA code prohibit the impairment of trust and require independence, secrecy, and restrictions of advertising. Punishment may be administered for false and unreasonable attestation.	Under CPA Law, the Minister of Finance is empowered to investigate violations and to assess penalties, including warning, suspension, or withdrawal from registration. The CPA has the right to vindicate himself or herself. The JICPA Punishment Committee also enforces ethical standards. The President of the JICPA determines penalties according to the views of the committee and the board.	Under the Securities and Exchange Act, if investors lose because of material errors in audited financial statements, the auditor or firm must compensate for an error unless they can prove lack of intention and the use of due care. Under the Commercial Law Code, the auditor must compensate client for breach of contract and for materiality false items in an audit report if the auditor cannot prove due care.	The auditor must use due care to detect causes of material difference in financial statements. The auditor must report actions that contradict the directors' duties to the statutory auditors of the client.
Hong Kong	The Hong Kong Society of Accountants has issued statements of professional ethics originally based on those issued by the Institute of Chartered Accountants in the United Kingdom, but in some cases updated based on AICPA's professional conduct.	The Hong Kong Society acts as the disciplinary body.	Criminal liability for auditors who willfully make untrue statements in the prospectus or who induce another person by fraudulent or reckless misrepresentation to invest money. The auditor is liable for damages to the client and in some cases to third parties for negligence resulting in financial loss. Negligence may also be treated as a criminal offense.	The auditor is not expected to search for fraud but must be aware of the possibility of it and investigate fully if there are grounds for suspicion.

Korea (South)	The Korean Institute of Certified Public Accountants (KICPA) has set standards resembling those followed in the U.S., although modified to meet local circumstances.	The KICPA enforces standards; serious infractions are referred to the Ministry of Finance. Licenses may be suspended for six months to two years. There have been increasing instances of fines or imprisonment as provided by law.	Auditors face legal liability for negligence and fraud. Suits by a third party and prosecution by the government for a fraudulent audit is increasing.	The auditor is not expected to detect fraud in the course of an audit. The KICPA and SEC have mandated extensive audit procedures to avoid fraud in accounting for cash and promissory notes.
Philippines	*The Code of Professional Ethics promulgated by the Board of Accountancy aims to provide for the maintenance of high standards of competence and integrity by CPAs.*	The Board of Accountancy may issue reprimands, or suspend or revoke registration certificates.	*The CPA has a liability to clients and third parties. As to clients, a CPA is liable for damages for his negligence and breach of contract to render professional services. As to third parties, a CPA is liable for losses which are caused by his fraud or gross negligence.*	*The auditor is not primarily responsible for the detection of fraud but if the auditor's examination indicates that some fraud may have occurred that could result in material misstatement of the financial statements, this would cause the auditor to extend his procedures to confirm or dispel this concern.*
Singapore	The rules of the Accountants Act call for integrity and confidentiality, and prohibit incompatible functions, advertising, encroachment on the business of others, certification of estimates, acceptance of benefits from service for clients without consent, and acts discreditable to the profession. The standards on independence parallel those set by the United Kingdom.	The Disciplinary Committee of the ICPAS and PAB may censor, expel, or suspend a member. It may also issue fines of up to $5,000 and the costs of an investigation.	There is liability for damages to the client and in some cases third parties for negligence in performing an audit, and criminal liablity for willfully making untrue statements in a prospectus. Negligence may also bring criminal liablity.	The auditor is expected to seek reasonable assurance that material fraud has not occurred; if material fraud has taken place, the auditor must ensure that the error is corrected or that its effect is indicated in the financial information. The Companies Act also requires reporting of fraud under certain circumstances to the Minister of Finance.

Exhibit 15.3 (*Continued*)

Country	Ethical Standards	Enforcement	Legal Liability	Responsibility for Detection of Fraud
Africa and Middle East				
Saudi Arabia	Ethical standards (which encompass U.S. GAAS requirements) as set by SOCPA	Ministry of Commerce	The auditor is liable for negligence. However, civil litigation against auditors is very rare. The Ministry of Commerce will penalize auditors who break regulations.	Responsibility exists only if the fraud is material to the financial statements taken as a whole.
Kenya	Ethical standards are given in Statements and in Section 28 of the Accountants Act (Cap 531 of the Laws of Kenya). A member of ICPA(K) must maintain integrity, professional independence and confidentiality, and show competence in all professional work.	Section 28 of the Accountants Act (Cap 531 of the Laws of Kenya)	The auditor is legally and professionally liable only when he or she fails to apply or incorrectly applies the required auditing standards.	The auditor is not responsible for failure to detect fraud or illegal acts. However, the auditor should plan his or her audit with reasonable expectation of detecting material misstatements resulting from irregularities or fraud.

Exhibit 15.3 (*Continued*)

for enforcement. For example, during 1990, IFAC issued a Code of Ethics for professional accountants that set forth fundamental principles of professional conduct. The fundamental principles include integrity, objectivity, professional competence, and due care, confidentiality, professional behavior, and compliance with international and national technical standards.[8] Since IFAC "believes that due to national differences of cultural, language, legal and social systems, the task of preparing detailed ethical requirements is primarily that of the member bodies in each country concerned,"[9] it remains to be seen how much influence these guidelines will have in the harmonization of ethical standards.

(b) Legal Liability and the Detection of Fraud. The auditor is usually held liable by the client for breach of contract, including the failure to carry out an audit in a timely and professional manner. The liability of the auditor to third parties varies greatly among the countries studied, but it usually stems from failure to perform the audit in accordance with established professional standards. For instance, simple negligence on the part of the auditor is normally not sufficient in the United States or Germany for a third party to win, but in other countries, such as Sweden, the United Kingdom, Japan, Hong Kong, Saudi Arabia, and Kenya, the auditor can apparently be held liable to third parties for simple negligence. In all countries, the auditor can be held liable for fraud or gross negligence.

The issue of the auditor's responsibility for detection of fraud and error is addressed in ISA No. 1, which places the responsibility for the prevention and detection of fraud and error on management. It holds that the auditor "is not and cannot be held responsible for the prevention of fraud and error." However, "In planning the audit the auditor should assess the risk that fraud and error may cause the financial statements to contain material misstatements and should inquire of management as to any fraud or significant error which has been discovered." And, "Based on the risk assessment the auditor should design audit procedures to obtain reasonable assurance that misstatements arising from fraud and error that are material to the financial statements taken as a whole are detected."[10]

Exhibit 15.3 indicates that this guideline most closely resembles the auditor's responsibility as defined in the United States, Canada, Mexico, the United Kingdom, Singapore, Japan, and Saudi Arabia. However, in most other countries, including Canada, France, Italy, the Netherlands, Hong Kong, Korea, and Kenya, the responsibility for detecting fraud is explicitly stated or limited to what might be discovered in the ordinary course of the audit.

15.6 INDEPENDENCE. Exhibit 15.4 summarizes the approaches to independence taken by the countries in this study, as well as the functions generally not allowed.All countries have a test of independence for the auditor, and most stress both the appearance and the fact of independence. But translation of these concepts into practice varies considerably. Most countries do not allow the auditor to be an employee or part of management, but some countries, such as Hong Kong, allow the auditor to sit on the board of directors in certain instances, and others, such as Korea, permit the

[8]International Federation of Accountants, 2001, p. 442.
[9]International Federation of Accountants, 2001, p. 439.
[10]International Federation of Accountants, 2001, pp. 79–80.

Country	Concept of Independence	Functions Generally Not Allowed
North and South America		
Argentina	Based on an objective definition of lack of independence, as opposed to general requirement of independence	*Company employee, partner, chairman, manager, consort or consanguinity relationship up to fourth degree of the company authorities.*
Canada	Defined by rules of professional conduct of the *Provincial* Institute of Chartered Accountants and by incorporating acts. *GAAS requires* the audit to be carried out *with* an objective state of mind. *The rules and conduct of Certified General Accountants require public practitioners to be independent.*	Serving in any function that lessens independence, taking part in decision making in a management consultant engagement, auditing a corporation where stock in the client is owned
Mexico	Prohibits a public accountant from acting as an auditor of a corporation when circumstances exist that may impair his or her objectivity and reduce his or her mental independence or give such an impression to the public. Statutory auditors are considered to be independent.	Not available.
United States	Must meet standards of independence in both fact and appearance.	The functions generally not allowed are described in the ET Section of the AICPA Professional Standards. Recently passed Sarbannes-Oxley legislation further defines independence to include a requirement that the auditor of publicly-owned companies not be allowed to provide consulting services and to add new requirement for the companies' audit committees.
Europe		
The Netherlands	In recent Dutch auditing literature, independence is described as functional independence, financial independence, and relational and mental independence.	The auditor cannot undertake any work affecting independence or impartiality (i.e., acting in a managerial capacity, accepting an executive appointment in business or industry, or acting as an insurance agent or broker).
United Kingdom	*Ethical guidance of RSB's emphasizes responsibility of auditor to avoid conflict of interest or compromise of independence; gives examples of situations likely to cause conflict. Professional persons must be, and must be seen to be, independent. The concept of 'independence' is not defined in law or standards.*	*The auditor must not be a director, partner or a shareholder of a client company; must not hold close personal relationship with a director, partner or shareholder.*

Italy	Must meet in both fact and appearance	A partner cannot be appointed as director or "statutory" for companies quoted on the stock exchange or for other entities required by law to be audited for at least three years prior to his or her appointment as auditor; and auditor cannot be a shareholder, employee or manager, or have any contractual commitment with the entity to be audited for at least three years prior to his or her appointment as auditor. *Change in auditing firm is compulsory every 9 years for listed companies.*
France	Form as well as substance of independence; relationships to avoid are detailed by law.	Receiving any special benefit from a client or holding an incompatible position as a board member, a part of management, or an employee. Statutory audits may not provide other services (i.e., consulting) in the same company.
Germany	Appearance as well as fact of independence. Relationships to avoid are detailed by law.	*An auditor must not audit a corporation if 1) he owns shares of or has done the accounting or preparation of financial statements for the client 2) he is or has been a legal representative, board member or employee of the client in the preceding three years, 3) is an owner, legal representative, board member or employee of an organization which controls the client or owns 20% or more shares outstanding of the client or which has done the accounting or preparation of financial statements for the client, 4) has earned more than 30% of his income from the client in each of the preceding three years.* *Similar rules apply to auditing partnerships/companies. Additionally they may not audit a corporation whose shares are listed in the .amtlicher Handel. segment of the German stock market if the audit done by one who has signed the Bestaetigungsvermerk in more than six of the preceding ten years.*
Sweden	The auditor must be independent in both fact and appearance.	Any financial interest in or together with a client, and any business interest other than auditing and associated activities.

Exhibit 15.4 Independence.

Country	Concept of Independence	Functions Generally Not Allowed
Asia and the Pacific		
Australia	The auditor must be, and must be seen to be, independent (i.e., free of any interest which is incompatible with objectivity).	Investment by members of the practice and their relatives in an audit client, either directly or via an intermediary, such as a trust or nominee. Accepting, making, or guaranteeing a loan outside the ordinary course of the client's business; acting as a receiver or a liquidator of an audit client or as a director of a company which exerts influence over an audit client; preparing the books of a company, except in exceptional circumstances; and under the Corporation Law, borrowing over $5,000, other than in housing loans made by the client in the normal course of its business.
Japan	Concept of independence (fair and impartial attitude) set forth in professional standards. An auditor should have no material conflict-of-interest relationship. Specific rules are set forth in CPA law and Ordinance of Ministry of Finance.	An auditor or spouse cannot be independent if serving as an official of the corporation or responsible for financial affairs within one year of an auditing report; employed within one year of an auditing report; holding a material interest in the corporation; connected closely, in present or past, with the corporation through duties as a government official; providing certain tax services.
Hong Kong	Appearance as well as fact of independence are required. Relationships to avoid are specified in the Companies Ordinance and in the Rules of Professional Ethics issued by the Hong Kong Society of Accountants. It is not allowed to have any financial interest in a client.	Serving as a director or an officer of the client company or as the partner or employee of an officer of the company, except when the company is private or a body corporate.
Korea (South)	"Financial independence" from audit clients is required; however, a CPA is permitted to have equity interest in the client up to *1* percent. *A CPA is not permitted to audit a client if he/she has been an employee within a year before initiative date of audit period*	Auditors are permitted to provide any and all kinds of services within a limited range of accounting, auditing, and consulting services.

Philippines	The public accountant accepts the responsibility of sustaining criteria that would be viewed as independent and unbiased by one with knowledge of all facts. In all matters relating to an engagement, an independence in mental attitude is to be maintained by the public accountant.	The following functions are not generally allowed: *an auditor with direct or material indirect financial interest in the enterprise; an auditor who had any joint, closely held business investment with the enterprise or any officer, director or principal stockholder which was material in relation to his or her firm's net worth; an auditor who was connected with the enterprise as a promoter, underwriter or voting trustee; an auditor who was a trustee for any pension or profit-sharing trust of the enterprise.*
Singapore	Independence and freedom of any obligation are required by the Statement of Auditing guidelines of the ICPAS; restrictions are specified in the Companies Act.	Serving as an officer of the company, as a partner, employer or employee of an officer, or as the person responsible for keeping the register of members or of holders of debentures for the company; holding a debt to the client or a related company of more than $2,500.
Africa and Middle East		
Saudi Arabia	The auditor and his or her staff must be completely independent, impartial, and objective.	Any function that impairs independence
Kenya	A member of ICPA(K) in public practice should be, or should be seen to be, free of any interest which might detract from objectivity and integrity in each assignment that he or she undertakes.	Not available

Exhibit 15.4. ***(Continued)***

auditor to have a small financial interest in a client. Although the United States is generally regarded as having the most stringent independence standards, it allows auditors to perform tax and consulting services for clients who are being audited without impairment of independence. Due to recent developments, the practice of providing certain consulting services to public companies will likely be disallowed in the future in the United States. In contrast, a firm in Japan cannot perform these functions for the same client for which it also serves as auditor, and in the Netherlands these tasks are not generally performed for an audit client, whereas in France they are not permitted in a statutory audit. The Eighth Company Law Directive gives discretionary power to member states to determine the conditions of independence for a statutory auditor. In practical terms, this action will probably lead to a variety of definitions of independence, because member states are likely to follow their existing philosophies of independence.

15.7 AUDIT REPORTS. IAG No. 13 provides guidelines for the concept of audit reports, recommending that the auditor's report contain the following basic elements: title, addressee, the date of the report, the auditor's address, and signature.[11] This recommendation that the auditor's unqualified report contain three paragraphs: an opening paragraph that identifies the financial statements and states management's and the auditor's responsibilities, the scope paragraph describes the nature of the audit, and the opinion paragraph that expresses the opinion on the financial statements. Exhibit 15.5 summarizes the form of the audit report for the countries contained in this survey.

As can be seen in Exhibit 15.5, Argentina, Canada, the United States, Italy, the United Kingdom, Japan, Hong Kong, Korea, the Philippines, Singapore, and Kenya comply substantially with this standard. Other countries diverge from these guidelines. France, for example, requires a report of related parties with no standard format, and, in the Netherlands, there is not a standard format but there is a reference to international auditing standards. In about half of the countries, such as Argentina, Japan, and the United States, the opinion states that the financial statements "present fairly," and in others, such as Germany and Sweden, reference is made to compliance with the country's laws.

From the varying degrees with which these countries conform to IAG No. 13, it is clear that substantial differences in how auditors communicate to users of financial information exist from country to country. For a user of the audited financial statements to be able to interpret the auditor's report of a particular country, it is necessary to know and to understand the auditing standards of that country.

15.8 SUMMARY. Although there are differences in auditing standards among the 18 countries surveyed, there are also substantial similarities. The differences that do exist stem from the dichotomy that exists between countries that rely on law for auditing standards and those that rely on professional bodies. Areas where this difference has an impact are in the identity of the auditor as a statutory auditor and professional accountant, the source of auditing standards, ethical standards and their enforcement, and the form and content of audit reports. Unique features in auditing standards tend to show up in countries such as Sweden, France, and Italy, which are

---

[11] International Federation of Accountants, 2001, pp. 212–213.

Country	Reporting Requirement
North and South America	
Argentina	Standard audit report formats have been issued by the Buenos Aires CPCE. Although not mandatory, they are generally used. The FACPCE sets the minimum data that must be included in an audit report. The important elements are: 1. The name of the reports audited and the related periods. 2. The conduct of the audit in accordance with auditing standards. 3. The auditing standards. 4. The opinion as to fairness of statements. 5. Statements presented in accordance with professional accounting standards. 6. The name of those requiring audit or services.
Canada	The standard auditor's report is very similar to a U.S. Report. However, Canadian standards require a clean opinion if there are inconsistencies or contingencies, provided that they are adequately disclosed in the financial statements.
Mexico	In all cases in which the name of the public accountant is associated with financial statements or information, he or she should express in a clear and unmistakable manner 1. The nature of his or her relation with such information. 2. His or her opinion on the same. 3. The important limitations, when applicable, that were imposed on the examination, the qualifications derived from them, the important reasons why an adverse opinion is expressed, or the reasons why a professional opinion cannot be expressed after an examination is performed in accordance with auditing standards. The auditor, when rendering his or her opinion on financial statements, should observe that 1. They were prepared in accordance with generally accepted accounting principles. 2. Such principles were applied on a consistent basis. 3. The information presented therein and in the related notes is adequate and sufficient for its reasonable interpretation.
United States	In a standard three-paragraph report, the auditor first identifies the company and financial statements being audited and states the responsibilities of management and the auditor. Second, the auditor must indicate the scope of the examination and whether or not the audit complied with generally accepted auditing standards and that is a sufficient basis for an opinion. Third, he or she must state whether the financial statements are presented fairly in accordance with GAAP and whether GAAP have been consistently observed in relation to reports of previous years. The auditor must express an opinion on the financial statement as a whole or assert that an opinion cannot be expressed.

(*continued*)

Exhibit 15.5. Audit Reports.

Country	Reporting Requirement
Europe	
France	The auditor must certify the financial statements or qualify the report following a standard format based on International Auditing Standards. A second report is required, detailing agreements entered into between the company and legally defined related parties. There is no standard format for this second report.
Italy	*The auditor's report consists of four main paragraphs. The first identifies the financial statements and defines the responsiblities of both the Directors and the Auditors. The second (or scope) paragraph includes the source of accounting standards used, the parts of the director's report necessary for a clear understanding of the responsibility. The third paragraph identifies any material departure or deviation from generally accepted accounting standards. The fourth paragraph is the opinion paragraph. A fifth paragraph might be present for emphasis on significant matters.*
The Netherlands	The wording is not specified by law. According to ISA 700 "The Auditors' Report on Financial Statements" which has been adopted by NIvRA the auditors' report includes among others both scope and opinion paragraphs. In the scope paragraph reference is made to the ISAs. In the opinion paragraph the auditor clearly states as to whether the financial statements give a true and fair view in accordance with the financial reporting framework and, where appropriate, whether the financial statements comply with statutory requirements.
Sweden	Chapter 10 of the Companies Act states that the auditor's report should include statements about 1. The preparation of the annual report in accordance with the Act. 2. The adoption of the balance sheet and income statement. 3. The proposal included in the administration report for disposition of the unappropriated earnings or deficit. 4. The discharge from the liability of members of the board of directors and the managing director.
United Kingdom	*The auditor's report sets out respective responsibilities of directors and auditor's scope of audit; basis of opinion and statement of opinion. By statute it must cover the balance sheet, profit and loss account, and related notes; by auditing standards it extends to other financial statements prescribed by accounting standards, such as the cash flow statement. The opinion is stated on whether the financial statements give a true and fair view and comply with statutory requirements. The scope section explains that auditors read other information contained in the audit report, including the corporate governance statement, and consider the implications for their report if they become aware of inconsistencies. The scope section also explains the auditor's responsibilities in relation to the directors' report, the accounting records, information and explanations required, and rules regarding the disclosure of directors' remuneration.*
Germany	*According to the German Commercial Code the auditor's report to the corporation must contain a description of the process and the result of the audit, including management's report, an estimation of future development, a statement of compliance with legal regulation and a statement explaining the company's risk management system. The auditor must also provide a summary in the Bestaetigungsvmerk that covers the content, type, and volume of the audit; an evaluation of the audit results; and statements as to whether or not the financial statements and management's report present a true and fair view.*

Asia and Pacific	
Australia	The standards report has the following format: We have audited the accounts of X Limited on pages ____ to ____, and the Statement by Directors in accordance with Australian Auditing Standards (scope paragraph). In our opinion the accounts of X Limited are properly drawn up in accordance with the provisions of the Companies (XXX) Code and so as to give a true and fair view of: (i) the state of affairs of the company at ____ 19____ and of the profit of the company for the year ended on that date; (ii) the other matters required by Section 269 of the Code to be dealt with in the accounts; and are in accordance with applicable approved accounting standards and Australian Accounting Standards (opinion paragraph).
Japan	The auditor's report must outline the scope of the audit performed and state an opinion on the financial statements, expressing whether the statements fairly present the results. It must also state matters that are also reported in the financial statements but that the auditor wants to call attention to.
Hong Kong	The auditor's report must state whether the balance sheet and profit-and-loss account have been prepared properly in accordance with the Companies Ordinance and whether they give a true and fair view of the state of affairs at the year's end and of the profit and loss for the year. The report must also express an opinion as to whether proper books of account have been kept, whether proper returns have been received from the branches, and whether the accounts agree with the books and returns. The report should be modified if the auditor has not received all required information and if disclosures about officers' and directors' remunerations are inadequate.
Korea (South)	The reporting standards and the standard format of the audit report are generally the same as those provided by the AICPA statements of auditing standards in the United States.
Philippines	The auditor's report must state whether the financial statements have been formed in accordance with GAAP and whether the principles have been applied in the same way during the current period as they were in the previous one. The report must express an opinion regarding the financial statements as a whole; when such an opinion cannot be expressed, the reasons should be stated. The report should also contain a clear indication of the character of the auditor's examination and of the degree of responsibility assumed by the auditor. Unless otherwise indicated in the report, informative disclosures are to be regarded as reasonably adequate. The wording is similar to reports in the United States before the adoption of SAS No. 50 by the AICPA.

Exhibit 15.5. *(Continued)*

Country	Reporting Requirement
Asia and Pacific (Continued)	
Singapore	The auditor's report must state whether the accounts and, when relevant, consolidated accounts give a true and fair view. The report must also express an opinion as to whether the accounting and other records, including the registers, have been kept properly for a fair presentation and for compliance with stipulations on disclosure in the Companies Act. Reference is made to statements of auditing standards in a similar format to International Auditing Standards.
Africa and Middle East	
Saudi Arabia	The auditor's report must refer in the scope paragraph to management's responsibility for financial statements and whether management has provided all information and explanations required, as well as to the auditing standards followed and whether the auditor has been able to attain a reasonable degree of assurance to express an opinion. The report must express an opinion as to fair presentation of financial statements in accordance with accepted accounting standards and state compliance with regulations for companies and articles of association of the enterprise. Minister of Finance further requires that all books of accounts must be maintained in Arabic. Compliance with this requirement must be stated in the report.
Kenya	The Kenyan Auditing Standard 2 specifies the contents of the auditor's report, which must include: 1. An appropriate title, such as "Auditors' Report." 2. The identity of the addressee, as required by the circumstances of the engagement and regulations. 3. Identification of the financial statements audited. 4. Reference to the auditing standards followed. 5. The audit opinion. 6. Any other information prescribed by statute or other specific requirements. 7. The date of the report. 8. The identity of the auditor.

Exhibit 15.5. (*Continued*)

closely tied to the legal system. The minimum qualifications to become an auditor can vary in both education and experience, as well as in the nature and content of professional examinations. The definitions of independence are fairly similar in the countries surveyed, but the actions that are deemed to violate independence can vary both in the financial relationships permitted between the auditor and client and in the nature of the services performed. Although half of the countries report an opinion based on a "true and fair view," and the rest report an opinion based on "present fairly," international auditing standards treat these terms as equivalent. Overall, there seems to be a trend toward harmonization of auditing standards based on international auditing standards.

SOURCES AND SUGGESTED REFERENCES

American Institute of Certified Public Accountants. *Professional Accounting in Foreign Countries Series*. New York: AICPA, 1987–1989. (Countries included are Argentina, Canada, France, Hong Kong, Italy, Japan, Mexico, the Netherlands, the Philippines, Sweden, and the United Kingdom.)

International Federation of Accountants. *IFAC Handbook: Technical Pronouncements*. New York: IFAC, 2001.

International Federation of Accountants. *Guidelines on Ethics for Professional Accountants*. New York: IFAC, 1990.

Needles, Belverd, (ed.). *Comparative International Auditing Standards*. Sarasota, FL: American Accounting Association, 1985.

Needles, Belverd E. Jr., Sridhar Ramamoorti, and Sandra Waller Shelton. "The Role of International Auditing Standards in the Improvement of International Financial Reporting." *Advances in International Accounting*, 2002.

Pomeranz, Felix. "The Responsibility of an American Accountant in the Audit of Foreign Locations." Paper presented in the Annual Distinguished Speaker Series at California State University at Long Beach, California, April 17, 1985.

"SEC Concept Release: International Accounting Standards." Release Nos. 33-7801, 34-42430; International Series No. 1215, February 18, 2000.

Smith, Brian. Secretary of the Forum of Firms. Interview conducted May 2002.

PART IV

INTERNATIONAL ACCOUNTING HARMONIZATION

CHAPTER 16

INTERNATIONAL FINANCIAL REPORTING STANDARDS

Paul Pacter

Deloitte Touche Tohmatsu

CONTENTS

16.1 INTRODUCTION. A business enterprise that receives capital from investors and creditors or one that is seeking new capital has an obligation to keep its capital providers informed about the company's performance, condition, and prospects. In a word, the business is *accountable* to its investors and creditors. It is also accountable to others who provide resources or an environment in which to operate, such as employees, governments, and the community at large. Providing this information is the role of financial accounting and reporting.

Historically, the rules for what financial information should be provided and in what format have evolved country by country. By the last quarter of the twentieth century, a mechanism for developing and adopting accounting standards had been established in most countries.

In some cases, standard setting has been the responsibility of the public accounting profession, often with enforcement of the standards achieved by law or government regulation. For example, accounting standards are set by private-sector professional accounting organizations in Austria, Brazil, Canada, Denmark, Hong Kong, Indonesia, Italy, the Netherlands, New Zealand, Philippines, South Africa, Sweden, Switzerland, and Taiwan.

In other cases, standard setting has been the responsibility of the government. For example, there are government-sponsored accounting standards boards in Argentina, China, Finland, France, Greece, Malaysia, Poland, and Saudia Arabia.

In a few countries, including Germany, Japan, the United Kingdom, and the United States, a private-sector standard setter has been established that is independent of the public accounting profession. The Australian board is private but appointed by and under the oversight of a government agency.

National accounting standards made sense when companies raised money in, and investors and lenders looked for investment opportunities in, their home country. But over 30 years ago, the accounting profession began to recognize the importance of a cooperative international effort in the development of accounting standards—and the benefits of a common global accounting language.

16.2 GLOBALIZATION OF CAPITAL MARKETS. Nowadays, investors seek investment opportunities all over the world. Similarly, companies seek capital at the lowest price anywhere. Almost every day you can open a business newspaper and read about a sizable cross-border merger. The problem that this creates for investors, of course, is that accounting differences can completely obscure the comparisons that they must necessarily make as they assess various investment opportunities.

In testimony before a United States House of Representatives committee in June 2001, Paul Volcker, former Chairman of the U.S. Federal Reserve Board and Chairman of the International Accounting Standards Committee (IASC) Foundation Board of Trustees, said: If markets are to function properly and capital is to be allocated efficiently, investors require transparency and must have confidence that financial information accurately reflects economic performance. Investors should be able to make comparisons among companies in order to make rational investment decisions. In a rapidly globalizing world, it only makes sense that the same economic transactions are accounted for in the same manner across various jurisdictions.

(a) Cross-Border Capital Raising Throughout the World. That the world's financial markets are globalized is undeniable. On many stock exchanges, foreign listings are a large percentage of total. Exhibit 16.1 sets out some representative statistics from late 2002.

Market	Percent of Listed Companies that Are Foreign
NASDAQ (U.S.)	11%
New York Stock Exchange	20%
Registered with the U.S. SEC—total	8% (approximately 1,400 foreign registrants out of 16,000 total registered companies)
London Stock Exchange	17% of the number of listed companies are non-U.K. 66% of market capitalization is non-U.K. companies.
Euronext	25%
Switzerland	36%
Germany	24%
Luxembourg	80%
New Zealand	24%
Australia	5%
Singapore	17%

Exhibit 16.1. Globalization of the World's Securities Markets in Late 2002.

(b) Cross-Border Capital Raising in the United States. In the United States, the 1,400 foreign registrants come from about 59 different countries. They are permitted to submit financial statements in their national generally accepted accounting principles (GAAP), provided that they add a reconciliation of income and net assets to U.S. GAAP. But despite the reconciliation, the financial statements and footnotes themselves, and all of the other financial data in the annual and quarterly reports, are prepared using the company's national GAAP—which means different recognition and measurement principles for assets, liabilities, and income from the principles that U.S. companies use, as well as different formats and disclosures. Clearly, for these foreign companies, comparability of most financial figures with similar U.S. companies is not possible, and the understandability of 59 different GAAPs to American investors is compromised.

(c) Cross-Border Securities Markets. Securities markets themselves are now crossing national boundaries. Euronext, for example, is a recent combination of the former Amsterdam, Brussels, Lisbon, and Paris stock exchanges. You can buy NASDAQ and London shares on the Stock Exchange of Hong Kong. American Exchange (Amex) shares are traded in Singapore. Merger talks continue among some of the world's largest stock exchanges.

(d) Investing via the Internet. The Internet now enables any investor anywhere to gather corporate financial data posted by companies all over the world and enter into securities purchase and sale transactions on line in markets and through brokers all over the world. In that environment, a single set of global accounting and financial reporting standards makes eminent sense.

16.3 ACCOUNTANTS INTERNATIONAL STUDY GROUP (1966–1977). Accountants and others have been aware of the problems of different sets of accounting standards for many years. As early as 1966, professional accountancy bodies in Canada, the United Kingdom, and the United States created an Accountants International Study Group (AISG) to develop comparative studies of accounting and auditing practices in the three countries in the hope that their respective local accounting standards board would work toward harmonization of any differences. AISG published a total of 20 studies through 1977, when it was disbanded.

16.4 FORMATION OF THE IASC (1973). In 1972, at the 10th World Congress of Accountants in Sydney, Sir Henry Benson of the United Kingdom put forward a proposal for an International Accounting Standards Committee (IASC). Representatives of the three AISG countries (Canada, the United Kingdom, and the United States) discussed the proposal at the Congress. Shortly thereafter, the proposal was raised with representatives of several other countries, including Australia, France, Germany, Japan, the Netherlands, and Mexico. Together, the nine countries agreed to form the IASC, and in 1973, the IASC opened its doors in London. Each of the countries had a voting seat on the IASC board.

The IASC board was empowered to establish International Accounting Standards (IASs). Each of the signatories to the agreement creating IASC agreed to use their best efforts to bring about adoption of IASs as their national GAAP.

16.5 ACHIEVEMENTS OF THE IASC (1973–2000). Through expansion, by 2000, the IASC's original nine sponsoring bodies had grown to encompass 152 professional accounting bodies in 112 countries—all of the members of the International Federation of Accountants (IFAC), which is the global association of national accounting professional bodies. The IASC board that established International Accounting Standards eventually grew to have 16 seats—each represented normally by two individuals plus a technical advisor. This meant that at least 48 people normally sat at the IASC board table deliberating technical issues. Thirteen of the 16 seats were held by individual countries or, in a few cases, pairs of countries. The other three seats were held by a global financial analysts organization, a global financial executives organization, and a Swiss industry federation.

(a) Structure. In addition to the 16 board seats (48 persons in all), a number of groups were represented around the board table as observers with the right of the floor. They were the European Commission (generally two persons), the U.S. Financial Accounting Standards Board (FASB) (one person), the Ministry of Finance of the People's Republic of China (two persons), the Basel Committee (one or two persons), and the International Organization of Securities Commissions (IOSCO) (up to five persons). Including the IASC staff, it was not uncommon for upwards of 70 people to be seated at the IASC board table.

A super-majority vote was required to publish an exposure draft (11 of the 16 IASC board members) and final Standard (12 of the 16).

(b) "Core Standards" and the "IOSCO Agreement." As a private-sector, nongovernmental body, the IASC had no power to enforce its standards. And since it was a global organization, it could not look to one national governmental agency to bring about widespread adoption and enforcement of its standards. In this regard, IASC differed from the FASB in the United States, whose standards are imposed on listed companies by the Securities and Exchange Commission (SEC), and also differed from the Accounting Standards Board in the United Kingdom, whose standards are imposed on companies via legislation (the Companies Act).

The International Organization of Securities Commissions (IOSCO) is the representative body of the world's securities markets regulators, including the U.S. SEC and about 100 similar organizations. High-quality financial information is vital to the operation of an efficient capital market, and differences in the quality of the accounting policies and their enforcement between countries leads to inefficiencies between markets. As regulators of capital markets, IOSCO members have a strong interest in financial reporting that is relevant, reliable, complete, and transparent.

Starting in the early 1990s, IOSCO took an active role in encouraging and promoting the improvement and quality of IAS. In 1985, IOSCO and the IASC agreed to work on a program of "core standards" that could be used by publicly listed enterprises when offering securities in foreign jurisdictions. The program identified 40 topics that IOSCO felt had to be addressed in the core standards before IOSCO could recommend International Accounting Standards to its member agencies.

In December 1998, the IASC completed the core set of Standards, and IOSCO immediately began a review of those Standards. The IOSCO review culminated in May 2000 in a public recommendation from IOSCO that its members allow foreign securities issuers to use International Accounting Standards, rather than requiring the member's national GAAP, possibly supplemented by additional disclosures. The full text of the IOSCO endorsement may be found on IOSCO's Web site at *www.iosco.org/news/.*

At about the same time both the Basel Committee of bank regulators and the G7 Finance Ministers similarly endorsed IAS. In its April 2000 *Report to G7 Finance Ministers and Central Bank Governors on International Accounting Standards*, the Basel Committee on Banking Supervision said: "The Committee expresses its support for the standards developed by the IASC. It will continue a close dialogue with the IASC and the banking industry to monitor future developments with care." The G7 Finance Ministers themselves issued a public statement saying: "We call upon the IASC to finalize by early 1999 a proposal for a full range of internationally agreed accounting standards. IOSCO, IAIS, and the Basel Committee should complete a timely review of these standards."

(c) Growing Pressure for Global Standards in the Late 1990s. The economic crisis that began in 1998 in certain Asian countries and spread to other regions of the world showed the need for reliable and transparent accounting to support sound decision making by investors, lenders, and regulatory authorities. Regulators and economic authorities around the world recognized this need.

The World Bank pushed countries to adopt IASs or develop national standards based on IASs. In some cases, they required IAS reporting as a condition for granting a loan. The U.S. Senate passed a resolution calling on the SEC to study the use of IASs in the United States. The European Commission began to see a common set of accounting standards as a critical pillar in building a single unified capital market in Europe, and after studying whether to develop their own set of standards they concluded that the better way to go would be to require European companies to use IASs.

The G7 Finance Ministers and Central Bank Governors also committed themselves to endeavor to ensure that private-sector institutions in their countries comply with internationally agreed principles, standards, and codes of best practice. They called on all countries that participate in global capital markets similarly to commit to comply with these internationally agreed codes and standards.

(d) Adoption of IASs Around the World. The goal of a single set of International Accounting Standards replacing national standards was lofty—and the creators of the

IASC in 1973 had recognized it as such. By the beginning of the twenty-first century, in only one of the nine original IASC countries (Germany) did even a relatively small number of listed companies use IASs as their primary basis of reporting to domestic investors. In four of the nine (France, Germany, the Netherlands, and the United Kingdom), nearly all listed companies will be required to do so by 2005, and even in those countries national GAAP are likely to remain for unlisted companies. In Australia, the government is considering a proposal to replace national GAAP with IASs. In the others (Canada, Japan, Mexico, the United States), the prospects that IASs will replace national GAAP for at least some domestic companies are still uncertain but—it is fair to say—those prospects are growing.

Even now, U.S. companies that are subsidiaries of companies in Europe, Australia, and wherever else international standards replace national GAAP are likely to have to prepare financial information using international standards. Similarly, U.S.-owned subsidiaries and investees in Europe, Australia, and elsewhere will soon have to comply with international standards.

Also, more and more, countries that continue to develop their own GAAP are adopting IASs almost verbatim (like South Africa, Singapore, Hong Kong, the Phillippines). And many smaller countries have stopped developing national standards altogether, relying instead on IASs as their national GAAP. Examples include Bahrain, Croatia, Cyprus, the Dominican Republic, Ecuador, Egypt (listed companies only), Haiti, Jamaica, Kenya, Malta, Nepal, Oman, Panama, Tajikistan, Tanzania, and the Ukraine, and the United Arab Emirates (banks only). For the past few years, foreign issuers and at least some domestic issuers in most European countries have been permitted to prepare IAS consolidated financial statements instead of national GAAP statements. Some countries already allow domestic companies to choose to follow IASs rather than national GAAP, for example, Hong Kong, Russia, and Switzerland.

A complete history of the IASC (and its recent replacement, the IASB) is set out in the appendix to this chapter.

(e) International Accounting Standards. From its inception in 1973 until it was reorganized into the International Accounting Standards Board (IASB) in early 2001, the IASC developed 41 standards. Many of these were revised one or more times over the years. Several were superseded or merged in with other standards. Exhibit 16.2 sets out a complete list of the IASs promulgated by the IASC. Those not identified as superseded continue in force.

(f) IASs Reflect a Principles-Based Approach. IASs reflect a principles-based approach to developing accounting standards, rather than a rules-based approach. Principles-based standards focus on establishing general principles derived from a conceptual framework, reflecting the recognition, measurement, and reporting requirements for the transactions covered by the standards. Few, if any, exceptions to the principles are provided for. By following a principles-based approach, IASs tend to limit additional guidance for applying the general principles to typical transactions, encouraging professional judgement in applying the general principles to other transactions specific to an entity or industry.

By having taken a principles-based approach, the IASC's standards tend to have far fewer application examples and "bright lines" than their U.S. counterparts. Also, the number of published Interpretations of IASs is minuscule as compared to the

IAS 1, Presentation of Financial Statements

IAS 2, Inventories

IAS 3, Consolidated Financial Statements. Originally issued 1976, effective January 1, 1977. No longer effective. Superseded in 1989 by *IAS 27* and *IAS 28*.

IAS 4, Depreciation Accounting. Withdrawn in 1999, replaced by IAS 16, 22, and 38, all of which were issued or revised in 1998.

IAS 5, Information to Be Disclosed in Financial Statements. Originally issued October 1976, effective January 1, 1997. No longer effective. Superseded by *IAS 1* in 1997.

IAS 6, Accounting Responses to Changing Prices. Superseded by *IAS 15*.

IAS 7, Cash Flow Statements

IAS 8, Profit or Loss for the Period, Fundamental Errors and Changes in Accounting Policies.

IAS 9, Accounting for Research and Development Activities. Superseded by *IAS 38* effective July 1, 1999

IAS 10, Events After the Balance Sheet Date

IAS 11, Construction Contracts

IAS 12, Income Taxes

IAS 13, Presentation of Current Assets and Current Liabilities. Superseded by *IAS 1*.

IAS 14, Segment Reporting.

IAS 15, Information Reflecting the Effects of Changing Prices

IAS 16, Property, Plant and Equipment

IAS 17, Leases

IAS 18, Revenue

IAS 19, Employee Benefits

IAS 20, Accounting for Government Grants and Disclosure of Government Assistance

IAS 21, The Effects of Changes in Foreign Exchange Rates

IAS 22, Business Combinations

IAS 23, Borrowing Costs

IAS 24, Related Party Disclosures

IAS 25, Accounting for Investments. Superseded by *IAS 39* and *IAS 40* effective 2001.

IAS 26, Accounting and Reporting by Retirement Benefit Plans

IAS 27, Consolidated Financial Statements and Accounting for Investments in Subsidiaries

IAS 28, Accounting for Investments in Associates

IAS 29, Financial Reporting in Hyperinflationary Economies

IAS 30, Disclosures in the Financial Statements of Banks and Similar Financial Institutions

IAS 31, Financial Reporting of Interests In Joint Ventures

IAS 32, Financial Instruments: Disclosures and Presentation

IAS 33, Earnings Per Share

IAS 34, Interim Financial Reporting

IAS 35, Discontinuing Operations

IAS 36, Impairment of Assets

IAS 37, Provisions, Contingent Liabilities and Contingent Assets

IAS 38, Intangible Assets

IAS 39, Financial Instruments: Recognition and Measurement

IAS 40, Investment Property

IAS 41, Agriculture

Exhibit 16.2. Complete List of International Accounting Standards (1973–2000).

number of Consensuses of FASB's Emerging Issues Task Force. Also, only a very few IASs address industry accounting issues, whereas many FASB statements deal with individual industries—and these are supplemented by specialized industry accounting guides developed by industry committees of the American Institute of Certified Public Accountants (AICPA).

(g) IASC Framework. In 1989, the IASC adopted a Framework for the Preparation and Presentation of Financial Statements. The Framework describes the basic concepts by which financial statements are prepared. It defines the objectives of financial reporting and the basic elements of financial statements (assets, liabilities, equity, income, and expenses). It sets out concepts of recognition and measurement of the elements. The Framework serves as a guide to the board in developing accounting standards and as a guide to resolving accounting issues that are not addressed directly in an ISA or International Financial Reporting Standard.

However, the Framework is not, itself, a Standard. Therefore, it does not establish enforceable standards for any particular accounting recognition, measurement, or disclosure matter. Nor does the Framework override any specific IASB Standard if there appears to be a conflict.

(h) IASC Due Process. The procedures followed by the IASC in issuing final Standards always included publishing an exposure draft (ED) for public comment. The ED was an IASC board document and required 11 affirmative votes of the board for issuance. For most agenda projects, the IASC appointed a steering committee of experts on the subject. Most often, the exposure draft was preceded by two documents prepared and issued by the steering committee—a Discussion Paper setting out the issues and a Draft Statement of Principles (DSOP) setting out the steering committee's tentative views.

(i) Interpretations. Recognizing the need for guidance on implementation questions that might arise as IAS moved into complex accounting areas, the IASC board in 1997 established a Standing Interpretations Committee (SIC). The SIC's role was to consider, on a timely basis, accounting issues that are likely to receive divergent or unacceptable treatment in the absence of authoritative guidance. The SIC considered accounting issues within the context of existing IASs and the IASC Framework. That is, it could interpret the meaning of existing requirements but it could not plow new ground.

The SIC followed a due process that included soliciting public input before reaching a final consensus. Once the SIC approved a final Interpretation, it was submitted to the IASC board, which had to approve the Interpretation by a vote of least 12 of its 16 members before the Interpretation took effect. In a few cases, the IASC remanded an Interpretation back to the SIC to be reworked. In a few other cases, the IASC did not adopt the final SIC Interpretation. Exhibit 16.3 sets out a list of all of the Interpretations issued by the SIC. Note that Draft Interpretations 4, 26, and 34 had been issued for public comment but were never finalized.

(j) Implementation Guidance. The IASC did not have a practice of publishing staff views or other detailed implementation guidance for its Standards and Interpretations. The one exception it made was with respect to IAS 39, Financial Instruments: Recognition and Measurement. When that Standard was issued in December 1998, the IASC recognized the need for practical guidance and formed an IAS 39 Imple-

SIC 1, Consistency—Different Cost Formulas for Inventories
SIC 2, Consistency—Capitalization of Borrowing Costs
SIC 3, Elimination of Unrealized Profits and Losses on Transactions with Associates
SIC 5, Classification of Financial Instruments—Contingent Settlement Provisions
SIC 6, Costs of Modifying Existing Software
SIC 7, Introduction of the Euro
SIC 8, First-Time Application of IASs as the Primary Basis of Accounting
SIC 9, Business Combinations—Classification either as Acquisitions or Unitings of Interests
SIC 10, Government Assistance—No Specific Relation to Operating Activities
SIC 11, Foreign Exchange—Capitalization of Losses Resulting from Severe Currency Devaluations
SIC 12, Consolidation—Special-Purpose Entities
SIC 13, Jointly Controlled Entities—Nonmonetary Contributions by Venturers
SIC 14, Property, Plant and Equipment—Compensation for the Impairment or Loss of Items
SIC 15, Operating Leases—Incentives
SIC 16, Share Capital—Reacquired Own Equity Instruments (Treasury Shares)
SIC 17, Equity—Costs of an Equity Transaction
SIC 18, Consistency—Alternative Methods
SIC 19, Reporting Currency—Measurement and Presentation of Financial Statements under IAS 21 and IAS 29
SIC 20, Equity Accounting Method—Recognition of Losses
SIC 21, Income Taxes—Recovery of Revalued Nondepreciable Assets
SIC 22, Business Combinations—Subsequent Adjustment of Fair Values and Goodwill Initially Reported
SIC 23, Property, Plant and Equipment—Major Inspection or Overhaul Costs
SIC 24, Earnings per Share—Financial Instruments that May Be Settled in Shares
SIC 25, Income Taxes—Changes in the Tax Status of an Enterprise or its Shareholders
SIC 27, Evaluating the Substance of Transactions in the Legal Form of a Lease
SIC 28, Business Combinations—"Date of Exchange" and Fair Value of Equity Instruments
SIC 29, Disclosure—Service Concession Arrangements
SIC 30, Reporting Currency—Translation from Measurement Currency to Presentation Currency
SIC 31, Revenue—Barter Transactions Involving Advertising Services
SIC 32, Intangible Assets—Web Site Costs
SIC 33, Consolidation and Equity Method—Potential Voting Rights and Allocation of Ownership Interests

Exhibit 16.3. Complete List of Final Interpretations (1997–2000).

mentation Guidance Committee (IGC). In its two years of existence, the IGC published approximately 250 questions and answers on various issues that had arisen in applying IAS 39. The Q&A are included in the annual bound volume of *International Accounting Standards.*

16.6 SHORTCOMINGS OF THE OLD IASC. Productive as it was, the IASC suffered from a number of shortcomings, including:

- Weak relationships with national standard setters
- Lack of convergence of IASs and major national GAAP after 25 years of trying
- Part-time board with a full-time workload
- Need for broader sponsorship than the accounting profession
- Lack of widespread recognition of its standards by regulators
- Shortage of resources

16.7 RESTRUCTURING OF IASC INTO IASB. Recognizing these problems, in 1998 the committee that was entrusted with oversight of the IASC undertook a comprehensive review of the IASC's structure and operations. That review was completed in 2000. The principal recommendations of the structure review were that:

- The large, part-time IASC should be replaced by a smaller and essentially full-time International Accounting Standards Board (IASB or "the Board").
- The new IASB should operate under a broad-based IASC Foundation (IASCF) whose trustees represented all regions of the world and all groups interested in financial accounting.
- The new IASB should have a Standards Advisory Council (SAC) to provide counsel to the board.
- The SIC should continue in a slightly modified form under the name of International Financial Reporting Interpretations Committee (IFRIC).

(a) Approval of the Proposed Restructuring. After some tweaking, the proposals received rapid and widespread support. In November 1999, the IASC board itself approved the constitutional changes necessary for its own restructuring. In May 2000, the Council of the International Federation of Accountants (IFAC) unanimously approved the restructuring. The constitution of the old IASC was revised to reflect the new structure. A new IASC Foundation was incorporated (under the laws of the U.S. state of Delaware), and its trustees were appointed. By early 2001, the members of the IASB and the SAC were appointed, and the new structure became operational. Later that year, the IASB moved into new quarters in London.

The IASB's budget of US$15 million per year is nearly five times that of the old IASC. The board meets monthly, except for August, usually for four days. Three or four times a year the board meets with the chairpersons of certain major national standard setters, with a goal of mutual information and identification of steps toward convergence of accounting standards. Seven of the members of the IASB have specific liaison responsibilities with these national standard setters. The liaison countries are Australia, Canada, France, Germany, Japan, New Zealand, the United Kingdom, and the United States. The board also meets three times a year with its Standards Advisory Council.

Exhibit 16.4 is a diagram of the new IASB structure.

(b) Key Responsibilities of the IASB. The IASB has 14 members, 12 of whom serve full-time and two part-time. The board's principal responsibilities are to:

- Develop and issue International Financial Reporting Standards and Exposure Drafts
- Approve Interpretations developed by the IFRIC.

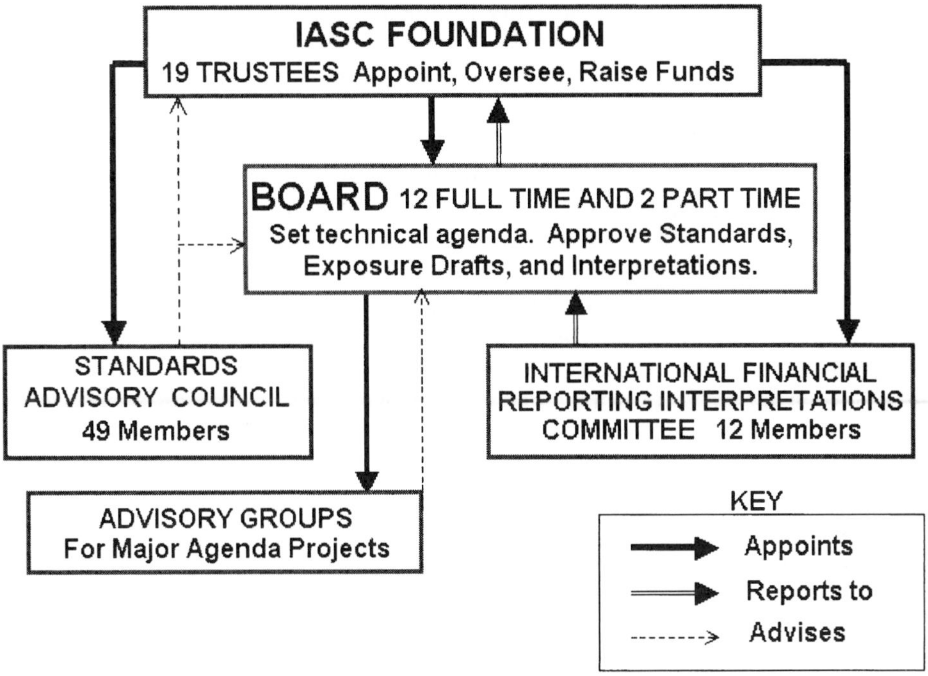

Exhibit 16.4. The IASB Structure Starting in 2001.

Note that the new name for standards issued by the IASB is International Financial Reporting Standards (IFRSs). In one of its earliest actions, the IASB voted to make clear that the IASs issued by the former IASC continue with full force and effect unless and until the IASB amends or replaces them. Therefore, the term IFRS encompasses IAS.

(c) Specific Objectives of the IASB. As set out in IASB's constitution, the board's objectives are:

- To develop, in the public interest, a single set of high-quality, understandable, and enforceable global accounting standards that require high-quality, transparent, and comparable information in financial statements and other financial reporting to help participants in the world's capital markets and other users make economic decisions
- To promote the use and rigorous application of those standards
- To bring about convergence of national accounting standards and IASs to high-quality solutions

In accomplishing its objectives, the IASB has complete responsibility for all technical matters including the preparing and issuing of IFRSs and EDs, both of which must include any dissenting opinions, and final approval of Interpretations by the IFRIC. The IASC Foundation trustees have no involvement in developing IFRSs. And IASB's use of the term *advisory groups* rather than the old IASC term *steering committees* reflects the purely advisory role of these groups—they no longer will "steer" technical projects in a direction supported by the "steering committee." Rather, they will serve as resources of expertise for the board.

(d) IASB Due Process. Before issuing a final Standard, the IASB must publish an ED for public comment. Normally, it will also publish a discussion document for public comment on major projects before it issues the ED.

The IASB has full discretion over its technical agenda. It may outsource detailed research or other work to national standard setters or other organizations. The board is responsible for establishing the operating procedures for reviewing comments on EDs and other documents. The IASB will normally form specialist advisory groups to give advice on major projects, though it is not required to do so. The IASB is required to consult the SAC on major projects, agenda decisions, and work priorities. The IASB will normally issue bases for conclusions with both final Standards and EDs. Although there is no requirement to hold public hearings or to conduct field tests for every project, the board must, in each case, consider the need to do so.

Standards and EDs are approved by simple majority vote (8 of the 14 IASB members). Dissenting opinions are included. Interpretations developed by IFRIC must also be approved by a simple majority vote of the IASB.

(e) Qualifications of IASB Members. The key qualification for board membership is technical expertise. The trustees also must ensure that the board is not dominated by any particular constituency or regional interest. To achieve a balance of perspectives and experience, at least five members must have backgrounds as practicing auditors, at least three as financial statement preparers, at least three as users of financial statements, and at least one as an academician. There is no required geographical mix.

(f) Standards Advisory Council. The International Accounting Standards Advisory Council has 49 members from 29 countries and five international organizations. The SAC provides a forum for organizations and individuals with an interest in international financial reporting to participate in the standard setting process. Members are appointed for a renewable term of three years and have diverse geographic and functional backgrounds.

The SAC normally convenes three times each year at meetings open to the public to:

- Advise the board on priorities in the board's work
- Inform the board of the implications of proposed standards for users and preparers of financial statements
- Give other advice to the board or to the trustees

(g) International Financial Reporting Interpretations Committee. The IFRIC (until 2002 known as the Standing Interpretations Committee) has 12 members appointed by the IASC Foundation trustees for terms of three years. IFRIC members are not salaried but their expenses are reimbursed. IFRIC meetings are open to public observation. Approval of draft or final Interpretations requires that not more than three voting members vote against the draft or final Interpretation. The IFRIC is chaired by a nonvoting chair who can be one of the members of the IASB, the Director of Technical Activities, or a member of the IASB's senior technical staff. (In fact, the Director of Technical Activities was appointed the chair of IFRIC.)

The IFRIC's responsibilities are to:

- Interpret the application of IFRSs and provide timely guidance on financial reporting issues not specifically addressed in IFRSs or IASs, in the context of the IASB's Framework, and undertake other tasks at the request of the Board;
- Publish Draft Interpretations for public comment and consider comments made within a reasonable period before finalizing an Interpretation
- Report to the board and obtain board approval for final Interpretations.

By allowing the IFRIC to develop Interpretations on financial reporting issues not specifically addressed in an IFRS or IAS, the new IASB constitution has broadened IFRIC's mandate beyond that of the former SIC.

16.8 WHO USES INTERNATIONAL ACCOUNTING STANDARDS? Exhibit 16.5 identifies some representative companies from among the thousands that prepare their financial statements using IASs as of 2002.

(a) Europe. In June 2000, the European Commission adopted a "Financial Reporting Strategy" for the 15 European Union (EU) member states and the three additional European Economic Area countries that would require "all listed EU companies to prepare their consolidated accounts in accordance with one single set of accounting standards, namely International Accounting Standards (IAS)." Listed companies in

AdidasSolomon	European Investment Bank	Nordic Investment Bank
Air Malta	Eutelsat	Novartis
Alianz	Gazprom	Petroleos de Venezuela
Amadeus Global	Great Nordic	Puma
AngloGold Ltd.	Gucci	Roche
Ashanti Goldfields	Gulf Bank	Rostelecom
Austrian Airlines	Henkel	RWE
Bank of Cyprus	Holderbank	Scandinavian Air System
Banka Slovenjie	Hong Kong Land	Schindler
Barbados Shipping	IOSCO	Shanghai Petrochem
Bayer	Jardine Matheson	Statoil (Norway)
Brierley Investments	Lufthansa	StoraEnso
China Petrochemical	Mandarin Oriental	Swatch
Commerzbank	Matav Hungary Telecom	Swiss Air
Consolidated Water	Mexican Maritime Transport	UBS
Czech Telecom	Movenpick	United Saudi Bank
Dairy Farm	Munich Re	Volkswagen
Danisco	National Bank of Kuwait	Wella AG
Dresdner Bank	Nestlé	World Bank
Emirates Bank	Nokia	Zurich Financial Services

Exhibit 16.5. Some Companies that Prepare IAS Financial Statements (2002).

the 10 additional countries that have been provisionally approved for EU membership starting in May 2004 would also have to follow IFRS.

To implement that strategy, in June 2002 the European Parliament adopted a regulation requiring all listed EU companies (including banks and insurance companies) to prepare consolidated accounts in accordance with IAS by 2005, at the latest. An EU member state may delay IASs to 2007 for an entity that currently uses U.S. GAAP as its primary GAAP or for an entity that has only listed debt securities and no listed equity. This IAS reporting requirement will affect approximately 7,000 listed enterprises, plus the subsidiaries, associates, and joint ventures of these entities.

EU member states can extend the IAS requirement to unlisted companies and to individual company accounts. The government of the United Kingdom, for example, has invited comment on whether to extend the European IAS requirement to nonlisted companies and/or to individual company (nonconsolidated) financial statements. Such extension might be on a voluntary basis or a compulsory basis.

(b) Australia. In July 2002, the Australian Financial Reporting Council (a governmental agency) formalized its support for adoption by Australia of International Accounting Standards by January 1, 2005. The FRC envisioned that the Corporations Act 2001 will be amended to require that the accounting standards applicable to reporting entities under the Act will be the standards issued by the IASB, and auditors' reports will refer to international standards rather than Australian GAAP. Consideration is also being given to retaining Australian GAAP but bringing it into line with IFRS.

(c) Russia. In 2002, the Prime Minister announced that all companies and banks in Russia will be required to prepare their financial statements in accordance with IASs starting, January 1, 2004.

(d) United States. In the United States, a foreign registrant may submit financial statements using IAS or national GAAP but a reconciliation of earnings and net assets to U.S. GAAP figures is required. In effect, this requires companies to "keep two sets of books." In February 2000, the U.S. Securities and Exchange Commission issued a Concept Release, *International Accounting Standards*, inviting views on whether and how IASs might be permitted for foreign registrants, and possibly domestic registrants as well. The matter continues to be under study by the SEC. The full text of the SEC's Concept Release can be found on the SEC's Web site at *www.sec.gov/rules/concept/34-42430.htm.*

In 2002, the United States Congress enacted the Public Company Accounting Reform and Investor Protection Act of 2002, also known as the Sarbanes-Oxley Act. The Act requires the SEC to conduct a study on the "adoption by the United States financial reporting system of a principles-based accounting system," including:

- The extent to which principles-based accounting and financial reporting exists in the United States
- The length of time required for change from a rules-based to a principles-based financial reporting system
- The feasibility of and proposed methods by which a principles-based system may be implemented
- A thorough economic analysis of the implementation of a principles-based system.

As a result of the Act, the FASB has invited comment on a proposal for a principle-based approach to U.S. accounting standard setting. The proposal addresses concerns about the increase in the level of detail and complexity in accounting standards.

The Sarbanes-Oxley Act permits the SEC to look to a private-sector accounting standard setter, such as FASB, provided that the standard setter "considers, in adopting accounting principles, . . . the extent to which international convergence on high-quality accounting standards is necessary or appropriate in the public interest and for the protection of investors."

(e) Convergence of IAS and U.S. GAAP. In October 2002, the FASB added to its agenda a short-term international convergence project conducted jointly with the IASB. The FASB also voted to authorize its staff to expand its research project on international convergence. With respect to the short-term project, the FASB established a goal of December 31, 2003, for issuance of a final Statement that would "eliminate or reduce many, if not all, of the differences to be addressed in that project."

Deloitte Touche Tohmatsu has published a detailed comparison of IASs and U.S. GAAP that is available without charge on their IASPlus Web site at *www.iasplus.com/dttpubs/pubs.htm.*

16.9 BENEFITS OF GLOBAL ACCOUNTING STANDARDS. Among the benefits often cited for a single set of global accounting standards are:

- Easier access to foreign capital markets
- Credibility of domestic capital markets to foreign capital providers and potential foreign merger partners
- Credibility to potential lenders of financial statements of companies from lesser-developed countries
- Lower cost of capital to companies
- Comparability of financial data across borders
- Greater transparency
- Greater understandability—a "common financial language"
- Companies need to keep only one set of books
- Reduced national standard-setting costs
- Ease of regulation of securities markets—regulatory acceptability of financial information provided by market participants
- Still can have local implementation guidance for local circumstances
- Standards are less susceptible to political pressures than national standards
- Portability of knowledge and education across national boundaries
- Consistent with the concept of a single global professional credential

In his testimony before the U.S. Senate Committee on Banking, Housing, and Urban Affairs in February 2002, IASB Chairman Sir David Tweedie put the case for a global accounting standard setter this way:

> Why have an international standard setter?
>
> - First, there is a recognized and growing need for international acco
> - Second, no individual standard setter has a monopoly on the be
>   ing problems.

- Third, no national standard setter is in a position to set accounting standards that can gain acceptance around the world.
- Lastly, there are many areas of financial reporting in which a national standard setter finds it difficult to act alone.

16.10 ACTIVITY OF THE IASB SO FAR. When it started its operation in 2001, the IASB was able to hit the ground running because there were a number of projects left in the pipeline from its predecessor. Exhibit 16.6 summarizes the IASB technical agenda projects at the end of 2002.

Any summary of the "current" activity of the IASB in a handbook such as this is bound to be out of date rather quickly. The best places to look for up-to-date information about IASB projects are two Web sites:

1. *www.iasb.org.uk*—IASB's own Web site
2. *www.iasplus.com*—An IASB-related Web site maintained by Deloitte Touche Tohmatsu

16.11 RECENT TRENDS IN INTERNATIONAL FINANCIAL REPORTING STANDARDS. The standards issued by the IASC in its last few years and the direction that the IASB has taken in its first few years allow the following observations about trends in international financial reporting standards:

- Greater use of fair value in measuring transactions:
  - Financial instruments (trading investments)
  - Impairment recognition (write-down to fair values)
  - Prohibition of pooling interests
- More fair values on the balance sheet:
  - Financial instruments (available for sale investments)
  - An entity's own debt (proposed by IASB in its IAS 39 revisions)
  - Investment property
  - Commodity inventories
  - Biological assets and agricultural produce
  - Property … ed in exchange for similar property
  - V… unds

… nponents of income: performance reporting becomes key.

… , cost deferrals, or general provisions:

… approach to pensions

… h to deferred taxes

… osses

… ng rules

… ms onto the balance sheet:

… ments, plans, and assumptions:

… policies

"Asset Ceiling" Amendment to IAS 19. This project has been completed. It resulted in an amendment to IAS 19, Employee Benefits, to correct an anomaly that, when applying IAS 19 in a falling equity market enterprises sometimes reported an asset and a gain as a consequence of an actuarial loss.

Business Combinations—Phase I. Phase I of this project addresses the definition of a business combination, the appropriate method of accounting for a business combination (purchase or pooling/merger accounting), and the accounting for goodwill and intangible assets. Consequential amendment to IAS 36 and IAS 38 will also result.

Business Combinations—Phase II. This project is addressing:

- Issues relating to application of the purchase method of accounting for a business combination.
- New basis accounting.
- Combinations of entities under common control.

Convergence Topics. This project is focusing on topics where one or more partner standard setters and the IASB have standards that are broadly similar but differ in a limited number of areas. The goal is to achieve convergence either by changes in IFRS or changes in the partners' standards. The principal focus is on reducing differences between IFRS and U.S. GAAP.

Consolidation (including Special Purpose Entities). This project is reconsidering the basis on which an entity should consolidate its investments including more rigorous guidance around the concept of "control." The project is expected to amend IAS 27, Consolidated Financial Statements and Accounting for Subsidiaries.

Disclosure and Presentation of Financial Activities. This project is updating the existing requirements (principally IAS 30) related to disclosing information and presenting financial statements that reflect the specific characteristics of the business activities of banks and other institutions whose business is to take deposits, grant credits, or provide other financing or investment services.

First-Time Adoption of International Financial reporting Standards. This project will provide guidance when an entity adopts IFRSs for the first time as its basis of accounting by an explicit and unreserved statement of compliance with IFRSs.

Improvements Project. The objective of an improvements project is to add clarity and consistency to the requirements of existing Standards issued by the IASC, eliminate some accounting choices, and help converge IFRS with major national GAAPs, notably U.S. GAAP.

Insurance Contracts—Phase I. This project addresses how existing IASs should be applied to insurance contracts.

Insurance Contracts—Phase II. Continuation of the former IASC project to develop a comprehensive standard on accounting for insurance contracts that is consistent with the conceptual framework definitions of assets and liabilities. This phase of the insurance contracts project is not constrained by existing IASs.

The Income Statment (Performance Reporting). This project addresses broadly the issues related to the display and presentation in the income statement of all recognized changes in assets and liabilities from transactions or other events except those related to transactions with owners as owners (sometimes called comprehensive income). Thus, it will consider items that presently are reported in the income statement, cash flow statement, and statement of changes in equity. Issues addressed in this project include distinguishing revenues and expenses from other sources of comprehensive income or expense, reporting of holding gains and losses, and distinguishing operating and nonoperating items.

Preface to International Financial Reporting Standards. This project is completed. It resulted in a revised preface to IASB Standards that sets out the board's objectives, its proce-

Exhibit 16.6. IASB Technical Agenda Projects: From IASB's Inception in 2001 through Late 2002.

dures for due process reflecting the IASB's new structure, and the scope, authority, and timing of application of International Financial Reporting Standards (IFRS). The Preface also reflects some Board decisions about the format and style of IFRS and clarifies that bold and nonbold type in IASB standards are of equal authority.

Concepts of Revenue Recognition, Liabilities, and Equity. This project addresses three interrelated issues:

- General principles for determining when revenue should be recognized in the financial statements.
- The distinction between liabilities and equity.
- Liability recognition, including guidance on whether an item meets the definition of a liability and, if so, the criteria for recognizing liabilities in the financial statements.

Revisions to IAS 39 and IAS 32. Revisions to IAS 32 and IAS 39 based on issues identified by the IAS 39 Implementation Guidance Committee and others. This project includes issues relating to derecognition of financial instruments and extending the use of fair valuation.

Share-Based Payment. This project seeks to develop a standard on all aspects of accounting for share-based payments to employees (including employee stock options and their repricing), suppliers, creditors, and others.

Exhibit 16.6. ***(Continued)***

    - Risk management policies
    - Sensitivity analyses
- Balance between relevance and reliability: shifting toward relevance
- Eliminate opportunities for "cherry picking" of income items, especially for financial instruments
- Avoid intent-driven accounting to the extent possible:
    - Consolidate even if decision to dispose
    - No accrual of planned restructurings after a business combination
    - Principles-based standards, with separate implementation guidance
- Eliminate accounting choices:
    - IASB's "improvement project" would eliminate many
- Convergence with U.S. GAAP.

16.12 MODEL FINANCIAL STATEMENTS AND DISCLOSURE CHECKLIST. The IASB does not publish model financial statements that conform to IFRS or a related disclosure checklist. However, model IAS statements and a disclosure checklist are available at the Deloitte Touche Tohmatsu IASPlus Web site at *www.iasplus.com/fs/fs.htm.*

16.13 INTERNATIONAL FORUM ON ACCOUNTANCY DEVELOPMENT. The International Forum on Accountancy Development was created in 1999 as a working group between the Basel Committee, the International Federation of Accountants, IOSCO, the large Accounting Firms, OECD, the United Nations, and the World Bank and regional development banks. The East Asian financial crisis was their impetus in forming the IFAD. The IFAD's mission is to improve market security and transparency, and financial stability on a global basis.

(a) Endorsement of IASs. The IFAD has endorsed Internationl Accounting Standards as the global benchmark: "All general-purpose financial information must be prepared using a single world-wide framework using common measurement criteria and fair and comprehensive disclosure. The framework must provide users with a transparent representation of the underlying economics of transactions. All of this must be done rigorously and on a consistent basis. The vision will not be achieved overnight and will require significant long-term efforts. National accounting standards of most countries should be raised with IAS as the benchmark or minimum standards."

(b) Annual IAS–National GAAP Comparisons. Under the auspices of the IFAD, the large accounting firms have annually published a comparison of approximately 60 national GAAP and IASs. The lastest comparison may be found at the IFAD's Web site at *www.ifad.net/.*

16.14 INTERNATIONAL ACCOUNTING STANDARDS FOR THE PUBLIC SECTOR. IASB's Preface to International Financial Reporting Standards notes that IFRSs are designed to apply to the financial reports of all profit-oriented entities. Although IFRSs are not designed to apply to not-for-profit or governmental activities, nonprofit and governmental entities "may find them appropriate." The Public Sector Committee (PSC) of the IFAC develops International Public Sector Accounting Standards (IPSASs) for financial reporting by governments and other public-sector entities. The PSC has issued a guideline stating that IFRSs are applicable to governmental business enterprises.

More information is available at the PSC Web site at *www.ifac.org/PublicSector.*

16.15 INTERNATIONAL AUDITING STANDARDS. The International Auditing and Assurance Standards Board (IAASB) is a committee of the IFAC that works to improve the uniformity of auditing practices and related services throughout the world by issuing pronouncements on a variety of audit and assurance functions and by promoting their acceptance worldwide. Until 2002, the IAASB was known as the International Auditing Practices Committee (IAPC).

IAASB pronouncements on audits and reviews of historical financial information are of two types:

1. International Standards on Auditing (ISAs)
2. International Auditing Practice Statements (IPSs)

The ISA on the auditor's report on financial statements requires that the auditor's opinion must clearly indicate the financial reporting framework used to prepare the financial statements (including the country of origin of the financial reporting framework when the framework used is not International Accounting Standards) and state the auditor's opinion as to whether the financial statements give a true and fair view (or are presented fairly, in all material respects) in accordance with that financial reporting framework and, where appropriate, whether the financial statements comply with statutory requirements.

More information is available at the IAASB Web site at *www.iaasb.org.*

16.16 PLANNED CERTIFICATION PROGRAM IN IAS/IFRS. The anticipated adoption of IAS/IFRS throughout Europe and elsewhere has created a demand for high-quality learning materials and training programs. The IASC Foundation Trustees are developing programs to train and examine individuals on their skills in financial reporting under IASs and IFRSs. The programs would carry the certificate "ISACF-approved training." Two levels of certification are envisioned: Application Level (Certification in IASs and IFRSs) and Advanced Level (Diploma in IASs and IFRSs).

SOURCES AND SUGGESTED REFERENCES

Alexander, David, and Simon Archer. *2002 Miller International Accounting Standards Guide.* Elsevier Science/Harcourt International, 2001, *www.harcourt-international.com.*

Choi, Frederick D. S., Carol A. Frost, and Gary K. Meek. *International Accounting,* 4th ed. Upper Saddle River, NJ: Prentice Hall, Inc., 2002, *www.prenhall.com/.*

Deloitte Touche Tohmatsu. *GAAP Differences in your Pocket: IAS and US GAAP.* Deloitte Touche Tohmatsu, 2002, *www.iasplus.com.*

Epstein, Barry, J., and Abbas Ali Mirza. *Wiley IAS 2003: Interpretation and Application of International Accounting Standards.* New York: John Wiley & Sons, February 2003, *www.wiley.com.*

Gernon, Helen, and Gary Kenneth Meek. *Accounting: An International Perspective,* 5th ed. New York: McGraw-Hill Higher Education, 2001, *www.mhhe.com.*

Gray, Sidney J., Stephen B. Salter, and Lee H. Radebaugh. *Global Accounting & Control: A Managerial Emphasis.* New York: John Wiley & Sons, 2001, *www.wiley.com.*

Haskins, Mark E., Kenneth R. Ferris, and Tom Selling. *International Financial Reporting and Analysis,* 2nd ed. New York: McGraw-Hill Higher Education, 2000, *www.mhhe.com.*

International Accounting Standards Board. *International Accounting Standards* (bound volume). Published annually by the IASB, London, *www.iasb.org.uk.*

International Accounting Standards Board. *Comprehensive Subscription Service.* Includes all final Standards and Interpretations, Exposure Drafts, the annual bound volume, three newsletters (IASB Insight, IASB Update, and IFRIC Update), and the Annual Review, *www.iasb.org.uk.*

Iqbal, M. Zafar. *International Accounting.* Mason, OH: Thomson/South-Western, 2002, *www.swcollege.com.*

Mackenzie, Bruce, and Andy Simmonds. *International Accounting Standards: A Guide to Preparing Accounts,* 3rd ed. London: AGB Professional Information, 2001, *www.abgweb.com.*

Nobes, Christopher, and R. H. Parker (eds.). *Comparative International Accounting,* 7th ed. Upper Saddle River, NJ: Prentice-Hall, Inc., April 2002, *www.prenhall.com.*

Roberts, Clare, Pauline Weetman, and Paul Gordon. *International Financial Accounting: A Comparative Approach,* 2nd ed. Prentice-Hall, Inc., 2002, *www.prenhall.com.*

Saudagaran, Shahrokh M. *International Accounting: A User Perspective.* Mason, OH: Thomson/South-Western, 2001, *www.swcollege.com.*

Stolowy, Herve, and Michael Lebas. *Corporate Financial Reporting: A Global Perspective.* London: Thomson Learning, 2002, *www.thomsonlearning.co.uk.*

APPENDIX: CHRONOLOGY OF IASC AND IASB

PRE-1973 EVENTS LEADING TO FORMATION OF IASC

1966

Proposal to create an Accountants International Study Group is agreed to by professional accountancy bodies in Canada, the United Kingdom, and the United States to develop comparative studies of accounting and auditing practices in the three nations.

1967

Accountants International Study Group is created. Precursor to IASC.

1968

First AISG study: Comparative accounting practices for inventories in Canada, the United Kingdom, and the United States. AISG published a total of 20 studies through 1977, when it was disbanded. Some were used by IASC in its early standards.

1972

- Proposal for IASC is put forward by Sir Henry Benson at 10th World Congress of Accountants in Sydney. Discussed with the three AISG countries (Canada, the United Kingdom, and the United States).
- Further discussions of the Benson proposal including representatives of Australia, France, Germany, Japan, the Netherlands, and Mexico.

INTERNATIONAL ACCOUNTING STANDARDS COMMITTEE (IASC) 1973–2000

1973

- Agreement to establish IASC signed by representatives of the professional accountancy bodies in Australia, Canada, France, Germany, Japan, Mexico, the Netherlands, the United Kingdom/Ireland, and United States.
- IASB opens an office at 3 St. Helen's Place, London.
- Paul Rosenfield (the United States, on secondment from AICPA) is appointed first Secretary of IASC.
- IASC holds its inaugural meeting 29 June, London.
- Sir Henry Benson elected first Chairman of IASC.
- IASC adopts its initial agenda of three technical projects: Accounting Policies, Inventories, Consolidated Financial Statements.
- Steering committees are appointed for the above three projects (the first IASC steering committees).
- First meeting of an IASC steering committee (IAS 1, Disclosure of Accounting Policies).
- IASC holds board meetings in London (2).

Exposure Drafts Published

None

Final Standards Published

None

1974

- First associate members of IASC are admitted: Belgium, India, Israel, New Zealand, Pakistan, and Zimbabwe.
- IASC holds board meetings in London (3) and Paris.

Exposure Drafts Published

- E1, Disclosure of Accounting Policies
- E2, Valuation and Presentation of Inventories in the Context of the Historical Cost System
- E3, Consolidated Financial Statements and the Equity Method of Accounting

Final Standards Published

None

1975

- Proposal to create an International Federation of Accountants (IFAC) to replace the International Coordinating Committee for the Accounting Profession (ICCAP).
- IASC holds board meetings in London (3) and Montreal.

Exposure Drafts Published

- E4, Depreciation Accounting
- E5, Information to Be Disclosed in Financial Statements

Final Standards Published

- IAS 1 (1975), Disclosure of Accounting Policies
- IAS 2 (1975), Valuation and Presentation of Inventories in the Context of the Historical Cost System

1976

- Joseph P. Cummings of the United States becomes chairman of IASC.
- "Group of Ten" Bank Governors funds an IASC project on bank financial statements.
- IASC bolds board meetings in London (2) and Washington.

Exposure Drafts Published

- E6, Accounting Treatment of Changing Prices
- E7, Statement of Source and Application of Funds
- E8, The Treatment in the Income Statement of Unusual Items and Changes in Accounting Estimates and Accounting Policies

Final Standards Published

- IAS 3 (1976), Consolidated Financial Statements
- IAS 4 (1976), Depreciation Accounting
- IAS 5 (1976), Information to Be Disclosed in Financial Statements

1977

- IASC Constitution is revised to add two seats to the IASC Board (in addition to the 9 founder countries), bringing the total to 11. Nine votes are required to adopt a Standard, giving the nine founder members substantial control. Also, this revised Constitution identified the standards-setting body as the "board" of the IASC, not a "committee."

- IFAC is formed.
- AISG is disbanded.
- IASC holds board meetings in London, Amsterdam, and Edinburgh.

Exposure Drafts Published

- E9, Accounting for Research and Development Costs
- E10, Contingencies and Events Occurring after the Balance Sheet Date
- E11, Accounting for Foreign Transactions and Translation of Foreign Financial Statements
- E12, Accounting for Construction Contracts

Final Standards Published

- IAS 6 (1977), Accounting Responses to Changing Prices
- IAS 7 (1977), Statement of Changes in Financial Position

1978

- John A. Hepworth of Australia becomes chairman of IASC.
- South Africa and Nigeria join board, increasing board size to 11.
- IASC holds board meetings in London (2) and Perth (Australia).
- For the first time, IASC rejects a proposed standard (based on E11, Accounting for Foreign Transactions and Translation of Foreign Financial Statements), and a new steering committee is appointed for a fresh start.
- IASC begins discussions with the International Federation of Accountants (IFAC) on "mutual commitments" regarding the relationship between the two bodies.

Exposure Drafts Published

- E13, Accounting for Taxes on Income
- E14, Current Assets and Current Liabilities

Final Standards Published

- IAS 8 (1978), Unusual and Prior Period Items and Changes in Accounting Policies
- IAS 9 (1978), Accounting for Research and Development Activities
- IAS 10 (1978), Contingencies and Events Occurring after the Balance Sheet Date

1979

- Allan V. C. Cook becomes Secretary of IASC.
- IASC meets OECD working group on accounting standards.
- IASC holds board meetings in London (2) and Mexico City.

Exposure Drafts Published

None

Final Standards Published

- IAS 11 (1979), Accounting for Construction Contracts
- IAS 12 (1979), Accounting for Taxes on Income
- IAS 13 (1979, Presentation of Current Assets and Current Liabilities

1980

- J. A. (Hans) Burggraaff of the Netherlands becomes chairman of IASC.
- IASC publishes a discussion paper on bank disclosures (project funded by "Group of Ten" Bank Governors).
- IASC holds board meetings in London, Berlin, and Dublin.
- United Nations Intergovernmental Working Group on Accounting and Reporting meets for first time. IASC proposes a cooperative working arrangement with UN group.

Exposure Drafts Published

- E15, Reporting Financial Information by Segment
- E16, Accounting for Retirement Benefits in the Financial Statements of Employers
- E17, Information Reflecting the Effects of Changing Prices
- E18, Accounting for Property, Plant and Equipment in the Context of the Historical Cost System
- E19, Accounting for Leases

Final Standards Published

None

1981

- Geoffrey B. Mitchell becomes Secretary of IASC. Title is changed to Secretary-General during his tenure.
- IASC Consultative Group is formed to advise IASC on agenda projects and priorities. Consultative Group members represent both accounting and nonaccounting organizations with an interest in financial reporting (stock exchanges, bankers, lawyers, business, unions, government, United Nations, World Bank, OECD, etc.). First meeting in October 1981.
- IASC begins a joint project on accounting for income taxes with standard setters from the Netherlands, the United Kingdom, and the United States.
- IASC holds board meetings in London (2) and Tokyo.

Exposure Drafts Published

- E20, Revenue Recognition
- E21, Accounting for Government Grants and Disclosure of Government Assistance
- E22, Accounting for Business Combinations

Final Standards Published

- IAS 14 (1981), Reporting Financial Information by Segment
- IAS 15 (1981), Information Reflecting the Effects of Changing Prices

1982

- Stephen Elliott of Canada becomes chairman of IASC.
- IASC and IFAC make mutual commitments. The IASC Board is expanded to up to 17 members, including 13 country members appointed by the Council of IFAC and up to 4 representatives of organizations with an interest in financial reporting. All members of IFAC are members of IASC. IFAC recognizes and will look to IASC as the global accounting standard setter. Special constitutional status of the 9 founder members of IASC is eliminated.
- IASC bolds Board meetings in London (2) and Amsterdam.

Exposure Drafts Published

- E23, Accounting for the Effects of Changes in Foreign Exchange Rates
- E24, Capitalization of Borrowing Costs

Final Standards Published

- IAS 16 (1982), Accounting for Property, Plant and Equipment
- IAS 17 (1982), Accounting for Leases
- IAS 18 (1982), Revenue Recognition

1983

- Italy joins IASC board.
- Expanded IASC board under the revised constitution takes effect.
- IASC holds board meetings in London, Edinburgh, and Paris.
- Title of senior staff executive changed from Secretary to Scretary-General

Exposure Drafts Published

E25, Disclosure of Related Party Transactions

Final Standards Published

- IAS 19 (1983), Accounting for Retirement Benefits in the Financial Statements of Employers
- IAS 20 (1983), Accounting for Government Grants and Disclosure of Government Assistance
- IAS 21 (1983), Accounting for the Effects of Changes in Foreign Rates
- IAS 22 (1983), Accounting for Business Combinations

1984

- Taiwan joins IASC board.
- IASC holds a formal meeting with the U.S. Securities and Exchange Commission.
- IASC holds board meetings in London, Toronto, and Dusseldorf.

Exposure Drafts Published

E26, Accounting for Investments

Final Standards Published

- IAS 23 (1984), Capitalization of Borrowing Costs
- IAS 24 (1984), Related-Party Disclosures

1985

- John L. Kirkpatrick of the United Kingdom becomes chairman of IASC.
- David Cairns becomes Secretary-General of IASC.
- IASC participates in an OECD forum on global accounting harmonization.
- IASC responds to SEC proposals for a multinational prospectus.
- IASC holds board meetings in London, Rome, and New York.

Exposure Drafts Published

E27, Accounting and Reporting by Retirement Benefit Plans

Final Standards Published

None

1986

- Financial analysts (International Coordinating Committee of Financial Analysts Associations) get a seat on the IASC board.
- IASC co-sponsors a conference with New York Stock Exchange and International Bar Association on the globalization of financial markets.
- IASC holds board meetings in London, Dublin, and Amsterdam.

Exposure Drafts Published

E28, Accounting for Investments in Associates and Joint Ventures

Final Standards Published

IAS 25 (1986), Accounting for Investments

1987

- Georges Barthes de Ruyter of France becomes chairman of IASC.
- IASC begins its Comparability and Improvements Project. Objective is to reduce or eliminate alternatives and make standards more detailed and prescriptive rather than flexible and descriptive of current practice.
- International Organization of Securities Commissions (IOSCO) joins the Consultative Group and supports the Comparability Project.
- IASC publishes its first bond volume of *International Accounting Standards.*
- IASC holds meetings in Sydney and Edinburgh.

Exposure Drafts Published

- E29, Disclosures in the Financial Statements of Banks
- E30, Consolidated Financial Statements and Accounting for Investments in Subsidiaries
- E31, Financial Reporting in Hyperinflationary Economies

Final Standards Published

IAS 26 (1987), Accounting and Reporting by Retirement Benefits Plans

1988

- Jordan, Korea, and the Nordic Federation (representing accounting bodies in Norway, Denmark, Sweden, Finland, and Iceland) join the IASC Board, replacing Mexico, Nigeria, and Taiwan.
- Financial instruments project started in conjunction with Canadian Accounting Standards Board.
- IASC published a survey on the use of IAS.
- FASB joins the Consultative Group and becomes an observer at the IASC board table.
- IASC holds board meetings in Dusseldorf, Toronto, and Copenhagen.

Exposure Drafts Published

Exposure Draft: Framework for the Preparation and Presentation of Financial Statements

Final Standards Published

None

1989

- European Accounting Federation (FEE) supports international harmonization and greater European involvement in IASC.
- IFAC adopts a public-sector guideline to require government business enterprises to follow IAS.
- IASC holds board meetings in Brussels and New York.
- IASC publishes its Framework for the Preparation and Presentation of Financial Statements.

Exposure Drafts Published

- E32, Comparability of Financial Statements
- E33, Accounting for Taxes on Income
- E34, Disclosures in the Financial Statements of Banks and Similar Financial Institutions
- E35, Financial Reporting of Interests in Joint Ventures

Final Standards Published

- IAS 27 (1989), Consolidated Financial Statements and Accounting for Investments in Subsidiaries
- IAS 28 (1989), Accounting for Investments in Associates
- IAS 29 (1989), Financial Reporting in Hyperinflationary Economies

1990

- Statement of Intent—Comparability of Financial Statements.
- Arthur R. Wyatt of the United States becomes chairman of IASC.
- European Commission joins the Consultative Group and takes a seat at the

IASC board table as an observer. Bank regulators and asset valuers also join the Consultative Group.

- A program to seek external funding is launched.
- IASC holds board meetings in Amsterdam, Paris, and Singapore.

Exposure Drafts Published

None

Final Standards Published

- IAS 30 (1990), Disclosures in the Financial Statements of Banks and Similar Financial Institutions
- IAS 31 (1990), Financial Reporting of Interests in Joint Ventures

1991

- IASC organizes a conference of national standard setters in conjunction with FEE and FASB.
- U.S. FASB indicates its support for international accounting standards.
- IASC holds board meetings in London, Milan, and Seoul.

Exposure Drafts Published

- E36, Cash Flow Statements
- E37, Research and Development Activities
- E38, Inventories
- E39, Capitalization of Borrowing Costs
- E40, Financial Instruments

Final Standards Published

None

1992

- IASC constitution revised.
- IASC holds board meetings in Madrid, Amman, and Chicago.

Exposure Drafts Published

- E41, Revenue Recognition
- E42, Construction Contracts
- E43, Property, Plant, and Equipment
- E44, The Effects of Changes in Foreign Exchange Rates
- E45, Business Combinations
- E46, Extraordinary Items, Fundamental Errors and Changes in Accounting Policies
- E47, Retirement Benefit Costs

Final Standards Published

Revision: IAS 7 (revised 1992), Cash Flow Statements

1993

- Eiichi Shiratori of Japan becomes chairman of IASC.
- India replaces Korea on board.
- IASC and IOSCO agree on a list of core standards.
- Comparability and Improvements project completed with approval of ten revised IAS. However, IOSCO did not endorse IAS at that time for use in cross-border securities offerings.
- South African Institute of Chartered Accountants decides that South African accounting standards should be based on IAS—existing South African GAAP to be revised.
- IASC holds Board meetings in Tokyo, London, and Oslo.

Exposure Drafts Published

None

Final Standards Published

Revisions:

- IAS 2 (revised 1993), Inventories
- IAS 8 (revised 1993), Net Profit or Loss for the Period, Fundamental Errors and Changes in Accounting Policies
- IAS 9 (revised 1993), Research and Development Costs
- IAS 11 (revised 1993), Construction Contracts
- IAS 16 (revised 1993), Property, Plant and Equipment
- IAS 18 (revised 1993), Revenue
- IAS 19 (revised 1993), Retirement Benefit Costs
- IAS 21 (revised 1993), The Effects of Changes in Foreign Exchange Rates
- IAS 22 (revised 1993), Business Combinations
- EIA 23 (revised 1993), Borrowing Costs

1994

- Board meets with standard setters to discuss E48, Financial Instruments.
- Accounting educators join Consultative Group.
- World Bank agrees to fund Agriculture Project.
- Establishment of IASC Advisory Council approved, with responsibilities for oversight and finances.
- IOSCO accepts 14 IAS and identifies some specific issues to be addressed in the remaining core standards (the so-called "Shiratori letters").
- FASB agrees to work with IASC on a joint earnings per share project.
- The G4+1 group, which includes IASC as the "+1," publishes its first study on Future Events.
- IASC holds Board meetings in Edinburgh and Budapest.

Exposure Drafts Published

- E48, Financial Instruments
- E49, Income Taxes

Final Standards Published

None

1995

- Michael Sharpe of Australia becomes chairman of IASC.
- Sir Bryan Carsberg becomes Secretary-General of IASC.
- IASC agrees with IOSCO to complete the core standards by 1999. IOSCO states that if the core standards are successfully completed, IOSCO will review them with the objective of endorsing IAS for cross-border offerings.
- First German companies report under IAS.
- Federation of Swiss Holding Companies takes a seat on the IASC Board.
- Malaysia and Mexico replace Italy and Jordan on Board. India and South Africa agree to share board seats with Sri Lanka and Zimbabwe, respectively.
- World Bank's accounting handbook states that "in the absense of any superior national standards, the Bank requires the use of IASs in the preparation of financial statements."
- European Commission supports the IASC/IOSCO agreement and concludes that IAS should be followed by EU multinationals.
- IASC holds board meetings in Dusseldorf, Amsterdam, and Sydney.

Exposure Drafts Published

- E50, Intangible Assets
- E51, Reporting Financial Information by Segment

Final Standards Published

New: IAS 32 (1995), Financial Instruments: Disclosure and Presentation

1996

- IASB accelerates its core standards program by one year, with completion planned by the end of 1998.
- International Association of Financial Executives Institutes joins IASC board. IOSCO takes a seat at the IASC board table as an observer.
- IASC starts a joint project on Provisions with United Kingdom Standards Board.
- A study by the EU Contact Committee finds IAS compatible with EU directives, with minor exceptions.
- U.S. SEC announces its support of the IASC's objective to develop, as expenditiously as possible, accounting standards that could be used for preparing financial statements used in cross-border offerings.
- U.S. Congress calls for "a high-quality comprehensive set of generally accepted international accounting standards."
- Australian Stock Exchange supports a program to harmonize Australian standards with IAS.
- World Trade Organization encourages successful completion of international accountancy standards.
- IASC holds Board meetings in Brussels, Stockholm, and Barcelona.

Exposure Drafts Published

- E52, Earnings per Share
- E53, Presentation of Financial Statements
- E54, Employee Benefits

Final Standards Published

Revision: IAS 12 (revised 1996), Income Taxes

1997

- Standing Interpretations Committee is formed. Twelve voting members.
- IASC and FASB issue similar EPS standards. IASC, FASB, and CICA issue new Segments standards with relatively minor differences.
- IASC discussion paper proposes fair value for all Financial Assets and Financial Liabilities. IASC holds 45 consultation meetings in 16 countries.
- Actuaries join Consultative Group.
- Arab Society of Certified Accountants calls for all of its 22 member countries to adopt IASs as their national GAAP (Dubai Declaration).
- APEC (Asia-Pacific Economic Cooperation) expresses its support of the efforts of the International Accounting Standards Committee to develop international accounting standards.
- Joint Working Group on financial instruments formed with national standard setters.
- People's Republic of China becomes a member of IFAC and joins the IASC Board as observer.
- IASC sponsors a conference of accounting standard setters from 20 countries in Hong Kong.
- FEE calls on Europe to use IASC's Framework.
- U.S. SEC reports to Congress on the outlook for successful completion of a set of international accounting standards that would be acceptable in the United States.
- IASC appoints a Strategy Working Party (SWP) to make recommendations regarding the future structure and operation of IASC following completion of the core standards. First meeting in April.
- IASC sets up its Internet Web site.
- IASC holds board meetings in London, Johannesburg, Beijing, and Paris.

Exposure Drafts Published

- E55, Impairment of Assets
- E56, Leases
- E57, Interim Financial Reporting
- E58, Discontinuing Operations
- E59, Provisions, Contingent Liabilities and Contingent Assets
- E60, Intangible Assets
- E61, Business Combinations

Final Standards Published

New: IAS 33 (1997), Earnings Per Share

Revisions:

- IAS 1 (revised 1997), Presentation of Financial Statements
- IAS 14 (revised 1997), Segment Reporting
- IAS 17 (revised 1997), Leases

Final Interpretations Published

- SIC 1, Consistency—Different Cost Formulas for Inventories
- SIC 2, Consistency—Capitalization of Borrowing Costs
- SIC 3, Elimination of Unrealized Profits and Losses on Transactions with Associates

1998

- Stig Enevoldsen of Denmark becomes chairman of IASC.
- New laws in Belgium, France, Germany, and Italy allow large companies to use IASs domestically in their consolidated financial statements.
- First official translation of IAS (German).
- IFAC/IASC membership expands to Latin America (new member bodies in Bolivia, Costa Rica, El Salvador, Guatemala, Honduras, and Nicaragua) as well as Haiti, Iran, and Vietnam, bringing membership to 140 bodies in 101 countries.
- IFAC Public Sector Committee begins a program to develop International Public Sector Accounting Standards based on IAS.
- Strategy Working Party proposes structural changes (including a bicameral standard-setting structure) and closer ties to national standard setters.
- In response to Asian financial crisis, the G8 Summit, the G7 ministers and central bank governors, the World Bank, and the IMF all call for rapid completion and global adoption of high-quality international accounting standards.
- International Federation of Stock Exchanges expresses support for IAS.
- IAS published on CD-ROM.
- IASC completes the core standards with approval of IAS 39 in December.
- IASC holds board meetings in London, Kuala Lumpur, Niagara-on-the-Lake, Zurich, and Frankfurt.

Exposure Drafts Published

- E62, Financial Instruments: Recognition and Measurement
- E63, Events after the Balance Sheet Date

Final Standards Published

New:

- IAS 34 (1998), Interim Financial Reporting
- IAS 35 (1998), Discontinuing Operations
- IAS 36 (1998), Impairment of Assets
- IAS 37 (1998), Provisions, Contingent Liabilities and Contingent Assets

- IAS 38 (1998), Intangible Assets
- IAS 39 (1998), Financial Instruments: Recognition and Measurement

Revisions:

- IAS 16 (revised 1998), Property, Plant and Equipment
- IAS 19 (revised 1998), Employee Benefits
- IAS 22 (revised 1998), Business Combinations
- IAS 32 (revised 1998), Financial Instruments: Disclosure and Presentation

Final Interpretations Published

- SIC 5, Classification of Financial Instruments—Contingent Settlement Provisions
- SIC 6, Costs of Modifying Existing Software
- SIC 7, Introduction of the Euro
- SIC 8, First-Time Applications of IASs as the Primary Basis of Accounting
- SIC 9, Business Combinations—Classification either as Acquisitions or Unitings of Interests
- SIC 10, Government Assistance—No Specific Relation to Operating Activities
- SIC 11, Foreign Exchange—Capitalization of Losses Resulting from Severe Currency Devaluations
- SIC 12, Consolidation—Special-Purpose Entities
- SIC 13, Jointly Controlled Entities—Nonmonetary Contributions by Venturers
- SIC 14, Property, Plant and Equipment—Compensation for the Impairment of Loss of Items

1999

- IOSCO begins its review of IASC core standards.
- IASC board meetings are opened to public observation. First public meeting is held in Washington in March.
- G7 Finance Ministers and IMF urge support for IASs to strengthen the international financial architecture.
- New IFAC International Forum on Accountancy Development (IFAD) commits to support use of International Accounting Standards as the minimum benchmark for raising national accounting standards worldwide.
- EC study finds no significant conflicts between IASs and the European Directives. EC adopts a financial services action plan that includes use of IASs as European GAAP.
- FEE reporting strategy for Europe strongly supports use of IAS in Europe without requiring compliance with EC Accounting Directives, plus phase-out of U.S. GAAP.
- Eurasian Federation of Accountants and Auditors plans adoption of IASs in CIS countries.
- Various meetings of the Strategy Working Party to discuss the comments on their initial proposal and to develop final recommendations. SWP publishes a revised proposal.

- IASC board unanimously approves restructuring into 14-member board (12 full-time) under an independent board of trustees.
- IASC board appoints a Nominating Committee, chaired by U.S. SEC Chairman Arthur Levitt, to select first trustees under new IASC structure.
- Looking beyond financial statements, IASC publishes a study of business reporting on the Internet.
- IASC holds board meetings in Washington, Warsaw, Venice, and Amsterdam.

Exposure Drafts Published

- E64, Investment Property
- E65, Agriculture

Final Standards Published

Revision: IAS 10 (revised 1999), Events after the Balance Sheet Date

Final Interpretations Published

- SIC 15, Operating Leases—Incentives
- SIC 16, Share Capital—Reacquired Own Equity Instruments (Treasury Shares)

2000

- Thomas E. Jones (U.K. citizen, career primarily in the United States) becomes chairman of IASC.
- SIC meetings open to public observation.
- Basel Committee expresses support for IAS and for efforts to harmonize accounting internationally.
- SEC issues a concept release inviting comments on the use of international accounting standards in the United States.
- As part of restructuring program, IASC board approves a new constitution.
- IOSCO recommends that its members allow multinational issuers to use IASC standards in cross-border offerings and listings.
- Nominating Committee announces initial trustees of the restructured IASC. Paul Volcker, former U.S. Federal Reserve Board Chairman, will chair the board of trustees.
- IASC member bodies approve IASC's restructuring and a new IASC constitution.
- European Commission announces a plan to require all EU listed companies to use IASs starting no later than 2005.
- Trustees name Sir David Tweedie (chairman of the U.K. Accounting Standards Board) as the first chairman of the restructured IASC board.
- Trustees announce search for new board members. Over 200 applications are received.
- IASC Board approves limited revisions to IAS 12, IAS 19, and IAS 39.
- IASC publishes first batch of Implementation Guidance Q&A on IAS 39.
- IAS 41, Agriculture, is approved at the last meeting of the IASC board (published in 2001).

- IASC holds Board meetings in Sao Paulo, Copenhagen, Tokyo, London.
- As one of its last official acts, the IASC board approves a Statement to the new IASC board commenting on projects to be carried forward and possible additional projects to be undertaken.

Exposure Drafts Published

- E66, Financial Instruments: Recognition and Measurement—Limited Revisions to IAS 39
- E67, Pension Plan Assets
- E68, Income Tax Consequences of Dividends

Final Standards Published

New: IAS 40 (2000), Investment Property
Revisions:

- IAS 12 (revised 2000), Income Taxes
- IAS 19 (revised 2000), Employee Benefits
- IAS 28 (revised 2000), Accounting for Investments in Associates
- IAS 31 (revised 2000), Financial Reporting of Interests in Joint Ventures

Final Interpretatons Published

- SIC 17, Equity—Costs of an Equity Transaction
- SIC 18, Consistency—Alternative Methods
- SIC 19, Reporting Currency—Measurement and Presentation of Financial Statements under IAS 21 and IAS 29
- SIC 20, Equity Accounting Method—Recognition of Losses
- SIC 21, Income Taxes—Recovery of Revalued Non-Depreciable Assets
- SIC 22, Business Combinations—Subsequent Adjustment of Fair Values and Goodwill Initially Reported
- SIC 23, Property, Plant and Equipment—Major Inspection or Overhaul Costs
- SIC 24, Earnings Per Share—Financial Instruments that May Be Settled in Shares
- SIC 25, Income Taxes—Changes in the Tax Status of an Enterprise or its Shareholders International Accounting Standards Board (IASB) Starting 2001

2001

- Trustees appoint the initial 14 members of the International Accounting Standards Board.
- In March 2001, IASC Trustees activate Part B of IASC's new constitution and establish a nonprofit Delaware corporation, named the International Accounting Standards Committee Foundation, to oversee the IASB.
- On April 1, 2001, the new IASB takes over from the IASC the responsibility for setting International Accounting Standards. New board holds its first meeting, adopts existing IASs and SICs, and deliberates its agenda and other issues.
- Trustees appoint 49 charter members to the IASB Standards Advisory Council. First SAC meeting is held in July.

- European Commission presents legislation to require use of IASC for all listed companies no later than 2005.
- EFRAG (European Financial Reporting Advisory Group) is created by the accounting profession, preparers, users, and national standard setters in EU countries to advise the European Commission on acceptability of individual IAS for Europe, as well as to respond to IASB comment documents.
- European Directives amended to allow compliance with IAS 39.
- IASB moves into new offices at 30 Cannon Street, London.
- IASB meets with chairs of those national accounting standards-setting bodies that have a formal liaison relationship with IASB—Australia/New Zealand, Canada, France, Germany, Japan, the United Kingdom, and the United States—to begin coordinating agendas and setting out convergence goals.
- IASB adopts its initial agenda of nine technical projects and agrees to have an advisory or monitoring role on 16 additional projects being worked on by partner national standard setters.
- Debate over IASB's stock options project reaches U.S. Congress.
- Seven largest accounting firms strongly endorse IAS for Europe.
- Trustees appoint the members of the restructured Standing Interpretations Committee.
- IFAD publishes GAAP 2000—a comparison of IASs and GAAP in 53 countries—as part of its effort to bring national GAAP up to an IAS benchmark.
- IASB holds board meetings in London (6), Washington, and Paris.

Exposure Drafts Published

Exposure Draft: Preface to International Financial Reporting Standards

Final Standards Published

New: IAS 41 (2001), Agriculture (approved by old IASC Board in December 2000).

Final Interpretations Published

- SIC 27, Evaluating the Substance of Transactions in the Legal Form of a Lease
- SIC 28, Business Combinations—"Date of Exchange" and Fair Value of Equity Instruments
- SIC 29, Disclosure—Service Concession Arrangements
- SIC 30, Reporting Currency—Translation from Measurement Currency to Presentation Currency
- SIC 31, Revenue—Barter Transactions Involving Advertising Services
- SIC 33, Consolidation and Equity Method—Potential Voting Rights and Allocation of Ownership Interests

2002

- IASB Chairman Sir David Tweedie and IASC Foundation Chairman Paul Volcker testify at U.S. Senate hearing on Accounting and Investor Protection Issues Raised by Enron and Other Public Companies.
- IASB issues its first exposure draft and final Standard on an accounting issue (IAS 19, Employee Benefits: The Asset Ceiling).

- SIC renamed to International Financial Reporting Interpretations Committee, with a mandate not only to interpret existing IAS and IFRS but also to provide timely guidance on matters not addressed in an IAS or IFRS.
- Europe adopts regulation requiring all listed companies, including banks and insurance companies, to prepare their consolidated accounts in accordance with IASs starting 2005.
- IASB board member Robert Herz is appointed chairman of the U.S. Financial Accounting Standards Board. John T. Smith, partner, Deloitte Touche Tohmatsu, replaces Mr. Herz on the IASB.
- IASB issues its first exposure draft of a Standard that will be in its new series of International Financial Reporting Standards: ED1, First-Time Application of International Financial Reporting Standards.

Exposure Drafts Published

- Exposure Draft: Amendment to IAS 19, Employe Benefits: The Asset Ceiling
- Exposure Draft: Improvements to International Accounting Standards
- Exposure Draft: First-Time Application of International Financial Reporting Standards
- Exposure Draft: Amendments to IAS 32, Financial Instruments: Disclosure and Presentation, and IAS 39, Financial Instruments: Recognition and Measurement
- Exposure Draft ED 2: Share-Based Payment
- Exposure Draft ED 3: Business Combinations
- Exposure Draft: Amendments to IAS 36 and IAS 38

Final Standards Published
Revisions:

- Preface to International Financial Reporting Standards (2002), replaced Preface to Statements of International Accounting Standards (1982)
- IAS 19 (Revised 2002), Employee Benefits

Final Interpretations Published
SIC 32, Intangible Assets—Web Site Costs

CHAPTER 17

EUROPEAN HARMONIZATION

Peter Walton

Open University Business School, United Kingdom

CONTENTS

17.1 INTRODUCTION. The harmonization of accounting within the European Union (EU) can be seen as a unique experiment in accounting, and one that reveals a great deal about the nature of accounting regulation and its relationship with cultural variables. Of course, accounting is just a very small part of a much wider program, and to some extent exhibits the same strengths and weaknesses as the overall project of political and economic harmonization. However, accounting harmonization in the EU has probably gone through one complete cycle, only to start up a new, and perhaps more promising, cycle. The first cycle went from initial, and perhaps naïve, enthusiasm, through practical difficulties, to disillusion and finally abandonment, having achieved some major objectives but failed in others. The second cycle has set out on a different track, using different instruments, and in a world which has moved on significantly.

In this chapter, the state of harmonization will be examined, in the first place by presenting a brief outline of the institutions of the EU, its accounting harmonization program and the effects of this on member states, and then reviewing the plans to harmonize audit, taxation, and the euro.

17.2 INSTITUTIONS

(a) Role of the Commission. A detailed knowledge of the institutional processes of the EU is not really necessary to understand harmonization, even if essential to a lobbyist. However, it is useful to have a grasp of the main institutions and their interrelationship. The permanent executive of the EU is the European Commission. The Commission itself consists of 20 members, nominated by member states (the larger states, such as the United Kingdom, have the right to nominate two commissioners), but the working brief of each commissioner is just one of the many decisions which are made by trade-offs between countries. Accounting and audit currently come under Internal Market Commissioner Frits Bolkestein. Commissioners have a five year term of office, renewable once. Most commissioners have been prominent national politicians before being appointed, and have held at least ministerial rank. Romano Prodi, for example, the current president of the Commission, was previously a prime minister in an Italian government.

The Commissioners are supported by permanent officials, organized into Directorates General. Accounting comes under Directorate General XV (DGXV) whose responsibilities include financial information, stock markets, and company law. The head of accounting within DGXV is a Belgian lawyer, Professor Karel Van Hulle (formally, his title is head of unit, financial information and company law).

The Commission has the sole right to initiate legislation and indeed to implement statutes once passed, but the process of approval of its proposals is tortuous. The two principal legislative institutions of the EU are the European Parliament and the Council of Ministers. Members of the European Parliament are directly elected in member states and the Parliament sits in Strasbourg. For the moment it has limited direct power, although in the longer term its powers are supposed to be increased. The Commission's legislative proposals are referred to the Parliament (as well as to the Council of Ministers and the Committee of Permanent Representatives—a standing committee of member states) for debate and Parliament's opinions are taken into account by the Commission in modifying these proposals.

(b) Role of the Council of Ministers. The decision-making power is increasingly being passed to the European Parliament from the Council of Ministers. This is not a single council, but rather a series of councils, each dealing with a different subject area and made up of the relevant ministers from member states, so a finance matter would be decided by the council of finance ministers, an agricultural matter by ministers of agriculture and so on. The presidency of the Council of Ministers rotates between member states every six months, and so the foreign minister of the member state is in effect head of the EU, and the individual ministers chair their respective subject councils. The rapid rotation means that no state ever sees through a decision from beginning to end, although states do try to make their mark by making some positive achievement during their presidency.

Theoretically, the Council of Ministers can accept or reject the Commission's proposals, but can amend them only with a unanimous vote. In practice, of course, the whole EU decision-making process operates through informal consensus seeking, with much behind the scenes negotiation before formal meetings. There are many trade-offs and temporary alliances between states along the lines of Country A, for example, agreeing to support Country B's position on beef subsidies, in return for Country B's support on a taxation question. In practice therefore, the Commission's proposals are widely debated and frequently modified in the process of arriving at a form which can command approval in the Council of Ministers. This can result in a major statute taking several years to be finalized, or in proposals being permanently stalled. Different company law proposals from DGXV have suffered both fates in the past.

Once passed by the Council of Ministers, the Commission oversees implementation of directives. However, the EU has its own court, the European Court of Justice, which is the final arbiter in terms of interpretation of an EU statute. Cases have been brought—and won—by private individuals who think that a member state has incorrectly applied European law, as well as by the Commission itself. In the past, the Commission has obtained judgment against Germany over its application of the Fourth Company Law Directive.

The EU governmental machinery is financed partly by a complex system of payments that differentiate between member states' economic capacities, and partly by the direct transfer of part of the product of the national value-added tax (VAT) rate. Opponents of European integration, known as "Euroskeptics", make much of what they describe as the fat Brussels bureaucracy, but in fact the Commission has fewer staff than many municipalities, and in the accounting area, for example, uses people seconded free of charge from the private sector to supplement its own officials.

(c) Evolution of the EU. The EU has gone through many stages since its creation with six members in 1957. Currently, it has 15 members, and it is widely expected that Poland, Hungary, the Czech Republic, and seven other countries will be admitted within the next five years. Views about Europe are usually sharply divided within each member state, without there being any pattern which correlates to the traditional political spectrum. Consequently, the input from individual states can vary in quality substantially every time there is a change of government. Currently, there is still a debate between those who wish to see the EU concentrate on improving integration within its existing borders, as opposed to those who wish to see it take on new members. This links to a debate about the extent to which power should be centralized or left in the hands of member state governments. Euroskeptic politicians frequently make emotional appeals about loss of sovereignty, while Europhiles query the extent of national autonomy in a global economy. This lack of agreement has led to what is called a "variable geometry" EU in which not all member states are participating, for example, in the single currency. This means that institutions related to the euro exclude some EU member states.

Historically, the integration process continued fairly strongly through the 1960s but started to lose momentum thereafter. It was revived by the "single-market" initiative which, through the Single European Act of 1986 placed emphasis on creating a "level playing field" for business and gave a new focus to harmonization. However, by the beginning of the 1990s, a new watershed had been reached which was marked by the Maastricht Treaty of 1992. This set in train a new political momentum but also recognized that there was no longer any political appetite for harmonization for harmonization's sake, even if the rhetoric perhaps suggested otherwise. This can be regarded as the beginning of the end for the first accounting harmonization program, even if this also set in train the process of movement towards a single currency, leading eventually to new emphasis on a single financial market and the second accounting harmonization program.

17.3 ACCOUNTING HARMONIZATION

(a) History. In the 1960s, the European Commission launched a program of harmonization of accounting. The basic process was to commission a technical report dealing with the subject area, then proceed to draft a statute, called a directive, which, once approved by the Council of Ministers, would have to be adopted by individual member states in their domestic legislation. It is a unique example of accounting harmonization imposed through the law. Fifteen or so company law Directives were drafted up until the end of the 1980s, but many of these remain stalled in the system. For example, the Fifth Directive, which deals with, among other things, the membership of company boards and includes employee participation, provoked sufficient opposition for it to remain blocked. The directives that had a major impact are the Fourth and Seventh, as regards accounting, and the Eighth as regards the audit profession. The Fourth Company Law Directive (78/660/EEC) deals with the form of individual company accounts, valuation rules, and the need for audit. The Seventh (83/349/EEC) addresses consolidated accounts.

The drafting of the Fourth Directive offers a fascinating case study in the difficulty of harmonizing regulations across contrasting cultural contexts, and also a good example of the incremental nature of much regulation drafting. In 1967, the Commission requested the accounting profession in the six member states to prepare a recommendation for a European company law for listed companies, with the stipulation that this should be based on existing best practice within the member states (France, Germany, Italy, Belgium, the Netherlands, and Luxembourg), rather than suggesting any new basis. The profession nominated a committee chaired by W. Elmendorff, an eminent German auditor, and its report, published in 1969, made a proposal based on the German 1965 law on public companies, at the time the most advanced statute within the six states.

The Elmendorff proposal reappeared in 1971as the first draft version of the Fourth Directive, but with the substantial change that it was to apply to all companies, not just publicly held companies. This rather draconian change, which involved applying German listed company rules to small private companies, was mitigated a little by recognizing that small (fewer than 50 employees) and medium-sized (fewer than 250 employees) companies could make slightly abbreviated disclosures. The size requirements, articulated around thresholds of balance sheet total, annual turnover, and average number of employees, have become a standard feature of European company law. The directive also required that both medium-sized and large companies should be subject to statutory audit, and left it to member states as to the audit status of small companies.

The evolution of the Fourth Directive was soon forced into a different direction because in 1973 Denmark, Ireland, and the United Kingdom joined the EU. These countries did not have the same regulatory traditions as Germany and also had existing regulations that could be claimed to be at least as up to date as the German model on which the first draft was based. What came to be a central conflict was that German accounting regulation has, since the nineteenth century, stipulated that the overall requirement in producing accounts is that they should be in accordance with accounting rules, while British and Irish regulation says that accounting rules can be set aside in achieving the over-riding objective of giving a true and fair view of the company's financial position.

There is evidence that the British position in the negotiations was partly a desire not to change existing U.K. law, and partly a resistance to "foreign" accounting, accompanied by a belief that insistence on a true and fair override would enable U.K. companies and their auditors to ignore German-style regulations, which they did not like. The arguments are not perhaps important in themselves, other than as evidence of the cultural and psychological obstacles to harmonization, but their effect was in the end to weaken the Fourth Directive.

The final version, approved by the Council of Ministers in 1978 (11 years after the initial report—a good example of the potential length of the institutional processes) said that accounts should both give a true and fair view and comply with accounting rules. The Directive also included numerous options, where member states could make choices about details of the regulations. For example, while the Directive contains an official format for the income statement, this can be presented horizontally in account form or vertically as a list, and ordinary operating expenses can be analyzed by nature (materials, depreciation, salaries, etc.) or by function (cost of goods sold, distribution, administration). In this way, German and British companies could continue to do the different things which they had always done, while still being officially "harmonized."

The Seventh Directive, which required that large companies produce consolidated accounts, had an easier passage through the drafting process. No new member states joined during the drafting. Of the original six members, only Germany had any regulations requiring companies to produce consolidated accounts, so there was no long history of well-established but different local rules, and the drafting committee made a conscious effort to align itself with the International Accounting Standards Committee (IASC) standards (the IASC came into being in 1973, too late to influence the Fourth Directive). This directive was passed in 1983.

(b) Impact of the Accounting Directives. There can be no doubt that the Fourth and Seventh Directives had a dramatic impact on financial reporting throughout the EU, without, for all that, producing accounting as harmonized as might have been hoped. While the Fourth Directive has many options, it did succeed in standardizing the approach to presenting income statements by separating out (1) the "ordinary" operating result, (2) financial income and expenses, and (3) the extraordinary result. Equally, the balance sheet format provided coherent, standard classifications and did away with dubious practices such as showing unpaid calls on stock as an asset. A minimum amount of supplementary information had to be provided in the notes to the accounts, including any modification of the economic result brought about by compliance with tax regulations.

This last is a particularly difficult issue in continental Europe because tax regulations have since the start of the twentieth century become progressively entwined with accounting rules. It is typical of this environment that companies can claim accelerated depreciation for tax purposes and also deduct certain provisions, provided that these deductions appear in stockholder accounts (with the idea that if the state gives tax concessions to help companies retain cash, the money should not be paid out in excessive dividends). This linkage causes expenses to be overstated and the Fourth Directive requires the degree of this overstatement to be disclosed in the notes. It is debatable how strictly this requirement is observed, but users will typically find remarks in notes about the application of tax rules. In addition, French and Italian rules provide for the difference between economic depreciation and tax depreciation to be shown as part of the extraordinary result.

The introduction of consolidated accounts was also a major advance. The only consolidation requirement in continental Europe had been that of Germany, which nonetheless allowed groups to exclude from consolidation any foreign subsidiaries. The Seventh Directive brought all EU members into line (even if Italy did not apply the rules until 1994) and also provided some forward-looking innovation in allowing that the criteria for consolidation should include not only ownership of a majority of voting stock, but also economic domination where the stock holding is a minority.

The major achievements of the harmonization program were to bring accounting in all the EU member states up to a good and reasonably uniform level. The program probably accelerated the development of accounting quite dramatically in a number of countries, and it also had the effect of providing a standard which influenced accounting in neighboring, non-EU countries.

There are, however, different cultural traditions within Europe about the role of accounting and how regulation should be articulated, and these take more time to harmonize, even if harmonization itself is in accordance with a long European tradition of borrowing and adapting regulations from neighbors. In particular, continental European accounting, largely inspired by French regulations issued as early as 1673, sees accounting as something to be regulated by the state, and mostly to suit state needs for regulating taxation and the economy. Against this, British and Irish accounting, like that of the United States, evolved in the wake of the industrial revolution in the nineteenth century as part of the apparatus of the capital markets, and is primarily oriented around providing economic information to investors. This contrast in approaches leads to the kind of uncomfortable compromises found in the Fourth Directive, even if time and experience have now shown how to move forward. It also leads to differences in the way in which the rules are applied, with tax-oriented countries likely to be much more prudent in their judgment in areas such as depreciation, provisions, and asset impairment.

At a detailed level, the harmonization process has produced its own disharmonies. In particular, member states did not scrap their existing accounting rules when adopting EU directives, but rather adapted the new rules to their existing ones, meaning that in no two countries do you find exactly the same rules, even if there is much common ground. For example, French accounts before the Fourth Directive were supposed to be "sincere and regular." The Fourth Directive says accounts should give a true and fair view, so current French law requires that accounts are sincere and regular and give a true and fair view.

In Germany, the Fourth Directive requirement that rules should be set aside if ultimately necessary to give a true and fair view (clause 2.5 of the Directive) was greeted with horror and not included in the German legislation, not least because in German law a general rule can never override a specific rule. In addition, the Germans have developed a view (known as separation theory) that the true and fair view applies to the notes to the accounts, while the income statement and balance sheet must comply with accounting rules at all times. Clearly, the true and fair view is not seen the same way in every country.

The extraordinary result is another area of hazard where different countries see it as having a different role. In France, the regulations require asset disposals and accelerated depreciation to be accounted for automatically as extraordinary items. U.K. standard setters have more recently tried to get rid of extraordinary items but are constrained by their existence in the Fourth Directive.

Equally, asset valuation is contentious: Germany applies strict historical cost rules, and if an asset is deemed to be impaired, its value is written down, with no requirement to adjust back to historical cost later when no longer impaired, if the write-back would result in higher taxable income—which is normally the case. France, Italy, and Spain permit revaluation above historical cost, but this is rarely done because such a revaluation has tax consequences, while U.K. companies practiced revaluation of real estate almost uniformly until the late 1990s, and some Dutch companies use replacement cost for tangible assets.

Another issue is the degree to which member states enforce harmonization. Germany is often criticized as having opted for a "soft" adoption. In particular, medium-sized companies, which prior to the Fourth Directive, were not audited in Germany, were hit by the Fourth Directive which required them to make substantial public disclosures of what had previously been seen as private information and to have an audit. However, the annual fine for not filing the accounts is trivial, so there is an estimated 90% noncompliance rate. Germany also uses a wider range of corporate legal vehicles than most EU states, including limited partnerships and similar devices with special tax implications. The Fourth Directive has been applied only to limited liability companies, however, so many small and medium-sized businesses that use other vehicles escape from its requirements.

(c) The End of the First Cycle. When the Commission started its harmonization program in the 1960s, internationalization of business was just beginning to gain momentum, and it was impossible to predict where this would lead. When the IASC was created it was part of a sudden and wider preoccupation with international harmonization in accounting which was also manifested at that time by the United Nations and the Organization for Economic Cooperation and Development (OECD), but even so, was not taken very seriously until at least 15 years later. However, the reality of international pressures and the need of European multinationals to be listed on several stock exchanges finally made it clear that the creation of a strong European regional level of accounting regulation was simply adding an unnecessary third tier, sandwiched between national regulations and the international capital markets. It should be noted that not all European accountants actually accept this view, and many still think strong EU accounting rules would effectively counter U.S. dominance of the markets.

It had also come to be realized that harmonization of individual company accounts is not necessarily very useful. On the one hand, the harmonization process is resisted because changing the measurement rules would mean changing the taxable profit in countries where the individual accounts are intimately involved in tax. On the other hand, it is not clear what advantage there is in harmonization, since small companies are not typically much involved in cross-border dealing, while large companies prepare consolidated accounts. Consequently, there are heavy costs for small companies associated with harmonization—EU measures affect at least 3 million small enterprises—and no obvious economic benefit.

The Commission, in a major policy announcement in November 1995 ("Accounting Harmonization: a New Strategy vis-à-vis International Harmonization"), recommended to member states that they pursue harmonization of consolidated accounting requirements through alignment on IASC standards, as far as that is compatible with the Seventh Directive. At the same time, the Commission decided, after many years of hesitation, to participate in IASC standard setting, although only as an observer. This landmark decision more or less fixed the end of the Commission's first program of accounting harmonization, while at the same time endorsing what has come to be an acceptance of a break of the link between individual company accounts and consolidated accounts, and in effect preparing the ground for the second cycle.

The Commission continued to work on accounting in a modest way. It issued in March 1998 its "Interpretative Communication Concerning Certain Articles of the Fourth and Seventh Council Directives on Accounting." This document dealt with a relatively large number of detailed points from the accounting directives "where authoritative clarification appears to be required." The exact legal status of this document is not clear, since it does not have the force of amending a directive, and the Commission specifies that it does not impose any obligation on member states nor prejudge any interpretation which the European Court of Justice might make.

In February 2000, the Commission published proposed amendments to the Fourth and Seventh Directives. These were finally passed in the latter part of 2001 (2001/65/EC), and had the limited objective of permitting the use of fair value as a measurement approach—necessary for the application of IAS 39 on financial instruments.

(d) Second Cycle. The Commission's second cycle could be said to have got under way in visible fashion during 2000 also. In April, the Council of Ministers gave approval to a proposal to develop a single European financial market, and then in June 2000 the Commission announced its new master plan: All European companies listed on a regulated exchange are to be required to account using International Financial Reporting Standards (IFRSs)[1] from 2005. This was to be achieved not through a new Directive (which would have to be enacted in member state law in due course), but rather through the mechanism of a Regulation. The latter has immediate force throughout the EU and entirely bypasses national statutes. The EU "Regulation on IAS" was passed by the Council of Ministers in June 2002, completing its passage through the EU institutions in record time.

This initiative has so far shown to have consequences in four different areas: (1) the need for companies to revise their internal systems by the end of 2003; (2) the need to create a mechanism for the EU to incorporate IFRSs into EU law; (3) revision at EU and national level of existing accounting rules for unlisted companies, and (4) the need for a review of compliance control procedures throughout the EU.

The Commission estimates that about 7,000 European companies will be concerned by the Regulation. European stock exchanges (and the IASB) generally require companies to provide only one year's comparative figures with the current result. This means that, outside of those European companies that are Securities and Exchange Commission (SEC) registrants, companies will have to have systems in place to capture information for 2004, which can be used to provide the comparatives for the first year of IFRS reporting in 2005. SEC registrants will have to have systems in place in 2003. However, a limited number of companies (essentially German ones such as DaimlerChrysler) that are currently using U.S. generally accepted accounting principles (GAAP) for their main accounts have been given a derogation to switch in 2007, but will also have to use IFRS from that time. Companies that have listed debt securities but not equity also benefit from this derogation.

The rules for transition to the use of IFRSs are currently contained in an IASC Interpretation, (SIC-8, issued in January 1998). The IASB is, however, preparing a standard that will replace SIC-8. The proposed standard was issued in exposure draft form during the second half of 2002. It is expected that the standard will require that companies that are applying IFRSs for the first time should restate assets and liabil-

[1]The International Accounting Standards Board (IASB) determined in its 2002 *Preface to IFRS* that the expression "IRFS" should, when used generically, be taken to encompass both the International Accounting Standards (IASs) issued by the International Accounting Standards Committee and the International Financial Reporting Standards issued by the IASB. The EU Regulation refers to IASs, not IRFSs, but we will use the expression *IFRSs*.

ities using IFRS rules as at the transition date (typically January 1, 2004 for a European listed company), giving rise to a one-time adjustment to retained earnings. However, past business combinations do not have to be restated, and fair value can be used for assets and liabilities if calculation of historical cost would require undue cost or effort.

Companies would be expected to produce a reconciliation statement to take users from the last year under the old accounting principles, to the same year restated according to IFRSs, and used as comparatives for the first IFRS year. A typical European company would be expected, therefore, to publish 2004 accounts under national rules in the normal way, then restate them under IFRSs, to be published both in a reconciliation statement and as previous-year comparatives alongside the 2005 figures.

A particular problem, which so far remains unresolved, is the reporting requirements for the significant number of listed European insurance companies. The IASB has no insurance accounting standard, although one is at an early stage of preparation. It seems highly unlikely that the IASB will have its standard for insurance contracts in place in time. Consequently, either the IASB will have to provide some sort of interim rule, such as recognizing existing practices (which are diverse), or the EU will have to provide a deferral of the Regulation for insurance companies.

(e) IFRS Endorsement Mechanism. Not the least problem posed by the use of IFRS in the EU is that the standards need to have legal force, and the Commission has been obliged to devise some mechanism whereby a private sector body, not under the control of the EU, can in effect write accounting law for Europe. This has proved controversial, and it remains to be seen how the arrangements will work out. The Commission and others have argued that, provided it intervenes upstream in the IASB's due process, its views can be taken into account in the formulation of IFRS and there is therefore no problem about the EU not having the opportunity to write its own standards.

In practice, the Commission has in the past had a difficult relationship with the IASC, only becoming an observer as late as 1995. Although France, Germany, and the United Kingdom are represented on the new IASB as "liaison standard setters," there is no EU representation as such. The Commission is not represented directly on the IASB or on the Standards Advisory Council (although it has observer status in the latter). In addition, the Commission does not have the staff to participate in depth in the IASB standard-setting process. The solution that has been put into effect has been for the Commission to call on the private sector to participate in the standard-setting process.

An organization called the European Financial Reporting Advisory Group (EFRAG) has been created by the private sector. This is supposed to coordinate input from national standard setters from the EU, to comment on discussion papers and exposure drafts, to participate in advisory committees when asked, and to liaise with the IASB in general. When a standard is issued, the EFRAG will provide a commentary to the Commission, which then submits the standard to member state representatives for endorsement.

EFRAG came into existence in June 2001. It has a supervisory board consisting of representatives of the bodies that are sponsoring it: the Fédération des Expert Comptables Européens (FEE—European Accountants Federation), the Union Confédérations de l'Industrie et des Employeurs d'Europe (UNICE—Europea ployers' Union), European Banking Federation, European Savings Banks

European Association of Cooperative Banks, Comité Européen des Assurances (insurance companies), European Association of Craft, Small and Medium-sized Enterprises, European Federation of Accountants and Auditors for small and medium-sized enterprises (SMEs), Federation of European Securities Exchanges, and the European Federation of Financial Analysts' Societies. The first secretary general of EFRAG is Paul Rutteman, a former technical partner in Ernst & Young with years of experience in European harmonization.

The executive organ of EFRAG is its Technical Expert Group (TEG). This body meets every month, under the chairmanship of Johan van Helleman, a former Shell executive and latterly chairman of the Dutch standard setter. The TEG is the body that deals with the day-to-day work of participating in IASB committees and discussing IASB literature. Although the TEG does not have a liaison member as such on the IASB, Tom Jones, IASB vice chairman, has taken on responsibility for liaison with them.

The procedure that has been worked out for endorsement is that the TEG will issue its opinion on each IFRS when issued and submit this to the European Commission. The Commission then assembles a committee of member state permanent representatives, called the Accounting Regulatory Committee (ARC). The ARC will then endorse (or not) the standard. At the same time, the European Parliament has the right to intervene, if it wishes, during a three-month period. If the Commission is not happy with the ARC's deliberations, it has the right to refer an issue to the Council of Ministers.

Clearly, the machinery for transmission of IFRS into EU law leaves plenty of room for manipulation, and it remains to be seen whether IFRS will have a clear passage from the IASB into the EU. TEG chairman Johan van Helleman, in an interview in *World Accounting Report*, has commented: "There is a strong feeling that we should take IFRS as they are. We could provide negative advice to the European Commission, but that should be a very great exception. We hope rather to have a European influence before the standards become final."[2] As far as the ARC is concerned, it is supposed to limit itself to taking a position as to whether or not a particular IFRS is compatible with European Directives. Clearly, it would be very damaging to IFRS if the EU were to start amending them for use in Europe.

(f) Future Harmonization. It may be that when the European Commission decided to adopt a stance of requiring the use of IFRS by listed companies, this was seen as an extension of their 1995 position, and the intention was to leave national GAAP untouched in the member states. However, it now seems unlikely that this will be the case. The effect of introducing IFRS looks likely to be to pull national GAAP toward IFRS and in effect introduce another wave of full harmonization, potentially affect-
... businesses, from the smallest to the largest.

... can be seen in a number of ways. Commentators have observed that
... ularly the larger ones, will want to adopt IFRS in order not
... citizens. Countries such as France are planning to leave
... repare consolidated accounts with a choice of IFRS or
... up accounts. Just as many U.S. companies that are not SEC
... S. GAAP, so it is expected that the same reasons that moti-

... rt, November 2001, p. 15.

vate in the United States will encourage unlisted European companies to use IFRS where they have that possibility.

Countries like the United Kingdom have a tradition of applying the same accounting standards to all except the very smallest incorporated entities, irrespective of listed status, and consequently, IFRS will in effect become national GAAP from 2005. The Accounting Standards Board in the United Kingdom has already started to amend national standards to bring them into line with IFRS. In Spain, the idea of adopting IFRS for all companies is under consideration.

The Commission has decided to facilitate this movement by proceeding with a further set of amendments to the Fourth and Seventh Directives. Unlisted companies that do not use IFRS, or are not allowed to do so (permitting use of IFRS by unlisted companies is a member state option at this time), will have to comply with the Fourth and Seventh Directives, which are not wholly compatible with IFRS. In June 2002, the Commission put a proposal to the Council of Ministers to proceed to a new set of amendments that would "bring EU accounting requirements into line with modern accounting theory and practice."[3]

The intention is to remove inconsistencies with IFRS, as well as remove the possibility of hiding liabilities in off balance sheet vehicles, and to call for more risk disclosure. The proposal also includes a specification of the issues to be mentioned in the audit report. However, the Commission observes that accounting is linked to taxation in many member states, and therefore the proposed amendments are expressed as Member State options, to permit individual states to move toward IFRS at "a pace appropriate to that individual country."

The Commission has also started to take an active interest in the idea of there being a small company version of IFRS. Some countries, such as the United Kingdom, Canada, and New Zealand, have in recent years given derogations to allow smaller entities to use simplified accounting standards. The UN Intergovernmental Working Group of Experts on International Standards of Accounting and Reporting (ISAR) has been working on an abridged form of IFRS to meet the needs of smaller business. Such a set of standards would be helpful in an EU environment since it would provide an intermediate stage that could be applied to all smaller business and still remain compatible with full IFRS. The IASB has in the past been reluctant to go down this path, but is expected shortly to start its own project in this area.

It is too early in the process to predict the outcomes with certainty, but it seems very likely that the use of IFRS by listed companies will be the catalyst for very many other enterprises to produce either full IFRS accounts, or national variants which are very close to IFRS.

17.4 AUDITING. The Commission had significantly, but probably unintentionally, affected the market for statutory audit as a result of the Fourth Directive. This caused many medium-sized companies in countries like Germany and Belgium to fall into the statutory audit net for the first time and therefore enlarged the market substantially. In Germany, this led to the creation of a second tier of audit professionals (*vereidigte Buchprüfer*) to be licensed to carry out audits on medium-sized companies, alongside the *Wirtschaftsprüfer*, because it was felt impossible to expand the number of the latter sufficiently quickly to meet demand.

---

[3]European Commission press release IP/02/799 of June 3, 2002.

However, the Commission first visited the idea of harmonizing the audit profession with the Eighth Directive (84/253/EEC) issued in April 1984. This dealt with the professional qualifications of auditors, insisting that they had at least three years' experience before qualifying and that the professional qualification should be equivalent to a university degree. The degree of professionalization throughout the EU was very varied, not least because the role of the auditor had developed historically in different ways in different states. Countries like Spain, Italy, and Greece had to undertake fairly radical restructuring of their different forms of the profession, leading to the establishment of official government registers of auditors.

The organization of the profession remains, however, extremely diverse throughout Europe. For example, the United Kingdom has six accounting bodies, members of four of which have ministerial approval to be statutory auditors, subject to having obtained the necessary training certificates. France has two bodies, but one is exclusively for auditors, and the other for those who provide accounting, tax, law and other services. Both bodies are subject to the control of ministries, but not the same one, and recognition as a statutory auditor goes automatically with membership of the audit body.

In Germany, however, there are three private-sector professional bodies in the same area of auditing, accounting, and tax. However, auditors have to be registered with a government agency, the *Wirtschaftsprüferkammer* (WPK—chamber of auditors), which awards a license to practice, and can withdraw this. Membership of the private sector *Institut der Wirtschaftsprüfer* (IdW—auditors institute) is optional, although the IdW issues audit standards and ethical codes. Equally, the IdW is a member of Federation des Experts-comptables Européens (FEE), the regional association, but the WPK is not, and is regularly opposed by the IdW when it applies for membership. There is an entirely separate body known as *Steuerberater* who provide accounting and tax advice to clients. These are regarded as "second tier," by the Wirtschaftprüfer, although they have been given access to audit through the new status of *Vereidigte Buchprüfer*. Steuerberater may take a supplementary exam and then register with the Wirtschaftsprüferkammer as auditors of medium-sized companies.

This very diverse range of structures is not about to change—accountants are very conservative people, at least at an institutional level. However, it makes common agreement on anything in the audit area quite difficult. However, FEE, the regional organization for the profession, maintains that, despite the different structures, the quality of audit is high and in most countries is carried out to worldwide standards. In 2002, it published a discussion paper which suggested that the European profession should systematically adopt International Standards of Auditing. A number of national bodies have also set up a working party to harmonize the content of professional examinations.

The Commission signaled a renewed interest in auditing matters in 1996, when it published a green paper on the role, position, and liability of the statutory auditor within the EU. This was followed by wide consultation, a conference, and then publication on May 7, 1998, of a "Communication" on the future of statutory auditing in the EU. The Communication announced the setting up of a Committee on Auditing whose role is to examine the comparability of auditing standards and to audit quality control systems and rules on auditor independence. The Commission said it hoped that harmonization could be achieved without legislation, but would not hesitate to introduce this if necessary.

The Commission's rationale for this initiative was that reliable financial statements are part of the mechanisms for the operation of a single market, but without common agreement on the role of the auditor and scope of the audit, there is some doubt as to what degree of reliability is being offered in different countries. The chosen solution was the Committee on Auditing, which includes representatives of member states, the auditing profession, and internal auditors, as well as representatives of user groups.

The first output from this committee was a Recommendation on Quality Assurance (2001/256/EC) published in November 2001. This recommended that all member states should institute a system of quality assurance for statutory auditors. The system could be based on either monitoring by a specialist agency or peer review, and could look at firms or individual auditors, but the cycle for full review of all auditors should be a maximum of six years. Quality assurance should be maintained in line with International Standard on Auditing (ISA) 220, "Quality Control for Audit Work."

This was followed in May 2002 by the Commission Recommendation on Statutory Auditors' Independence in the EU. This says the statutory auditor must be independent in mind and appearance. It proposes a principles-based approach where the auditor should assess both risks to independence and safeguards against these. There is a detailed discussion of the nature of these risks, how different tasks might interact with them, and what safeguards should be in place. There is no systematic proscription of nonaudit work. The Recommendation, however, calls for disclosure of fees received by the audit firm from the audit client, analyzed as between audit work, other assurance work, tax advisory services, and other nonaudit services. At least two years should elapse before a "key audit partner" can take up a "key management position" with an audit client. Key audit partners should spend no more than seven years as part of the audit team of a particular client that is a "public interest entity."

Different countries have in the past had markedly different approaches to independence. In Germany and France in particular, the statutory auditor is expressly prohibited from carrying out nonaudit work for audit clients. While in practice the Anglo-Saxon concept of the profession as offering a wide range of services has gained ground and devices exist for effectively circumventing the independence rules, there is still considerable opposition to such concepts. Questions of auditor independence and corporate governance structures were included in the ill-fated Fifth Directive, and while the climate may have changed, the area is not the easiest on which to make progress. The Recommendation does not bind member states. The only area where the Commission has moved toward compulsory harmonization is the audit report, where the 2002 proposed amendments to the accounting directives (see above) include details of the necessary content of the statutory audit report.

17.5 CAPITAL MARKET ENFORCEMENT. The Commission launched a Financial Services Action Plan in 1999, which set out a package of legislation for building a single financial market in the EU. This is primarily aimed at unifying the legal framework on issues such as market abuse, prospectuses and regulations governing financial conglomerates and pension funds. However the Commission has no concrete plan to legislate on the issue of surveillance of the financial reports of listed companies. The Lamfalussy Report, endorsed by the EU Heads of Government in March 2001, laid out the recommendations of the so-called Committee of Wise Men created by the Commission to review the streamlining of the European securities markets. However, while it recommended that enforcement should be improved, it suggested that this should be done by cooperation between national stock exchange regulators, rather than through any EU-wide regulator. The Committee of European Securities Regulators (CESR) has been set up for this purpose.

An FEE discussion paper on enforcement of IFRS within Europe reviews the situation. It says that "ideally global standards require global enforcement" but comes to the conclusion that "a single enforcement system, even at a European level, is an unrealistic goal at present." Enforcement systems throughout the EU differ widely. Only two countries, Italy and France, have SEC-style stock exchange surveillance agencies. The U.K. system, although considerably reformed in recent years, does not have any mechanism for systematic checking by the oversight authorities that accounting standards are followed. It does have the Financial Reporting Review Panel, but this body, while effective in what it does, examines only those financial reports that outsiders refer to it. Most European countries simply rely on the statutory auditors to ensure that the appropriate accounting principles are complied with.

FEE's recommendations are that all member states review their enforcement procedures and, in view of the short period before IFRSs come into force, those without any enforcement system adopt the review panel model as providing the least costly immediate solution. At the same time the accountants' regional body believes that it is essential to create a coordination unit for enforcement bodies. Common procedures need to be worked out and arrangements made for close consultation with the IASB and the International Financial Reporting Interpretations Committee to deal with emerging issues and implementation issues.

17.6 TAXATION. If resistance to change is fairly strong within national audit bodies, this is nothing to the governmental resistance to any change in taxation, and therefore to any harmonization of taxation. Nonetheless, different taxation remains a major factor in business decisions, and for that matter impacts on accounting measurements, partly through the distorting affect of tax concessions and partly through the fact that taxes are levied in different ways. For example, in many EU countries, if depreciation is to be claimed as a deduction against revenues, it must appear in the accounts for the amount claimed. Where the tax authorities will accept accelerated rates, this means that the companies must apply these, thereby in countries like Italy, France, and Germany reporting higher depreciation on new assets than in countries like the Netherlands and the United Kingdom.

There are also structural differences, with a wide range of different taxes. One comparative study noted that France had as many as 76 different taxes, while at the other end of the spectrum Spain had only 19. Some differences have a major impact on accounting measurements. France, for example, funds its social security system (health and unemployment) exclusively from payroll taxes, while the United Kingdom does not link the source of tax to the spending budget. France has significantly higher payroll taxes, which appear as part of personnel cost, while the U.K. equivalent makes apparently higher profits but pays more income tax.

The Commission has reviewed taxation a number of times, the most recently in 1992 in the Ruding Report. This took the view that steps should be made to harmonize taxes because of the distorting effect on the single market, but so far very little has been done. In 1998, Austria and Germany manifested a political will to do something to resolve the complex patchwork of different taxes throughout Europe, but the task is very difficult and appears to have run into the sand. Aside from the fact that the existing framework is built up of compromises between different interests and objectives reached in different countries over the years, there are very real fears that harmonization would lead to a severe destabilizing of economies.

Countries which think they have relatively low tax regimes, such as the United Kingdom, fear that they might be obliged to increase taxes, thereby making products more expensive and the economy less competitive. Countries with high tax regimes fear the social unrest that may be generated by attempts to cut back public expenditure to take account of reduced tax income, as was experienced in some member states during the period when they were trying to reduce public borrowing to meet the entry requirements for the single currency.

A committee of the European Parliament has also been looking into a list of tax practices in individual member states that might be deemed to be anticompetitive. For example, Ireland offers a ten-year income tax holiday to companies setting up there. This clearly offers a tax incentive whose object is to persuade inward investment to locate in Ireland rather than in any other member state. The role of tax havens is also being questioned, with places like Jersey and the Isle of Man now being considered to have negotiated an overly privileged relationship with the EU since they are broadly within its customs tariff wall but free from the constraints of membership.

At the same time, there is no doubt that the diverse taxation regimes are a bigger obstacle to a single market than financial accounting, and that these are part of the regulatory package which means that some EU member states are more interesting for inward investors than others.

17.7 THE EURO. Many skeptics thought that a single European currency would never be achieved, and that if achieved, would not last. It remains to be seen how successful the experiment will be, but the initial introduction of the currency has passed without any major disruption. The single currency is arguably the most important individual development since the founding of the European Economic Community in 1957, not only because of its economic consequences, but also because it is the first major initiative that does not involve all member states, thereby excluding a small group of members from a development which is at the heart of the EU. The 11 participants in the European Monetary Union are: Germany, France, Italy, Spain, Ireland, the Netherlands, Belgium, Luxembourg, Finland, Austria, and Portugal.

It has been expected that the single currency will itself accelerate the movement toward harmonization, simply because differences that express themselves in price differentials between countries will become more visible. It is thought that this visibility is likely to lead to calls for harmonization but is also likely to lead to competition that will itself damage the economies of uncompetitive states and force them to react. However, there is very little obvious manifestation of this so far. A number of companies that trade across borders have revised their prices to have a single euro price, but there is little evidence that the new currency is having the harmonizing effects which were predicted.

As far as the investment market is concerned, here again the euro is expected to heighten the ease of comparisons, as well as removing currency risk from investments within the Eurozone, thereby encouraging cross-border investment. However, the effects are likely to be slower since many investors prefer corporate debt investment to equity, and many continental European funds have restrictions on placing their funds outside their home market, apart from the depressed state of the equity markets. Even so, the pressures are growing for a restructuring of the stock exchanges, and the euro will increase the momentum. Although it is arguable that the individual stock exchanges are themselves the biggest obstacle to a single financial market in the EU.

This points to another area where the effects of the euro are not yet clear, the effect on the surrounding countries who are not members of the Eurozone. The idea of a single price list throughout Europe, if it becomes a reality, could mean that companies outside are forced to price in euros, and stock exchanges like London are forced to list both sterling and euro prices, with the consequence that the euro becomes the effective trading currency, wherever one is based in Europe (just as the U.S. dollar is the effective currency in a number of countries outside the United States). This kind of effect can be seen with Swiss companies now wanting to publish group accounts denominated in euros instead of Swiss francs.

17.8 CONCLUSION. Between 1965 and 1995, the EU conducted probably the greatest individual experiment in legally based accounting harmonization the world will ever know, and has now set off on a new cycle. Its initiatives in this area have affected the accounts of millions of companies, have changed the way accounts are presented not only within its borders but outside, and have consumed countless millions of man-hours in discussing, approving, and then implementing these changes. The cost has never been calculated, but must amount to many billions of dollars. What does it tell us about harmonization?

First, that changing the rules does not necessarily mean that countries change their attitudes to accounting, so that what is necessary is not only a rule change but a "hearts and minds" campaign, which persuades people that the change is useful. In the case of the EU, it is not certain that changing the way small and medium-sized companies approach their accounts has been shown to be useful. It may well be that the Commission should have stuck to its original idea, that the Fourth Directive should have applied to listed or large companies and left the rest alone.

A second point is that the new regulations in the first cycle were adopted and adapted to work into existing national regulations, they did not replace the existing rules, and therefore countries after harmonization had certain points in common, but also retained many of their old differences. It has always been the case in European accounting regulation that where countries have borrowed each others' rules, which happens frequently, they have then adapted them to suit local circumstances and national culture, thereby changing them quite substantially. It remains to be seen whether the approach of using IFRS in the second cycle will succeed in stopping local variations.

A third point is that changing accounting is in itself not enough. Different accounting rules are only one reason why accounts look different, there are other differences such as different accounting objectives, different auditing rules, and different taxation. Beyond these technical aspects there are also issues such as corporate and investor expectations which do not correspond in all countries, with the effect that management priorities are different and what they prioritize in the annual report is also different.

Assessed overall, one might come to the conclusion that the initial impetus for accounting harmonization was ideologically based—the construction of a single Europe for its own sake. It consequently ran into a number of implementation problems because accountants on the ground saw no reason to change in order to respond to someone else's vision of a greater Europe. Subsequently, the mood changed and companies became much more aware of a market need driven by the internationalization of business. However, the EU instead of gaining from this new perception, also lost as far as writing its own accounting rules was concerned in that the market pressure is for global standards, and makes regional standards redundant. It is remarkable, for example, how quickly Germany reacted to its multinationals' needs to have internationally-based consolidated accounts by changing the law in a matter of months in 1997–1998, when it labored over introducing the Fourth directive for nearly ten years in the 1980s.

The second cycle of harmonization seems to be quite different in that it primarily addresses the needs of the capital market participants to have transparent, comparable information to improve the effectiveness of investment decisions. By adopting IFRS, the Commission avoids both the need to develop its own rules, and the problem that once they are enshrined in EU law it is an extremely long process to amend them. If unlisted companies take the same route, this will probably be motivated by their own wish for that, rather than because harmonization has been forced on them.

However, the new cycle is far from being without many dangers. Politicians may find it difficult not to intervene in the endorsement process, or at least use the threat of intervention as a bargaining chip, so the passage on IFRS into the EU may be problematic. After that, there will be the questions of enforcement and interpretation of IFRS, where once again national habits and preferences are likely to come to the fore.

SOURCES AND SUGGESTED REFERENCES

Alexander, D., and S. Archer, (eds.). *European Accounting Guide*, 5th ed. Gathersburg, NY: Aspen Publishing, 2003.

"The European Endorsement Mechanism." *World Accounting Report*, November 2001.

FEE. *Discussion Paper on the Enforcement of IFRS within Europe*. Brussels, April 2002.

Hoogendoorn, M. "Accounting and Taxation in Europe—A Comparative Overview." *European Accounting Review*, Vol. 5 Supplement, 1996, pp. 783–794.

Messina, M., and P. Walton. "The Impact of Government on Company Cash Flows in France and the United Kingdom." *Journal of International Accounting, Auditing and Taxation*, 1998, pp. 273–293.

Stitt, I. P. A. "Corporate Taxation in the EC." *British Tax Review*, 1993, pp. 75–89.

Van der Tas, L. "Evidence of EC Financial Reporting Practice: The Case of Deferred Taxation." *European Accounting Review*, Vol. 1, No. 1, 1991, pp. 69–104.

Van Hulle, K. "Harmonization of Accounting Standards in the EC: Is It the Beginning or Is It the End?" *European Accounting Review*, Vol. 2, No. 2, 1993, pp. 387–396.

Van Hulle, K. "The True and Fair Override in the European Accounting Directives." *European Accounting Review*, Vol. 6, No. 4, 1997, pp.711–720.

Walton, P. "Harmonization of Accounting in France and Britain: Some Empirical Evidence." *Abacus*, 1992, pp. 229–254.

Walton, P., (ed.). *European Financial Reporting—A History*. San Diego: Academic Press, 1995.

Walton, P., A. Haller, and B. Raffournier, (eds.). *International Accounting*, (2nd ed.). London: Thomson Learning, 2003.

Weetman, P., and S. Gray. "A Comparative Analysis of the Impact of Accounting Principles on Profits: The USA versus UK, Sweden and the Netherlands." *Accounting and Business Research*, Autumn 1991, pp. 363–379.

PART V

REPORTING ISSUES

CHAPTER 18

CONSOLIDATED FINANCIAL STATEMENTS AND BUSINESS COMBINATIONS

James R. Ratliff

New York University

CONTENTS

18.1 INTRODUCTION. Corporate structures have become increasingly complex in the last several years. Some companies have diversified into additional lines of business through internal growth and acquisitions while others have consolidated, concentrating on their core and more profitable businesses. Many companies of all sizes have expanded into foreign markets, frequently through newly formed entities. Accounting rule makers and regulators are more and more focused on how to account for these business combinations and under what circumstances consolidated financial statements should be prepared. This chapter will concentrate on how to account for business combinations and under what circumstances consolidated financial statements should be prepared. First to be discussed is the preparation of the consolidated financial statements.

18.2 DEFINITIONS. Some definitions are:

- *Acquisition.* A business combination in which one entity (the acquirer) obtains control over the net assets and operations of another (the acquiree) entity in exchange for the transfer of assets, the incurrence of liabilities, or the issuance of equity.
- *Business combinations.* The bringing together of separate enterprises into one economic entity as a result of one enterprise uniting with or obtaining control over the net assets and operations of another.
- *Consolidated financial statements.* The financial statements of a group presented as those of a single enterprise.
- *Goodwill.* The excess of the cost of a business accounted for by the purchase method over the fair value of the net assets.
- *Minority Interest.* That part of the net results of operations and net assets of a subsidiary attributable to interests that are not owned, directly or indirectly through subsidiaries, by the parent.
- *Pooling-of-interest method.* An accounting method used for business combinations, which is predicated upon a mutual exchange and continuation of ownership interests in the combining entities. It does not result in the establishment of a new basis of accountability.
- *Purchase method.* An accounting method used for business combinations, which recognizes that one combining entity was acquired by another. It establishes a new basis of accountability for the acquiree.
- *Subsidiary.* A subsidiary is an entity that is controlled directly or indirectly by another entity, its parent. As discussed in section 18.5(a) control may be defined in a number of different ways. The key feature is that it is controlled by a single entity. A subsidiary may be organized as a corporation or a partnership.

18.3 FUNDAMENTAL ISSUES

(a) Relevant and Informative Accounting. The primary purpose of financial reporting is to provide the reader with useful information about the reporting entity (including the accounting for investments in subsidiaries) that helps users make rational investment, credit, or economic decisions. The accounting for investments in subsidiaries should be evaluated from this viewpoint:

- Does the Statement of Financial Position give relevant information related to the assets, liabilities, and equity of the reporting enterprise, including the assets it controls and the liabilities it incurs through the ownership of subsidiaries?

- Does the Income Statement give relevant information about the revenues, expenses, gains and losses of the reporting entity, including the revenues and gains it earns and the expenses and losses it incurs through the ownership of subsidiaries?
- Does the Statement of Cash Flows give relevant information about the cash inflows and outflows or the reporting entity, including the cash inflows and outflows that arise from subsidiaries and any restrictions on the free movement of cash among the entities?
- Do the financial statements taken as a whole give relevant information about the businesses in which the enterprises participates and the risks to which it is subject, including the business and risk that it participates in through its investments in subsidiaries?

(b) Different Legal Forms of Investment. Should the legal form of an investment affect the accounting for that investment? A company can participate in business and operations through various forms. A given business might be conducted through a division or a branch of the company, through a subsidiary, or through a joint venture. Ideally, the accounting for the different forms of investments should differ only if the legal form has a material impact on the parent company's risk or rewards from the investment.

(c) Transactions Between Investor and Investee. The final fundamental issue is the proper accounting for transactions between the investor and investee. If the investor contributes or sells assets to the investee, or vice versa, is it appropriate for the transferor to record a gain? Is it appropriate for the transferee to record the asset at an amount different from the amount at which the transferor recorded it? Some accountants believe that recording such transactions at current fair values provides the most useful information; others believe that the related-party nature of these transactions creates the potential for accounting abuses and oppose recognition of asset write-ups.

18.4 DESCRIPTION OF ACCOUNTING METHODS

(a) Full Consolidation. In full consolidation the assets, liabilities, revenues, expenses, gains, losses, and cash flows of the investor and the investee are combined in the investor's financial statements. The interests of outside investors in the investee is labeled "minority interest" and is shown as a liability or an item between the liabilities and owners' equity in the statement of financial position. The interest of the minority stockholders in the net income of the investee is shown as a deduction from net income, typically labeled "minority interest in net income." The result of full consolidation is to present the financial statements of the parent company and its subsidiaries as if they were a single company.

(b) Pro rata, or Proportionate, Consolidation. In pro rata, or proportionate, consolidation the investor's proportionate interest in the asset, liabilities, revenues, expenses, gains, losses, and cash flows of the investee is combined with the similar items of the investor without distinguishing the amounts. Accordingly, no "minority interest" is shown on the financial statements. This method is used more often when accounting for joint ventures.

(c) Equity Method. Another name for this method is one line consolidation. In the equity method of accounting for investments the investor's statement of financial po-

Assume that Parker International acquired 80% of the common stock of MNO Corp. on January 1, 2001 (at the beginning of the current year) for $800,000. On the date of acquisition, the book value of the net assets of MNO was $800,000, which also equaled their fair value. The first two columns in the solution are the Statement of Financial Position and the Income Statement for Parker International and MNO Corp. as of December 31, 2001 and for the year then ended. While this is an illustration of the four methods discussed above it must be remembered that the methods are not interchangeable. Specific conditions must be taken into consideration when determining the method to be used. The investment in MNO is recorded on the books of Parker International using the equity method.

Solution:

Observe that the Net income is the same under all the methods except the cost method. Since no dividends were paid by MNO, Parker would not report any income from its investment in MNO under the cost method. The minority interest is recognized on the statements when the full consolidation method is used. Minority interest is not recognized when the proportionate consolidation method is used as only the parent's share of the assets and liabilities of MNO are reported under the proportionate consolidation method.

Exhibit 18.1. Comparison of Methods of Reporting Investments.

sition reflects the investor's proportionate interest in the net assets of the investee as a single amount, typically labeled "equity in net assets of investee," and in which the investor's income statement reflects the investor's proportionate interest in the net income of the investee as a single amount, typically labeled "equity in net income of investee." As the investee earns income, the investor includes its proportionate share in income and increases the balance of the investment (equity in net assets). As the investee declares dividends the investor reduces the balance of the investment.

(d) Cost Method. This is a method of accounting for the investments in which the investor's statement of financial position reflects its investment in the investee at original cost. The investor records income as the investee declares dividends out of net accumulated earnings of the investee since the investor's purchase of its investment. Dividends in excess of the net accumulated earnings are accounted for as a reduction of the investment.

(e) Comparison of Methods. The first three methods generally result in the same shareholders' equity and net income with minor exceptions but the presentation of the financial statements is quite different, as illustrated in Exhibit 18.1. The cost method results in different stockholders' equity and net income, because the investor does not record the investee's undistributed income. For purposes of illustration, Exhibit 18.1 applies all four accounting methods to a single investment. In reality the four methods can not be used interchangeably in accounting for a single investment.

18.5 ACCOUNTING FOR INVESTMENTS IN SUBSIDIARIES

(a) Definitions of Control. A parent–subsidiary relationship is a prerequisite for the preparation of consolidated financial statements. A subsidiary is defined as an entity that is controlled by another entity. Therefore, the definition of control is of primary concern in determining whether or not consolidated financial statements should be prepared. The definitions of control fall into two categories: legal control and economic control.

Definitions of control based on legal control look to specific objective conditions that demonstrate the ability of the parent to control the subsidiary. Examples of legal control include:

- Ownership of a majority voting interest in the subsidiary
- Ownership of a majority of the equity securities of the subsidiary
- Ability by contract, proxy, or otherwise, to appoint a majority of the subsidiary's board of directors

Economic control is a more subjective concept than legal control. Some examples of economic control are:

- The control of legally independent entities by a mutually agreed system of central and unified management
- The right to direct the operating and financial policies of the enterprise through either a controls contract or provisions in the enterprises' Articles

This concept relies on a subjective determination of when the operation of a group of entities is sufficiently unified to constitute economic control.

(b) Triumph of Full Consolidation. The full consolidation has emerged throughout the world as the predominant method of accounting for investments in subsidiaries in the primary financial statements. Accounting rule makers and regulators have come to accept that the financial statements of a parent and its subsidiaries should report the financial position, results of operations, and cash flows as if they were one legal entity. Multiple subsidiaries may be formed for tax, legal, or other reasons, but they function as a single economic unit and should report as one. Proponents of full consolidation recognize that members of the group may operate in a decentralized manner and that management of the various subsidiaries may be given broad authority to run their business with minimum supervision by the parent. The subsidiaries, however, operate for the benefit of the group and will be able to continue to operate in a decentralized manner only as long as they serve the needs of the group. The parent retains the power to control the subsidiaries whether they exercise it or not.

The alternatives to full consolidation, the equity method and the cost method have become less acceptable over time, because they potentially obscure the nature and extent of operations conducted by the subsidiaries and the parent's control over them. If the equity method is used, the parent reports its share of the subsidiary income or losses but does not display the subsidiary assets or liabilities. In the United States, the equity method is acceptable only when a company has significant influence over another company but does not have control. When the cost method is used, the parent does not report its share of the undistributed income and, of even greater concern, does not report its share of subsidiary losses. The cost method thus provides a means to conceal losses by transferring loss operations to existing or newly created subsidiaries. In the United States the cost method is generally accepted accounting principles (GAAP) only when a company invests in another company but neither has control or significant influence. It is true that footnote disclosures can partially compensate for the deficiencies of the equity or cost method; however, information in the footnotes commands less attention than the information contained on the face of the financial statements. Further information in the footnotes generally is excluded from financial statement databases.

Full consolidation, however, does not solve all of the problems. Creditors in the individual entities in the consolidated group need separated financial statements to reveal the resources that are available for the repayment of their loans. Consolidated financial statements may also need footnote disclosure to explain restrictions on the transfer of cash or other assets between the members of the group.

(c) Required Accounting for Investment in Subsidiaries. This section describes the accounting requirement in the United States, Canada, the European Union, the United Kingdom, Japan, and the requirements of International Accounting Standards.

(i) United States. The primary guidance in the United States is FASB Statement No. 94, "Consolidation of All Majority-Owned Subsidiaries. Statement No. 94 requires the parent to fully consolidate all companies in which it "has a controlling financial interest through direct or indirect ownership of a majority voting interest." SFAS 94 contains two exceptions to this rule: (1) if control is likely to be temporary, or a long-term investment position is not contemplated, such as when a majority interest is acquired for the purpose of facilitating other business deals and not with a meaningful commitment to the acquired company; and (2) if the control does not rest with the majority shareholders. If the subsidiary is in legal reorganization or in bankruptcy, control may not rest with the parent company management, but with fiduciaries, such as bankruptcy trustees or creditors. Similarly, effective control of foreign subsidiaries may rest with the foreign government, in cases where foreign exchange restrictions, controls, or other governmentally imposed restrictions are so severe that they cast significant doubt on the parent's true ability to control the subsidiary. If the subsidiary were not consolidated because control does not rest with the majority shareholders, it would generally be accounted for by the cost method.

Rule 3A-02 of SEC Regulation S-X is substantially similar to Statement No. 94. Rule 3A-02 differs in two respects:

1. It requires full consolidation of majority-owned "entities," which includes non-incorporated entities.
2. It notes that, in certain rare circumstances, it may be necessary to consolidate an entity fully notwithstanding the lack of majority ownership, "because of the existence of a parent-subsidiary relationship by means other than record ownership of voting stock."

In 1989, the SEC staff became increasingly concerned about special-purpose entities (SPEs):

> Certain characteristics of those transactions raise questions about whether SPEs should be consolidated (notwithstanding the lack of majority ownership). . . . Generally, the SEC staff believes that for nonconsolidation . . . to be appropriate, the majority owner (or owners) of the SPE must be an independent third party who has made a substantive capital investment in the SPE, has control of the SPE, and has made a substantive capital investment in the SPE, and has substantive risks and rewards of ownership of the

assets of the SPE (including residuals). Conversely, the SEC staff believes that nonconsolidation . . . [is] not appropriate . . . when the majority owner of the SPE makes only a nominal capital investment, the activities of the SPE are virtually all on the sponsor's or transferor's behalf, and the substantive risks and rewards of the assets or the debt of the SPE, rest directly or indirectly with the sponsor or transferor.[1]

In 1995, the FASB issued an Exposure Draft (ED), "Consolidated Financial Statements: Policy and Procedures" and in 1999 issued a revised ED, "Consolidated Financial Statements: Purpose and Policy." The 1999 ED addresses only consolidation policy issues while the 1995 ED deals with both consolidation policy and procedures. This section discusses the consolidation policy changes proposed in the 1999 ED.

According to the 1999 ED, " The purpose of consolidated financial statements is to report the financial position, results of operations, and cash flows of a reporting entity that comprises a parent and its affiliates essentially as if all of their assets, liabilities, and activities were held, incurred and conducted by a single entity with one or more branches or divisions. What binds separate legal entities into a single reporting entity is the parent's decision-making authority, direct or indirect, over each of the entities in the group and the parent's consequent ability to direct their activities, including the use of their assets."[2]

The purpose of consolidated financial statements as stated in the 1999 ED differs little in substance from language used in earlier pronouncements, What is new is the reference to decision-making authority as the basis of control, without specific regard to the ownership of voting shares.

The 1999 ED would still require the consolidation of all controlled companies but it would change the definition of control. Control would no longer be defined as the majority ownership of the voting stock of the entity. The ED provides the following definition of control: "Control—the ability of an entity to direct the policies and management that guide the ongoing activities of another entity so as to increase its benefits and limit its losses from that other entity's activities, For purposes of consolidated financial statement, control involves decision-making ability not shared with others."[3]

This definition and the ensuing discussion in the 1999 ED recognize two versions of control, legal control and effective control. Legal control involves the unconditional ability to select a majority of an entity's governing board, and is typically indicated by direct or indirect control of a majority of the entity's voting shares. Effective control achieves the needed decision-making ability by other means, typically a large minority ownership position and other factors that enable the parent to dominate the entity's governing board and, accordingly its decision-making process.

Determining whether effective control exists is largely a matter of judgment. The ED provides implementation guidance consisting of presumptions of effective control in business organizations and ten specific examples of applying the notion of effective control when the conclusion is not obvious.

The ED suggests that the presumptions of effective control exists when an entity (including its subsidiaries):

---

[1]FASB, EITF Abstracts, 1990.

[2]Paragraph 7, 1999 ED.

[3]Paragraph 6, 1999 ED.

- Possesses a large minority voting interest that produces a majority of the votes typically cast in the election of a corporation's governing board with other voting interests being generally dispersed
- Possesses the unilateral ability to obtain a majority voting interest in a corporation's governing board, such as the ownership of options, including those embedded in convertible securities, which if exercised produce such a majority voting interest
- Is the general partner in a limited partnership in which no other group of limited partners can remove the general partner or dissolve the limited partnership

The ED also proposes to adopt the economic approach to preparing consolidated financial statements, in particular the treatment of minority interests as part of consolidated shareholders' equity.

(ii) Canada. The primary guidance in Canada is Section 1590 of the CICA Handbook. Section 1590 defines a subsidiary as "an enterprise controlled by another enterprise (the parent) that has the rights and ability to obtain future economic benefits from the resources of the enterprise and is exposed to related risks." *Control of the enterprise* is defined as:

> The continuing power to determine its strategic operating, investing and financing policies without the co-operation of others . . . An enterprise is presumed to control another when it owns, directly or indirectly, an equity interest that carries the right to elect the majority of the members of the other enterprise's board of directors, and is presumed not to control the other enterprise without such ownership.

Control does not exist if an enterprise is acquired "with the clearly demonstrated intention that it be disposed of in the foreseeable future." In addition, control does not exist, even when one enterprise has majority voting rights in a second enterprise, if a statute or agreement imposes "severe" long-term restrictions" on the ability of the second enterprise to distribute earnings to the first enterprise or undertake other transactions with the first enterprise. "For example, the imposition of severe foreign exchange or currency export restrictions over a foreign subsidiary may indicate that control has been lost."

A parent is required to fully consolidate all subsidiaries. Certain disclosures are required if an enterprise concludes that it does not control another enterprise despite ownership of majority voting rights or concludes that it does control another enterprise despite not owning majority-voting rights.

(iii) European Union. Guidance on the preparation of consolidated financial statements in the European Union is found in the Seventh Directive. These requirements are legally enforceable for all EU member countries once they have been introduced into each country's national laws. As of 1992 all of the member countries have adopted the Directive. The Directive generally requires parents to prepare financial statements that account for investments in subsidiaries by the full consolidation method. The Directive provides a framework for the preparation of these statements with numerous options in two areas: which parent undertakings are required to present consolidated financial statements and what constitutes a parent–subsidiary relationship.

Consolidation is required under Article 1 of the Directive when any of the following circumstances apply:

- The investor corporation holds a majority of the shares with voting rights.
- The investor corporation has a shareholding and the right to appoint a majority of the board of directors.
- The corporation has a dominant influence as a result of a contract.

The Directive permits the following parent relationships not to be reported in consolidated financial statements:

- Parent undertakings that are not companies incorporated with limited liability
- Parent undertakings that are themselves subsidiaries of a higher-level parent, if the higher-level parent prepares financial statements that fully consolidate the intermediate parent
- Parent undertakings that are purely passive holding companies, that is, are not involved directly or indirectly in the management of their subsidiaries and are not represented on the subsidiaries' boards of directors
- Small parent undertakings that fall below certain size thresholds

The Seventh Directive permits member states some flexibility in defining control, and thus in defining the subsidiaries that are to be fully consolidated. The first four relationships listed below are defined by the Directive as constituting control and thereby creating a parent–subsidiary relationship. Relationships five and six may be defined by member states as constituting control.

1. The parent has majority voting rights in the subsidiary.
2. The parent is a shareholder and has the right to appoint or to remove a majority of the subsidiary's directors.
3. The parent has the right to exercise a dominant influence over the subsidiary under a contract or pursuant to the subsidiary's bylaws, and local law permits such a contract or bylaw provision. Member states may prescribe that the parent also must be a shareholder. (These contract or bylaw provisions may not be permitted in some member states.)
4. The parent is a shareholder but controls alone, by agreement with the other shareholders, a majority of the voting rights of the subsidiary. (Member states may enact more detailed provisions concerning the form and content of the agreement.)
5. The parent is a shareholder, and a majority of the subsidiary's directors holding office since the beginning of the preceding year have been appointed solely by the parent's exercise of its voting rights. This condition would not result in a parent–subsidiary relationship if another entity were parent under relationship 1, 2, or 3 above. A member state electing this option may require that the parent hold at least 20% of the subsidiary's shares.
6. A parent holds a "participating interest" (long-term equity interest of 20% or more), and either exercises dominant influence over the subsidiary or manages the subsidiary on a unified basis with itself. (A member state could define a "participating interest" to exist at a lower level of ownership.)

Furthermore, consolidation may be required by individual member states where there is a shareholding and a dominant influence or unified management in practice. Some of the options available to the EU member states are:

- Group corporations may include those managed on a unified basis or dominantly influenced.
- Requirements to consolidate may be restricted to parents that are corporations.
- Financial holding corporations may be exempted.
- "Small groups" may be exempted from consolidation, except listed corporations.
- EU groups may be exempted if owned by non-EU parents that prepare "equivalent" accounts.
- Exclusion of subsidiaries from consolidation is permitted on the basis of immateriality, long-term restrictions, expense, or delay.
- Pooling of interests accounting is permitted.
- Proportional consolidation is permitted.

(iv) United Kingdom. Requirements for consolidated financial statements in the United Kingdom conform to the Seventh Directive. The statutory requirements are contained in the Companies Act of 1985 as amended by Companies Act of 1989. The accounting requirements are contained in the Accounting Standards Committee SSAP1, "Accounting for Associated Companies," as amended by the Accounting Standards Board Interim Statement "consolidated Accounts" and by the Accounting Standards Board Financial Reporting Standard FRS2, "Accounting for Subsidiary Undertakings.

(v) Japan. The Securities and Exchange Law requires listed companies, over-the-counter traded companies, and companies that have filed registration statements in the past under the Securities and Exchange Law to prepare both parent-company-only statements and consolidated financial statements. A subsidiary is defined as a corporation in which a parent has direct or indirect ownership of a majority voting interest by standards issued by the Business Accounting Deliberation Council. Subsidiaries are not to be consolidated if (1) control does not rest with the majority owner, (2) the subsidiary is not a going-concern enterprise, or (3) control is temporary. Subsidiaries would also be excluded from consolidation if the result would mislead readers of the consolidated financial statements. Subsidiaries could also be excluded from consolidation if they are so immaterial that exclusion for the consolidated statements would not prevent reasonable judgement on financial position or operating results of the group of consolidated companies. This excluded subsidiary would generally be accounted for by the use of the equity method.

(vi) International Accounting Standards. International Accounting Standards Committee IAS No. 27, "Consolidated Financial Statements and Accounting for Investments in Subsidiaries," requires full consolidation of all subsidiaries, with the following exceptions:

1. A parent is exempted from presenting consolidated financial statements if it is itself a wholly or virtually wholly owned subsidiary of a parent that presents consolidated financial statements.

2. A subsidiary should be excluded from consolidation if
   a. Control is intended to be temporary because the subsidiary is acquired and held exclusively with a view to its subsequent disposal in the near future, or
   b. The subsidiary operates under severe long-term restrictions that significantly impair its ability to transfer funds to the parent.

Subsidiaries excluded from consolidation should be accounted for in accordance with IAS No. 25, "Accounting for Investments." This pronouncement permits long-term investments to be accounted for at cost, lower of cost or market, or fair value.

IAS No. 27 defines *control* as "the power to govern the financial and operating policies of an enterprise so as to obtain benefit from its activities."

(d) Exclusion of Subsidiaries From Full Consolidation. While the predominant method of accounting for investments in subsidiaries is full consolidation, under certain circumstances subsidiaries should be excluded from consolidation. The four most common reasons for exclusion from consolidation are: immateriality, control not resting with the legal owners, control being temporary, and significantly different lines of business.

(i) Control Not Resting With Legal Owners. If a subsidiary is in bankruptcy, control might not rest with the legal owners but with a bankruptcy trustee; in this situation, the legal owners should not consolidate the subsidiary. Likewise, if a foreign subsidiary is severely restricted in terms of its business operations or its distribution of earnings by government restrictions or foreign currency controls, the parent should not consolidate the subsidiary. If consolidation is inappropriate for these reasons, the parent in all probability also does not have significant influence and therefore the subsidiary should be accounted for by the cost method.

(ii) Control Is Temporary. This exemption would generally apply to newly acquired subsidiaries. Most authorities believe that if a parent has consolidated a subsidiary in the past, it should continue to do so until the subsidiary is sold or otherwise disposed of. The subsidiary continues to be controlled until the sale and consolidation aids in comparability with past periods. However, if a subsidiary has been purchased with the intention of reselling, there are good arguments for the nonconsolidation of the subsidiary. This lack of control is discussed in the FASB Exposure Draft, "Consolidated Financial Statements: Purpose and Policy," issued in February 1999. This ED states:

> A subsidiary shall be consolidated unless a parent's control is temporary at the date that control is obtained. Control of a newly acquired subsidiary shall be considered temporary if at the date of acquisition the parent either has committed to a plan to relinquish control of that subsidiary or is obligated to do so and it is likely that loss of control will occur within one year.

(iii) Significantly Different (Nonhomogeneous) Lines of Business. This is still a controversial topic. The trend is toward full consolidation. The United States, Canada, the United Kingdom, and the IASC rules require consolidation regardless of the lines of business. However, many accountants argue that the issuance of parent financial statements that account for subsidiaries in significantly different lines of business by

the use of the equity method and the issuance of separate financial statements of the nonconsolidated subsidiaries is more meaningful.

Those opposed to the consolidation of businesses in nonhomogeneous lines of business may be confusing and also may obscure important information. Companies in financial businesses have different assets, liabilities, revenues, expenses, and financial ratios than those in manufacturing and commercial business. The users of financial statements could have a better understanding of the financial conditions of the group if the parent's financial statements consolidate only the subsidiaries with similar financial and accounting characteristics and present separate financial statements for entities with significantly different financial and accounting characteristics.

Proponents of the full consolidation of all controlled subsidiaries believe that full consolidation presents more meaningful financial information. They agree that users of financial statements are interested in the performance of individual business units, but they believe that the appropriate response is to issue consolidated statements that include all controlled subsidiaries along with either segment information or separate financial statements for the various business units.

In the United States, the Financial Accounting Standards Board (FASB) has recognized that information on the different segments of a business is important to the user. Accordingly, the Board issued FASB Statement No. 131, "Disclosures About Segments of an Enterprise and Related Information." This Statement requires the disclosure of information about the operating segments of a company as supplemental information in the consolidated financial statements. Some level of segment reporting is required in most of the industrial countries.

(e) Subissues in Accounting for Subsidiaries. A number of subissues exist concerning how to implement full consolidation. Some of these subissues will be discussed in this section.

(i) Conceptual Approach to Consolidation. The first issue is the selection of a conceptual approach to consolidation. The question is essentially one of entity definition. Should the focus of consolidation reporting be on the parent, the total business entity, or on some other construct?

PARENT THEORY OF CONSOLIDATION. Currently, the generally accepted consolidation practices have followed the parent theory of consolidated statements. This approach considers the consolidated statements to be no more than an extension of the parent company financial statements. The consolidated statements are not intended to be of a significant benefit to the minority interest. The cost principle is followed in that only the parent's share of the assets acquired and the liabilities assumed is reported in the fair value evidenced by the parent's cost. The minority interest continues to be carried at book value, since no transaction occurred, and hence no cost incurred for this portion. Minority interest is treated basically as creditors.

Major characteristics of the parent theory can be summarized as follows:

- Fair values are assigned only to the portion of the assets and liabilities acquired by the parent. The minority interest share of the assets and liabilities is continued to be carried at their book value.
- Goodwill reported on the consolidated statements relates only to the parent's interest.

- Minority interest in the subsidiary reflects the minority interest's share of the book value of the stockholders' equity.
- Minority interest in the subsidiary generally appears in the noncurrent liability section of the consolidated statement of financial position. The consolidated stockholders' equity relates only to the controlling interest.

ENTITY THEORY OF CONSOLIDATED FINANCIAL STATEMENTS. The entity theory of consolidated financial statements is referred to by the FASB as the economic unit approach/full consolidation method. The is the principal alternative to the parent company approach. The viewpoint of this theory is that consolidated financial statements should reflect the total business entity. The resources of the subsidiary controlled by the consolidated entity relate to both the controlling and to the minority shareholders. All of the assets acquired and liabilities acquired in the purchase transaction are valued at their values. Major characteristics of the entity theory of consolidated financial statements may be summarized as follows:

- Fair values are assigned to all of the subsidiary's assets and liabilities including the portion attributed to the minority (noncontrolling) interest.
- Goodwill is derived from the total fair value that is inferred from the price paid by the parent for its fractional interests, and pertains to both the controlling and noncontrolling shareholders.
- Minority interest in the subsidiary reflects the minority's share of the total fair value of the subsidiary's stockholders' equity.
- Minority interest in the subsidiary is separately disclosed and is included within the consolidated stockholders' equity.

MODIFIED ENTITY THEORY. This theory is also known as the economic unit approach/purchased goodwill method. Under this theory, the identifiable assets and liabilities of the subsidiary are recorded at their fair value in the consolidated statement of financial position, and the appropriate portion is reflected in the minority interest. Goodwill, however, is viewed as a premium paid by the parent for the value of the control over the subsidiary. When viewed in this way, goodwill accrues only to the parent, not to the noncontrolling shareholders, thus no goodwill is attributed to the minority interest. The goodwill calculated under this theory would be the same as the goodwill calculated under the parent company approach.

(ii) Elimination of Intercompany Profits. Under both the parent company and economic entity approaches, all intergroup transactions and related profits are eliminated in consolidation. If the subsidiary is not wholly owned, the profit elimination may be allocated between the majority and minority shareholders. There is, however, controversy over when the allocation of the profit elimination is appropriate. Most accountants believe that in the sale from the parent to the subsidiary (downstream sale), all of the eliminated profit should be charged to the majority owners and that allocation is appropriate only in sales from the subsidiary to the parent (upstream sales).

(iii) Push-Down Accounting. Controversy also exists over how purchased subsidiaries should report in their separate financial statements. The general rule is that the adjustments to the fair value of assets and liabilities are made only on consoli-

dated working papers and are not recorded on the books of the subsidiary. If separate financial statements are issued by the subsidiary, they report the subsidiary's original book values.

This practice is now being questioned in the United States, especially with reports that have to be made to the Securities and Exchange Commission (SEC). Under Staff Accounting Bulletin (SAB) No. 54, "Application of `Push Down' Basis of Accounting in Financial Statements of Subsidiaries, Acquired by Purchase," when a change in ownership involving substantially all (generally at least 95%) of an acquired company's stock occurs, it establishes a new basis of accountability for the acquired company, equal to the cost of the acquisition.

Under push-down accounting, the new owner's cost of the acquired company is "pushed down" to the acquired company by recording the fair value of the assets and liabilities on the acquired company's books. This procedure assures that the acquired company's separate financial statements report the same valuation reflected in the consolidated financial statement. This procedure is criticized by some, however, because it permits an entity to revalue its assets and liabilities based on an ownership change rather than on a purchase transaction made by the entity.

18.6 BUSINESS COMBINATIONS

(a) Overview. There are two methods of accounting for business combinations: (1) the purchase method and (2) the pooling-of-interest method (international accounting standards use the term *uniting of interest*). Under the purchase method, an acquisition of one entity by another is deemed to have occurred and, therefore, a new basis of accounting is established for the assets and liabilities of the acquired entity. Under the pooling-of-interest method, the combined companies are deemed to have fused their interest and therefore the assets and liabilities are carried forward at their book values. It is as if the combined companies have always been one.

In practice, only a small minority of companies worldwide uses the pooling-of-interest method. In the United States, pooling is not permitted for business combinations initiated after June 30, 2001, nor is it permitted in Australia, Brazil, or Japan. Interestingly enough, it is required under certain circumstances in Canada, France, Sweden, and the United Kingdom. In most countries there are specific conditions that must be met before the pooling-of-interest method can be in accounting for a business combination. In all countries that permit the pooling method, the pooling-of-interest method and the purchase method are not alternative methods for reporting of a specific business combination.

The treatment of goodwill arising in a purchase is different among the various countries. In the United States, goodwill must be capitalized and written off only when it has been determined to be impaired. In some other countries, goodwill is capitalized and then subsequently amortized. In others, goodwill is charged off immediately against earnings or equity.

(b) Purchase Accounting. The purchase method is used to account for a business combination when there is an acquisition of one company by another.

From an accounting standpoint, the purchase creates a new accounting basis for the assets and liabilities of the company being purchased. It is to be considered the same as if the acquiring company had acquired each individual asset and assumed each individual liability of the acquired company and their fair values. Thus, under purchase accounting the acquisition of a company is no different than the acquisition of any other asset at its fair value. It is the application of cost accounting to the purchase of assets and the assumption of liabilities. In a purchase, the revenues and expenses of the acquired company from its business operations accrue to the acquiring company from the date of acquisition.

The purchase price of the acquisition must be allocated among the various assets that are acquired, net of any liabilities assumed in the transaction in accordance with the fair values of those assets. Fair values must be allocated to all identifiable assets and liabilities whether they were or were not recorded on the books of the acquired company. If the fair value of the net assets equals the acquisition price, the allocation is straightforward. However, in most acquisitions, the fair value of the net assets and the acquisition price are not equal. If the acquisition price exceeds the fair value of the identifiable net assets, that excess must be allocated to goodwill. Likewise, if the fair value of the acquired identifiable net assets exceeds the purchase price, that excess must be allocated to negative goodwill.

The acquisition should be accounted for as the cost paid or incurred. Cost is the amount of cash paid or the fair value of other consideration given to the stockholders of the acquired company. Cost also includes transaction costs such as legal fees, accounting fees, investment banking charges, and so on. Depending on the terms of the acquisition agreement cost may also include some contingent considerations. Exhibit 18.2 illustrates the accounting for a business combination under the purchase method.

(c) Pooling of Interest. In a pooling of interest, unlike a purchase, an acquisition of an another entity has not been deemed to have taken place. Instead, a pooling accounts for the business combination as a uniting of the ownership interest of two companies. For a business combination to be accounted for as a pooling, it must be effected by the exchange of common stock, which would keep the resources of the combined entities undistributed. A business combination may not be accounted for as a pooling of interest if the consideration paid is cash. Since an acquisition has not been deemed to have occurred, no new basis of accounting for the assets and liabilities has been established. The assets and liabilities are carried over to the new combined company at their book values.

Since an acquisition has not taken place, theoretically there is no purchase price. Since there is no purchase price, no "excess" of purchase price arises in the transaction so there is no goodwill. The treatment of the revenues and expenses of the combined companies also differs from the treatment in a purchase. In a pooling, the revenues and expenses of the combined companies for the year includes the revenue and expenses of both of the constituents for the entire period being reported. Exhibit 18.3 illustrates the accounting for a business combination under the pooling-of-interest method.

(d) Required Accounting for Business Combinations. This section discusses the required accounting standards in various jurisdictions.

(i) United States. On June 21, 2001, the FASB issued Statement No. 141, "Business Combinations," and FASB Statement No. 142, "Goodwill and Other Intangible Assets." These statements drastically change the accounting for business combinations, goodwill, and intangible assets. Statement No. 141 supercedes APB Opinion No. 16,

Assume that the Packer Corp. acquires Summit Corp. on December 31, 2001 for a purchase price of $1,200,000. The condensed financial statements of Summit for as of December 31, 2001, and for the year then ended are given below;

Income Statement
For the Year Ended
December 31, 2001

Sales	$400,000
Expenses	(240,000)
Net income	$160,000

Statement of Financial Position
December 31, 2001

	Book Value	Fair Value
Cash	$100,000	$100,000
Accounts receivable	400,000	380,000
Inventory	650,000	675,000
Property, plant and equipment, net	1,150,000	1,195,000
Total Assets	2,300,000	2,350,000
Accounts payable	530,000	530,000
Long-term debt	790,000	740,000
Other liabilities	50,000	50,000
Total Liabilities	1,370,000	1,320,000
Common stock	620,000	
Additional paid-in-capital	190,000	
Retained earnings (including net income of $140,000 for the year ended 12/31/01	120,000	1,030,000
Total Equity	930,000	1,030,000
Total Liabilities and Equity	$2,300,000	$2,350,000

Assume that the accounts receivables' fair value has been determined after a reassessment of the allowance for doubtful accounts; the fair value of inventory and property, plant and equipment have been determined after the review of current replacement cost; and the fair value of long-term debt is based on the present value at current market rate of interest.

Solution: Packer Corp. would make the following journal entry to record the acquisition:

Cash	100,000	
Accounts receivable	380,000	
Inventory	675,000	
Property, plant and equipment	1,195,000	
Goodwill	170,000	
Accounts payable		530,000
Long-term debt		740,000
Other liabilities		50,000
Cash		1,200,000

Each of the assets acquired and assets assumed has been recorded at their fair value. The goodwill of $170,000 is calculated as the difference between the amount paid for Summit of $1,200,000 and the fair value of the net assets of Summit of $1,300,000. If financial statements were prepared immediately after the acquisition the statement of financial position would show the combined amounts of Packer Corp. accounts and Summit Corp. accounts. The combined statement of financial position would also reflect the $170,000 Goodwill. The income statement, however, will reflect only the revenues and expenses of Packer Corp. without any of the revenues or expenses of the Summit Corp.

Exhibit 18.2. Purchase Method.

Assume the same facts as in Exhibit 18.2 except that instead of the $1,200,000 cash being paid to MNO, Packer Corp. issued the stockholders of Summit Corp. 120,000 shares of Packer Corp. common stock on December 31, 2001. On that date the common stocks of Packer Corp. were selling for $10 per share.

Solution: The Packer Corp. would make the following entry to record the pooling on its books:

Cash	100,000	
Accounts receivable	400,000	
Inventories	650,000	
Property, plant and equipment	1,150,000	
Accounts payable		530,000
Long-term debt		790,000
Other liabilities		50,000
Retained earnings		120,000
Common stock		120,000
Additional paid-in capital		690,000

The individual assets and liabilities of Summit Corp. are recorded at book values. The $10 fair market value of Packer Corp. common stock is irrelevant even though the stockholders of Summit will receive common stock with a fair value of $1,200,000 just as they did when they received cash in Exhibit 18.2. The stock issued by Packer in the business combination is recorded at its $1 par value. The credit to additional paid-in capital represents the difference between par value of the stock issued by Packer and the $810,000 of stated capital on the books of Summit. It should also be noted that since this is a pooling no goodwill was recorded as part of the entry recording the business combination. It should also be noted that the $120,000 retained earnings of Summit is carried over to the books of the combined companies. This is consistent with the assumption that Packer and Summit interest have been fused, rather than being an acquisition of Summit by Packer.

Exhibit 18.3. Pooling-of-Interest Method.

"Business Combinations," and amends or supersedes a number of interpretations of APB No. 16. Statement No. 141 eliminates the pooling-of-interest method of accounting for business combinations in the United States except for qualifying business combinations initiated prior to January 1, 2001. However, it carries forward without reconsideration the guidance in APB No. 16 related to the purchase method of accounting. Statement No. 142 supersedes APB Opinion No. 17, "Intangible Assets." Under Statement No. 142, goodwill and indefinite-lived intangible assets are no longer amortized but are reviewed at least annually for impairment. This section will concentrate on the accounting standards set forth in SFAS No. 141, "Business Combinations."

Statement No. 141 states that "business combination occurs when an entity acquires net assets that constitute a business or acquires equity interests of one or more other entities and obtains control over that entity or entities. For the purpose of this statement, the formation of a joint venture is not considered a business combination.

Since the Statement requires the purchase method to be used, it becomes necessary to identify the acquiring entity in each business combination. Identifying the acquirer is relatively straightforward when the combination is effected solely through the distribution of cash, other assets, or incurring debt. It can be difficult in a stock-for-stock transaction when the combining companies are of relatively the same size. Accordingly, the Statement points out that "in identifying the acquiring entity in a combination effected through an exchange or equity interests, all pertinent facts and circumstances shall be considered." Some of these considerations are:

- Consideration should be given to the relative voting rights in the combined entity after the combination. The combining entity whose owners as a group retained or received the larger portion of the voting rights is generally the acquirer. Consideration should be given to unusual or special voting arrangements and options, warrants, or convertible securities.
- Consideration should be given to the existence of a large minority voting interest in the combined entity when no other owner or organization group of the original group of owners has a significant voting interest. The acquiring entity is generally the combining entity whose single owner or organized group of owners holds the large minority interest in the combined entity.
- Consideration should be given to the composition of the governing body of the combined entity. The combining entity that has the ability to elect or appoint the governing board is generally the acquirer.
- Consideration should be given to the composition of the senior management of the combined entities. The combining entity whose senior management dominates that of the combined entity is generally the acquirer.
- Consideration should be given to the terms of the exchange of equity securities. The combining entity that pays a premium over the market value of the equity securities is generally the acquirer.

The most significant change in the purchase price allocation is the criteria established in Statement No. 141 to recognize intangible assets apart from goodwill. Statement No. 141 defines intangible assets as assets (not including financial assets) that lack physical substance. It then provides specific criteria for recognizing those intangible assets. Criteria for the recognition of intangible assets in a business combination are:

- The intangible asset arises from contractual or other legal rights, regardless of whether those rights are transferable or separable from the acquired entity or from other rights or obligations.
- If the intangible asset does not arise for a contractual or other rights it is to be recognized apart from goodwill only if it is capable of being separated or divided from the acquired entity and sold, transferred, licensed, rented, or exchanged (regardless of whether there is an intent to do so). An intangible asset that cannot be sold, transferred, licensed, rented, or exchanged individually is considered separable if it can be sold, transferred, licensed, rented, or exchanged in combination with a related contract, asset or liability.

The Statement specifically states that an assembled workforce is not an intangible asset to be recognized apart from goodwill.

(ii) International Accounting Standards. International Standards permits the use of both purchase method and the pooling-of-interest (uniting of interest) methods of accounting for a business combination. International Standards, however, set very strict criteria for the use of the pooling method. International Accounting Standard No. 22 defines a uniting of interest as a business combination in which the shareholders of

the combining enterprises combine control over the whole, or effectively the whole, of their respective net assets and operations to achieve a continuing mutual sharing in the risks and benefits attaching to the combined entity such that neither party can be identified as the acquirer.

The Standards set three tests that must be met before the combination can be accounted for as a pooling. These tests are:

1. The shareholders of the combined entity must achieve a continuing mutual sharing of the risks and benefits attaching to the combined entity.
2. The basis of the transaction must be principally an exchange of voting common shares of the entities involved.
3. The whole, or effectively the whole, of the net assets and operations of the combining entries are combined into one entity.

The first of these three criteria relates to the continual sharing of risks and benefits by the combined shareholder groups. To meet this test, the following must occur according to the IAS:

- The substantial majority, if not all, of the voting common shares of the combining entities are exchanged or pooled.
- The fair value of one entity is not significantly different from that of the other entity.
- The shareholders of each entity maintain substantially the same voting rights and interest in the combined entity, relative to each other, after the combination as before.

IAS 22 states that "the shareholders of the combining enterprises join in a substantially equal arrangement to share control over the whole, or effectively the whole, of their net assets and operations." Further, it states that to achieve such a mutual sharing of risks and benefits, "the fair value of one enterprise [cannot be] significantly different from that of the other." This makes it seem that merger of entities of at least somewhat differing sizes can be accounted for as poolings if other terms stated are met.

The Standing Interpretations Committee (SIC) has offered a set of observations that support the notion that true unitings of interests rarely occur in practice. SIC 9 notes that business combinations must be accounted for as either acquisitions or unitings of interest, and that most such transactions are expected to be acquisitions, with only those for which an acquirer cannot be identified qualifying for unitings of interests accounting.

(iii) Business Combinations in Other Countries. Only the purchase method of accounting for business combinations is permitted in Australia, Canada, Japan, Mexico, and South Africa. Accounting in these countries does not permit the use of the pooling-of-interest method under any circumstances. Canada has adopted basically the same standards as the United States. In Israel, pooling accounting is in theory allowed in very special circumstances, but it is almost never used in practice. In Hong Kong, pooling is permitted, but no specific guidance exists, and therefore it is almost never applied. In the Netherlands and New Zealand pooling is permitted only when

the constituent entities are of such relatively the same size that the acquiring and acquired entities cannot be distinguished from each other. In the United Kingdom, Germany, Sweden, Italy, Belgium, Singapore, and Korea, and under European Directives, pooling treatment is available for business combination in which shares of stock are exchanged to effect the transaction regardless of the relative sizes of the combining entities.

In all jurisdictions, purchase accounting is permitted but with varying ways of computing and accounting for goodwill. In Australia, Belgium, Canada, Hong Kong, Germany, Israel, Korea, Mexico, Singapore, and South Africa, goodwill is calculated as the excess of purchase price over the fair value of identifiable net assets. In Japan, goodwill represents the residual amount after the excess of the purchase price over the aggregate book value of net assets acquired has been allocated primarily to tangible fixed assets. Thus, not all assets and liabilities will be stated at their individual fair value after the acquisition has taken place. The EDs do not explicitly address the manner in which goodwill would be allocated.

CHAPTER 19

FAS 133: ACCOUNTING FOR DERIVATIVE INSTRUMENTS

Jeffrey B. Wallace

Greenwich Treasury Advisors LLC

CONTENTS

19.1 INTRODUCTION Financial Accounting Standard (FAS) 133 is a substantial body of work, reflecting the inherent complexity of derivatives and the enormous range of possible hedging situations. It also reflects a Darwinian evolutionary process. The hedgers and their advisors repeatedly create hedges and derivative-like instruments structured to take maximum advantage of FAS 133's ambiguities and exceptions, with amendments and DIG issues evolving to fix the holes that are being exploited. As a result, the Financial Accounting Standard Board's (FASB's) latest FAS 133 compendium, the "Green Book," encompasses 800 pages.

Many of the Green Book pages, however, deal with limited exceptions to the general concepts of FAS 133. This chapter will develop those general concepts by first summarizing the historical developments related to FAS 133 and why it is such a revolutionary document. The basic concepts of FAS 133 are then introduced: derivative definition, the three different hedge types, hedge documentation, effectiveness testing, and termination risk. The three important exceptions to the effectiveness tests are then reviewed as well as the rules surrounding option hedging. The chapter ends with a review of the ways to minimize reported profit and loss (P&L) ineffectiveness and forecast error.

19.2 HISTORICAL BACKGROUND. Prior to FAS 133, U.S. generally accepted accounting principles (GAAP) on derivatives consisted of over 20 years of inconsistent, incremental, and inadequate attempts at measurement and disclosure. Derivatives could be accounted for on the basis of historic cost, which was often zero, or fair value. Foreign exchange (FX) options were allowable hedge instruments, but forward contracts were not. Synthetic instrument accounting reigned unchecked. Seven-year floating LIBOR-to-fixed interest rate swaps magically transformed a commercial paper portfolio into long-term fixed-rate debt. Derivative gains and losses could be classified as liabilities and assets, respectively, but were most often entirely ignored. No GAAP existed for commodity hedging.

In June 1998, the FASB issued FAS 133. This controversial pronouncement adopted the simple premise that foreign exchange, interest rate, and commodity derivatives represent assets and liabilities, and should be recorded as such at their fair value on the balance sheet. Synthetic instrument accounting—viewing a derivative hedge and the underlying instrument as one whole instrument—was completely abolished. Instead, all derivative hedges must be documented and proven to be a highly effective hedge of the underlying hedged position. If not, then any changes in the fair value of the derivative are to be recorded in current earnings. In addition, while a hedge may be highly effective, the change in value on the hedge may not fully offset the change in the hedged underlying, and that difference—hedge ineffectiveness—must be reported currently into earnings.

For the first time, U.S. GAAP is requiring hedging *performance*, rather than hedging *intent*, as the criterion for evaluating whether deferral accounting of the derivative gain or loss is appropriate. With FAS 133, deferral hedge accounting is a privilege, not a right, and that privilege must be earned in a rigorous fashion.

As a result, two surveys by the Association for Finance Professionals have shown that U.S. corporate derivative hedging is now lower than the activity prior to FAS 133. "Macro" or portfolio hedges are no longer done. Arguably, the FASB has achieved its goal of eliminating the speculative, "closet" hedging that existed in the 1990s. No longer can companies speculate and hide derivative losses in the financial statements to the detriment of the investors who relied upon them.

The original FAS 133 statement was vague in explaining how to determine whether hedges were highly effective and how any ineffectiveness might be calculated. To deal with these and other implementation issues, the Derivative Implementation Group (DIG) was formed, consisting largely of the then Big 5 national office derivative experts plus some industry representatives. By the spring of 1999, it was clear that too many issues still needed resolution, FAS 133–compliant systems were nonexistent, and Y2K was consuming scarce corporate resources. Thus, FAS 137 was issued in May 1999, postponing the mandatory implementation date for FAS 133 for one year.

In June 2000, the FASB issued FAS 138, which corrected some obvious deficiencies in FAS 133. Consistent with widespread hedging practices, FAS 138 allows the netting of cash flow FX exposures under certain restricted circumstances as well as allowing for the first time cross-currency interest rate swap hedging of foreign currency debt. In addition, FAS 138 modified interest rate hedging, changing it from the hedging outright interest rate, including the credit spread, to hedging a "benchmark" interest rate. Eliminating the requirement to account for the credit spread eliminated a significant source of interest rate hedging ineffectiveness.

With continued guidance from the DIG, the FASB has published 175 "FAS 133 Implementation Issues." These implementation issues, commonly called DIG issues, represent the FASB Staff's (but not the Board's) views on FAS 133, are organized into 11 distinct categories, and are commonly referred to using the FASB Staff's alphanumeric designations, for example, F7 or G20.

DIG issues have continued to be revised and new issues addressed since December 2001, albeit at a much slower pace, and the DIG itself has been disbanded. It is useful to visit occasionally the FASB Web site at *www.fasb.org* and browse the section entitled DIG (Derivatives) for new or revised DIG issues, the FASB study material on FAS 133, and to be put on the FASB's e-mail notification list for new FAS 133 changes.

In a substantial attempt to plug more holes, the FASB published a new draft amendment to FAS 133 in May 2002. It dealt largely with a revised definition of a derivative and provided additional rules for separating ("bifurcating") derivatives from a host contract. Highly technical and criticized in its dissent section as inadequate by some Board members, in September 2002 the Board decided not to approve the amendment. The next steps now rest with the FASB Staff. It is not clear when, if ever, there will be another amendment to FAS 133 and what changes that amendment might involve.

What is clear, however, is that the Board continues to view FAS 133 as an important first step toward its long-term objective of having all financial instruments—derivative and nonderivative—measured at fair value (Paragraph 247). Standing as it does between historical cost accounting and fair value accounting, FAS 133 is a hybrid document that admirably tries, but does not always succeed, in reconciling the differences between two fundamentally different accounting models.

19.3 FAS 133 OVERVIEW. Yet, despite amendments and numerous DIG issues, the original statement established a robust accounting framework that has not been amended or changed, only clarified. FAS 133 defined for the first time what a derivative is, and then using that definition, proscribes that:

- All derivatives must be fair valued on the balance sheet, including those that are embedded in host contracts that are not normally fair valued under U.S. GAAP. In the latter case, the derivative must be bifurcated from the host contract and then fair valued as if it were a stand-alone derivative.
- There are three types of hedging relationships: fair value (FV) hedges, cash flow (CF) hedges, and net investment (NI) hedges for four kinds of allowable risks: entire change in fair value, the change in fair value attributable to FX risks, the change in fair value attributable to changes in the benchmark interest rate, and the change in fair value due to creditworthiness of the instrument being hedged. These hedging relationships must be fully documented at the inception of the hedge and are more fully described in Section 19.7.
- All hedging relationships must be "highly effective." If not, then the hedge relationship must be terminated, and the net change in the value of the derivative is immediately and fully recorded in current earnings.
- If highly effective, the change in the fair value of the derivative is allocated, in accordance with the hedge documentation, into three possible components: the "effective portion," the "ineffective portion," and "the excluded portion."

Changes in the ineffective and excluded portions are always recognized immediately in earnings, regardless of the type of hedging relationship.

- If the hedge is an FV hedge, the "effective portion" is also recognized currently in earnings. However, the hedged item is also fair valued on the balance sheet, with the change in fair value also going into earnings, where it will be offset by the change in the effective portion of the derivative.
- If the hedge is a CF hedge, then the effective portion is recognized in Other Comprehensive Income (OCI) and then recorded on an *after-tax* basis in Accumulated Other Comprehensive Income (AOCI), a retained earnings account, in accordance with FAS 130. The AOCI is reclassed into earnings when the underlying hedged item impacts earnings.
- If the hedge is an NI hedge, the effective portion is also recognized in OCI and then recorded in AOCI on an after-tax basis, again in accordance with FAS 130. However, the AOCI is reclassed into earnings only when the subsidiary is subsequently sold or liquidated.
- Hedge relationships can be voluntarily or involuntarily terminated. The latter occurs when the hedge relationship fails the highly effectiveness test or when the underlying hedged forecast is no longer probable or the hedged firm commitment is no longer firm.

Anyone trying to understand FAS 133 must have a copy of the 800-page Green Book, which is a clear statement of FAS 133 as amended as of December 10, 2001. In it, 133 various paragraphs are annotated with references to specific DIG issues, which are also included in the bound volume. In addition, FAS 130, "Reporting Comprehensive Income," should also be obtained, due to interactions between FAS 130 and FAS 133 regarding the accounting for cash flow and net investment hedges in the statement of comprehensive income.

The best way to first read FAS 133 is to start with the initial Summary before the Statement and then skip to Appendix C: Background Information and Basis for Conclusions. This will help provide a useful context for reading the Statement itself. In addition, these DIG Issues are particularly useful in understanding how the Statement should be applied (in alphabetical order): C10–11, E1–10, E17–19, F2, F5, G2–3, G7, G9, G15–16, G20, G22–23, H6–11, H15, and K1.

The biggest cause for confusion in understanding FAS 133 is its use of the term *fair value.* At times, fair value means fair market value, as in how an economist or bank trader would mark-to-market a derivative or financial instrument, and is always used in this sense for fair valuing a derivative on the balance sheet. However, in the effectiveness testing, fair value is best understood as a technical accounting term whose definition can vary considerably depending on the actual hedge documentation.

Depending on the type of hedging relationship and the derivatives used, there are at least 64 different definitions of fair value that can be used in the effectiveness tests. In addition, there are some exceptions, for example, the shortcut method and the hypothetical derivative method, that extend the number of permutations beyond 64. However, many of these permutations are clearly unsuitable, and the number of relevant permutations is in the teens. Selecting the appropriate effectiveness test requires an understanding of the likely distribution of that particular effectiveness test, and managing the trade-offs between:

- Termination risk, that is, the likelihood that the hedge will fail to be highly effective
- P&L ineffectiveness risk, resulting from an imperfect hedge of the underlying hedged item
- Forecast error risk related to cash flow hedging of probable forecasts, where the derivative gain/loss on any error forecast error amount is immediately recognized in income

Necessarily, certain issues cannot be covered in this chapter. The most important issue concerns bifurcating derivatives that are embedded in host contracts, although the main elements are discussed in Section 19.4. Three other major areas not covered are the disclosure requirements, which are listed in Paragraphs 44–47 (this and all subsequent Paragraph references refer to paragraphs in FAS 133 per the amended December 10, 2001, Green Book); the substantial body of DIG issues involving commodity hedging; and taxes. Regarding the latter, all cash flow and net investment hedges must be tax-effected per FAS 130 and there are numerous FAS 133 book–U.S. tax differences. The Sources and Suggested References Section lists an article by Peter Connors that is an excellent introduction to the tax issues.

19.4 DERIVATIVE DEFINITION. Per FAS 133, Paragraph 6, a derivative is a "financial instrument or other contract with all three of the following characteristics:

a. It has (1) one or more underlyings and (2) one or more notional amounts or payment provisions, or both. These terms determine the amount of the settlement or settlements, and in some cases, whether or not a settlement is required.

b. It requires no initial net investment or an initial net investment that is smaller than would be required for other types of contracts that would be expected to have a similar response to changes in market factors.

c. Its terms require or permit net settlement. It can be readily settled net by a means outside the contract, or it provides for delivery of an asset that puts the recipient in a position not substantially different from net settlement."

An underlying is a specified interest rate, security price, commodity price, foreign exchange rate, index of prices or rates, or other variable. A notional amount is the face or principal value of the instrument. Examples of derivatives include: FX forward contracts, FX options, interest rate caps and collars, interest rate swaps, forward rate agreements, cross-currency interest rate swaps, and so on.

However, there are a number of exceptions as to what qualifies as a "FAS 133 derivative." These are listed in Paragraph 10 and include:

- "Regular-way" security trades, that is, normal security trades executed on an exchange
- Normal purchase and sales contracts involving the sale or purchase of something other than a financial instrument
- Certain insurance contracts
- Certain financial guarantee contracts
- Certain contracts not traded on an exchange, such as a weather-related derivative
- Derivatives that serve as impediments to sales accounting

There are also some other important exceptions listed in Paragraph 11 involving derivative contracts of the company's own stock or contingent consideration in a business combination. The Paragraphs 10–11 exceptions are supplemented by numerous DIG issues.

An even more complicated area is embedded derivatives, in which there is a derivative meeting the Paragraph 6 definition that is part of a "host contract" containing other contractual flows that do not in their entirety qualify as a Paragraph 6 derivative. In these situations, per Paragraph 12, the embedded derivative must be birfurcated from the host contract and accounted for as a derivative instrument under FAS 133 if, and only if, all of the following conditions are met:

- The economic characteristics and risk of the embedded derivative instrument are not clearly and closely related to the economic characteristics of the host contract.
- The host contract, including the embedded derivative, is not remeasured at fair value under otherwise applicable GAAP, with changes in fair value reported in earnings as they occur.
- A separate instrument with the same terms as the embedded derivative instrument would, pursuant to paragraphs Paragraphs 6–11, be a derivative under FAS 133.

An example of an embedded derivative would be a Standard & Poor's (S&P) 500 stock option embedded in a bond. A stock index option is not clearly and closely related to the normal interest nature of a bond. However, a convertible bond, where the bond is convertible to the stock of the bond issuer, would not be considered an embedded derivative due to the Paragraph 11 exclusion of derivatives related to the company's own stock.

Overall, the intent of Paragraphs 6–16 and over 30 DIG issues (B1–33) is to apply FAS 133's marking-to-market requirements to stand-alone financial derivatives as well as to derivatives deliberately "hiding" in host contracts that are not clearly and closely related to the host contract. At the same time, the Board wants to exclude bifurcating derivative-like instruments that are not normally considered derivatives and should not be marked-to-market. Nonetheless, embedded derivatives remain an elusive concept that has not been well defined to anyone's satisfaction.

19.5 THE THREE FAS 133 HEDGE TYPES. An FAS 133 hedge relationship is documented and identifies an allowable hedged item's financial risk(s) and a qualified hedge instrument. The hedge instrument is normally a derivative, but in certain cases can be an FX balance sheet exposure. Exhibit 19.1 shows the three types of FAS 133 hedge relationships and how they interrelate with each other.

Exhibit 19.2 summarizes the major differences in the accounting for these three hedge types.

19.6 TERMINATION EVENTS. If a hedge relationship fails the retrospective highly effective test, then the hedge is terminated, and the deferred gain or loss on the derivative is recognized currently in earnings and then reported as a separate item in the footnotes in the annual report. For this reason, nearly all corporates will only do hedge accounting if they are very certain that the hedge will indeed be highly effective. Section 19.9 discusses the issues involved.

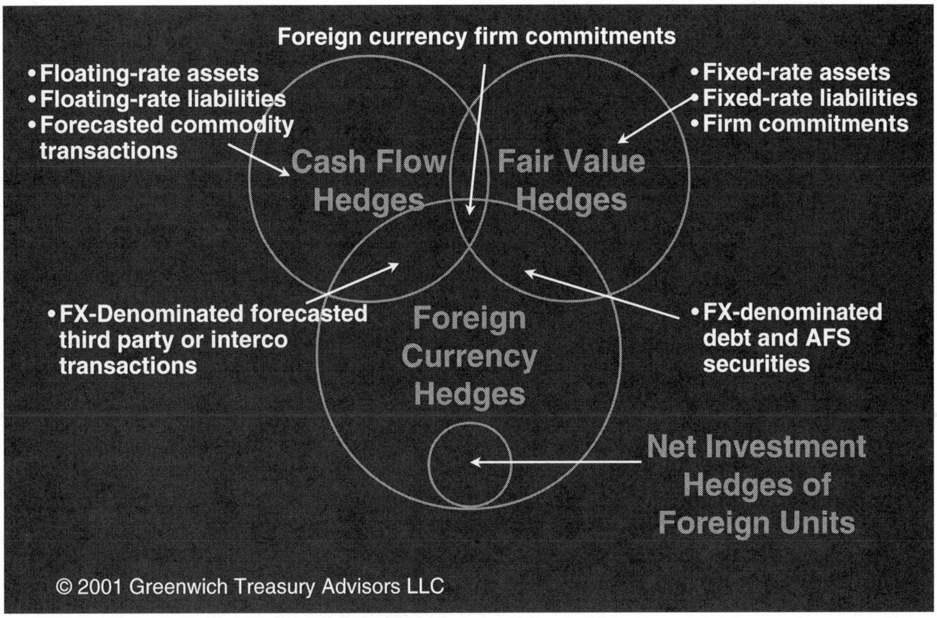

Exhibit 19.1 FAS 133 Hedge Types.

In total, there are five different accounting treatments, depending on how the hedge is terminated and what kind of hedge it is:

1. An FV hedge fails the highly effective assessment (Paragraph 26).
   - Amounts previously recorded as of the last assessment (which was highly effective) remain deferred. If it is known exactly when the FV hedge failed the highly effective test, can defer the change in fair value on the hedged item up to the last day (week, month, etc.), it was highly effective.
   - If it is not known when exactly the hedge failed, then there is no marking-to-market of the hedged item for the current period, and the entire current period change in fair value of the hedge instrument goes to P&L (Paragraph 26).
2. The firm commitment side of an FV hedge is no longer firm or the FV hedged item no longer exists (Paragraph 26).
   - Any amounts recorded on the balance sheet related to the change in fair value of the *hedged item* are reversed out to P&L (Paragraph 26).
   - Per Paragraph 44.a.(2), this is an annual report footnote disclosure item.
3. A CF hedge fails the highly effective assessment (Paragraph 32.b.).
   - Amounts previously recorded in AOCI as of the last assessment (which was highly effective) remain deferred. If it is known exactly when the CF hedge failed the highly effective test can defer the change in fair value on the hedged item in AOCI up to the last day (week, month, etc.) it was highly effective.
   - If it is not known when exactly the hedge failed, then there is no adjustment to AOCI, and the entire current period change in fair value of the hedge instrument goes to P&L (Paragraph 32).

Category	Fair Value Hedges	Cash Flow Hedges	Net Investment Hedges
Hedged Item	Booked fixed IR exposures or a foreign currency firm commitment	Anticipated or variable FX, interest rate, or commodity exposures	Equity position of a foreign affiliate
Foreign Exchange Example	Forward contract hedge of FC firm commitment	Option hedge of a forecasted intercompany FC sale	Forward contract hedge of Japanese subsidiary's equity
IR Example	Fixed debt swapped floating	Floating debt hedged with an interest rate cap	N/A
Foreign currency B/S exposures allowable hedge instruments	Yes	No	Yes
P&L accounting for the hedge instrument	Yes	First to OCI, then to AOCI and then to P&L only when the hedged exposure is recorded in P&L	No, only to OCI-CTA and then to AOCI-CTA
B/S accounting for the hedge instrument	Fair market value	Fair market value	Fair market value
P&L accounting for the hedged item	Immediately to P&L	Only when normal GAAP would require booking of hedged item to P&L	Only at subsidiary liquidation
B/S accounting for the hedged item	Fair value	Only when normal GAAP would require booking to the B/S	Normal FAS 52 rules for CTA
Measurement of hedging ineffectiveness	FAS 133 rules	FAS 133 rules	FAS 52's ecomomically effective rules as revised by H6–H11
Period that hedging ineffectiveness is measured	Current period	Cumulative from hedge inception	Current period

Exhibit 19.2. Summary of FAS 133 Accounting by Hedge Type.

4. The forecast side of a CF hedge is no longer probable (Paragraph 33).

- Any amounts recorded in AOCI related to the forecast error amount are immediately reversed out of AOCI and recorded in P&L (Paragraph 33 and G3)
- Paragraph 32 provides a two-month grace period for forecast error. In other words, a forecast that fails to happen by the defined hedged period is given an additional two months to happen before the derivative gain or loss on the forecast error amount must be recognized in earnings.
- Per Paragraph 44.b.(4), this is an annual report footnote disclosure item.

5. Voluntary termination by the company (Paragraph 25.c. for FV hedges and Paragraph 32.c for CF hedges).
   - If an FV hedge, then amounts previously recorded on the balance sheet related to the hedged item remain fixed on the balance sheet (no reversal).
   - If a CF hedge, amounts previously recorded in AOCI remain in AOCI until the underlying hedged item impacts P&L.
   - If an NI hedge, the amounts previously recorded in AOCI Cumulative Translation Adjustment (CTA) remain there until all CTA amounts are reversed (e.g., at unit liquidation).
   - There is no explicit FAS 133 requirement to document voluntary termination. Market practice is to append a one-page document to the existing hedge documentation stating that the hedge was voluntarily terminated on a specific day, and providing the details of the mark-to-market on the derivative on that day and the resulting termination accounting.

Regarding voluntary terminations, the ability to voluntarily take hedges on and off at will without impacting prior deferral amounts means that all kinds of dynamic hedging strategies are implicitly allowed. However, since all prior deferred amounts remained deferred, FAS 133 prohibits entities from terminating their profitable hedges (i.e., cherry picking) so that selective hedge profits could be reported into current earnings.

In any type of termination, if any derivatives from the terminated hedges are still outstanding, then they should be continued to be fully marked-to-market on the balance sheet, with any subsequent change in fair value recorded in earnings.

19.7 HEDGE DOCUMENTATION. FAS 133 requires that at the time an entity designates a hedging relationship that it documents the method it will use to assess the hedge's effectiveness in achieving offsetting changes in fair value or offsetting cash flows attributable to the risk being hedged. The hedge documentation can be thought of as a mathematical algorithm for calculating numbers that are recorded in specific income statements, and comprehensive income and balance sheet accounts. The algorithm is to be so precise that anyone reading the documentation could apply it and arrive at the same numbers.

The appropriateness of a given method for assessing hedge effectiveness depends on the nature of the risk being hedged and the type of hedge instrument being used. An entity should use similar effectiveness methods for similar hedges (Paragraph 62). Thus, one could not use a time value–intrinsic value effectiveness method per Paragraph 63.a for certain European option hedges and use G20's assumption of perfect option effectiveness for other European option hedges.

Unlike the Paragraph 20 and Paragraph 28 requirements for FV and CF hedge documentation, respectively, there's no similar paragraph for NI hedge documentation. FAS 133's NI hedging follows closely FAS 52's NI hedging requirements, which do not have any specific documentation requirements. However, DIG Issues H6–11 specifically deal with NI hedging, disallowing previously acceptable FAS 52 NI hedges as well as requiring effectiveness testing for cross-currency interest rate swap NI hedges. As a result, market practice is to document NI hedges as thoroughly as what FAS 133 requires for FV and CF hedges.

Summarizing Paragraph 20 and Paragraph 28 as well as two fundamental DIG Issues, E7 and E8, the following items must be specified in the hedge documentation at the inception of the hedge:

1. Risk management objective and strategy for undertaking the hedge transaction (Paragraph 20.a. and Paragraph 28.a.).
   - Boilerplate text taken from the company's risk management policy, which must exist.
2. Description of the hedged item (Paragraph 20.a. and Paragraph 28.a.).
   - For effectiveness purposes, the hedge item's maturity and financial characteristics must be known so that it can be fair valued for at effectiveness measurement purposes.
   - An FV hedge of firm commitment must include a reasonable method for recognizing in earnings the asset or liability representing the gain or loss on the hedged firm commitment (Paragraph 20.a.(1)). This could be spot-to-spot, forward rate-to-forward rate or fair market value.
   - If it is an unrecognized firm commitment or a forecasted transaction, one may want to have some sort of company internal reference number to allow easy tracking of what happens to the commitment or forecast.
3. The hedged item's hedged risks (Paragraph 20.a. and Paragraph 28.a.).
   - Allowable risks are overall change in fair value or in cash flow; or one or more of these allowable component risks: benchmark interest rate risk, FX risk, or credit risk of the obligor.
   - If the benchmark interest rate, then must indicate whether the benchmark interest rate is the Treasury rate or the LIBOR rate for U.S. dollar instruments or the appropriate benchmark, per market practices, for nondollar instruments.
   - If it is FX or commodity risk, one must choose whether the hedged item's FX risk being hedged is the risk of changes in (a) spot-to-spot movements (Paragraphs 165–172); (b) forward rate-to-forward rate movement (Paragraphs 121–126); (c) the entire change in the derivative's fair value (i.e., present value using forward rates, Paragraphs 140–143), or (d) in cash flow hedges, the variability in expected cash flows beyond (or within) a specified level (or levels) on an option pricing model basis (G20).
4. Description of the hedge instrument (Paragraph 20.a. and Paragraph 28.a.)
   - If it is a balance sheet exposure, then it will be remeasured only on a spot-to-spot basis. Balance sheet exposures can be allowable hedge instruments only for foreign currency firm commitments in FV hedge relationships and in NI hedges.
   - If a derivative, then the documentation should state how it will be fair valued, that is, marked to market, whether via a pricing model or by market quotes.
5. Amounts, if any, that are excluded from the assessment of hedge effectiveness (Paragraph 20.a.(1) and Paragraph 28.a.(1)).
   - Per Paragraph 63, three exclusions are possible—but not mandated—under certain circumstances. In each circumstance, any changes in the excluded component would be included currently in earnings, together with any ineffectiveness that results under the defined method of assessing ineffectiveness:

- If the effectiveness of a hedge with an option contract is assessed based on changes in the option's intrinsic value (IV), the change in the time value (TV) of the contract would be excluded from the assessment of hedge effectiveness. TV = fair market value (FMV) of option less IV (Paragraph 63.a.). IV can be calculated in one of two ways: the spot rate less the strike rate (Paragraph 162) or the forward rate less strike rate (E19), both results applied against the principal amount of the option. However, per Paragraph 162, IV cannot be negative. Per E19, additional aspects of an option's time value can also be excluded: theta, vega, and rho. However, these "Greek" exclusions are rarely used in practice because of G20.
- If the effectiveness of a hedge with an option contract is assessed based on changes in the option's minimum value, that is, its intrinsic value plus the effect of discounting, the change in the volatility value of the contract would be excluded from the assessment of hedge effectiveness. Volatility Value = FMV of the option less minimum value, which is the present value of IV (Paragraph 63.b.) Again, IV can be calculated in the two ways noted above. This definition of the excluded amount is very rarely seen in practice.
- If the effectiveness of a hedge with a forward or futures contract is assessed based on changes in fair value attributable to changes in spot prices, the change in the fair value of the contract related to the changes in the difference between the spot price and the forward or futures price would be excluded from the assessment of hedge effectiveness. This is called forward contract TV = contract forward rate – spot rate (Paragraph 63.c).

6. Prospective assessment methodology (Paragraph 20.a.(1) and Paragraph 28.a.(1).).

- As explained in E7, upon designation of a hedging relationship (as well as on an ongoing basis), the entity must be able to justify an *expectation* that the relationship will be highly effective over future periods in achieving offsetting changes in fair value or cash flows.
- That expectation, which is forward-looking, can be based on dollar-offset (or simulations thereof) as well as regression or other statistical analysis of past changes in fair values or cash flows as well as on other relevant information.
- Other relevant information could be that the critical terms of the hedged item and the hedge instrument are the same (G9).
- Per F5, the period of the expectation that the hedge will be highly effective can be less than the maturity of the hedged item.

7. Retrospective Assessment Methodology (Paragraph 20.a.(1) and Paragraph 28.a.(1).).

- At least quarterly, the hedging entity must determine whether the hedging relationship has been highly effective in having achieved offsetting changes in fair value or cash flows through the date of the periodic assessment. Per E7, that assessment can be based on the dollar-offset method or regression or other statistical analysis of past changes in fair values or cash flows.
- Per Paragraph 71, all foreign currency hedges, whether fair value, cash flow, or NI, can be done on an after-tax basis (i.e., "grossing-up" the derivative notional so that after-taxes of both the derivative and hedge item offset exactly). This would need to be documented here if so documented in the prospective assessment documentation.

8. Retrospective Assessment Testing Frequency (Paragraph 20.b. and Paragraph 28.b.).

- Determines how frequently the retrospective assessment test and the calculation of hedge ineffectiveness will be tested and calculated.
- Per Paragraph 20.b. and Paragraph 28.b., retrospective assessment is required at least quarterly. User can choose daily, weekly, monthly, or quarterly.

9. Period used for the Retrospective Assessment (E7 and E8).

- The period used for calculating the change in fair value for the dollar-offset method or the period in which the statistical analysis will be performed.
- Allowable options, per E8, are period by period or cumulative. If the former, period cannot exceed three months (i.e., could be 1 day, 1 week, or 1 month).
- If the latter and the dollar-offset method is used, the period starts from the inception of the designation of the hedge.
- If the latter and statistical analysis is used, then:

  a. Per E7, if an entity elects at the inception of a hedging relationship to utilize the same regression analysis approach for both prospective considerations and retrospective evaluations of assessing effectiveness, then during the term of that hedging relationship those regression analysis calculations should generally incorporate the same number of data points.

  b. If statistical analysis was not used for prospective assessment, then the cumulative period is from the inception of the designation of the hedge.

See the Appendix for sample documentation for these common hedges:

- Forward contract foreign currency CF hedging of future sales
- Perfect interest rate swap FV hedge of fixed rate debt

19.8 CALCULATING THE CHANGE IN FAIR VALUE OF THE HEDGED INSTRUMENT AND THE HEDGED ITEM. The above documentation requirements uniquely determine which of 64 theoretically possible calculations are used for calculating the "change in fair value of the hedged item's hedged risk(s)" and the "change in the fair value of the hedge instrument." There are four different ways to calculate the "change in fair value" of the hedge item's hedged risk(s): fair market value, spot-to-spot, forward rate-to-forward rate, and using an option pricing model (the latter per G20 for cash flow hedges only).

There are also four different ways to calculate the "change in fair value" of the hedge instrument: fair market value with no excluded amounts or fair market value less any of the three allowable excludible amounts, as defined in Section 19.7 (e). As noted in that Section's commentary, if option hedging is done, there are two different ways to calculate intrinsic value. Finally, these calculations can be done on a pretax or posttax basis.

Thus, the 64 = 4 different ways for the hedged item's hedged risks times 4 different ways for the hedge instrument times 2 different ways for intrinsic value times 2 different ways for taxes. These definitions are then used consistently in that hedged relationship's calculations of the prospective *highly effective test* (HET), the retrospective HET, and the measurement of ineffectiveness for P&L and footnote reporting purposes.

These are the basic rules of the game, and like any game, there's no point in arguing about the rules—it's how you play with the rules. Of course, it wouldn't be FAS 133 if there weren't some exceptions. These exceptions involve relaxation of the strict requirements of the highly effective tests, and are discussed in Section 19.11. Please note that these exceptions must always be specified in the hedge documentation.

19.9 THE TWO HIGHLY EFFECTIVE TESTS. There are two kinds of HET methodologies—the dollar-offset method and statistical analysis—which can be used for prospective and retrospective HETs. However, one does not have to use the same methodology prospectively and retrospectively; there is no requirement for consistency (E7).

The dollar-offset method is simply the change in the fair value of the hedge instrument as specified in the documentation by the change in the fair value of hedged item's hedged risk, again as specified in the documentation. This ratio, typically calculated as a percentage, should be within a range of 80 to 125% or 80 to 120%. Otherwise, the hedge is not highly effective and should be terminated. In practice, many use the 80 to 125% range, which was articulated by the SEC at their 1995 Annual Accounting Conference. The FASB clearly prefers 80 to 120%.

A key parameter in calculating the dollar-offset is whether the changes are calculated over the current assessment period or cumulatively since inception. Both are acceptable per E7. The cumulative period is recommended since that ratio over a longer period should be more stable than the ratio over a shorter period and thus less likely to fall outside of the range. There is a risk, particularly in complex interest rate hedging, that small changes in interest rates will cause small changes in the dollar-offset's numerator and denominator that will result in large numbers wildly outside the 80 to 125% range, even though the small changes are immaterial by themselves.

Regarding statistical analysis, as E7 notes, "The application of a regression or other statistical analysis approach to assessing effectiveness is complex. Those methodologies require appropriate interpretation and understanding of statistical inferences." Regression analysis is the most common statistical method. Briefly, Paragraph 75 allows regressing on price levels, rather than changes in prices, since one could have highly correlated prices, but not highly correlated price changes.

If a regression analysis is done, market practice agrees that the R^2 must be 80% or better to be considered highly effective. One important factor to consider is the time period over which the regression analysis should be conducted. Clearly, one would want a period sufficiently long to "dampen" any current period volatility that could cause an R^2 to be less than 80%.

An alternative to regression analysis is a value-at-risk–like approach that is known as either the "volatility reduction method" or the "variance reduction method" or "VRM." It calculates the reduction in the volatility after the hedge compared to the volatility of the hedged item alone using this formula:

$$1 - \frac{\left[\text{Standard deviation of the hedged item } \textit{and} \text{ the hedge instrument}\right]}{\left[\text{Standard deviation of the unhedged hedged item}\right]}$$

As with regression analysis, this statistic is calculated over an historic time period using historic rates, consistent with how both changes are defined in the hedge documentation, which is generally going to be on a full market value basis. If this was greater than some agreed-upon parameter, say 80% (in words, the volatility of the position has been reduced by the hedge by 80%), then the hedge relationship would pass this HET. Please see the excellent articles on statistical analysis in the Sources and Suggested References section at the end of this chapter for more detailed explanations of what is involved, including the statistic complexities, in using both regression analysis and VRM.

As a general rule, it is better to use any kind of statistical test, rather than the dollar-offset method, for hedging relationships in which there is basis risk or relatively large imperfect matching of the critical terms or, especially, when there is portfolio hedging. The dollar-offset test is inflexible, making no adjustment for when there is a period of financial market distress, such as the 1998 Asian/Russian ruble crisis. During volatile financial markets, a statistical approach may allow a hedge to be considered highly effective, while the dollar-offset test might well cause the hedge to be considered ineffective and then terminated. An $R^2 \geq 80\%$ requirement is not a restrictive test for most reasonable hedges.

19.10 MEASURING INEFFECTIVENESS. Assuming that the retrospective assessment methodology has shown the hedge to be highly effective, there may still be some hedge ineffectiveness that needs to be recorded in current earnings. The actual calculation of any hedge ineffectiveness is based on the extent to which *an exact offset* is not achieved as specified in Paragraph 22 of Statement 133 (for FV hedges) or Paragraph 30 (for CF hedges) between the documented change in the fair value of the hedged item and the documented change in the fair value of the hedge instrument.

For fair value hedges, this is a current period test, that is, FV hedging ineffectiveness is the difference between the current period changes in fair value of both sides of the hedging relationship. For CF hedges, it is "the lesser of the two cumulatives test," which is based on cumulative changes in fair value since hedge inception (Paragraph 30.b, see Paragraph 141 for an example). It is a complex test, and the text that follows assumes a full understanding of the Paragraph 141 example. The test is designed to record into cumulative P&L only the difference between the cumulative change in value of the derivative less the cumulative change in the value of the hedged item if, and only if, the absolute value of the cumulative change in the derivative is greater than the absolute value of the cumulative change in the hedged item.

The Board's intent with this test is to ensure that if change in the derivative is greater than the change in the underlying, the difference will be recorded in earnings. However, in the case where the change in the underlying was greater than the change in the derivative, the Board wanted this difference *not* to be booked in the financial statements. The Board's rationale was that since CF hedges always have a forecast hedged position that would not ordinarily be booked currently in the financial statements, any forecast "excess" over the change in the fair value of the derivative should not be booked either. Section 19.13, Minimizing Ineffectiveness, discusses the implications of this asymmetric test.

As discussed earlier, the actual calculations of the changes in fair value of the hedge item's hedged risk(s) and of the hedge instrument is one of 64 possible ways defined in the hedge documentation, and it is these definitions of the changes in fair value that are used to calculate the actual amount of ineffectiveness. Thus, we can then allocate the change in the true fair market value of the hedge instrument into three possible components:

1. The excluded amount, if any, per the hedge documentation, which goes to P&L.
2. The ineffective amount is calculated using the ineffectiveness measurement tests described above, depending on whether it is an FV or a CF hedge. See H6–11 for ineffectiveness tests related to NI hedges.
3. The effective amount is the residual, equal to the change in the net present value of the hedge instrument from the prior period, less any current period excluded amounts less any current period ineffectiveness.

For CF hedges, the effective amount goes to OCI and then AOCI. For FV hedges, the effective amount goes to P&L. Thus, for FV hedges, it may seem that the calculation of the three components is not strictly necessary because everything goes to P&L. However, year-end footnote disclosure for FV hedges (as well as for CF hedges) requires reporting, by type of hedge, of the year's cumulative excluded amounts and cumulative ineffective amounts.

19.11 THREE HET EXCEPTIONS. There are three exceptions to the use of the dollar-offset and statistical analysis for determining whether a hedge is highly effective:

1. When the critical terms of the hedge instrument and the hedged position are the same
2. The shortcut method for interest rate swaps
3. The hypothetical derivative method

DIG Issue G9 allows the "assumption" that a CF hedge is fully effective if the terms of the derivative hedge are such that the changes in the derivative's fair value are expected to *completely offset* the expected changes in the cash flows of the hedged risk on an ongoing basis.
At a minimum, the following critical terms must be the same:

- The notional amount of the derivative is equal to the notional amount of the hedged position.
- The maturity of the derivative equals the maturity of the hedged position.
- The underlying index of the derivative matches how the changes in the fair value of the hedged position are calculated.
- The fair value of the derivative is zero at inception.

If so, then G9 requires that the equivalence of the critical terms is explicitly stated in the documentation and that there is an ongoing assessment both prospectively and retrospectively that the critical terms have remained the same. If the terms have changed, then either of the two highly effective tests must be applied as well as the calculation of any hedge ineffectiveness. Since many entities do "perfect" hedging, G9 is welcome relief from the burdensome detailed record keeping that FAS 133 requires.

The shortcut method for interest rates swaps is described in Paragraphs 68 to 69. They apply to both fair value interest rate swap hedges of fixed rate debt and cash flow interest rate swap hedges of floating rate debt. Essentially, if—and only if—the interest rate swap matches the underlying debt perfectly in all respects (including any call provisions), then the swap can be assumed to be perfectly effective, and there is no need to do any highly effective testing nor calculate any hedge ineffectiveness.

If it is an FV hedge, the swap is fully marked-to-market on the balance sheet, with an offset to earnings. At the same time, the debt is "fair valued" (i.e., not marked-to-market) by an amount exactly equal to the mark-to-market on the swap, with the change in the mark-to-market going to earnings. Since the two amounts going to earnings are identical, there is no earnings impact. If it is a CF hedge, the swap is also fully marked-to-market on the balance sheet with the offset going to AOCI. For both kinds of hedges, reported interest expense is equal to the debt interest plus the net interest flows on the swap.

The shortcut treatment is a very desirable method because it simplifies the FAS 133 accounting and provides essentially the same answers as synthetic instrument accounting. For more information on how the shortcut treatment can be applied and not applied in a number of circumstances, see DIG Issues E4, E6, E10, E15–E16, and F2. E15 deals with the inability to apply shortcut treatment of debt acquired in a business combination. F2 deals with the related issue of the proper accounting for interest rate swaps that hedge debt for a shorter term than the debt itself.

The last exception, the hypothetical derivative method, is a powerful FAS 133 effectiveness technique that was first explicitly introduced in DIG Issue G7. It was needed for those situations in which the interest rate swap does not perfectly match the terms of the underlying debt. Without the shortcut method, any interest rate swap hedge, even a perfect swap, would fail either highly effective test. The change in the fair value of the derivative would not sufficiently offset the change in the fair value of the underlying debt because fair valuing the debt would involve fair valuing the principal repayment. The derivative, of course, has no principal repayment to fair value.

Thus, G7 developed a new method in which the hedged debt for effectiveness testing purposes could be treated as if it was a hypothetical derivative that mirrored all of the terms of the debt, but without the principal repayment cash flow. This eliminates the artificial ineffectiveness caused by the principal flow. The changes in the mark-to-market of both the hypothetical derivative and the real derivative are then used with the dollar-offset or statistical analysis to test for high effectiveness. If highly effective, then any ineffectiveness is the difference between the two mark-to-markets.

The hypothetical derivative method is an elegant solution to the problem of developing reasonable effectiveness tests. By analogy, it can be used in cross-currency interest rate swap (CCIRS) hedging, which while permitted by FAS 138, cannot be done using the shortcut method, which applies only to pure interest rate swaps. H8 requires that ineffectiveness be calculated when a CCIRS is used as a NI hedge. H8 uses a forward contract as the hypothetical derivative for the underlying NI position. G20 uses a European option as the hypothetical derivative when option hedges are used.

The hypothetical derivative method is actually not a new concept. It was implicit in the original FAS 133 statement regarding the hedging of forecast foreign exchange exposures. One of the allowable definitions for the change in the fair value of the foreign exchange exposure is the change in its fair market value, which can only be calculated assuming a hypothetical forward contract with the same maturity of the exposure with a forward rate that gives the hypothetical forward an initial zero cost.

19.12 OPTION HEDGING. Except for rare circumstances when they are used to hedge embedded purchased options under Paragraph 20.c, FAS 133 requires that *written* options must be fully marked-to-market, with gains and losses recorded in earnings. In Paragraph 20(c)(1), the FASB states, "A combination of options (e.g., an interest rate collar) entered into contemporaneously shall be considered a written option if, either at inception or over the life of the contracts, a net premium is received in cash or as a favorable rate or other term."

Provided that the effectiveness tests are passed, FAS 133 allows hedge accounting for single purchased options and net purchased options (i.e., combinations of purchased and written options), including zero cost collars. In E2 and E5, a net purchased option is defined as a combination of options that satisfies these four conditions at all times:

1. No net premium is received.
2. The components of the combination of options are based on the same *exact* underlying (i.e., the exact index, see also G22).
3. The components of the combination of options have the same maturity date.
4. The written option component's notional is not greater than the notional amount of the purchased option component (see also E18).

Originally issued in April 2001 and finalized that August, DIG Issue G20, "Assessing and Measuring the Effectiveness of a Purchased Option Used in a Cash Flow Hedge," eliminates FAS 133's original bias against option hedging. Prior to G20, changes in the time value of option hedges were reported in earnings. The result was not only unpredictable earnings volatility but also additional reporting complexity and confusion.

G20 states that if the hedging instrument is "(a) . . . a purchased option or a combination of only options that comprise either a net purchased option or a zero-cost collar, (b) the exposure being hedged is the variability in expected future cash flows attributed to a particular rate or price beyond (or within) a specified level (or levels), and (c) the assessment of effectiveness will be based on total changes in the option's cash flows (that is, the assessment will include the hedging instrument's entire change in fair value), the hedging relationship *may be considered* to be perfectly effective (resulting in recognizing no ineffectiveness in earnings) if the following conditions are met:

1. The critical terms of the hedging instrument (such as its notional amount, underlying, and maturity date, etc.) completely match the related terms of the hedged forecasted transaction (such as the notional amount, the variable that determines the variability in cash flows, and the expected date of the hedged transaction).
2. The strike price (or prices) of the hedging option (or combination of options) matches the specified level (or levels) beyond (or within) which the entity's exposure is being hedged.
3. The hedging instrument's inflows (outflows) at its maturity date completely offset the change in the hedged transaction's cash flows for the risk being hedged.
4. The hedging instrument can be exercised only on a single date, its contractual maturity date."

Prior to G20, nearly all nonvanilla or exotic options were not acceptable FAS 133 hedges because their payoffs were too nonlinear to satisfy the effectiveness tests. However, when an option fails any of the four G20 conditions above, G20 provides for effectiveness testing between the actual option and a "hypothetical derivative" that does satisfy all of the four G20 conditions.

This will make more kinds of nonvanilla options acceptable 133 hedges because the effectiveness tests will be comparing the pricing of the actual option against the hypothetical option, and they should be more closely related.

19.13 MINIMIZING INEFFECTIVENESS. The best way to minimize hedge ineffectiveness is to match the hedge instrument perfectly with the hedge exposure, and then declare that since the critical terms are the same, we can assume that the hedge is 100% effective, as discussed earlier. Obviously, this is not always practical.

If it is a cash flow hedge, another approach is to take advantage of the asymmetric lesser of the two cumulatives ineffectiveness test. As discussed in Section 19.10, if the cumulative change in the fair value of the hedging derivative is less than the cumulative change in the fair value of the hedged position, then no ineffectiveness is recognized

There are two ways this can be generally achieved. Document that the derivative is hedging a notional exposure greater the notional value of the derivative or have the derivative's maturity be less than the documented maturity of the exposure. By having the documented exposure either larger or later than the derivative, the change in the fair value of the exposure will be generally greater than the change in the fair value of the derivative.

Of course, there are some risks with these approaches. A smaller-than-necessary derivative may lead to underhedging of the true economic risk. Or, if the notional amount of the exposure is artificially inflated, forecast error risk is increased. Having the derivative mature before the exposure's expected maturity runs the price risk of having to subsequently rollover the derivative at some unknown rate to fully cover the entire forecast exposure period. In all cases, the highly effectiveness tests must be passed first before the hedge ineffectiveness is calculated, so if the differences in notional amount or maturity are too large, the HET may fail, causing the hedge to terminate.

Monte Carlo simulations are another way to manage ineffectiveness. For example, one could run 2000 or so Monte Carlo simulations on the ineffectiveness statistic, which in complicated hedging situations is usually the difference between the change in the fair market value of both sides, to develop a probability distribution of the ineffectiveness. Then, in a VAR-like approach, the 5% tail could be examined to determine the maximum amount of ineffectiveness with 95% confidence to see if this amount of ineffectiveness is acceptable.

In complex IR portfolio hedging, simulations could be used to evaluate the ineffectiveness risk of different hedge ratios, that is, using different derivative notionals to determine which one minimizes ineffectiveness and economically hedges the exposure. A similar process could be done with exotic option hedging against the hypothetical option per G20. The hypothetical option could be documented to have any strike rate, and simulations could be run to determine which hypothetical strike best minimizes ineffectiveness with the real option.

19.14 MINIMIZING FORECAST ERROR RISK. When a hedged forecast is no longer considered probable to occur, the net G/(L) in accumulated OCI is immediately reclassified into earnings on the forecast error amount. Paragraph 33 (amended) allows a two-month grace period *after* the exposure maturity in the documentation. This is not necessarily a great boon because often companies are hedging consecutive months, and when they do so, they often state in the documentation that the hedged forecast represents the first x dollars (or yen or whatever) occurring in the month. Thus, if there is a forecast shortfall in June, to use it up in July would require the July actual to more than cover the July hedge's forecast, and then any actual over the documented July hedge exposure could be applied against the June shortfall.

Per Paragraph 494, a pattern of forecasted transactions not occurring would call into question the entity's ability to accurately predict transactions and thus the propriety of using cash flow hedge accounting. In other words, too many forecast errors and cash flow hedge accounting could be taken away from you.

A long hedge period for the forecast to error is one of the best ways to minimize forecast error. So rather than hedging forecasts that occur in a given month, it is better to hedge quarterly or semiannual forecasts. Wide hedge periods are quite possible; Paragraph 460 uses a six-month hedge period and G16 uses a *five-year* hedge period. However, both of these citations are examples of a single forecasted event. Most hedging of forecasts is hedging a portfolio of forecast transactions, such as forecast foreign currency sales or purchases. FAS 133 allows cash flow hedging of a portfolio, and requires that the hedged risk of the portfolio components share the same risk exposure. However, unlike fair value portfolio hedging, in which sharing the same risk exposure is explicitly defined (Paragraph 21.a.(1)), there is no such definition for cash flow portfolios. In practice, companies have been able to hedge quarterly forecasts, especially if they are doing their hedge assessments for effectiveness on a quarterly basis and their internal forecasting is done on a quarterly basis.

Another way to minimize forecast error risk is to aggregate like forecasts together for hedge documentation purposes. A company with export sales in euros to France, Germany, Belgium, and so on should not have individual hedge documentations for export sales to each country. Instead, aggregate all of the euro export sales together, and write the hedge documentation on that amount. Note that Paragraph 40.a. discusses how FX exposures of a group of operating units with the same functional currency can be aggregated and hedged.

Another way to reduce forecast error risk is to lower the hedge ratio. For example, say a company forecasts £100 of sales to the United Kingdom for a given period. Many companies will hedge only a portion of the £100, say 80%. In the hedge documentation, they would say that they were hedging the first £80 of sales for the given period. If they have significant concerns about the validity of the forecast, they might hedge only £60 and minimize the risk for FAS 133 purposes of forecast error. However, they are also risk underhedging the actual sales, which is a true economic risk. In these circumstances, a useful approach is to hedge in layers or tiers. In this approach, the first hedge is for a small amount, say 20 to 40%. Then, as the forecast gets closer and closer and there is more confidence in the forecast, then hedge in progressing stages, say 20% at a time, until the forecast is perhaps 90 to 100% hedged with one month out. This progressive hedging would simply require more hedge documentation for each new hedge.

APPENDIX: SAMPLE HEDGE DOCUMENTATION

For the hedge documentation that follows, note the following assumptions:

- The period for the frequency of the retrospective effectiveness testing is quarterly. It could in fact be any period less than a quarter (e.g., a month or a day).

- The documented hedging objectives are supported by the written risk management strategy.
- AOCI related to hedges of sales and of inventory are reclassed to sales and cost of goods sold, respectively. FAS 133 does not require a specific P&L item for such reclassification, but it must be disclosed in the footnotes (Paragraph 44 and K4).
- All forecasts are assumed to be probable. Auditors may require additional documentation supporting that assumption.
- At the end of each sample hedge documentation below, there is a section to be filled in that will cause the hedge to comply with the IRS requirements. While not required by FAS 133, nearly all hedges by U.S. entities must be documented for IRS purposes. IRS documentation includes nearly all of the same elements that FAS 133 requires, but there are additional requirements depending on the hedge's tax regime. Best practice is to use the same documentation for both book and tax, appending the necessary IRS documentation at the end of the 133 documentation.

A. DOCUMENTATION FOR FORWARD CONTRACT FOREIGN CURRENCY CF HEDGE OF FUTURE SALES

Documentation preparation date: January 2, 200X

Risk Management Objective and Strategy

General International, Inc. (HedgeCo), a U.S. dollar (USD) functional currency entity, forecasts that it will have intercompany sales to General International Japan K.K (Buyer) in April 200X in the amount of Japanese yen (JPY) 3,300,000,000. These intercompany sales are invoiced in JPY and therefore HedgeCo is exposed to variability in expected future USD cash flows as a result of foreign currency movements between the JPY and the USD.

In accordance with HedgeCo's risk management strategy, HedgeCo's risk management objective is to reduce the variability in functional currency-equivalent cash flows from forecasted nonfunctional currency intercompany sales that are caused by changes in foreign currency exchange rates. This objective is met by entering into a foreign currency forward contract to sell the Japanese yen forward and buy US dollars at a specific rate on the last day of the month of the forecasted intercompany sale.

Type of FAS 133 Hedge

Cash flow.

Hedged Item

For this Hedge Relationship, HedgeCo designates as the hedged item the first JPY 3,300,000,000 of its forecasted JPY-denominated intercompany sales to Buyer during April 200X. Based on historical trends (see attached), the amount of forecasted Hedged Item is probable to occur.

Hedged Item's Hedged Risk

For this Hedge Relationship, HedgeCo designates the above Hedged Item's Hedged Risk as the risk of changes in the net present value of Hedged Item's functional-currency-equivalent cash flows, calculated on a forward rate basis, attributable to changes in the JPY/USD foreign currency exchange rate.

Hedge Instrument
For this Hedge Relationship, Parent designates the following foreign currency forward contract as the Hedge Instrument:

Trade Execution Date:	January 2, 200X
In the Name of:	HedgeCo
Counterparty:	XYZ Bank
Notional Amounts:	PY 3,300,000,000 against USD 30,275,229.36
Forward Rate:	JPY 109.00/USD
Maturity Date(s):	April 30, 200X
Contract Type:	Forward contract to sell JPY/buy USD
HedgeCo Contract Number:	101

Period for the Retrospective Effectiveness Test
HedgeCo will perform, as discussed below, the Retrospective Effectiveness Test quarterly.

Prospective and Retrospective Effectiveness Test/Measurement of Ineffectiveness
The critical terms of the Hedged Item and the Hedge Instrument are identical:

- The notional amount of the Hedge Instrument equals the notional amount of the Hedge Item.
- The maturity date of the Hedge Instrument is in the month that the Hedge Item is forecasted to occur.
- The currency pair of the Hedge Instrument and the Hedged Item's Hedged Risk are the same (i.e., JPY/USD).

In addition, the change in the fair value of the Hedged Instrument will be assessed based by HedgeCo on changes in fair value attributable to changes in forward exchange rates calculated on a net present value basis using the LIBOR swap curve. The change in the fair value of the Hedged Item's Hedged Risk will also be assessed based by HedgeCo on changes in fair value attributable to changes in forward exchange rates calculated on a net present value basis using the LIBOR swap curve. In other words, for HedgeCo's assessment of hedge effectiveness, the calculation of the changes in the fair value of the Hedge Instrument is identical to the calculation of the change of the fair value of the Hedged Item's Hedged Risk.

Assumption of No Ineffectiveness
Thus, in accordance with FAS 133, paragraph 65, HedgeCo assumes automatic effectiveness of the Hedge Instrument designated as a cash flow hedge of the Hedged Item's Hedged Risk, and will not conduct effectiveness testing of this Hedge Instrument nor measure any hedge ineffectiveness during the life of this Hedging Relationship.

Quarterly Accounting
However, in accordance with the requirements of Statement No. 133 Implementation Issue G9, HedgeCo will verify at each quarterly assessment testing date that the critical terms of the Hedging Relationship have remained the same.

U.S. Tax Documentation Requirements
Optimal documentation to be filled in by HedgeCo's Tax Department.

B. PERFECT INTEREST RATE SWAP FAIR VALUE HEDGE

Documentation preparation date: December 31, 200X

Risk Management Objective and Strategy
General International, Inc. (HedgeCo), a U.S. dollar (USD) functional currency entity, has a six-year USD 100,000,000 fixed-rate note (Fixed Debt), and thus is exposed to variability in expected future fair values of the debt as a result of long-term USD interest rate movements. In accordance with HedgeCo's risk management strategy, HedgeCo's risk management objective is to reduce the variability in the fair value of its fixed-rate debt that are caused by changes in long-term interest rates. This objective is met by entering into a pay floating/receive fixed interest rate swap that effectively stabilizes the fair value of the Fixed Debt.

Type of FAS 133 Hedge
Fair value.

Hedged Item
For this Hedge Relationship, General International designates as the hedged item all the fixed interest flows of the fixed debt that bears interest at $8\frac{7}{8}\%$ p.a., payable on June 30 and December 31 for the years 200X+1 to 200X+6, with payment of the principal amount due on December 31, 200X+6.

Hedged Item's Hedged Risk
For this Hedge Relationship, HedgeCo designates the above Hedged Item's Hedged Risk as the risk of changes in the net present value of Hedged Item's fair value, calculated by present valuing the interest flows using a LIBOR swap curve, attributable to changes in LIBOR interest rates, the designated benchmark interest rate.

Hedge Instrument
For this Hedge Relationship, HedgeCo designates the following interest rate swap as the Hedge Instrument:

Trade Execution Date:	December 31, 200X
In the Name of:	General International, Inc.
Counterparty:	XYZ Bank
Notional Amount:	USD 100,000,000
Pay Floating LIBOR Rate	Six-Month LIBOR
Receive Fixed	6.5% [N.B.: there's no need to match the fixed rate]
LIBOR Reset Dates:	June 30 and December 31
Maturity Date:	December 31, 200X+6
Contract Type:	Interest Rate Swap
HedgeCo Contract Number:	102

Period for the Retrospective Effectiveness Test
HedgeCo will perform, as discussed below, the Retrospective Effectiveness Test quarterly.

Prospective and Retrospective Effectiveness Test/Measurement of Ineffectiveness
The critical terms of the Hedged Item and the Hedge Instrument are identical, and the Hedge relationship meets all of the requirements of Statement FAS 133, paragraph 68 for fair value interest rate swap hedges:

- The notional amount of the Hedge Instrument equals the principal amount of the Hedge Item.
- The fair value of the Hedge Instrument is zero at the inception of this Hedging Relationship.
- The formula for calculating the net settlements of the Hedge Instrument is the same for each settlement.
- The maturity date of the Hedge Instrument is the date that the Hedge Item matures.
- The fixed interest rate sides of the Hedged Item and Hedge Instrument are identical.
- All flows of the Hedged Item are designated as being hedged.
- There is no floor or cap on either the Hedged Item or the Hedge Instrument
- The repricing dates of the Hedge Instrument match the interest payments dates of the Hedged Items.

Accordingly, HedgeCo will apply the shortcut method in accounting for the Hedge Instrument. As a result, HedgeCo will not conduct effectiveness testing of this Hedge Instrument nor measure any hedge ineffectiveness during the life of this Hedging Relationship.

Quarterly Accounting
However, in accordance with the requirements of Statement No. 133 Implementation Issue G9, HedgeCo will verify at each quarterly assessment testing date that the critical terms of the Hedging Relationship have remained the same.

As a fair value hedge, the Hedged Instrument will be marked to market on a quarterly basis, using a LIBOR swap curve, with changes in fair value recorded in P&L, less adjustments for any accrued interest expense. In accordance with Paragraph 68 of FAS 133, the change in fair value of the Hedged Item will exactly equal the change in the fair value of the Hedge Instrument, with the offset to P&L, less adjustments for any accrued interest expense.

U.S. Tax Documentation Requirements
[Optional documentation to be filled in by HedgeCo's Tax Department]

SOURCES AND SUGGESTED REFERENCES

Althoff, John, and John Finnerty. "Testing Hedge Effectiveness." *FAS 133 and the New Derivatives Landscape*, Henry Davis, (ed.). New York: Institutional Investor, 2001.

Connors, Peter. "FAS 133 Raises Complex Tax Issues for Corporate Treasurers." *FAS 133 and the New Derivatives Landscape*. Henry Davis, (ed.). New York: Institutional Investor, 2001.

Financial Accounting Standards Board. *Accounting for Derivative Instruments and Hedging Activities, Statement of Financial Accounting Standards No. 133, as Amended and Interpreted*. Norwalk, CT: Financial Accounting Standards Board, 2001.

Financial Accounting Standards Board. *Statement of Comprehensive Income, Statement of Financial Accounting Standards No. 130*. Norwalk, CT: Financial Accounting Standards Board, 1997.

Financial Accounting Standards Board. *Examples Illustrating Application of FASB Statement No. 138*. Norwalk, CT: Financial Accounting Standards Board, 2000.

Kalotay, Andrew, and Leslie Abreo. "Testing Hedge Effectiveness for FAS 133: The Volatility Reduction Method." *Journal of Applied Corporate Finance*, Winter 2001. Available at *www.kalotay.com*.

Kawaller, Ira, and Reva Steinberg. "Hedge Effectiveness Testing Using Regression Analysis." *AFP Exchange*, September/October 2002.

Kawaller, Ira, and Association for Finance Professionals. *The Impact of FAS 133 on the Risk Management Practices of End Users of Derivatives*. Bethesda, MD: Association for Financial Professionals, 2002. Available at *www.kawaller.com*.

Kwun, David. "Hedging Cross-Currency and Interest Rate Exposures under FAS 133." *FAS 133 and the New Derivatives Landscape*. Henry Davis, (ed.). New York: Institutional Investor, 2001.

Royall, Robert. "Use of Regression in Assessing Hedge Effectiveness." *FAS 133 and the New Derivatives Landscape*. Henry Davis, (ed.). New York: Institutional Investor, 2001.

Wallace, Jeffrey. "The Dual Spot vs. the Dual PV Methods." *GTANet*, No. 1, February 2001. Available at *www.greenwichtreasury.com*.

Wallace, Jeffrey. "Option Hedging under G20." *GTAnet*, No. 2, October 2001. Available at *www.greenwichtreasury.com*.

CHAPTER 20

ACCOUNTING FOR THE EFFECTS OF INFLATION

Harold E. Wyman

Florida International University

CONTENTS

20.1 INFLATION UNDERMINES THE KEY ACCOUNTING PRINCIPLE OF HISTORICAL COST. Existence of a high rate of inflation related to transactions recorded under the historical cost principle undermines the economic validity of the basic accounting statements. Companies with multinational operations must be concerned with the effects of inflation, even though their principal operations are in a country where inflation is not a significant problem. Failure to recognize the accounting distortions that inflation causes can lead to a misunderstanding of reported financial results. This causes problems in both financial accounting and managerial accounting.

20.2 INFLATION AROUND THE WORLD. According to statistics from the International Monetary Fund, a significant number of countries had inflation in 2000. In Exhibit 20.1, inflation rates for various countries are presented. The more industrialized

Consumer Price Index
95 = 100

	1996	1997	1998	1999	2000
United States	2.9	2.3	1.6	2.1	3.4
Canada	1.6	1.6	1.0	1.7	2.7
Australia	2.6	0.3	0.8	1.5	4.5
Japan	0.1	1.7	0.7	(0.3)	(0.7)
New Zealand	2.3	1.2	1.3	(0.1)	2.5
Denmark	2.1	2.3	1.8	2.4	2.9
France	2.0	1.2	0.7	0.6	1.7
Germany	1.5	1.8	1.0	0.7	2.0
Greece	8.2	5.5	4.7	2.7	3.1
Ireland	1.7	1.5	2.4	1.6	5.6
Italy	4.0	2.0	2.0	1.7	2.5
Spain	3.6	1.9	1.8	2.3	3.5
United Kingdom	2.4	3.2	3.4	1.6	3.0
Poland	20.2	15.9	11.7	7.3	9.0
Turkey	80.3	85.8	84.6	64.9	54.9
Egypt	7.2	4.6	4.2	3.1	2.7
Israel	11.3	9.0	5.4	5.2	1.1
Argentina	0.2	0.5	0.9	1.2	(0.9)
Chile	7.0	6.5	5.3	3.3	3.6
Ecuador	24.4	30.6	36.1	52.3	96.1
Mexico	34.4	20.6	15.9	16.6	9.5
Paraguay	9.8	7.0	11.5	6.8	8.9
Peru	11.5	8.6	7.3	3.5	3.7
Uruguay	28.3	19.9	10.8	5.6	4.8
Venezuela	99.9	50	35.8	23.6	16.2

Source: International Financial Statistics: International Monetary Fund.

Exhibit 20.1. Inflation in the World.

nations generally have less inflation than other countries. Notice that although most of the Latin American countries have significant inflation, it is present in many countries from a diversity of regions such as Turkey. If 1996, 1997, 1998, 1999, and 2000 are compared, it can be seen that inflation rates by country are erratic on a year-to-year basis. An inspection of Exhibit 20.1 would lead to the conclusion that most multinational companies probably have operations in some countries with high inflation because there are so many of them.

20.3 INFLATION, HYPERINFLATION, AND HIGHLY INFLATIONARY. Both the International Accounting Standards Board (IASB) and the Financial Accounting Standards Board (FASB) have defined a concept for severe inflation. The IASB calls it "hyperinflation," which is indicated by such characteristics as:

(a) The general population prefers to keep its wealth in non-monetary assets or in a relatively stable foreign currency. Amounts of local currency held are immediately invested to maintain purchasing power;

(b) The general population regards monetary amounts not in terms of the local currency but in terms of a relatively stable foreign currency;

(c) Sales and purchases take place at prices that compensate for the expected loss of purchasing power during the credit period, even if the period is short;

(d) Interest rates, wages, and prices are linked to a price index; and

(e) The cumulative inflation rate over three years is approaching or exceeds 100%. (IAS No. 29, IASC, 1989).

The purpose of the IASB definition is to indicate which enterprises should present primary financial statements that are stated in terms of the measuring unit current at the balance sheet date. This requires use of a general price level index, whether the financial statements are based on a historical cost approach or a current cost approach.

The FASB has defined a "highly inflationary" economy as one that has cumulative inflation of approximately 100% or more over a three-year period.[1] The purpose was to define those foreign operations of companies for which the current exchange rate method of translation was not appropriate. In the case of foreign operations in "highly inflationary" economies, the historical exchange rate is used in place of the current rate. Since the FASB does not require the primary statements of the foreign operation to be restated for "hyperinflation," there must be a presumption that using historical exchange rates based on the U.S. dollar somehow accounts for inflation. This is debatable, since inflation rates measure the price of goods and services within an economy, while exchange rates measure the trade conditions between two different economies.

An economic theory proposes that exchange rates will maintain purchasing power parity between two economies. This depends upon exchange rates adjusting for the differences in purchasing power between two economies with different rates of inflation. Thus, if foreign statements were price level adjusted and converted at current rates, the results might approach an inflation adjustment, if purchasing power parity held. However, the use of the FASB method for highly inflationary economies does not adjust for inflation; it ignores it.

20.4 ECONOMIC CAUSES OF INFLATION. *Inflation* has been defined by Paul Samuelson in this fashion: "Inflation occurs when the general level of prices and costs is rising—rising prices for bread, gasoline, cars; rising wages, land prices, rentals on capital goods."[2] The Keynesian economists and the monetarists differ in their view of the causes of inflation. The Keynesians cite two major causes of inflation: "demand-pull," where aggregate demand is greater than supply, and "cost-push." In demand-pull, there are shortages of products in periods of high demand, and this leads to increased prices. In cost-push, labor, material, energy, or other input factors rise and lead to higher prices.

The monetarists, primarily Milton Friedman, hold the theory that the supply of money is the primary factor determining aggregate demand and that control of inflation is through controlling the money supply. The Keynesians believe that inflation is controllable with fiscal policies.

There is also an international aspect to inflation. The trade deficits that the United

---

[1]FAS No. 52, paragraph 11, FASB, 1981.

[2]Samuelson, 1985, p. 226.

States has been running up have increased dollar balances abroad, which has an impact on the world economy similar to an increase in the money supply, given the importance of the U.S. dollar in world trade.[3] Also, domestic inflation in developing countries leads to devaluation of their currency under the floating exchange rates in effect since 1971. This makes the imports they need to develop their economies cost more, which leads to further inflation—a vicious circle.

20.5 MANAGERIAL IMPLICATIONS OF INFLATION. The literature on the managerial implications of inflation is significant. It includes two monographs by Alan Seed III of Arthur D. Little. One was published by the Financial Executives Institute (FEI) in 1978: *Inflation: Its Impact on Financial Reporting and Decision Making*. The other was published by the National Association of Accountants in 1981: *The Impact of Inflation on Internal Planning and Control*. The FEI also published *Coping with Inflation: Experiences of Financial Executives in the UK, West Germany and Brazil* in 1981. The Institute of Management Accountants (IMA) (formerly the (National Association of Accountants (NAA)) also has available a monograph, Inflation and Managerial Decision Making, by Denise Breden and Robert DeMichiel, which does not show a publication date but, judging from the dates of citations, was issued after 1983.

Seed's 1981 work devotes three chapters to "Management Accounting Issues and Practices." They are titled "Strategic Planning and Budgeting Issues," "Management Control Issues," and "Planning and Control Practices." The work by Breden and DeMichiel for the IMA has a chapter titled "The Impact of Inflation on Managerial Decision Making." The chapter covers the following topics: Strategic Planning, Capital Budgeting, Budgets and Cost Management, Pricing, Inventory, Performance Evaluation, Management Evaluation, and Dividend Policy. The following paragraphs draw heavily on the previously cited works. (For an in-depth treatment of management and control issues in a hyperinflationary environment, see Chapter 27.)

(a) Strategic Planning. Inflation must be considered in strategic planning because of the changes in specific prices and uncertainty about the amount and timing of these changes. This has an effect on business unit analysis, preparation of financial projections, portfolio analysis, the selection of financial strategies, and evaluation of capital expenditures. The long-term planning inherent in developing strategy exposes the planner to a greater possibility of inflation than would a shorter time horizon.

Even such developed economies as the United States, which is not considered at this time to have an inflation problem, have a significant decline in the purchasing power of the monetary unit if the time span is long enough. For example, from 1985 to 2000 the cumulative inflation rate in the United States was 59.9% and the cumulative loss in purchasing power was 37%, as shown in Exhibit 20.2. Notice that the inflation per year varied from 5.3% to 1.6% in a very irregular manner. This is what makes prediction of amount and timing of price changes difficult to forecast, even for an economy with a relatively low rate of inflation.

Strategy is developed from a business unit analysis. Seed[4] gives the Arthur D. Little format for this, as follows:

---

[3]Seed, 1978, p. 7.
[4]Seed, 1981, p. 68.

Period	Consumer Price Index 1995 = 100[a]	Consumer Price Index 1995 = 100[b]	Purchasing Power[c]	Cumulative Loss of Purchasing Power[d]	Inflation %[e]
1985	70.6	100.0	1.00		
1986	71.9	101.8	0.98	–0.02	1.8
1987	74.6	105.7	0.95	–0.05	3.8
1988	77.6	109.9	0.91	–0.09	4.0
1989	81.4	115.3	0.87	–0.13	4.9
1990	85.7	121.4	0.82	–0.18	5.3
1991	89.4	126.6	0.79	–0.21	4.3
1992	92.1	130.5	0.77	–0.23	3.0
1993	94.8	134.3	0.74	–0.26	2.9
1994	97.3	137.8	0.73	–0.27	2.6
1995	100.0	141.6	0.71	–0.29	2.8
1996	102.9	145.8	0.69	–0.31	2.9
1997	105.3	149.2	0.67	–0.33	2.3
1998	107.0	151.6	0.66	–0.34	1.6
1999	109.3	154.8	0.65	–0.35	2.1
2000	112.9	159.9	0.63	–0.37	3.3

[a]Consumer Price Index 1995 = 100
[b]Converted Index 1985 = 100
[c]Purchasing power in terms of 1985 dollars. (Reciprocal of column 2)
[d]Cumulative loss of purchasing power (1 – column 3)
[e]Inflation per year change from one year's index in column 1 to the next year's index.

Exhibit 20.2. Loss of Purchasing Power in United States Dollars (Index 1995 = 100). ***Source:*** **International Financial Statistics: International Monetary Fund.**

STRATEGIC BUSINESS UNIT INDICES AND RATIOS

Indices (Base Year = 100)
Industry throughput (units)
Business unit's product throughput (units)
Business units's sales (dollars)
Profit after taxes
Net assets

Cost and Earnings (per $ Sales)
Cost of goods sold
Research and development
General administration
Other income and expenses
Profit before taxes
Profit after taxes
Return on net assets

Investment (per $ Sales)
Receivables
Inventories
Current liabilities
Working capital and other assets
Total net assets

Funds Generation and Deployment
Operating cash flow (per $ sales)
Change in assets (per $ sales)

Percent internal deployment (change in assets ÷ operating funds flow)

This is a historical cost-accounting-oriented analysis subject to the deficiencies in dealing with inflation mentioned at the beginning of this chapter. The goal of the business unit should be to earn an appropriate *real* rate of return on assets. Consequently, the inflation generated holding gain, or loss, should be eliminated from profits, and the asset base used as a divisor in calculating the return on assets should also be adjusted for inflation. In addition to inflation adjusted rates of return, the strategic business unit analysis should also be adjusted to eliminate the growth in sales revenues and expenses due to inflation.

(b) Financial Projections. The need for financial projections to assist in strategy selection gives the analyst an opportunity to depart from the historical cost accounting convention. The effects of inflation must be incorporated into any financial projection. Financial projections are quite often presented in both nominal currency and currency with a constant purchasing power.

In countries with high rates of inflation or in the case of foreign subsidiaries subject to strong variations in exchange rates, it cannot be assumed that one need only change the nominal currency projections. The presence of rapid change in an economy can have market effects that change the underlying assumptions used in the constant dollar projections. For example, with an extremely high rate of inflation in consumer prices, if wage levels are not keeping pace, there is often a shift in consumer preference to goods possibly at the lower level of the price scale, away from mid-sized cars to smaller cars. The same situation can occur when the exchange rate moves against the local currency. This causes an inflationary rise in prices of imported goods, which leads to shifts in consumer goods to domestic goods, where they can be substituted.

Implicit in the preceding analysis is the need for multinational strategic business units to consider inflation rates in the foreign country or countries, inflation rates in the home country, and exchange rates between the two in making strategic financial projections. Each of these must be incorporated in the calculation of projections in such a manner that it may be easily changed to reflect changing conditions.

(c) Portfolio Analysis. At the corporate level, where management is dealing with a portfolio of strategic business units (SBUs), it is also essential to consider the effects of inflation. Using the Boston Consulting Group's growth share matrix, as shown in Exhibit 20.3, we can see that strategy for a strategic business unit is partially determined by market growth.[5]

Unless the analyst has adjusted market growth for inflation to arrive at "real" growth, the company could embark on the wrong strategy. For example, if apparently high market growth for a low market share SBU is adjusted for inflation to a low real market growth, the company should be following a "divest" strategy instead of the "build" strategy that a high market growth, unadjusted, would signal. With a high market share, the company could be holding when it should be harvesting.

[5]Shank, 1989, p. 33.

Strategy

Market Growth		Market Shares: Low	Market Shares: High
	High	Build	Hold
	Low	Divest	Harvest

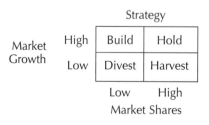

Exhibit 20.3. Growth/Share Matrix.

(d) Financial Strategies. Inflation causes an increase in the cost of capital goods, which can be more rapid than the company's ability to generate cash flows to replace the capital goods, particularly machines. The consequences of this situation are any of the following, alone or in combination: some replacements must be deferred, external financing must be increased, or other uses of funds, such as dividend payments and discretionary expenses, must be curtailed. Martin V. Alonzo, Vice-President and Controller of AMAX,[6] suggests the following strategies for beating inflation:

Investment

- Explore, buy and develop natural resources and build capital facilities as a hedge.
- Take advantage of recessionary periods and negotiate better engineering, construction and labor contracts.
- Be prepared to buy used facilities.
- Look for "buys" in the stock market.
- Forecast higher future selling prices to justify new investments.

Financing

- Borrow as much long-term debt as you can for as long as you can.
- In lease–finance transactions, retain residual equipment values.

Operating

- Use last-in, first-out (LIFO) inventory valuation method.
- During periods of oversupply increase inventory.
- Negotiate long-term purchase contracts.
- In new technology development, design away from energy-based processes because of anticipated escalating energy costs.
- Measure performance in real terms by converting operating results via use of GNP deflator and wholesale price index.

(e) Capital Expenditure Evaluations. The traditional discounted cash flow methods for evaluating capital expenditures, net present value, and internal rate of return have to be modified in an inflationary environment. There are two aspects to this: consideration of inflation in the cash flow projections and incorporation of inflation in the required rate of return. In practice, there have been several ways for doing this.

Some companies use nominal dollars based on anticipated inflation in specific cash flow elements for each year of the project. In this method, an inflation-adjusted cost of capital is used as the hurdle rate. Other companies select specific elements to adjust, for example, the amounts of capital expenditures, but use constant dollars to project cash flows from operations on the premise that cost increases will be offset by revenue increases; in practice, this is sometimes difficult to achieve. Finally, some companies project all expenditures and other elements of cash flow in constant dollars and use a cost of capital that excludes inflation. If the inflation rate is high, the method cited first is preferable.

---

[6] *Management Accounting*, March 1978, pp. 57–58.

Working capital terminal values need to be adjusted for inflation, just like the other cash flow elements in the project. Because inflation is a significant factor in the capital expenditure analysis, it is desirable to do a sensitivity analysis using different rates of inflation in the cash flow and cost of capital analysis.

(f) Operating Planning and Budgeting. Traditional planning and budgeting control systems produce information which is misleading during periods of high inflation. Budgets and plans should be adjusted for inflation where it is an important factor, and these should be revised and reviewed more frequently. Trends used to project short-run performance should be deflated for the effects of specific inflation to see the "real" trend which can then be adjusted for future anticipated inflation.

Firms should look for productivity measures that are in physical units, to avoid the effects of inflation. Those familiar with the learning curve calculation will remember that learning is based on inflation deflated costs.[7] In analyzing results, one should separate the effect of differences caused by prices from the effect of differences which represent performance.

According to Breden and DeMichiel,[8] some European companies use quarterly standard costs based on average material purchase costs and a forecast of key overhead elements. Revenue and other expense budgets are calculated by indexing each month in the quarter. Monthly reports compare actual to the budget. In Brazil, standard costs are adjusted during the year by indices on a monthly basis. The indices are specific for a variety of costs and revenues.

(g) Management Reporting and Performance Evaluation. Just as inflation influences the plans and budgets against which results are measured, it also influences management's perspective on analyzing actual results. Performance trends should be analyzed, after the effect of inflation has been removed. Profit analyses should be based on profits, which are calculated after considering the replacement costs of inventory and fixed assets (through replacement cost depreciation). Holding gains should be removed, and returns on investment should be calculated based on current costs or constant dollars.

A number of methods may be used to separate the noncontrollable impact of inflation from controllable operating results.[9] For example, one method is to identify the inflation effect in the actual results reported. To do this, the difference between assumed and actual price levels is calculated and removed to get at the controllable variance. Another method entails use of a "price adjusted flexible budget." In this case, the budget, not actual results, is adjusted for price level changes. The first step is to modify the budget for volume—a flexible budget—and then the flexible budget is increased for noncontrollable changes in the price of the input factors—costs.

(h) Pricing. When a company thinks its prices are sufficient to cover the costs of inflation and earn a profit, it may not be doing so. The solution is to take into account the income tax effect. A price to recover replacement cost can be calculated by taking the cost of a product and increasing it for the effects of inflation.

Prices will probably have to be changed more frequently where there is high inflation. They should be changed at least as often as the operating cash cycle, but, if

---

[7] Kaplan and Atkinson, 1989, p. 142.
[8] Breden and Demichiel, pp. 53–54.
[9] Seed, 1981, pp. 86–87.

the company has not estimated the inflation of the replacement cost correctly and the difference is significant, then the company will have to make mid-cycle adjustments.

(i) Inventory Valuation. Because the references cited concerning the managerial implications of inflation are by U.S. authors, there is a heavy emphasis on using LIFO for inventory valuation. This is only of significance for U.S. companies and other companies with U.S. operations, because LIFO is not acceptable elsewhere.

Working with the first year of operations in the hypothetical example, we can see the difference between FIFO—first-in, first-out—the most used inventory method outside the United States, and LIFO.

	FIFO	LIFO
1. Revenue	$115,400	$115,400
2. Cost of goods sold	100,000	112,000*
3. Profit	15,400	3,400
4. Taxes at 40%	6,160	1,360
5. Profit after taxes	$ 9,240	$ 2,040
6. Cash flow (#1 – #4)	$109,240	$114,040

*Higher because of 12% inflation.

The cash flow from LIFO would be sufficient to pay for the $112,000 replacement cost of inventory and leave $2,040 available for dividends. Under FIFO, it would not be sufficient to replace inventory. Every company operating in the United States whose inventory costs are increasing should use LIFO, but some companies are reluctant to report the lower profits after taxes that are a consequence of LIFO.

(j) Dividend Policy. Dividend policy and cash flow analysis are closely linked during periods of high inflation. As was evident from the preceding FIFO example, the company does not have enough cash to replace the inventory that was sold, let alone consider paying a dividend, even though there were apparent profits.

According to Alfred Rappaport,[10] measurement of distributable cash is a useful concept in calculating the funds available for dividends in an inflationary environment. Distributable cash is the maximum amount that the company can distribute to its stockholders during a period without impairing its operating capability or business capacity.

Three measurements are required to determine distributable cash:

1. Cash required for increases in costs of productive capacity.
2. Cash required for increases in net working capital.
3. Cash available from increased debt capacity.

Since the cash required for increases in net working capital is deducted in determining cash flow from operations, under the recent FASB statement on cash flows,[11] those companies operating in the United States need only deduct the first and third items to arrive at distributable cash.

---

[10]Rappaport, *Harvard Business Review*, January–February 1979.
[11]FAS No. 95, FASB, 1987.

Companies operating in other countries should give serious thought to adapting a cash flow statement to supplement the income statement and balance sheet. This is particularly true if they are operating in inflationary environments, because looking at profits alone can be deceptive.

20.6 MEASUREMENT APPROACHES TO INFLATION ACCOUNTING. Financial accounting standard setters in different countries have developed two basic approaches for dealing with inflation in financial statements. There are differences in the way the two methods are applied and whether they are used in the primary statements or as supplementary data.

In one method, called "constant dollar," general price level indices are used to adjust historical cost accounting records into monetary units of the same general purchasing power. Inflation effects are eliminated by changing the units of measure from the historical monetary unit, with different purchasing power at different dates, into a monetary unit with the same purchasing power. In practice, the GNP (Gross National Product) price level deflator developed by governmental economists has been suggested as the best measure of purchasing power in an economy. It measures the relative prices of all goods and services in the economy.

In contrast, the other general method, called, variously, "current cost," "current value," or "replacement cost," attempts to arrive at an economic value for past transactions. Current cost is used by the United States and is described in FAS No. 89.[12] The FASB requires only the restatement of inventories and property, plant, and equipment. The current cost of inventories is the current cost of purchasing the goods concerned or the current cost of the resources required to produce the goods. The current cost of property, plant, and equipment is the current cost of acquiring the same service potential of the asset owned. This considers operating cost and physical output capacity.

As applied in the United States, there are several ways to calculate this current cost.[13] It may be applied to single items or broad categories, as appropriate. The current cost may be calculated by:

- *Indexation.* Either externally generated price indices for the class of goods or services being measured or internally generated price indices.
- *Direct pricing.* Current invoice prices; vendors' price lists, quotes, or estimates; or standard manufacturing costs that reflect current costs.

Current value has been used in the Netherlands, based on the Limperg theory,[14] which says that the underlying assumption of the enterprise is continuity, whereby assets have to be replaced by building, equipment, and inventories that perform a similar economic function.

> For goods produced and sold, current value is the sum of the values of the factors of production consumed at the moment of exchange (sale). For capital goods—inventories and fixed assets—value is, for all practical purposes, measured at the moment of statement (balance sheet) presentation, annually or quarterly, although continuous recording

---

[12]FAS No. 89, FASB, 1986, p. 11.
[13]FAS No. 89, paragraph 19, FASB, 1986.
[14]Enthoven, 1982, p. 27.

is required. The cost to be incurred at the moment of sale to replace the product sold is the product's current value.[15]

The Dutch system is very close to the U.S. system, but by replacement they mean replacement by an asset that can perform a certain task. The replacing asset does not have to be technically identical to its predecessor, and the concept of reproduction cost of existing assets does not fit into the current value theory, nor does replacement cost of existing capacity, because it presupposes an ideal situation. According to Enthoven,[16] the current value method "closely resembles the U.S. concept of `replacement cost of existing assets.' The current value of assets does not imply replacement by an asset with an identical capacity and identical specifications."

Companies with debt, whose repayment is fixed in amount, benefit from borrowing and investing in goods whose value increases with specific price inflation or, in the case of constant purchasing power indexation, from being factored upward with general price levels. In the United States, a gain or loss on the net monetary position is calculated based on the difference between monetary assets and monetary liabilities. A net monetary liability position will show a profit from inflation. Both the Netherlands and the United Kingdom calculate a "gearing" adjustment. *Gearing* is the U.K. term for leverage.

To understand the U.K. gearing adjustment, one needs to be familiar with the Statement of Standard Accounting Practices (SSAP) No. 16 definition of monetary working capital. This is the aggregate of trade accounts and notes receivable, prepayments, and inventories not subject to the cost-of-sales adjustment, less trade accounts and notes payable and accruals. The monetary working capital adjustment is computed based on a change in a relevant index applied to each element of the monetary working capital. Thus, the index for receivables should reflect the current cost of items included in the applicable cost of goods and services sold, and the index for payables should reflect the cost of items financed by the payables.

The gearing adjustment is determined by multiplying the aggregate of three adjustments—an adjustment to depreciation, to cost of sales, and to the monetary working capital—by the ratio of net borrowings to net operating assets. Net borrowings are the excess of all liabilities and provisions fixed in monetary terms, other than those in monetary working capital and those that are in substance equity capital, over the aggregate of all current assets, other than those subject to a cost-of-sales adjustment and those included in monetary working capital. Net operating assets are the fixed assets, inventory (stock), and monetary working capital presented in an historical cost balance sheet.

In summary, there are two general ways recommended to handle the problem of inflation. One uses general price levels; the other uses specific price levels. Both have to take account of the effect of inflation gains or losses on monetary assets and liabilities. The current or replacement cost method attempts to put an economic value on the transaction. The general price level method adjusts the unit of measure. From a practical standpoint, the current price level method has an advantage in that it is more objective and can be audited objectively. The current or replacement cost method is more subjective, and its advocates would say it is more relevant.

---

[15]Enthoven, 1982, p. 28.

[16]Enthoven, 1982, p. 29.

20.7 U.S. INFLATION ADJUSTMENTS. The U.S. method of adjusting for inflation started in 1979 with the issuance of FAS No. 33.[17] Over the years, eight additional standards were issued, covering special industries and special problems. The information required by FAS No. 33 was mandatory, effective for fiscal years ending on or after December 25, 1979. Mandatory reporting ended with FAS No. 89 for financial statements issued after December 2, 1986, which said, "A business enterprise that prepares its financial statements in U.S. dollars and in accordance with U.S. generally accepted accounting principles is encouraged, but not required, to disclose supplementary information on the effects of changing prices."[18] In all cases, whether required or encouraged, the reporting was always in supplementary statements.

Samples of the format for U.S. supplementary disclosures appear in Exhibits 20.4 and 20.5. Notice that in Exhibit 20.4 the major adjustments to income from continuing operations are for cost of goods sold (inventory) and depreciation, and that current cost is the basis for reporting income. The gain or loss on monetary assets is a gain from being in a net monetary liability position. Also, the inventory, property, plant, and equipment increased more on a specific price basis than if their increase had been measured by the general price level.

A foreign currency translation adjustment is shown as a loss due to a decline in the value of the foreign currency investment in an overseas subsidiary. The foreign currency declined against the dollar during the year, causing a translation loss. The historical translation loss was remeasured in units of constant purchasing power to arrive at the figure reported in Exhibit 20.4.

Four separate items are reported in Exhibit 20.4: income from continuing operations, gain from purchasing power on net amounts owed, the effect of increases in specific prices over the general price level, and the foreign currency translation adjustment. The FASB does not provide guidance on what is commonly called the "bottom line." In effect, the user must decide which of the three items additional to income should be considered income. A strong case could be made for considering the gain on net monetary liabilities as an income item, because the interest expense paid to achieve this gain has been deducted to calculate net income. The other two items could be considered as equity adjustments, but this is for the user to decide.

An alternative recommended presentation of the same data given in Exhibit 20.4 is shown in Exhibit 20.5. The figures reported are much the same, but Exhibit 20.5 gives more information, because the user can see directly which items have been adjusted and by how much without having to refer back to the primary statements.

Three different methods of showing a five-year analysis, required in the past under FAS No. 33 and encouraged under FAS No. 89, are permitted. In all three the past current-cost information has been adjusted for changes in purchasing power so that everything is expressed in the average purchasing power of the dollar in the most recent statement year. A better method for countries with high inflation would be to express the financial data in terms of end-of-year purchasing power, since it would be the most recent data and would match the purchasing power of the measurements in the balance sheet at that date.

In terms of user ease, the format in Exhibit 20.6 would be preferable, since it presents both reported data and adjusted data. It shows the before-adjustment and after-

---

[17]FAS No. 33, FASB, 1979.

[18]FAS No. 89, FASB 1986, paragraph 3.

For the Year Ended December 31, 2006
In Thousands of Average 2006 Dollars

Income from continuing operations, as reported in the primary income statement	$22,995
Adjustments to reflect current costs	
Costs of goods sold	(8,408)
Depreciation expense	(9,748)
Income from continuing operations adjusted for changes in specific prices	$4,839
Gain from decline in purchasing power of net amounts owed[b]	$2,449
Increase in specific prices (current cost) of inventory and property, plant, and equipment held during the year[c]	$25,846
Effect of increase in general price level	5,388
Excess of increase in specific prices over increase in the general price level	$20,458
Foreign currency translation adjustment[d]	$ (624)

[a]The condensed financial information in this schedule compares selected information from the primary financial statements with information that reflects effects of changes in the specific prices (current cost) of inventory and property, plant, and equipment expressed in units of constant purchasing power. The current cost amounts for inventory and cost of goods sold reflect actual manufacturing costs incurred in 20X6. The current cost amounts for major components of property, plant, and equipment were determined by applying specific price indexes to the applicable historical costs. For assets used in U.S. operations, Producer Price Indexes and Factory Mutual Building Indexes were used; for assets used in foreign operations, appropriate indexes for each country were used. The current cost information is expressed in average 20X6 dollars as measured by the CPI-U.

[b]The purchasing power gain on net amounts owed is an economic benefit to the enterprise that results from being able to repay those amounts with cheaper dollars.

[c]During 20X6, the specific prices (current cost) of inventory increased by $9,108 and of property, plant, and equipment by $16,738. The total increase of $25,846 exceeded the increase necessary to keep pace with general inflation. At December 31, 20X6, the current cost of inventory was $65,700 and of property, plant, and equipment, net of accumulated depreciation, was $89,335 (both measured in December 31, 20X6 units of purchasing power). Those amounts are higher than the amounts in the primary statement of $63,000 for inventory and $45,750 for property, plant, and equipment, net of accumulated depreciation; therefore, it is reasonable to expect income from continuing operations on a current cost basis for 20X7 to remain significantly below that reported in the primary statements.

[d]Current cost amounts for foreign operations are measured in their functional currencies, translated into dollar equivalents using the average exchange rate for the year, and restated into constant units of purchasing power using the CPI-U. Essentially, the foreign currency translation adjustment is the effect of changes in exchange rates during the year on shareholders' equity. The negative translation adjustment indicates that, overall, the dollar has increased in value relative to the functional currencies used to measure the foreign operations of the enterprise.

Exhibit 20.4. Statement of Income from Continuing Operations Adjusted for Changing Prices.[a]

adjustment earnings per share for five years. Looking at Exhibit 20.6, one can see why the required reporting under FAS No. 33 was not popular with management. In every year, adjusted earnings per share were considerably lower than the reported figures, and in two years the reported earnings were adjusted to losses. Dividends

For The Year Ended December 31, 20X6
In Thousands of Dollars

	As Reported in the Primary Statements	Adjusted for Changes in Specific Prices (Current Cost)
Net sales and other operating revenues	$275,500	$275,500
Cost of goods sold	197,000	205,408
Depreciation expense	10,275	20,023
Other operating expenses	14,685	14,685
Interest expense	7,550	7,550
Income tax expense	22,995	22,995
	252,505	270,661
Income from continuing operations	$ 22,995	$ 4,839
Gain from decline in purchasing power of new amounts owed[b]		$ 2,449
Increase in specific prices (current cost) of inventory and property, plant, and equipment held during the year[c]		$ 25,846
Effect of increase in general price level		5,388
Excess of increase in specific prices over increase in the general price level		$ 20,458
Foreign currency translation adjustment[d]	$ (295)	$ (624)

[a]The condensed financial information in this schedule compares selected information from the primary financial statements with information that reflects effects of changes in the specific prices (current cost) of inventory and property, plant, and equipment expressed in units of constant purchasing power. The current cost amounts for inventory and cost of goods sold reflect actual manufacturing costs incurred in 20X6. The current cost amounts for major components of property, plant, and equipment were determined by applying specific price indexes to the applicable historical costs. For assets used in U.S. operations, Producer Price Indexes and Factory Mutual Building Indexes were used; for assets used in foreign operations, appropriate indexes for each country were used. The current cost information is expressed in average 20X6 dollars as measured by the CPI-U.

[b]The purchasing power gain on net amounts owed is an economic benefit to the enterprise that results from being able to repay those amounts with cheaper dollars.

[c]During 20X6, the specific prices (current cost) of inventory increased by $9,108 and of property, plant, and equipment by $16,738. The total increase of $25,846 exceeded the increase necessary to keep pace with general inflation. At December 31, 20X6, the current cost of inventory was $65,700 and of property, plant, and equipment, net of accumulated depreciation, was $89,335 (both measured in December 31, 20X6 units of purchasing power). Those amounts are higher than the amounts in the primary statements of $63,000 for inventory and $45,750 for property, plant, and equipment, net of accumulated depreciation; therefore, it is reasonable to expect income from continuing operations on a current-cost basis for 20X7 to remain significantly below that reported in the primary statements.

[d]Current-cost amounts for foreign operations are measured in their functional currencies, translated into dollar equivalents using the average exchange rate for the year, and restated into constant units of purchasing power using the CPI-U. Essentially, the foreign currency translation adjustment is the effect of changes in exchange rates during the year on shareholders' equity. The negative translation adjustment indicates that, overall, the dollar has increased in value relative to the functional currencies used to measure the foreign operations of the enterprise.

Exhibit 20.5. Statement of Income from Continuing Operations Adjusted for Changing Prices.[a]

In Thousands of Dollars, Except for Per Share Amounts

	Year ended December 31				
	20X6	20X5	20X4	20X3	20X2
Total revenue					
As reported	$275,500	$239,800	$219,100	$194,800	$193,100
Adjusted for general inflation[a]	$275,500	$247,500	$240,000	$235,500	$265,000
Income (loss) from operations					
As reported	22,995	11,097	4,756	9,977	11,847
Adjusted for specific price changes[a]	4,839	1,660	(2,102)	(4,663)	1,261
Purchasing power gain from holding net monetary liabilities[a]	2,449	7,027	5,432	1,247	6,375
Excess of increase in specific prices of assets over increase in the general price level[a]	20,458	2,292	3,853	8,597	3,777
Foreign currency translation adjustment					
As reported	(295)	(276)	(396)	(138)	76
Adjusted for specific price changes[a]	(624)	(386)	(454)	(293)	127
Net assets at year-end					
As reported	47,700	28,000	20,179	18,819	11,980
Adjusted for specific price changes[b]	92,027	67,905	60,409	56,966	55,705
Per share information:					
Income (loss) from operations					
As reported	$15.33	$7.40	$3.17	$6.65	$7.90
Adjusted for specific price changes[a]	3.23	1.11	(1.40)	(3.11)	.84
Cash dividends declared					
As reported	2.00	2.00	2.00	2.00	2.00
Adjusted for general inflation[a]	2.00	2.06	2.19	2.42	2.75
Market price at year-end					
As reported	36	38	41	23	25
Adjusted for general inflation[a]	35	39	43	27	32
Average consumer price index[c]	298.4	289.1	272.4	246.8	217.4

[a]In average 20X6 dollars.
[b]Net assets adjusted for specific price changes include inventory and property, plant, and equipment at current cost and all other items as they are reported in the primary financial statements. No adjustment has been made for the lower tax basis applicable to the current cost amounts included in net assets.
[c]For purposes of this illustration, although the years for which information has been provided are nonspecific, the actual 20X2–20X6 average index numbers have been applied.

Exhibit 20.6. Five-year Comparison of Selected Financial Data.

were paid far in excess of adjusted earnings, and the stable cash dividend actually declined in terms of its purchasing power. Although Exhibits 20.4 through 20.6 represent an example rather than results of an actual company, the characteristics cited above were representative for firms reporting under FAS No. 33.

20.8 INFLATION ADJUSTMENTS IN THE NETHERLANDS. Dutch accounting permits current cost accounting but does not require it. Thus, Dutch companies have a choice between current cost and historical cost. Contrary to widespread belief, historical cost accounting is more common than current-cost accounting in Dutch financial reporting. N. V. Phillips has been the most cited example of a user of current cost reporting although they have recently reverted to historical cost accounting in the published financial statements. Heineken is now the only major Dutch company using current-cost accounting in external financial reporting.[19] Exhibits 20.7 through 20.9 are based on an earlier version of Phillips's published financial statements.[20]

Notice that in Exhibit 20.7 the current cost income is reconciled to the historical cost income. A major factor in determining the net profit is the large charge against income for an "Addition to revaluation surplus realized for financing with Shareholders' interests." This is described as part of the gearing adjustment explanation in the companies footnotes, as follows:

---

[19]Nobes and Parker, 2000, p. 168.
[20]Enthoven, 1982.

Millions of Euros	2005		2004	
Sales		42,411		36,536
Costs and expenses:				
Cost of sales	–32,209		–27,633	
Selling and general expenses	–8,009	–40,218	–7,059	–34,692
Trading profit		2,193		1,844
Revaluation included in costs		710		663
Trading profit on the basis of historical cost		2,903		2,507
Financing charges		–1,977		–1,225
Miscellaneous income and charges		–21		59
Tax on profit		–181		–452
Profit after tax on the basis of historical cost		724		889
Addition to revaluation surplus realized for financing with shareholders' interests		–354		–345
Profit after tax		370		544
Share in net result of nonconsolidated companies		86		95
Minority interests		–134		–115
Profit before exceptional items		322		524
Exceptional income and charges				
Elimination of provision for lifetime risks of fixed assets as from January 1, 2005	540		–600	
Restructuring provision	–525			
Tax on exceptional income and charges	20		290	
Reduction of United Kingdom tax provision		35	131	–179
Net profit		357		345

Exhibit 20.7. Combined Statement of Results.

Millions of Euros	2005		2004	
Assets		42,411		36,536
Property, plant, and equipment				
Current value	28,819		27,433	
Depreciation	–13,672		–13,613	
		15,147		13,820
Intangible assets		30		82
Investments in nonconsolidated associated companies		1,747		1,518
Sundry noncurrent cost		1,058		630
Stocks				
Factory stocks	6,840		6,625	
Commercial stocks	6,789		6,335	
	13,629		12,960	
Advanced payments by customers	–1,255		–986	
		12,374		11,974
Accounts receivable				
Trade debtors	9,900		9,532	
Discounted bills	–452		–451	
	9,448		9,081	
Other accounts receivable	895		665	
Prepaid expenses	738		624	
		11,081		10,370
Liquid assets				
Marketable securities	165		143	
Cash at bank and in hand	1,128		1,190	
		1,293		1,333
		42,730		39,727
Capital and Liabilities				
Shareholders' interests				
Ordinary share capital	1,806		1,705	
Reserves	10,785		9,846	
		12,591		11,551
Deferred gearing adjustment		1,556		1,435
Minority interests		1,620		1,419
Deferred tax liabilities due to revaluation		1,722		1,675
Long-term liabilities and provisions				
Provisions	3,540		3,523	
Convertible debenture loans	471		493	
Convertible private loans	—		400	
Other debenture loans	2,151		1,770	
Other long-term liabilities	3,871		3,257	
		10,033		9,443
Short-term liabilities and provisions				
Provisions	1,864		1,405	
Bank credits	3,837		3,676	
Accounts payable	6,543		6,358	
Tax on profit	300		371	
Accrued expenses	2,345		2,085	
Profit available for distribution	275		129	
Distribution out of retained profit	34		180	
		15,198		14,204
		42,730		39,727

Exhibit 20.8. Combined Statement of Financial Position.

Current Value

The valuation of the fixed assets, that is, property, plant, and equipment, and stocks, as well as the depreciation and consumption respectively thereof, is based on current value. Within the context of the aim of achieving continuity, this is, in principle, the replacement value and in certain cases, the lower net realizable value.

The replacement value is determined with due regard to the function of the relevant assets and the place where they are employed, taking technological developments into account. For calculating the replacement value, the current prices of specific assets are used, or, if this is not possible, use is made of indices for groups of assets, the price level development of which is determined by similar influences.

Insofar as fixed assets and stocks are considered to be financed with shareholders' interests, changes occurring in the replacement value as a result of fluctuations in the local price level (revaluation) are credited or debited directly to revaluation surplus. Where fixed assets and stocks are considered not to be financed with shareholders' interests, the change in the replacement value is included as a deferred gearing adjustment. This is transferred to the profit-and-loss account in proportion to the depreciation of the fixed assets and the consumption of the stocks concerned.

The deferred taxation on the total revaluation is shown as deferred tax liabilities due to revaluation and is temporarily deducted from the revaluation surplus and the deferred gearing adjustment. The amounts thus deducted from these accounts are added to revaluation surplus or the deferred gearing adjustment again when the fixed assets are depreciated and stocks are consumed and these taxes are simultaneously accounted for in the profit-and-loss account.

Exhibit 20.9. Principles of Valuation.

> The addition to the Revaluation surplus realized because of financing with Shareholder's interests. This relates to the part of the revaluation realized on fixed assets and stocks considered to be financed with Shareholder's interests.[21]

Assets in Exhibit 20.8 are shown at their current value, as described in the footnotes to the financial statement. The relevant portion of the footnotes is reproduced as Exhibit 20.9. The deferred gearing adjustment is a significant figure in the capital and liabilities section of the balance sheet. It is explained in the footnotes, as follows: "The Deferred gearing adjustment relates to the revaluation not yet realized on the fixed assets and stocks that has arisen from changes in the price level, in so far as these assets are considered not to be financed with Shareholder's interests the adjustment is shown net of Deferred tax and the amount applicable to Minority interests."

20.9 BRAZILIAN EXAMPLE OF INFLATION ADJUSTMENTS. In the past, Brazil was subject to many years of hyperinflation. Recommended inflation accounting in Brazil is covered by two sets of reporting options, one from Brazilian Corporate Law and the other from the Brazilian Securities Exchange Commission. Permanent assets and stockholder's equity are to be restated using a price index supplied by the federal government.

The net difference between the adjustments to permanent assets and to stockholder's equity accounts is reported in current income as a monetary gain or loss. This can be illustrated by looking at an example from Choi, Frost, and Meek,[22] given in Exhibit 20.10.

[21]Enthoven, 1982, p. 103.

[22]Choi, Frost and Meek, 2002, p. 266.

Historical Amounts			Inflation Corrected Amounts Assuming a 25% Rate of Inflation		
Balance Sheet	*1/1/X5*	*12/31/X5*	*12/31/X5*		
Current assets	R$ 150	R$ 450	Current assets		R$ 450
Permanent assets	1,600	1,600	Permanent assets		2,000[a]
Provision for Depreciation	(200)	(200)	Provision for		
			Depreciation	(300)	
			Monetary correction	(75)[b]	
			Correction of historical Charge to P&L	(25)[c]	(400)
Total	R$ 1,550	R$ 1,750	Total		R$ 2,050
Current liabilities	R$ 50	R$ 50	Current liabilities		R$ 50
Long-term debt	400	400	Long-term debt		400
Equity:			Equity		
Capital	800	800	Capital		800
			Capital reserve		200[d]
Reserves	300	300	Reserves		375[e]
Profit of period		200	Profit of period		225
Total	R$ 1,550	R$ 1,750	Total		R$ 2,050

Exhibit 20.10. Brazilian Example of Inflation Adjustments.

(*continued*)

Historical Amounts			Inflation Corrected Amounts Assuming a 25% Rate of Inflation		
Income Statement					
Year Ended 12/31/X5			*Year Ended 12/31/X5*		
Operating Profit		R$ 500	Operating Profit		R$ 500
Depreciation of period (historical)		100	Depreciation of period	100	
			Correction of depreciation	25	125
Trading profit		400	Trading profit		375
			Inflationary loss:		
Exchange loss on foreign debt		(100)	Exchange loss on foreign debt	(100)	
Monetary correction on local debt		(100)	Monetary correction on local debt	(100)	
			Gain on correction of balance sheet	50[f]	(150)
Net profit		R$ 200	Net profit		R$ 225

[a]Represents the original R$1,600 plus a 25% (R$400) adjustment.
[b]25% of the original R$300.
[c]25% of the period's depreciation expense (typically based on the average value of fixed assets).
[d]25% of the original capital balance of R$800.
[e]Represents the original R$300 plus a 25% (R$75) adjustment.
[f]Gain on correction of the balance sheet:

Correction of permanent assets	R$ 400	
Correction of depreciation allowances	(75)	325
Correction of capital	(200)	
Correction of reserves	(75)	(275)
		50

Exhibit 20.10. *(Continued)*

Notice in footnote f6, that the R$325 net gain on permanent assets adjusted upward for inflation, is greater than the net adjustment to capital and reserves, R$275, resulting in a R$50 gain on the correction. This gain is reported on the income statement. Also, note that when permanent assets are revalued, both the depreciation and the provision for depreciation are adjusted.

20.10 STATUS OF ACCOUNTING STANDARDS AND PRACTICES ON INFLATION IN THE WORLD AND MAJOR COUNTRIES. The International Accounting Standards Board issued IAS No. 15, "Information Reflecting the Effects of Changing Prices," which recommends that large publicly traded enterprises disclose information using any method that adjusts for the effects of changing prices. According to IAS No. 15[23] (paragraph 20), the minimum disclosures are:

> (a) the adjustments to or the adjusted amounts of depreciation of property, plant and equipment and cost of sales that are necessary to reflect the effects of changing prices.
>
> (b) adjustments relating to monetary items, the effect of borrowing, or equity interests described in paragraphs 15 = N17, when such adjustments are taken into account in determining income under the method adopted; and
>
> (c) the overall effects on results of adjustments made to reflect the effects of changing prices.
>
> In addition, under the current cost approach the current cost of property, plant and equipment and of inventories are relevant and are disclosed.

The reference in the preceding quote to paragraphs 15 to 17 relates to a discussion, the essence of which is that, under current cost methods, income is recognized after the operating capacity of the enterprise has been maintained (paragraph 15). A different point of view, also discussed, maintains that it is not necessary to recognize in the income statement the replacement cost of assets if they are financed by borrowing (paragraph 20). There is also a discussion of the application of a general price index to the shareholders' interests (paragraph 17). The effective date of the standard was for financial statements covering periods beginning on or after January 1, 1983. In IAS No. 15, no examples were presented.

Subsequently, the IASB published another standard on inflation adjustments, IAS No. 29, "Financial Reporting in Hyperinflationary Economies," dated July 1, 1989. This standard emphasizes that, in a hyperinflationary economy, financial results in a local currency without restatement are not useful. IAS No. 29 explains that it is a matter of judgment when restatement becomes necessary but that hyperinflation is indicated by such characteristics as mentioned earlier in this chapter.

The standard explains that, in a hyperinflationary economy, financial statements, whether on a historical cost basis or a current cost approach, are useful only if they are expressed in terms of the measuring unit current at the balance sheet date. Thus, IAS No. 29 applies to the primary financial statements.

The restatement requires the use of a general price index that reflects changes in general purchasing power, and IAS No. 29 suggests that all enterprises in the same country use the same index. Both historical cost and current cost statements require restatement, as well as the determination of a gain or a loss on the net monetary position. No examples were given.

---

[23]IAS No. 15, paragraph 20.

The Fourth Directive of the European Economic Community retains the historical cost perspective but allows member states to authorize the use of replacement value measurements or other methods based on current or market values. Any difference arising from this must be aggregated and shown as a "revaluation reserve" in owners' equity.

Among the major countries in the world that have addressed the inflation issue, the United States' experience with FAS No. 33 and FAS No. 89 has been covered earlier. The United States required some companies to report current cost/constant dollar information from 1979 to 1985. The standard was only applied to those companies with either

> (a) Inventories and property, plant, and equipment (before deducting accumulated depreciation, depletion, and amortization) amounting in aggregate to more than $125 million; or
>
> (b) Total assets amounting to more than $1 billion (after deducting accumulated depreciation).[24]

The United Kingdom required inflation adjustments with SSAP No. 20, "Current Cost Accounting" for accounting periods starting on or after January 1, 1980. The standard extended to a far broader range of companies than the U. S. standard, because it applied to all listed and unlisted companies meeting any two of the following criteria: sales of £5 million or more, total assets of £2.5 million or more, and 250 or more employees.

The major differences between the U.K. standard and FAS No. 33 were twofold. First, the U.K. standard required only current cost, unlike the U.S. standard that dealt with current cost and constant dollars. Second, the U.K. standard required both a current cost income statement and a balance sheet, while, as we have seen earlier in this chapter, the U.S. standard had an income statement focus.

The U.K. standard gave latitude in the presentation of the inflation-adjusted data, as follows:[25]

> This requirement to include current cost information in addition to historical cost accounts or historical cost information can be complied with by:
>
> (a) presenting historical cost accounts as the main accounts with supplementary current cost accounts which are prominently displayed; or
>
> (b) presenting current cost accounts as the main accounts with supplementary historical accounts; or
>
> (c) presenting current cost accounts as the only accounts accompanied by adequate historical cost information.

Treatment of the gain or loss on the net monetary position was also different from the United States, where a single figure was calculated based on a general price level index. In the United Kingdom, a monetary working capital adjustment was calculated, recognizing the effect of specific price changes on the total amount of monetary working capital (trade receivables less trade payables). A gearing adjustment based on the ratio of total debt to total capitalization was evidence that it was not nec-

---

[24]FAS No. 33, paragraph 23, FASB, 1979.

[25]SSAP No. 16, paragraph 48.

essary to recognize the additional replacement cost of assets in the income statement to the extent they were financed by debt. In June 1985, SSAP No. 20 was suspended and withdrawn in April 1988.[26]

20.11 INFLATION AND TRANSLATION. The issues of inflation and translation have been treated in FAS No. 33, FAS No. 52, FAS No. 70, and FAS No. 89. The seminal work on inflation, FAS No. 33, was issued before FAS No. 52; then FAS No. 89 made the information requirement optional.

The latest information, from FAS No. 89, discusses the translate-restate method. A foreign subsidiary first adjusts depreciation in local currency to a current cost basis and then calculates a current cost income, which is translated into dollars at the average exchange rate during the year.[27] These dollar figures are then consolidated into the parent's balance sheet. The U.S. consolidated figures are then restated into constant dollars.

Under the restate-translate method, current cost in the local environment is determined and restated to reflect the effects of general inflation in the local currency, before translation.[28] Both translate–restate and restate–translate are allowed by FAS No. 70.[29] Since the results will almost certainly be different, one has to decide which exercise gives the better information. Restate-translate has the advantage that local currency statements are developed which reflect both current cost and general price level adjustments in the local currency. Translate-restate requires only one set of restatements for price level adjustments and is thus simpler.

Under hyperinflation, neither method is used and the financial statements of the foreign entity shall be remeasured as if the functional currency were the reporting currency.[30] Therefore, if an economy has a cumulative inflation of approximately 100 percent or more over a three-year period, nonmonetary assets are translated at historical dollar exchange rates. In effect, the dollar becomes the reporting currency. There is no easy adjustment for hyperinflation, but an example will show that there are many possibilities.

Suppose a U.S. company invests $1,000 in a Latin-American country when the exchange rate is 33,000 Fc to $1. A year later the foreign asset has a current cost of 70,000,000 Fc, the local inflation has been 100%, the U.S. inflation has been 5%, and the exchange rate is 72,600 Fc to $1. These assumptions incorporate experience with hyperinflationary economies, where it is not uncommon for assets to increase in value faster than the government statistics which give the "official" price level index and the exchange rate outraces both asset values and government statistics because it is influenced by future expectations. Given these facts for one asset only, we can see several possible valuations:

	Fc	*Rate*	*U.S.$*
Historical cost	33,000,000	(33,000)	1,000
Price level indexed	66,000,000	(72,600)	909
Historical cost U.S. indexed	33,000,000		1,050 (+5%)
Current cost	70,000,000	(72,600)	964

[26]Nobes and Parker, 2000, p. 400.
[27]FAS No. 89, paragraph 80, FASB, 1986.
[28]FAS No. 89, paragraph 80, FASB, 1986.
[29]FAS No. 70, paragraph 4, FASB.
[30]FAS No. 52, paragraph 11, FASB, 1981.

Unless translation rates adjust to reflect the specific price inflation or the general price level shifts (purchasing power parity), the assets value is misstated, even though the historic rate was used. Thus, the translation method for hyperinflationary economies presented in FAS No. 52 is a translation device, but it does not adjust for inflation.

20.12 ISSUES IN IMPLEMENTATION AND INTERPRETATION. This chapter has shown a variety of approaches to inflation accounting. The two major themes are constant dollar reporting and current cost. Yet we have seen some differences between how the two methods were implemented. Any method that concentrates on current cost exclusively is taking an entity viewpoint; that is, it is important to measure the situation of the reporting entity. Unless these results are adjusted for changes in general price level, the shareholders' viewpoint is ignored.

An entity could be successful with an operating profit after applying current cost adjustments, but its capacity to pay a dividend could be far less than needed to pay the investors a dividend which would permit them to maintain their purchasing power. Put simply, one would be interested to know that the current cost of one's home had gone up 10% but disappointed if the cost of living had gone up 20%. Many current cost applications ignore this point.

Another issue has been the interpretation of the gain or loss on net monetary assets. This was described for the United States, and gearing adjustments for Dutch and U.K. companies were discussed. One can go through the calculations of the gearing adjustment, but an alternative is to consider the gain or loss on the net monetary position as an offset to interest income and expense. Simply put, if you gain in purchasing power from borrowing, you are paying for that in a higher interest cost, due to the inflation component. Therefore, it would make sense to deduct the purchasing power gain from the interest cost.

References to purchasing power parity have been made earlier and in reference to assumptions in FAS No. 52. Even if purchasing power parity held in the long run, there would be short-run adjustments to reach parity that would influence translated statements. If one chose to ignore this, there would still be the problem that purchasing power parity was the exchange rate which equated purchasing power in two economies.

Returning to the example of the Latin-American investment, if purchasing power parity held at the beginning of the year for the 33,000 rate, then a rate of 62,857 would be needed to maintain purchasing power parity. The calculation is as follows:

Purchasing power beginning	33,000Fc	$1
Inflation	100%	5%
Purchasing equivalent end	66,000Fc	$1.05

66,000Fc ÷ $1.05 = 62,857Fc—the purchasing power parity rate

Notice that a purchasing power parity rate would translate the restated foreign currency assets into restated U.S. assets correctly. To argue that using the historic rate adjusts for inflation because of purchasing power parity ignores the fact that the basic U.S. historical cost was not adjusted for inflation. Thus, FAS No. 52 for hyperinflationary economies ignores inflation.

20.13 THE FUTURE OF ACCOUNTING FOR INFLATION. Countries containing the major financial accounting standard setters in the world have not had high inflation rates recently. Thus, the United States and the United Kingdom could drop their inflation adjustment requirements on the grounds that inflation was not a problem for them. Yet, high rates of inflation persist in many areas of the world (see Exhibit 20.2). Those who must continually cope with the problems of inflation have the abandoned requirements of the United States and United Kingdom to guide them. In the future, given the growing U.S. government's budget deficit inflation could return as an issue, even though, as Exhibit 20.3 showed, on a cumulative basis, it has never gone away. The issues with respect to U.S. standard setting for inflation were put into excellent perspective by David Mosso in his dissent to FAS No. 89[31]

> Mr. Mosso dissented to the issuance of Statement 33 and he dissents to its recision, both for the same reason. He believes that accounting for the interrelated effects of general and specific price changes is the most critical set of issues that the Board will face in this century. It is too important either to be dealt with inconclusively as in the original Statement 33 or to be written off as a lost cause as in this Statement.
>
> The basic proposition underlying Statement 33—that inflation causes historical cost financial statements to show illusory profits and mask erosion of capital—is virtually undisputed. Specific price changes are inextricably linked to general inflation, and the combination of general and specific price changes seriously reduces the relevance, the representational faithfulness, and the comparability of historical cost financial statements.
>
> Although the current inflation rate in the United States is relatively low in the context of recent history, its compound effect through time is still highly significant. High inflation rates prevail in many countries where United States corporations operate. Rates from country to country vary from time to time. Those distortive influences on financial statements will now go unmeasured and undisclosed.
>
> Although Statement 33 had obvious shortcomings, it was a base on which to build. It represented years of due process—research, debate, deliberations, decisions—and application experience. As last amended, it had made significant progress in eliminating alternative concepts and methodologies. Its recision means that much of that due process and application experience will have to be repeated in response to a future inflation crisis. That will entail great cost in terms of time, money, and creative talent and, because due process does not permit quick reaction to crises, it risks loss of credibility for the Board and loss of initiative in private sector standard setting.

SOURCES AND SUGGESTED REFERENCES

Alonzo, Martin V. "Corporate Strategy for Combating Inflation." *Management Accounting*, March 1978, pp. 57–58.

Booz, Allen, and Hamilton. *Coping with Inflation: Experiences of Financial Executives in the UK, West Germany and Brazil.* New York: Financial Executives Institute, 1981.

Breden, Denise, and Robert DeMichiel. *Inflation and Managerial Decision Making.* New York: National Association of Accountants, (no date).

Choi, Frederick D. S., Carol Ann Frost, and Gary K. Meek. *International Accounting*, 4th ed. Upper Saddle River, NJ: Prentice Hall, 2002.

Enthoven, Adolph J. H. *Current Value Accounting*. Dallas: Center for International Accounting Development, the University of Texas at Dallas, 1982.

Evans, Thomas G., Martin E. Taylor, and Robert J. Rolfe. *International Accounting and Reporting*, 3rd ed. Houston, TX: Dame Publications, Inc., 1999.

Financial Accounting Standards Board. Statement of Financial Accounting Standards No. 33, "Financial Reporting and Changing Prices." Stamford, Conn.: FASB, 1979.

---

[31]FAS No. 89, paragraph 4, FASB, 1986.

——. Statement of Financial Accounting Standards No. 52, "Foreign Currency Translation." Stamford, Conn.: FASB, 1981.

——. Statement of Financial Accounting Standards No. 70, "Financial Reporting and Changing Prices: Foreign Currency Translation." Stamford, Conn.: FASB, 1982.

——. Statement of Financial Accounting Standards No. 89, "Financial Reporting and Changing Prices." Stamford, Conn.: FASB, 1986.

——. Statement of Financial Accounting Standards No. 95, "Statement of Cash Flows." Stamford, Conn.: FASB, 1987.

Gernon, Helen, and Gary K. Meek. *Accounting: An International Perspective*, 5th ed. New York: Irwin McGraw-Hill, 2001.

The Institute of Chartered Accountants in England and Wales. Statement of Standard Accounting Practice No. 20, "Current Cost Accounting." London: ASC, 1980.

International Accounting Standards Committee. International Accounting Standard No. 15, "Information Reflecting the Effects of Changing Prices." London: IASC, 1982.

——. International Accounting Standard No. 29, "Financial Reporting in Hyperinflationary Economics." London: IASC, 1989.

Iqbal, M. Zafar. *International Accounting: A Global Perspective*, 2nd ed. Cincinnati, OH: South-Western, 2002.

Kaplan, Robert S., and Anthony A. Atkinson. *Advanced Management Accounting*, 2nd ed. Englewood Cliffs, NJ: Prentice Hall, 1989.

Nobes, Christopher, and Robert Parker. *Comparative International Accounting*, 6th ed. Essex, England: Pearson Education Limited, 2000.

——. *Comparative International Accounting*. New York: St. Martin's Press, 1985.

Rappaport, Alfred. "Measuring Company Growth Capacity During Inflation." *Harvard Business Review*, January–February 1979.

Samuelson, P., and W. Nordhaus. *Economics*, 12th ed. New York: McGraw-Hill, 1985.

Seed III, Allen H. *Inflation: Its Impact on Financial Reporting and Decision Making*. New York: Financial Executives Institute, 1978.

——. *The Impact of Inflation on Internal Planning and Control*. New York: National Association of Accountants, 1981.

Shank, John, and Vijay Govindarajan. *Strategic Cost Analysis*. Homewood, IL: Irwin, 1989.

CHAPTER 21

ASSET SECURITIZATION

Lisa Filomia-Aktas

Ernst & Young LLP

CONTENTS

21.1 WHAT IS SECURITIZATION? Securitization is the process of transforming predictable cash flows into securities. These securities are tradable and have greater liquidity than the cash flows themselves. Thus, securitization facilitates the creation of markets for financial claims that would otherwise not be marketable. Securitization also allows for the repackaging of cash flows into different buckets (also called tranches) with respect to seniority and timing of repayment. Tranches are sized to minimize funding costs within the needs and requirements of investors.

For investors, securitization makes it possible to invest in tradable financial claims

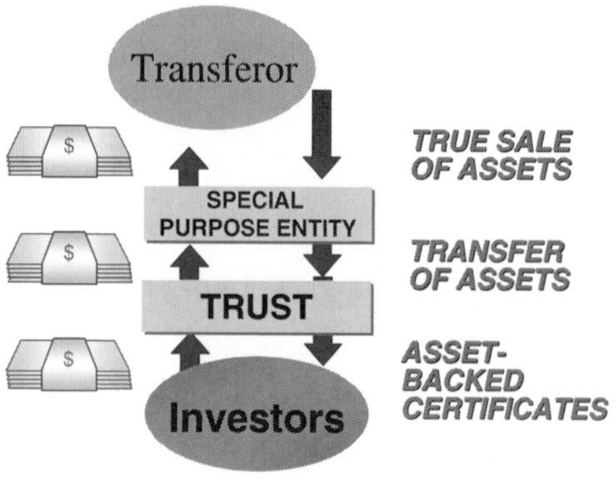

Exhibit 21.1. Typical Securitization Transaction.

with attractive returns. For borrowers, securitization provides an alternative funding source with lower costs of funds compared with other forms of financing. By playing a role in improving the efficiency of the financial system and increasing credit availability, securitization is an integral and vital part of today's economy.

A typical securitization transaction is structured in Exhibit 21.1.

In a typical asset-backed securitization, the transferor (also known as the "sponsor" or "issuer") bundles together financial assets (e.g., accounts receivable or loans) from a number of customers (or borrowers). The sponsor then forms a special-purpose entity (SPE) (sometimes referred to as a special-purpose vehicle or a special-purpose company) to buy the assets from the sponsor. In most structures, a second transfer of the assets to a trust occurs and the trust issues the asset-backed securities. It is the combination of the two entities and transfers (a two-step transaction) that typically is necessary to accomplish legal isolation.

The issuance of the asset-backed securities provides funds for the purchase of the receivables from the transferor. Such securities are in the form of beneficial interests in the receivables or the cash flows the receivables will generate and, accordingly, are backed solely by the assets in the trust due to the legal isolation. Beneficial interests may comprise either a single class of securities having debt or equity characteristics or multiple classes of interests, some having debt characteristics and others having equity characteristics. The sponsor also may retain an interest in the assets transferred (e.g., the residual interest) and may service the receivables, performing such duties as collecting principal and interest from the customer (or borrowers), investigating delinquencies, foreclosing and liquidating collateral of defaulted loans and remitting principal and interest to the asset-backed security holders, guarantors, trustees or others that provide services for the structure.

The following list contains terms commonly employed in securitization transactions:

- **Beneficial interests:** Rights to receive all or portions of specified cash inflows to a trust or other entity, including senior and subordinated shares of interest, principal, or other cash inflows to be "passed-through" or "paid-through," premiums due to guarantors, commercial paper obligations, and residual interests, whether in the form of debt or equity (FASB Statement No. 140, paragraph 364).

- **Financial asset:** Cash, evidence of an ownership interest in an entity, or a contract that conveys to a second entity a contractual right (a) to receive cash or another financial instrument from a first entity or (b) to exchange other financial instruments on potentially favorable terms with the first entity (FASB Statement No. 140, paragraph 364).
- **Interest-only strip:** A contractual right to receive some or all of the interest due on a bond, mortgage loan, collateralized mortgage obligation, or other interest-bearing financial asset (FASB Statement No. 140, paragraph 364).
- **Qualifying SPE:** A special-purpose entity that qualifies for specific accounting treatment under FASB Statement No. 140.
- **Special-Purpose Entity:** A legal entity with a specific, limited purpose.
- **Transfer:** The conveyance of a noncash financial asset by and to someone other than the issuer of that financial asset. Thus, a transfer includes selling a receivable, putting it into a securitization trust, or posting it as collateral but excludes the origination of that receivable, the settlement of that receivable, or the restructuring of that receivable into a security in a troubled debt restructuring (FASB Statement No. 140, paragraph 364).
- **Transferee:** An entity that receives a financial asset, a portion of a financial asset, or a group of financial assets from a transferor (FASB Statement No. 140, paragraph 364).
- **Transferor:** An entity that transfers a financial asset, a portion of a financial asset, or a group of financial assets that it controls to another entity (FASB Statement No. 140, paragraph 364).

21.2 REASONS FOR ORIGINATORS TO SECURITIZE.

The securitization structure is intended to provide significant advantages to the originator of the financial asset, which includes providing an alternative source of funding, reducing cost of funds, creating risk transparency, and increasing the return on asset and return on equity by moving the assets and related funding off balance sheet.

(a) Alternative Source of Funding.

One of the greatest advantages of securitization is the creation of tradable securities from illiquid financial claims. In many cases, originators are limited to a few sources of funds such as unsecured debt, asset-based funding, or sale/syndication. These types of financing usually carry higher costs than securitization as it relies on the creditworthiness of the originators rather than on the financial claims.

Securitization of financial claims also provides the originator with a way to receive payment for the financial claims earlier than the scheduled collection date of those financial claims. This helps originators to carry on their business and to generate new financial claims.

(b) Cost of Funds.

In the financial markets, higher-rated debt commands lower rates. Through the isolation of the financial claims in a "bankruptcy-remote" entity, asset diversification, tranching, and overcollateralization, securitization provides for the issuance of highly rated securities and, in many cases, securities that are rated higher than the originator itself. This tends to reduce the costs of funds to the originator when compared to traditional forms of financing.

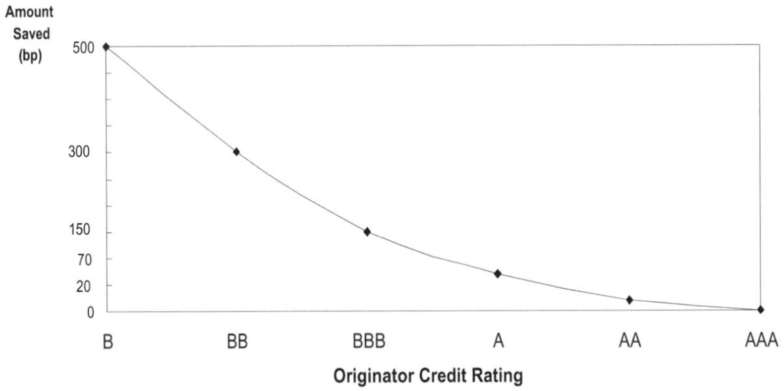

Source: Ernst & Young Structured Finance Advisory Services.

Exhibit 21.2. Savings from Securitization.

The "bankruptcy remoteness" of the financial claims is an important factor in the ability of the originator to offer the securities at lower rates. The fact that an investor's claim over the cash flows of the assets is not exposed to the originator's other obligations, which emerge from the originator's possibly risky ongoing business, makes it possible for the rating agencies to look to the financial claims quality and not the originator's credit quality in assigning ratings. This could be significant in many cases to companies that carry ratings lower than "AAA" and could raise cheaper funds through the process of securitization.

As illustrated in Exhibit 21.2, savings from securitization increase as the originator's rating decreases. However, it should be noted that the spread saved through securitization could widen or shrink at different points in time as a result of the economy and the company.

(c) Risk Transparency. The predictable nature of the cash flows of financial claims allows investors to measure risk associated with their investment more easily and with greater accuracy. In addition, in many structures, assets and related liabilities can be matched, eliminating the need for hedges.

(d) Off-Balance-Sheet Financing. In many securitization transactions, the financial claims and related funding are moved "off balance sheet" and replaced by cash and other assets. This helps improve the originator's balance sheet and the financial ratios used to measure the originators' financial health. For example, securitization allows banks to release capital and reduce the reserve requirements by exchanging illiquid financial claims, which are considered to be the risky assets, for cash and unrated first loss securities. This in turn increases the bank's lending abilities and, subsequently, its profitability.

21.3 EVOLUTION OF SECURITIZATION. The first securitization transactions date back to the early 1970s and involved pass-through mortgage securities guaranteed by the Government National Mortgage Association (Ginnie Mae). In order to promote

1985	$1.2	1997	$185.1
1988	$14.3	2000	$217.0
1991	$50.1	2001	$280.0
1994	$75.3	2002	$305.0 (estimated)

Source: The Bond Market Association.

Exhibit 21.3. Public Asset-Backed Market Volumes.

an active secondary market for home mortgages, the U.S. government established Ginnie Mae to guaranty the mortgage pass-through securities of various Ginnie Mae–approved private institutions. The Ginnie Mae guarantees created a readily tradable mortgage-backed securities market because they were government backed and guaranteed and accordingly carried AAA credit ratings.

The original Ginnie Mae transactions were followed by similar transactions of the Federal Home Loan Mortgage Corporation (Freddie Mac) and Federal National Mortgage Association (Fannie Mae) in the early 1980s. However, with time, investors wanted more diverse maturity products and cash flows, which led to the development of CMOs (multiclass mortgage pass-throughs). The Tax Reform Act of 1986 allowed mortgage security pools to elect the tax status of a Real Estate Mortgage Investment Conduit (REMIC) and, since 1986, most mortgage securitizations have been issued in REMIC form to create tax and accounting advantages for the issuers. The first nonmortgage securitization occurred in 1985 when Sperry Corporation securitized computer lease receivables, soon to be followed by the growth of the asset-backed securities market. The growth of the public asset–backed securities market is depicted in Exhibit 21.3.

As the market developed, various asset classes were securitized, such as credit cards and home equity loans. Currently, any asset with a predictable cash flow can be securitized. Exhibit 21.4 indicates the approximate percentage share that each asset class represents out of the current public ABS market.

21.4 SECURITIZATION PROCESS. A securitization transaction typically starts with an originator's[1] decision to securitize its financial assets. The originator then selects an underwriter and together they assemble the rest of the financing team. The under-

[1]An entity that originates financial assets (or purchases the financial assets from entities that originate them) in the course of its business.

Home Equity	34%	Student Loans	5%
Auto	31%	Mfg. Housing	3%
Credit Cards	21%	Leases	3%

Source: Dow Jones Interactive.

Exhibit 21.4. Public ABS by Asset Class.

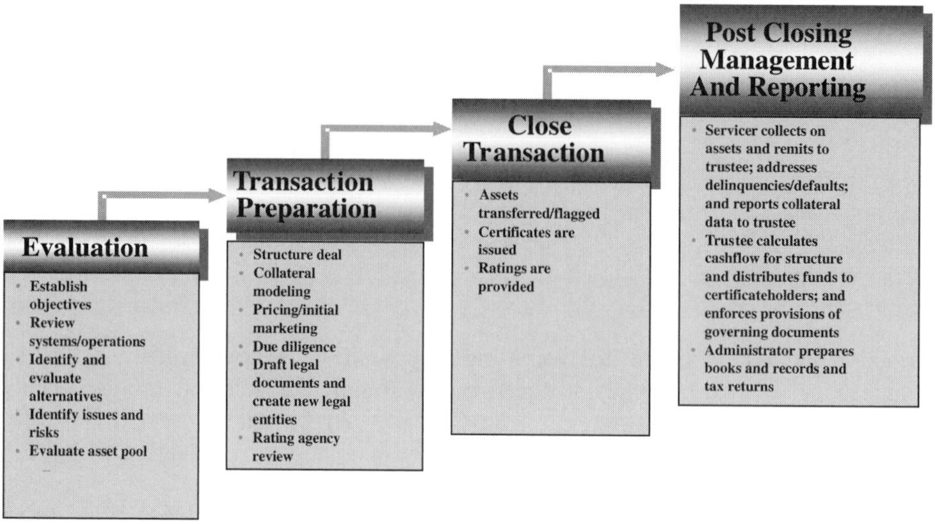

Exhibit 21.5. Phases of the Securitization Process.

writer and issuer coordinate the assembly of a collateral pool and related data. The rating agencies or financial guarantors then determine the required credit enhancement. The attorneys draft legal and disclosure documents. Exhibit 21.5 depicts the four phases of a securitization transaction and the primary aspects undertaken in each phase.

During the evaluation phase, the originator determines whether securitization is the most appropriate option (e.g., would asset based funding or a sale/syndication provide better economics?) and identifies any issues that need to be addressed (e.g., can the systems provide the required information?). Once securitization is chosen, the transaction is structured, the optimal assets are selected, and the rating agencies perform due diligence. It generally takes between eight to sixteen weeks to close a transaction, depending on such factors as whether the deal is public or private and the availability of data. The securitized pool of assets will need to be tracked separately from other assets serviced by the servicer.

21.5 STRUCTURAL ASPECTS. Most securitization structures involve the sale of a pool of financial claims by the originator to a "bankruptcy-remote," wholly owned special-purpose entity in a manner that qualifies as a legal "true sale,"[2] in exchange for cash and retained interests in the financial claims (generally the residual interest). The SPE then transfers the financial claims to a trust or other type of special purpose

[2]This first step is designed to be judged a true legal sale, in part because the originator does not provide "excessive" credit protection. In addition, the special purpose entity typically has a board of directors that is independent of the originator and is not permitted by its charter to undertake any other business or to incur any liabilities. Its dedication to a single transaction and the other circumstances surrounding it makes it extremely unlikely that it would enter bankruptcy and, even if it did, that a receiver could reclaim the transferred assets. This transfer is intended to legally isolate the transferred assets from the transferor/originator.

entity, which credit enhances the pool to obtain the high credit rating sought by third-party investors on their interests. The credit enhancement can be provided in a variety of ways such as by establishing a spread account (in which certain collateral collections are retained in the SPE to support repayment to the investors before being distributed to the originator), by purchasing a financial guarantee (wrap), or using a senior/subordinate structure (in which the subordinate holders' financial interests are junior to the senior holders—that is, the subordinate holders assume more of the economic risks). The trust that issues the securities transfers the cash it raises from investors to the first SPE, which simultaneously transfers the cash to the originator.

Typically, an SPE has the following characteristics: an entity that is created to accomplish a narrow and well-defined objective (e.g., to effect a lease, research and development activities, or a securitization of financial assets) that takes the form of a corporation, trust, partnership or unincorporated entity. SPEs often are created with legal arrangements that impose strict and sometimes permanent limits on the decision-making powers of their governing board, trustee, or management over the operations of the SPE. Frequently, the provisions specify that the policy guiding the ongoing activities of the SPE cannot be modified, other than by its creator or sponsor (i.e., they operate on so-called autopilot). As a result, SPEs do not typically have employees or the day-to-day operations of a normal corporation.

The originator will usually be the servicer of the financial claims, as it already has the resources and expertise necessary to manage the financial claims. During the term of the transaction, the servicer bills and collects payments on the financial claims, on behalf of the SPE.

21.6 ACCOUNTING

(a) History. Since the time of the first securitization transactions, the determination of whether the transfer of assets in a securitization should be accounted for as a sale or a secured borrowing has been challenging. FASB Statement No. 77, "Reporting by Transferor for Transfers of Receivables with Recourse," issued in 1983, and FASB Technical Bulletin No. 85-2, "Accounting for Collateralized Mortgage Obligations," issued in 1985, led to confusion and inconsistency in accounting practices for financial asset transfers. FASB Technical Bulletin No. 85-2 provided that a sale of assets by an entity to an SPE that issued debt securities should be recorded as a borrowing if the seller obtained any of the securities issued by the SPE. However, in accordance with FAS 77, if an entity sold assets to an SPE that issued certificates/participations (equity type instruments as opposed to debt securities), the transaction was to be accounted for as a sale even if the originator obtained any of the securities or retained recourse.

As a result of that confusion, FASB decided to adopt a financial components approach that focuses on control and recognizes that financial assets and liabilities can be divided into a variety of components. In June 1996, the FASB issued FASB Statement No. 125, "Accounting for Transfers and Servicing of Financial Assets and Extinguishments of Liabilities" (FAS 125), which provided accounting and reporting standards for sales, securitizations, and servicing of receivables and other financial assets, secured borrowing and collateral transactions, and the extinguishments of liabilities. FAS 125 applied to transactions occurring after December 31, 1996.

Almost immediately after the FASB issued FAS 125, constituents began asking for reconsideration and clarification of certain of its provisions, even beyond the guidance provided in the FAS 125 Implementation Guide. In response to the growing need for reconsideration and clarification, the FASB agreed that amendments to FAS 125 were necessary and decided that a replacement would be more user friendly than simply amending the FAS 125 guidance. As a result, FASB Statement No. 140, "Accounting for Transfers and Servicing of Financial Assets and Extinguishment of Liabilities" (FAS 140) was issued in September 2000.

FAS 140 retained the concepts of FAS 125 but the ground rules for determining whether a transfer of financial assets constitutes a sale or secured borrowing were clarified.

(b) U.S. Accounting Overview. FAS 140 is based on a financial-components approach that focuses on control of the financial components of the assets. Under this approach, the accounting for a financial asset is determined for each of the components that are contractually created and accounted for based on the interests transferred and interests retained. Following a transfer of financial assets, an entity recognizes the assets it controls and liabilities it has incurred, and derecognizes financial assets for which control has been surrendered and all liabilities that have been extinguished. Transfers of nonfinancial assets are governed by other accounting literature discussed below.

For example, if an entity transfers a loan receivable in a transaction in which a third party has acquired control over the future principal payments but the seller retains control over future interest payments, FAS 140 would consider the entity to have sold the "principal" component of the loan and to have retained the "interest" component. If the seller in this example also has guaranteed the third-party investor that the debtor will make all contractually required principal payments, the seller would recognize a liability for the financial guarantee contract it has provided the investor.

Under this model, components of the transferred asset, or newly created instruments require separate accounting recognition. For example, an interest rate swap might exist in a transfer of financial assets that qualifies as a sale even though no formal interest rate swap agreement exists. This can occur in situations in which financial assets are securitized and the rate paid to investors is determined on a basis different than the rate paid by the debtor. For example, a swap is deemed to exist where a fixed rate receivable is sold to an investor that receives all payments made by the debtor except that the interest payments are converted to a variable rate of interest. In this situation, the economic components of the transfer result in the creation of an interest rate swap.

The components of a financial asset are determined based on the contractual components that are created as a result of the transfer. For example, consider a transfer of a portfolio of fixed rate receivables in which the buyer is to receive the first 90% of all principal collections, a variable rate of interest, and receives a guarantee of principal and interest collections. In this case, the transferor would be viewed as retaining a single retained interest that represents a combined principal-only strip, interest rate swap, and financial guarantee contract. It would not separately account for the three financial components retained. However, each of the three components that are combined into the retained interest will impact the cash flow that will result from the retained interest and, therefore, its fair value. Therefore, the importance of carefully understanding each aspect of a transfer involving financial instruments cannot be overemphasized.

Under FAS 140, a transferor/originator is considered to have surrendered control over transferred assets and, therefore, to have sold the assets (to the extent that consideration other than beneficial interests in the transferred assets is received in exchange), only if all of the following conditions are met:

- *Legal isolation.* The transferred assets have been isolated from the transferor/originator—put presumptively beyond the reach of the transferor/originator and its creditors, even in bankruptcy or other receivership.
- *Right to pledge or exchange.* Each transferee (or, if the transferee is a QSPE (see 21.5), each holder of its beneficial interests) has the right to pledge or exchange the assets (or beneficial interests) it received, and no condition both constrains the transferee (or holder) from taking advantage of its right to pledge or exchange and provides more than a trivial benefit to the transferor/originator.
- *Effective control criteria.* The transferor/originator does not maintain effective control over the transferred assets through either an agreement that both entitles and obligates the transferor/originator to repurchase or redeem them before their maturity or the ability to unilaterally cause the holder to return specific assets, other than through a clean-up call.

Transfers of financial assets in which the transferor/originator has no continuing involvement with the transferred assets or with the transferee have not been controversial. However, transfers of financial assets often occur whereby the transferor/originator has some form of continuing involvement either with the assets that have been transferred or with the transferee. Typical examples of continuing involvement include recourse provisions relating to the assets transferred, servicing arrangements, and agreements or options to repurchase or reacquire the transferred assets. Transfers of financial assets with continuing involvement raise questions about whether the transfers should be accounted for as sales or as secured borrowings. The three criteria above establish the standard for determining when the transfer of financial assets should be considered a sale or as a secured borrowing.

(c) Sale Criteria

(i) Legal Isolation. The facts and circumstances surrounding the transfer of assets must provide reasonable assurance that the transferred assets would be beyond the reach of the transferor/originator, or the powers of a bankruptcy trustee or other receiver (e.g., the Federal Deposit Insurance Corporation for FDIC insured entities or the SPCE for broker-dealers) for the transferor/originator or any of its affiliates. Derecognition of transferred assets is appropriate only after all available evidence that either supports or questions the isolation assertion has been considered and found to provide reasonable assurance that the transferred assets would be beyond the reach of the powers of a bankruptcy trustee or other receiver for the transferor/originator or any of its consolidated affiliates. However, if the transferor/originator has continuing involvement with the transferred assets, the assistance of legal counsel likely will be required. Typically, a "true sale/nonconsolidation" opinion is obtained from a bankruptcy attorney. Statement of Auditing Standards No. 73, "Use of Specialist's Opinion Required in Most Securitization Transactions," provides guidance on reviewing the legal opinion and indicates that a "would be" true

sale level of assurance is required. The "would be" opinion is the highest level of assurance an attorney can give. In addition, the opinion should indicate that the SPE would not be consolidated with the transferor by a bankruptcy court.

(ii) Right to Pledge or Exchange. In assessing whether this criteria for sales treatment under FAS 140 has been met, the first question that should be addressed is whether the transferee (or the beneficial interest holders of a QSPE) is constrained from pledging or exchanging its purchased assets (or the beneficial interests) in such a way as to keep it from obtaining all or most of the cash inflows associated with its ownership. In implementing FAS 125, issues arose concerning the types of constraints on the transferee's right to pledge or exchange transferred assets which preclude sale accounting and whether a transferee must obtain either the right to pledge transferred assets or the right to exchange them or whether a transferee must obtain both rights for the transfer to qualify for sale accounting. This issue was resolved in FAS 140 as the emphasis is on providing the transferee with the ability to obtain all or most of the cash flows, not on the method of doing so (i.e., whether it can either exchange or pledge).

The second question that should be addressed if one concludes that the transferee or the holder of a QSPE's beneficial interest is constrained is whether or not the constraint provides more than a trivial benefit to the transferor/originator.

The following is a list of examples of provisions that would typically be considered constraining:

- A prohibition on the transferee's subsequent sale of its interests
- A prohibition on the sale to a competitor, if that competitor would be the only willing buyer for the type of asset concerned
- A right for the transferor/originator to buy back the transferred assets that are "deep in the money" at the time of transfer

Some conditions do not constrain a transferee (or beneficial interest holders) from pledging or exchanging the assets (or beneficial interests) and therefore do not preclude a transfer subject to such a condition from being accounted for as a sale. For example, a transferor/originator's right of first refusal on the occurrence of a bona fide offer to the transferee or beneficial interest holder from a third party presumptively would not constrain a transferee, because that right in itself does not enable the transferor/originator to compel the transferee to sell the assets and the transferee would be in a position to receive the sum offered by exchanging the asset, albeit possibly from the transferor/originator rather than the third party. However, a transferor's right of first refusal when the transferor holds the residual interest in the transferred assets is a constraint that provides more than a trivial benefit to the transferor and would preclude sale treatment. Further examples of conditions that presumptively would not constrain a transferee (or beneficial interest holder) include:

- A requirement to obtain the transferor/originator's permission to sell or pledge that is not to be unreasonably withheld
- A prohibition on sale to the transferor/originator's competitor if other potential willing buyers exist
- A regulatory limitation such as on the number or nature of eligible transferees

(as in the case of securities issued under Securities Act Rule 144A or debt placed privately)

- Illiquidity, for example, the absence of an active market

These provisions should be considered in connection with the other provisions and restrictions in the transaction or rights retained by the transferor/originator, as they may not constrain the transferee (or beneficial interest holder) individually, but may as they work in combination with other aspects of a transaction.

Whether a constraint is of more than a trivial benefit to the transferor is not always clear, but as transferors presumably incur costs if they impose constraints, since transferees pay less than they would pay to obtain the asset without constraint, imposition of a constraint by a transferor typically results in more than a trivial benefit to the transferor.

For example, a provision in the transfer contract that prohibits selling or pledging a transferred loan receivable not only constrains the transferee but also provides the transferor with the more-than-trivial benefits of knowing who has the asset, a prerequisite to repurchasing the asset, and of being able to block the asset from finding its way into the hands of a competitor for the loan customer's business or someone that the loan customer might consider an undesirable creditor. Transferor-imposed contractual constraints that narrowly limit timing or terms, for example, allowing a transferee to pledge only on the day assets are obtained or only on terms agreed with the transferor, also constrain the transferee and presumptively provide the transferor with more-than-trivial benefits. Additionally, a condition not imposed by the transferor that constrains the transferee may or may not provide more than a trivial benefit to the transferor. For example, if the transferor refrains from imposing its usual contractual constraints on a specific transfer because it knows an equivalent constraint is already imposed on the transferee by a third party, it presumptively benefits more than trivially if it is aware at the time of the transfer that the transferee is constrained. However, the transferor cannot benefit from a constraint if it is unaware at the time of the transfer that the transferee is constrained.

(iii) Effective Control Criteria. Under FAS 140, if the transferor/originator has any ability to unilaterally reclaim specific transferred assets on terms that are potentially advantageous to the transferor/originator—whether through a removal-of-accounts provision, the ability to cause the liquidation of the special purpose entity, a call option, forward purchase contract, or other means—sale treatment is precluded because, in those circumstances, the transferor/originator would still effectively control the transferred assets. The transferor/originator maintains effective control by being able to initiate action to reclaim specific assets with the knowledge that the transferee cannot sell or distribute the assets because of restrictions placed on it.

A right to reclaim specific transferred assets by paying fair value for the assets when reclaimed generally does not maintain effective control, because it does not convey a more than trivial benefit to the transferor/originator. However, a transferor/originator has maintained effective control if it has such a fair value right and also holds the residual interest in the transferred assets because it can unilaterally cause their return. For example, if a transferor/originator can reclaim such assets by purchasing them in an auction at the termination of the transaction/QSPE, and thus at what might appear to be fair value, then sale accounting for the assets it can reclaim would be precluded. Such circumstances provide the transferor/originator with a more than trivial benefit and effective control over the assets, because it can pay any price it chooses in the auction and recover any excess paid over fair value through its residual interest.

Some rights to reacquire transferred assets (or to acquire beneficial interests in transferred assets held by a QSPE), although they do not constrain the transferee, may result in the transferor maintaining effective control over the transferred assets through the unilateral ability to cause the return of specific transferred assets. Such rights preclude sale accounting. For example, an investor in a beneficial interest with an attached call would not be constrained because, by exchanging or pledging the asset subject to that call, it would be able to obtain substantially all of its economic benefits. However, an attached call could preclude sale accounting as it may result in the transferor maintaining effective control over the transferred asset(s) because the attached call gives the transferor the ability to unilaterally cause whoever holds that specific asset to return it. In contrast, transfers of financial assets subject to calls embedded by the issuers of the financial instruments, for example, callable bonds or prepayable mortgage loans, do not preclude sale accounting. Such an embedded call does not result in the transferor maintaining effective control, because it is the issuer rather than the transferor who holds the call.

If the transferee is a QSPE, it is constrained from choosing to exchange or pledge the transferred assets. As such, any call held by the transferor is effectively attached to the assets and could—depending on the price and other terms of the call—maintain the transferor's effective control over transferred assets through the ability to unilaterally cause the transferee to return specific assets. For example, a transferor's unilateral ability to cause a QSPE to return to the transferor or otherwise dispose of specific transferred assets at will or, for example, in response to its decision to exit a market or a particular activity, could provide the transferor with effective control over the transferred assets. As a result, the transfer of receivables with a right to reacquire those associated with a specific division or operating unit will not generally be treated as a sale.

The effective control criteria also precludes sale accounting for transfers of financial assets subject to an unconditional removal-of-accounts provisions (ROAP) that allows the transferor to specify the assets removed. The most common example of a ROAP is the right to specify accounts to be removed from credit card master trusts. The effective control criteria also precludes sale accounting for transfers of financial assets subject to a ROAP in response to a transferor's decision to exit some portion of its business. The FASB reached this conclusion because such provisions allow the transferor to unilaterally remove specified assets from the QSPE, which demonstrates that the transferor retains effective control over the assets.

Certain other types of ROAPs that are commonly found in securitization structures are permissible. For example, a ROAP is permitted if it allows the transferor to remove specific financial assets after a third-party cancellation, or expiration without renewal, of an affinity or private-label arrangement on the grounds that the removal would be allowed only after a third party's action (cancellation) or decision not to act (expiration) and if it could not be initiated unilaterally by the transferor. Also, a ROAP is permitted that allows the transferor to randomly remove transferred assets at its discretion, but only if the ROAP is sufficiently limited (i.e., to excess assets) so that it does not allow the transferor to remove specific transferred assets, for example, by limiting removals to the amount of the transferor's retained interest and to one removal per month.

A clean-up call, however, is permitted as an exception to the effective control criteria. A clean-up call is an option held by the servicer or its affiliate, which may be the transferor, to purchase the remaining transferred financial assets, or the remaining beneficial interests not held by the transferor, its affiliates, or its agents in a QSPE (or in a series of beneficial interests in transferred assets within a QSPE), if the amount of outstanding assets or beneficial interests falls to a level at which the cost of servicing those assets or beneficial interests becomes burdensome in relation to the benefits of servicing.

(d) Consolidation. Once it is concluded that the transfer meets the three sale criteria discussed above, the transferor/originator must determine whether the SPE that holds the assets and issues the beneficial interests must be consolidated. If a transfer is accounted for as a sale and the SPE is subsequently consolidated in the transferor's consolidated balance sheet, then the result would be that the transferor continues to recognize the transferred assets.

The first and most typical way for the transferor/originator in a securitization to avoid consolidating the SPE, is to structure the SPE as a qualifying SPE (QSPE). FAS 140 provides that a QSPE should not be consolidated in the financial statements of a transferor or its affiliates. This does not exempt beneficial interest holders other than the transferor from consolidating the SPE should they be deemed to have control. Any entity that is not a transferor of financial assets to a QSPE, including a transferor that transfers financial assets to an SPE that does not meet the qualification criteria, should consider other guidance on consolidation policy (FAS 94, EITF Topic D-14, EITF 90-15, and related guidance).

(e) Qualifying Special-Purpose Entities (QSPEs). FAS 140 provides detailed guidance on the criteria to be a QSPE. The concept of a QSPE is intended to be restrictive. Under FAS 140, a QSPE must meet four broad conditions. The QSPE must be demonstrably distinct from the transferor, restricted as to its permitted activities, limited as to the types of assets it can hold, and limited as to its ability to sell or otherwise dispose of noncash financial assets.

(i) Demonstrably Distinct Nature of a QSPE. A QSPE is demonstrably distinct from the transferor if the transferor cannot "unilaterally" decide to change the QSPE and at least 10% of the beneficial interest issued by the QSPE are held by outside parties (i.e., parties that are not the transferor, its affiliates, or its agents).

(ii) Activities of a QSPE. The activities of a QSPE must be significantly limited, fully described in the legal documents that established the SPE or created its beneficial interests, and changeable only with the consent of the majority of the outside beneficial interest holders.

A QSPE may not have discretion over its activities and it may not engage another entity to make such decisions. Instead all of the QSPE's activities must be "preprogrammed" at the inception. Because of its limited activities, a QSPE may be described as "brain dead" or running on "autopilot."

(iii) Assets a QSPE May Hold. A QSPE may hold financial assets transferred to it that are passive in nature, passive derivative financial instruments that pertain to beneficial interests, financial assets (e.g., guarantees) that would reimburse it if others were

to fail to adequately service financial assets transferred to it or to timely pay obligations due, servicing rights related to assets that it holds, nonfinancial assets obtained in connection with the collection of financial assets that it holds (but only temporarily), and cash collected from assets that it holds and investments purchased with that cash (i.e., relatively risk-free instruments) pending distribution to holders of beneficial interests. A QSPE may not purchase assets from the market (unless it is temporarily investing its cash collections).

(iv) Selling of Noncash Financial Assets Held by a QSPE. A QSPE may sell noncash financial assets only in automatic response to certain conditions. The conditions include the occurrence of an event that (1) is specified in the legal documents, (2) is outside the control of the transferor, and (3) causes the fair value of the financial assets to decline by a specified degree below the fair value of those assets when the SPE obtained them; exercise by a BIH (other than the transferor) of a right to put that holder's beneficial interest back to the SPE; exercise by the transferor of a call or a removal-of-accounts provision (ROAP—a call that empowers the transferor to reclaim assets subject to certain restrictions) specified in the legal documents; or termination of the SPE or maturity of the beneficial interests in those financial assets on a fixed or determinable date that is specified at inception. As one can see, a QSPE has no discretion as to whether assets may be sold.

(f) Decision Tree. Exhibit 21.6 provides an example of a decision tree.

(g) Initial Accounting/Gain-on-Sale Calculation. Upon completion of a transaction that satisfies the conditions to be treated as a sale and avoids consolidation, the gain or loss from such sale needs to be determined in accordance with FAS 140. The gain or loss will be recognized on the portion of the assets sold and the interests retained will be recorded at an allocated book value. FAS 140 requires that on completion of a sale of financial assets, the previous carrying amount is to be allocated between the assets sold and any retained interests based on their relative fair values at the date of transfer. Retained interests in transferred assets consist of portions of the assets that existed prior to the transfer that the transferor continues to hold subsequent to the transfer. The most common examples include a servicing contract with respect to the transferred assets, or a portion of the principal balance or interest collections from the transferred assets.

Recognition of gains or losses on the sale of financial assets is not elective and the transferor may not defer in the balance sheet a gain or loss resulting from the sale of financial assets.

The following example illustrates the gain-on-sale calculation for a transfer that meets the sale criteria.

Example: Assume a financial institution sells a portfolio of loans with a principal amount and net carrying amount of $1,000 to an SPE for $900 cash and a residual interest. The financial institution will also continue to service the loans for a contractual servicing fee of 2% of the outstanding balance annually. The principal and interest collections will be used to pay the investors first. Any remaining cash flow after losses, prepayments, and expenses will be paid to the residual holder.

Exhibit 21.7 summarizes the calculation. The first step is to determine the components—the interests sold and the interests retained. In this example, the financial institution retained the residual interest and the servicing. The next step is to calculate

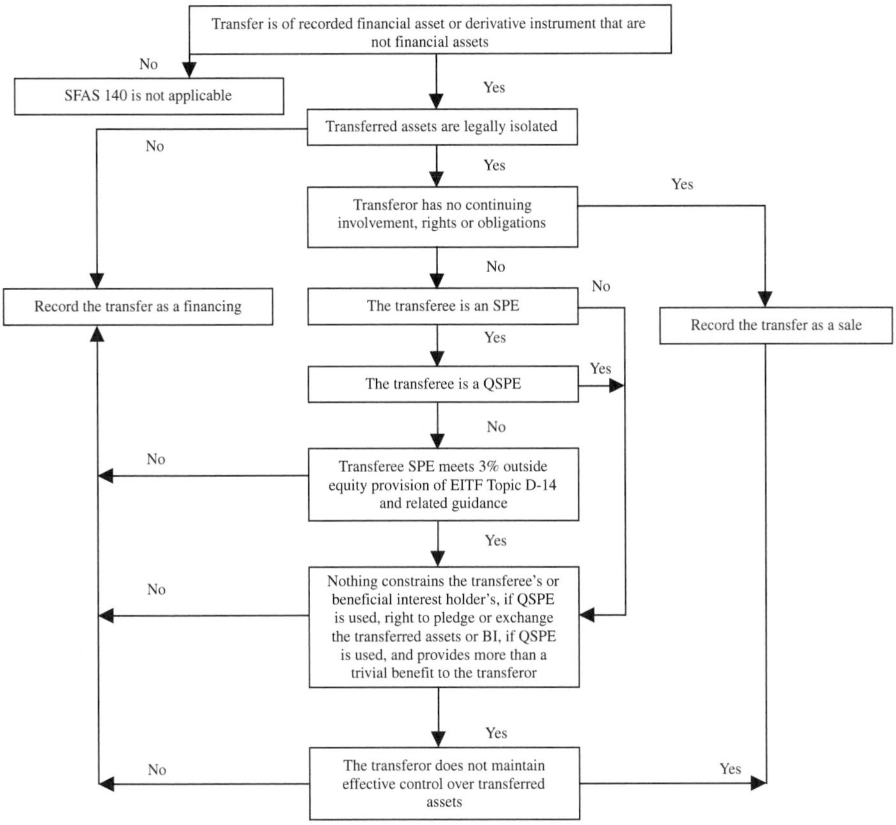

Exhibit 21.6. Decision Tree Example.

the fair value of each component. The proceeds received, the $900 of cash, represents the fair value of the interest sold. The fair value of the residual interest is determined through a discounted cash flow analysis. The cash flows to the residual holder are estimated based on the contractual cash flows of the assets, assumptions such as losses

	Fair Value of Financial Components	Percentage of Total Fair Value	Allocated Carrying Amount	Gain-on-Sale
Loans Sold	$ 900.00	80.82%	$ 808.18	$91.82
Residual Interest	188.52	16.94%	169.38	
Servicing Asset	25.00	2.24%	22.25	
	$1,113.62	100.00%	$1,000.00	
			Less Expenses	($5.00)
			Net Gain	$86.82

Exhibit 21.7. Gain-on-Sale Calculation.

and prepayments, and the cash flow waterfall with the transaction. The discount rate used to present value the estimated cash flows is commensurate within the risk of the residual interest. The fair value of the residual interest is $188.52 in this example.

Under FAS 140, an entity that contracts to service financial assets that it does not own generally will be required to recognize either a servicing asset or a servicing liability. A servicer of financial assets commonly receives the benefits of servicing—revenues from contractually specified servicing fees, late charges, and other ancillary income, including "float"—as compensation for performing the servicing activities and incurring the related costs of servicing the assets. When the benefits of servicing are more than adequate compensation for a servicer performing such servicing, the contract results in a servicing asset. Adequate compensation is defined as the amount of benefits of servicing that would fairly compensate a substitute servicer should one be required, that includes the profit that would be demanded in the marketplace. A servicing contract with adequate compensation would be able to be transferred to a substitute servicer without a corresponding payment or receipt. If the benefits of servicing are not expected to adequately compensate a servicer for performing the servicing, the contract results in a servicing liability. In the case of a transfer of assets accounted for as a sale, a servicing liability would serve to reduce the net proceeds of the sale, thus decreasing the gain on the sale or increasing the loss. A servicing asset would be treated as a retained interest in the securitized asset and, therefore, initially would be carried at an amount based on its allocated book value. FAS 140 clarifies that servicing assets and liabilities are not to be netted for financial reporting purposes. Rather, they are to be treated separately as assets and liabilities. Since the 2% contractual servicing fee in this example is more than adequate compensation, a $25 fair value resulted.

FAS 140 also requires that a transferor recognize any newly created assets obtained and liabilities incurred in a transaction. These items usually would include put or call options held or written, guarantee or recourse obligations, forward commitments to deliver additional receivables (e.g., in connection with reinvestment provisions of some credit card securitizations), swaps (e.g., provisions that convert interest rates earned by the transferee from the fixed rate paid by the debtor to a variable rate), and servicing liabilities, if applicable. These items would be initially measured at fair value. Expenses such as accounting, legal and underwriting fees reduce the gain.

(h) Subsequent Accounting. FAS 140, with certain notable exceptions concerning servicing assets and liabilities and financial assets subject to prepayment as discussed below, does not provide guidance about the subsequent accounting for items that are recorded as a result of applying its provisions. Accordingly, assets and liabilities recorded as a result of applying FAS 140 will be treated in accordance with existing generally accepted accounting principles (GAAP) applicable to the item. Some of the items emanating from transfers of financial assets may be debt securities that are addressed by FASB Statement No. 115, "Accounting for Certain Investments in Debt and Equity Securities" (FAS 115) or derivative financial instruments that are addressed by FAS 133, "Accounting for Certain Derivative Instruments and Certain Hedging Activities" (FAS 133).

FAS 140 provides that interest-only strips, loans, other receivables, retained interests in securitizations, or other financial assets that can contractually be prepaid or settled in such a way that the holder would not recover substantially all of its recorded investment (except for instruments that are within the scope of FAS 133) shall be recognized like an investment in debt securities classified as available-for-sale or trading under Statement 115. Accordingly, changes in the value of these instruments will be included in equity (other comprehensive income) until realized when they are considered available-for-sale. However, if the instruments are designated as trading, changes in fair value will be included in income immediately. Financial assets subject to prepayment risk may not be classified as held-to-maturity securities.

In late 2000, EITF Issue No. 99-20, "Recognition of Interest Income and Impairment on Purchased and Retained Beneficial Interests in Securitized Financial Assets," was issued which discusses how a transferor/originator that retains an interest in securitized financial assets or an enterprise that purchases a beneficial interest in securitized financial assets, should account for interest income and impairments while the assets are held.

EITF 99-20 adopts the prospective method for recognizing interest income. Under EITF 99-20, the holder of a beneficial interest should recognize the excess of all future cash flows estimated at the initial transaction date over the initial carrying amount as interest income over the life of the beneficial interest using the effective yield method. The holder of a beneficial interest should continue to periodically (e.g., quarterly) update the estimate of future cash flows attributable to the beneficial interest. If such evaluation results in a change (favorable or adverse taking into account both the timing and amount) in cash flows from the cash flows previously projected, then the amount of accretable yield should be recalculated and recognized prospectively as a change in the amount of periodic accretion recognized over the remaining life of the beneficial interest.

The interest must also be assessed for impairment each period. If there is an adverse change in the estimated future cash flows and the fair value is lower than the carrying amount, an impairment has occurred. The asset should be written down with the amount reflected in the income statement.

In the example above, the residual interest would be accounted for like a debt instrument classified under FAS 115 and the income and impairments would be accounted for in accordance with EITF 99-20.

FAS 140 requires that a servicing asset or liability be amortized to income or expense in proportion to and over the period of estimated net servicing income or net servicing loss. However, if the fair value of a servicing liability subsequently increases above the carrying amount (e.g., because of significant changes in the amount or timing of actual or expected future cash flows from the cash flows previously projected), the servicer should revise its earlier estimates and recognize the increased obligation as a loss in earnings. A servicing asset or liability should be assessed for impairment.

For a more detailed example of the initial gain-on-sale accounting and the subsequent accounting refer to the Appendix.

(i) Consolidation of SPEs. As discussed earlier, securitization transactions typically involve the use of a QSPE, however due to the requirements of certain deals, the SPE cannot qualify as a QSPE. This is commonly found with transactions which actively manage the assets such as arbitrage deals.

The existing accounting literature[3] focuses on control of/over an entity to determine whether an investor should consolidate the financial statements of an investee (i.e., the SPE). The consideration of control over an entity also presumes that the controlling entity also has the substantive risks and rewards of ownership. Although much of the guidance is specific to leasing SPEs, it has been consistently used in evaluating all types of SPEs in determining consolidation treatment. Holders of the equity of the SPE generally are considered to have the substantive risk and rewards of ownership, unless the equity in the SPE is not considered substantive. The current practice is to consider three percent equity as being substantive.

A frequent issue that arises when there is not substantive equity in the SPE is whether a sponsor of an SPE should consolidate the SPE in its consolidated financial statements. There is a rebuttable presumption that the transferor/sponsor should consolidate the SPE in the absence of clear evidence to the contrary. Consolidation of the SPE would result in continuing to recognize the transferred assets in the transferor's consolidated balance sheet. Determining when a company is a transferor to an SPE is usually straightforward. However, much more judgment is involved in determining the sponsor of an SPE.

The following is a list of items provided in a Securities and Exchange Commission (SEC) speech in December 2000 that are commonly considered when determining whether the company is the SPE sponsor:

- *Purpose.* What is the business purpose of the SPE?
- *Name.* What is the name of the SPE?
- *Nature.* What are the types of operations being performed (for example, lending or financing operations, asset management, and insurance or reinsurance operations)?
- *Referral rights.* Who has, and what is the nature of, the relationships with third parties that transfer assets to or from the SPE?
- *Asset acquisition.* Who has the ability to control whether or not asset acquisitions are from the open market or from specific entities?
- *Continuing involvement.* Who is providing the services necessary for the entity to perform its operations and who has the ability to change the service provider (e.g., asset management services, liquidity facilities, trust services, financing arrangements)?
- *Placement of debt obligations.* Who is the primary arranger of the debt placement and who performs supporting roles associated with debt placement?

---

[3]FASB Statement 94, "Consolidation of All Majority-Owned Subsidiaries"; EITF Topic D-14, "Transactions Involving Special-Purpose Entities"; EITF Issue 90-15, "Impact of Nonsubstantive Lessors, Residual Value Guarantees, and Other Provisions in Leasing Transactions"; EITF Issue 96-21, "Implementation Issues in Accounting for Leasing Transactions Involving Special-Purpose Entities"; EITF Issue 96-16, "Investor's Accounting for an Investee When the Investor Has a Majority of the Voting Interest but the Minority Shareholder or Shareholders Have Certain Approval or Veto Rights"; EITF Issue 97-1, "Implementation Issues in Accounting for Lease Transactions, Including Those Involving Special-Purpose Entities"; EITF Issue 97-2, "Application of FASB Statement No. 94 and APB Opinion No. 16 to Physician Practice Management Entities and Certain Other Entities with Contractual Management Arrangements"; and EITF Issue 98-6, "Investor's Accounting for an Investment in a Limited Partnership When the Investor Is the Sole General Partner and the Limited Partners Have Certain Approval or Veto Rights."

- *Residual economics.* Who receives the residual economics of the SPE including all fee arrangements?
- *Fee arrangements.* Who receives fees for asset management, debt placement, trustee services, referral services, and liquidity/credit enhancement services? How are the fee arrangements structured?
- *Credit facilities.* Who holds the subordinated interests in the SPE?

In order for transferors/sponsors of SPEs to avoid consolidating an SPE, the guidance requires that independent third parties: make substantive equity investments, typically an amount equal to a minimum of 3% of the fair value of the assets; have voting control of the SPE; and have the substantive risks and rewards of ownership of the assets of the SPE. In evaluating the consolidation criteria for SPEs, some of the common issues that need to be evaluated include:

- Is the capitalization of the SPE adequate at all levels particularly when multi-tiered SPE structures are utilized, assets held by the SPE are volatile, and/or derivatives are utilized?
- Does the owner's interest represent a residual equity interest in legal form?
- Is the equity holder truly subordinate to the debt holders?
- How are profits and losses allocated? Does the equity holder have both upside and downside potential? Is the equity investor an independent third party?
- Who has actual control over the management and activities of the SPE?
- Are the risks and rewards of ownership retained by the third party equity investor for the entire term of the SPE?

(j) Proposed Accounting for SPEs. The FASB is in the process of developing an Interpretation of FASB Statement No. 94, "Consolidation of All Majority-Owned Subsidiaries," and Accounting Research Bulletin No. 51, "Consolidated Financial Statements," which is expected to be issued in the latter part of 2002. The Interpretation will provide guidance for determining when an entity, the *Primary Beneficiary*, should consolidate another entity, an SPE, that functions to support the activities of the Primary Beneficiary. The proposed Interpretation is similar to current practice because it requires that an SPE be consolidated by another entity if the SPE is nonsubstantive and supports the activities of that other entity. The guidance in the proposed Interpretation:

- Expands the situations in which an entity is considered to be an SPE.
- Provides that interests in an SPE that are exposed to significant variability in returns for reasonably possible outcomes are used to determine which entity is the SPE's Primary Beneficiary.
- Identifies parties that shall be considered one and the same as the Primary Beneficiary for applying the requirements of the Interpretation.
- Requires an SPE's Primary Beneficiary to consolidate an SPE covered by the Interpretation unless the investment by independent, third party equity owner(s) provide the SPE with the ability to fund or finance its operations without assistance from or reliance on the Primary Beneficiary. The Interpretation presumes that condition would not exist if the level of the investment is less than 10% of

the total assets of the SPE, unless there is clear and compelling evidence to the contrary. (Prior to the proposed Interpretation, practice interpreted 3% to be sufficient equity.)

- Requires an SPE's Primary Beneficiary to consolidate an SPE unless the SPE's equity owner(s) bears all of the exposure to the first dollars of loss and its potential rewards are unlimited.

(k) Bifurcation Issues. The FASB is also expected to issue an amendment to FAS 133 in the latter part of 2002, which may require, in certain situations, the holders of beneficial interests in SPEs/QSPEs to bifurcate their interest into a debt or equity host and a derivative. For example, when fixed rate assets are transferred to a QSPE that issues floating rate senior beneficial interests and a residual interest, the residual interest would be required to be recorded as a debt instrument and an interest rate swap.

21.7 DISCLOSURES FOR SECURITIZATION TRANSACTIONS AND RELATED ASSETS. In response to growing concern expressed by analysts and investors over the adequacy of disclosures surrounding financial asset transfers, particularly the securitization of financial assets, the FASB developed disclosures to help users adequately assess the risk involved with such transactions.

If the entity has securitized financial assets during any period presented and accounts for that transfer as a sale, for each major asset type (e.g., mortgage loans, credit card receivables, and automobile loans) it should disclose:

- Its accounting policies for initially measuring the retained interests, if any, including the methodology used in determining their fair value (i.e., quoted market prices, prices for similar assets, or other valuation techniques)
- The characteristics of the securitization (a description of the transferor's continuing involvement with the transferred assets, including, but not limited to, servicing, recourse, and restrictions on retained interests) and the gain or loss from the sale of financial assets in the securitization
- The key assumptions (which may be disclosed as a range for multiple securitizations of a single asset type) used in measuring the fair value of retained interests at the time of securitization (including, at a minimum, quantitative information about discount rates, expected prepayments including the expected weighted-average life of prepayable financial assets, and anticipated credit losses, if applicable)
- Cash flows between the securitization SPE and the transferor, unless reported separately elsewhere in the financial statements or notes (including proceeds from new securitizations, proceeds from collections reinvested in revolving-period securitizations, purchases of delinquent or foreclosed loans, servicing fees, and cash flows received on interests retained)

If the entity has retained interests in securitized financial assets at the date of the latest statement of financial position presented, for each major asset type (e.g., mortgage loans, credit card receivables, and automobile loans) it should disclose:

- Its accounting policies for subsequently measuring those retained interests, including the methodology (whether quoted market prices, prices based on sales of similar assets or liabilities, or prices based on valuation techniques) used in determining their fair value. This disclosure should include whether the assets are classified as trading or available for sale, how the yield on the asset is recorded and a discussion of how impairment is assessed and measured.

- The key assumptions used in subsequently measuring the fair value of those interests (including, at a minimum, quantitative information about discount rates, expected prepayments including the expected weighted-average life of prepayable financial assets, and anticipated credit losses, including expected static pool losses, if applicable)
- A sensitivity analysis or stress test showing the hypothetical effect on the fair value of those interests of two or more unfavorable variations from the expected levels for each key valuation assumption independently from any change in another key assumption, and a description of the objectives, methodology, and limitations of the sensitivity analysis or stress test.
- For the securitized assets and any other financial assets that the transferor manages together with them:
    - The total principal amount outstanding, the portion that has been derecognized, and the portion that continues to be recognized in each category reported in the statement of financial position, at the end of the period
    - Delinquencies at the end of the period
    - Credit losses, net of recoveries, during the period
    - Disclosure of average balances during the period is encouraged, but not required

In the wake of the collapse of Enron Corporation, in early 2002 the SEC issued a financial reporting release (FR-61), which provides specific considerations for Management Discussion and Analysis (MD&A) disclosures. The SEC release was in direct response to a December 31, 2001, petition from the Big Five firms, which was endorsed by the American Institute of Certified Public Accountants (AICPA).

FR-61 focuses on disclosing arrangements with unconsolidated entities that affect liquidity or the availability of or requirements for capital resources, including:

- Relationships that are contractually limited to narrow activities that facilitate the registrant's transfer of or access to assets
- To extent of reliance on off-balance-sheet arrangements where those entities provide financing, liquidity, or market or credit risk support for registrant, engage in leasing, hedging, or expose the registrant to liability that is not reflected on the face of the financial statements
- Contingencies that are reasonably likely to affect liquidity and their effects
- Business purpose and activities
- Economic substance
- Key terms and conditions of any commitments
- Initial and ongoing relationships with the registrant and its affiliates
- Registrant's potential risk exposures resulting from its contractual or other commitments.

Other disclosures to consider include:

- Total amount of assets and obligations of the off-balance-sheet entity, with a description of the nature of its assets and obligations, and identification of the class and amount of any debt or equity securities issued by the registrant
- The effects of the entity's termination if it has a finite life or it is reasonably likely that the registrant's arrangements with the entity may be discontinued in the foreseeable future
- Amounts receivable or payable, and revenues, expenses, and cash flows resulting from the arrangements
- Extended payment terms of receivables, loans, and debt securities resulting from the arrangements, and any uncertainties as to realization, including repayment that is contingent on the future operations or performance of any party
- The amounts and key terms and conditions of purchase and sale agreements between the registrant and the counterparties in any such arrangements
- The amounts of any guarantees, lines of credit, standby letters of credit or commitments or take or pay contracts, throughput contracts or other similar types of arrangements, including tolling, capacity, or leasing arrangements that could require the registrant to provide funding of any obligations under the arrangements, including guarantees or repayment of obligors of parties to the arrangements, make whole agreements, or value guarantees.

21.8 VARIATIONS OF SECURITIZATION AND RELATED ACCOUNTING. Structured products continue to evolve. In the early 1980s, most transactions were collateralized by high-yield bonds and loans. Today, securitized assets include mortgage-backed securities, asset-backed securities, real estate investment trusts (REITS), and future cash flows. The following discusses two variations of securitization transactions: collateralized debt obligations and the securitization of future cash flows.

(a) Overview of Collateralized Debt Obligations. One of the structured products that has been widely used in the market is the collateralized debt obligation (CDO). CDOs are privately placed securitizations that were created in the late 1980s, which borrowed their structural template from another structured product—collateral mortgage obligations (CMOs). The collateral may include several different types but usually contains bonds, loans, or/and other assets. These structures may be called CBOs, collateralized bond obligations; CLOs, collateralized loan obligations; and CFOs, collateralized fund obligations.

CDOs may be structured as either a Cash Flow CDO or Market Value CDO. Cash Flow CDO structures use the ongoing cash flow from the underlying collateral pool to serve as the repayment of interest and principal on the securities. Market Value CDO structures use ongoing cash flow proceeds from the sale of the underlying collateral to serve as the repayment of interest and principal on the securities.

Cash flow structures are the dominant CDO form in terms of issuance volume. These are commonly broken down into arbitrage and off-balance-sheet transactions. Arbitrage structures are the most common cash flow form and capture the positive spread between a portfolio of high-return, high-risk assets and lower-cost, highly rated securities (liabilities) issued to purchase the underlying collateral portfolio. The second cash flow structure—an off-balance-sheet transaction—was created to reduce regulatory capital constraints by securitizing balance sheet assets. However, off-balance-sheet CDOs are also used to increase lending capacity and lower funding costs.

Market value structures—as opposed to cash flow structures—trade the underlying collateral to realize positive gains for the payment of liability interest and principal. Market value structures are "trading portfolios."

As discussed previously, under FAS 140, the transferor of assets to a CDO that is a QSPE does not have to consolidate the CDO on its balance sheet. Market Value CDOs generally will not be QSPEs because of the asset manager's ability to actively trade the CDOs assets. In addition, CDOs which purchase assets in the market (assets are not transferred to it) will not be QSPEs. Balance sheet CDOs are often structured as QSPEs so that the transferor can retain the CDOs equity but still obtain sale treatment for the assets.

(b) Overview of the Sale of Future Cash Flows. In addition to the securitization of financial assets (asset backed security [ABS], mortgage backed security [MBS], and CDOs), various forms of future cash flows such as operating leases or royalties can be securitized. Funding for these transactions is obtained based on the future cash flow stream expected. Perhaps the most famous transaction involving the securitization of future cash flows was the 1997 "Bowie Bonds" transaction, in which rock star David Bowie issued $55 million in securities backed by revenues from the future sales of his early albums.

Since the sale of future cash flows is not a sale of financial assets, the accounting for such transactions is governed by EITF No. 88-18, "Sale of Future Revenues," instead of FAS 140. According to EITF 88-18, if the seller has significant continuing involvement in the generation of the cash flows due to the investor, the proceeds received from the sale should be recorded as debt and amortized under the interest method.

21.9 INTERNATIONAL SECURITIZATION. During 2001, the worldwide ABS market was approximately $328 billion with United States issuance accounting for over 75% of the total. However, Europe, which issued over $50 billion in 2001 is now evolving into a viable and rapidly advancing securitization market as a result of recent legal and regulatory changes and the introduction of the Euro. Competitive and regulatory pressures on institutions are mounting in Europe, which have led to more focus on measures such as return on equity (ROE) and on efficient balance sheet management. As a result, securitization is expected to become one of the most important sectors in the European banking business.

Japan currently holds the third largest securitization market in the world and has grown rapidly in the past few years. In 2001, Japanese issuance totaled $22 billion. Securitization market participants believe Japan has the potential to replace Europe as the second largest market, but they are of the opinion that there is limited opportunity in the other Asian countries because the markets are too small.

In Canada, commercial paper conduits have historically been the driving force in the Canadian ABS market, which was stagnant in 2001. However, market participants believe that with tightening credit standards at banks, and the possibility of future downgrades, securitization is becoming a more important component of Canadian issuers' funding strategies as Canadian borrowers are denied access to Canada's highest-rated corporate commercial paper market.

In Latin America securitization issuance was approximately $7 billion in 2001 with

Brazil remaining the predominant player. However, due to the problems in Argentina, the immediate future of the Latin American securitization market is uncertain.

(a) International Accounting Standards. The International Accounting Standards Committee (IASC) issued IAS 39, "Financial Instruments: Recognition and Measurement," in March 1999. IAS 39 became effective for financial statements covering financial years beginning on or after January 1, 2001.

The guidance in IAS 39 is similar to U.S. GAAP in most areas. The concepts within the two frameworks are very comparable, with the primary difference being that U.S. GAAP involves more extensive detail regarding application of the principles than international accounting standards (IAS). The implementation guidance is also considerably more developed within U.S. GAAP than is the case with IAS. The primary differences between IAS 39 and the concepts embodied within U.S. GAAP include:

- U.S. GAAP requires a financial asset to be legally isolated from a transferor to allow it to be derecognized by that enterprise (a "true sale at law" concept). This concept applies even when the enterprise is in bankruptcy. IAS 39 has no such requirement.
- U.S. GAAP includes a concept of a "qualifying special-purpose entity," which, if used in connection with a securitization, avoids considerations about whether risks and rewards have been transferred to determine who should consolidate the SPE. IAS 39 does not differentiate between types of special purpose entities, and all securitization structures must include a transfer of the risks and benefits of ownership to achieve derecognition.
- The treatment of gains and losses on subsequent measurement of available-for-sale financial assets is different in that IAS 39 provides an option to record such gains and losses either directly in equity or to report them in net profit or loss for the period. U.S. GAAP requires all gains and losses on available-for-sale investments to be reported as a separate component of equity.

(b) Japanese GAAP. The Japanese accounting rules for securitization of financial assets are also very similar to FAS 140. According to Japanese GAAP, a financial asset should be derecognized if the contractual right that represents the financial asset is exercised, if the right is lost, or if control over the right is transferred to others. Control over the contractual right that represents the financial asset is transferred to others when all of the following conditions are met:

- The transferee's contractual right on the transferred financial asset is legally secured from the transferor and its creditors.
- The transferee can enjoy benefits in an ordinary manner directly or indirectly from the contractual right on the transferred financial asset.
- The transferor, in substance, does not have a right and an obligation to repurchase the transferred financial asset before the maturity date of the asset.

Like IAS 39, perfection against the originator of the assets is not required so that there remains still risk of offset of transferred assets with transferor's obligations (if the transferor is also the originator of the financial assets). Paragraph 31 of Implementation Guidelines to Accounting Standards for Financial Instruments issued by Japanese Institute of Certified Public Accountants (JICPA Guidelines) notes that "legally secured" in the first point above should be assessed considering:

- Whether the transferor can revoke the transfer based on an agreement or a circumstance
- Whether the trustee can nullify the transfer of the financial asset when the transferor is in bankruptcy procedures under the Japanese Bankruptcy Law, the Japanese Corporate Reorganization Law, the Japanese Composition Law, and other similar laws

The transferee's right is deemed to be legally secured under the current legal environment, if the transfer of the financial assets can be perfected against all third parties except for the issuer of the assets.

In addition to the legal isolation difference from U.S. GAAP, Japanese GAAP does not yet incorporate all of the QSPE rules from FAS 140 such as the permissible activities of QSPE.

(c) Canadian GAAP. Accounting Guideline 12, "Transfers of Receivables" (AcG-12), provides the accounting and reporting standards for sales, securitizations and servicing of receivables and other financial assets under Canadian GAAP. AcG-12 adopts substantially the same approach as that set out in FAS 140, although the scope of AcG-12 is narrower than that of FAS 140. The Canadian Institute of Chartered Accountants (CICA) attempted to conform AcG-12 as closely as possible to FAS 140 but several GAAP differences continue to remain because of pre-existing differences in other GAAP. The primary differences between AcG-12 and FAS 140 are:

- While both AcG-12 and FAS 140 explicitly exempt a transferor from consolidating a QSPE to which the transferor has transferred receivables, if the special purpose entity in not qualifying, the transferor must look to other applicable guidance to determine whether it should be consolidated. Since the consolidation rules are different in Canada and the United States, in some circumstances entities will be compelled to consolidate nonqualifying SPEs for U.S. GAAP purposes but not for Canadian GAAP and vice versa.
- U.S. GAAP provides specific guidance for accounting for retained interests (FAS 115 and EITF 99-20), whereas AcG-12 states that an entity should analyze the substance of a retained interest and account for that interest as a loan or an investment in accordance with Section 3025, Impaired Loans, and Section 3050, Long-Term Investments and disclose its accounting policies. Accordingly, under Canadian GAAP retained interests are generally recorded at amortized cost.
- EITF 99-20 requires the transferor to recognize the excess of all cash flows attributable to the retained interest at the transaction date over the initial investment as interest income over the life of the retained interest using the effective yield method. Canadian companies have tended to follow a similar model for recognition of income from retained interests for Canadian GAAP. However, other patterns of income recognition may also be accepted in practice.

- Under Canadian GAAP, entities accounting for their investment in retained interests as a long term investment would record a write down of the interest if there is "other than temporary" impairment. This approach appears to be more prevalent in Canada. If accounted for as a loan, entities would review the criteria in Section 3025 when assessing impairment. The amount of any write down would be measured by discounting the expected future cash flows at the effective interest rate inherent in the retained interest.

SOURCES AND SUGGESTED REFERENCES

"European Securitisation Issuance Soars to Another Record in 2001." European Securitisation Forum, The Bond Market Association, March 1, 2002.

Corrigan, Colleen. "Can ABS Kickstart Japanese Market?" *Asset Securitization Report.* Thomson Financial, May 13, 2002.

EITF Issue No. 88-18. "Sale of Future Revenues."

EITF Issue No. 99-20. "Recognition of Interest Income and Impairment on Purchased and Retained Beneficial Interests in Securitized Financial Assets."

Ernst & Young Financial Reporting Developments FASB Statement No. 140, "Accounting for Transfers and Servicing of Financial Assets and Extinguishments of Liabilities."

FASB. Consolidation of Certain Special-Purpose Entities—an interpretation of ARB No. 51 (Exposure Draft—Proposed Interpretation).

FASB Statement No. 140, "Accounting for Transfers and Servicing of Financial Assets and Extinguishments of Liabilities."

"Latin America: A Rough 2001, but a Solid Year in Issuance." *Asset Securitization Report.* Thomson Financial, January 7, 2002.

APPENDIX

This Appendix provides an example of the gain-on sale calculation and subsequent accounting sections.

III. Cash Flows Anticipated at Time of Securitization

A. Loan Cash Flow

Year Ending December 31,	Beginning Balance	Cash Credit Losses	Interest at 15%	Scheduled Principal	Prepayments	Ending Balance	Total Cash
	(A)	(B)	(C)	(D)	(E)	(A) − (B) − (D) − (E)	(C) + (D) + (E)
20X1	$ 1,000.00	10.00	$ 148.50	$ 148.50	$ 17.00	$ 824.50	$ 314.00
20X2	824.50	10.00	122.18	165.30	13.14	636.06	300.61
20X3	636.06	10.00	93.91	183.31	9.00	433.75	286.22
20X4	433.75	10.00	63.56	201.77	4.54	217.44	269.87
20X5	217.44	10.00	31.12	207.44	—	—	238.56
		$ 50.00	$ 459.26	$ 906.32	$ 43.68		$ 1,409.26

B. Cash to Senior Interest

Year Ending December 31,	Beginning Balance	Principal (1)	Interest at 6%	Ending Balance	Total Cash
	(A)	(B)	(C)	(A) − (B)	(B) + (C)
20X1	$ 900.00	159.66	$ 54.00	$ 740.34	$ 213.66
20X2	740.34	169.24	44.42	571.11	213.66
20X3	571.11	179.39	34.27	391.72	213.66
20X4	391.72	190.15	23.50	201.56	213.66
20X5	201.56	201.56	12.09	0	213.66
		$ 900.00	$ 168.28		$ 1,068.28

(1) Each period principal represents the payment on the principal for a $900 investment based on 5 yr, constant payment and constant 6% interest rate. There is no bullet payment assumed.

C. Subordinated Interest

Year Ending December 31,	Cash Flow to SPE from Loans	Servicing Paid by SPE	Cash to Senior Interest	Cash to Subordinate Interest	Fair Value of Subordinate Interest at 18.00%
	(A)	(B)	(C)	(A) − (B) − (C)	
20X0					$188.62
20X1	314.00	$20.00	$213.66	$80.34	142.23
20X2	300.61	16.49	213.66	70.47	97.36
20X3	286.22	12.72	213.66	59.84	55.05
20X4	269.87	8.68	213.66	47.54	17.42
20X5	238.56	4.35	213.66	20.55	—
	$ 1,409.26	$ 62.24	$ 1,068.28	$ 278.74	

Appendix A. Securitization.

D. Servicing Asset

Year Ending December 31,	Contractual Cash Receipt (1)	Adequate Compensation (1)	Net (1)	Fair Value of Servicing Interest at 10% Discount
				25.00
20X1	$ 20.00	$ 10.00	$ 10.00	17.50
20X2	16.49	8.25	8.25	11.00
20X3	12.72	6.36	6.36	5.74
20X4	8.68	4.34	4.34	1.98
20X5	4.35	2.17	2.17	—
	$ 62.24	$ 31.12	$ 31.12	

(1) Applied to the outstanding principal asset balance.

VI. Gain on sale (Pre-Tax)

A. Basis Allocation

	Market Value	% Market Value	Allocated Basis
Sold senior interest	$ 900.00	80.82%	$ 808.18
Retained interests:			
Subordinate interest	$188.62	16.94%	169.38
Servicing	25.00	2.24%	22.45
	213.62	19.18%	191.82
	$ 1,113.62	100.00%	$ 1,000.00

B. Pre-Tax Gain (Loss)

Sales proceeds	$ 900.00
Basis allocated to senior interest	(808.18)
Transaction expenses	(5.00)
Pre-tax income	$ 86.82

C. Accretable Yield on Subordinated Interest

Estimated cash flows (undiscounted)	$ 278.74
Allocated basis	169.38
Accretable yield	$ 109.37

D. Subordinated Interest Amortization (according to EITF 99-20)

Year Ending December 31,	Beginning Basis	Accretion at 23.92% (2)	Cash Receipts	Ending Basis	Fair Value of Subordinate Interest at 18%	Unrealized Gain/(Loss)
	(A)	(B)	(C)	(A) + (B) − (C)	$ 188.62	19.24
20X1	$ 169.38	$ 40.51	$ 80.34	$ 129.54	142.23	12.69
20X2	129.54	30.98	70.47	90.05	97.36	7.31
20X3	90.05	21.54	59.84	51.75	55.05	3.30
20X4	51.75	12.38	47.54	16.59	17.42	0.83
20X5	16.59	3.97	20.55	(0.00)	—	—
		$ 109.37	$ 278.74			

(2) Yield that results in present value of subordinate cash flow equal to allocated basis.
If assumptions change during transaction, the yield on the subordinate interest would be adjusted in accordance with EITF 99-20.

E. Servicing Interest Amortization (according to EITF 99-20)

Year Ending December 31,	Beginning Basis	Contractual Cash Receipt	Amortization (3)	Ending Basis
	(A)		(B)	(A) − (B)
20X1	$ 22.45	20.00	7.21	$ 15.23
20X2	15.23	16.49	5.95	9.29
20X3	9.29	12.72	4.59	4.70
20X4	4.70	8.68	3.13	1.57
20X5	1.57	4.35	1.57	(0.00)
		$ 62.24	$ 22.45	

(3) In proportion to the estimated servicing income (i.e. $7.21 = 20/62.24 * 22.45)

Appendix A. ***(Continued)***

F. Journal Entries and Balance Sheet

Journal entries

20X0

		Debit		Credit
Cash	$	895.00		
Subordinated Interest (AFS)		169.38		
Servicing Asset		22.45		
Loans			$	1,000.00
Gain from securitization				86.82
To record the sale				
Subordinated Interest (AFS)	$	19.24		
Unrealized gain			$	19.24
Record the SFAS 115 AFS adjustment				

Balance sheet

Assets			Liabilities and Equity		
Cash	$	895.00	Equity	$	1,000.00
Subordinated Interest (AFS)		188.62	Unrealized gain		19.24
Servicing Asset		22.45	Retained earnings		86.82
	$	1,106.07		$	1,106.07

Income Statement

Income			Expense		
Gain from securitization	$	86.82	Other	$	—
Interest Income		—	Servicing Expense		—
Servicing Income		—			
	$	86.82		$	—

20X1

		Debit		Credit
Cash	$	80.34		
Subordinated Interest (AFS)			$	39.84
Interest Income on Subordinated Interest				40.51
Record accretion on Subordinated Interest and interest received from SPE				
Cash	$	20.00		
Servicing Expense		7.21		
Servicing Income			$	20.00
Servicing Asset				7.21
Amortize Servicing Asset and record the contractual servicing fee				
Unrealized gain	$	6.56		
Subordinated Interest (AFS)			$	6.56
Record the SFAS 115 AFS adjustment				

Balance sheet

Assets			Liabilities and Equity		
Cash	$	995.34	Equity	$	1,000.00
Subordinated Interest (AFS)		142.23	Unrealized gain		12.69
Servicing Asset		15.23	Retained earnings		140.12
	$	1,152.81		$	1,152.81

Income Statement

Income			Expense		
Gain from securitization	$	—	Other	$	—
Interest Income on Subor		40.51	Servicing Expense		7.21
Servicing Income		20.00			
		$60.51		$	7.21

20X2

Cash	$	70.47		
Subordinated Interest (AFS)			$	39.49
Interest Income on Subordinated Interest				30.98
Record accretion on Subordinated Interest and interest received from SPE				
Cash	$	16.49		
Servicing Expense		5.95		
Servicing Income			$	16.49
Servicing Asset				5.95
Amortize Servicing Asset and record the contractual servicing fee				
Unrealized gain	$	5.38		
Subordinated Interest (AFS)			$	5.38
Record the SFAS 115 AFS adjustment				

Balance sheet

Assets			Liabilities and Equity		
Cash	$	1,082.30	Equity	$	1,000.00
Subordinated Interest (AFS)		97.36	Unrealized gain		7.31
Servicing Asset		9.29	Retained earnings		181.64
	$	1,188.95		$	1,188.95

Income Statement

Income			Expense		
Gain from securitization	$	—	Other	$	—
Interest Income on Subor		30.98	Servicing Expense		5.95
Servicing Income		16.49			
	$	47.47		$	5.95

20X3

Cash	$	59.84		
Subordinated Interest (AFS)			$	38.30
Interest income				21.54
Record accretion on Subordinated Interest and interest received from SPE				
Cash	$	12.72		
Servicing Expense		4.59		
# Servicing Income			$	12.72
Servicing Asset				4.59
Amortize Servicing Asset and record the contractual servicing fee				
Unrealized gain	$	4.01		
Subordinated Interest (AFS)			$	4.01
Record the SFAS 115 AFS adjustment				

Balance sheet

Assets			Liabilities and Equity		
Cash	$	1,154.86	Equity	$	1,000.00
Subordinated Interest (AFS)		55.05	Unrealized gain		3.30
Servicing Asset		4.70	Retained earnings		211.31
	$	1,214.61		$	1,214.61

Income Statement

Income			Expense		
Gain from securitization	$	—	Other	$	—
Interest Income on Subor		21.54	Servicing Expense		4.59
Servicing Income		12.72			
		$34.26			$4.59

Appendix A. ***(Continued)***

20X4

Cash	$	47.54		
Subordinated Interest (AFS)			$	35.16
Interest income				12.38

Record accretion on Subordinated Interest and interest received from SPE

Cash	$	8.68		
Servicing Expense		3.13		
Servicing Income			$	8.68
Servicing Asset				3.13

Amortize Servicing Asset and record the contractual servicing fee

Unrealized gain	$	2.47	
# Subordinated Interest (AFS)			$2.47

Record the SFAS 115 AFS adjustment

Balance sheet

Assets			Liabilities and Equity		
Cash	$	1,211.08	Equity	$	1,000.00
Subordinated Interest (AFS)		17.42	Unrealized gain		0.83
Servicing Asset		1.57	Retained earnings		229.23
	$	1,230.06		$	1,230.06

Income Statement

Income			Expense		
Gain from securitization	$	—	Other	$	—
Interest Income on Subor		12.38	Servicing Expense		3.13
Servicing Income		8.68			
	$	21.05		$	3.13

20X5

Cash	$	20.55		
Subordinated Interest (AFS)			$	16.59
Interest income				3.97

Record accretion on Subordinated Interest and interest received from SPE

Cash	$	4.35		
Servicing Expense		1.57		
Servicing Income			$	4.35
Servicing Asset				1.57

Amortize Servicing Asset and record the contractual servicing fee

Unrealized gain	$	0.83	
Subordinated Interest (AFS)			0.83

Balance sheet

Assets			Liabilities and Equity		
Cash	$	1,235.98	Equity	$	1,000.00
Subordinated Interest (AFS)		—	Unrealized gain		—
Servicing Asset		—	Retained earnings		235.98
	$	1,235.98		$	1,235.98

Appendix A. (*Continued*)

CHAPTER 22

SEGMENTAL AND FOREIGN OPERATIONS DISCLOSURES

Lee H. Radebaugh

Brigham Young University

Donna L. Street

University of Dayton

CONTENTS

22.1 INTRODUCTION. The 1950s and 1960s were characterized by a trend toward significant diversification, both by line of business and geographic area. In more recent years, diversification has continued for multinational corporations (MNC), particularly in regard to geographic activity. Accordingly, questions have surfaced as to whether consolidated financial statements are adequate where the corporation's operations comprise different activities in different geographic locations with different profitability, risk, and growth characteristics.

To the extent that the financial statements of the reporting entity do not represent the nature of that entity's activities worldwide in a transparent manner, there appears to be a need for reporting disaggregated information in segmental reports so that overall performance, risks, and future prospects can be better evaluated by investors and other users. This chapter examines the history of segmental reporting on a global basis and discusses current developments in segmental reporting. In addition, segment reports of several corporations are provided to illustrate alternative forms of segmental reporting.

22.2 EVOLUTION OF SEGMENTAL DISCLOSURE STANDARDS

(a) Demand for Information. In the case of an MNC, there are a variety of forces brought to bear on management that determine the level of disclosure that will be provided regarding the operations of the firm. These forces, both domestic and international, are summarized in Exhibit 22.1.

Although six major groups are identified in Exhibit 22.1 that influence disclosure, this chapter focuses on two of these groups of financial statement users: investors and governments. After describing the needs of these different user groups, the chapter examines the major segment reporting standards in existence today and reviews gen-

Source: Lee H. Radebaugh and Sidney J. Gray. *International Accounting and Multinational Enterprises,* 5th ed. New York: John Wiley & Sons, Inc., 2002, p. 132.

Exhibit 22.1. Multinational Corporations: Participants and Pressures for International Harmonization.

eral disclosure practices. The chapter also discusses the pros and cons of additional disclosure to the firm and discusses items of segmental data which firms should consider providing on a "voluntary" basis to better satisfy the needs of financial statement users.

The major impetus for segmental disclosures has been the needs of capital markets. During the 1950s and 1960s, the view was that financial statement analysis was difficult as firms were diversifying and thereby adding different lines of business to their traditional lines. A disaggregation of these diverse lines of business through segmental reporting would allow investors to better predict the risk and return of the firm.

Governments have also been influential in a variety of ways. As discussed later in this chapter, the initial segment reporting requirements in the United States were developed by the government rather than the accounting profession. In the United States, this governmental influence resulted from concern about the increase in the conglomerate movement.

Other sources of government influence are evident in the activities of the United Nations (UN) and the Organization for Economic Cooperation and Development (OECD), where governments are preeminent in their influence. Interest in segmental reporting within UN and OECD agencies has revolved primarily around the influence of the MNC in host countries.

(b) Influential Factors in the United States. The movement to disaggregate financial statements accelerated rapidly during the 1960s when the merger movement was in full swing. During the late 1950s, more than 60% of mergers took place between firms in the same line of business. By the late 1960s, same industry mergers had dropped to less than 50%.

The 1960s was a time of great discussion about the inadequacy of existing financial reporting standards and guidelines, especially in the case of conglomerates. The U.S. Senate Subcommittee on Antitrust and Monopoly and the Securities and Exchange Commission (SEC) both conducted a series of hearings that resulted in a call for "the kind of information needed to evaluate the experience and prospects of conglomerate companies."[1]

At the same time, a number of private-sector studies on segmental information were conducted. The most important basic studies were conducted by Mautz for the Financial Executives Institute and by Backer and McFarland for the National Association of Accountants (now the Institute of Management Accountants). These studies surveyed bankers, financial analysts, and investment advisors to determine the advantages and disadvantages of increased disclosures. These two studies formed the empirical basis for most of the discussion leading to segmental disclosure standards.

Mautz's definition of a diversified company identifies the reasons for additional disclosures. A diversified company is one "which either is so managerially decentralized or lacks operational integration, or has such diversified markets that it may experience rates of profitability, degrees of risk, and opportunities for growth which vary within the company to such an extent that an investor requires information about these variations in order to make informed decisions."[2] Thus, the key is that differ-

---

[1]Rappaport and Lerner, 1969.

[2]Mautz, 1968.

ent segments of a business may experience differences in the rates of profitability, degrees of risk, and opportunities for growth.

As noted earlier, concern for investors drove much of the discussion regarding segmental disclosures in the United States. Backer and McFarland asked financial analysts to identify the major reasons for using segmental data, and identified the following reasons: "(1) segment reports are wanted to provide knowledge of what businesses a company is in and the relative size of the several components, (2) sales and contributions to enterprise profit are wanted in forecasting consolidated profits, and (3) . . . appraisal of the success which management of a company has had in making acquisitions."[3] The view of analysts, at least as related to the first point, was that performance is affected by risk and prospects for future growth of earnings and that this performance differed significantly by industry.

In spite of the concern expressed by the investing public, as noted previously, the initial U.S. segment reporting requirements came from the government, not the accounting profession. The government seemed to be interested in information regarding growth and market concentration of firms in different product lines to facilitate public-policy decisions. As noted in congressional hearings,

> The relative profitability of different divisions and product lines should be brought out in order to appraise the competitive tactics utilizing diversification. We are operating in almost complete ignorance in this area when we do not know even the sales of many of the major firms in different lines, let alone the profitability or losses incurred in these lines. We cannot reach a judgment which is supportable in proposing legislation or changes in public policy.[4]

Surprisingly, there was little concern exhibited over geographic disclosures; most of the attention was initially focused on lines of business. As pointed out by Mautz,

> The one geographical distinction that appears reasonably clear is that between domestic and foreign operations, although even this one is questioned in practice. Once a company engages in activities within the boundaries of two or more sovereign powers, conceptually it can be concluded that the independence of those two powers subjects the company to different risks of regulation and expropriation, not to mention local customs which may influence profit levels and growth potential. The differences between operating, for example, in the United States and in some emerging country in Africa are quite apparent. On the other hand, the differences between operating in the United States and Canada or England are much less apparent. In any event, the problem of reporting foreign activities by American business companies has been dealt with elsewhere, and this particular problem seems to be satisfactorily covered by generally accepted accounting principles. Thus, it is unnecessary to regard this kind of activity as a method of diversification requiring attention in this study.[5]

While Mautz did not view foreign disclosures as a pressing issue, Backer and McFarland found that financial analysts were concerned about the disclosure of pertinent information on foreign subsidiaries. Analysts were interested in several items of geographic information, including sales and income earned in different countries or major world areas.

---

[3]Baker and McFarland, 1968, pp. 7–12.

[4]Id., p. 12.

[5]Mautz, 1968, p. 9.

(c) Demand for Information by Governments. The U.S. SEC was definitely concerned about the activities of conglomerates and indicated that the government needed more information on which to base policy decisions. Thus, the concern for investors was mixed with policy concerns over the conglomerate movement.

The spread of multinationalism has created additional issues. Governments are increasingly concerned over the activities of their firms abroad and the activities of foreign firms operating in their countries. These concerns have given rise to demands for information. Some of the demands have been issued by individual governments, but others have been, and are, currently being developed in regional and international forums, such as the European Union (EU), the OECD, and the UN.

There are several ways in which MNCs impact both home and host societies, and governments are interested in information that will help evaluate the impact of MNCs. The economic impact of a MNC occurs primarily through a balance of payments and growth and employment effects. The flow of goods occurs through importing and exporting, while capital flows occur through investments and the return on those investments, usually by way of dividends, royalties, management fees, and so on.

Because of the high degree of integration between a parent company and its subsidiaries abroad, there are usually a number of different financial flows that take place. One such flow that is politically explosive involves the payment of intracompany accounts. The transfer price established on these intracompany transactions is subject to manipulation due to the absence of a market mechanism. Hence, the price not only impacts the flow of money to satisfy the intracompany obligation but also can help determine the profitability of the transactions and, therefore, the taxes that will be collected by the respective governments. The nature of the transfer price is an important piece of information for a government.

The growth and employment effects of the MNC on the host country relate to the degree to which investment merely displaces existing business capacity or actually develops new capacity. In addition, new investment abroad can replace investment in the home country or alternatively can serve as an outlet for parts and components produced in the home country. Thus, governments are interested in the degree of investment undertaken by the MNC at home and abroad and the type of activities the firm is involved in.

22.3 SEGMENTAL STANDARDS IN THE UNITED STATES. In 1969, the SEC issued the first major segmental reporting requirements in the United States. The required disclosures were limited to sales and profit information for industry segments and related only to SEC registrants. Sales and profits (or losses) had to be disclosed for the most recent five-year period for each industry which accounted for 10% or more of the firm's sales or profits before income taxes and extraordinary items.

In 1973, two events occurred that increased the pressure for segmental disclosures. First, the New York Stock Exchange recommended that the SEC disclosures be included in the corporate annual report to shareholders, in addition to the 10K annual report. That requirement became effective in 1974. Second, the FASB decided to include disaggregated information in one of the Board's studies. Statement No. 14, "Financial Reporting for Segments of a Business Enterprise," followed in December 1976. The standard applied to all public and nonpublic enterprises-virtually all firms that issue financial statements according to generally accepted accounting principles (GAAP). The standard applied only to annual, not interim, financial statements.

Statement of Financial Accounting Standard (SFAS) 14 required companies to disclose certain information related to operations in different industries, foreign operations, export sales, and major customers. Industry segments were determined by grouping products and services by lines of business. The required disclosures for industry segments included: revenues, operating profit or loss, identifiable assets, depreciation and amortization, capital expenditures, equity method income, and investment in equity-method investees. SFAS 14 also required that revenues, operating profit, and identifiable assets be disclosed for foreign operations. In regard to major customers, where applicable companies were required to disclose the fact that revenues for any one customer accounted for 10% of total revenues and the amount of revenues from any such customer. Additionally, companies were to identify the segment(s) reporting the revenues.

In a 1993 position paper, the Association for Investment Management and Research (AIMR) noted that segment information is important but that SFAS 14 was inadequate. It argued:

> FAS 14 requires disclosure of line-of-business information classified by "industry segment." Its definition of segment is necessarily imprecise, recognizing that there are numerous practical problems in applying that definition to different business entities operating under disparate circumstances. That weakness in FAS 14 has been exploited by many enterprises to suit their own financial reporting purposes. As a result, we have seen one of the ten largest firms in the country report all its operations as being in a single, very broadly defined industry segment.[6]

The potential for improving segment reporting was also strongly expressed in the report *Improving Business Reporting—A Customer Focus.*[7] Improvements in SFAS 14 disclosures of business segment information were listed as the Committee's first recommendation. The Special Committee's list of the most important improvements needed in segment reporting included:

- Greater number of segments for some enterprises
- More items of information about segments
- Segmentation that corresponds to internal management reports
- Consistency of segment information with other parts of an annual report

As a result of the AIMR position paper, the report of the AICPA Special Committee on Financial Reporting, and other comments on SFAS 14, the FASB and Accounting Standards Board (AcSB) of the Canadian Institute of Chartered Accountants jointly developed "Reporting Disaggregated Information about a Business Enterprise." The new North American standard was issued in 1997 and became effective for fiscal years beginning after December 15, 1997.

(a) General Objectives of SFAS Statement No. 131. As noted above, an important aspect of the new North American standard is that public business enterprises must provide disaggregated information for operating (reportable) segments based on management's organization of the enterprise. Additionally, enterprise wide informa-

---

[6]AIMR, 1993, p. 60.

[7]American Institute of Certified Public Accountants Special Committee on Financial Reporting, 1994.

tion must be supplied based on products and services, the geographic areas in which the company operates, and major customers. The objective of the standard is to provide information about the different types of business activities of an enterprise to help users of financial statements:

- Better understand the enterprise's performance
- Better assess its prospects for future net cash flows
- Make more informed judgments about the enterprise as a whole

Two important aspects of the new standard include: (1) how management chooses to disaggregate the company into operating segments and (2) the items of information that are required to be disclosed for each operating segment.

(b) Operating Segments. An operating segment is defined by the FASB as a component of an enterprise:

- That engages in business activities from which it earns revenues and incurs expenses.
- Whose operating results are regularly reviewed by the enterprise's chief operating decision maker to assess the performance of the individual segment and make decisions about resources to be allocated to the segment.
- For which discrete financial information is available that is generated by or based on the internal financial reporting system.

Two or more operating segments may be aggregated into a single operating segment if aggregation is consistent with the objective and basic principles set forth in SFAS 131, the segments have similar economic characteristics, and the segments are similar in each of the following areas:

- The nature of the products and services
- The nature of the production process
- The type or class of customer for their products and services
- The methods used to distribute their products or provide their services
- If applicable, the nature of the regulatory environment

Separate information must be reported for any operating segment that meets any one of the following quantitative thresholds:

- Its reported revenue is 10% or more of the combined revenue of all other reportable segments.
- The absolute amount of its reported profit or loss is 10% or more of the greater, in absolute amount, of (1) the combined reported profit of all operating segments that did not report a loss or (2) the combined reported loss of all operating segments that did not report a loss.
- Its assets are 10% or more of the combined assets of all operating segments.

Information about operating segments that do not meet any of the above thresholds may be disclosed separately. Alternatively, operating segments that do not meet any of the quantitative thresholds may be combined to produce a reportable segment but only if the operating segments share a majority of the aggregation criteria listed above. At least 75% of total consolidated revenue must be included in reportable segments; other business activities that are not included in reportable segments may be disclosed in an "all other" category. While no limit is established in SFAS 131, the FASB indicates that as the number of reportable segments increases above 10 the company should consider whether a practical limit has been reached.

Under SFAS 131, operating segments may be based on products and services, geographic areas of operations, a combination of products and services and geographic location (mixed), or regulatory environments. The method used must be disclosed. Based on a study of U.S.-based Global 1000 companies,[8] it was found that most of these companies are managed by line of business and accordingly disclose operating segments based on products and services.

As noted above, operating segments are determined based on a company's management structure. As anticipated by the FASB, it was found that, in comparison to reporting under SFAS 14, determination of segments based on the management approach has resulted in a significant improvement in the consistency of segment information with other sections of the annual report. Also as anticipated by the FASB, research reveals that the number of operating segments reported by U.S.-domiciled Global 1000 companies increased significantly under SFAS 131 and that several companies that had claimed to operate in one line of business under SFAS 14 now provide operating segment disclosures.

(c) Information Provided for Reportable Operating Segments. In comparison to SFAS 14, SFAS 131 represents an increase in the items of segment information required to be disclosed. Since the information is available for both internal and external uses, the FASB argues the additional cost of preparation should not be substantial. However, the cost of publication and competitive disadvantage are potential issues that merit consideration.

The major categories of information that must be provided for each operating segment include:

- Information about segment profit or loss and certain revenues and expenses included in segment profit or loss (to include revenues, interest revenue, interest expense, depreciation/depletion/amortization, amount of noncash items other than depreciation/amortization that are included in the determination of segment profit/loss, unusual items, equity in the net income of investees accounted for by the equity method, income tax expense/benefit, and extraordinary items)
- Information about segment assets (to include assets, expenditures for additions to segment assets, and the amount of investment in equity method investees included in segment assets)

Under SFAS 131, the segment data represents information generated for internal purposes, not the information used in preparing the enterprise's general-purpose fi-

---

[8]Street, Nichols, and Gray, 2000.

nancial statements. Adjustments made to the internal financial information in preparing the general purpose financial statements are not included in the segment information.

(d) Information about Products and Services and Geographic Areas. If not provided as part of the operating segment data, SFAS 131 also requires disclosure of enterprise wide data based on products and services and geographic region. This includes information on revenues from each product and service or each group of similar products and services. Required disclosures for geographic regions include:

- Revenues from external customers (1) in the enterprise's country of domicile and (2) in each other country from which the operating segment derives material revenues or for all foreign customers in total if revenues from external customers in no individual foreign country is material.
- Long-lived assets located (1) in the enterprise's country of domicile and (2) in each other country in which the company holds material assets or for all foreign countries if the assets held in no individual foreign country are material.

While SFAS 14 required companies to disclose profit data by geographic region, this information is no longer required under SFAS 131. A study of U.S. based Global 1000 companies,[9] found that SFAS 131 accordingly resulted in a loss of geographic profit information. In 1997 under SFAS 14, 85% of the companies in the sample reported geographic profit data. This declined to 15% in 1998 under SFAS 131.

On a more positive note, the study found that almost all the companies in the sample reported geographic data for the country of domicile following the issuance of SFAS 131. Additionally, the research revealed an increase in the number of sample companies providing country specific data (i.e. from 4% under SFAS 14 to 28% under SFAS 131). For example, in 1997 Kellogg reported segment data for the United States, Europe, and Other. In 1998 under SFAS 131, the company reported enterprise-wide data for the United States, United Kingdom, and Other. The latter finding of the study is of considerable importance to financial statement users as another study[10] suggests that country specific geographic segment data make it possible to more accurately predict sales than do more aggregated geographic data.

In a study of U.S.-based Global 1000 and *Fortune* 500 companies,[11] a comparison was made of forecast errors for models utilizing SFAS 131 geographic sales data to forecast errors for models utilizing SFAS 14 geographic sales data. Its findings indicate a significant improvement in the predictive accuracy of geographic sales disclosures provided under SFAS 131 and suggests this enhanced predictability may be associated with the revised requirements that companies report sales for the country of domicile and for each individually material country.

On a less positive note, research[12] also indicates that the aggregation problem has not been fully resolved, as many U.S. companies continue to provide data based on

---

[9]Nichols, Street, and Gray, 2002.
[10]Nichols, Tunnell, and Waldrup, 1996.
[11]Behn, Nichols, and Street, 2002.
[12]Nichols, Street, and Gray, 2002.

a highly aggregated continental or multi-continental basis. In line with SFAS 131 guidelines, many companies now utilize the United States/Other categorization for their geographic enterprise-wide data. For example, in 1998 both Colgate and Gillette utilized the geographic grouping of United States and Other; the "Other" segment accounted for 72% and 62%, respectively, of sales for these two U.S. multinationals.

(e) Information about Major Customers. If 10% or more of the revenues of an enterprise is derived from transactions with a single customer, the enterprise must disclose that fact, the total amount of revenues from each such customer, and the identity of the operating segment or segments earning the revenues. The enterprise need not disclose the identity of a major customer or the amount of revenues that each segment derives from that customer.

(f) Interim Information. Under SFAS 131, certain financial information must be disclosed about an enterprise's operating segments in condensed financial statements of interim periods. For each operating segment, interim disclosure requirements include: revenues, a measure of profit or loss, and total assets for which there has been a material change from the amount disclosed in the last annual report.

Reporting segment data in the interim accounts represents a major change in segment reporting. The new requirements represent the FASB's response to user requests for interim data.

(g) Illustration. Exhibit 22.2 illustrates the 2001 segment reporting provided by Black and Decker, which is managed principally by products and services. Black and Decker's reportable operating segments include: Power Tools and Accessories, Hardware and Home Improvement, and Fastening and Assembly Systems. As required by SFAS 131, the company discloses the following items for each of the three reportable segments: sales, profit, depreciation and amortization, income from equity-method investees, capital expenditures, segment assets, and investment in equity-method investees. In addition, Black and Decker provides enterprise-wide information (i.e., sales) for eight product groups. Geographic enterprise-wide data includes segment sales for the United States, Canada, Europe, and Other countries and segment assets (property, plant, and equipment) for the United States, United Kingdom, and Other countries. The company additionally acknowledges the existence of a major customer.

Another interesting example of segment reporting under SFAS 131 is provided by the 2001 accounts of Kellogg Company. The company is managed in two major geographic divisions, the United States and International, with the International segment further delineated into Europe, Latin America, Canada, Australia, and Asia. Kellogg's reportable operating segments under SFAS 131 consist of the United States, Europe, and Latin America. For each reportable operating segment, Kellogg reports sales, operating profit, charges for Keebler amortization expense, depreciation and amortization expense, interest expense, income taxes, assets, and additions to long-lived assets. Additionally, Kellogg reports supplemental enterprise-wide data on geographic sales and long-lived assets for three geographic regions that include the United States, United Kingdom, and Other foreign countries. Supplemental enterprise-wide data also includes the disclosure of sales information for several products. The enterprise-wide data on products is provided in a matrix format as illus-

The Corporation has elected to organize its businesses based principally upon products and services. In certain instances where a business does not have a local presence in a particular country or geographic region, however, the Corporation has assigned responsibility for sales of that business's products to one of its other businesses with a presence in that country or region.

The Corporation operates in three reportable business segments: Power Tool and Accessories, Hardware and Home Improvements, and Fastening and Assembly Systems.

Operating Business Segments (Millions of Dollars)
Year Ended 12/31/2001

	Power Tools & Accessories	Hardware & Home Improvement	Fastening & Assembly Systems	Total	Currency Translation Adjustment	Corporate, Adjustments , & Eliminations	Consolidated
Sales to unaffiliated customers	$3121.1	$784.7	$492.4	$4398.2	$(65.1)	$ —	$4,333.1
Segment profit (loss)	252.4	59.1	69.9	381.4	(5.5)	(28.3)	347.4
Depreciation and amortization	87.2	33.6	14.7	135.5	(1.9)	25.8	159.4
Income from equity method investees	13.2	—	—	13.2	—	2.1	15.3
Capital expenditures	87.0	33.1	15.9	136.0	(2.0)	.8	134.8
Segment assets	1605.9	517.2	307.6	2430.7	(65.5)	1649.0	4014.2
Investment in equity method investees	37.6	—	.1	37.7	(1.1)	(2.7)	33.9

Enterprise Wide Data (Millions of Dollars)

Composition of sales by product group for 2001 (Millions of Dollars)	
Consumer and professional tools and product service	$2284.4
Consumer and professional accessories	314.7
Electric lawn and garden products	285.4
Electric cleaning and lighting products	122.1
Household products	47.5
Security hardware	547.3
Plumbing products	255.2
Fastening and assembly systems	476.1
Total	$433.1

Exhibit 22.2. Illustration of SFAS 131 Segmental Data Provided by Black and Decker.

Composition of sales to unaffiliated customers between those in the United States and those in other locations for 2001*	
United States	$2796.2
Canada	140.2
Total North America	2936.4
Europe	1057.4
Other	339.3
Total	$4333.1

*The Corporation markets its products and services in over 100 countries and has manufacturing sites in ten countries. Other than in the United States, the Corporation does not conduct business in any country in which its sales in that country exceed 10% of consolidated sales.

Composition of property, plant, and equipment between those in the United States and those in other countries as of the end of 2001.	
United States	$425.2
United Kingdom	72.1
Other countries	190.2
Total	$687.5

Major Customers
Sales to Home Depot, a customer of the Power Tools and Accessories and the Hardware and Home Improvement segments, accounted for $861.8 million of the Corporation's consolidated sales for the year ended December 31, 2001.

Exhibit 22.2. **(*Continued*)**

Enterprise Wide Data (Millions of Dollars)

Product information for 2001 from external customers	
United States	
Retail channel cereal	$2481.9
Snacks	2263.5
Other	1383.6
International	
Cereal	2432.2
Convenience foods	292.1
Consolidated	8853.3

Exhibit 22.3 Illustration of the Matrix Format of Segmental Reporting as Provided by Kellogg.

trated in Exhibit 22.3. In the matrix, Kellogg provides data on three products within the U.S. geographic region and two products within the International geographic region. Matrix reporting will be further discussed later in this chapter. Kellogg also discloses that its largest customer, Wal-Mart Stores, Inc. and its affiliates, accounted for approximately 11% of consolidated sales during 2001, comprised principally of sales within the United States.

Wal-Mart's 2001 segment reporting illustrates the concept of mixed operating segments. The company states that operating segments are identified "based on management responsibility within the United States and geographically for all international units." Wal-Mart's three operating segments include two product lines (Wal-Mart Stores and SAM's CLUB) and a geographic region (International). For each operating segment, the company discloses revenues from external customers, intercompany real estate income, depreciation and amortization, operating income, and assets. Supplemental enterprise-wide level data is provided for the two geographic regions (United States and Other); disclosures include long-lived assets excluding goodwill and additions to long-lived assets. Supplemental enterprise-wide level data is also provided for the ASDA subsidiary (within the International segment); disclosures include sales and long-lived assets.

22.4 GLOBAL BENCHMARK: IAS 14 REVISED. The International Accounting Standards Committee (IASC) was founded in 1973 with the objective of harmonizing accounting standards worldwide. During the late 1990s in the interest of international harmonization, the IASC worked closely with the FASB and AcSB in developing International Accounting Standard 14 Revised (IAS 14R). Accordingly, the current North American and International segmental reporting standards are similar in many respects. Before discussing IAS 14R, we will consider its predecessor.

The original version of IAS 14 was issued in 1981 and required that firms disclose sales, profits, and identifiable assets for each significant geographic and line-of-business segment.[13] Unfortunately, IAS 14 allowed companies to exercise considerable judgment in determining what was significant. The standard was also criticized for

[13]IASC, 1981.

permitting too many alternative interpretations in an attempt to accommodate its diverse constituencies. By 1990, the OECD, the International Organization of Securities Commissions (IOSCO), and a UN working group had recommended that the IASC incorporate additional disclosure items and correct implementation issues for IAS 14.[14]

While voicing strong support for segment reporting, international analysts' organizations also indicated there was much room for improvement.[15] Analysts argued that:

- Many companies hide behind broad definitions arguing they do not have industry segments.
- Geographical areas blend too many diverse countries.
- More items of data for each segment should be reported.
- The organizational units by which the business is managed and the segments for which data are reported are not articulated as important criteria for reporting segments in financial statements.

Following completion of the IASC's Comparability Project in the mid-1990s, the IOSCO announced it would review IAS and consider endorsing the standards for cross-border listings pending completion of a comprehensive set of core standards. The IOSCO's list of core standards included segment reporting. Additionally, as noted above, the North Americans were revisiting segment reporting. Hence, the time was right for the IASC to revise IAS 14 and work alongside the United States and Canada in the interest of international harmonization.

(a) General Objectives of IAS 14R. The objective of IAS 14R is to establish principles for reporting segmental information to include information about different types of products and services and different geographic areas in which the enterprise operates. Segmental information should assist financial statement users to:

- Better understand the enterprise's past performance
- Better assess the enterprise's risks and returns
- Make more informed judgments about the enterprise as a whole

(b) Primary Segments under IAS 14R. IAS 14R adopts a two- tier approach and requires information both by business and geographic region.[16] For the identification of primary segments, IAS 14R utilizes the management approach. However, in contrast to the North American standard, the IASC imposed a risk and rewards qualification. Each primary segment determined via the management approach must exhibit similar risk or reward characteristics; otherwise, the groupings are modified based on the risk and rewards approach.

A business or geographic segment should be considered as a reportable segment if a majority of its revenue is earned from sales to external customers and:

---

[14]Albrecht and Chipalkatti, 1998.
[15]McConnel and Pacter, 1995.
[16]IASC, 1997.

- Its revenue is 10% or more of the total revenue of all segments, or
- Its segment result is 10% of more of the combined result of all segments in profit or the combined result of all segments in loss, whichever is greater in absolute amount, or
- Its assets are 10% or more of the total assets of all segments

If a segment does not satisfy any of the above thresholds, a company may still elect to designate it as a reportable segment. Alternatively, the segment may be combined with other similar segments that do not satisfy the above thresholds. Criteria to consider when determining whether segments are similar and hence may be combined include:

- Similarity of economic and political conditions
- Relationships between operations in different geographic areas
- Proximity of operations
- Special risks associated with operations in a particular area
- Exchange control regulations and
- The underlying currency risks

Reportable segments must account for at least 75% of the total consolidated enterprise revenue. Otherwise, additional reportable segments must be identified, even if they do not satisfy the 10% thresholds listed above.

A study of the pre- and post-IAS 14R disclosures of a sample of companies preparing IAS-based financial statements,[17] found a significant increase in the consistency of segment information with other sections of the annual report. This result is associated with the requirement that primary segments now be determined based on the management approach.

Although the study did not find a significant increase in the average number of primary segments reported under IAS 14R, several of the companies in the sample provided primary segment disclosures under IAS 14R that had previously claimed to operate in one line of business thereby representing a significant improvement. On a less positive note, the study found that under IAS 14R several companies continue to claim to operate in one line of business while the annual report taken as a whole suggests the existence of multiple line of business segments, thereby suggesting these companies are not adhering to the spirit of the standard.

(c) Secondary Segments. Under IAS 14R, primary segments are determined based on the internal organization of the enterprise. If the primary tier is based on business/geographic segments, the second tier is based on geographic/business segments. If the company's organizational structure resembles neither business segments nor geographic segments, IAS 14R requires the company to choose between business segments and geographic segments for its primary and secondary tiers. In contrast to the North American standard, mixed segments (see above discussion of Wal-Mart's segmental reporting) are not allowed.

---

[17]Street and Nichols, 2002.

(d) Information Required for Primary and Secondary Segments. The disclosure requirements of IAS 14R and the North American standards are very similar. For primary segments, IAS 14R disclosure requirements include: revenue, result, assets, liabilities, capital expenditures, depreciation, noncash expenses other than depreciation, and equity method income. For secondary segments, IAS 14R requires disclosure of revenue, assets, and capital expenditures. One study[18] found that a benefit of the revision of IAS 14 has been a significant increase in the number of items of information disclosed for each primary and secondary segment.

The study noted that of considerable concern is the finding that under IAS 14R, when geographic regions constitute the secondary segments, many companies continue to utilize the broad, vague geographic groupings for which the original version of IAS 14 was often criticized. An example is provided by the geographic groupings (secondary segments) reported by Bayer (see Exhibit 22.4). Analysts argue that disaggregated data based on geographical areas that blend too many diverse countries are of limited usefulness.

IAS 14R also encourages disclosure of segment cash flow information and allows for matrix reporting. A matrix presentation gives information on the interrelationship of the line of business and geographic segments. Hence, within each line of business a company reports data for each geographic region. Examples of matrix reporting are provided later in this chapter.

(e) IAS 14R and SFAS 131 Compared. While IAS 14R and the North American standards are similar, there are important differences in addition to those noted above. IAS 14R requires a standardized measure of segment result for all segments, whereas the North American approach allows for the disclosure of any profitability measure that is used internally. In addition, IAS 14R requires that segment information be prepared according to the accounting policies adopted for the consolidated financial statements, whereas the North American approach accepts internally reported information, even if it is prepared using accounting standards that differ from GAAP (i.e., those used in the consolidated accounts).

(f) Illustration. Exhibit 22.4 utilizes Bayer's 2001 segmental reporting to illustrate the disclosure requirements of IAS 14R. In addition to IAS 14R required and recommended disclosures, Bayer provides a considerable number of voluntary disclosures. These voluntary disclosures will be further discussed in Section 22.5.

As noted in Exhibit 22.4, Bayer Group is managed on the basis of 14 business groups, which for the purpose of reporting primary segments are aggregated into seven segments. For each primary segment, Bayer provides the following required disclosures: sales, intersegment sales, operating result, total assets, equity-method income, capital expenditures, amortization and depreciation, and liabilities. Bayer additionally reports segmental data for four geographic regions. The required disclosures include: sales, total assets, and capital expenditures.

As noted previously, IAS 14R recommends the disclosure of segment cash flow data. While Bayer discloses "gross cash flow" for both primary business segments and secondary geographic segments, the information may be of somewhat limited usefulness as it ties back to "gross cash provided by operating activities" in the con-

---

[18] Id.

In accordance with IAS 14 (Segment Reporting), a breakdown of certain data in the financial statements is given by segment and geographical region. The segments and regions are the same as those used for internal reporting. The aim is to provide users of the financial statements with information regarding the profitability and future prospects of the Group's various activities. To allow a more accurate appraisal of continuing operations, the discontinuing operations are shown separately.

The Bayer Group is managed on the basis of business groups, which are aggregated into reportable segments according to economic characteristics, products, production processes, customer relationships and methods of distribution. There are currently 14 business groups, which are aggregated here into 7 reportable segments.

KEY DATA BY SEGMENT (1)

	Health Care		Agriculture		Polymers Chemicals		
Reportable Segments	Pharmaceuticals & Biological Products	Consumer Care & Diagnostics	Crop Protection	Animal Health	Plastics & Rubber	Polyurethanes, Coatings & Colorants	Chemicals
Euros in millions—2001							
Net sales (external)	5,729	4,104	2,708	988	5,581	5,207	3,749
• Change in euros	–6.7%	+5.6%	+10.3%	–1.1%	–4.0%	+2.6%	+9.9%
• Change in local currencies	–6.7%	+5.0%	+10.7%	–1.1%	–5.0%	+2.1%	10.0%
Intersegment sales	38	2	102	5	116	138	456
Other operating income	62	49	102	13	87	51	53
Operating result before exceptionals	383	388	453	172	288	146	271
Return on sales before exceptionals	6.7%	9.5%	16.7%	17.4%	5.2%	2.8%	7.2%
Exceptional items	(332)	(47)	0	0	(50)	(100)	(68)
Operating result	51	341	453	172	238	46	203
Return on sales	0.9%	8.3%	16.7%	17.4%	4.3%	0.9%	5.4%
Gross cash flow	229	534	550	163	587	614	379
Capital invested	5,352	3,799	3,884	645	6,405	8,051	4,774
CFROI	4.2%	14.0%	13.9%	22.8%	8.9%	7.5%	7.7%
Equity-method income	0	0	0	0	0	0	0
Equity-method investments	16	0	0	0	27	773	13
Total assets	5,303	3,956	3,488	734	5,867	7,493	4,216
Capital expenditures	415	267	215	49	592	492	483
Amortization and depreciation	364	291	247	40	482	604	334
Liabilities	1,869	1,271	1,130	379	1,339	2,311	1,797
Research and development expenses	1,242	252	292	98	134	186	114
Number of employees (as of Dec. 31)	26,800	14,900	10,900	3,900	17,900	15,100	19,500

Exhibit 22.4. Illustration of IAS 14R Segmental Data Provided by Bayer.

KEY DATA BY SEGMENT (2)

Segments	Reconciliation	Continuing Operations	Discontinuing Operations	Bayer Group
Euros in millions—2001				
Net sales (external)	872	28,938	1,337	30,275
• Change in euros		+1.1%		–2.2%
• Change in local currencies		+0.8%		–2.5%
Intersegment sales	(857)			
Other operating income	63	480	340	820
Operating result before exceptionals	(246)	1,855	76	1,931
Return on sales before exceptionals		6.4%		6.4%
Exceptional items	(16)	(613)	293	(320)
Operating result	(262)	1,242	369	1,611
Return on sales		4.3%		5.3%
Gross cash flow	(230)	2,826	97	2,923
Capital invested	556	33,466	1,392	34,858
CFROI		8.3%		8.2%
Equity-method income	12	12	14	26
Equity-method investments	158	987	179	1,166
Total assets	4,933	35,990	1,049	37,039
Capital expenditures	40	2,553	64	2,617
Amortization and depreciation	41	2,403	113	2,516
Liabilities	9,616	19,712	307	20,019
Research and development expenses	170	2,488	71	2,559
Number of employees (as of Dec. 31)	3,000	112,000	4,900	116,900

Exhibit 22.4. **(*Continued*)**

KEY DATA BY REGION

Regions	Europe	North America	Asia/ Pacific	Latin America/ Africa/ Middle East	Reconciliation	Continuing Operations	Discontinuing Operations	Bayer Group
Euros in millions—2001								
Net sales (external)—by market	11,659	9,473	4,660	3,146		28,938	1,337	30,275
Net sales (external)—by point of origin	12,999	9,806	3,817	2,316		28,938	1,337	30,275
• Change in euros	+0.6%	+1.1%	+1.5%	+3.4%		+1.1%		–2.2%
• Change in local currencies	+0.5%	–1.9%	+7.3%	+2.5%		+0.8%		–2.5%
Interregional sales	3,154	1,927	226	116	(5,423)			
Other operating income	312	70	48	50		480	340	820
Operating result before exceptionals	1,707	23	241	219	(335)	1,855	76	1,931
Return on sales before exceptionals	13.1%	0.2%	6.3%	9.5%		6.4%		6.4%
Exceptional items	(272)	(278)	(14)	(30)	(19)	(613)	293	(320)
Operating result	1,435	(255)	227	189	(354)	1,242	369	1,611
Return on sales	11.0%	–2.6%	5.9%	8.2%		4.3%		5.3%
Gross cash flow	2,037	632	312	225	(380)	2,826	97	2,923
Capital invested	16,355	12,808	2,711	1,607	(15)	33,466	1,392	34,858
CFROI	12.5%	4.7%	11.3%	14.5%		8.3%		8.2%
Equity-method income	12	0	0	0		12	14	26
Equity-method investments	351	618	2	16		987	179	1,166
Total assets	17,298	12,652	3,132	1,834	1,074	35,990	1,049	37,039
Capital expenditures	1,620	560	255	118	0	2,553	64	2,617
Amortization and depreciation	1,227	918	150	104	4	2,403	113	2,516
Liabilities	9,769	6,407	1,382	673	1,481	19,712	307	20,019
Research and development expenses	1,559	690	68	9	162	2,488	71	2,559
Number of employees (as of Dec. 31)	64,600	23,200	12,600	11,000	600	112,000	4,900	116,900

Exhibit 22.4. ***(Continued)***

solidated cash flow statement. Hence, segmental "gross cash flow" represents operating results adjusted for income taxes currently payable, depreciation and amortization, change in long-term provisions, and gains on retirements of noncurrent assets. A more useful disclosure would perhaps be to disclose cash flow provided by operating activities for each segment (see the Oerlikon-Buhrle Group example provided in Section 22.5).

22.5 OTHER SEGMENT REPORTING STANDARDS. Historically, segmental reporting requirements in most countries have been somewhat limited. However, as the "international benchmark" was raised with the issuance of IAS 14R and the new North American standards, some major countries responded with efforts to converge with these internationally recognized segmental reporting standards. For example, effective for fiscal years beginning on or after April 1, 1998, Japan modified its guidelines[19] to come more in line with the original U.S. segment reporting standard (SFAS 14). As part of its IASC convergence project in 2000, Australia issued a new standard that removes differences with IAS in regard to segmental reporting.[20] Additionally, in 1998, Germany passed the "Law for Control and Transparence in Companies" and the "Law for Improved Equity Raising Capabilities."[21] One important change associated with the new laws was that segment reporting became mandatory for fiscal years beginning after December 31, 1998. *GAAP 2001*[22] notes no significant differences between the current German segment reporting requirements and IAS 14R.

As of 2002, the European Union's (EU) Fourth Directive only required companies to disclose sales revenues for geographic and industry segments. Additionally, no specific guidelines were supplied regarding what constitutes a segment. However, segmental reporting in the EU will be significantly impacted in 2005 when the use of IAS, including IAS 14R will increase notably. In March 2002, the European Parliament voted to require all EU listed companies, by 2005 at the latest, to prepare consolidated accounts in accordance with IAS. Hence, all EU listed companies will eventually adopt IAS 14R. Additionally, countries based in Central and Eastern Europe that hope to soon join the EU must now consider the significance of the EU regulation.

22.6 COST/BENEFIT CONSIDERATIONS. Given the different segment reporting standards and practices that exist, a firm must consider several issues as it determines the form and extent of its segmental disclosures.

(a) Benefits of Segmental Disclosures. Analysts argue that segment data is "essential, fundamental, indispensable, and integral to the investment analysis approach."[23] These important users of financial statement data contend that segment data enables the user to better understand an enterprise's past performance and facilitates judgments about the enterprise as a whole including a better assessment of risks and prospects.

---

[19]Chapman, 1999.

[20]Andersen, BDO, Deloitte Touche Tohmatsu, Grant Thornton, KPMG, PricewaterhouseCoopers, 2002.

[21]Miller European Accounting Guide, 1999.

[22]Andersen et. al., 2000.

[23]AIMR, 1993.

As the disclosure requirements of SFAS 131 and IAS 14R are relatively new, academic researchers have not yet had an opportunity to comprehensively examine the predictive ability and value relevance of these new standards. However, as prior research has provided evidence that segment data is useful, it is logical to anticipate that future research will support analysts' view that the segmental data provided by SFAS 131 and IAS 14R is indeed highly useful. For example, prior research indicates that earnings forecasts based on line of business data are more accurate than those based on consolidated earnings.[24] While results have been mixed, recent research also indicates segment based forecasts outperform consolidated based forecasts. Additionally, there is some evidence that disclosure of both line of business and geographic segment data result in a decrease in market assessments of risk of the disclosing company. Research also supports a significant relationship between geographic disclosures and market risk assessments.

(b) Costs of Segmental Disclosures. Although well-defined segmental disclosures might help potential investors better understand the firm and thus make better investment decisions, there are costs associated with providing these disclosures externally. A major cost that must always be considered in relation to requiring added disclosure is the cost of compiling, processing, and disseminating the information. However, in regard to SFAS 131 and IAS 14R, most of the required disclosures are already collected internally. As operating/primary segments are based on the company's organizational structure, management already receives considerable information on these segments. Hence, it is easy for management to disclose a subset of that information in the annual report.

A second and more persuasive argument is the cost of competitive disadvantage, especially in the disclosure of profit information. This argument is posed more by MNCs than any other argument. The reason for the concern is based on the wide disparity of standards and practices across and within countries. Another competitive problem exists for firms that are single-industry firms operating in different geographic regions. By providing sales and profit information for different geographic regions, they might be allowing more diversified competitors to learn a great deal about them.

22.7 VOLUNTARY DISCLOSURES. In addition to the disclosures currently required by FASB Statement No. 131 and/or IAS 14R, other pieces of segmental data may be useful to financial statement users. Yet, research[25] indicates that voluntary disclosures provided by companies applying SFAS 131 and IAS 14R, respectively, are very limited.

As noted previously, IAS 14R requires the disclosure of segment liabilities. In the Exposure Draft preceding SFAS 131, the FASB (1996) stated that disclosure of segment assets and liabilities together with interest revenue and interest expense included in segment profit/loss would provide information about the financing activities of the segment, but SFAS 131 does not require U.S. companies to report segment liabilities. A study[26] found that very few of the U.S. based Global 1000 companies voluntarily disclosed segment liabilities. Hence, in regard to segment liabilities, with

---

[24]See Radebaugh and Gray, 2002 for a review of this literature.

[25]Street, Nichols, and Gray, 2000 and Street and Nichols, 2002.

[26]Street, Nichols, and Gray, 2000.

few exceptions, users of U.S. GAAP financial statements are missing information viewed as useful by both the FASB and IASC (now IASB).

IAS 7, "Cash Flow Statements," notes that disclosing cash flow information for each industry segment and geographic segment is relevant to understanding the enterprise's overall financial position, liquidity, and cash flows.[27] Accordingly, IAS 7 and IAS 14R both encourage, but do not require, disclosure of segment cash flow information. In the Exposure Draft preceding SFAS 131, the FASB noted that the Board considered requiring disclosure of operating cash flow for each operating segment; however, the Board eventually elected not to require the disclosure.[28] Studies have found that few of the companies following U.S. GAAP or IAS disclose segment cash flow data. Hence, with few exceptions, the users of U.S. GAAP and IAS financials are denied access to information viewed as useful by the FASB and IASC (now IASB).

In the Exposure Draft preceding SFAS 131, the FASB argued that disclosure of research and development (R&D) included in segment profit/loss would provide users with information about the operating segments in which an enterprise is focusing its product development efforts. The Board also noted that disclosure of R&D had been requested by a number of financial statement users and was specifically requested in both the AICPA's Special Committee report and the AIMR's 1993 position paper. Yet, neither SFAS 131 nor IAS 14R require disclosure of R&D by segment. Again, users are denied access to potentially useful information as studies,[29] found that few companies following U.S. GAAP or IAS disclose R&D data by segment.

While research indicates the disclosure of voluntary segmental data by U.S. GAAP and IAS GAAP companies is limited, there are notable exceptions. For example, as illustrated in Exhibit 22.4, Bayer, which prepares financial statements in accordance with IAS, provides several pieces of voluntary data in its 2001 accounts. Voluntary disclosures for Bayer's line of business–based primary segments include: multiple measures of segment profitability and segment assets, R&D, number of employees, gross cash flow, and select ratios (return on sales and cash flow return on investment). While only three items of information are required to be disclosed for Bayer's secondary segments, which are based on geography, the company provides all items required for primary segments plus those listed above.

While the IASC (now IASB) and FASB argue that segment cash flow data is useful, as noted in section 22.3, Bayer's disclosure of "gross cash flow" may be of somewhat limited use. A more useful format for providing segment cash flow data is provided by the 1999 segmental disclosures of Oerlikon-Buhrle Group (now Unaxis) as illustrated in Exhibit 22.5. In its 1999 accounts, Oerlikon-Buhrle, which at the time was in the process of discontinuing several industry segments, disclosed funds from/used by operations, funds from/used by investing activities, and funds from/used by financing activities for each of the company's primary segments. The segment cash flow data ties to the company's consolidated cash flow statement.

As noted previously, IAS 14R allows companies to utilize matrix reporting. The IASC argues that a "matrix presentation," whereby both line of business segments

---

[27] IASC, 1997.

[28] Street, Nichols, and Gray (FASB Statement No. 131 companies) and Street and Nichols (IAS 14R companies).

[29] Street, Nichols, and Gray, 2000 and Street and Nichols, 2002.

	Core Businesses	Oerlikon Contraves Defense	Bally	Oerlikon-Buhrle Immobilien	Pilatus	Zurich	Total
Orders received	2040	289	329	45	417	33	3153
Orders on hand	756				145		901
Sales by region							
Switzerland and Liechtenstein	64	44	52	45	28	33	266
EU countries	915	36	150		53		1154
North America	457	26	74		230		787
Asia	385	39	39		73		536
Other areas	72	11	14		51		148
	1893	156	329	45	435	33	2891
Sales by location							
Switzerland and Liechtenstein	369	112	74	45	226	33	859
EU countries	918	22	150				1090
North America	413	18	71		204		706
Asia	191	4	28				223
Other areas	2		6		5		13
	1893	156	329	45	435	33	2891
Capital expenditures in fixed assets							
Switzerland and Liechtenstein	32	4	1	31	5	1	74
EU countries	48	1	2				51
North America	37						37
Asia	6						6
Other areas	1						1
	124	5	3	31	5	1	169

Exhibit 22.5. Illustration of Matrix Reporting Format and Disclosure of Segmental Cash Flow Data Provided by Oerlikon-Buhrle Group 1999 Accounts (in CHF Millions).

	Core Businesses	Oerlikon Contraves Defense	Bally	Oerlikon-Buhrle Immobilien	Pilatus	Zurich	Total
Number of employees							
Switzerland and Liechtenstein	1835				996	198	3029
EU countries	3458						3458
North America	1247				45		1292
Asia	560						560
Other areas	24				3		27
	7124				1044	198	8366
Net assets	773				205	37	1015
—Assets	1509				319	41	1869
—Liabilities	736				114	4	854
Shareholder's equity including minority interest	882				143	40	1065
R&D	150	15			23		188
Operating result	111	–29	–30	15	12	1	80
Result before taxes	67	–27	–29	11	16	0	24
Income taxes	–13	0	2	–4	–3	0	–18
Net income/loss including minority interest	54	–27	–27	7	13	0	6
Funds from/used by							
Operations	122	–36	–42	–7	12	4	53
Investing activities	138	80	–23	–66	–7	0	122
Financing activities	157	–82	–22	22	3	–3	75

Exhibit 22.5. ***(Continued)***

and geographical segments are presented as primary segment formats with full segment disclosures on each basis, will often provide useful information if an enterprise's risks and rewards are strongly affected both by differences in line of business and the geographic areas in which it operates. A matrix form of presentation gives information on the interrelationship of the line of business and geographic segments. Hence, within each line of business a company reports data for each geographic region. As IAS 14R allows, but does not require matrix reporting, the information is provided only on a voluntary basis. A study[30] identified very few instances of matrix reporting in a review of the segmental reporting of IAS companies. This is unfortunate as both risk and expected return are dependent on the extent to which specific industry activities are committed to specific countries. A matrix presentation provides a more accurate assessment of business prospects. This is because the effect of changes in political, economic, or social conditions in any country will depend on the specific lines of business conducted by the MNE in the country concerned.

As illustrated in Exhibit 22.5, the Oerlikon-Buhrle Group utilizes matrix reporting in its 1999 accounts. Within each of six line of business based primary segments, the company discloses sales by region, sales by location, capital expenditures, and number of employees for five geographic regions. As of the 2002 accounts, the restructured company (now UNAXIS), continues to utilize matrix reporting. In the 2002 accounts, within each of four line of business–based primary segments (Information Technology, Surface Technology, Components and Special Systems, and Other), the company discloses the same four items of segmental data for four geographic regions (Japan and Asia/Pacific, Europe, North America, and Other areas).

22.8 THE FUTURE. In June 2002, the IASB announced that the Board's new program of technical projects would include segment reporting. The focus of the segmental reporting project is to achieve convergence on a topic "on which the IASB believes that a high-quality solution is available from existing international and national accounting standards." Our review of the segmental reporting standards of the IASB and its standard setting partner the FASB indicates several possible modifications to IAS 14R and FASB Statement No. 131 that should be considered in this important effort to converge the two standards.

The U.S. FASB should consider expanding U.S. disclosure requirements to include: (1) liabilities for operating segments and (2) operating profit for geographic segments. Both the IASB and FASB should consider requiring the disclosure of cash flow information and R&D for primary/operating segments. Additionally, both standard setters should further consider the merits of encouraging or requiring matrix reporting.

Several changes should additionally be considered in regard to geographic segments. The IASB should consider modification of the guidelines regarding identification of geographic segments to move more in line with SFAS 131, which requires disclosure of geographic data for the country of domicile and any country responsible for a material portion of total sales or assets. Given the number of companies that continue to report geographic segments based on broad vague regions, both the IASB and FASB should reconsider the advice of the American Accounting Association's

[30]Street and Nichols, 2002.

Financial Accounting Standards Committee, which recommended that geographic segments for sales should be determined based along country boundaries or operations in each of the seven major industrialized countries of the world.[31]

SOURCES AND SUGGESTED REFERENCES

Andersen, BDO, Deloitte Touche Tohmatsu, Ernst & Young, Grant Thorton, KPMG, and PricewaterhouseCoopers. *GAAP 2001: A Survey of National Accounting Rules Benchmarked against International Accounting Standards*, 2002.

Albrecht, W. B., and N. Chipalkatti. "New Segment Reporting." *CPA Journal*, May 1, 1998.

American Institute of Certified Public Accountants (AICPA). *Improving Business Reporting—A Customer Focus*. Report of the AICPA Special Committee on Financial Reporting, 1994.

Association for Investment Management and Research. *Report of Association for Investment Management and Research Corporate Information Committee Including Evaluation of Corporate Financial Reporting in Selected Industries for the Year 1991-92*. New York: AIMR, 1993.

Backer, Morton, and Walter B. McFarland. *External Report for Segments Of A Business*. New York: National Association of Accountants, 1968.

Barth, M. E., T. B. Bell, D. W. Collins, G. M. Crooch, J. A. Elliott, T. J. Frecka, E. A. Imhoff, W. R. Landman, and R. G. Stephens. American Accounting Association Financial Reporting Standards Committee Response to the FASB Discussion Memorandum, "Reporting Disaggregated Information by Business Enterprises, Accounting Horizons, September 1994, pp. 75–82.

Barth, M. E., T. B. Bell, D. W. Collins, G. M. Crooch, J. A. Elliott, T. J. Frecka, E. A. Imhoff, W. R. Landsman, and Bruce K. Behn, Nancy B. Nichols, and Donna L. Street. "The Predictive Ability of Geographic Segment Disclosures: SFAS 131 versus SFAS 14." *Journal of International Accounting Research*, Vol. 1, 2002.

Chapman, Paul. "Accounting Standards Are Not Just a Technicality." *Independent Business Weekly*, May 19, 1999.

Financial Accounting Standards Board. *Statement of Financial Standards No. 14: Financial Reporting for Segments of a Business Enterprise*. Stamford, CT: Financial Accounting Standards Board, 1976.

Financial Accounting Standards Board. *Proposed Statement of Financial Accounting Standard: Reporting Disaggregated Information About a Business Enterprise*. Stamford, CT: FASB, 1996.

Financial Accounting Standards Board. *Statement of Financial Accounting Standards No. 131: Disclosures about Segments of an Enterprise and Related Information*. Stamford, CT: FASB, 1997.

International Accounting Standards Committee. *International Accounting Standard No. 14: Reporting Financial Information by Segment*. London: IASC, 1981.

International Accounting Standards Committee. *International Accounting Standard No. 14R: Reporting Financial Information by Segment (Revised)*. London: IASC, 1997.

Mautz, R. K. *Financial Reporting by Diversified Companies*. New York: Financial Executives Research Foundation, 1968.

McConnell, P., and P. Pacter. "IASC and FASB Proposals Would Enhance Segment Reporting." *CPA Journal*, August 1, 1995.

Miller European Accounting Guide. "Germany: Recent and Expected Future Developments," 1999.

Nichols, Nancy B., Donna L. Street, and Sidney J. Gray. "Geographic Segment Disclosures in the United States: Reporting Practices Enter a New Era." *Journal of International Accounting, Auditing, and Taxation*, Vol. 9, No. 1, 2000, pp. 59–82.

[31]Barth, Bell, Collins, Crooch, Elliott, Frecka, Imhoff, Landman, and Stephens, 1994.

Nichols, D., L. Tunell, and B. Waldrup. "An Exploratory Study of the Effect on Forecast Accuracy of Using Different Geographic Segment Data Sources." *Journal of International Financial Management and Accounting*, Vol. 7, 1996, pp. 125–136.

Radebaugh, Lee H., and Sidney J. Gray. "Multinational Corporations: Participants and Pressures for International Harmonization." *International Accounting and Multinational Enterprises*, 5th ed. New York: John Wiley & Sons, Inc., 2002, pp. 132.

Rappaport, Alfred, and Eugene M. Lerner. *A Framework for Financial Reporting by Diversified Companies.* New York: National Association of Accountants, 1969.

Street, Donna L., and Nancy B. Nichols. "LOB and Geographic Segment Disclosures: An Analysis of the Impact of IAS 14 Revised." *Journal of International Accounting, Auditing, and Taxation*, Vol. 11, 2002, p. 2.

Street, Donna L., Nancy B. Nichols, and Sidney J. Gray. "Segment Disclosures under SFAS 131: Has Business Segment Reporting Improved?" *Accounting Horizons*, September 2000, pp. 259–285.

CHAPTER 23

CORPORATE ENVIRONMENTAL AND SOCIAL REPORTING

Carol Adams
Monash University
Geoffrey Frost
University of Sydney
Sidney J. Gray
University of New South Wales

CONTENTS

23.1 INTRODUCTION. This chapter is concerned with the public reporting of environmental and social information—this may be disclosure within the annual report, a special environmental (or other titled) report, or on the company Web page. The predominant feature is that it is reporting by the company targeted to the general users of such information, and is not specific reporting to regulators on a specific issue. For example, there are mandatory reporting guidelines such as the Toxic Release Inventory (TRI) in the United States. Such reporting is not covered in this chapter because it is reporting for a specific regulator and was not initiated to improve reporting to the general public.

23.2 ENVIRONMENTAL REPORTING

(a) Reporting Regulations. Until recently, disclosure on environmental performance has been predominantly a voluntary undertaking that on occasion fell within the jurisdiction of various accounting standards due to the materiality of the event. However, the past few years have seen the introduction of mandatory reporting requirements in a number of countries. The following is a brief description of mandatory environmental reporting requirements in a selection of countries.

(i) United States. Registrants to the U.S. Securities and Exchange Commission (SEC) are required to disclose material information to actual and potential shareholders related to environmental performance, compliance and liabilities. In this context, the SEC Regulation S-K Item 101, Item 103, and Item 303 require disclosure of material information on environmental performance. Regulation S-K Item 101 (Description of Business) requires registrants to disclose the material effects of complying or failing to comply with environmental requirements on capital expenditures, earning and competitive position. Regulation S-K Item 103 requires that SEC registrants disclose, on at least a quarterly basis, pending procedures or proceedings known to be contemplated by a governmental authority such as the Environmental Protection Agency (EPA). Such disclosure is qualified by the concept of materiality. Regulation S-K Item 303 (Management Discussion and Analysis of Financial Condition and Results of Operations) requires the disclosure of environmental contingencies that may reasonably have a material impact on net sales, revenue or income from continuing operations.[1]

(ii) Australia. In 1998, Australia introduced the requirement that companies mandatorily disclose their environmental performance. The initial introduction of s.299(1)(f) of the Corporations Act was controversial due to its introduction requiring broad consultation, and hence was subject to a government inquiry after enactment. Despite considerable opposition from corporations and associated legal and accounting firms, the provision remains. Section 299(1)(f) of the Australian *Corporations Act* states:

> 299. Annual Directors' Report—General Information
>
> (1) General information about operations and activities:
>
> The Directors' Report for a financial year must:
>
> . . .
>
> (f) if the entity's operations are subject to any particular and significant environmental regulation under a law of the Commonwealth or of a State or Territory—details of the entity's performance in relation to environmental regulation.

The key to disclosure under s.299(1)(f) is that it relates to significant regulation, which was not defined in the Corporations Act. The Australian Securities and Investment Commission (ASIC) have determined that significant does not necessarily mean material (which is the basis of the SEC's regulations). However, ASIC also did not provide a definition of significant. This has resulted in companies recognizing and listing the regulations by which they must abide. Prior research[2] has indicated that the introduction of s.299(1)(f) has resulted in a significant increase in the level

---

[1]Environmental Protection Agency, 2001.
[2]Frost, 2001.

of disclosure of environmental information by Australian companies, particularly in the area of acknowledgement of breaches in environmental regulations. (See Exhibit 23.1)

(iii) Denmark. Denmark has required mandatory environmental reporting since 1996, with approximately 3,000 companies now required to publish a "green account." Green accounts were introduced as an amendment to the Environmental Protection Act in June 1995 and states in s.35a(1):

Performance in relation to environmental regulation

BHP Billiton Limited's performance in relation to environmental regulation during 2001 (i.e. 12 months from 1 July 2000 to 30 June 2001) is measured by:

- the number and amount of fines and prosecutions incurred by BHP Billiton Limited's world wide operations (Table 1); and
- the number of environmentally significant incidents (including non-compliances) that occurred in BHP Billiton Limited's world wide operations. There were no significant incidents (i.e. severity rating 3 or above) reported for 2001, based on BHP Billiton Limited's internal severity rating scale (tiered 1 to 5 in terms of increasing severity).

Table 1: Fines and Prosecutions (2001)

BHP Business	Fines and Prosecutions
Minerals	• La Plata mine, New Mexico Coal, US, in July 2000 received a fine of US$1,210 regarding an Office of Surface Mining inspection in March 2000, and subsequent Notice of Violation relating to road use and maintenance, and sediment control measures. • Tower mine, Illawarra Coal, NSW, Australia, in March 2001 received two fines of $1,500 each for failure to comply with EPA licence conditions regarding recording of water flow rates. • Appin mine, Illawarra Coal, NSW, Australia, in June 2001 received a $1,500 fine for failure to comply with EPA licence conditions regarding recording of water flow rates.
Petroleum	• Liverpool Bay, UK, in November 2000, received a fine of £40,000 following an oil spill of 345 bbls in June 1998.
Steel	• Chullora Service Centre, NSW, Australia, received a $1,500 fine for contravening a license condition (late submission of certificate) in August 2000. • Port Kembla steelworks, NSW, Australia, in October 2000 received three fines of $1,500 each for sinter plant stack opacity exceedences. • Port Kembla steelworks, NSW, Australia, in February 2001 received 10 fines of $1,500 each. These related to various offences, including failure to carry out emission surveys, fugitive dust emissions, emissions from a blocked standpipe cap, and sinter plant stack opacity exceedences.
Transport and Logistics	• None

Exhibit 23.1. Disclosure from BHP Billiton Annual Report—Mandatory Requirement.

> The Minister for Environment and Energy can lay down rules on the duty of listed companies periodically to prepare green accounts. The statement of accounts shall indicate the significant consumption of energy, water and raw material and the type and quantity of pollutants . . . forming part of the production process, which are discharged from the enterprise to air, water and soil or form part of products and waste.

In December 1995, the Ministry for Environment and Energy issued statutory order No. 975 which provided detail of the specific information to be provided.

The Danish government in 1999 undertook a review of the effectiveness of the legislation, which included the analysis of 550 green accounts, interviews with managers responsible for green accounts, people with a background or interest in green accounts, the EPA, neighbors of polluting enterprises, and consumers.[3] Regarding the environmental reporting law generally, the review concluded positively. Of most interest, the review found that approximately "50% of the firms who undertook environmental reporting believed that they had achieved financial benefits which arose from the producing of the accounts which compensated for the costs involved."[4] At the same time it was noted that the distribution of costs and benefits did, however, result in "winners and losers" and it was concluded that evidence from the review of the Danish law "points towards this form of environmental accounting as having significant benefits." [5]

(iv) Netherlands. In 1997, the Environmental Management Act was extended to incorporate environmental reporting. The environmental reporting decree in the Netherlands has required that companies from 1999 produce two sets of environmental accounts: one for the authorities and another for the general public. The Act (through sections 12.1 to 12.10) sets out that companies licensed by the province and which have a substantial environmental impact can be required to produce each year an environmental report for the authorities (government report) or an environmental report for the general public (public report). While the report to the authorities is specifically targeted to meet regulators' needs, the public report is intended for all stakeholders.

The specific categories on which disclosure is required include:

- The nature of the establishment and the activities and processes in the establishment
- The adverse effects on the environment caused by the establishment including a summary of relevant quantitative data
- The technical, organizational, and administrative measures taken by the facilities installed in respect of the establishment in order to protect the environment
- Information on the main changes that have taken place in the reporting year in relation to the previous reporting year
- Developments that may reasonably be expected in the next reporting year

(v) Norway. The Norwegian Law of Accounts (introduced as an extension to the Norwegian Accounting Act in 1998) requires the disclosure of environmental information within the Directors' Report, if a firm has a significant environmental impact.[6]

---

[3]Bebbington 1999.
[4]Id, p. 4.
[5]Id.
[6]Kolk, 1999.

The environmental reporting requirement is through regulations on corporate financial disclosures and responsibilities to shareholders. The basis of the regulation is further analysis of activities of the enterprise in an environmental context, and to provide an overview of the environmental obligations. From the accounts it should be possible to understand which ambitions and targets the company has set, and what environmental limitations are expected from the authorities.

(b) Overview of Regulations. Mandatory reporting can be classified as that which focuses on the financial risks associated with the impact on the environment or regulations that require a "full account" of a company's impact on the environment (these are classified in Exhibit 23.2). Those regulations that focus on the financial may be seen as a bridge between existing accounting regulations and the increasing importance of environmental issues. The requirement for "full" disclosure of environmental impacts to external stakeholders is much less usual, with a number of countries requiring components of full disclosure but only to government agencies for monitoring environmental performance and to collate inventories of environmental impact (e.g., the TRI in the United States). The disclosure of impact has typically been dealt with through voluntary environmental reporting guidelines.

(c) Voluntary Guidelines. The introduction of mandatory environmental reporting guidelines has been relatively recent for many countries, whereas there is a plethora of guidelines or voluntary standards on the reporting of environmental and social issues. Exhibit 23.3 lists some of these guidelines or standards and gives a web address for further information.

Many of these guidelines argue for further voluntary disclosure by companies on their environmental performance, suggesting that such disclosure improves public perception of the company's performance (further discussion on voluntary environmental reporting is undertaken below). Further discussion on selected guidelines is undertaken in a latter section.

(d) Voluntary Disclosures. The voluntary reporting of social and environmental information by companies has a long history. A 1982 study[7] observed that U.S. Steel had engaged in social reporting for over eight decades. A similar study[8] of an Australian company (BHP) also observed the existence of social reporting over an ex-

[7]Hogner, 1982.
[8]Guthrie and Parker, 1989.

Country	Regulation Type	Disclosure Requirement
United States	Corporate	Compliance and liabilities
Australia	Corporate	Compliance
Denmark	Environment	Resource consumption
Netherlands	Environment	Environmental impact
Norway	Accounting	Targets and regulations

Exhibit 23.2. Mandatory Regulations.

Full Name of Standard	Abbreviation Used	Further Information
AccountAbility 1000 Series	AA1000S	*www.accountability.org.uk*
Amnesty International's Human Rights Guidelines for Companies	Amnesty	*www.amnesty.org.uk/business/pubs/hrgc.shtml*
Agence de Rating Social et Environmental sur les Enterprises	ASPI	*www.arese-sa.com/*
Dow Jones Sustainability Group Index	DJSGI	*www.sustainability-index.com/*
ECCR/ICCR Benchmarks for Global Corporate Responsibility	ECCR/ICCR	*www.web.net/~tccr/benchmarks/*
Eco-Management and Audit Scheme	EMAS	*europa.eu.int/comm/environment/emas/*
Ethical Trading Initiative Base Code	ETI	*www.ethicaltrade.org*
EU Eco-label criteria	Eco-label	*europa.eu.int/comm/environment/ecolabel*
Forest Stewardship Council's Principles and Criteria for Forest Management	FSC	*www.fscoax.org*
FTSE4Good Selection Criteria	FTSE4Good	*www.ftse4good.com*
Global Reporting Initiative Guidelines	GRI	*www.globalreporting.org*
IFOAM Basic Standards	IFOAM	*www.ifoam.org*
International Organization for Standardization ISO 9000 & 14000	ISO9000/14000	*www.iso.ch*
Organisation for Economic Co-operation and Development Guidelines for Multinational Enterprises	OECD	*www.oecd.org/daf/investment/guidelines/*
Social Accountability 8000	SA8000	*www.sai.org*
SIGMA Guidelines	SIGMA	*www.projectsigma.com*
Global Sullivan Principles	Sullivan	*www.revleonsullivan.com*
UN Global Compact	UN GC	*www.unglobalcompact.org*
WHO/UNICEF International Code on Marketing of Breastmilk Substitutes	WHO / UNICEF	*www.who.int/nut/documents/code_english.PDF*

Source: Forstater et al. "Mapping Standards for Corporate Social AccountAbility," AccountAbility, 2002.

Exhibit 23.3. Standards and Guidelines on Aspects of Environmental, Social, and Ethical Reporting.

tended period. The development and adoption of voluntary environmental reporting has however been a more recent phenomenon with both studies identifying such disclosure occurring from the 1970s. Since that time there has been considerable academic research on both environmental and social reporting.

In the examination of the extent of reporting on environmental issues, a study of U.S. companies observed that disclosure was not complete when compared to an index, and that disclosure bore little relationship with actual environmental performance.[9] Results from more recent research still observe no association with measures of disclosure levels and selected measures of performance.[10] What has however become apparent is that the number of firms including some environmental disclosure has increased, as well as the quantity of information provided[11] and the inclusion of environmental performance data (see, for example, Exxon Mobil).

Prior research has, however, predominantly focused on the annual report as the source of environmental reporting. But companies today use many alternate mediums to communicate on environmental performance, from their Web site to stand-alone environmental reports. A study[12] has shown that where companies have adopted alternate reporting mediums such as an environmental report, there has been a subsequent decrease in the information disclosed within the annual report.

Current global environmental reporting trends with respect to the use of environmental reports have been tracked by KPMG's International Survey of Corporate Sustainability. KPMG defines *reports* as environmental, health and safety, social, community and sustainability reports, and a combination of these. The results of their most recent survey[13] indicated a "significant change in the number, scope and quality of reports." The survey of reporting practices focused upon the Global *Fortune* Top 250 companies from the Global *Fortune* 500, and the Top 100 companies in 19 countries, and found that 45% and 23%, respectively, produced a report. The majority of these reports were classified as Environment, Health, and Safety Reports.

23.3 SOCIAL AND ETHICAL REPORTING

(a) Regulations. Very few countries have any regulations concerning reporting on social and ethical issues other than with respect to employment conditions and pay. Perhaps one of the most promising developments in terms of its potential to improve corporate social responsibility and accountability is the European Commission's Green paper on Corporate Social Responsibility published in July 2001. The Green Paper aimed to:

> . . . launch a wide debate on how the European Union could promote corporate social responsibility at both the European and international level, in particular how to make the most of existing experiences, to encourage the development of innovative practices, to bring greater transparency and to increase reliability of evaluation and validation. It suggests an approach based on the deepening of partnerships in which all actors have an active role to play. (para 7)

Particular concerns within the Green Paper are:

- The role of stakeholders, particularly employees, in promoting socially responsible practices
- Integration of corporate responsibility issues into day-to-day management and strategic planning

---

[9]Wiseman, 1982.
[10]Fekrat, Inclan, and Petroni, 1996.
[11]Gamble, Hsu, Kite, and Radtke, 1995; Gray, Kouhy, and Lavers, 1995.
[12]Frost, 2001.
[13]KPMG, 2002.

- Ensuring that corporate social responsibility standards are respected throughout supply chains
- Improving the extent and quality of verification
- Increasing the volume of socially responsible investment

While the Green Paper aimed to stimulate debate on new ways of promoting corporate social responsibility (para 93), it does *not* suggest that the outcome must be increased legislation. However, this may indeed be an outcome in some Member States. France became the first EU country to react to the Green Paper through legislation with the introduction of mandatory reporting in February 2002. As well as information on environmental impacts, reports must include information on how they cooperate with trade unions, civil society, neighborhood communities, and non-governmental organizations (NGOs) (*www.environnement.gouv.fr*).

(b) Guidelines. In contrast to the scarcity of mandatory reporting requirements there is a plethora of guidelines or voluntary standards on social and ethical issues. Exhibit 23.3 above lists some of these guidelines or standards and gives a web address for further information.

A report for the European Commission's Directorate General (EC DG) on Employment and Social Affairs prepared by AccountAbility[14] groups the guidelines or standards into four groups: aspirational principles and codes of practice (i.e., those that lack an external audit mechanism); guidelines for management systems and certification schemes; rating indices typically used by socially responsible investment agencies; and accountability and reporting frameworks. Examples in each category, together with information on the level of involvement of various stakeholders, are shown in Exhibit 23.4.

The AccountAbility 1000 (AA1000) framework[15] differs from other guidelines in that its focus is on the *processes* of reporting rather than on *what* should be reported. Two particularly important parts of this process are the involvement of stakeholders and governance structures. Robust processes involving stakeholders are important if accountability to stakeholders is to be achieved. Sound governance structures are important to ensure that stakeholders are heard, that responsibilities are clear, and that social and ethical issues are included in strategic planning and day-to-day decision making.[16] AA1000 is described as an "integrating" guideline and the framework sets out the extent to which the key stages of the process model (stakeholder engagement, planning, accounting, auditing and reporting, and embedding) are incorporated into other social and ethical standards. Other surveys of standards and guidelines on corporate social reporting can be found in Exhibit 23.5.

Perhaps the best-known guidelines on social reporting are the GRI guidelines.[17]

---

[14]Forstater et al., 2002.
[15]AccountAbility, 1999.
[16]Adams, 2002a.
[17]Global Reporting Initiative, 2000.

	Organizations Involved						
	Old Organizations					New Organizations Formed	
Standard	Government/ Multilateral Body	Business/ Business Grouping	Technical Standards Organization	NGO/NGO Grouping	Commercial Ratings Body	New Standards Body	Multisector Partnership
Aspirational Principles and Codes of Practice							
UN GC	•	✓✓					•
Amnesty				•			
ETI	✓✓	✓✓✓		✓✓✓			•
Sullivan		✓✓		✓✓✓		•	
OECD	•	✓	✓	✓			
WHO/UNICEF	•	✓		✓			
ECCR/ICCR				•			
Management Systems and Certification Schemes							
SA8000	✓✓	✓✓✓		✓✓✓		•	
ISO	✓	✓	•	✓			
EMAS	•						
EU Eco-label	•						
FSC		✓✓✓		✓✓✓		•	
Rating Indices							
DJGSI		✓		✓	•		
FTSE4Good		✓		✓	•		
ASPI		✓		✓	•		
Accountability and Reporting Frameworks							
GRI	✓✓	✓	✓	✓✓✓	✓	•	
AA1000S	✓	✓✓✓	✓	✓✓✓	✓	•	

Source: Forstater et al. "Mapping Standards for Corporate Social AccountAbility," AccountAbility, 2002.

NB Abbreviations used are detailed in Exhibit 23.3.

Key to symbols: • — Institutional home; ✓✓✓ — Involved at governance level; ✓✓ — Involved as member or supporter; ✓ — Included in consultation; blank space — No involvement.

Exhibit 23.4. Types of Standard/Guideline and Types of Organizations Involved.

They prescribe the issues which companies should report on and say little about process. They cover a range of sustainable development issues. These were extended in the draft sustainability reporting guidelines released for public comment in April 2002.[18]. Although the GRI guidelines require stakeholder consultation, there is little guidance as to the form it should take. This must be addressed if stakeholder dialogue is to be a robust exercise in enhancing trust and minimizing risk rather than simply a

[18]Id.

Box 1: Existing CSR Standards Surveys

- Comparison of Selected Corporate Social Responsibility-Related Standards, BSR (2001) compares 7 key standards. *www.bsr.org*
- ILO Business and Social Initiatives Database. An exhaustive database of documents relating to CSR including standards, searchable by sector, country and type of initiative. *http://oracle02.ilo.org:6060/vpi/vpisearch.first*
- Maquila Solidarity Network Codes Resources. Compares major multistakeholder labour codes. www.maquilasolidarity.org/resources/codes/index.htm
- OECD Codes of Corporate Conduct Inventory looks at 233 voluntary codes. *www.oecd.org/ech/act/codes.htm*
- Private Initiatives and Labour Standards: A Global Look, ILO (1998) reviews 215 codes and standards in relation to labour issues. *www.unglobalcompact.org/un/gc/unweb.nsf/content/ilostudy.htm*
- The SIGMA Standards Overview, Sigma Project (2001) gives an overview of 21 standards. *www.projectsigma.org.uk*
- U.S. Council for International Business Compendium of Corporate Responsibility Initiatives (2001). Outlines the 20 of the major international standards. *www.uscib.org/docs/01_10_24_cr_compendium.pdf*

Source: Forstater et al. "Mapping Standards for Corporate Social AccountAbility," AccountAbility, 2002.

Exhibit 23.5. Surveys of CSR Standards.

legitimating exercise which companies can hide behind in the way that they did with the Sullivan Principles.[19] The case of ICI in the United Kingdom illustrates that simply telling companies *what* they should report on is insufficient to ensure accountability.[20]

As well as guidelines, reporting award schemes also have an influence on the quality of corporate social reporting. In the United Kingdom, the Institute of Social and Ethical AcccountAbility (ISEA) and the Association of Chartered Certified Accountants (ACCA) run a joint awards scheme covering social reporting only, the Social Reporting Awards. This scheme started in 1999 and in 2001 there were 26 entries for the awards.[21]

(c) Disclosures

(i) General. A wide variety of Key Performance Indicators (KPIs) covering social issues are used in company reports. It is often not clear whether they cover all the issues considered to be material by shareholders. Some companies use indicators derived from internal data only, while others include KPIs based on stakeholder views of various issues obtained through questionnaire surveys. KPIs used by Shell are shown in Exhibit 23.6 and include: safety statistics; number of countries in which their operations have staff forums and grievance procedures; country of origin of

[19]Arnold and Hammond, 1994.
[20]Adams, 2002b.
[21]ACCA, 2002.

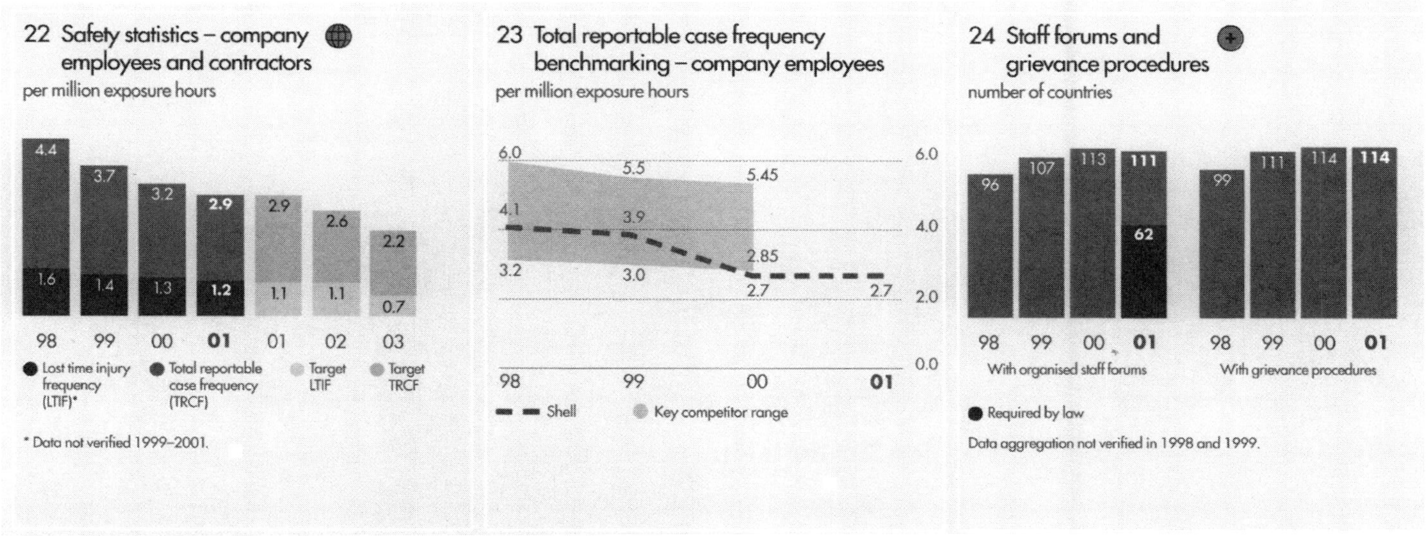

Exhibit 23.6. KPIs on P36 of the Shell Report, 2001.

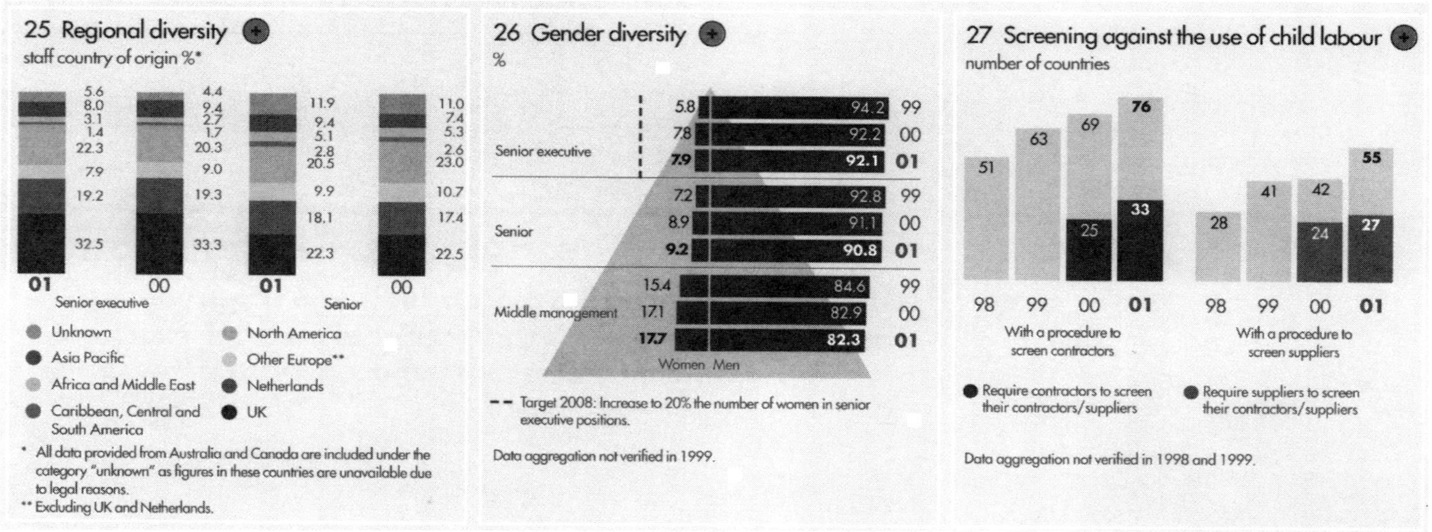

Exhibit 23.6. (*Continued*)

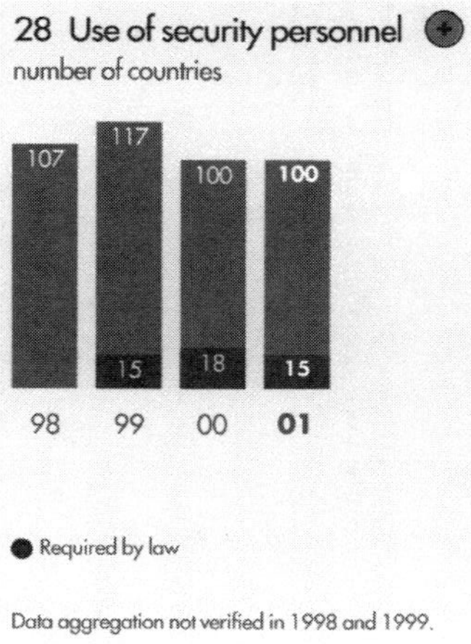
28 Use of security personnel
number of countries
107
117
100
100
15
18
15
98
99
00
01
Required by law
Data aggregation not verified in 1998 and 1999.

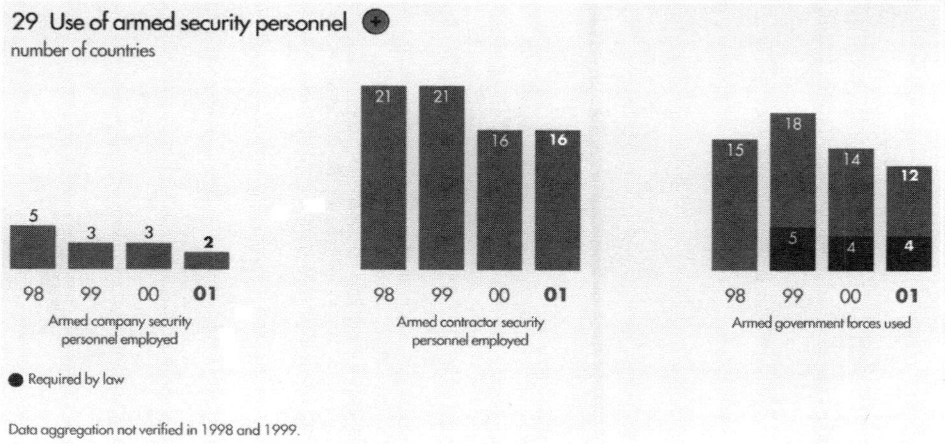
29 Use of armed security personnel
number of countries
5
3
3
2
98
99
00
01
Armed company security personnel employed
21
21
16
16
98
99
00
01
Armed contractor security personnel employed
15
18
14
12
5
4
4
98
99
00
01
Armed government forces used
Required by law
Data aggregation not verified in 1998 and 1999.

Exhibit 23.6. (*Continued*)

staff at senior executive and senior levels; gender balance at senior executive, senior, and middle management levels; numbers of suppliers to screen against the use of child labor; and use of security personnel.

(ii) Equal Opportunities. Reporting on equal opportunities issues worldwide is generally very poor.[22] Novo Nordisk's reporting on this represents best practice (see Exhibit 23.7). It provides quantified data and shows the representation of ethnic minorities in the population as well as in the company itself. The representation of women is shown at various levels in the hierarchy and employees have been consulted on their views.

[22]Adams and Roberts, 1995.

Target

Each Executive Vice President and Senior Vice President has to establish a plan with targets for their organisation to address equal opportunities issues in 2002.

Gender Representation in Management
Another indicator of equal opportunities is the extent to which men and women are perceived to have equal career opportunities. At Novo Nordisk, we are pursuing the goal of increasing the representation of women at management level. The table below illustrates the current status of women in management. One of the parameters of our succession planning system is to increase the number of women candidates selected as successors for vacant management positions.

In our employee survey, eVoice 2001, we asked our employees to state on a scale from 1 to 5 the extent to which they see men and women as having equal opportunities at Novo Nordisk. Of the more than 80% employees who returned the eVoice questionnaire, 67% responded positively to this statement. However, men tend to agree more than women with the statement that Novo Nordisk is pursuing equal opportunities. About three quarters, or 73%, of the male respondents responded positively, compared to 60% of the female respondents.

Dealing with Harassment or Other Discriminatory Behaviour in the Workplace
Any employee who believes he or she has been or is being harassed or discriminated against should promptly take action. The EO Toolbox offers a series of steps to either confront the person doing the harassing, or report the behaviour to superiors or to the Human Resources department.

If the issue is not resolved, as a final solution the issue may be brought to the attention of the Novo Nordisk Ombudsman. He will be responsible for investigating the issue, hearing the parties involved and suggesting a satisfactory solution.

Representation of Men/Women as at 1 January 2001

NN Top Management (Danish Organisation)	Total	Men	Women
CEO/Executive Vice Presidents	5	5	0
Senior Vice Presidents	13	11	2
Vice Presidents/ Senior Principal Scientists	174	137	37
Managers/Principal Scientists	752	527	225

Representation of Immigrants/Descendants of Immigrants as at 1 January 2001

	Representation of Immigrants/Descendants of Immigrants	Of Which from LDC[1]	Representation of Immigrants/Descendants of Immigrants at Management Levels	Of Which from LDC[1]
Novo Nordisk Denmark	5.6%	1.5%	6.0%	0.8%
Denmark Total[2]	7.3%	3.9%	—	—

These figures are the only obtainable approximation to ethnicity allowed by Danish law.
These figures will continue to be collected as part of future evaluation of equal opportunities programmes.

[1]Less Developed Countries (UN definition).
[2]The figures represent the population group 15–65 years of age.

Exhibit 23.7. Men, Women, and Immigrants on P36 of Novo Nordisk's Reporting on the Triple Bottom Line, 2001.

(iii) Community. The activities of companies have a major impact on local communities. The German chemical company Henkel takes particular care in consulting local communities. Exhibit 23.8 provides details of the number of complaints received by the company and the nature of those complaints.

Complaints from Neighbors	**1999**	**2000**
(Complaints attributable to Henkel)		
Number of sites covered	*107*	*127*
Sites that received complaints	22	21
Sites that received more than 5 complaints	4	4
Number of Complaints	**88**	**82**
Of these, due to		
– odor	52	43
– noise	29	33
– dust	7	6
Improvement Measures Initiated	**76**	**55**
Cause Already Eliminated	**34**	**42**

External Certification

Facility audits by independent auditors are an important instrument for ensuring compliance with SHE requirements and thus for reducing risks. SHE audits by independent Henkel experts are a key instrument in this context. In addition, Henkel Group companies in all regions of the world also have their environmental management systems certified to international standards by accredited external verifiers, if this yields competitive advantages in the market. By the end of 2000, 41 major production sites had been certified under the Eco-Management and Audit Scheme (EMAS) of the European Union and/or to the international ISO 14001 standard. These sites account for 46 percent of Henkel's total production. Furthermore, two of the four business sectors and Cognis have adopted the long-term objective of achieving certification of all their production sites.

Production Sites Certified to International Standards

Belgium	Henkel Belgium, Herent	▒
	Henkel-Ecolab, Tessenderlo	▒
Brazil	Cognis Brasil, Jacarei	▒
	Henkel Loctite Adesivos, Itapevi	▒
	Henkel Loctite Adesivos, Jacarei	▒
	Henkel Surface Technologies Brasil, Diadema	▒
China	Henkel Chemicals, Guangzhou	▒
Denmark	Henkel-Ecolab, Valby	▒
France	Henkel-Ecolab, Châlons-en-Champagne	▒
	Henkel-France, Châlons-en-Champagne	▒
	Henkel France, Reims	▒
Germany	Cognis Deutschland—Grünau, Illertissen	▒■
	Cognis Deutschland—Neynaber, Loxstedt	▒■
	Cognis Deutschland—Stalo, Lohne	▒
	Henkel Bautechnik, Unna	▒■
	Henkel Fragrance Center, Krefeld	▒■
	Henkel, Düsseldorf-Holthausen*	■
	Henkel Genthin, Genthin	▒
	Henkel Oberflächentechnik, Herborn-Schönbach	▒■
	Henkel Teroson, Heidelberg	▒
	Kepec Chemische Fabrik, Siegburg	■
	Lang Apparatebau GmbH, Siegsdorf	▒
	Thompson-Siegel, Düsseldorf-Flingern	▒
Great Britain	Henkel Consumer Adhesives, Winsford	▒
Hungary	Henkel Magyarország, Vác	▒
India	Henkel SPIC India, Karaikal	▒
Ireland	Cognis Ireland, Cork	▒
	Henkel-Ecolab, Bray	▒
	Loctite Ireland, Ballyfermot	▒
	Loctite Ireland, Tallaght	▒
Italy	Henkel S.p.A. Divisione Surface Technologies, Caleppio di Settala	▒
Netherlands	Henkel-Ecolab, Nieuwegein	▒
Poland	Henkel Polska, Racibórz	▒
Puerto Rico	Loctite Puerto Rico, Sabana Grande	▒
Slovenia	Henkel-Ecolab, Maribor/Studenci	▒
Spain	Cognis Ibérica, Barcelona/Zona Franca	▒■
	Cognis Ibérica, Terrassa	▒
	Henkel Adhesivos, Santa Perpétua	▒
	Henkel Ibérica, La Coruña	▒
	Henkel Ibérica, Montornés	▒
Sweden	Henkel Surface Technologies Nordic, Mölndal	▒■

*The largest production facility of Cognis Deutschland GmbH occupies part of the site.

▒ ISO 14001

■ EMAS (EU Eco-Management and Audit Scheme)

Exhibit 23.8. Complaints from Neighbors from P16 of Henkel's Safety, Health, and Environment Report, 2000.

(iv) Verification. As mentioned earlier, there is concern that company reports do not fairly reflect their activities and impacts and that they may be used as a public relations and legitimating exercise. A recent trend with the issue of the separate report on social or environmental issues is the inclusion of some form of verification statement. A recent survey by KPMG of global mining companies found that 38% of companies surveyed produced a separate report, and that of the Canadian and Australian companies 40% included some form of external verification (or audit). An external audit is no guarantee that reports will not be used as a legitimating exercise. For external audits to add value from a stakeholder perspective, they must be conducted by appropriately qualified people who both understand the audit process and accept the ethical, social and environmental responsibilities of companies.[23] They must also be carried out using generally accepted auditing guidelines and, crucially, the criteria for qualification of the audit report must be clear. At present there are no guidelines that adequately cover the ethical, social and environmental audit process. There is an urgent need for their development and enforcement for companies operating globally. AccountAbility published a consultation document on the issue in June 2002 and plans to develop a full assurance standard following the consultation period.

At present, many companies do not provide an assurance statement and where they do the scope of the work is often limited. For example, the scope of the work, which is determined by the company itself, carried out by KPMG on ICI's 1999 report was limited to one part of the reporting process. The Ernst & Young audit report of BP dated March 12, 2001, provides an example of an audit much broader in scope. The terms of reference included, for example, reviewing "a selection of external media sources for reports relating to BP's adherence to its policies, as a check on the appropriateness of the information reported and statements made in the report" (*http://www.bp.com*).[24]

The increase in reporting on the Internet, whereby companies can change their disclosures frequently, further emphasises the need to define the scope of such audits. There is concern that much of the data on the Internet is not audited. The Ernst & Young report of BP specifically includes publication on the Internet and, unusually, provides some comfort:

> BP periodically updates the report to provide information on company activities and to reflect progress in performance. As and when new assertions, statements and performance data are published by BP, they are reviewed by Ernst & Young. The date appearing on the Ernst & Young statement shows the last date at which information has been reviewed and attested to by Ernst & Young in accordance with our terms of reference. (*http://www.bp.com*)

The assurance statements of the Cooperative Bank and Novo Nordisk in Exhibits 23.9 and 23.10 currently represent examples of best practice.

23.4 SUSTAINABILITY/TRIPLE BOTTOM LINE REPORTING. An emerging trend in corporate reporting is the integration of accounting and reporting of social, environ-

---

[23]See Ball et al., 2000; Kamp-Roelands, 1999; and Owen et al., 2000.

[24]Adams, 2002b.

auditor's statement: *ethics etc ...*

Richard Evans, March 26, 2001

ethics etc ... is an independent social accounting consultancy based in Newcastle upon Tyne. The audit of The Co-operative Bank 2000 Partnership Report has been undertaken by Richard Evans. He is a certified Member of the Institute of Social and Ethical AccountAbility and currently a director and council member. He has had a significant role in the development of corporate social and ethical accounting since 1992 and in founding and establishing ISEA.

Responsibilities of the Directors and the Auditor. The directors of The Co-operative Bank plc are responsible for the content, truthfulness and scope of the Partnership Report. They have signed off the final version of the report on which my audit is based and have undertaken to provide me with unlimited access to all the information and bank staff I considered necessary for me to assess the accuracy, completeness and balance of the reported facts and opinions.
The auditor's responsibility is to assure the bank's shareholders, customers, employees, suppliers, local communities, society and fellow co-operators that The Partnership Report is trustworthy and gives a balanced account of the bank's performance.
The auditor's duty is to consider the interests of these partners and not those of the bank's managers and directors. The auditor is entirely responsible for the content of the auditor's report, which the directors have agreed to publish in full.

Basis of the Auditor's Opinion. The assessment I have made is based on my own investigation of the accuracy of statements made and the data included in the report and of the bank's honesty in reporting partners' and commentators' opinions. I have continued my investigations of the last three years into the management practices, data systems, and partner dialogue processes which support the bank's ethics, values, social responsibility policies and ecological principles.
I have commented below on some of the issues that arose during this audit. In all my investigations the bank has disclosed original data requested and allowed me free access to management files, reports by internal and independent specialists, and to staff and partner representatives. I am confident that no material information has been deliberately withheld.
In assessing the Partnership Report I have followed the principles set out in The Institute of Social and Ethical AccountAbility's AA1000 Framework Standard for social and ethical accounting, auditing and reporting. I have also referred to the GRI Sustainability Reporting guidelines (June 2000), statutory guidelines for company reporting and, for auditing principles, to the Statement of Auditing Standards published by The Auditing Practices Board.

Scope of the Audit Process. I have:

- audited the data, commentary and opinions on pages 2–67;
- selected two projects and written the reviews on pages 70–73;
- considered the content of the expert assessments on delivering value, social responsibility and ecological sustainability on pages 79–85 and find the views expressed consistent with my own findings.

The Audit. The bank has made good progress in following up issues raised in my last auditor's report and the recommendations made to managers in the course of carrying out the previous systems review and audit. The main actions are referenced below under the progress report headings.
This report has increased the transparency of the process by providing references, accessible on the bank's website, to underlying supporting data. It has also made a first, and noteable attempt, to provide a cost/benefit analysis in a number of areas where the bank has pursued an ethical and ecological agenda beyond minimum legislative requirements. I recognise that this is neither easy, because there are no accepted standards for such reporting in place, and will be controversial, because it challenges traditional limits to corporate transparency. The bank is to be commended and encouraged for its initiative.

Delivering Value. The bank's equity shareholder, its customers and suppliers can all draw satisfaction from the continued good performance of the bank in delivering value. As was signalled last year, staff have faced a year of considerable and continuing change with the implementation of new people policies and practices. New staff surveys designed to monitor the impact on employees have, as recommended last year, made use of broad based consultation with staff and their representatives. The changes in survey methodology have produced results, in this section of the report, where some targets set under

Exhibit 23.9. Auditor's Statement from Co-operative Bank Partnership Report, 2000 (Pages 76–78).

the previous system have not been achieved. It is the bank's view, and the auditor's that the new surveys have produced a more realistic view of staff opinions. While staff continue to value the banks' ethical position, the quality of training and enjoy working for the bank; the surveys have identified issues around salaries, changes in benefits and career development that need to be addressed in future reports.

Social Responsibility. The foundation of the bank's social responsibility is its Ethical Policy. Training has taken place in the last year to increase the number of Ethical Advocates throughout the bank and to increase staff awareness. Most notably, "Ethics in Action" has been incorporated as one of the four key competences in every staff member's role statement, and is being incorporated in departmental business plans.

Screening of new-to-bank business, suppliers and business customers has moved well clear of simple compliance with the Ethical Policy. This has inevitably raised issues around the discretion bank staff exercise in ethical areas that are not specifically included in the current Ethical Policy Statement. The bank has satisfied the auditor that appropriate action is being taken on two fronts. The revision of the Ethical Policy scheduled for 2002 has involved broader consultation with customers on the issues to be included in the pending customer ballot. Corporate Affairs and the Ethical Policy Unit will undertake further consultations with independent specialists and internally around issues where staff are required to exercise discretion because the issues are not explicitly covered by the Ethical Policy, or where a balance between social and ecological acceptability is at issue.

A potential weakness in the screening of new business not covered by a relationship manager is that applicants are required to self-certify their compliance with the bank's Ethical Policy. This does not exempt them from the bank's normal screening and referral systems. However, the bank's Internal Audit Department recently added to their existing inspection of relationship managed business an ethical quality control and inspection procedure for non-relationship managed accounts. This has identified some process discrepancies which have been addressed and will be monitored and reported, if necessary, in future reports.

The bank has increased the percentage contribution of pre-tax profits to charitable causes and remains well ahead of the other clearing banks. It has also launched its new Community Involvement Policy with clear application procedures and funding criteria. However, it has not yet developed adequate monitoring systems for measuring and reporting outcomes and impacts.

I drew attention to the need for more systematic public reporting on the bank's Health and Safety performance last year. Two new indicators have been included in this report and the systems for health and safety management are now being integrated across the whole bank.

The implementation and training programme around the Diversity and Dignity at Work policies are welcomed. **smile**, the new Internet bank has been successful in attracting, through targeted recruitment, a good racial mix in its staff. Other parts of the bank remain out of line with the racial mix in the community, and require action.

Ecological sustainability. Recomendations contained in my last auditor's report that more specific performance targets are introduced—and that CO_2 emissions, water consumption and reducing paper usage are reported more fully—have all been addressed. This focus on targets is welcomed as well as the review of priorities in ecological impact reporting and the cost/benefit analysis. All these help to define a more integrated view of the bank's ecological footprint. For a more detailed analysis, which the audit endorses, please refer to Jonathon Porrit's assessment on pages 84–85.

Auditor's Opinion. On the basis of the audit work I have carried out and the review of supporting data and management systems, I believe the Partnership Report fairly represents the bank's economic, social and ecological impact on its partners, society and the environment.

ethics etc ...

Exhibit 23.9. (*Continued*)

mental, and economic issues, which has been referred to as the "triple bottom line,"[25] or "sustainability reporting."[26] Elkington argues: "Today we think in terms of a 'triple bottom line,' focussing on economic prosperity, environmental quality, and—the element which business has preferred to overlook—social justice."[27] The Global

[25]Elkington, 1997.

[26]Global Reporting Initiative, 2000.

[27]Elkington, 1997, p. 70.

Verification Statements

As an innovation, this year we have adopted a triple approach to the quality assurance of our Report. A broader overview that seeks to provide stakeholders with some assurance of the relevance and completeness of the Report and its underlying processes. A formal external verification that focuses on the accuracy of the quantitative data. And a high-level assurance engagement of our environmental information system, CATCH. The scope of these independent statements also covers the additional information in the Internet report.

Statement from Simon Zadek

This Statement focuses on the completeness and relevance of Novo Nordisk's Triple Bottom Line report, and on the company's underlying learning and capacity to work with longer-term 'stretch' goals and targets. In the Internet report is a description of the Review's approach.

On substantive issues, significant advances have been made in the area of 'access to health.' Its approach reflects the company's fundamental business principles, builds on WHO's recommendations, and was accentuated and accelerated by the Danish debate following the legal case brought by the pharmaceutical industry against the South African government concerning intellectual property rights. Learning from this should in the future inform its overall approach to risk assessment and management. The company has further progressed its approach to animal care, deepening its engagement to include challenging and also productive dialogue with activists. Incremental progress has been made in environmental management and performance, and there is a renewed need to explore new opportunities and strategic directions. Considerable progress has been made in handling labour standards in supply chains, and the weight now given to this in supplier screening is to be commended. Also notable are further developments in the company's global approach to equal opportunities.

On accounting and reporting, the strategic dilemmas approach has proved valuable in exploring the link between values, governance, and strategy. The commitment to account for licensees, contractors, and suppliers is a welcome development. The greater focus on the crucial area of health-related impacts is a significant development, although the company might reflect on how best to satisfy growing demands from stakeholders for greater transparency about health-related R&D activities.

The report complies with the main GRI Reporting Guidelines, and the underlying accountability process has been consistent with AA1000 principles.

Overall, Novo Nordisk continues to be a leader in public reporting, and can sustain this by considering future developments in the following areas.

- Further development of reported long-term strategic goals and associated targets.
- Continuing this year's effective approach that reports performance in the context of strategic dilemmas.
- Annual reporting on progress in its 'access to health' initiatives.
- Reporting on how R&D policy and practice fits within the Novo Charter.
- Report on internal incentive and career development in relation to social and environmental policies and performance.
- Strengthening engagement with mainstream investment community about risks and opportunities associated with social and environmental performance.
- Extension of quality assurance process to all report-based corporate communications about social and environmental issues and performance.

London, 1 March 2002

Dr. Simon Zadek

Statement from Deloitte & Touche

Agreed upon procedures related to the 'Report' and supporting documentation
We have been engaged to perform certain agreed upon procedures on the Novo Nordisk Triple Bottom Line Report 2001 and the related supplementary information on the Novo Nordisk website (all referred to as the 'Report'). Our work has been performed according to Professional Guidance applied to State Authorised Public Accountants in Denmark. The scope of the agreed upon procedures was agreed with the management of Novo Nordisk.

- We interviewed corporate officials at corporate headquarters and employees at a sample of sites, responsible for compiling data (environmental, social and economic data) for the Report, and we analysed and tested samples of supporting documentation.
- We ascertained whether the data collection procedures, as described in 'Scope of Report,' were used at corporate level to collect figures from reporting units. We compared the figures in the Report on investments and costs pertaining to environmental work to the source documentation presented to us. We assessed whether figures collected this way are appropriately reflected in the Report.
- We reviewed the internal control procedures established at corporate level to verify relevant figures submitted from reporting units. On a test basis, we compared the 2001 figures reported from a sample of two reporting units, Kalundborg and Bagsværd, to the source documentation supporting the submitted figures.

The agreed-upon scope and work performed preclude us from stating an opinion as to whether all figures in the Report are complete and accurate.

We find that Novo Nordisk applied detailed data collection procedures for the purpose of collecting 2000 and 2001 figures from the reporting units for inclusion and appropriate reflection in the Report, and made reasonable endeavours at corporate level to verify the figures. For the two reporting units identified above, submitted figures were consistent with the source documentation presented to us.

High-level assurance engagement on the environmental information system (CATCH)
We have been engaged to perform a high-level assurance engagement of CATCH. CATCH is a corporate level system as asserted in 'Scope of Report' and in detail in the Internet version of the Report. The Report and the assertion are the responsibility of and have been approved by Novo Nordisk's management. Our responsibility is to express an opinion on the assertion based on our engagement. Our work has been performed according to Professional Guidance applied to State Authorised Public Accountants in Denmark.

Our engagement included, on a test basis, an examination of the evidence supporting the assertion and performance of other such procedures, as deemed necessary by us. We believe that our examination provides a reasonable basis for our opinion.

In our opinion, in all material respects, CATCH is functioning as described in 'Scope of report,' and the system ensures an appropriate data collection process at corporate level.

Copenhagen, 1 March 2002

DELOITTE & TOUCHE
Statsautoriseret Revisionsaktieselskab

Preben J. Sørensen
State Authorised Public Accountant (Denmark)
Environment & Sustainability

Exhibit 23.10. Verification Statements on P66 of Novo Nordisk's Reporting on the Triple Bottom Line, 2001.

Reporting Initiative (GRI) published its *Sustainability Reporting Guidelines in 2000* "to design and build acceptance of a common framework for reporting on the linked aspects of sustainability—the economic, the environmental and the societal."[28] The key stated aims of the GRI guidelines are to facilitate decision making, to meet stakeholder needs and to provide a management tool. Organizations that integrate their reporting in this way argue that it improves reputation, decision making, performance, and risk management and builds good relationships with key stakeholders.[29] They also claim that it facilitates the ability to attract, motivate and retain high-quality staff and facilitates innovation, creativity and learning which allows a faster response to changing customer needs.[30] KPMG,[31] in their latest survey of Corporate Sustainability Reporting, noted a move away from the separate reporting solely focusing on HSE or environmental issues, to include performance in social or community development. This was seen as an initial movement toward more integrated sustainability reports on social, environmental, and economic performance information. Novo Nordisk provides an example of best practice (see Exhibit 23.11).

23.5 SUMMARY. Corporate social and environmental reporting has evolved considerably over the last few years. Most notable has been the increased formal involvement by government regulators, which has progressed from providing general guidance on the type of information suggested as useful, to the introduction of mandatory reporting requirements, specifically on environmental issues. This has corresponded with the development and acceptance internationally of more comprehensive voluntary guidance statements such as AA1000 and GRI. Such guidance statements have been utilized to provide the basis of country specific guidance statements and the formulation of individual corporate reporting policies. AccountAbility are also developing detailed assurance guidelines.[32]

Second, while many recent studies have noted a significant increase in the quantity of disclosure on social and environmental issues, the most significant change that has occurred over recent years has been the adoption of a broader range of reporting mediums. Traditionally, the annual report has been the primary source of information on corporate performance. However, with the advent of the Web, and the move toward more tailored reporting as observed through the issue of stand-alone environmental and community reports, companies now have the ability to more strategically approach external reporting and provide an emphasis on stakeholder involvement.

Finally, the reporting of social and environmental information is heading for a transformation with companies now exploring the integration of various performance measures. This is highlighted with companies experimenting with triple bottom line reporting and issuing sustainability reports. Hence, internationally we could expect that social and environmental reporting will become more comparable in the future with greater intervention by regulators, but with companies producing information more tailored to identified users and also more integrated to provide a more complete overview of corporate performance.

---

[28]Global Reporting Intiative, 2000, p. 1.
[29]Adams, 1999.
[30]Nelson, Singh, and Zollinger, 2001.
[31]KPMG, 2002.
[32]AccountAbility, 2002.

Following Up Targets

Novo Nordisk is committed to continuous improvement in our environmental, social and economic performance. Setting high objectives and targets and reporting on progress in meeting those goals are core elements of the Novo Nordisk Way of Management. The table shows how targets were met in 2001. For details, see the Internet version of this report.

Section		Target	Status
Integrated	2001	Develop a set of key performance indicators for social responsibility and the other elements of the Triple Bottom Line, p. 10	• • •
Social	2001	Complete the initial review of social responsibility and develop a strategy for implementation, p. 8	• • •
	2001	Ensure that there is no significant increase in the frequency of occupational injuries at work and wherever possible continue to achieve reductions, p. 30	• • •
	2001	Collect background information from each production unit and country on factors that have relevance to the number of accidents reported, p. 30	•
	2001–02	Develop business strategies for equal opportunities in the workplace, p. 35	• •
	2001–02	Engage in dialogue with selected key suppliers and carry out pilot projects regarding social considerations in supplier and contractor evaluation, p. 38	• • •
	2001–02	Investigate how Novo Nordisk can improve the health of people in the organisation	• •
	2001–02	Conclude and communicate the findings of the DAWN (Diabetes Attitudes, Wishes and Needs) study to uncover behavioural, social and psychosocial aspects of diabetes, p. 26	• • •
	2001–02	Initiate the development of a 'sustainable business model' for helping people with diabetes in poor countries to gain access to diabetes care, p. 20	• •
	2001–02	Assist in the development and implementation of national diabetes strategies, p. 26	• •
Environmental	2001	Increase the eco-productivity for energy by 4 percentage points, p. 52	• • •
	2001	Increase the eco-productivity for water by 5 percentage points, p. 52	•
	2001–02	Further involve employees in the implementation of ISO 14001 globally, p. 50	• •
	2001–02	Improve methods for reporting transport emissions and use the results to reduce the environmental impact, in co-operation with our transport suppliers, p. 55	• •
	2001	Continue working towards the replacement and/or removal of antibiotic resistance marker genes in our production strains, p. 49	• • •
	2001	Establish Novo Nordisk principles for the future use of human materials in drug discovery and development as part of implementing the Council of Europe's Convention on Human Rights and Biomedicine, p. 44	• • •
	2001	Remove animal testing for the product control of 29 selected material codes, p. 40	• •
	2001–02	Implement improvements in the housing conditions for experimental animals in consideration of the needs of the animals, p. 40	• •
	2001	Formalise and further develop an internal ethical review process for experiments on animals, p. 40	• • •
	• • •	achieved	
	• •	progress made	
	•	not achieved, included in new targets	

Exhibit 23.11. Targets and Progress Against Target from P9 of Novo Nordisk's Reporting on the Triple Bottom Line, 2001.

SOURCES AND SUGGESTED REFERENCES

ACCA. ACCA UK awards for sustainability reporting. London: ACCA, 2002.

AccountAbility. AccountAbility 1000 (AA1000) Framework: Standard, Guidelines and Professional Qualification, 1999.

AccountAbility. AA1000 Assurance Standard: Guiding Principles, AccountAbility, 2002.

Adams, C. A. "The Nature and Processes of Corporate Reporting on Ethical Issues." *CIMA research monograph*, 1999, 64 pp.

Adams, C. A. "Factors influencing corporate social and ethical reporting: moving on from extant theories." *Accounting, Auditing and Accountability Journal*, Vol. 15, No. 2, 2002a, pp. 223–250.

Adams, C. A. The Reporting—Performance Portrayal Gap In ICI. Working paper, 2002b.

Adams, C. A., and C. B. Roberts. "Corporate Ethics: An Issue Worthy of Report?" *Accounting Forum*, Vol. 19, No. 2/3, 1995, pp 128–142.

Arnold, P., and T. Hammond. "The Role of Accounting in Ideological Conflict: Lessons from the South African Divestment Movement." *Accounting, Organisations and Society*, Vol. 19, No. 2, 1994.

Ball A., D. L. Owen, and R. Gray. "External Transparency or Internal Capture? The Role of Third-Party Statements in Adding Value to Corporate Environmental Reports." *Business Strategy and the Environment*, Vol. 9, No. 1, 2000.

Bebbington, J. "Compulsory Environmental Reporting in Denmark: An Evaluation." *Social & Environmental Accounting*, Vol. 1, No. 2, 1999.

Elkington, J. *Cannibals with Forks: The Triple Bottom Line of 21st Century Business*. Oxford: Capstone, 1997.

Environmental Protection Agency. "U.S. EPA Notifying Defendants of Securities and Exchange Commission's Environmental Disclosure Requirements." *Enforcement Alert*, Vol. 4, No. 3, October 2001.

Fekrat, A. M., C. Inclan, and D. Petroni. "Corporate Environmental Disclosures: Competitive Disclosure Hypothesis using 1991 Annual Report Data." *International Journal of Accounting*, Vol. 31, No. 2, 1996, pp. 175–195.

Forstater M., T. Swift, C. Nacamuli, and P. Monaghan. "Mapping Standards for Corporate Social Responsibility; for the EC DG Employment and Social Affairs." *AccountAbililty*, 2002.

Frost, G. "An Investigation of the Introduction of Mandatory Environmental Reporting in Australia." *British Accounting Association Annual Conference*. Nottingham, England. March 26–28, 2001.

Gamble, G. O., K. Hsu, D. Kite, and R. R. Radtke. "Environmental Disclosures in Annual Reports and 10Ks: An Examination." *Accounting Horizons*, Vol. 9, No. 3, September, pp. 34–54.

Global Reporting Initiative. *Global Reporting Guidelines on Economics, Environmental, and Social Performance. Access at http://www.globalreporting.org/GRIGuidelines/June2000/June2000Guidelines8X11.pdf.*

Global Reporting Initiative. Draft Sustainability Reporting Guidelines, GRI, 2002, *www.globalreporting.org*.

Gray, R., R. Kouhy, and S. Lavers. "Corporate Social and Environmental Reporting." *Accounting, Auditing and Accountability Journal*, Vol. 8, No. 2, 1995, pp. 47–77.

Guthrie, J., and L. D. Parker. "Corporate Social Reporting: A Rebuttal of Legitimacy Theory." *Accounting and Business Research*, Vol. 19, No. 6, 1989, pp. 343–352.

Hogner, R. H. "Corporate Social Reporting: Eight Decades of Development at U.S. Steel." *Research in Corporate Social Performance and Policy*, Vol. 4, 1982, pp. 243–250.

Kamp-Roelands, N. "Audits of Environmental Reports: Are We Witnessing the Emergence of Another Expectation Gap." Koninklijik Nederlands Instituut van Registeraccountants, 1999.

Kolk, A. "Evaluating Corporate Environmental Reporting." *Business, Strategy and the Environment*, Vol. 8, 1999.

KPMG. "Focus on the Mining Sector: Preview of KPMG's International Survey of Corporate Sustainability Reporting 2002." KPMG Global Sustainability Services, 2002.

KPMG. "Mining: A Survey of Global Reporting Trends." KPMG, 2001.

Nelson, J., A. Singh, and P. Zollinger. "The Power to Change: Mobilising Board Leadership to Deliver Sustainable Value to Markets and Society." SustainAbility/International Business Leaders Forum, London, 2001.

Owen, D. L., T. A. Swift, C. Humphrey, and M. Bowerman. "The New Social Audits: Accountability, Management Capture or the Agenda of Social Champions?" *European Accounting Review*, Vol. 9, No. 1, 2000.

Wiseman, J. "An Evaluation of Environmental Disclosures Made in Corporate Annual Reports." *Accounting, Organizations, and Society*, Vol. 7, No. 1, 2001, pp. 53–63.

CHAPTER 24

CORPORATE GOVERNANCE IN EMERGING MARKETS: AN ASIAN PERSPECTIVE

Judy Tsui

The Hong Kong Polytechnic University

Tony Shieh

City University of Hong Kong

CONTENTS

24.1 BACKGROUND. The 1997 Asian financial crisis was probably the single most devastating economic event of this century. Currencies across the region lost more than 50% of their value in many cases because of unexpectedly weak performance in the corporate sector. The stock markets plummeted by about an average of 40%. The crash in Indonesia and Malaysia was more catastrophic than in Hong Kong and Taiwan—the main stock price index fell 52% in Malaysia and 37% in Indonesia between 1996 and 1997. Though a long list of factors such as high levels of debt, corrupt lending policies, nonmarket criteria for credit allocation, distorted incentives for project selection, and monitoring have been identified as causes for the crisis, it is clear that the crisis would not have been that severe if there were confidence in corporate governance and financial transparency in these corporations. Poor corporate governance has been singled out as a major culprit for the Asian financial crisis.[1] Johnson et al.[2] also presented evidence that the weakness of legal institutions for corporate gover-

---

[1]International Finance Law Review, 2001.
[2]Johnson et al., 2000.

nance had an important effect on the extent of depreciations and stock market declines in the Asian financial crisis. Hong Kong experienced less shock (i.e., only a 20% drop in stock price index as compared to the other Asian capital markets) and this is probably because of the corporate governance mechanisms already in existence at that time which included more financial disclosures and transparencies than the other capital markets in Asia.

International institutional investors clearly regarded weak corporate governance, inadequate financial disclosure and a lack of corporate transparency as a cause of the Asian financial crisis. In particular, Tripathi made the following point: "Pressure from multilateral agencies on the global market for more disclosure of financial data is rising. Asian companies that want to tap international capital markets will have to meet more stringent reporting requirements."[3]

Given the above backdrop, corporate governance is the most topical issue that concerns governments including relevant policy makers, regulators, professional bodies, and institutes such as the accounting profession, securities, and directors institutes. The governments and their related policy-making units have made a great deal of efforts since 1997 to enhance their requirements or disclosures to improve their corporate governance standards. Hong Kong's Financial Secretary in its 2000 Budget Speech has put corporate governance as the forefront driver of his priorities for Hong Kong's future economic development and initiated a Corporate Governance Review to be implemented by the Standing Committee on Company Law Reform. Malaysia has recently implemented its Code on Corporate Governance in 2000.

Having considered the key economic driver of corporate governance in the region, the next section outlines the theoretical underpinning for unique agency problems in the emerging markets in Asia.

24.2 ECONOMIC INCENTIVES FOR LACK OF CORPORATE GOVERNANCE AND TRANSPARENCY. In the agency view, managers are expected to act opportunistically at the expense of the shareholders' interests.[4] The agency problem arises from the separation of ownership and control in modern corporations. This is the fundamental problem that faces modern corporations—the potential for managers to act opportunistically given that it is not possible to write contracts to cover every contingency and the difficulties of monitoring and enforcing contracts.[5] Manifestations of these opportunistic behaviors may be seen in terms of the lack of corporate disclosures and manipulation of accounting earnings. Managers have a range of economic incentives for managing earnings.[6] For example, explicit compensation contracts that link compensation to reported earnings under a bonus plan create incentives for managers to manipulate earnings.[7] However, it is impossible to write contracts that cover every contingency in the business environment. The difficulties associated with writing contracts to cover every possible situation and monitoring as well as enforcing these contracts becomes significant because of the agency problem. The implementation of effective corporate governance mechanisms seems to offer a solution to monitor and reduce these opportunistic behaviors.

---

[3]Tripathi, 1998.

[4]Jensen and Meckling, 1976; and Fama and Jensen, 1983.

[5]Tsui and Gul, 2000.

[6]Id.

[7]Coase, 1937; Holstrom and Tirole, 1989; and Jensen and Meckling, 1992.

In Asia, one unique institutional feature that is different from the other developed economies such as the United States and the United Kingdom and distinguishes itself from the above agency problem is the concentration of ownership. Though there are many different variations on concentrated ownership in Asia, there is a predominance of family or state-owned businesses in these emerging markets. Claessens et al.[8] found that there is evidence of expropriation of minority shareholders' wealth by majority or controlling shareholders in East Asian countries. While recognizing this unique feature that may have resulted in corporate successes in the East Asian economies in the past, the challenge is to implement effective corporate governance mechanisms to balance the interests between majority and minority shareholders.[9] The recent McKinsey Report[10] urged that the distinct ownership structure such as the importance of family-owned businesses in emerging markets should be recognized more explicitly. Otherwise, this unique ownership structure could continue to act as an impediment to corporate governance reform.

Apart from the ownership structure that would set the scene for the unique agency problems in the emerging markets, it is important to understand the underlying legal framework that defines the rights of shareholders, in particular, those of the minority shareholders. La Porta et al.[11] examined the legal protection of investors and found that common law countries offer considerably more protection to investors than civil law countries. Their results also showed that countries with more concentrated ownership of shares are associated with less investor protection. Amongst the several emerging markets examined, in this study, common law countries such as Hong Kong, India, Malaysia, Singapore, and Thailand offer more investor protection than civil law countries such as Indonesia, Philippines, Korea, and Taiwan.

The above theoretical analysis on ownership structure and legal systems forms the basis of our understanding on corporate governance regimes in the emerging markets. The next section presents the analytical framework to understand different corporate governance regimes in this region.

24.3 CORPORATE GOVERNANCE REGIMES. Rajan and Zingales[12] pointed out that corporate governance systems in East Asia are relationship-based as opposed to the arms-length market-based systems in the developed economies such as the United States. Market-based systems are characterized by diverse shareholding. They posited that market-based systems by definition require more transparency as a guarantee of protection to investors which are more diverse. By contrast, relationship-based systems which have more owner/managers are designed to disclose less information and thus resulting in a preservation of opacity. This has the effect of protecting the relationship and the companies from the threat of competition. However, it is expected that this would lead to less transparency and disclosures.

These relationship-based systems are evident in many Asian countries. For example, in Korea, the existence of chaebols controlled by family members and linked to influential politicians and bankers has contributed to the lack of financial transparency.[13] Similar problems also exist with the huge Japanese conglomerates or

[8] Claessens et al., 1999.
[9] Jordan, 1999.
[10] McKinsey & Company, 2001.
[11] LaPorta et al., 1998.
[12] Rajan and Zingales, 1998.
[13] Gul and Kealey, 1999.

keiretsus with their close banking ties.[14] In Hong Kong, listed companies may also be characterized as family owned. The unique institutional arrangements which engender these relationship-based systems must be recognized in implementing corporate governance mechanisms.

The above distinct corporate governance system in Asia with its unique ownership structure and legal system shed light on the notion that the market-based corporate governance system in the developed economies may not be effective in the emerging economies. The following section gives a detailed comparison on the different types of corporate governance regimes in the emerging markets.

(a) Different Types of Corporate Governance Regimes in Emerging Markets. In order to understand the different types of corporate governance regimes in the emerging markets, it is necessary to appreciate the institutional, legal, and political environments that would impose constraints on the implementation of an optimal solution to an effective corporate governance regime. The following categorizes and describes the different types of corporate regimes in the emerging markets.

1. *Market-based corporate governance regime.* The market-based regime is the one that characterizes efficient equity markets and dispersed ownership,[15] Examples of the countries classified as market-based regimes are developed economies such as the United States, the United Kingdom, Canada, and Australia. These countries have well-developed capital markets and diffusely owned corporations. As mentioned above, these systems by definition require transparency as a guarantee of investor protection.[16]

   Though Claessens et al.[17] identified Japan as having the largest share of widely held firms, followed by Korea and Taiwan, it is nonetheless classified as non–market based in terms of the corporate governance regimes in Asia.
2. *Family-based corporate governance regime.* Emerging markets in general have high concentrated ownership, particularly family ownership. It should be noted that the agency problems that stem from the conflicts of interest between owners/managers and minority shareholders are different in the emerging markets.[18] Using a sample of 67 Hong Kong listed companies, Gul et al.[19] documented that family control is associated with lower audit fees. This is consistent with the view that family firms are subject to fewer typical agency problems or separation between managers and shareholders than nonfamily firms. However, such concentrated ownership of a large proportion of the corporate sector could lead to the suppression of minority rights and could adversely affect the economic development of these markets characterized by weak enforceability of these legal and regulatory institutions.[20] Johnson et al.[21] presented evidence to show that the weakness of these legal institutions for corporate governance had

[14]Gul, 1999.
[15]McKinsey & Company, 2001.
[16]Rajan and Zingales, 1998.
[17]Claessens et al., 2000.
[18]Shleifer and Vishny, 1997.
[19]Gul, Tsui, and Chen, 1998.
[20]Claessens et al., 2000.
[21]Johnson et al., 2000.

accentuated the extent of depreciations and stock market declines in the Asian financial crisis.

Overall, the nine East Asian countries all have high family ownership, approximately on average about 50% except Japan.[22] For example, Indonesia has the highest concentrated family ownership of about 72%, Malaysia and Thailand both score about 67% and 62% respectively. Hong Kong, Singapore, and Taiwan are also classified as family-based corporate governance regimes. Hong Kong documents that 53% of all listed companies in Hong Kong have one shareholder or one family group holding more than 50% of issued capital.[23] Singapore has very high concentrated ownerships both in family and state scoring 55% and 24% respectively.[24] Taiwan's 90% of total companies consists mainly of small- and medium-sized enterprises (SMEs) and family-control remains a dominant characteristic even in large corporations.[25]

This unique family ownership has led to a relationship-based corporate governance regime whereby less transparency on corporate governance practices such as disclosure of financial information is expected than in market-based regimes.

3. *Bank lending corporate governance regime.* Banks in emerging markets are characterized by the government which intervened extensively in lending decisions. This has led to little interest in deriving good disclosure from the companies. Examples are Korea, Indonesia, and Malaysia, where the government would act as a *de facto* guarantor for loans extended to companies in targeted industries.

   Gul and Kealey's[26] study highlighted the lack of financial transparency in Korean chaebols which are controlled by family members and linked to influential politicians and bankers.[27] Similar problems also existed with the huge Japanese conglomerates or keiretsus with their close banking ties.[28]. These lending decisions of these banks were made primarily on the basis of relationship rather than on an objective assessment of the prospects of the company. These banking lending relationships generally characterize the lack of effective corporate governance mechanisms and lack of transparency in these bank lending corporate governance regimes.

4. *Government affiliated corporate governance regime.* Another significant relationship based corporate governance system is the government affiliated regime. China has very high state ownership with 64% and 65% of total shares issued on Shanghai and Shenzhen markets, respectively.[29] Lin[30] also stated that the non–freely tradeable state and legal person shares together account for the majority of these listed companies in China.

---

[22]Claessesn et al 2000.

[23]Hong Kong Society of Accountants, 1995, 1997.

[24]Claessens et al., 2000.

[25]Taiwan Securities and Future Institute, 2001.

[26]Gul and Kealey, 1999.

[27] Korea's 30 largest chaebols had very high average debt–equity ratios (348% in 1995, 519% in 1997). Some chaebols' debt–equity ratios even exceeded 1000%. Korean banks continued their lending to high debt–equity firms with some even with negative equity suggesting that the financial institutions were not making their lending decisions based on the chaebols' financial performance (Joh, 2001).

[28]Gul, 1999.

[29]Shanghai Securities Exchange Year Book, 1998.

[30]Lin, 2000.

Singapore came second to China in terms of the proportion of state ownership (i.e., 23.5% in East Asia).[31] The Singapore government directly or indirectly controls up to 80% of the listed companies in Singapore.[32] This government ownership has been reduced in the 1990s through a privatization program. Malaysia's state ownership is also relatively high (i.e., about 13%).[33] The above government-affiliated listed companies no doubt have affected the corporate governance regime in China, Singapore, and Malaysia in the past decade or so. With the emergence of the World Trade Organization in China and the need for East Asian countries to attract foreign capital such as institutional investors, the governments of these countries have made extra strides to develop codes of corporate governance to overcome the inherent difficulties arising from government ownership.

In conclusion, the distinct relationship-based corporate governance regimes in terms of family ownership, bank lending relationships and government ownership in emerging markets could result in less financial transparency leading to possibility of earning manipulations by corporate managers to expropriate wealth from the minority shareholders. The next section describes the recent developments of corporate governance and financial disclosures in the emerging markets.

(b) Recent Developments of Corporate Governance and Financial Disclosures in Emerging Markets. Given the inadequate financial disclosures and lack of effective corporate governance mechanisms in the relationship based corporate governance regimes, reliable and quality financial reporting and disclosures are of paramount importance to enhancing corporate governance standard and practices. This is consistent with the OECD Principles of Corporate Governance which state that: "The corporate governance framework should ensure that timely and accurate disclosure is made on all material matters regarding the corporation, including the financial situation, performance, ownership, and governance of the company."[34]

Timely and accurate financial disclosures are emphasized because of the possible earnings manipulations by corporate managers.[35] Managers can conceal financial information by a range of methods because accounting standards provide managers with considerable latitude and discretion in financial reporting. Johnson et al.[36] also showed that managerial agency problems can make countries with weak legal systems vulnerable to the effect of a sudden loss of investor confidence. The lack of transparency and the low quality of available information precipitated a crisis of confidence which led to rapid and massive outflows of capital out of many Asian countries during the financial crisis.

It should be recognized that while better disclosures may not have prevented the Asian financial crisis, it would probably have provided earlier warnings to policy makers, businesses and investors and may even have allowed them to develop better responses and strategies. Therefore, one of the fundamental corporate governance mechanisms in relationship-based systems in the emerging markets is the reliability

---

[31]Claessens et al., 2000.
[32]Mak and Chng, 2000.
[33]Claessens et al., 2000.
[34]OECD Principles of Corporate Governance, 1999.
[35]Tsui and Gul, 2000.
[36]Johnson et al., 2000.

and timeliness of financial information and disclosures. This notion is also supported by McKinsey & Company's 2001 Emerging Market Investor Opinion Survey.[37] Three major areas where reform in emerging markets were identified as priorities: "Accountancy Standards. The accuracy of accounts is the first priority of investors, the timeliness and coverage of accounts taking second priority." Other priorities identified for the emerging markets are the enforceability of legal rights and the maintenance of an effective regulatory system.

Recent reforms in many jurisdictions in emerging markets had already begun to strengthen the disclosure regimes for listed companies to adequately protect investors and to ensure greater accountability by a company's board and management. Some countries have commenced converging their accounting and auditing standards with international accounting standards. The following section discusses the recent developments in accounting and auditing standards in the emerging markets.

(c) Development of Accounting Standards. Changes in accounting standards in emerging markets are being implemented to better protect shareholders. Nestor[38] pointed out that one of six trends in OECD member countries that have profound impact on the global corporate governance landscape is the harmonization of financial reporting standards. The continuing convergence of International Accounting Standards (IAS) and U.S. GAAP had also encouraged an increasing number of countries in the emerging markets to either harmonize, converge or directly adopt IAS as their domestic accounting standards or as alternative to their domestic accounting standards. Exhibit 24.1 gives evidence of the different ways in which the emerging markets have adopted IAS. Based on the above analysis, the following section discusses

[37]The McKinsey Emerging Market Investor Opinion Survey 2001 was undertaken by the corporate governance team in McKinsey & Company. Forty-six private equity investors were surveyed during International Finance Corporation's Global Equity Conference. They had approximately US$5 billion assets under management, 90% of which was invested in emerging markets (McKinsey, 2001).

[38]Nestor, 2002.

Panel A **Adopted IAS or Allow Domestic and Foreign Companies Following IAS to be Listed on Their Exchanges**		**Panel B** **Allow Foreign Companies Following IAS to be Listed on Their Exchanges**	
Country	Exchange	Country	Exchange
China	Shanghai Stock Exchange	Hong Kong	Stock Exchange of Hong Kong
		Japan	Tokyo Stock Exchange
		Malaysia[a]	Kuala Lumpur Stock Exchange
		Singapore	Stock Exchange of Singapore
		Taiwan[a]	Taiwan Stock Exchange
		Thailand	The Stock Exchange of Thailand

[a]Reconciliation to local GAAP is required.

Source: IASC Web site, *www.iasc.org.uk.*

Exhibit 24.1. International Accounting Standards in Emerging Markets.

the unique factors that contribute to the effectiveness of corporate governance regime in the emerging economies.

24.4 UNIQUE FACTORS ON EFFECTIVENESS OF CORPORATE GOVERNANCE REGIME IN EMERGING MARKETS. The above analysis clearly indicates that effective corporate governance regimes in the emerging markets need to take into consideration the legal and regulatory framework and the respective roles that they play. In some of these jurisdictions, disclosure and listing regulations were insufficient to ensure the availability of complete, accurate and timely financial and nonfinancial information.[39] For example, some countries had weak disclosure rules on cross-shareholdings, cross-guarantees, and related-party transactions. In other jurisdictions such as Japan, the requirements for consolidated financial statements for corporate groups were inadequate.

Stock exchanges and regulatory authorities such as the Securities and Futures Commission and Monetary Authority in emerging markets are also playing their role to enhance better accountability and transparency of their listed companies and amend their listing rules aimed at improving corporate governance practices. Since the Asian financial crisis, developing economies have taken great efforts to improve their disclosure requirements as well.

The Stock Exchange of Hong Kong, for example, has proposed 30 amendments to the Listing Rules in its recent consultation paper currently soliciting views from all the stakeholders and the public. Some of the major proposed changes are:[40]

- Quarterly reporting to be required and be released within 45 days of quarter end, and to contain a balance sheet.
- One-third of board members must be independent nonexecutive directors (INEDs), with a minimum of two INEDs on the board.
- Disclosure on the following is required in the annual reports:
  - A report on corporate governance practices prepared by the companies' board of directors.
  - Any deviation from the minimum standards of the Code of Best Practice on Corporate Governance will have to be disclosed.
  - Disclosure on the number of audit committee meetings held during the year with a record of attendance
  - Disclosure on individual director's remuneration.
- Any director's contract exceeding three years will require the approval of minority shareholders.

Other emerging markets are also changing their legal and regulatory requirements. South Korea passed a new law in 2001 that specified at least one-third of independent directors must be on the board and required the establishment of audit committees. Companies in China are now required to file quarterly reports starting from 2003 and Singapore is set to tighten quarterly reporting deadlines from within 60 days in 2003 to within 45 days by 2004.

---

[39] OECD, 2001.
[40] CLSA, 2002.

Many East Asian countries have issued codes or guidelines on corporate governance. Malaysia and India, for example, require companies to devote a section of their annual reports to the implementation of corporate governance principles, along with a detailed compliance report. Recently, jurisdictions such as Hong Kong, Malaysia, and Singapore, have also established "secondary" markets to cater to young and high-growth companies. Given the higher risks associated with these small, start-up companies, these markets require more disclosures to protect investors.

The Securities and Futures Commission usually is the front-line regulator of listing related matters and oversees the performance of the stock exchange. It has the responsibility to enhance market efficiency and improve transparency. After the Asian financial crisis, many countries have revamped their listing requirements. Codes of best practices of corporate governance have been formulated with more requirements for independent directors and the like. Apart from the front-line regulator, Monetary Authorities usually require more financial disclosures as well as more stringent corporate governance requirements.

Private sector bodies such as societies of accountants in emerging economies have also responded to the demand for better financial transparency and good corporate governance. The Hong Kong Society of Accountants (HKSA), for example, recommended changes in regulations such as the role and responsibilities of board of directors, improving financial reporting and audit. The HKSA also advocated recommendations covering board membership including the inclusion of finance directors on boards, the establishment of board subcommittees such as audit committee and remuneration committee.

Based on the above analysis, a strong disclosure system must be underpinned by an effective legal and regulatory framework. With a few exceptions, the regulatory framework in the region lacked the institutional capacity and effective and credible sanctions to ensure that companies complied with the relevant regulations and that accounting and auditing self-regulatory organizations were diligent in ensuring their members applied the relevant disclosure standards.

Apart from the effective legal and regulatory framework that needs to be improved for good corporate governance, it is of paramount importance that the quality of independent nonexecutive directors in the board and the three board subcommittees must be assured. Against a background of relationship based corporate governance system whereby the INEDs are usually connected to the companies, the quality of the independent nonexecutive directors is even more important.

24.5 CONCLUDING COMMENTS. Emerging market corporate governance reform has not progressed very substantially despite the willingness of policy makers and investors to press for change. First, corporate governance reform needs to devote more emphasis to driving change through institutional reform of capital markets and underlying structure of property rights to complement practical improvements to governance at the corporate level. Second, the importance of concentrated ownership such as family owned businesses, government affiliated corporations in emerging markets should be recognized more explicitly. Without the proper incentives, a relationship based system could continue to act as a major obstacle to corporate governance reform. One should recognize that developing economies have a distinct legal and regulatory framework and unique ownership structure that are markedly different from those that prevail in the developed capital markets such as the United

States and the United Kingdom. Any adoption of corporate governance mechanisms from market-based system to relationship-based system must be done with extreme caution.

SOURCES AND SUGGESTED REFERENCES

Credit Lyonnais Securities Asia. "Corporate Governance in Emerging Markets." *CG Watch*, CLSA Emerging Markets, 2002.

Claessens, S., S. Djankov, J. P. H. Fan, and L. H. P. Lang. "Expropriation of Minority Shareholders: Evidence from East Asia." *World Bank Policy Research Paper* 2088, March 1999.

Claessens, S., S. Djankov, and L. H. P. Lang. "The Separation of Ownership and Control in East Asian Corporations." *Journal of Financial Economics*, Vol. 58, 2000, pp. 81–112.

Coase, R. "The Nature of the Firm." *Economica*, Vol. 4, November 1937, pp. 386–405.

"Corporate Governance in Hong Kong: The Road to Reform Following the Asian Financial Crisis." *International Financial Law Review*. London, 2001, pp. 53–59.

Fama, E. F., and M. C. Jensen. "Separation of Ownership and Control." *Journal of Law & Economics*, June 1983, pp. 301–325.

Gul, F. A. "The Asia Financial Crisis, Accounting Earnings Manipulation and Corporate Governance." Working Paper. City University of Hong Kong.

Gul, F. A., and B. Kealey. "Chaebol, Investment Opportunity Set and Corporate Debt and Dividend Policies of Korean Companies." *Review of Quantitative Finance and Accounting*, Vol. 13, 1999, pp. 401–416.

Gul, F. A., J. Tsui, and C. J. P. Chen. "Agency Costs and Audit Pricing: Evidence on Discretionary Accruals." Working Paper. City University of Hong Kong.

Holstrom, B. R., and J. Tirole. "The Theory of the Firm." Chapter 2 in R. Schmalensee, (ed.), *Handbook of Industrial Organization*. Amsterdam: North-Holland, 1989, pp. 63–133.

HKSA. First Report of the Working Group on Corporate Governance, 1995.

HKSA. Second Report of the Corporate Governance Working Group, 1997.

Jensen, M. C., and W. H. Meckling. "Theory of the Firm: Managerial Behavior, Agency Costs and Ownership Structure." *Journal of Financial Economics*, Vol. 3, 1976, pp. 305–360.

Jensen, M. C., and W. H. Meckling. "Specific and General Knowledge and Organizational Structure." Chapter 9 in L. Werin and H. Wijkander, (eds.), *Contract Economics*. Oxford: Basil Blackburn Ltd, 1992, pp. 251–274.

Joh, S. W. "Korean Corporate Governance and Firm Performance." Working Paper. Korea Development Institute, June 2001.

Johnson S., P. Boone, A. Breach and E. Friedman. "Corporate Governance in the Asian Financial Crisis." *Journal of Financial Economics*, Vol. 58, 2000, pp. 141–186.

Jordan, C. "Corporate Governance in Asia and the Asian Financial Crisis: Evidence of the Impact and Current Trends." OECD Conference on Corporate Governance in Asia: A Comparative Perspective, March 1999.

La Porta, R., F. Lopez-de-Silanes, A. Shleifer, and R. W. Vishny. "Law and Finance." *Journal of Political Economy*, Vol. 106, No. 6, December 1998, pp. 1113–1155.

Lin. C. "Challenges in Corporate Governance Development in China." OECD Development Centre Informal Workshop on Corporate Governance in Developing Countries and Emerging Economies, April 2000.

Mak, Y. T., and C. K. Chng. "Corporate Governance Practices and Disclosures in Singapore: An Update." OECD/World Bank 2nd Asian Roundtable on Corporate Governance, 2000.

McKinsey & Company. "Giving New Life to the Corporate Governance Reform Agenda for Emerging Markets." *McKinsey Emerging Market Investor Opinion Survey*, 2001, pp. 1–6.

Nestor, S. "Corporate Governance Trends in the OECD Area: Where Do We Go from Here?" OECD Web site, *www.oecd.org*.

OECD Principles of Corporate Governance 1999. Organization for Economic Co-operation and Development.

OECD. "Asian Corporate Governance White Paper." Asian Roundtable on Corporate Governance, 2001.

Rajan, R. G. and L. Zingales. "Which Capitalism? Lessons from the East Asian Crisis." Working Paper. University of Chicago.

Shanghai Securities Yearbook 1998. Shanghai Academy of Social Science Publishing House.

Shleifer, A. and R. Vishny. "A Survey of Corporate Governance." *Journal of Finance*, June 1997, pp. 737–783.

Taiwan Securities and Future Institute. *Corporate Governance in Taiwan*, December 2001.

Tripathi, S. "A Different World." *Far Eastern Economic Review*, August 13, 1998, p. 49.

Tsui J., and F. A. Gul. "Corporate Governance and Financial Transparencies in the Hong Kong Special Administrative Region of The People's Republic of China." OECD/World Bank/Asian Development Bank The Second Asian Roundtable on Corporate Governance, 2000.

CHAPTER 25

MULTINATIONAL BUDGETING AND CONTROL SYSTEMS

Frederick D. S. Choi

New York University

Gerald F. Lewis

Mobil Corporation (retired)

CONTENTS

25.1 INTRODUCTION. The budgeting and control process for a multinational company is basically no different from that for domestic operations, except that it must recognize diverse environments as well as the addition of one major element—the impact of currencies.

In this chapter, two broad areas of budgeting and control systems will be discussed—capital budgeting and operations budgeting, or profit planning. In both cases, the process is one that forms part of a company's overall planning process.

Many companies have express or implied mission or vision statements—objectives which they wish to achieve. These may be financial or operational in nature; financial objectives run the gamut from achieving specific rates of return to reducing the debt/capital ratio to a given percentage, while operational objectives include entering into additional countries, introducing new products, increasing market penetration, or containing costs and expenses, and so forth. The capital budget ratios cash disbursements for such assets as buildings, machinery, equipment, and other long-term projects. The profit plan sets income targets that, together with investment (capital) expenditures and financing transactions, will hopefully meet or exceed the annual segments of the company's overall multiyear objectives.

As indicated above, both capital budgeting and profit planning in a multinational environment are not fundamentally different from those for domestic operations. The two factors that will, however, pervade this chapter are nationalistic and currency aspects—matters that do not apply to purely domestic operations. Additional factors affecting the capital budgeting decision are described in Chapter 4.

When we talk about nationalist factors, we mean the legal and behavioral elements that are present in dealing with operations in other countries. The most obvious element is that the operations are carried out in a number of countries, each of which has its own laws, specific jurisdictions, tax statutes, and operating practices that differ from those in the United States. Thus, while the chairman or managing director of a foreign subsidiary company "reports" nominally to a domestic senior executive, in fact, he or she is subject to the laws of his or her country and, in all likelihood, to the power and control of a local board of directors or equivalent supervisory body. Genuine diplomacy being a desired necessity, we shall refer to foreign subsidiaries as "affiliates." In fact, executives and other employees abroad neither regard themselves as "foreigners" nor look upon their company as a "subsidiary," since it is incorporated in their own country and is, therefore, independent. The American parent's 100% or majority ownership is looked upon as a relationship aspect that requires constant negotiation and renegotiation, particularly in the budgeting processes.

The currency factor is perhaps the most visible difference between domestic and multinational budgeting. It requires the forecasting of exchange rates for, first establishing capital budgets and profit plans and, second, controlling them later on.

25.2 FORECASTING EXCHANGE RATES

(a) Floating Exchange Rates. The present environment of floating exchange rates has accentuated the importance of accurately forecasting exchange rates, although some would say that the combination of "accurate" and "forecasting" is a contradiction in terms. Nevertheless, the forecasting process has imposed a discipline—first, to identify and quantify those economic, political, and social variables which influence a currency's value and, second, to predict the direction, magnitude, and timing of a currency's change in value.

Briefly stated, forecasting techniques follow either the traditional, fundamental approach or the more recent technical, analytical approach.

(b) Fundamental Approach. The fundamental approach has evolved from classical economics. In applying this technique, management (usually, the treasurer) assesses certain economic and sociopolitical variables of a nation to predict the economy's performance and how such performance will affect the supply of, and demand for, that nation's currency. Economic variables include domestic monetary and fiscal policy, inflation rates, unemployment, development of natural resources, international trade competitiveness, and capital flows. Sociopolitical variables include the general attitude of government and population towards the private business sector, the system of government, its involvement in the commercial sector, labor relations, and the degree of political stability. The forecaster must also be aware of the sensitivity of each variable and its relative importance with respect to the time horizon projected. Relevant variables should be forecast for the times of interest to management in the budgeting process, for example, one, three, or five years.

(c) Technical Approach. Technical analysis has developed from the study of international money market behavior in an attempt to predict cyclical trends in the demand and supply of individual currencies. This forecasting technique concentrates more on predicting the timing of exchange rate movements than on the underlying fundamentals per se. By forecasting when a shift in currency values is expected, the user of technical analysis expects to be in a position to hedge accordingly. Technical analysts often postulate that the market adjusts too swiftly to changes in fundamental variables to make a forecast based on fundamentals meaningful. They argue that it is best to observe the signals which mark a change in market mentality and to climb on board before the market leaves them behind. Fundamentalists have often argued that this game plan is little better than the "school of fish" theory, which states that a fish is best protected if it swims with the maintream and in the center of the school out of a predator's reach.

Regardless of the forecast discipline employed, the ability to predict exchange rates accurately remains particularly important, given the degree of volatility in the present floating-rate system. From a practical point of view, management must decide whether it wants to forecast exchange rates on the basis of one of the aforementioned theories or whether it concludes that exchange rates cannot be forecast and that, therefore, the current exchange rates (at the time of initiating a particular budget cycle) should be used for the forward period (an exception would be made for hyperinflationary countries, where the fundamental theory would be adopted).

25.3 THE MULTINATIONAL ORGANIZATION

(a) Corporate Structure. Before more specific budgeting and control systems are presented, a basic corporate structure must be established. In actuality, corporate structures vary widely, from a strong parent company with numerous subsidiaries taking directions from the parent company to a parent company which, in effect, is literally a holding company which ties together virtually independent subsidiaries. Thus, practices depend upon the corporate culture developed within the companies.

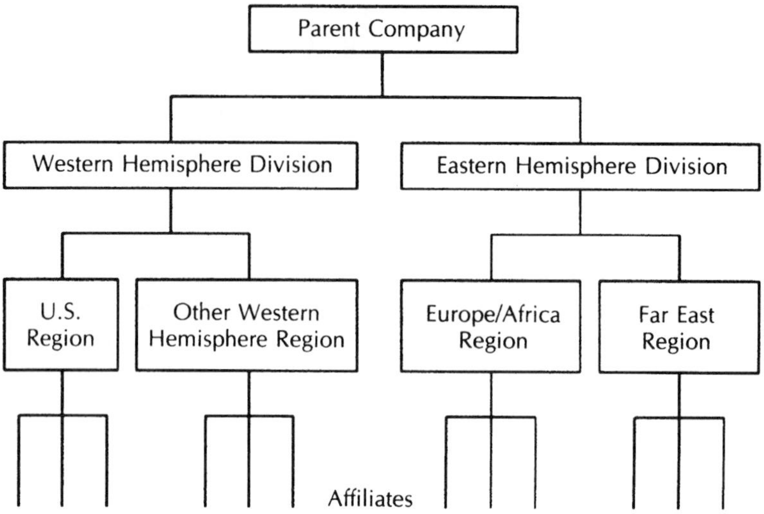

Exhibit 25.1. Corporate Organization.

(b) Corporate Level and Operating Divisions. For purposes of this chapter, we may at times refer to the parent or holding company as the "corporate" level. The subsidiaries or affiliates are usually grouped together under operating divisions for delegated guidance and control. Broadly speaking, operating divisions may be geographically oriented (Exhibit 25.1) or functionally organized (Exhibit 25.2). Frequently, there is an additional management layer, a "region" between the operating division and a number of affiliates. Of course, there are numerous other possibil-

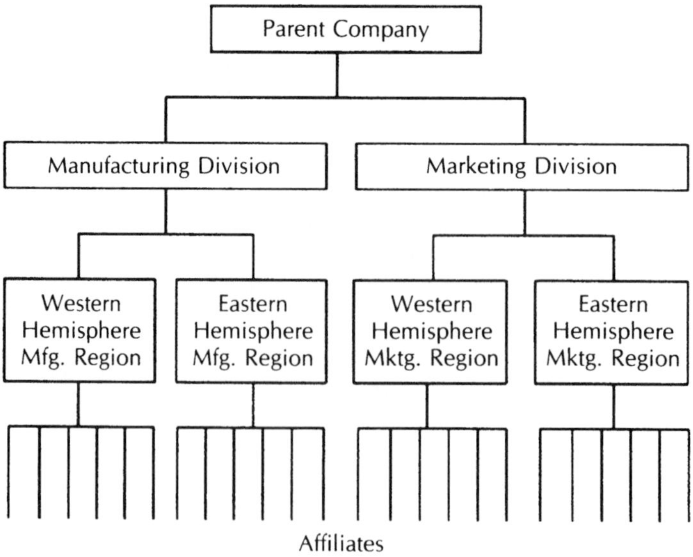

Exhibit 25.2. Corporate Organization.

ities. For example, there may be dual parent companies (as in the case of Royal Dutch/Shell); there may be affiliates reporting directly to the parent company; or, for one product line, the company may be organized geographically, but for another product line, a functional organization may be more suitable.

In the following discussion, we will assume that the parent company, operating divisions, and regions use the U.S. dollar to express financial results, regardless of the physical location of operations and affiliates. To designate the parent company orientation, the letters *PC* will be applied when referring to the parent company's and other management levels' U.S. dollar accounting.

The affiliates, on the other hand, operate, of course, in their respective local currencies, referred to as "LC."

25.4 BASIC APPROACHES TO CAPITAL BUDGETING AND PROFIT PLANNING

(a) Basic Approaches. When examining the methods and procedures used for capital budgeting and profit planning, we find two basic approaches: top-down and bottom-up.

If the corporate level determines the perimeter of the capital budget, the total amount of dollars to be spent, and then allocates portions to division, regions, and affiliates, this constitutes a top-down approach. If, conversely, the corporate level asks the affiliates to determine their capital requirements and proposed net income, and the regions and divisions merely aggregate the affiliates' proposal, we refer to this process as a bottom-up approach.

(b) Guidance. In practice, these two approaches are frequently combined. At the corporate level, the overall perimeters will be determined. In discussions with the next level of organization—the divisions—"guidance" will be given, suggesting to the divisions the total budgets to be given to the regions, as well as the net income expected to be generated by each region. In the meantime, the affiliates have prepared their own capital requirements, together with net profit and cash generation assumptions. The only firm guidance the affiliates receive are the assumptions regarding exchange rates to be used so that local plans can be converted into U.S. dollars.

(c) Local Conditions. After the affiliates' plans have been completed, taking into account local needs and operating conditions, negotiations between affiliate managements and regional managements take place to determine the final budgets and net profits to be proposed by the affiliates to the divisions and corporate management. The process will be described in more detail as we separate the capital budgeting procedures from those used for profit planning.

25.5 BUILDING THE CAPITAL BUDGET

(a) Objectives. Prior to the establishment of a capital budget, it is important that the company determine its long-range objectives and prepare a strategic plan that specifies timing horizons and overall capital requirements. In a multinational company, objectives and capital needs are then suggested for each country and each major affiliate or function within the countries.

(b) Annual and Total Requirements. Frequently, a negotiating period is needed during which the corporate level negotiates with the division, the division with the region, and, finally, the region with the affiliates what capital projects will eventually yield the desired objectives. To enable the affiliates to do the necessary preparatory work, two dimensions of all proposed capital projects are considered: the total cost of the project and the timing of cash expenditures to complete the project. For purposes of capital budgeting, the total cost, which may stretch out over several years, is included; for purposes of cash budgeting, the annual funds required are essential to determine the annual overall financing aspects.

(c) Interface between Objectives and Capital Budget. It is desirable, but not absolutely necessary, to prepare objectives for a three- or five-year period in sufficient detail, that is, stating requirements for each major program or project, so that the first forward year's data can—and frequently do—form the capital budget for that year. The remaining years of the objectives will then represent preliminary indications, which will be fleshed out in subsequent cycles.

(d) Determination of Exchange Rates. The reason for making Year 1 of the objectives the capital budget for Year 1 is the complexity caused by the need to set the exchange rates for each country's use in the objectives and capital budgeting process. It is recommended that the exchange rates be fixed at the beginning of that process; otherwise, a lot of time will be consumed in discussions (arguments) between a region and an affiliate as to which rate is to be used for what purpose. Precise rates fluctuate and frequently change daily. We shall see how we can cope with the reality of floating exchange rates when we discuss the control aspects of budgeting.

(e) Capital Budgets Illustration. We are now at the point where we want to put together the objectives and, within the objectives, details of the first forward year's capital budgets for Affiliate B in Region A. Let us assume that "appropriate" levels were agreed upon between the parent company and the division, as well as between the division and Region A. The levels for each affiliate are then negotiated between Region A and its affiliates. The end result of negotiations between the various management levels is an overall budget of PC 10,000 for Affiliate B, based on an exchange rate of PC 1 = LC 2 (see Exhibit 25.3).

(i) Functional Elements. The functional elements of such a budget would then be hammered out between Region A and Affiliate B, with the affiliate putting together detailed project-by-project proposals that may or may not add up to the required LC 20,000 level. This bottom-up approach frequently leads to changes in the total affiliate's budget, in which case further negotiations up the line take place and the corporation's overall objectives, capital budget, and related cash flow projections are changed. In other situations, an affiliate may be requested to come forward with projects that, with the possible addition of a contingency amount, will add up to the predetermined total.

To complete the illustration, Exhibit 25.3 also shows the full objectives cycle for Affiliate B. The data for 20X1 and 20X2 are worked out similarly to the procedures described in the preceding paragraph, except that sometimes a summary rather than a project-by-project approach is used. It should be observed that, in determining objectives levels, we maintained the exchange rate at PC 1 = LC 2 for the three forward

AFFILIATE B
Capital Budget
20X0

	PC	Exchange Rate	LC
Manufacturing	3,000	PC 1 = LC 2	6,000
Marketing	5,000		10,000
Transportation	2,000		4,000
Total	10,000		20,000

Objectives
20X0–20X2

	20X0		20X1		20X2	
	PC	LC	PC	LC	PC	LC
Manufacturing	3,000	6,000	2,000	4,000	2,000	4,000
Marketing	5,000	10,000	4,000	8,000	6,000	12,000
Transportation	2,000	4,000	1,000	2,000	3,000	6,000
Total	10,000	20,000	7,000	14,000	11,000	22,000

Exhibit 25.3. Capital Budget and Objectives.

years; it is the recommended practice, as forecasting different exchange rates for each year will not make the forecasts more "accurate."

(ii) Timing of Cash Expenditures. A few additional observations about capital budgeting in a multinational environment may be appropriate. The timing of cash expenditures of major projects becomes even more crucial than in a domestic environment. As the parent company's strategies are put together, all matters are considered in terms of the parent company's currency, say the U.S. dollar. If, for example, we are in favor of a project costing $2 million for Country X, with the financing in local currency to be spread over the next two years, a conscious decision must be made as to how to deal with the vagaries of exchange rate fluctuations. The cost of the project is likely to be more than $2 million or less than that amount, but it is most unlikely to come in at exactly $2 million. The company may want to consider hedging in such a way that the exchange rate is locked in; this is a financial decision, separate and apart from capital budgeting.

(iii) Regional Budget Retention. In the multinational environment, there is a budget technique which is utilized to overcome major uncertainties, not only those related to fluctuating exchange rates. These uncertainties may relate to cash availability problems, to changing market conditions, to procurement difficulties, and to many other situations. Under such circumstances, the region or higher corporate level may wish to retain budget funds for release at a later time. Exhibit 25.4 illustrates the capital budget for the Europe region, showing individual country budgets for the United Kingdom, France, Germany, and Italy, adding up to PC($) 35,000. However, the total

EUROPE REGION
Capital Budget
20X0

	PC ($)	LC
Affiliate C (United Kingdom)	10,000	6,000
Affiliate D (France)	8,000	45,000
Affiliate E (Germany)	12,000	20,000
Affiliate F (Italy)	5,000	6,000,000
Affiliates total	35,000	
Region control	10,000	
Region total	45,000	

Exhibit 25.4. Capital Budget.

Europe region budget is PC($) 45,000; the region maintains "control" over PC($) 10,000 which, during the budget year, may be transferred to one or more of the affiliates, reducing the region control budget by the amounts so transferred and increasing the affected affiliates' budgets accordingly. If we assume that PC($) 4,000 was transferred to Affiliate E and PC($) 6,000 to Affiliate F during 20X0, the final budget allocation is shown on Exhibit 25.5 in both PC($) and the LCs of the affected countries, using the same exchange rates as were used in the original capital budget.

25.6 CONTROLLING THE CAPITAL BUDGET

(a) Budget Controls. In controlling capital budgets, it is customary to examine three aspects of the budget periodically, say quarterly: the capital budget itself, appropriations against the capital budget (how much of the budget was authorized for actual implementation), and capital budget expenditures. We have illustrated a control aspect of the capital budget itself in our discussion of the region control procedure shown on Exhibits 25.4 and 25.5; otherwise, increases or decreases in the capital budget are usually a matter determined by the corporate level. Controls of capital ex-

EUROPE REGION
Capital Budget—Revised
20X0

	PC ($)	LC
Affiliate C (United Kingdom)	10,000	6,000
Affiliate D (France)	8,000	45,000
Affiliate E (Germany)	16,000	27,000
Affiliate F (Italy)	11,000	13,200,000
Total	45,000	

Exhibit 25.5. Capital Budget—Revised.

penditures are a function of the corporate treasurer's overall cash controls, which are not related to the capital budgeting process per se. We will therefore concern ourselves with budget appropriations only as they pertain to the real "control" aspects of capital budgeting.

(b) Status Report Illustration: Fixed Exchange Rates. Exhibit 25.6 illustrates a year-end status report, based upon the capital budget shown in Exhibit 25.3. At that stage, we determined that the exchange rate would be PC 1 = LC 2. In quarterly performance reporting, appropriations against the budget would use the same exchange rate. For the full year, both the manufacturing and marketing budgets were underappropriated in terms of PC and budget-based LC, while the transportation budget was overappropriated (presumably, the necessary approvals had been obtained, and appropriations were, therefore, in line with expectations as far as the region, division, and parent company were concerned). Normal expectations are that budgets, in total, will not be overappropriated.

From the affiliate's point of view, shown as "Memo: Local Analysis" in Exhibit 25.6, the situation was different; while directionally manufacturing and transportation appropriations reflected the same indications as in the report to the region, marketing overappropriated its budget, a situation which was probably reported to the region as being due to a weakening of the LC currency. Internal company control procedures usually specify whose approval is required to authorize such local company overappropriations; up to a certain level, no higher-level authorization may be

AFFILIATE B
Capital Budget Status Report
Appropriations
Year Ended December 31, 20X0

	PC			LC (Budget Basis)		
	Actual	Budget	Variance	Actual	Budget	Variance
Manufacturing	2,750	3,000	250	5,500	6,000	500
Marketing	4,750	5,000	250	9,500	10,000	500
Transportation	2,250	2,000	(250)	4,500	4,000	(500)
Total	9,750	10,000	250	19,500	20,000	500

Memo: Local Analysis

	LC		
	Actual	Budget	Variance
Manufacturing	5,700	6,000	300
Marketing	10,400	10,000	(400)
Transportation	4,800	4,000	(800)
Total	20,900	20,000	(900)

Note: The actual exchange rate used in the local analysis is PC 1 = LC 2.2.

Exhibit 25.6. Capital Budget Status Report: Appropriations.

needed. If, however, the local currency exchange rate strengthens compared to the budgeted exchange rate assumption, higher-level authorization normally would be required.

The reporting mechanism discussed in the foregoing paragraphs represents a control approach that stresses parent company (including division and region) emphasis on the total company budget, with relatively weak control needs over local variances due to fluctuating exchange rates.

(c) Status Report Illustration: Current Exchange Rates. A different control environment exists if the parent company wants to exercise more direct controls over an affiliate's budgets, including all the vagaries of changing exchange rates. In that case, the budgeted exchange rate is used for the capital budget only, while appropriations (like expenditures) are recorded as the exchange rate in force on the day, or in the month, of recording the appropriation.

This approach has the advantage of coming somewhat closer to real "actual" data, but it has the disadvantage that budgets have to be adjusted and projects may have to be abandoned solely because of shifts in the exchange rate.

The difference between the two control approaches depends, of course, upon the degree and frequency of exchange rate changes. If we use the same LC data as were illustrated in Exhibit 25.6 and if we assume that the average actual exchange rate in 20X0 was PC 1 = LC 2.2, the results are those shown in Exhibit 25.7 (the LC amounts are the same as the "Local Analysis" in Exhibit 25.6). Comparing the two exhibits, we note that, while the PC amounts are different, the direction of the variances from budget are the same and, as before, marketing underappropriated its budget in PC terms, while in actuality, in LC terms, a higher amount was appropriated than had been budgeted.

(d) Assessment of Alternative Approaches. No preference can be expressed for one or the other alternative control approach. Capital budgets represent intended capital programs. Other considerations entering into a decision regarding which control pro-

AFFILIATE B
Capital Budget Status Report
Appropriations
Year Ended December 31, 20X0

	PC			LC		
	Actual	Budget	Variance	Actual	Budget	Variance
Manufacturing	2,600	3,000	400	5,700	6,000	300
Marketing	4,700	5,000	300	10,400	10,000	(400)
Transportation	2,200	2,000	(200)	4,800	4,000	(800)
Total	9,500	10,000	(500)	20,900	20,000	(900)

Note: The actual exchange rate is PC 1 = LC 2.2.
The budget exchange rate is PC 1 = LC 2.

Exhibit 25.7. Capital Budget Status Report: Appropriations.

cedure to use include the sources of financing and actual capital expenditures. If financing normally takes place in the PC country and funds are sent to the affiliate, the former approach—freezing the exchange rate—may be an adequate and simpler procedure. If the affiliate is essentially self-financing, reporting budget appropriations at current rates rather than fixed exchange rates provides a more accurate and meaningful presentation; moreover, in dealing with hyperinflationary countries, a fixed exchange rate approach is entirely unrealistic and leads to distorted results.

25.7 BUILDING THE PROFIT PLAN

(a) Income Forecasting: The Profit Plan. In the preceding sections, we observed the close relationship between the long-range objectives and the capital budgets, especially those for the first forward year. A full set of objectives contains not only capital projections for the next three to five years but also income levels and cash flow forecasts. Here we want to concentrate on income forecasting.

While it was appropriate and time saving to use the first year of the objectives as both the starting and ending point for the capital budget, this approach does not work equally well for the profit plan or operating budget. A top-down/bottom-up dialogue was used to pass down guidance from the corporate level via division and region to the various affiliates, with the affiliates building up the details of capital projects and programs to "meet" the corporate guidelines. The affiliates, no doubt, participated in establishing income levels in the objectives, but other than agreeing on broad economic perimeters—revenues, total costs and expenses, margins, taxes, and the resulting net income—a detailed buildup of all data does not normally occur.

(b) Development of the Profit Plan. In building a profit plan for the next forward year, it is important to establish the reasons for this exercise. The profit plan is frequently used as a target for, and commitment by, management. It is a vital forecast for the company's cash management, overall operating decisions, and maximizations of intracorporate transactions, and it frequently serves as a yardstick against which bonuses are calculated. It is, therefore, necessary to be as specific as possible within each affiliate when establishing underlying assumptions. It is often advisable to start literally from the bottom up, that is, involving the lowest level of the organization in determining realistic estimates for such data as volumes, prices, new products, and recurring and nonrecurring expenses, which, in turn, may be variable or nonvariable (fixed), and so on. Also, the likely economic conditions for each country—and sometimes for areas within a country—as well as income and other tax rates must be established by the various levels within each affiliate's organization. These assumptions are then presented to region management for its concurrence or suggested changes. As was the case in establishing capital budget details, there is an almost continuous negotiation process going on to make sure that region and affiliates think along the same lines.

(i) Local Currency-Based Income Statement. The affiliate's profit plan is then fleshed out and cast into a local income statement format. At this stage, we have monetary and volumetric data in the detail required by local management to run the local operation efficiently, but, because of the use of LC and local accounting conventions, higher management levels, for example, the region, will be unable to understand and to evaluate the profit plan. Some additional procedures must now be carried out.

AFFILIATE B
Profit Plan
Year ended December 31, 20X0

	PC	Exchange Rate	LC
Before-tax income:			
Manufacturing	310	PC 1 = LC 1	310
Marketing	225		225
Transportation	75		75
Administration	(40)		(40)
Total	570		570
Income tax	(285)		(285)
Net income	285		285

Exhibit 25.8. Profit Plan.

(ii) Conversion of Income Statement to U.S. Basis. The next step is to convert the LC-based local income statement into one that is based upon the parent company's income statement, in our case, U.S. "generally accepted accounting principles." By this time, the parent company, division, and region have determined the currency exchange rate to be used for individual affiliates. After having converted the LC-based local income statement into a PC-based income statement based on U.S. generally accepted accounting principles (the parent company's currency is the U.S. dollar), one final step may be necessary. Frequently, there are charges by the parent company that need to be allocated to the affiliate, and these have to be incorporated, both before and after tax, in the PC-based income statement.

To give us a basis for comparing results with profit plan, let us assume that Affiliate B's planned net income is LC 285, as shown in Exhibit 25.8. This exhibit shows functional pretax income, for which each function's general manager is responsible; income tax is then applied on a total affiliate basis. An alternative method would be to calculate the tax for each function; this can lead to some distortions due to allocated expenses, headquarters charges, and so on, and the need to cope with tax credits arising from loss operations in one function, creating credits that can be offset against taxes arising from profitable operations of other functions. (For a further discussion of international tax considerations, see Chapter 30.)

(iii) An Affiliate's Profit Plan. Affiliates prepare detailed underlying plans, one of which is illustrated in Exhibit 25.9. To facilitate the analysis of results later in this chapter, the exhibit shows a conventional income statement, and we will refer to the marketing function, a profit center of Affiliate B, as LC Company. In both Exhibits 25.8 and 25.9, we have assumed a planned exchange rate of LC 1 = PC 1.

25.8 PROFIT PLANNING CONTROLS

(a) Periodic Income Reports. Throughout the year, control reports are prepared at intervals required by the various levels of management and the corporate parent.

AFFILIATE B—MARKETING
(LC COMPANY)
Profit Plan
Year Ended December 31, 20X0

	LC
Revenues	1,000
Beginning inventory	(500)
Purchases	(500)
Total	(1,000)
Ending inventory	500
Cost of sales	(500)
Gross profit (gross margin)	500
Expense	(200)
Interest	(25)
Depreciation	(50)
Before-tax income	225

Note: The company determined an exchange rate of LC 1 = PC 1.

Exhibit 25.9. Marketing Profit Plan.

Thus, for example, it is likely that LC Company, the marketing function of Affiliate B, will have prepared its profit plan in monthly installments and will compare its actual results against the profit plan on a monthly basis. While Affiliate B, in total, will do similarly, it is possible that the region requires only quarterly results and comparisons with the profit plan. If a company has numerous affiliates, it may be too costly and, from a materiality point of view, insufficiently important to obtain monthly data from small affiliates, such as those in some less developed countries, while results from significant operations in some of the larger countries may need the parent company's attention on a monthly basis.

Quarterly income comparisons are necessary, not only because of managerial considerations, but also because Securities and Exchange Commission (SEC) filings of corporations listed on the major U.S. stock exchanges require a commentary by management of the previous quarter's results. While these commentaries pertain to a comparison of the current quarter's results with those of the same quarter of the previous year, the method used for analysis is the same as that used for comparison with the profit plan.

Let us assume now that we have reached the end of Year 20X0 and that we want to compare why the results for the year differed from those planned and, further, attribute the differences to operating factors, on the one hand, and to currency factors, on the other.

(b) Income Comparison. Exhibit 25.10 shows the income statement for Affiliate B by function. Management also knows that the profit plan reflected a currency conversion of LC 1 = PC 1, whereas the actual exchange rate during 20X0 and at year-end 20X0 was LC 1 = PC 0.9, a local currency depreciation of 10%. Looking at the PC columns in Exhibit 25.10, we note that the total administrative expense exactly

AFFILIATE B
Income Statement
Year Ended December 31, 20X0

	LC			PC		
	Actual	Plan	Variance	Actual	Plan	Variance
Before-tax income						
Manufacturing	340	310	30	295	310	(15)
Marketing	360	225	135	279	225	54
Transportation	80	75	5	71	75	(4)
Administration	(40)	(40)	0	(36)	(40)	4
Total	740	570	170	609	570	39
Income tax	(370)	(285)	(85)	(185)	(285)	100
Net income	370	285	85	424	285	139

Exhibit 25.10. Income Statement.

equalled the profit plan in local currency; thus, the negative variance shown in PC must be fully attributable to currency factors. Indeed, the administrative expense in PC is 10% below the profit plan, the result of local currency depreciation. In those functions where the actual performance differed from the profit plan in LC, we have to perform some variance analysis to separate the currency factor from one or more operating factors. To illustrate this separation, we shall analyze the performance of the marketing function (LC Company), which shows favorable variances of LC 135 and PC 54, respectively.

(c) Variance Analysis. Variance analysis can be made relatively simple, or it can be extended to include detailed and sophisticated approaches, depending upon the requirements of managements. For illustrative purposes, we use a relatively simple approach, which is explained in detail, while the more sophisticated methods are only alluded to later in this chapter.

The two most common variances used by financial analysts are volume and price variances. We need these to analyze both revenues and costs, and the method is the same whether we deal with realizations or cost of sales. One way of arriving at a volume variance in revenues is to multiply the change in sales volume by the unit selling price of the base period. Similarly, when we wish to establish the volume variance arising out of costs, we multiply the change in cost volume by the base period's unit cost. The base period is the period against which we make our comparison, be it the prior year, the prior month, or the profit plan.

To arrive at the revenue price variance, we take the change in selling price and multiply it by the current period's sales volume. The cost price variance is computed similarly; the change in unit cost is multiplied by the current period's volume. It is more descriptive to call the price variance, relating to cost of sales, a cost rate variance.

The foregoing variances give us the explanation as to what happened to the margin or gross profit realized in our business. In the simplest variance analysis, one more aspect needs to be accounted for: expenses. The easiest method is to compare current period expenses with those of the comparison period and call the result an expense variance.

This methodology provides only a very basic variance analysis. More sophistication is frequently desirable and necessary. The price variance relating to revenues can easily be broken down into variances arising from price changes at the port of entry (assuming third-party market prices are available) and the prices achieved at the final destination. Similarly, the volume variances can be divided between a true volume variance and the variance which arises from a change in the mix of products sold. A more elaborate variance analysis approach will include the change in volume-related expenses as part of the volume variance. The cost rate variance can be calculated in such a way that management can ascertain the effect of a cost rate change based on current or replacement costs, segregating them from those which are due to the vagaries of the inventory valuation system. Finally, the expense variance can be made more useful by differentiating between fixed expenses, maintenance, gain or loss on exchange, gain or loss on the sale of assets, and so forth.

To simplify our illustration, we use only the four basic variances (volume, price, cost rate, and expenses); any other approach would make the understanding of currency impacts more complicated. The formulas suggested are those that have been found most useful by many businesses. While other formulas are possible, no statement can be made as to the most correct calculation, as much depends upon the results that a given manager wishes to concentrate on or achieve.

To arrive at an evaluation as to what the effects of currency are on income, it is necessary to go through the conventional variance analysis and then ascertain by difference how currency movements affected the stated results. Again, we have to establish a convention to determine the base on which we make our comparisons. Comparisons made against the currency translation in force during the base period are the most practical. Thus, for example, if the exchange rate in our profit plan was LC 1 = PC 1, all local currency results in the profit plan are translated at that rate. In our example, we assume that the LC has depreciated by 10% and that the actual exchange rate in year 20X0 and at year-end 20X0 was LC 1 = PC 0.9.

(d) Local Variance Analysis: Illustration. First, it is necessary to establish the variance analysis as it would be done by the local subsidiary or affiliate. Exhibit 25.11 presents the income statement of LC Company for the year ended December 31, 20X0. In the profit plan, it was assumed that the company would sell 1,000 units at LC 1; unit cost was LC 0.50; it planned expenses, interest, and depreciation of LC 200, LC 25, and LC 50, respectively. Actual results for 20X0 showed that the company's sales rose to 1,200 units at a selling price of LC 0.95 per unit; its cost had dropped to LC 0.40 per unit. Expenses rose to LC 220, and interest charges, to LC 30; depreciation was the same as planned.

The first column of the variance analysis is a total column and shows the variances between the actual results and the profit plan for each item in the income statement. The volume variance for revenues is computed by multiplying the change in sales volume (200) by the base period (profit plan) selling price of LC 1, which results in a variance of LC 200. The related volume variance applying to cost of sales is ascertained by multiplying the change in volume (200) by the base period unit cost of LC 0.50. The result indicates that volumes added LC 100 to the company's costs. Therefore, our net volume variance is LC 100, relating to gross profit and before-tax income. To identify the price variance, we take the actual volume of 1,200, multiply it

LC Company
Income Statement
Year Ended December 31, 20X0

	Actual	Plan	Total	Volume	Price	Cost Rate	Expense
			Variance Analysis (LC)				
Revenues	1,140	1,000	140	200	(60)		
Beginning inventory	(400)	(500)	100				
Purchases	(480)	(500)	20				
Total	(880)	(1,000)	120				
Ending inventory	400	500	(100)				
Cost of sales	(480)	(500)	20	(100)		120	
Gross profit	660	500	160	100	(60)	120	
Expense	(220)	(200)	(20)				(20)
Interest	(30)	(25)	(5)				(5)
Depreciation	(50)	(50)	0				
Before-tax income	360	225	135	100	(60)	120	(25)

Exhibit 25.11. Income Statement.

by the change in selling price (a negative LC 0.05), and obtain a negative price variance of LC 60. The cost rate variance is LC 120, which we obtain by multiplying the actual volume of 1,200 with the positive change in cost of LC 0.10. Finally, the negative expense variances of LC 20 and LC 5 are shown in the last column.

The analysis of these results shows that the company improved its before-tax income by LC 135, which is made up as follows:

	LC
Higher volumes accounted for	100
Lower prices reduced earnings by	(60)
Cost rate lower by	120
Expenses higher by	(25)
Before-tax income improved by	135

As mentioned previously, in many situations it is unnecessary, meaningless, or very difficult to extend the variance analysis to include the tax line. In most business situations, management can affect transactions in terms of pretax realizations and outlays only. Prices to customers are always stated on a pretax basis, and merchandise is normally paid for on a pretax basis. Moreover, tax calculations are frequently complex; companies avail themselves of accelerated depreciation for tax purposes, but not always for book purposes. In the United States and some other countries, depletion allowances for tax purposes have a different basis from that used for shareholder reporting purposes; various inventory systems, such as stock relief in the United Kingdom or LIFO valuation in many other jurisdictions, apply to tax calculations but do not always find reflection in book income (to mention just a few of the literally dozens of book/tax adjustments that multinational companies face). Consequently, the variance analysis frequently stops on the before-tax income line, and we follow this convention in this chapter.

The variance analysis, illustrated in Exhibit 25.11, shows details of revenues and cost of sales; these details are of importance when we discuss the impact of changing exchange rates later on. At times, companies are managed with attention being concentrated on the gross margin, or gross profit, by upper-level management. Local details above the gross profit line are regarded as responsibilities of the affiliates themselves rather than of the region, the division, or the parent company. In the discussion that follows, we will assume that all upper levels of management are, indeed, interested in revenue and cost details.

(e) Variance Analysis for Parent Company Use. Exhibit 25.12 extends the example just discussed to the parent company by showing how LC Company's results would be reflected in the parent company's statements, if we assume an exchange rate of LC 1 = PC 1 in the profit plan against a rate of LC 1 = PC 0.9 for actual 20X0 results.

(i) Functional Currency Determination. We have to introduce one additional element—the concept of "functional currency." Under FASB No. 52, the parent company determines the currency basis (functional currency) to be used for translation purposes: either (1) the parent company's currency or (2) the affiliate (local) company's currency. The illustration in Exhibit 25.12 is based on the concepts included in FASB No. 52, where the functional currency is the currency of the parent company. For example, if PC Company is located in the United States and LC Company in Turkey, assuming a hyperinflationary economy in that country, FASB No. 52 requires that the U.S. dollar be used as the functional currency.

(ii) Analysis If Functional Currency Is That of Parent Company. The data in the PC column follow logically from the above exchange rate assumptions. Two lines need further explanations. The beginning inventory has to be converted at the historical rate of exchange in compliance with FASB No. 52. For the purposes of this illustration, we are assuming that inventories are valued on a FIFO basis and that the profit plan rate is the same as the historical rate, namely LC 1 = PC 1. The actual ending inventory has an average exchange rate of LC 1 = PC 0.9, as the old inventories have been used up and only the latest inventories are held in stock. The other line that shows an unusual exchange rate conversion is the one showing the depreciation expense; that item also follows the requirement of an historical conversion rate (which in our example is LC 1 = PC 1) if the functional currency is the currency of the parent company, regardless of whether the exchange rate has changed since the assets were acquired originally.

Before considering the variance analysis of the parent company, we restate our principle of using the base period (profit plan) exchange rate as that which underlies our comparison. It reinforces the highly desirable result that the basic variance analysis at the parent company office will look the same as that obtained by the local subsidiary or affiliate. Thus, if we look at the variance analysis columns of Exhibit 25.12, we see that the results of the analysis—the bottom line for volume, price, cost, and expense—are exactly the same as those of Exhibit 25.11, except that all data are stated in PC. This is solely due to an assumption of a base period exchange rate of LC 1 = PC 1. In all real situations, this is most unlikely, but proportionately the results will always have to be the same.

LC COMPANY
Income Statement
Year Ended December 31, 20X0

	Actual			Plan			Variance Analysis (PC)					
	LC	ER	PC	LC	ER	PC	Total	Volume	Price	Cost Rate	Expense	Currency
Revenue	1,140	0.9	1,026	1,000	1.0	1,000	26	200	(60)			(114)
Beginning inventory	(400)	1.0	(400)	(500)	1.0	(500)	100					
Purchases	(480)	0.9	(432)	(500)	1.0	(500)	68					
Total	(880)		(832)	(1,000)		(1,000)	168					
Ending inventory	400	0.9	360	500	1.0	500	(140)					
Cost of sales	(480)		(472)	(500)		(500)	28	(100)		120		8
Gross profit	660		554	500		500	54	100	(60)	120		(106)
Expense	(220)	0.9	(198)	(200)	1.0	(200)	2				(20)	22
Interest	(30)	0.9	(27)	(25)	1.0	(25)	(2)				(5)	3
Depreciation	(50)	1.0	(50)	(50)	1.0	(50)	0					
Before-tax income	360		279	225		225	54	100	(60)	120	(25)	(81)

Notes: The functional currency is the currency of the parent company:
LC—local company currency
ER—exchange rate
PC—parent company currency.

Exhibit 25.12. Income Statement.

Continuing with our illustration: if we go through the results of our total revenue differences of PC 25, the volume and price variances of PC 200 and a negative PC 60, respectively, do not add up to the total of PC 25. Since we have previously established that these identified variances are the appropriate ones calculated by the local company, the balance, a negative PC 114, must be due to currency. (This amount can be calculated: the planned exchange rate was one-ninth higher than the actual rate, or 11.11%; 11.11% of PC 1,025 equals PC 114.) In other words, the weakening of the local currency versus the parent company currency has resulted in a translation into fewer parent company currency units. Exactly the opposite is the case for cost of sales and expenses.

Our final conclusion here is that, from the parent company's point of view, the total variance of PC 54 shows the same factors as the ones noted in Exhibit 25.11, only this time expressed in parent company currency, and that the difference in exchange rates has caused the overall results to be lower by PC 81. This indicates that, when a local company's currency depreciates in relation to the parent company currency, and where margins are positive, the translation process will result in lower earnings, as shown in this illustration. By the same token, the opposite would happen if the local currency appreciated.

The summary presentation of the variance factors is:

	PC
Higher volumes accounted for	100
Lower prices reduced earnings by	(60)
Cost rate lower by	120
Local gross profit (margin) improved by	160
Expenses higher by	(25)
Local factors accounted for an earnings improvement of	135
Weakened local currency caused currency losses of	(81)
Before-tax income improved by	54

Each one of these factors may be analyzed further. It is, for example, possible to segregate the currency effect between ordinary, or pure translation, and dual currency accounting. Dual currency accounting is practiced for such factors as inventories and fixed assets where books are kept in both LC and PC.

In this example, the dual currency accounting effect would be PC 45, which is arrived at as follows: the opening inventory was converted at a rate of LC 1 = PC 1, whereas the actual 20X0 exchange rate was LC 1 = PC 0.9, with the effect of reducing costs by PC 40. Similarly, depreciation was held constant, while a translation at the current rate would have reduced the charge by PC 5. Altogether, as our overall currency variance is a negative PC 81 and dual currency accounting explains PC 45 of the variance, the pure translation effect between the two quarters is a negative PC 36.

(iii) Analysis If Functional Currency Is That of Local Company. While the foregoing example converted the LC results into PC, using the principles of FASB No. 52, when the functional currency is PC, Exhibit 25.13 uses the same LC data but converts them into PC results, using LC as functional currency, and all elements are converted at the actual 20X0 exchange rate (LC 1 = PC 0.9). It should be noted that only two elements change (when compared with PC as functional currency): inventory and depreciation.

LC COMPANY
Income Statement
Year Ended December 31, 20X0

	Actual			Plan			Variance Analysis (PC)					
	LC	ER	PC	LC	ER	PC	Total	Volume	Price	Cost Rate	Expense	Currency
Revenue	1,140	0.9	1,026	1,000	1.0	1,000	26	200	(60)			(114)
Beginning inventory	(400)	0.9	(360)	(500)	1.0	(500)	140					
Purchases	(480)	0.9	(432)	(500)	1.0	(500)	68					
Total	(880)		(792)	(1,000)		(1,000)	208					
Ending inventory	400	0.9	360	500	1.0	500	(140)					
Cost of sales	(480)		(432)	(500)		(500)	68	(100)		120		48
Gross profit	660		594	500		500	94	100	(60)	120		(66)
Expense	(220)	0.9	(198)	(200)	1.0	(200)	2				(20)	22
Interest	(30)	0.9	(27)	(25)	1.0	(25)	(2)				(5)	3
Depreciation	(50)	0.9	(45)	(50)	1.0	(50)	5					5
Before-tax income	360		324	225		225	99	100	(60)	120	(25)	(36)

Notes: The functional currency is the currency of the local company:
LC—local company currency
ER—exchange rate
PC—parent company currency.

Exhibit 25.13. Income Statement.

The analytical procedures are exactly the same as those just illustrated, and the volume, price, cost rate, and expense variance continue to reflect the same relationships after translation into PC, as they did in the original LC example. There is, however, a change in the currency variance between Exhibits 25.12 and 25.13.

If PC is the functional currency, the currency variance is a negative PC 81; if LC is the functional currency, the currency variance is a negative PC 36. The difference of PC 45 is, of course, the currency effect of using historical currency rates (dual currency accounting) for purposes of Exhibit 25.12—a situation which no longer applies under the assumptions for Exhibit 25.13. (The negative currency variance of PC 36 can be arrived at independently by multiplying the pretax income of PC 324 with the 11.11% change in currency values.) It is evident that, in those situations where LC is used as functional currency, we achieve an improved analysis of results, as the currency variance represents a true measure of the effect of the changed currency values without being encumbered with accounting conventions which have little meaning in the eyes of management.

The results of the variance analysis, if LC is the functional currency, are therefore the following:

	PC
Higher volumes accounted for	100
Lower prices reduced earnings by	(60)
Cost rate lower by	120
Local gross profit (margin) improved by	160
Expenses higher by	(25)
Local factors accounted for an earnings improvement of	135
Weakened local currency caused currency losses of	(36)
Before-tax income improved by	99

(f) Assessment of Variance Analysis Approaches. Variance analysis is a methodology which explains the differences in results when we are comparing two income statements; the technique is the same, whether we compare actual income with the profit plan or one period with another, say the same quarter of the previous year. Such analysis serves as a "control," not only over operations, but also over currency effects. By substituting different exchange rates in the profit plan statements, ranges of currency exposure can be established which, in turn, permit hedging decisions to be made. On the operational side, all levels of management can arrive at conclusions as to future actions to be taken on the basis of what volume or price variances reveal. For example, a negative price variance may cause management to probe into the possibility and effects of raising unit prices; a negative cost rate variance may suggest a need for better inventory controls or a change in suppliers.

The recommended basic methodology is not affected by any revision of the techniques for translating local currency statements. The examples show that the basic operational variances are the same, regardless of whether the parent company's or the subsidiary (local) company's currency is selected as functional currency; only the variance attributable to changes in currency relationships differs in line with the translation technique employed. The portion of the analysis which deals with the operational events that occurred in the country in which LC Company was located will not be affected, regardless of which currency is selected as functional.

(g) Other Profit Plan Control Aspects. Up to this point, we have concerned ourselves with the financial aspects of profit plans, their determination, currency affects, and controls. One most important factor in profit planning and controls must be added: operating statistics. Most plans and subsequent periodic control reports include a host of operating nonfinancial data. We may need volume assumptions for each product or line of merchandise. We may have to establish labor hours and machine usage hours. Other plans may include capacity utilization data. Depending upon industry and lines of business, operating statistics may tell managements in a succinct manner what happened and, to some managers, the conversion of these data into financial elements may be of secondary importance. More generally, operating details furnish the basis for simple explanations of the variances discussed above, particularly volume variances.

25.9 SUMMARY. In this chapter, we have discussed some major aspects of capital budgeting and profit planning in a multinational environment. In both areas, we have to come to grips with the planning process of the corporation which desires to implement appropriate procedures for, first, establishing and, later, controlling the end results of the planning process.

Perhaps we can summarize the essential features of multinational budgeting and controls. There must be a clear-cut organizational structure, from the parent company at the top to the operating functions of each affiliate at the bottom. There has to be a strong communications link between the various levels to search out ideas, reach appropriate conclusions, and arrive at capital spending and income levels that straddle the fine line between the availability of funds and the generation of new cash sources via the income route. Capital budgets and profit plans must be put together and fully understood in both the parent company's currency and that of each affiliate. There must be adequate reference points to enable all management levels to establish periodic controls; in the capital budgets, major projects or programs should be listed; the profit plan should display the results of specific volume, price, and expense targets, to name just a few. For all plans, currency exchange rate assumptions must be agreed upon among the various management levels.

The types and frequency of control reports depend upon the varied requirements of the managements involved; the control reports should present data that fulfill the "need to know" by management.

CHAPTER 26

DYNAMIC PERFORMANCE MEASUREMENT SYSTEMS FOR A GLOBAL WORLD: THE COMPLEXITIES TO COME

Stephen J. Mezias
New York University
Patrice Murphy
New York University
Ya-Ru Chen
New York University
Mikelle A. Calhoun
New York University

CONTENTS

26.1 INTRODUCTION. The growing intensity of global competition has been widely documented, both with respect to the structure and strategy of transnational organizations[1] and the effects on behavior in organizations.[2] In order to compete more effectively in global markets, increasing numbers of firms are establishing

---

[1]Bartlett and Ghoshal, 1989.
[2]Adler, 1992.

physical operations outside their home nation. Cross-national operations permit closer contact with customers in markets outside the organization's home base, access to local labor markets, and penetration of political systems, which may be crucial in shaping the environment for trade. The globalization of business has spurred growth in new organizational forms such as alliances, joint ventures, and virtual corporations, as well as the more traditional multinational corporation (MNC).

Every year, *Fortune* publishes a list of "the world's most admired companies." In the current, extremely volatile, world environment, "this year's winners have in common . . . global reach and vision."[3] The author, Jeremy Kahn, explained that "as the planet shrinks, many organizations are clearly struggling to find the right balance between localization and globalization, between the organization's culture and that of the countries in which the corporation operates."[4] Kahn noted that we have moved from a time when international operations were viewed as of little value to a time when "[p]ower has shifted to business units responsible for performing a given function globally, and the empasis is on optimizing processes worldwide."[5]

Indeed, there has been increasing attention to the need for coordination between units in different geographic locations of companies that have operations dispersed across the globe.[6] The rising tide of international operations may suggest that managerial experience in dealing with operations outside the home country is essential for the development of organizational leaders.[7] A large body of empirical evidence has confirmed that cultural variables affect the success of many common management strategies,[8] including attempts by organizations to assess the performance of their multinational operations. The general importance of the issue of assessing the performance of global units and subsidiaries is highlighted by the specific situations of firms in the United States and Canada. For these firms, trade liberalization and other forces have made even more acute the need to address the issues of globalization and trade liberalization.[9] However, the kind of information and analysis that management needs in making such decisions remains unclear.

In a recent article in *CFO, The Magazine for Senior Financial Executives*, the problems encountered by firms seeking to evaluate potential and existing foreign operations were presented.[10] According to the author, the task of determining a requisite level of performance is complicated because "multinationals can find themselves confronted with hyperinflation, currency risks, and volatile, underdeveloped capital markets." [11] When Timothy Smith, director of capital and business planning for the Latin American unit of General Motors Corporation "tried to determine how accurately [GM's hurdle] rates reflected the cost of operating in the parts of the world for which his unit was responsible, he came up empty-handed. And that was unsettling."[12] Explaining his reaction further, Smith stated: "We thought we had been

---

[3]Kahn, 1998, p. 207.

[4]Id., p. 226.

[5]Id.

[6]Black, Gregersen, and Mendenhall, 1992.

[7]Bowman, 1986.

[8]For example, see Erez, 1992, 1986; Cheng, 1995; Cox, Lobel, and McLeod, 1991; and for reviews, see Adler, 1992; Bhagat, Kedia, Crawford, and Kaplan, 1990.

[9]De Grandpre, 1989.

[10]Meyers, 1998.

[11]Id.

[12]Id.

doing well, but we also felt that we didn't really have any basis on which to judge ourselves."

The GM example suggests a need for consideration of the issues involved with identifying appropriate "hurdles" for entry into a new country as well as the complications encountered when trying to measure the performance of existing international locations. The hurdle rate and the company's perceptions of its ability to meet or exceed it have clear implications for the decision to enter a foreign market; it also sets the standard for evaluation of future performance of the foreign operation. Obviously, the need to develop an appropriate measure or hurdle to use for making decisions regarding proposed or existing foreign operations is great. Meyers, in his *CFO* article, pointed out that "[g]etting the numbers right is critical to making good investment decisions and accurately compensating offshore managers."[13] Smith has posited that it might make more sense "for multinationals to determine what level of returns equity investors are demanding in foreign markets today, and then invest only in those markets. . . . If GM isn't earning a rate of return in Brazil comparable to what [could be made] investing in a Brazilian fund, then [GM is] not doing a service to any U.S. investor."[14]

Yet, in the domain of hurdle rate calculation, as with other forms of measuring or assessing foreign operations, success has been, at best, mixed. History has been a primary source of guidance, and many corporations have relied on capital asset pricing models, marked up to reflect the perceived increase in risk related to the particular foreign market.[15] Although limited, a recent survey of such practices suggested some surprising results. Companies were asked how they calculated the cost of capital and set hurdle rates in assessing, evaluating, and comparing their operations around the world. The survey found that a "follow-the-leader" mentality exists and that "none of the surveyed firms had developed a methodology for setting international hurdle rates."[16] Most firms reported that the evaluation, measurement, and assessment of foreign operations tended to vary with current strategy rather than be held to some regular standard based on some calculation of rates of return.[17]

Global companies continue to struggle with the question of how to evaluate and assess their foreign operations; for example, Hewlett-Packard recently decided to abandon its previous pricing policy and adopt a global pricing initiative.[18] Elizabeth Smith, the former director of finance and administration at Levi Strauss's Greek affiliate, reported some of the difficulties of her experience in managing foreign operations. She argued that there can be many frustrating business practices encountered by a foreign office—many of which can affect financial practices and the bottom line.[19] The varying practices result in a number of differences that make it difficult to compare operations in one country to operations in another country. The problematic individual experiences of companies continuing to struggle with the search for appropriate performance measures or assessment techniques for foreign subsidiaries is reflected by a study of a large number of companies with foreign operations. Only

---

[13]Id.
[14]Id.
[15]Id.
[16]Id.
[17]Id.
[18]Anonymous, 1994.
[19]Anonymous, 1995.

one measure was believed to give reliable information for comparing operations in multiple countries: profitability as indicated by the ratio of selling, general, and administrative expenses to sales.[20] Where other measures are used, either by necessity or choice, they must be adjusted to render them comparable, which is likely to be a fairly complex process. This is reflected in the experience of Thomas Schoewe, senior vice president and CFO of Black & Decker Corporation, who offered the following characterization of the process: "If somebody thinks there's a cookie-cutter recipe for this, I'd like to see the results."[21]

As this brief discussion makes clear, management accountants have had mixed success in creating comparable financial controls for the multiple operations of multinational enterprises. From the perspective of many financial managers, traditional concerns, such as translation of financial information into the home currency, political risk, and the uncertainty of financial markets abroad, have not yet been resolved in a satisfactory manner. At the same time, a new set of challenges for management accountants has arisen in connection with the need to develop dynamic performance measurement and financial controls. Though more recent than globalization, these challenges loom large in a contemporary vision of the role of financial management and control. They can be dated to two articles that appeared in *The Harvard Business Review* at the beginning of this decade that called for a broadening of the traditional conceptualization of the role of financial and management control. The first, by Robert Eccles, forcefully made the point that new strategies and competitive realities demand new measurement systems.[22] The second, by Robert Kaplan and David Norton, summarized some practical steps for dealing with these new strategies and competitive realities in terms of the notion of the balanced scorecard.[23]

Despite the fact that many of the firms that have struggled with constructing new performance measures are also struggling with globalization, there has been very little recognition of the additional complexity that dynamic performance measures can introduce into the global financial management conundrum. Our plan in this chapter is to begin this process of recognition by reporting on some data from various locations of an American multinational. These data result from an attempt by this multinational to create dynamic performance measurement systems for one of its divisions in locations throughout the world. In doing this, our hope is to begin to scratch the surface of the complexity that is to come in global management accounting.

We will proceed as follows. First, as a model of dynamic performance measurement systems, we focus on adaptive aspiration levels as first introduced in *A Behavioral Theory of the Firm.*[24] Second, having introduced the notion of adaptive aspirations, we examine data from several sites to assess the parameters of this model. Finally, we close with a discussion of some implications of the different findings from these various sites for the complexity of performance measurement and management accounting.

26.2 ADAPTIVE ASPIRATIONS. The assumption that organizations set goals, or aspiration levels, and compare their actual performance to their goals, is common in be-

---

[20]Wallace and Walsh, 1995.
[21]Meyers, 1998.
[22]Eccles, 1991.
[23]Kaplan and Norton, 1992.
[24]Cyert and March, 1963.

havioral models of organizational learning since Cyert and March.[25] Typically, this literature develops the proposition that performance above or below aspiration level affects the likelihood of observable organizational change because performance relative to aspiration levels defines the organization's perceptions of success and failure. Change in behavior is more likely when performance is below aspiration level, or perceived as failure. This is a typical outcome of trial-and-error learning; behavior that is associated with success tends to be repeated, while behavior that is associated with failure tends not to be repeated.[26]

(a) Arguments Concerning Aspiration Levels. The original statement of the behavioral theory of the firm summarized much of the basic thinking that has developed into this conventional wisdom on the role of aspirations in decision making. For example, Cyert and March wrote, "[m]ost organization objectives take the form of an aspiration level rather than an imperative to maximize or minimize."[27] The main implication of this argument is that one of the most important determinants of firm behavior is whether the experience of the recent past is coded as success or failure; this is determined by whether actual performance is below (failure) or above (success) aspiration level. This work focused on how aspiration levels frame action so that organizational behavior varies significantly according to whether performance has exceeded or fallen below target. In particular, the original statement of the behavioral theory of organizational learning focused on how performance relative to a target affected search behavior and the possibility of organizational change. Cyert and March described this process: "Search within the firm is problem oriented. A problem is recognized when the organization either fails to satisfy one or more of its goals or when such a failure can be anticipated in the immediate future. So long as the problem is not solved, search continues. The problem . . . is solved by discovering an alternative that satisfies the goals."[28] A central argument of this perspective is that aspiration levels mediate perceptions of success and failure. These perceptions are important because failure is a trigger for search and change. A second core argument concerning aspiration levels in the behavioral theory is that they adapt to experience. Cyert and March argued that "the aspiration level changes in response to experience."[29] Furthermore, they predicted that performance relative to this aspiration level would influence strategic choice. Thus, aspiration levels are one possible mechanism by which organizations may try to ensure that measures of performance are dynamic, at least in the sense that they change over time in response to experience.

(b) Role of Aspiration Levels. It is also important to recognize that the role of aspiration levels takes on additional significance when we recognize that these levels are not fixed. Rather, they are continually adapting to performance feedback. The implications of this have been explored by March[30] and March and Shapira.[31]

---

[25]Id.
[26]Levitt and March, 1988.
[27]Cyert and March, 1993, p. 32.
[28]Id., p. 28.
[29]Id., p. 32.
[30]March, 1988.
[31]March and Shapira, 1992.

If aspirations adapt quickly to the level of past performance, or even exceed this level due to optimism, then decision makers will be in a failure decision context most of the time. This suggests a high level of risk taking but also actions influenced by psychological forces such as escalation of commitment and external attribution. If aspirations adapt slowly to performance feedback, however, a success decision context results. This suggests a low level of risk taking and psychological forces such as internal attributions and complacency in the belief that success will continue.

We suspect that the role of aspirations as a framing mechanism for organizational decisions is quite broad. We see the impact of this variable on both decision-maker cognition and the behavior of organizational systems. In terms of cognition, the use of aspirations to code performance outcomes as positive or negative serves a cognitive simplification function.

By allowing decision makers to code performance as satisfactory or not satisfactory, aspiration levels simplify the decision-making process. Not only does this simple categorization of performance outcomes provide frames of reference, but these frames of reference may cue certain schemas in the minds of decision makers that can influence their choices in a wide variety of ways.[32] Cognitive schemas and associated responses are cued through a process of categorizing situations. Certain schemas are linked with certain types of situations. Given the prevalence of categorizing situations as successes or failures, decision makers are likely to have developed schemas for responding to success situations and failure situations. Thus, performance relative to aspiration serves to elicit an array of responses associated with either success or failure.

In terms of the impact of aspirations on organizational systems, we suspect that aspirations serve to both absorb actual variations in performance and to motivate organizational participants. Because aspirations adapt to actual performance, large aspiration–performance discrepancies will be tempered by the fact that target levels of performance move toward actual performance outcomes. Furthermore, to the extent that aspiration formation is optimistic, organizations will frequently find themselves with negative performance gaps that motivate continued effort. As a result of these two systemic effects, we would expect to observe patterns of organizational action that are relatively consistent over long periods of time.[33] Lant and Mezias[34] have demonstated this effect in simulation studies. They also show how large changes in organizational action can occur in organizations characterized by adaptive aspirations when significant environmental changes occur.

26.3 A FIELD STUDY OF ADAPTIVE ASPIRATIONS. As our review of the literature on behavioral theories of organizational learning has indicated, there are many interesting questions of importance that remain open. In particular, we believe there has been a real shortage of field work to examine the processes by which organizations exhibit the behaviors that have been the focus of models of organizations as experiential learning systems.

In the next section, we illustrate some of the complex dynamics that may emerge

---

[32]Lant, 1992; Milliken and Lant, 1991.

[33]Tushman and Romanelli, 1985.

[34]Lant and Mezias, 1992.

in a system of performance management characterized by adaptive aspirations with a field study of aspiration level setting at a large American multinational.

We believe that aspiration levels may be a plausible vehicle for understanding how companies go about implementing the kinds of dynamic performance measures that have attracted much recent attention. Furthermore, we are motivated by the observation that empirical exploration of how aspirations in organizations are actually formulated has been limited. We have collected data on goals and budgets for individuals, groups, departments, and divisions over time at several sites in multiple countries: We use data from these sites to estimate and compare one model of aspiration level updating.[35] Patterns over time such as those highlighted in the experimental literature might emerge, or some new finding might be uncovered. In addition, by comparing these goals and budgets across hierarchical levels and within hierarchical levels over time, we hope to shed some light on the dynamics of goal setting in complex organizations. The present study tests a specific model of aspiration adaptation, the attainment discrepancy model.[36]

According to the attainment discrepancy model, individuals and groups adapt their aspiration levels using a simple decision rule of adjustment to feedback on performance compared with aspiration level. The model can be summarized as:

$$AL_{i,t} = \alpha_0 + \alpha_1 AL_{i,t-1} + \alpha_2[P_{i,t-1} - AL_{i,t-1}] \tag{1}$$

where $AL_{i,t}$ is aspiration level for the *i*th person or units in the current period, $AL_{i,t-1}$ is the aspiration level for that entity in the previous period, and $P_{i,t-1}$ is its performance in the previous period.

The attainment discrepancy model predicts that aspiration levels will be a function of at least two variables: previous aspiration level and actual performance during the previous period. The specific functional form shown in equation (1) was found by Lant to provide the best description of aspiration-level adaptation. It models aspiration level as a function of previous aspiration level and attainment discrepancy, with a single period lag. In equation (1), attainment discrepancy showns as $P_{i,t-1}$ $AL_{i,t-1}$ is equal to the actual performance of the *i*th unit or person minus the aspiration level for that entity. Thus, the model can be restated as follows:

$$AL_{i,t} = \beta_0 + \beta_1{}^* AL_{i,t-1} + \beta_2 P_{i,t-1} \tag{2}$$

where $\beta_1{}^* = \alpha_1 - \alpha_2$ and $\beta_2 = \alpha_2$ from equation (1). In order to avoid having $AL_{i,t-1}$ enter the stimated equation twice, the parameter estimates in this study are developed using the model in equation (2). For purposes of comparison with previous results, we will restate the estimated parameters from equation (2) in terms of the parameters in equation (1) in the discussion. We test the attainment discrepancy model using field data on group goals, determined in the context of an American financial service organization's retail operations.

Our focus in reporting results from this model will be to provide examples of the very different kinds of processes of aspiration-level adaptation that may take place in multiple sites in different nations that are all part of a single division of a large American financial services company.

---

[35]Lant, 1992; Glynn, Lant, and Mezias, 1991.

[36]Lant and Montgomery, 1987; Glynn, Lant, and Mezias, 1991; Lant, 1992.

26.4 THREE PRELIMINARY ANALYSES

(a) The Data. Quantitative records of objectives kept over time and revised after receiving reports of performance with respect to those objectives have been collected at several sites. Regressions to estimate the parameters in equation (2) are reported below. What follows is a brief outline of several research questions related to the measurement of performance at this company along with a presentation of results from some preliminary analyses. In discussing these three questions, data reported will concern six different measures used at four different sites.

(b) Empirical Confirmation of the Adaptive Process. A first obvious question is whether the attainment discrepancy model, confirmed using experimental subjects[37] and groups of executives and master's degree students taking a graduate marketing course,[38] will be confirmed using field data. To test this, data from the goals of the retail units for total deposits at one site were collected. At this particular site, the distribution of deposit goals, which were stated in local currency, seemed very skewed; examination of the distribution of the log of these goals revealed a distribution that better conformed with the assumptions of the general linear model. In addition, several of the retail units had recently been converted from being franchise operations to being wholly owned units of the company. This change in status was indicated by a dummy variable called Branch Conversion in the analysis. The results are reported in Exhibit 26.1; as can be seen by inspection of the results, they are roughly consistent with those found in the past research. First, there is a significant, positive constant; β_0 is greater than zero at the 0.01 level. Second, there is a significant effect from previous aspiration level; as predicted, β_1 is greater than zero, also at the 0.01 level. Third, performance in the previous period has a significant effect; β_2 is greater than zero at the 0.05 level. Finally, the control variable for the conversion of retail units is also significant; the parameter measuring the effect of being among those observations β_3 indicates that they have a slighltly higher intercept than the other observation ($p < 0.05$).

---

[37]Glynn, Lant, and Mezias, 1991.
[38]Lant and Montgomery, 1987; Lant, 1992.

Measure: Annual branch goals for liabilities stated in local currency.

Data: 102 usable observations were obtained.

Predictor Variable	**Coefficient**
Constant	2.270**
Log of Previous Aspiration Level	.452**
Log of Previous Performance Level	.078*
Branch Conversion	.177*
*p < 0.05	**p < 0.01

Restated Model:

$$\text{LogGoal}_t = 2.270 + .530\ \text{LogGoal}_{t-1} + .078\ (\text{LogPerf}_{t-1} - \text{LogGoal}_{t-1}) + .177\ \text{BrConv}$$

Exhibit 26.1. Goals for Deposits.

Measure: Annual cost center goals for costs, stated in local currency.

Data: 95 usable observations were obtained.

Predictor Variable	**Coefficient**
Constant	.709
Log of Previous Aspiration Level	–.077
Log of Previous Performance Level	.975**
*p < 0.05	**p < 0.01

Restated Model:

$$\text{LogGoal}_t = .709 + .175\ \text{LogGoal}_{t-1} + .975\ (\text{LogPerf}_{t-1} - \text{LogGoal}_{t-1})$$

Exhibit 26.2. Goals for Costs.

(c) Aspiration Levels Through the Balance Sheet. We also became interested in the question of how pervasive the phenomenon of adaptive aspirations was in the organization. Perhaps the goals for deposits we chose are an aberration, and most goals at the organization do not follow an adaptive process. To answer this question, we decided to follow adaptive goals through the balance sheet by examining those that pertained to costs, revenues, and overall profitability. The analysis for costs is reported in Exhibit 26.2, which represents estimation of equation (2) using the log of annual goals stated in local currency for all cost centers at one of the sites. As with the analysis of deposits, logs were used to satisfy the distributional assumptions of the general linear model. Interestingly, the results for costs indicate that neither the constant nor the previous aspiration level has a significant effect on the current level of aspiration. Rather, it is the log of actual cost performance—that is, the log of costs actually incurred by each center—that is the best predictor of subsequent goals for that cost center. Thus, these goals seem to adapt to performance without reference to past goals and with an intercept that is not significantly different from zero. For revenues, we examined sales of mortgage products at one of the sites measured in local currency and subjected to a logarithmic transformation, once again for distributional reasons (Exhibit 26.3). As with the analysis of deposits, there had been recent transformations at some of the units, and this is reflected in the coding of a dummy variable to indicated these transitions. For sales, as with de-

Measure: Annual branch goals for mortgage products stated in local currency.

Data: 102 usable observations were obtained.

Predictor Variable	**Coefficient**
Constant	1.729**
Log of Previous Aspiration Level	.196*
Log of Previous Performance Level	.389**
Branch conversion	.167*
*p < 0.05	**p < 0.01

Restated Model:

$$\text{LogGoal}_t = 1.729 + .585\ \text{LogGoal}_{t-1} + .389\ (\text{LogPerf}_{t-1} - \text{LogGoal}_{t-1}) + .167\ \text{BrConv}$$

Exhibit 26.3. Goals for Sales.

Measure: Quarterly goals for profitability stated in local currency.

Data: 89 usable observations were obtained.

Predictor Variable	Coefficient
Constant	.251**
Log of Previous Aspiration Level	.725**
Log of Previous Performance Level	.198**
*p < 0.05	**p < 0.01

Restated Model:

$LogGoal_t = .251 + .923\ LogGoal_{t-1} + .198\ (LogPerf_{t-1} - LogGoal_{t-1})$

Exhibit 26.4. Goals for Profits.

posits the model is exactly as fitted by Lant.[39] There is a significant constant that is greater than zero, a significant, positive coefficient on past aspiration, and a significant, positive coefficient on past performance. Once again, the control variable for the conversion of units indicates that this population should have a higher intercept. To examine profitability goals, we used 89 observations on goals for the profitability of individual units (Exhibit 26.4). Once again, a logarithmic transformation was done for distributional reasons. In this estimation as with that for revenues, the model is as estimated in previous work: The results indicate a significant, positive constant, a significant, positive effect from past aspiration, and a significant, positive effect from past performance.

We believe that this evidence that adaptive aspirations characterize all sides of the balance sheet indicates how pervasive a phenomenon the process represents. Furthermore, given that a large number of different measures at sites in different locations around the world have displayed outcomes consistent with an adaptive process, we feel confident in concluding that the phenomenon is quite pervasive, at least in this one organization.

(d) Adaptive Aspirations at the Boundary and in the Technical Core. The last of the preliminary analyses reported here concern different locations in the organization in terms of whether they are in the organization's technical core or in the boundary spanning unit.[40] Specifically, we are interested in how these different locations might affect whether aspiration levels would follow the adaptive process we have discussed. Proposition 2.1 of Thompson[41] summarizes the basic argument: Organizations seek to seal off their technical cores from environmental influences. They do this by surrounding the technical core with input and output components, smoothing input and output transactions by buffering and leveling, adapting proactively to anticipated environmental fluctuations, and rationing to handle unanticipated environmental fluctuations. Quite simply, the technical core is the part of the organization where uncertainty is purposely minimized and the contingencies that adaptive aspirations are designed to handle are intentionally moved away by design of task and structure. The

[39] Lant, 1992.
[40] Thompson, 1967.
[41] Id., p. 19.

contrast with boundary spanning units is extreme. Thompson described the contrast as follows: "Whereas coordination is a central problem for the technical core of the organization, adjustment to constraints and contingencies not controlled by the organization is the crucial problem for boundary spanning components."[42]

In terms of our study, the units that provide service and support to the retail units are closer to the technical core. There is no entry and exit of customers as exists in the retail unit; contact with customers is channeled in ways that categorize the problem and route the contact to the point most equipped to handle the inquiry. Thus, we would expect that the goals of the units in the technical core would have some of the same characteristics that Lant[43] ascribed to aspirations under a rational expectations process. Based on her discussion, this would imply that the coefficient on previous aspiration level would be zero. By contrast, the retail units are directly accessible to nonemployee customers whose inquiries cannot be effectively controlled or routed in person as they can by remote communication. Thus, we would expect these units to follow a process as specified in equation (2).

To examine aspirations at the technical core, we examined the volume of manned calls per month at one of the sites where the unit under study engaged in solely a support function; the results are reported in Exhibit 26.5. To examine the boundary spanning units, we once again examined the sales volume of a consumer product at a site that had retail operations. Control variables were also included for size (measured in units of 10 millions of local currency) and branch manager tenure in the organization (measured in quarters). The results are reported in Exhibit 26.6. The negative constant is not significantly different from zero, and there is a significant, positive coefficient for both previous aspiration level and previous performance level, a significant positive effect for branch size, and a nonsignificant effect for tenure. Taken together, Exhibits 26.5 and 26.6 show that, as predicted, the coefficient on previous aspiration is not significant for the unit at the technical core, while it is significant for goals set by units that are at the boundary of the organization.

26.5 CONCLUSION. As indicated, the results here are only preliminary. We are not yet ready to present results with sufficient precision to justify a thorough review of the larger question of how performance evaluations are changing in response to in-

[42] Id., p. 81.

[43] Lant, 1992, pp. 627–628.

Measure: Monthly goals for divisional performance on number of manned calls.

Data: 27 usable observations were obtained.

Predictor Variable	Coefficient
Constant	7.764**
Log of Previous Aspiration Level	.028
Log of Previous Performance Level	–.307
*p < 0.05	**p < 0.01

Restated Model:

$$\text{LogGoal}_t = 7.764 + .279\ \text{LogGoal}_{t-1} + .307\ (\text{LogPerf}_{t-1} - \text{LogGoal}_{t-1})$$

Exhibit 26.5. Goals for Manned Calls (technical core).

Measure: Annual branch goals for life insurance products stated in local currency.

Data: 102 usable observations were obtained from 2 years of data on 102 branches.

Predictor Variable	**Coefficient**
Constant	.938**
Log of Previous Aspiration Level	.404**
Log of Previous Performance Level	–.396**
Branch Conversion	.103
*p < 0.05	**p < 0.01

Restated Model:

$$\text{LogGoal}_t = .938 + .800\ \text{LogGoal}_{t-1} + .396\ (\text{LogPerf}_{t-1} - \text{LogGoal}_{t-1}) + .103\ \text{BrConv}$$

Exhibit 26.6. Goals for Other Sales (boundary spanning units).

creasing pressures for more dynamism and rapid globalization. However, we do feel confident that these data are suggestive of the complexity of the performance evaluations problem faced by financial managers in global corporations. First, it seems quite clear that performance measurement systems are being allowed to adapt to local conditions. At some sites, total liabilities were the focus of quantitative goals for performance; at other sites, sales of particular products, such as life insurance or mortgage products, were the focus. At another site, actual behaviors like numbers of manned calls were the targets; while at yet another, total costs were the item controlled. We have no doubt that there are conditions under which it makes perfect sense to allow performance monitoring to adapt to what is important in the local environments of various sites in a global company. However, it is also true that combining these various measures of performance into a coherent vision, as the advocates of dynamic performance measures would suggest is necessary, is likely to be a fairly complicated process.

Even from the point of view of traditional management accounting concerns, the overall performance picture is likely clouded by this multitude of measures. The parameters by which goals for sales of products, goals for profitability, and goals for total costs adjust over time are quite distinct. Similarly, the process that seems to govern the setting of goals for units and personnel at the technical core seems to be quite distinct from the process that governs the setting of goals for boundary spanners. We have no doubt that clever budgets can get all these numbers to balance, even after the myriad of currency translations and other considerations imposed by the purely global aspects of the transactions. However, it is not at all clear that balancing the numbers and eliciting the best performance need to or even can coincide. Furthermore, as experiments with feedback in simple supply chains have shown, misperceptions of inputs in dynamic decision-making contexts is pervasive.[44] The stringing together of the results of operations using a variety of performance measures from a variety of locations creates complexities that may very well have similar effects. Further analysis of the experience of multinational companies as they try to globalize their increasingly dynamic performance measurement systems is clearly in order. While the results reported here are far too preliminary to provide conclusive evidence concerning the scope of the problem, they are certainly suggestive of the need to con-

[44]Sterman, 1989.

sider the implications of dynamic performance measures for the quality of decision making in the context of global financial management.

SOURCES AND SUGGESTED REFERENCES

Adler, N. J. *International Dimensions of Organizational Behavior*, 2nd ed. Belmont, CA: Wadsworth, 1992.

Anonymous. "The Price Is Right at Hewlett-Packard." *Financial Executive*, Vol. 10, 1994, pp. 22–25.

——. "When in Athens, Stop and Smell the Peaches." *Financial Executive*, Vol. 11, 1995, pp. 50–51.

Bartlett, C., and S. Ghoshal. *Managing Across Borders: The Transnational Solution.* Boston: Harvard Business School Press, 1989.

Bhagat, R., B. Kedia, S. Crawford, and M. Kaplan. "Cross Cultural Issues in Organizational Psychology: Emergent Trends and Directions for Research in the 1990s." In C. Cooper and I. Robertson (eds.), *International Review of Industrial and Organizational Psychology*, Vol. 5. New York: John Wiley & Sons, 1990, pp. 59–99.

Black, J., H. Gregersen, and M. Mendenhall. *Global Assignments: Successfully Expatriating and Repatriating International Managers.* San Francisco: Jossey-Bass, 1992.

Bowman, E. H. "Concerns of CEOs." *Human Resource Management*, Vol. 25, 1986, pp. 267–285.

Cheng, C. "New Trends in Reward Allocation Preference: A Sino/US Comparison." *Academy of Management Journal*, Vol. 38, 1995, pp. 408–424.

Cox, T., S. Lobel, and P. McLeod. "Effects of Ethnic Group Cultural Differences on Cooperative and Competitive Behavior in a Task Group." *Academy of Management Journal*, Vol. 34, 1991, pp. 827–847.

Cyert, R. M., and J. G. March. *A Behavioral Theory of the Firm.* Englewood Cliffs, NJ: Prentice Hall, 1963.

——. *A Behavioral Theory of the Firm*, 2nd ed. Englewood Cliffs, NJ: Prentice Hall, 1993.

De Grandpre, A. Jean. "Does Business Need to Adjust Its Agenda?" Financial Executive, Vol. 5, 1989, pp. 28–32.

Eccles, Robert G. "The Performance Measurement Manifesto." *Harvard Business Review*, Vol. 69, No. 1, 1991, pp. 131–137.

Erez, M. "Congruence of Goal-Setting Strategies with Sociocultural Values and Its Effects on Performance." *Journal of Management*, Vol. 12, 1986, pp. 83–90.

——. "Interpersonal Communication Systems in Organizations and Their Relationships to Cultural Values, Productivity and Innovation." *Applied Psychology: An International Review*, Vol. 41, 1992, pp. 43–64.

Glynn, M. A., T. Lant, and S. J. Mezias. "Incrementalism, Learning, and Ambiguity: An Experimental Study of Aspiration Level Updating." In J. L. Wall and L. R. Jauch (eds.), *Best Paper Proceedings of the Academy of Management Meetings.* Madison, WI: Omnipress, 1991, pp. 384–388.

Kahn, Jeremy. "The World's Most Admired Companies." *Fortune*, October 26, 1998, pp. 206–226.

Kaplan, Robert S., and David P. Norton. "The Balanced Scorecard—Measures That Drive Performance." *Harvard Business Review*, Vol. 70, No. 1, 1992, pp. 71–79.

Lant, T. K. "Aspiration Level Updating: An Empirical Exploration." *Management Science*, Vol. 38, 1992, pp. 623–644.

Lant, T. K., and S. J. Mezias. "An Organizational Learning Model of Convergence and Reorientation." *Organization Science*, Vol. 3, 1992, pp. 47–71.

Lant, T. K., and D. Montgomery. "Learning from Strategic Success and Failure." *Journal of Business Research*, Vol. 15, 1987, pp. 503–518.

Levitt, B., and J. G. March. "Organizational Learning." *Annual Review of Sociology*, Vol. 14, 1988, pp. 319–340.

March, J. G. "Variable Risk Preferences and Adaptive Aspirations." *Journal of Economic Behavior and Organization*, Vol. 9, 1988, pp. 5–24.

March, J. G., and Z. Shapira. "Variable Risk Preferences and the Focus of Attention." *Psychological Reivew*, Vol. 99, 1992, pp. 172–183.

Meyers, Randy. "GM Remeasures the Bar in Latin America: Connecting International Hurdle Rates to Investor Expections." *CFO, The Magazine for Senior Financial Executives*, Vol. 5, No. 14, May 1998, p. 77.

Milliken, F. J., and T. K. Lant. "The Effect of an Organization's Recent Performance History on Strategic Existence and Change: The Role of Managerial Interpretations." In P. Shrivastava, A. Huff, and J. Dutton (eds.), *Advances in Strategic Management*, Vol. 7, Greenwich, CT: JAI Press, 1991, pp. 129–156.

Sterman, J. "Modeling Managerial Behavior: Misperception of Feedback in a Dynamic Decision-Making Experiment." *Management Science*, Vol. 36, No. 3, 1989, pp. 321–329.

Thompson, James, D. *Organizations in Action.* New York: McGraw-Hill, 1967.

Tushman, M. T., and E. Romanelli. "Organizational Evolution: A Metamorphosis Model of Convergence and Reorientation." In L. L. Cummings and B. M. Staw (eds.), *Research in Organizational Behavior*, Vol. 7, Greenwich, CT: JAI Press, 1985, pp. 171–222.

Wallace, Wanda A., and John Walsh. "Apples-to-Apples Profits Abroad." *Financial Executive*, Vol. 11, 1995, pp. 28–31.

CHAPTER 27

FINANCIAL REPORTING IN HYPERINFLATIONARY ENVIRONMENTS: A TRANSACTION ANALYSIS FRAMEWORK FOR MANAGEMENT*

Frederick D. S. Choi

New York University

CONTENTS

27.1 INTRODUCTION. Control issues dominate management concerns in high inflation environments. Financial reporting limited to unadjusted accounting data may result in distorted or illusory profits which are useless, possibly even harmful, to management.

In this chapter, we will show how financial statements presented in soft currency tend to distort operating results reducing comparability over time and providing unreliable performance measures for managerial planning and control decisions.

U.S. generally accepted accounting principles (U.S. GAAP) are used by many multinational business enterprises (U.S. and non-U.S.) that operate in inflationary environments around the world. While U.S. GAAP provide useful guidelines in preparing hard currency statements, they are poorly adapted to meet the reporting needs of firms operating in high inflation countries.[1]

In consolidating the accounts of foreign subsidiaries, Statement of Financial Accounting Standards No. 52 (SFAS 52)[2] mandates use of the current rate translation method whenever the functional currency of the parent company's foreign affiliate is

*The author wishes to thank Ronald R. Gunn, Finance and Administrative Director of BS Continental, for his assistance with the previous edition of this chapter.

[1]Coopers & Lybrand, 1989.

[2]Financial Accounting Standards Board, 1982.

deemed to be the local currency. This treatment acknowledges the parent's (assume for the moment a U.S. parent) interest in the local currency performance of the foreign affiliate since the latter is viewed as an autonomous operation; that is, a foreign operation that happens to be owned by a U.S. parent. The temporal translation method is prescribed when the functional currency is deemed to be the parent currency. This treatment, which recognizes both transaction and translation gains and losses in consolidated income, acknowledges the parent company's interest in the dollar utility of the foreign affiliate's activities. The affiliate is viewed as an extension of the parent company as its operations are integrally related to the latter's; that is, a U.S. operation that happens to be located abroad. An exception to the current rate translation method occurs whenever a foreign subsidiary is located in a high inflation environment. In this instance, the parent currency is deemed to be functional and the temporal translation method employed. Being domiciled in a hard currency environment, the parent is understandably interested in seeing what operating results generated in soft currency amount to in hard currency terms.

Under the temporal translation method, monetary items are translated to parent currency at the exchange rate prevailing at the financial statement date, nonmonetary items at rates that preserve their original measurement bases in local currency, and income statement items at exchange rates that correspond with the dates of the underlying transactions. If revenue and expense transactions are voluminous, an average rate may be used to provide an approximation of the actual rates existing during the period.

In high-inflation environments, financial statements prepared in conformity with U.S. GAAP tend to distort economic reality by:

- Overstating or understating revenues and expenses
- Misstating interest income or expense
- Reporting large translation gains or losses which are difficult to interpret
- Leaving unresolved the implicit interest problem
- Distorting performance comparisons over time

As a consequence, management is generally provided with an unreliable basis upon which to intelligently manage a business. There is often a need for parallel controls in order to obtain useful management data.[3] The cost of such dual reporting systems are nontrivial, especially in today's competitive environment.

In a world of zero inflation, enterprise income could be measured either as the difference between revenues and expenses or, utilizing the Hicksian concept of income, as the change in owners' equity during the period, barring any additional investments or withdrawals by the owners. Both measures would be identical and would accurately describe what transpired during the period. This would not be the case in a world of changing prices. Differences between the two income measures are attributable to gains and losses associated with holding monetary assets when performance measures are couched in terms of local currency and/or exchange gains and losses when performance measures are couched in terms of parent (hard) currency. In a high-inflation environment, balance sheet comparisons; that is, net asset comparisons, measured on

[3]Jacque and Lorange, 1984.

a consistent basis and controlling for capital increases or deductions and dividends, are generally a more accurate method of profit determination. Owing to changing commodity, currency, and credit prices, the income statement is often just a best attempt to explain what has taken place from one balance sheet to the next.

Understandably, many companies operating in high-inflation environments have not fared well in explaining what actually transpired during the period based on reported earnings numbers. Coopers & Lybrand (C&L) state the problem thusly:[4]

> Hard currency income statements prepared by the traditional FASB Statement No. 52 monetary/nonmonetary method tend to display a large translation gain or loss. Commonly, this is one of the larger items in the income statement. The gain or loss reflects so many features . . . that it is remarkably difficult to analyze. Management is often highly perplexed by this item. Some managements . . . have been known to persuade their head offices . . . that they should be judged on net income before the "extraneous" translation loss.

In fact, the item is not all extraneous but pertains to various lines of the income statement. A business cannot be managed intelligently unless the translation gain or loss is reallocated to its various sources.

27.2 MANAGEMENT REPORTING FRAMEWORK. Our reporting model is premised on the following conviction: management's objective of maximizing the value of the firm should be framed in terms of a currency that holds its value. Accordingly, the best way to measure the performance of an affiliate located in a hyperinflationary environment is to do so in terms of hard currency.[5] Our model also implicitly assumes that inflation rates, exchange rates, and interest rates are interrelated, although this assumption is not critical to our proposal.

In accounting for foreign currency transactions, a common reporting convention is to record revenues and expenses at exchange rates prevailing at the financial statement date, although use of average rates are also common. For month-end closing, this entails using the month-end rate. We argue that local currency transactions should be reported (valued) at the exchange rate prevailing on payment date. This reporting mode provides the best measure of a transaction's intrinsic value as this is the date that the transaction in question is tracked in hard currency. Recording a transaction at any other date muddles the measurement process by introducing gains or losses in the purchasing power of money or implicit interest into the picture. In a perfectly competitive market, all local currency transactions would be made for cash. However, under conditions of imperfect competition and inflation, it will prove advantageous for buyers to delay payment as long as possible and for sellers to accelerate collections. The date at which payment is effected will be determined by the competitive strengths of the contracting parties. The recommended reporting treatment produces reported numbers that are reliable, economically interpretable, and symmetric in the sense that two economically similar transactions (for example, one foreign, one domestic) produce the same financial statement numbers when the trans-

[4] Coopers & Lybrand, op. cit.

[5] Interviews with financial executives of U.S.-based multinationals as well as subsidiary managers suggest that this assumption is consistent with corporate practices at the micro level. It also appears consistent with practices at the macro level. Witness the recent trend of more and more Latin American countries pegging their currencies to the U.S. dollar. Moffett and Friedland, 1995.

actions are translated to a common currency.[6] In short, the model employs "accrual accounting" with a "cash accounting" mentality.

As we highlighted earlier, translation of soft currency income statements to hard currency per FAS 52 tends to give rise to large translation gains or losses. Commonly, these gains or losses are one of the larger items in the income statement.

In the following analysis we focus on the translation gains and losses generated by FAS 52. While many would attribute these gains and losses to foreign exchange risk; that is, the translation of a monetary asset or liability position in Turkish lira by a devalued exchange rate, we will show that the translation gain or loss is really due to an improper accounting for events that occurred "above the line." In a hyperinflationary environment, conventional accounting treatments often distort the underlying economics of a firm's efforts and accomplishments. Our model seeks to minimize such distortions. We examine the following areas:

- Sales Revenue
- Expenses, including Cost of Sales
- Gross Margins

Exhibit 27.1 contains our working assumptions. Inflation and lira (TL) devaluation is 30% per month or 1.2% per work day. Accordingly, the general price level index

[6]The notions of economic interpretability and symmetry are discussed in more rigorous fashion in Beaver and Wolfson, 1992.

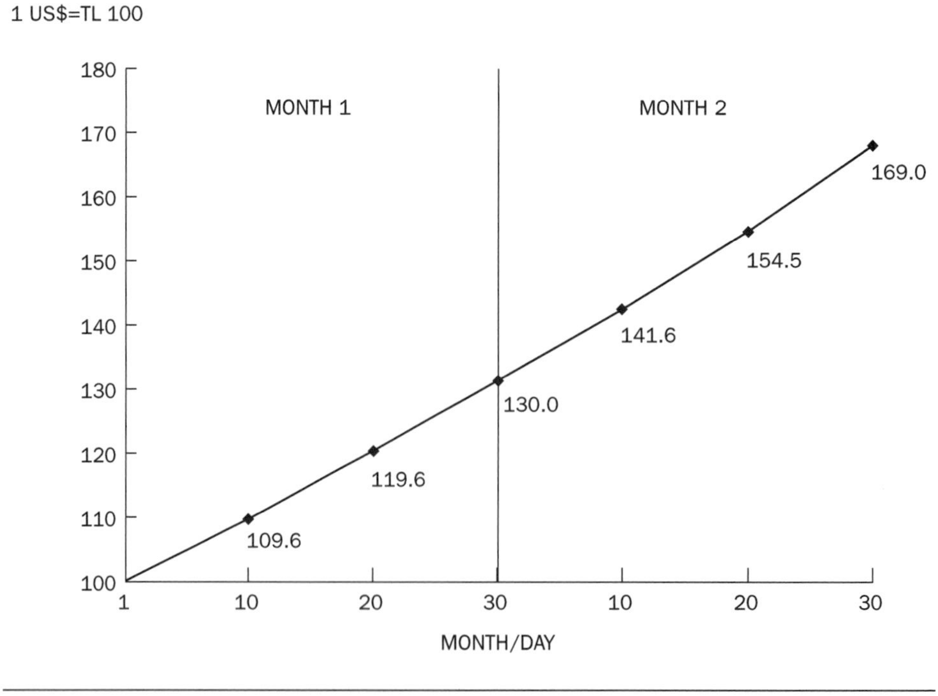

Exhibit 27.1. Inflation and TL Devaluation = 30%/Month (1.2%/Work Day).

rises from 100 on the first day of month one to 169.0 by the end of the second month. The exchange rate on Day 1 is $1 = TL100. At month's-end it is $1 = TL130.

27.3 SALES REVENUE. To illustrate our proposed treatment of sales revenues, assume that the firm sells TL2,000,000 worth of merchandise in Month 1, with varying invoice dates and payment terms. Assuming monthly preparation of financial statements, we illustrate the conventional practice of recording the sales transaction at the month-end exchange rate regardless of when the sale is invoiced during the month or when payment is received. While many firms also use the average rate, the principles demonstrated here remain the same whether month-end or average rates are employed. The sales figure reported using the month-end exchange rate would be TL2,000,000/130 = $15,385 (use of the average rate would produce a sales figure in dollars of TL2,000/115 = $17,391).

In our first scenario, assume that the sale is invoiced on Day 1 of Month 1, with payment immediately being received in cash = TL2,000,000/TL100 = $20,000. Conventional treatment would measure the transaction at month end rather than when cash is received. The economic basis of the transaction however, is the cash that has actually been received on the invoice date. In this instance revenues would be understated by 30% or $4,615 determined as follows:

Actual	$20,000
Reported	15,385
Variance	$4,615

In keeping with the translation methodology associated with FAS 52, this $4,615 understatement of sales would be offset by an equivalent nonoperating translation gain appearing below the line.[7]

In the next scenario, assume instead that the sale is invoiced on Day 5, with the client being offered 25 days payment terms. Based on our model, the transaction would be booked on the same day that payment is received. From an economic point of view, there would be no variance and no nonoperating translation gain or loss.

Actual	$15,385
Reported	$15,385
Variance	$0

From a control perspective, management should be able to elicit from the salesperson what the expected profit margin is on the day the sale is made. The salesperson should not have to wait until the books are closed to know that. The information to make this determination is already at hand as invoices in hyperinflationary environments will clearly state the date the customer has to pay.

In the following example, assume that the client is invoiced on Day 30 with pay-

[7]Assume that the firm in question begins the period with a $10,000 equity investment and immediately converts this cash balance to saleable inventories. The goods are marked up 100% over cost and sold for cash the next day. In this case, the aggregate exchange adjustment would be $4,615 determined either as a plug when preparing the end of period translated balance sheet, or as a positive aggregate translation adjustment comprising the gain on the hard currency cash balance.

ment being required a month later. From an economic point of view the firm is collecting \$11,834(= TL2,000,000/TL169). The accounting system reports a figure of \$15,385 resulting in a variance of \$3,551.

Actual	\$11,834
Reported	\$15,385
Variance	\$3,551

In this case, the conventional reporting system overstates sales by 23.1% with the positive variance being offset by an equivalent nonoperating translation loss below the line. This scenario is probably the most common in practice as businesses customarily send out invoices at or near month's-end. While home offices may not be happy with the implications of this analysis for reported performance, market efficiency suggests that reliance on fictitious gains permitted by generally accepted accounting principles is self-delusory.

The magnitude of the dispersions associated with differing invoicing and payment terms is set forth in Exhibit 27.2. Depending on sales terms, sales can be overstated or understated by significant proportions.

Why are we concerned with these distortions? Traditional reporting systems could induce suboptimal behavior on the part of the sales force. For example, there is no motivation for a company's sales force to improve payment terms. If sales are recorded at the end-of-month rate, some sales personnel may be unconcerned whether they are paid in cash or in 30 or 60 days. In an inflationary environment, the sooner money is in hand the better. One might argue that payment terms are dictated from the top and thus minimize this possibility. However, with sales personnel often numbering in the hundreds, management may not be in a position to personally monitor all competitive pricing terms. Under these conditions, it is important to have in place a system that encourages the sales force to act in the best interests of the company.

Traditional reporting systems also provide no motivation for the sales force to invoice and ship earlier in the month. Again with sales being recorded at end-of-month rates, the time of delivery is of no consequence to the salesperson. Yet, even a day's delay in shipment could be costly; for example, 1.2% of exchange losses plus inter-

TL\$2,000,000 Sales in Month 1
Varying Invoice Dates and Payment Dates

	Invoice Day	Payment Terms	Today's Measure	Proposed Measure	Diff.	%
A	1	Cash	15,385	20,000	4,615	30.0%
B	5	5 days	15,385	18,248	2,863	18.6%
C	5	15 days	15,385	16,722	1,337	8.7%
D	5	25 days	15,385	15,385	0.000	0.0%
E	10	30 days	15,385	14,124	–1,261	–8.2%
F	20	30 days	15,385	12,945	–2,440	–15.9%
G	30	30 days	15,385	11,834	–3,551	–23.1%

Exhibit 27.2. Dispersions Associated with Differing Invoicing and Payment Terms.

est in our example. Another glance at Exhibit 27.2 shows that bonuses and commission payments will be based on inflated sales values whenever payment terms are lagged to the subsequent period.

Perhaps the most serious shortcoming of traditional reporting systems is that they may encourage results manipulation. Assume now that exchange rates at the end of each of the next three months are as follows:

End-of-month	130
End-of-month	169
End-of-month	220

In this example, a salesperson gets together with a favored customer and arranges the following: deliver and invoice TL2,000,000 of a product on Day 30 of Month 1 at TL2,500,000 with 60-day payment terms instead of invoicing at TL2,000,000 on the same date with 30-day payment terms. The attractiveness of this arrangement is not hard to fathom. Under conventional reporting methods the revised sales value would be $19,231 (=TL2,500,000/TL130) versus $15,385 (=TL2,000,000/TL130) under traditional measurements, an additional sales "pick-up" of almost $4,000 or 25%. From the customer's point of view, the actual cost of the purchase will be only $11,364 (=TL2,500,000/TL220) versus $11,834 (=TL2,000,000/TL169), a cost savings that is hard to resist, other things the same. Indeed, under these circumstances, the customer is likely to be the one initiating such a proposal.

Under the proposed reporting system the incentives for such arrangements to occur are lessened. In reporting the sales transaction at the exchange rate prevailing on the payment date, the transaction would be recorded at $11,364 rather than $11,834. From the selling firm's perspective, the better alternative would be to invoice the sale at TL2,000,000 with 30-day payment terms. The reporting system proposed here provides the salesperson with the incentive to take this proper course of action.

Our model thus encompasses using the actual or forecasted exchange rate prevailing on the day of payment to record local currency transactions. Those dates are generally in the accounts receivable system (that is, already on sales invoices) and thus this reporting system is readily implemented. To reiterate, the idea is to use "accrual accounting" while maintaining a "cash accounting" mentality. Some have argued, and correctly so, that sales and expenses in hyperinflationary environments have built into them an implicit interest rate. Hence, the need to discount local currency transactions to their present values prior to translation. Our model emphasizes the difference in the exchange rate between the invoice date and the collection date. This exchange differential automatically incorporates the implicit interest differential (the International Fisher Effect[8]). Under our reporting framework, there is no need to think about what the interest rate is or worry about how to calculate an appropriate

[8]Under a freely floating system of exchange rates, spot rates of exchange are theoretically determined by the interrelationships between national rates of inflation, interest rates, and forward rates of exchange, usually expressed as premiums or discounts from the spot rate. If the forecasted rate of inflation in Turkey one month ahead is 30% higher than in the United States, the lira can be forecast to decline in value by 30% relative to the dollar. By the same token, interest rates for maturities of comparable risk can be expected to be 30% higher on Turkish securities than on comparable U.S. securities. For an extended discussion of these relationships, see Eiteman and Stonehill, 1995 and Gunter Dufey and Ian Giddy, Chapter 6 of this volume.

discount rate. After all, it is the exchange rate difference that operating management is concerned with.

What would happen if the customer delays payment beyond the promised payment date? In our reporting framework, normal payment conditions would be reflected in reported sales and gross margins. Thus, if a customer agrees to pay on a certain date, the transaction would be booked at the exchange rate prevailing on the agreed payment date. Thus, the salesperson knows at the time of sale what his profit margin will be. If payment takes place after the promised date, the loss in dollars would be reported below the line as a translation loss and partially or totally attributed to the line of business or sales segment that is responsible for its incurrence. That loss however, would likely be compensated by interest income as original sales terms would normally include a penalty and interest for delayed payments. The latter would appear as additional interest or miscellaneous income below the line. Alternatively, the loss could be backed out of reported gross margin to reflect a sale that was realized in hard currency later than expected.

27.4 OPERATING EXPENSES INCLUDING COST OF SALES. In applying our model to expenses, we embrace the same environmental assumptions that we employed with respect to revenues (see Exhibit 27.1); namely monthly inflation and lira devaluation of 30%. We contrast with our proposed reporting model the traditional accounting treatment accorded a TL1,000,000 expense under varying invoice dates and payment terms. We again assume the use of month-end rates to record the expense transactions. Use of average rates would produce similar results.

In our first scenario, assume that the firm is invoiced on the first day of the month with a cash payment. Our model would record the expense when cash payment is made; the traditional model would record it at month's end.

Actual	TL1,000,000/TL100 =	$10,000
Reported	TL1,000,000/TL130 =	$ 7,692
Variance		$ 2,308

In this instance the expense would be understated by 30%. The understated expense, in turn, would be offset below the line by a nonoperating translation loss.

In the next scenario, assume the firm is invoiced on Day 5 and given 25 days in which to remit payment. Because payment is made on the same date as the measurement date, there would be no variance and the reported expense would reflect the underlying economics of the transaction. In our experience, this situation is the exception rather than the norm.

Assume now that the firm is invoiced on Day 30 and given 30 days payment terms. In this case, reported expenses would be overstated by $1,775 or 23.1% determined as follows:

Actual	TL1,000,000/TL169 =	$5,917
Reported	TL1,000,000/TL130 =	7,692
Variance		($1,775)

This variance of $1,775 would be offset by a translation gain appearing below the line. Additional outcomes based on other invoice dates and payment terms are illustrated in Exhibit 27.3.

TL$1,000,000 Expenses in Month 1
Varying Invoice Dates and Payment Dates

	Invoice Day	Payment Terms	Today's Measure	Proposed Measure	Diff.	%
A	1	Cash	7,692	10,000	2,308	30.0%
B	5	5 days	7,692	9,124	1,432	18.6%
C	5	15 days	7,692	8,361	669	8.7%
D	5	25 days	7,692	7,692	0.000	0.0%
E	10	30 days	7,692	7,062	–630	–8.2%
F	20	30 days	7,692	6,472	–1,220	–15.9%
G	30	30 days	7,692	5,917	–1,775	–23.1%

Exhibit 27.3. Over or Understatement of Expenses.

Reliable expense figures are critical for many reasons including outsourcing studies, make versus buy decisions, results evaluation, and numerous performance measures within the firm. Since a firm may be reporting numbers in detail by cost centers, branch offices, and various lines of business, it is important for local management to have numbers that are useful and reliable on a day-to-day basis, not distorted numbers based on simple averages of what transpired during the period. In Exhibit 27.3, we illustrated an example where expenses were overstated by 23%; in another, expenses were understated by 30%. During any reporting period, it may very well turn out that some expense overstatements are offset by expense understatements so that on balance average expenses are a satisfactory depiction of what actually transpired in the aggregate. We reiterate once again, however, that management decisions are often not made on overall results. They are based on detailed costs that together contribute to the overall picture.

Another compelling reason why the proposed reporting framework merits management attention is the avoidance of results manipulation. Assume in our previous example that a salesperson or purchaser arranges with a supplier to have promotional supplies (to be charged to the salesperson's/purchaser's account) delivered on the first day of Month 2 with payment being made on the 10th, rather than having delivery take place on the last day of Month 1 with the same payment date. By delaying the transaction by a day, the salesperson can significantly skew reported results in his favor. In this instance the traditional reporting model would record an expense of $5,917 versus $7,692 or 30% less. This understatement would, as before, be offset by an equivalent nonoperating translation loss.

Last day delivery	TL1,000,000/TL130 = $7,692
Delivery a day later	TL1,000,000/TL169 = $5,917

Under the suggested reporting framework, it would not matter when delivery is taken as the transaction would always be recorded when payment is made. Hence, the transaction would be reported at $7,062 (=TL1,000,000/TL141.6) regardless of whether delivery occurs in month one or two. This encourages an astute salesperson to improve his reported results by arranging for immediate delivery while postponing payment as long as possible. The longer payment is postponed, the lower the cost.

Accounting now leads the salesperson in the right direction. It also discloses when the salesperson has made the wrong decision. For proper performance measurement in a hyperinflationary environment, management must reclassify the translation gains or losses reported under Statement 52 back to the related expense lines to reflect soft currency costs in hard currency terms.

In using forecasted exchange rates to book soft currency transactions, we are cognizant of the fact that the firm may experience variances caused by unexpected rate changes; that is, forecast errors. Under the proposed reporting framework the future exchange rate can be modified at any time. Assume for example that we are projecting an exchange rate of TL169 = $1 two months into the future per Exhibit 27.4. The actual rate turns out to be TL174, a distortion of about 3% over a two-month period. Exhibit 27.5 illustrates what would happen to our assumed TL1,000,000 expense in our last example which assumed invoicing on Day 30 of Month 1 with 30 days payment terms.

In this case the actual expense turns out to be $170 less (=$5,917 – $5,747) than the firm thought it was going to be. A practical expedient, and one that minimizes user confusion, especially for exchange rate variances that are small, would be to leave the original number unchanged and simply let the variance fall below the line as a nonoperating translation gain. Under today's traditional reporting system, the translation gain that would have been reported below the line is $1,945 (=$7,692 – $5,747). The translation gain that would be reported under the proposed model, as a

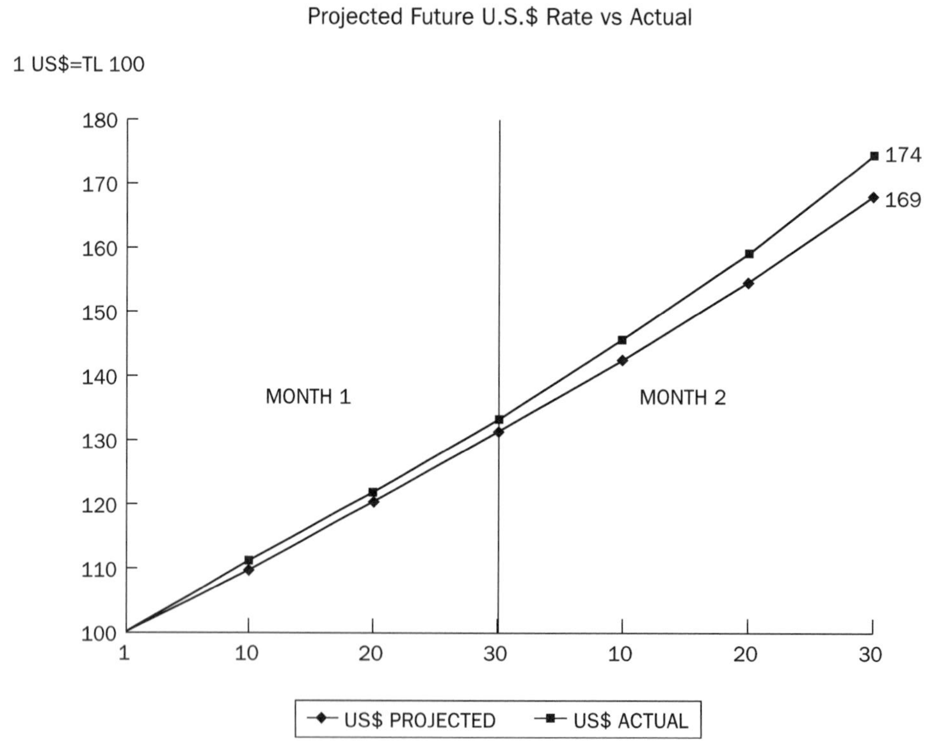

Exhibit 27.4. Unexpected Rate Changes.

Invoice on Month 1, Day 30; Payment Term 30 Days				
	Traditional Measure	Proposed Measure	Diff.	%
At 169 Forecast	7,692	5,917	–1,775	–23.1
At 174 Actual	7,692	5,747	–1,945	–25.3

Exhibit 27.5. Effect of Rate Changes on Operating Expenses.

consequence of the unexpected rate change, is $170. This represents a 91% improvement over what would have been. Alternatively, the proposed reporting system, in enabling management to trace all translation gains and losses on an individual transactions basis, allows the firm to go back and retroactively correct the original entry. This may prove cost effective to do if the exchange rate variance proves to be unacceptably large as a result of a sudden price freeze or a maxi-devaluation.

Reporting cost of goods sold is based on the same concepts that we have enumerated with respect to expenses in general. However, since costs are passed through inventories, it is more complicated to go back and make retroactive corrections to reported expenses when future exchange rates are projected incorrectly.

The importance of having accurate numbers in the case of cost of sales cannot be overemphasized. It is critical in determining a firm's "drop dead rate," that is, the lowest price a firm is willing to quote a client before turning down the business. This is especially important if a firm has excess capacity or must match competitors' prices. Traditional methods of reporting cost of goods sold can result in tremendous distortions.

27.5 GROSS MARGINS. Let us now examine the distortions traditional reporting practices have on gross margins. In the following example, assume that our Turkish affiliate purchases an item of inventory for TL1,000,000 and sells it for TL2,000,000 in the same month. The traditional reporting model would report a gross margin of 50% determined as follows:

Sales	TL2,000,000/130 =	$15,385
Cost of Goods Sold	TL1,000,000/130 =	7,692
Gross Margin		$ 7,693
Gross Margin %		50.0%

In the first scenario, assume that the inventory is purchased on the last day of the month on account with payment due in 30 days. The item is sold the same day for cash. While traditional reporting would continue to report a gross margin percentage of 50%, the proposed accounting treatment reveals that the gross margin on the sale is really 61.5%:

Sales	TL2,000,000/130 =	$15,385
Cost of Goods Sold	TL1,000,000/169 =	5,917
Gross Margin		$ 9,468
Gross Margin %		61.5%

Assume instead that the inventory is purchased on Day 30 for cash and immediately sold with 30 days payment terms. In this case, the gross margin percentage would be only 35% versus the customarily reported 50%:

Sales	TL2,000,000/169 =	$11,834
Cost of Goods Sold	TL1,000,000/130 =	7,692
Gross Margin		$ 4,142
Gross Margin %		35.0%

Can anyone properly run a business with such distortions?

27.6 CONCLUSION. U.S. generally accepted accounting principles are poorly adapted to meet the needs of companies operating in hyperinflationary environments such as Latin America, Eastern Europe, or the Far East. Traditional reporting systems report large exchange gains or losses which are difficult to interpret, mismatches revenues and expenses, greatly overstates interest income and expense, and does not resolve the implicit interest problem. As a consequence, management is provided a poor information base for planning and control decisions.

These deficiencies can be largely overcome. The transactions-based reporting model described here:

- Allocates translation gains and losses back to the specific revenues and expenses to which they are related
- Provides both headquarters and subsidiary management with numbers that will lead to better decisions
- Eliminates the need for parallel controls
- Facilitates performance comparisons over time
- Is consistent with U.S. GAAP

The proposed reporting framework will not eliminate entirely all translation gains or losses. Some translation losses will inevitably persist owing to missed collections, forecasting errors, unprotected bank balance floats, and delays in identifying other possible causes. However, the gains can be significant. We have observed instances where companies adopting the proposed reporting framework in Brazil have managed to reduce their translation losses by 96, and in some instances, 100%. With a little additional effort, conventional accounting data can be transformed into information that is useful to management.

SOURCES AND SUGGESTED REFERENCES

Beaver, William H., and Mark A. Wolfson. "Foreign Currency Translation and Changing Prices in Perfect and Complete Markets." *Journal of Accounting Research*, Autumn 1992, pp. 528–550.

Brooke, James. "New Money No Innovation in Brazil." *New York Times*, July 9, 1994, p. C-1.

Collins, Terence R. "Risk Management in Hyperinflationary Environments." In F. D. S. Choi, *Handbook of International Accounting*. New York: John Wiley & Sons, 1991, pp. 28.1–28.24.

Coopers & Lybrand. *Reporting Reality From High-Inflation Countries*. New York: Coopers & Lybrand (U.S.A.), 1989.

Eiteman, David K., Arthur I. Stonehill, and Michael Moffett. *Multinational Business Finance*, 7th ed. Reading, MA: Addison-Wesley Publishing Company, 1995.

Financial Accounting Standards Board. *Statement of Financial Accounting Standards No. 52*. "Foreign Currency Translation." Stamford, CT: FASB, 1982.

Goldman Sachs. *The Global Currency Analyst*. New York: Goldman Sachs, June 2000.

International Accounting Standards Committee. *International Accounting Standards No. 29*. "Financial Reporting in Hyperinflationary Economies." London: IASC, 1989.

Jacque, Laurent L., and Peter Lorange. "The International Control Conundrum: The Case of 'Hyperinflationary' Subsidiaries." *Journal of International Business Studies*, Fall 1984, pp. 185–201.

Moffett, Matt, and Jonathan Friedland. "Mexican Peso Collapse Presents Stark Choices to Latin Economies." *Wall Street Journal*, January 6, 1995, p. A1.

Schieneman, Gary S. "High Inflation Environments: Discerning Fact from Fiction." *Smith New Court International Accounting Research*, August 13, 1991, unpaginated.

Seed III, Allen H. *The Impact of Inflation on Internal Planning and Control*. New York: National Association of Accountants, 1981.

CHAPTER 28

INTERNATIONAL INFORMATION SYSTEMS*

Jon A. Turner

New York University

CONTENTS

---

*The author is grateful for the support provided by the American Academy in Rome in revising this chapter.

28.1 INTRODUCTION

(a) Intended Audience. This chapter is intended for professionals and managers interested in the use of information technology (IT) in international firms. Some knowledge of IT is assumed. A brief glossary of terms is provided at the end of this chapter as an aid to those readers with little exposure to technology. Readers who feel uncomfortable with the description of technology presented here and would like to have more knowledge of concepts should consult a practical book on technology and its management.[1]

(b) Role of Information Technology (IT) in the International Firm. Executives manage largely on the basis of information. Managers in international firms typically require a greater quantity of more diverse information than do their domestic counterparts because information from foreign subsidiaries and from headquarters must be combined with local information for many activities and decisions. In order for information from foreign subsidiaries to be understood and aggregated it must conform to both local and global needs, and be qualified by particular knowledge about how it has been gathered. Due to increasing time pressures of international competition, in order to speed up the process, there is a tendency to use a firm's technology infrastructure for the exchange of information between and among a firm's headquarters and its subsidiaries.

Four factors govern the amount of information that is transmitted between a subsidiary and its headquarters: the type, maturity, and scope of business activity at the subsidiary, and the decision authority of local management. Type of activity can be divided roughly into two categories: services and manufacturing. Services, because they are heavily information intensive, tend to require that more information be transmitted among organizational units than does manufacturing. The more mature a foreign subsidiary, that is, the more globally integrated it is, the greater the amount of information it exchanges with other organizational units. The greater the scope of activity at the subsidiary, the greater the amount of information communicated to headquarters and the other subsidiaries. Conversely, the greater the decision authority of local managers, the less information exchanged with headquarters.

Information may be used for a variety of *purposes* within a firm ranging from describing a structured business transaction, such as an order, to communicating an in-

---

[1]McNurline & Sprague, 1989; Vaskevitch, 1993.

formal message that might be an answer to a previously asked question. It is useful to distinguish among three types of business information: transactions, reports, and messages. Transactions are structured business communications that describe basic business activity, such as the transferring of funds among accounts or the payment of an outstanding invoice. These are generated where the business activity, that is, sale, takes place (often at the subsidiary) and transmitted to where the information is processed (possibly the subsidiary, more often headquarters or a regional processing center). Great care must be taken to ensure that all transactions can be accounted for and that no unauthorized transactions are entered into the system. Thus, these systems require extensive *controls.* Manufacturing firms tend to produce more structured business transactions than do service firms. Reports are predetermined information groupings, such as a monthly accounting statement, that are provided in response to a request. Reports may be either *periodic* in that they are produced at set intervals, or *ad hoc* where they are provided when needed. They are produced by running an application program to extract information from a database. Messages are point-to-point information transmissions consisting of text, graphics, or video media, sent over the firm's technology infrastructure (i.e., a network). Messages require that the sender know or be able to obtain the network address of the recipient.

Not all information is of the same *class* and the classes are often treated differently. Three useful classes are corporate, local, and personal. Corporate data is official shared data that describes important corporate activity. Corporate data often comes from a corporate application and database, such as General Ledger, or the Human Resources system and implies that agreement has been reached across the corporation as to the exact meaning of the data contained in the system. Data of this class is formally defined, and it can only be created and changed by authorized personnel, for example, by a payroll clerk in the human resources department changing an employee's monthly pay rate. Some corporate data may be confidential, such as salaries, product sales figures, and customer lists, while others may be available generally within the firm. In contrast to corporate data, local data concerns only the organizational unit that generates it, for example, a report of the inventory level for an item in a subsidiary's warehouse. Local data, because of differences in meaning, create difficulties in aggregation and reporting to headquarters and in exchange with other subsidiaries (*in inventory* may not mean the same thing among subsidiaries). Personal data refers to data generated by an individual for his or her own use, such as a client report or spread sheet analysis. As a general rule, the report or message should indicate the class of information upon which it is based and even the specific data source.

Regarding the importance of an international firm's technology infrastructure, Bartlett and Goshal[2] observe that companies operating globally will be at a serious disadvantage if they are unable to firmly control their worldwide operations and manage them in a globally coordinated manner. A firm's technology infrastructure is the vehicle for accomplishing this global control and management.

(c) Differences between Domestic and International Firms. The differences between domestic and international firms place significant demands on their information sys-

---

[2]Bartlett and Goshal, 1987.

tems. These differences can be grouped into three categories: factors that affect the design of systems, factors that affect the operation of systems, and factors that affect government regulation.

(i) Factors Influencing System Design. In a domestic environment, there is usually a single language used for business activities. While it is often presumed that English is the universal language of information technology, the reality is that many countries prefer to use their own language at the "interface"[3] level of a system. (The difficulty here is the character set that the operating system and the application system support.) Most of the common systems used in the United States support only 128 characters.[4] This creates difficulty in representing extra alphabetic characters. For example, the Danish alphabet contains three additional characters, and many languages contain inflection marks that are not part of the 128-character set. The major system developers, have moved to an expanded 256-character set, which incorporates many of these additional characters, but the issue is complicated, for example, in the handling of non-Western languages, such as Japanese, Chinese, and Arabic. This is not simply a problem of transliteration. Not only does the system have to accommodate the internal representation of these symbols but the fonts supported by printer and displays, and the dictionaries in word processors need to be coordinated. Apple has gone further than most companies in modifying its operating system to produce different country-specific systems from a common core and there is a major international standardization effort underway in this area.

Another difficult representation problem is currency. Most domestic environments consist of a single currency. But international firms need to handle a variety of currencies and be able to convert among them. The issue is complicated by volatility in exchange rates and the timing of these conversions needs to be specified and consistent. This places additional demands on systems that aggregate financial information from subsidiaries in different countries.

(ii) Factors Influencing System Operation. A domestic environment often operates in one or at most three time zones. This means that there are times during a 24-hour period when a system can be brought down for maintenance or for other support activities without incurring adverse operational effects. In anticipation of operating in such an environment, a system may be designed not to accept inputs during these periods and to instead perform internal maintenance activities, such as updating translation tables. Operational staffing may be reduced greatly during such periods. However, systems that support worldwide activities must be prepared to accept inputs 24 hours a day. Such 24-by-7 systems, for example an online trading or a funds transfer system, need to be designed so that all maintenance activities can be done at the same time that operational processing is taking place.

Systems operating in different countries often create severe support demands. Not

---

[3]The "interface level" means the inputs to or outputs from a system. It includes the display screens and reports that are produced from an application system, the screens that are used for data input, and the workstation keyboard.

[4]Called the ASCII character set. It contains the 26 capital letters and 26 lowercase letters of the English alphabet, the 10 Arabic numerals 0–9, and 66 special characters, including punctuation and monetary symbols.

only are there issues as to where support staffs should be located (at each site or at a regional center, or some combination of the two) but differences in language and culture complicate staffing and training. If the systems have been customized for country-specific requirements (either language or functionality), it places additional demands on the support staff. Additionally, because of equipment availability, the technology infrastructure used in each country may be different. This further complicates support because it broadens the range of equipment with which the repair staff needs to be familiar, and replacement parts may be difficult to obtain. One strategy that can be followed is to outsource some support to local vendors with coordination and oversight remaining as internal functions (see section 28.5(a)(iii), Outsourcing).

(iii) Factors Influencing Regulation. Domestic firms face one regulatory environment while international companies face many. This is particularly the case with regard to data privacy and Trans-Border Data Flow issues (TBDF) (see section 28.5).

(d) Types of International Business Activity. International firms differ in the complexity of their business activities. The simplest is for a company to *export products* to customers in foreign countries. While some new business activities may have to be supported, such as customs clearance and international shipment, the demands placed on a firm's technology infrastructure by exporting goods are minor. When the firm's employees *market and sell* in each foreign country (direct sales) business activities such as invoicing, sales support, inventory, accounts payable and receivable all need to be supported. This can be done by capturing data in the foreign country and transmitting it to a central location for processing or by processing the data locally in the host country. The choice between these two alternatives depends on how restrictive the host country is to the transfer of data across its borders, how easily a firm's key operational systems can be modified to run in host countries, and issues around timing, that is, when the results of the processing are needed.

Deciding to place *direct production* facilities in foreign countries increases the technology support required. Now, in addition to marketing activities, all of the production functions, such as production scheduling, manufacturing, bill of materials processing, inventory, computer-aided design (CAD), and computer integrated manufacturing (CIM) need to be supported. Because each of these systems tends to be customized for a particular production facility containing specific equipment, it is impractical to run these systems on remote computers. A decision to produce in foreign countries implies a *local* technology infrastructure and *local* support.

When a firm has fully autonomous subsidiaries in foreign countries with their own presidents and boards of directors, they probably also have their own technology infrastructure. This implies a complete set of application systems and a complete technology infrastructure in each country. As a firm grows, competing in many markets around the world, it will become increasingly attractive to coordinate activities globally in order to gain advantages of scale and scope. This requires that autonomous technology infrastructures in each country be interconnected and that applications be coordinated and shared. This places great demands on the planning and operation of a firm's technology.

(e) Differences between Service and Manufacturing. Services are becoming an increasingly important part of the U.S. economy accounting for well over half of the nation's GNP and employing over 80% of the workforce.[5] These trends have put the United States in the position of being a net exporter of services internationally. Similar changes are taking place in the other world markets, for example, in Europe, and the world market for services is growing at a rate twice that of product trade.

A number of factors distinguish service from manufacturing, including intangibility, inseparability of production and consumption, heterogeneity, and perishability, which affect a firm's technology infrastructure. Probably *intangibility* is the key differentiating factor. A manufacturing firm, in producing a physical product, needs to attend to the product during its development, production, and support life cycle. A service firm, however, just needs to deliver its service, be that consulting, advertising, or the like. This reduces greatly the number of application systems that are needed and the volume of transaction activity when compared with a manufacturing firm, although it may place additional demands on the sophistication of the technology used, for example, being able to handle multimedia, or to support World Wide Web (WWW) publishing.

Another difference between service and manufacturing firms is that service firms tend to be less capital intensive. This explains, partially, the rapid move to fully autonomous service subsidiaries in foreign countries. A major motive for a service firm going abroad is to service home country clients in foreign countries.

In a study of technology among international service and manufacturing firms, Deans and Kane[6] found that different profiles existed. Service firms were most concerned with data security and equipment utilization and least concerned about local cultural constraints. Manufacturing firms, on the other hand, were most concerned about educating senior personnel and international protocol standards while being least concerned about currency restrictions and exchange rate volatility. These differences probably reflect differences in business activities between service and manufacturing firms as well as differences in the characteristics of their technology infrastructures. For example, the more homogeneous nature of service staffs when compared to the range of job classifications in manufacturing may account for manufacturing's concern about educating senior staff. Since many service employees come from the home country, local culture is less of an issue for them.

A study by Kane (1986) suggests that multinational companies organize their data processing operations differently domestically than they do internationally. In the United States, 42% of their data processing operations are centralized[7] while 30% are decentralized. Abroad, these firms have only 17% of their data processing centralized, while 59% is decentralized. The proportion organized in a distributed manner is about the same in both cases 28 versus 24%. Interestingly, 22% of these multinational companies had centralized domestic data processing organizations and decentralized data processing in their foreign subsidiaries. The conclusion is that data processing in domestic multinational firms tends to be centralized while it is more likely to be decentralized in these firms' foreign subsidiaries. Part of the explanation for this may

---

[5]Deans & Kane, 1992.

[6]Id.

[7]Centralized computing would be where all work was sent to one, or a few, locations for processing. Decentralized computing is where each major organizational unit has its own computing resources. Distributed computing makes use of a network to route processing to an appropriate location where the job is run. In distributed processing, a portion of an application may run locally while another portion runs remotely, elsewhere on the network.

be that the foreign subsidiaries are younger and also that at the time these firms' international telecommunications were established, communications costs were higher, making it more economic to have local processing support. In comparing service and manufacturing firms, Kane found that 66% of the multinational manufacturing firms had decentralized data processing, while only 33% of the service firms were decentralized. Eleven percent of the manufacturing firms had centralized data processing, while 52% of the service firms were centralized. These patterns in organizing technology support probably reflect the differences in needs between service and manufacturing firms; manufacturing must have its technology close at hand, while service firms can afford to have it provided remotely.

28.2 FACTORS DRIVING THE USE OF IT IN THE MULTINATIONAL COMPANY. A variety of factors have made the use of IT a key ingredient in the successful multinational firm. As Hammer[8] notes, the basic for managerial decision making in the past was to minimize cost or to achieve economies of scale in production. Now, product or service quality, ability to respond quickly to customer needs, and reduced time-to-market are as important as cost. Six factors have made the use of IT particularly attractive for international firms in pursuit of these goals.

(a) Global Markets. With improvement in data communications (increased data rates, improved quality, and reduced costs) and in international transportation, along with a general lowering of international tariffs, markets have become more global. This tendency becomes pronounced as regional markets develop (for example, the EC) and with political changes in Eastern Europe. King and Sethi[9] have noted that increases in global trade have been followed closely by rapid growth in service transactions, international monetary transactions, and foreign direct investment. In this environment, IT becomes one of the key factors that determines success.

In global markets, firms tend to locate production close to the most effective labor pool, close to raw materials, or to take advantage of government regulations. A key problem for firms operating globally is coordination. IT and particularly data communication can be used to exchange information resulting in improved coordination. For example, Banker's Trust Corporation uses an integrated office system to better coordinate the activities of their Asia Pacific Division. With the system, the time to craft and receive approval on financial proposals was reduced on average from 15 to 3 days.[10]

(b) Timeliness. As McFarlan[11] notes, the required response time for firms operating in global markets is shrinking dramatically. Companies in the automobile and construction industries have been able to reduce their design cycles by upwards of 60% through the use of a combination of automated design equipment (CAD) directly connected to the systems of their suppliers and customers (see section 28.5(a)(i), "Interorganizational Systems"). McFarlan reports that a $30 million investment in manufacturing and information technology by a U.K. chemicals company transformed what had been a 10-week order entry and manufacturing cycle down to two days.

---

[8]Hammer, 1990.
[9]King and Sathi, 1992.
[10]Turner, 1986.
[11]McFarlan, 1992.

This reduction in order entry and manufacturing cycle time permitted the firm to make-to-order, reducing inventory carrying costs to only those of work-in-process and removing the uncertainty around demand forecasts.

(c) Need for Organizational Flexibility. IT is altering the relationship among scale, automation, and flexibility. Large-scale production is no longer essential to achieve the benefits of automation. As a result, barriers to entry in a number of industries are falling. After installation of a flexible manufacturing system, BMW can build customized cars on the normal assembly line, with their own tailored gearbox, transmission, interior, and custom features. The increasing flexibility in performing many tasks combined with the falling costs of designing products (often due to the use of CAD) has resulted in many opportunities to customize products and to serve small market niches.

Because of differences in labor and raw material cost or local government regulation, it is often advantageous for global firms to move operations from a plant in one country to a plant in another. Having a standardized and flexible production line facilitates these shifts. When the product is the same throughout the world (e.g., Coca-Cola) or is provided by subsidiaries through the world (e.g., real estate listings and sales), IT can reduce greatly individual subsidiary costs and foster common levels of quality.

(d) Quality. Led by the Japanese automakers, product and service quality has become a key strategic factor for many firms. Maintaining track of faults, establishing a quality control program, and monitoring of production can permit the identification of a part or manufacturing process that requires redesign. This monitoring and diagnostic activity is heavily information intensive.

(e) Customer Focus. It is no longer enough for a firm to produce a quality product. A customer's needs, preferences, and desires must also be considered. This, in turn, requires capturing large quantities of data about customers, either by direct solicitation or by purchasing marketing databases. Firms that service traveling customers—airlines, hotels, rental car and credit card companies—find it necessary to have worldwide customer databases. So do firms that serve customers that demand integrated worldwide service. The creation, maintenance, access, and distribution of these customer databases places significant demand on a firm's technology infrastructure.

(f) Custom Products and Services. Reduction in product development and manufacturing cycle-times (see section 28.2(b), Timeliness) along with the collection and distribution of extensive customer information (see section 28.2(e), Customer Focus) has permitted firms to customize their products and services.

(g) Industry Transformations. Major shifts in industry structure is one consequence of this rapidly changing international environment. For example, in the late 1970s McKesson, in order to compete better with drugstore chains, introduced the ECONOMOST order entry and inventory system for their customers, mostly individually-owned retail outlets. Cost savings from the system (in terms of lower administrative costs and larger value per order) were passed on to the individual proprietors permitting them to compete more effectively with the chains. Over time, the industry became more concentrated with a number of the chains going out of business.[12] The individual proprietors prospered.

28.3 THE INTERNATIONAL ENVIRONMENT FOR INFORMATION TECHNOLOGY.

The demands of the international environment differ significantly from those a technology manager would face when operating domestically.

(a) Demands of the International Environment. Four factors have been identified as being important in an international environment: legal, environmental, political, and cultural. *Legal* factors include the legal tradition of a country and the extent to which laws are applied equitably. This involves assessing the effectiveness of the legal system. Patent, copyright, and trademark laws are particularly important as are those laws that apply, specifically, to business. *Environmental* factors include the state of the economy in the country, the level of economic development, per capita income and literacy level. A technology manager needs to assess the availability of local workers in the job categories that will be needed, and their wage levels. The nature of competition in the host country needs also to be understood. The *cultural* environment includes the customs, norms, values, and beliefs held generally in the host country. Language, and whether the language of the parent company will be understood in the host country offices, how customers and staff are motivated, status symbols, and religious beliefs must be considered when deciding on an office setting and staff. Finally, the *political* system of the host country needs to be understood including the form of government, its stability, the strength of opposition parties, and the extent of social unrest. Particularly important is the government's attitude toward foreign firms.

While many of these factors are of concern when operating domestically, workers tend to automatically take them into account in their home country due to considerable shared knowledge. In a foreign country, these issues need to be explictly considered. This requires considerable learning.

(b) Levels of Complexity in International Business. At least three levels of complexity need to be considered when managing technology internationally. First, the domestic environment in which the firm is based (the *home* country) places a set of constraints and considerations on operations. Second, each foreign, or *host* country adds a set of considerations which must be taken into account. Third is the international dimension where issues are considered globally. For example, a policy to use certain equipment in one country, may make no sense when the total foreign needs of the company are considered.

28.4 CENTRAL CHALLENGES AND STRATEGIES.

Global companies face challenges and follow strategies that are different than those of firms operating within one country.

(a) Challenges. The challenges of global companies revolve around two basic needs. First is the necessity of resolving differences in *culture* and to manage effectively *headquarters–region–subsidiary relations.* Second is the need to coordinate and control activities *globally.*

---

[12]Clemmons and Row, 1988.

(i) Global vs. Local Tensions. It has been shown convincingly that managers in different environments not only have different ways of analyzing and resolving problems but also different information needs on which they base business decisions. This creates a fundamental dilemma for global companies: managers at headquarters are likely to want different decision information than managers in the region or the local country use. Not only this, but the basis for decision making may be fundamentally different. This points out one of the difficulties of using common systems across a global company.

(ii) Cultural Differences. A heterogenous cultural environment makes it more difficult to share common resources among units. It means products and IT applications require extensive customization to accommodate language and currency differences, for example. There is some evidence, however, that both workers and customers are becoming more alike and that cultural distinctions are lessening through the homogenization of needs and desires as a result of global communication (e.g., TV, Internet, and fax) and travel.

Distinctions also exist in styles of systems development. For example, Ives and Jarvenpaa report,

> that the French were skilled in data modeling and in the more theoretical aspects of systems development. Other interviewees reported the English to be well trained in the use of structured development methodologies, while the Germans were seen as excellent project managers. Singaporeans were described by one interviewee as extremely hard working, skilled, and willing to take on any task assigned. Another manager described them as the consultants of Asia. Australia, on the other hand, was seen as lacking in systems skills.[13]

(iii) Headquarters–Region–Subsidiary Relations. The primary tension between headquarters and subsidiaries is over *control* and *integration.* Subsidiaries desire to act locally so that they can better meet the needs of their (local) customers. In more general terms, organizations must maintain freedom of action when faced with challenges in their environment—threats from competitors or market opportunities, for example. The subsidiary is itself a complex organization and if every action must be cleared with a higher level, reaction time is slowed and resources are wasted in endless communication. Headquarters, thinking more globally, wants commonalty and conformity among its subsidiaries—a nice, neat structure. For them the challenge is to successfully integrate subsidiaries into the larger organization. This integration becomes more complex as the number of different subsidiaries (breadth) and their scope (diversity) increases.

(iv) Alignment of Business and IT Strategies. One of the most difficult challenges faced by firms, whether or not operating globally, is the *alignment* of their IT and business strategies. The goal should be that the IT strategy is consistent with and supports the business strategy. Thus, a globally integrated firm should follow either a coordinated global operation strategy or a cooperation strategy (see section that follows).

---

[13]Ives and Jarvenpaa, 1991, p. 45.

(b) Global Business Strategy and IT. Some business strategies are more dependent than others on timely, accurate, and complete information on overseas operations. There are two broad strategy options for running international operations: *country specific* and *globally integrated.*

(i) Country Specific. When coordination needs are relatively light, home offices often concede considerable autonomy to foreign business. These country specific strategies minimize reporting and information flows between home office and subsidiary. Information technology, under these conditions, is primarily used locally and is probably decentralized.

(ii) Globally Integrated. As competition increases and firms search for economies of scale and scope globally, their needs for coordination and control increase. This creates greater demand for information flow between home office and subsidiaries. Bartlett and Ghoshal[14] identify four broad strategies that an international firm may pursue:

1. Multinational—where foreign subsidiaries are operated nearly autonomously or in loose federation so as to sense and response quickly to diverse local needs and national opportunities.
2. Global—where worldwide activities are closely coordinated from headquarters so as to capitalize on economies associated with standardized product design and world scale manufacturing.
3. International—that exploits parent company knowledge through worldwide diffusion and adoption.
4. Transnational—which seeks to retain local flexibility while simultaneously achieving global integration and efficiencies along with worldwide diffusion of innovations. As Bartlett and Ghoshal put it, "Dynamic interdependence is the basis of a transnational company, one that can think globally and act locally."[15]

The development of a successful international business over time corresponds to the progression from multinational to transnational strategies. This progression from simple to more complex organization requires increased information for coordination and control and, correspondingly, places greater emphasis on IT in relation to other firm activities.

(c) Global IT Strategies. Four generic strategies have been identified for the management of IT globally[16] related to a firm's global business strategy (see section 28.3(b)).

(i) Independent Global Operations. Subsidiaries pursue independent system initiatives mirroring the more general multinational strategy of minimum control from headquarters. Technology choices reflect the influence of local vendors as well as prevailing national communication standards and offerings. Technology platforms,

---

[14]Bartlett and Ghoshal, 1987.
[15]Id., p. 69.
[16]Ives and Jarvenpaa, 1991.

databases, and applications are largely nonintegrated. The strength of this strategy is local responsiveness. Its weakness is the lack of integration which has the potential to severely impede efforts to implement global business strategies.

(ii) Headquarters Driven. Headquarters imposes corporate wide IT solutions on subsidiaries. This is particularly useful for global firms that strive for worldwide efficiencies. Advantages are that centralized IT provides for the coordination and control needed for efficient operations throughout the firm along with some efficiencies of its own. Bringing together headquarters and subsidiary systems staffs may result in some organizational learning. Disadvantages are the clash of this one corporatewide IT solution with local needs and customs, especially if there is not a strong global business push, and the threat of local rejection.

(iii) Cooperative. Headquarters attempts to influence rather than control the IT choices of its subsidiaries. Personnel are exchanged regularly and joint application development efforts are initiated. Subsidiaries modify applications developed by headquarters. This approach closely parallels the more general international strategy that seeks to rapidly disseminate corporate innovation. Advantages are that systems developed this way are more likely to be adopted, and the organizational learning that results from sharing ideas. Disadvantages are the time and effort required for coordination and the variability of outcomes that results from indirect control.

(iv) Integrated. IT applications that reach across national boundaries to meet a firm's diverse objectives. Systems are integrated using international standards and a planned, common IT architecture that meets the needs of various sized organizational units operating in diverse environments. Application modules are divided into common and locally tailored parts. Data entities are shared worldwide and universal data dictionaries and databases are developed. Innovation, in this setting, is a two-way street with headquarters benefiting from the knowledge of subsidiaries as well as the reverse. Few companies have reached this level of development.

28.5 NEW BUSINESS PARADIGMS: USING IT TO TRANSFORM ORGANIZATIONS

(a) Changing External Information Flows. Traditionally, information flows have gone vertically, up the hierarchy, or horizontally among members of a work group, or to subsidiaries, but they have all remained within a *single* firm's boundaries. When transactions needed to be sent externally, hard copy was used, for example, sending them by fax. A new class of interorganizational systems has emerged that *link* together, electronically, independent organizational entities. These systems have the potential of creating new organizations, altering the structure of industries, and changing the economics of business.

(i) Interorganizational Systems. SABRE, American Airlines' travel reservation system, was started in the late 1960s to better manage American's aircraft seat inventory. Specifically, American desired to tie passenger information directly to a seat number on a flight. Because of the size and complexity of the system (a heavy data communications load combined with a huge transaction volume, a large database, and the need to be highly reliable), it was beyond the technology at the time and it took many years to develop.

Forced by competitor moves to make the system available to travel agents in the mid-1970s, American observed an increase in sales volume that offset additional costs. American then began to list auto rentals and hotel reservations (i.e., the products of other travel related companies) in the system. Over time these listings were replaced with electronic links to the auto company's or hotel's reservation systems, thus making SABRE an *interorganizational* system. And American, too, began to list the flights of other airlines for a fee. When deregulation of the airline industry occurred in the late 1970s, American found itself in possession of information about passenger demand and preferences which its competitors did not have. This situation permitted it to structure rates and schedule flights in a profitable manner. In fact, the airline reservation system is so profitable, that the president of American Airlines said recently that if he had to sell either the reservation system or the airline he would sell the airline.

(ii) Electronic Data Interchange. Electronic data interchange (EDI) is the electronic transfer of business information from a computer application in one company to a computer application in another company using standards to structure the data needed to carry out the transaction.[17] An example would be a buyer sending a purchase order as an EDI transaction directly to a supplier's order entry system. Invoices, delivery notices, bills of lading, and customs declarations are examples of business transactions that can be exchanged in electronic form between computers rather than as written communication through the mails, or by fax. The key concepts here are the exchange of *structured* business information among firms without *human intervention.* Two categories of advantages result. The first one comes from the elimination of the exchange of paper documents among firms and the clerical steps involved in handling them. The second one occurs when the complete work process is restructured.

EDI is growing rapidly in Europe and Asia, but less so in the United States. This is because with only three times zones and no customs barriers there is less of an incentive in America to install these systems than in the remainder of the world. Keen[18] reports that EDI has doubled the speed of trucks crossing Europe; there is less time waiting at customs and handling paperwork. Hong Kong (Tradelink) and Singapore (TradeNet) have established EDI value-added networks to position their cities better in the wider world trading network. Hong Kong has over 100,000 trading firms each sending between 2,000 and 10,000 documents a year. SWIRE, a typical trading company, has 300 employees, of whom 120 work on documentation, handling nearly one half million bills of lading per year, supported by the same number of shipping papers comprised of 7 to 8 documents each.[19]

EDI IMPACTS. The direct impacts of EDI include *labor savings* in data transcription, control, error investigation and correction; *fewer delays* in data handling; and *reduced time* to transmit and process data. These are reflected in improved inventory management, better control of transportation and distribution, reduced administrative costs (frequently by a factor of 10 in per-document costs), better cash management,

[17]Keen, 1991.
[18]Keen, 1992.
[19]Id.

and improved trading partner relations. The indirect benefits of EDI result from a closer integration among related functions within different organizations and as a result of the restructuring of activities that often result when EDI is introduced. As DeLuca et al. observe,

> It is not the replacement of paper by electronic messaging which provides EDI's strategic capabilities, but the associated changes in operation and function within and between organizations which EDI links make possible.[20]

For example, Levi Strauss, through its LeviLink system, has vertically integrated the company's entire apparel manufacturing and marketing cycle (including inventory replenishment, management and reconciliation of purchase orders, receipt of goods, processing and payment of invoices, capture of point-of-sale information, and the analysis of market trends). It is this focus on integration across organizational functions and between firms that distinguishes EDI from other forms of electronic communication.[21]

Two trends are apparent with EDI: *desourcing* and *partnering*. Desourcing refers to the tendency of firms using EDI to reduce the number of suppliers they deal with because of improved reliability of suppliers that results from better information flows. Partnering is tighter vertical integration (alliances) among corporations.

EDI STANDARDS. The standardization of documents (i.e., business transactions) is a necessary accompaniment to the replacement of physical transport of paper and magnetic media by electronic transmission. The X12 standard, developed by the American National Standards Institute (ANSI), and the GTDI standard developed in England and Europe are being replaced by the EDIFACT (Electronic Data Interchange for Administration, Commerce and Transport) standard currently under development by a United Nations Joint European and North American (UN-JEDI) working party. A full range of structured business documents (e.g., purchase order, invoice, bill of lading, etc.) is being developed.

(iii) Outsourcing. Traditionally, firms have provided their IT resources internally. That is, they create a group, within their firm, to provide the needed computing and communications services for the remainder of their company. Recently, there has been a move to outsource much of this activity. For example, both Eastman Kodak and Continental Bank have outsourced their *complete* IT functions.

Firms outsource their IT services (or portions of them) for several reasons. First, a firm can often obtain equivalent or better IT service from an outside provider because of lower production costs that come about through economies of scale, or just as a result of competition. Second, a firm may outsource as an incentive alignment mechanism. That is, to send a signal to internal providers of service that they need to become more competitive. Third, a firm may outsource in order to acquire technical skills or capability that do not exist internally. Fourth, a firm may outsource IT so it may focus its internal resources on its core competencies. When IT is not a core business activity, it may be outsourced so that management attention and other scarce resources can be focused on business activities that are central to the mission of the

---

[20]DeLuca et al., 1992, p. 279.

[21]Id.

firm. Fifth, firms may outsource in order to align their IT strategy with the business life cycle of their products and services.

Outsourcing provides an attractive way for a firm to acquire various types of IT services in different countries. Obtaining equipment service, processing capacity, or network services locally may be preferable to retaining permanent staff in each country in which the firm operates.

(iv) Internet. The Internet was funded initially by the U.S. government (Advanced Research Projects Agency, DOD) in the late 1960s.[22] The goal of the project was to develop a robust data communications architecture that would be highly tolerant to loss of communications lines and other failures. Initially used to tie computer science departments in the United States together so they could share computing and other resources, its open set of protocols was expanded and enhanced to encompass many data communications functions (e.g., electronic mail, distributed processing, file transfer, etc.). Because these standards were in the public domain, they were adopted by many manufacturers of data communications equipment until, over time, they have become a worldwide standard. This happened almost by default. The result has been the creation of a worldwide data communications resource that is usable in almost any country in the world.

It is now commonplace for software developers to post software updates on their FTP (File Transfer Protocol) servers for downloading by their customers. They then list the availability of these updates on their WWW (World Wide Web) server Web page and may also send e-mail notification of the availability of the update to their customers, directly. Some suppliers even provide customers with a small program that periodically checks for the availability of updates to their software and can download and apply them automatically. Not only does this result in faster availability of the update, but it also reduces the cost to the developer, by removing most of the costs associated with distributing the update.

The Internet is a distributed network run cooperatively. Internet addresses are unique, and the Internet shares a set of common protocols. Organizations pay the cost of connecting to the network (usually involving some network equipment, such as a router and a leased high-speed telephone line). Individuals can connect to the network through an ISP (Internet service provider) and pay a monthly fee of about $20 per month in the United States. The common bond is that all computers connected to the Internet use the same protocols (e.g., TCP/IP), and they obtain their Internet address from a common network addressing authority.

With an Internet address, one can:

- Send and receive e-mail (electronic mail) messages from anyone else who has an Internet e-mail address. In addition, documents, pictures, or video can be attached to the message.
- Post (publish) a Web page that contains whatever information the individual or company cares to provide. For example, a company may provide a brief description of itself, a list of products or services offered, pictures of them, and a means for purchasing their products online. This requires an online Web server and some electronic commerce software.

[22]Then called the ARPANet.

- Read information posted by others on their Web page.
- Download/upload documents, data, or programs from an online FTP server .
- Search for information on the Web using a search engine, such as Google.
- Highlighted text (or a button) on a Web page or another Internet document, written in HTML (Hypertext Mark Up Language), may be linked to data stored on a computer located anywhere on the Internet. Thus, a company can create a description of a product on its Web page composed of segments, such as text, a picture, a drawing, or even a video with sound, that is stored on another computer connected anywhere on the Internet (see, for example, *www.bmw.com*, where you can get the feel of driving a Z3 roadster). This simplifies greatly the creation of attractive visual displays.

There are search engines on the Internet for locating information of all sorts. This makes the Internet a powerful research tool.

The Internet has already changed the way that many firms present themselves to the public. It has created new opportunities for electronic commerce, in, for example, online auctions, the ability to purchase airline and related travel services online, and as an alternate channel for communicating with suppliers. An industry has sprung up for creating Web pages and in managing their content. And with increased attention to security, the Internet has become an alternative to private data networks.

((b) Changing Internal Information Flows. Although there are many ways of organizing workers, a hierarchical structure is most common in the United States. A hierarchy is described by the (average) number of workers reporting to a supervisor (manager) at the next higher level—called "span of control," and number of levels in the organization. Normally, spans of control vary from four to eight workers reporting to one manager, and large organizations may have three to ten levels.

In hierarchies, which have been called "command and control" organizations, directives (or commands) flow from the top to the bottom, where they are executed, and information flows from the bottom, where it is gathered or generated, to the top. As commands and information move from level to level they become distorted. Drucker[23] notes that the primary function of middle management is communication—to pass commands down the hierarchy to workers who will act on them and to transmit information up the hierarchy to top management where, presumably, decisions will be made. By substituting IT for middle management, accuracy and timeliness of information can be improved, responsiveness increased, and labor costs reduced. The use of IT in this manner has been one of the drivers of organizational downsizing.

(i) Knowledge-Based Organizations. Drucker's[24] vision for the structure of organizations that deal with knowledge intensive tasks, such as those in consulting, finance, and publishing, is that the work will be accomplished by small, self-organizing groups of professionals. These groups will be highly interconnected by data communications and augmented by various technology based tools which will allow their members independence in when and where they work, and will permit them to lever-

---

[23]Drucker, 1988.
[24]Id.

age their knowledge and skills. In these organizations, knowledge will be at the bottom rather than at the top, and decisions will be made where the work is performed. Knowledge-based organizations (KBOs) will be much flatter (fewer levels) and leaner than hierarchies. The role of top management will be to provide a business vision for coordination and synchronization, and to develop an organization's culture, rather than making decisions and providing direction as they do now. Drucker likens KBOs to hospital emergency room teams and string quartets in that they will be organized around the work to be performed (a project-driven organization). An implication of these new organization forms is that they will require the rethinking of traditional management processes, such as supervision, control, and employee development.

(ii) Reengineering Organizations. Hammer[25] maintains that businesses are not taking advantage of technology because they tend to follow current procedures when building IT applications rather than rethinking the way their work is performed. He notes that the division of labor has gone too far—most workers perform only part of a job and spend needless effort in coordination. Many tasks that are done are unnecessary; they have simply been handed down over time. To cope with this situation, firms should examine their basic business activities so as to recognize those that truly add value. These activities should be retained and others discarded. Organizations and business processes should be redesigned to give workers complete jobs, to capture information once, and to place decision-making authority where the work is performed. This leads to a case form of work organization where workers handle complete cases or are responsible for all of the contact with a class of client.

(iii) Groupware. The model behind most office support software is a *single* user; in *groupware*, the model changes to *multiple* users. An implication of this is that people can *share* information. Groupware is computer application software that supports people working together, cooperatively. One of the most widely used Groupware products is **Notes,** developed by the Lotus Corporation (now part of the IBM Corporation).

LOTUS NOTES. Notes is a client-server software product that has facilities for constructing a distributed database of documents that workers can share. Authorized users can change the database and changes are propagated among the Notes servers by a process called replication. A document may contain text, graphics, or video. Users can customize the way a database appears by altering their view of it. Notes also includes e-mail with attachments, and strong security provisions for logging on to the network and for accessing information on a Notes server.

INTRANET. An alternative to a proprietary groupware product, such as Notes, is an intranet, the use of Internet protocols and programs (see section 28.5(a)(iv)) within a firm in order to share information. Intranets have become popular because of the large number of free and commercial products available for the construction of Web pages (compound multiobject databases that can be shared), Web servers, and Web browsers. Since almost everyone who uses the Internet has a Web browser, it is a convenience to use that software to read internal as well as external information.

---

[25]Hammer, 1990.

(iv) End-User Computing. Prior to 1982, the high cost and performance attractiveness of mainframe computers resulted in computing services, in most firms, being provided centrally. In that manner, scarce IT resources (equipment and skilled labor) could be more easily shared and fixed costs spread more widely. However, the demand for new and modified applications outstripped the supply of system building resources resulting in backlogs for development and modification stretching out two to four years in many firms. Clearly this situation was unacceptable.

Information centers (ICs), introduced by IBM Canada in the early 1980s provided some relief by making access to data easier. The notion behind an IC was that if terminal equipment, powerful database query languages, and consulting assistance were made available to users, they could produce their own reports, reducing somewhat the demand for new systems and, hence, the backlog in systems development. But ICs still used large central computers and expensive telecommunications.

In parallel with ICs, the first personal computers (PCs) were introduced into businesses around 1982. Used first for stand-alone (that is, unconnected to other computers) text processing and data analysis work, PCs soon became interconnected through local area networks (LANs) permitting resources (information and equipment) to be shared and expanding the range of business related activities that could be performed on them. As more PC applications were developed and the cost of equipment decreased while performance increased, wide scale diffusion occurred. Professionals performing functional activities, such as lawyers and accountants, became skilled in the application of technology—purchasing packaged software, configuring it to assist them in their work, and sometimes even writing their own programs in a macro-computer language. This *shift* in the *locus of control* and knowledge about computing from centralized, professional support groups to end users has changed fundamentally the technical power structure in many organizations. Rather than technology being the province of a small elite, it is, today, far more widely dispersed.

This, in turn, has promoted a distributed architecture for technology infrastructure and is particularly well suited to international firms. Often called *client/server* computing, this architecture divides an application into two portions: one that resides on a workstation, called the *client*; the other running on another machine on the network called a *server.* The advantage of this arrangement is that the client portion of the system, which runs locally on a worker's machine, is much smaller than the whole application and it can be tuned to provide quick response for the worker. The server portion, which is often the most complicated, need only be installed on one or a small number of servers on the network. The client and server portions of the application communicate with each other by sending messages over the network using a standard protocol. Thus a server may be located in a regional processing center while clients are running on workstations in many different countries, providing customized local service (e.g., having display screens in local languages).

A key issue for management is the effective use and coordination of this distributed technology infrastructure. First off, client/server computing is a complicated architecture. Then, there is a *tension* between the *freedom* needed to create innovative applications that have truly beneficial effects, the *coordination* required for interoperability (which permits resource sharing), and the *support* (consulting and maintenance) necessary to leverage end-user technology activities. All of this becomes more difficult internationally.

28.6 ISSUES IN THE GLOBAL MANAGEMENT OF IT. A variety of issues are specific to the management of technology internationally.

(a) Trans-Border Data Flow. Trans-border data flow (TBDF) is the transmission of data in machine-readable form, such as a data file in ASCII format, between two countries. The medium used for transmission is unimportant. Whether TBDF is an issue for a particular firm depends on the *laws governing data transmission* in the sending and receiving countries and the *type of data* being transmitted. The Scandinavian countries, Germany, the Netherlands, Brazil, China, and Singapore have regulations governing data flow across borders.[26] Of most concern is human resource and payroll data.

The basic issues concerning TBDF are: *individual privacy*, and *economics*. Countries are concerned that private information about individuals contained in a computer database may be used in a manner that compromises that individual's privacy. When this information is transmitted beyond a country's borders, the country loses some jurisdiction over the data and may have a more difficult time protecting the rights of its citizens. For example, medical records are usually considered to be confidential. If a worker's medical records are transferred from the country in which he is working to another country and then disclosed in a manner that embarrasses the worker, he may be unable to seek redress in the courts due to privacy laws in effect in the second country. In such a situation, the worker may have difficulty taking legal action against the company unless the transmission of the data to the second country was explicitly prohibited.

The economic concern stems from a desire to promote local work activities. If processing of data is done in the host country, local jobs are created, hardware and software are purchased and configured, work space is rented, people are hired, and value is created. If the processing is done in another country, this value is lost to the host country.

Fortunately, payroll and human resource records systems, the two classes of applications most vulnerable to TBDF regulation, or to be in violation of local privacy legislation, do not lend themselves to global use. Only the transnational firm may have need for an integrated worldwide skills inventory system. As a general rule, firms need to provide the same level of security and access to personnel data stored abroad as is required by the most stringent privacy legislation in all of the countries in which they operate.

Originally predicted as the trade war of the 1990s, the control of trans-border data has not become a major issue.[27] Part of the reason is that many of the laws and regulations governing TBDF are vague and difficult to enforce. Also, as countries have tended to work together to remove trade barriers among goods and services, they have been less inclined to erect new barriers to the flow of data. A strategy followed by some firms is to inform responsible officials in local countries as to what they intend to do and ask if this presents difficulties.

---

[26]See, for example, the French Data Processing, Data Files, and Individual Liberties Act of 1978 and the Swedish Data Act of 1973.

[27]Ives and Jarvenpaa, 1991.

(i) Key Issues. Key TBDF issues include:

- Requirements to use locally manufactured equipment, software, and services. This may be more costly and it may compromise a firm's standardization strategy.
- Requirements to process certain types of data locally. This may affect cost and it may mean that data from different geographic locations may be processed in different ways, compromising aggregation and consistency.
- Restrictions on data that may be transmitted among countries. The implication may be that applications running in a country may run with incomplete data.
- Increased tariffs that increase costs.
- Government intervention including the requirement to register databases and intrusive monitoring procedures.

(ii) Management Strategies. One strategy that an international firm can follow is to track closely procedures and new regulations related to TBDF in the countries in which it operates. Often, it is useful to create an internal task force that assesses the regulations of each country in which the firm operates and assesses the extent to which the firm is in compliance with these regulations. Some firms assign this responsibility to the Director of Telecommunications, who stays informed through special reports, journals, professional literature, and professional associations, such as the International Telecommunications User Group. Sometimes the monitoring of compliance is part of an overall political risk-assessment program.

TBDF usually takes one of two forms. Either it is extensively *processed* information, or as *raw* data. Interestingly, raw data tends to be more highly scrutinized and regulated by local authorities than is processed information. When there are restrictions in the transfer of raw data, a firm should process data within the host country.

(b) Local Telecommunications. Keen observes that, "International telecommunications is a morass of regulatory, nationalistic and economic complexities."[28] Telecommunications traffic is expected to grow significantly, with much of this in mobile communications. Telecommunication costs vary widely worldwide and this is becoming a key factor in determining facility location. The fundamental blockage to leveling costs are the PTTs (Poste Telegraphe et Telephoniques), the government or quasi-government monopolies that provide telecommunications in various countries. In certain countries, it is not unusual to wait months or even years for a private telephone line to be installed. And high-capacity lines, such as T1, T3, and ISDN, can take even longer. Sometimes there are limitations as to what can be connected to the line. Many countries have begun to break up and to privatize their PTTs, which are naturally unwilling to see their cartels dissolved.

There is some evidence that the quality and reliability of foreign telephone networks is much lower than that available in the United States and that effective data transfer speeds are less, although this situation is changing. Traveling workers with their notebook computers may notice that dial tones and timings of signals are different than in the United States. This may require that the modems of their comput-

---

[28]Keen, 1992, p. 599.

ers be programmed with special "initialization strings." Traveling workers need to take proper power and telephone jack plugs with them and they should be certain not to plug their modem telephone line into a digital telephone system (often found in newer hotels and office buildings) as this will severely damage their computers. It is best to ask specifically for an analog telephone line or to use the telephone line connected to a fax machine.

(c) IT Architecture and Standards. How should a worldwide IT architecture be structured? IT architecture refers to the use, configuration, and location of IT resources including protocols, network structure, software, equipment, data, and staff. Alavi and Young[29] note that a firm's IT architecture should be related to its overall strategy. Strategy in this sense could be thought of as having two components: a firm's business strategy and its international strategy. With regard to an international strategy, firms following a *country-specific* or a *multinational strategy* would be best with independent IT facilities at both subsidiary and headquarters locations since these units function relatively independently of each other (this corresponds to the Independent global operations strategy of section 28.4(c)(i)).

Multinational firms often come about through financial investment in existing organizations which then become subsidiaries. As a result, the technology architecture of these firms is likely to be different from one another because they have been developed independently by each subsidiary and in the headquarters. Additionally, because subsidiaries operate relatively independently, with the exception of financial data, which is necessary to determine firm performance, a low level of data integration is needed among them. Since a relatively small amount of data need be transferred between headquarters and subsidiaries and among subsidiaries, direct low capacity data telecommunications links should be sufficient.

Firms following a *global* strategy with strong central control may well have central IT facilities at headquarters that are shared with subsidiaries along with some local IT support (this corresponds to the headquarters-driven strategy of section 28.4(c)(ii), although it might also be the cooperative strategy of section 28.4(c)(iii). Databases may be firmwide, often refered to as *enterprise* databases and be maintained centrally at headquarters. Since firmwide data needs to be collected globally, the telecommunications architecture would be a vertical hierarchy, with subsidiaries connected to regions where data are aggregated, and regions transmitting aggregated data to headquarters. Ives and Jarvenpaa[30] note that establishing locations for international data centers presents challenges of overlapping work hours, local labor regulations, potential theft and sabotage, and unreliable power sources.

A *transnational* strategy suggests independent coordinated IT facilities at subsidiaries and headquarters (this corresponds to the integrated strategy of section 28.4(c)(iv)). Since this strategy is predicated on rapid firm wide response to local opportunities, information exchange becomes critical. The data architecture of such a firm would be distributed for convenience and fast response, but coordinated, with a network topology providing a high degree of connectivity among subsidiaries and headquarters.

Note that as firms evolve and shift their strategies, they may want to change their

---

[29]Alavi and Young, 1992.

[30]Ives and Jarvenpaa, 1991.

IT architecture to better match their new approach. This implies that an international firm that has not reached the advanced state of being fully standardized and distributed in its equipment, software, data, and staff will be under continual pressure to evolve in this direction. And this pressure is likely to be greater than that on a domestic firm of the same size in the same business.

Extensive work had been done on communications and other technical standards which forms the basis of interoperability among hardware and software produced by different manufactures. For example, TCP/IP (Transmission Control Protocol/Internet Protocol) has become the dominant communications protocol, worldwide. To the extent a firm can adopt the leading standard in each area, it makes it easier to assemble software and equipment in different locations that work together. When operating in a foreign country, it is well to know the standards and protocols that are used in that country.

If an international firm desires the flexibility of moving its staff to different locations worldwide, there are strong advantages in standardizing the office application software (text processors, spreadsheets, presentation, and database software, and firm specific applications) and their communications infrastructure. For example, when fully standardized, a professional who is transferred from New York to the London office can then expect to encounter the same set of office tools in both locations. If the firm had an integrated communications architecture with a common e-mail directory service, only one administrative change need be made in the directory database to indicate the real address of the e-mail server the worker will now be using in London. The actual e-mail address used by others inside and outside of the firm to send messages to him would not change.

This pressure for interoperability suggests that equipment and software in various categories should be the same throughout a firm. At a minimum careful consideration should be given as to how equipment and software in various categories will operate together. For example, if managers at headquarters use Apple Macintoshes, then it is desirable for them to be used also at subsidiaries so that managers traveling encounter familiar computer applications and can easily share data and hardware (e.g., a dock for a notebook computer, or a power adapter). To deal with this issue, many companies adopt *standard* platforms and software. As a firm operates in more geographic locations, fewer suppliers are able to provide support at all locations. This reduces the number of candidates on which to standardize. Additionally, a firm operating globally can be faced with high prices for local hardware, lack of hardware, lack of local service for products, the absence of an authorized distributor, and long lead times for acquiring equipment and spare parts. All of this needs to be taken into consideration when deciding on standards.

(i) Central versus Distributed Systems. In the 1970s when there were significant economic advantages to large main-frame computers, most corporate data processing was centralized. What remote teleprocessing that did exist came from terminals connected to the computer by leased telephone lines. While various schemes were developed to make better use of communications lines (such as combining the data from a number of terminals using a multiplexer) setting up a worldwide computing and communications network was an expensive proposition. It needed to be justified by a large volume of business transaction processing. In the 1980s, the telecommunications companies (telecoms) began to offer *packet switched* data services, that reduced the cost of sending data between machines. By the mid-1980s the power and

reliability of PCs had increased to the point where they began to replace computer terminals in business applications.

Local area networks (LANs) were developed to *interconnect* personal computers and to *share* data files, programs, printers, and other resources. Workers on a LAN could exchange e-mail and send each other copies of documents and spreadsheets that they may have developed on their computers. The success of departmental LANs encouraged firms to tie their LANs together, as long as they were close enough, for example, in one building, using communications devices called bridges. These LANs could be further interconnected using communications services provided by the telecoms, called wide area network (WAN) services.

(ii) Private versus Public Networks. It used to be that the only way to obtain reliable data communications was for a firm to construct its own private data network. A firm would lease a line from a private telephone company or from a PTT in a foreign country in order to connect two locations, for example, a subsidiary and headquarters. The firm had to then provide the equipment on both ends of the line. This made sense when a firm could use most of the data capacity between two locations, but it was expensive when less information needed to be exchanged. Now, with the acceptance of the Internet, firms can connect foreign (and domestic) locations together using off-the-shelf communications equipment (routers, switches, hubs, etc.) and open Internet protocols. Thsy still need to subscribe to a service to gain entry, but many companies will already have this gateway in place. The incremental cost to route data to a home office or other remote location over the Internet may be minimal. Care needs to be taken with the security of the data and the internal network.

(iii) Network Management. While distributed networks have many advantages in terms of reliability and responsiveness, they require active management. It is not unusual for an international firm to establish its own network management center, where network performance is monitored on a 24-hour basis. In addition, because distributed applications lack the unified controls of applications that run on a single processor, they have to be specially tuned and monitored in order to insure their performance.

(iv) Security. Security is a problem in distributed networks. One approach is to insure that unauthorized external access to the network is prevented by the use of a firewall. Another is to see that passwords are changed frequently and that equipment manufacturers' default passwords are never used. A third is to give the responsibility for monitoring the status of network security to someone other than the head of telecommunications. Users should own their own data and take an active interest in security.

(d) Applications. As firms move toward global and transnational strategies, there is pressure for commonalty among applications software. It is unlikely that an application system developed at one subsidiary (or headquarters) will meet the needs of other subsidiaries without significant *participation* from the other units—both IT staff and functional area representation—in its development, and extensive local modification. It takes considerably *longer* for an information technology project to be completed when the team developing it is from different countries, and the resulting software is more complex. Consequently, firms are often reluctant to allocate the extra resources needed to build integrated application systems.

Ives and Jarvenpaa[31] report that application packages designed to run in one country may be incompatible with their counterparts designed to run in another country. In some countries, local disregard of copyright restrictions have caused vendors to retreat from the market. Due to unavailability of software, firms may have to buy packages in one country and then distribute them to subsidiaries in another.

Evolving standards (see section 28.6(c)) are the key to worldwide application development. It is essential to adopt a number of standards for hardware, software and communications consistent with the regulatory constraints and supply of technology in different geographic regions.

28.7 CONCLUSION. Information technology is one of the key factors in the management of international firms. IT permits the better coordination of worldwide operations. IT forms the basis of new products and it has been used to transform industries. International firms that do not invest heavily in an IT infrastructure fail to do so at their risk. IT is no longer a luxury; it is a necessity. In the future the importance of IT to the international firm will only increase.

GLOSSARY OF TERMS

Application program. Application programs are computer programs that perform business activities. For example, an accounting application might perform the General Ledger processing of a firm including the capturing of expense and income, the posting of these to firm accounts and the production of monthly statements. Application programs may be packaged software provided by a software developer and then customized to the needs of a firm or they may be developed internally, or under contract to the specific needs of the firm.

Computer-aided design (CAD). A set of programs for producing two-dimensional drawings and converting these into three-dimensional projections. The programs provide automation of many design functions, especially in the translation of the design representation from one form to another.

Database. A collection of data managed by a Database Management System (DBMS). DBMS have facilities for the definition of a database, design of the system including screens and reports, loading of the database, modification and change to the database, and its operation.

Firewall. A computer placed between a firm's Internet gateway and its internal network that blocks unauthorized traffic.

Media. Media comes in many forms, each with its own format. What is transmitted is one or more characters of data. A translator is required in order to interpret a received character and produce the proper representation.

Text. Text, numeric, and special characters in either the ASCII 128 character or 256 format.

---

[31] Id.

Graphics and Pictures. Graphs, graphic images, and presentations in bit mapped formats such as GIFF and TIFF.

Multimedia. Video images including audio in a format such as QuickTime.

Local Area Network (LAN). LANs are clusters of workstations, printers, file servers, and communications devices operating together that support a work group. The equipment is wired using special cabling (that has a finite length on the order of thousands of feet) and a networking program is run on all equipment that routes information among the devices. Each device on the network has its own network address. A network protocol, such as Ethernet that runs at 100M–1G bytes of data per second, is used to break a message up into data packets and to place the packet on the network. The device receiving the data packet acknowledges receipt. If the sending device does not receive a receipt within a certain period of time it retransmits the data.

Wide Area Network (WAN). WANs are networks composed of devices or other networks, often LANs, tied together by communications services provided by telecoms or PTTs. A firm with a number of locations at which LANs are running may want to interconnect these LANs into a single network so that information can be sent easily to any employee.

Operating System.[32] The operating system is a special purpose program, often provided by the manufacturer of a workstation, that makes the resources of the workstation available to the user. It consists of a file system, resource management, and task management. Application programs use the facilities of the operating system when using system resources.

SOURCES AND SUGGESTED REFERENCES

Alavi, M., and G. Young. "Information technology in an international enterprise: an organizing framework," in S. Paluia, P. Paluia, and R. Zigli (eds.), *The Global Issues of Information Technology Management.* Harrisburg, PA: Idea Publishing, 1992.

Bartlett, C. A., and S. Ghoshal. *Managing Across Borders: The Transnational Solution.* Cambridge, MA: Harvard Business School Press, 1987.

Center for Research on Information Technology and Organization (CRITO). "Globalization of E-Commerce." University of California at Irvine, 2002.

DeLuca, R., P. Clark, J. Gricar, T. Imai, D. McCubbrey, and P. Swatman. "The International Significance of Electronic Data Interchange," in S. Paluia, P. Paluia, and R. Zigli (eds.), *The Global Issues of Information Technology Management.* Harrisburg, PA: Idea Publishing, 1992.

Clemmons, E., and M. Row. "McKesson Drug Company." *MIS Quarterly*, Vol. 5, No. 1, 1988.

Deans, P. C. and M. Kane. *International Dimensions of Information Systems and Technology.* Boston: PWS-Kent Publishing Company, 1992.

Drucker, P. F. "The Coming of the New Organization." *Harvard Business Review*, January–February 1988, pp. 45–53.

[32]The major operating systems for workstations are Microsoft Corporation's Windows, Apple Computer Corporation's OSX, and the Open Source Linux. The major operating systems for servers are Sun Computer Corporation's Solaris (UNIX), Microsoft Corporation's NT, and Open Source Linux.

Hammer, M. "Reengineering Work: Don't Automate, Obliterate." *Harvard Business Review*, July–August 1990, pp. 104–111.

Ives, B., and S. Jarvenpaa. "Applications of Global Information Technology: Key Issues for Management." *MIS Quarterly*, March 1991, pp. 33–49.

Kane, M. J. "A Study of the Impact of Transborder Data Flow Regulation on Large United States-Based Corporations Using an Extended Information Systems Interface Mode." Unpublished Ph.D. dissertation. University of Southern California, 1986.

Keen, P. G. W. *Shaping the Future: Business Design through Information Technology.* Cambridge, MA: Harvard Business School Press, 1991.

——. "Planning Globally: Practical Strategies for Information Technologies in the Transnational Firm," in S. Paluia, P. Paluia, and R. Zigli (eds.), *The Global Issues of Information Technology Management.* Harrisburg, PA: Idea Publishing, 1992.

King, W., and V. Sethi. "A Framework for Transnational Systems," in S. Paluia, P. Paluia, and R. Zigli (eds.), *The Global Issues of Information Technology Management.* Harrisburg, PA: Idea Publishing, 1992.

McFarland, W. "Multinational CIO Challenge for the 1990s," in S. Paluia, P. Paluia, and R. Zigli (eds.), *The Global Issues of Information Technology Management.* Harrisburg, PA: Idea Publishing, 1992.

McNurlin, B. C., and Ralph H. Sprague, Jr. *Information Systems Management in Practice*, 2nd. ed. Englewood Cliffs, NJ: Prentice Hall, 1989.

Turner, J. A. *The Organization of Work with Integrated Office Systems: A Case Study in Commercial Banking.* A working paper. Center for Research on Information Systems, New York University, 1986.

Vaskevitch, D. *Client–Server Strategies.* San Mateo, CA: IDG, 1993.

PART VI

INTERNATIONAL TRANSFER PRICING AND TAXATION

CHAPTER 29

TRANSFER PRICING FOR INTERCOMPANY TRANSACTIONS

Robert Feinschreiber

Feinschreiber & Associates

Margaret Kent

Feinschreiber & Associates

CONTENTS

29.1 INTRODUCTION. A multinational enterprise by its inherent nature has facilities of many types located in many locations in the world. Transfer pricing is a field of analysis that reflects the determination of profits of each such portion of the enterprise. The profits of each portion of the business are most typically structured through intercompany transactions, including intercompany sales, licensing, leasing, and the like. Transfer pricing is a field of analysis that reflects the price of goods, services, or intangible transfer between these entities, or, as an alternative, the determination of profits of entity for that activity having taken place within the enterprise.

(a) Transfer Pricing as a Decision-Making Process. Transfer pricing for an enterprise is a complex decision-making process. The process itself reflects many inputs and reflects many constituencies of the enterprise. The inputs typically include diverse activities, including the cost of construction, marketing efforts, taxation, market share goals, and many other inputs of this type including human behavior specialists, international tax practitioners, industrial engineers, and economists and many others. The constituencies typically include shareholders, employees, and customers.

The decision-making process typically involves inputs from various segments of the business. The transfer pricing decision is viewed differently by persons who can see one segment of the entire picture. It is rare that a person can see the entire picture and act on that picture.

(b) Tax and Nontax Considerations. Some outsiders to a business view the business as making unilateral decisions, viewing the executives as having no goal than maximizing short-term profitability of the worldwide business determined on an after-tax basis. These outsiders neglect to consider that businesses often use pricing structures designed to compete with outside interests, compete with executives in terms of executive compensation, and deal with long-term interest of suppliers. What makes the field of transfer pricing interesting is that the revenue authorities in many jurisdictions are such outsiders described above.

A business can view transfer pricing as a zero-sum analysis except for executive compensation and taxation, as profits would be the same regardless of the legal entity of physical location where the profits occur. Some businesses view the zero-sum features of transfer pricing as an excuse to avoid top level transfer pricing adjustments. Other businesses split transfer pricing issues among transfer pricing tax executives and executive personnel.

(c) Ascertaining Who Is at Risk. Transfer pricing decisions most typically take place among executives located in and representing affiliates in an enterprise or their own interest. This pricing decision affects the profitability of each legal entity within the affiliated group and the tax that is to be paid on the profits of each legal segment of the business.

Transfer pricing is, at the outset, a business decision and a tax decision. Income tax payments are a significant cost for most multinational businesses. and transactions between affiliated entities are an important part of this income tax exposure. Global transfer pricing is an analytical approach that enables a business to control its income tax cost on a worldwide basis. This global transfer pricing approach focuses only on transactions with related parties, so that relationships with independent entities are ignored. Other relationships, such as business partnerships between unrelated entities, remain a threshold inquiry for the tax collectors.

(d) Foreign Country Participation in Transfer Pricing. More than 30 countries have somewhat standard approaches toward transfer pricing, typically through the Organization for Economic Cooperation and Development (OECD). Such countries include the following:

Argentina	Germany	Poland
Australia	India	Russia
Belgium	Indonesia	Sweden
Brazil	Italy	Singapore
Canada	Japan	Switzerland
Chile	Kazakhstan	South Africa
China	Korea	Spain
Czech Republic	Malaysia	United Kingdom
Denmark	Mexico	United States
Finland	Netherlands	Venezuela
France	New Zealand	

(e) Basics of the Transfer Pricing Inquiry. Global transfer pricing is complex and requires significant analytical inputs. A company seeking to use global transfer pricing should be able to answer the first ten inquiries, using this information as a starting point for each country in which the company does significant business:

1. What transfer pricing methods are acceptable in the country?
2. What priority is there among transfer pricing methods?
3. What penalties can the country impose on your company?
4. When can you reduce the penalty that could otherwise be imposed?
5. What type of information must you provide to the tax collector?
6. Can you set up a pricing agreement with the tax collector in advance?
7. What adjustments and set-offs are required after a pricing adjustment?
8. When can you use a cost sharing agreement with your affiliates?
9. What is the effective tax rate in your configuration in that country?
10. What is the effective withholding rate for international payments?

Transfer pricing issues impact both the businesses that may have to pay the taxes and the tax collectors that expect to collect the taxes. Quite fortuitously, and by design, transfer pricing rules across international borders are much more similar than they are different. These differences, however, lead to substantial tax consequences. Most differences typically lead to double taxation but these differences occasionally lead to tax-saving opportunities.

(f) Transfer Pricing Reference Materials. Information about U.S. transfer pricing policies and practices is readily convenient. While other references are available, the *Transfer Pricing Handbook* (John Wiley & Sons, 2001) has grown in stature among international tax practitioners. The third edition of the *Handbook*, edited by Robert Feinschreiber, is a two-volume series and includes a comprehensive supplement.

In addition, John Wiley & Sons, Inc. published its companion volume *International Transfer Pricing—A Country by Country Guide*, edited by Robert Feinschreiber.

29.2 TRANSFER PRICING METHODOLOGIES.

Governments most typically make their transfer pricing analysis on a legal entity basis so that transfer pricing focuses primarily on the legal ownership and control of legal entities. Very little attention is paid to branches or divisions from a transfer pricing perspective. The tax collector may examine contractual relationships, corporate partnerships, and other activities.

(a) Transfer Pricing Methodologies. Transfer pricing, for tax purposes, depends on pricing in and of itself or on a split of net income among affiliated entities. Thus, transfer pricing has two often conflicting objectives:

1. Determining an equitable share of the profits between taxing jurisdictions
2. Determining equitable prices for intercompany transactions

Most countries focus on the pricing or transactional approach and away from a profit split approach. Global trading is used for financial institutions.

(b) Specific Methods. The "standard" transfer pricing methods include:

- Comparable uncontrolled price method
- Resale price method
- Cost-plus method
- Profit split

Countries do differ in their pricing methods, especially when it comes to the profit split alternative. There are many variations and cost accounting methods in determining "cost." Value-based costing comes into play in determining the "plus." Brazil's transfer pricing methods differ most significantly from other countries.

(c) Comparability Analysis. Some countries impose a priority in determining the applicable transfer pricing method. Other countries, including the United States, impose no specific priority. Their goal is to determine the best transfer pricing method, using parameters such as the following as part of a comparability analysis:

- Functions of the business in each country. Activity-based costing has an important role here.
- Contract terms—including purchasing terms, licensing, and so forth
- Risks—everything from bankruptcy to currency devaluation to slip-and-fall

- Economic conditions—including riots, hyperinflation, tax incentives and the like
- Property or services in each country

(d) U.S. Transfer Pricing. In practice, transfer pricing in the United States is based on the comparable profits method (CPM), which focuses on the U.S. activities of the business. This approach seeks comparative data between ostensibly similarly situated enterprises in the United States. Three comparable profits methods are in widespread use:

1. The ratio of operating profits to sales
2. The ratio of gross profits to sales
3. The ratio of operating profits to operating assets

Economists make a number of adjustments to establish the CPM. These adjustments include:

- Inventory adjustments
- Accounts receivable
- Accounts payable
- Foreign exchange risk

(e) Comparable Profits Method and SIC Codes. The taxpayer or the IRS frequently applies the easiest transfer pricing method, which is often the formulary CPM. The taxpayer or the IRS auditor often applies the CPM procedure by going to the Standard Industrial Classification (SIC) code and doing the following:

- Using the four-digit Standard Industrial Classification (SIC) code applicable to the business
- Including other businesses in that SIC code
- Preparing and utilizing CPM comparative formulas

At the present time, the SIC approach for transfer pricing is being abused and is fraught with difficulty. The six most serious transfer pricing problems for the taxpayer or the IRS examiner are:

1. The initial selection of SIC may be determined by a staff person in the company who is unfamiliar with the ramifications of SIC selection or with transfer pricing.
2. Such individual may not be adequately familiar with the operations of the business to adequately select the SIC code.
3. A four-digit SIC code is too broad-based, and encompasses activities vastly different from the taxpayer under examination.
4. The SIC process does not adequately effect changes in the taxpayer's business. Many businesses continue on with the SIC code by habit rather than by further analysis.
5. The SIC process does not contain an established process for changing a busi-

ness's SIC Code.

6. The SIC code may become obsolete or obsolescent as high technology moves rapidly. Multiyear data would not be available under any event.

(f) Substantiating Transfer Pricing. A taxpayer can avoid a detailed transfer pricing audit by preparing and retaining primary documents and background documents. The documents must be prepared in the ordinary course of business, and cannot be prepared specifically for audit. Contemporaneous documentation includes:

- Business overview
- Organizational structure
- Section 482 documentation
- Method selection
- Rejected methods
- Controlled transactions
- Comparables
- General index

29.3 TRANSFER PRICING PENALTIES IN THE UNITED STATES. The United States has a complex transfer pricing penalty regime that is separate from penalties that could apply to taxpayers in other contexts and from the special penalty rules that could apply to foreign-owned U.S. corporations. These penalties are not deductible in determining gross income. There are, in fact, two transfer pricing penalties:

1. Transaction penalty
2. Net adjustment penalty

There are two penalty levels:

1. Substantial valuation misstatement penalty—20%
2. Gross valuation misstatement penalty—40%

All penalties apply to Section 482–related tax underpayments. Each type of penalty can apply at either of the two levels mentioned above. The penalty applies to the tax, not to underpayment itself. "Tax underpayment" is the difference between the result reflected on the tax return and the results as finally determined.

(a) Substantial Misstatement Penalty. The substantial valuation misstatement penalty applies if price stated is twice as much as the true price or is half as much as true price. Consider the two examples:

1. The parties select an intercompany price of $4,000.
   The true price was $8,000.
   The 20% substantial valuation misstatement penalty applies to the difference.
2. The parties select an intercompany price of $4,000.
   The true price was $2,000
   The 20% substantial valuation misstatement penalty applies to the difference.

(b) Gross Misstatement Penalty. The gross valuation misstatement penalty applies if the price stated is four times as much as the true price or is one quarter as much as true price. Consider the two examples:

1. The parties select an intercompany price of $4,000.
   The true price was $16,000
   The 40% gross valuation misstatement penalty applies to the difference.
2. The parties select an intercompany price of $4,000.
   The true price was $1,000
   The 40% gross valuation misstatement penalty applies to the difference.

(c) Net Adjustment Penalty. The net adjustment penalty is the most significant of the two transfer pricing penalties, especially for large and medium-sized multinationals. In contrast to the transactional penalty, which is determined on a transaction-by-transaction basis, the net adjustment penalty is determined on an aggregate basis. There are two levels in applying the net adjustment penalty:

1. Substantial valuation misstatement penalty and
2. Gross misstatement penalty.

The substantial valuation misstatement applies to the net adjustment penalty if the net Section 482 adjustment is the lesser of the following:

1. $5 million
2. 10% of gross receipts

(d) Substantial Valuation Misstatement Net Adjustment Penalty. The substantial valuation misstatement net adjustment penalty could be recharacterized in the following manner:

- Gross receipts of less than $50 million—valuation based on 10% of gross receipts.
- Gross receipts of $50 million—valuation of $5 million
- Gross receipts of more than $50 million—valuation of $5 million

The gross valuation misstatement applies to the net adjustment penalty if the net Section 482 adjustment is the lesser of the following:

- $20 million
- 20% of gross receipts

The gross valuation misstatement net adjustment penalty could be recharacterized in the following manner:

- Gross receipts of less than $100 million—valuation based on 20% of gross receipts
- Gross receipts of $100 million—valuation of $20 million
- Gross receipts of more than $100 million—valuation of $20 million

29.4 FOREIGN-OWNED BUSINESSES DOING BUSINESS IN THE UNITED STATES. Foreign-owned U.S. companies that are doing business in the United States could be subject to two U.S. tax regimes. The business has a dual tax responsibility if:

- A business is engaged in intercompany transactions, and
- A principal shareholder of the business is foreign

The two U.S. tax regimes include:

1. Transfer pricing
2. Foreign-owned U.S. corporation reporting and record keeping

These two regimes have different objectives, and, as such, interrelate on specified occasions. This portion of the chapter specifically addresses the rules for foreign-owned U.S. corporations.

(a) Responsibilities Imposed. The U.S. tax law imposes extensive responsibilities on the foreign-owned U.S. corporations. The U.S. tax law also imposes responsibilities on the foreign owners, but these responsibilities are only derivative (i.e. the responsibilities relate to the parent–subsidiary relationship), and limited in scope. This peculiar relationship toward the foreign owners exists because the United States recognizes that its long arm of the U.S. tax law is limited by international law concepts, and does not apply directly to the foreign owners. The full responsibility falls on the U.S. subsidiary because the U.S. courts have power over this subsidiary because of its presence in the United States.

Foreign-owned U.S. corporations have two responsibilities:

1. To prepare and retain specified records
2. To file specified documents with the IRS

The foreign-owned U.S. corporation provisions may potentially have the following impact on the U.S. company:

- May cause the U.S. company to be subject to penalties
- May require the U.S. company to enter into an authorization agreement with the foreign owners
- May subject the U.S. company to a summons
- May subject the U.S. company to special harsh penalties for non-compliance

(b) Reporting Requirements. Foreign-owned U.S. corporations must file Form 5472 on an annual basis to reflect intercompany transactions with *each* affiliate. For example, a foreign-owned business has four subsidiaries overseas and three subsidiaries in the United States. Assume that each entity in the United States does business with the four subsidiaries of the parent and the parent itself. Each U.S. entity would have to file five Forms 5472. Since there are three U.S. subsidiaries, 15 Forms 5472 would be needed in all.

The term *U.S. owner* is broader than the ownership and control of a subsidiary. In fact, the tax rules require that the U.S. company reflect a shareholding of 25% or more. The relevant term is a *reporting corporation.* Partnerships and branches are treated in the same manner as branches.

Form 5472 must reflect U.S. dollars, even if principal currency was not the U.S. dollar. U.S. currency tax rules are used to determine the U.S. tax amount. Nevertheless, Form 5472 is an information return, not a tax return. Section 6038A permits the reporting corporation to use approximations. Estimates are considered reasonable if the estimates range between 75% and 125% of the actual amount. The IRS and the courts determine this actual amount.

The English language must be used for all purposes in preparing documents and filing the requisite forms to the IRS. The businesses can use foreign language documents and retain documents overseas, but the business must be prepared to translate these documents into English and have these documents made available to the IRS. The reporting party and the foreign-related party can contest in court the amount and the extent of the documents sought by the IRS.

The IRS could request virtually every record that exists and some records that do not exist. Instead of requiring all of these records, the Treasury Regulations enable the reporting corporation to prepare and retain 100 or so separate records. The Treasury provisions call this provision a "safe harbor," and a part of the contemporaneous documentation rules. Nevertheless, tax practitioners' view these provision as an "unsafe harbor." Preparing less than all of the documents may enable the IRS to expand rather than contract its investigation. The section 6038A safe harbor provisions have no parallel in the section 482 provisions. Section 482 has no safe harbors.

(c) Specific Database Requirements. There are six components to the section 6038A safe harbor provisions:

1. Original entry books and transaction records
2. Profit and loss statements
3. Pricing documents
4. Foreign country and third-party filings
5. Ownership and capital structure records
6. Records of loans, services, and other nonsale transactions

The reporting corporation is obligated to prepare and retain many types of records. In some cases, the reporting corporation has an obligation to create records if these records otherwise did not exist. This rule applies to original entry books and transaction records.

Original entry book and transaction records include:

- General ledgers
- Sales journals
- Purchase order books
- Cash receipts books; cash disbursement books
- Bank statements; canceled checks
- Workpapers
- Purchase invoices; sales contracts

(d) Six Reporting Levels. The U.S. tax rules require more reporting for big companies and for big transactions than they do for small businesses and for small transactions. There are six reporting levels in all.

1. By type of transaction	$50,000
2. Related-party gross payments	$5,000,000
3. U.S. gross receipts	$10,000,000
4. Gross receipts—penalty exclusion	$20,000,000
5. Significant industry segments	$25,000,000
6. High profit test	$100,000,000

(e) Penalties on Foreign-Owned U.S. Corporations. The specific rules for foreign-owned U.S. corporations contain three penalties:

1. Initial penalties
2. Additional penalties
3. Noncompliance penalties

It is important to note that these specific penalties that can apply to foreign-owned U.S. corporations are separate from the penalities that could apply to section 482 transfer pricing. As such, foreign-owned U.S. corporations that made transfer pricing errors are subject to two penalty regimes. These penalties are not deductible in determining gross income.

The penalties for foreign-owned U.S. corporations are based on the number of Forms 5472 required to be filed, which for a typical large multinational can be more than 100 Forms 5472 per year. If ten U.S. subsidiaries of the foreign parent have the requisite transactions with foreign subsidiaries, 100 Forms 5472 must be filed and up to a hundred $10,000 penalties could be assessed for such failures, $1 million in total. The inital penalties are imposed on an annual basis.

The IRS can impose an initial penalty on a reporting corporation that fails to comply with:

- The reporting requirements imposed by Section 6038A
- The record maintenance requirements imposed by Section 6038A

The initial penalty is $10,000, and can be imposed for each such failure. Nevertheless, the penalty does not apply to minor failures. Instead, the penalty is imposed if the information required is "substantially incomplete." Three specific failures invoke the initial penalty:

1. Failure to furnish the information return, Form 5472, within the time and manner prescribed by the regulations
2. Failure to maintain records under the record maintenance rules, or failing another party to maintain records under the record maintenance rules
3. Failure to meet the requirements for records outside the United States within the requisite time period

Additional penalties can apply if the IRS notifies the reporting corporation in writing that the reporting corporation failed to meet its compliance obligation and this failure continues for 90 days. At that point, the additional penalty begins to apply. The additional penalty is $10,000 for each 30-day period. A fraction of the 30-day period is treated as the entire 30-day period.

More penalties can apply if the IRS requests the requisite tax information, but the reporting corporation is not forthcoming in providing this information. In that situation, the IRS can deny all deductions claimed. In addition, criminal penalties may apply for the reporting corporation that fails to file a tax return or files a false or fraudulent tax return.

A reporting corporation might be able to escape from penalties if the reporting corporation can demonstrate the following:

- The reporting corporation has reasonable cause for its actions or inaction.
- The reporting corporation has substantially complied with the record-keeping and reporting obligations.
- The reporting corporation has proven the facts and circumstances were such to deny the penalty.
- The reporting corporation acted in good faith.
- The reporting corporation's failure was due to an honest misunderstanding.

29.5 INTRODUCING THE ADVANCE PRICING AGREEMENT PROCESS. The United States has long advocated advance pricing agreements (APAs). Similar advanced agreements are available in more than 20 countries. There are two types of APAs:

1. Unilateral APAs—between the taxpayer and the Internal Revenue Service
2. Bilateral APAs—between the taxpayer and the Internal Revenue Service, the foreign taxpayer, and the foreign tax authorities

The APA procedure in the United States involves the following steps:

1. One or more prefiling conferences
2. Paying a fee for the APA
3. The APA request for an APA
4. An establishment of critical assumptions in the APA
5. The APA agreement itself
6. Preparation of annual report to the IRS describing APA activities
7. Audit-limiting activities
8. Record retention
9. Continuation of the APA
10. Cancellation of the APA

A global transfer pricing analysis most often reduces income tax payments In one or more jurisdictions, making the entire effort invariably worthwhile for the business as a whole.

29.6 PROPOSALS FOR REVISING THE TRANSFER PRICING AUDIT STRUCTURE. The IRS is now in the process of modifying its transfer pricing procedures, as the 1993 regulations have proved to be deficient in a number of respects, including documentation, examination procedures, and methodologies. These modifications will be taking place through revised audit procedures as well as possibly through changes to the regulations themselves.

29.7 USING DATA SOURCES. There are many occasions in which the IRS fails to seek, obtain, or utilize potential data sources. In short, we are suggesting that there may be occasions in which Information Document Requests (IDRs) are too narrowly focused. Here are two situations in which the IRS may benefit from expanding the IDR process.

(a) International Merger Example. Consider, as an example, the situation of an IRS international examiner and the transfer pricing economist seeking information about an international merger. The two entities had been independent, but the U.S. entity and a foreign subsidiary face intercompany transfer concerns for the first time because of this merger. The merger that is under review by the IRS had previously been subject to the Hart Scott Rodino (HSR) premerger notification requirements with the Department of Justice (DOJ) and the Federal Trade Commission (FTC).[1]

It would be in the interests of the IRS to seek, obtain, and utilize these HSR premerger filings. The filings should provide the international examiner and the transfer pricing economist with information that should be quite useful in the transfer pricing context, especially as to industry segments and competitors. In this regard, the international examiner and the transfer pricing economist should be able to interpret the importance of second request filings, the investigation process, and third-party involvement in the HSR process.

(b) Engineering Economy Example. The international examiner is dependent on receiving and utilizing engineering data under a number of scenarios (see Section 29.8, Cost Issues, Excess Capacity, and Cost Structures Overseas, for one such example). We suggest that the transfer pricing economist be involved in the interpretation of engineering data in coordination with the needs of the international examiner until the transfer pricing coordinator(s) serve this role.

In our view, having a transfer pricing coordinator would be beneficial to the IRS, as the transfer pricing coordinator could better identify or confirm data sources that should exist before the IRS makes the effort to seek, obtain, and utilize these data sources. The transfer pricing coordinator and other high-level transfer pricing personnel should benefit from education and cross-training that would bring these untapped data sources to light.

(c) Divisional Tax Accounting and Intracompany Transfer Pricing. Tax considerations are the central focus of the transfer pricing regulations, to the exclusion of the business considerations other than taxation that impact transfer pricing. As such, it is our suggestion that the transfer pricing regulations take into account such business facets as division and profit center accounting, autonomous transactions, vertical integration, and the like.[2]

---

[1]Thomas E. Johnson, "Antitrust Customs, Gray Market, and Other Nontax Transfer Pricing Considerations," *Transfer Pricing Handbook* #2, 3rd ed., edited by R. Feinschreiber (New York: John Wiley & Sons, 2001): Section 85.2.

[2]Robert Feinschreiber, "Business Facets of Transfer Pricing," *Transfer Pricing Handbook* #1, 3rd ed., edited by R. Feinschreiber (New York: John Wiley & Sons, 2001): Section 1.5.

The fact of the matter is that businesses may be making transfer pricing decisions for other reasons than worldwide tax minimization. Tax issues, though clearly important, have declined in comparative importance as tax rates have declined during the 1990s and beyond.

For example, the transfer pricing regulations fail to recognize that many multinational businesses operate on a two-tier system, an official intercompany transfer price and an informal intracompany transfer pricing system. This two-tier system occurs most often in the context of work-in-process goods, as there is often no true market for these goods.

The transfer pricing regulations fail to address intermediate goods, such as work-in-process inventories. At the present time, the taxpayers and the IRS have been reticent in seeking and applying this intracompany data because the transfer pricing regulations do not address this product area.

29.8 COST ISSUES, EXCESS CAPACITY, AND COST STRUCTURES OVERSEAS. Many multinational businesses transfer their products among affiliated enterprises by using a full standard cost system or by using a full actual cost system.[3] As a practical matter, manufacturers both inside and outside the United States have to address excess production capacity issues from a cost accounting perspective, for addressing allocation and apportionment considerations, and for addressing transfer pricing considerations. The treatment of excess capacity is likely to be an allocation and apportionment issue under Regulation Section 1.861-8 when the excess capacity takes place within the United States and as a transfer pricing issue when excess capacity takes place in a foreign facility, thus creating nonparallel treatment.

Our concern is that such intercompany transfers produce a significant level of contemporaneous documentation, but the IRS rarely takes the opportunity to analyze this data, and, as a result, the data is ignored or lost. Consider the following two examples.

(a) Example. X Corporation is a manufacturer in Country X. X's factory has the capacity of producing 10,000 widgets per year. X produces and sells 4,000 units for sale in the United States and produces and sells 4,000 units for sale in Country X during year 1. The remaining 2,000 units are not produced and became excess capacity for year 1. The variable cost of production is $1,000 per unit. Overhead is $5 million. X Corporation sells the widgets to its U.S. affiliate for $1,800 each. The U.S. affiliate makes use of extensive marketing intangibles and sells the widgets to ultimate customers for $2,000 each.

Assume that X Corporation treats excess capacity costs as attributable to X's exports under local law and pursuant to the transfer pricing rules of Country X. Exports to the United States would bear 60% of the overhead costs (4,000 export units plus 2,000 excess capacity units divided by 10,000 units) or $3 million (60% × $5 million). The $3 million would be divided by the 4,000 export units, or $750 per unit. Total costs would be $1,750 ($1,000 in variable costs plus $750 for overhead.) Corporation X would show profits of $200,000 ($50 × 4,000 units) for its U.S sales.

In contrast, domestic sales in Country X would bear 40% of the overhead costs (4,000 domestic units divided by 10,000 units) or $2 million (40% × $5 million). The

---

[3]Robert Feinschreiber, "Business Facets of Transfer Pricing," *Transfer Pricing Handbook* #1, 3rd ed., edited by R. Feinschreiber (New York: John Wiley & Sons, 2001): Section 1.13.

$2 million would be divided by the 4,000 domestic units, or $500 per unit. Total costs would then be $1,500 ($1,000 in variable costs plus $500 for overhead.) Corporation X would then show profits of $1,200,000 ($300 × 4,000 units) for its domestic sales, assuming the $1,800 price.

The international examiner reviews the $1,800 intercompany transfer, the marketing intangibles of the U.S. affiliate, and the sale to the ultimate customer of $2,000. The U.S. corporate tax director exclaims, "The entire profit is $250 per unit, of which $200 is in the United States. Do you want blood from a stone?" The international examiner views the transaction as a resale transaction, and elects not to pursue the matter further in light of the company's SIC code. The U.S tax director makes no mention of the cost shift overseas, and in fact the U.S. tax director may not know of that cost shift.

(b) Example Postscript. It is our view that the IRS does not have the facility to pay adequate attention to overseas cost structures.[4] There are two reasons for this gap:

1. The transfer pricing economist, being trained in marginal costing, is well suited to analyze the business's cost system, and the transfer pricing economist is well equipped to examine a crucial component of the cost system—excess production capacity. Nevertheless, the transfer pricing economist rarely, if ever, has the opportunity to delve into the specifics of the business cost system under review. In addition, the transfer pricing economist for the most part lacks the skill set to address allocation and apportionment issues under Regulation Section 1.861-8.
2. International examiners and attorneys lack the skill set to address cost systems or excess production capacity. Nevertheless, international examiners have the facility and skill set to address allocation and apportionment issues under Regulation Section 1.861-8. As a practical matter, the international examiner is unlikely to have the opportunity to address excess capacity issues, as these issues are likely to be buried within the company's cost accounting system.

29.9 ADVANCE PRICING AGREEMENTS.

It is our belief that the central transfer pricing issues for taxpayers and the IRS is foregone opportunities on the part of both parties as well as with their foreign counterparts.[5]

(a) Unilateral, Bilateral, and Multinational Agreements. We support the APA process, whether unilateral, bilateral, or multilateral. It is our belief that the acceleration of the APA process should be a goal of the United States as well as a goal of U.S. taxpayers. The best way to achieve this goal is through increased use of e-mail and Internet technologies to access and review databases of the business originating from disparate locations.

---

[4]Todd J. Wolosoff and Maja M. Arcyz, "Cost Plus Method," 18.5.

[5]Robert Feinschreiber, "Using Advance Pricing Agreements for Transfer Pricing," *Transfer Pricing Handbook* #2, 3rd ed., edited by R. Feinschreiber (New York: John Wiley & Sons, 2001): Section 77.1. *See also*, E.Miller Williams, Jr., "Evaluating Whether to Use the Advance Pricing Agreement Program," *Transfer Pricing Handbook* #2, 3rd ed., edited by R. Feinschreiber (New York: John Wiley & Sons, 2001): Section 78.1.

It is our belief that the central transfer pricing issues for taxpayers and the IRS is foregone opportunities on the part of both parties as well as with their foreign counterparts. We support the advance pricing agreement process, whether unilateral, bilateral, or multilateral.

(b) Competent Authority Considerations. We believe that the competent authority process is too slow to be effective, whether on the part of the taxpayer in dealing with the IRS, or with the IRS in dealing with the IRS's foreign counterparts.[6] We favor a change in the competent authority process and in the bilateral APA process that would bring the following parties to the table:

- The taxpayer
- The IRS
- The foreign affiliate of the U.S. taxpayer
- Tax authorities of the foreign government

We recognize the IRS's position that they view the competent authority process as being government to government, and that taxpayers are being told to "butt out." In our view, a number of taxpayers have lost the respect of the competent authority process because of the IRS's viewpoint and the slowness of the process itself.

29.10 GRAY MARKET CONSIDERATIONS. Gray market sales begin when a manufacturer sells its products to retailers in different locations. The sales price differs sharply from one location to another.[7] A purchaser buys the product from the retailer at the lower cost then available at the low cost jurisdiction. The purchaser makes use of this pricing differential by reselling the goods into a higher priced jurisdiction at a higher price. This price is still lower than the price charged by the manufacturer/seller in that second market.

All too often, IRS examiners, upon viewing a scheme or device that seems unusual to them, suspect that the taxpayer has concocted a device that has as its primary purpose the saving of taxes. The facts are often otherwise. In the gray market situation, these schemes or devices may be designed for nontax purposes, such as a device to siphon off the manufacturer's profits.

Misdirection of sales—whether inadvertent or not—becomes crucial. These schemes may have tax ramifications that the IRS is likely to miss because the IRS is looking elsewhere. Here the examiner is reviewing the manufacturer and the seller in a quest for transfer pricing adjustments, but the purchaser who resold the goods unbeknown to the manufacturer caused the potential adjustments.

(a) Example. V Corporation, headquartered in country V, produces kimonos in country V and sells kimonos in two countries, Country V and in Country J, for $25 each. In addition, V Corporation sells 200,000 kimonos in the United States, of which

---

[6]Paul C. Rooney, Jr., Darren R. Fortunato, and Nelson Suit, "Competent Authority," *Transfer Pricing Handbook* #2, 3rd ed., edited by R. Feinschreiber (New York: John Wiley & Sons, 2001): Section 74.1.

[7]Thomas E. Johnson, "Antitrust, Customs, Gray Market, and Other Nontax Transfer Pricing Considerations," *Transfer Pricing Handbook* #2, 3rd ed., edited by R. Feinschreiber (New York: John Wiley & Sons, 2001): Section 85.6.

100,000 are sold to Y Corporation, a U.S. company, at a price of $9 each, or $900,000 in total. V Corporation and Y Corporation are totally independent.

Y Corporation exports the kimonos to its subsidiary J Prime in Country J, incurring a shipping charge of $1 per unit for the kimonos, or $100,000 in total shipping charges. Y Corporation sells the kimonos for $11 each, reflecting gross sales of $1,100,000, costs of $9 each or $900,000, shipping expenses of $1 per unit or $100,000, and earns a profit of $1 per unit or $100,000.

J Prime then resells the kimonos for $20 each in Country J, thus undercutting V Corporation's sales price of $25 in country J. J Prime's revenue is $2 million, 100,000 kimonos × $20 each. J Prime is a discount operation, and has no intangibles. The gross income from the transaction is $2 million. Net income to J Prime is $2,000,000 minus the $900,000 purchase price for the kimonos and $100,000 for the shipping of the kimonos, or a net of $1,000,000. The U.S. portion of the profit is $100,000, one-tenth of the total.

The international examiner examines the Form 5472 for V Corporation[8] and the Form 5471 for Y Corporation to determine whether these businesses are related parties. The analysis is inconclusive. Nevertheless, the international examiner believes that V Corporation and Y Corporation might be affiliates, and examines whether the initial sales price of the kimonos of $9 is at arm's length. The international examiner compares sales to V Corporation and sales to others in the United States and concludes the transactions with Corporation V are in fact at arm's length.

The international examiner undertakes a SIC code analysis and establishes that Y Corporation earns a comparable return on investment of its U.S. activities. As such, the international examiner proposes no adjustment against Y Corporation.

(b) Suggestions. We suggest that the underlying purpose of Y Corporation's activities was to develop a gray market structure against V Corporation, to take advantage of V Corporation's high profitability in Country J. That having been said, there is a transfer pricing issue. The U.S. activities of the Y Corporation group are only one-tenth of the total profits, and a significant portion of that profit is in purchasing the kimonos in the United States. We note that the United States transfer pricing regulations recognize marketing intangibles, but these regulations do not take purchasing intangibles into account.

29.11 CORPORATE GOALS AND STRUCTURE.

International examiners view the decision-making process of a worldwide corporation as a monolith, seeking to maximize after-tax returns on investment. All too often, this perception is not correct, as the worldwide business tends to have divergent goals, including:[9]

- Executives may be paid and evaluated based on a defined segment of the overall business. Each such executive normally would seek to maximize his or her income and profits, which may differ from the maximization goals of the entire business.

---

[8]Robert Feinschreiber, "Overview of Foreign-Owned U.S. Corporations," *Transfer Pricing Handbook* #2, 3rd ed., edited by R. Feinschreiber (New York: John Wiley & Sons, 2001): Section 54.1.

[9]Robert Feinschreiber, "Business Facets of Transfer Pricing," *Transfer Pricing Handbook* #1, 3rd ed., edited by R. Feinschreiber (New York: John Wiley & Sons, 2001): Section 1.17.

- Pricing adjustments tend to be made after the fact rather than being contemporaneous with the events that would precipitate change. Obsolete data can change the pricing method being selected.

29.12 DETERMINING WHO OWNS THE INTANGIBLES. Transfer pricing professionals, whether within the IRS or private practitioners, expend considerable effort in determining whether a particular intangible is owned by a U.S. business rather than owned by its foreign affiliates.[10] These professionals most typically undertake this transfer pricing analysis with a view toward ascertaining the applicable arm's length licensing rate. These transfer pricing professionals, however, expend much less effort in ascertaining whether the business owners or the business owns the intangibles. The intangibles may initially begin with the business owner, and these intangibles remain with the business owner, never having been transferred to the business itself.

(a) When Does the Intangible Issue Arise? This intangible ownership issue most typically arises in either of two contexts:

1. Capital gains or reorganization context, in the event of a sale or disposition of the business
2. Estate planning

As a practical matter, the intangible ownership issue infrequently arises in the transfer pricing context. The failure of the IRS to actively address this intangible ownership issue in the transfer pricing context has become more serious in light of taxpayer victories in *Martin Ice Cream v. Commissioner*[11] and *Norwalk v. Commissioner.*[12]

(b) Case Law. In *Martin Ice Cream*, the father (a shareholder) had extensive marketing contacts and marketing expertise, which he used to introduce ice cream to supermarkets. The Tax Court recognized marketing contacts and marketing expertise as being intangible assets. The Tax Court concluded these marketing rights were the property of the father and these rights did not belong to the corporation.

In *Norwalk*, two accountants set up an accounting corporation, which had employment agreements, a covenant not to compete, and protection over client records. The agreements terminated and the corporation liquidated. The IRS asserted that the market-based intangibles were assets of the corporation, subject to tax under Section 336. The Tax Court held that these assets were owned by the shareholders themselves, and that no tax was applicable.

(c) Three Scenarios. Consider three scenarios for intangible ownership in the context of potential transfer pricing issues.

1. The IRS is likely to have the requisite data in two of the four basic fact patterns to address transfer pricing concerns.

---

[10]Robert Feinschreiber, "Comparable Uncontrolled Transaction Method for Intangibles," *Transfer Pricing Handbook* #1, 3rd ed., edited by R. Feinschreiber (New York: John Wiley & Sons, 2001): Section 39.1.

[11]110 T.C. 189 (1998).

[12]T.C. 279 (1998).

2. One basic fact pattern indicates that a licensing structure would unlikely be used, as the structure would be disadvantageous to the business and to the business owner.
3. One basic fact pattern indicates that licensing would be advantageous to the business and to the business owner, but that the IRS is ill prepared to address that particular situation.

As we shall see, the latter situation, in which the IRS is ill prepared, is most plentiful, especially as tax advisors are increasingly advocating licensing structures in light of *Martin Ice Cream* and *Norwalk.*

(d) How Taxpayers Would Structure Licensing Arrangements. In the first scenario, the business owner is an U.S. resident, the business is located in the United States, and the business is profit making. Here it is in the interest of the business owner and the business to charge for the intangibles through a license arrangement. The taxpayer is siphoning off a portion of the business's profits in lieu of declaring and paying dividends.

This licensing transaction in the first scenario is a wholly domestic matter. In fact, the impetus for these transactions is to achieve state tax savings when the business owner moves to a low or no state income tax jurisdiction. As a practical matter, the IRS is unlikely to address the licensing matter from the transfer pricing viewpoint because the IRS views transfer pricing as an international issue. At present, the only bar to imposing excessive royalty amounts is the risk to the business owner that the IRS will view part or all of the payments as imputed dividends.

(e) Additional Licensing Scenarios. In the second scenario, the business is incurring persistent losses. Licensing would cause the business owner to reflect personal licensing income despite a business's deficit in earning and profits. In that situation, it would be in the business owner's interest not to license the intangibles. In addition, the value of the marketing intangibles would be open to question.

In the third scenario, the business owner is located in the United States and the business is located outside the United States. The business owner and the business, operating together, would consider the business's deductibility of license fees, withholding rates, effectively connected status of the business owner, and taxability of licensing amounts accrued or received in the United States, after considering foreign tax credit and similar issues. In any event, the IRS should have this information, including transfer pricing information, through the filing of Form 5271.

29.13 LIFE-CYCLE BUSINESS ANALYSIS. The transfer pricing regulations fail to address a number of transfer pricing issues, among them being the life cycle of an ongoing business.[13] As transfer pricing practitioners, we have seen that international examiners and transfer pricing economists have different approaches to the business life cycle:

- We have found that international examiners, for the most part, are not attuned to business cycle analysis. The international examiner tends to ignore life-cycle

[13]Robert Feinschreiber, "Life-Cycle Analysis and Transfer Pricing," *Transfer Pricing Handbook* #1, 3rd ed., edited by R. Feinschreiber (New York: John Wiley & Sons, 2001): Section 37.1.

analysis because, quite simply, the transfer pricing regulations do not directly address life-cycle analysis.

- In contrast, transfer pricing economists within the IRS have a different skill set, making them, for the most part, quite familiar with this business cycle analysis. In essence, the transfer pricing economist treats business cycle analysis as a given.

As such, because of the disparity between the approaches of the international examiner and the transfer pricing economist, the taxpayer desperately needs the attention of the transfer pricing economist.

(a) Life-Cycle Analysis Under IRS Audit. Life-cycle analysis reflects activities that are dynamic and continuous, and have many gradations, such as:

- Start up
- Growth
- Maturity
- Decline
- Termination

Transfer pricing, by its nature, comes to be an issue in the middle three life-cycle phases. The third of these three life-cycle phases, the decline phase, becomes problematical in the transfer pricing context, because the international examiner relies on (or, from our standpoint, overrelies on) the prior years' data base.

(b) Declining Businesses and the CRT Example. Consider, for example, a business that produces cathode ray tube (CRT) computer monitors. This CRT industry is declining, as flat screen monitors are becoming increasingly prevalent. This decline in CRT's means increased emphasis on engineering and production, as efficiency becomes the byword. Prior data is no longer relevant in ascertaining subsequent year results, but the international examiner, not being attuned to life-cycle analysis, chooses to ignores this life-cycle issue.

29.14 OVERRELIANCE ON EXTERNAL DATA. Over the past decade, transfer pricing analysis has become increasingly dependent on external data. Both taxpayers and the IRS have viewed the CPM as the transfer pricing method of choice. As a result, both taxpayers and the IRS expend considerable time and effort in including or excluding corporate data that could or could not be treated as comparables.

This quest for comparables has become increasingly suspect. The data being sought by taxpayers and the IRS is accounting and financial data, as opposed to tax data. This accounting data is coming under increasing scrutiny after the Enron–Andersen debacle for three reasons:

1. The populace and the financial community's increasing distrust of the accounting rules prescribed by the Securities and Exchange Commission (SEC) and by the Financial Accounting Standards Board (FASB).
2. The populace and the financial community's increasing challenge to the independence of the financial auditors.

3. The populace and the financial community's increasing distrust of the data and the financial statements being presented, in part because of document destruction.

As a result of these events external to the transfer pricing process, the taxpayer or the IRS that relies on comparables is on dangerous ground. It has now become much easier for the transfer pricing litigator to challenge the comparables presented by the opposition. The transfer pricing regulations make reference to the reliability of data, and this issue itself may be the issue in transfer pricing litigation.

It is our view that events external to the transfer pricing process will impact forum selection and will impact taxpayer challenges to the IRS's comparables. More taxpayers may find refuge with the District Court and avoid both the Tax Court and the Claims Court to secure their right to trial by jury, to better challenge the comparables being presented by the IRS as part of the comparable profits method.[14] These events are part of the fallout to the recent accounting and financial failures to be sure, but we suggest the IRS return to the traditional transfer pricing methodologies or develop new methodologies such as the "comparison of functions employed" discussed later in this analysis.

29.15 DEPENDENCE ON SIC CODE ANALYSIS. All too often, the selection of an SIC for a business is often made by the lowest functionary of that business, the person who knows least about the current business or the future plans of the business. Nonetheless, the international examiner may seize upon the SIC code and force the business into the mold of that SIC code so as to secure a ready transfer pricing comparable.[15]

(a) SIC Issues. The following SIC code issues are likely to arise:

- The SIC code being selected by the taxpayer may not be correct.
- The SIC code may change over time, making the original SIC code no longer relevant.
- The business could be better reflected by having a number of SIC codes.

We believe that the IRS should undertake an initial review of the SIC code being selected by the taxpayer. Further, we find that both taxpayers and the IRS would benefit from establishing parameters for having more than one SIC code. We suggest that such parameter be analogous to the segmental analysis under Section 1.6038-3(c)[16] or to high-profit segments under Section 1.6038-3(c)(6),[17] addressing return on assets.

(b) Difficulties Caused By the Comparable Profits Method. The CPM forces each taxpayer to be categorized into a narrow category such as an SIC code. The examiner

---

[14]Robert J. Cunningham, "Litigating Transfer Pricing Cases," *Transfer Pricing Handbook* #2, 3rd ed., edited by R. Feinschreiber (New York: John Wiley & Sons, 2001): Section 69.1.

[15]Barbara N. McLennan, "Finding and Applying Arm's-Length Comparables under the Comparative Profits Method," *Transfer Pricing Handbook* #1, 3rd ed., edited by R. Feinschreiber (New York: John Wiley & Sons, 2001): Section 11.1.

[16]Robert Feinschreiber, "Significant Industry Segments," *Transfer Pricing Handbook* #2, 3rd ed., edited by R. Feinschreiber (New York: John Wiley & Sons, 2001): Section 60.1.

[17]Robert Feinschreiber, "High Profit Test," *Transfer Pricing Handbook* #2, 3rd ed., edited by R. Feinschreiber (New York: John Wiley & Sons, 2001): Section 61.1.

partakes in this process. Both the taxpayer and the examiner spend much of their time questing for comparables. The company and the comparables may rely on questionable codification, possibly erroneous numbers, and the possibility the comparables may be erroneous. We agree that the comparable profits method is the method of last resort for transfer pricing purposes.

Each business believes that its business is unique and special. The quest for comparables is antithetical with that belief. A better result would be to examine each segment or division of a business to determine the profit split. This process requires staffing, and we suggest that the profit split analysis be first developed by the taxpayer in each instance.

(c) Jingoism Can Shift Transfer Pricing Results. The CPM assumes that the data used would be neutral between jurisdictions, that U.S. manufacturers could be equated with foreign manufacturers, and that U.S. resellers could be equated with foreign manufacturers. In fact, a multinational organization has a tendency to shift profits to the home country. There are two facets of this tendency:

1. Pure patriotism—decisions made independent of the tax effects
2. Tax decision making—taking the cost of withholding into account

The transfer pricing regulations have not come to grips with the jingoism shift. The shift can be significant if, for example, all manufacturers are located in one country and the retailers are located in a different country. Return for a moment to the kimono example.

Assume that all of the kimonos are produced outside the United States, that very limited profits are left in the United States, and virtually all of the profits are located in the country of the manufacturer. These results will be distortive to a new U.S. manufacturer of kimonos. The same situation could well occur in any industry when most of the manufacturers are located overseas except for the tested party, or when all of the manufacturers are located in the United States except for a foreign-located tested party.

29.16 SELECTION OF THE BEST TRANSFER PRICING METHOD. It is our view that many international examiners give short shrift to the best method process, thus ignoring functional analysis and risk in particular. We believe that the CPM is not automatically the best transfer pricing method.[18] Instead, the traditional transfer pricing methods may be more fully applicable.

All too often, it appears to us that the CPM is chosen because it is easier for the international examiner to apply it solely because of the availability of SIC code database. As litigators, it is our view that disparity between the Regulations as to best method provisions and present audit techniques leads to increased vulnerability on the part of the IRS.

29.17 "COMPARISON OF FUNCTIONS EMPLOYED" METHODOLOGY. We believe the Regulations approached the creation of viable profit split regulations at the

---

[18]Barbara N. McLennan, "Finding and Applying Arm's Length Comparables under the Comparative Profits Method," *Transfer Pricing Handbook* #1, 3rd ed., edited by R. Feinschreiber (New York: John Wiley & Sons, 2001): Section 11.1.

time that the Treasury promulgated the former temporary transfer pricing regulations.[19] Nevertheless, the Regulations stepped back from these particular profit split provisions. The Treasury did not carry these provisions forward when the Treasury promulgated the final transfer pricing regulations, thus creating a gap in the need to have viable profit split regulations.

The profit split methods, as now constituted, are difficult to perform and are rarely applied. Nevertheless, we continue to believe in the potential efficacy of profit split methods. In response to that need for viable profit split transfer pricing methodologies, we are proposing one of the most important potential transfer pricing methodologies—a profit split based on a comparison of the functions being performed, which we term the *functions employed comparison* (FEC). This transfer pricing method could permit the taxpayer and the IRS to develop an arm's length price that is wholly independent of external data sources.

There would be three steps in computing the FEC method:

1. Compute the composite rate of return.
2. Sever transfer pricing transactions from nontransfer transactions.
3. Make economic adjustments.

We believe the FEC method could be effectuated by the IRS under audit, with the first two steps being effectuated by international examiners plus an assist from cost accountants. Transfer pricing economists would undertake the final step. We further suggest that the IRS develop a new form that could be used to better effectuate the FEC method.

(a) Begin with Composite Return on Investment. The first step in applying the functions employed comparison, at the outset, would be to apportion total composite income or profits, determined on a net basis, using a constant rate of return concept. This income would be apportioned based on total assets where these amounts are determined on a worldwide basis.

$$IR/RW = IA/RA = IB/RB$$

A and B are portions of the worldwide business, W is income and assets determined on a worldwide business, I is income, and R is the amount of assets. This inquiry does not end the transfer pricing process, but instead would be the beginning point. Adjustments to this process take place later.

Assume that the enterprise has activities in two locations, Location A and Location B. Assets are $2 billion in Location A and $4 billion in Location B, or $6 billion in total, and that overall profits for the enterprise are $900 million. It is then appropriate to apportion the $900 million profit to $300 million in Location A and $600 million in Location B to equate the returns of each location (e.g., a 15% return at each location)

---

[19]Richard M. Hammer and Robert Feinschreiber, "Profit Split Methodologies," *Transfer Pricing Handbook* #2, 3rd ed., edited by R. Feinschreiber (New York: John Wiley & Sons, 2001): Section 47.2.

The formula would be reflected as follows:

Worldwide	Location A	Location B	Return on Investment
$\frac{\text{900 million}}{\text{6 billion}}$	$\frac{\text{300 million}}{\text{2 billion}}$	$\frac{\text{600 million}}{\text{4 million}}$	15%

(b) Severing Transfer Pricing Transactions from Non-Transfer Transactions. The first step in the functions employed method implicitly treats transfer pricing transactions in the same manner as transactions that are not subject to the transfer pricing provisions. The second step in the functions employed method would be to sever the transfer pricing transactions from transactions that are independent from the scope of the transfer pricing regulations. Economic adjustments would then provide the third step.

The concept underlying the severing process is that a business has limited flexibility to arrange nontransfer transactions. In contrast, the business has extensive versatility in adjusting, or attempting to adjust transactions that are subject to the transfer pricing regulations.

This second step in the functions employed method has three substeps:

1. The IRS (or the taxpayer) would sever for tax accounting purposes the assets used for transfer pricing purposes from assets that are used for other than transfer pricing purposes.
2. The IRS (or the taxpayer) would then divide dual use assets on a pro rata basis.
3. The IRS (or the taxpayer) would then sever for tax accounting purposes the income for transfer pricing purposes from the income for other than transfer pricing purposes. Total income or profits is determined on a deemed basis, based on the first step of the analysis; income not subject to transfer pricing is the actual amount; income subject to transfer pricing is the residual amount.

Return to our example in which Location A has assets of $2 billion and is deemed to have income of $300 million. In this scenario, assets subject to transfer pricing are $1 billion and assets not subject to transfer pricing are $1 billion, taking dual-use assets into account. Now let us assume that income not subject to transfer pricing is $200 million. This amount would be determined on the actual records of the business. The income subject to transfer pricing analysis is the deemed total income of $300 million, less the income of transactions not subject to transfer pricing of $200 million, or $100 million in total.

The return on investment data for Location A would appear as follows:

	Transactions Not Subject to Transfer Pricing	Transactions Subject to Transfer Pricing	Total
Income	$200 million	$100 million	$300 million
Assets	$1 billion	$1 billion	$2 billion
Return	20%	10%	15%

Now we turn to our example in which Location B has assets of $4 billion and is deemed to have income of $600 million. In this scenario, assets subject to transfer pricing are $1 billion and assets not subject to transfer pricing are $3 billion, taking dual-use assets into account. Now let us assume that income not subject to transfer pricing is $300 million. This amount would be determined on the actual records of the business. The income subject to transfer pricing analysis is the deemed total income of $600 million, less the income of transactions not subject to transfer pricing of $300 million, or $300 million in total.

The return on investment data for Location B would appear as follows:

	Transactions Not Subject To Transfer Pricing	Transactions Subject To Transfer Pricing	Total
Income	$300 million	$300 million	$600 million
Assets	$3 billion	$1 billion	$4 billion
Return	10%	30%	15%

(c) Recombining the Transfer Pricing Transactions

	Location A	Location B	Total
Income	$100 million	$300 million	$400 million
Assets	$1 billion	$1 billion	$2 billion
Return	10%	30%	20%

(d) Making Economic Adjustments. The final step in the FEC transfer pricing method would be to make economic adjustments, including accounts receivable, accounts payable, inventories, risks, currency adjustments, life-cycle analysis, market intangibles, technology licensing rates, and so forth. Here, the transfer pricing economist would begin with the differences in rate of return in Location A and in Location B and would contrast functions and risks between these two locations. Finally, the transfer pricing economist should ascertain whether the functions employed method is in fact the best transfer pricing method in this situation.

29.18 USING TOTAL OPERATING EXPENSES. We suggest the total operating expense method as an alternative to the return on assets method. Under this approach, total operating expenses for each branch, segment, division, or subsidiary would be determined. These total operating expense amounts would be allocated, and would serve as the denominator of an apportionment fraction. The numerator of the fraction would be the total operating expenses of that branch, segment, division, or subsidiary.

Total operating expenses are the denominator of the Berry ratio, gross profit divided by total operating expenses.[20] The second step in this process would be to sever transfer pricing transactions from nontransfer pricing transactions. The third step in this process would be to make economic adjustments.

(a) Gross Operating Expense Computations. The first step in the transfer pricing process would be to combine the gross operating expense amounts to the branches, segments, divisions, or subsidiaries. Assume that a corporation has two divisions, Division C and Division D.

[20]Charles H. Berry, "Berry Ratios," *Transfer Pricing Handbook* #1, 3rd ed., edited by R. Feinschreiber (New York: John Wiley & Sons, 2001): Section 20.1.

$$\frac{\text{Division C Profit}}{\text{C Operating Expenses}} + \frac{\text{Division D Profit}}{\text{D Operating Expenses}} = \frac{\text{Total Profit}}{\text{Total Operating Expenses}}$$

$$\frac{200{,}000}{500{,}000} + \frac{800{,}000}{1{,}500{,}000} \qquad \frac{1{,}000{,}000}{2{,}000{,}000}$$

(b) Severing Nontransfer Pricing Transactions from Transfer Pricing Transactions. The second step in the gross operating expense computation is to sever nontransfer pricing transactions from transfer pricing transactions. Consider the results for Division C and for Division D.

Division C

Nontransfer Pricing	Transfer Pricing	Total
$\frac{100{,}000}{300{,}000}$	$\frac{100{,}000}{200{,}000}$	$\frac{200{,}000}{500{,}000}$

Division D

Nontransfer Pricing	Transfer Pricing	Total
$\frac{600{,}000}{1{,}000{,}000}$	$\frac{200{,}000}{500{,}000}$	$\frac{800{,}000}{1{,}500{,}000}$

(c) Recombining the Transfer Pricing Transactions

	Division C	Division D	Total
Income	100,000	200,000	300,000
Operating Expenses	200,000	500,000	700,000
Ratio	50%	40%	

(d) Economic Analysis. The final step in the operating expense transfer pricing method would be to make economic adjustments, including accounts receivable, accounts payable, inventories, risks, currency adjustments, life-cycle analysis, market intangibles, technology licensing rates, and so forth. Here, the transfer pricing economist would begin with the difference in income in operating expenses of 50% in Division C in contrast with 40% in Division D. Finally, the transfer pricing economist should ascertain whether the operating expense method is in fact the best transfer pricing method in this situation.

29.19 TAX MALPRACTICE ATTORNEY AS YOUR ALLY. As IRS officials, you may find that you may have an unlikely ally, the plaintiff's tax malpractice litigator in a malpractice claim against directors, officers, or tax professionals[21] The plaintiff's tax malpractice litigator may be attacking the same practices that take place in a business as would you, especially if the business or its tax advisors have gone amuck. In essence, in some situations, the plaintiff's tax malpractice litigator can serve as an

---

[21]Robert Feinschreiber, "Malpractice Risk in Transfer Pricing," *Transfer Pricing Handbook* #2, 3rd ed., edited by R. Feinschreiber (New York: John Wiley & Sons, 2001): Section 89.1.

adjunct to the IRS, just as a professional investigator (PI) serves as an adjunct to the police in securing data that might be unavailable to the IRS.

29.20 DEVELOPING THE STANDARD INITIAL TRANSFER PRICING INFORMATION DOCUMENT REQUEST. Audits have been decreasing as a percentage of taxpayer returns during the past few years because of IRS staffing shortages. These shortages may have led to a kinder, gentler IRS but have severely challenged the veracity of America's taxing system. Charles Rossotti, Commissioner of Internal Revenue, is making strong steps to fill this gap.

It is our belief that overall tax compliance would benefit from meeting the IRS staffing needs and from the IRS agents' greater use of information document requests. Such a need is for a standard information document request in the transfer pricing context.

We have prepared such a standard transfer pricing information document request for the IRS as part of our presentation to IRS officials. This was part of our presentation concerning "documentation, examination procedures, and methodologies" so recently praised by Mr. Rossotti and by Treasury Secretary Paul O'Neill. In preparing these standard transfer pricing information document requests for the IRS, as practitioners we are mindful of the time and effort in preparing and retaining such documentation.

(a) Initial Transfer Pricing Information Document Request. The following provisions apply for Part I of the Initial Transfer Pricing Information Document Request.

(i) Profit and Loss Statement. A profit and loss statement includes records that pertain to profit and loss. These records requested herein reflect the following:

- Profit or loss statements of the taxpayer and all related parties (the related-party group) that meet required parameters and
- Profit or loss statements of the taxpayer and all related parties (the related-party group) attributable to U.S.-connected products or services that meet required parameters.

The definition of profit and loss statement is taken from Treasury Regulation Section 1.6038A-3(c)(2)(ii). This definition of a profit and loss statement is broader for the Initial Transfer Pricing Information Document Request than it is for the Treasury Regulation Section 1.6038A-3(c)(2)(ii) definition. This broader definition enables the IRS to determine whether the taxpayer is complying with other facets of Section 6038A, Section 482, and Section 6662. Treasury Regulation Section 1.6038A-3(c)(2)(ii) seeks records that are material. The Initial Transfer Pricing Information Document Request treats these documents as tentative material in the first instance, pending future examination by the IRS.

(ii) Related Party. A related party meets one of three definitions:

- A related party is a party that is a direct or indirect shareholder of the taxpayer,
- A related party is a party that is a direct or indirect subsidiary of the taxpayer, or
- A related party is a party that is acting in concert with the taxpayer as otherwise as defined under Section 267(b), Section 707(b)(1), or Section 482.

A party is to be treated as related party based on 25% direct or indirect common ownership. Corporations filing a consolidated federal tax return can elect to treat the consolidated tax return as one entity. This definition of related party is taken from Treasury Regulation Section 1.6038A-1(d). The Initial Transfer Pricing Information Document Request affirmatively addresses the 25% threshold in Treasury Regulation Section 1.6038A-1(d). The definition of a related party is broader in the Initial Transfer Pricing Information Document Request so as to test whether the taxpayer is complying with the requirements of Treasury Regulation Section 1.6038A, Section 482 and Section 6662.

(iii) Related-Party Group. A related-party group encompasses the taxpayer and all related parties, whether foreign or domestic. This definition of related-party group is taken from Treasury Regulation Section 1.6038A-3(c)(2)(ii), which deals with profit and loss statements, and with Treasury Regulation Section 1.6038A-1(d), which deals with the definition of related-party group. This definition of related-party group is taken from Treasury Regulation Section 1.6038A-3(c)(4), the existing records test. Treasury Regulation Section 1.6038A-3(c)(4) determines the materiality of the records by their presence of these records.

(iv) U.S.-Connected Products or Services. U.S.-connected products or services means products or services that are imported to or exported from the United States by transfers by the taxpayer and any of its related parties. For this purpose, exports are added to each other and are not subtracted. The definition of "U.S.-connected products or services" is taken from the definition of that term as specified in Treasury Regulation Section 1.6038A-3(c)(7)(i). The Initial Transfer Pricing Information Document Request terminology is somewhat broader than the comparable term in the regulations. The Initial Transfer Pricing Information Document Request refers to all related parties, but Treasury Regulation Section 1.6038A-3(c)(7)(i) applies only to "foreign" related parties.

(v) Application of "U.S.-Connected Products or Services." The taxpayer is to make the following adjustments in determining U.S.-connected products or services:

- Gross up all licensing amounts to reflect the rights or assets giving rise to the licensing amounts.
- Gross up all lease amounts to reflect the assets giving rise to the leasing amounts.

Licensing and leasing are often determined on a net basis. Information requested here is designed to better equate licensing and leasing with the sale of goods.

(vi) Industry Segment. Industry segment means a segment of the related-party group's combined operations that is engaged in providing a product or service, or a group of related products or services, where the product or service is directed primarily to customers that are not members of the related-party group. The definition of "industry segment" is taken from the definition of industry segment in Treasury Regulation Section1.6038A-3(c)(7)(ii).

(vii) Gross Revenues of an Industry Segment. Gross revenues of an industry segment means gross receipts in the nature of earning gross income that pertain to that seg-

ment. Gross revenues are taken into account before taking returns or allowances, and are taken into account before determining the cost of goods sold or operating expenses. "Gross revenues" do not include borrowings, lendings, or the receipt of passive dividend income.

The definition of the gross revenues of an industry segment is taken from the definition of the gross revenues of an industry segment in Treasury Regulation Section 1.6038A-3(c)(7)(ii).

(viii) Worldwide Gross Revenues. Revenues of the taxpayer and the related-party group are to be determined reflecting worldwide gross revenues on an aggregate basis, whether the activities giving rise to the income are located within the United States or are located outside the United States.

(ix) Operating Profit of the Industry Segment. The operating profit of the industry segment is the gross revenue of the industry segment minus all operating expenses of the industry segment. The following items cannot be added to or subtracted from operating profit:

- Revenue earned at the corporate level and not derived from operations of any industry segment, such as passive income.
- General corporate expenses, except as allocated and apportioned under Treasury Regulation Section 1.861 et seq.
- Interest expense
- Domestic and foreign income taxes

This definition of operating profit of the industry segment is taken from the definition of "operating profit of industry segment" in Treasury Regulation Section 1.6038A-3(c)(7)(v).

(x) Worldwide Operating Profit. Worldwide operating profit of the taxpayer and the related-party group are to be determined reflecting worldwide operating profit on an aggregate basis, whether the activities giving rise to the income are located within the United States or are located outside the United States.

(xi) Operating Expenses of the Industry Segment. Operating expenses as to an industry segment include all expenses of the segment, except for

- General corporate expenses, except as allocated and apportioned under section 1.861 et seq.
- Interest expense
- Domestic and foreign income taxes

This definition of operating expenses of the industry segment is extracted from the term *operating expenses* in Treasury Regulation Section 1.6038A-3(c)(7)(v) but is not further defined in that section.

(xii) Worldwide Operating Expenses. Worldwide operating expenses of the taxpayer and the related-party group are to be determined reflecting worldwide operating ex-

penses on an aggregate basis, whether the activities giving rise to the income are located within the United States or are located outside the United States.

(xiii) Return on Assets. Return of assets is determined by dividing operating profit by identifiable assets that generated or gave rise to the income.

(xiv) Identifiable Assets of an Industry Segment. Identifiable assets of an industry segment include tangible and intangible assets exclusively used by that industry segment and an allocation of all nonexclusive assets, using any reasonable and consistent method. This definition of identifiable assets of an industry segment are taken from Treasury Regulation Section 1.6038A-3(c)(7)(iv).

(b) Existing Records

1. Specify the entity(ies) for which the taxpayer created or compiled a profit and loss statement and/or balance sheets for internal accounting purposes.
2. Specify the entity(ies) for which the taxpayer created or compiled a profit and loss statement and/or balance sheets for management purposes.
3. Specify the entity(ies) for which the taxpayer created or compiled a profit and loss statement and/or balance sheets for disclosure to shareholders.
4. Specify the entity(ies) for which the taxpayer created or compiled a profit and loss statement and/or balance sheets for disclosure to financial institutions.
5. Specify the entity(ies) for which the taxpayer created or compiled a profit and loss statement and/or balance sheets for disclosure to government agencies, whether foreign or domestic.
6. Specify the entity(ies) for which the taxpayer created or compiled a profit and loss statement and/or balance sheets for disclosure to any other persons.

The preceding requirements are directly taken from the existing records test in Treasury Regulation Section 1.6038A-3(c)(4). Treasury Regulation Section 1.6038A-3(c)(4) speaks of profit and loss statements. Our position is that the IRS, having been authorized to acquire profit and loss statements, has the authority to obtain balance sheets for the same entity.

7. The taxpayer is to transmit all of the previously mentioned profit and loss statements and/or balance sheets to the international examiner within ___ days after receiving the IDR.

The following standards apply to profit and loss statements and balance sheets: As a general matter, when a taxable year is under review, the taxpayer must submit the profit and loss statement, the balance sheet preceding the year being reviewed, and the balance sheet after the year being reviewed. All such profit and loss statements and balance sheets shall be submitted to the international examiner under this provision:

- Whether or not the profit and loss statement and balance sheets are compiled or certified,
- Whether or not the taxpayer applies uniform inventory capitalization,

- Whether the taxpayer applies methods of amortization or depreciation, or
- Whether the taxpayer properly allocates and apportions expenses.

(c) Industry Segments

(i) Preparation of Documents and the Supplying of Documents. For each such industrial segment, prepare and supply to the Internal Revenue Service the following statements for the year under review, including

- The profit and loss statement of the related-party group
- The balance sheet for the related-party group immediately preceding the year under review
- The balance sheet for the related-party group immediately after the year under review

Such statements are to be determined for each industry segment of the business for which the amount of gross revenue earned by the related-party group from the provision of U.S. products or services within the industry segment is $25 million or more for the taxable year.

(ii) Selecting Industrial Segments. The taxpayer is to provide the IRS with information and documents in a manner that maximizes the number of industrial segments in which U.S. products or services within the industry segment are $25 million or more for the taxable year.

The taxpayer is to select industrial segments with due regard to its product lines, products, models and related party services.

The Initial Transfer Pricing Information Document Request is broader than the Treasury Regulations in three respects:

1. Treasury Section 1.6038A-3(c)(5)(I)(B) limits the industrial segment analysis to those industry segments that are 10% of the worldwide gross revenue of the affiliated group's combined industry segments,
2. Treasury Regulation Section 1.6038A-3(c)(6)(I)(B) speaks of $100 million segments under the high profit test,
3. The return of assets test under Treasury Regulation Section 1.6038A-3(c)(6)(ii) addresses segments having worldwide operations of 15% or more, and a return on assets that is at least 200% of the return on assets earned by the group in all industrial segments combined.

The Initial Transfer Pricing Information Document Request is designed in part to test whether the taxpayer meets the above-mentioned segment requirements.

(iii) Complying and Supplying Profit and Loss Statements and Balance Sheets. The taxpayer is instructed to use the following rules for complying and supplying profit and loss statements and balance sheets for purposes of this analysis:

- The profit and loss statements must reflect the consolidated revenue and expense of all members of the related party group. Thus, raw materials might be used by one party and finished goods might be sold by a different party, but all records are to be combined for this purpose.

- Financial statements are to be kept under U.S. accounting principles.
- Any reasonable method may be used to allocate the related party groups' worldwide costs to the revenues generated by the sales of those products or services. The taxpayer must provide an explanation of its accounting methods, including the manner is which costs are allocated.

The preceding requirements as to profit and loss statements are taken from Treasury Regulation Section 1.6038A-3(c)(2)(ii).

(iv) Taxpayers Are to Complete the Following. Specify the following amounts reflecting the entire business of the taxpayer and the related party group as a whole for the year under review:

1. Worldwide gross revenues
2. Worldwide operating expenses
3. Worldwide operating income
4. Worldwide gross assets

Specify the following information for each industrial segment for the year under review:

1. Gross revenues of the industrial segment, determined on a worldwide basis
2. Operating expenses of the industrial segment, determined on a worldwide basis
3. Operating income of the industrial segment, determined on a worldwide basis
4. Gross assets of the industrial segment, determined on a worldwide basis, based on identifiable assets

Amounts provided in items 1 through 4, together with amounts provided in the information requested as to worldwide activities of the taxpayer and related-party group provide the IRS with comparative data that may lead the international examiner to request subsequent Transfer Pricing Information Document Requests.

Specify the following information for the same industrial segment as to U.S.-connected products or services, determined on a worldwide basis, for the year under review:

5. Gross revenues of the industrial segment as to U.S.-connected products or services, determined on a worldwide basis
6. Operating expenses of the industrial segment as to U.S.-connected products or services, determined on a worldwide basis
7. Operating income of the industrial segment as to U.S.-connected products or services, determined on a worldwide basis
8. Gross assets of industrial segment as to U.S.-connected products or services, determined on a worldwide basis, based on identifiable assets

Amounts provided in items 5 through 8, together with amounts provided in items 1 though 4, provide the IRS with comparative data that may lead the international examiner to request subsequent Transfer Pricing Information Document Requests.

Specify the following information for the same industrial segment in the United States as to U.S.-connected products or services for the year under review:

9. Gross revenues of the industrial segment in the United States as to U.S.-connected products or services
10. Operating expenses of the industrial segment in the United States as to U.S.-connected products or services
11. Operating income of the industrial segment in the United States as to U.S.-connected products or services
12. Gross assets of the industrial segment in the United States as to U.S.-connected products or services, based on identifiable assets.

Amounts provided in items 9 through 12, together with amounts provided in items 5 though 8, provide the IRS with comparative data that may lead the international examiner to request subsequent Transfer Pricing Information Document Requests.

Signify whether or not you have retained all records pertaining to the transfer pricing documentation:

Yes ______
No ______

Treasury Regulation Section 1.6038A-3(g) requires the taxpayer to maintain records "so long as they may be relevant and material to determine the correct tax treatment."

29.21 TRANSFER PRICING INFORMATION DOCUMENT REQUEST FOR ACQUISITIONS

(a) Introduction. A person who is engaged in a merger, consolidation, or merger transaction (merger transaction) must generally report this merger transaction to the Federal Trade Commission (FTC) and to the Department of Justice (DOJ). The information pertaining to this merger transaction should generally be of interest to the Internal Revenue Service (IRS), as information regarding the merger could address either or both of the following issues:

1. The reorganization issues of taxability, basis, and carryover of attributes
2. To assess whether, and to what extent, the merger transaction causes parties to undertake related-party transactions that are properly under IRS scrutiny under Section 482

Transfer pricing issues arise in two contexts in conjunction with FTC–DOJ reporting:

1. Erstwhile independent transactions between independent parties may well become related-party transactions, making these transactions subject to IRS scrutiny as a result of a merger.
2. The report filed with the FTC and DOJ in conjunction with a forthcoming merger may reveal existing related-party structures that the IRS previously had no occasion to observe.

This article examines the potential database and examination opportunities that the IRS now will have in the context of Section 482 transfer pricing as to merger transactions that are already subject to FTC–DOJ review. Robert Feinschreiber and Margaret Kent conducted this study at the request of the IRS. The Treasury and IRS previously asked Feinschreiber & Associates to further its review of the U.S. transfer pricing methodologies, databases, and audit techniques.

(b) Background. Statutes require that each person that is subject to Section 7A of the Clayton Act, section 15 U.S.C. Section 18a, as added by Section 201 of the Hart Scott Rodino Antitrust Improvements Act of 1976, and rules promulgated thereunder must file a notification form with the FTC and DOJ. The form is termed Notification and Report Form for Certain Mergers and Acquisitions (Notification Form). The Notification Form is the appendix to 16 C.F.R. Part 803, and is FTC Form C4. The Notification Form is 15 pages in length and requires extensive specific attachments. Much of the information furnished to the FTC and the DOJ is through supplemental requests that the FTC and DOJ might make. This supplemental information can significantly add to information already provided through the Notification Form.

The acquiring party must pay a filing fee to the Federal Trade Commission, which can range from $45,000 to $280,000. It is our strong suspicion that the acquiring party, on discovering this fee, will not be complaining about the cost of obtaining an IRS ruling. We strongly suggest to the IRS that this phase of the transfer pricing information document request should be used only when the aggregate total amount of assets and voting stock to be held as a result of the acquisition are $50 million or more. Robert Feinschreiber and Margaret Kent suggest to the IRS that it additionally employ a standard transfer pricing information document request that has different parameters from assets and voting stock, that of U.S.-connected goods or services.

(c) Objectives. Robert Feinschreiber and Margaret Kent suggest to the IRS that it use a standard transfer pricing information document request form that would tie into the information provided by FTC Form C4. The international examiner would be the person at the IRS who would initiate this standard transfer pricing document request. We visualize that much of the information obtained by the international examiner would be funneled though to the transfer pricing economists. The transfer pricing economists would then utilize much of the information to make necessary economic adjustments as part of this audit review.

Robert Feinschreiber and Margaret Kent then suggest that the IRS employ such a standard transfer pricing information document request form to achieve this objective. This suggested standard form is published as part of this analysis. Robert Feinschreiber and Margaret Kent presented this analysis at the first instance to international examiners, transfer pricing economists, and IRS counsel for the southeast region on May 10, 2002, in Atlanta.

(d) Examination of the Notification Form. Many tax practitioners, including those engaged in a mergers and acquisitions tax practice, are unfamiliar with the FTC–DOJ Notification Form. Fewer merger and acquisitions tax practitioners are familiar with the transfer pricing implications of the FTC–DOJ filing. This portion of the article addresses the issues that tie-in antitrust issues to transfer pricing tax issues. The Notification Form itself comprises eight detailed items together with some preliminary information about the filer and the certification by the filer of what is being included in the form.

The Notification Form delineates eight specific items as follows:

1. The person filing the Form
2. Parties and the transaction
3. Specific issues affecting the transaction
4. Specific items relied on and filed
5. Detailed information reflecting the North American Industry Classification System—United States, 1997
6. Shareholders, holdings, and entities
7. Dollar revenues and geographic market information
8. Prior acquisitions

As we shall see, all eight items in the Notification Form have transfer pricing implications, but the fourth and fifth items in particular are specifically relevant to Section 482 transfer pricing. The Notification Form can apply to domestic–foreign mergers, to foreign–domestic mergers, to domestic–domestic mergers, and, in limited circumstances, to foreign–foreign mergers. As a result, the Notification Form is broader than the scope of both Form 5471 and Form 5472 together. Section 482 transfer pricing can encompass domestic–foreign mergers, foreign–domestic mergers, domestic–domestic mergers, and foreign–foreign mergers.

(i) Person Filing the Form. Item 1 in the Notification Form seeks the headquarters address of the party filing the Form, which can be an acquiring person or an acquired person. The Form can be filed on behalf of a foreign person pursuant to 16 C.F.R. 803.4, or filed on behalf of the ultimate parent entity pursuant to 16 C.F.R. 803.2(a).

Item 1(h) designates an individual located in the United States for the limited purpose of receiving issuance of a request for additional information or documents. Section 1.6038A(e)(1) and Treas. Reg. Section 1.6038A-5(b)(1) require the reporting corporation to specify an agent in the United States for tax purposes. Both the FTC–DOJ provision and the Treasury provision provide analogous responsibilities to the U.S. counterpoint, but the specific party may be different.

(ii) Parties and the Transaction. Item 2(a) requests the filer to provide ultimate parent entities of all acquiring persons and the ultimate parent entities of all acquired persons. The IRS can use this information as a starting point to ascertain related party relationships for section 482 transfer pricing. Item 2(b) addresses the type of transaction contemplated or undertaken, but the Form permits the preparer to select more than one box.

Item 2(c) specifies the notification threshold, the size of the transaction, as being \$50 million, \$100 million, or \$500 million. Item 2(d) addresses value of the voting securities, the percentage being acquired, the value of the assets to be held as a result of the acquisition, and the total value of the assets. Item 2(e) addresses the identification of the party making the fair market valuation.

(iii) Specific Items Affecting the Transaction. Item 3(a) requires the preparer to describe the acquisition. The instructions specify that the preparer must include the

name and mailing address of each acquiring and acquired person, whether or not required to file the Notification. Item 3(b) speaks to the assets to be acquired and the assets held by the acquiring person. Item 3(c) addresses the specifics of a voting stock acquisition, including the dollar value of securities in each class. Item 3(d) requires the preparer to include a copy of the acquisition contract or agreement, or an intent to merge or acquire.

(iv) Specific Items Relied Upon and Filed. Item 4 requires just three types of items: documents filed with the SEC, annual financial reports, and "studies, surveys, analyses, and reports." This third group within item 4 should be specifically of interest to the international examiner seeking to review transfer pricing transactions and by the transfer pricing economist. The instructions to item 4(c) speak of the following categories of economic documentation, all of which will be relevant to Section 482 transfer pricing:

- Market shares
- Competition
- Competitors
- Markets
- Potential for sales growth
- Expansion into product or geographic markets

The information concerning competition should be relevant to an international examiner seeking to set up an adjustment based on the comparable profits method. All too often, some international examiners seek the course of least resistance and reach too quickly to the SIC manual, relying on the taxpayer's representation of its primary SIC code. The list of competitors in 4(c) is likely to be far more relevant.

The acquiror will most frequently prepare such economic documentation to justify and support the acquisition. The acquiror prepares the Notification and Report Form with a view toward obtaining a preclearance "all clear" from the FTC and DOJ. In this regard, the acquiror is likely to emphasize the heavy competition on the part of the business's competitors, the strength of these competitors, and the limited market share even after the acquisition takes place.

Such a study is likely to reflect market intangibles, the impact of intellectual property such as patents, trademarks, and the like. The studies may reflect intended economies of scale and an "efficiency" argument. All of this information will be of great interest to the international examiner and to the transfer pricing economist.

(v) Detailed Information Reflecting the North American Industry Classification System (NAICS)—United States, 1997. At the present time, taxpayers and the IRS rely on the CPM to compute the most easily determined transfer pricing method, though not necessarily the best method. The CPM relies heavily on the SIC system, but the NAICS system is to ultimately replace the SIC system.

Item 5(a) requests dollar revenues by industry. This information is to be reflected by use of the six-digit NAICS industry code. Item 5(b)(i) requests dollar revenues by manufactured products. This information is to be reflected by the use of the ten-digit NAICS code.

Both the industry data and the manufacturing products data refer to 1997 total dollar revenues. We believe that the Form may be in error in calling for 1997 data. The year 1997 indicates the NAICS promulgation, but this information may not necessarily be relevant to antitrust issues that the Form is designed to address.

Item 5(b)(ii) seeks information about products added or deleted, described by the ten-digit NAICS product code. A business may be selling part of its operations or cease certain activities in its quest for antitrust clearance. Additions typically reflect scalar economies or other efficiencies than an increase in transfer pricing transactions.

Item 5(b)(iii) seeks dollar revenues by manufactured product class. Item 5(c) seeks dollar revenues by nonmanufacturing industry. The manufactured product classes are determined at the seven-digit NAICS level. The dollar revenues for the nonmanufacturing industry can be determined by the six-digit NAICS code. The instructions for the Form indicate that industries for which the dollar revenues totaled less than one million dollars in the most recent year may be omitted. Item 5(d) addresses the acquisition in the context of a joint venture, including contributions, contracts, credit guarantees, consideration, business description, and dollar revenues.

(vi) Shareholders, Holdings, and Entities. Item 2(a) had addressed information concerning the ultimate parent entities of all acquiring persons and the ultimate parent entities of all acquired persons. In contrast, item 6(a) seeks information concerning entities within the person filing the Notification, most typically the subsidiaries of the person filing the notification. The instructions to item 6(a) specify that the person seeking the Notification may omit entities with total assets of less than $10 million. Item 6(b) seeks shareholders of the parent seeking the Notification. The instructions to item 6(b) specify that shareholders include the ultimate parent, and that holders need not be listed for entities with total assets of less than $10 million. Item 6(c) seeks information as to the holdings of the person filing the Notification.

(vii) Dollar Revenues and Geographic Market Information. Item 7(a) seeks dollar revenues, specified by the six-digit NAICS code and description. Item 7(b) requests the name of each person who derived dollar revenues. Item 7(c) requests geographic market information. Of the three items, geographic market information is most significantly related to the transfer pricing inquiry. As a general matter, the geographic information required by item 7(c) is significantly more detailed than required for transfer pricing purposes, but this information can be used to challenge or substantiate assertions made for transfer pricing purposes.

(viii) Previous Acquisitions. Item 8 seeks information concerning previous information from the acquiring persons. For each such acquisition, the acquiring persons are to supply the following:

- The name of the entity acquired
- The headquarters of the entity prior to acquisition
- Whether the acquiring person acquired securities or assets
- The consummation date of the acquisition
- The six-digit NAICS code in which the acquired entity derived dollar revenues

Item 8 has two safe harbors, a $1 million exclusion and a $10 million exclusion. The person filing the Notification is to reflect each six-digit NAICS code for which the filer derived dollar revenues of $1 million or more in the most recent year. The acquired issuer either derived revenues of $1 million or more in the recent year or derived revenues of $1 million or more in the most recent year attributable to the acquired assets. The $10 million amount applies to joint ventures.

The material in italics explains the background for the request is for IRS use only. The international examiner may opt to exclude this material in issuing the standard transfer pricing information document request.

29.22 PROPOSED SECOND STANDARD TRANSFER PRICING INFORMATION DOCUMENT REQUEST

(a) Classification. This information document request seeks information regarding revenues, expenses, U.S.-connected products and services, and net income for lines of commerce, determined under the North American Industry Classification System—United States, 1997, the 1997 NAICS Manual published by the Executive Office of the President, Office of Management and Budget.

(b) Consistency. All information sought pursuant to this information document request shall be prepared in conjunction with the information otherwise requested and submitted pursuant to the Notification and Report Form for Certain Mergers and Acquisitions, 16 C.F.R. Part 803—Appendix.

(c) Applicability. The information document request seeks detailed information regarding each acquisition of assets or voting stock that is $50 million or more, based on the aggregate total of assets and voting stock to be held as a result of the acquisition. Information pertaining to acquisitions of less than $50 million, based on the aggregate total of assets and voting stock to be held as a result of the acquisition, are exempt.

(d) Information Requested. Information requested is to be determined under two NAICS levels:

1. Unless otherwise specified, the information sought must be reflected at the six-digit NAICS national industry code level.
2. Activities pertaining to manufacturing operations (as defined by NAICS Sections 31 through 33) must be submitted at the seven-digit NAICS product class and at the ten-digit NAICS product code level.

(e) U.S.-Connected Products or Services. U.S.-connected products or services means products or services that are imported to or exported from the United States by transfers by the taxpayer and any of its related parties. For this purpose, exports are added to each other and are not subtracted. The definition of "U.S.-connected products or services" is taken from the definition of that term as specified in Treasury Regulation Section 1.6038A-3(c)(7)(i). The Second Transfer Pricing Information Document Request terminology is somewhat broader than the comparable term in the regulations. The Second Transfer Pricing Information Document Request refers to all related parties, but Treasury Regulation Section 1.6038A-3(c)(7)(i) applies only to "foreign" related parties.

(f) Gross Revenues. Gross revenues means gross receipts in the nature of earning gross income. Gross revenues are taken into account before taking returns or allowances, and are taken into account before determining the cost of goods sold or operating expenses. "Gross revenues" do not include borrowings, lendings, or the receipt of passive dividend income.

The above definition is taken from the definition of the gross revenues of an industry segment in Treasury Regulation Section 1.6038A-3(c)(7)(ii).

(g) Operating Income. Operating income is gross revenue minus all operating expenses. The following items cannot be added to or subtracted from operating profit:

- Revenue earned at the corporate level and not derived from operations, such as passive income
- General corporate expenses, except as allocated and apportioned under Treasury Regulation Section 1.861 et seq.
- Interest expense
- Domestic and foreign income taxes

This definition of operating profit is taken from the definition of "operating profit of industry segment" in Treasury Regulation Section 1.6038A-3(c)(7)(v).

(h) Operating Expenses. Operating expenses include all expenses of the segment, except for the following expenses:

- General corporate expenses, except as allocated and apportioned under Section 1.861 et seq.
- Interest expense
- Domestic and foreign income taxes

This definition of operating expenses is extracted from the term "operating expenses" in Treasury Regulation Section 1.6038A-3(c)(7)(v) but is not further defined in that section.

(i) General Information. A taxpayer is to provide the following information:

1. Indicate your taxpayer identification number.
2. Specify each acquisition initiated during the tax year under review.
3. Specify each acquisition in process during the tax year under review.
4. Specify each acquisition completed during the year under review.
5. Specify each acquisition initiated during the tax year under review that was subject to the Notification and Report Form, 16 C.F.R. Parts 801–803.
6. Specify each acquisition in process during the tax year under review that was subject to the Notification and Report Form, 16 C.F.R. Parts 801–803.
7. Specify each acquisition completed during the tax year under review that was subject to the Notification and Report Form, 16 C.F.R. Parts 801–803.
8. Indicate the intended tax treatment of each 16 C.F.R. Part 801–803 transaction completed during the year of issue.

9. Indicate the intended tax treatment each of the 16 C.F.R. Part 801–803 fee.
10. Enclose a copy of each Form 16 C.F.R. Part 803–Appendix filed or required to be filed in the taxable year of issue. Include any supplemental information included in Form 16 C.F.R. Part 803—Appendix. Include all information requested by the FTC or the DOJ.

(j) NAICS Reporting. Specify the following information for each sixth digit, seventh digit, or tenth digit NAICS classification under FTC Form C4 item 5 for the year under review.

11. Gross revenues
12. Operating expenses
13. Operating income

(k) U.S.-Connected Products or Services. Specify the following information for each sixth digit, seventh digit, or tenth digit NAICS classification under FTC Form C4 item 5 for the year under review.

14. Gross revenues
15. Operating expenses
16. Operating income

Amounts provided in items 1 through 4 provide the IRS with comparative data that may lead the international examiner to request subsequent Transfer Pricing Information Document Requests.

Prior versions of portions of this analysis appeared in the May or June 2002 edition of *Corporate Business Taxation Monthly* (Panel Publishers), edited by Robert Feinschreiber and Margaret Kent, and in *Mergers and Acquisitions: The Monthly Tax Journal* (Panel Publishers), edited by Robert Feinschreiber and Margaret Kent. This analysis was undertaken in part at the request of the Internal Revenue Service. A significant portion of this analysis remains embargoed by the Internal Revenue Service.

CHAPTER 30

INTERNATIONAL TAXATION

Paul M. Bodner

Attorney-at-Law

CONTENTS

30.1 INTRODUCTION. The term *international taxation* is a misnomer in that there is not an independent body of law that applies to international business transactions. Instead, the United States and other countries apply general tax rules to domestic companies operating abroad and to foreign businesses investing locally, supplemented by special provisions. The United States has the most complex tax system in the world, and especially complex are the provisions that deal with international business activities. This chapter summarizes these U.S. tax rules and assumes that the reader has a basic understanding of U.S. federal income taxation. A chapter of equal length could be written on the tax laws of our major trading partners.

30.2 OVERVIEW

(a) Methods of Taxation. With the possible exception of cost of goods sold, taxation is the largest expense of any business. Taxes can take many forms, and a variety of methods have been used to categorize taxes. There are direct taxes that are clearly recognizable and can be found on a financial statement, such as income taxes. In addition, there are indirect taxes, such as consumption taxes, whether they be a state or local sales tax, which is common in the United States, or a value-added tax, which is more common outside the United States; property or capital taxes; excise taxes; estate and gift taxes, employment taxes, and so-called user fees, a term that may be more politically acceptable than the term *tax*. Although international business tends to focus on income taxes, other taxes, especially consumption type taxes, may have an important impact on a business activity. Although estate and gift taxes impact on individuals rather than on business entities, because they can impact on employees who are transferred into a foreign country, they impact on the employer. Consumption taxes affect the cost of assets purchased by a business entity, and, when they take the form of a transfer tax, they often dictate the means of buying and selling businesses. For example, the relative importance of transfer taxes in Europe often necessitates the purchase of a business taking the form of a purchase of shares of stock rather than the underlying assets, whereas, in the United States, the relative lack of significance of transfer taxes, except when real property is involved, leads to more flexibility in the purchase and sale of businesses. Despite the importance that nonincome taxes can have on a business enterprise, businesses tend to focus more on income taxes, since these taxes can most easily be affected by tax planning. Consequently, this chapter focuses on United States international income taxation. However, the reader should be aware that nonincome forms of taxation are also important, as is foreign taxation.

(b) Classical versus Integration. The United States has (as this chapter is written) the so-called classical system of taxation. This means that there is a tax at the corporate level, with a second tax at the shareholder level, when the corporate profits are either distributed as a dividend to the shareholders or the shareholders sell their investment in the underlying corporation. There is a trend in most of the other developed nations away from the classical system of taxation to an integrated or imputation type of taxation. This means that the corporate tax and the shareholder taxes are integrated in such a fashion so that only one tax is levied on the profits. In most cases, there is a lack of full integration but only a partial integration. This integration can take several forms. In some countries, such as Germany, retained profits are taxed at a higher rate than distributed profits. In other countries, such as the United Kingdom, shareholders receive a credit for some of the underlying corporate taxes. (This system was abolished for distribution on or after April 16, 1999. In addition, the general corporate tax rate was reduced to 30%, with lower rates for small companies.) This can best be understood by the following simple example:

A U.K. corporation is subject to a 33% corporate tax. When it distributes a dividend to its shareholders, a portion of that dividend (currently, 25/75) is remitted to the U.K. tax authorities as an Advance Corporation Tax, or ACT. This ACT serves a dual purpose: it serves as a credit against the mainstream corporate tax, and it can also be claimed as a credit by the shareholder against its tax liability on the received dividends. If the U.K. shareholder were to receive a dividend of 75 with an ACT of 25, it would report a total dividend of 100 (75 + 25) with a tax credit of 25 against the individual income tax liability on that 100. By this means, the United Kingdom have partially integrated its corporate and shareholder income taxes.

Depending on the form that integration takes, it has a potential of favoring local investors and discriminating against foreign investors. Consequently, the United

States has sought bilateral relief through income tax treaties where the foreign country has an imputation system that discriminates against American investors while favoring local investors.

(c) Who Is Subject to Tax? Countries typically exercise jurisdiction either over the taxpayer or over the income or property. The United States claims both jurisdictions. Thus, it taxes American corporations and citizens on their worldwide income—income earned from sources within the United States, as well as income earned from foreign sources. In addition, it taxes foreign corporations and foreign residents on income earned from sources within the United States or property located within the United States. Some countries only exercise taxing jurisdiction on income from sources within a country and exempt or spare from taxation income earned outside their borders. Although many countries exercise only this "source-jurisdiction," the methods of determining source are not uniform. In addition, those countries that claim taxpayer jurisdiction do not apply this method in a uniform way. For example, most countries tax residents but not citizens who are not residents, whereas the United States taxes its U.S. citizens working abroad even if they are not resident in the United States.

Because jurisdiction on the basis of jurisdiction over the taxpayer as well as jurisdiction over income or property can lead to double taxation, a method has to be created that would avoid a multiplicity of taxes that would discourage international activities. In the United States, this takes the form of a foreign tax credit (discussed below), or tax sparing, for a specified amount of income earned by U.S. citizens working abroad.

(d) Determination of Tax Base. In determining the magnitude of a country's tax, one tends to focus on tax rates. It is, however, at least equally important to focus on how the tax base is determined. One only has to think back to the 1986 Tax Reform Act in the United States, in which tax rates were lowered; however, the tax liability of most taxpayers increased, because the tax base was expanded by means of eliminating deductions for certain expenditures. Consequently, in analyzing the tax impact on an anticipated business activity, it is necessary to determine both the tax base and the tax rate. We, therefore, distinguish between statutory tax rates and effective tax rates. Business is generally interested in effective tax rates, that is, the tax burden on its income as determined under its method of accounting.

(e) Rates. There has been a worldwide tendency, starting in the United Kingdom and spreading to the United States and then the rest of the world, for income tax rates to decline, with a corresponding base broadening, in order to maintain the level of taxes raised by the government. In analyzing the impact of income taxes on business profits earned by a U.S. corporation in a foreign country, one should consider not only the direct income taxes paid on that business activity but also the possibility of additional taxes paid when the profits are repatriated to the United States. Consequently, there can be a difference in the effective tax on retained profits and repatriated profits.

30.3 U.S. TAXATION OF A FOREIGN OPERATION

(a) Foreign Branches of U.S. Corporations. Because the United States exercises taxing jurisdiction over the worldwide income of U.S. corporations, the income derived by a foreign branch of a U.S. corporation is subject to U.S. tax in the same manner as income derived from sources within the United States. However, in order to prevent international double taxation, the United States grants primary taxing jurisdiction to the country from where the income is derived. The tax can then either be deducted or claimed as a tax credit, as described in section 30.4.

(b) Foreign Subsidiaries of U.S. Corporations. In general, the United States does not tax income earned by foreign subsidiaries of U.S. corporations until such income is repatriated to the United States. There are several exceptions to this general rule in addition to income earned by certain Canadian and Mexican subsidiaries that are included in a consolidated federal income tax return. (Note that such Canadian and Mexican corporations must meet certain requirements in order to be so included.) The most important exception applies to those foreign corporations that are controlled by U.S. shareholders and derive certain types of "tainted" income. These corporations are called "controlled foreign corporations," and the provisions that are applied to them are known as "Subpart F." Prior to the Revenue Act of 1962, corporations formed subsidiaries in tax havens, such as Panama and the Bahamas. These corporations purchased goods manufactured by the U.S. patent and resold the products to customers throughout the world. Since Internal Revenue Code Section 482 (discussed in the prior chapter) was not as rigidly enforced in those days as it is now, these tax haven corporations were able to claim, free from any tax, a significant portion of the overall profit. These profits were then used to earn investment type income or perhaps were even loaned to the parent company. If the corporation was no longer needed, it was sold or liquidated and capital gains treatment was claimed. The Revenue Act of 1962 introduced Subpart F into the Internal Revenue Code, and, in the ensuing years, these Subpart F provisions were modified and generally tightened so as to snare more and more types of income within its net. These provisions tax the U.S. shareholder on tainted types of income derived by controlled foreign corporations even before the income is repatriated. A correlative provision of the Internal Revenue Code treats the untaxed income derived after 1962 as a dividend when the foreign corporation is liquidated or sold.

The term *tainted* income is not a term of art but one that is used to describe categories of income that must be included in the U.S. shareholder's income. The major component of this tainted income is "Subpart F income." However, it also includes the controlled foreign corporation's increase in earnings invested in U.S. property as well as certain other types of income that in earlier years was excluded from immediate taxation as long as the income was reinvested in prescribed activities. Thus, in earlier years, certain income earned in less developed countries was excluded from the Subpart F provisions if that income was reinvested in less developed countries, and shipping income was excluded from the definition of Subpart F income if the income was reinvested in qualified shipping assets. When those amounts are disinvested, they are included in "tainted" income.

Subpart F income has five components, and its major component, foreign base company income, also has five subdivisions. They are:

1. Foreign base company income:
   - a. Foreign base company sales income
   - b. Foreign base company services income
   - c. Foreign base company shipping income

   d. Foreign base personal holding-company income
   e. Foreign base company oil-related income
2. Insurance income
3. Illegal bribes, kickbacks, and other payments paid by, or on behalf of, the corporation, directly or indirectly, to an official, employee, or agent of a government
4. Boycott income
5. Income derived from certain countries, such as Libya

The provisions contain "words of art" that form a special vocabulary by which international tax practitioners communicate with one another. The Subpart F provisions provide that, if a foreign corporation is a "controlled foreign corporation" (CFC) for an uninterrupted period of 30 days or more during the taxable year, every "person" who is a "U.S. shareholder" and owns stock in such corporation on the last day of the corporation's year must include in gross income its pro rata share of the corporation's tainted income, whether or not such income is distributed.

A CFC is a foreign corporation in which more than 50% of the total combined voting power or fair market value is owned directly, indirectly, or constructively by "U.S. shareholders" on any day during the taxable year. A "U.S. shareholder" is a "U.S. person" who owns, directly, indirectly, or constructively, 10% or more of the foreign corporation, such as U.S. corporations, citizens, and residents of the United States.

A special definition applies to foreign insurance companies. For purposes of taking into account certain income derived from the insurance of U.S. risks and risks earned outside the country of the foreign corporation's organization, the term *CFC* includes a foreign corporation of which more than 25% of the total combined voting power is owned, directly, indirectly, or constructively, by U.S. shareholders during any day during the taxable year. If the foreign insurance company insures the risks of related persons, then, in determining whether the 25% of total voting power test is met, shares owned by all U.S. persons are counted, even if they own less than 10% of the CFC stock. For these provisions to apply, the gross amount of premiums with respect to U.S. risks or related-party risks must exceed 75% of the gross amount of all premiums or other consideration with respect to all risks.

The most common of the five components of Subpart F income is foreign base company income. Certain exclusions apply to this foreign base company income.

A *de minimis* rule applies: If foreign base company income is less than the lesser of 5% of the CFC's gross income or $1 million, the CFC is deemed not to have any foreign base company income. Certain income from a related party that is organized in the same country as the CFC is excluded from foreign base company income. For this purpose a related person includes not only subsidiaries but also corporations that are controlled by the same shareholder that controls the CFC. For this purpose, control means 50% or more of either voting power or fair market value.

Foreign base company sales income is income derived in connection with (1) the sale or purchase of personal property if (2) a related person is involved in either the sale or the purchase, (3) the property is produced outside the CFC's country of incorporation, and (4) the property is used outside the CFC's country of incorporation. For example, a Panamanian subsidiary of a U.S. corporation purchases goods from its U.S. parent and resells the property to customers located in Europe; the profits derived by the Panamanian corporation are foreign base company sales income. However, if the Panamanian corporation were to sell the property in Panama for use in Panama, then foreign base company sales income would not be generated. In addition, if the Panamanian corporation were to manufacture the property in Panama and then sell it to related parties, foreign base company sales income would not be generated, because the property would have been produced in the CFC's country of incorporation. Substantial transformation is required before property is treated as having been produced by the selling corporation. Regulations provide a safe harbor rule that, if the conversion cost, consisting of direct labor and factory burden, equals 20% or more of the total cost of sales, then the property is considered to be manufactured within the CFC's country of incorporation. Mere packaging, labeling, or minor assembling operations do not constitute production. There is an exception for sale of certain agricultural commodities that are not grown in the United States in commercially marketable quantities. Such agricultural commodities are excluded from the foreign base company sales income provisions. Accordingly, a CFC can purchase or sell cocoa from or to a related person without generating foreign base company sales income. This is so, regardless of where the cocoa is used or grown, as cocoa is not grown in the United States in commercially marketable quantities.

Under certain branch rules, if sales or purchasing activities are conducted by a branch outside the CFC's country of incorporation and the tax effect is substantially the same as if the branch were a wholly owned subsidiary, the income attributable to the branch activities is treated as income derived by a wholly owned subsidiary of the CFC. Consequently, it could be considered foreign base company sales income.

Foreign base company services income is income derived from services performed for, or on behalf of, a related party when the services are performed outside the CFC's country of incorporation. Services directly related to the sale by the CFC of property manufactured by it and performed prior to the time of sale, or services related to an offer to sell such property, are subject to the foreign base company sales rules rather than the services income rules. Foreign base company services income is described by the following example.

CFC A enters into a contract with an unrelated person to drill an oil well in a foreign country. Domestic Corporation P owns all the outstanding stock of A, which employs a relatively small clerical and administrative staff and owns the necessary well-drilling equipment. Most of the technical and supervisory personnel who will oversee the drilling of the oil wells of A are regular employees of P, perhaps temporarily employed by A. In addition, A hires on the open market unskilled and semiskilled laborers to work on the drilling project. The services performed by A under the well-drilling contract are performed for, or on behalf of, a related person, because the services of technical and supervisory personnel that are provided by P are a substantial assistance in the performance of the contract. They assist A directly in the execution of the contract and provide A with skills that are a principal element in producing the income in the performance of such contracts.

Foreign base company shipping income is income derived from, or in connection with, the use of any aircraft or vessel in foreign commerce. This includes charter income, hiring (or leasing for use) of an aircraft or vessels, as well as performance of services related to the use of such aircraft or vessels. Where the CFC has an investment in a lower-tier shipping company, foreign base company shipping income includes dividends and interest (as well as gains from sales of stock) of lower-tier corporations.

Subpart F foreign personal holding company income includes investment type income, such as dividends, interest, rents, and royalties, as well as gain from the sale of securities and the excess of gains over losses from a sale or exchange of property that gives rise to dividends, interest, royalties, rents, and annuities or which does not give rise to any income (e.g., land held for capital appreciation). Also included in foreign personal holding company income is net income from a national principal contract and payments in lieu of dividends under an equity securities agreement, for tax years beginning after August 5, 1997. An exception is made for inventory or dealer property, as well as certain bona fide hedging transactions and active business gains or losses by producers, processors, merchants, or handlers of commodities. Also included is the excess of foreign currency gains over losses attributable to certain foreign exchange transactions, except those that are directly related to the business needs of the CFC. Rents and royalties derived in the active conduct of a trade or business and received from unrelated persons are excepted from the definition of Subpart F foreign personal holding company income. In addition, certain income received from related persons is excepted. Dividends and interest are excepted if the related payor is organized in the same foreign country and has a substantial part of its assets used in its trade or business located in that country. Rents and royalties attributable to property used in the CFC's country of organization are excepted. These exceptions do not apply to any interest, rent, or royalty to the extent it reduces the payor's Subpart F foreign personal holding company income. This includes original issue discount and commitment fees. Subpart F insurance income includes all income from the insurance or reinsurance in connection with risks located in a country other than the CFC's country of organization. This includes insurance or reinsurance on property located outside the CFC's country of organization, life insurance on the lives of individuals residing outside the CFC's country of organization, and risks occurring outside the CFC's country of organization. Captive insurance companies can avoid these Subpart F provisions by electing to treat related-person insurance income as income effectively connected with the conduct of a U.S. trade or business and thus subject to regular U.S. tax. Income derived by banks and finance companies are excluded.

The boycott income provision of Subpart F income is designed to affect those taxpayers that participate in, or cooperate with, an international boycott. The provision applies if as a condition of doing business directly or indirectly with a country or with a government, a company, or a national of that country, the taxpayer agrees to refrain from:

- Doing business within a country which is the object of an international boycott or with the government, companies, or nationals of that country
- Doing business with any U.S. person engaged in trade within another country which is the object of an international boycott or with the government, companies, or nationals of that country
- Doing business with any company whose ownership or management is made up, in whole or in part, of individuals of a particular nationality, race, or religion or remove (or refrain from selecting) corporate directors who are individuals of a particular nationality, race, or religion
- Employing individuals of a particular nationality, race, or religion
- Shipping or insuring products on a carrier owned, leased, or operated by a person who does not participate in, or cooperate with, an individual boycott

These provisions are primarily directed at the Arab boycott of Israel. Periodically, the IRS issues a notice listing countries that may require participation in, or cooperation with, an international boycott. Boycotts sanctioned by the United States are not affected by this provision, such as the boycotts of Cuba and Libya.

Taxpayers can elect an exception from foreign base company income if that income is subject to a foreign tax of at least 90% of the maximum U.S. corporate tax rate. If a CFC is engaged in a trade or a business within the United States, any item of income from U.S. sources that is effectively connected with a conduct of that U.S. trade or business is excluded from Subpart F income, unless the income is exempt from taxation or subject to a reduced rate of tax under an income tax treaty.

Even if the CFC does not have Subpart F income, U.S. shareholders are subject to a tax on their pro rata share of a CFC's increase in earnings and profits invested in U.S. property. *U.S. property* is very broadly defined as

- Tangible property located in the United States
- Stock of a domestic corporation
- Obligation of a U.S. person (including the guarantee of such obligation)
- Any right to use in the United States:
  a. A patent, copyright, invention, model, design, secret formula, or process.
  b. Any other similar property right which is acquired or developed by the CFC for use in the United States.

Although the definition of U.S. property is extremely broad, the tax law then excludes from the term *U.S. property* the following items:

- Obligations of the United States
- Money and bank deposits
- Assets acquired in normal commercial transactions without any intention of permitting them to remain in the United States, for example, accounts receivable
- Certain transportation equipment used predominantly outside the United States, for example, aircraft used in foreign countries
- Assets of an insurance company equivalent to the unearned premiums or ordinary and necessary reserves for the proper conduct of its insurance business attributable to certain contracts
- Stock or obligations of an unrelated corporation (for this purpose, a corporation is considered related if 25% or more of the total combined voting power is owned by the U.S. shareholders of the CFC directly, indirectly, or constructively)
- Any movable property (other than a vessel or aircraft) used for the purpose of exploring, developing, removing, or transporting resources from or under ocean waters in the U.S. continental shelf, such as drilling platforms
- Assets equal to the earnings or profits accumulated after 1962 and excluded from Subpart F income as income effectively connected with a conduct of a U.S. trade or business
- Property held by a foreign sales corporation that is related to its export activities
- Any indebtedness (other than indebtedness arising in connection with the sale of, or processing of, property) which is either collected within the period de-

scribed in regulations or matures within that period but is not collected within such period solely by reasons of the debtor's inability or unwillingness to pay

- Certain assets of securities and commodities dealers acquired in the ordinary course of business, effective for tax years beginning after December 1, 1997.

Amounts previously included in income as Subpart F income are not taxed again as either an increase in earnings invested in U.S. property or when actually distributed. Thus, the same income will not be taxed twice.

Although this income is subject to U.S. taxation, the actual U.S. tax on that income can be mitigated by the foreign tax credit provision discussed in section 30.4.

Generally, when a U.S. shareholder sells its investment in an affiliated company, the gain qualifies as capital gain. However, a special rule provides for gains from the sale of CFCs. A U.S. shareholder that owns 10% or more of the total combined voting power of the CFC, at any time during the five-year period ending on the date of the sale or exchange, treats as a dividend any gain recognized on the sale or exchange, to the extent of the earnings and profits of the CFC attributable to the stock sold that were accumulated while the stock was held by the U.S. shareholder and while the foreign corporation was a CFC. If the gain is taxed as a dividend, then the foreign tax credit provisions apply. Because of the impact of the foreign tax credit provisions, in most cases, treatment of all or a portion of the gain as a dividend results in a lower federal income tax than treatment of the gain as a capital gain.

In order to enable the Internal Revenue Service to monitor the activities of controlled foreign corporations, an information return is filed by U.S. persons as an attachment to their federal income tax return. This information return not only reports items of Subpart F income but also provides information to the Internal Revenue Service that it may also use to identify transactions between the U.S. taxpayer and controlled foreign corporations.

30.4 FOREIGN TAX CREDIT. Because the United States taxes domestic corporations on their worldwide income, income earned both within and without the United States is subject to tax. Just as the United States exercises taxing jurisdiction over foreign corporations doing business within the United States, foreign countries exercise similar jurisdiction over U.S. corporations doing business within their borders. Thus, a U.S. corporation doing business within a foreign country will often be subject to both U.S. and foreign taxation. This potentially prohibitive double taxation would inhibit U.S. business from expanding outside the United States. To remove this obstacle, Congress had a choice of either completely exempting foreign income from U.S. taxation or permitting domestic corporations to reduce or eliminate the U.S. tax on their foreign source income by the amount of foreign income tax paid. The United States has chosen this latter alternative through the use of the foreign tax credit system. A domestic corporation may, on an annual basis, elect either to claim the foreign income tax as a deduction, just as it deducts state and local income taxes, or to claim the foreign tax as a credit. The foreign tax credit can be claimed only to the extent of U.S. tax attributable to the net foreign source income. This is achieved by the foreign tax credit limitation discussed below. The effect of the foreign tax credit limitation is that the taxpayer pays a combined U.S. and foreign income tax equal to the higher of the effective U.S. and foreign taxes. However, if a taxpayer is subject to the alternative minimum tax, the credit cannot exceed 90% of the alternative minimum tax.

The economic effect of claiming a foreign tax as a credit rather than as a deduction can be seen from the following example. Assume that T, a U.S. corporation, derives $1,000 of income from foreign sources. Further assume that this income is subject to a $200 foreign tax. T's total tax is determined as follows:

	Tax Deduction	Tax Credit
Foreign taxable income	$1,000	$1,000
Foreign tax paid	200	
Taxable income—U.S. purposes	$ 800	$1,000
U.S. tax @ 35%	$ 280	$ 350
Less: foreign tax credit		200
Resultant U.S. tax		$ 150
Total tax burden	$ 480	$ 350
Effective tax rate	48%	35%

A credit is granted only for income taxes paid or accrued to a foreign country or a U.S. possession. To qualify as an income tax, a tax must be a tax on income as that term is used in U.S. tax laws. Although a tax based on estimated income or gross receipts is not creditable, taxes withheld from dividends, royalties, and interest are considered taxes in lieu of income taxes and are therefore creditable.

The purpose of the foreign tax credit is to avoid double taxation of foreign source income. It is not intended to reduce U.S. tax on U.S. source income. Thus, the foreign tax credit is limited to the U.S. tax attributable to foreign source income. The tax credit is limited to the proportion of the U.S. tax that the taxpayer's taxable income from foreign sources bears to its entire taxable income for the year. The following formula is used:

$$\text{Foreign tax credit limitation} = \frac{\text{Foreign source taxable income}}{\text{Worldwide taxable income}} \times \text{U.S. tax before credits}$$

The formula can be applied to the following fact pattern. T earned $1,000 of foreign source taxable income and $9,000 of U.S. source taxable income. It paid $400 of foreign income taxes. Its foreign tax credit limitation is computed as follows:

$$\frac{\$1{,}000}{\$1{,}000 + \$9{,}000} \times \$3{,}500\ (\$10{,}000 \times 35\%) = \$350$$

The foreign tax credit is the lesser of the foreign income taxes paid or accrued (i.e., $400) and the foreign tax credit limitation (i.e., $350) or $350.

A separate foreign tax credit limitation applies to taxes on the following types of income:

- Passive income
- High withholding tax interest
- Financial services income

- Shipping income
- Dividends from each 10% to 50% U.S.-owned foreign corporation

For earnings after 2002, the look-through rules discussed below will apply. For distributions of pre-2003 earnings, the separate foreign tax credit limitation provisions will continue to apply.

- Dividends from a domestic international sales corporation (DISC) or former DISC
- Taxable income attributable to foreign trade income of a foreign sales corporation (FSC)
- Distribution from an FSC (or former FSC) out of earnings and profits attributable to foreign trade income or qualified interest or carrying charges
- Foreign oil–related income
- Other income (general basket)

The foreign tax credit limitation is limited to the U.S. tax on the foreign source taxable income of each of the baskets. Foreign source taxable income is foreign source gross income less the appropriate deductions. Foreign source gross income is reduced by the expenses, losses, and deductions properly allocable to the foreign source income plus a ratable share of expenses, losses, and deductions that cannot definitely be allocated to any item or class of gross income. There are comprehensive regulations that describe how to do this. The interpretation of this provision is one of the major areas of dispute between taxpayers and the IRS.

Look-through rules apply for purposes of categorizing income of a U.S. taxpayer received either in the form of interest or dividends paid by U.S.-owned foreign corporations or included in income under the Subpart F provisions. Under these look-through rules, income is categorized as either U.S. source income or placed in the appropriate foreign tax credit limitation basket based upon the underlying income of the foreign corporation. To the extent the CFC has separate limitation income, the dividend, interest, rent, or royalties received by the U.S. taxpayer from the related controlled foreign corporation is categorized in the appropriate separate limitation basket category. Here is an example. The CFC's income is as follows:

1. High withholding tax interest	$ 25
2. Shipping income	20
3. Passive income	10
4. General basket income	45
Total	$100

The CFC paid a $100 dividend. The $100 dividend is divided into the four limitation baskets as if the CFC were a conduit—that is, high withholding tax interest of $25, shipping income of $20, passive income of $10, and general basket income of $45.

Any amount included in income as Subpart F income is divided in an identical manner. Thus, in the previous example, the portion of the income that is Subpart F income is divided among the baskets as if a dividend had been paid. Similar look-through rules apply to interest, rents, and royalties from CFCs to a 10% U.S. shareholder.

Passive income is income of a kind that would be Subpart F foreign personal holding company income if derived by a CFC, as described in section 30.3. However, exceptions are made for passive income subject to a different special limitation, such as high withholding tax interest, export financing interest, high taxed income (i.e., income which after allocation of expenses is subject to a foreign tax in excess of the U.S. rate), and foreign oil and gas extraction income.

Financial services income is income derived in the active conduct of a banking, financial, or similar business or derived by an insurance company from the investment of its unearned premiums or on its ordinary and necessary reserves. Exceptions are provided for export financing interest and high withholding tax interest.

Export financial interest is interest derived from financing the sale (or other disposition) for use or consumption outside the United States of any property manufactured, produced, grown, or extracted in the United States by the taxpayer or a related person if not more than 50% of the fair market value of the exported property is attributable to products imported into the United States. Such income is included in the general limitation basket.

High withholding tax interest is interest subject to a foreign withholding tax of 5% or more, determined on a gross basis, unless such interest qualifies as export financing interest.

A domestic corporation may be entitled to claim credits not only for foreign taxes that it actually pays but also for foreign taxes paid by its foreign affiliate to the extent attributable to dividends received by the domestic corporation or included in income under the Subpart F provisions. A domestic corporation that owns 10% of the voting stock of a foreign corporation in which it receives a dividend is deemed to have paid a proportion of any foreign income taxes paid or is deemed to have paid by the foreign corporation. The "deemed paid" foreign tax credit is a substitute for the dividend received deduction available for dividends received from domestic corporations.

A credit is available for foreign income taxes paid by a first-tier foreign corporation if the domestic corporation owns at least 10% of the voting stock of the foreign corporation. In addition, if the first-tier corporation owns at least 10% of the voting stock of a second-tier foreign corporation, the domestic corporation can be deemed to have paid the foreign income taxes of the second-tier foreign corporation. If the second-tier foreign corporation owns at least 10% of the voting stock of a third-tier foreign corporation, the domestic corporation can be deemed to have paid the foreign income taxes of the third-tier foreign corporation. However, the domestic corporation must have an overall indirect interest of at least 5% in both the second and third-tier foreign corporations. Effective for tax years beginning after August 5, 1997, these provisions have been extended to fourth, fifth, and sixth tiers. To determine a 10% ownership requirement, only direct ownership is recognized. The ownership test must be met on the day the dividends are received.

Foreign income tax deemed paid

$$= \frac{\text{Dividend}}{\text{Post-1986 undistributed earnings of the foreign corporation (after income taxes)}} \times \text{Creditable taxes}$$

Assume that P, a U.S. corporation, owns F, a French corporation. F has post-1986 profits of 100,000 euros. It paid $20,000 of French taxes during this period, translated from euros at the exchange rate on the date the taxes were paid. F pays a dividend to P of 20,000 euros. The deemed paid credit is computed as follows:

$$\frac{€20{,}000}{€100{,}000} \times \$100{,}000 = \$20{,}000$$

The foreign income tax deemed paid is included in income. The dividend is translated into U.S. dollars at the rate in effect at the time the dividend is received. Assume that the rate is €1 to 1 US$. P's taxable income is as follows:

Dividend received	$20,000
Foreign tax deemed paid	20,000
Total income	$40,000

For years prior to 1987, the denominator is earnings and profits computed annually.

If the foreign income taxes paid or accrued exceed the foreign tax credit limitation, the excess must be carried back two years and forward five years. A credit cannot be carried to a year in which a deduction for *foreign* income taxes is claimed. These carryover rules apply separately to each limitation basket. If a taxpayer has an overall foreign loss (i.e., its expenses attributable to foreign source income are in excess of that foreign income), it must keep track of that overall foreign loss. In a later year, foreign source income, to the extent of the overall foreign loss, must be recategorized as U.S. source income. The amount of otherwise foreign source income that is recategorized as U.S. source income is the lesser of the amount of the overall foreign loss or 50% of the foreign taxable income for the year. Taxpayers can elect to have a higher percentage apply. These rules are applied separately to each of the foreign tax credit limitation baskets. Losses in a foreign tax limitation basket are allocated on a proportionate basis among (and thereby reduce) the foreign income baskets in which the entity earns income in a loss year. If a foreign loss is allocated to another basket and if a loss basket has income in a subsequent taxable year, then, to the extent of the losses allocated to a different basket, the subsequent income is allocated to those different baskets.

This complex provision was enacted because Congress was concerned that taxpayers would conduct their foreign activities in branch form during the initial start-up years when the foreign activities are operating at a loss, using the loss to reduce their U.S. taxable income. Then, in a later year, when the foreign activities are profitable, the foreign tax credit would eliminate the U.S. tax. The following is an example of this:

	Foreign Source Taxable Income	Foreign Tax
Year 1	($1,000)	0
Year 2	$1,000	$350
Total	0	$350

In this example, the $1,000 loss in Year 1 would save $350 of U.S. taxes, and no U.S. tax would be paid on the Year 2 income because of the foreign tax credit. By converting the Year 2 income to U.S. source income, the foreign tax credit limitation in Year 2 is zero. This concept applies to each of the foreign tax credit limitation baskets.

30.5 TRANSFER PRICING. Internal Revenue Code Section 482 authorizes the Commissioner of Internal Revenue to distribute, apportion, or allocate gross income, deductions, or allowances between or among related taxpayers. These rules are discussed in detail in the prior chapter. The effect of this Internal Revenue Service power is applied before all the other rules discussed in this chapter are applied. The purpose is to prevent the evasion of taxes by such devices as shifting of profits, the making of fictitious sales, and other methods frequently adopted for the purposes of "milking." This section prevents the arbitrary shifting of income and deductions among controlled corporations and places such corporations on a tax parity with uncontrolled corporations.

Section 482 applies when there are two or more organizations, trades, or businesses owned or controlled by the same interest. It becomes operative when the activities result in either evasion of taxes or a failure to reflect income clearly. To determine ownership or control by the same interest, the regulations look to the reality of the control. The regulations find that a presumption of control arises if income or deductions have been arbitrarily shifted. The evasion of taxes or the failure to reflect clearly income may be intentional or unintentional. Transactions between or among related parties are subject to special scrutiny to see if there was a failure to reflect income clearly. If there was such a failure, income or deductions can be shifted by the IRS from one entity to another. The theme of the regulations is to require related parties to deal with each other at arm's length, that is, as they would with unrelated parties. The regulations describe what is meant by "arm's length" in five types of transactions: loans or advances, performance of personal services, use of tangible property, transfers of, or the use of, intangible property, and sale of tangible property. In some of these specific types of transactions, the regulations provide safe havens or safe-haven rules. A taxpayer that conforms to these safe-haven rules automatically has a defense against a Section 482 allocation, since the transaction is deemed to be at arm's length.

(a) Specific Transactions

(i) Loans. The Section 482 regulations provide safe-haven interest rates that apply to U.S. dollar loans. For loans or advances entered into after May 8, 1986, the safe-haven rates are provided by the Internal Revenue Service on a monthly basis and are known as the applicable federal rate. The AFR varies, depending upon whether the loan is short term, medium term or long term, and whether interest is paid monthly, quarterly, semiannually, or annually. The AFR in effect at the time the loan is entered into applies. The safe-haven range is 100% of the AFR (lower limit) to 130% of the AFR (upper limit). If the rate charged is less than the lower limit, then the IRS may raise the rates to the lower limit. If the rate charged is higher than the upper limit, then the IRS may lower it to the upper limit. If the rate charged is within this range, the IRS must accept it.

The interest period begins on the date the indebtedness arises. However, for indebtedness arising in the ordinary course of business from sales, leases, or the rendition of services, or any other similar extension of credit that is not evidenced by a written instrument requiring payment of interest, the interest period is not required to begin until the first day of the third calendar month (fourth calendar month if debtor is located outside the United States) following the month in which the trade receivable arises. unless the taxpayer can demonstrate that regular trade practice permits a longer period. This interest-free period does not apply to simple loans or advances of money. Taxpayers may establish a more appropriate rate which takes into account all the relevant factors. The following is an example.

Suppose T, a U.S. taxpayer, lends $1,000 to its foreign subsidiary interest-free. The IRS can compute interest income to T based on the AFR. The foreign subsidiary, as a correlative adjustment, has an interest deduction.

(ii) Services. Where an entity performs personal services for a related entity and the services are not an integral part of the trade or business of either of the entities, a mere reimbursement of actual costs is permitted. However, where the personal services are an integral part of the trade or business of either, a profit must be added to the change. The regulations do not provide a safe-haven profit rule. An arm's-length charge for such services would be the amount that would have been charged by unrelated parties performing the same services in a comparable transaction. An arm's length charge is required where:

- Either party receiving the services or the party performing the services is engaged in a trade or business of providing similar services to unrelated parties. This also applies where the party performing the services is a member of a group and another member of the group performs, as one of its principal activities, such services for unrelated parties.
- The services performed are one of the principal activities of the party performing the services.
- The party performing the services is clearly capable of doing so and the services are a principal element in the recipient's operations.
- The recipient of the services has received a benefit or a substantial amount of services from related entities during the taxable year. Services other than manufacturing, production, extraction, or construction services are presumed not to be a principal activity of the party performing them if during the taxable year all the direct and indirect costs (including the cost of services constituting manufacturing, production, extraction, or construction) for the taxable year attributable to related entities do not exceed 25% of the performing entity's total cost (excluding cost of goods sold).

(iii) Use of Tangible Property. A safe-haven formula applies to leases entered into before August 7, 1986, or pursuant to a binding written contract entered into before May 9, 1986. After that date, there is no safe-haven formula for leases.

(iv) Use of Intangible Property. The regulations do not provide a safe-haven rule for royalties. An amount charged in similar transactions involving unrelated parties is considered an arm's length charge. The IRS can adjust the royalty rate to ensure that the royalty is commensurate with the income derived from the use of intangible property. In lieu of providing a royalty on the transfer of intangible property, taxpayers can have a cost-sharing arrangement.

(v) Sales. The most difficult area in Section 482 and the one with the largest potential impact is intercompany pricing. These provisions are described in detail in the prior chapter.

(b) Internal Revenue Service Activities. In recent years, the Internal Revenue Service has focused a great deal of attention on transfer pricing issues, and Congress has been granting the Internal Revenue Service greater authority to develop the information that it claims it needs to administer this provision properly. All taxpayers are required to maintain records and documents relevant to the determination of their transfer pricing prior to the filing of their tax return and, if requested, to furnish these records to the Internal Revenue Service within 30 days of the IRS request. Initial requests for information necessary to an IRS audit are generally submitted to the taxpayer in the form of IDRs. The IRS is empowered, for the purposes of ascertaining the correctness of any return, or making a return where none has been made, to determine the tax liability of any person or to collect any such liability, (1) to examine any books, papers, records, or any other data that may be relevant or material to such inquiry, (2) to summon the person liable for tax or required to perform the act, or any officer, employee, or such person having possession, custody, or care of books of account containing entries related to the business of the person liable for tax or required to perform the act, or any other person the IRS may deem proper to appear before the IRS at a time and place named in the summons and to produce such books, papers, records, or other data, and to give such testimony under oath, as may be relevant or material to such inquiry, (3) to take such testimony, from the person concerned, under oath, as it may be relevant or material to such inquiry. Through the use of whatever information the IRS obtains, it will generally attempt to construct, through economic analysis and other means, what it believes to be an appropriate arm's-length price and, to the extent this price differs from the price actually charged in the transaction under review, to make appropriate adjustments to the tax liability of the taxpayer.

The IRS primarily focuses on U.S. subsidiaries of foreign multinationals and tax-haven subsidiaries of U.S. multinationals.

30.6 FOREIGN CURRENCY ISSUES. The 1986 Tax Reform Act introduced, for the first time, a comprehensive set of rules governing the taxation of foreign currency gains and losses. These provisions, which provide greater certainty for the tax treatment of normal commercial transactions, are based on the functional currency concept of FAS No. 52. Under this concept, all determinations have to be made in the taxpayer's functional currency.

(a) Functional Currency and Qualified Business Unit. The functional currency is automatically the U.S. dollar, except for a "qualified business unit" (a self-contained foreign operation or QBU), in which case it is a currency:

- Used to keep the books and records
- Of the economic environment in which a significant part of the business unit's activities generating revenues and expenses are conducted
- Used to borrow or lend

A QBU that would otherwise be required to use a hyperinflationary currency as its functional currency must use the U.S. dollar as its functional currency.

(b) Transactions. For transactions in other than the functional currency, a disposition of foreign currency results in the recognition of gain or loss. The foreign exchange gain or loss is accounted for separately from any gain or loss attributable to the underlying transaction, except in the case of certain integrated financial transactions. This is known as the "dual transaction theory." As an example, let us assume that a U.S. exporter sells its products for a designated amount of foreign currency units. It determines the selling price at the translation rate on the day of the sale. When it collects its payment, the foreign currency exchange rate on the date of payment and the date the account receivable were set up are different. There is a foreign currency gain or loss.

Gain or loss is generally not recognized until there is a closed and completed transaction, such as the collection of an account receivable. The foreign currency gain or loss is generally ordinary income or loss (U.S. or foreign source).

The IRS has issued regulations providing for the integration of certain financial transactions, such as where a taxpayer borrows or lends foreign currency and enters into a hedging transaction in the same day on which the underlying foreign currency transaction is entered into. By this means, any foreign exchange gain or loss on the underlying loan is offset by gain or loss on the hedging contract. By integrating the two, the hedge gain or loss becomes an addition or reduction of interest income or expense.

Generally, foreign currency gains or losses are allocated between U.S. and foreign sources by reference to the residence of the taxpayer or qualified business unit on whose books the asset or liability is reflected. Accordingly, for a U.S. corporation, the gain or loss would come from the United States. A special rule applies to certain related party loans that have to be marked to market annually. On foreign currency loans that bear interest at a rate at least 10 percentage points higher than the applicable rate for midterm federal obligations at the time the loan is made and that are made by U.S. persons or a related foreign person to a 10% owned foreign corporation, any interest income is treated as U.S.-source income to the extent of any loss on the loan caused by the marking to market. In addition, to determining foreign exchange gain or loss on foreign currency transactions, such as loans and purchase and sale of goods, foreign currency translation losses have to be accounted for.

(c) Translations

(i) Branch. If a U.S. taxpayer conducts its activities in a foreign country through a branch, it has to translate the branch results into U.S. dollars. Except for hyperinflationary economies, the branch's taxable profits are first determined on the basis of its functional currency. The functional currency is then converted into U.S. dollars using the weighted average exchange rate for the taxable period. Any repatriations to the United States are translated at the rate in effect at the time of the repatriation. Foreign income taxes are translated at the rate in effect at the time the tax is paid and then added to the foreign taxable income or "grossed-up." The foreign taxes can then be claimed as a credit, as described in section 30.4. On remittances, any exchange gain or loss is recognized to the extent that the value of the foreign currency differs from its value when earned.

(ii) Subsidiary. Actual and deemed dividends related to the sale of a foreign subsidiary are translated at the exchange rate on the date the dividend is included in in-

come. Deemed distributions under Subpart F are translated at the weighted average exchange rate for the foreign corporation's taxable year. Investments in U.S. property are translated at the rate in effect on the last day of the taxable year. Deemed-paid foreign taxes are translated into U.S. dollars using the exchange rate on the date the tax was paid.

(d) Hyperinflationary Economies. A QBU, whose functional currency is a hyperinflationary currency, must use the U.S. dollar as its functional currency. The taxpayer uses the "dollar approximate separate transactions" method of accounting. Under this method, profit and loss or earnings and profits are computed under the following four-step approach:

1. Prepare a profit-and-loss statement in the QBU's hyperinflationary currency.
2. Make the adjustments necessary to conform this profit-and-loss statement to U.S. accounting and tax principles.
3. Translate the amount of hyperinflationary currency into U.S. dollars in accordance with prescribed regulations.
4. Adjust the result in dollar profit and loss or earnings and profits to reflect the amount of the currency gain or loss determined under the regulations.

In general, the amounts shown on a profit-and-loss statement are translated into dollars at the average exchange rate for each month of the taxable year, with special rules provided for translating items of inventory, cost of goods sold, depreciation, depletion, amortization, and prepaid items. Amounts representing allowance for depreciation, depletion, and amortization are translated at the average exchange rate for the translation period in which the cost of the underlying asset was incurred, with prepaid expenses and income translated at the average rate for the translation period during which they were paid or received.

These rules, which are complex, are similar to generally accepted accounting principles but are not identical. In general, the accounting rules provide greater flexibility than permitted by the tax rules. Consequently, preparers of the tax return cannot rely on accounting department calculations but must refine these calculations to take into consideration these special tax rules.

30.7 U.S. TAXATION OF A FOREIGN CORPORATION

(a) Overview. Foreign corporations are subject to U.S. taxation on certain investment income from U.S. sources and on business income that is "effectively connected" with a U.S. trade or business.

(i) Investment Income. U.S.-source investment income is subject to a 30% gross receipts tax if it is not effectively connected with the conduct of a U.S. trade or business. Income subject to this 30% flat-rate tax includes:

1. Fixed or determinable annual or periodic income
2. Timber, coal, or iron ore royalties
3. Original issue discount
4. Gains from the sale or exchange of intangible property, such as patents and

copyrights, to the extent that the gains are contingent on the productivity, use, or disposition of the property sold and thus economically similar to royalties

Certain income is exempt from this 30% gross receipts tax in order to encourage foreign investment in the United States. The exempt income includes interest on bank deposits if the interest is not attributable to a U.S. trade or business. Another similar exemption is interest that qualifies as "portfolio interest." This is certain targeted bonds that are sold only to foreign investors and that cannot be owned by U.S. corporations, citizens, or residents. In addition, the interest cannot be received from a corporation or a partnership in which the recipient has a 10% or greater interest and cannot be received by a bank. This portfolio interest exception is designed to cover Eurodollar bonds sold to the public outside the United States and eliminates the need for utilization of expensive structures that typically have included utilizing finance companies organized in the Netherlands or Netherlands Antilles. At present, if a foreign corporation has a U.S. subsidiary and it sells the shares of the U.S. subsidiary, the gain is not subject to U.S. taxation unless the subsidiary constitutes a "U.S. real property interest."

In many cases, this 30% gross receipts tax is reduced to a lower rate or completely exempted by an income tax treaty between the United States and the country of residence of the foreign investor.

(ii) Business Income. Business income that is effectively connected with the conduct of a U.S. trade or business is taxed at the normal U.S. rates. The income attributable to U.S. trade or business is income that is effectively connected with the conduct of a U.S. trade or business and sometimes referred to as "ECI (effectively connected income)." Deductions are allowed to the extent they relate to the ECI. Complex regulations are used to determine when expenses of a foreign corporation are attributable to ECI.

(b) U.S. Trade or Business

(i) Definition. In order for a foreign corporation to be engaged in a U.S. trade or business, there must be a significant amount of business activity in the United States. The term *trade or business* is not defined in the tax law but is based upon specific facts and circumstances of the taxpayer. Foreign investors, other than dealers, can trade in stocks, securities, and commodities in the United States without being engaged in a trade or business in the United States.

(ii) Effectively Connected Concept. A foreign corporation that is engaged in trade or business within the United States is taxed at the regular corporate rate on income that is "effectively connected" with the conduct of that trade or business. This effectively connected concept applies to four types of income:

1. Gain or loss from the sale or exchange of capital assets
2. Fixed or determinable annual or periodic income
3. Gain or loss in the disposition of U.S. real property interest
4. All other income, gain, or loss

All income from U.S. real property interest is automatically considered ECI. U.S.

source capital gains and fixed or determinable income are only ECI if they are attributable to a U.S. trade or business. Fixed or determinable annual periodic income refers to interests, dividends, rents, wages, and similar types of income. For nonfinancial institutions, the primary determination of whether such income is ECI is based upon the "asset use" test. Under this test, if the asset is held by the U.S. trade or business, or has some type of direct relationship to the U.S. trade or business, then the income generated by that asset is ECI. The "business activities" test is used by financial institutions. If the business activities that generated the income are performed by personnel associated with a U.S. office, then the income is ECI.

(c) Branch Profits Tax. As indicated at the beginning of this chapter, the United States has the classical system of taxation, that is, income taxed both at the corporate level and the shareholder level. Thus, income earned by a U.S. corporation is subject to U.S. tax, and, when the income is paid out as a dividend, it is subject to a second tax at the shareholder level. Once such income is paid out as a dividend to a foreign shareholder, the dividend will constitute U.S. source fixed or determinable annual or periodical income and will thus be subject to a 30% or lower treaty rate of tax.

A branch profits tax is designed to subject a U.S. branch of a foreign corporation to the same level of tax that would be paid if the business activities were performed in subsidiary form rather than as a branch of a foreign corporation. This is done by imposing a 30% or lower treaty rate of tax on a foreign corporation's "dividend equivalent amount." This amount is the foreign corporation's effectively connected earnings and profits that are not reinvested in the United States but are instead repatriated to the foreign head office. This means that if a foreign corporation had 100 of effectively connected income before corporate tax, it would pay a corporate tax of 35 and then 19.5 [30% of (100 – 35)] for a total tax burden of 54.5. Just as many income tax treaties reduce the rate of tax on dividend, many treaties either reduce the branch profits tax or prevent the United States from imposing the branch profits tax. These treaties are overridden by internal law if the foreign corporation is not a "qualified resident" of the treaty country. A foreign corporation is not a "qualified resident" if it is not owned by residents of that country or residents of the United States. Thus, for example, if residents of a nontreaty country owned all the stock of a Dutch corporation, which in turn had a branch in the United States, the Dutch corporation would not be considered a "qualified resident," and thus the United States could impose the branch profits tax. In addition to the tax on the dividend equivalent amount, there is a branch level interest tax that operates in such a fashion as to treat interest paid by a U.S. branch of a foreign corporation as if it were paid by a U.S. subsidiary of the foreign corporation. Consequently, such interest paid to foreign investors would be subject to the 30% U.S. tax unless reduced or eliminated by an income tax treaty.

30.8 INCOME TAX TREATIES

(a) United States and Income Tax Treaties. The United States has entered into many income tax treaties. The express purpose of these treaties is to eliminate international double taxation and render mutual assistance in tax enforcement.

(b) General Effects. The U.S. foreign tax credit goes a long way towards eliminating international double taxation of U.S. taxpayers. Many countries avoid international double taxation by not taxing their taxpayers on foreign source income. To a large extent, the income tax treaties determine the amount of tax to be paid to the country where the income is produced and the amount to be paid to the taxpayer's country of residence. It does this by providing for reduced rates of tax or complete exemptions from tax for certain specified items of income. For example, under internal law, interest paid by a U.S. payor to a foreign recipient is subject to a 30% U.S. withholding tax. Under the U.K.–U.S. income tax treaty, this tax is eliminated.

Treaties often contain limitation on, or expansion of, benefits if certain conditions are met. Consequently, tables comparing tax rates contain numerous footnotes. Accordingly, the following table, without footnotes, is illustrative only and should not be relied on.

	Withholding Rate on Interest Payment
Nontreaty	30%
Australia	10%
Belgium	15%
Canada	15%
France	0
Germany	0
Japan	10%
The Netherlands	0
Switzerland	5%
United Kingdom	0

Each treaty is slightly different from others and is a result of binational negotiation between the United States and the treaty partner. In order to prevent a resident of a non-treaty country from using, for example, the United Kingdom treaty to invest in the United States, anti-conduit provisions were enacted. If a Saudi Arabia investor were to lend money to a United Kingdom corporation that lent it to the United States subsidiary, the anti-conduit provisions treat the loan as coming directly from Saudi Arabia.

PART VII

INTERNATIONAL AUDITING

CHAPTER 31

MANAGING THE AUDIT RELATIONSHIP IN AN INTERNATIONAL CONTEXT*

Norman R. Walker
PricewaterhouseCoopers LLP

Seymour Jones
New York University

CONTENTS

31.1 INTRODUCTION. Professional accountants in their role as auditors perform an indispensable service in the financial reporting process. As independent outside experts, they audit management's financial representations and attest to their fairness. In doing so, they assure investors and other readers of published financial statements that the information they are using is fairly stated and relatively unbiased. This, in turn, contributes to the operational and allocational efficiency of the capital formation process.

---

*The author acknowledges the assistance of Ryan Hipscher (Deloitte and Touche, LLP) for the revision of this chapter.

Managing the audit relationship can be a challenging process for both the reporting entity as well as for the auditors seeking appointment. This is particularly true for international companies with worldwide operations as audit and accounting requirements vary from country to country.

Selecting auditors involves:

- Clearly identifying management expectations of the auditors
- Assessing the qualifications of the candidates
- Establishing the deliverables or terms of reference

Maintaining a successful relationship with auditors further involves evaluating performance, both the company's and the auditor's, and providing feedback in both directions.

Throughout the process of selecting and maintaining a relationship with auditors, communications are the most critical success factor. The challenges to successful communications for international companies and their auditors are many—language differences, time differences and distance, different and changing accounting and reporting requirements from country to country, and, most importantly, the differences in national cultures.

Further, an international company may need financial statements all stated in U.S. generally accepted accounting principles (GAAP), whereas local auditors may not be familiar with such principles, thus requiring auditors from the U.S. to complement local auditors. A goal for international companies is to have financial statements in both U.S. GAAP and in International Accounting Standards by the middle of this decade. After reading this chapter the reader should be better able to manage the selection and continuing relationship with auditors.

31.2 ESTABLISHING EXPECTATIONS. It is particularly important that companies focus on their expectations of their auditors if they wish to obtain the maximum value from the relationship. This should include clearly identifying those expectations and communicating them to the auditors.

The Sarbanes-Oxley Act of 2002 recently enacted in the United States is expected to impact the services auditors may provide and the responsibilities of audit committees, and managements of companies. The Act addresses matters of corporate governance as well as the scope of services and professional responsibility of external auditors. The Act, which applies to all public companies reporting to the Securities and Exchange Commission (SEC), requires, among other things, certification of the financial statements by the company's CEO and CFO, audit committee composition solely of "independent" directors one of which must be a "financial expert" and the following which affect the function of the audit committee and the relationship between the external auditor and the audit committee and management:

- All audit services must be preapproved by the audit committee.
- The audit committee is exclusively responsible for retention, compensation, and oversight of the external auditor.
- Preapproval of all nonaudit services to the extent that such nonaudit services are permitted and disclosure of such services
- Audit committees are to have the authority to engage independent counsel and professional advisors

- Impermissible nonaudit services include:
  - Financial information systems design and implementation
  - Legal and expert services
  - Internal audit outsourcing services
  - Appraisal/valuation services
  - Human resources (HR) and management services
  - Investment banking, investment advisor and broker dealer services
  - Legal and expert services unrelated to the audit
  - Bookkeeping
  - Any other services that the newly constituted Public Company Accounting Oversight Board may deem impermissible
- The lead engagement partner of the external auditing firm and the lead review partner must be rotated every five years. (It is further anticipated that this provision may ultimately be extended to other members of the audit team.)
- The external auditor must report to the audit committee its assessment of the critical accounting policies and practices of the company as well as any disagreements with management
- The audit committee is required to review and discuss with management and the external auditors the effectiveness of the company's internal control structure and procedures and the auditors will be required to attest to management's internal control assessment, which in turn is to be disclosed in the company's annual report.
- Prohibition of improper influence on the conduct of audits by directors or management

(a) Scope of Services. There are several dimensions to the question of what services the auditors are to provide. The annual audit of the group financial statements is the obvious starting point, which, together with other aspects of the scope of possible services, is discussed next.

(i) The Audit

SINGLE OR MULTIPLE AUDITORS. Predominant practice is to appoint a single audit firm to perform an audit sufficient in scope to issue an opinion on the group financial statements. With operations in many locations and countries and possibly in different businesses, the audit of an international company's group financial statements requires communication and a high degree of coordination between the auditors involved as well as a clear understanding of their respective responsibilities. These auditors also require leadership, organization, and control by those who are responsible for the audit at the group or parent company level.

There are distinct advantages to appointment of a single audit firm as auditors to all subsidiaries in a group:

- The engagement partner at the group level is responsible for coordinating all service to the company. The company can look to one person to initiate action to meet their needs throughout the world.
- Comprehensive and timely reporting to the parent company's audit committee

as well as board of directors is greatly facilitated. Such matters as scope of work, audit findings, proposed audit reports, internal control, and other recommendations and fees can be reported promptly and efficiently for all locations.

- All of the offices of the audit firm throughout the world *should* subscribe to a common service philosophy and audit approach. If they do, they can work more effectively with each other in identifying and meeting the company's needs and resolving questions on auditing and accounting, format and content of reports, deadlines and billing arrangements. This compatibility contributes to audit efficiency because:
  - All offices act in harmony providing the most effective service to the group.
  - Information flows freely between offices, individual partners, and staff without unnecessary formality.
  - Full advantage can be taken of opportunities to restrict audit scope at selected locations and to work with internal auditors. Also, audit scope can be communicated to other offices with less difficulty and less chance of misunderstanding.
  - The principal office can more effectively monitor and control group audit fees by prompt receipt of details on estimated and actual time and expenses.
  - The company can choose to negotiate fees with the auditors on a worldwide basis or an individual location basis. If multiple auditors are involved, fee negotiations necessarily are required with each audit firm.

If more than one audit firm is used, there is also a question of divided responsibility for the opinion of the group financial statements. In circumstances where multiple audit firms are selected, as a minimum, the principal auditor generally must audit a majority of the group to issue a report on the group financial statements. What constitutes a majority of the group is determined by reference to the most appropriate criteria in the circumstances. Group consolidated assets and revenues are normally appropriate; however, net assets and earnings may also be important.

In some countries, the principal auditors are required to assume sole responsibility for the group audit report, even though other auditors examined part of the group. In other countries, the principal auditor has the option of indicating the division of responsibility by reference to the other auditors in his report. The predominant practice is for the principal auditors to refer to the other auditors if those auditors audit operations that are material to the group financial statements. In either case, the other auditors remain responsible for the performance of their work and for their own reports. A key consideration here is whether the audit committee and management wish to have sole responsibility for the audit of the group financial statements vested in a single firm of auditors.

While it is not particularly common because of certain country requirements companies sometimes select audit firms to perform an audit jointly. In these circumstances, a single audit report may be issued over the signature of both firms or separate reports may be issued on the same set of financial statements. Any company expectations in this regard must be clearly set forth to the audit firm candidates at the outset, because firms may choose to accept such an engagement only in exceptional circumstances or because of local requirements.

STATUTORY AUDIT REQUIREMENTS OUTSIDE THE PARENT COMPANY'S COUNTRY. Many countries impose statutory audit requirements on subsidiaries or other business units located in that country. Frequently, these requirements extend only to companies that meet certain size requirements, normally total assets, annual revenue, or turnover and, occasionally, number of employees. The most common practice is to have most or all statutory audit requirements fulfilled by the audit firm responsible for auditing the group consolidated financial statements (i.e., the principal auditors).

However, this is not a requirement, even in circumstances where the audit committee, management and the board of directors of the company desire to have responsibility for the audit of the group financial statements vested in a single firm of auditors. Depending on the significance of individual operations to the group financial statements, the principal auditor may require audit procedures to be performed for those operations only occasionally or not at all. In effect, the audit scope is established in the context of the consolidated group financial statements. In such circumstances, the statutory audit requirements for those operations may be fulfilled either by the principal auditors or other auditors.

REVIEWS OF INTERIM FINANCIAL INFORMATION. If reviews of quarterly or semiannual financial information are required or desired by the company, there are several questions that must be addressed:

- Are the reviews to be performed on a "timely" basis, that is, contemporaneously with and immediately following the preparation of the interim financial information, or on a basis to coincide with completion of the annual audit?
- Are written reports to be issued?
- If such reports on the reviews are to be issued, will they be available to shareholders or otherwise publicly?

INTERIM FINANCIAL REPORTING. The timing of work to be performed by the auditors will vary depending on the answers to these questions. For public companies based in the United States, the SEC now requires timely prefiling reviews of interim financial information. Additionally, the extent of the interim review procedures is established in the context of the group financial statements, so the auditor may require procedures to be performed at some operating units or locations only occasionally or not at all.

Further, the extent of reporting to the company on the results of the reviews may vary from the standard written reports prescribed by professional standards to oral or informal reporting to management or the board of directors on the results of the review and related observations that the auditors have for the company. The SEC does not require written reports or reviews of interim financial information from auditors.

OTHER REPORTING REQUIREMENTS. Frequently, there are statutory or other reporting requirements for the parent company or individual subsidiaries beyond those involved in the audit of the group financial statements. Such requirements may result from contractual requirements (e.g., lease or other debt agreements) or statutes of individual countries. The latter area includes audits of employee benefit plans for which reporting standards have been increasing significantly in recent years, thus requiring greater efforts on the part of both companies and their auditors. In addition, countries other than the United States are now also requiring audits of such plans.

Further, reporting on compliance with legal regulations, company bylaws, proper handling of correspondence and minutes of meetings, and so on, may be required as in Colombia or a tax compliance "audit" may be required as in Mexico. In these cases, materiality standards may not apply and the penalties, and hence the risk, faced by the auditor in the event of an error in the reports or underlying information may be significant. Accordingly, the company's expectations of its auditors in these areas must be clearly understood by them.

RELIANCE ON INTERNAL AUDIT. Internal audit capabilities at international companies range from very little to very extensive. Similarly, the focus of internal audit functions can range from project or program audits to systems and controls audits to full financial statements audits. Some companies desire that their external auditors place the maximum reliance possible, within the requirements of applicable professional standards, on their internal audit group. In other cases, international companies want their external auditors to place little or no reliance on their internal auditors. The effect on the scope of the external auditor's work from placing reliance on the internal auditors can be very significant, resulting in a similarly significant effect on external audit fees.

The degree to which external auditors are able to rely on the work of internal auditors is based on several factors, including:

- The degree of independence of the internal auditors within the company, that is, do they report directly to the audit committee or only to management
- Their competence and their experience
- The relevance of their work to the external auditors
- How responses to their reports are monitored and implemented

When the evaluation of each of these factors is very positive, the key issue becomes a question of allocation, within the confines of applicable professional standards, of the total audit effort between external and internal auditors.

TIMING. Expectations as to timing of auditors' work and reporting are crucial to a company's successful relationship with those auditors. Audit firms are normally flexible and able to meet company desired timing for work and reporting. However, the concentration of December 31 year ends among companies, particularly in the United States, results in a peak load or "busy season" in the months of January through March. Most audit firms desire to move as much work as possible out of the busy season. In any event, the company's expectation for timing of the audit and related reporting must be clearly set forth. This includes:

- Opinion and earnings release dates
- Publishing dates for printed annual reports and reports filed with governmental agencies
- Audit committee and annual meeting dates

(ii) Business Advice. Historically, auditors have provided general business advice to companies that they were serving on a variety of matters, including the effectiveness of the company's operations and organization, financial structure, internal control policies, and regulatory matters. More recently, some companies have received only

reports on the audit and reports on internal control or other matters as required by professional standards. This latter approach is sometimes referred to as a "commodity" purchase approach.

However, the challenges facing companies today, particularly international companies, are tremendous. Business environments are changing, in many cases rapidly, all around the world.

Auditors normally perform business risk assessments, obtain evidence as to the design and operation of control systems, and evidence with respect to specific transactions for all significant company operations worldwide. Further, auditors normally bring extensive experience with other companies, both in the same businesses and in other businesses to their task.

This combination of activities involved in performing an audit of the group financial statements, together with their extensive expertise from around the world, positions auditors to be a valued business advisor with respect to accounting matters to international companies.

While it is less common for companies to focus on and articulate their expectations in the area of business advice than in the area of the specific audit requirements discussed above, it is no less critical to a successful and valued relationship between the company and their auditors. It is also common practice for the auditors to present the audit committee with a management letter at the conclusion of the audit.

Typical areas where business advice might be sought include:

- Internal controls
- Cash management and treasury matters
- Management reporting and monitoring
- Stock options and other forms of incentive compensation
- Inventory management and accounting
- Business combinations (acquisitions)

The distinction between business advice that can be expected as a normal outgrowth of the audit process and tax projects that are discussed below is normally the amount of incremental time required on the part of the audit firm. Advice or recommendations to *consider* various courses of action generally flow from knowledge gained through the audit and prior experiences. Recommendations to *implement* specific courses of action or changes usually require a specific additional commitment of the audit firm's resources and would be considered a separate project.

(iii) Performance Evaluation. During the course of performing an audit, the auditors will work closely with finance, accounting, and internal audit personnel at all significant operations. The extent to which management wishes to receive an evaluation from the auditor regarding the personnel they have worked with varies from company to company. In some cases, management wishes only to be informed of extreme negative performance, that is, a negative exception basis. In other cases, management wants more thorough reporting of both positive and negative performance. Further, expectations may differ from operation to operation within a single company. In all cases, evaluating and reporting on performance of individuals is a delicate undertaking and must be performed with great care. Again, the company's expectations in this area must be clearly addressed. It is now required for the company

to also evaluate the auditor in accordance with the Sarbanes-Oxley Act previously discussed above.

(iv) Taxes. As part of the audit of the group financial statements, the auditors are required to determine whether or not the impact of taxes, both income and other taxes, has been presented fairly in those financial statements. Beyond this requirement, and depending upon the company's internal expertise in the area of taxes as well as other factors, the company may wish to involve the external audit firm in a variety of other tax planning and tax compliance activities of the company. These activities may vary from country to country and may also cover employees' personal taxes, particularly in the case of employees on international assignments.

While many companies receive significant tax services from their auditors, that is not always the case. If the engagement of auditors is to include such tax services on a recurring basis, the company's expectations should be clearly delineated.

(b) Communications. As indicated in the introduction to this chapter, communications are the most critical success factor for international companies in selecting and maintaining a relationship with their auditors. The sections, which follow, discuss four aspects of communications, namely participants in the communications process, content, form, and frequency.

(i) Participants in the Communications Process. Communications between an international company and their auditors is a "many to many" process. From the company's perspective, the board of directors, audit committee, chief executive officers, and/or managing directors, financial management, including finance and accounting officers, and legal counsel are all-important in the communications process. Communications are with individuals in the above positions or with those responsibilities at both the parent company and subsidiary or significant operating unit level.

From the auditor's perspective, the key individual in the communications process is normally the overall engagement partner at the parent company level. However, the tax and other partners who may be serving the company at the parent company level as well as the partners serving subsidiary companies or major operating units are also important to the process. In fact, a major challenge faced by the overall engagement partner on a day-to-day basis is to keep abreast of important communications between the auditors and the company on a worldwide basis.

Effective communications between auditors in various locations serving an international company involve a balancing act in meeting the apparently divergent needs of a multinational holding company and its subsidiaries. This balancing act may involve either professional issues or client relations matters. International companies must make their expectations in this regard very clear. The ultimate responsibility of the auditor normally must be to the parent or holding company. The needs of the parent company and the auditors' responsibility to the parent company must be paramount.

(ii) Content. The content or nature of communications between international companies and their auditors varies from statutorily required opinions and formal recommendations on matters of internal control to a variety of matters that assist in maintaining an effective working relationship. This latter area includes:

- Engagement letters
- Plans for the audit

- New financial reporting and accounting matters
- Business advice, including changes in taxation and governmental regulation
- Personnel evaluations
- Progress reports and significant matters noted during the conduct of the audit

It is fundamental to an audit that the auditors have access to all relevant information underlying the company's financial statements. Beyond this, it is very important that the company communicate their expectations in all areas discussed in this section clearly and succinctly to their auditors if they expect their expectations to be fully satisfied.

(iii) Form. At the heart of communications between a company and its auditors are written reports or presentations. The value of written communications in avoiding miscommunications cannot be overestimated. Even in meetings that feature oral presentations and discussion, written communications often form the underlying basis for the meeting.

The combination of significant distances and differences in time zones has long been recognized as a challenge to effective communications in international companies and among the auditors serving those companies. To overcome this hurdle, financial management from the parent company together with the engagement partner and managers for the parent company have visited major subsidiaries and led meetings with the subsidiaries' financial and operating management and engagement partners and managers serving the subsidiary. This form of communication can be characterized by viewing the parent company financial management and engagement partners/managers as the hub of a wheel and the visits to the subsidiaries as spokes on the wheel.

More recently, many international companies and their auditors have conducted meetings on a worldwide or regional basis that bring both financial management and auditors from all subsidiaries together with the financial management and auditors from the parent company level. While such meetings entail the commitment of time and economic resources, the advantages to be gained are numerous.

From the company's perspective, the opportunity to:

- Describe their business vision and discuss their specific needs
- Address the priority issues, opportunities, and threats to be faced both in the short term and in the long term
- Discuss the related actions planned or underway
- Outline the methods used to measure success
- Relate what is expected from their auditors

From the auditor's perspective, the opportunity to:

- Gain insights into the company's needs
- Express their perspective on controls over the financial reporting process
- Secure feedback on the company's expectations
- Improve communications with the company's decision makers
- Promote the exchange of ideas and experiences
- Subdue time and space barriers

These meetings can be viewed as the rim on the wheel discussed in the preceding paragraph. Personal acquaintance can go a long way to removing the barriers to effective communication.

(iv) Frequency. As with the nature of communications, the frequency of some communications between a company and its auditors is required by professional standards or statutory regulation and the frequency of such communications (e.g., audit committee meetings) follows naturally from the audit process. With respect to other communications, the expectation is normally to avoid surprises. This means early communication of any matters that could present a significant problem for the company or jeopardize the timeliness or success of completion of the services being provided. The watchword for both the company and auditors should be "when in doubt, communicate." While the volume of communications encountered through the in-basket (either paper or electric) and phone mail can be daunting, that will never be a satisfactory explanation in hindsight for the failure to communicate an important matter on a timely basis.

(c) Consistency of Service. With few exceptions, companies seek a consistently high level of service from their auditors, both over time and at all locations around the world where the companies are being served. However, it is useful to recognize the factors that can impact achieving a consistent high level of service.

First and foremost is a commitment on the part of both the company and the auditors to a consistent high level of service. The most able audit organization in the world will have difficulty overcoming a severe lack of cooperation from an international company. Responsiveness to the needs of the auditors, whether they be for access to key individuals, information, or answers to questions raised is crucial to the auditor's success in consistently delivering high quality services.

Another factor that must be considered in establishing an expectation for a consistent level of service worldwide is the availability of top quality people in some parts of the world. For a variety of reasons, international companies may have significant operations in areas of the world where the supply of well-trained financial personnel is extremely limited. This can impact both the company and the auditors in those locations. Traditionally, both parties have sought to address this situation by sending individuals from areas where there is an ample supply of financial expertise to those locations where there is not. While this may meet the immediate need, the approach is also not without its drawbacks. Specifically, it is difficult to assimilate the national culture and business environment in these locations quickly. It may not by possible for the expatriates to gain acceptance into the business community with the insights and understandings that such acceptance brings, except over a fairly long period of time.

Both with respect to consistency over time and consistency from location to location, a critical element is feedback from the company to the auditors on their performance. Simply put, the auditors need to know, for better or for worse, how they're doing. The company should commit to providing feedback on a periodic basis that is consistent in coverage with the scope of services being provided by the auditors. While the specific performance measures to be included in the feedback may vary from company to company, they typically would include subjects such as:

- Sensitivity to the company's needs
- Business perspective

- Technical knowledge and expertise
- Proactivity
- Coordination of services
- Engagement team characteristics
- Fees and cost control
- Communication

As already mentioned, the last performance measure, communication, is probably most important.

31.3 ASSESSING THE QUALIFICATIONS OF THE CANDIDATES.

There are numerous criteria that can be used to assess the qualifications of the firms being considered for selection as auditors. Some of the criteria may be assessed fairly objectively and it is likely that different companies assessing the same firm of auditors would make a similar assessment. In other cases, the assessments are very subjective and different companies might make very different assessments of the same firm. A company's assessment of a particular firm may differ substantially based on the engagement team proposed by that firm.

It is almost always useful to adopt a relatively straightforward quantitative framework for assessing a firm's qualifications. Such a framework might entail rating each of the criteria for each of the firms on a scale of, say, 1 to 5 or 1 to 10. A further step would be to group the criteria into those that are most important, of moderate importance, or of lesser importance, and assign a rating of 1, 2, or 3 to the criteria within those groups, respectively. As useful as the quantitative framework may be in focusing the assessment of the firms, it must be recognized that the final decision may come down to a subjective choice between the top competitors. That choice may not be the firm with the best quantitative score.

(a) Criteria.

The criteria discussed in the following paragraphs form the basis for the selection of auditors by international companies. The criteria are not necessarily presented in the order of their importance, as that is a relative judgment and, in all likelihood, will differ from company to company. However, in virtually every case, each of these criteria should be taken into consideration as well as others that individual companies may identify.

(i) Experience in Serving International Companies.

Experience in serving similarly configured international companies is invaluable to auditors in providing high quality service to a new international company client. This is important both for the offices serving the parent company as well as for offices serving subsidiaries or other major operating units, or in the vernacular of audit firms, both the office sending instructions and the office receiving instructions.

Further, the partners and managers assigned to the engagement teams at both the parent company level and the subsidiary level should have verifiable experience serving international companies in their particular industries. While it may not be the most important factor, it is, nonetheless, very desirable for the engagement team to have experience both as a team sending instructions as well as a team receiving instructions. Such experience clearly benefits effective communications and the anticipation of potential problems in carrying out their respective assignments.

Relevant direct international experience is a definite plus for all partners and managers serving an international company. Such experience includes tours of duty in locations outside of one's home country as well as specific client assignments of more than brief duration outside one's home country. Such tours and assignments should benefit the engagement team members and, hence, the company immeasurably in understanding the business environments in different countries and in becoming aware of the impact the national cultures have on how business is conducted.

Foreign language proficiency is desirable. In fact, since international companies often operate in many countries, numerous languages are encountered and multiple foreign language capability would be very beneficial. Unfortunately, individuals' foreign language capabilities are often limited to a single additional language at the day-to-day working level. The prevalence of English as a common language in business mitigates some of the potential language problems. In some situations (e.g., Japanese and Chinese), the use of interpreters is fairly common. If the interpreters have worked with auditors frequently they can compensate for what otherwise would be, literally, "lost in translation." With the significant increase in the amount of non-U.S. companies that have been entering the U.S. capital markets, certain professional service firms have established practices of placing U.S. trained professionals in various locations to serve these non-U.S. companies. Oftentimes, these professionals assist the local offices with providing "invaluable on the ground quality service" to engagement teams serving subsidiaries of U.S. companies in those locations.

(ii) Coverage of Company Locations. An audit firm's ability to deliver quality service is directly related to whether they have full time partners and staff in close proximity to an international company's subsidiaries or other significant operating units. The option of flying professional staff in to provide recurring services is rarely successful. Obtaining and maintaining a deep understanding of the company's business operations and being fully responsive to the company's needs are quite difficult on a fly-in basis. Such arrangements should be avoided wherever possible.

(iii) Knowledge of the Company's Industries. Knowledge of the company's industries rarely rates below the highest level when considering criteria for the selection of auditors. Such knowledge is vital to assessing risk in the audit process and understanding management's perspective in addressing issues and challenges they face.

If the auditors understand the critical success factors in the company's industries as well as the company's specific operations, they are better able to assess audit risk with respect to the company's reported financial position, results of operations, and cash flows. Further, this knowledge contributes directly to the auditor's ability to provide valued business advice, as discussed above.

It is not reasonable to expect the same depth and breadth of industry and business knowledge at every company location around the world. However, the auditors should have or be willing to relocate such experience to directly serve the parent company. In addition, it is important to identify backup capability within the auditor's organization in the event that the company should need to draw on that capability for whatever reason.

(iv) Communications Capabilities. As stressed throughout this chapter, communications are the most important link for international companies in having a successful relationship with their auditors. Electronic mail, facsimile and phone mail communi-

cations tools have become commonplace for virtually all organizations. They have contributed to vastly improved communications as compared to years ago. The ability to send electronic documents, analyses, and files between the company and their auditors and between the auditors serving the parent company and those serving the subsidiaries and vice versa should be expected. The ability to communicate in this fashion enhances both the timeliness of communication as well as the efficiency of the audit process.

While video conferencing has not been used extensively to date in communications between companies and their auditors at various locations around the world, the audit organization's views and expectations on that communications form should be assessed. In light of the expense and time involved in extensive global travel and in view of the effectiveness of video conferencing, particularly for people who have worked together on a face-to-face basis in the past, video conferencing capability should be carefully considered by international companies in working with their auditors in the future.

(v) Working with Internal Auditors. For international companies who have the expectation that their external auditors will rely on the work of internal auditors to more than insignificant extent, it is important to assess the external audit firms' approach to relying on internal audit and their track record in that regard. This assessment should be specific to the particular engagement team proposed at the parent company level. Further, if the company has internal audit activity both in the parent country and in other countries around the world, the external auditor's record should be evaluated with respect to working with internal audit in a comparable manner.

Companies may also wish to consider whether the external auditors are familiar with the professional standards promulgated by internal audit professional organizations and whether the external auditor could evaluate and make recommendations for the quality of internal audit practice in the company.

(vi) Continuity. Knowledge of the company, its industries and businesses on the part of the service providers is a key ingredient. Rarely can such knowledge be gained in the course of a single year's audit engagement. In fact, experience indicates at least two years' experience is normally necessary for the partners serving a company to be in a position to provide the greatest value to the company. Professional standards in some countries limit the period of time that professionals can serve a specific company, generally five to seven years for partners, (see new U.S. requirements in section 31.2), and other periods for managers or other professional staff. Within these limitations, it generally behooves a company to keep the engagement partners for as long as possible and to obtain a "fresh look" periodically through the rotation of other professionals assigned to the engagement team.

Again, companies should seek verification of an audit firm's track record in providing continuous service at the partner and manager level from existing clients, particularly international companies in similar situations.

(vii) Responsiveness and Quality of Advice and Recommendations. Over time, the evaluation of the success of a relationship with an audit firm will often come down to judgment about the responsiveness and quality of the advice and recommendations received from the auditors. There are several factors which are considered in making those judgments:

- Early identification of issues or opportunities and communication of those matters to the audit committee and appropriate members of the company's management
- Timely and appropriate responses to specific needs:
  - if the need is urgent, the response reflects the urgency
  - bringing the right resources within the audit firm to bear and getting the benefit of that firm's whole knowledge base
- Quality of both written and oral reports and recommendations:
  - Demonstrate an in-depth knowledge of the specific circumstances and the overall business
  - Concise and understandable
  - Sensitive to company's culture and style
  - Represent sound advice

Assessing such factors during the initial selection process requires reviewing actual reports issued (names deleted where appropriate) by the audit firms and discussions with clients of the firms. These discussions should include both existing and former clients, as the latter may have some very enlightening and sometimes surprising perspectives on the responsiveness and quality criteria.

(viii) Plans for Serving the Company. The starting point for providing professional services to an international company is the preparation of an overall or strategic plan for those services. Such a plan is imperative for effectively and efficiently serving a worldwide company. Each final candidate in the selection process should prepare and present their strategic plan to the company.

There are several aspects of such plans that the company's evaluation should be directed to:

- Does the plan reflect and respond to the expectations of the company as discussed earlier in this chapter?
- Does the plan demonstrate an understanding of the company's operations, including business strategies and operating plans?
- Does the plan reflect reasonable assessments of the relative levels of business and audit risk associated with various company operations?
- Are financial reporting and accounting areas involving a significant degree of subjectivity identified?
- Does the plan include a commitment of professional resources commensurate with the services to be provided?
- Are the preliminary decisions about the overall audit approach at the parent company and significant subsidiaries or other operating units consistent with the assessments of business and audit risk, control environment and information systems environment? Are those decisions responsive to specific company expectations?

The depth of knowledge obtained by auditors during a proposal process will be substantially less than after having provided significant services to the company. Nevertheless, the strategic plan presented during the proposal should demonstrate persuasively to the company that the audit firm is proceeding on a sound basis. Further, it should confirm the company's assessment of the understanding and meeting of the company's needs, as well as the responsiveness and quality of the audit firm's oral and written reports or presentations referred to above.

(ix) Chemistry. The most subjective criterion involved in the assessment process is determining how well the proposed engagement team fits with the international company's culture and style. It must be recognized that over time members of both the engagement team and company management will change and a fit for today may not be a fit for tomorrow.

To properly assess this criterion requires that quality time be spent with the proposed engagement team members during the assessment process. While part of this time may be represented by formal meetings and discussion, often informal contracts provide a very good basis for making the assessment. Traveling with engagement team members to visit subsidiaries or significant company operations around the world is frequently a good way to foster such informal contracts.

Engagement team members should demonstrate a healthy respect for the company's culture and style. This aspect encompasses interpersonal relations, conversational language, punctuality, dress, social contacts, format for meetings, enthusiasm, and energy level, and so on. Again, in the initial selection of auditors, the most useful source of such information is from current and former clients. Particularly with respect to this criterion, the evaluation should be specific to the proposed engagement team members.

Many international companies have a large number of partners and managers from the audit firm providing service on a worldwide basis. It is useful to have the managing director and financial management at significant subsidiaries also assess the chemistry of their local engagement team partners and managers. However, the key focus should be on the parent company engagement team partners and managers because the involvement with them will be the most extensive and they will set the tone for the worldwide engagement teams. In fact, the parent company engagement partner should have considerable influence over the initial selection and any subsequent changes in the partners serving the company on a worldwide basis. The parent company engagement partner has overall responsibility for the performance of the worldwide team.

(x) Cost. The competitiveness of the marketplace for professional services provided by audit firms is well known to all participants, worldwide. The fees paid to audit firms by an international company will, first and foremost, reflect the expectations discussed in the previous section of this chapter and will vary considerably from international company to international company. Within that context, audit firms are very competitive, both at the time of initial selection as well as on a continuing basis. This latter point reflects the fact that, while audit firms realize it is costly, particularly in terms of time, for international companies to change audit firms, such changes have and will continue to take place if the value received by the international companies is not commensurate with the fees being charged.

Whatever the level of the international company's expectations with respect to its auditors, the efficiency with which the services are delivered will be strongly influenced by the coordination and cooperation between the company and the auditors. Such coordination and cooperation are important not just with respect to the internal auditing activity, but with respect to operating as well as financial and accounting personnel. The lack of availability of key operating personnel to provide the necessary understanding of the company's operations and explanations for the financial impacts of those operations can significantly affect the efficiency of the audit process.

Historically, fees for audit services were generally negotiated and agreed upon by financial management and the engagement partners at the individual operating unit level. Such an approach had the advantage from the company's perspective of being able to match closely the value of services received with the fees paid for those services. However, across large international companies, apparent anomalies in fee levels could result between operating units that would appear to require similar levels of service. See section 31.2 for requirements under the Sarbanes-Oxley Act to have the audit committee have exclusive responsibility for retention, compensation and oversight of the external auditors.

More recently, many international companies have negotiated and agreed upon a single worldwide fee. Negotiations normally were between the financial management at the corporate or parent company level and the audit firm's engagement partner at the comparable level. The global fee was then allocated by the audit firm to the various offices serving the international company. The global approach has the obvious benefit of overall cost control but also entails the risk of not fairly reflecting circumstances and differences in individual operating units.

An example of the latter can occur in highly inflationary countries. In those countries, rates of inflation do not necessarily correspond to the devaluation of the local currency versus hard currencies at the official exchange rates. Typically, companies have tended to fix the audit fees in those countries in a hard currency. If the devaluation does not properly match the inflation, the impact on the audit firm in that country can be severe and unwarranted. In such circumstances, it is desirable, if not imperative, to allow local adjustment of the fee after the services have been provided and inflation/devaluation factors are known in order to maintain a productive working relationship between the auditors and the company.

In the final analysis, there are three questions that audit committees of international companies must answer in judging the fees paid to auditors:

- Is the value received commensurate with the fee being paid?
- Are the fees reasonably competitive?
- Are the fees commensurate with the scope of work required?

If the answers to the first and third questions are no, the second question is not relevant. If the answers to the first and third questions are yes but the answer to the second question is no, the international company will undoubtedly seek an adjustment from their auditors. In all but rare cases, an appropriate adjustment will be agreed.

31.4 ESTABLISHING THE TERMS OF REFERENCE OR DELIVERABLES. The final step in the process is to formalize the terms of reference or deliverables in an engagement letter or memoranda of services to be provided by the audit firm selected.

(a) Rationale. While engagements have been undertaken by auditors on the basis of an oral or handshake agreement only, the extent and complexity of providing professional services to an international company requires more formal arrangements. The process of establishing expectations and assessing the qualifications of the firms normally involves considerable discussions over several weeks' time. The number of individuals involved in receiving services in an international company as well as the number of partners responsible for the delivery of services for the audit firm can be very large. Further, the individuals involved on both sides will, over time, change. In such circumstances, it is necessary to clarify through a written document the understandings that have been reached and thereby avoid misunderstandings of the intended arrangements at a later date.

(b) Content. All significant objective aspects of the company's expectations discussed in the first section of this chapter should be included in the terms of reference. Such items would include:

- Auditing standards to be complied with during the engagement
- All audit and related reports to be received
- Reliance on an anticipated coordination with internal audit and the accounting functions
- Tax projects, if applicable
- Timing of work and related reporting

The commitment of company resources for clerical and administrative support should also be clearly spelled out. Such assistance can be critical in meeting reporting deadlines and providing service in the most efficient manner possible.

Fee arrangements including the timing and amounts of billings, to whom bills should be submitted, any special approval requirements and payment terms should be included. While such matters may seem mundane, they can be a disruption to an otherwise strong working relationship between an international company and its auditors.

A final matter to consider for inclusion in the terms of reference is the company's plan for reviewing the performance of the audit firm. A brief description of the timing and focal points of the performance review will be useful to both parties. With respect to timing, a review should be performed after the first year. Taking the time to provide such feedback will be very beneficial to the audit firm and allow them to make what will inevitably be necessary corrections in their approach to serving the company. After the initial year, reviews every two or three years would be optimal.

31.5 CONCLUSION. Changing audit firms is time consuming and inherently inefficient with respect to at least the first (if not the second and third) annual audit after the change. International companies have more at risk in this regard because of the worldwide nature and extent of their needs.

As stated in this chapter, the keys to maintaining a successful relationship between an international company and its auditors, and thus avoiding a change, are:

- Clearly identified expectations
- Careful assessment of qualifications
- Thorough evaluation of performance
- Communications, communications, communications!

Valued, mutually beneficial relationships have historically been maintained by international companies and their auditors for decades. Adherence to the matters above are at the heart of those successful relationships.

In 2002, a newly designated International Auditing and Assurance Standards Board (IAASB), assumed responsibility from its predecessor, the International Auditing Practices Committee, for the promulgation of International Standards on Auditing (ISAs). The IAASB operates under the auspices of the International Federation of Accountants and is seeking to have the ISAs adopted by the European Union and to obtain the endorsement of the International Organization of Securities Commissions.

It is expected that in time underlying countries' auditing standards and the ISAs will be harmonized to a large extent and ISAs will be the required standards in many countries.

CHAPTER 32

INTERNAL AUDITING

Seymour Jones*

New York University

CONTENTS

32.1 INTRODUCTION. This chapter explains internal auditing, how it has evolved over the past 50 years, and how it must continue to evolve in the future to accommodate not only the changing business environment but the public impact on the auditing profession's independence when external auditors perform such services for audit clients. This chapter also emphasizes the internal audit function in international companies.

Factors such as business developments, and a history of financial disasters influence the public's internal audit expectations and hence development. While there is no worldwide generally accepted method of internal auditing, there is a growing body of knowledge about what internal auditing should encompass. The Institute of Internal Auditors (IIA) has made great progress in helping to develop a comprehensive body of knowledge about internal auditing.

Other factors, such as the location of a company's corporate headquarters influence management's view of the internal audit function. Branches and subsidiaries of foreign companies, even when located in another country, will follow corporate di-

*The author acknowledges the prior work on this chapter by Penelope A. Flugger and the assistance of the Internal Audit Services Group of PricewaterhouseCoopers.

rectives for internal auditing depending upon headquarter's policies for controlling foreign subsidiaries.

32.2 ROLE OF INTERNAL AUDITING IN BOTH NATIONAL AND INTERNATIONAL ENVIRONMENTS. The historic basic role of internal audit has been to test on an interim basis the operations of internal controls within a business organization to see that they are operating effectively and efficiently. The external auditors are also concerned with the effectiveness of internal controls because it is the primary basis on which they base their audit strategy, that is, the nature, timing and extent of their substantive audit tests. What are internal controls? In essence they are systems of checks and balances to determine whether management's policies and procedures are being carried out effectively, whether financial transactions are being reported properly, and whether the assets of the organization are being protected. Internal controls on an entity-wide basis consist of the "tone at the top," the accounting system, risk evaluation and monitoring by management.

An effective internal audit department became part of the overall internal control structure within an organization. It was important, therefore, to recognize that the internal auditors would not only be part of management but also a check on management. To achieve this objective it was recognized that a certain "independence" would be required of the internal audit function. Internal auditors function best when they are required to report directly to the Board of Directors and/or the Audit Committee of the Board of Directors. In many situations, the internal auditors report to both executive management and the Board and/or Audit Committee. When the internal audit functions properly its work may be relied on by the external auditors in developing their audit plan and in reducing their control testing in connection with their audit.

In the current post-Enron business environment it is imperative that internal auditors focus their attention on "tone at the top," that is, how top management conduct themselves with regard to policies of the organization including such matters as personal expenses, related-party transactions, and self-dealing. If top management does not observe policies with respect to protecting a company's assets, how can all of the employees be expected to comply with protective policies.

In the United States, the internal audit professional has grown from being a verifier of data and fraud identifier to being a member of the management team. The auditor is an active participant in the risk management process. For example, internal auditors are also used as active participants in acquisitions and divestitures because internal audit resources can be leveraged to avoid costly consultants' fees, identify potential problems, and prevent unnecessary expenditures. Auditors are also becoming "management advisors charged with developing new process flows and controls in the redesigned operation as well as gathering and reporting key performance information and monitoring operations stability during the transition."[1]

The internal auditing function can be executed in many ways. Some companies consider it essential for management trainees to spend time in internal audit if they are being groomed for management positions. For example, General Electric feels management trainees cannot advance within their company if they have not spent some time in the audit function. Some companies also consider the internal audit ex-

---

[1]Trampo, 1998.

perience a prerequisite to advancement. Truly progressive companies realize the value that internal audit brings to the management process.

Fortunately, the number of companies valuing the contributions being made by internal auditors is increasing. In the United States, the increased pressure on audit committees to provide independent reviews have in some cases led to greater recognition of the internal audit function.

There are distinct differences in internal audit practices between countries as well as companies, so it is difficult to generalize about internal audit practices globally or even within the United States. This is largely due to the different national context within which internal auditing operates. There is a relationship between how management perceives internal audit's role and the major area of internal audit work. In some countries, where management is reported to have a deeper understanding of the business value of internal auditing, operational audits are considered as important as financial audits and internal control reviews.

The scope of internal audit work also reflects the different business priorities in each country. In Japan, highly industrialized and heavily populated, internal auditors emphasize compliance audits that address environmental management, hazardous substances, and product and service safety. Australian businesses, however, have responded to increased competition by adopting a quality perspective in their attempt to provide customer value. As a result, internal auditors undertake a significant amount of quality systems audit work.[2]

For example, some companies still have their internal auditors function as detectives/verifiers. Auditors mainly count and reconcile financial records, and their work supports that of external accountants. Others have their internal auditors establish their programs in concert with public accountants' needs, but emphasis is also placed on helping management identify business risks and analyze cost–benefit trade-offs.

Internal auditing, also referred to as management auditing, is generally thought of as the periodic evaluation of internal controls and management efficiency and effectiveness. Early on, internal auditors focused on protection of company assets and the detection of fraud. As noted in the 1963 National Industrial Conference Board Report, "Auditors concentrated most of their attention on examination of financial records and on the verification of assets that were most easily appropriated. A popular idea among management people a generation ago was that the main purpose of an auditing program was to serve as a psychological deterrent against wrongdoing by other employees." [3]

The internal audit role has changed considerably, adapting to significant changes in the world of business. Technology has allowed many manual tasks to be automatically checked. Furthermore, businesses' need to curtail costs and increase efficiency took on greater importance. Cost versus benefit trade-off was quickly evident in management's expectations of the internal audit function. To offset the costs of attracting qualified individuals to the internal audit function, it was important for auditors to provide input valued by management, such as operational reviews.

The IIA best described the broad role of internal auditing in its 1957 Statement of Responsibilities of Internal Auditing. According to that publication, the management services provided by internal auditors include:

---

[2]Flescher, 1991.

[3]Id.

- Reviewing and appraising the soundness, adequacy, and application of accounting, financial, and operational controls
- Ascertaining the extent of compliance with established policies, plans, and procedures
- Ascertaining the extent to which organizational assets are accounted for and safe-guarded from losses of all kinds
- Ascertaining the reliability of accounting and other data developed within the organization
- Appraising the quality of performance in carrying out assigned responsibilities

There are various ways these responsibilities can be modified and executed. An internal auditor can have a large staff, located centrally or dispersed throughout the world. The staff can have numerous specialists for areas such as products, technology, or compliance requirements. Conversely, the audit staff can be mainly generalists that hire specialists via external auditors or consulting firms to provide required skills. Some companies have totally outsourced their internal audit function to external accounting firms. This trend is fueled by the growing interest in general outsourcing, the belief that public accountants have deep knowledge and skill in performing the audit function, and the realization that internal audit salaries may have to increase significantly to attract qualified individuals.

In recent years, the major accounting firms have created Internal Audit Services departments to service both audit clients and nonaudit clients in response to outsourcing needs of companies. However, there has grown to be a perception that the external audit function has compromised its independence (a key standard under generally accepted auditing standards) when it undertakes the internal audit function for an audit client. It has been alleged that as a result of such undertaking the external auditors become too closely associated with management of the company. Studies have indicated that users of financial statements, such as credit grantors have greater confidence in the independence of outside auditors, when they use different staffs for the external and internal audit functions. Nevertheless, the American Institute of Certified Public Accountants (AICPA), under pressure from the Securities and Exchange Commission (SEC) and the audit failure environment resulting from the Enron case and others, has set forth guidelines in its Interpretation 101-13 under Rule of Conduct 101, Extended Audit Services. These guidelines indicate that independence would not be impaired if the audit firm did not offer to act and does not act in a capacity equivalent to a member of client management or as an employee. Pressure still exists from regulators and congressional sources for public accounting firms to disassociate their internal audit services for publicly held audit clients. Nevertheless, it has been held by certain users of financial statements that benefits may be derived from having the external audit firm perform internal audit functions. Such benefits include greater understanding of the business and the key audit risks and therefore improved overall audit quality. Nevertheless,the Sarbanes-Oxley Act of 2002 prohibits the performance of internal audit services by audit firms for their public company audit clients. It is quite clear, however, that the major accounting firms will nevertheless continue to perform internal audit services for nonaudit clients and nonpublic companies.

Regardless of whether internal audit services are outsourced or handled internally, the role of internal audit must be sufficiently dynamic to accommodate the changing views of management, the need to provide continuous value and innovation, a focus on sensitivity to risk and controls, and an emphasis on business strategy. All of these requirements have forever changed the role of internal audit, and, consequently, the expectation gap between management and the internal audit function is narrowing as companies go through periods of dynamic growth and ever increasing change.

There is no one perfect way to execute the internal audit function internationally. Some companies are organized on a decentralized basis and employ local auditors for full-service branches that handle their own accounting. In such cases, the home office expects local management to handle all financial problems, including local inflation and changes in foreign exchange issues, in reliance on the knowledge of local management to plan for all contingencies. Accordingly, top management and audit committees believe that they are best served by local auditors who understand the local environment and the related customs and regulations. The drawback to this method involves a more restrictive advancement pattern for internal auditors hired locally.

Some international organizations have centralized control over their foreign operations to the extent that key financial decisions, including planning for inflation and foreign exchange issues, are dictated and controlled by the home office. In such situations the internal control function is centralized, and the internal audit function is similarly centralized or regional auditors are employed for this function. As a result, more experienced personnel and/or specialists in areas of foreign exchange planning may be employed. However, the drawback to this methodology is a lack of understanding of local customs, language, and related issues.

It is evident that either of the foregoing techniques can be successful. It all depends on how top management enforces its own policies. Indeed, a system that works in one market or under one type of management may not work for another.

The impact of technology has been pervasive. In the world of internal auditing, auditors have to become proficient in technology. They also have to be able to audit new applications, become experts in testing data security, and use of audit application modules, and teach other auditors how to take advantage of the data that technology makes available.

32.3 HISTORY. It was not until the late nineteenth and early twentieth centuries that the internal auditing profession began to develop to support the growth of business. Surprisingly, the growth of internal auditing actually took place outside the United States. Many European countries enacted regulations that referred specifically to internal audit functions and requirements. One of the early U.S. users of the internal audit function was the railroad; with operations spread out across the country, owners could not oversee daily operations and sought help.

What did these internal auditors do? It varied, as there were no standards or guidelines. The needs and views of their employers, more than the generally accepted practices of a profession, shaped their actual day-to-day activities. In fact, anyone could sign on to be an internal auditor. There were neither generally accepted qualifications nor professional standards. Early auditors were verifiers of assets, reconciling inventory and cash to accounting records. Some companies concentrated auditors' attention on ensuring that rules and regulations were being followed. In many cases, internal auditors concentrated on investigating frauds, an initial foray into what is now known as forensic accounting.

Forensic accountants/auditors tend to work in a difficult environment. People do not like being accused of wrongdoing, nor do they like being investigated for wrongdoing. Auditors are constantly challenged and put on the defensive. It can result in a situation that is perceived to have no long-term benefits, unless one uncovers all the facts to convict someone or recover missing assets. Conversely, the satisfaction of discovering incriminating facts can be enormous.

Since early on, internal auditors as well as external auditors have held that the detection of fraud is not their responsibility. However, the external auditors had to materially change their views in April 1997 when Statement on Auditing Standard (SAS) No. 82 was effected. SAS No. 82, "Consideration of Fraud in a Financial Statement Audit," recognizes that, while management is responsible for the prevention and detection of fraud, auditors are responsible for minimizing the risk of fraud. Auditors have to concern themselves with the control environment and the steps taken to monitor that environment. They have to be skeptical. This essentially conforms to the role they are expected to assume in implementing the Committee on Sponsoring Organizations (COSO) guidelines discussed below.

The IIA outlines the internal auditor's responsibility for the detection of fraud in their "Standards for the Professional Practice of Internal Auditing" as follows:

> In conducting an audit assignment, the internal auditors' responsibilities for detecting fraud are to:
>
> (a) Have sufficient knowledge of fraud to be able to identify indicators that fraud may have been committed. This knowledge includes the need to know the characteristics of fraud, the techniques used to commit fraud, and the types of fraud associated with the activities audited.
>
> (b) Be alert to opportunities, such as control weaknesses, that could allow fraud. If significant control weaknesses are detected, additional tests conducted by internal auditors should include tests directed toward identification of other indicators of fraud. Some examples of indicators are unauthorized transactions, override of controls, unexplained pricing exemptions, and unusually large product losses. Internal auditors should recognize that the presence of more than one indicator at any one time increases the probability that fraud may have occurred.
>
> (c) Evaluate the indicators that fraud may have been committed and decide whether any further action is necessary or whether an investigation should be recommended.
>
> (d) Notify the appropriate authorities within the organization if a determination is made that there are sufficient indicators of the commission of a fraud to recommend an investigation.

Internal auditors are not expected to have knowledge equivalent to that of a person whose primary responsibility is detecting and investigating fraud. Also, audit practices alone, even when carried out with due professional care, do not guarantee that fraud will be detected.

During the twentieth century, the aspects of a "true profession" began to develop. Auditors began to concentrate much more on management controls and preventive measures rather than investigative techniques. The difference is simply that detective measures assess after the fact, whereas preventive measures consider what are available alternatives to prevent that occurrence. There are a number of cost–benefit tradeoffs that auditors are expected to bring to bear when problems are identified. In early times, auditors felt that they just had to identify problems without offering solutions. That has changed. As members of the management team, auditors have learned to help managers consider the alternatives.

It is fair to say that the auditor of the early twentieth century still served as an in-house policeman of sorts. Internal auditors might discover fraud and defalcations more quickly than external auditors could. The mere existence of the audit function and the threat of the arrival of the internal auditors were, in many instances, viewed as a strong deterrent to anyone who might think of misappropriation.

In the early 1940s, the changing U.S. regulatory environment began to change the internal auditors' responsibilities. They began to be viewed as an arm of management, that is, someone who could identify actions needed to improve operating controls that would also reduce waste and improve efficiency.

At the time, two events in the United States helped to elevate the status of the internal auditing profession. The first was a book on the internal audit profession by Victor J. Brink. The second, while subtler in effect, was the establishment of the IIA.

The IIA's mission is to be the primary professional association, organized on a worldwide basis, dedicated to the promotion and development of the practice of internal auditing.

The IIA is committed to:

- Providing, on an international scale, comprehensive professional development activities, standards for the practice of internal auditing, and certification
- Researching, disseminating, and promoting to its members and to the public throughout the world, knowledge and information concerning internal auditing, including internal control and related subjects
- Establishing meetings worldwide in order to educate members and others as to the practice of internal auditing as it exists in various countries throughout the world
- Bring together internal auditing and promoting education in the field of internal auditing

This recognition of the profession was supported by initiatives that were a cornerstone of the overall World War II effort—efficiency and effectiveness. These were two objectives that the internal audit profession were asked to foster in corporate America. Because of our nation's emphasis on productivity, auditors shifted the emphasis of their programs from what were considered financial audits to what is now known as *operational audits.* As a result, management began to develop an understanding of what the internal audit function could accomplish as well as an appreciation of how its activities could contribute to business success. The idea that the internal audit profession could contribute to business success did more for the profession then many fully appreciate.

After the war years, the profession continued to develop and grow, partially as a result of internal audits' perceived benefits and partially as a result of the increasing cost of the external audit function. Internal auditors were viewed as a vehicle for reducing or controlling external audit costs. In addition, the regulatory emphasis on corporate governance enhanced the prestige of the internal audit function. Internal auditing received its greatest support in the bank regulatory area and in those industries subject to Department of Defense reviews (e.g., aerospace). The litigious U.S. environment prompted audit committees and boards of directors to rely on internal auditors to aid them in protecting themselves from charges of not being diligent with respect to executing their duties.

In 1977 the U.S. Congress passed the Foreign Corrupt Practices Act (FCPA).

While the main purpose of this legislation was to make bribery or facilitating payments to foreign officials illegal, it had a number of other effects. The legislation stressed the importance of internal controls and the documentation of policies and procedures with the objective of detecting illegal payments. The excuse that "management did not know" was no longer acceptable because the law said you had to have a system that would let you know. The increased liability led many organizations to increase the size of their internal audit staffs and to pay more attention to the latter's recommendations. Some of this was window dressing encouraged by legal counsel, but many auditors took advantage of the law to improve their own company's understanding of the need for a corporate code of conduct and general documentation.

In 1987, the Treadway Commission report was issued. The Commission's official name was the National Committee on Fraudulent Financial Reporting. The Committee was a defensive measure on the part of the U.S. accounting profession that feared that Congress might enact harsh legislation as a result of a number of corporate failures related to fraudulent financial reporting. Major conclusions of the Treadway Commission were that (1) every public company should have an internal audit function, and (2) there should be a corporate audit committee made up of nonmanagement directors. These conclusions enhanced the image of the internal audit profession and resulted in more emphasis being placed on the internal audit function.

The Treadway Commission was supported by the five major accounting organizations and became known as COSO (the Committee of Sponsoring Organizations). The Commission's recommendations included the following:

> The Commission recommends that the organizations sponsoring the Commission work together to integrate the various internal control concepts and definitions and to develop a common reference point. This guidance would build on the Commission's recommendations, help public companies judge the effectiveness of their internal controls, and thus help public companies improve their internal control systems. The sponsoring organizations should determine the most appropriate means for providing the additional guidance.

COSO eventually came out with a document, "Internal Control—Integrated Framework." This pioneering document put down in one place a consensus on what constituted a framework for internal controls. It had a significant impact on the auditing profession because of the clear picture it gave as to management's responsibilities for controls. Prior to this document, many business managers argued that they could delegate their responsibilities for internal controls to internal auditors. They contended that the blame for failures was on the auditors for not reporting a missing control.

Added importance was attributed to this document when the national Sentencing Guidelines made explicit financial penalties that individuals and corporations would be subject to for not establishing the right control environment. Specifically, failure to establish the proper environment exposed individuals and corporations to a doubling and more of fines.

During 1999, after much pressure from the Securities and Exchange Commission (SEC), various organizations changed their requirements for audit committees. Essentially, such committees were in substance expected to exercise a responsible oversight function. While none of the literature specifically referred to the assistance that audit committees should seek from internal auditors, in those companies with existing internal audit functions, the internal auditors are becoming trusted advisors to the audit committee of the board of directors.

32.4 HOW CORPORATE AMERICA AND EXTERNAL AUDITORS ACTUALLY VIEW THE INTERNAL AUDIT FUNCTION. Views as how internal auditors can assist management in meeting the requirements of regulatory bodies, such as the SEC, the Department of Defense, and the banking regulators (i.e., the Federal Reserve, the Comptroller of the Currency, the Federal Deposit Insurance Corporation, and numerous state regulatory agencies) have been rapidly evolving. As banking regulators have been constrained from growing their own budgets, they have put pressure on financial institutions to improve the quality of their internal audit functions. In conjunction with these efforts, external accountants have informed cost-conscientious managers that better internal audit functions enable the former to reduce their efforts and, accordingly, the fees they charge. There have been numerous situations where this has indeed been borne out. However, there are those who argue that this has not been substantiated. It is quite possible that the increased use of internal auditors for other management functions reduce their time spent on testing the system of internal control and therefore the ability of external auditors to rely on the internal audit work to effectively reduce the scope of their own audit testing of the various systems.

The task of substituting internal audit efforts for external audit work has been more successful with external regulators who do not have the financial and staffing resources that corporations do. Regulators have put pressure on corporations to put more money into their internal audit functions. This allows regulators to focus on the effectiveness of the internal auditor's work versus performing the work themselves. In fact, more recently, bank regulators have asked that the internal audit work not be performed by the external auditors lest their independence be impaired.

As indicated previously, both external and internal auditors have argued that they should not be responsible for the detection of fraud. They feel that management has a comparative advantage here. Differences of opinion notwithstanding, the question of fraud became significant in the 1980s. Frauds that drew widespread attention related to savings and loan associations, commercial banks, defense industries, as well as insider trading activities. In the public view, these frauds were so blatant that it was difficult to understand how the auditors could distance themselves from them.

Accordingly, auditors have adjusted their view on fraud. However, if they focus totally on fraud, auditors will lose their value and credibility. Nevertheless, they are resident experts that can help managers understand how frauds occur. As the conscience of the organization, auditors are the best investigators of fraud. The biggest mistake is to have a manager responsible for the area where fraud occurs, overseeing the investigation. From a legal defense, as well as a corporate message, the independence issue comes into play.

The following discussion provides a hypothetical case. The number one hotshot trader who has made millions for the firm is having a bad month. He fraudulently adjusts his positions to hide the fact that he is having losses in the month that the compensation committee is setting bonuses. His intention is to adjust his reported results next month so that the firm is not out of money and his compensation is not adversely impacted. If his manager reviews the facts and realizes how difficult it may be to replace the trader, he may look the other way.

Should not some independent individuals, such as the internal auditors, who are executing the corporate culture gather the facts here? Managers have to be consistent in their signaling of corporate messages. If the trader were retained, the informal message would be "You can get away with anything if you make money for the firm." Consequently, it will be harder to keep drawing the line on what is acceptable behavior and what is not. This is a classic case of "tone at the top," to be monitored and reported on by the internal audit staff directly to the board of directors and/or its audit committee. Unfortunately, a recent international case involving the mismanagement of derivatives by an Asian trader was reported to the board of directors in London but the board failed to act. The internal auditors had nevertheless done their job.

The fraud challenge presents internal auditors with opportunities. Proper response to the challenge sells control recommendations. In the long run, proper response by the internal auditors and the organization not only builds professional credibility but also helps organizations to sidestep dangers and significant losses. The auditor who chooses to be part of the fraud solution can look forward to continuing professional challenge and a firm place in the management structure of an organization.

32.5 REGULATION AND THE LACK THEREOF IN THE INTERNAL AUDIT PROFESSION. The requirements for entering the internal audit profession might still be unclear. It takes a special person to be successful in this profession and to really enjoy it. Although it takes a unique person to do an outstanding job in this area, not all companies appreciate that. The truly visionary company does. However, there are still a number of companies who keep their internal audit function only because it is a necessary cost of doing business in the eyes of the regulators.

While the IIA has done a wonderful job of advancing the profession, there are still a number of individuals and companies who do not subscribe to the standards the IIA has published. There is no requirement, such as is true of the public accounting profession, that one must be certified or be subject to peer review to function in an internal audit capacity. However, the IIA has undertaken research to suggest a body of knowledge that is necessary to be successful.

As of March 1, 1999, the IIA's Competency Framework for Internal Auditing (CFIA) became available. A significant finding of the study is the need for a universal definition of the profession. Associations worldwide report that a great deal of uncertainty exists about the total number of practicing internal auditors. This is partly attributed to variations in definitions of internal auditing around the globe. This lack of definition also hampers management's understanding of, and respect for, the profession and its practitioners. In recognition of the need for a formal definition, after the formal exposure process, the board of directors of the IIA adopted the following definition of internal auditing:

> Internal auditing is an independent, objective assurance and consulting activity designed to add value and improve an organization's operations. It helps an organization accomplish its objectives by bringing a systematic, disciplined approach to evaluate and improve the effectiveness of risk management, control, and governance processes.

Should there be competency standards? The author believes we should have guidelines and an authoritative source to help identify what is needed in the function. Professional certification might indeed be an answer. The arguments here are no different from the overall argument about the ability of our current testing methodologies to identify the best in class.

32.6 BOARD OF DIRECTORS/AUDIT COMMITTEES AND THE INTERNAL AUDITORS. As directors have become aware of their increased liability to protect shareholders, they have often looked for sources to provide them with independent assurance that the information they receive from management is fair and accurate. At first, directors turned to the external independent accountants. However, as they became aware that external accountants really focus on a much higher level of materiality in connection with their audit of the annual financial statements, directors have increasingly turned to internal auditors. The apparent conflict of interest here is that management hires the internal auditors, compensates them, and evaluates them.

Can individuals who report to management really report on management, especially if the report may not be favorable? The answer should be yes, of course they can based on professionalism. The challenge to corporate governance structure in business today is to maintain the proper "tone at the top." That is where there is a real risk exposure. Boards of directors need to ask themselves whether "Enron" could happen in their own companies and an essential protective device is to have an active aggressive internal audit function that can assist the Boards in monitoring the internal control environment in their companies. This is particularly true today because the Sarbanes-Oxley Act of 2002 requires management certification of financial statements and internal control reporting.

Auditors who bring very negative information have to be strong and have a good set of facts. The difficulty with the facts, except in a case of outright fraud, is that they can be viewed differently. Auditors can present evidence that management does not implement controls previously agreed to. Management can contend that they did not implement the controls for cost or reorganization reasons, to name a few. Audit committee chairmen need to understand the conflict that exists if management controls salaries, budgets, and promotions of the internal auditors who are expected to report independently.

The IIA in response has provided a number of tools on the issue of ethics. There is a Code of Ethics, a Standard for the Professional Practice of Internal Auditing, and a position paper on whistle-blowing and consultation with peers. To quote the IIA, "Serving as the conscience of an organization is one facet of the internal auditor's function. A strong sense of ethics is required to fulfill this responsibility. Like any skill or ability, a strong sense of ethics requires training and understanding. Regular reviews of the basic tenets of feedback is a mechanism that can prevent the pendulum of ethics from being either in the black/white only world, or in the one where telltale gray is more dominant than necessary."[4]

32.7 QUALIFICATIONS FOR AN INTERNAL AUDITOR. Owing to pressure from the IIA and its support, the number of schools offering courses in internal auditing is increasing. In the past, most have considered public accounting qualifications as appropriate background for internal auditing. Should internal auditors be generalists or specialists? Do they have to be certified public accountants? How important is it that internal auditors understand the industry they work in? Is internal auditing a training ground for young people, or is it a place for only really experienced people? The answer is, "So much depends on how the function is run."

The author believes that you need very bright, inquisitive staff and the right type of management and training. Sprinkling that with specialists and experience will only help to improve the quality of the function. Nothing succeeds like experience in training bright auditors.

---

[4]Flescher, 1991, p. 104.

The IIA introduced the concept of certification for the internal audit function in 1974. A number of individuals globally have achieved certification, and this does help in setting certain standards for auditing. However, there are a significant number of internal auditors in the world who are not members of the Institute, have not taken any audit courses, and do not understand financial statements. Does that make them inadequate auditors? It depends on how they are being used in the function. It is important that management understand the internal audit responsibilities and the importance of independence in executing those functions.

It is to be hoped that the CFIA project will help in defining the competency requirements at various levels—entry, experienced, and manager. This will help provide guidance to schools in developing appropriate courses toward a degree or specialization in internal auditing.

32.8 EVALUATING THE INTERNAL AUDIT FUNCTION. Evaluation of the internal audit function is not easy. The head of the function should spend some time with management early on and agree on what are the criteria for success. A balanced scorecard approach, which combines some financial as well as project-driven measures, should help. There should exist an ability to bring in outside evidence for comparison with others in the industry. One option is to ask independent accountants to evaluate how well the internal audit function is being performed. Other options include relying on the IIA guidelines or hiring qualified members of the Institute to evaluate the internal audit function. A common drawback of all these approaches is that if management still does not believe in the quality of the function, outside evidence is not that helpful. The recognition of the internal audit function as "the best" by external peers will not always convince management. The use of external auditors to evaluate internal auditors may have drawbacks. Until recently, many external auditors did not understand the full scope of what the internal auditors should be doing. If the internal auditors were not doing what the external auditors were doing, the external auditors tended to give a negative review of the work performed by the internal auditors. In many cases, such reviews focused more on the documentation and training process rather than on the outcome of their work. External auditors, being acutely aware of how the lack of clear documentation processes has hurt in litigation, tend to spend more time refining the process than focusing on the outcome of the work of internal auditors.

Using a peer internal audit function in the evaluation process has a number of pluses. One is that the profession is evaluated on factors they should be evaluated on. Second, peers tend to be a friendlier audience, although this approach still does not help to overcome the gulf between management and the internal auditors.

In 1986, IIA established the Quality Assurance Review Service (QARS) with the object of providing internal audit directors with the assurance that they were in compliance with standards. A quality assurance review is conducted by volunteer members of the IIA. They receive training at headquarters in Altamonte Springs, Florida, prior to conducting their reviews. The average duration of a quality assurance review of an internal audit department is about one week.

32.9 VIEWS OF INTERNAL AUDITING MUST CHANGE. Management's views of internal audit in general are guarded. Too many business managers do not appreciate the way their various business units can work with the internal auditors and tend to view the latter as a necessary evil. A game develops wherein managers do not communicate with auditors, and auditors try to catch managers doing something wrong. There is nothing to be gained by this. All that is accomplished is wasted energy and negative output. The organization is the loser in the process. Other managers truly see the auditors as team members. The major public accounting firm of PricewaterhouseCoopers offers ten imperatives to help the internal audit function succeed in a post-Enron world:

1. Sharpen dialogue with top management and directors in order to clearly establish the value-added objectives of internal audit (i.e., strategic issues, risk management and protection of company assets).
2. Realign to meet key stakeholders' expectations (stockholders, executive management, external auditors and regulators).
3. Think and act strategically.
4. Expand audit coverage to include "tone at the top," the conduct of executive management in protecting the company.
5. Assess and strengthen expertise for complex business auditing.
6. Leverage technology in high-risk areas.
7. Focus on enterprise risk management capabilities.
8. Make the audit process dynamic, changing with changed business conditions.
9. Strengthen quality assurance processes.
10. Measure the enhanced performance against expectations of stakeholders.

If everyone begins to view the internal audit function as a truly challenging experience for which only the best and brightest are selected, the company will have a truly outstanding function. The function will work with management in helping them fulfill their responsibility for maintaining strong internal controls.

Internal auditors have five main stakeholders—the board of directors, the outside auditors, senior management, operating management, and regulators. It is important that the audit function clearly define how it will interact with each of these groups.

As can be gathered from discussion on hiring the best and brightest, the cost of a top internal audit function is significant. If the function is considered as purely detective, managers will question that cost, to the detriment of the overall organization. However, if auditors are accepted on the risk assessment team and make their contribution in controlling exposures, their costs will be considered more than acceptable.

32.10 COSO'S VIEWS OF THE CONTROL ENVIRONMENT AND THE IMPACT ON INTERNAL AUDITING. As indicated previously, COSO, which included representatives of the IIA, public accounting profession, the American Accounting Association, the Institute of Management Accountants, and Financial Executives International, undertook to define the elusive framework of internal control and to set some guidelines of what would be considered an appropriate framework. That effort helped to clarify management's responsiblity. One of the historic discussions has always been to ascertain who is the keeper of corporate internal controls. Is it the internal auditors, the external auditors, or both? Managers had a hard time accepting responsibility for something they could not define.

What the COSO document did was to help internal auditors turn to an authoritative source in explaining to managers their role in the internal control process. The

COSO process looks to a review of a business's objectives, control objectives, measures to evaluate risk, procedures to monitor those objectives and risks, and reporting on the effectiveness of those measures and their employment. It also requires an overview of the effectiveness of the process. In the COSO presentation, managers and their staff do the evaluation, not internal auditors. The internal auditors actually spend more time reviewing management's evaluation. Although a subtle change, we begin to see a shift to a partnership where the internal auditors help managers assess their risks.

This process shift also helped auditors from an efficiency aspect. Managers had to present why they believed they had the appropriate control environment. The internal auditors assessed the process by which management came to this conclusion. Much of the detail audit work shifted to the business because they had to provide the evidence that they had the appropriate control and risk measures and that those measures were being monitored and reported on to the appropriate supervisory levels.

32.11 FUTURE OF INTERNAL AUDITING. The new internal auditing model focuses on risk. Instead of viewing a business process within a system of internal control, today's auditor views the business process within an environment of risk. This shift in focus emphasizes the future as opposed to the past and is more likely to address the full range of issues that concern management.

An analysis of the way in which organizations are changing suggests ways that internal audit will have to adapt. Reengineering changes the way in which employees work. Changing technology alters the way we control work. Virtual organizations are gaining in importance. Regulatory compliance is here to stay.

What does the future of internal auditing look like?

The current business environment requires a leaner and more flexible approach to internal control. Many companies have addressed this challenge through reengineering and new information systems, creating entirely new types of businesses to manage and control. Senior managers can no longer impose structured internal control systems on their organizations; such systems are too costly both in terms of people and in terms of competitive advantage. Instead, senior executives must manage and control as an active team member in their organization's business processes, providing real-time responses to current business challenges.

How can senior managers gauge how they are changing with their processes? A good diagnostic is to start by asking a few simple questions. What have we done to ensure that:

- People in the organization are behaving the way intended?
- We are identifying our real risks and being alerted to critical changes?
- The internal and external data we rely on for critical decisions are accurate?
- Critical information and assets are protected?
- Regulations are followed?

Underlying all of these questions is the ultimate question—are we setting the right tone at the top?

32.12 SUMMARY. Internal auditing has entered a period of extreme challenge. Internal auditors must involve themselves in things that are happening in a company as they are evolving. They must become knowledgeable about the complex issues affecting their company operations. They have to identify risks that business managers might not be aware of.

The internal auditor has moved from being a policeman or an indicator of what is going wrong in an organization to being a member of the management team, which ensures that the organization continues to grow and prosper. In order for the internal audit function to generate benefit to the corporation, auditors have to help managers assess risk and provide practical solutions to minimize those risks. Auditors can no longer point out the problem and walk away from the solution. They have become part of the solution.

If the internal auditor's role changes to that of participating on the management team, what does that imply about the perception of the function and its role in the organization by stakeholders? Internal auditors still have to assume a role that ensures they are not part of the business and that they are independent. Yes, they will be involved in making suggestions on managing the business and they will have to take responsibility for bad advice. This role should not interfere with their independence but puts them in the position of being consultants to management in areas where they have exceptional expertise. They will still have the responsibility for bringing bad news even when operations management disagrees. Internal auditors will need to embrace a code of conduct and ethical standards to help them in deciding what steps to take in their dual capacity of both reporting on and advising to operations management.

At the same time, the profession must continue to grow. The requirements of internal auditing will continue to be refined and defined on a global basis. Certification may become essential to fulfillment of the internal audit function.

The internal auditor, having reached a higher level of compensation and recognition in a corporation, must realize that with rewards there are risks. If the internal auditors do not perform, not only can they be fired but also they may eventually be sued by managers, the boards of directors, or regulators. If the internal auditor truly wants to be an adviser just as the chief financial officer is, he or she must perform at a high level and continue to grow with the corporation.

The good news is that the internal auditor has moved into a senior financial management position. The work internal auditors perform has been recognized as critical to the success of companies for which they work. Their insight into the risk management process is important, and their advice is sought after. The internal auditor is no longer a detective, a necessary evil to prevent fraud. Rather, the internal auditor is a trusted adviser who takes a proactive approach to risk management that progressive managers have learned to need and benefit from.

It is clear that to deliver value internal auditors' capabilities and resources must be aligned with stakeholder value expectations. The adoption of best practices on a global basis is particularly critical where the corporate organization is operating on a multinational basis, be it centralized or decentralized, in order to ensure proper risk assessment and effective control by top management.

SOURCES AND SUGGESTED REFERENCES

Flescher, D. L. *The IIA: 50 Years of Progress Through Sharing*. Institute of Internal Auditors, 1991. "Internal Audit Checklist." *Journal of Accounting*, 1997, p. 91.

Internal Auditor—50th Anniversary. Institute of Internal Auditors, June 1991, pp. 1–148.

The Institute of Internal Auditors, 249 Maitland Avenue, Altamonte Springs, Florida 32701–4201, *www.theiia.org*.

Lambrix, Robert J., and Suren S. Singhivi. *Global Finance 2000, A Handbook of Strategy and Organization*. The Conference Board, 1996.

Trampo, John. "Thriving in Change." *Journal of Accounting*, April 1998, pp. 33–36.

"Will CFIA Transform Internal Auditing?" *IIA Today*, May/June 1998.

INDEX